C0-AVB-932

# Data Processing for Business and Management

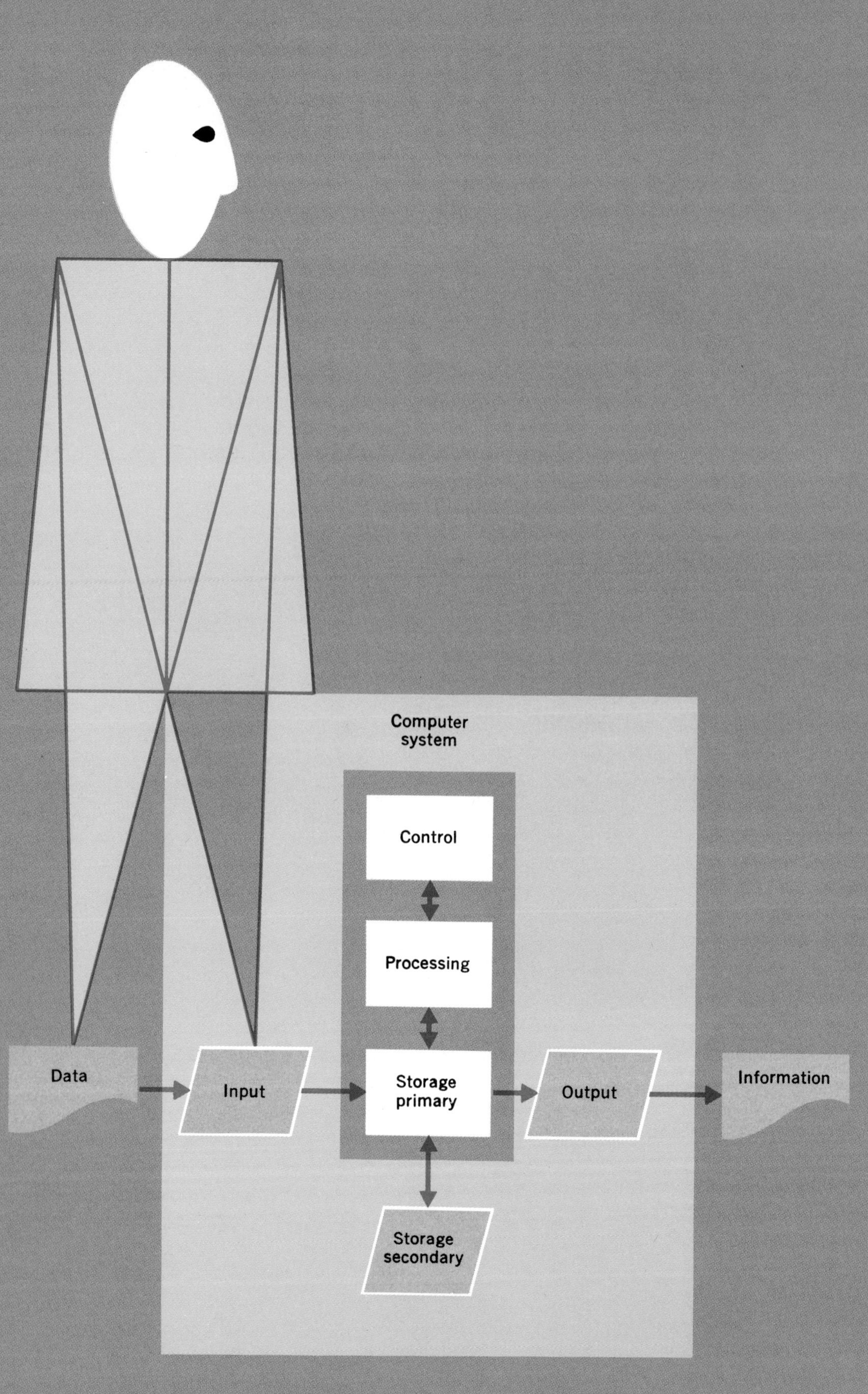
Computer system
Control
Processing
Data
Input
Storage primary
Output
Information
Storage secondary

# DATA PROCESSING FOR BUSINESS AND MANAGEMENT

***ROBERT J. THIERAUF, Ph.D., C.P.A.***

**Associate Professor of Management**
**Chairman, Department of Management and Industrial Relations**
**Xavier University, Cincinnati, Ohio**

*Edited by*

*DANIEL W. GEEDING, Ph.D., C.P.A.*

Assistant Professor of Management
Xavier University, Cincinnati, Ohio

**JOHN WILEY & SONS, INC. / NEW YORK · LONDON · SYDNEY · TORONTO**

*Cover:* A magnetic core plane beneath a four n-channel MOSFET (metal oxide-semiconductor Field Effect Transistor). Both provide 4k bits of storage; however, the MOSFET chip units run at twice the speed for half the price. Courtesy of IBM.

This book was set in Vega by York Graphic Services, Inc., and printed and bound by Halliday Lithographers. The designer was Bob Goff; the drawings were done by the Wiley Illustration Department. The editor was Elaine Miller. Robert Kamen supervised production.



***Library of Congress Cataloging in Publication Data:***

Thierauf, Robert J.
Data processing for business and management

Bibliography: p.

1. Electronic data processing—Business.
I. Title.
HF5548.2.T44    658.4'0028'54    72-5376
ISBN 0-471-85872-2

Printed in the United States of America

10 9 8 7 6 5 4 3 2 1

# PREFACE

The field of business data processing has grown unusually fast during its brief history. Generally, the quantity of books published in the established areas—punched cards, computers, and programming—has kept pace with the rapid advances of the field. However, the quality of many of these publications has been mediocre, since demand often preceded the actual writing. Only recently has the dust begun to settle on this new emerging field, allowing more time for a thorough treatment of the subject matter. This book is a balanced study and analysis of data processing for business and management. Where possible, material has been summarized to highlight important factors.

There can be many approaches to this subject. One extreme is to survey all possible material on data processing, including all languages used in computer programming, and to review numerous data processing systems. This approach is simply a survey of the field and nothing more. From the student's viewpoint, a superficial treatment contributes little to his understanding of the computer field. Another extreme is to restrict the subject matter to one or two aspects of data processing. Concentration on the particular features of one computer, the equipment itself, or the programming aspects might be undertaken. From this viewpoint the student's initial encounter with data processing is disadvantageous because his knowledge becomes outdated as the computer studied is replaced by another. The two extremes—one being too comprehensive and the other being too narrow in presentation—can be avoided by taking a balanced approach. This is the kind of approach that I take.

The major areas covered are systems, punched cards, essentials of computers, computer programming, programming languages, time sharing, the feasibility of data processing, and the human element. Emphasis is placed on the FORTRAN language, since it is possible to have a student program the computer in less time when compared to other programming languages. Also, many schools require that the student solve a wide range of business and scientific problems for which FORTRAN is well suited, especially when using time-sharing terminals.

Essentially this book concentrates on the material covered in an introductory course on business data processing. My purpose is to provide the student with a working knowledge of the data processing field. A thorough understanding of this material is an excellent starting point for one who is considering additional study. Also the material is suitable for one whose only formal exposure to the subject will be an introductory course.

This text is appropriate for any time period—one or two quarters (semesters) in a course covering an introduction to computers or the fundamentals of data processing. If it is used for a survey course of one quarter, Chapters 11 and 12 on FORTRAN and Chapters 13 to 15 on the feasibility study can be dropped. Two quarters or one semester normally will allow coverage of the entire book. The text can be utilized for a full academic year in conjunction with selected data processing manuals. With this approach, the book is used as a general guide for the computer course. Chapters can be supplemented with various computer and language manuals. No matter what approach is taken, the text is flexible enough to accommodate most classroom situations.

The structure of the book follows a logical sequence for a comprehensive treatment of data processing for business and management. The major areas covered are as follows.

*Prologue, Evolution of Data Processing for Business and Management.* The prologue surveys the historical background of data processing as well as important developmental factors of computers.

*Part I, Introduction to Business Data Processing.* Chapter 1 discusses basic data processing concepts and the various types of systems developed for computers. Emphasis is placed on real-time management information systems, operating in a management control center environment.

*Part II, Data Entry and Punched Card Equipment.* Chapters 2 and 3 cover the fundamentals of data entry and punched card equipment. Also, punched card applications are set forth.

*Part III, Electronic Data Processing.* The fundamentals of flowcharts and decision tables are investigated in Chapter 4; Chapter 5 explores the input-storage-processing-control-output (ISPCO) cycle concept of computers. In Chapter 6, computer data codes are covered with emphasis on the binary and hexadecimal systems. Also the execution of computer instructions is explored. Computer equipment and related devices or hardware are presented in the next chapter. Chapter 8 is devoted to optical character recognition equipment and applications. In Chapter 9, computer communications and time sharing are covered.

*Part IV, Programming Languages.* The field of computer programming, known as computer software, is the subject matter for Chapter 10. COBOL, BASIC, PL/1, and RPG are explored along with an orderly method for programming and implementation. The FORTRAN IV language is the subject of discussion in Chapters 11 and 12. Typical FORTRAN programs are illustrated for several functional business areas and management reports in a real-time management information system environment.

*Part V, Implementing and Controlling Data Processing.* The feasibility study is the subject matter for this part of the book (Chapters 13 to 15). Included in the material is a discussion of the exploratory survey, systems analysis, systems design, equipment selection, and systems implementation. Data processing systems controls, particularly those for computers, are discussed in Chapter 16.

*Part VI, Data Processing and Its Impact on the Firm.* Chapter 17 deals with the key to success in business data processing: the human element. The past, present, and future thrusts of data processing are presented in Chapter 18. In addition, the relationships of mathematical models in operations research to computers are discussed.

*Epilogue, A Last Look at Data Processing for Business and Management.* The epilogue takes a final look at data processing from the viewpoints of the individual, the group, management, the organization structure, the firm, and society.

In an undertaking of this magnitude, I am deeply indebted to the many people who have contributed their time and effort to make this publication possible. I am grateful to Ronald J. Kizior of Loyola University (Chicago) and William H. Charlton of Villanova University for suggesting organizational and writing improvements. I sincerely thank Keith Carver, Sacramento City College; Daniel Dell, University of Cincinnati; Ronald W. Eaves, California State Polytechnic College; William J. Keys, Long Beach City College; and Marvin Kushner, The City University of New York for their helpful suggestions.

At Xavier University, I thank the following faculty members: Robert Breyer, John F. Niehaus, Robert C. Strunk, and J. Michael Thierauf. I am particularly grateful to Daniel W. Geeding who undertook the laborious job of editing the original manuscript. Finally, I thank the many students who have contributed valuable ideas to the manuscript, and particularly: Paul J. Binko, James F. Goughenour, Donna M. Krabbe, Brother Peter J. Maurer, R. David Meade, T. Kenneth Roussil, Daniel V. Schnur, and Thomas J. Wood.

Xavier University, 1972 *Robert J. Thierauf*

# CONTENTS

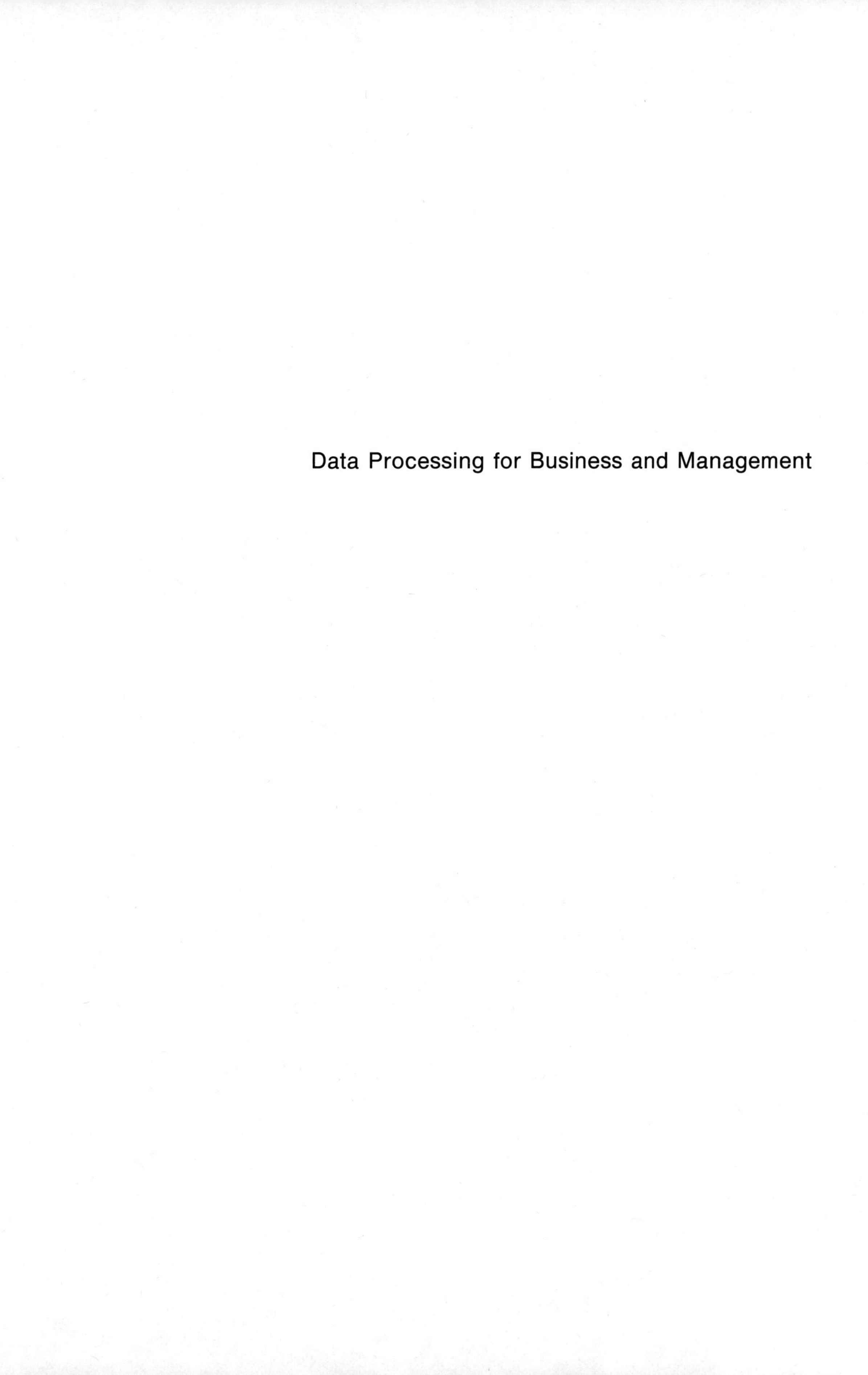

Data Processing for Business and Management

## PROLOGUE

# Evolution of Data Processing for Business and Management

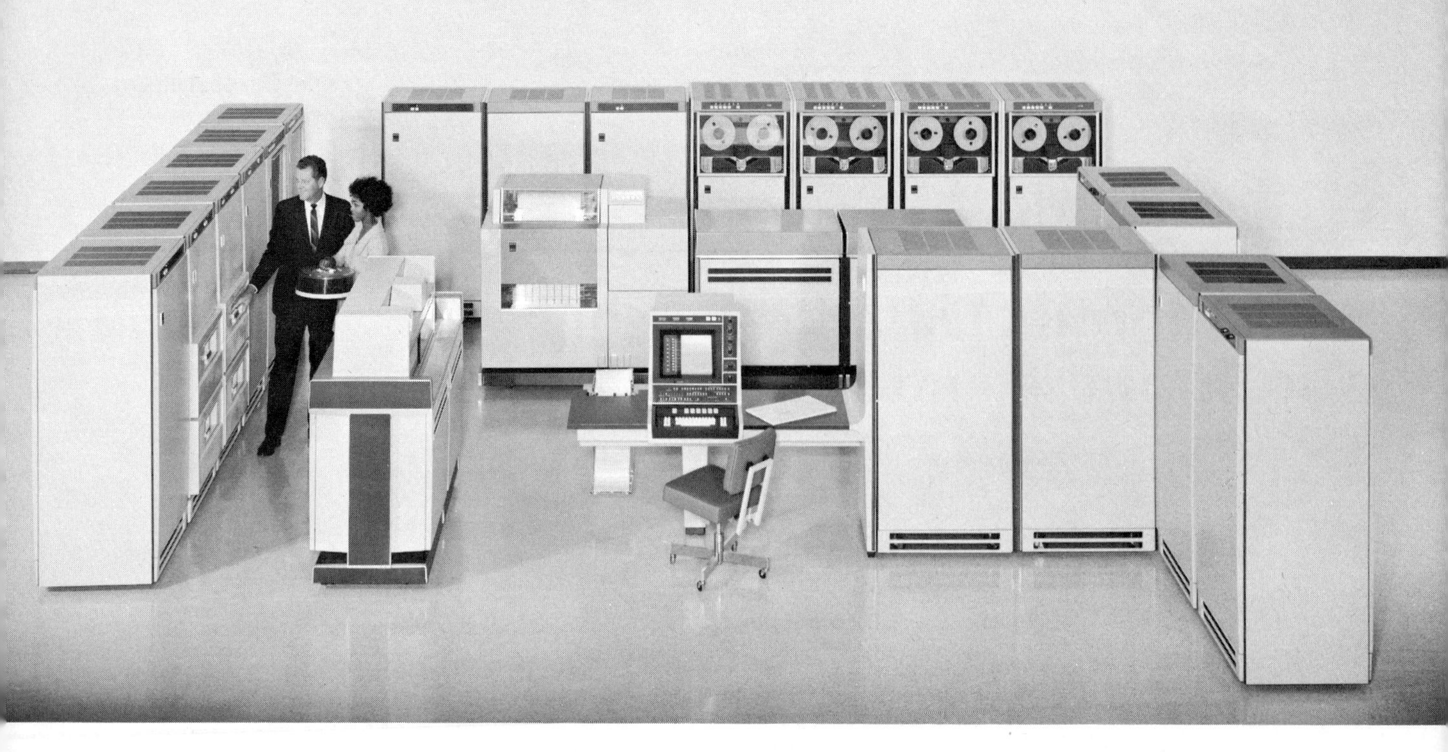

*The evolution of manual entry computing devices has spanned several centuries. However, the development of punched card equipment and computers has been more rapid. The 20th century has witnessed the introduction and use of several computer generations. Pictured is a typical current-generation computer. (Courtesy The National Cash Register Company.)*

Although "business data processing" has come into common usage only recently, it originated many centuries ago. Its origin is difficult to state with absolute certainty. Throughout recorded history, business and government activities have created this need. When business data processing officially began, it enabled man to express the concept of numbers in symbolic form. The numbering systems that have been documented over the years have varied from civilization to civilization. Although several of these are discussed in this chapter and in succeeding chapters, there will be more systems in the future to take advantage of advancing technology.

Basically, the prologue concentrates on key historical aspects of business data processing. A brief review of significant past events in data processing places recent developments into proper perspective. The growth of this function over the years demonstrates how essential business activities reach a point where manual or mechanical means do not always give timely feedback and results to those who need such information. In addition to detailing the history of punched card machines and computers, the past and current generations of computers are explored.

## HISTORY OF BUSINESS DATA PROCESSING

*The history of business data processing began when families joined with other families to form tribes.*

Business data processing began when families joined with other families to form tribal groups. These groups, in turn, grew into small nations where trade ultimately became the means of exchange. Since the need for business transactions began prior to recorded history, some method of record keeping had to be developed by the populace. These methods varied based upon the type of people and the number of transactions. As trading activity increased, written records and number systems were developed to record business transactions.

### History of Numbering Systems

*Important numbering systems have been developed by many civilizations. They started with pictographic writing.*

The oldest surviving written records date back to the period from 3700 to 3000 B.C. They consist of pictographic writing on clay tablets made by the Sumerians (predecessors of the Babylonians). Additional archeological findings have shown clay tablets in the Sumerian language, dating from 3000 to 2600 B.C. The wet clay tablets were marked with the cut end of a reed and placed in the sun or baked in an oven for a permanent record. Since this method of writing produced wedge-shaped marks, such writing was called cuneiform (from the Latin *cuneus*—meaning wedge). Other cultures, including the Babylonian and Assyrian, used clay tablets for recording data.

*Babylonian numerals were formed by pushing the end of a stylus into clay.*

***Babylonian Numerals.*** Most of the first business records on clay tablets were recorded by the Babylonians beginning about 2600 B.C. Since Babylon was a commercial center at that time, records of receipts, disbursements, and similar business transactions were scratched on slabs of wet clay with a wedge-shaped stick (stylus). Representative Babylonian symbols and their decimal number equivalents are shown in Figure P-1. The symbol that represented the value of 1 was formed by pushing the end of the stylus into clay. Their other symbol was formed by turning the stylus for a value of 10.

*Egyptian numerals consisted of symbols that represented common objects of the day.*

***Egyptian Numerals.*** About 3000 B.C. the ancient Egyptians discovered and perfected the use of the papyrus (the word "paper" is derived from papyrus) and the calmus (sharp-pointed pen made from the reed plant) to record data. Using the reedlike plant which grew along the banks of the Nile River, they cut the pith of this plant into strips. Arranging them crosswise into layers, the Egyptians soaked

| | |
|---|---|
| V | 1 |
| V V | 2 |
| V V V | 3 |
| V V V V | 4 |
| V V V<br>V V | 5 |
| V V V<br>V V V | 6 |
| V V V V<br>V V V | 7 |
| V V V V<br>V V V V | 8 |
| V V V V V<br>V V V V | 9 |
| < | 10 |
| < < | 20 |

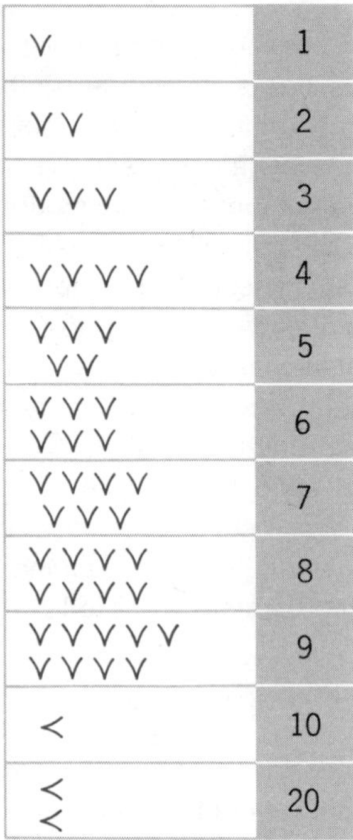

Figure P-1 Babylonian numeral symbols and decimal number equivalents.

*Roman numerals employed a straight-line method to form their values.*

them in water, pressed them, and dried them, obtaining a durable thin sheet that could be used for writing.

The Egyptian system of writing numerals is shown in Figure P-2. Position of the Egyptian numerals made no difference when writing a value. Each numeral was written repeatedly until the quantity shown added up to the amount desired. For example, the number 214 was written: 𓍢𓍢𓎆𓏺𓏺𓏺𓏺. To represent the number 40, four of the heel bone pictures were written in succession.

When contrasting the clay tablets (and stylus) of the Babylonians and the papyrus (and calmus) of the Egyptians, there should be no doubt about the problems encountered with the former method. Although the clay tablets were stored in jars and arranged in some logical order, they were cumbersome to say the least. The papyrus offered a practical medium for recording data. It was the most widely used ancient writing material until its gradual replacement by parchment during the 3rd and 4th centuries.

Another important recording device was the tablet book, which consisted of from two to ten sheets of wood coated with wax and tied together. Records were scratched on the waxed surface with a metal stylus. This device was used extensively by the Greeks and Romans for record keeping. This method had its disadvantages since there were limitations on the size of leaves and the number that could be bound together. Also, the records were not permanent since the wax could be rubbed off and used again.

***Roman Numerals.*** The next step in the development of recording data was the Roman numerals. For the first time in recorded history, a straight-line method was used to form all values; this is shown in Figure P-3. The Romans used a bar at the top of the numerals to indicate that the numeral was to be multiplied by 1000. This enabled them to write large values.

Although paper can be traced back to the 2nd century B.C., it was not available to the rest of the world until the 8th century A.D. when it was discovered by the Arabs. In Europe, the manufacture of paper originated during the middle of the 12th century by the Moors in Spain. This paper manufacturing process moved to the great countries of Europe—Italy, France, Germany, and England. By the second half of the 14th century, the use of paper had gained a strong foothold in western Europe.

An interesting development of business records was the wooden tallies used in England during the Dark Ages. It served as the basis for collecting taxes from

| Object Represented | Egyptian Numeral | Decimal Number |
|---|---|---|
| Vertical staff | 𓏺 | 1 |
| Heel bone | 𓎆 | 10 |
| Coiled rope | 𓍢 | 100 |
| Lotus flower | 𓆼 | 1000 |
| Bent reed | 𓂭 | 10,000 |
| Burbot fish | 𓆐 | 100,000 |
| Surprised man | 𓁨 | 1,000,000 |

Figure P-2 Egyptian numeral symbols and decimal number equivalents.

| ROMAN NUMERAL | DECIMAL NUMBER | ROMAN NUMERAL | DECIMAL NUMBER |
|---|---|---|---|
| I | 1 | $\overline{I}$ | 1,000 |
| V | 5 | $\overline{V}$ | 5,000 |
| X | 10 | $\overline{X}$ | 10,000 |
| L | 50 | $\overline{L}$ | 50,000 |
| C | 100 | $\overline{C}$ | 100,000 |
| D | 500 | $\overline{D}$ | 500,000 |
| M | 1000 | $\overline{M}$ | 1,000,000 |

Figure P-3 Roman numeral symbols and decimal number equivalents.

the people. Data for determining the revenue to be collected from each taxpayer was included in a record called the Doomsday Book. Although the notching of sticks was a primitive form of recording data, the wooden tallies were used until 1826 when they were abolished by an act of Parliament.

***Hindu-Arabic Numerals.*** The most important of all ancient number systems for our present use come from the Hindu-Arabic system (Figure P-4). Although the Hindu numbers date from about 500 A.D., a comparable date for the Arabic numbers is 900 A.D. The advantage of this combined system was that the zero symbol was

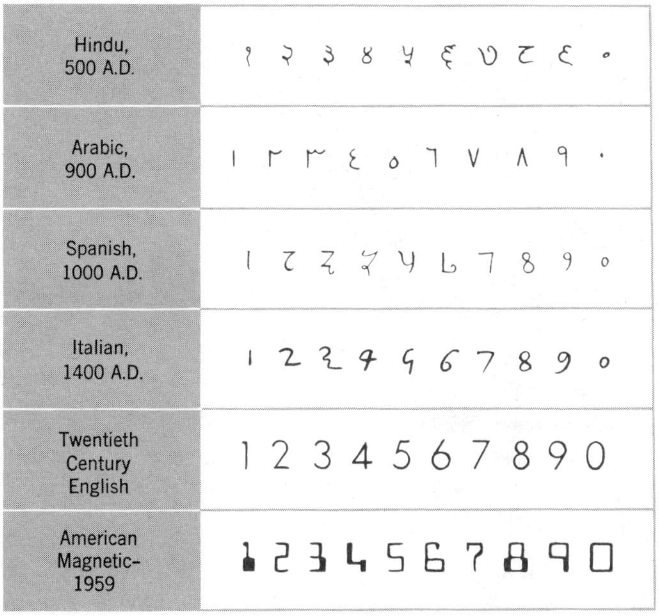

| | |
|---|---|
| Hindu, 500 A.D. | |
| Arabic, 900 A.D. | |
| Spanish, 1000 A.D. | |
| Italian, 1400 A.D. | |
| Twentieth Century English | 1 2 3 4 5 6 7 8 9 0 |
| American Magnetic–1959 | 1 2 3 4 5 6 7 8 9 0 |

Figure P-4 Evolution of numbers. (Courtesy The National Cash Register Company.)

*Hindu-Arabic numerals consisted of values comparable to our present decimal system. They used a zero symbol to indicate positional values in a column of figures.*

an integral part of numbers that utilized a fixed base and positional notation. The Hindu system used 9 symbols and a zero. This system allowed all the beads in the first row of the computing device to have a value of 1, the next row to have a value of 10, the next to equal 100, and so forth. In effect, the Hindus were the first to apply the use of a zero symbol to indicate the positional value in a column of figures. For the first time, a set of numbers could be manipulated to perform addition, subtraction, multiplication, and division as it is known today.

Numerous refinements have been made over the centuries to form our present decimal system.

***Present Numerals.*** As indicated in Figure P-4, the Spanish (1000 A.D.) and Italians (1400 A.D.) refined the decimal number system for carrying on the increased trade during the Middle Ages. These developments have resulted in the following systems.

1. Present decimal system or base 10 system—0 through 9.
2. Binary system or base 2 system—0 or 1.
3. Hexadecimal system or base 16 system—0 through 9 and A through F.
4. Other numbering systems.

All present numbering systems are capable of being converted from one system to another. (These systems will be discussed at some length in Chapter 6).

**History of Manual Entry Computing Devices**

The first manual entry computing device employed the principles of the abacus.

The history of manual entry computing devices is as fascinating as the history of recording methods and numbering systems. It originated with the predecessor of the abacus, about 3000 B.C. in the Tiger-Euphrates Valley. This early device consisted of a clay board with a number of grooves into which pebbles were inserted. The pebbles were moved from one side to the other for counting. The abacus in its present form was invented in China about 2600 B.C. Records indicate that the Egyptians used it many centuries before the coming of Christ. The word "abacus" is derived from the Greek word *abax* which means calculating table. The word "calculate" is derived from the pebbles or calculi on the wires of the abacus.

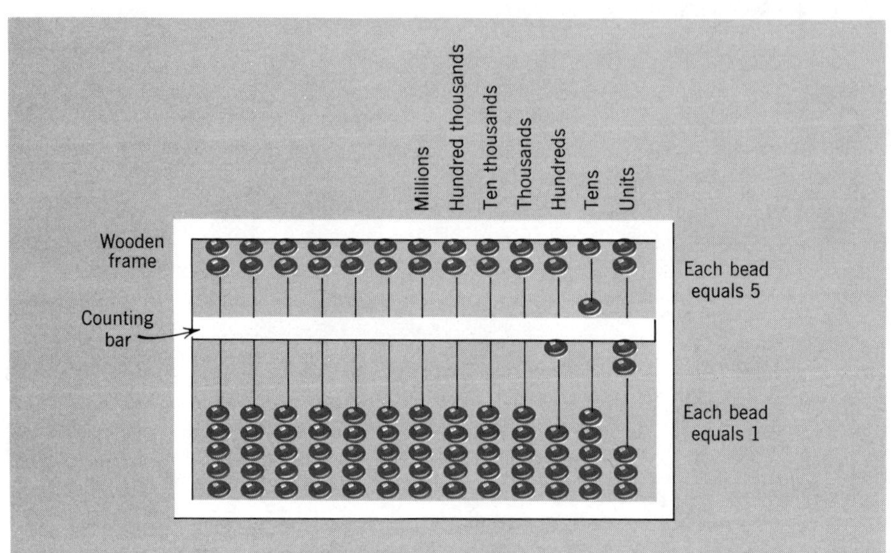


Figure P-5 Chinese abacus.

An abacus consists of beads that are pushed against a counting bar for determining calculated values.

***Abacus.*** A typical abacus, shown in Figure P-5, consists of several rows of beads that can slide back and forth on the wires. It is divided by a counting bar. The top row of beads have a value of 5 when pushed against the counting bar while each lower bead has a value of 1. Just as in the decimal system, moving to the left results in a higher order position, that is, from units, tenths, hundreds, and so forth. The value of 152 is illustrated in Figure P-5. The four principal calculations of arithmetic can be performed on the abacus as well as other mathematical calculations. The Oriental method of learning to operate the abacus depends upon memorizing long lists of rules. When memorized, they come to mind just as readily as our multiplication tables for the decimal system.

Several thousand years elapsed before more advanced methods for performing calculations were developed. This lag was caused mostly by the use of Roman numerals throughout Europe. The acceptance of the Arabic numeral system around 1200 A.D., which was a much simpler means of calculating, provided the necessary impetus for developing important advances in computing devices during the seventeenth century.

*Napier's bones were a mechanical arrangement of strips of bone that could be used to perform direct multiplication.*

***Napier's Bones.*** From 1614 to 1617, John Napier, a Scotch mathematician developed two different methods of simplifying multiplication and division, the first being computing rods (called Napier's Bones) with direct multiplication tables. It was a mechanical arrangement of strips of bone on which numbers were printed (Figure P-6). When brought into combination, these strips could perform direct

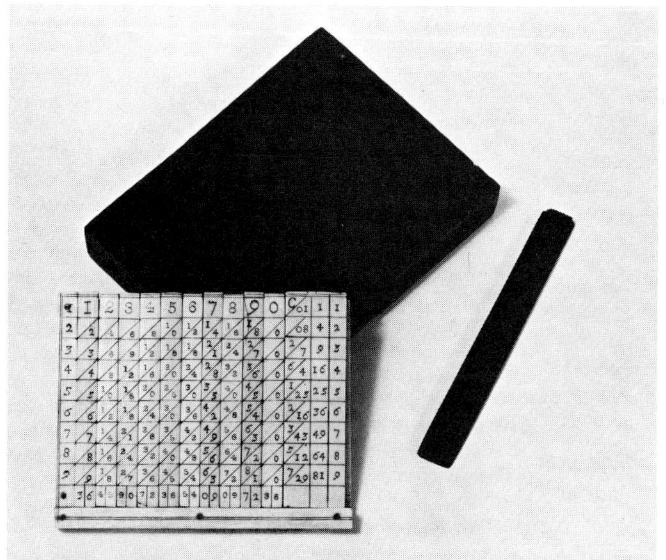

Figure P-6 Napier's Bones. (Courtesy International Business Machines Corporation.)

multiplication. For example, to multiply 8 × 123 in Figure P-6, we list from right to left the sums of the diagonals found in the 8th row for columns 1, 2, and 3. Thus, the units position would be 4, the tens position would be 2 + 6 = 8, the hundreds position would be 1 + 8 = 9 for a total of 984.

The second method developed by Napier relates to his computing the first logarithmic tables. The use of logarithms (base *e*) shortens to simple addition and subtraction those calculations involving multiplication and division. It also facilitates the extraction of roots and raising to powers.

*The slide rule, developed by W. Oughtred, approximates an answer.*

***Slide Rule.*** Using the logarithm tables developed by Napier, a British mathematician by the name of William Oughtred invented the slide rule around 1630. The slide rule performs multiplication and division through addition and subtraction of logarithmic units. Although the first such device was circular in nature, a rectilinear device was produced a few years later. This is the slide rule as it is known today. Whereas the abacus is correct to the final digit (like a digital computer), the slide rule is accurate only insofar as the precision of its physical parts will allow. Thus the slide rule makes approximations (like the analog computer).

*The first adding machine was a development of B. Pascal.*

***First Adding Machine.*** The first true adding machine was invented in 1642 by Blaise Pascal at the age of 19. When the young Pascal saw his father's arithmetic problems as a tax collector in Normandy, he developed a numerical wheel and rachet calculator (Figure P-7). Its principle was one of using cogged wheels for

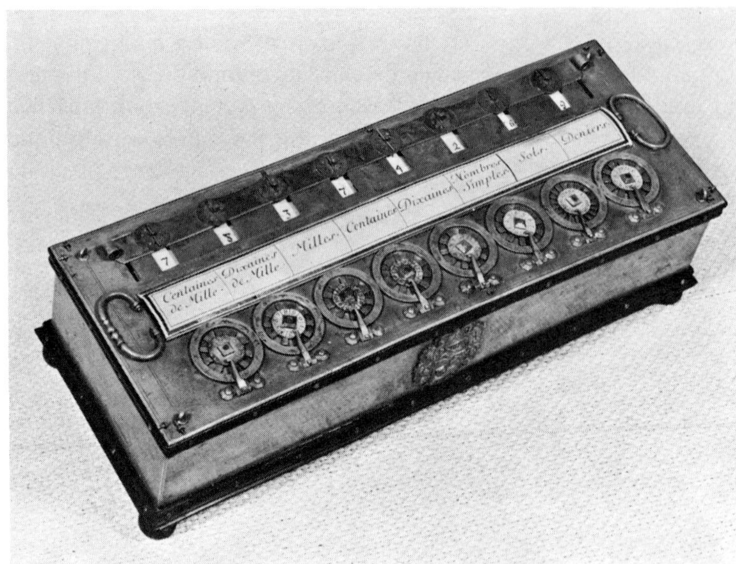

Figure P-7 Pascal's adding machine. (Courtesy International Business Machines Corporation.)

totaling sums. The machine registered values by the rotation of the wheels, numbered 1 through 9. A lever was used to perform the carry from one wheel to the next when the capacity of the first was exceeded. By repeated selection and operation for each digit to be added, the corresponding drums were rotated through cycles to indicate an accumulation of values. The action of a numbered wheel 0 through 9 and the ability to carry a value to a higher order numbered wheel are the fundamentals for most calculating machines up to the present time. Also, Pascal's adding machine proved that subtraction can be accomplished by turning dials in reverse and that multiplication can be performed by repeated addition.

*The first of the calculating machines was constructed by G. Leibniz.*

***Initial Calculating Machines.*** The last important contribution of the 17th century was by Gottfried Wilhelm von Leibniz in 1694. Although it is reported that he independently discovered the principles of the calculus about the same time as Newton, he developed a machine to do all known mathematical calculations of his time. Shown in Figure P-8, this machine has the capacity to perform the four basic arithmetic functions and extract square roots. Its operating technique was based on the concept of a stepped cylinder, an ingenious device used in countless machines from his day up to the present. The cylindrical drum had 9 teeth of increasing length along its surface. As the drum rotated, a gear sliding on an axis parallel to that of the drum engaged some of the teeth being rotated on an equivalent number of steps.

The problem with the above machines, developed in the 17th century, was that great care had to be used for accuracy. Additional attempts were made in the next

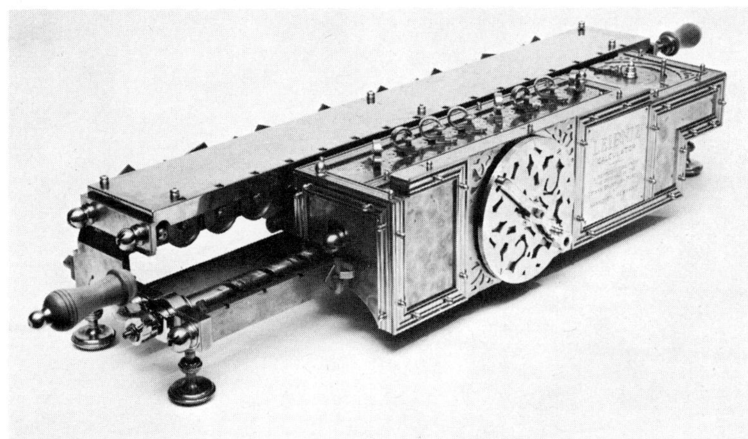

Figure P-8 Leibniz calculating machine. (Courtesy International Business Machines Corporation.)

century to produce a reliable machine. However, it was not until 1820 when Charles Xavier Thomas of Colmar, France constructed his Arithmometer, the first really practical application of Leibniz's principle. The major improvement over current machines was the addition of a crank that would feed data into the machine. This machine was the first such equipment to be manufactured by a firm established for this purpose. Some of these machines were brought to the United States, which had a stimulating effect on the continuing development of computing devices in this country.

In 1850, D. D. Paramalee obtained a United States patent for the first key-driven adding machine. Since only a single column of data could be added at a time, the equipment was very limited. Several years later (1857), Thomas Hill developed the first key-driven, four-process calculating device. For his work, he is often referred to as "the father of desk calculators in the United States."

In the 1870's, two parallel inventions took place. Frank S. Baldwin (from the United States) and Willgodt T. Odhner (from Europe) developed equipment that improved upon the design of the Leibniz stepped-cylinder calculator. They used a thin but solid device rather than a cylinder to serve as the wheel to be rotated. This was accomplished by adding teeth to the edge of the wheel. Each tooth was assigned a certain value (from 0 through 9). Shown is Figure P-9 is Odhner's calculator whose design marked the beginning of the calculator industry in the United States.

*The add-list machine of W. S. Burroughs combined the features of adding to a printing device.*

***Add-List Machine.*** The next important phase in calculating devices was the combining of adding to a printing device. The first rudimentary listing machine was developed by E. D. Barbour in 1873. Sometime later (1884), William S. Burroughs developed an adding-listing machine (Figure P-10) which had a 90-key keyboard to accommodate a column of values up to 9 decimal digits and was crank operated. The machine was patented in 1888 and was successfully marketed in 1891. The Burroughs Company that exists today was the manufacturer. This piece of equipment represented a significant advance since it had the ability to record, total, and calculate.

*The cash register of J. Ritty was an important advancement in computing devices.*

***Cash Register.*** About the same time, the cash register (Figure P-11) was invented by James Ritty. This device was developed and marketed by John H. Patterson, who founded the National Cash Register Company in 1884. Another device, developed by Dorr E. Felt in 1887, was the first successful key-driven

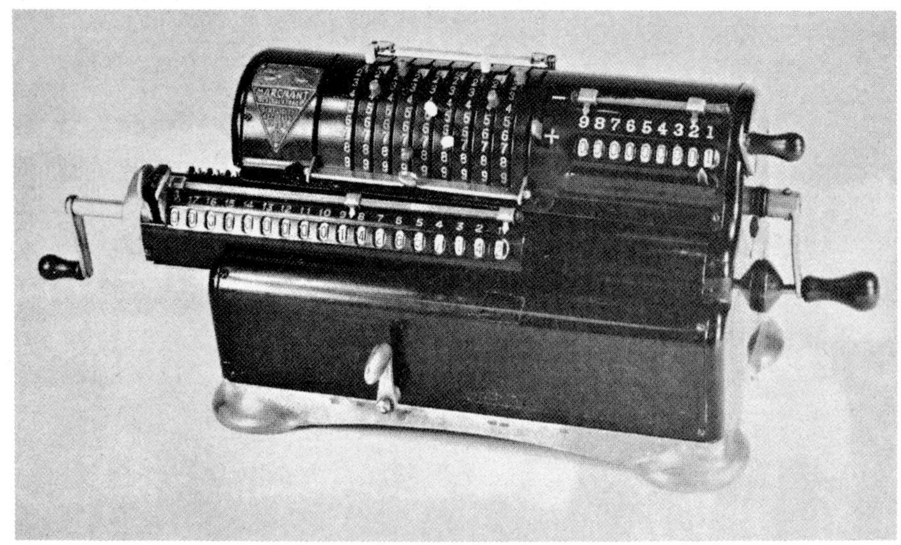


Figure P-9 Odhner calculator, 1878. (Courtesy International Business Machines Corporation.)

multiple-order calculator. It was known as the "Macaroni Box" and was the forerunner of the present "comptometer." A company (Felt and Tarrant) was founded to manufacture these machines. In 1889 Felt incorporated a listing feature to the machine, which resulted in one of the first practical devices of its kind.

*The 10-key adding machine, developed by H. Hopkins, replaced the full keyboard of prior machines.*

***10-Key Adding Machine.*** The first machine to perform multiplication by a direct method instead of repeated addition was developed by Léon Bolleé in 1887. It had a multiplying piece consisting of a series of tongued plates, representing the ordinary multiplication table up to "9 times." Within a few years Elgli marketed the "Millionaire" machine (Figure P-12) patented by Otto Steiger in 1893. It was based

Figure P-10 First practical adding-listing machine. (Courtesy Burroughs Corporation.)

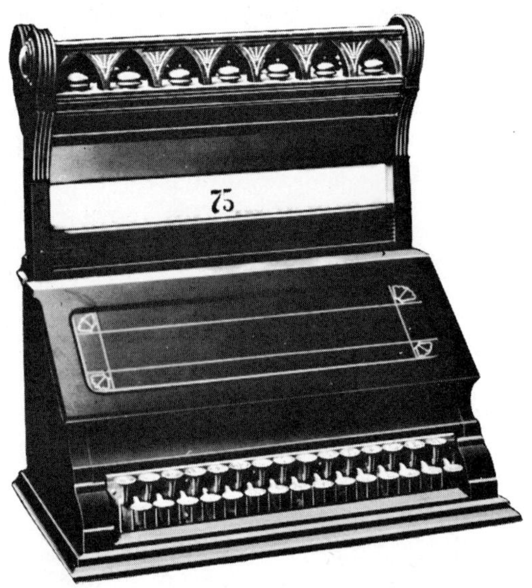


Figure P-11 Original cash register invented in 1879. (Courtesy The National Cash Register Company.)

Figure P-12 "The Millionaire," the first successful direct multiplying machine, 1899. (Courtesy International Business Machines Corporation.)

on the mechanical multiplication table developed by Bolleé. The device required only one turn of the handle for each figure of the multiplier and provided for automatic shift to the next position. About the same time (around 1900), Hubert Hopkins of the United States developed the first practical billing machine utilizing a direct multiplication technique based on that developed by Bolleé. In 1901, Hopkins developed the first adding machine to use 10 keys instead of utilizing the "full keyboard" concept.

*The combined efforts of J. Monroe and F. Baldwin produced the first keyboard-rotary calculator.*

***Keyboard-Rotary Calculator.*** The combined efforts of Jay R. Monroe and Frank S. Baldwin (mentioned earlier) produced, commercially, the first successful keyboard-rotary calculator in 1911 (Figure P-13). This represented 40 years of work by Baldwin who invented his first computing device back in 1872. It became known as the Monroe Calculator and was a nonprinting calculator. Its speed in performing all four basic arithmetic functions made it a success. Monroe and Baldwin founded the Monroe Calculating Machine Company in 1912, which is now a division of Litton Industries.

In the same year, Oscar and David Sundstrand established a firm for the manufacture of their 10-key adding machine. The use of 10 keys increases the speed of operation over a full keyboard machine.

*Accounting machines were, and still are, widely employed for processing business transactions.*

***Accounting Machines.*** In 1909 the first accounting machine was developed for the National Cash Register Company by Charles F. Kettering. It had the ability to sort data into a number of columns via a tabulating carriage in addition to the functions of recording, calculating, and summarizing. By the end of World War I, the impact of the accounting machine on the business firm was considerable.

The first electromechanical calculating machines came on the market around 1920. Most of them were similar to those outlined previously, except for improve-

Figure P-13 First Monroe keyboard machine. (Courtesy Litton Industries.)

ments in engineering, speed, and facility of operation. Additional models have been placed on the market over the years, the advances being more in appearance than in mechanical design.

*Present calculators utilize microminiature circuits to perform desired calculations.*

***Present Calculators.*** Small, desk-sized electronic calculators were introduced in the 1960's by most manufacturers of calculating equipment. These machines utilize microminiature integrated circuits to perform the calculations desired in millisecond (thousandth of a second) speeds. These minute parts replaced most of the mechanical parts which allow the equipment to operate noiselessly. As shown in Figure P-14, data are printed for visual output.

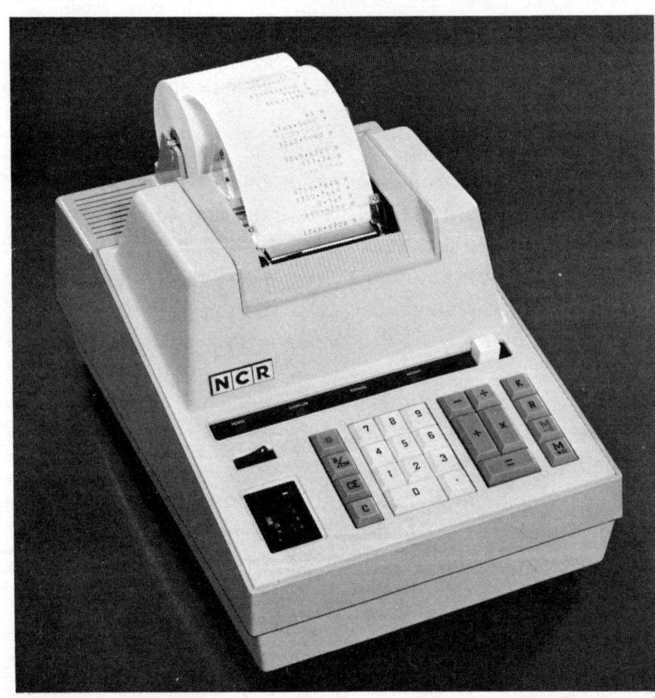


Figure P-14 NCR electronic printing calculator. (Courtesy The National Cash Register Company.)

*Manual entry computing devices are quite limited in their abilities to handle data processing operations.*

***Limitations of Manual Entry Computing Devices.*** Despite the increased ability of these machines over the years, they are still quite limited as indicated by the following characteristics.

1. Failure to give timely management information as needed.
2. Slow speed as a result of manual keyboard entry.
3. Subject to human errors of omission and commission.
4. Operate independently of other pieces of data processing equipment.

In order to remedy these problems, newer equipment—basically punched card equipment and computers—have been developed to overcome the inherent limitations of manual entry computing devices.

**History of Punched Card Machines**

*The punched card concept was initially employed by J. Jacquard for automating textile equipment.*

During the period 1725–1745, two Frenchmen, Basile Bouchon and M. Falcon, developed textile-weaving equipment which used punched holes in either paper strips or cardboard to control the weaving of cloth. Another Frenchman, Joseph Marie Jacquard, went a step further and invented an automatic loom, thereby revolutionizing the weaving industry. Weaving was under the control of punched cards in that cards could be punched for each type of woven design. A hole in the card corresponded to a lifted thread while a blank represented a depressed thread, comparable to the binary system (on or off condition) for computer systems. In order to operate the loom, cards were strung together with loops of string to form a continuous chain, shown in Figure P-15. By 1812, thousands of these

Figure P-15 Jacquard automatic weaving loom, utilizing punched cards. (Courtesy International Business Machines Corporation.)

automated looms were used in France alone. Updated models of Jacquard looms are widely used today for the production of cloth.

*C. Babbage utilized the punched card principle in his "analytical engine."*

***Babbage's Analytical Engine.*** In the 19th century, an initial attempt to utilize the punched card principle in a mathematical application was undertaken by Charles Babbage. After spending almost a decade on the "difference engine," designed to calculate and print mathematical tables, he turned his efforts to a machine called the "analytical engine" (Figure P-16). The input data were processed by using flexible

Figure P-16 Babbage's analytical engine. (Courtesy International Business Machines Corporation.)

arithmetic controls that performed the calculations required. His device included a memory unit, capable of storing 1000 numbers. The device stored data in the form of holes punched in cards and had an output mechanism that could print like a typewriter or punch holes in cards. It also had the ability to machine check the data for errors. Unfortunately, the technical sciences of the day were not advanced enough for practical implementation of his analytical engine.

*The success of punched cards is attributable to Dr. Hollerith. He developed the necessary equipment to process the 1890 census.*

***Hollerith Method.*** The success of punched cards by Jacquard many years before in the weaving industry did not inspire anyone else, other than Babbage, to further the development of this technique until the 1880's. Dr. Herman Hollerith, a noted statistician at the time, started experimenting with new ideas in compiling data for the U.S. Census Bureau. In 1880, he was engaged by the Census Bureau to find a more practical way of handling census data. At that time the census method required writing data on cards which necessitated hand sorting to arrive at various desired classifications. Obviously, this method was extremely time consuming. The

1880 census report was not completed until 1887. It was estimated that the next census (1890) would take approximately 10 years to compile. This time lag would not have permitted the reallocation of Congressional seats as required every 10 years by the Constitution of the United States.

Initially, Hollerith experimented by punching data into a roll of paper that utilized a ticket punch for punching the required holes. Since the paper did not work out satisfactorily, he substituted a 3 × 5 inch card, which was divided into squares approximately $\frac{1}{4}$ inch in size. This served as the basis for recording the 1890 census data and came to be known as a "unit record" of information. The census data were punched into cards in the form of holes that were cut by a hand-operated punch. The cards, in turn, were positioned one by one in a frame over mercury-filled cups. Rows of telescoping pins that descend on the surface of the cards dropped through the holes into the mercury. Each contact completed an electrical circuit that caused a corresponding pointer to move one position on a dial. This contact also opened a given box lid for filing the card. It was hand-filed according to the given characteristics found in the card data. With the ability to tabulate cards at the rate of 50 to 75 a minute, it was possible to complete the 1890 census in one-third of the time required for the 1880 census, which relied on manual methods completely. Thus the card punch, a manual feed card reader, tabulator with dials for counting results, and a sorting box were the first pieces of equipment found in a punched card installation (Figure P-17).

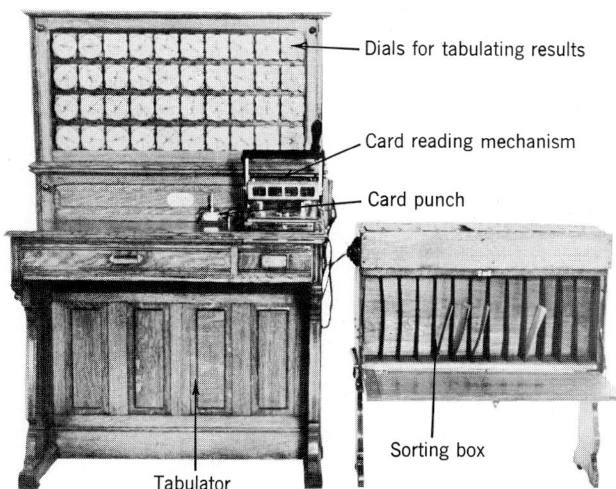


Figure P-17 Hollerith tabulating machine for 1890 census. (Courtesy International Business Machines Corporation.)

*Dr. Hollerith is the founder of the successful International Business Machines Corporation.*

***Formation of IBM.*** Dr. Hollerith adopted his census tabulator to business applications by forming the Tabulating Machine Company in 1896. In 1911, this firm was merged with two others into the Computing-Tabulating-Recording Company. By 1914, the new firm had four basic machines in operation. These included a key punch for punching holes in cards (Figure P-18), a hand-operated gang punch for punching duplicated data into a number of cards (Figure P-19), a sorter for arranging cards into selected groups (Figure P-20), and a tabulating machine for adding the punched cards. In 1924 the firm's name was changed to the International Business Machines Corporation, by which it is known today.

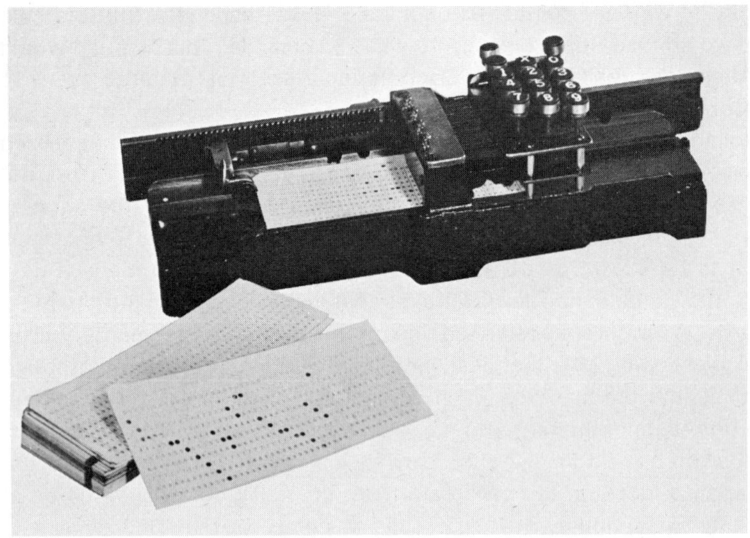

Figure P-18 Early key-driven card punch. (Courtesy International Business Machines Corporation.)

*J. Powers continued the punched card developmental work of Hollerith at the Census Bureau.*

***Powers Method.*** After Hollerith resigned from the Census Bureau to explore the commercial potentials of his equipment, James Powers was selected to continue developmental work of data processing equipment. He developed several concepts that were different from those of Hollerith. In the area of key punching with the Hollerith method, a hole was punched into a card each time a key was struck. If the operator had made an error, it was too late to correct it. With Powers' method, no punching took place until the keys had been depressed for all data. At that time, all data were punched simultaneously into the card. In effect, the Powers' method allowed for correcting a mispressed key before punching occurred. Another contribution of Powers was to have metal pegs drop down through the round holes and make contact with pieces of metal to set up electrical circuits. Under the Hollerith system, brushes were used to read rectangular holes in the card. Another basic difference between the two systems was the coding of decimal digits, alphabetic

Figure P-19 Early hand-operated gang punch. (Courtesy International Business Machines Corporation.)

Figure P-20 Early vertical punched card sorter—sorting on a column digit at a time. (Courtesy International Business Machines Corporation.)

characters, and special characters. Powers' equipment was produced by the government for the 1910 census.

*Like Hollerith, Powers formed his own firm which is now the UNIVAC Division of the Sperry Rand Corporation.*

***Formation of Remington Rand.*** The success of his developments at the Census Bureau prompted Powers to leave in 1911 and form the Powers Accounting Machine Company in the same year. This firm was eventually merged with the Remington Rand Corporation in 1927 which, in turn, was merged to form the Sperry Rand Corporation in 1955.

*Advances in punched card equipment made it possible to handle many business data processing activities.*

***Advances in Punched Card Machines.*** The adoption of punched card machines or EAM (Electric Accounting Machine) equipment by business was slow at the beginning of the 20th century. With important advancements occurring in the late 1920's and the early 1930's, the number of punched card installations began to increase. The advances included the increased capacity of punched cards to 80 (IBM) and 90 (RR) columns, the ability to multiply figures, and the handling of alphabetic information versus only numeric information previously. By 1936, the equipment was sufficiently advanced to handle the largest accounting operation—the United States social security system. The initial operation was to set up accounts for 30 million people. Within one year, the agency was processing large numbers of accounts daily. During the next 20 years, the system had added almost 100 million new accounts.

Additional developments from the 1930's to the present have resulted in more speed, flexibility, and utility of punched card machines. Basically, these developments have come from the International Business Machines Corporation and the Sperry Rand Corporation. The present state of punched card development is covered comprehensively in Chapters 2 and 3.

*Although punched card equipment is a significant advance over manual entry computing devices, it is not the complete answer to a firm's data processing needs.*

***Limitations of Punched Card Machines.*** Even though punched card equipment represents considerable advances over manual methods, several significant limitations are apparent.

1. Machine speeds are limited by their electromechanical ability.
2. Most equipment performs a special function rather than many functions.
3. Manual transfers of cards from one machine to another are needed.
4. Machines have limited programming and internal storage capabilities.

The conclusion to be drawn is that punched card machines are not the complete answer to most business data processing needs. This is the rationale for the successful development of computers.

## DEVELOPMENT OF ELECTRONIC COMPUTERS

*The basic concepts of computers were first conceived in 1786 by J. H. Miller.*

Although the actual development of electronic computers is a recent event, an automatic computer was first conceived in 1786 by J. H. Miller, a German engineer. Because of the engineering and manufacturing difficulties of undertaking the project, he developed his ideas on paper. His machine was devised to generate data for functions (involving their differences) based upon algebraic formulas. But more importantly to the development of computers were the ideas of the analytical engine by Babbage. Its basic concepts have proved to be the fundamental basis for the development of modern computers. Since his analytical engine is considered the forerunner of today's electronic computers, some writers have bestowed upon Babbage the title of "grandfather of modern computers."

*The first analog computer was developed by Dr. V. Bush at M.I.T.; it was completed in 1942.*

***First Analog Computer.*** In 1925, Dr. Vannevar Bush and some associates at the Massachusetts Institute of Technology constructed a large scale analog computer. (A type of calculating machine that operates with numbers represented by directly measurable quantities.) Basically, it was a mechanically operated computer with some electrical power. Ten years later, the same group started to develop an improved machine with greater capabilities. It was formally completed in 1942 but not announced until the end of World War II.

***Bell Model 1—Semiautomatic Computer.*** Another important concurrent activity in computer development took place at the Bell Telephone Laboratories. Dr. George R. Stibitz began work on the Bell Model 1 in 1937. It was completed in 1939. Being a semiautomatic computer, the Bell Model 1 used telephone relays to perform its computations. It was not an electronic computer in the real sense since it used electrical relays rather than electronic circuits. Later, revisions to this basic relay-type computer were completed by the Bell Telephone Laboratories as well as by other firms and institutions.

*The combined efforts of Dr. H. Aiken and IBM produced the first general purpose digital computer, marketed in 1944 for scientific work.*

***Mark I—First General Purpose Digital Computer.*** Of all the work performed on the development of digital computers in the 1930's, the first important work was undertaken by Dr. Howard Aiken as a Harvard graduate student in 1935. He designed a machine whose function was to prepare mathematical tables by automatically performing a set sequence of arithmetic operations. (His work paralleled those concepts and ideas developed by Babbage some 75 years earlier.) When some initial work had been completed, he went to the International Business Machines Corporation for both financial and technical help on his proposal. In 1937, he received both. The Mark I or the Automatic Sequence Controlled Calculator (ASCC) was the result of their efforts and proved to be the largest relay calculating device ever constructed.

The Mark I was designed to follow automatically a series of instructions punched in paper tape $3\frac{1}{4}$ inches wide. Being a digital computer, it stored numbers in devices called registers. All machine operations were performed electromechanically by wheel counters and relays, many of which were adaptations of standard production parts from IBM's punched card equipment. The Mark I could perform 23-digit additions and subtractions in three tenths of a second and could multiply two 23-digit numbers in about six seconds. Under automatic control of the paper-tape program, it could produce intermediate and final answers to a problem on punched cards or electric typewriter. It was publicly announced by the International Business Machines Corporation in 1944, becoming the first of a series of Mark computers to be marketed in subsequent years. Although the Mark I was the first successful digital computer ever to be completed, it was designed for scientific work where a long series of complex mathematical equations and problems had to be solved. The original Mark I was retired in 1959 after 15 years of continuous operations.

*The building of the first electronic computer (ENIAC) was a joint effort of Drs. J. Eckert and J. Mauchly. The on-off switching circuits of vacuum tubes were used to represent numbers.*

***ENIAC—Introduction of Electronic Circuitry.*** While the foregoing were essentially relay-type computers for scientific work, the first truly electronic computer was begun in 1943 at the Moore School of Electrical Engineering at the University of Pennsylvania. Dr. J. Presper Eckert, an electrical engineer, and Dr. John Mauchly, a physicist, developed the ENIAC (Electronic Numerical Integrator and Calculator) which was, at that time, the most complex electronic device in the world. The machine eliminated the need for moving parts, such as electrically controlled counter wheels, to represent digits and numbers. Instead, they adapted electronic flip-flop circuits and used electronic pulses to cause a change in vacuum tubes—on and off type switches with the "on" and "off" representing numbers. Since electronic pulses can move thousands of times faster than electromechanical devices, the concept behind the ENIAC was a real breakthrough in the development of computers for business applications.

The first high-speed electronic computer was installed in the Ballistic Research Laboratory at the Aberdeen Proving Grounds, Aberdeen, Maryland in 1946 (Figure P-21). It contained over 18,000 vacuum tubes and was capable of performing 5000, 10-decimal-digit calculations a second and multiplying at a speed of 300 calculations

Figure P-21 ENIAC, the first all-electronic digital computer, 1946. (Courtesy UNIVAC Division of the Sperry Rand Corporation.)

a second. The computer weighed over 30 tons and required more than 1500 square feet of floor space.

***Advances—ENIAC.*** When comparing the ENIAC to prior equipment developments—in particular, electromechanical computers and punched card equipment—the following significant advances were found.

1. Fast motion of electrons replaced slow movements of switches.
2. Much faster operating speeds (300 multiplications per second versus one per second for other machines).
3. Several operations could be combined into a single pass on the ENIAC.

Many of the major objections to earlier equipment had been answered by the first general purpose digital computer. Even though the machine was designed mainly for solving ballistics problems, it contained advancements that were adopted in computers designed for business applications.

***Deficiencies—ENIAC.*** Despite the significant advances, the ENIAC was still deficient for several reasons.

1. It lacked internal storage facilities.
2. It experienced difficulty reading instructions since they had to be hand wired (similar to wiring a control panel on punched card equipment).
3. It had to be tested extensively in order to have accurate output.

From these viewpoints, the machine was inflexible. To overcome these difficulties, it was necessary to have its program stored in a high-speed internal storage unit, referred to as primary storage or memory.

The stored program concept was developed in the 1940's by Dr. John von Neumann. He suggested in 1945 that operating instructions as well as data be stored inside the computer memory and that the computer be made to modify these instructions under program control. Subsequent computers were developed in the United States and Great Britain based on his important concepts. In fact, he set forth the concepts that were to fix the pattern of computer design for the subsequent decades in electronic data processing. For his invaluable contributions, he has been bestowed the title of "father of modern computers" by those in the field.

*The second computer (EDVAC), designed by Eckert and Mauchly, was an internally stored program machine.*

***EDVAC—Internally Programmed Machine.*** The second computer designed by Eckert and Mauchly was a completely internally programmed machine, designed to overcome a major limitation of the ENIAC. It was called the EDVAC (Electronic Discrete Variable Automatic Computer) and was started in 1946 and completed in 1952. The EDVAC was smaller in size (3500 vacuum tubes) than the ENIAC, but larger in capability. Not only was the machine a stored program machine but it also utilized the binary system for both data and instructions. The first program was a sorting routine designed by Dr. von Neumann who worked closely with Eckert and Mauchly.

***IAS.*** The outgrowth of the collaboration among these three men, together with the Moore School of Electrical Engineering and the Institute of Advanced Study of Princeton University, resulted in a proposal to the U.S. Ordinance Department to produce the IAS computer. This project was completed in 1952. Essentially, the computer was a punched paper tape input/output system that included such features as the binary number system, parallel arithmetic, and instruction commands. Credit for the basic principles used in the IAS computer goes to von Neumann.

***EDSAC.*** While the foregoing represent developments in the United States during the middle of this century, comparable advances were underway in England. The EDSAC (Electronic Delayed Storage Automatic Computer), utilizing many of the ideas proposed for the EDVAC, was constructed under the direction of M. V. Wilkes at the Mathematical Laboratory of the University of Cambridge in 1949. Mercury delay lines were used for storage, while input was in the form of punched paper tape and output was to a tape punch or teleprinter. In reality, the EDSAC represented the first stored program electronic computer.

***ACE.*** A second English computer that employed the ideas from the EDSAC and von Neumann was started in 1945 and completed in 1950 at the National Physics Laboratory in London. It was named the ACE (Automatic Computing Engine). Punched card input/output, delay line storage, and less than 1000 vacuum tubes comprised its major characteristics. The ACE was faster and more reliable than the EDSAC. Its notable contribution was the "two address code" for instructions. Each instruction contains both the location of the number or address to be operated upon plus the location of the next instruction. This programming procedure reduces the time needed to execute a computer program.

***Whirlwind I.*** The development of computer technology was given a significant boost by the construction of the Whirlwind I computer system at the Massachusetts Institute of Technology under the direction of Dr. Jay W. Forrester. In addition to being a stored program computer, it was capable of performing 32 distinct operations, including all arithmetic operations, shifting, and branching. Further developments included components found on many computer systems today.

Other computer projects were undertaken by various individuals, universities, and firms. However, the foregoing events represent the more important ones up to the early part of the 1950's. As can be seen from these developments, the most significant ones occurred in the United States and Great Britain, which provided the necessary thrust for the first-generation of business computers, starting with the UNIVAC I. The highlights of significant developments that led to the introduction of punched card equipment and computers are depicted in Figure P-22.

It should be pointed out that although many of the commonly used data processing terms are not discussed in considerable detail in this chapter, they will be covered in some depth in future chapters. A passing reference to these many computer terms will give the reader an overview of recent developments in a business data processing environment.

## FIRST-GENERATION COMPUTERS

*The contract for the first business computer—UNIVAC I —was received in 1951.*

The first firm to offer a business computer commercially was the Electronic Control Company, founded in 1946 by Eckert and Mauchly who resigned their positions at the University of Pennsylvania. (As noted previously, their firm ultimately became the UNIVAC Division of the Sperry Rand Corporation.) They were able to procure a contract from the National Bureau of Standards and proceeded to develop the UNIVAC I (UNIVersal Automatic Computer) in 1951.

***UNIVAC I.*** The UNIVAC I computer was a direct descendent of the ENIAC and the BINAC computer systems. Storage had a capacity of 1000 words of data or instructions, each consisting of 12 coded decimal digits or characters. The UNIVAC I (Figure P-23) could perform 45 different operations, handle alphabetic characters, and check for errors. The principal recording medium used to read and write data out of the system was metal-based magnetic tape.

The first UNIVAC, which was delivered to the Bureau of the Census, proved

| YEAR | INVENTOR | SIGNIFICANT DEVELOPMENT | DESCRIPTION |
|---|---|---|---|
| 3000 B.C. | — | Abacus | Calculating device |
| 1617 | Napier | Napier's Bones | Multiplication device |
| 1642 | Pascal | Adding machine | First mechanical adding machine |
| 1694 | Leibniz | Calculating device | First mechanical calculating machine |
| 1786 | J. H. Miller | — | First conceived idea of a scientific computing machine (on paper only) |
| 1842 | Babbage | Difference engine | Machine for calculating tables by means of differences |
| 1850 | Babbage | Analytical engine | Theoretical design for a stored program digital computer |
| 1890 | Hollerith | Punched card reader, punch, and sorter (80 columns) | Development of EAM equipment for processing census data |
| 1910 | Powers | Punched card, sorter, and tabulator (90 columns) | Further developments of EAM equipment |
| 1925 | Bush | Analog computer | First analog computer—basically it was mechanically operated |
| 1939 | Stibitz | Bell Model 1 | First semiautomatic computer, relay-type |
| 1944 | Aiken | Mark I | First general purpose digital computer |
| 1946 | Eckert, Mauchly | ENIAC | First use of electronic circuitry in a computer system |
| 1949 | Wilkes | EDSAC | First stored program electronic computer in England |
| 1950 | National Physics Laboratory (London) | ACE | First use of two address code |
| 1952 | Eckert, Mauchly | EDVAC | First use of acoustic delay line memory and binary mode in the United States |
| 1951–1952 | Remington Rand | UNIVAC I | First commercially available business computer |
| 1953 | Forrester | Whirlwind I | First use of magnetic-core memory |

Figure P-22 Significant historical developments for punched card machines and computers.

Figure P-23 UNIVAC I, first-generation electronic data processing system. (Courtesy UNIVAC Division of the Sperry Rand Corporation.)

to be a "real workhorse." The computer was used almost continuously, that is, 24 hours a day, 7 days a week for over 12 years before it was shipped to the Smithsonian Institute for exhibit. Because of its outstanding features—speed, memory capacity, and reliability, this model was sold to business firms. The General Electric Appliance Park in Louisville, Kentucky, became the first business user of the UNIVAC I in October 1954. During its life cycle, 48 UNIVAC I computer systems were installed.

After the UNIVAC I, the second production model computer was the CRC 102 (NCR 102), manufactured in 1952 by the Computer Research Corporation. The firm was absorbed later by the National Cash Register Company. The 102 was basically a scientific computer, meaning that it was not intended for business data processing.

The third piece of equipment available in the computer market was the IBM 701, developed in 1952. Despite the fact that it was a scientific-oriented computer, it helped the IBM Corporation develop a staff for selling business-oriented computers. In 1953, the IBM 702—a small, commercially oriented computer—and the IBM 650—a general-purpose computer with special business capabilities—were introduced. These were followed by a series of other models, specifically, the IBM 305, 704, 705, and 709.

***IBM 650.*** Of the several first-generation computers produced, the IBM 650 was the most successful, the first business application taking place in December 1954. It was capable of serving the needs of both scientific and business applications. During its lifetime, there were well over 1000 IBM 650's installed. Among its important features were vacuum tubes for electrical switches, magnetic drum memory, 2000 addressable words of 10 characters each, and punched card input/output. The wide acceptance of the 650 and other models established IBM as the leading producer of computers by 1955, a position it holds today.

*The most popular model of the first-generation computers was the IBM 650.*

The entry of computer manufacturers during the first-generation period was not restricted to Sperry Rand, National Cash Register, and IBM. Other large manufacturers included Burroughs, General Electric, Honeywell, and RCA. Still other firms entered the field. However, the foregoing list represents the important names in the field.

### Beginning Developments of Computers (First-Generation)

*Important developments of the first-generation computers (1952–1957) included:*
- *vacuum tubes*
- *magnetic drum and magnetic core*
- *buffering*
- *random access processing*
- *machine languages*

The first-generation of computers began in 1952 and lasted for six years. In retrospect, the success of the first-generation computers can be attributed to their ability in overcoming basic limitations experienced with the earlier experimental models. Their most important developments are given below.

***Vacuum Tubes.*** Although most of the first-generation computers were punched-card oriented, they employed vacuum tubes in their circuitry. This necessitated a need for considerable electric power. Regardless of the computer size, an enormous amount of heat was produced by the computer system. Air conditioning and humidity control overcame this problem.

***Magnetic Drum and Magnetic Core Utilized for Primary Storage.*** Magnetic drum was used initially for primary storage where the computer's program and data to be operated on are located. It was later replaced, to a limited degree, by magnetic core since core is much faster than drum.

***Buffering.*** Another important feature was buffering, which controls input, processing, and output in some logical sequence. Buffers serve as a temporary storage device for data being read in or out of the computer system. They allow the computer system to read in data or read out data more quickly since data are always available internally within the system. This is opposed to stopping the program each time and instructing it to perform the desired read, write, or print operation.

***Random Access Processing.*** A most important innovation of this first-generation period was immediate accessibility to stored data. In this random type of computer processing system, magnetic disk files were used for secondary storage or on-line computer files. For this generation, most machines could process data only in some serial or sequential order. Data had to be accumulated for some period of time and then processed. The time lag between the receipt of data and the final processing might take several days. On the other hand, the random concept of data processing allowed those business transactions to be posted as they occurred. In this manner, business data could always be up-to-date.

***Machine Languages.*** The programming of internally stored programs in primary storage was in the form of machine language. This refers to coding the individual program steps in terms of the language designed by the computer engineer.

The above significant developments and others for the first-generation computer are found in Figure P-28 along with succeeding generations.

## SECOND-GENERATION COMPUTERS

*The most popular model of the second-generation computers was the IBM 1401.*

With the rapid development of technological advances in electronic and solid-state physics, a second-generation of computers was developed. A proliferation of computer models to fit most small-, medium-, and large-scale requirements were marketed. The IBM 1401 (Figure P-24) led the field with over 17,000 installations. Two other models—IBM 1410 and 1440—proved to be popular models as well as the 1620's, 7070's, 7080's, and 7090's. Models that sold well for other manufacturers were: Burroughs—B-200 series, General Electric—GE-225, Honeywell—H-400, National Cash Register—NCR 315 and 500, Radio Corporation of America—RCA 301 and 501, Sperry Rand—SS 80/90 and UNIVAC 1004.

### Continuing Developments of Computers (Second-Generation)

The second-generation of computers were sold from 1958 to 1963, lasting 6 years like the first-generation. Many important developments were noted during this period. The most significant ones are discussed.

Figure P-24 IBM 1401 RAMAC, second-generation electronic data processing system. (Courtesy International Business Machines Corporation.)

*Important developments of the second-generation computers (1958–1963) included:*
- *transistors and diodes*
- *expanded magnetic core*
- *magnetic tape*
- *magnetic disk pack*
- *real-time and time-sharing capabilities*
- *modular or building block concept*
- *symbolic languages*

***Transistors and Diodes.*** The second-generation employed transistors, diodes, and printed circuit-board type wiring. These technical advances in the machine's components generated less heat, were more reliable, and were reduced in size. Not only was it possible to reduce significantly the physical size of the computer's hardware, but it also permitted an increase in efficiency, greater operating power, and lower cost per unit of throughput.

***Expanded Magnetic Core.*** For primary storage, magnetic core was extended to most computers. Internal operating speeds were also increased by improved core technology. However, a few computers did utilize a magnetic drum memory.

***Magnetic Tape.*** While many of the first-generation machines were card oriented, the second-generation made great use of high-speed magnetic tape units for reading and writing data. Magnetic tapes provided massive secondary data storage even though the data had to be processed sequentially. In addition, magnetic tape units provided storage at a very low cost—a most important consideration for the growth of computer systems.

***Magnetic Disk Pack.*** Further advances were made in the concept of random access data processing. Removable disk packs were developed. They allowed machine-readable files (secondary storage) to be stored for quick insertion into disk drives, comparable to that of magnetic tape files. Thus, files of accounts payable, accounts receivable, and inventory can always be available for processing current transactions.

***Real-Time and Time-Sharing Capabilities.*** Data transmission and communication devices were developed during this period for sending and receiving data from both local and remote data processing centers. By combining these devices and techniques within a computer system that utilized on-line storage devices, the concept of "on-line real-time" data processing was introduced. The SABRE system of American Airlines brought this concept into reality. With its reservation system, it is possible to inquire about the status of a specific flight and get an instantaneous feedback on the availability of the flight in question. Since this gigantic endeavor, the on-line real-time concept has been applied further to the implementation of management information systems. In a similar manner, enthusiasm for time sharing spread in the early 1960's to academic and research institutions, in particular, Dartmough College. Here, faculty and students developed a time-sharing program for a medium-sized GE computer and invented a simple programming language, called BASIC.

***Modular or Building Block Concept.*** The modular or "building block" concept was developed for designing internal circuitry and major pieces of equipment in computer systems. This permitted systems to be expanded as more capacity was needed. A system could be expanded with the growth pattern of the firm rather than being replaced completely by a new data processing system.

***Symbolic Languages.*** Significant improvements were made in programming. Instead of using the instructions and data codes defined by the computer designer, a symbolic representation of these was developed to simplify the programming process. For example, if the machine language operation code for add is 25, the symbolic representation might be ADD.

Other improvements for the second-generation computers included those relating to peripheral devices, such as increasing the speed of reading cards, punching cards, and printing output. Still other advances included built-in error detection and correction devices and improved programming techniques. The latter improvement reduced the need for computer operator intervention. The foregoing second-generation developments are shown in Figure P-28.

## THIRD-GENERATION COMPUTERS

*For third-generation computers, IBM continued to dominate the number of installations with its System/360 series.*

The third-generation computers represented additional technological advances from 1964 to 1969. IBM announced their System/360 series in 1964 as did RCA with their Spectra 70 series. All major equipment firms—Burroughs, Control Data, General Electric, Honeywell, National Cash Register, and Sperry Rand—developed a third-generation computer series line. (A typical third-generation NCR computer is shown in Figure P-25.) Many of these firms introduced small-scale computers to meet the needs of the smaller firm. The System/3 of IBM (Model 10 introduced in 1969) is such a system. Furthermore, the arrival of the mini-computer made some type of fast computing power available to even the smallest of firms. Many of these computer systems are operating currently.

### Continuing Developments of Computers (Third-Generation)

*Important developments of the third-generation computers (1964–1969) included:*
- *integrated circuits*
- *thin film and faster core memories*
- *expanded real-time and time-sharing capabilities*
- *multiprogramming and multiprocessing*
- *extension of building block concept*
- *higher-level languages*

Past advances, for the most part, were expanded and improved upon in the third-generation of computers. This will be apparent in the following sections.

***Integrated Circuits.*** Monolithic integrated circuitry and hybrid integrated circuitry were developed to replace much of the solid-state circuitry. Monolithic circuitry refers to placing all the elements of a circuit (transistors, resistors, and diodes) on one chip at a time. It was used in some models of RCA's Spectra 70 series. The hybrid circuitry, sometimes called "solid logic technology" (SLT), means producing transistors and diodes separately and then soldering them into place. This circuitry was used in the first of the third-generation computers—introduced in April 1964 by IBM for their System/360 series. These SLT components, shown in Figure P-26, require low voltage, produce very little heat, and are considerably more reliable than their counterparts in the past. Likewise, their size is extremely small, making it feasible to reduce the size of the computer's hardware. But more importantly, these miniaturized components reduce the electrical travel time within the circuits, thereby, increasing internal operating speeds.

***Thin Film and Faster Core Memories.*** By no means was the advancing technology limited to the computer's circuitry. Improved manufacturing techniques included the printing of circuits instead of wiring them. Thin film and faster core memories were introduced to increase internal operating speeds as well as to lower costs of production. Operating speeds are measured in billionths of a second.

Figure P-25 NCR century 100 third-generation electronic data processing system. (Courtesy The National Cash Register Company.)

Figure P-26 Solid logic technology (SLT) component. (Courtesy International Business Machines Corporation.)

Massive data storage capabilities became available to provide reliable and high-speed access to stored data.

***Expanded Real-Time and Time-Sharing Capabilities.*** Expansion in the areas of data collection, data communication, and data transmission permitted the utilization of remote terminals and display units that are on-line with a centralized computer facility. Not only are on-line real-time systems practical for most business firms but they are also very practical for smaller firms who can utilize time-sharing services for "now" information. In effect, the cost of having a computer to solve important business problems was low enough for any user, depending on the amount of sophistication required.

***Multiprogramming and Multiprocessing.*** Multiprogramming and multiprocessing techniques made significant strides with the third-generation computers. Executive control programs were developed which permitted several programs to be processed, in what appears to be simultaneous operation. This is known as multiprogramming. In addition to having this capability, computers are able to communicate with each other through multiprocessing. This allows computers of the same or related firms to communicate with each other so as to utilize the additional processing capacities of those machines that might otherwise stand idle.

***Extension of Building Block Concept.*** Another important characteristic was the expansion of the building block concept. There was greater upward and downward compatibility of components, which permitted greater flexibility in expanding computer systems without altering the basic systems. Most manufacturers incorporated this concept in their third-generation equipment. Of particular importance to the user is the ability to handle both business and scientific applications with equal facility. Many times, justification for the large outlays necessary for conversion to these new systems revolved around this issue.

***Higher-Level Languages.*** Refinements were also forthcoming in the area of computer programming. The introduction of new languages, such as PL/1 for the IBM System/360, increased the level of programming. Improvements upon established procedure-oriented languages—BASIC, COBOL, and FORTRAN—decreased the time it took to get a program operating. The use of time-sharing devices for computer testing helped to close the widening gap between the equipment and its effective utilization.

These and other significant developments for third-generation computers are set forth in Figure P-28.

## CURRENT-GENERATION COMPUTERS

*The current-generation computers are sometimes referred to as the 3.5-generation.*

The previous advancements are extremely impressive over the last two decades in the field of computer data processing. However, the current generation, sometimes called the 3.5-generation, has an equally impressive list of achievements. In June 1970, IBM announced its systems for the 1970's, the System/370 which is the successor to the highly successful System/360.

*Competition among equipment manufacturers has become more intensive for the current-generation computers.*

***Current Computer Series.*** Besides the IBM System/370—Models 135, 145, 155, 165 and 195—other computer manufacturers introduced new computer lines in 1970 and 1971. Honeywell Information Systems (which absorbed General Electric's computer operations, excluding time-sharing operations, in 1970) introduced three new systems—Models 115/2, 1015, and 2015. Burroughs new 700 line includes four series of models—B4700, B5700, B6700, and B7700. Its computer line incorporates the latest version of monolithic integrated circuits. RCA's new family of computers are the RCA 2, 3, 6, and 7. Monolithic circuitry technology has also been applied, which is the same basic Spectra architecture of their third-generation computers. However, their computer operations were absorbed by UNIVAC in 1971.

The National Cash Register Company expanded its Century computer line to include the Century 50 and 300 series, designed for small- to large-sized computer systems. UNIVAC's most recent additions are the large-scale system, the 1110, and the medium-scale system, the 9700. With these new families of 3.5-generation computers, true fourth-generation computers are not expected until the latter part of the 1970's. However, competition may cause an earlier announcement date.

*A measurement of current- and future-generation computers is in terms of mips (million instructions per second).*

***Current Supercomputers.*** The current offerings of the 3.5-generation machines are not restricted to small-, medium-, and large-scale computers. In fact, important gains have been made in the supercomputer field. Million instructions per second (mips) is the computer measurement of the 1970's as a variety of supercomputers are being marketed. These massive machines had been the exclusive province of the Control Data Corporation for several years after unhappy experiences by IBM with Stretch and UNIVAC with Larc in the late 1950's. IBM reentered with its giant 360/195 computer system. The 195 and CDC's 7600 supercomputer both operate at the rate of approximately 15 million instructions per second.

Control Data has marketed its STAR (STring ARay) processor which operates at about 100 mips. Its speed approximates the operating range for the stripped-down Illiac IV, built by Burroughs under a contract from the Advanced Research Projects Agency for the University of Illinois. Although these speeds are very impressive, Control Data expects a 1000 mips computer by the middle of the 1970's or a kilo mips computer while IBM is said to be planning a 250 mips entry about the same time or shortly thereafter.

IBM has calculated that the cost of 100,000 multiplications on the IBM 704 (first-generation) was $1.38 while the same cost on the IBM 7090 (second-generation) was $0.25. The same cost with the third-generation machines is a few pennies. Comparable costs for current computers noted above are considerably less, especially when a supercomputer is used as a benchmark.

*The computer utility concept is analogous to any present-day utility firm, such as gas and electric. It provides all the services needed for data processing operations.*

***Computer Utility Concept.*** The need for this super-computing ability is apparent in the computer utility concept. A computer utility is a data processing service organization that provides a wide range of computer services—time sharing, remote batch processing, and local batch processing—through its large-scale computing power, large data banks, and vast data communication networks. In reality, the computer utility surpasses in capability what can be achieved with most individual in-house computer systems. Such firms as Control Data, through its network of national and international data centers (CYBERNET), are making sizable gains in implementing this enlarged concept of the traditional service bureau. Control Data's CYBERPAK allows customers to acquire the equivalent of from $\frac{1}{16}$ to a complete CDC super-scale computer system with full support services and a wide range of proprietary application packages. Thus, a computer utility acts like any other utility firm (such as gas, electric, and water). It provides all the computer services that are needed for an automated data processing system within the firm.

For small businesses, the largest computers in the world are now as accessible as the nearest telephone plug. In real estate, for example, there is a data bank with instant readings on available properties across the country. Likewise, there is Telecredit's credit checking service for merchants. Also, there is General Electric's Medinet package of data processing services for hospitals. The computer utility concept thus makes a computer accessible to the smallest user.

*Important developments of the current-generation computers (1970–present) include:*
- *microscopic integrated circuits*
- *microprogramming*
- *faster memories and mass storage*
- *improved software*

**Current Developments of Computers (Current-Generation)**

Current-generation advances for the 1970's are equal in importance to those of the prior three generations. In addition to the fast speeds of large-scale computers noted previously, many of the more important advances are noted below. By no means do these features represent the end-state of computer developments. When compared to those envisioned in the 21st century, these may be small by comparison.

***Microscopic Integrated Circuits.*** The IBM System/370 series employs microscopic integrated circuits or monolithic systems technology (MST). These tiny chips have fewer connections and pack more circuits on their surfaces (8 times more) than previous components in the 360 series. For example, the chips used in the Model 155 contain 2 to 8 complete circuits, operating in the billionth of a second range. These microscopic circuits make greater operating speeds possible. The computing process of the System/370 line is several times faster than its predecessor, System/360. The IBM System/370 Model 165 is shown in Figure P-27.

Figure P-27 IBM System/370 Model 165, current-generation electronic data processing system. (Courtesy International Business Machines Corporation.)

Perhaps, the most impressive advancement of the current System/370 line is Model 145, a medium-sized computer. It is the first electronic computer with a main memory and all of its circuitry made entirely of monolithic circuits or silicon chips—each one-eighth inch square—that carry more than 1400 microscopic memory circuit elements. The significance of this semiconductor memory lies in the switch from the former memory storage made of little donut-shaped magnetic cores, allowing an enormous reduction (about 50%) in storage space and power requirements. The result is much the same as if, in a large filing system, a new process was introduced that reduced the size of file cards automatically to microscopic proportions for storage but made them instantly retrievable in fully readable form.

In addition to the MST circuits, several manufacturers are now building computers that employ large-scale integration (LSI). These tiny chips are usually no more than one-tenth of an inch square. Each is a maze of microscopic electronic circuits that can contain more than 5000 transistors or electronic switches. Burroughs Corporation employs LSI circuits in its Illiac IV which is able to do the work accomplished by 128 third-generation computers.

***Microprogramming.*** An important advancement of the 3.5-computer generation is greater application of microprogramming. The third-generation, such as the IBM System/360 and RCA Spectra 70's, used it to achieve downward compatibility, that is, to develop rather complex control sequences that permit a small computer to have the same instruction repertoire that is used in larger machines of the same

| SIGNIFICANT DEVELOPMENTS OCCURRED IN THE FOLLOWING AREAS: | FIRST-GENERATION COMPUTERS 1952–1957 (6 YEARS) | SECOND-GENERATION COMPUTERS 1958–1963 (6 YEARS) | THIRD-GENERATION COMPUTERS 1964–1969 (6 YEARS) | CURRENT-GENERATION COMPUTERS 1970–PRESENT |
|---|---|---|---|---|
| Switching devices | Vacuum tubes | Transistors and diodes | Integrated circuits | Miscroscopic integrated circuits |
| Primary storage | Magnetic drum<br>Magnetic core ⟶ | ⟶ | ⟶<br>Thin film ⟶ | ⟶<br>⟶<br>Large scale integration |
| Internal operating speeds | Milliseconds | Microseconds | Nanoseconds ⟶ | ⟶<br>Picoseconds (under development) |
| Secondary storage | Magnetic drum ⟶<br>Magnetic tape ⟶<br>Magnetic disk ⟶ | ⟶ | ⟶<br>Magnetic strip ⟶ | ⟶<br>Laser mass storage |
| Buffering | Input/Output devices | Input/Output channels ⟶ | ⟶ | ⟶ |
| Processing modes | Sequential ⟶<br>Random access ⟶ | ⟶<br>Real-time ⟶<br>Time sharing ⟶<br>Multiprocessing ⟶ | ⟶ | ⟶ |
| Building block concept | | Modularity ⟶ | ⟶ | ⟶ |
| Programming | Machine languages | Symbolic languages<br>Multiprogramming ⟶ | ⟶<br>Higher-level languages ⟶ | ⟶<br>Microprogramming |
| Outside processing | Service bureau ⟶ | ⟶ | ⟶<br>Time-sharing centers ⟶<br>Computer utility ⟶ | ⟶ |

Figure P-28 Significant computer developments—past and present. The arrow (⟶) denotes continued use and improvement.

line. Basically, microprogramming involves the very rapid assembly and use of complex control or processing routines.

***Faster Memories and Mass Storage.*** Other important advances include the associative memory and the laser mass storage. An associative memory is one whose storage locations are identified by their contents rather than by their positions. It can show a substantial improvement in operations that are performed on large amounts of data. For example, it is estimated that sorting comprises from 25 to 50% of the overall computer workload for business data processing systems. When one realizes that in terms of present-day technology the production cost ratio of associative memories to conventional memories is about 4 to 1, and that with large-scale integration (LSI) the cost ratio is about 2 to 1, it becomes clear that associative memories have a tremendous potential for certain functions.

Laser mass secondary storage is a magnetic tape strip medium in which small holes are burned by the laser beam. The holes are not refillable, which means that the storage lacks the ability to erase or rewrite. However, where records are fixed or can be updated in ledger form—that is, the user can leave blanks anywhere in his records and later add information—a laser memory system can store literally many billions of bits of data for an on-line reference.

***Improved Software.*** The foregoing advances are basically hardware. Corresponding improvements have been made in software (programs and routines) although they are not as noticeable. For example, 14 new instructions have been added to the IBM System/360 repertoire for the System/370. Present 360 software can be run on the 370 series, except for a few time-dependent or device-dependent programs. A system generator (SYSGEN) run is all that is required to convert to the System/370.

Further advances appear to be very promising. Projected for release by IBM in the mid-1970's is an automated programming system that optically scans a flowchart. It will be capable of producing simple FORTRAN instructions.

As with the previous generations of computers, the foregoing significant developments and others are summarized in Figure P-28.

## SUMMARY

The evolution of recording techniques and manual entry computing devices has been a long and gradual process over the centuries. The same cannot be said for punched card machines and electronic computers. The first punched card system was developed by the Bureau of the Census for its 1890 census. Variations of these basic pieces of equipment are used today.

In the area of computers, the basic concepts of computers were formulated much earlier. The technology of the day did not permit their implementation. The advancing technology of the 20th century permitted the building of the first analog computer, followed by the digital computer. In a relatively short period of time, the first commercial computer—the UNIVAC I—was installed in 1954 for business data processing. The advances in the electronic data processing field from that time to the present day has exceeded the inventors' wildest dreams. Despite the explosive growth of the computer industry today, there appears to be no end in sight. The projected computer market today may prove to be small in comparison with sales of the 21st century. At that time, the computer field is expected to be the largest of all industries.

## *QUESTIONS*

1. What brought about the development of numbering systems over the centuries? Explain.
2. How important was the development of the abacus? Explain.
3. Explain the method of calculating using Napier's Bones.
4. Contrast the devices developed by Pascal and Leibniz.

5. If Charles Babbage never actually finished the machinery on which he worked, of what importance are his contributions?
6. (a) What was the first application of punched cards?
   (b) What type of equipment was used?
7. Enumerate the important contributions of the following pioneers in the development of data processing equipment:
   (a) Frank Baldwin and Willgodt Odhner
   (b) William Burroughs
   (c) James Ritty
   (d) Dorr Felt
   (e) Jay Monroe
   (f) Howard Aiken
   (g) J. Eckert and John Mauchly
   (h) John von Neumann
8. What are the basic differences between the Hollerith method of punched cards and that of Powers?
9. Were the first computers analog or digital machines?
10. What were the basic limitations of the first computers? How were they overcome?
11. What are the principal developments that distinguish each generation of electronic computers?
12. What impact have the principal developments of electronic computers had on business? Discuss.

# I

# INTRODUCTION TO BUSINESS DATA PROCESSING

## CHAPTER ONE

# Business Data Processing Concepts and Systems

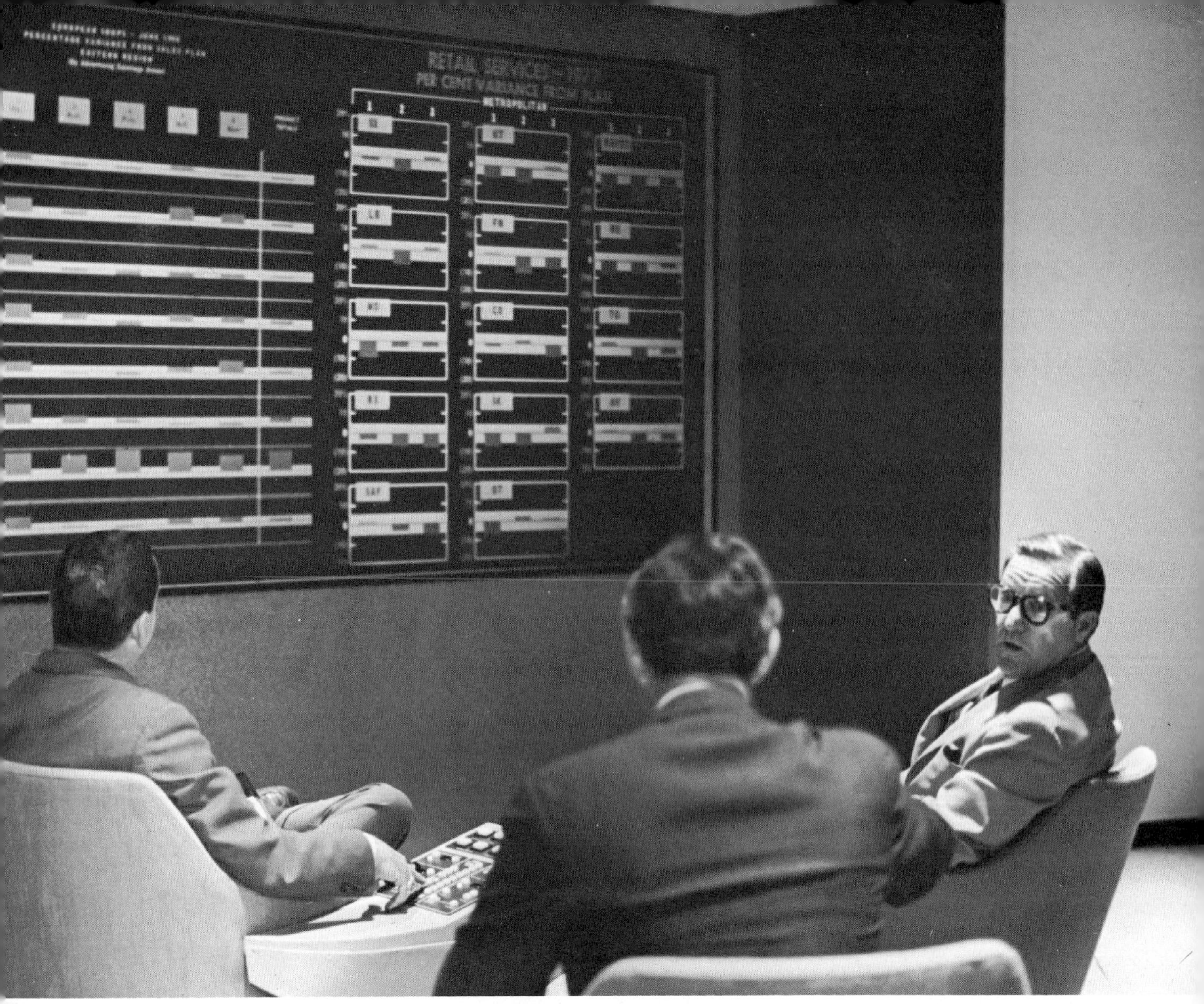


*Before undertaking an investigation of business data processing, it is helpful to have an understanding of its basic principles and concepts. This background provides a foundation for exploring the important approaches to business data processing systems, in particular, real-time management information systems (MIS). The management control center, illustrated for real-time MIS, will become an integral part of the decision-making process via its "paperless" output. (Courtesy Information Management International Corporation.)*

"Business data processing system" has several meanings to those in the field of EAM (electric accounting machines—punched card equipment) and EDP (electronic data processing—computers). If applied on the microlevel to business activities, it has the general connotation of manual and mechanical office procedures. When used on the intermediate level, it is applicable to procedures that involve the computer, though not too intensively. Although the foregoing approaches are of interest to us, the more important meaning of business data processing system is its application to the business as a whole, that is, to employ modern methods, procedures, and computer technology. From this macro viewpoint, business systems are management systems since they provide meaningful information with which to plan, organize, direct, and control the firm's operations.

Although our concern is an evaluation of business data processing systems—specifically management information systems (MIS)—it should be pointed out that past data processing systems were concerned with the internal operations of the firm. A management information system places additional emphasis on data describing the economic environment in which the firm operates. Of prime importance is information about markets in which the firm operates, current knowledge of its customers and competitors, availability of capital, capabilities of available personnel, knowledge concerning sources of supply, and other important matters affecting the firm. Thus, an all inclusive discussion of management information systems must consider both internal and external data.

This chapter defines data processing terms, explores the sources of internal data, discusses the basic data processing functions and important basic systems concepts, and reviews several specific types of business data processing systems. A desirable approach to business data processing is investigated—specifically, the total systems concept. A real-time management information system, the closest to the total systems concept in use currently, is related to other systems for comparative analysis. Also, future design considerations for business data processing systems are discussed.

## BUSINESS DATA PROCESSING—BASIC TERMS

*Business data processing centers around moving large amounts of data from input to output or storage with very little manipulation.*

Many activities in business firms, governmental agencies, education institutions, and the like revolve around the processing of business and scientific data. Throughout this book, the subject matter is oriented toward business data processing and not scientific data processing. Most business operations require the handling of large quantities of data. The problem, then, is one of utilizing fast and efficient procedures to handle these data. This is particularly true in terms of reading, storing, and printing out the required results. On the other hand, scientific data processing usually does not require the reading or printing of large quantities of data. Instead, it requires extremely fast handling and manipulation of data in the form of complex and drawn-out calculations. Thus, business data processing is concerned with moving large amounts of data from input to output or storage with very little manipulation while scientific data processing does just the reverse; it employs small amounts of input and output and makes great use of calculative ability.

*Data are unstructured facts that provide the necessary inputs to a system.*

***Data.*** The term "data" (plural of datum) is defined as unstructured facts. It is the unstructured raw material of data processing. As shown in Figure 1-1, it provides the necessary inputs to a system.

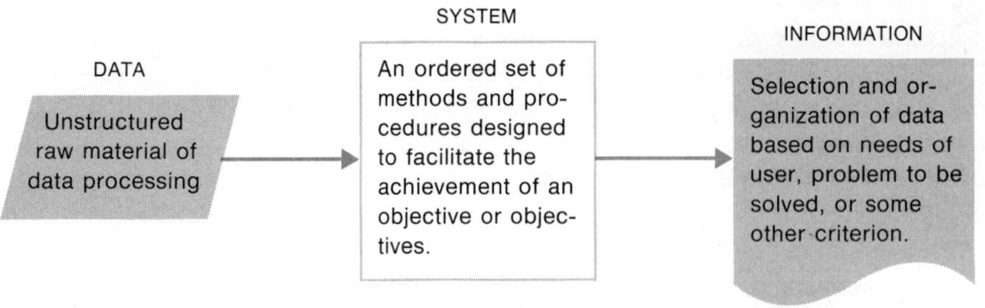


Figure 1-1 An effective data processing system extracts the required data to produce meaningful information.

*Information is selected data that is meaningful output from a system.*

***Information.*** Information can be defined as selected data. The selection and organization process may be based upon the needs of the user, particular problem to be solved, or some other criterion. Information, as illustrated in Figure 1-1, is the output of a system. For example, a telephone book is a collection of data. A specific number in that book becomes information when a user refers to it.

*A system is an ordered set of methods and procedures that facilitates the achievement of an objective(s).*

***System.*** A system is basically defined as an ordered assemblage of methods and procedures designed to facilitate the achievement of an objective or objectives. To state it more simply, it is a means of accomplishing something. The primary function of a data processing system is the conversion of data to information that will further the firm's objectives (Figure 1-1). If the information compiled by the system does not enhance its objectives, there is little point in making the conversion. Otherwise, information is compiled for its own sake.

## BUSINESS DATA PROCESSING SYSTEM DEFINED

*Business data processing system is the handling, manipulating, and recording required to convert business data into timely and meaningful information.*

Since our concern is business data processing, it can be described in a very broad sense; that is, it is the processing of any business data. A business data processing system is defined as the handling, manipulating, and recording required to convert business data into timely and meaningful information in order to help the firm accomplish its objectives. In the past, these tasks were referred to as "record keeping." The advent of punched card equipment, computers, and more sophisticated data processing equipment have witnessed the replacement of the term "record keeping" with "business data processing system."

## INFORMATION AND THE MANAGEMENT FUNCTIONS

As was demonstrated in the Prologue, the demands of the times brought about the need for processing business data in order to extract meaningful information. When information needs are considered in light of the real world today, they are classified as those that originate inside the firm and those that are external to the firm. Both these broad categories are vital to the firm's operations.

*Information is vital for performing the management functions of:*
- *planning*
- *organizing*
- *directing*
- *controlling*

Information, as depicted in Figure 1-2, is essential for effectively performing the management functions of planning, organizing, directing, and controlling. It is of vital importance for short-, intermediate-, and long-term goals. Management needs a fairly accurate measurement of the sales and cost factors of its business enterprise. It must continuously strive in two directions at the same time; that is, it must maximize its income through higher selling prices and/or larger inventory turnover and minimize the costs of its products and/or services. In short, it wants that combination of selling prices, turnover, costs, and profit per unit that will provide

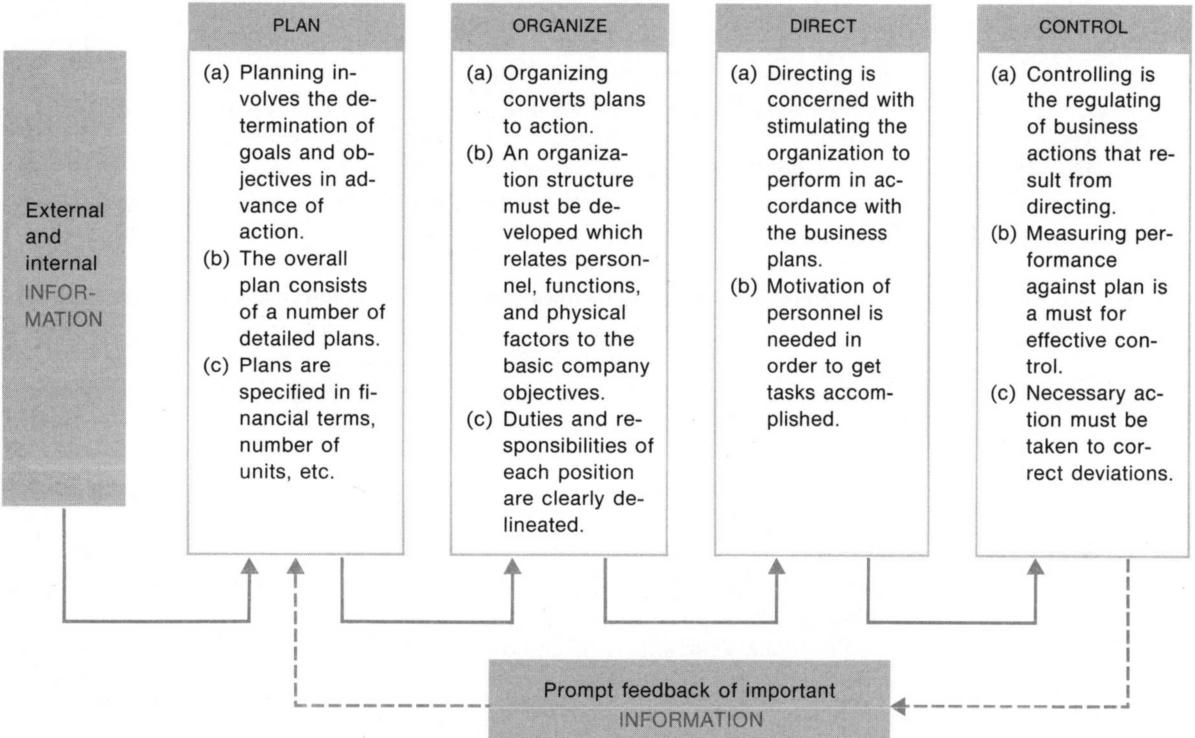


Figure 1-2 Information is vital for performing the management functions effectively.

the highest return on its stockholder's capital. Given adequate knowledge of these essential facts, management can rely more on deductive or analytical judgment and less on guesses and intuitive judgment, which it uses when many of the relevant facts are missing. It should be remembered that many wrong decisions over time have been the result of insufficient or inadequately processed information. Thus the need for accurate and timely information is paramount.

*Planning involves the determination of goals and objectives.*

***Planning Function.*** The act of planning may be quite informal for a small firm. In medium- and large-sized firms, it is generally very formal where there is an overall scheme that consists of a number of detailed plans. To be specific, planning activities for a typical manufacturing firm include decisions concerning product lines, marketing activities, inventories, purchasing, research, production, manpower, financial resources, exports, and similar items. For a complete business plan, the physical levels as well as the corresponding dollar amounts need to be determined. This information is captured quantitatively in flexible budgets—another name for a formalized plan. While the budgets for the coming year will be extremely detailed, the ones for the next several years will be more general. Nevertheless, the starting point for budgets is reliable current financial information. Before the plans can be finalized, they must be coordinated with the firm's objectives, policies, and procedures to insure compatibility.

***Organizing Function.*** Once the plans are placed into effect, there must be a mechanism or organization that is adapted to the execution of these plans. An

*Organizing is concerned with developing a logical framework or structure to carry out the plans.*

organization structure must be developed which relates people, functions, and physical factors to the basic objectives. Duties and responsibilities must be clearly set forth within this framework. Demand for reliable information is just as great for this function as for the planning function.

*Directing involves the motivation and stimulation of organization members toward accomplishing the plans.*

***Directing Function.*** Directing or activating the firm is equal in importance to the other managerial functions. It is concerned with motivating or stimulating the organization to undertake action according to the business plan. As such, it deals with the dissemination of information in the form of orders and the acceptance and execution of these orders. Whatever action results from the directing function forms the basis for inputting information to the control function.

*Controlling is comparing actual results with the original plans and taking corrective action where necessary.*

***Controlling Function.*** Without the necessary information for proper coordination of the firm's activities, management will find it difficult to control according to the plans. Control consists mainly of overseeing and comparing actual results with those that were originally forecast. Control devices can include the following: use of standards; variances from the budgeted amounts; return on investment analysis; breakeven, cost, volume, and contribution analyses; and ratio analyses. These typical management control devices permit a comparison of actual data with planned data, indicating favorable or unfavorable results. Management is concerned with those variances—over and under—that exceed a stated percent. This timely information provides feedback to the appropriate levels of management for review and action.

*Feedback is forwarding critical information to the proper personnel for modifying the plans.*

***Feedback Principle.*** The information feedback principle is one of the most important management concepts because it governs everything performed by individuals, groups, and machines in the process of adjusting to one another. (The familiar mechanical example of this principle at work is the common thermostat where temperature and furnace interact continually to keep heat at a predetermined level.) For this principle to operate effectively, there is a great need for accurate information.

*External information is furnished to:*
- *customers*
- *vendors*
- *governmental agencies*
- *stockholders*
- *unions*

***Usefulness of External Information.*** If internal information is accurately compiled, there should be no problem in meeting external demands. These include processed output to various governmental agencies, stockholders, unions, and other legitimate bodies. Some of the firm's reports must be furnished to governmental agencies. These include: income taxes—federal, state, and local; witholding taxes—federal and state; social security taxes—employees and employer; sales taxes; and manufacturer's excise taxes. Business firms must also furnish annual reports to stockholders, render invoices to customers, and pay bills of creditors.

*Internal information can be a source of power in that it gives management the ability to out-maneuver their competitors at critical times.*

***Usefulness of Internal Information.*** For effective internal operations and external reporting, reliable information is a must. There is a growing awareness that accurate and timely business information is a vital resource of the firm and that an improved business data processing system is a means of providing the needed information. Many top managers are finding that information is a source of power. It gives them the ability to out-maneuver their competitors at critical times, especially with the introduction of newer and better products. If the business data processing system does not have access to the information necessary for management to run its own operations effectively, an "out-of-control" condition may result from which the firm might never recover. An examination of those firms who have experienced difficult times over the years will verify this important point.

## SOURCES OF DATA

*Internal sources of data operating within the firm include:*
- *marketing*
- *research and development*
- *engineering*
- *manufacturing*
- *purchasing*
- *receiving*
- *stock control*
- *shipping*
- *accounting*
- *personnel*

Having answered the question of why the firm processes data, it is advisable to investigate the sources of data operating within the firm before examining the basic data processing functions. Data are generated as result of daily operations and interaction with other functions. Although most activities are related to other internal functions, there is a need to relate activities to external groups, namely, customers, vendors, bank(s), and governmental agencies. As indicated in Figure 1-3, there are several basic business operations to be found in a typical manufacturing firm. Because these key operations are interrelated, large masses of data are generated on literally hundreds of different forms in medium and large firms. Many of these operating forms serve as a basis for producing reports that are necessary in making managerial decisions.

The chart in Figure 1-3 illustrates more than the basic flow of goods through a firm. It shows other important activities—the information flow necessary to produce the goods. Likewise, there is the important feedback of critical information to the

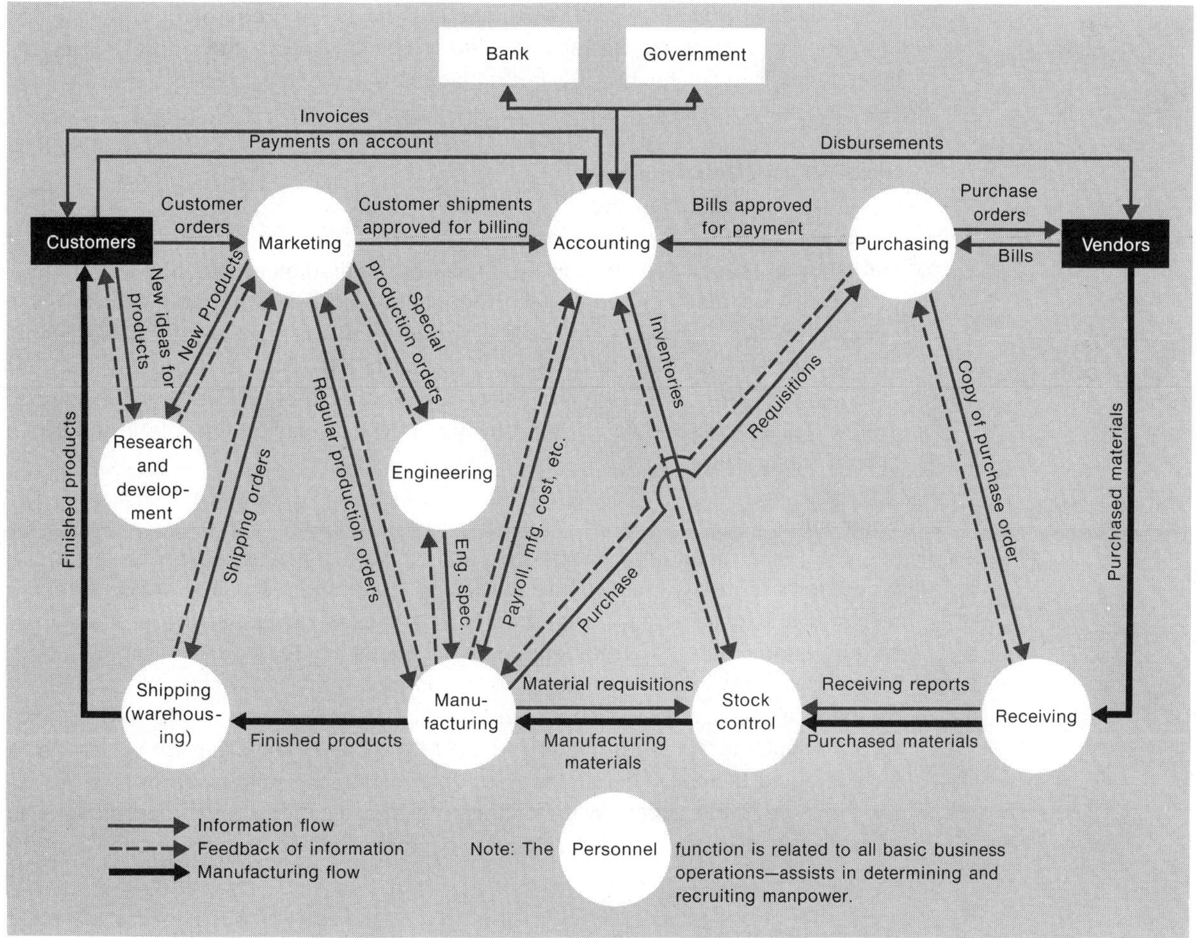


Figure 1-3 The sources of data for the basic business operations of a typical manufacturing firm.

appropriate levels of management for controlling operations. These important aspects regarding information will be set forth below along with the source of data for each basic operation. Even though this chart shows the operations of a manufacturing firm, many of these are found in other firms that market goods and services.

### Marketing

*Marketing sources of data are:*
- *sales orders*
- *sales slips*
- *contracts*
- *bids*
- *back orders*
- *change orders*

The primary job of the marketing department is to contact potential customers and sell merchandise through salesmen, advertising, and special promotions. If products are sold by a salesman, a multicopy *sales order* is originated by him or the order section of the marketing department. Copies are distributed as follows: original copy to customer for acknowledging order; duplicate copies to the salesman and to the manufacturing, stock control, shipping, and accounting departments. In addition, the marketing department may prepare other forms, such as *contracts, bids, back orders,* and *change orders*.

Retail sales other than regular cash transactions are recorded normally on a *sales slip* and are prepared by sales personnel. The original copy is given to the customer and other copies are distributed to the shipping, stock control, and accounting departments. Other sales documents can be prepared by various types of selling institutions. No matter what kind of firm is involved, the marketing department generally starts the product information flow in the firm, thereby being an initial source of data within the firm.

### Research and Development

*R & D source of data is the research and development order.*

Often the marketing department receives inquiries regarding a new product. It will initiate a *research and development* (*R & D*) *order* for its development if marketing prospects look promising. Similarly, the marketing research section may have their own ideas on what new products should be developed. This, too, will result in an R & D order. Other times, another firm will want to utilize the talents and expertise of the firm for pooling research talents. This is necessary in order to obtain a larger contract which neither firm is capable of undertaking individually. In the final analysis, research and development can play a vital role in the firm's growth rate.

### Engineering

*Engineering sources of data are:*
- *engineering blueprints*
- *bills of materials*

Before manufacturing operations can commence, it is necessary to design the products as agreed upon by the marketing department in conjunction with the research and development department. This means designing the product from scratch after which the engineering specifications are forwarded to the manufacturing department. The *engineering blueprints* form the basis for producing the parts, subassemblies, frames, and the like. The requirements for the product to be manufactured are summarized on *bills of materials.* This forms the basis for exploding bills of materials, that is, determining the number of detailed items for the production order. With engineering specifications and appropriate bills of materials prepared, these data can be forwarded to the production control department.

### Manufacturing

The manufacture of finished products involves many steps. Not only must plant, equipment, and tools be provided but also appropriate personnel must be hired

Manufacturing sources of data are:
- production orders
- purchase requisitions
- materials requisitions
- periodic production reports
- tool orders
- material usage reports
- material scrappage reports
- inspection reports
- labor analysis reports
- cost analysis reports
- production progress reports

and trained to utilize the manufacturing facilities. Raw materials and goods-in-process must be available as needed. Production must be planned, scheduled, routed, and controlled for output that meets certain standards. The effective management of this area, then, is a study unto itself.

The firm's products can be produced for finished goods in anticipation of demand, manufactured upon receipt of customer's orders, or some combination of the two. If goods are being produced to order, a sales order copy, in many cases, may be the *production order* (regular or special). The usual arrangement is to have the production planning or control department initiate action on factory orders. The production order is also distributed to the stock control, shipping, and accounting departments. The original copy is kept in the production department files.

Referring to Figure 1-3, manufacturing materials can be obtained from within or outside the firm. If a *purchase requisition* is prepared, it is forwarded to the purchasing department for vendor purchase. On the other hand, if materials are available from the stock control department, a *materials requisition* is prepared. Other records and forms, found within the manufacturing function, are *periodic production reports, tool orders, material usage reports, material scrappage reports, inspection reports, labor analysis reports, cost analysis reports,* and *production progress reports.*

**Purchasing**

Purchasing sources of data are:
- requests for quotation
- purchase orders

The purchasing function is concerned with procuring raw materials, equipment, supplies, utilities, as well as other products and services required to meet the firm's operating needs. Depending upon the size of the firm, the purchasing function is generally centralized in one department—the purchasing department. Its basic purpose is to service those basic operations, especially manufacturing, that must buy from the outside. The procurement process generally begins with the completion of the purchase requisition which is prepared in duplicate. One is forwarded to the purchasing department and one is retained by the originator.

Based on the purchase requisition form, the purchasing department locates and determines the supplier(s) from whom the order is to be filled. If the desired information is not available, the buyer may send a *request for quotation* to prospective vendors. Once the outside supplier has been determined, a *purchase order* is typed and mailed to the vendor. It contains the items to be shipped, prices, specifications, terms, and shipping conditions. Generally, the original is forwarded to the vendor and duplicate copies are distributed to the purchasing, receiving, stock control, accounting, and preparing departments.

**Receiving**

Receiving sources of data are:
- receiving reports
- inspection records

As soon as goods are received from suppliers, they are checked and verified against the copy of the original purchase order by the receiving department. Once the receiving clerk is satisfied that the goods correspond to those on the purchase order, he prepares a *receiving report,* noting any discrepancies between the order and actual material received. Sometimes, an *inspection record* may be prepared by the receiving department along with the receiving report. Copies of both are sent to those departments, namely, purchasing, stock control, manufacturing, and accounting that have need of such information. A carbon copy is retained by the receiving department.

Goods are delivered by the receiving department to the stock control department or any other department who has ordered them. Generally, the department that physically takes possession of the materials acknowledges receipt by signing a copy of the receiving report.

### Stock Control

*Stock control source of data is the inventory or stock records.*

The function of the stock control or the stores department is to store and protect all materials and supplies that are not required for current usage. The transfer-in of materials from an outside vendor to the stores department is documented by the receiving report mentioned earlier. The transfer-out of goods to the manufacturing department is authorized by the materials requisition, also noted previously. Materials are issued in response to current manufacturing needs.

A most important source of data is the *inventory records* or *stock records* maintained by the department. Since it is responsible for materials in and out of stock, it has all the necessary data for determining inventories. Stock records may be in the form of visual records, punched cards, or computer storage. If stored on-line, input/output devices are generally used in keeping inventory data up-to-date.

Stock control has the added function of replacing stock when it reaches a minimum level, which is often referred to as a reorder point. The stores clerk prepares a purchase requisition for the specific materials and forwards it to the purchasing department for appropriate action. In essence, the stock control department is an important source of data. It keeps the basic business functions operating in a manner that is compatible with the firm's objectives.

### Shipping

*Shipping sources of data are:*
- *shipping orders*
- *bills of lading*

Once the customer order has been manufactured or finished goods are available in the warehouse, they are ready for shipment. The finished products must be packed, labeled, and transported to the customer. The *shipping order,* which authorizes shipment, is delivered with or in advance of the goods. If delivery is made directly to the customer, he will acknowledge receipt of goods by signing a copy of the shipping order which is then filed in the shipping office.

Shipments that are made via public carriers must be accompanied by a *bill of lading* which is actually a contract between the consignor and the carrier. There is one copy each for the customer and the public carrier, and a third copy is filed in the shipping department as proof of shipment.

### Accounting

*Accounting sources of data are:*
- *customer invoices*
- *cash receipts journal*
- *statement of accounts*
- *time cards*
- *payroll checks*
- *voucher checks*

After the required basic business operations have been performed by the shipment of finished products, the accounting department must prepare *customers' invoices*. These not only serve as a record of charges but also are the basis on which the seller can legally claim payment for goods or services. Generally, the first two copies are sent to the customer while remaining copies are distributed to the marketing department, salesman, and held in the accounting department's billing file.

Depending upon the terms of the invoice, payments are received from customers which are deposited in the firm's bank account. These payments are recorded in the *cash receipts journal* as documented evidence of their receipt by the firm. Periodically, *statement of accounts* are mailed to inform customers on the status of their accounts. The usual time for mailing statements is at the end of each month. Whenever there are a large number of accounts, cycle billing is used to spread the workload throughout the month with approximately 20 cycles (which corresponds roughly to the number of working days in a month).

In addition to billing and collecting, the accounting department is concerned with disbursing funds, the major types being for payroll and for goods and services. *Time cards* are the originating source for paying salaries and wages. They may also be used for making labor distribution charges to various departments. *Payroll checks* and *earnings statements* are the net result of payroll procedures.

The second type of disbursements involves checking the vendor's invoice against the purchase order and receiving reports initially. Upon approval of payment by the purchasing department, *voucher checks* are prepared. A voucher check is a check with an attached voucher that contains sufficient space for date, purchase order number, vendor number, description, amount, discount, and net payment. The first copy is mailed to the payee on designated days of the month according to stated terms of the vendor's invoice and duplicate copies are used for data processing. When processing is complete, they are filed.

The foregoing accounting functions are not complete until all legitimate governmental forms have been prepared and the proper voucher checks drawn for the respective amounts due. Federal, state, and local governments require the preparation of specific tax forms. These include *federal income tax returns, reports on social security taxes withheld* (employer and employee), *federal and state unemployment compensation returns, state income tax returns, personal property tax returns,* and *city income tax returns.* Other governmental information returns that form the basis for statistical data on the United States are also required. In the final analysis, government requirements can place a substantial load over and beyond the normal data needed for the firm's internal operations.

### Personnel

*Personnel sources of data are:*
- *personnel history and promotion records*
- *personnel requisition forms*

Although the personnel function is not shown graphically in Figure 1-3, it is interconnected with all the basic business operations shown. Its basic task is to determine personnel needed in the present and future, thereby recruiting the necessary manpower. Placing the right man in the right job can be an arduous task. However, this undertaking can be lightened by having a combined personnel and payroll file on-line which can assist in recruiting personnel internally for new positions before going to outside sources. Various personnel forms can be employed for this function, such as *personnel history and promotion records* and *personnel requisition forms*. The type of forms will vary, depending upon the prevailing conditions.

## BASIC DATA PROCESSING FUNCTIONS

*Basic data processing functions can be defined in two ways:*
- *input-storage-processing-control-output (ISPCO) cycle*
- *originating-recording-classifying-manipulating-summarizing-communicating (data processing) cycle*

Having explored the sources of data operating within the firm, we shall now discuss the basic data processing functions or steps necessary to produce the required information for the firm's functional areas. From the time input data are received and until they are available in their final output form, there is a processing cycle that the data must pass through for meaningful output. As will be seen, there are two ways of describing the basic data processing functions.

### ISPCO Cycle

*Input-storage-processing-control-output (ISPCO) cycle is a meaningful way of identifying the important elements of a computer system.*

The input-storage-processing-control-output (ISPCO) cycle is a meaningful way of identifying the essential elements of a data processing system. Regardless of the system employed—manual, mechanical, punched card, or computer—these operational functions must be performed. Data must be processed through a controlled system in order to produce usable information.

When applying the ISPCO cycle concept to a computer system, its major components are linked together, as illustrated in Figure 1-4. These components are given below.

1. *Input* data are read by various reading devices.
2. *Storage* is available as high speed, primary storage (used for storing program instructions and data) or slower secondary storage (used for storing file data).
3. *Processing* of program instructions and data is accomplished through the arithmetic/logical unit.
4. *Control* over processing is provided by the computer's control unit.
5. *Output* information is produced by various recording and printing devices.

This cycle approach will be discussed in detail in Chapter 5.

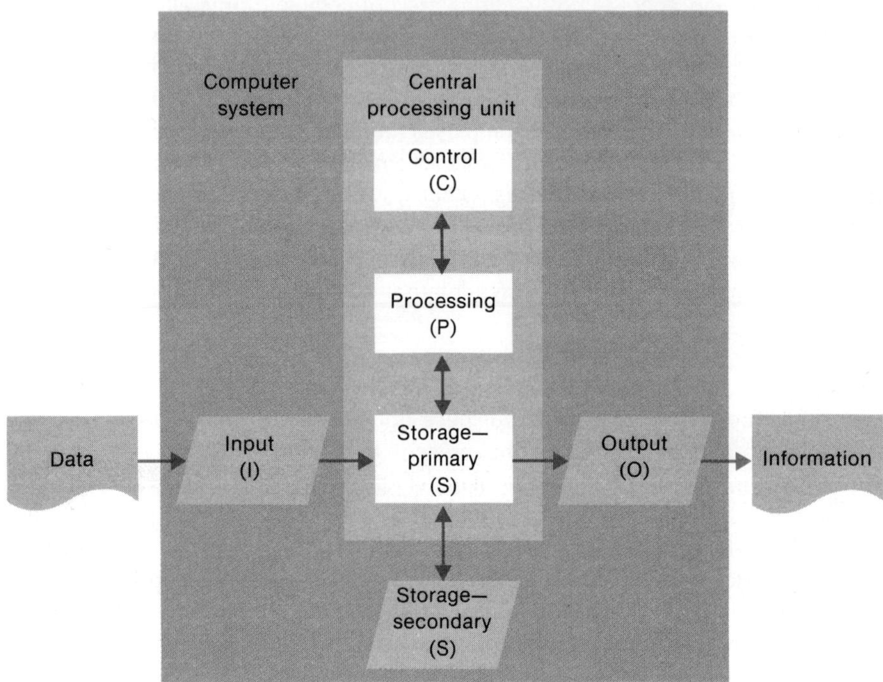


Figure 1-4 Input-storage-processing-control-output (ISPCO) cycle is a meaningful way of identifying the major components of a computer system.

### Data Processing Cycle

*Originating-recording-classifying-manipulating-summarizing (report preparation)-communicating is a useful way of explaining the basic steps in the data processing cycle.*

Another way of explaining the basic data processing functions is in terms of the data processing cycle. Its sequence of basic functions which can also be applied to any system are listed below.

1. originating
2. recording
3. classifying
4. manipulating
5. summarizing—report preparation
6. communicating

Each of these functions will be explained.

Upon close examination, both of the above approaches to the firm's basic data processing functions are comparable. Input refers to originating and recording while processing that is controlled relates to classifying and manipulating. Storage and output are linked to summarizing—report preparation and communicating since stored data are retrievable for summarizing output. The purpose of output is to communicate required information so that appropriate action can be taken. These relationships are depicted in Figure 1-5.

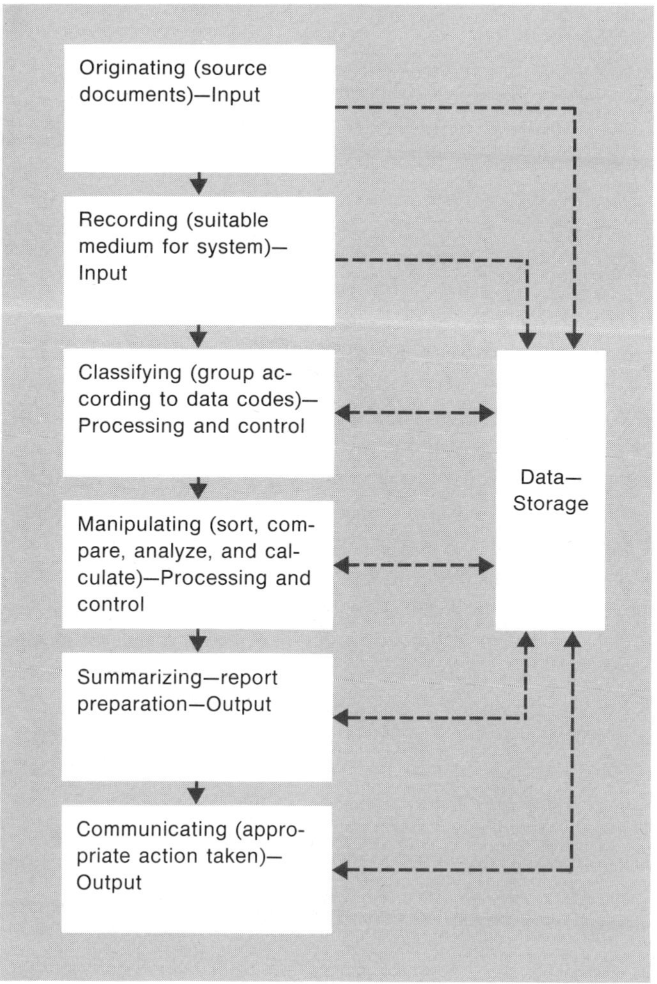


Figure 1-5 Basic functions or steps in the data processing cycle and the ISPCO cycle.

*Originating is the capture of data on a source document at the time a transaction occurs.*

***Originating.*** The basic input for any business data processing system originates on various business forms, more commonly known as source documents. Data are initially captured on a source document at the time a transaction occurs. As noted previously, common input documents are: payroll time cards, sales orders for billing customers, receipt forms for merchandise received, materials requisitions, and the like. Input documents are related not only to accounting and finance but also to marketing, manufacturing, purchasing, engineering, personnel, research and development, and related functions, depending upon the nature of the firm's products and/or services. However, these originating forms have two points in common: they form the basis for further data processing and they verify that a transaction has occurred.

Since business forms become the basis of input to the data processing system, it is necessary that the data be as clear and accurate as possible. Another important consideration relates to the sequence of data on the input form. Data should be arranged in the same order as that desired in the transcription. In this manner, it is possible to speed up the next step—the recording process—as well as to increase accuracy. Also, the sequence on the document should follow the natural order required in the processing procedure.

*Recording is the process of converting data from the source document into a form that is acceptable to data processing equipment in the next sequence of operations.*

***Recording.*** Having captured the data accurately on source documents, it is generally necessary to record them onto another medium. This may necessitate the conversion from a written form to punched holes in cards or paper tape or to magnetized spots on tapes or disks. The conversion may involve making a manual entry or entering data through the keyboard of a bookkeeping machine or using an input-output terminal. In data collection systems, data are captured by the input of cards and badges on which fixed data have been prerecorded in a machine-acceptable language. Variable data are entered by turning dials, knobs, or other kinds of manual settings. Still other recording methods—cash registers, imprinters, and data communication devices—are available for capturing the original data. No matter what form of conversion takes place, data from the source document are recorded in a form that is acceptable to the data processing equipment available in the next sequence of operations.

During the recording process, every effort should be made to verify the accuracy of critical data. Some form of internal control—internal check and internal accounting control over input data—should be made an integral part of the recording function. Not only should individuals check on one another so that no one person has complete control over one operation, such as payroll (internal check), but also totals accumulated throughout the recording process should be checked against those tabulated previously in order to insure accuracy (internal accounting control).

In addition to the verifying function, editing and duplicating are important parts of the data recording function. Editing is defined as the process of selecting important data for recording and discarding the irrelevant data. On the other hand, duplicating is the process of reproducing the same machine-processable data. This may be necessitated by the internal needs of the system or if timing dictates that two or more sets of data be duplicated. This is particularly true of some punched card operations. Time may be of the essence in processing critical data.

*Classifying is the process of identifying one or more common characteristics usable for grouping data.*

***Classifying.*** Data may need to be classified after they have been recorded in a machine-processable form. Classifying is the process of identifying one or more common characteristics usable for grouping data. Classes of data might be product line, geographic location, sales territory, division, department, price range, type of cost, and so forth. It should be noted that the appropriate classification is usually anticipated; that is, classifications are generally determined before the recording process begins.

An essential part of classifying is coding. Coding is the conversion of data to some symbolic form in order to save space, time, and effort during the recording process. It includes numbers, the alphabet, or an appropriate combination. The use of a series of numbers for coding automatically classifies the data according to some logical sequence. For example, numbers 1 through 12 represent the months of the year and customer numbers are used in place of names.

***Manipulating.*** Even after data have been properly recorded and classified on

*Manipulating is the process of sorting, comparing, analyzing, and calculating data in some meaningful manner before proceeding to the next step—summarizing.*

some meaningful basis, they are generally still unsuitable for use. The data must be manipulated before they can be summarized, reported, and communicated to the proper individuals. The basic data manipulating functions are sorting, comparing, analyzing, and calculating.

*Sorting* is the process of arranging data into some desired order, being dependent upon a key or field contained in each item. It may be performed manually, mechanically with bookkeeping machines, electromechanically with punched card equipment, or electronically with computers. The sorting task is determined by the length of the fields and the number of items to be sorted. Like other steps in the data processing cycle, sorting is simplified by expressing certain data in coded form.

The degree of *comparing* and *analyzing* is a function of the equipment utilized. The order relationship and the relative value of data, respectively, are capable of being determined before making the necessary calculations. *Calculating* is the process of performing arithmetic operations that convert data into a final form for summarizing if the application calls for it. Thus, data must generally be manipulated in some meaningful manner before proceeding to the next step in the data processing cycle.

*Summarizing-report preparation is the process of totaling numerical data so that its important highlights are emphasized.*

***Summarizing—Report Preparation.*** The need to summarize data is apparent since management needs to know, at periodic intervals, certain overall information about the results of business operations. Basically, summarizing is the process of totaling numerical data in order to emphasize its highlights. In this respect, totaling is dependent on the sorting process, since data have been ordered in some meaningful sequence for totaling. In general, summarizing goes one step further by providing aggregate values that can be compared to other values for management action.

The net result of the data processing cycle—originating, recording, classifying, manipulating, and summarizing—is processed information, commonly referred to as output. The output medium may be typewritten copy, printed forms, punched cards, punched paper tapes, magnetic tapes, magnetic disks, or many other output mediums from a business data processing system. In the final analysis, the most important output is accurate and timely reports for all phases of the firm's operations. These may be reports on production, sales analysis, inventory, finance, and the like. The output is contingent upon the design of the system and the corresponding needs of company personnel—management and nonmanagement alike.

*Communicating is the dissemination of information produced by the data processing system to the respective user or users for taking appropriate action.*

***Communicating.*** Of all the steps found in the data processing cycle, the communicating function is the most important from a management point of view. The communication function is directed toward the assembly and transmission of information throughout the data processing system so that appropriate action can be taken. Generally, the distribution of data results is in the form of reports to the user. However, communicating can mean the transmitting of information in the form of data communications. It is now possible to transmit all pertinent data between a wide variety of input/output devices that are connected directly to the data processing system or by means of telegraph circuits, telephone circuits, or microwave networks. This method allows communication between close and distant points.

***Storage of Data.*** An important feature of the communicating function is the storage of the data upon completion of the processing cycle. Data are generally stored so that they can be easily retrieved. Likewise, an advanced business data processing system stores the information and associates it with previously stored information in order to provide a frame of reference for its next step, that of making a decision. The results of its decision are automatically transmitted to an output device so that appropriate action can be taken when and where the need arises.

The foregoing steps in the data processing cycle are common elements in which any data processing system can be subdivided (Figure 1-5). From the standpoint of the system employed—manual, bookkeeping, punched card, or computer—it matters little. The functions of data processing remain basically the same although there may be substantial differences in methods, procedures, and equipment employed.

## BASIC BUSINESS DATA PROCESSING SYSTEMS

*Two basic approaches to business data processing systems are:*
- *batch processing*
- *on-line processing*

There are two basic approaches to business data processing systems: batch processing and on-line processing. Using the batch approach, transactions are accumulated and processed periodically. The items in a batch may be in sequential or random order. Using the on-line approach, records are stored on-line and updated as the transactions occur. Peripheral equipment or on-line devices are in direct communication with the central processing unit and are used to reflect current activities introduced into the data processing system. The requirements of a computer system capable of processing on-line data are considerably different from those used in batch processing.

Peripheral file storage devices of computer systems can be of two types—sequential access and direct or random access. In sequential access files, the data are stored in some predetermined order. Before a record can be read, say in the middle of the file, all preceding records must first be read, as in magnetic tape files. When operating with direct access file equipment, the unit is capable of locating and reading any record without having to read other records in order to obtain the desired one. On-line computer devices that have this ability are magnetic drums, magnetic disks, magnetic strips, magnetic cards, bulk core, and laser mass storage.

### Batch Processing

*Batch processing systems utilize:*
- *sequential access files*
- *direct access files*

The batch processing approach is characterized by the periodic processing of transactions accumulated over a period of time. It is normally associated with records that are maintained on punched cards or on magnetic tape.

***Sequential Access Files.*** When the files are the sequential access type, the entire master file is updated each time it is processed on a computer system. This requires sorting all input data according to the same sequence of the master file (Figure 1-6). Batch processing with sequential access file storage is ideally suited for payroll and accounts payable applications. It usually costs less to process batches than to process each transaction, as it occurs, immediately on-line. However, for other processing runs that require timely information for immediate decisions, the on-line approach may be justified.

***Direct Access Files.*** Batch processing is not limited to sequential access files. The batch approach can also use direct or random access file devices. The most common form of random access storage is the disk file which allows the direct updating of the desired record. For applications involving few transactions relative to the size of the master file, this approach is widely used. An added advantage of direct access over the sequential access approach in the batch processing mode is that there is no need to sort the input data. Thus, certain advantages of direct access over sequential access batch processing make it a logical candidate for certain critical business applications.

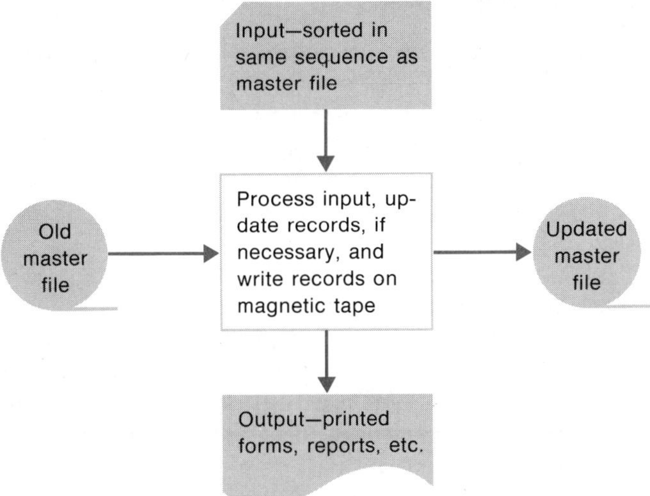


Figure 1-6 Batch processing with sequential access file storage—magnetic tape.

## On-Line Processing

*On-line processing systems employ direct access files.*

Of the two basic business data processing systems, the trend continues to be toward more on-line processing. Transactions and inquiries into the system are processed as they occur, generally in no particular order with respect to each other. Data stored on-line in direct access files are always up-to-date to reflect the current operating status of the firm whether it be marketing, manufacturing, finance, accounting, personnel, engineering, or research and development.

***Direct Access Files.*** In an advanced on-line processing system, called on-line real-time (OLRT) system, all data and inquiries are processed as they occur. Each originating point for transactions has an input/output terminal connected to the computer. The terminal is used to send data and to receive responses from the central computer complex. All information is stored in direct access file devices that are available at all times for immediate interrogation (Figure 1-7). Present

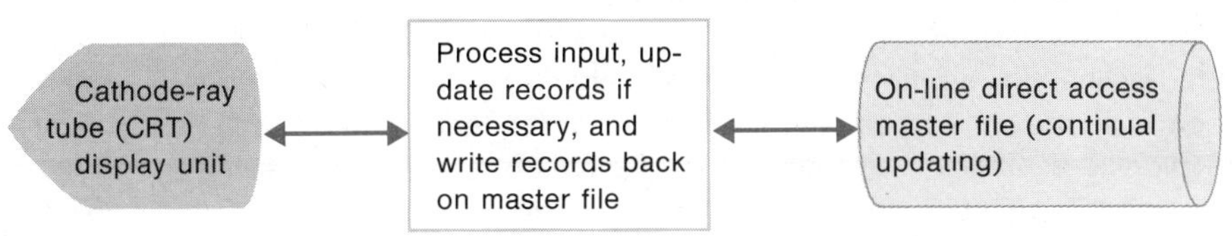


Figure 1-7 On-line processing with direct access file storage—magnetic drum.

applications include accounts receivable, airlines' reservation systems, bank deposit and withdrawal accounting, hotel accounting and reservations systems, law enforcement intelligence systems, patient hospital records, savings and loan deposit accounting, and stock market information. By no means do these applications exhaust those presently in operation, those currently being installed, or those being contemplated. On-line processing with direct access file storage is decidedly the continuing direction of business data processing system developments.

## BUSINESS DATA PROCESSING SUBSYSTEMS

*A business data processing system consists of a number of subsystems that function on various operating levels.*

Going beyond the basic business data processing systems delineated above, it is common to think in terms of a system and its subsystems. From this point of view, a business data processing system can be fully investigated for a more thorough understanding. A business data processing system has been defined as a group of interrelated activities or functions that operate to achieve some objective(s). One of its essential characteristics is the number and levels of subsystems.

*Each subsystem interacts with other subsystems for accomplishing data processing tasks.*

***Importance of Subsystems.*** Each component (activity or function) is called a *subsystem* that, in turn, interacts with other components (subsystems) for accomplishing the firm's objectives. As shown in Figure 1-8 for a typical manufacturing firm, there are seven major subsystems. Each of these functions generate information to assist the other subsystems while carrying out its own function. Implied in the activities of these major subsystems are organizational objectives that complement one another. Moving down to the intermediate subsystem for accounting, we have another level of subsystems that interact with each other. They are represented by connecting lines. (A comparable manufacturing breakdown for this level includes production plans, routings, schedules, inventories, engineering information, quality reports, and manufacturing management reports.) The lowest level for the accounting subsystem, called the minor subsystem, is shown only for payroll. Again, there is an interdependency among the functions to be performed so that the desired data are processed and information is forthcoming on the results of operations. A system, then, involves relationships between and among subsystems on a higher, lower, or equal level for the many functions operating within the firm.

*Subsystems involve relationships between and among subsystems of similar and dissimilar functions.*

***Interdependence of Subsystems.*** Since subsystem interdependencies are not restricted to activities revolving around one function of the firm and those on the same level, many subsystems are related to other subsystems on a higher or lower level. Although this is not shown in Figure 1-8, these relationships become quite complex. For example, payroll and personnel functions are frequently integrated through a computer data processing system. In such a system, payroll, formerly performed separately in each plant, is consolidated at one location. By the same token, related functions, such as payroll and personnel, which worked cooperatively but separately from one another, are consolidated by creating a single on-line computer file to serve both. Integration of the new employee file allows the firm to prepare payroll checks, test the consequence of payroll changes as labor union negotiations progress, project the number of new employees for the coming year after evaluating the current personnel status, prepare the required governmental reports on the employees, and answer similar requests. Thus, a system can involve relationships between and among subsystems of similar and dissimilar functions. These relationships can have a direct or indirect bearing on the behavior and performance of other subsystems. Furthermore, they can, and generally do, affect the performance of the overall system.

## BUSINESS DATA PROCESSING SYSTEMS CONCEPTS

Now that the basics of business data processing systems have been explored, it will be helpful to investigate their underlying concepts. An understanding will help the reader to obtain an overview of the various approaches to past, present, and future business data processing systems. Although many systems concepts have been developed over the years, the discussion will center around the more important

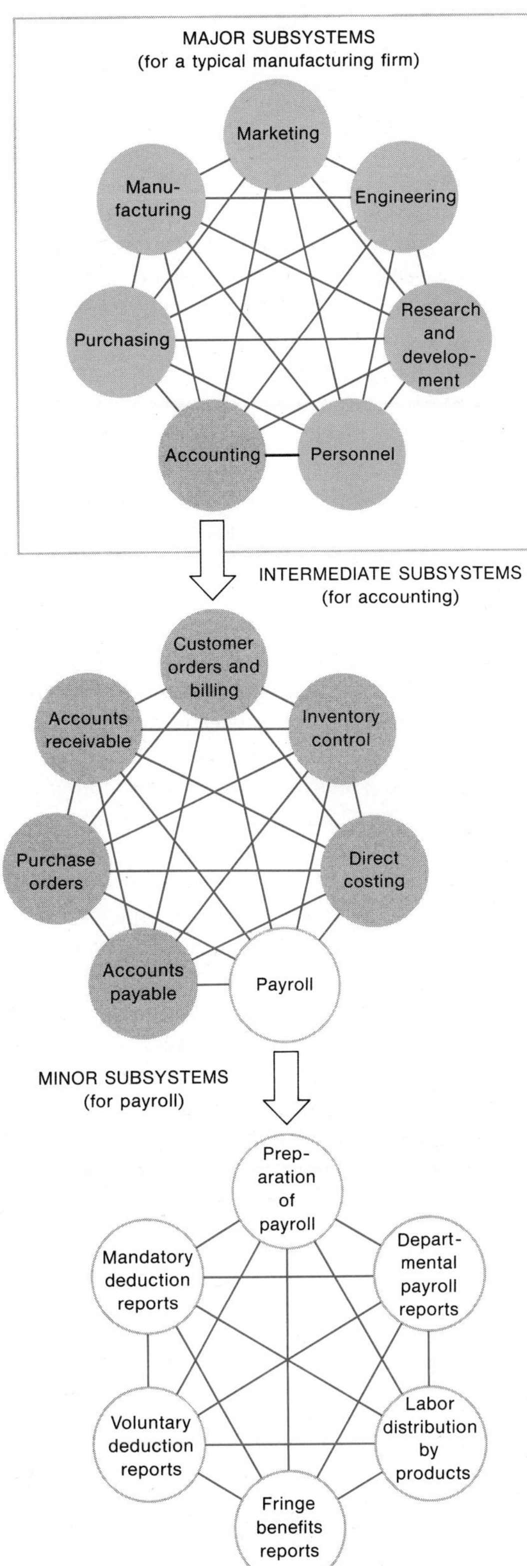


Figure 1-8 Major, intermediate (accounting), and minor (payroll) subsystems for a typical manufacturing firm.

*Important business data processing system concepts include:*
- *the systems concept of data processing*
- *the total systems concept*
- *the management information systems concept*
- *the modular systems concept*

ones. These include the systems concept of data processing, the total systems concept, the management information systems concept, and the modular systems concept. As time passes, advanced concepts of data processing will supplement the current listing.

**The Systems Concept of Data Processing**

The systems concept of data processing is concerned with the best possible system to carry out the firm's objectives. The relationships of the subsystems and how they affect the performance of the overall system are emphasized. In essence, the systems concept is a basic analytical approach for viewing the system and its related subsystems as a whole.

*The systems concept of data processing is an analytical approach for viewing the system and its subsystems. Among its characteristics are:*
- *subsystems compatibility*
- *feedback of timely information*
- *flexibility of system*

***Subsystems Compatibility.*** As each subsystem is broken down and relationships examined, it, too, can be analyzed by the same means as it is subdivided into more component parts. When the lowest level of the subsystem has been developed, it will be compatible with the overall system as well as enhance the goals of the system. The systems concept, then, requires downward as well as upward compatibility of subsystems that comprise the entire system for a firm's data processing needs.

***Feedback of Timely Information.*** When viewing the firm in terms of the systems concept, we immediately recognize the information needs for operating the various subsystems in an efficient and coordinated manner. The more complex and sophisticated the subsystems are, the more important the information system becomes. When the entire system, including its many levels of subsystems, are thoroughly investigated and understood, the conclusion is that the traditional methods and procedures are much too narrow in perspective. The systems concept is concerned with "management informations systems" or "now" operating informations systems that transcend traditional accounting reports. Instead of being concerned with only historical accounting data, they feed back timely information to meet the needs of management. It makes little sense to feed back frequent information on a few minor subsystems for corrective action when the most important ones are experiencing "out of control" conditions.

***Flexibility of System.*** The systems concept of data processing requires the design of an integrated system that will satisfy the firm's information needs. The idea of integration can be carried one step further. Management must have an information system that is capable of adapting itself to the changing environment of the day. Otherwise, the firm will be unable to cope with the pace of changes emanating from outside and inside the firm. The business data processing system, then, must be adaptable and responsive to the firm's dynamic environment.

**The Total Systems Concept**

*The total systems concept views the firm in terms of its information system, the decision-making process, the organization structure, and other relevant factors so that the objectives of the firm are reached.*

The systems concept of data processing, when enlarged further, encompasses important interrelationships among the following:

1. the information system
2. the decision-making process
3. the organization structure itself

Logically, one cannot design an effective information system without considering the decisions that must be made and where these decisions are located within the framework of the firm. When these important factors are combined in a manner that encompasses and enhances the objectives of the firm, it is known as the "total systems concept."

This concept also includes being guided by sound policies and controlled by logical procedures that are integrated into the many subsystems. Mechanization with advanced equipment is systems-oriented rather than isolated and problem-oriented; thus, patchwork of the system is eliminated. Furthermore, the total systems concept is oriented toward performing methods and procedures as economically as possible, giving timely and correct information to the right personnel, and protecting the integrity of the information by effective internal control.

*In a highly idealized state, the total systems concept has all the firm's inputs and outputs automatically coordinated; however this level of sophistication has not yet been obtained.*

***Inputs and Outputs—Automatically Coordinated.*** The total systems concept, when carried to a high degree of application, tends to be utopian. In this highly idealized state, all the firm's inputs and outputs are automatically coordinated. Markets would be automatically gauged, incoming orders would result in the proper allocations of labor and materials, production and inventories would be appropriately adjusted, and finances would reflect the current operations. Management would have to be concerned only with exceptions, reported instantaneously by devices that provide feedback for making the appropriate adjustments, In essence, an elaborate self-adjusting mathematical model would be necessary to oversee such a system. Although this highly idealized total systems concept has been unattainable by business in the past, a few scattered applications are leaning in this direction, in particular, airline reservation systems and gasoline refinery control systems.

*The total systems concept extends beyond the firm to other firms in the manufacturing and marketing process.*

***Extends Beyond the Firm.*** The total systems concept need not be restricted to the confines of the firm. When it encompasses other firms, all important business data are communicated back and forth between suppliers, manufacturers, wholesalers, retailers, customers and, in some cases, competitors. This total system is much larger than that of one firm where company boundaries are not too meaningful. Even though this approach has not been implemented, future designers of business data processing systems must consider these possibilities as their ultimate goals. Thus the highest degree of sophistication for the total systems concept envisions having all the inputs and outputs for a series of firms automatically coordinated. The demand response of customers will be relayed instantaneously back to raw material suppliers who will forward the goods to the manufacturers for further processing. The completed products, in turn, will be shipped via the proper distribution channels so that sellers will have the right product available at the proper time and place for their customers.

*Basically, the total systems concept is defined as an approach to data processing that views the firm as a single unit, although it is composed of many interrelated subsystems.*

***Total Systems Concept Defined.*** Having set forth various ways of viewing the total systems concept, it is rather difficult to state a precise definition with which all data processing personnel will agree. However, the following definition is a general one that encompasses the essentials set forth previously. The *total systems concept* is defined as an approach to data processing that views the firm (and possibly other firms) as a single unit. It is composed of many interrelated subsystems that function effectively and efficiently together so that accurate and timely information can be produced for management decision making. This leads to the overall optimization of the firm's objectives and profits at all times.

### The Management Information Systems Concept

The most important systems design concept today is one referring to a *management information system* (MIS), sometimes called a management information and control system (so called because of its output—information reports and control reports). Even though it is possible to have a noncomputerized management infor-

The management information systems concept centers around generating management information for all functional areas of the firm as opposed to accounting only.

mation system, this book stresses the computer as an essential part of it. External and internal information is channeled into this single, centralized computer system. In this manner, output generated by such a system will be meaningful and effective for management's decisions.

***Common Data Base.*** Basically, a computerized management information system means capturing originating data as close to their source as possible, feeding the data directly or almost directly into the computer system, and permitting the system to utilize common files (a data bank or data base) that can service several different output (Figure 1-9). In this type of environment, a single piece of information is

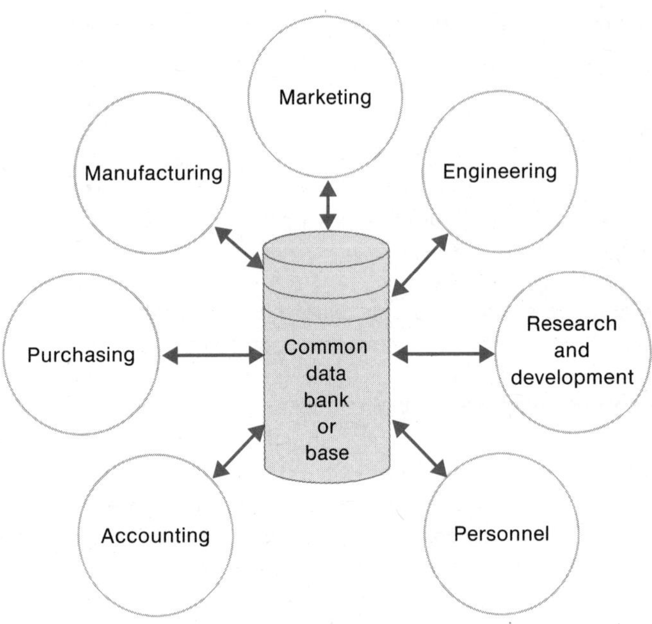


Figure 1-9 An essential part of a management information system is a common data bank or data base.

An essential part of MIS is a common data bank or data base where data elements are entered once and are available to serve all data processing requirements.

entered into the data processing system only once in its history. From then on, it is available to serve all requirements until its usefulness is exhausted. Under these ideal conditions, adequate and correct information can be presented to managers in a coordinated rather than in a segmented fashion. Likewise, such a system provides the required information on a timely basis to help management plan, organize, direct, and control the firm's activities. Thus the output of a management information system is report-oriented, being position- or department-oriented for meeting specific managerial requirements. In other words, a management information system is not an improved accounting reporting system, but rather an orderly flow of timely information for meeting specific management needs.

Control reports are standard output for MIS where actual results are compared to plans or standards.

***Control Reports.*** Control reports produced by this system include those necessary to service the basic business functions of the firm. Among these are sales forecasting, shipping and warehousing, finished goods replenishment, production control, materials management, manufacturing cost control, personnel skills and manning control, and management incentives. Other reports include short- and long-range financial and operating budgets, monthly financial and operating statements, and various historical data for short-run to long-range planning. Sales and order entry statistics, including sales quotas, salesmen's compensation, purchasing, manufacturing, and shipping, are additional examples of output that provide input to many other systems. An essential part of any management information system is feedback which shows what has happened to the financial plan in view of actual results to date or what would happen if hypothetical changes were made in the plan. Control reports, then, are concerned with monitoring actual results via feedback in order to determine whether the firm's functions are proceeding in accordance with plans and standards.

*A management information system is defined as a group of subsystems that fulfill the managerial requirements of planning, organizing, directing, and controlling the functional areas of the firm in conformance with the firm's objectives.*

***Management Information Systems Concept Defined.*** Based upon the foregoing, a *management information system* can be defined as a collection of subsystems and related program parts (modules) that are interconnected in a manner which fulfills the information requirements necessary to plan, organize, direct, and control business operations. It is a system for producing and delivering timely information that will support management in accomplishing its specific tasks in an enterprise. Among the many benefits of such a system to the firm are: faster and better information, greater facility to carry out managerial functions, improved decision making, more effective use of manpower and facilities, prompt communication, very little need to re-create data, elimination of peak period volume reports, and prompt correction of out-of-control conditions (management by exception). In addition, an advanced management information system should be computer-based, integrated with all subsystems, accessible through a common data bank or data base, utilize terminals at on-site and remote locations, timely through use of communications capability, and interactive between the user and information available.

For a management information system to qualify as excellent in terms of speed, the system should be capable of sending the information to the user within the operational time span in which it is needed to make the right decision or to take the appropriate action. To qualify as excellent in content, the data should be relevant to the user's needs in terms of the problem under study. Using the criterion of costs, the management information system should compare favorably with alternative methods available and with the benefits mentioned above. Additional criteria for measurement of MIS can be employed. However, the foregoing qualifications highlight the essential considerations for converting to such a system. Additional comments on MIS will be found in subsequent sections in this chapter (Integrated Management Information System and Real-Time Management Information System).

### The Modular Systems Concept

*The modular systems concept is a method of breaking down a system and its programs into their lowest level component parts so that modules can be logically grouped for implementation and ease of making changes.*

As a means of obtaining systems design objectives now and in the future, EDP personnel have found it necessary to formulate the modular system concept. Under this concept, separate but detailed information system modules are identified. For example, referring to Figure 1-8, the minor subsystems for payroll would consist of many program modules to produce the desired reports. The advantage of this modularizing approach at a very low level within a computer program is the ability to develop a system, and applications within it, in an orderly and planned fashion. Just as important is the capability to change individual program modules without the need to reconstruct or redo the entire computer program and related methods and procedures. Also, this modularity or building block systems concept allows programming personnel to test each subsection (containing several modules) of the final program separately.

***Modular Programming Languages.*** The modular concept in programming, allowing for a discrete task to be performed, is quite compatible with many of the

*The modular concept is evident in certain programming languages, such as PL/1.*

programming (procedure-oriented) languages being offered today. Among these are FORTRAN and PL/1 while the newer version of COBOL (not yet officially sanctioned) is oriented around a functional processing module concept.

*Firms are writing several hundred independent computer program modules that can be brought together to form a number of programs for specific applications.*

***Modular Programs.*** Some of the more progressive firms in the field are writing a set of several hundred independent computer program modules that are capable of utilizing a common data base. To generate a specific application program, the desired modules are tied together by the programmer through master control blocks which are written for each application. These modules can be integrated into any kind of management information system or storage and retrieval system. Thus, program-structuring and data-structuring must be sufficiently flexible, yet at the same time complete and consistent in order to permit the use of the modular systems concept.

To utilize this concept effectively, business applications must specify the interacting functions between modules. Otherwise, many program modules will have been developed and available but not used in one of the firm's applications. An important characteristic for this systems concept is to integrate the modules as they are developed. To illustrate, it would be advisable to integrate the modules required for the various computer programs in accounting (Figure 1-8) with the firm's budgets before developing other program modules for marketing, manufacturing, purchasing, engineering, personnel, and research and development. However, once program modules have been written for all areas of the firm, the task of updating programs is minimal. Only the individual program modules requiring correction need be changed. New program modules can be tested before inserting them in the required program(s).

## APPROACHES TO BUSINESS DATA PROCESSING SYSTEMS

*Approaches to business data processing systems that have and are being employed include:*

- *custodial accounting*
- *responsibility reporting*
- *integrated data processing*
- *integrated MIS*
- *real-time MIS*

In order to understand the present direction of on-line real-time systems within business and industry today, it is advantageous to review the past approaches to data processing systems. Prior to the first decade of computers, custodial accounting systems were widely used to produce meaningful information. Basically, the accent was on producing historical data.

***First Computer Decade (1952–1961).*** With the advent of the computer, the total systems concept was advocated by those selling computer equipment. Attempts to achieve a company-wide total system were unsuccessful during the first decade of computers. However, the concept proved to be a desired goal for data processing systems in the future. The total systems concept was finally shelved as being completely unrealistic and unobtainable when consideration was given to the hardware, software, and system design capability of the time. In its place, more manageable systems were developed, namely, responsibility reporting systems and integrated data processing systems.

***Second Computer Decade (1962–1971).*** In the second computer decade, the integrated data processing systems concept was replaced by integrated management information systems. Toward the end of the decade, real-time management information systems came to the forefront. This change has brought the total systems concept back into the limelight. The reason is that an on-line real-time MIS approach is a starting point for future advanced systems that encompass the basic tenets of the total systems concept.

***Third Computer Decade (1972–1981).*** Within the third computer decade, the real-time management information systems concept is expected to reach its height.

Its replacement will be a "data managed system"[1] or a comparably named system that has a broader viewpoint of management decisions. Instead of being concerned with lower and middle levels of management decisions, the data managed system will accent all levels—from the highest to the lowest—in order to maximize all the available resources within the firm. This systems concept will depend upon sophisticated mathematical modeling of operations research to optimize the firm's overall results. Much hard work must be accomplished before the data managed system concept can be operational and capable of achieving its goals. The implementation of this concept will put the data processing systems designer much closer to realizing the total systems concept. In essence, all input and output will be automatically coordinated through a series of interrelated mathematical models for all firms whose operations are interrelated.

### Custodial Accounting System

*Custodial accounting system is concerned with reporting historical information.*

In general, information systems prior to the introduction of computers have been concerned with the historical facts of the firm. There has been very little concern for control of operations day-by-day, hour-by-hour, and so forth. The accent was centered on what had occurred and not on what might be done to control current operations. This attitude led to what is now termed "custodial accounting."

The designers of custodial accounting systems were not concerned about the basic needs of management, that is, obtaining feedback of critical information for comparing actual performance with a predetermined plan or standard. However, the blame should not be placed entirely on the systems designers. In many cases, managers were not trained to utilize such information. Consequently, they did not ask that timely management reports be provided.

*The major deficiency of custodial accounting is that information is generated too late for meaningful analysis.*

***Deficiencies of Custodial Accounting.*** For custodial accounting systems, manual methods, bookkeeping equipment, and punched card equipment were utilized in processing the batched data. The major subsystems were treated as separate entities where record keeping was concerned. There was no attempt to integrate records that might serve several functions at the same time. Not only was there a proliferation of excess records in the firm but it also generally took a long time to produce historical reports. By the time data were assimilated, it was much too late for meaningful analysis. In total, the custodial accounting system approach had more bad points than good points. It is no wonder that systems designers initially became overly enthusiastic about the total systems concept.

The important characteristics of custodial accounting systems, as well as other approaches to business data processing systems, are summarized in Figure 1-14.

### Responsibility Reporting System

*Responsibility reporting system accumulates historical information according to the various activities and levels of responsibility.*

An outgrowth of custodial accounting was the preparation of reports on the basis of responsibility assignments. A responsibility reporting system goes a step further by accumulating historical data for specific time intervals according to the various activities and levels of responsibility. The basis for determining responsibility and, in turn, holding the individual accountable is the firm's organization structure. Responsibility reporting is concerned with activities that are directly controllable by the individual. Although noncontrollable costs are included in the reports distributed, the manager is held accountable for unfavorable deviations of controllable

[1] P. D. Walker and S. D. Catalamo, "Where Do We Go from Here with MIS?" *Computer Decisions,* September 1969, p. 36.

costs from the predetermined plans or the budget. A typical set of reports in a responsibility reporting system (manufacturing firm) is found in Figure 1-10.

*Budgets are used for comparison to actual cost at all levels of responsibility.*

***Utilization of Budgets.*** Under responsibility reporting, each manager, regardless of his level, has the right to participate in the preparation of the budget by which he is evaluated monthly. The budget is constructed from the top level of management to the lowest level, that of a foreman, department head, or supervisor. Only in this manner can the individual be held responsible and accountable for costs that he controls directly.

*Computers are capable of producing more timely responsibility reports than other equipment.*

***More Timely Reports.*** The adoption of this type of reporting system required too much time when manual methods and bookkeeping machines were used. Even with punched card equipment, the problem of preparing detailed cards, handling the cards manually, and running off the reports is a time-consuming task. The utilization of a batch processing computer system to perform the required manipulation of data and storage of prior data expedited the preparation of the reports, similar to those found in Figure 1-10. The speed with which the computer system could prepare detailed responsibility reporting output made the information more meaningful. Instead of waiting weeks under an older accounting system, management had extremely meaningful reports in their hands within a week after the close of a period. With the operations relatively fresh in their minds, they were able to review results, even though it should have been done sooner.

*Responsibility reporting is an improvement over custodial accounting for several reasons:*

- *individuals are held accountable for results*
- *reports are more timely*
- *reports are more detailed*

***Improvement of Responsibility Reporting over Custodial Accounting.*** The responsibility reporting system is an improvement over the custodial accounting system in several ways. There were more detailed reports and were on a more timely basis. Also, the various levels of managerial reports show not only what has happened but also who is responsible for unfavorable as well as favorable deviations from the established plans.

### Integrated Management Information System

*Integrated MIS was an outgrowth of earlier integrated data processing systems.*

As business data processing utilized computers in the accounting area, initial business applications were discrete and were processed individually. There were several reasons for this approach. First, computers were regarded as large accounting machines that represented only a further mechanization of the data processing function by the accounting and finance section. For example, payroll was first designed and programmed, followed by accounts receivable, then inventory, and so forth. Second, this piecemeal approach was the result of following the organizational boundaries that have traditionally existed in the firm. Third, these early installations were justified not on the basis of giving management more information and control over their entire operations, but on the basis of the computer's ability to perform accounting jobs faster and more economically. Because of the stress on accounting applications, the electronic data processing system generally became a part of the accounting department within its existing framework. Generally, the other two major functions—marketing and manufacturing were processed on the computer only after all or most feasible accounting applications were operating.

*Integration of subsystems led to the development of integrated MIS that cuts across the entire firm.*

***Integration of Subsystems.*** An examination of the responsibility reporting approach indicates that it centered primarily around the accounting function. The reason for this direction is based upon the foregoing facts regarding earlier computers. As time passed, systems designers recognized that operations go considerably beyond the accounting aspects. They saw the great need for a system that integrates all the subsystems of the firm's operations that can be logically inter-

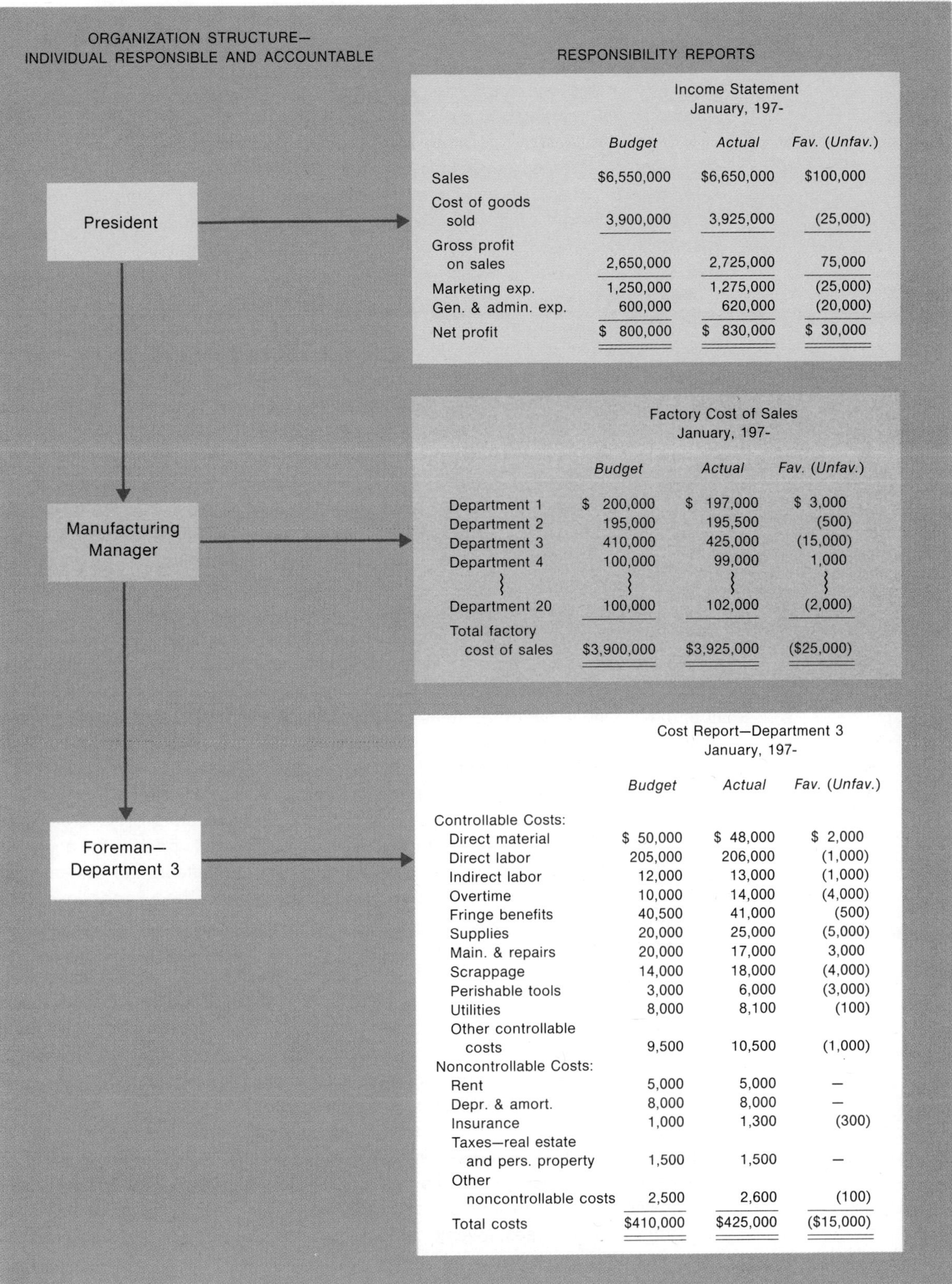


Income Statement
January, 197-

| | Budget | Actual | Fav. (Unfav.) |
|---|---|---|---|
| Sales | $6,550,000 | $6,650,000 | $100,000 |
| Cost of goods sold | 3,900,000 | 3,925,000 | (25,000) |
| Gross profit on sales | 2,650,000 | 2,725,000 | 75,000 |
| Marketing exp. | 1,250,000 | 1,275,000 | (25,000) |
| Gen. & admin. exp. | 600,000 | 620,000 | (20,000) |
| Net profit | $ 800,000 | $ 830,000 | $ 30,000 |

Factory Cost of Sales
January, 197-

| | Budget | Actual | Fav. (Unfav.) |
|---|---|---|---|
| Department 1 | $ 200,000 | $ 197,000 | $ 3,000 |
| Department 2 | 195,000 | 195,500 | (500) |
| Department 3 | 410,000 | 425,000 | (15,000) |
| Department 4 | 100,000 | 99,000 | 1,000 |
| ⋮ | ⋮ | ⋮ | ⋮ |
| Department 20 | 100,000 | 102,000 | (2,000) |
| Total factory cost of sales | $3,900,000 | $3,925,000 | ($25,000) |

Cost Report—Department 3
January, 197-

| | Budget | Actual | Fav. (Unfav.) |
|---|---|---|---|
| Controllable Costs: | | | |
| Direct material | $ 50,000 | $ 48,000 | $ 2,000 |
| Direct labor | 205,000 | 206,000 | (1,000) |
| Indirect labor | 12,000 | 13,000 | (1,000) |
| Overtime | 10,000 | 14,000 | (4,000) |
| Fringe benefits | 40,500 | 41,000 | (500) |
| Supplies | 20,000 | 25,000 | (5,000) |
| Main. & repairs | 20,000 | 17,000 | 3,000 |
| Scrappage | 14,000 | 18,000 | (4,000) |
| Perishable tools | 3,000 | 6,000 | (3,000) |
| Utilities | 8,000 | 8,100 | (100) |
| Other controllable costs | 9,500 | 10,500 | (1,000) |
| Noncontrollable Costs: | | | |
| Rent | 5,000 | 5,000 | — |
| Depr. & amort. | 8,000 | 8,000 | — |
| Insurance | 1,000 | 1,300 | (300) |
| Taxes—real estate and pers. property | 1,500 | 1,500 | — |
| Other noncontrollable costs | 2,500 | 2,600 | (100) |
| Total costs | $410,000 | $425,000 | ($15,000) |

Figure 1-10 A responsibility reporting system for a typical manufacturing firm.

related. The system must integrate men, machines, money, materials, and management in conformity with the firm's policies, methods, procedures, and objectives. The net result is a unified and integrated data processing system, later upgraded to an "integrated management information system" by specifying output required for each level of management.

*The output of integrated MIS is directed toward operating management where periodic financial reports are a by-product of information processed to control current operations.*

***Reports to Assist Operating Management.*** An essential characteristic of an integrated data processing system is that records kept for one purpose may actually have several other uses. Related elements in different processing activities are coordinated by common procedures and work flows. As a result, the whole business system is interrelated. Formerly, developing financial statements was the primary interest of the data processing system. But when an integrated system is installed, the major concern is producing reports that will assist operating management. The periodic financial reports are secondary, being a by-product of the information processed to assist in controlling current operations. From this standpoint, data processing records can serve several uses, thereby reducing costs of obtaining essential managerial reports.

*Flexibility in terms of responsiveness to a changing environment is an important part of integrated MIS.*

***Responsive to Changes—Flexibility.*** An integrated information system does not require a computer. However, a computer can facilitate meeting the essential requirements of such a system. This is particularly true because a computerized system can respond to external influences and conditions as well as to internal requirements. Activities, methods, procedures, responsibilities, and the like are continually changing. It is easier to effect changes with computer systems since many of these can be programmed without the need for retraining personnel with new equipment and procedures. Thus, flexibility is generally an important part of an integrated data processing system.

*Integrated MIS relegates routine decision making to the computer.*

***Performs Routine Decision Making.*** A true integrated management information system produces more than a mechanical linking of the various functions of the firm. It aids management by taking over routine decision making. If a manager can define his decision criteria, they can be computerized. Thus, management can concentrate its efforts on those areas that are not routine.

*An integrated management information system is illustrated in Figure 1-11 for a typical manufacturing firm.*

***Integrated MIS Illustrated.*** Essential characteristics of integrated MIS are illustrated in the following example. The introduction of a customer order creates an open order file that forms the basis for preparing invoices and updating the accounts receivable files at a later time. The customer order also affects the raw material orders, manpower scheduling, production scheduling, finished goods inventory, shipping orders, sales commissions, and marketing forecasts. Incoming orders, through their effect on inventory levels, may trigger an automatic computer reordering subroutine through the issuance of a purchase order. The reorder quantity is based on reorder levels and quantities determined by mathematical formulas designed into the system. The purchase orders, in turn, create a liability, requiring payment to vendors. In such a system, the operational aspects of order entry billing, accounts receivable, inventory control, purchasing, and accounts payable are interwoven. This example is illustrated in Figure 1-11.

In addition to the foregoing parts of this integrated management information system, Figure 1-11 contains other important data. It shows data input from major business functions being sent to a computer system on some predetermined periodic basis. Inputs in previous periods have resulted in master files of data relating to customers, employees, inventories, and all other business phases accumulated from previous processing cycles. As current data are processed on-line, the appropriate master files are updated, whereby documents, forms, and reports are prepared automatically. The kinds and number of control reports and information reports generated from the basic data are dictated by the needs of management and the capabilities of the equipment.

*Major characteristics of integrated MIS are:*
- *backward-looking control system*
- *integrated subsystems*
- *common data bank*
- *single-source data for multiple usage*
- *operating level reports*
- *routine decision making*
- *batch processing oriented*
- *flexibility*

***Major Characteristics of Integrated MIS.*** An integrated management information system is a network of related subsystems that are interwoven for performing the functional activities of a firm. Activities that are common to all departments are stored in a single data bank. Transactions that affect more than one application area are captured only once and then processed in a manner that is appropriate for all users of information. The essentials of this system—single-source data for multiple usage, routine decision making, batch processing computer orientation, and flexibility—are capable of uniting the firm's essential activities for achieving its objectives. When viewed from this perspective, it is a considerable improvement over prior systems.

*The basic deficiency of integrated MIS and prior systems is that they are backward looking. These systems look to past history before reports are produced and important feedback occurs.*

***Deficiencies of Integrated MIS and Prior Systems.*** Even though the integrated management information system rectified the problem of being accounting-oriented and is an information system that provides feedback in the form of reports through its various subsystems, it is still deficient in one important respect. Data must be accumulated for a period of time before processing is feasible. Whether sequential or random access files are utilized, there is still the problem of time lag. For this reason, all prior systems, whether they are custodial accounting, responsibility reporting, or integrated management information systems, are called "backward-looking control systems." The methods, procedures, and equipment look to past history before reports are produced for important feedback. What is needed is a system that looks to the present and future and is termed a "forward-looking control system." Such an approach to data processing is found in a "real-time management information system."

### Real-Time Management Information System

*Real-time management information system centers around data stored on-line where information can be extracted, processed, and fed back to the appropriate source in time to change or control the operating environment.*

An essential characteristic of a real-time management information system is the on-line real-time concept. All information is "on-line," that is, all data are sent directly into a computer system as soon as it comes into being. The whole operation is in "real-time," which means data are processed and fed back to the appropriate source in sufficient time to change or control the operating environment. Basically then, any system that processes and stores data or reports them as they are happening is considered to be an on-line real-time system. Company personnel will receive a response from the system in time to satisfy their own real-time environmental requirements. The response time may range from a fraction of a second to minutes, hours, and days, depending on the attendant circumstances.

To illustrate the concept of real-time in a business data processing system, the production planning department has developed a computerized on-line daily scheduler. Since all variable manufacturing data are entered as they occur, the on-line data base for this function as well as others is always up-to-date. Before the start of each day, the computerized scheduler simulates the activities of the factory for that day. Knowing what has occurred during the previous day, that is, where jobs are backed up or behind schedule and where production bottlenecks are currently occurring, this manufacturing simulation model can determine what will happen as the day begins and, thereby, alerts the foremen and plant supervisor about critical areas that need immediate attention. A response, then, has been fed back in sufficient time to control the upcoming manufacturing activities.

***Integration of All Subsystems.*** A real-time system must be integrated in order

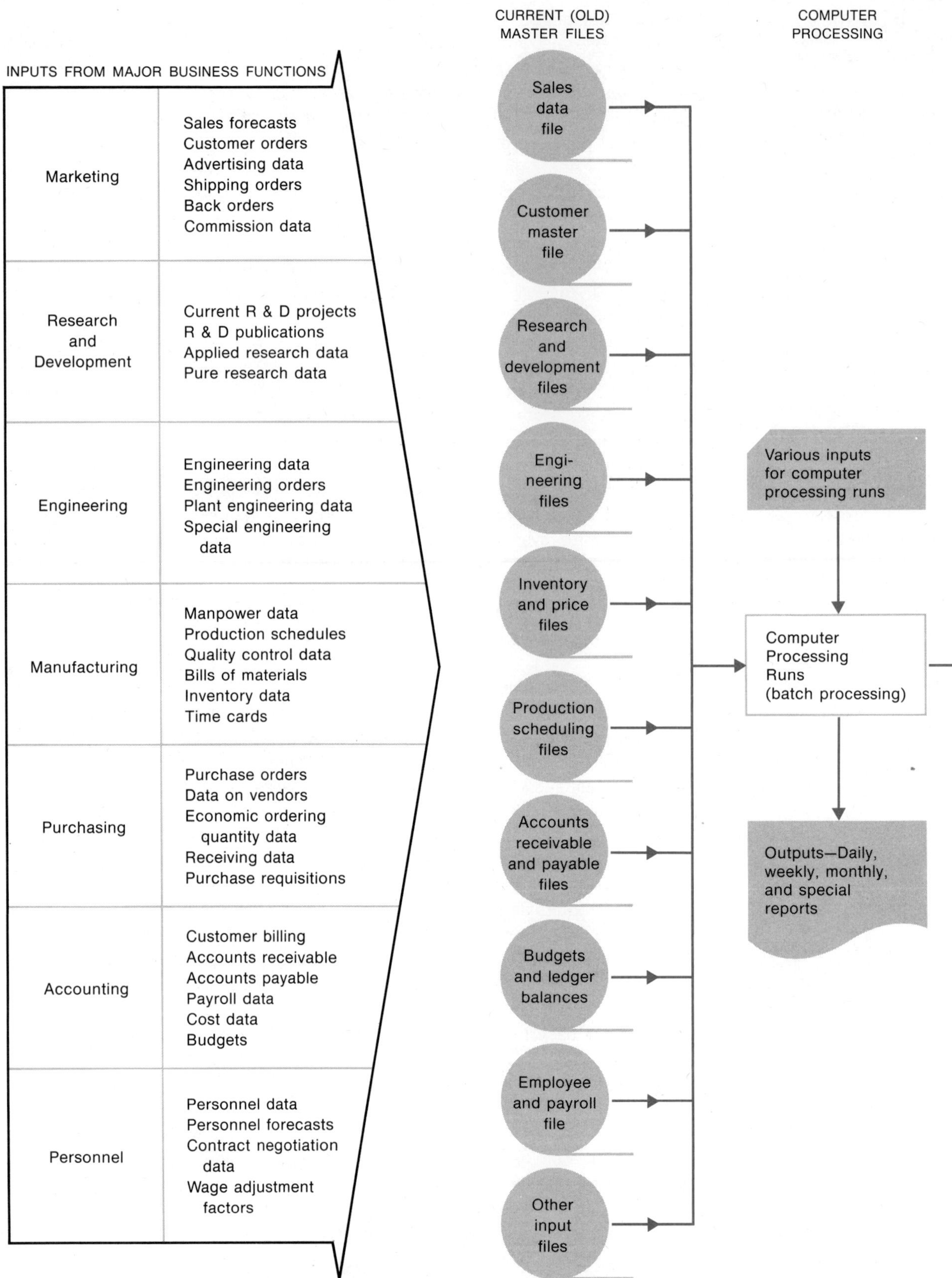


Figure 1-11 Integrated management information system for a typical manufacturing firm-data stored on magnetic tapes can be used for more than one report.

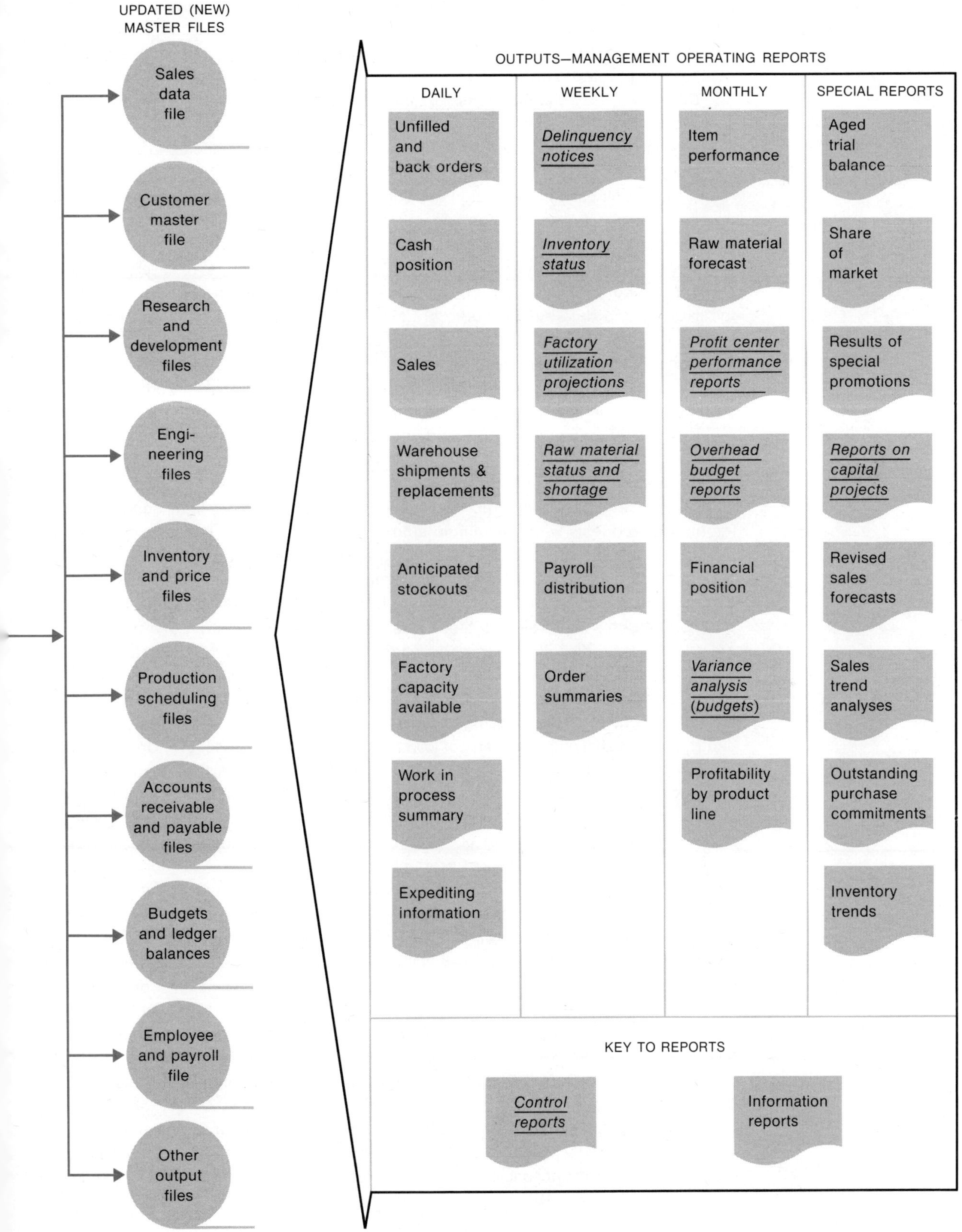

UPDATED (NEW) MASTER FILES

- Sales data file
- Customer master file
- Research and development files
- Engineering files
- Inventory and price files
- Production scheduling files
- Accounts receivable and payable files
- Budgets and ledger balances
- Employee and payroll file
- Other output files

OUTPUTS—MANAGEMENT OPERATING REPORTS

| DAILY | WEEKLY | MONTHLY | SPECIAL REPORTS |
|---|---|---|---|
| Unfilled and back orders | *Delinquency notices* | Item performance | Aged trial balance |
| Cash position | *Inventory status* | Raw material forecast | Share of market |
| Sales | *Factory utilization projections* | *Profit center performance reports* | Results of special promotions |
| Warehouse shipments & replacements | *Raw material status and shortage* | *Overhead budget reports* | *Reports on capital projects* |
| Anticipated stockouts | Payroll distribution | Financial position | Revised sales forecasts |
| Factory capacity available | Order summaries | *Variance analysis (budgets)* | Sales trend analyses |
| Work in process summary | | Profitability by product line | Outstanding purchase commitments |
| Expediting information | | | Inventory trends |

KEY TO REPORTS

*Control reports* — Information reports

*Integration of all subsystems is an important requirement for real-time MIS.*

to be effective. Data acquired from one source are often used in many subsystems. If this approach is not used, there is much wasted motion and extra cost since each subsystem must treat the same data without taking advantage of processing accomplished by other subsystems.

*Common data base elements are data-oriented and not business function-oriented. For example, inventory data can be used to serve many departments as opposed to just one department.*

***Common Data Base Elements.*** The integrated data accumulated from the many detailed on-line transactions are commonly referred to as the data base elements or the organization's data base. In addition to having all data collected in one place (basically secondary on-line storage), a firm's data base must be data-oriented rather than business function-oriented. The same inventory data base may be used by a number of departments, such as manufacturing, production control, inventory control, purchasing, and finance. In another example, a data base element is an employee skill number that can assist in preparing weekly payroll, referencing personnel records, filling new job openings, preparing contract negotiations, and the like. Thus, a data base for a firm refers to elements or data bits in a common storage medium that form the foundation for all information provided to management and nonmanagement personnel alike.

*The data base should be so structured that the data elements can be used for as many different outputs as possible.*

***Structure of Common Data Base.*** Before the organization's data base can be structured in a meaningful manner, it is first necessary to identify the information requirements of management. Second, the data base elements must be fully identified, that is, where they are located, how they are obtained, how large they are, and what their specific contents are. The last requirement dictates that relationships among the data base elements be clearly known so that they can serve many information requests with a minimum amount of programming. The data elements should be capable of being related to as many different outputs as possible, in particular, those needed for timely managerial reports (Figure 1-12). In order to extract the desired information as is or with modification from the data base or on-line computer files, retrieval techniques in the form of multipurpose programs are needed for a close interaction between the computer and the individual.

*Real-time MIS output is geared to satisfy the needs of lower and middle management.*

***Reports to Lower and Middle Management.*** Designing a structured data base for accommodating the various levels of management (lower, middle, and top) is a formidable task for the systems designer. Currently, systems designers are concentrating on satisfying the needs of lower and middle management for organizing, directing, and controlling the firm's activities around the established plans, being in conformity with the firm's objectives. Thus, real-time management information systems are focused on the following areas: improved forecasting for all phases of the firm, optimum marketing budget, improved shipping schedules and service to customers, better utilization of production facilities, improved vendor performance, higher return on short-term assets, and improved negotiations with labor. Other outputs found in a real-time MIS for a typical manufacturing firm are given in Figure 1-12. By no means will middle or lower managers restrict their activities within the confines of the firm. They will use computers to consider external data that have been included in the system and assist in decision making for tactical business decisions. (Tactical refers to optimizing decisions at the middle management level while strategic is accomplishing the same at the top management level.)

*Numerous teletypewriters and visual display devices are capable of sending and receiving information in an on-line real-time environment.*

***On-Line Input/Output Devices.*** In addition to the on-line computer files (data base elements) and outputs mentioned earlier, there are a number of on-line input/output devices that are located through the firm's operations. Teletypewriters and visual display devices are capable of sending as well as receiving information that relate to any of the basic business operations set forth previously in Figure

1-3. They may be many miles away from one another, but are linked through a data communication network for producing information that is forward looking.

The real-time system, for example, may be so designed that input data from an I/O device will trigger a production order when inventory reaches a predetermined level. The number of units to be produced will be based on an economic order quantity (mathematical model). The computer program will scan the present production schedules of the many plants scattered throughout the country and determine which plant will produce the order, based on its capacities and previous production commitments. Likewise, the computer program will indicate to which warehouse the products will be shipped, based upon proximity to the factory and level of present inventory. During this on-line process, the computer files are updated simultaneously to reflect these changing conditions. In essence, feedback on the various activities is concerned with present and future conditions, a very important feature of the real-time management information system.

*Real-time MIS has the capability of handling remote batch processing for applications not suited for real-time processing.*

***Remote Batch Processing.*** An examination of Figure 1-12 reveals other devices, such as mini-computers, analog computers, and magnetic tape that provide input for the system. This large computer system is capable of handling remote batch processing for applications that are not ideal candidates for real-time processing. In effect, a real-time MIS computer is capable of handling remote input/output devices as well as remote batch processing, the question being which is best suited for the activity.

*Major characteristics of real-time MIS are:*

- *forward-looking control system*
- *real-time processing*
- *integrated subsystems*
- *commonality of on-line files*
- *common data base*
- *remote I/O terminals*
- *man-machine interface*
- *output directed to lower and middle management*
- *real-time exception reporting*
- *remote batch processing*

***Major Characteristics of Real-Time MIS.*** There are many essential characteristics of a real-time management information system. Real-time MIS, being a forward-looking control system, maintains data base elements on-line which are available to the central processing unit when needed. The firm's data base is always updated as events occur and can be interrogated from many I/O terminals. With source data being entered as they happen, the real-time approach reduces repetitious recording, makes data available to all subsystems needing them, and reduces the error in conflicting reports that arise from varying coding or interpretations and unsynchronized timing. As a result, all departments work with the same information, thereby making it possible to tie in their decisions with those of other functions. Also, information stored on-line can be obtained upon request from a number of locations at a distance from the main computer system. It is possible to process data in real-time so that output may be fed back almost instantaneously to control current operations. The on-line computer's ability to interact with people on a timely basis with important information is its greatest asset. Management can be made aware of trends, exceptions, and results of recent decisions in order to initiate corrective action that meets predetermined business plans. Environmental feedback alerts the manager as to how the total business is operating, favorably or unfavorably, in relation to internal and external conditions.

*Real-time MIS fails to provide top management with essential information for long-range or strategic planning.*

***Deficiency of Real-Time MIS.*** Even though lower and middle managers can obtain updated information about the firm's basic business operations through some kind of input/output device, the same cannot be said for top management with a real-time management information system. Although the system does respond to the managerial needs of the first two levels, it falls short of the information desired by top-level executives. Those in top management are responsible and accountable for the full range of business activities. Their principal task revolves around long-range planning or strategic planning, which is reviewing long-run studies made by staff personnel. No matter what name is used for future planning, a real-time system does not provide long-range information per se. However, it does respond with

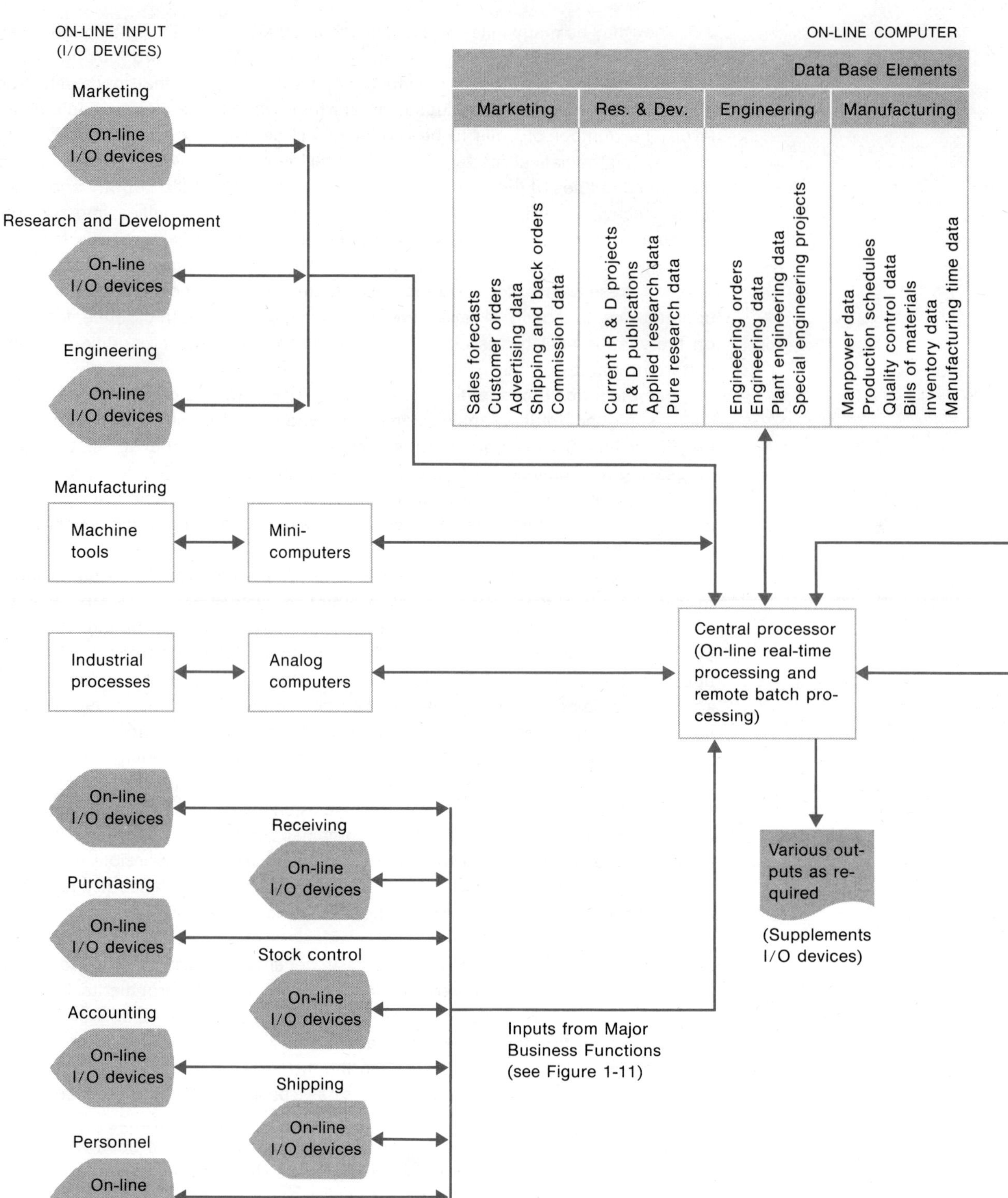


Figure 1-12 Real-time management information system for a typical manufacturing firm-data base elements stored on-line can be used for more than one report.

FILES

| and Programs | | |
|---|---|---|
| Purchasing | Accounting | Personnel |
| Purchase orders<br>Data on vendors<br>Economic ordering quantity data<br>Receiving data<br>Purchase requisitions | Customer billing<br>Accounts receivable<br>Accounts payable<br>Payroll data<br>Cost data<br>Budgets and general ledger data | Personnel data<br>Personnel forecasts<br>Contract negotiation data<br>Wage adjustment factors |

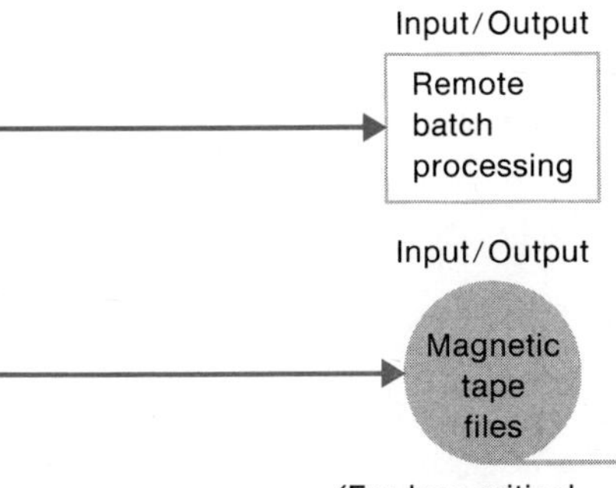


(For less critical and voluminous files)

Outputs—Management Operating Reports (see Figure 1-11)

ON-LINE OUTPUT—TYPED OR VISUAL
(I/O Devices)

**Marketing**
Customer order status
Back order status
Finished products available for sale

**Research and Development**
Research references for review
Graphic displays
Pure and applied research results

**Engineering**
Plotted engineering data
Results of mathematical calculations
New engineering designs

**Manufacturing**
Production order status
Inventory levels on specific items
Production control data

**Purchasing**
Purchase order status
Results of vendor comparison

**Receiving**
Shipments received over quantities ordered
Unshipped items from vendors on orders
Cancellations of purchase orders

**Accounting**
Net profit to date
Expense accounts exceeding budget
Accounts receivable status on individual accounts
Credit check
Accounts payable by vendors
Overdue invoices

**Stock Control**
Items available in stock
Location of stock items

**Personnel**
New personnel needs
Payroll forecasts
Available personnel from within to fill new job openings

**Shipping**
Routing information
Data on location of goods to be shipped

immediate feedback on present operations which is essential to modify future plans.

The data base required for top management needs must be restructured to accommodate them. The very structure, then, of a real-time management information system is not compatible with the full requirements of top management. For example, detailed information is needed for past, current, and future sales—cost performance that can be related to a financial simulation model which will produce an optimum mix of resources for producing a desired level of profits and return on investment.

### Future Management Information System

The major deficiency of real-time management information systems, which is the lack of output oriented toward top management, can be overcome by reworking its structure. This is shown in Figure 1-13.

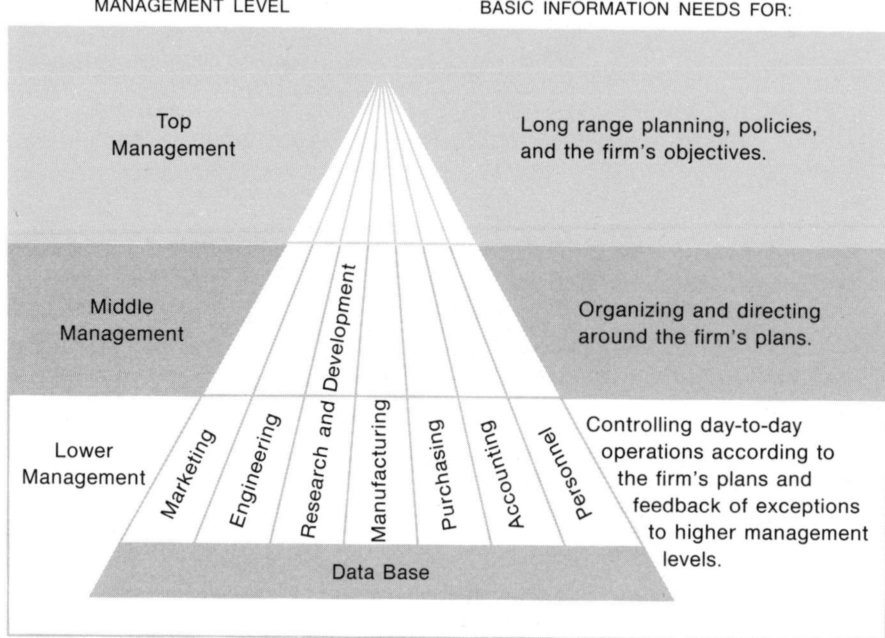


Figure 1-13 Vertical structure of major functions for a future management information system.

*Future management information systems will have to be more vertical in structure in order to accommodate the information needs for all levels of management.*

***Vertical Structure.*** The structure of a future management information system will have to be more "vertical" rather than "horizontal" in nature, being based on the data managed systems concept (suggested name given previously). For this approach to become operational, the systems designer must determine how the data base elements form a common data base for the important needs of all management levels. He must answer such questions as: Are current data, being utilized for lower management day-to-day decisions, valid when projected for the long run? Can the marketing, manufacturing, finance, and other business functions utilize the same inventory figures as those needed by top management for long-range planning? But even more basically, are the requirements for top management so different as to be incompatable with lower and middle management needs? Such questions present a new challenge to the information systems designer. Not only must he integrate a company data base that will serve all functions (subsystems) effectively but he must also be capable of servicing all levels of management with their respective information needs. Thus, data, sufficient to answer questions in the short or intermediate runs, may not be adequate for the long run.

*Future management information systems will employ very complex mathematical models that encompass all or many of the firm's functional subsystems.*

***Extensive Use of Complex Mathematical Models.*** Considerable development work is essential before the next major step can be initiated in the area of management information systems. In the past, the integrated MIS has relied on batch processing while, presently, the real-time MIS is geared to an on-line real-time response for important control information. Although the firm has hardware and software available to achieve the current phase of management information systems, the same is not completely true for the next important data processing thrust. Even though present-level mathematical business models are adequate for the present state of data processing, the same cannot be said for newer systems. The systems designer must be capable of understanding very complex mathematical models that encompass all subsystems of the firm. This is a necessary prerequisite for an effective and efficient overall mathematical model of the firm that relates the lower, middle, and top management needs in a logical manner. In essence, there must be a marriage of data processing with operations research so that sophisticated, overall mathematical models can be developed. Without these combined efforts, the business systems analyst will not be able to utilize the forthcoming advancements in software and hardware.

*Future MIS will approach the total systems concept.*

***Approaches Total Systems Concept.*** Future management information systems will be approaching the total systems concept. Despite the fact that the total systems concept tends to be utopian when carried to its highest level of achievement, it is still a goal to which future management information systems can aspire.

As indicated previously, the various approaches to data processing are summarized in Figure 1-14. Their important characteristics are set forth for comparative purposes.

## MANAGEMENT CONTROL CENTER

*The current trend is toward management control centers where a wide variety of management information can be viewed in a decision-making environment.*

In keeping with the continuing advances in management information systems, equipment manufacturers have developed large display devices that are capable of showing current operating and financial information (Figure 1-15). Whether this location is called a "management control center" (MCC) or a "decision room" is purely academic. Its importance lies in its ability to call up a wide variety of management information in a decision-making environment. Instead of searching manual files and cluttering up the office with extra paperwork, top-level executives can obtain the required information now. They can, for example, obtain sales figures for any time period together with comparable figures for previous periods. Current production schedules, the number of pending orders, status of back orders, amounts of accounts receivable and payable, profit analysis by periods and products, equipment utilization, and divisional performance factors are additional information that is available. By no means do the foregoing exhaust the possible applications for a management control center.

### Benefits of Management Control Center

The benefits from a management control center are many for present and future business data processing systems. Data will always be current, accurate, and in

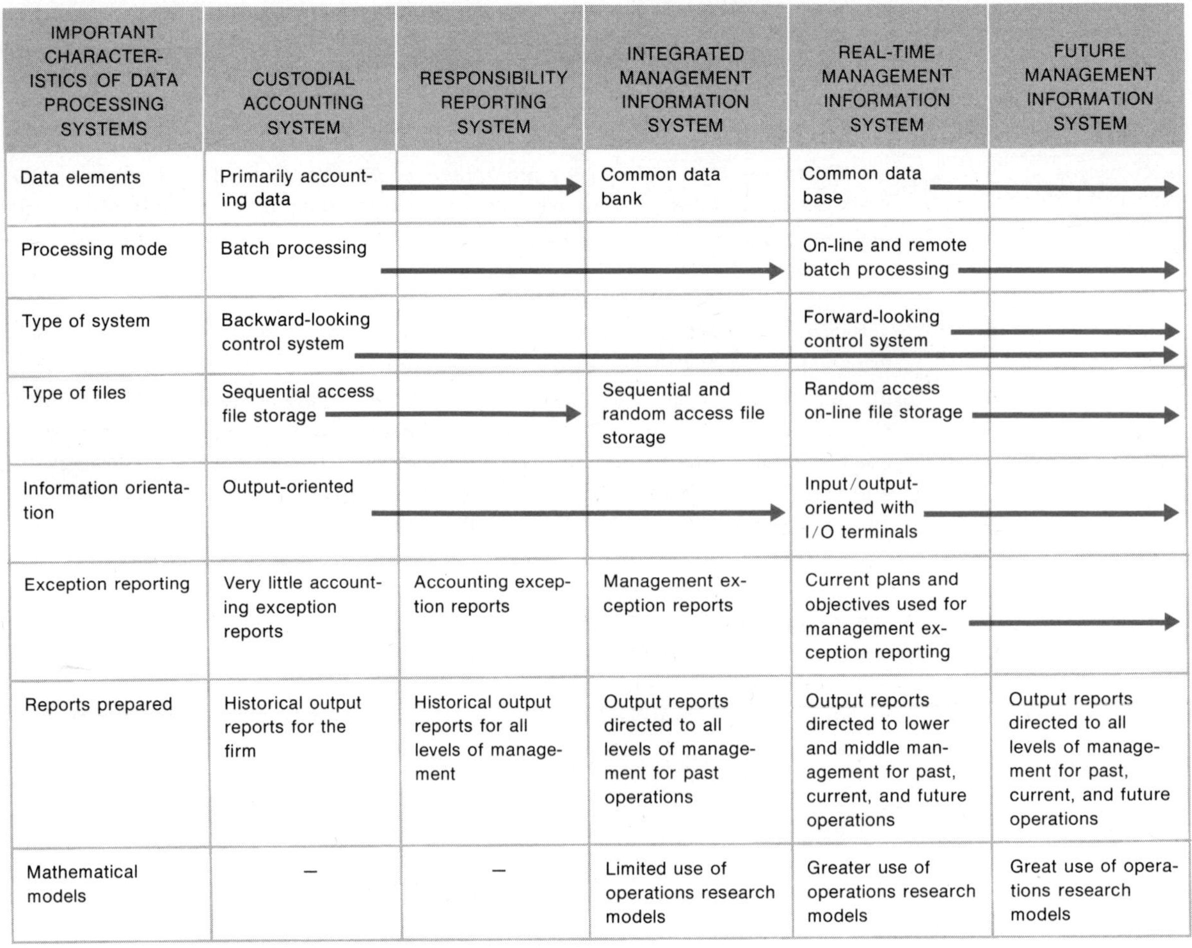

| IMPORTANT CHARACTERISTICS OF DATA PROCESSING SYSTEMS | CUSTODIAL ACCOUNTING SYSTEM | RESPONSIBILITY REPORTING SYSTEM | INTEGRATED MANAGEMENT INFORMATION SYSTEM | REAL-TIME MANAGEMENT INFORMATION SYSTEM | FUTURE MANAGEMENT INFORMATION SYSTEM |
|---|---|---|---|---|---|
| Data elements | Primarily accounting data → | → | Common data bank | Common data base → | → |
| Processing mode | Batch processing → | → | → | On-line and remote batch processing → | → |
| Type of system | Backward-looking control system → | → | → | Forward-looking control system → → | → → |
| Type of files | Sequential access file storage → | → | Sequential and random access file storage | Random access on-line file storage → | → |
| Information orientation | Output-oriented → | → | → | Input/output-oriented with I/O terminals → | → |
| Exception reporting | Very little accounting exception reports | Accounting exception reports | Management exception reports | Current plans and objectives used for management exception reporting → | → |
| Reports prepared | Historical output reports for the firm | Historical output reports for all levels of management | Output reports directed to all levels of management for past operations | Output reports directed to lower and middle management for past, current, and future operations | Output reports directed to all levels of management for past, current, and future operations |
| Mathematical models | — | — | Limited use of operations research models | Greater use of operations research models | Great use of operations research models |

Figure 1-14 Important characteristics of the various approaches to business data processing systems. The arrow (⟶) denotes continued use and improvement.

*The important benefit of a management control center is paperless output of management information utilizing exception reporting.*

a form well suited for fast evaluation. Graphs, charts, indexes, and the like on the large display screen will keep the information to a minimum, thereby, increasing management's understanding. Pages and pages of tabular information can be condensed into one projected display picture. Exception reporting will reduce the amount of data for possible viewing. The use of computer-generated displays will further reduce the need for paper reporting. The speed and simplification of reporting will allow the executive considerable time for performing the tasks for which he was employed. The problem of being bogged down with paperwork will be greatly reduced since the management control center is a very large output device for management.

Although current applications for a management control center are numerous, they can be characterized as operational and tactical applications, designed to meet the needs of lower and middle management respectively for the short run. This pertains to the real-time management information systems that are currently in use. What is needed are applications at the highest level (strategic) that utilize the real potential of a computer. For example, planning and evaluating new products over

Figure 1-15 Management control center with executive armchair control panel (closeup above) reduces the need for paper reports. (Courtesy Information Management International Corporation.)

their life cycle, allocating available factory capacity in the most efficient manner throughout the firm, and setting long-range plans and objectives for the firm are areas where answers are invaluable to top management. This is basically the approach that will be forthcoming from future management information systems.

### Combines Operations Research with Data Processing

*The management control center will provide the proper environment for combining operations research with data processing operations.*

Before strategic applications can be commonplace when utilizing the output from a management control center, senior systems analysts who possess both operations research and data processing skills are needed. They provide the required link between top management and the computer system. These expert business analysts will be capable of programming sophisticated mathematical models and running them on on-site and remote input/output devices. Once the program is operational, both top management and the business analyst can sit down and simulate the actual operating conditions in the management control center. The executive can request new output information based on changes in the parameters and constraints of the problem. Within the wide range of capabilities for a specific computer model, top management will have answers that were heretofore unobtainable.

### Team Approach—Top Management and Staff Specialists

The senior analyst must be a capable mathematican although this is not necessary for top management. The manager must know what the various quantitative tools are capable of accomplishing and what their inherent limitations are. He must be able to understand what the staff specialist is attempting to achieve by a particular model and to discuss the appropriateness of alternative models. Also, he must understand the variables in the model and whether the relationships among the

*The interaction of the staff specialist (knowledgeable about computers and operations research) and the top manager will result in more exacting and far-reaching decisions in a management control center environment.*

variables make sense. In effect, the top manager cannot utilize an analytical OR model wisely unless he has knowledge about the assumptions made, what the computer-mathematical analysis is expected to achieve, and how conclusions are adaptable to changing conditions and intangible factors.

A high-level problem that makes great use of this team approach is one dealing with planning and evaluating new products over their life. The business analyst develops a series of mathematical models for evaluating a new product and its related marketing program. The models allow management to vary operating conditions, assumptions, variables, market penetrations, cost factors (manufacturing, distribution, and marketing), consumer acceptance, and like items. Included in this venture analysis model are leading indicators of the United States economy and probable reaction by competitors which are interrelated with the firm's data. With this wide assemblage of data, the analyst can simulate the introduction of the product from the research and development phase, through the start-up point, then to manufacturing, distribution, and marketing, and through its point of decay. Over the product's life cycle, profit analyses can be generated. The top executive can have the analyst vary the inputs stated above for comparison of outputs. The purpose of the venture analysis approach is not only to test how the product will perform over its life under one stated set of conditions but also to test the product under a variety of operating conditions. This means that top management will be more analytical and more exacting when it reaches its final decision in a management control center environment.

## SUMMARY

The sources of data provide the necessary input for the firm's basic data processing functions, which can be subdivided two ways:

1. input-storage-processing-control-output (ISPCO cycle),
2. originating-recording-classifying-manipulating-summarizing (report preparation)-communicating (data processing cycle).

Both of these approaches are basically the same if they are examined closely. They are found in any type of system, ranging from manual methods to sophisticated management information systems.

Several different approaches to data processing have been, are being, or will be designed by system analysts for managerial use. Before the dawn of the computer age, management was fact-minded rather than information-oriented. To state it another way, management was accounting-oriented in terms of reports rather than toward information for controlling all of the firm's basic business functions. It dealt with today's problems in the light of yesterday's results. This approach, represented by the custodial accounting system, was appropriate for the times. The structure of the firm and its markets were static and changes came gradually. As a result, today's problems were not too different from those of yesterday. With the arrival of the computer, management found it could produce many more accounting reports for a more comprehensive approach to this area. This led to the development of a responsibility reporting system that was capable of producing accounting-oriented reports for all levels of management.

These accounting-oriented approaches satisfied management during the life of first-generation computers. The dynamics of the ever-changing business world, the volume and complexity of data for producing needed managerial information, and the awakening of the computer's potential by personnel in the data processing field provided the initial thrust for better systems design. About the same time, management began to realize that the information potential of the computer had not really been exploited. Based upon the initial developments, integrated data processing systems came into being and were further refined into integrated management information systems. While this type of system is batch- and output-oriented, the next development stage is the real-time management information system that is currently in vogue. It is input- and output-oriented, making great use of I/O devices for on-line processing in real-time. With the ability to obtain information now, it is often called a forward-looking control system. Feedback received now can be the focal point of controlling present and future operations.

Future management informations systems are directed toward the total systems concept, the ultimate in automating data processing operations that are internal and external to the firm. Top management, with the aid of business systems analysts (well versed in data processing and operations research) will utilize game theory, Bayesian statistics, PERT networks, decision trees, and similar quantitative techniques to minimize the risk of doing business. They will be able to do this, and more, on the basis of up-to-date information retrieved from the computer's data base. The end result of all this systems activity is that important information will be displayed by a management control center. The center will be capable of displaying critical answers to problems under study regardless of whether they are well structured or poorly structured. The potential of the computer should be more fully realized for effective management at all levels. Thus the managers of tomorrow will utilize the computer as today's managers use the telephone.

## *QUESTIONS*

1. Define the following terms:
   (a) a business data processing system
   (b) subsystem
   (c) data
   (d) data base
   (e) information
   (f) sources of data
   (g) management by exception
   (h) total systems concept
2. (a) What are the basic sources of data to be found in any firm, regardless of the system employed?
   (b) What are the basic data processing functions to be found in any firm, regardless of the system employed?
3. (a) What basic data processing function is the most important from a systems point of view?
   (b) Answer (a) from a management point of view.
4. Why is the concept of a business data processing system so important to a manager? Explain.
5. Differentiate between basic computer access file systems and basic data processing systems.
6. (a) Distinguish between a custodial accounting system and a responsibility reporting system.
   (b) How does a responsibility reporting system effect better control in a business firm than a custodial accounting system?
7. Discuss the importance of feedback in a business data processing system.
8. What are the essential differences between an integrated data processing system and an integrated management information system?
9. Distinguish between a backward-looking control system and a forward-looking control system.

10. Distinguish between a batch processing system and an on-line real-time processing system.
11. Which of the two basic methods utilized in processing business data is most common today? Why?
12. Discuss the essential characteristics of a real-time management information system.
13. How do future management information systems differ from those currently in use?
14. Since systems designers turned from accounting-oriented systems to information systems many years ago, what must be the next trend in business data processing systems?
15. What are the essential differences between future management information systems and the total systems concept carried to the highest degree of implementation?

# II

# DATA ENTRY AND PUNCHED CARD DATA PROCESSING

## CHAPTER TWO

# Data Entry and Punched Card Equipment

*The initial phase of automated business data processing centered around punched card equipment. Continuing developments are causing changes in data entry from punched card input to other means of input. These include keyboard data entry onto magnetic disk and tape as illustrated. (Courtesy Honeywell Information Systems.)*

In the past, firms have relied heavily on two types of equipment for business data processing: punched card machines and computers. Today, there is greater emphasis on the latter, combined with optical character recognition equipment, source data collection devices, and on-line input/output devices. Even though the trend is away from punched card machines, there are still a substantial number of them in operation in addition to many small, card-oriented computer systems. There are, for example, approximately 600,000 key punches and verifiers operating in the United States presently, with about 80% of these in clusters of 14 units or more. Thus, an understanding of punched card machines contributes to a comprehensive overview and knowledge of the entire data processing field.

This chapter (and Chapter Three) goes beyond an explanation of the various punched card machines that have been utilized. It also focuses on data entry devices that circumvent the need for punched cards when the data are initially captured from the source document. This current approach eliminates unnecessary processes, thereby reducing the cost of the data processing system while increasing its speed. As time passes, better methods will be discovered to replace or supplement contemporary advances in data entry equipment.

## THE UNIT RECORD PRINCIPLE

*The unit record principle refers to a unit of recorded data and its storage medium, such as punched card, punched paper tape, and magnetic tape.*

Source documents used to record daily business activity vary widely in their size, content, and arrangement of data. Uniformity is not present because of the specific requirements of the firm's departments and functions; hence, it is not possible to gather and process the data as they are. Rather, information must be processed in some logical order whether it be a manual system, a punched card system, or some computer system. For a punched card system, original documents must be first converted into a machine-readable form before processing can occur. The punched card serves as such a form and is commonly referred to as a *unit record,* that is, a unit of recorded data. In data processing installations, the unit record principle is applicable to other storage mediums, such as punched paper tape and magnetic tape.

*The unit record concept requires that data from the source document be transferred to a machine-processable medium. This allows the repeated usage of data for various data processing runs.*

***Data Recorded Once.*** The important feature of the unit record concept is that the data from the source document are recorded once in some machine-processable medium. Once the data are transferred to a unit record, they are in a permanent form that can be used repeatedly for a variety of processing runs. For punched cards, it may be necessary to have more than one punched card to represent a document or transaction. Under this circumstance, it is necessary to have a set of cards, consisting of a master card and one or more trailer cards. The most used information should appear in the master while less frequently used data should be punched into the trailer card(s). If this procedure is followed, file handling and manipulation will be kept to a minimum.

***Unit Record Illustration.*** One way to visualize a unit record (punched card) is to think in terms of a single customer sale. A typical sale results in the following accounting entries: recording amount in the sales register, relieving finished goods inventory, posting to the accounts receivable ledger, posting to the salesman account, and posting to the commission records. Using manual or bookkeeping machine methods, these entries require copying and recopying the same set of data for different accounting records. Under the unit record principle, all data relating to the sale are keypunched and key verified into one punched card that is used over and over again for all accounting entries. Likewise, this same sales card can be used to produce various sales reports and to age accounts receivable. In this manner, all recopying and regrouping of accounting data are performed automatically by punched card equipment which is faster and less costly than manual entry or posting machine methods.

*Generally, economies are available with punched card equipment when cards are processed on approximately six different runs.*

***Justification of Unit Record Equipment.*** Punched card or unit record equipment is a most economical method of processing business data if the data cards are used many times. The cutoff point for justifying punched card machines varies by installation but, as a general guideline, the punched card should be used about six times. The rationale is that pegboard manual methods, especially in accounting, allow us to obtain three records for the price of one writing. Likewise, it should be obvious that it is faster to write and correct a record than to keypunch and key verify the same set of data. Thus, considering these factors, punched card economies are available with unit record equipment when punched cards are processed on approximately six different runs. Generally, the attendant circumstances must be analyzed to determine the specific cutoff point for a particular application.

## THE PUNCHED CARD

The holes in the punched card can be used for many purposes. The results that can be obtained from the punched holes are given below.

- It will add itself to something else.
- It will subtract itself from something else.
- It will multiply itself by something else.
- It will divide itself into something else.
- It will list itself.
- It will reproduce itself.
- It will classify itself.
- It will select itself.
- It will print itself on the card.
- It will produce an automatic balance forward.
- It will file itself.
- It will post itself.
- It will reproduce and print itself on the end of a card.
- It will be punched from a pencil mark on the card.
- It will cause a total to be printed.
- It will compare itself to something else.
- It will cause a form to feed to a predetermined position, or to be ejected automatically, or to space from one position to another.

*Punched cards available today include:*
- *80 column card*
- *90 column card*
- *96 column card*

The 80 or 90 column card is a thin piece of cardboard that measures $7\frac{3}{8}$ by $3\frac{1}{4}$ inches and .007 inches thick. (These dimensions correspond to our paper currency in the period of development of the punched card, and so were chosen arbitrarily for the punched card.) On the other hand, the more recent 96 column card is approximately one-third the size of the present 80 or 90 column card. The corners may be either sharp or rounded, depending upon the application. Generally, one corner is cut to keep the cards right end up during processing.

In the following sections, the IBM punched cards—80 and 96 columns—and their related machines will be discussed since these installations are, by far, the most common. Today, the RR 90 column card equipment has become almost extinct because of the acceptance of the IBM cards as the industry standard.

While the introduction of the 96 column card by IBM in 1969 has brought the question of standardization into sharp focus again, the general principles discussed are readily applicable to all punched card systems, regardless of their card column capabilities.

### 80 Column Card

The 80 column card, shown in Figure 2-1, is divided into 80 columns (numbered 1 through 80), going from left to right. Each column, in turn, is divided into 12 rows

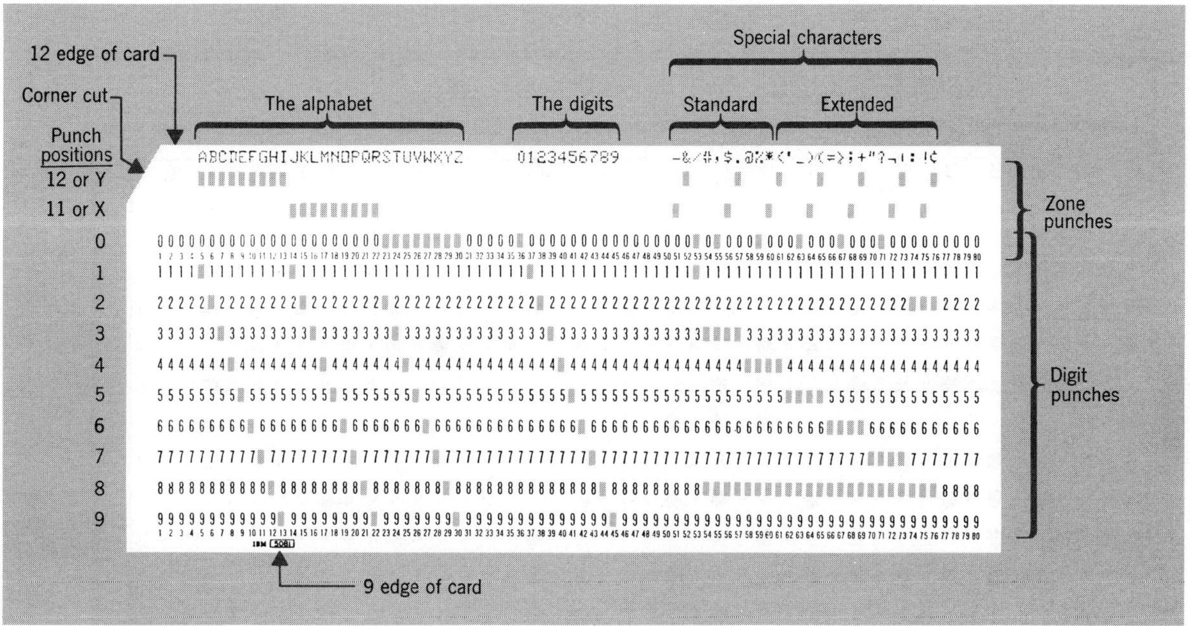


Figure 2-1 80 column punched card.

*The 80 column card employs one punch for numerics and two punches for alphabetics. The entire card's width is used for punching column by column data.*

or punching positions. The punching positions, from the top of the card to the bottom, are 12 or Y, 11 or X, and 0 through 9. While the top three punching positions of the card—12, 11, and 0—are the zone punches, the 0 through 9 are the digit punches. It should be noted that the zero punch position may be either a zone punch or the digit 0. The top edge of the card is called the "12 edge" and the bottom of the card is the "9 edge" while the printed position of the card is called the face. The edge of the card is important since some machines process cards 9 edge first while others process cards 12 edge first.

If a numeric is to be coded, say 5, the position 5 is punched out. All other numerics are punched in a like manner. For the alphabetic characters A through Z, more than one punch is required in each column. The alphabetic combinations have a logical structure, as can be seen in Figure 2-1. The first nine letters (A through I) are coded with the 12 punch and a digit. For example, the C is a combination 12 or Y punch and a digit punch 3. Likewise, the letters J through R use the 11 or X punch combined with an appropriate digit. The letters S through Z utilize the 0 punch and consecutive digits, starting with digit 2. Special characters are shown at the right-hand side of the card in Figure 2-1. They are recorded by one, two, or three punches in a column.

*The 90 column card employs one or two punches for numerics and two or three punches for alphabetics. Only half of the card's width is used for punching column by column data.*

### 90 Column Card

The Remington Rand card contains 90 columns, 45 columns in the upper half of the card and 45 columns in the lower half. The numerics 0, 1, 3, 5, 7, and 9 are coded in the card by having the appropriate position punched. However, the numerics 2, 4, 6, and 8 require two punched holes in the card, a combination of the appropriate 1, 3, 5, and 7 punch plus the 9 punch, as shown in Figure 2-2.

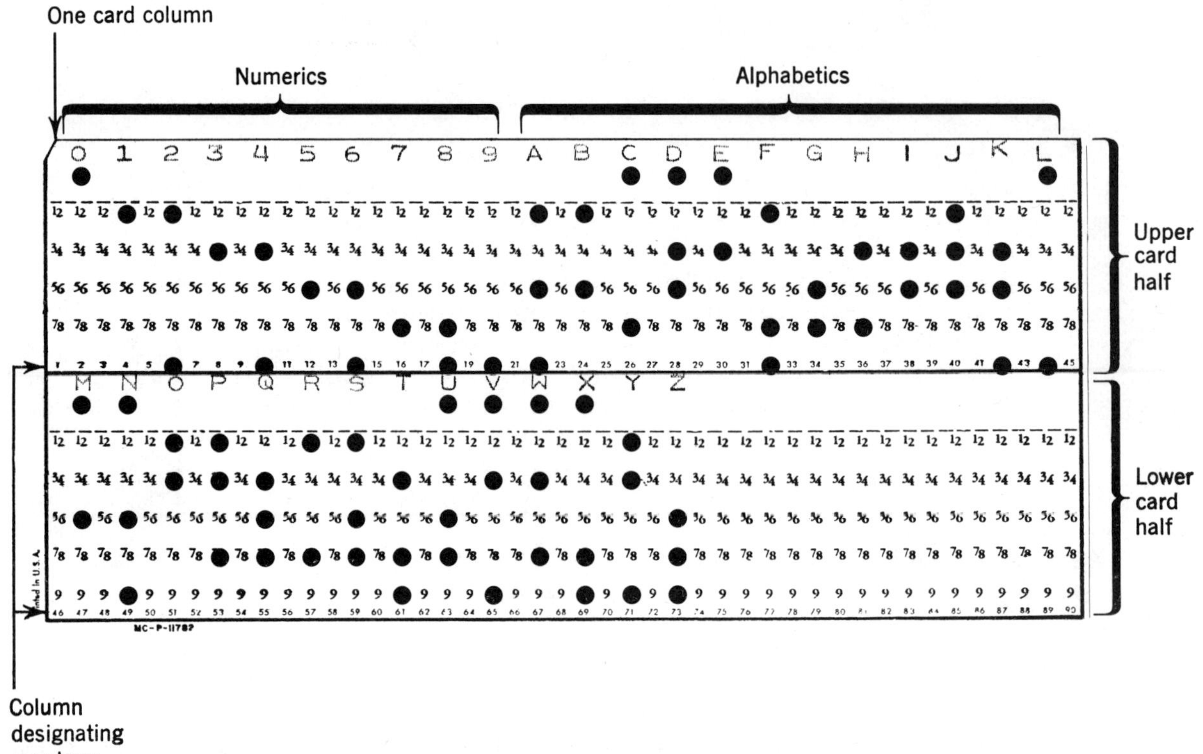


Figure 2-2 90 column punched card.

As noted above, there is a logical framework for the alphabetic characters in a 80 column card. The same cannot be said for the 90 column card, as seen in Figure 2-2.

### 96 Column Card

The size and structure of the 96 column card is different from the two punched cards discussed above. It can hold 16 more characters than an 80 column card (a 20% increase) and up to 128 characters can be printed on the face of the card (a 60% increase over an 80 column card). These differences for a card about one-third the size of the 80 column card are shown in Figure 2-3. Regarding the card's structure, the punching area is divided into three parts: upper half—columns

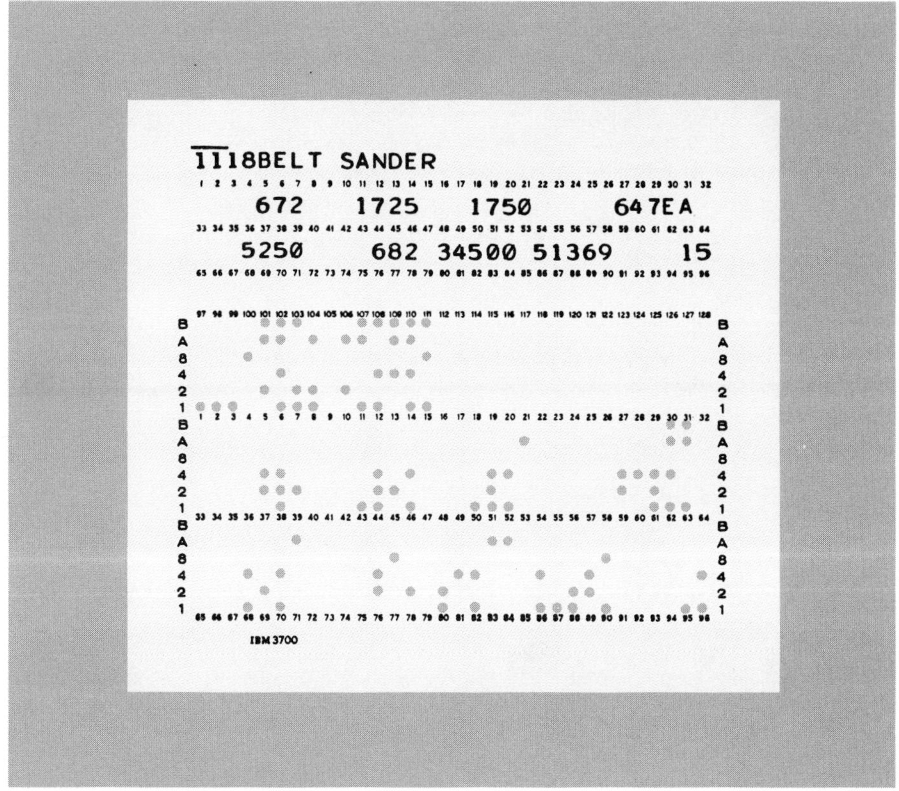


Figure 2-3 96 column punched card.

*The 96 column card employs the 6-bit binary coded decimal system. The 8-4-2-1 are for numerics and the B-A-8-4-2-1 are for alphabetics. Only one-third of the card's width is utilized for punching column by column data.*

1 through 32, middle half—columns 33 through 64, and lower half—columns 65 through 96.

***6-Bit BCD System.*** The method of coding data into the card is the 6-bit binary coded decimal (BCD) system or B-A-8-4-2-1. (More will be said about the BCD system in Chapter 6.) The B-A combination represents the zone punches while the numerics are used for the digit punches and the alphabetics. The comparable schemes for the 96 column card and the 80 column card are shown in Figure 2-4.

The BCD system is one of the most common variations of the binary system, employing only the four binary positions of 1, 2, 4, and 8. Any numeric from 0 through 9 can be represented by a combination of these four values. The value 3 is a combination of binary 2 and 1 positions while the value 7 is represented by binary 4, 2, and 1 positions, as shown in Figure 2-4. In a similar manner, any alphabetic characters can be represented by a combination of zone and numeric punches. The zone or binary punches for the alphabetic characters A through I are a 1 1 combination (12 zone punch for 80 column card), J through R are a 1 0 arrangement (11 zone punch), and S through Z are a 01 combination (0 zone punch). Also, the binary numeric positions that appear for 0 to 9 are applicable again to the three sets of alphabetics (the same is true of the 80 column card). For example, a C is represented by two binary 1's for the zone positions (96 column card) versus a 12 zone punch position (80 column card) and by binary values 0 0 1 1 (value of 3) for the numeric positions (96 column card) versus a 3-digit punch position (80 column card). Again, reference is made to Figure 2-4 for this comparison.

| STANDARD 80 COLUMN | | | STANDARD 96 COLUMN | | | | | |
|---|---|---|---|---|---|---|---|---|
| CHARACTER | CARD ZONE | CODE—DIGIT | BCD ZONE | | CODE—NUMERIC | | | |
| | | | B | A | 8 | 4 | 2 | 1 |
| 0 | | 0 | 0 | 1 | 0 | 0 | 0 | 0 |
| 1 | | 1 | 0 | 0 | 0 | 0 | 0 | 1 |
| 2 | | 2 | 0 | 0 | 0 | 0 | 1 | 0 |
| 3 | | 3 | 0 | 0 | 0 | 0 | 1 | 1 |
| 4 | | 4 | 0 | 0 | 0 | 1 | 0 | 0 |
| 5 | | 5 | 0 | 0 | 0 | 1 | 0 | 1 |
| 6 | | 6 | 0 | 0 | 0 | 1 | 1 | 0 |
| 7 | | 7 | 0 | 0 | 0 | 1 | 1 | 1 |
| 8 | | 8 | 0 | 0 | 1 | 0 | 0 | 0 |
| 9 | | 9 | 0 | 0 | 1 | 0 | 0 | 1 |
| A | 12 | 1 | 1 | 1 | 0 | 0 | 0 | 1 |
| B | 12 | 2 | 1 | 1 | 0 | 0 | 1 | 0 |
| C | 12 | 3 | 1 | 1 | 0 | 0 | 1 | 1 |
| D | 12 | 4 | 1 | 1 | 0 | 1 | 0 | 0 |
| E | 12 | 5 | 1 | 1 | 0 | 1 | 0 | 1 |
| F | 12 | 6 | 1 | 1 | 0 | 1 | 1 | 0 |
| G | 12 | 7 | 1 | 1 | 0 | 1 | 1 | 1 |
| H | 12 | 8 | 1 | 1 | 1 | 0 | 0 | 0 |
| I | 12 | 9 | 1 | 1 | 1 | 0 | 0 | 1 |
| J | 11 | 1 | 1 | 0 | 0 | 0 | 0 | 1 |
| K | 11 | 2 | 1 | 0 | 0 | 0 | 1 | 0 |
| L | 11 | 3 | 1 | 0 | 0 | 0 | 1 | 1 |
| M | 11 | 4 | 1 | 0 | 0 | 1 | 0 | 0 |
| N | 11 | 5 | 1 | 0 | 0 | 1 | 0 | 1 |
| O | 11 | 6 | 1 | 0 | 0 | 1 | 1 | 0 |
| P | 11 | 7 | 1 | 0 | 0 | 1 | 1 | 1 |
| Q | 11 | 8 | 1 | 0 | 1 | 0 | 0 | 0 |
| R | 11 | 9 | 1 | 0 | 1 | 0 | 0 | 1 |
| S | 0 | 2 | 0 | 1 | 0 | 0 | 1 | 0 |
| T | 0 | 3 | 0 | 1 | 0 | 0 | 1 | 1 |
| U | 0 | 4 | 0 | 1 | 0 | 1 | 0 | 0 |
| V | 0 | 5 | 0 | 1 | 0 | 1 | 0 | 1 |
| W | 0 | 6 | 0 | 1 | 0 | 1 | 1 | 0 |
| X | 0 | 7 | 0 | 1 | 0 | 1 | 1 | 1 |
| Y | 0 | 8 | 0 | 1 | 1 | 0 | 0 | 0 |
| Z | 0 | 9 | 0 | 1 | 1 | 0 | 0 | 1 |

Figure 2-4 Comparison of 80 column card code and 96 column binary coded decimal (BCD) code.

*The most frequently used punched cards, other than 80, 90, or 96 column cards, are:*
- *edge-notched*
- *edge-punched*
- *perforated*

**Other Card Types**

There are several additional punched card types that have been widely used by business. Among these are edge-notched cards, edge-punched cards, and perforated cards. Each is discussed below.

***Edge-Notched Card.*** The edge-notched card is encoded by notching the edge instead of punching all or part of it. An example is found in Figure 2-5. Note the four positions labeled 7, 4, 2, and 1 for coding each digit of information. For example, the value 4 is coded by a 4 notch and a value 8 is punched by notching the 7 and 1 positions. Cards are sorted by inserting a needle through the position examined, resulting in all edge-notched cards falling out. This method allows for sorting cards in some specified order.

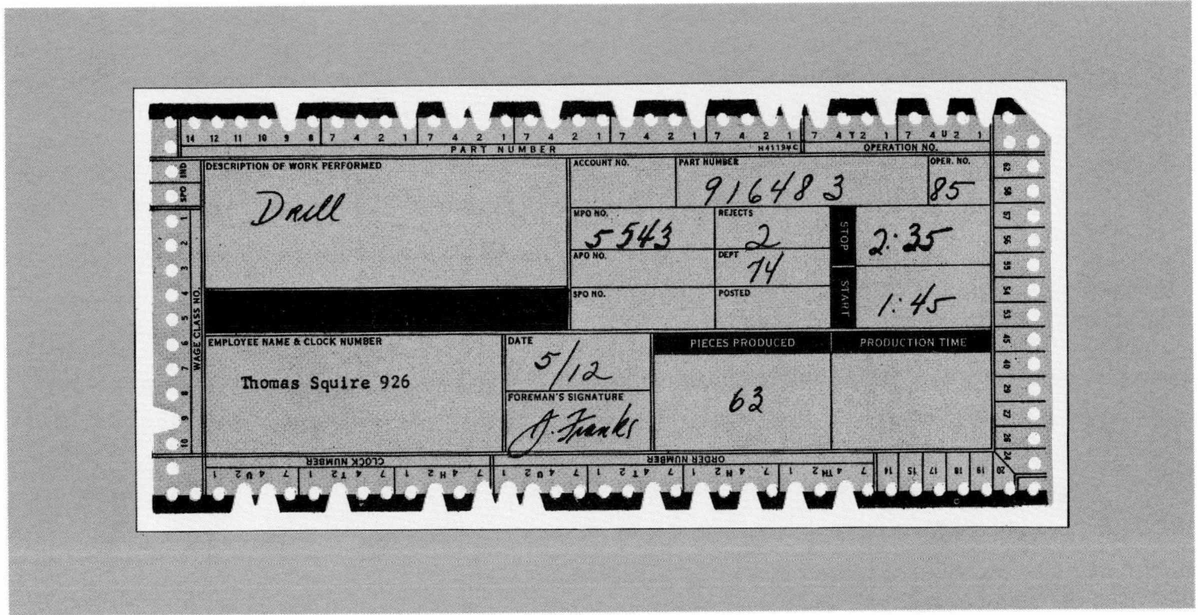


Figure 2-5 Edge-notched card. (Courtesy Litton Automated Systems.)

Another example of an edge-notched card is found in Figure 2-6. Teeth along the bottom edge of the card are selectively notched with a specific numeric or alphabetic code. This code forms the basis for selecting file cards that can be in any random or sequential order. The metallic element at the lower left-hand corner of the card interacts magnetically with the selector during the search cycle and provides the means by which selected cards are automatically delivered to the operator.

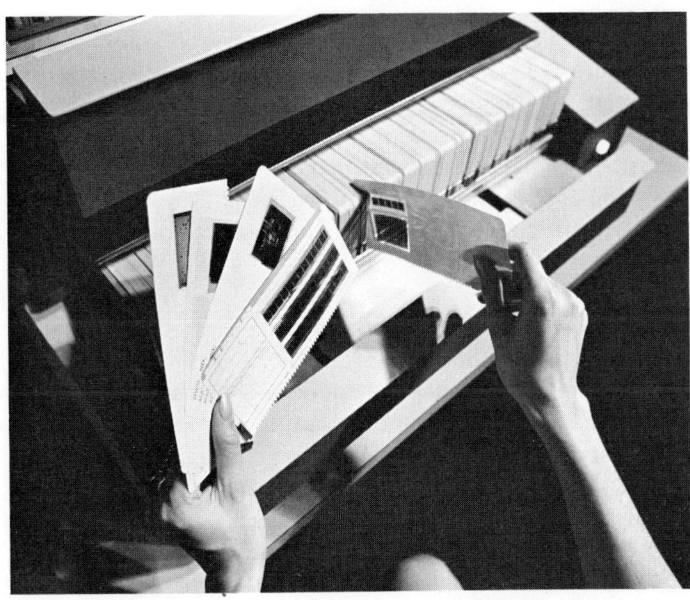

Figure 2-6 Edge-notched card. (Courtesy Access Corporation.)

***Edge-Punched Card.*** Closely related to edge-notched cards are edge-punched cards. As shown in Figure 2-7, the card is punched along the lower edge with rows of small holes. The basis for punching is the same as for punched paper tape (see Chapter 3 for additional information). The Flexowriter, produced by Friden, Inc., or other comparable equipment is needed to prepare edge-punched cards. These, in turn, must be read by special equipment and converted to other media (such as 80 column cards or punched tape) before further processing can be undertaken.

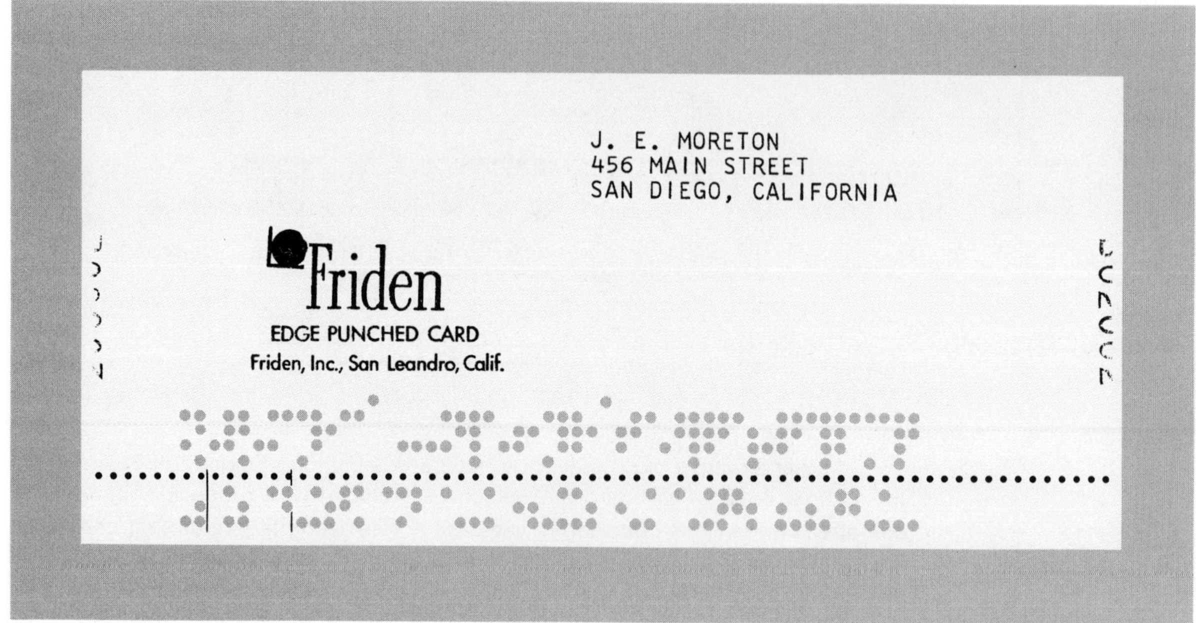


Figure 2-7 Edge-punched card. (Courtesy Friden, Inc.)

***Perforated Card.*** A punched card used widely for customer billing is the perforated card, shown in Figure 2-8. The card is a full-size 80 column card. It is perforated and consists of two sections—one section to be returned with payment (51 columns) and a smaller section to be retained by the customer (29 columns). When returned by the customer, the 51 column section is read by a special attachment to punched card equipment. As an alternative, the smaller 29 column section could be returned. Again, special equipment is needed to read the punched data.

## FIELDS OF INFORMATION

*One or more columns that are grouped together to record a specific amount of information is called a field of information.*

For most information punched into one of the foregoing cards, more than one column will be required. Examples are found in Figures 2-9 and 2-10. In the 80 column card, 12 columns are adequate for all customer names while 5 columns are necessary to handle customer numbers. The number of columns required for the sales accounting card depends on the data being analyzed. Thus, when a number of column data are grouped together to record a specific piece of information, this group of columns is called a *field of information*.

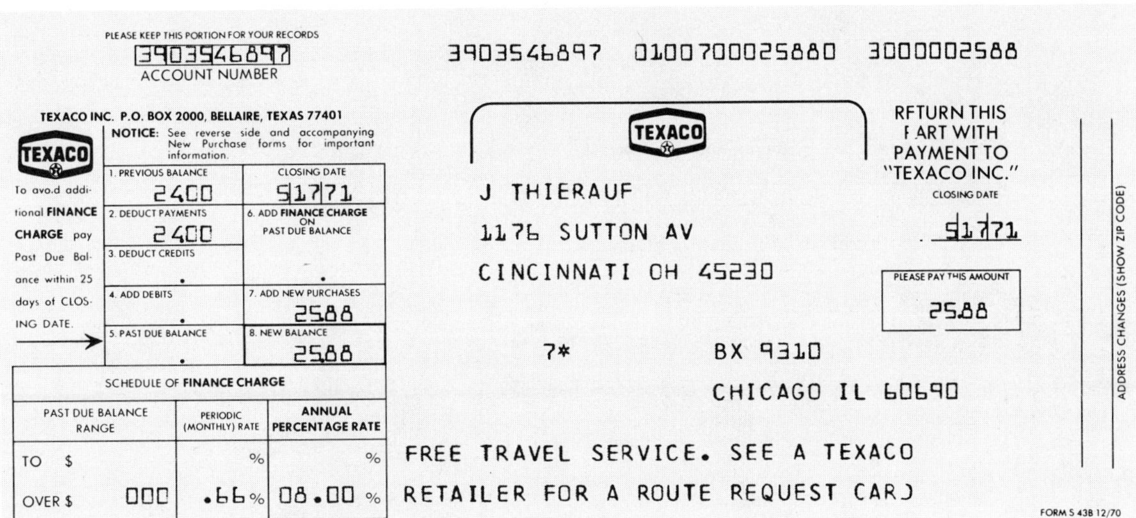

PLEASE KEEP THIS PORTION FOR YOUR RECORDS

3903546897

ACCOUNT NUMBER

3903546897 0100700025880 3000002588

TEXACO INC. P.O. BOX 2000, BELLAIRE, TEXAS 77401

NOTICE: See reverse side and accompanying New Purchase forms for important information.

TEXACO

To avoid additional FINANCE CHARGE pay Past Due Balance within 25 days of CLOSING DATE.

| 1. PREVIOUS BALANCE | CLOSING DATE |
|---|---|
| 2400 | 5 17 71 |
| 2. DEDUCT PAYMENTS | 6. ADD FINANCE CHARGE ON PAST DUE BALANCE |
| 2400 | |
| 3. DEDUCT CREDITS | |
| . | . |
| 4. ADD DEBITS | 7. ADD NEW PURCHASES |
| . | 2588 |
| 5. PAST DUE BALANCE | 8. NEW BALANCE |
| . | 2588 |

SCHEDULE OF FINANCE CHARGE

| PAST DUE BALANCE RANGE | PERIODIC (MONTHLY) RATE | ANNUAL PERCENTAGE RATE |
|---|---|---|
| TO $ | % | % |
| OVER $ 000 | .66 % | 08.00 % |

TEXACO

J THIERAUF

1176 SUTTON AV

CINCINNATI OH 45230

7* BX 9310

CHICAGO IL 60690

FREE TRAVEL SERVICE. SEE A TEXACO RETAILER FOR A ROUTE REQUEST CARD

RETURN THIS PART WITH PAYMENT TO "TEXACO INC."

CLOSING DATE 5 17 71

PLEASE PAY THIS AMOUNT 2588

ADDRESS CHANGES (SHOW ZIP CODE)

FORM S 438 12/70

Figure 2-8 Perforated card—used widely for billing.

The length of the field of information is determined by the maximum number of characters to be entered. Data, such as dates, names, and locations can use considerable space. Coding is the best way to use card space effectively, especially in a card already crammed with data fields. Digits 1 through 12 can be utilized to designate months, customers can be given account numbers to replace names, and zip codes can be utilized to replace city and state. Although

NEW MEX CO 59751 41 143 968 13 067 1231 12349 00040 11202 0003320

| CUSTOMER NAME | CUST. NO. | LOCATION ST. | LOCATION CITY | TRADE CLASS | BRANCH | SALESMAN NO. | DATE MO. | DATE DAY | INV. NO. | QUANTITY | COMMODITY NO. | ITEM AMOUNT | INVOICE AMOUNT |
|---|---|---|---|---|---|---|---|---|---|---|---|---|---|

Sales Accounting

IBM

Figure 2-9 80 column card illustration of fields.

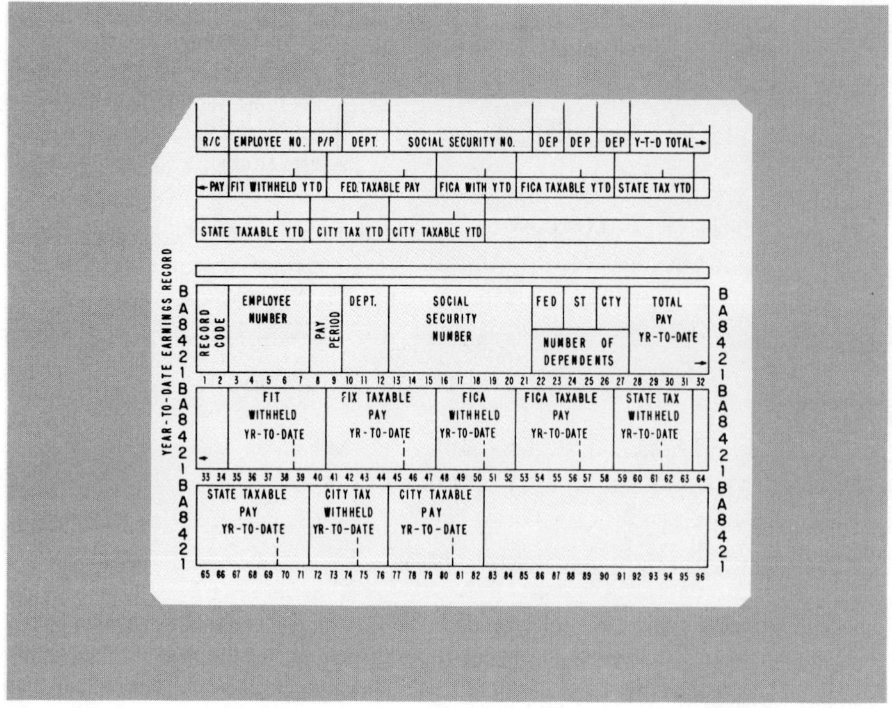


Figure 2-10 96 column card illustration of fields.

data processing equipment can read coded data, there are limits to coding. The individual must be able to identify the code readily if human intervention or action is necessary within the system. For example, it makes no sense to produce customer invoices containing only a customer number if the invoice must be mailed to the customer. Common sense dictates the best coding approach.

## CODING METHODS

*An efficient coding method should encompass these factors:*

- *contain as few digits as possible*
- *be comprehensive in coverage*
- *allow for future growth*
- *be simple enough for visual interpretation*

Several coding methods have been developed for data processing systems. Among these are:

1. sequence coding
2. block coding
3. group coding
4. significant digit coding
5. mnemonic coding

No matter what coding system is used, it should include the following factors. The code should contain as few digits as possible in order to conserve space; the code should be comprehensive in coverage; and the coding scheme should allow for additional capacity for future expansion, including space within the coding structure to add new items. Also, the coding structure should be simple so that the code is clearly identifiable by visual analysis.

*Sequence Coding Example:*

| | |
|---|---|
| *Bolts* | *1020* |
| *Braces* | *1021* |
| *Clamps* | *1022* |
| *Nuts* | *1023* |
| *Screws* | *1024* |
| *Washers* | *1025* |

***Sequence Coding.*** In the sequence coding method, numbers are assigned sequentially to items that have already been arranged in some order. This approach is useful for any limited list of accounts, names, products, and the like where the only concern is the application of simple code numbers and where arrangement of data is not important. The cutoff point for a sequential coded list is about 25 to 35 items and where there is complete assurance that no new items will be added. It will be seen below that this method is a part of other coding methods.

*Block Coding Example:*

| | |
|---|---|
| *Bolts* | *1100–1199* |
| *Screws* | *1200–1299* |
| *Braces* | *1300–1399* |
| *Clamps* | *1400–1499* |
| *Nuts* | *1500–1599* |
| *Washers* | *1600–1699* |

***Block Coding.*** Under the block coding method, blocks of numbers in sequence, other than tens, hundreds, and thousands are utilized to represent classifications of data. Any number of items can be included in a block, giving flexibility without wasting space. Room for future expansion should be provided within each group by leaving open (unassigned) numbers. Thus, an important feature of this method is that block coding allows more groups with fewer digits than other methods.

*Group Coding Example:*

| | |
|---|---|
| *Bolts* | *1100* |
| *Screws* | *1200* |
| *Braces* | *2100* |
| *Clamps* | *2200* |
| *Nuts* | *3100* |
| *Washers* | *4100* |

***Group Coding.*** Group coding segregates major and minor classifications by coding in groups of thousands, hundreds, and tens. All coded items have the same number of digits. However, the extreme left digit is the basis for the major classification while each succeeding digit to the right identifies more and more detailed classifications.

*Significant Digit Coding Example:*

| | |
|---|---|
| *Bolts 2″* | *1102* |
| *Bolts 3″* | *1103* |
| *Screws 6″* | *1206* |
| *Screws 8″* | *1208* |
| *Braces 45°* | *2145* |
| *Braces 90°* | *2190* |

***Significant Digit Coding.*** Significant digit coding uses one or more of the digits to indicate the specific nature, size, weight, or some other quantitative factor of each item. An important feature of this coding method is that it reduces confusion and errors by incorporating visual recognition right into the code. This coding method is suitable for coding long lists of inventory items, but is not as flexible as regular group coding where another number can be easily assigned. After a period of time, the code endings become less meaningful and the system degenerates into one analogous to regular group coding.

*Mnenomic Coding Example:*

| | |
|---|---|
| *Bolts 2″* | *BLT02* |
| *Bolts 3″* | *BLT03* |
| *Screws 6″* | *SCR06* |
| *Screws 8″* | *SCR08* |
| *Braces 45°* | *BRC45* |
| *Braces 90°* | *BRC90* |

***Mnemonic Coding.*** The last of the most commonly used coding methods is mnemonic symbols. This is a combination of numbers and letters that is helpful to the eye or ear. Mnemonic symbols are used extensively where it is advantageous to memorize code designations. Any time a coding system contains alphabetic codes, more time will be spent sorting cards on punched card equipment, not to mention the inability to collate alphabetic information on some machines. Since the 80 column sorter can read only one punch per column at a time, alphabetic coding requires two passes per column on the sorter, one for the zone punch and one for the digit punch. This limitation of punched card machines is not applicable to computers.

## BASIC TYPES OF CARDS

*Basic types of cards available are:*

- *transcript*
- *dual*
- *mark-sensed*
- *stub*
- *short*
- *continuous form*
- *multipurpose*
- *summary*
- *aperture*

Cards utilized by a data processing installation vary widely, depending on the application. The type of card is a function of the system's manual and machine operations that are anticipated. Although cards vary in content and design, all have a place within a business data processing installation. There are many different types; the more basic ones are explained below.

***Transcript Cards.*** Transcript cards are punched from information previously recorded on another document. The key punch operator reads the source document and depresses the appropriate keys for transcribing the data. Any punched card, such as the one shown in Figure 2-9, is a transcript card since the information is punched from the original source document.

***Dual Cards.*** Dual cards are punched from information written previously on the card itself. This type of card serves the dual function of being a source document and a machine-processable card. Daily time tickets, master address cards, and inventory cards are common examples where values are recorded on the card in pen or pencil. Later, they are keypunched and key verified.

***Mark-Sensed Cards.*** Mark-sensed cards, like the one shown in Figure 2-11, are automatically punched from electrically sensed electrographic pencil marks (recorded on the face of the card) by using a punched card reproducer. This equipment senses the electrographical marks and converts them to punched holes. Examination of a marked-sensed card reveals that the capacity of the 80 column card is 27 mark-sense columns. If the pencil-marked data are not to be recorded

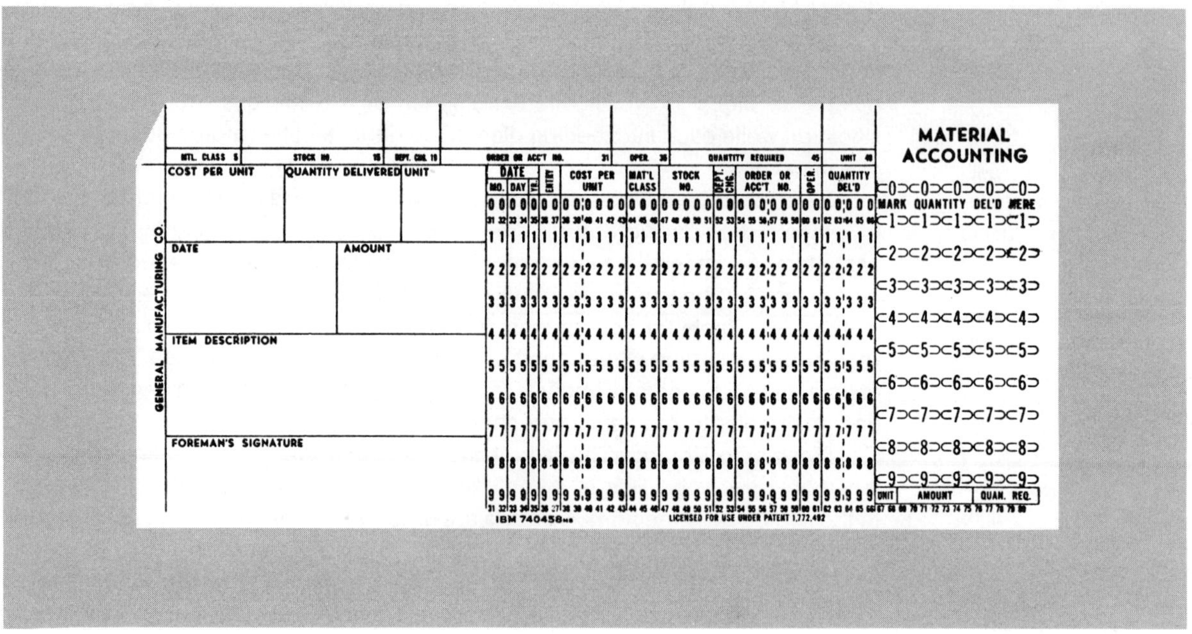


Figure 2-11 Mark-sensed card.

in the card containing the markings but punched into another card(s), both sides can be used for mark-sensing. This raises the capacity of the card to 54 mark-sense columns. It should be pointed out that the mark-sensed card must be processed twice when reading from both sides of the card.

***Stub Cards.*** Stub cards are available with a perforated stub on either the right or left end of the card. When the smaller section of the card has been detached, a regular-sized punched card remains. They are used in situations that require tags, labels, or stubs. Stub cards are utilized for monthly loan payments and are bound into a packet form that resembles a checking account book.

***Short Cards.*** Short cards, as shown in Figure 2-8, are 80 column cards with perforations for detaching the stub. Even though the cards are less than regular size after detaching the stub, machines are adaptable to process them. Oil companies and utilities make great use of short cards for payments on account.

***Continuous Form Cards.*** Continuous form cards which are attached at top and bottom to other forms are readily processable in standard form-feeding devices. Cards of this type are generally prenumbered and prepunched for internal control reasons.

***Multipurpose Cards.*** Multipurpose cards contain many card formats that can serve the same or different applications of the firm's data processing system. These cards are quite common since the number of cards kept in stock is minimized. There is one word of caution: with too many formats in one card, the readibility of the card decreases as more formats are added. This is apparent in Figure 2-12.

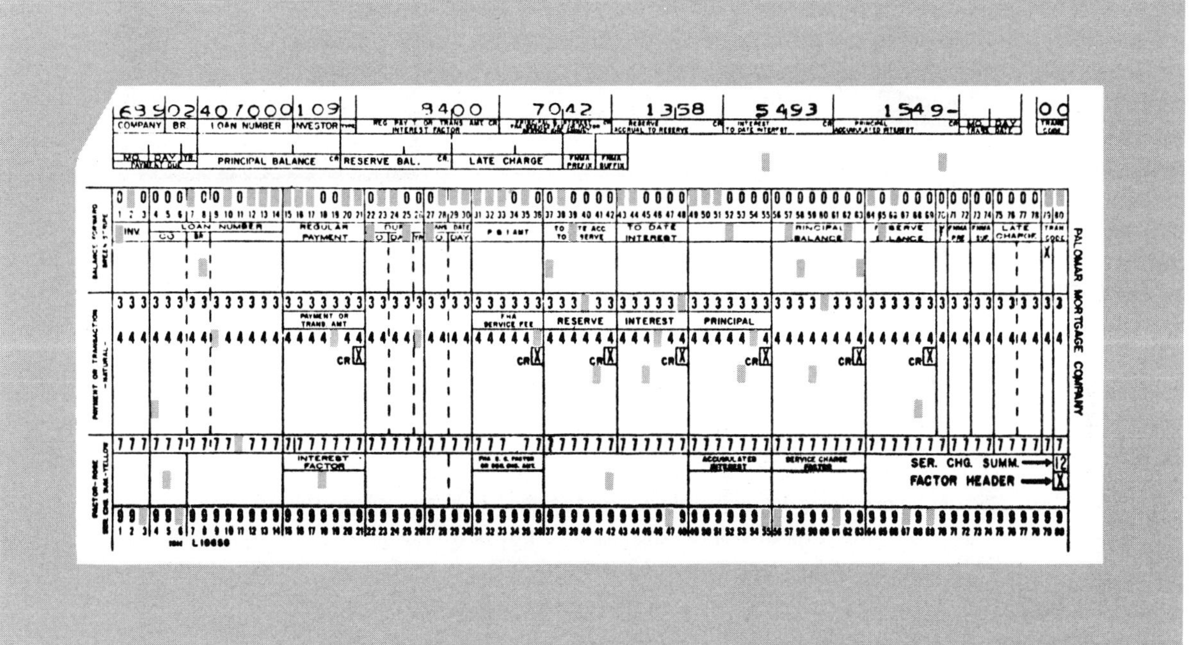


Figure 2-12 Multipurpose card.

***Summary Cards.*** Summary cards are punched automatically with totals that have been accumulated by some data processing equipment, such as the summary punch. Like transcript cards, these cards do not have any physical features that distinguish them from other types of cards. An example of a summary card is the sales invoice card that is created after detail billing cards have been totaled on punched card equipment.

***Aperture Cards.*** Aperture cards are ordinary 80 column cards (Figure 2-13) with rectangular openings designed to accommodate microfilm frames. The filmed images can be used in conjunction with viewing devices and enlarged paper copies can be made from the cards. Data concerning the microfilm frame can be key-punched and interpreted. This permits aperture cards to be collated, reproduced, and sorted just like any other punched card. An important use for this card type is the storage and retrieval of engineering drawings and sketches.

## CARD DESIGN

Card design is the process of determining the pattern of data to be placed on a punched card. In order to produce an optimum design, it is essential to have a thorough knowledge and understanding of the output, principally reports, to be

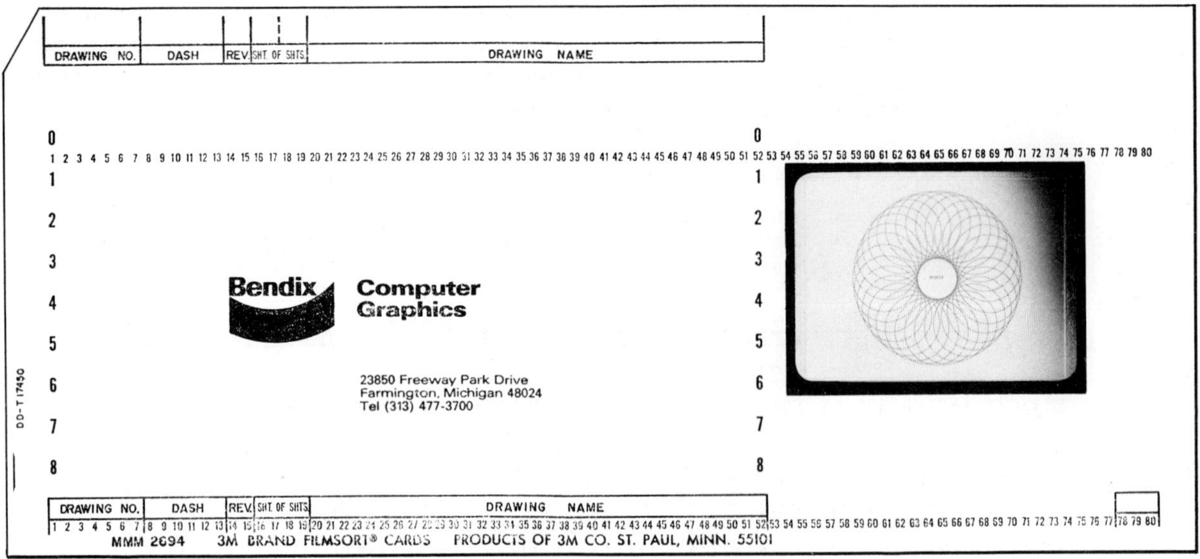


Figure 2-13 Aperture card. (Courtesy Bendix Computer Graphics.)

*Good card design entails these principles:*
- *alignment*
- *punching sequence from source documents*
- *placement of types of information*
- *methods of punching*

prepared from the cards. Once that has been determined, one is ready to begin the actual design of the card or cards necessary for the application.

*The first card design principle is that of alignment, that is, a field of information in one card is placed in the same column or columns in other cards.*

***Alignment Principle.*** If the firm has other cards already designed or if several new cards are being designed or redesigned simultaneously, a very important data processing principle must be followed. This is the *alignment principle* which states that a given item or field of information in a new card should always be placed in the same columns as assigned to other cards. This alignment of fields assures that common data necessary for sorting, collating, and controlling procedures will be compatible when all cards are used together. Wiring of punched card equipment is immeasurably facilitated when common fields of information are placed in the same columns on all punched cards. For example, the manipulation of payroll data, the aging of accounts receivable, or the preparation of inventory summaries are relatively easy tasks for punched card equipment if common fields are aligned.

*The second card design principle concerns the punching sequence from a source document. Reading by the key puncher occurs from left to right and from top to bottom of the page.*

***Punching Sequence from Source Documents.*** When designing a punched card, consideration must be given to the task of the key punch operator. It is desirable that the key punch operator be able to read needed information from the source document by scanning from left to right and from top to bottom of the page (as is the custom in normal reading). If the card is not designed in this manner, it not only makes accuracy more difficult to achieve but also contributes to unnecessary operator fatigue. A properly planned card design, then, will simplify the operator's task and will result in improved accuracy and increased output.

***Types of Information.*** Since the amount of data that can fit on a single punched card is limited to 80 characters, it is necessary to select the most important data to be included. As stated above, the contents are largely dependent on the output. Even though the data requirements vary by application, there are basically three types: reference, classification, and quantitative. *Reference* data indicate the original sources of data and their relationship to other data, such as batch number, invoice

*The third card design principle concerns the layout of informational data. Generally, reference, classification, and quantitative data are placed from left to right.*

number, or account number. The second type, *classification* data, allows for grouping and summarization of comparable data, such as by geographic area or by state. The last basic type is *quantitative* data, which may be added, subtracted, multiplied, or divided. Examples include sales amount or inventory on hand. Generally, reference information should be placed to the left of the card, classification data in the center of the card, quantitative information to the right of the card.

*The fourth card design principle concerns methods of punching. This refers to the means by which fields are to be punched, that is, keypunched, duplicated, calculator punched, etc.*

***Methods of Punching.*** The fourth consideration for card design is methods of punching. This means that the method by which a field of information is to be punched, that is, keypunched, duplicated, calculator punched, and the like, must be determined. All similar punching operations should be grouped logically in order to simplify the job of wiring and eliminate unnecessary skipping on the key punch machine.

No matter how hard the systems designer tries to mesh all four considerations of card design (alignment principle, punching from source documents, types of information, and methods of punching), not all requirements can be fully met. An intelligent compromise is necessary to resolve the resulting conflicts.

## DATA ENTRY AND PUNCHED CARD EQUIPMENT

*The major types of data entry and punched card equipment to be covered are:*
- *data recording*
- *verifying*
- *reproducing*
- *interpreting*
- *sorting*
- *collating*
- *calculating*
- *card proving*
- *reporting*

The processing capabilities of punched card equipment include all those necessary for performing basic business data processing functions within the firm. They include data recording, verifying, reproducing, posting, interpreting, sorting, collating, counting, computing, listing, summarizing, printing, and communicating. To meet these data processing functions, punched card machines are designed to be flexible and variable. Regarding flexibility, the equipment is capable of performing more than one function to meet the data processing requirements. This flexibility is available through the wiring unit (control panel) since different wired panels can be programmed for varied applications. In a similar manner, punched card machines are variable in that many combinations of equipment can perform the given data processing applications, some of which will be more efficient than others in getting the specific task accomplished.

The punched card equipment, discussed in the following material, is basically that of the International Business Machines Corporation. Other large manufacturers of data processing equipment have developed and marketed numerous equipment devices that either compete directly with IBM or represent advances in the field of data entry equipment. The appropriate method and manufacturers will be noted on the following pages.

*Data recording—the process of capturing data from input documents and sources—comprises these methods:*
- *manual punch*
- *mark-sensing*
- *punching as a by-product*
- *card punch*
- *data recorder*
- *keyboard to magnetic tape*
- *magnetic data inscriber*
- *keyboard data entry system*

### Data Recording

Today, there are several methods for capturing data from originating documents and sources. Data recording techniques include: manual punching, mark-sensing using a reproducing punch, punching as a by-product, keypunching with a card punch machine, keypunching to magnetic tape, magnetic data inscribing, keyboard data entry recording, and similar methods. Of these several methods, the keypunch method has been the most widely used. Data punching directly onto magnetic disk and tape has replaced many key punch machines and has saved considerable time and expense. This trend will continue because it benefits the firm.

***Manual Punch.*** The simplest method of data punching is to punch out (manu-

Manual punching is the process of punching holes manually in a prescored card.

ally) holes on a prescored card. Figure 2-14 shows the IBM Information Recorder 3000. An attached stylus is used to punch out prescored areas in the card. The entire application format is contained on a replaceable overlay that permits the unit to be used for any number of applications simply by changing overlays. Every other column is skipped on the card to preserve its strength. This provides only 40 columns of card capacity. In addition to Figure 2-14, there are other portable punches available, some of which are electrically powered.

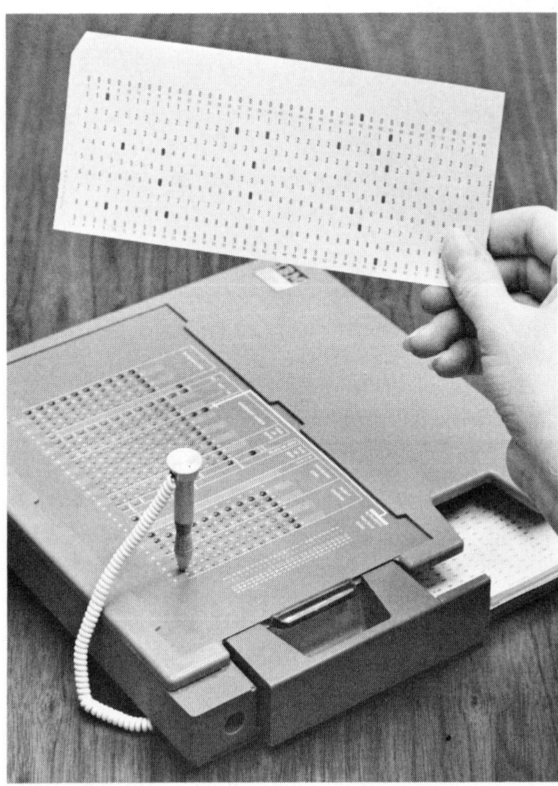

Figure 2-14 IBM Information Recorder 3000. (Courtesy International Business Machines Corporation.)

Manual punching is used for market research, quality control, work sampling, time reporting, school censuses, medical claims, and balloting purposes. The number of possible applications is limited only by the caliber of the operator. The outstanding advantage of this method is the ability to record data without having to operate punched card equipment.

Mark-sense method employs the reproducing punch to read special electrographic pencil marks on mark-sensed cards.

***Mark-Sensing.*** The mark-sensing method utilizes the reproducing punch (refer to Figure 2-32 later in the chapter) to read the marks of a special electrographic pencil for punching holes in the card. An alternative method in processing mark-sensed cards is to utilize optical scanning equipment that does not require a special lead pencil. Under either method of processing mark-sensed cards, the field operator, such as a public utility meter reader or delivery man, marks the appropriate spaces on the card (see Figure 2-11). If a reproducing punch is used, data are punched in selected columns of the same card from which they were read. A mark-sensed card is an example of the dual card discussed previously.

Punching as a by-product is an additional punched output that is produced automatically by some data processing operation.

***Punching as a By-Product.*** The 2201 Flexowriter, shown in Figure 2-15, is an example of punching as a by-product of another operation. This unit is basically a typewriter that can be cable-connected to provide more input sources and output in the form of punched paper tape, tabulating cards, and edge-punched cards. The Flexowriter has the flexibility and reliability needed for purchase orders, sales orders, production orders, personnel records, and other applications. In addition to this off-line unit, several manufacturers provide similar optional input and output attachments to their bookkeeping machines.

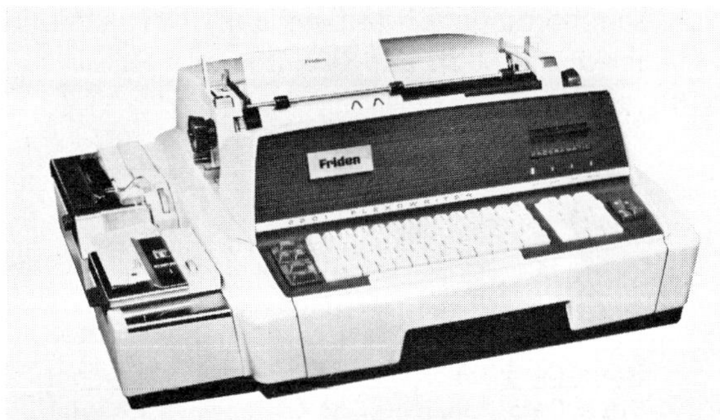


Figure 2-15 2201 Flexowriter with edge-punched card attachment. (Courtesy Friden, Inc.)

The more advanced off-line equipment of this type can be used for several operations. Shown in Figure 2-16 is the L 3000 Window Accounting Computer by Burroughs which combines billing and general accounting compatibilities with the ability to be an on-line computer terminal. This combination gives flexibility to the user since he can meet changing data processing requirements without buying new equipment. This unit operates with a wide range of peripheral devices for input and output of information to process a variety of accounting applications. The L 3000

Figure 2-16 L 3000 Window Accounting Computer. (Courtesy Burroughs, Inc.)

utilizes micrologic, also known as firmware, which is a software concept that performs the basic logic and arithmetic functions that are usually performed by the hardware on data processing equipment. It is programmed in COBOL (the common business programming language) internally on a small disk memory.

*Card punch converts data entered by the operator through the keyboard into punched holes.*

***Card Punch.*** The most common method of converting source data into punched cards is the use of the card punch or key punch machine. Basically, the operator of this machine reads a source document and transcribes the data into punched holes by depressing the appropriate keys on the keyboard. In order for the operator to perform an efficient job during keypunching, the key punch feeds, positions, and ejects cards automatically. The card punch stores two different card formats and operates in the 10 to 15 stroke per second range. Shown in Figure 2-17 is the IBM 29 Card Punch (older models include the IBM 24 and 26). It is available in nine different models (see Figure 2-18).

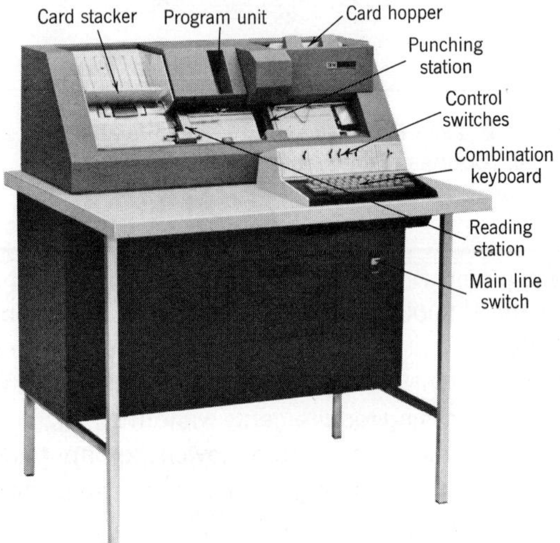


Figure 2-17 IBM 29 Card Punch. (Courtesy International Business Machines Corporation.)

| MODEL | NAME | KEYBOARD | FEATURE |
|---|---|---|---|
| A 11 | Basic Card Punch | 12-character | |
| A 12 | Basic Card Punch | 64-character | |
| A 21 | Basic Card Punch | 12-character | Print |
| A 22 | Basic Card Punch | 64-character | Print |
| B 11 | Left-Zero Insertion Card Punch | 12-character | |
| B 12 | Left-Zero Insertion Card Punch | 64-character | |
| B 21 | Left-Zero Insertion Card Punch | 12-character | Print |
| B 22 | Left-Zero Insertion Card Punch | 64-character | Print |
| C 22 | Interpreting Card Punch | 64-character | Print |

*Note:* 12 characters—numeric only, 64 characters—numeric, alphabetic, and special characters.

Figure 2-18 IBM 29 Card Punch-nine different models.

The operation of the IBM 29 Card Punch is discussed in the appendix to this chapter. The use of the program unit and program codes are also covered.

*The data recorder functions like a card punch.*

***Data Recorder.*** A 1970 addition to 80 column card punching is the IBM 129 Card Data Recorder, equally capable of verifying cards. Resembling the IBM 29 Card Punch, it has a memory that serves as a buffer before the cards are punched. This new technology means that the operator can key data continuously while another card is being punched and stacked. Since corrections can be made before a card is punched, the entire card does not have to be repunched because of a single mistake. In addition, the 129's memory will store up to six different card formats, enabling the operator to change from one format to another without interrupting the work flow. Options include an "accumulate" feature that will total selected card fields plus a count of key strokes and cards. Having the familiar 29 keyboard, an operator does not need extensive training in order to use it.

The IBM 5496 Data Recorder (Figure 2-19) is the basic punching device for

Figure 2-19 IBM 5496 Data Recorder. (Courtesy International Business Machines Corporation.)

the 96 column card. Three characteristics distinguish it from earlier IBM card punches: buffered storage, four control program levels, and the ability to punch directly from data written on the face of the card. Buffered storage stores the complete contents of a card image before any punching or printing takes place. This feature permits the operator to correct any known errors before the card is punched and printed as well as to increase the productivity of the operator by about 10%. Regarding the second characteristic, from one to four programs can be loaded into the Data Recorder by reading prepunched program cards. Four program level function keys are found on the keyboard. In addition, programming provides control of field lengths, automatic skipping, automatic duplicating, upper/lower shifting functions, and field or word erase operations.

*The keyboard to magnetic tape device converts data entered by the operator via the keyboard onto magnetic tape.*

***Keyboard to Magnetic Tape.*** The above punching devices are capable of handling large volumes of input. However, there is a considerable amount of time and expense involved. During the past several years, manufacturers have developed input equipment to remedy these deficiencies. Among the various pieces of equipment to record data directly onto magnetic tape are the 6401 Mohawk Data-Recorder (Figure 2-20) and the Honeywell Keytape (Figure 2-21).

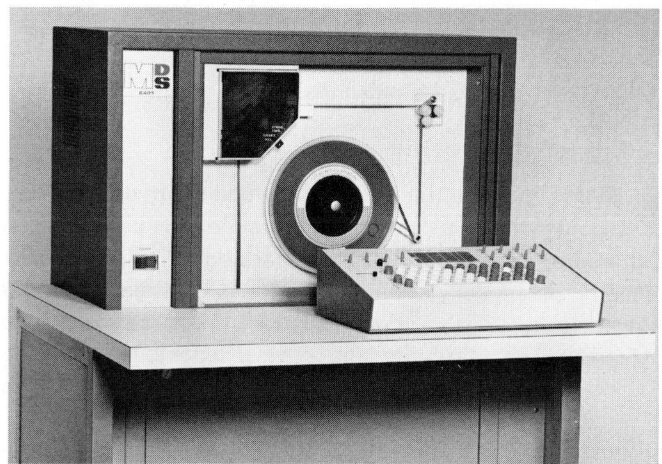


Figure 2-20 Mohawk 6401 Data-Recorder. (Courtesy Mohawk Data Sciences Corporation.)

Figure 2-21 Honeywell Keytape. (Courtesy Honeywell Information Systems.)

During data entry with the Mohawk 6401 Data-Recorder, a complete record is key entered and stored in the magnetic core memory before it is released to the magnetic tape. This feature simplifies and speeds up error correction. Errors sensed by the operator while keying data from the originating document can be corrected immediately by backspacing in memory and keying in the correction. The same correction method is applicable to verification. Programming for this unit is stored electronically as compared to the electromechanical punched card program unit discussed previously. Studies for the 6401 Data-Recorder indicate that operator's productivity is increased by approximately one-third over regular punching methods. These improvements in operator efficiency primarily result from quicker setup, simpler verification, and quieter operation.

***Magnetic Data Inscriber.*** The IBM 50 Magnetic Data Inscriber (Figure 2-22)

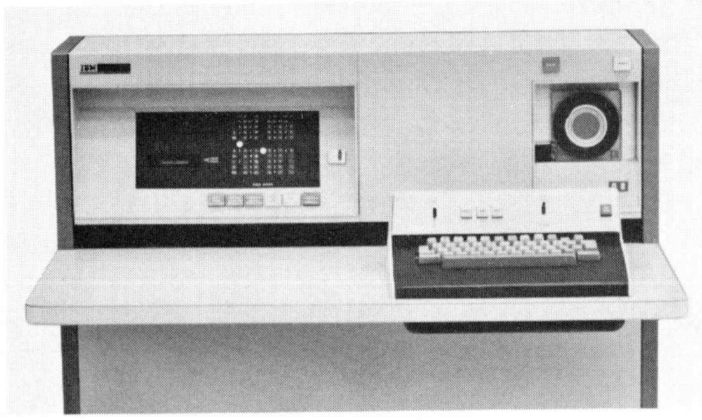

Figure 2-22 IBM 50 Magnetic Data Inscriber. (Courtesy International Business Machines Corporation.)

*Magnetic data inscriber converts input data entered by the operator onto a magnetic tape cartridge.*

prepares or verifies a magnetic tape cartridge from source document data entered through an operator-controlled keyboard. The recording is incremental, that is, it is written directly onto the sprocket-fed magnetic tape cartridge. Eight selectable program levels are provided. The capacity of each cartridge is equivalent to about 275 punched cards and each cartridge is compatible with IBM's magnetic tape Selectric typewriter. Each small plastic cartridge tape provides input to the IBM 2495 reader which, in turn, feeds the information into the computer at 900 characters a second.

The keyboard to cartridge approach is technically similar to keyboard to magnetic tape units with the cartridge being an intermediate between the keyboard and the computer compatible input. This intermediate step adds considerably to cost. However, this approach is economically justified in many applications involving formatted text editing and updating where the tape is used for format presentation and the operator enters the record data into that format.

*Keyboard data entry system consists of many data entry stations that are linked together for recording data onto magnetic disk and/or magnetic tape.*

***Keyboard Data Entry System.*** Despite the immediate benefits available for the keyboard to magnetic tape devices discussed above, someone must gather the magnetic tapes from the many data input devices and process them on the computer for a merge and a sort operation of the input data. To overcome this processing problem, manufacturers have developed sophisticated keyboard data entry systems, one of which is the Key Processing System developed by the Computer Machinery Corporation (Figure 2-23).

Figure 2-23 Key Processing System. (Courtesy Computer Machinery Corporation.)

*Computer-controlled data entry.* A computer-controlled keyboard input system is more efficient and less expensive than key punches or keyboard to magnetic tape machines. As data are entered through the keyboard (up to 32 individual keystations), they are processed by the system's shared computer and stored on a magnetic disk in locations appropriate to the keystation of original entry. Once recorded data are verified either by rekeying and comparing within the computer or by automatically balancing control totals to the totals derived from the original keying operation, completed batches can be transferred automatically from the disk onto a single reel of magnetic tape. Finally, this tape reel is the input for any computer batch processing run. In order to visualize the simplicity of this keyboard data entry system over keypunching and keyboard to magnetic tape, a comparison of input data processing methods is depicted in Figure 2-24. The result is time and cost savings for the user.

*Many data entry stations linked together.* A similar approach is the data input system of the Logic Corporation. Data are entered from a keyboard having a standard 64 character IBM 29 key punch machine layout. The system is capable of time sharing the input from 60 or more data stations. An easy to read alphanumeric display panel shows the operator, in English, the program number, record length, the last character entered and column number, record number, data availability, verification status, and terminal operating mode (Figure 2-25). The software

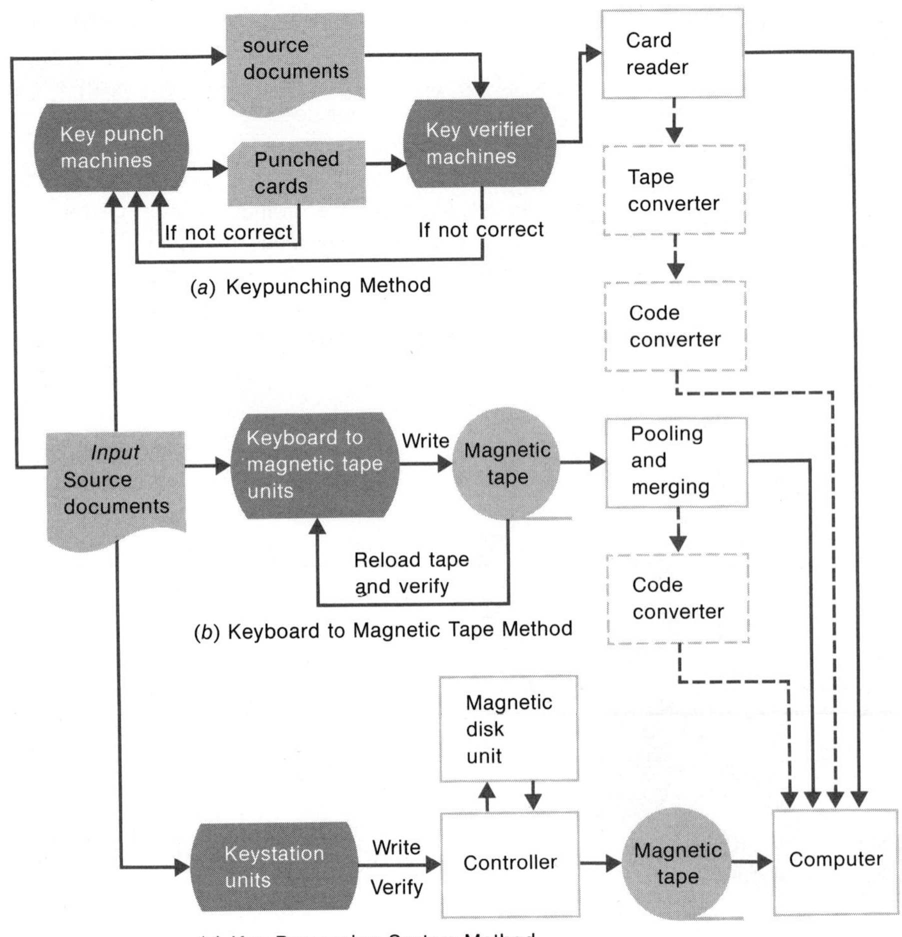


Figure 2-24 Three different methods of preparing data for computer entry. (*a*) Keypunching. (*b*) Keyboard to magnetic tape. (*c*) Key processing system.

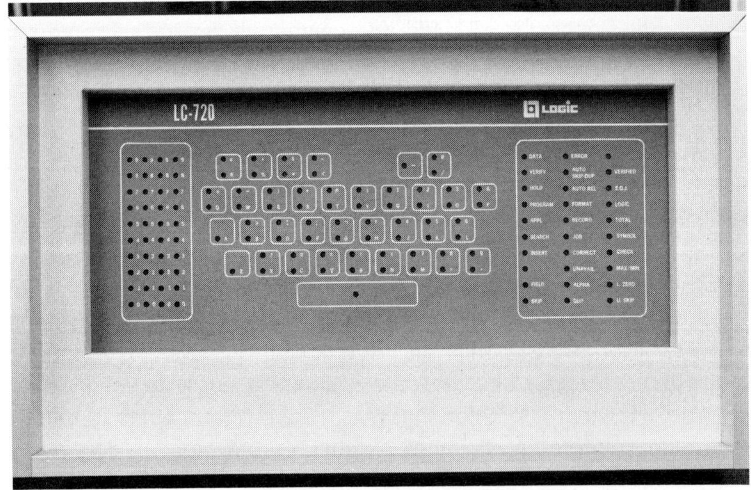


Figure 2-25 Alphanumeric display panel for LC-728 Data Station. (Courtesy Logic Corporation.)

programs for controlling data entry functions, such as formatting, record size or length, duplication, skipping, backspacing, and error corrections are stored in the system's central processor and are accessible under control of any and all operators directly from the keyboard. The system is capable of storing 30 or more different format programs, as well as complete variable record size or length designed to meet the user's requirements. Shown in Figure 2-26 are the major components of the computer data input system for producing the desired outputs.

*Extensive editing capabilities.* The LC-720 system makes it possible to check

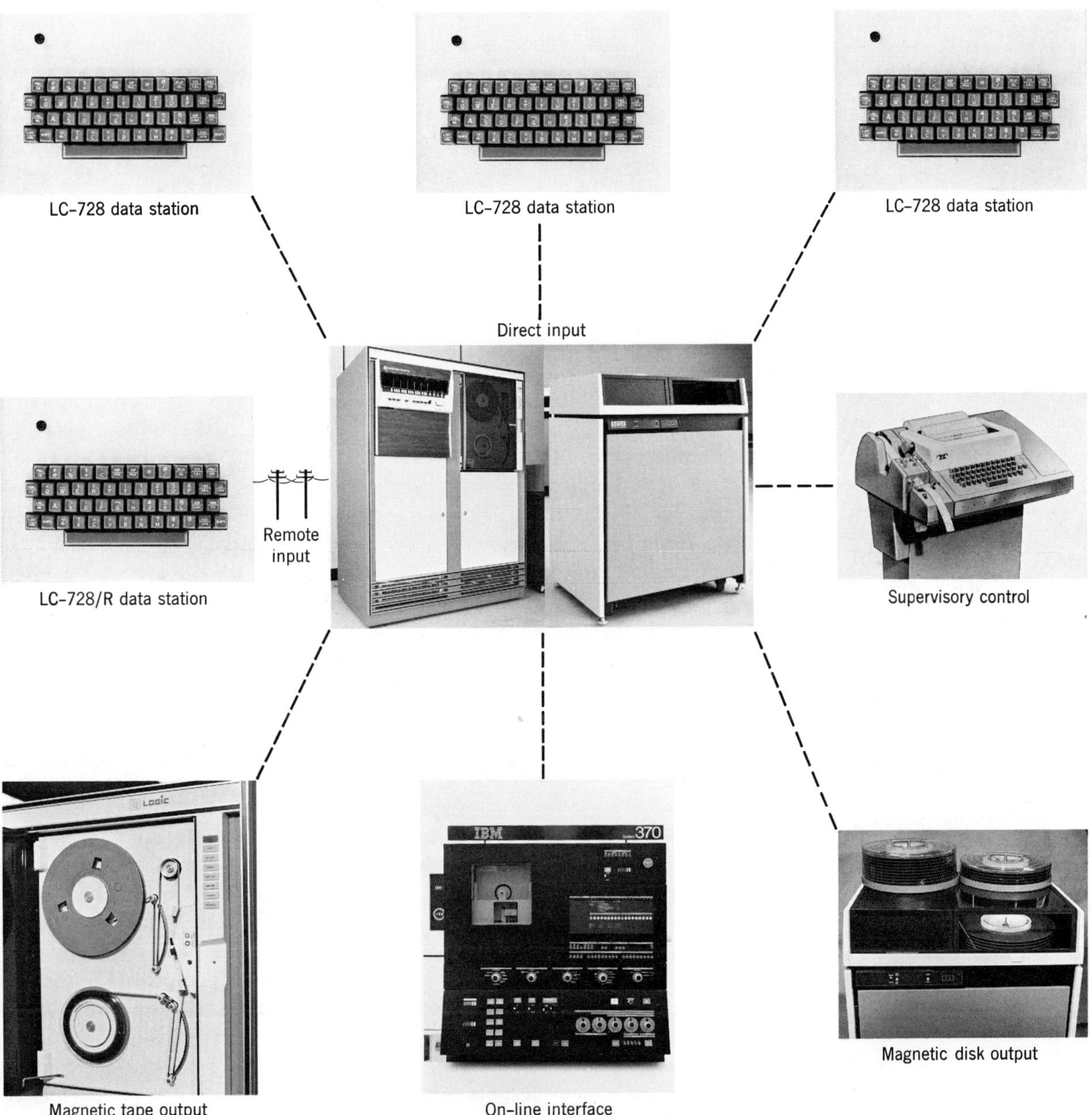


Figure 2-26 LC-720 Key Disk System. (Courtesy Logic Corporation.)

and verify part of the data during the initial data entry pass. Computer checks available include the check digit, limit check, control totals, and alphanumeric check. Also, automatic checking of quantity, price, extensions, subtotals, and totals is available.

After records have been stored on the magnetic disk, each record can be individually retrieved from the disk and verified in the normal manner. If an error is detected, the keyboard locks, an error tone is heard, and a red error light on the keyboard glows. Entry of the correct character for proper verification or correction of the original entry is accomplished by keyboard control.

### Verifying

*Verifying is a method of checking the accuracy of data punched. Its methods are:*

- *visual check*
- *batch totals*
- *key verifier*
- *self-checking digit*

*Visual check is the least desirable method of verifying punched data.*

Once the cards have been punched, it is usually desirable to check their accuracy before sending them on for further processing. This is particularly true in order to determine the accuracy of critical data, such as sales amount, amount of payment received, account number, and inventory amount. Incorrect data can only result in inaccurate and unusable reports, resulting in garbage-in and garbage-out (GIGO). The process of checking the accuracy of the punching operation so that this condition does not occur is called *verification*.

***Visual Check.*** There are several methods of verifying the card's accuracy. The first is to take the cards that have been punched and interpreted and to check visually what has been printed on the top of each card against the source document. This method is not recommended since there is a tendency to speed up the operation at the expense of accuracy. The eye is not as accurate as some type of mechanical or electronic verification method. Likewise, a malfunction of the interpreting equipment could indicate incorrect cards when actually the data have been punched correctly.

*Batch totals refer to a method whereby data are grouped and totaled on some logical basis for comparison with predetermined figures.*

***Batch Totals.*** Another approach to verification is processing cards on an electric accounting machine, printing calculator, or similar piece of equipment by batches and comparing the printed output totals with the original batch totals. This method can be slow since those batches that do not agree with the original batches must have the incorrect cards repunched as well as rerunning the batch for a printout. For example, a large number of accounts receivable payment cards could be sorted by batches and then printed on some off-line equipment. An error could be located quickly since input figures have been grouped on the same basis as the printout.

*The key verifier is widely used for determining the accuracy of data previously punched. Its operation is somewhat similar to a card punch.*

***Key Verifier.*** The most widely used verifying method is the card verifier machine, such as the IBM 59 Card Verifier (Figure 2-27). The verifier looks similar to the card punch, but does not punch holes. As the second operator or verifier duplicates the original card punching process by reading from the same source document and depressing the same keys (as the first key punch operator did), the card verifier compares each depressed key with the punched hole already in the card. This is accomplished by the sensing mechanism which has 12 pins rather than 12 punching dies. If the entire card is correct, then a notch is put in the extreme right-hand portion of the card between the 0 and 1 horizontal punching positions (Figure 2-28). However, if a verifier key is depressed and a difference is found between it and the card (indicates an error), the keyboard locks immediately and a red light comes on. The operator has two more chances to obtain agreement between the verifying and original keypunching. If there is none after three tries, the top of the card is automatically notched in the column of the error (Figure 2-29). This method identifies the column error so that the card punch operator can prepare a new card to replace

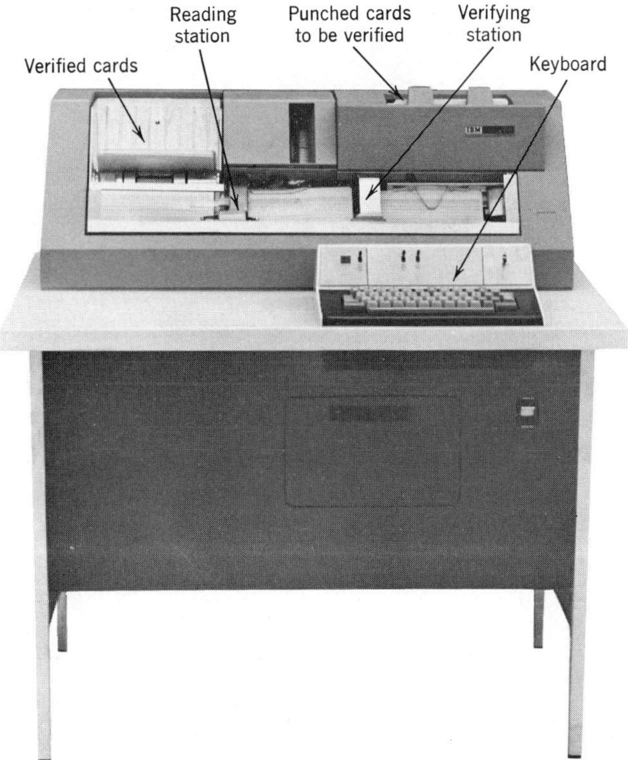


Figure 2-27 IBM 59 Card Verifier. (Courtesy International Business Machines Corporation.)

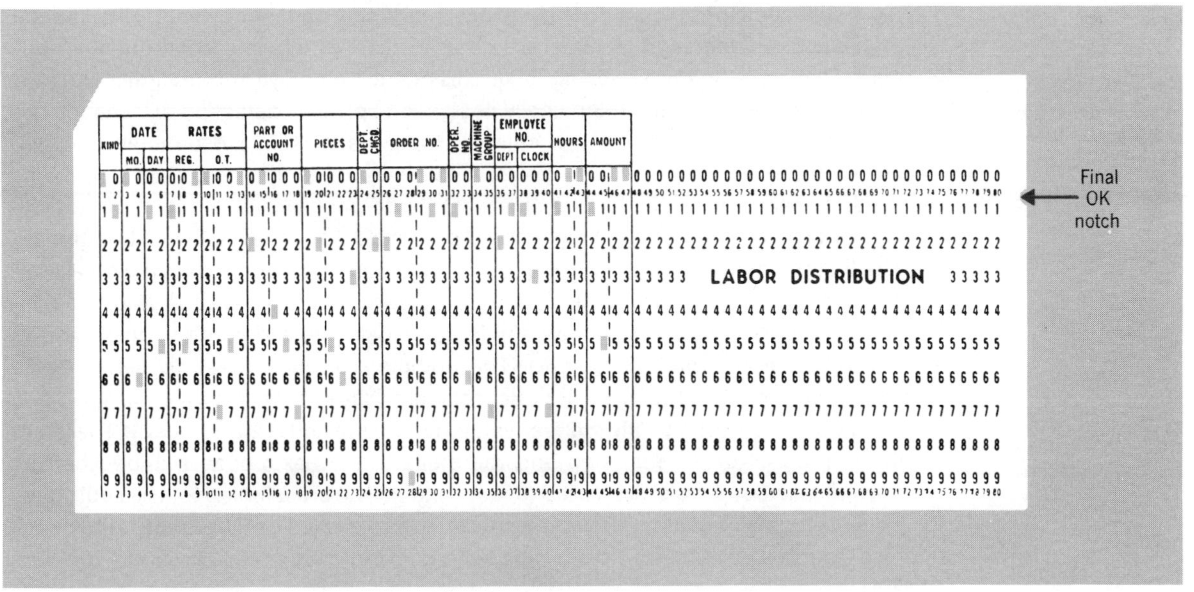


Figure 2-28 Verified card.

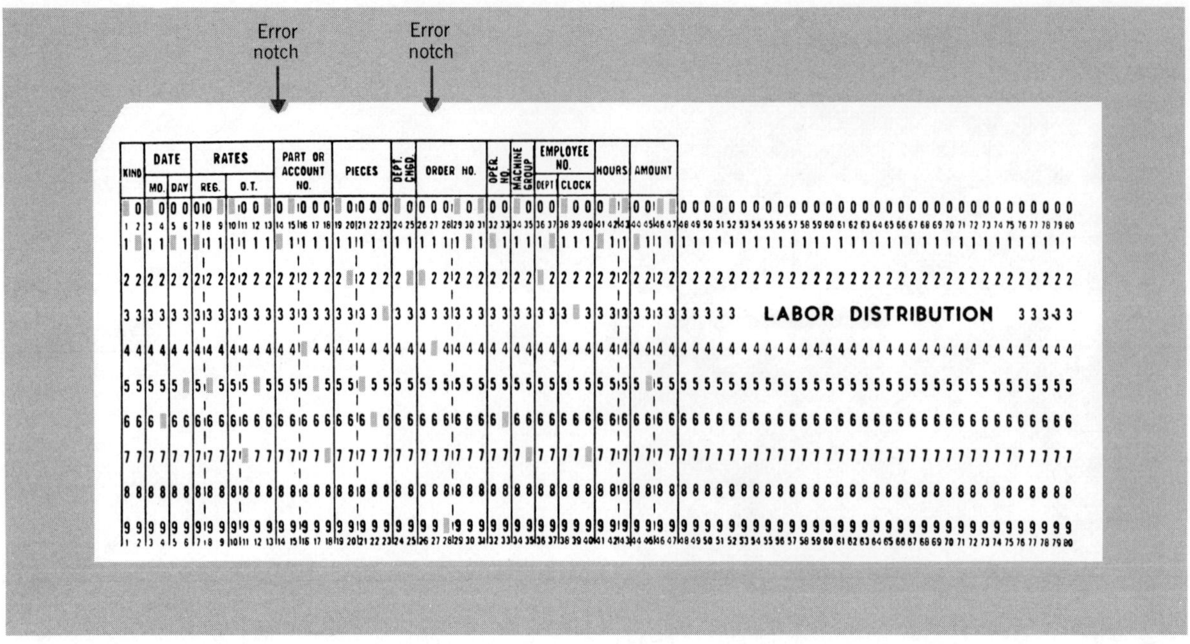


Figure 2-29 Error card.

the one punched in error. It should be noted that an error can occur at the key punch or at the key verifier.

When cards are removed from the card stacker, all correct cards that have been notched on the right-hand side can be easily identified. If not notched, the error cards will stand out. These can be removed, corrected by repunching new cards, and returned to the group after repunching and verifying. Figure 2-30 summarizes the verification procedure found in most punched card equipment installations.

*The self-checking digit method is one which employs an extra digit to detect incorrect digits within a number.*

***Self-Checking Digit.*** A special type of verification for reference numbers and classification is the self-checking digit. This method employs information in the form of an extra digit that is mathematically designed to provide detection of transposition or substitution of digits within a number. Paper tape and card punching devices are currently available that will perform this checking of critical data, one being the self-checking number feature on the 29 Card Punch (Model A only). This feature is controlled by special punching in the program card and is available in two models. The first (Modulus 10) is designed primarily to detect the incorrect keying of a single digit (most common error) and a single transposition. The second (Modulus 11) is designed to detect mispunches, single transpositions, and double transpositions.

*Self-checking digit procedure*. The arithmetic process used to generate the check digit for the Modulus 10 model requires that every other value in the basic code number, starting with the first value, be multiplied by 2 (first step). The digits in the product of the first step and the digits in the basic code number that are not multiplied by 2 are crossfooted (second step). The crossfooted total is subtracted from the next higher number—ending in zero (third step). The difference is the check digit (fourth step). An example of this self-checking digit method is found in Figure 2-31.

*Self-checking digit on card punch*. The procedure for the self-checking digit

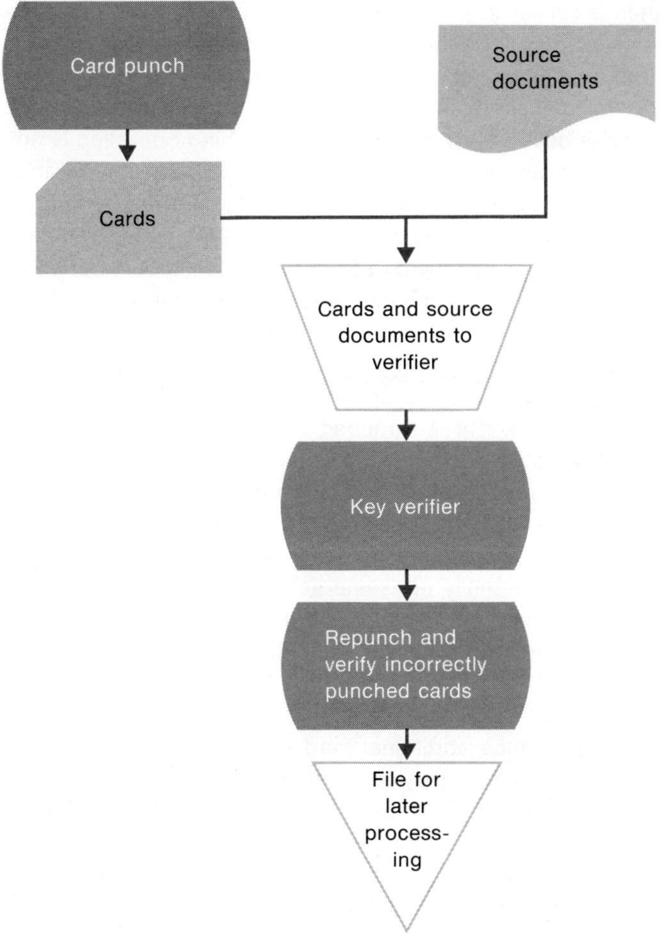


Figure 2-30 Verification procedure using a key verifier.

| | | | | | | |
|---|---|---|---|---|---|---|
| Basic code number | 3 | 0 | 7 | 5 | 9 | |
| Every other value of basic code number, starting with the first value | 3 | | 7 | | 9 | |
| Multiply by 2 | | | | | ×2 | |
| Value (first step) | 7 | | 5 | | 8 | |
| Digits not multiplied by 2 | | 0 | | 5 | | |
| Crossfoot values (second step) | 7 | +0 | +5 | +5 | +8 | = 25 |
| Next higher number ending in zero | | | | | | 30 |
| Subtract crossfooted total (third step) | | | | | | −25 |
| Check digit (fourth step) | | | | | | 5 |
| Self-checking number | 3 | 0 | 7 | 5 | 9 | 5 |

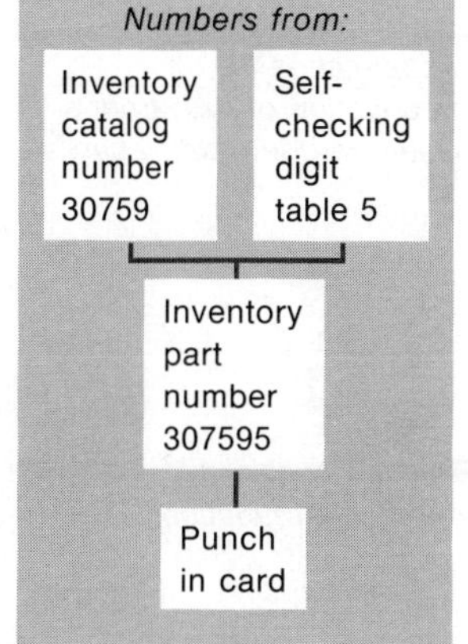


Figure 2-31 IBM 29 Card Punch—Modulus 10, self-checking digit.

on the IBM 29 Card Punch is similar to that of key verification. When the operator keys and punches the number, including the check-digit position, as it appears on the source document, internal calculations verify the accuracy of the keying—the validity of the self-checking number. If the number on the originating document is correct and the number has been keyed correctly, the punching operation is not interrupted (an 11-hole is automatically punched in column 81). On the other hand, if the number is recorded on the source document incorrectly or if the number is punched incorrectly, an error is indicated after the last digit of the self-check field is punched. A red light appears on the keyboard (a 12-hole is automatically punched in the check-digit column) and the keyboard locks. After the red light is turned off, the keyboard is unlocked, and the error card is released by pressing the error reset key. The normal correcting procedure is to duplicate the correctly punched fields of the error card into a new card up to the self-checking number field in error. The entire self-check field is repunched. If it is punched as recorded on the source document and the keyboard locks again, the cause of the error is the same document that must be routed for manual correction before attempting to repunch.

Verifying punched cards is a standard function of the IBM 5496 Data Recorder (96 column). Verified cards are notched at the trailing edge near the bottom. The self-check Modulus 10 or 11 is essentially the same as that offered on other IBM card punches. Cards with self-check field(s) that are correctly keyed are indicated with a punch in the B-bit of the first tier adjacent to column 32.

### Reproducing

*Reproducing is a method of duplicating additional cards. Its methods are:*

- *reproduce*
- *gangpunch*
- *emit*
- *other automatic punch operations*

It is often necessary to reproduce additional card sets since the original set may be worn, other processing operations may occur at the same time, or for similar reasons. Likewise, partial changes may have to be made on entire sets of cards or original records may have to be partially changed on a continuing basis in order to keep them up-to-date. To use key punching methods would be slow, costly, and error prone. For this reason, a reproducing punch or reproducer is a basic machine needed in any punched card installation.

*Reproduce is the automatic duplication of all or part of the data in one card into another card.*

***Reproduce.*** Automatic punching operations include reproducing, gangpunching, and emitting. Reproducing is the automatic duplication of all or part of the data in one card into another card. Data can be punched into the same location as punched on the original card or fields of data can be rearranged for a new card format. The comparing feature of the machine that proves agreement between originals and reproductions verifies the accuracy of the reproduction.

*Gangpunch is the reproduction of data from a master card into detail cards.*

***Gangpunch.*** There are two types of gangpunching: single master gangpunching and interspersed gangpunching. The first type uses one master card placed in front of a deck of blank or detail cards to produce all other cards desired. Where groups of data decks are desired from a number of master cards containing different data, the function is generally referred to as interspersed gangpunching. Under the latter method, the master cards are interspersed into a deck of blank or detail data cards. As a master card is read, the desired data to be reproduced will be placed in all the cards that follow until another master card is read.

*Emit is a specialized reproducing function.*

***Emit.*** Another reproducing function is the use of the reproducing punch with a special device, called the emitter. It can be wired to punch automatically into any position of any column without the necessity of reading a comparable punch from another card.

***Other Automatic Punch Operations.*** The reproducing punch is capable of punching important data when wired in conjunction with other punched card machines. The connecting of the automatic punch and an electric accounting machine permits the transfer of accumulated detail cards by the EAM equipment to the reproducer for punching summary cards. The total or summary cards can be used for various purposes without having to repeat the processing of the detail cards. Additional functions that can be handled by the reproducing punch include mark-sensing, double-punch and blank-column (DPBC) detection, and end-printing (interpreting some of the data punched in a card and printing it across the end of the card).

*The reproducing punch can be cable connected to certain punched card equipment for punching summary cards.*

The equipment available for automatic punching include four IBM models: the 514, 519, 528, and 549. The IBM 514 Reproducing Punch is similar to the 519 Document-Originating Machine (Figure 2-32) which will be discussed below. While

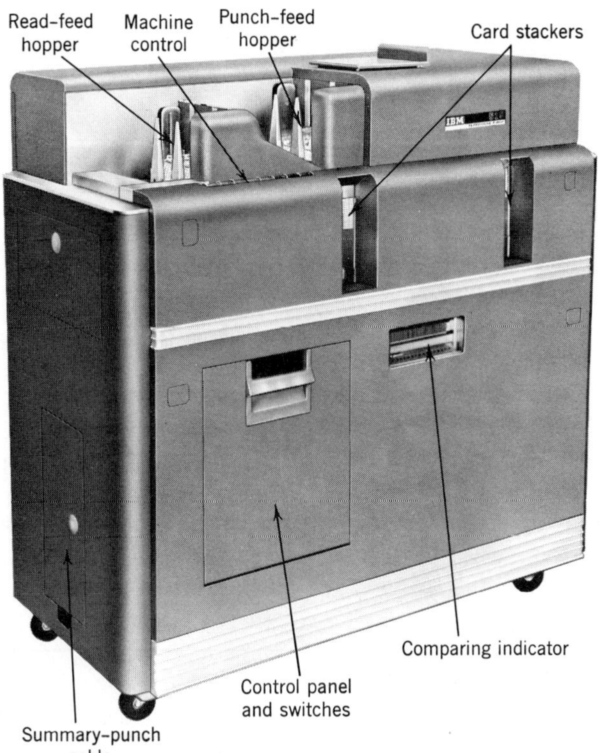


Figure 2-32 IBM 519 Document-Originating Machine. (Courtesy International Business Machines Corporation.)

the IBM 528 Accumulating Reproducer is a high-speed punch that performs addition and subtraction in conjunction with gangpunching, reproducing, and summary punching, the IBM 549 Ticket Converter is utilized for converting or transcribing sales data from ticket stubs to punched cards and other automatic punching operations.

***Operation of Reproducer.*** The IBM 519 Document-Originating Machine can be acquired with features that enable it to perform all of the automatic punching operations (reproducing, gangpunching, emitting, summary punching, mark-sensing, DPBC detection, and end-printing). All operations can be performed at the rate of 100 cards a minute. The relationship of the read unit and the punch unit and the sequence in which cards pass the operating stations is shown in Figure

*The reproducer has the capability of reading cards from one or both of the feed units and punching the desired output.*

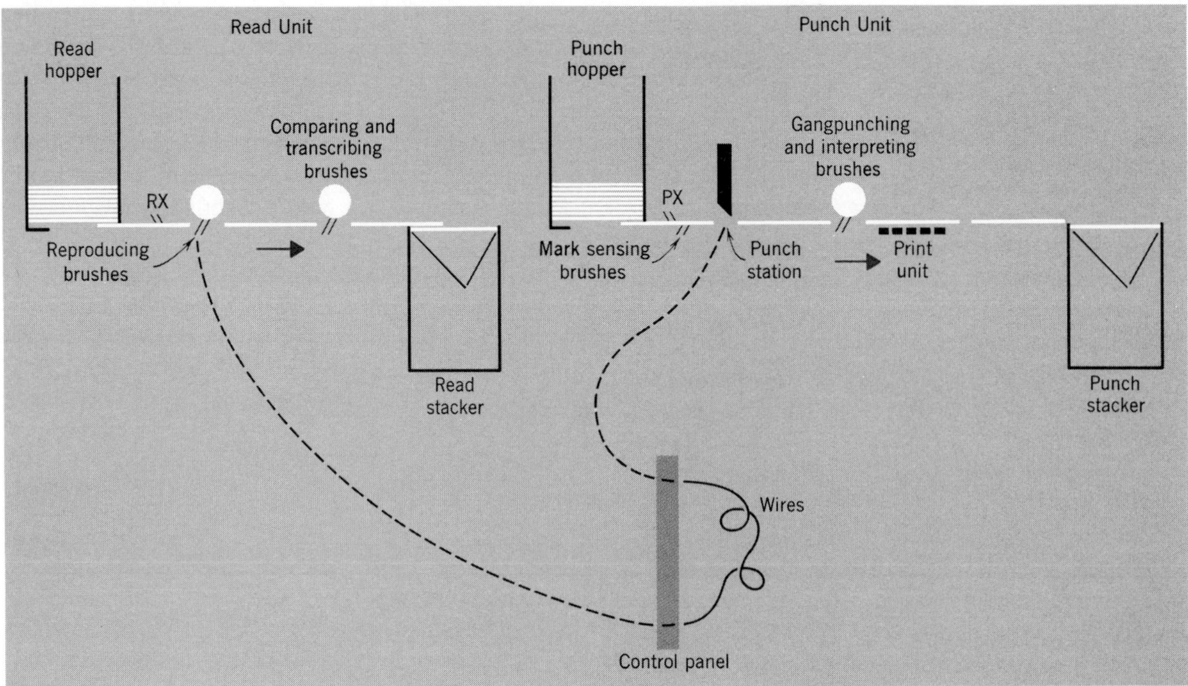


Figure 2-33 Schematic showing paths of cards during reproducing operation performed on the IBM 519 Document-Originating Machine. (Courtesy International Business Machines Corporation.)

2-33. Cards may be fed from one or both of the feed units, depending on the application being used.

As cards are fed into the read unit, they first pass the six read-X brushes (noted as RX in Figure 2-33) which can be set to read up to six selected card columns. These brushes read X (11 zone) punches which control the reading of data from the card. At the next station in the read unit, 80 reproducing brushes sense the contents of the card. The last station is a set of 80 comparing and transcribing brushes that represent the next cycle in the reading unit.

Examination of Figure 2-33 indicates that the punch unit has a similar set of six brushes, only this time they are six punch-X brushes. They read X (11 zone) punches which identify the master cards that control the subsequent punching and feeding operations. In the illustration, the machine is equipped with mark-sensing brushes (the next station in the punch unit) which read the marks on the card for punching into the same card. The punch station, the third one, consists of 80 punch dies where the top of each card passes the punch die first, resulting in the 12 position row being punched, the 11 position, and on through the last or 9 position. The last stations are the 80 gangpunching and interpreting brushes and the print unit, if this feature has been installed.

If both the read and punch feed units are being utilized, cards are fed simultaneously from both units. For example, master cards are fed into the read unit and blank cards are positioned in the punch hopper. As automatic reproducing occurs, comparison can be made between the one card in the reading unit and another card in the punching unit (or between cards at the two stations in the reading unit) if the machine has the comparing feature installed. This comparison provides for error detection if the punched holes in both cards differ. When there is a difference between the punching in both cards, the machine stops and the compare light goes on. The comparing indicator points out the position where the error has occurred. In this manner, all incorrectly punched cards can be detected before further processing occurs.

**Interpreting**

*Interpreting is a method of printing desired information in a certain order on a punched card.*

A card punch, containing a print unit, is capable of printing the information being punched along the top of the card, directly above the respective punched holes. Many times, data are desired in a different order or not all of the data are desired at the top of the card (selective printing). In these cases, an interpreter is needed, such as the IBM 548 Interpreter or 557 Alphabetic Interpreter (Figure 2-34).

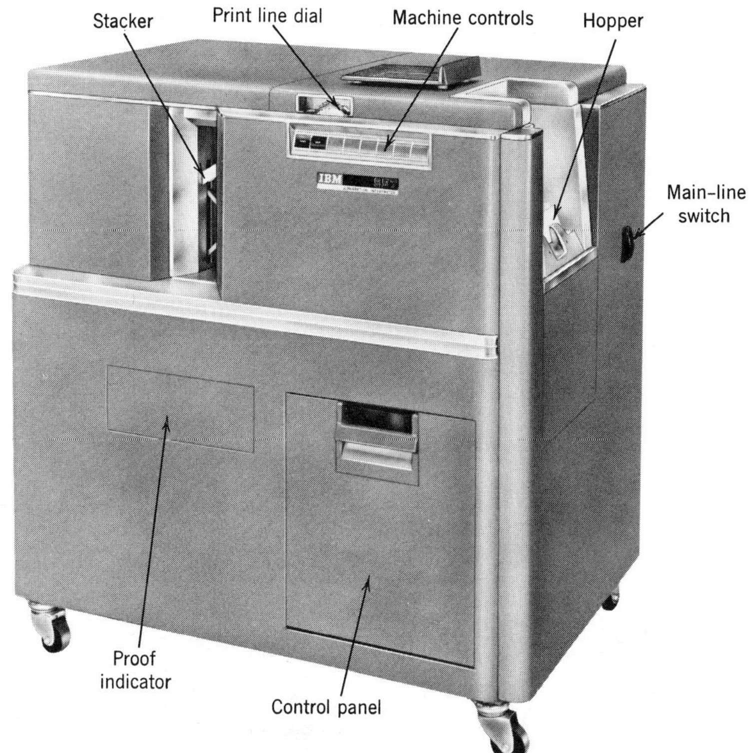


Figure 2-34 IBM 557 Alphabetic Interpreter. (Courtesy International Business Machines Corporation.)

The 557 Alphabetic Interpreter is capable of printing up to 60 columns of punched data on any of 25 printing lines on the face of an 80 column card. The limit of 60 characters across the card is caused by the print being larger than that on the 29 Card Punch. The arrangement of printed data on a card is determined and controlled by wiring the control panel.

***Selective Line Printing.*** When the machine is equipped with special features, such as the selective line printing, it becomes an automatic line finding, ledger posting machine while retaining all of its usual interpreting capabilities. The IBM

*Selective line finding is a special feature on the interpreter that allows it to read data from one card and print it on another card.*

557 has the ability to read data from one card and print it on another card. An application of this feature is the area of installment loan accounting where the payment transaction card is posted directly onto the history ledger card, shown in Figure 2-35. Other applications include: inventory ledgers, payroll earnings records, claims histories, and mortgage loans.

| NAME | DAY | TYPE LOAN | NUMBER | OFFICE | DEALER | SEC | TERM | MO. MATURITY | YR. MATURITY | AMOUNT OF LOAN | DISCOUNT | PROCEEDS | REGULAR PAYMENT |
|---|---|---|---|---|---|---|---|---|---|---|---|---|---|
| DAVIDSON H | 2 | 7 | 69059 | 6 | 5 | 7 | 18 | | | 1166 76 | 66 76 | 1100 00 | 6482 |

| DATE PAID MO. | DAY | YR | PRESENT BALANCE | AMOUNT OF REGULAR PAYMENT | AMOUNT OF IRREGULAR PAY'T | LATE CHARGE | NEW BALANCE | NOTICES 1st | 2nd | 3rd |
|---|---|---|---|---|---|---|---|---|---|---|
| 3 | 4 | | 1166 76 | 64 82 | | | 1101 94 | | | |
| 4 | 1 | | 1101 94 | 64 82 | | | 1037 12 | | | |
| 5 | 3 | | 1037 12 | 64 82 | | | 972 30 | | | |
| 6 | 4 | | 972 30 | 64 82 | | | 907 48 | | | |
| 7 | 2 | | 907 48 | 64 82 | | | 842 66 | | | |

(SEE REVERSE SIDE FOR ADDITIONAL INFORMATION)

IBM

INSTALLMENT LOAN HISTORY LEDGER CARD

Figure 2-35 Installment loan history ledger card. (Courtesy International Business Machines Corporation.)

## SUMMARY

Within this chapter, the basic machines—key punch, key verifier, reproducer, and interpreter—in a punched card installation have been treated. Once data are captured correctly on cards, the cards can be used over and over again. The cards can be sorted into groups, merged with another group of cards, matched with another group, and so forth. These functions will be discussed in detail in the next chapter. The ability to realign groups of cards quickly and inexpensively is essential for an efficient operation, in particular, to produce timely and meaningful reports for management. This basic data processing approach is one of applying the "management by exception" concept, which reports unfavorable as well as favorable deviations from the original plans for immediate managerial action.

Punched cards not only serve as input to punched card systems but they are also needed for many computer systems. Since most computer systems operate more efficiently without card input, many batch processing users have gone to some type of keyboard data entry system whereby input data, taken from source documents, are never recorded on punched cards. Instead, data are recorded directly from the original source onto magnetic disk or tape in order to eliminate costly processing steps and delays. This trend has made substantial changes in business data processing and will continue to do so in the future. Coupled with the growth of on-line input/output devices, optical character recognition equipment and more sophisticated data collection systems, these more direct input techniques will continue to grow at the expense of punched card equipment.

## QUESTIONS

1. (a) Relate the punched card to the unit record principle.
   (b) Relate the unit record principle to the design of an efficient punched card data processing system.
2. How do punch codes for the 80, 90, and 96 column cards differ?
3. How do fields of data differ from columns of data?
4. Of the coding methods given, which is (are) the commonly used?
5. Review the basic types of punched cards. Which one(s) is (are) the most used?
6. What are the four essential requirements for card design?
7. Since a card may contain many fields of data, how does one determine the order of the fields of information?
8. How can data processing clerks be helped to distinguish quickly among the many cards that are needed for a punched card system?
9. Describe briefly each of the basic methods set forth in this chapter for data recording.
10. What is the purpose of the program unit on the card punch? What functions does it control?
11. What are the shortcomings of key punch machines versus a keyboard data entry system?
12. (a) An operator makes a mistake when keypunching from the source document. When the card is verified, what happens?
    (b) Is it possible that the error may not be detected during key verification? Explain.
13. Why is the verifying procedure followed shortly after a batch of cards has been keypunched from originating documents?
14. Explain the significance of the self-checking digit and how it works.
15. What functions can be performed by the reproducer? Explain each.
16. What is meant by posting interpreting?
17. Is there a general rule to follow regarding the feasibility of converting from a manual system to a punched card system? If so, explain.
18. Explain why the GIGO principle is so important in punched card machine data processing.

## APPENDIX TO CHAPTER TWO

### IBM 29 CARD PUNCH

The IBM 29 Card Punch is a widely used key punch. Many equipment manufacturers have employed the standard 64 character 29 Card Punch layout for multiple data entry stations. Because of its widespread use, the operations of the card punch, the program unit, and program coding are covered below.

#### Operation of Card Punch

*The card punch punches one column at a time as data are entered through the keyboard.*

The IBM 29 Card Punch (Figure 2-17) operates in the following manner. Cards are fed face forward with the 9 edge down from the card hopper (upper right), which has a capacity of about 500 cards. The first two cards to be punched must be fed by key depression, but all other cards in the hopper can be fed automatically by setting an automatic feed switch. As the second card is fed, column 1 of the first card is automatically positioned at the punching station. While the initial card is being punched with data from the source document, the second card remains at its right. After the last column of the first card passes the punching station, the second card moves into position at the punching station. The third card in the card hopper, then, feeds down to the card bed. While the second card is being punched, the first card is moving to the left—past the reading station. After the second card has been punched and moved to the reading station, the first card is fed automatically into the card stacker (upper left) and the third card is ready for punching at the punching station. This process is completed for all remaining cards. All cards are ultimately deposited in the card stacker which holds about 500 cards and are in the same sequence as punched. The main line switch is turned off automatically when the stacker is full.

***Card Visibility.*** During the course of the punching operation, it should be noted that the operator does not see the card column being punched and interpreted. Figure 2A-1 indicates the area of the card that is visible when column 15 is being

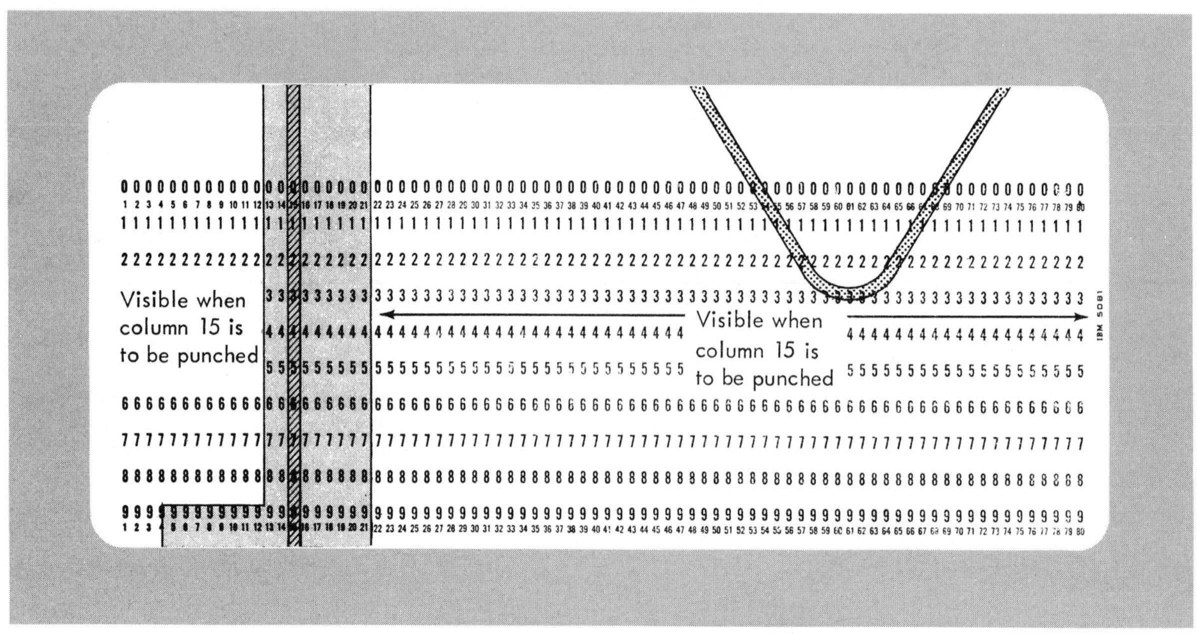


Figure 2A-1 Card visibility at the punch station.

*The key punch operator does not see the card column being punched and interpreted.*

punched. However, the operator is able to determine the position of cards passing the punch and read station by means of a column indicator that identifies the next column to be punched. Column numbers appear on the base of the program drum which turns synchronously with the cards being punched and read.

*The program unit assists the key punch operator. Basically, it controls:*
- *skipping*
- *duplicating*
- *numeric/alphabetic shift*

***Program Unit.*** The program unit, depicted in Figure 2A-2, is a device that permits some programming to assist the key punch operator. It controls *automatic skipping* over columns not to be punched, *automatic duplicating* of repetitive data, *shifting from numeric to alphabetic* and vice versa, *automatic insertion of zeros* to the left of the first significant digit in numeric fields (Model B only), controls the *skipping of fields* that are not to be interpreted (Model C only), and the *elimination of overpunches* from amount field columns (Model C only). These operations are controlled by the program card wrapped around the program drum, as in Figure

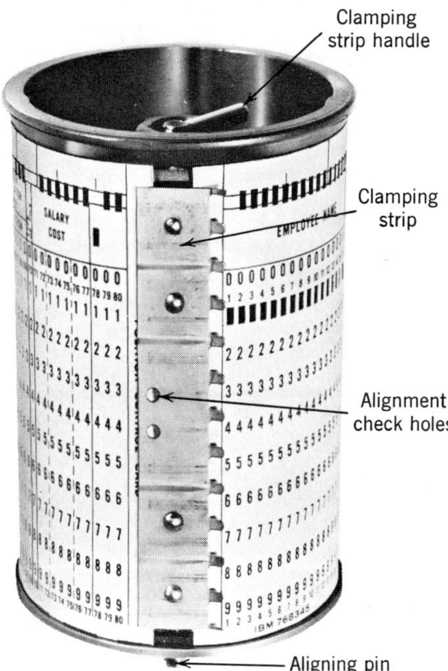


Figure 2A-2 Program drum for IBM 29 Card Punch and IBM 59 Verifier. (Courtesy International Business Machines Corporation.)

2A-2. Generally, a separate program card must be prepared for each different series of cards being punched. On the 29 Card Punch with two program levels (one program drum), the program card can contain two totally different 80 column programs. Either program can be selected by setting a program selection switch. If it is desired to utilize both program levels for control punching on a single card, alternating from program to program can be made by program selection keys on the keyboard.

*The card punch duplication feature can be controlled from the keyboard or under program control.*

***Duplication Feature.*** The card punch can duplicate common data from any card into the following card. This duplication feature can be controlled from the keyboard or under program control automatically, as stated previously. This approach reduces manual keying of repetitive data, such as dates and numbers. The duplication feature also facilitates error correction during punching. When an error is made, the operator need not repunch the whole card, but can duplicate all correctly punched fields into the next card and reenter the field(s) punched in error. The program control permits duplication of fields without concern for column number.

### Program Codes

*Program card codes instruct the key punch what operation it must perform when passing the punch dies.*

The program card is punched with code numbers that indicate to the key punch what it must perform for each of the card columns when passing the punch dies. A listing of program codes for all three models (A, B, and C) of the IBM 29 Card Punch is found in Figure 2A-3. The holes of the program card are detected by tiny starwheels that ride only on the top of the card as it rotates in unison with the card being punched. As a starwheel drops into a hole in the program card, it causes the key punch machine to perform one of the steps outlined in Figure 2A-3.

| PROGRAM ONE ROW | FUNCTION | PROGRAM TWO ROW | WHERE PUNCHED | USED ON |
|---|---|---|---|---|
| 12 | Field Definition | 4 | Each column except first | Models A, B, C |
| 11 | Start Auto-Skip | 5 | First column only | Models A, B, C |
| 0 | Start Auto-Duplicate | 6 | First column only | Models A, B<br>Model C only when in punch mode |
| 0 | 11/12 Elimination | 6 | Necessary column only | Model C only when in interpret mode |
| 1 | Alphabetic Shift | 7 | Each necessary column | Models A, B<br>Model C only when in punch mode |
| 2 | 8-Column Left-Zero Field | 8 | First column only | Model B only |
| 3 | 7-Column Left-Zero Field | 9 | First column only | Model B only |
| 2,3 | 6-Column Left-Zero Field | 8,9 | First column only | Model B only |
| 1,2 | 5-Column Left-Zero Field | 7,8 | First column only | Model B only |
| 1,3 | 4-Column Left-Zero Field | 7,9 | First column only | Model B only |
| 1,2,3 | 3-Column Left-Zero Field | 7,8,9 | First column only | Model B only |

Figure 2A-3 Program codes for IBM 29 Card Punch—Models A, B, and C. (Courtesy International Business Machines Corporation.)

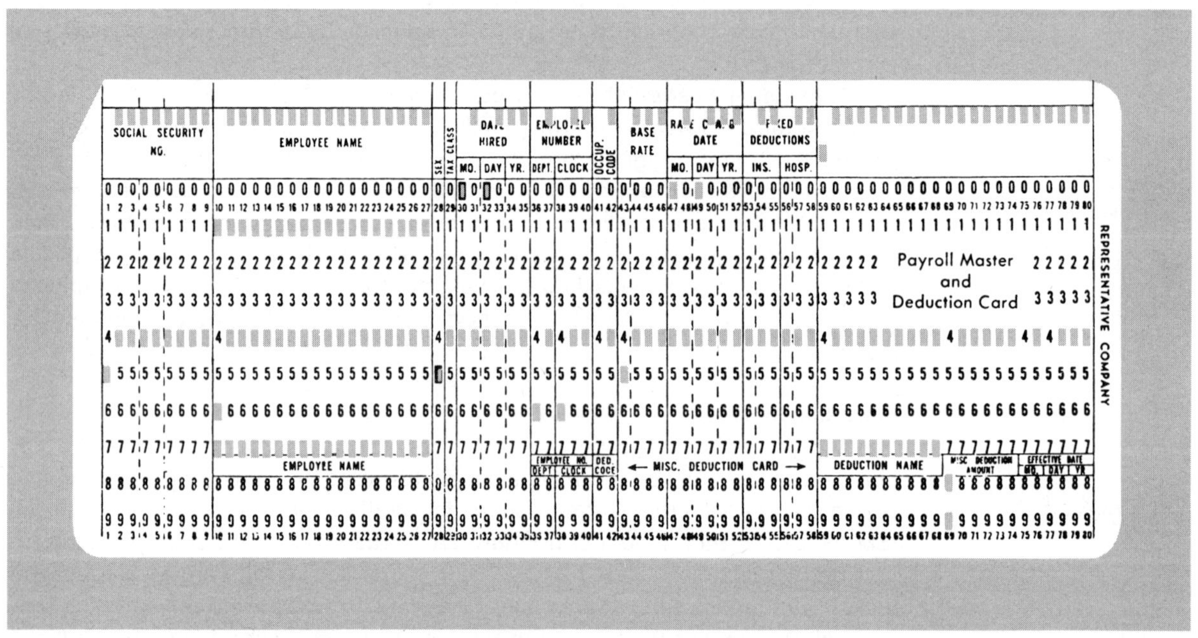


Figure 2A-4 Program card—multiple functions for IBM 29 Card Punch. (Courtesy International Business Machines Corporation.)

**Program Card Illustration**

In order to understand program codes for a multifunction (two) program card (Figure 2A-4), program one for the payroll master card has row 12, columns 2 through 9 punched for field definition of social security number (numeric to be punched manually) and row 12, columns 11 through 27 punched for field definition of employee name plus row 1, columns 10 through 27 for alphabetic shift (alphabetic to be punched manually). Referring to program two for the deduction card, row 5, column 1 is the first column of the program card and row 4, columns 2 through 9 call for automatic skipping, that is, no data are to be punched in columns 1 through 9. For the second field, row 6, column 10 denotes the first column of this data and row 4, columns 11 through 27 are the required spaces for employee name. The equivalent alphabetic shift (alphabetic to be punched automatically) for program two is row 7, columns 10 through 27. The remaining columns in the example have been programmed in a similar manner. Refer to Figure 2A-5 for programming of the remaining columns.

| COLUMNS | FIELD HEADING | NORMAL PROGRAM | ALTERNATE PROGRAM |
|---|---|---|---|
| 1–9 | Social Security No. | Manual punch | Automatic skip |
| 10–27 | Employee Name | Manual punch, alphabetic | Automatic duplicate, alphabetic |
| 28 | Sex | Manual punch | Automatic skip |
| 29 | Tax Class | Manual punch | |
| 30–35 | Date Hired | Automatic duplicate | |
| 36–40 | Employee Number | Manual punch (Department and Clock coded as separate fields for error correction and zero suppression)* | Automatic duplicate (Department and Clock coded as separate fields for zero suppression)* |
| 41–42 | Occupation Code or Deduction Code | Manual punch | Manual punch |
| 43–46 | Base Rate | Manual punch | Automatic skip |
| 47–52 | Rate Change Date | Automatic Duplicate | |
| 53–58 | Fixed Deductions | Manual punch (Insurance and Hospitalization coded as separate fields for error correction and zero suppression)* | |
| 59–68 | Deduction Name | Automatic skip | Manual punch, alphabetic |
| 69–74 | Misc. Ded. Amount | | Manual punch (left-zero insertion field) |
| 75–80 | Effective Date | | Manual punch |
| Month and day in each date field are coded as separate fields for zero suppression*<br>*Left-zero print switch off | | | |

Figure 2A-5 Program table for payroll master and deduction card per Figure 2A-4. (Courtesy International Business Machines Corporation.)

*A method of preparing program cards is to punch one card for each punching row and duplicate this information into a single card.*

***Preparation of Program Cards.*** The best method for preparing the combination payroll master and deduction program card is to punch a master deck of cards. This deck would consist of at least 12 cards, one for each punching row. After the master deck has been punched, each card would be duplicated, one at a time, into a single card. The resulting card will be the program card. This method circumvents the problem of duplicating other than standard multiple punch combinations which cause damage to the punching mechanism if attempted through the keyboard.

## CHAPTER THREE

# Punched Card Equipment
*(Continued)*

*Punched card equipment is capable of producing various outputs. However, it is being replaced by punched card and other type computer systems. (Courtesy International Business Machines Corporation.)*

Punched card data processing is based upon the unit record principle; that is, one card is utilized for encoding the essential data of each transaction. Initially, data are recorded and verified through some type of data recording device or automatic punching, as indicated in the previous chapter. The next major steps are sorting, collating, calculating, proving, and printing output data, which are discussed in this chapter. In addition, the advantages and limitations of punched card machines when compared to prior systems are discussed. Fundamentals of punched paper tape conclude the chapter.

## SORTING

*Sorting is the process of arranging a deck of cards into a numerical or alphabetical sequence.*

After cards have been punched and verified, they must be arranged into some meaningful sequence to facilitate further processing. The process of arranging a deck of cards into a numerical or alphabetical sequence is called *sorting*. Cards are sorted into a sequence according to some field of data previously punched in each card of the deck. Even after the cards have been arranged into some meaningful order, it may be necessary to re-sort the cards a number of times for many other reports. For example, total sales cards for the month can be sorted by product code and model, branch and product, region and end use, state and country, dealer, to name a few. In essence, sorting is the most frequently used classification function in punched card operations.

The IBM system of punched card records makes it possible to arrange cards numerically or alphabetically. The sorter is also capable of multiple-field sorting, block sorting, and single-column selecting. The IBM 84 Sorter (Figure 3-1) operates at a rated speed of 2000 cards per minute or 2000 cards per one column pass in a minute. It has brushless sensing, radial stackers, a vacuum-assist feed, and solid

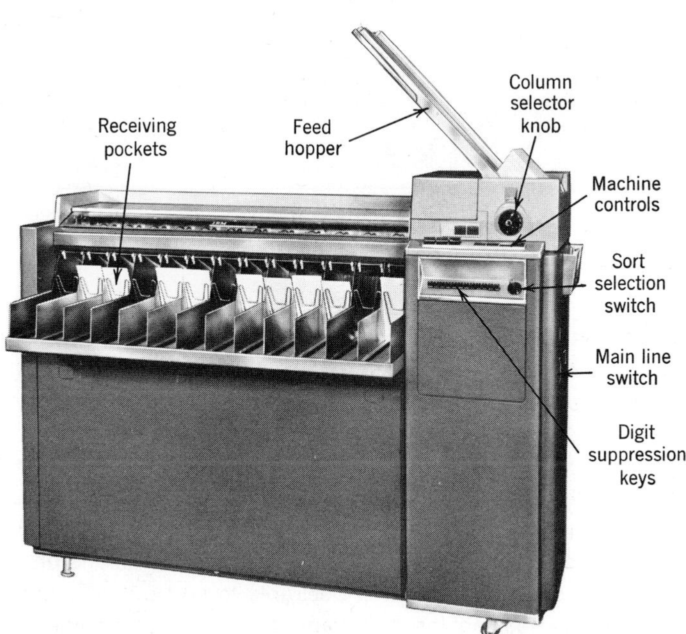


Figure 3-1 IBM 84 Sorter. (Courtesy International Business Machines Corporation.)

state circuitry. Other sorters are the IBM 83 Sorter, operating at 1000 cards per minute, and the IBM 82 Sorter at 650 cards per minute.

*The presence of a punched hole establishes an electrical impulse that pushes down a selector pin and separates the chute blades, thereby sending the card to the appropriate pocket.*

**Operation of Sorter**

Sorting on the 83 model is accomplished by placing cards in the feed hopper and setting the sort brush to the column desired for sorting. The brush may be set on any one of the 80 columns desired by rotating the column selector knob. The next step is to depress the start key. As cards pass through the sorter, the presence of a punch is detected by the sort brush dropping through the hole and making contact with the roller. This establishes an electrical impulse that pushes down a selector pin and separates the chute blades, as shown in Figure 3-2. This method directs the card to the appropriate pocket. Sorting continues in this manner until the feed hopper becomes empty, one of the stacker pockets is filled, or the stop key is depressed.

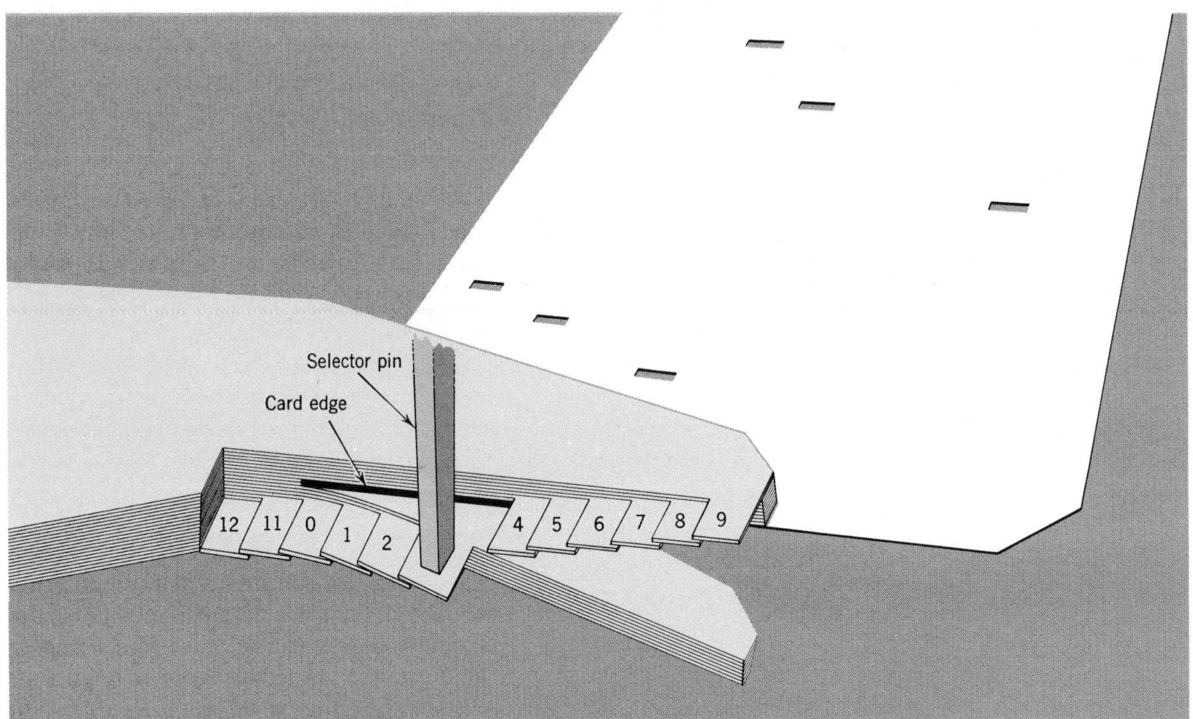


Figure 3-2 Schematic of chute blades for IBM 83 Sorter. (Courtesy International Business Machines Corporation.)

*Sorting patterns for an 83 model are:*
- *numerical*
- *zone*
- *alpha-1*
- *alpha-2*
- *alphanumerical*

**Sorting Patterns**

The sorting patterns for the 83 model are summarized in Figure 3-3. There are 13 receiving pockets (9 through 0, 11, 12, and reject), arranged from left to right and 12 digit-suppression keys corresponding to the 12 punching positions on an IBM 80 column card. Some applications make it desirable to sort out only those cards containing certain digits, leaving the remaining cards in their original se-

| SORT SELECTION SWITCH SETTING | POCKETS | | | | | | | | | | | | REJECTS REGARDLESS OF EDIT | ERRORS (WHEN EDIT OR EDIT-STOP IS ON) |
|---|---|---|---|---|---|---|---|---|---|---|---|---|---|---|
| | 9 | 8 | 7 | 6 | 5 | 4 | 3 | 2 | 1 | 0 | 11 | 12 | | |
| Numerical (N) | 9 | 8 | 7 | 6 | 5 | 4 | 3 | 2 | 1 | 0 | 11 | 12 | Blanks | Multiple-punched cards (incl. letters) |
| Zone (Z) | | | | | | | | | | 0 | 11 | 12 | Any card without a zone punch | Any card with more than one zone punch |
| Alpha-1 (A-1) | I | H | G | F | E | D | C | B | A | 0 S–Z | 11 J–R | | Blanks and cards with a 12-zone punch but no digit punch. Digits 1 to 9. | Any card with more than one zone punch or with more than one digit punch |
| Alpha-2 (A-2) | R,Z | Q,Y | P,X | O,W | N,V | M,U | L,T | K,S | J 0–1 | | | | Cards with 0 or 11-zone only. Blanks. Letters A to I, and 12-zone spec. char. Digits 1 to 9. | Same as A-1 |
| Alpha-numerical (A-N) | 9 | 8 | 7 | 6 | 5 | 4 | 3 | 2 | 1 | 0 (digit) | 11 J–R | 12 A–I | Blanks, 0-zone (S–Z) | Same as A-1 |

This pattern is based on cards being fed face down, 9 edge first.

Figure 3-3 Sorting pattern for the IBM 83 Sorter. (Courtesy International Business Machines Corporation.)

quence. Digit-suppression keys make this type of sorting feasible. There are also five positions for the sort selection switch that determines the sorting pattern. The function of each switch setting as shown in Figure 3-3 is set forth below.

1. Numerical (N): Cards are sorted on the first punch read; blank cards fall into the reject pocket.
2. Zone (Z): Cards are sorted on the zone (0, 11, and 12) punches only. Cards without a zone punch fall into the reject pocket.
3. Alphabetic-Sort 1 (A-1): Cards punched with a digit and a 12-zone (letters A through I) sort on the digit punches 1 through 9. Cards with an 11-zone fall into the 11-pocket while cards with a 0-punch fall into the 0-pocket. Blank cards and cards with a 12-zone punch, but no digit punch fall into the reject pocket.
4. Alphabetic-Sort 2 (A-2): Cards punched with an 11-zone and a digit (J through R) or a 0-zone and a digit (S through Z) sort on the digit punches. Cards with a zero or 11-punch only, cards with a digit punch only, cards punched with letters A through I, special characters, and blank cards fall into the reject pocket.
5. Alphanumerical (A-N): Cards with a digit punch (0 through 9), but no zone punch fall into their respective pockets. Cards with an 11-zone punch (J-R) fall into the 11-pocket and cards with a 12-zone punch (A-I) fall into the 12 pocket. Blank cards and a 0-zone punch (S-Z) fall into the reject pocket.

For a more complete understanding of Figure 3-3, the various sorting operations that can be performed are discussed below.

## Numerical Sorting

*The general rule for numerical sorting (80 column) is to sort the lowest order position of a field first and then go on to sort succeedingly higher order positions.*

Since the sorter will sort only one column at a time, the rule to follow is always to sort the lowest order position of a field first and then go on to sort succeedingly higher order positions. Upon completion of the first pass for the selected column, cards are removed from the pockets in ascending sequence, 0 through 9 for a numerical sort. The cards are arranged in numerical sequence according to the lowest order position of the field, as shown in the illustration for the first pass (Figure 3-4). The cards are replaced in the hopper and the column selector knob is moved

| RANDOM ORDER | FIRST PASS | SECOND PASS | THIRD PASS | FOURTH PASS |
|---|---|---|---|---|
| 4050 | 4050 | 2038 | 2038 | 1955 |
| 3198 | 7371 | 4050 | 4050 | 2038 |
| 1955 | 5083 | 1955 | 5083 | 3198 |
| 7371 | 9274 | 8469 | 3198 | 4050 |
| 9274 | 1955 | 7371 | 9274 | 5083 |
| 5083 | 6596 | 9274 | 7371 | 6596 |
| 8469 | 3198 | 5083 | 8469 | 7371 |
| 2038 | 2038 | 6596 | 6596 | 8469 |
| 6596 | 8469 | 3198 | 1955 | 9274 |

Figure 3-4 An illustration of numerical sorting.

to the second lowest order position of the field. The second sort arranges the cards according to the tens column, the third pass by the hundreds column, and the fourth pass by the thousands column. For higher order fields, this process is repeated.

After each pass, the operator can always test the sorting accuracy by sighting through the cards from each pocket. Since all cards in the 1-pocket should have a 1 punch in this position, he should be able to see light through the deck for that particular position. In like manner, all sorted positions can be checked as they are removed. An alternative is to push a small sort needle through the position in order to test the accuracy of the sort.

*Numerical sorting for a 96 column card is a $1\frac{1}{2}$ pass sort versus a 1 pass sort for an 80 column card.*

While the 80 column card requires one pass for numerical sorting, the IBM 5486 Card Sorter (Model 1 operates at 1000 cards per minute and Model 2 operates at 1500 cards per minute), shown in Figure 3-5, requires a two-phase numeric sort for the 96 column card. During phase 1, the even digits 0, 2, 4, 6, and 8 are selected into the 1/0, 3/2, 5/4, 7/6, and 9/8 stackers respectively, as shown in Figure 3-6*a*. The cards from the reject stacker are run through the sorter during phase 2. The odd digit cards fall on top of the even digits as illustrated in Figure 3-6*b*. All other characters and blank cards are again selected into the reject pocket. It should be noted that since only half the cards were run through on the second pass, this is called a $1\frac{1}{2}$ pass sort rather than a 2 pass sort. Another way of looking at the Model 1 is to think of the 1000 cards per minute sorter as a 667 (1000/1.5) card per minute machine when full numeric fields are being sorted.

## Alphabetical Sorting

Two sorts on an 80 column card must be performed on each column of the field before going onto the next one. As in numerical sorting, the right-hand column (lowest order position of field) must be sorted first. This separates the cards by the numerical position of the punching since the cards enter the machine 9-edge

Figure 3-5 IBM 5486 Card Sorter. (Courtesy International Business Machines Corporation.)

*The basic rule of numerical sorting is also followed for alphabetical sorting, except that two passes (numeric and zone) are required for each column.*

first and the numerical punch is read first. Before moving to the next column, the zone position (0, 11, and 12) is sorted by setting the sort selection switch toward the center of the selection switch group. This switch disconnects the digit circuits 1 through 9 so that on this second sort of the same column, all cards fall into the 0-, 11-, and 12-pockets. Cards punched A through I are in the 12-pocket; J through R are in the 11-pocket; and S through Z are in the 0-pocket, resulting in all cards being in alphabetic sequence for each pocket.

*Alphabetical sorting for a 96 column card is a $2\frac{1}{2}$ pass sort versus a 2 pass sort for an 80 column card.*

The alphabetic sort requires three phases or $2\frac{1}{2}$ passes per column for a 96 column card. This is depicted in Figure 3-7. If the 5486 Card Sorter has the special alphabetic sorting procedure, the alphabetic sort only can be reduced to 2 passes.

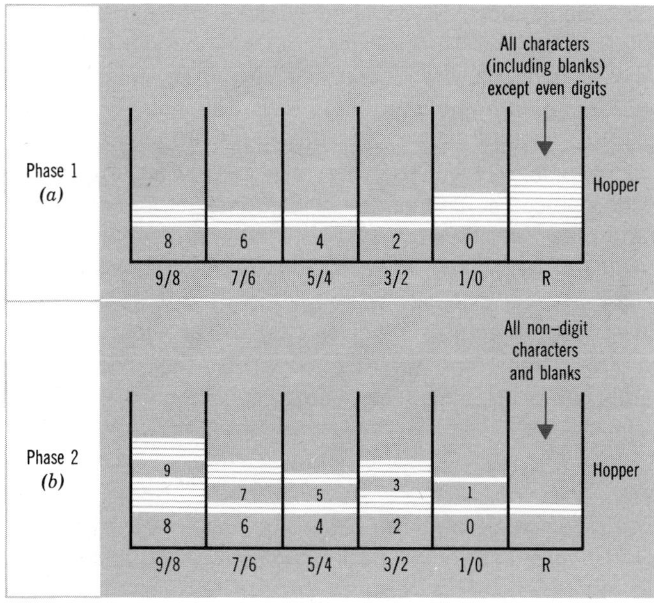


Figure 3-6 Numeric sort, phase 1 (*a*) and phase 2 (*b*).

| | 9/8 | 7/6 | 5/4 | 3/2 | 1/0 | R | |
|---|---|---|---|---|---|---|---|
| After zone sort | 9 ↑ 0 | Z ↑ S | R ↑ J } | I ↑ A | | | Hopper |
| After phase 2 | IRZ 9 | GPX 7 | ENV 5 | CLT 3 | AJ 1 | Blanks Special char. | |
| After phase 1 | HQY 8 | FOW 6 | DMU 4 | BKS 2 | } 0 | 13579 AJCLTEN VGPXIRZ Blanks Special char. | |

Figure 3-7 Alphabetic sort on IBM 5486 Card Sorter.

### Multiple-Field Sorting

*The general rule for multiple-field sorting is to start with the lower order field first and then the lowest order position within that field.*

When data are to be sorted into sequence by several fields of information for a specific run, it is necessary to determine the relationship of these fields. The general rule for multiple-field sorting is to start with the lower order field first and then the lowest order position within that field. In effect, the sorting procedure starts with the minor field (least important), proceeds through the (increasingly important) intermediate field, and finally to the major field (most important) of data. An example would be the sorting procedure necessary to prepare a monthly sales report where region number is punched in column 15, branch number in columns 16 and 17, and salesman number in columns 18 and 19. The sort procedure would proceed from column 19 to 18 to 17 to 16, and finally to 15 when utilizing the multiple-field sorting principle.

### Block Sorting

*The general rule for block sorting is to sort on the highest order field or column first before sorting on the lowest order position.*

Block sorting is a procedure used where large volumes of data are to be arranged in some meaningful sequence. The handling of so many cards would make the multiple-field method of sorting too awkward and time consuming since all cards must be sorted on one column before going on to the next. The method for block sorting entails breaking the large card deck down into blocks of data, sorting on the highest order field or column first. Other sorters can be utilized to continue the regular sorting procedure. Block sorting may be also advisable for average size group of cards since the first sorted block can be processed on other equipment while all succeeding blocks are being run. The need for block sorting is dependent upon the effective utilization of other pieces of equipment in order to speed up the processing of data in the firm. Referring to the sales example above, it might be advisable to sort on column 15—region number (9 regions). These 9 blocks could be sorted on different machines at the same time, thereby speeding up the sorting process.

### Single-Column Selecting

In some applications, it may be desirable to select those cards having one or several punches in a particular column. Under this condition, the single-column selecting procedure can be utilized. This requires the use of special selection

*Single-column selecting is a method of selecting certain cards without disturbing the sequence of other cards in the file.*

switches that provide a way of selecting certain cards without disturbing the sequence of other cards in the file. Mechanically, this is no more difficult than regular sorting. In the sales analysis example, a marketing manager may want specific information about regions 3 and 5 only. By utilizing the selection switches, these sales cards can be selected for pockets 3 and 5 of the sorter respectively while all remaining cards fall into the reject pocket. The selected cards can then be processed further per the individual's instructions.

## COLLATING

*Collating is the process of comparing two files of cards simultaneously in order to match or combine them into one file.*

The arranging of cards in a meaningful sequence has definite limitations since only one column can be checked at a time and only one deck can be processed at a time. What is needed is a machine that is capable of handling more complex functions and, at the same time, is more flexible than the sorter. The machine that supplements the sorter for processing needs is the *collator*. Its basic function is feeding and comparing two files of cards simultaneously in order to match them or combine them into one file. The collator has the added capability of detecting and separating those cards from the first file that do not have a matching card in the second file. Likewise, it is used for card sequence checking and selecting.

Depending upon the requirements of a punched card installation, several collators are available. They are divided into two basic types: numeric and alphabetic. Numeric collators are IBM Types 77, 85, and 88 while alphabetic ones are Types 87 and 88 (fully transistorized solid-state machines). The IBM 88 Collator (Figure 3-8) can process numeric only unless a special alphabetic collating device is installed. The alphabetic collators can process either numerical or alphabetic data

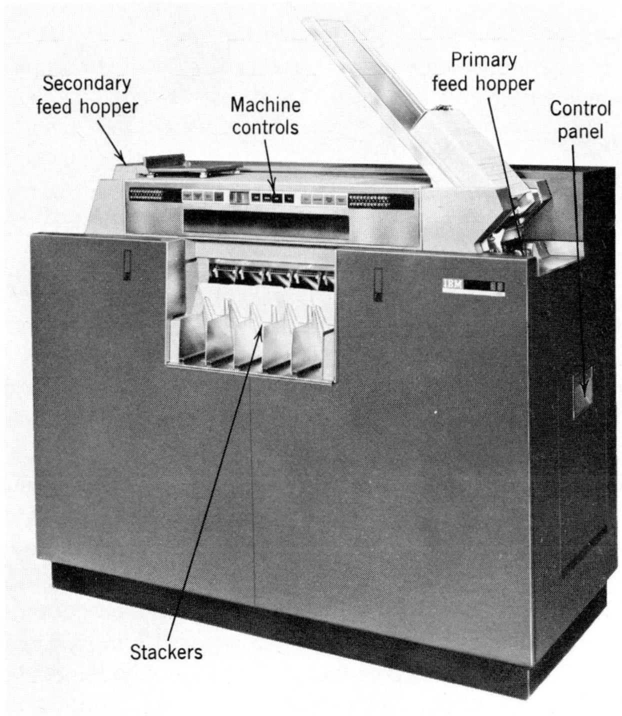


Figure 3-8 IBM 88 Collator. (Courtesy International Business Machines Corporation.)

and are similar in appearance, basic operations, and speeds. Speeds range from 650 to 1300 cards a minute. There are 5 radial stackers with a 1000-card capacity each and the machine is equipped with a primary file feed device, capable of holding 3600 cards.

### Operation of Collator

*The collator feeds cards from two different hoppers and compares their contents for appropriate action.*

The two feed units, shown in Figure 3-8, are called the primary feed and the secondary feed. In the primary feed hopper, cards are placed face down with the 9-edge toward the throat of the machine. The cards in the secondary feed hopper are placed face down with the 12-edge toward the throat of the machine, as depicted in Figure 3-9. Each station consists of 80 reading brushes that can be wired to read any of the card columns. The control panel fits into a rack on the side of the machine.

As cards are fed from the primary feed hopper, they pass the primary sequence read station and then the primary read station. The same procedure holds true for the secondary feed. After the cards have been read, they can be directed to any one of the five pockets, as indicated in Figure 3-9. The selection of the appropriate pocket depends on the processing operation being performed.

### Card Selecting

*The collator has the capability of selecting certain cards without affecting the sequence of other cards.*

The selecting task of the collator is very similar to that of the sorter, the difference being that the collator can select on more than one card column at a time. The selected card may be an X-card, a no-X card, the first card of a group, the last card of a group, a single-card group, a zero-balance card, a card with a particular number, a card out of sequence, or any other card conforming to a pattern set up by control panel wiring. When any of the above cards are desired, the collator selects them without disturbing the sequence of the other cards. For example, all cycle billing accounts receivable cards having a zero balance are to be selected so that special promotion material can be mailed to them for the purpose of reactivating their accounts. The sequence of all other accounts receivable cards is not disturbed by this card selection run.

### Sequence Checking

*Sequence checking is a method of checking whether or not cards are arranged in the proper ascending or descending sequence.*

A file of cards can be checked to determine if the cards are arranged in the proper ascending or descending sequence. This test is one of sequence checking which may be performed independently or in conjunction with other operations—selecting, merging, and matching. The two sets of brushes in each feed make it possible to compare each card with the card ahead. The comparison may be a high-, an equal-, or a low-sequence condition. The results of the checking operation can be used to perform various functions, such as stopping the machine for a card out of order, separating all cards out of sequence, recognizing a change in control groups, or identifying the first and last cards of a group.

Since a file is normally in ascending sequence, the cards are in order if any card is either higher than or equal to the card ahead. However, if a card is lower than the card ahead (a step-down condition), an error in sequence is indicated. This error is known as a low-sequence condition. Figure 3-10 illustrates three different errors in sequence. The step-down card 3 is out of order (*a*); the card 9 preceding the step-down card is out of order (*b*); and the step-down card 3 and the two cards 4 and 5 following it are out of numerical sequence (*c*). Sequence checking is frequently used for checking the order of data before computer processing.

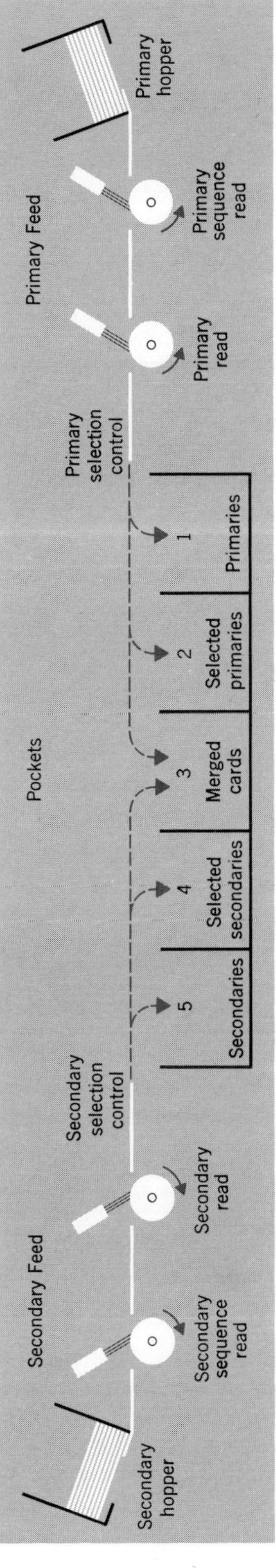


Figure 3-9 Schematic for path of cards through IBM 88 Collator. (Courtesy International Business Machines Corporation.)

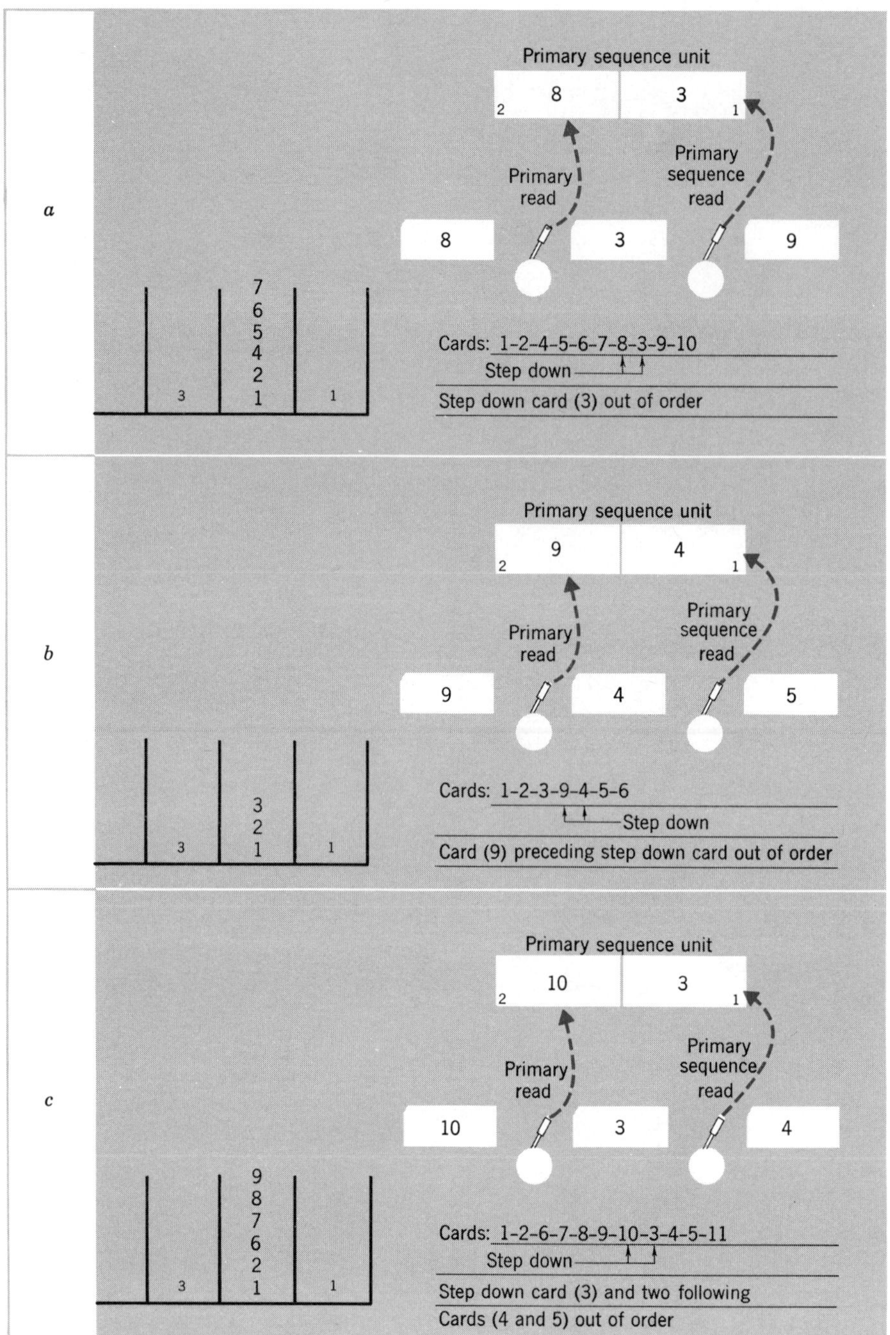


Figure 3-10 Three types of sequence checking errors.

## Merging

*Merging is the process of combining two card decks already in sequence into one deck of cards.*

When two decks of cards are already in sequence and are combined to produce one deck of cards, it is known as merging. The merging function is performed on a collator by placing one of the two sequenced decks in each of the primary and secondary feed hoppers. The merging of cards from the two hoppers is controlled by impulses from the primary and secondary brushes.

The cards in one file are compared with those in the other to determine which card should precede the other into the merged pocket. To illustrate (Figure 3-11), a card in the master file (primary feed) is compared with a card in the detail file (secondary feed) to determine which card should be moved to the merged file. Since the master and detail cards are both of equal value (*a* and *c* conditions), the master

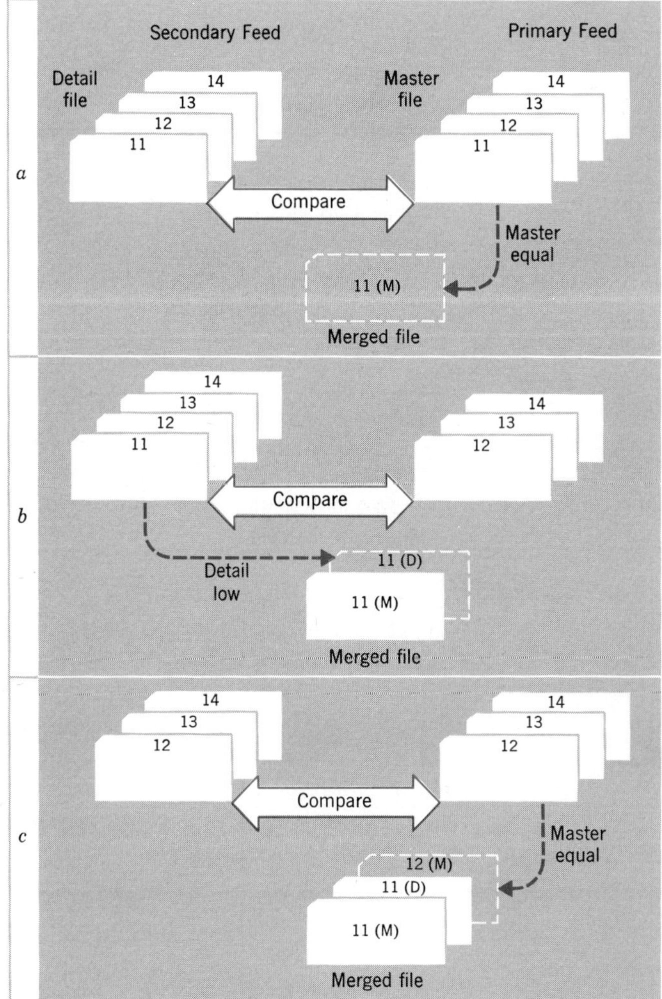


Figure 3-11 Merging operations of master file with detail file.

file card will be fed to the merged pocket first. If the number of the master file card is the lower in the comparison (not shown), it is selected as an error and fed to one of the other pockets. Similarly, other error conditions that can occur are provided for through programming of the control panel. On the other hand, if the number of the detail file is lower than the master card during the comparison (*b* condition), it will be fed to the merged pocket behind the master file card. As can be seen from the foregoing, it is important that the deck of cards be placed in the appropriate feed hoppers.

### Matching

*Matching is the process of comparing one deck of cards against another and extracting those cards that do not match.*

Instead of merging the two files into one file as above, cards that do match remain in the two original groups while cards in either file that do not match are separated. The matching operation requires using both the comparing unit and the sequence units for comparing four cards simultaneously. As the cards pass the primary and secondary reading stations and are compared, those that match are normally stacked in pockets 2 and 4, respectively. The unmatched primary and secondary cards are normally stacked in pockets 1 and 5, respectively. After the matching operation has been completed, the four files are in numerical sequence. Matching is widely used for comparing a master file to a detail file in order to insure that both decks are identical.

### Merging with Selection

*Merging with selection (match-merging) is the process of combining two ordered card decks and selecting those cards that do not match.*

Merging with selection, sometimes called match-merging, is a combination of the procedures described in the two preceding sections—matching and merging. Under this method, matching cards are merged together rather than being left in their original two groups. As with a matching operation, all unmatched cards from the primary and secondary feeds are fed into separate pockets. At the end of the operation, there are three separate groups of cards: one merged deck of cards and two selected or unmatched card groups.

Match-merging is utilized quite extensively for combining master and detail file cards, such as payroll files and inventory files. Not only does merging with selection bring the two decks together but it also selects a master card without a detail card and vice versa. The discrepancy between the two files is usually caused by human carelessness when additions or deletions are made to files.

### Editing

*Editing is the process of checking for double punching errors and blank columns.*

To assure accuracy of input data, cards should always be checked for double punching errors and blank columns. Up to 22 columns in each feed can be edited for these errors. Since the Type 88 Collator is a numerical machine, double-punch detection is automatic for every position read into the comparing unit. However, a switch for each position must be wired to detect unpunched columns. When the double-punch blank-column (DPBC) switch is wired and either error is detected, card feeding stops. The DPBC light goes on and a check light indicates the feed containing the error card. Editing can also be used to check computer input before processing occurs.

## CALCULATING

*Punched card calculators perform the four basic arithmetic operations.*

Most punched card installations have electric accounting machines to produce various reports. Their arithmetic ability is generally restricted to addition and subtraction. For this reason, there is need for a machine that performs all four arithmetic operations (addition, subtraction, multiplication, and division), namely, the calculating punch. It is designed to read several fields of information on a card, perform calculations based upon these data, and punch the results either in the card from which the data are read or in designated cards that follow. Of the several types in use—IBM 602, 604, and 609—only the IBM 609, shown in Figure 3-12, will be discussed.

The solid-state 609 Calculator performs operations at the rate of 200 cards a minute, permitting 110 milliseconds for calculating, and is capable of delay punching

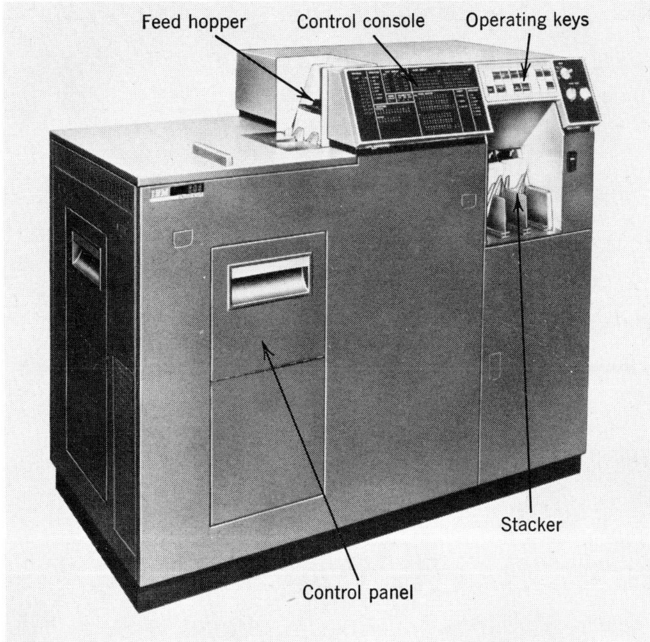


Figure 3-12 IBM 609 Calculator. (Courtesy International Business Machines Corporation.)

in any card needing added time for complex calculations. The maximum size of input or output data for any one program step is ordinarily six digits. Control panel wiring is necessary to execute the various program steps. A problem should first be analyzed to determine the best use of core storage and the sequence of the program to be executed by the calculating punch.

### Operation of Calculator

*Basically, the calculator reads punched card data, performs the arithmetic operations, and punches the results into the same card.*

Cards are placed face down, 12-edge first in the feed hopper and pass three stations—an 80 column reading station, a punching station, and a second reading station (Figure 3-13). At the first reading station, selected punched data on the card are read. Calculations are performed after reading the card and while it moves to the punching station. The calculated results are punched into the same card as it passes the punching station. As the card passes the second reading station, data can be read for the purpose of gangpunching or for double-punch and blank-column (DPBC) checking.

Numerous applications can be found for the calculating punch, such as calculating payroll or inventories and exploding bills of materials for production.

## CARD PROVING

*Card proving equipment can sort data, total figures for control purposes, and prove data before entry into a system.*

The primary objective for any punched card data processing system is to maintain an efficient operation, that is, operating at full capacity with a minimum of manual intervention. The card proving machine is designed to assist in achieving this objective. It can be used to prove punched card data before entry into a system, thereby substantially reducing error correction costs. Similarly, it can be utilized to total critical fields that can be compared to established control and hash totals. Also, it can sort cards into sequence before processing. Thus the card proving

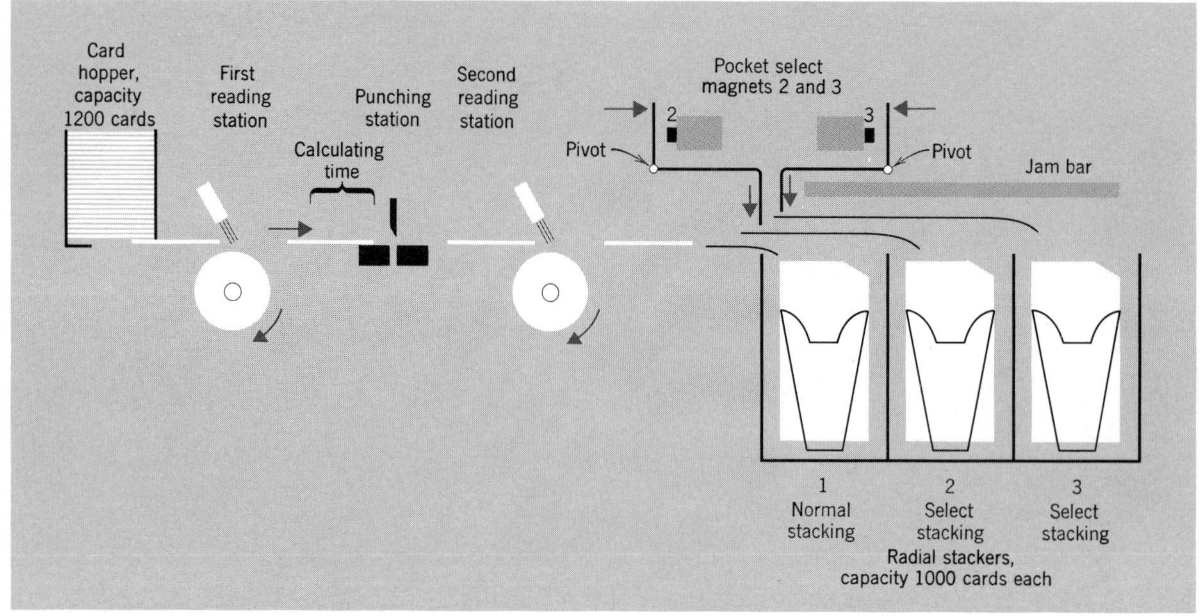


Figure 3-13 Card feed schematic for IBM 609 Calculator. (Courtesy International Business Machines Corporation.)

machine has the capability of proving, controlling, and sorting which is normally accomplished on three separate pieces of punched card equipment.

*The 108 card proving machine performs functions that are normally accomplished on several punched card machines.*

**Card Proving Machine**

IBM equipment for this function is available in two models: the 101 and 108. The IBM 101 Electronic Statistical Machine, which operates at a speed of 450 cards a minute, performs the following operations: sorting, counting, accumulating, editing, printing, and crossfooting. On the other hand, the IBM 108 Proving Machine (Figure 3-14) operates at the rate of 1000 cards a minute. Arithmetically, the 108 can perform addition, subtraction, manual totaling, automatic totaling, progressive totaling, total transfer, crossfooting totals, and balance testing. Its normal functions include: regular sorting, selective sorting, multiple columns selection, numeric sequence checking, alphabetic sequence checking, comparing, and editing operations. An output typewriter and card punch can be cable-connected to the 108 Card Proving Machine for printing and summary punching.

As indicated in Figure 3-14, the IBM machine is very similar in appearance and operation (Figure 3-15) to the card sorter. It has 13 pockets—12 for sorting cards and 1 for reject cards. A display panel is used to locate errors quickly. Cards are placed in the feed hopper face down, 9-edge toward the throat. Any one of the 49 columns of a card, in conjunction with the control panel wiring, can be sorted by using the two selection switches.

One of the most popular applications for the machine is the preediting of punched cards before computer processing. Double-punched columns, blank columns, incorrect batch and control totals, invalid codes, sequence errors, and other errors and irregularities can be selected by the Card Proving Machine. This preediting phase can save lost computer time and extensive corrections to computer files.

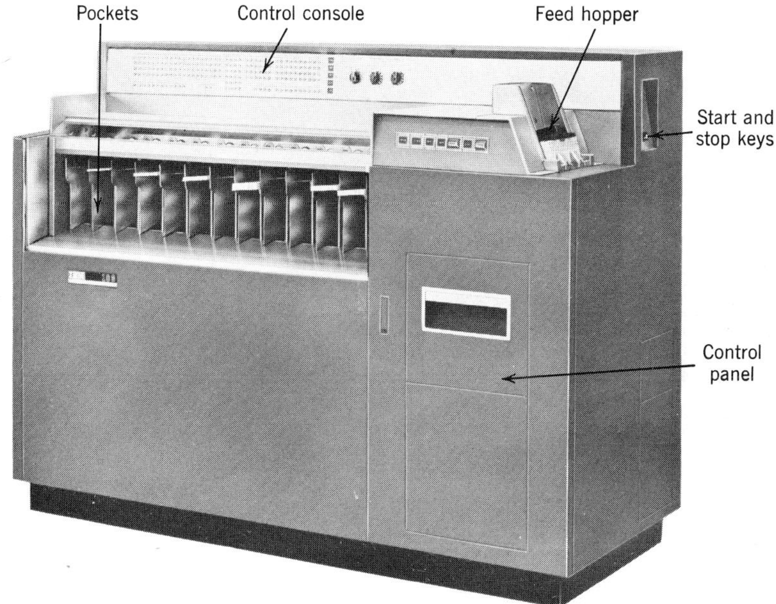


Figure 3-14 IBM 108 Card Proving Machine. (Courtesy International Business Machines Corporation.)

## Card Controller

*The 1001 Card Controller, a high-speed, multipurpose machine, is similar to the 108 Card Proving Machine.*

Somewhat similar to the IBM 108 Card Proving Machine is the UNIVAC 1001 Card Controller (Figure 3-16). Being a high-speed, multipurpose machine, it is capable of being programmed since there are 256 characters of core storage and a variable sequence of program steps. All operations, however, are directed through wiring of a removable connection panel. The 1001 Card Controller feeds cards at speeds up to 1000 cards a minute. Since it has two card-input stations and seven

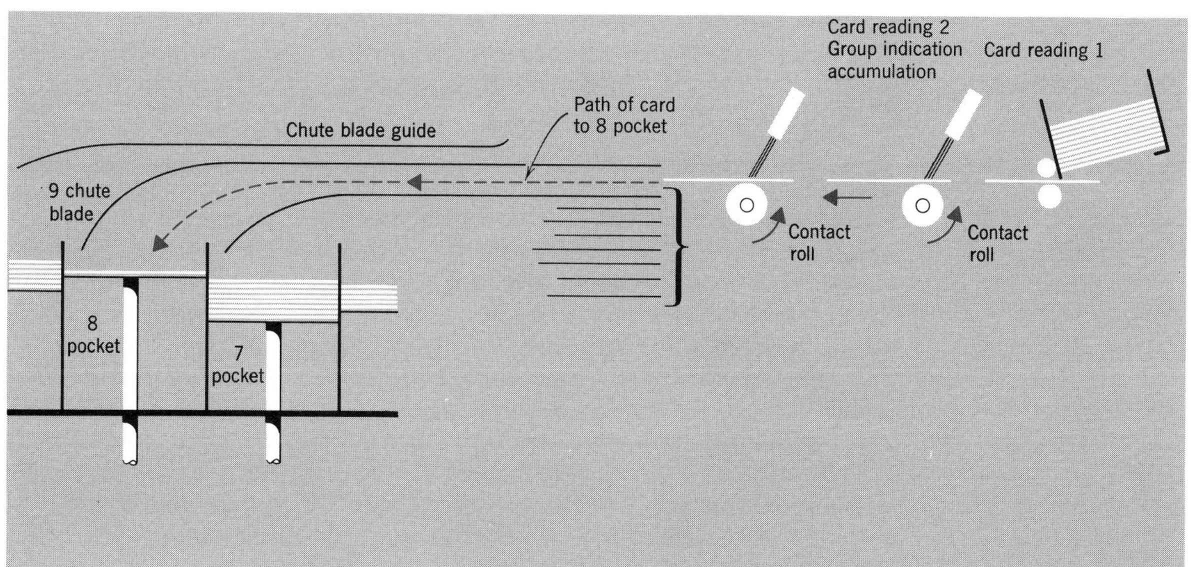


Figure 3-15 Schematic showing path of cards through IBM 108 Card Proving Machine. (Courtesy International Business Machines Corporation.)

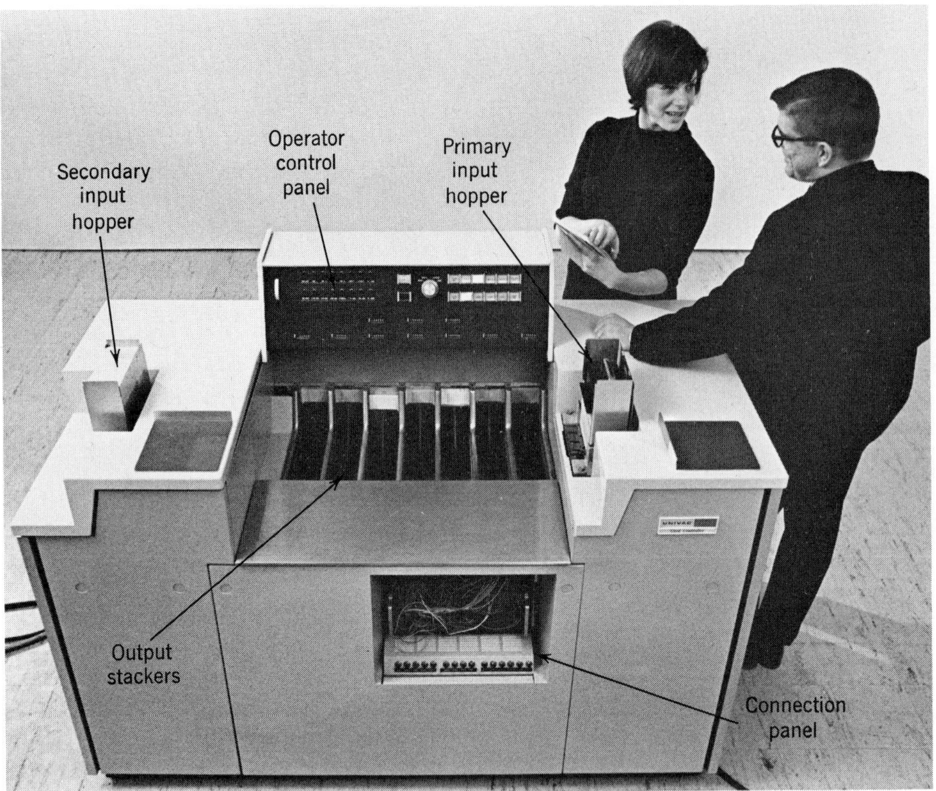


Figure 3-16 UNIVAC 1001 Card Controller. (Courtesy UNIVAC Division of the Sperry Rand Corporation.)

output stackers, it can handle most collating operations. Basically, its principal function is to arrange card files into groups or sequences required for further processing.

## REPORTING

*Reporting refers to the output function of punched card equipment.*

Once data have been converted from source documents to punched cards and have been manipulated in some meaningful order, they are ready for the last step—converting punched cards into a printed report, statement, invoice, check, or analysis on an accounting machine. This end result, for example, may be a customer statement, shipping notice, aging of accounts receivable, bills of materials, or sales reports. The accounting machine may prepare output for external or internal usage. Regardless of usage, the accounting machine handles most reporting functions required of a punched card information system. It is available in several different models, but they differ basically in their input/output speeds, accumulating capacity, and special features offered.

### Accounting Machines

The IBM accounting machine line includes these basic models: the 402, 403, 407, 408, and 409. The 402 and 403 Accounting Machines are comparable pieces of equipment. Both operate at speeds of 100 lines per minute for detail printing.

*IBM accounting machines have been and are widely used to produce meaningful output.*

The printing unit consists of two sections of typebars, the left section containing 43 typebars of alphanumeric print while the right section has 45 typebars that print numeric data only. Their basic difference is that the 402 is capable of printing only one line from a card whereas the 403 is capable of printing three lines from a single card. This operation is referred to as multiple-line print (MLP). This added feature on the 403 Accounting Machine is extremely helpful when printing name, address, city, state, and zip code. The printing operation can be speeded up by having one card for a complete name and address versus three cards required on a 402.

***Printing and Counters.*** The IBM 407 Accounting Machine (Figure 3-17) prints information from 120 printwheels with each printwheel containing 47 different characters. It can read cards at the rate of 150 per minute while it adds, subtracts, and prints 18,000 characters per minute. Amounts can be added or subtracted in 112 counter positions (126 or 168 are also available), which are arranged in 20 groups of 3, 4, 6, and 8 positions each. A 3-position counter can total up to 999, a 4-position counter can total up to 9999, and so forth. Counters can be used individually or combined in any manner to accommodate a larger number of digits.

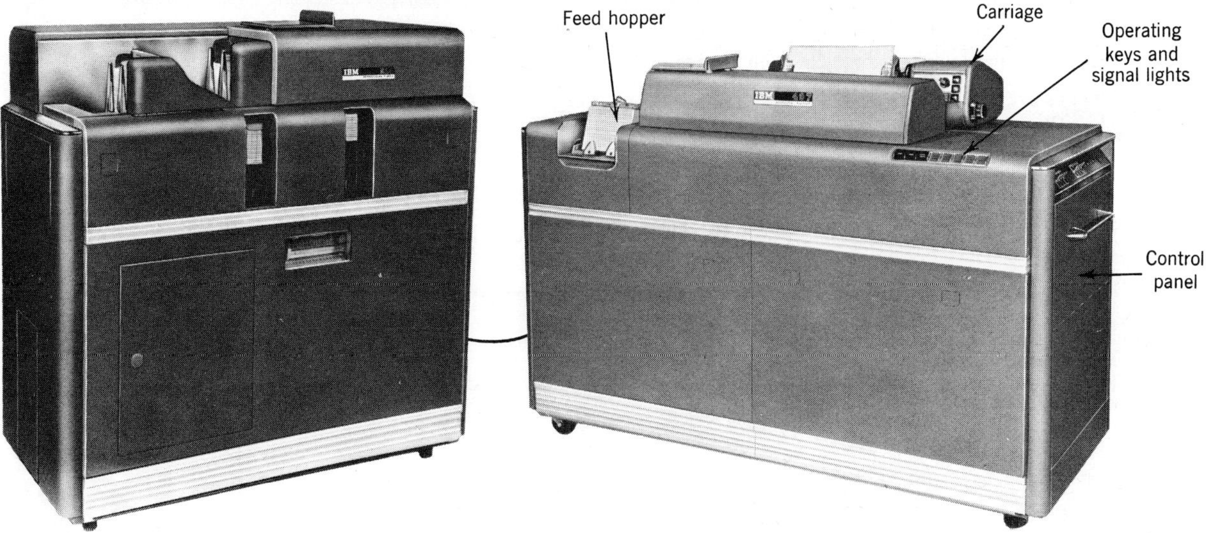


Figure 3-17 IBM 407 Accounting Machine with attached IBM 514 Summary Punch. (Courtesy International Business Machines Corporation.)

*Counters in accounting machines are utilized to accumulate values for printing desired information.*

*Program steps available with the 407 Accounting Machine are:*
- *minor*
- *intermediate*
- *major*

***Program Steps.*** A standard 407 is capable of handling three program steps, referred to as *minor program, intermediate program,* and *major program*. The printing of totals, the advancing of the form in the carriage, the punching of a card by the summary punch are examples of operations accomplished by one program step. To further clarify the printing of totals, accounting might want an expense distribution by department or branch as indicated in Figure 3-18. The minor program will accumulate totals for each subsidiary ledger account number, the intermediate program for each general ledger account number, and the major program for the department or branch. These totals are printed when the machine compares and finds a difference between the number at the first reading station and the number at the next reading station. When subtotals are taken for each "amount," it is

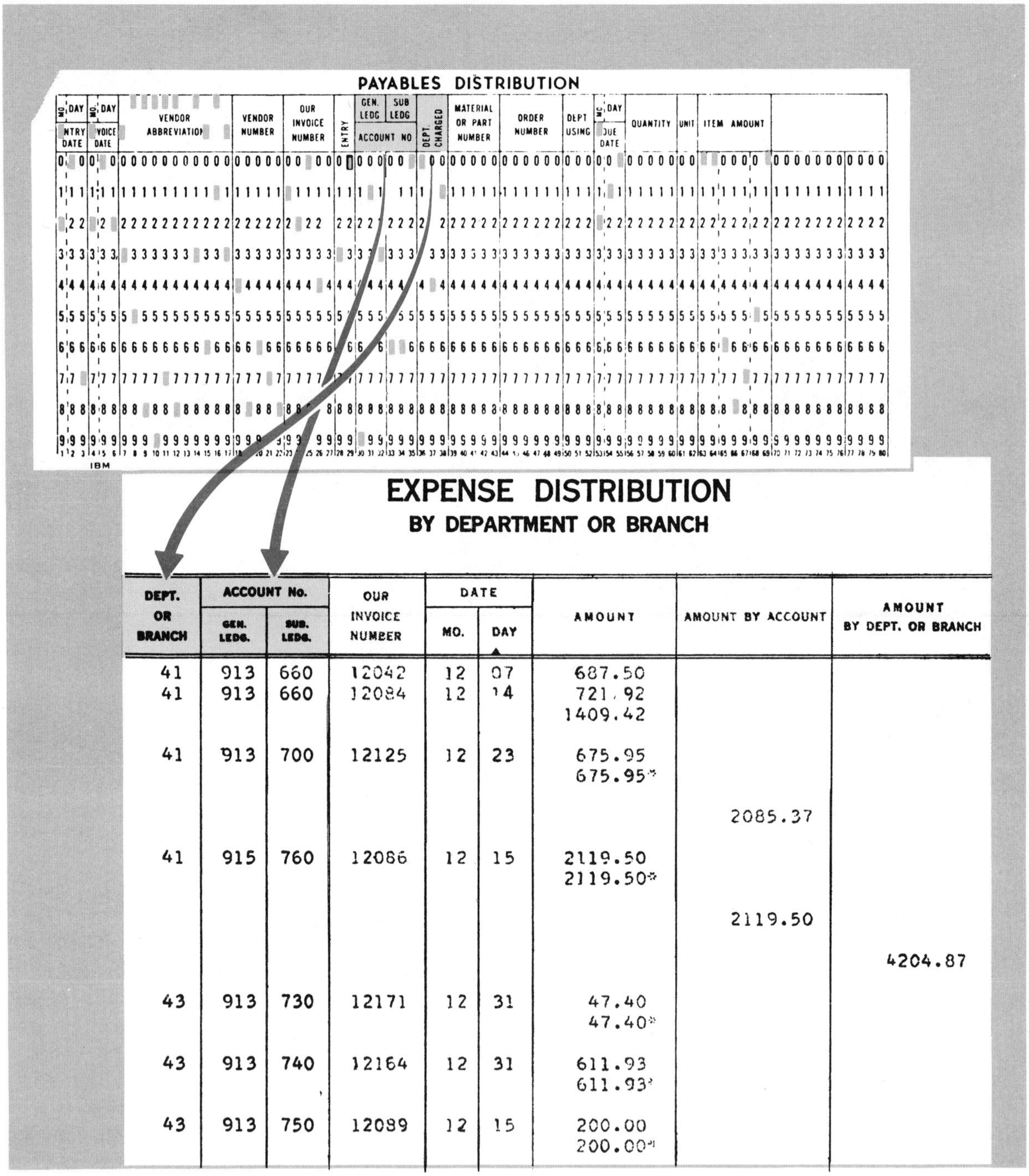

## PAYABLES DISTRIBUTION

MO DAY ENTRY DATE | MO DAY INVOICE DATE | VENDOR ABBREVIATION | VENDOR NUMBER | OUR INVOICE NUMBER | ENTRY | GEN. LEDG / SUB LEDG ACCOUNT NO | DEPT. CHARGED | MATERIAL OR PART NUMBER | ORDER NUMBER | DEPT USING | MO DAY DUE DATE | QUANTITY | UNIT | ITEM AMOUNT

IBM

## EXPENSE DISTRIBUTION
### BY DEPARTMENT OR BRANCH

| DEPT. OR BRANCH | ACCOUNT No. | | OUR INVOICE NUMBER | DATE | | AMOUNT | AMOUNT BY ACCOUNT | AMOUNT BY DEPT. OR BRANCH |
|---|---|---|---|---|---|---|---|---|
| | GEN. LEDG. | SUB. LEDG. | | MO. | DAY | | | |
| 41 | 913 | 660 | 12042 | 12 | 07 | 687.50 | | |
| 41 | 913 | 660 | 12084 | 12 | 14 | 721.92 | | |
| | | | | | | 1409.42 | | |
| 41 | 913 | 700 | 12125 | 12 | 23 | 675.95 | | |
| | | | | | | 675.95* | | |
| | | | | | | | 2085.37 | |
| 41 | 915 | 760 | 12086 | 12 | 15 | 2119.50 | | |
| | | | | | | 2119.50* | | |
| | | | | | | | 2119.50 | |
| | | | | | | | | 4204.87 |
| 43 | 913 | 730 | 12171 | 12 | 31 | 47.40 | | |
| | | | | | | 47.40* | | |
| 43 | 913 | 740 | 12164 | 12 | 31 | 611.93 | | |
| | | | | | | 611.93* | | |
| 43 | 913 | 750 | 12089 | 12 | 15 | 200.00 | | |
| | | | | | | 200.00* | | |

Figure 3-18 Detail printed report: minor, intermediate, and major program steps on IBM 407 Accounting Machine.

necessary to accumulate a total for each "amount by account" and, in turn, total an "amount by department or branch." The machine must be instructed to accumulate these figures or they will be destroyed when they are read out. The only way these values can be saved is by instructing the machine to "roll" totals from one counter to another while the subtotals are read out. Thus, it follows that each total—minor, intermediate, and major—in the illustration will require a separate counter.

*X-punch and no X-punch are used to separate a plus value from a minus value.*

***X-Punch.*** Many times, the amounts to be added and subtracted will be contained in the same card field although this was not true in Figure 3-18. To distinguish between debit and credit amounts, an X-punch can be used for the credit in column 80 (or column near the end of the card) and none for the debit (no X-punch) or vice versa. In this manner, the accounting machine can perform the arithmetic operation desired and/or print the amount in the proper column. For example, in Figure 3-19, the item amount field represents sales on NX-cards (no X-punch column 78) and returns and allowances on X-cards (X-punch in column 78). The control-panel wiring for this X selection is shown later in the chapter (Figure 3-25).

*Forms can be positioned in the machine automatically by a tape-controlled carriage.*

***Tape-Controlled Carriage.*** In addition to the above program control, forms can be positioned in the machine automatically by a tape-controlled carriage, together with control panel wiring. The printing unit can be set up for operation by inserting a prepunched tape in the tape control mechanism. For each processing run, the tape corresponds to the length of the business form it is to control (Figure 3-20). The tape, then, controls the feeding, spacing, automatic skipping to various parts on the form, and ejecting of forms.

*Values read by an accounting machine at the first and second reading stations are compared under program control to indicate a change in cards.*

***Operation of Accounting Machine.*** Cards are placed in the hopper with the 9-edge toward the throat and are fed into the 407 Accounting Machine from the bottom, under control of the feed rolls. As indicated in Figure 3-21, each card is positioned at the first, then at the second reading stations. Values at the first and second reading stations are compared under program control to indicate a change in the two cards. At each reading station, 960 possible punching positions are directly under 960 stationary reading brushes and directly above the 960 metal segments. Any hole that is punched in the card allows its corresponding brush to make contact with a metal segment. The electrical impulse resulting from this contact is transmitted from the commutator, as it rotates, to the brushes in that position. There are 80 commutators at each reading station that rotate together. These commutators transmit impulses to the brushes in their corresponding position. The brushes transmit these impulses to the control panel where they can be utilized to control a specific machine function, such as printing a line. If a line is to be printed under program control, special purpose wires take the impulse from the control panel to the printwheels. The impulse causes a selected printwheel to be activated for printing the desired number, letter, or special character on the form. Cards can be held at the reading station for any given number of cycles, after which they move around the stacker drum into the stacker. When the stacker becomes full, the machine halts. Likewise, as soon as the last card is fed, the machine stops automatically. The remaining cards in the machine must be fed into the stacker by pressing the start key.

*A computing device for multiplying and dividing can be attached to the accounting machine.*

***Computing Device.*** The IBM 402, 403, 407 Accounting Machines have a wide selection of features, one of them being the computing device. For this feature, the various models are called computing accounting machines. The computing device can be used for all arithmetic operations—addition, subtraction, multiplication, and division. Certain multiple computations are capable of being per-

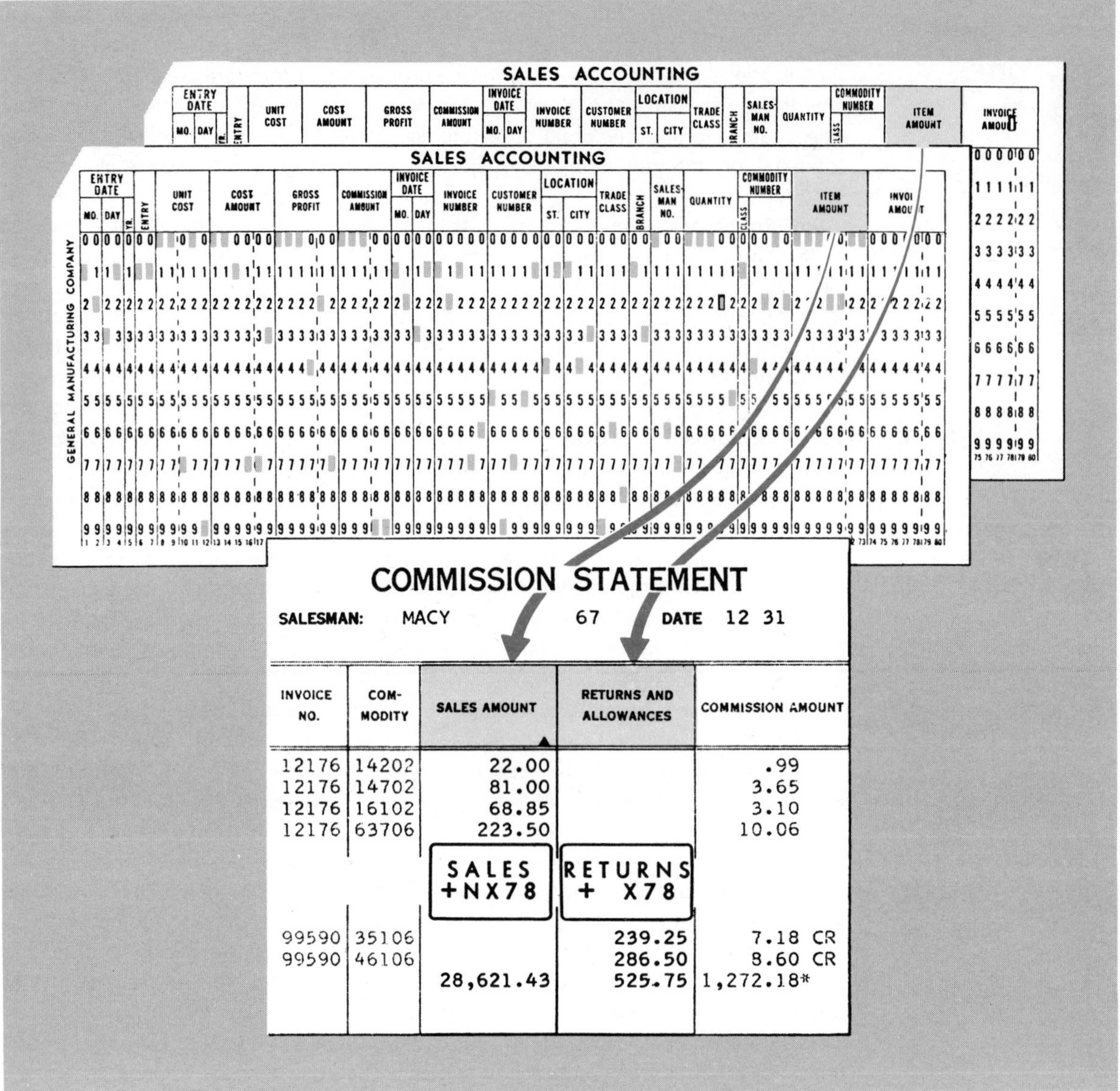


COMMISSION STATEMENT

SALESMAN: MACY 67 DATE 12 31

| INVOICE NO. | COM-MODITY | SALES AMOUNT | RETURNS AND ALLOWANCES | COMMISSION AMOUNT |
|---|---|---|---|---|
| 12176 | 14202 | 22.00 | | .99 |
| 12176 | 14702 | 81.00 | | 3.65 |
| 12176 | 16102 | 68.85 | | 3.10 |
| 12176 | 63706 | 223.50 | | 10.06 |
| | | SALES +NX78 | RETURNS + X78 | |
| 99590 | 35106 | | 239.25 | 7.18 CR |
| 99590 | 46106 | | 286.50 | 8.60 CR |
| | | 28,621.43 | 525.75 | 1,272.18* |

Figure 3-19 Selection—under control of X-punch.

formed in one machine cycle without interfering with other accounting machine functions. These computations do not delay the processing of normal accounting machine operations. More complex applications, involving a series of computations, can be performed during additional machine cycles. This considerably slows down normal operating speeds of the machine. When the computing device is not being used for other computations, it can total crossfooted amounts from a variety of inputs—fields read from a card, counter output, storage unit output, and output from the computing device. Up to six fields from a card can be totaled into one register (in the computing device) during the machine cycle in which a card is read. The

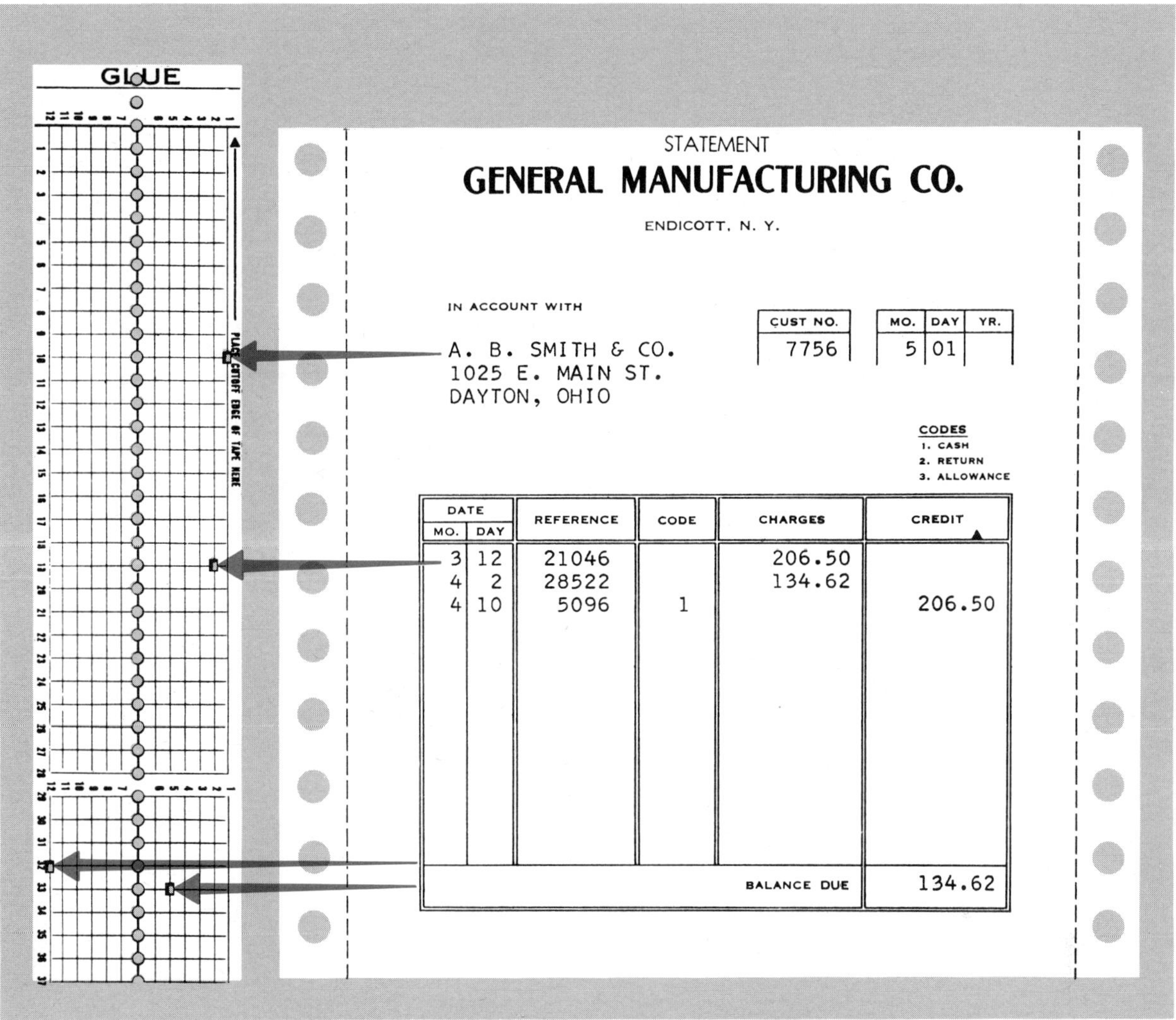


Figure 3-20 Control tape punching for predetermined printing locations on the IBM 407 Accounting Machine.

crossfooted fields can be all negative, all positive, or combinations of negative and positive amounts.

*Accounting machines are available for processing cut-card and continuous forms.*

***Card-and Continuous-Form Carriage.*** The IBM 408 Accounting Machine with card-and continuous-form carriage automatically processes cut-card forms or continuous forms. It is well suited for the preparation of punched card or post card documents, such as utility bills, premium notices, and checks. Various lengths of cards with various-sized stubs, ranging from a 51 column card up to an 80 column card with an 80 column stub, can be accommodated. The machine can feed two separate cards side by side. With multiple-line printing, the 408 can print from 120 printing positions at a speed of 150 lines per minute.

***Card Punching.*** The IBM 409 (Figure 3-22) Accounting Machine performs all operations of the 408 and more. It has the ability to combine the cut-card form carriage with the card punching feature. This permits printing and punching card

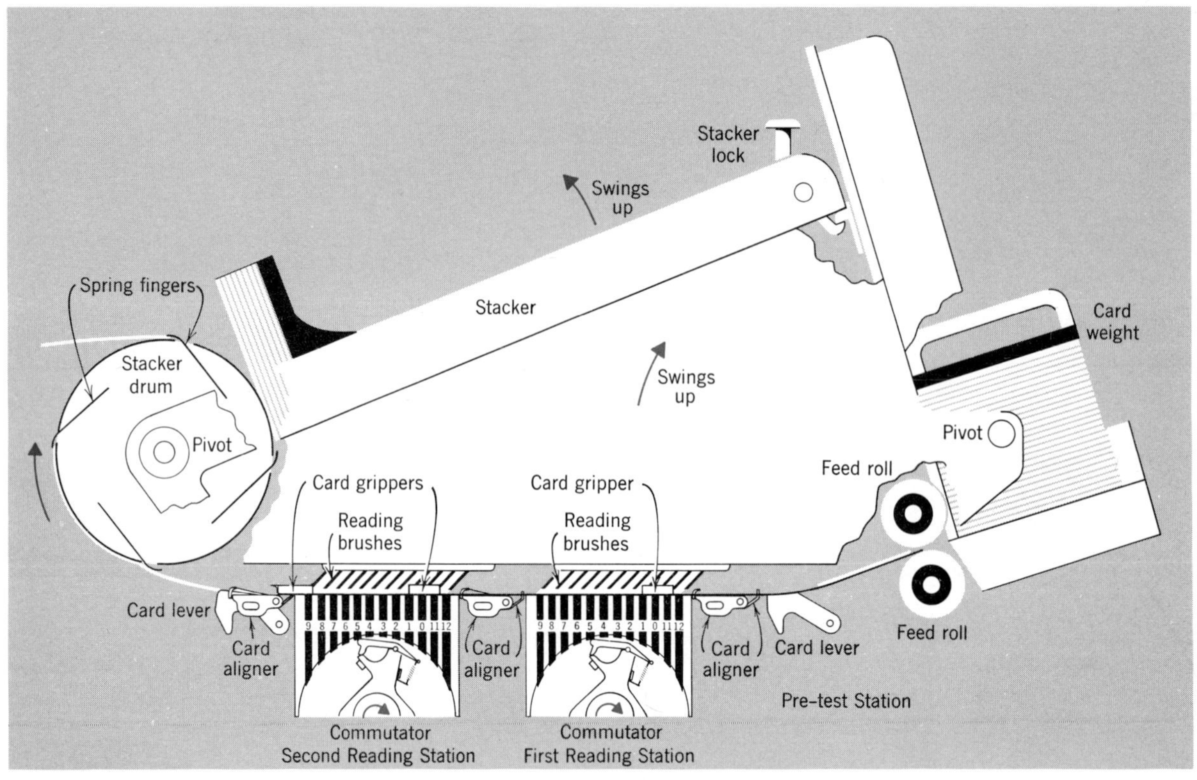


Figure 3-21 Feed unit schematic on IBM 407 Accounting Machine. (Courtesy International Business Machines Corporation.)

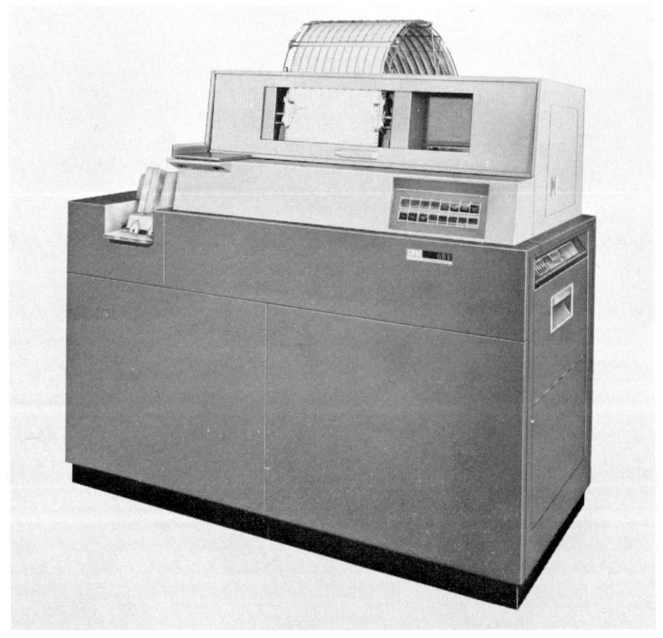

Figure 3-22 IBM 409 Accounting Machine. (Courtesy International Business Machines Corporation.)

*Accounting machines are obtainable that combine the card punching feature with cut-card form processing.*

documents during the same pass of the file without loss of time. Cards are punched in the carriage feed immediately after ejection from the print station and during the eject cycle. Columns 1 through 24 of the card can be punched with either alphabetic or numeric data or the 0-1 code combination. Continuous forms can also be processed in the 409, but only cut-card forms can be punched.

### Summary Punch

*A summary punch can be cable-connected to an accounting machine for punching summary information.*

Accounting machines not only have the ability to accumulate numerical values in counters for detail printing and group printing, but they are also capable of preparing summary cards for use in carrying balances forward for the next processing run. These total cards are punched by connecting an automatic punch to the accounting machine via a cable (see Figure 3-17). As the accounting machine prints a total and its corresponding information, the same data can be transferred to the summary punch which simultaneously punches a summary card. Numerous applications have been found for this combination of accounting machine and summary punch. Several applications will be discussed at the end of this chapter.

### Card Processor

The UNIVAC 1004-II Card Processor (Figure 3-23) combines into one unit the functions of card reading, arithmetic processing, high-speed printing, and card punching (optional). It comes in an 80 and a 90 column version with the unique

Figure 3-23 UNIVAC 1004-II Card Processor with optional card punch. (Courtesy UNIVAC Division of the Sperry Rand Corporation.)

*The card processor, comparable to the accounting machine, has these features:*
- *core storage*
- *programming steps*
- *arithmetic operations*

ability of accepting interspersed 80 and 90 column cards. Data cards are read at a rate of 300–400 per minute, printing is performed at 600 lines per minute, and cards are punched at the rate of 200 per minute. A comparison of the effective speed of the 1004 as against the 407 goes beyond the stated speeds. At 300 cards per minute, the ratio would appear to be 2 to 1 in favor of the 1004. However, this ratio may well be larger if summary punching is involved since the 1004 normally does not take extra time for summary punching. Furthermore, it can print totals without involving extra time.

***Core Storage.*** The processing section of the 1004 Card Processor houses the magnetic core storage and control circuitry required to accomplish the various machine operations. Core storage, having the capacity of 961 individually addressable positions, is allocated as follows: 80 for read storage, 80 for punch storage, 132 for print storage, and 669 for working storage. The working storage area may be augmented by positions unused for read, print, or punch storage in certain situations. It should be noted that storage is used exclusively for data and not for program instructions.

***Programming Steps.*** The logical operation of the machine is under the control of a series of instructions wired on the control panel. The program for a given job consists of a series of steps directing the system to perform some arithmetic, transfer, or logical operations. For a standard 1004 Card Processor, there are 31 steps with provision for optional increase to 62 steps.

***Arithmetic Operations.*** Arithmetic operations are performed through a one-digit serial adder. Results are stored in memory as they are developed and accumulations of any size can be accommodated. Commands provided include add and subtract—both algebraic and absolute. Multiply and divide are accomplished by subroutines within a program.

***Card Processor Applications.*** The UNIVAC 1004-II Card Processor is generally used to support and supplement operations of various size computer systems. Billing, special reports, and balancing are common applications that can be adequately handled. For example, special reports are often dependent upon their timeliness. Information, available in cards, may lose its significance if it cannot be analyzed and reported today. By means of a report generator panel, a special report can be produced in a matter of hours. These requests may be "one time" information requests from management personnel in the accounting, marketing, and production areas.

## CONTROL PANEL WIRING

*Control panel wiring provides flexibility in terms of producing varied output.*

As can be seen from the foregoing material, varied forms of output can be obtained by the accounting machines and card processors. To a great degree, this is achieved by the flexibility in control panel wiring. Control panels can be easily removed from and inserted into the machine for the job to be processed. The panels range from a very simple one for an interpreter to complex ones for some applications of reporting.

*Electrical impulses are produced by reading brushes and are sent via internal and external wiring under program control to the typebar for producing printed information.*

***Overview—How Printing Is Controlled.*** An overview of how printing is controlled on an accounting machine is illustrated in Figure 3-24. The impulse is taken from the reading brush through internal wiring to the control panel's hubs. Hubs are the holes in the control panel into which external wires are inserted. The exit hubs are those from which impulses are emitted from reading cards while entry hubs are those into which impulses can be sent for printing data. (When connecting hubs, an exit and an entry hub must be connected to accomplish any function.) Once the external connecting wire has been joined with the proper exit and entry hub on the control panel, the impulse is channeled back through internal wires to the typebar which causes a selected typebar to print the desired character.

***Control Panel Diagrams.*** In order to wire a control panel correctly, control panel diagrams are used. They are paper representations of the actual control panels and

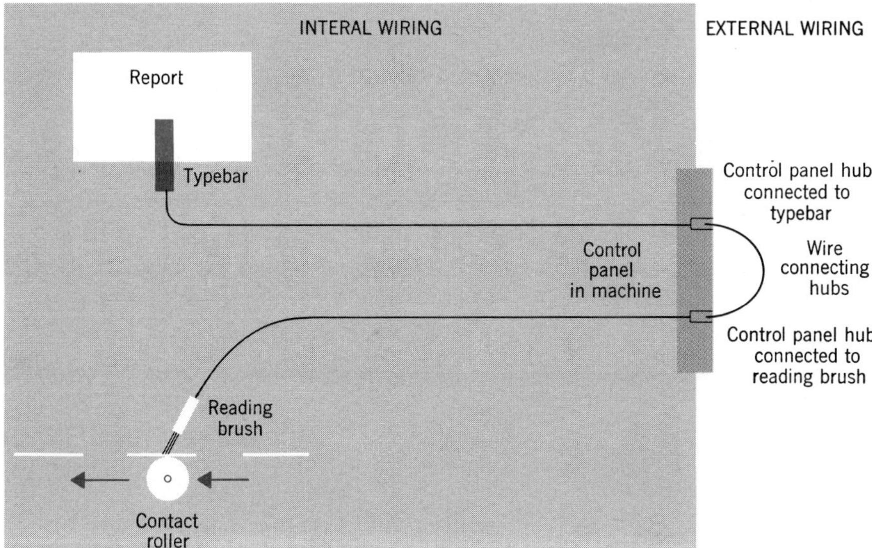


Figure 3-24 Internal and external wiring to cause printing on an accounting machine.

*Control panel diagrams are representations of the actual control panels and serve as work sheets for the job being planned.*

serve as work sheets for the job being planned. Not only can one work more quickly with a pencil than actual wires but also the completed diagram serves as documentation for future reference. Panels that are frequently used are kept permanently wired while infrequently used ones are disassembled and rewired as the need arises. Shown in Figure 3-25 is a sample control panel diagram for an IBM 407 Accounting Machine. Referring to Figure 3-19—the printing of the commission statements—only the wiring for control of the counters is illustrated.

The details of panel wiring go beyond the scope of this book. Several programmed learning and self-study guides are available for wiring punched card equipment. Likewise, the appropriate manufacturer should be consulted for scheduled classes on the specific piece of equipment.

## ADVANTAGES OF PUNCHED CARD EQUIPMENT OVER MANUAL AND MECHANICAL METHODS

*There are several important advantages of punched card equipment over manual and mechanical methods.*

The advantages of punched card machines over manual and mechanical methods, such as adding machines and calculators, are numerous. The most significant ones are listed below.

1. Improved control over operations.
2. Emphasizes standardization.
3. Accurate and uniform handling of data.
4. Cost can be lower.

***Improved Control Over Operations.*** Improved control over the firm's operations, resulting in better decisions, is a significant advantage of punched card equipment over prior methods. Since more timely reports can be generated with a punched card information system, management is better able to practice "management by exception." Exceptions can be detected by the programming ability of the machines, thereby minimizing the need for review of all information. With the ability to manipulate cards many different ways, reports are decidedly easier to produce. The flexi-

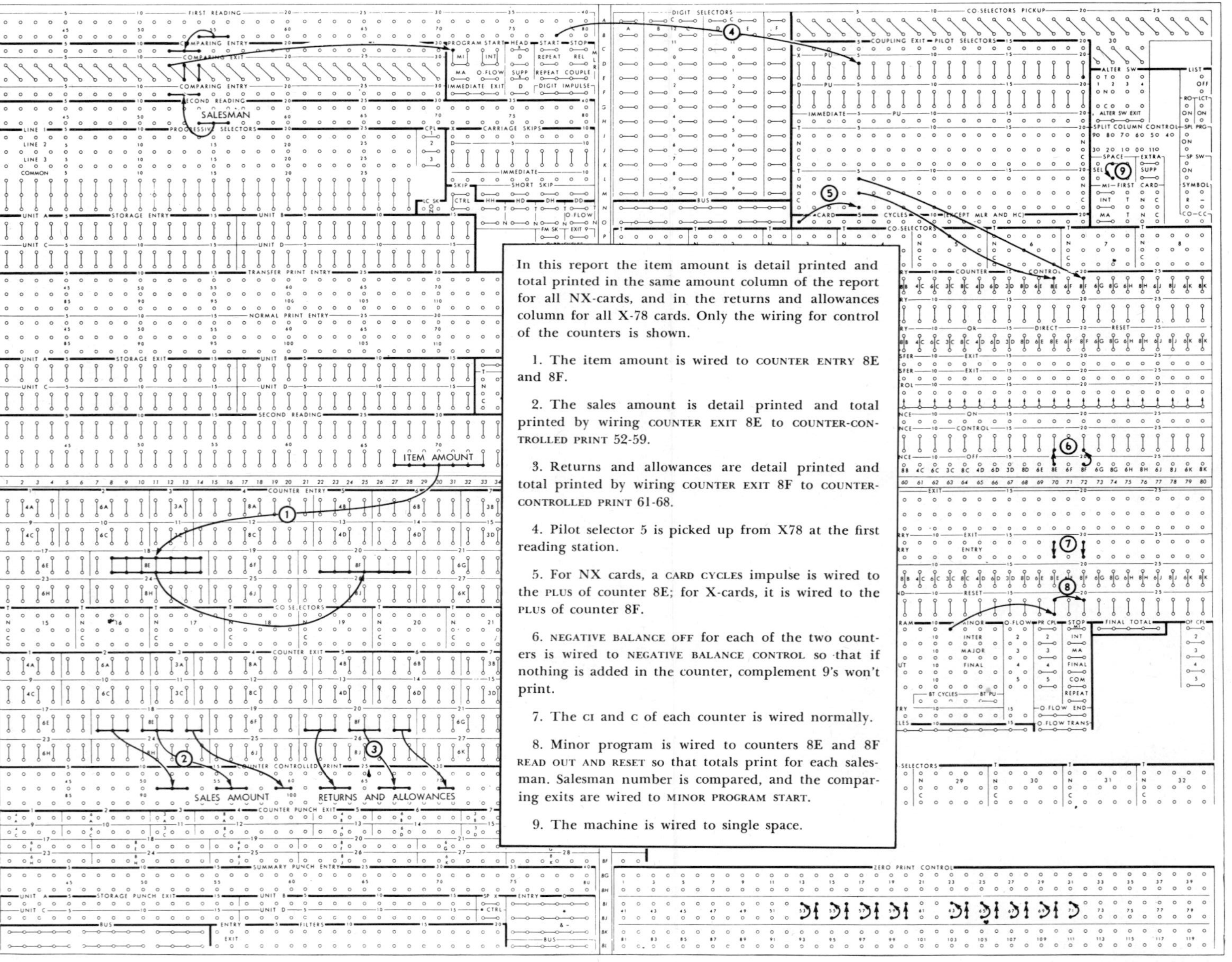

SALESMAN
ITEM AMOUNT
SALES AMOUNT
RETURNS AND ALLOWANCES
In this report the item amount is detail printed and total printed in the same amount column of the report for all NX-cards, and in the returns and allowances column for all X-78 cards. Only the wiring for control of the counters is shown.
1. The item amount is wired to COUNTER ENTRY 8E and 8F.
2. The sales amount is detail printed and total printed by wiring COUNTER EXIT 8E to COUNTER-CONTROLLED PRINT 52-59.
3. Returns and allowances are detail printed and total printed by wiring COUNTER EXIT 8F to COUNTER-CONTROLLED PRINT 61-68.
4. Pilot selector 5 is picked up from X78 at the first reading station.
5. For NX cards, a CARD CYCLES impulse is wired to the PLUS of counter 8E; for X-cards, it is wired to the PLUS of counter 8F.
6. NEGATIVE BALANCE OFF for each of the two counters is wired to NEGATIVE BALANCE CONTROL so that if nothing is added in the counter, complement 9's won't print.
7. The CI and C of each counter is wired normally.
8. Minor program is wired to counters 8E and 8F READ OUT AND RESET so that totals print for each salesman. Salesman number is compared, and the comparing exits are wired to MINOR PROGRAM START.
9. The machine is wired to single space.


Figure 3-25 Printing commission statements (Figure 3-19)—wiring for control of counters only on IBM 407 Accounting Machine. (Courtesy International Business Machines Corporation.)

bility of the control panels permits output to be produced that is physically not possible with clerks and mechanical machines. Thus the advantage of better control through feedback with more timely reports is reason alone for utilizing punched card equipment.

***Emphasizes Standardization.*** Punched card data processing requires standardization since the cards used in unit record processing are relatively small and hold a limited amount of information. This requirement of punched card equipment has forced personnel to be economical with the design and content of the cards as well as type of data. Standardization in terms of output for one functional area as input for another function has helped to break down empires within the firm and integrate the firm's operations. Data processing operations that cut across several departments require standardization for an efficient operation.

***Accurate and Uniform Handling of Data.*** Punched card systems are more accurate once the data have been captured on cards and checked for correctness. There is less chance of error as the same cards are moved from one machine to the next without repunching the data or having to refer back to the original source document. Since the data are not subject to the whims of employees, the output will be consistent at all times. The punched card equipment will process cards at the same rate while employees tend to work according to how they feel. In reality, machines are more reliable than people and handle data on a uniform basis.

***Costs Can Be Lower.*** Depending upon the punched card installation, costs can be measurably lower than with manual or mechanical methods. This is particularly true when producing meaningful reports. More sophisticated and timely reports can be produced at lower costs for better decisions that directly affect net profits. Even in those cases where data processing costs are higher with punched card equipment, many times the extra cost is more than offset by cost savings resulting from the improved feedback of critical operating information. Thus the cost of a punched card information system cannot be viewed by itself.

## LIMITATIONS OF PUNCHED CARD EQUIPMENT

*Limitations of punched card equipment has caused many firms to replace them with computers.*

Despite the foregoing advantages, punched card equipment has the following limitations when compared to other data processing methods.

1. Excessive card handling.
2. Undetected errors.
3. Difficulty in handling numerous exceptions.
4. Potential personnel problems.
5. Slow and inflexible.

***Excessive Card Handling.*** An excessive amount of card handling is experienced. Because each machine can perform only certain limited functions, the cards must be moved physically from one machine to another as the processing cycle continues. Often, the same card data are read over and over by different machines which slows the processing.

***Undetected Errors.*** The repeated handling of cards can lead to errors of omission or commission and the work must be rerun. The dropping of cards, mutilated cards, and the like can slow down the processing steps by requiring reruns. Errors can go undetected for some time before they are noticed. With manual and mechanical methods, a constant visual review and addition or deletion of data brings error conditions to light much faster.

***Difficulty in Handling Numerous Exceptions.*** A punched card system is limited in that it cannot handle too many exceptions. It is also much easier to make a correction with a pen or pencil versus punching a new card. Many times, one master card will do for a manual system while over 100 punched cards are needed to perform the same job.

***Potential Personnel Problems.*** The caliber of personnel required is much higher as are the training costs. A punched card system tends to be impersonal since numbers are used in place of names. Although the firm is subject to the whims of individuals, punched card equipment is subject to mechanical failures. Just as critical breakdowns can put the firm temporarily out of business, the same can be said for a disgruntled employee who throws away a master file or removes wires from a control panel.

***Slow and Inflexible.*** Many firms have outgrown punched card information systems. They have found that punched card equipment is slow and inflexible when compared to computer systems. For the reasons set forth above, punched card equipment has several inherent limitations, many of which have prompted firms to install electronic data processing systems.

## PUNCHED PAPER TAPE

*A punched paper tape is a continuous recording medium compared to the fixed length of punched cards.*

Just as punched cards are required for inputs to and are produced as outputs from many data processing systems, the same can be said for punched paper tape. The basic difference is that paper tape is a continuous recording medium as compared to punched cards which have a fixed length. Many mechanical devices have been adopted to produce *punched paper tape* as a by-product of recording transactions. This tape, in turn, is capable of being transmitted to another location, converted to another processing medium such as punched cards and magnetic tape, used as input to a computer processing system, and the like. As a machine-processable form of data processing, punched paper tape is an essential medium of communication from input to desired outputs for some firms.

### Codes

*Paper tape codes refer to the arrangement of punched holes in the tape.*

The arrangement of punch holes along the length of the paper tape is referred to as the "code." Paper tape codes come in 5-, 6-, 7-, and 8-channel codes. The term "channel" means that the impressions or holes representing data are made in imaginary channels which run the length of the tape. The number channel code is the number of channels used in recording the data, sometimes called channel width.

*The 5-channel tape is the oldest of the codes in use today.*

***5-Channel Tape.*** The 5-channel tape utilizes the telegraph code, developed by Jean Maurice Emile Baudot in 1870. Since this code has been used so extensively in teletype transmissions to this day, it is often referred to as the teletype code. Upon inspection of Figure 3-26, there appears to be no logical order to the code. However, the code was developed on the basis of using fewer holes for the letters and numbers most frequently used at the time. This coding scheme is based on the French language. It is easy to understand why the code has little apparent relationship to our English letters.

The number of code combinations in a 5-channel tape is 2 to the fifth power ($2^5$) or 32. By setting 6 combinations aside as signals for the equipment to execute basic machine functions, such as space and carriage return, 26 are left for basic code combinations.

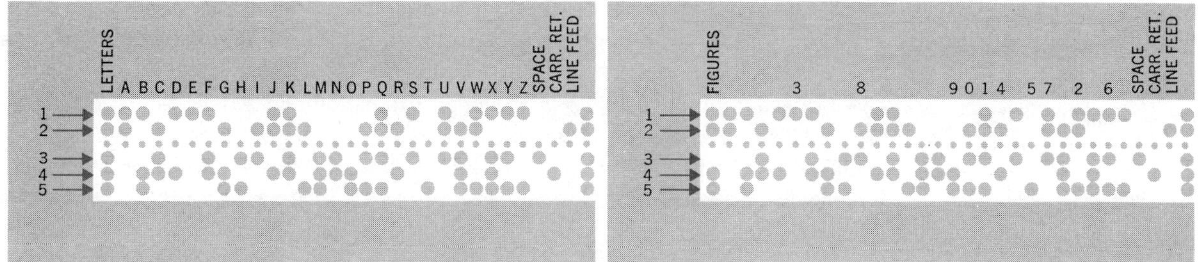


Figure 3-26 Baudot paper tape code—5-channel. (Courtesy International Business Machines Corporation.)

The teletype keyboard is similar to that of the typewriter, having the ability to "shift" to produce either of two type characters. With this shifting system, the number of available codes has doubled from 26 to 52 plus 6 for a total of 58 positions.

*The 8-channel tape uses the binary coded decimal (BCD) system.*

***8-Channel Tape.*** Of the three remaining codes (6, 7, and 8 channel), the 8 channel is most commonly used. Data for this code are punched in 8 parallel channels, as shown in Figure 3-27. Starting with the top channel and proceeding to the

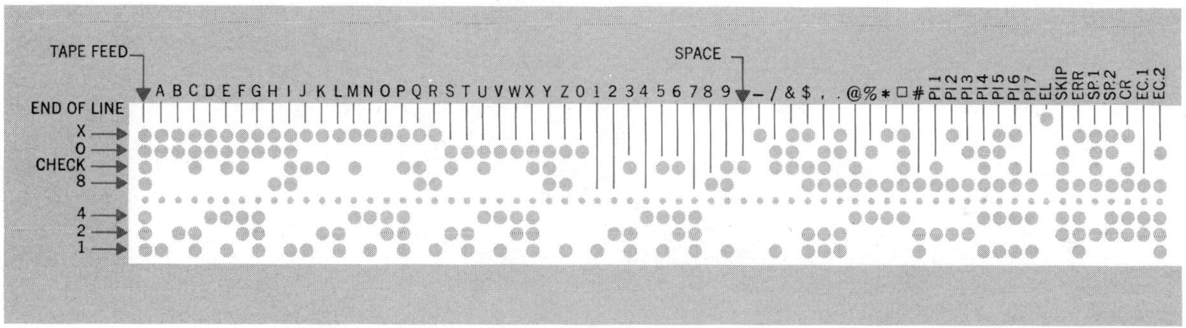


Figure 3-27 Punched paper tape code—8-channel. (Courtesy International Business Machines Corporation.)

bottom channel the codes are: end of line (carriage return); X and 0 (for alphabetic characters); check (for check bit); and 8, 4, 2, and 1 (numerical channels). The 8-channel code uses the binary coded decimal system, using the X and 0 for the zone punches in 80 column cards and the 8, 4, 2, and 1 for the digit punches. The "check" position is used to check on each character received in order to determine if the bit combinations represent valid data. The method for assuring accuracy in each column of the punched tape is to punch all columns with an odd number of holes. Since about half the number of characters are expressed in the BCD system by an even number of punches, it is necessary to add a check punch to produce an odd number of holes. When the data are transmitted, the columns that do not add up to an odd figure indicate that there is an error in transmission. For that reason, this type of checking is called "parity checking."

## Machines

*Machines capable of producing punched paper tape are:*

- *typewriters*
- *adding machines*
- *cash registers*
- *bookkeeping-accounting machines*

There are several mechanical devices capable of producing punched paper tape, the most important ones being *typewriters, adding machines, cash registers,* and *bookkeeping-accounting machines*. The automatic typewriter, such as the Friden Flexowriter with punched paper tape output, can produce an original document and punch the tape as a by-product. In the area of adding machines, the add punch machine (Figure 3-28) lists each item and, at the same time, automatically punches a tape (numeric amounts only) for processing at a later time. The cash register is comparable to the add punch machine in terms of output. Many bookkeeping-accounting machines are or have been wired for auxiliary punched paper tape and similar attachments. The EBS/1231 Accounting Machine in Figure 3-29 has a perforated paper tape reader and punch plus an edge-punched card reader. Output in terms of paper tape or other machine-processable media of the foregoing machines is available for subsequent data processing operations.

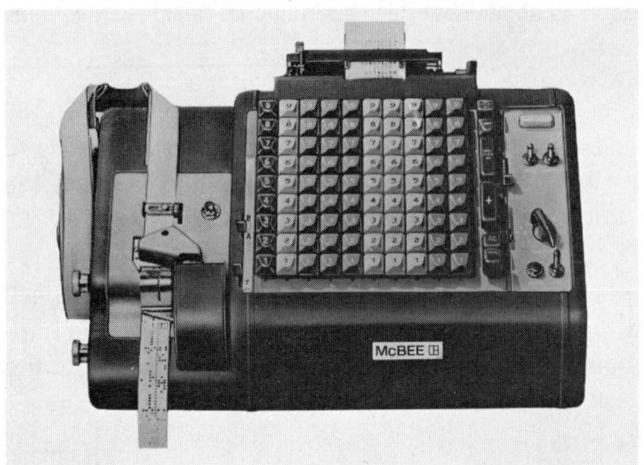


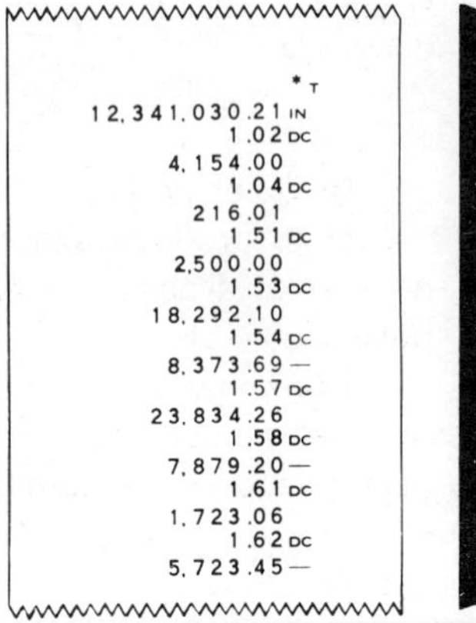


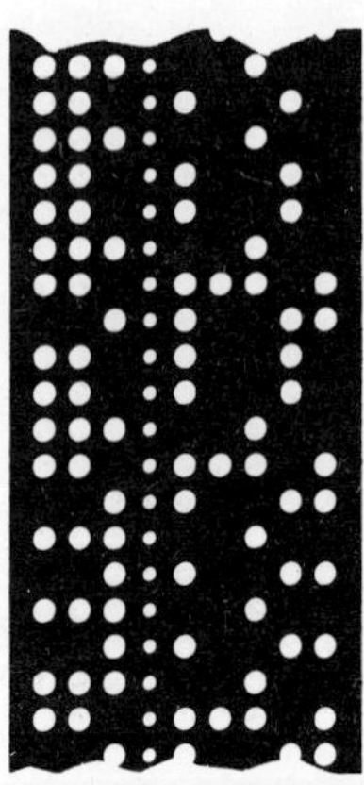

Figure 3-28 Punched paper tape adding machine. (Courtesy McBee Systems, Division of Litton Industries.)

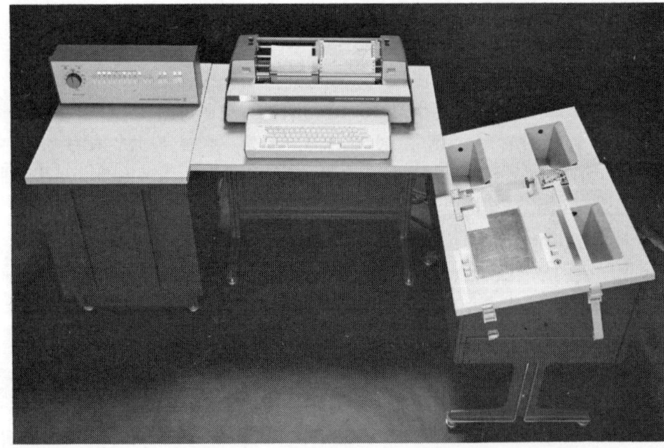

Figure 3-29 EBS/1231 Accounting Machine. (Courtesy Automated Business Systems, Division of Litton Industries.)

## SUMMARY OF OFF-LINE EQUIPMENT

The major pieces of off-line equipment set forth in this chapter and the preceding one are summarized in Figure 3-30. These are termed off-line because they operate independently of the computer. They are not connected in an on-line mode

Data recording:
- Information recorder
- Mark sensing (using reproducer)
- Flexowriter
- Card punch
- Data recorder
- Keyboard to magnetic tape
- Magnetic data inscriber
- Keyboard data entry system

Verifying:
- Key verifier
- Batching (using accounting machine)
- Self-checking digit attachment

Reproducer
Interpreter
Sorter
Collator
Calculator
Card proving machine
Card controller

Reporting:
- Accounting machine
- Summary punch
- Card processor

Punched paper tape:
- Typewriter
- Cash register
- Adding machine
- Bookkeeping—accounting machines

Figure 3-30 Summary of off-line equipment—data entry, punched card, and punched paper tape.

*Data entry and punched card equipment are defined as off-line since they can operate independently of the computer.*

with the computer system. In some cases, they provide the necessary data for direct entry into the EDP system. In other cases, the data are processed completely on punched card equipment without the need for computer processing. Depending upon the data processing environment, off-line equipment may or may not be an important part of the firm's methods and procedures in producing the required output.

## PUNCHED CARD APPLICATIONS

*Common punched card applications center around:*
- *payroll*
- *accounts receivable*
- *inventory*
- *other accounting areas*

Over the years, many business applications have been found for punched card equipment. Initially, the government made great use of punched card machines in tabulating census data. As these benefits became known to business and industry, there was a rush on the part of many firms to replace manual systems with punched card systems.

### Payroll

Payroll was one of the first applications for punched card equipment. It was common to see a large installation concentrating on this selected accounting function.

### Accounts Receivable

As time passed, firms added more punched card equipment to integrate several phases of the accounting function. For example, the billing of customers (printed invoice based upon input of name and address cards, terms card, detail item cards, ship-to cards, and the like) resulted in an accounts receivable card being punched on a summary punch connected to an accounting machine. This accounts receivable card or total charges for items billed formed the basis for a current accounts recievable file. At any time, all accounts receivable cards represent the amount of receivables outstanding. Periodically (say once a week), these unpaid cards are processed for an aged accounts receivable listing.

### Inventory

The above detail item cards used in customer billing provide the means for determining the new ending inventory balances. The beginning inventory plus receipts of merchandise into finished goods inventory less item cards of shipped finished goods give a new inventory balance. This balance is not only listed on the inventory printout but also is punched into a card by connecting the accounting machine to a summary punch. The new updated card balances become the input for the next period's processing run.

### Other Applications

Punched cards are widely used for accounts payable, vouchers payable, cash disbursements, fixed assets, securities, and preparation of financial statements. Although many punched card installations are accounting-oriented, others are directed toward the marketing, manufacturing, and/or personnel functions. Punched card machines have been applied to various types of sales analysis. Most firms have been able to produce new sales analysis reports that were not economically feasible under manual operations. The detail cards that have been used in billing have become an integral part of production control for many firms. In a similar manner, master payroll cards have been utilized by personnel to classify the skills possessed by the firm's employees; this has served as a basis for recruiting new personnel that have skills needed by the firm. It is rather difficult to conceive any major area in a firm that has not felt the impact of punched card machines.

### Feasibility of Punched Card Applications

*Feasibility of punched card equipment is based upon the repeated use of cards created in the system.*

Whether it is in the area of accounting, marketing, manufacturing, or personnel, the feasibility of punched card machines lies in their ability to reuse the cards created somewhere in the data processing chain of events. To create a card and use it once violates a fundamental principle of effective punched card data processing. Since it costs more to create a punched card than to prepare the comparable data manually, the punched card must have several uses before it is economically sound. Thus, a basic premise for using punched card equipment is one that relies heavily upon the repeated use of most cards created in the system. Otherwise, the use of punched cards only once or twice, for the most part, will not reap the benefits of punched card equipment since additional managerial reports are not being produced for more effective planning and control of operations. A firm would be better off retaining its manual system.

## SUMMARY

The operations of data recording, verifying, reproducing, and interpreting in the prior chapter plus those of sorting, collating, calculating, proving, and reporting in this chapter are the basic ones to be found in any punched card information system. Even though punched card equipment is being replaced by other equipment, an understanding of unit record or punched card data processing and data entry systems is extremely helpful for the study of computer data processing systems. In addition, this concentrated punched card study will be beneficial when this area is compared to computers. The advantages of computer batch processing and on-line processing will be more apparent after having reviewed the fundamentals of punched cards than if the subject matter had not been covered.

A typical punched card case study is presented in the appendix to this chapter. The purpose of the example is twofold. First, the capability of punched card equipment is demonstrated. Second, the major functional steps of any punched card information system are illustrated, that is, input, storage, processing, control, and output (ISPCO cycle).

## *QUESTIONS*

1. (a) Describe the basic rule to follow in regular sorting.
   (b) What are the basic types of sorting?
2. (a) A field of information, containing 8 digits of numeric data in an 80 column card, must be sorted. If there are 20,000 cards and the sorter operates at a speed of 1000 cards per minute, what will be the time required to complete the sort? Add card handling time as 20 percent of machine time.
   (b) How would your answer to (a) differ if the field contained alphabetic information?
   (c) Answer (a) and (b) for a 96 column card whose sorting speed is also 1000 cards per minute.
3. List and explain the basic functions of a collator.
4. Why must two feed hoppers be used for merging on the collator whereas only one is needed for sequence checking?
5. Explain why the collator does not eliminate the need for a sorter.
6. What functions are performed by a card calculating punch?
7. How does a card proving machine differ from a sorter and a collator?
8. How many program steps are available for the IBM 407 Accounting Machine? What is their function?
9. (a) What is the basic function of an accounting machine?
   (b) What is the basic function of a counter on an accounting machine?
10. How can a 12-digit total be accommodated on an accounting machine if the largest counter has only 8 positions?
11. How does the UNIVAC 1004-II Card Processor differ from the IBM 407 Accounting Machine?
12. How important is the summary punch in a punched card installation?
13. How is programming effected on most punched card equipment? Explain.
14. Of the many advantages attributed to punched card equipment, select the most important ones from a manager's point of view.
15. What is the relationship of "management by exception" to punched card accounting? Explain.
16. List several machines that are capable of producing punched paper tape as a by-product of another operation.
17. What are the most suitable areas for punched card equipment? Enumerate.

## *APPENDIX TO CHAPTER THREE*

### PUNCHED CARD CASE STUDY

The Midwestern Publishing Company is a young, aggressive enterprise that publishes and distributes a monthly magazine entitled *Small Business News*. This magazine presents current financial, regulatory, and economic trends to owners and managers of small businesses. The company and its publication have grown rapidly since its inception at the end of World War II. Growth projections for the near future are considered to be very promising.

Presently, Midwestern supplies 86,000 subscribers with timely issues of *Small*

*Business News*. Circulation has been growing at the net rate of 600 subscriptions per month for the past year. The increase in circulation prompted Midwestern's management to examine closely its procedures and methods for maintaining timely and up-to-date subscriber information. As a result of this review, Midwestern acquired (on a lease basis) an IBM punched card installation. The equipment complex consists of the following machines.

| *Equipment* | *Number* |
|---|---|
| IBM 029 Card Punch | 4 |
| IBM 059 Card Verifier | 2 |
| IBM 557 Interpreter | 1 |
| IBM 084 Sorter | 1 |
| IBM 088 Collator | 1 |
| IBM 519 Reproducer | 1 |
| IBM 609 Calculating Punch | 1 |
| IBM 402 Accounting Machine | 1 |

The principal application that has been designed for the punched card installation is the Subscriber Records System. The primary goal of the Subscriber Records System is to maintain data records on each subscriber for the purposes of prompt circulation of the publication, immediate response to changes of address, customer inquiries, and prompt financial processing—sales invoicing and accounts receivable. The main part of the Subscriber Records System is a set of interrelated master files on 80 column punched cards. The following describes briefly each of the files: its organization, its primary function, and its present size.

**Subscriber Master Name and Address File**

The master name and address file contains one 3-card entry for each subscriber. A set of cards contains the subscriber's name and mailing address. The first card of the set contains the name of the subscriber; the second card contains the first address line; and the third card contains the last address line or the city (town), state, and zip code. An entry always consists of three cards. This file is in sequence, major to minor, on subscriber number and card code. The master name and address file contains 86,000 entries or 258,000 cards. The primary function of this file is to produce the labels that are affixed to the publication at the time of mailing. Also, the name and address data serve to identify subscribers for other meaningful reports to management.

**Subscriber Profile File**

The master subscriber profile file contains one card for each subscriber. Each entry consists of certain data elements that, taken together, establishes a "profile" of the subscriber. The file is in sequence on subscriber number, the key data element. The primary reason for the profile file is to have a card file that is small enough to handle effectively with punched card equipment. The profile file consists of 86,000 cards (as opposed to 258,000 cards in the master name and address file). This file is used, to a large extent, in many of the processing procedures in this punched card study.

**Subscriber Address Change**

Whenever a subscriber changes his address, he is assigned a new subscriber number and his old number is removed from active use. In order to relate the new and old subscriber numbers, a cross-reference subscriber file (in alphabetical order) has been established. Each entry (one card per subscriber address change) consists of these data elements: new subscriber number, old subscriber number, date of change. When an address change is processed, the old subscriber number is also preserved in a special field in the profile entry.

## SUBSCRIBER RECORDS SYSTEM

The Subscriber Records System is comprised of several applications. These procedural areas are: new subscribers, change of addresses, renewals, and cancellations. The procedures and systems flowcharts for the handling of new subscribers will be covered. The numbered items in the narrative corresponds to the procedural steps found in Figures 3A-1 and 3A-2.

### New Subscribers Procedure

The initial step in the new subscribers procedure is checking the cross-reference subscribers file in order to determine that the subscriber is new. Also, a subscriber number is assigned to the new subscription and a count of source documents is determined (1). After this screening process, the subscription source document is forwarded to the keypunch section. The master name and address cards plus the master subscriber profile card are keypunched and key verified (2). Source document batches are held in a temporary storage file, available for ready reference if needed. Daily, the keypunched cards are sorted on subscriber number (3) and are run on the accounting machine for a listing of new subscribers (profile and name and address) received during the prior day (4). Before sending the list of new subscribers to the accounts receivable department, a manual comparison is made between the count of new customers in steps (1) and (4). Any discrepancies are investigated immediately (5).

Since each card contains a card code, the master subscriber profile cards are extracted from the master name and address cards on a sorter. The profile cards (code 4) are selected into the number 4 pocket while the name and address cards (codes 1, 2, and 3) fall into the reject pocket, still in subscriber number sequence (6). The name and address cards are used for preparing an address label (utilizes an accounting machine) so that an invoice can be mailed to the subscriber (7). Before sending the labels to the accounts receivable department, a count of new subscribers name and address labels is compared manually with the count established in step (5) to check further on the accuracy of new subscriber processing. New name and address cards are merged with the present master name and address file on subscriber number (8). At this step, the control log for the master name and address file is updated to reflect the number of cards for subscriber entries added to the file. The updated master name and address file is the basis for preparing monthly labels in mailing the monthly magazine.

After extracting the subscriber profile cards per step (6) above, they are reproduced (9), interpreted (10), and filed manually in the cross-reference subscriber (alphabetic) file (11). The original cards are sorted on subscription type code—standard, special, promotional, student, and complementary (12). A total count is again performed to insure accuracy of data handling and is compared to the totals established in step (5). The master subscription rate file is merged with the original subscriber profile cards (13) for gangpunching the appropriate rate into the new profile cards. After punching the rate into the new profile cards (14), the master

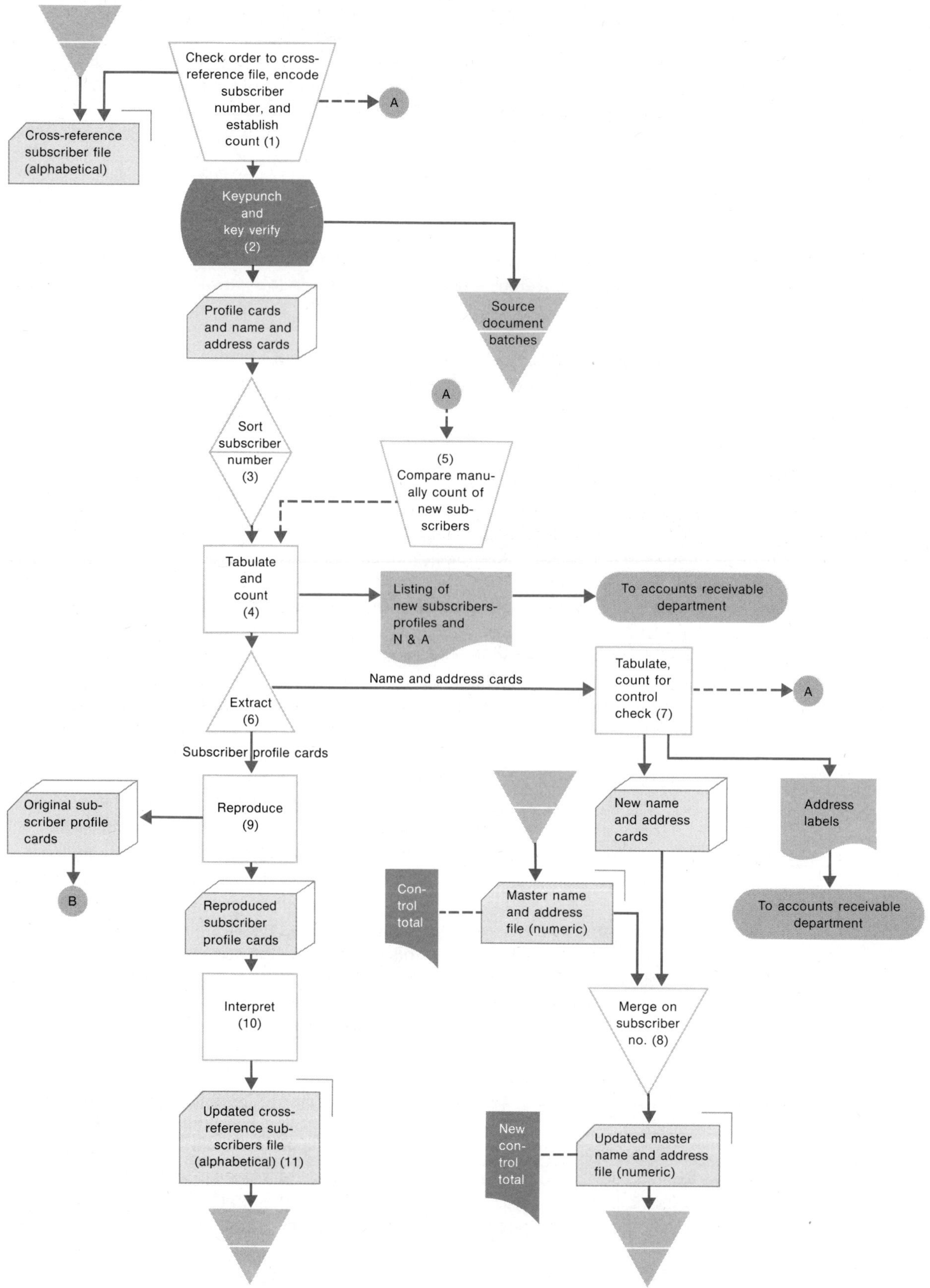


Figure 3A-1 New Subscribers System flowchart (continued per Figure 3A-2).

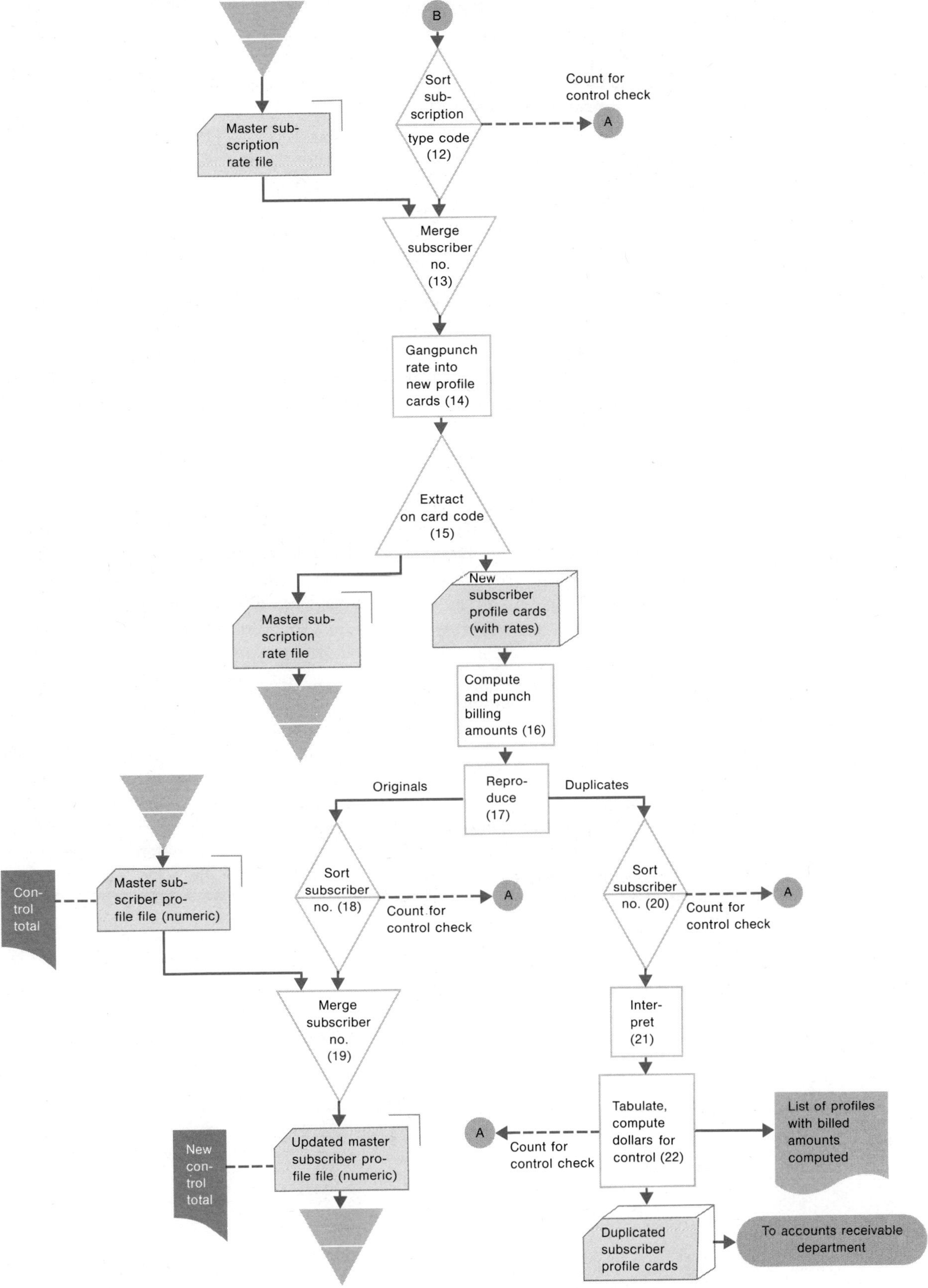


Figure 3A-2 New Subscribers System flowchart (continued from Figure 3A-1).

rate file is separated on card code from the subscribers profile cards (15). While the master subscription rate cards are returned to file, the subscribers profile cards (with the appropriate rates) are processed on the calculating punch. The number of months times the monthly rate which equals the amount to be billed is punched into the subscriber profile card (16).

Before further processing of the new subscriber profile cards occurs, it is necessary to reproduce this deck of cards (17). The original deck is sorted into sequence by subscriber number (18) and a manual comparison is again performed to check the card count per step (5). The master subscriber profile file is merged with the new subscriber profile cards for an updated file (19). All duplicate numbers are selected and corrective action taken to resolve the error. The updated file is returned to a storage cabinet and addition to the control logs is completed. The duplicate profile card from step (17) above is sorted by subscriber number (20) and compared to the control total established in step (5) previously. After the duplicate set of profile cards are interpreted (21), a listing of new subscriber profiles is run on the accounting machine (22). This printout includes the subscriber number, the number of months subscribed, the monthly rate, and the total billing amount as well as count control totals (compare with totals determined previously) and grand total billing amount. It is forwarded to the accounts receivable department along with the duplicated subscriber profile cards.

The new subscriber procedure has resulted in the updating of the master subscriber profile card file, the master name and address card file, and the cross-reference subscriber file. Likewise, it has provided name and address labels for billing purposes, a report of the billing amounts per subscriber, and cards to be used in the billing procedure of the accounts receivable section. Although the above procedure is complete for new subscribers, many other areas could have been selected for implementation. Typical punched card procedures for this case study could have been applied to the areas of accounts receivable, address changes, renewals, and cancellations.

It should be noted that throughout the case study, there were numerous processing points where errors can occur and corrective action could be initiated. The operations manager is responsible for establishing policies, practices, and procedures regarding error detection and correction. The quality of the outputs—the reports, the punched card data, the labels, the analyses, the working lists, and so forth—is only as good as the quality and accuracy of the input data. Thus, controls are essential to assure that all data in the files are accounted for continually. As data are added to, removed from, and changed in the files, it is vital that quantitative file changes are controlled.

## *QUESTION*

Suggest areas for improvement in the processing of new subscribers, as set forth in the punched card case study.

# III

# ELECTRONIC DATA PROCESSING

## CHAPTER FOUR

# Flowcharts and Decision Tables

*Flowcharts and decisions tables both have their place in systems analysis and design work. The illustrated flowchart was computer prepared. (Courtesy International Business Machines Corporation.)*

In this chapter, flowcharts and decision tables are discussed since they are the tools of the systems analyst and programmer. These charts and tables are applicable to punched card equipment as well as to computers. They provide the basis for setting forth on paper the logical thinking of systems personnel and the structure of the system to be installed. Likewise, charts and tables provide the basis for reviewing a system.

## FLOWCHARTS

Flowcharting is a technique used widely for a better understanding of existing or proposed methods, procedures, and systems. Basically, it is a diagramatic representation of a series of events.

### Characteristics of Flowcharts

*A flowchart is a visual representation of end-to-end activities.*

A *flowchart* is a symbolic or pictorial representation of data flow within the firm. It is extremely useful when working with punched card equipment since data must be processed through several machines before desirable output is produced. The need for a visual display of end-to-end activities becomes more acute when accurate and detailed directions are necessary for a computer system. To provide this direction, the flow of data and paper work from the input stages through the many intermediate stages, including involved computer programs, to the final outputs must be explicitly detailed for effective implementation.

### Values of Flowcharts

*The important values of a flowchart are:*
- *aids understanding*
- *effective communicator*
- *permanent record*

It has been said that "a picture is worth a thousand words." The same can be said for a flowchart since it is a picture of some part of a data processing system.

***Aids Understanding.*** A flowchart shows explicitly what is happening, in what order, and has the ability to detect gaps in procedures or overlaps in system activities. It is much easier to comprehend what is occurring with diagrams than with a written description. When one is forced to diagram on paper the steps involved in a data processing procedure, errors or omissions stand out.

***Effective Communicator.*** Another value of the flowchart is that it is an effective communicator to other personnel. The interworkings of a new method, procedure, or system can be communicated to other interested parties. Likewise, a chart is a succinct presentation of data flow to management and operating personnel for controlling the varied activities of the firm. Thus, a second value of the flowchart is its use to communicate to personnel other than the originator.

***Permanent Record.*** A third value of flowcharting is that it is a permanent record which does not depend on oral communication. Since the chart is written, it is available for review purposes in terms of accuracy and completeness. It also provides a basis for analyzing and comparing present and proposed systems so that efficiency, cost, timeliness, or other relevant factors may be improved. Regardless of the purpose in developing a flowchart, it serves as a basis for system documentation, now and in the future.

### Flowchart Symbols

Over the years, there has been a concerted attempt to standardize flowcharting symbols. The rationale for standardization is that it allows anyone to accurately interpret the work of another. This is particularly important today because of the

*Standard flowchart symbols lessen confusion as to the exact meaning intended.*

high job mobility of systems personnel. It may well be that the person preparing the flowchart today may not be the one interpreting it tomorrow. If standard flowcharting symbols are used, the amount of confusion as to the exact meaning intended is kept to a minimum. To alleviate the problem of nonstandardization in the past, the United States of America Standards Institute (USASI), formerly the American Standards Association (ASA), has developed a standard set of flowcharting symbols. Although the flowchart standards were approved in 1965, they were not published at that time because of conflicts with a proposed international standard. The flowchart symbols, set forth in this chapter, are the revised set of symbols approved and published in June 1966.

*USASI flowchart symbols include:*
- *basic (4)*
- *specialized—I/O, file and processing (13)*
- *additional (2)*

***Types of Symbols.*** The flowchart symbols developed by the United States of America Standards Institute are shown in Figure 4-1 while Figure 4-2 gives payroll examples of each flowchart symbol. In both illustrations, there are four basic symbols (input/output, process, flowline, and annotation), thirteen specialized symbols (punched card, punched tape, document, magnetic tape, manual input, display, communication link, on-line storage, off-line storage, decision, predefined process, auxiliary operation, and manual operation), and two additional symbols (connector and terminal). These last two symbols are optional since other symbols can be used in their place.

In addition to the USASI flowchart symbols, the International Standards Organization (international counterpart of the USASI) and IBM have developed other

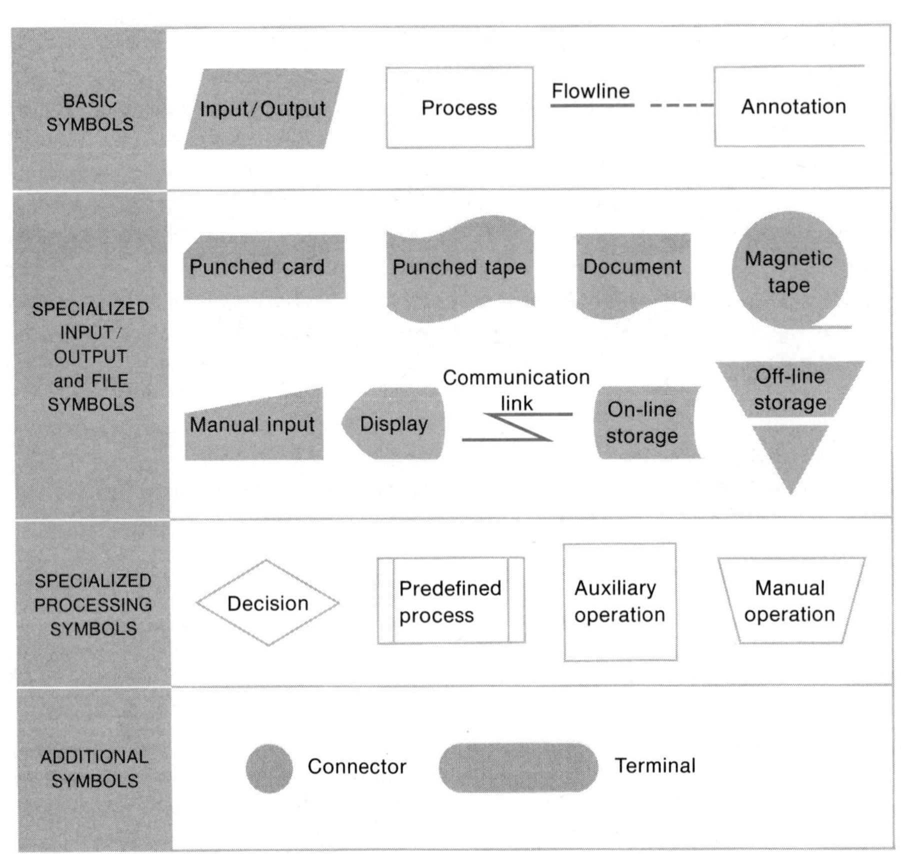


Figure 4-1 USASI flowchart symbols.

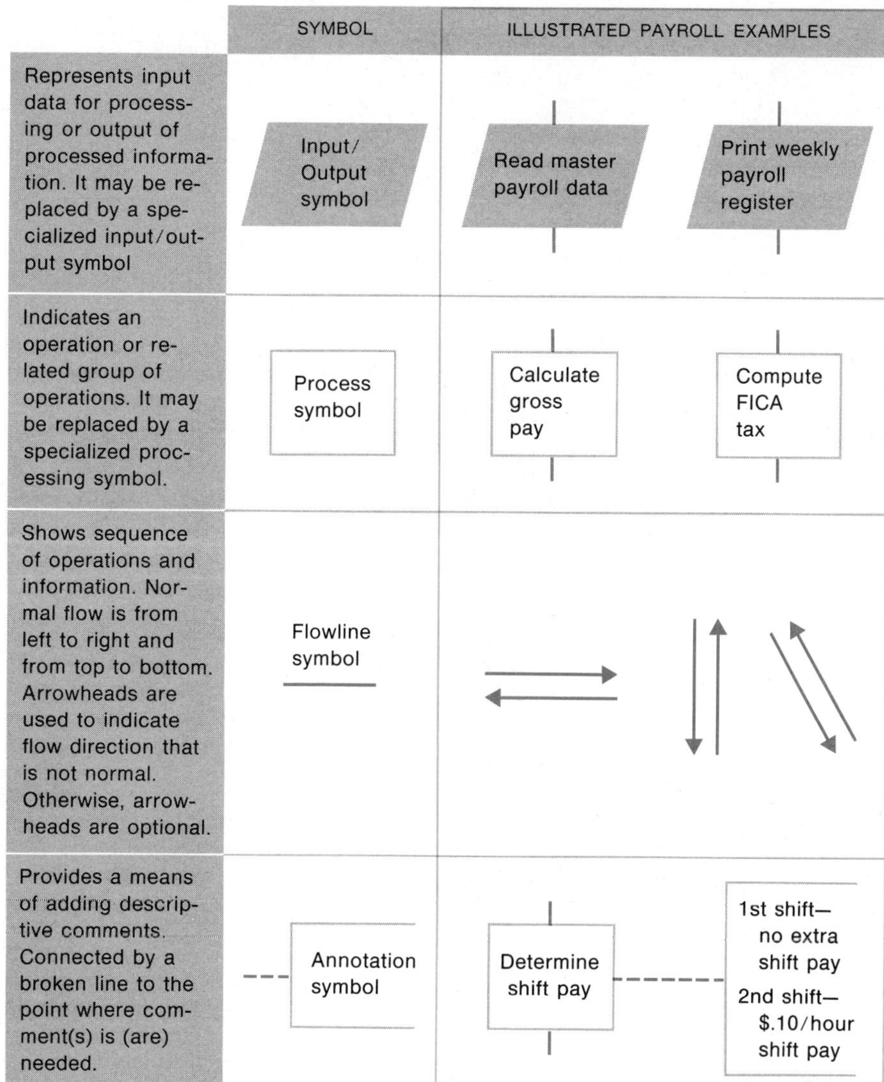

SYMBOL
ILLUSTRATED PAYROLL EXAMPLES
Represents input data for processing or output of processed information. It may be replaced by a specialized input/output symbol
Input/ Output symbol
Read master payroll data
Print weekly payroll register
Indicates an operation or related group of operations. It may be replaced by a specialized processing symbol.
Process symbol
Calculate gross pay
Compute FICA tax
Shows sequence of operations and information. Normal flow is from left to right and from top to bottom. Arrowheads are used to indicate flow direction that is not normal. Otherwise, arrowheads are optional.
Flowline symbol
Provides a means of adding descriptive comments. Connected by a broken line to the point where comment(s) is (are) needed.
Annotation symbol
Determine shift pay
1st shift— no extra shift pay
2nd shift— $.10/hour shift pay


Figure 4-2 USASI flowchart symbols and illustrated payroll examples.

*International flowchart symbols include:*
- *input/output and file (5)*
- *processing (5)*
- *additional (3)*

*Flowcharts normally flow from left to right and from top to bottom.*

symbols. These complement the USASI standard symbols and are shown in Figure 4-3. It should be noted that several of the flowchart symbols are primarily for punched card equipment. These include the processing symbols of keying, sorting, merging, collating, and extracting.

***Flow of Symbols.*** No matter what combination of above flowchart symbols are used, flowcharts are constructed to follow our natural tendency to read from left to right and from top to bottom. At times, it is desirable to deviate from this pattern in order to achieve symmetry and to emphasize important points. Solid flowlines are drawn to indicate the direction of the flow while dotted flowlines depict a transfer of information as well as annotated information. In either case, flowlines can be drawn horizontally, vertically, or diagonally, as needed, for a meaningful flowchart.

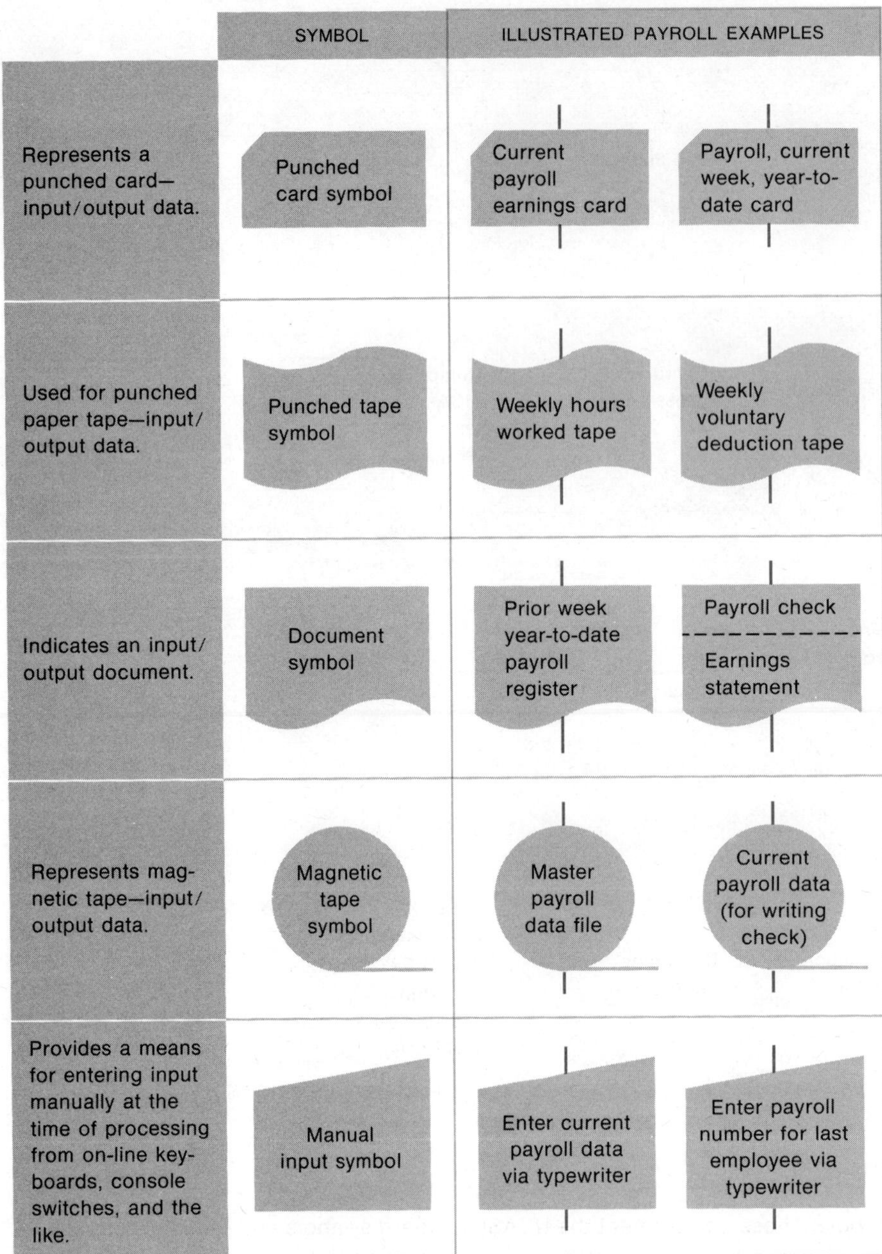

SYMBOL
ILLUSTRATED PAYROLL EXAMPLES
Represents a punched card—input/output data.
Punched card symbol
Current payroll earnings card
Payroll, current week, year-to-date card
Used for punched paper tape—input/output data.
Punched tape symbol
Weekly hours worked tape
Weekly voluntary deduction tape
Indicates an input/output document.
Document symbol
Prior week year-to-date payroll register
Payroll check
Earnings statement
Represents magnetic tape—input/output data.
Magnetic tape symbol
Master payroll data file
Current payroll data (for writing check)
Provides a means for entering input manually at the time of processing from on-line keyboards, console switches, and the like.
Manual input symbol
Enter current payroll data via typewriter
Enter payroll number for last employee via typewriter


Figure 4-2 (continued) USASI flowchart symbols and illustrated payroll examples.

## TYPES OF FLOWCHARTS

*Data processing needs dictate which type of flowchart(s)* is (*are*) *to be used.*

There are several types of flowcharts found in a data processing installation. Among the most used are:

1. system flowchart
2. program flowchart
3. modular program flowchart
4. document flowchart

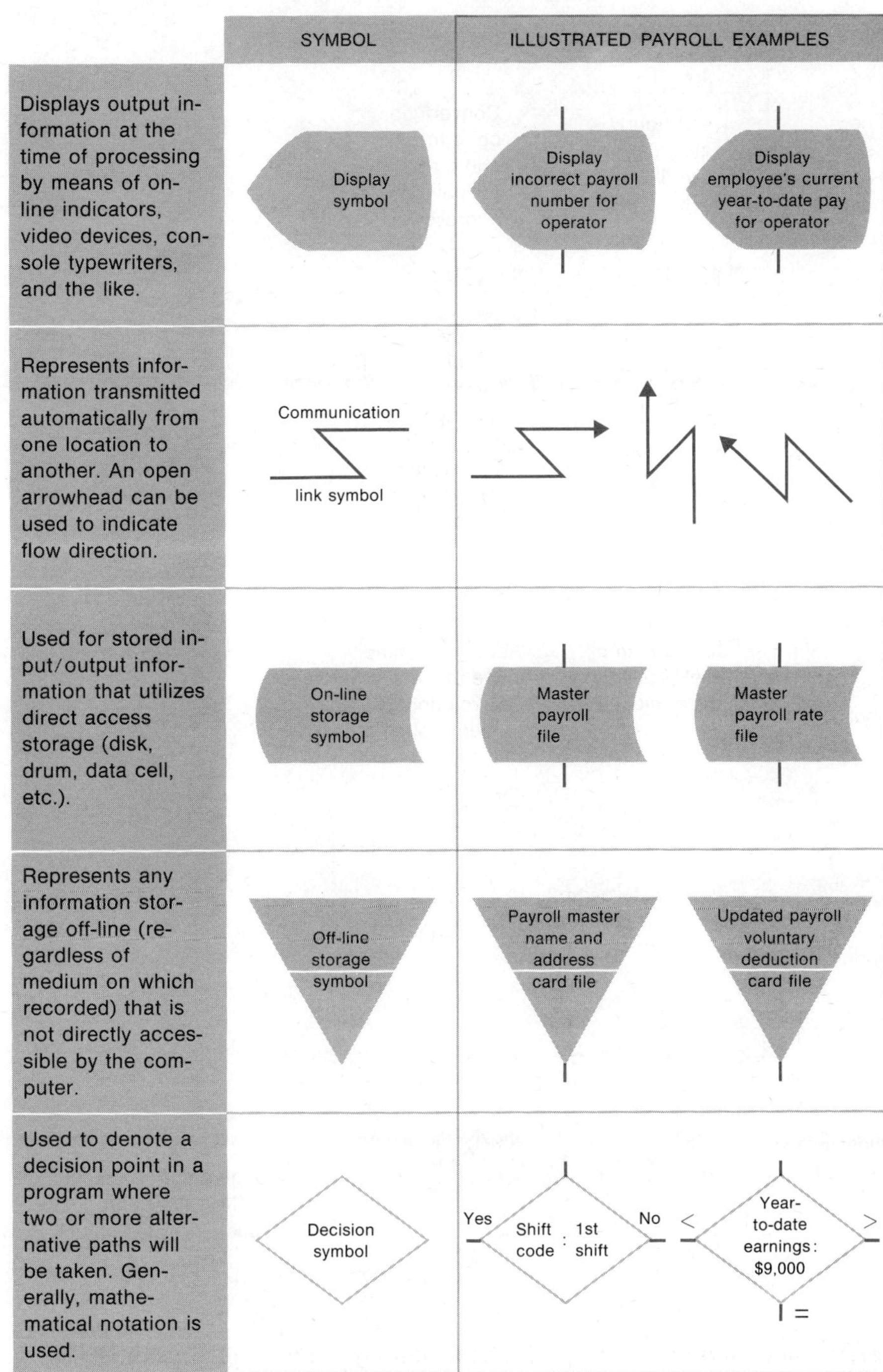

SYMBOL
ILLUSTRATED PAYROLL EXAMPLES
Displays output information at the time of processing by means of on-line indicators, video devices, console typewriters, and the like.
Display symbol
Display incorrect payroll number for operator
Display employee's current year-to-date pay for operator
Represents information transmitted automatically from one location to another. An open arrowhead can be used to indicate flow direction.
Communication link symbol
Used for stored input/output information that utilizes direct access storage (disk, drum, data cell, etc.).
On-line storage symbol
Master payroll file
Master payroll rate file
Represents any information storage off-line (regardless of medium on which recorded) that is not directly accessible by the computer.
Off-line storage symbol
Payroll master name and address card file
Updated payroll voluntary deduction card file
Used to denote a decision point in a program where two or more alternative paths will be taken. Generally, mathematical notation is used.
Decision symbol
Yes
Shift code : 1st shift
No
<
Year-to-date earnings : $9,000
>
=


Figure 4-2 (continued) USASI flowchart symbols and illustrated payroll examples.

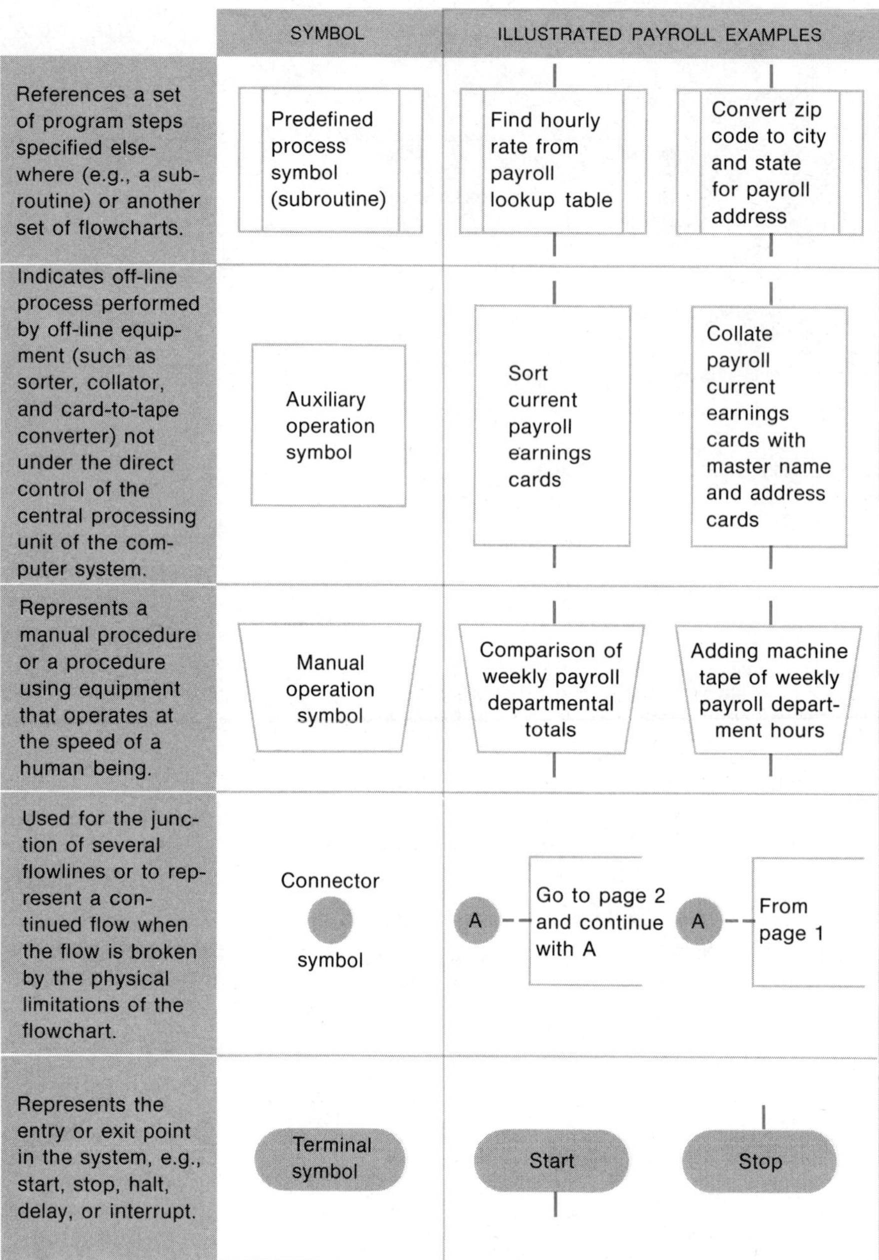

| | SYMBOL | ILLUSTRATED PAYROLL EXAMPLES | |
|---|---|---|---|
| References a set of program steps specified elsewhere (e.g., a subroutine) or another set of flowcharts. | Predefined process symbol (subroutine) | Find hourly rate from payroll lookup table | Convert zip code to city and state for payroll address |
| Indicates off-line process performed by off-line equipment (such as sorter, collator, and card-to-tape converter) not under the direct control of the central processing unit of the computer system. | Auxiliary operation symbol | Sort current payroll earnings cards | Collate payroll current earnings cards with master name and address cards |
| Represents a manual procedure or a procedure using equipment that operates at the speed of a human being. | Manual operation symbol | Comparison of weekly payroll departmental totals | Adding machine tape of weekly payroll department hours |
| Used for the junction of several flowlines or to represent a continued flow when the flow is broken by the physical limitations of the flowchart. | Connector symbol | A — Go to page 2 and continue with A | A — From page 1 |
| Represents the entry or exit point in the system, e.g., start, stop, halt, delay, or interrupt. | Terminal symbol | Start | Stop |

Figure 4-2 (continued) USASI flowchart symbols and illustrated payroll examples.

A system flowchart depicts the flow of data through all parts of a data processing system with a minimum of detail. Generally, it shows where input enters the system, how it is processed and controlled, and how it leaves the systems in terms of storage and output. On the other hand, a program flowchart or modular program flowchart is more detailed and is needed to supplement a system flowchart for a computer-oriented system. Since a computer must be directed according to a detailed set of instructions called a program (stored internally in the computer), these flowcharts are a necessity for programming computer applications. The document flowchart

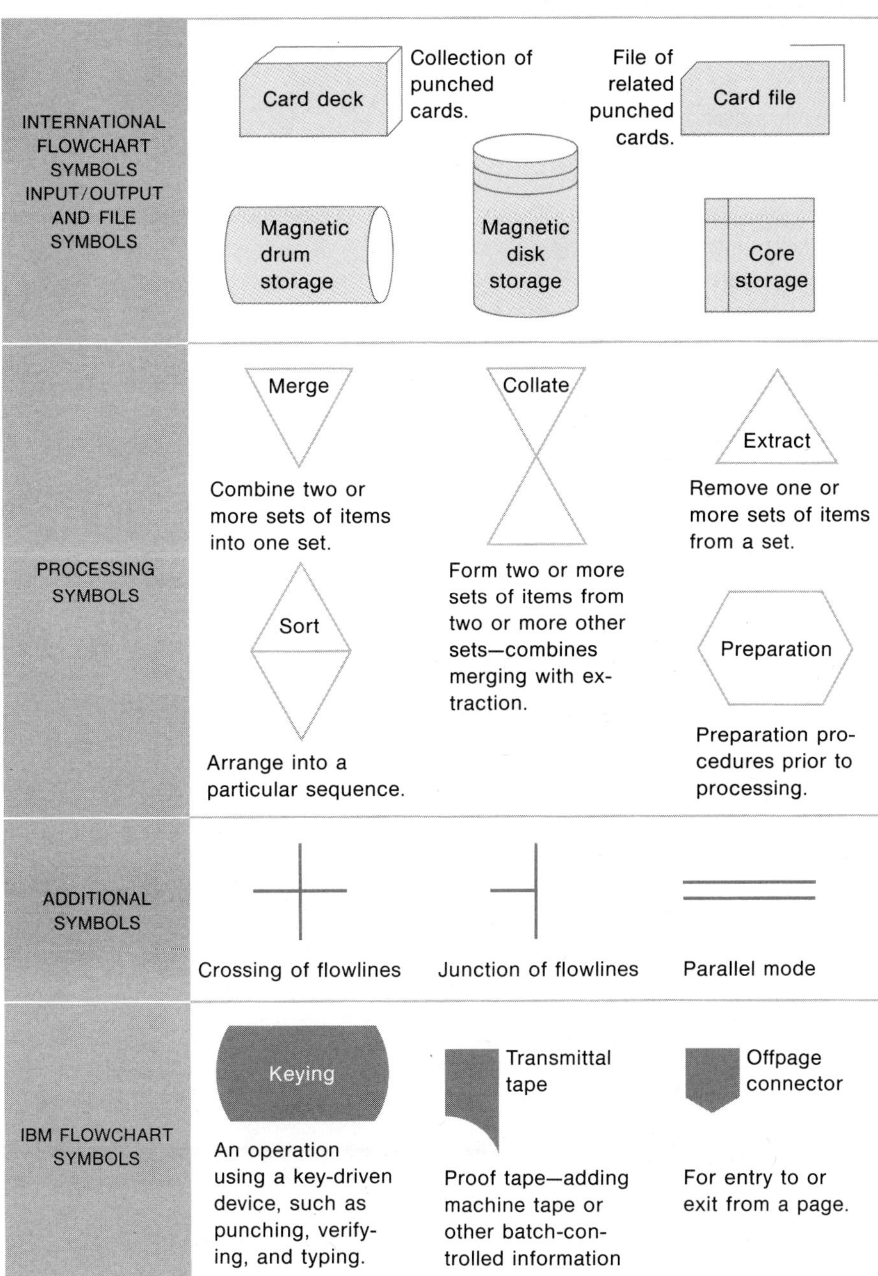
INTERNATIONAL FLOWCHART SYMBOLS INPUT/OUTPUT AND FILE SYMBOLS
Card deck
Collection of punched cards.
File of related punched cards.
Card file
Magnetic drum storage
Magnetic disk storage
Core storage
PROCESSING SYMBOLS
Merge
Combine two or more sets of items into one set.
Collate
Form two or more sets of items from two or more other sets—combines merging with extraction.
Extract
Remove one or more sets of items from a set.
Sort
Arrange into a particular sequence.
Preparation
Preparation procedures prior to processing.
ADDITIONAL SYMBOLS
Crossing of flowlines
Junction of flowlines
Parallel mode
IBM FLOWCHART SYMBOLS
Keying
An operation using a key-driven device, such as punching, verifying, and typing.
Transmittal tape
Proof tape—adding machine tape or other batch-controlled information
Offpage connector
For entry to or exit from a page.

Figure 4-3 International and IBM flowchart symbols.

is an additional flowcharting technique that is available to systems analysts for showing the flow of data processing documents within the firm.

Within the framework of the various type flowcharts, there are no formal rules for determining the level of detail to include. The amount of detail will depend upon the purpose for which the flowchart will be used. However, for a successful installation of any data processing equipment, there comes a point where all methods and procedures must be flowcharted in detail in order for the system to be implemented. Likewise, this lowest level of detail forms the basis for issuing data processing instructions to company personnel and is necessary for documentation of the system.

### System Flowchart

*A system flowchart depicts the sequence of major activities that comprise a complete operation.*

*System flowcharts,* sometimes referred to as procedural flowcharts, show the sequence of major activities that normally comprise a complete operation. They are generally prepared to assist all company personnel, in particular the systems analyst, in understanding some specific data processing operation as well as obtaining an overview of the operation itself. Before a system flowchart can be drawn, the data processing area under study must be clearly defined. Questions relating to the type and number of inputs (source documents), exceptions, transactions, files, and reports, must be answered. Similar questions refer to the relationship of the area under study to other functional parts of the data processing system, the timeliness of data, and the source of various data. Answers to these typical questions provide the necessary information for the initial system flowchart.

A very simple system flowchart, illustrated in Figure 4-4, involves the procedures necessary to maintain an individual's bank account at a minimum level of $200.

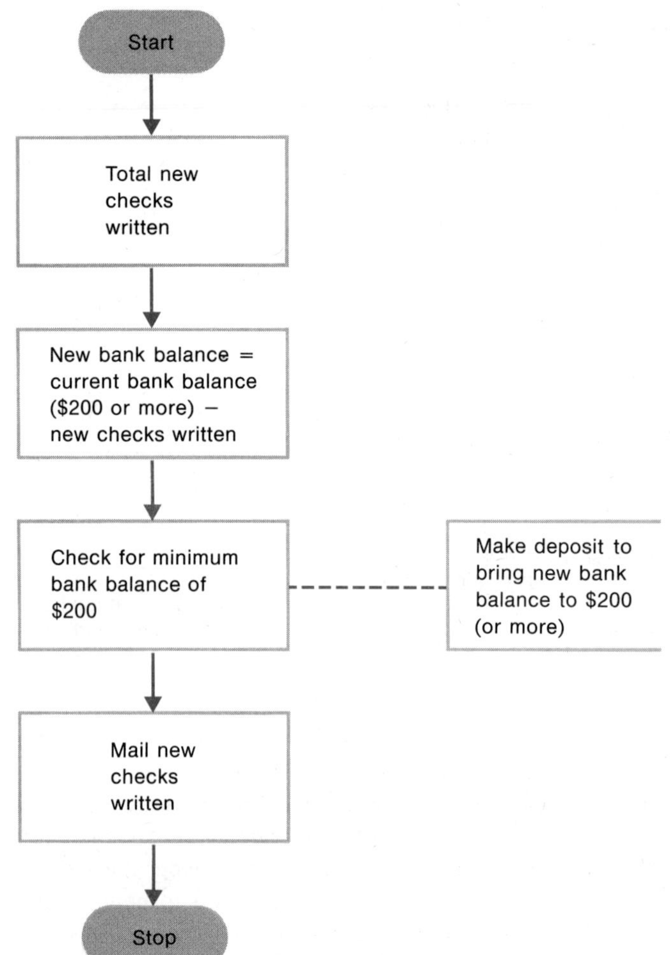


Figure 4-4 System flowchart for maintaining an individual's bank balance at a level of $200 or more.

The purpose of maintaining this amount is to save monthly banking charges as well as charges on each check written. The initial procedure is totaling the new checks written and subtracting them from the current bank balance for a new bank balance. A comparison is made to $200 (cutoff point for saving bank charges). If the new bank balance is greater than or equal to $200, checks are mailed and processing is completed. However, if the comparison results in a less-than condition, a deposit must be made to bring the new balance up to a level of $200 (or more). Checks are then mailed and processing ends.

***Payroll Illustration.*** From the first overall flowchart, additional flowcharts can be drawn so that each major operation is broken down into its subprocedures. The detailed procedures can be related to each other and to the entire system by the information flow between and among them. The punched card system flowchart for the preparation of a weekly payroll voluntary deduction register is illustrated in Figure 4-5. Its overall punched card system flowchart for weekly payroll processing is shown in Figure 4-6.

The procedural steps for the system flowchart in Figure 4-5 include the following. Payroll clerks in the accounting section complete the authorized voluntary deductions forms for new employees and existing employees (1). The voluntary payroll deduction forms are forwarded to the keypunch section for keypunching (2) and key verification (3). The current payroll voluntary deduction card file is added to the new punched cards and then sorted by employee payroll number (4). The current payroll earnings cards, produced in a prior procedure (A), are matched against the updated payroll voluntary deduction cards on a collator (5). All unmatched cards are selected and extracted into a separate pocket for immediate investigation by the payroll section (6). While matched current payroll earnings cards are forwarded to the appropriate section for handling the current week, year-to-date payroll procedure (C), matched updated voluntary deduction cards are fed into an off-line accounting machine for a printout (7). The output is sent to the payroll group and held for checking purposes against other payroll reports to be prepared at a later time (8). Finally, the updated payroll voluntary deduction card file is forwarded to another procedure of the weekly payroll processing system (D).

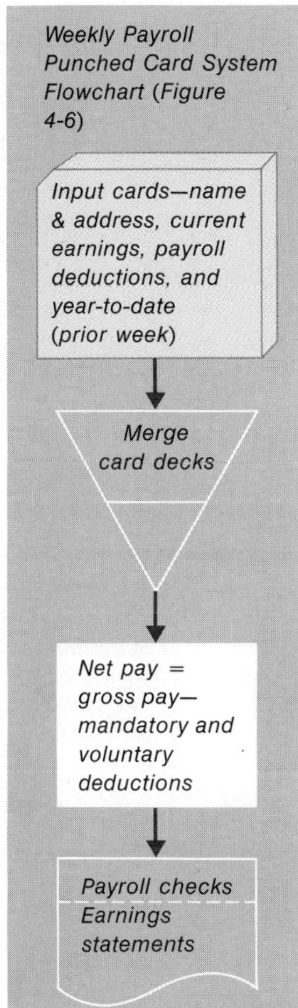


The overall punched card system flowchart, shown in Figure 4-6, indicates that several cards are merged together at various processing points in order to produce the following reports.

1. Weekly payroll hours and earnings (by employees and departments).
2. Weekly payroll voluntary deduction register.
3. Current week's year-to-date payroll register.
4. Current week's payroll earnings register.

The ultimate goal of this payroll processing is to print the payroll checks and earnings statements. It should be noted that procedures (A), (C), and (D) in Figure 4-6 are referenced to Figure 4-5.

Solid lines in the overall flowchart represent processing procedures. On the other hand, dotted lines indicate a comparison of values as procedures (A) through (*E*) are completed. In effect, the regular and overtime hours as well as amounts in procedure (A) should agree with those figures generated in procedure (E).

### Program Flowchart

*Program flowcharts,* sometimes referred to as block diagrams, describe the specific steps and their sequence for a particular computer program. When a

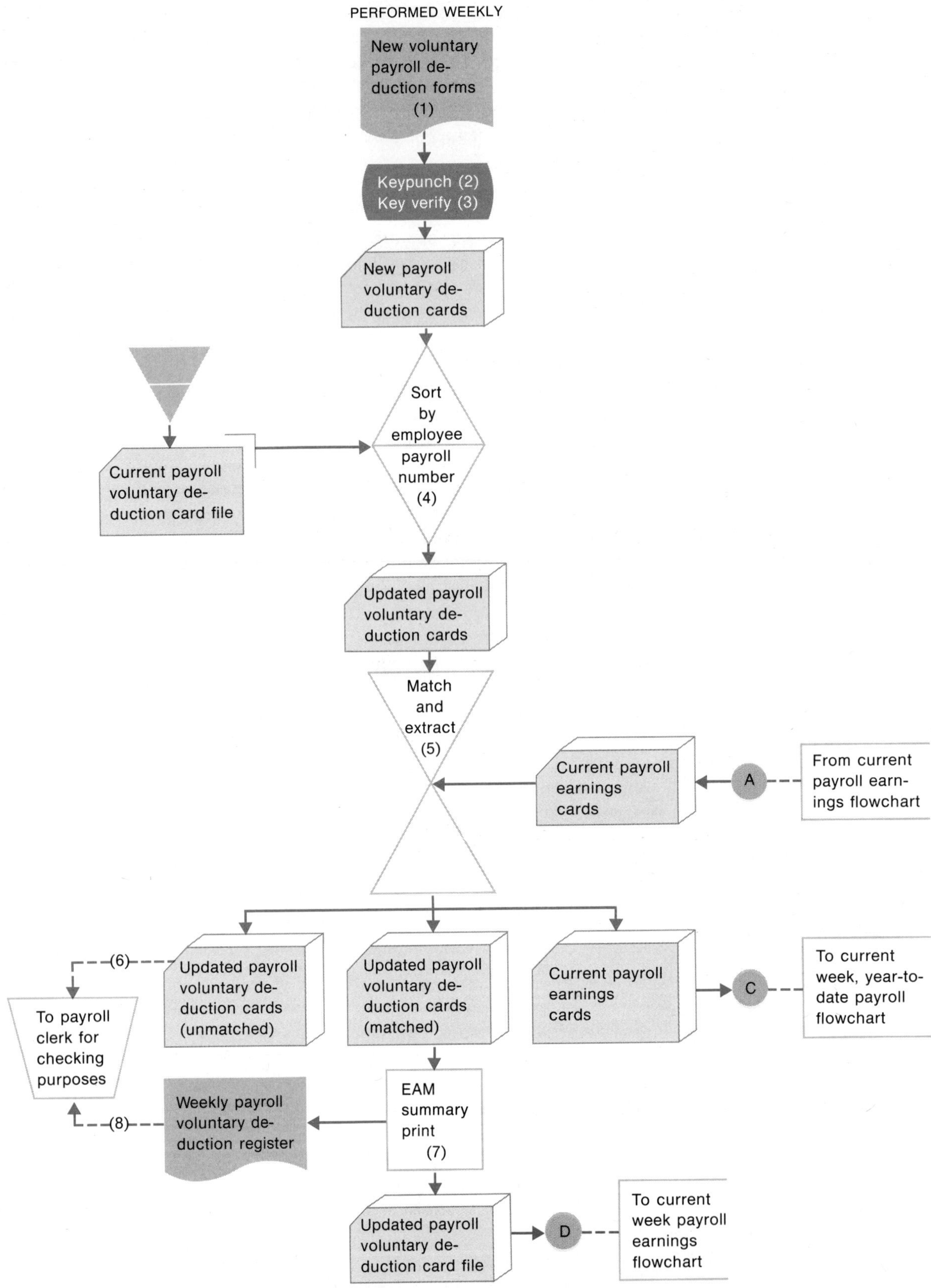


Figure 4-5 Weekly payroll voluntary deduction register punched card system flowchart—refer to (B) in Figure 4-6.

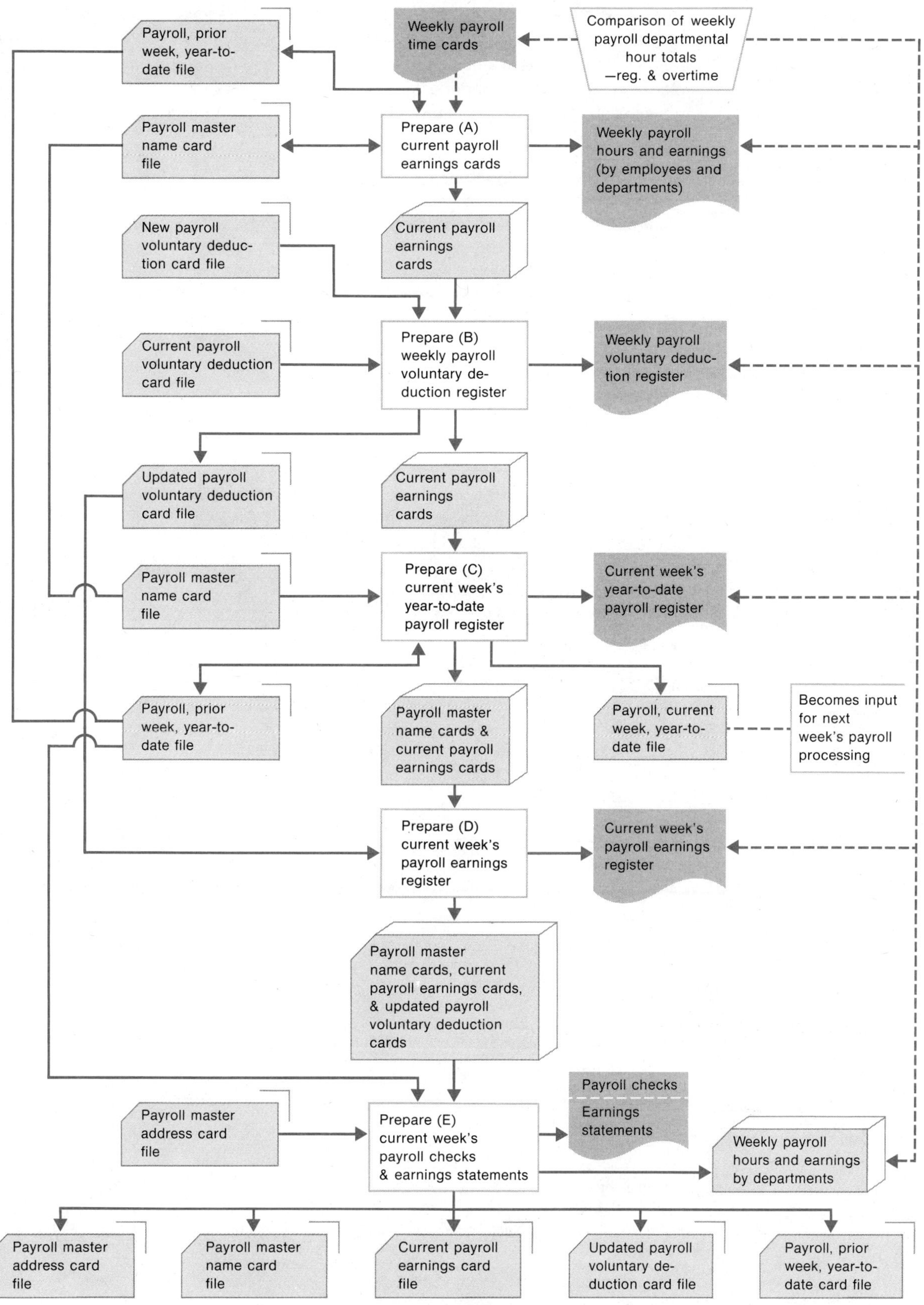

Payroll, prior week, year-to-date file
Weekly payroll time cards
Comparison of weekly payroll departmental hour totals —reg. & overtime
Payroll master name card file
Prepare (A) current payroll earnings cards
Weekly payroll hours and earnings (by employees and departments)
New payroll voluntary deduction card file
Current payroll earnings cards
Current payroll voluntary deduction card file
Prepare (B) weekly payroll voluntary deduction register
Weekly payroll voluntary deduction register
Updated payroll voluntary deduction card file
Current payroll earnings cards
Payroll master name card file
Prepare (C) current week's year-to-date payroll register
Current week's year-to-date payroll register
Payroll, prior week, year-to-date file
Payroll master name cards & current payroll earnings cards
Payroll, current week, year-to-date file
Becomes input for next week's payroll processing
Prepare (D) current week's payroll earnings register
Current week's payroll earnings register
Payroll master name cards, current payroll earnings cards, & updated payroll voluntary deduction cards
Payroll checks
Earnings statements
Payroll master address card file
Prepare (E) current week's payroll checks & earnings statements
Weekly payroll hours and earnings by departments
Payroll master address card file
Payroll master name card file
Current payroll earnings card file
Updated payroll voluntary deduction card file
Payroll, prior week, year-to-date card file

Figure 4-6 Weekly payroll punched card system flowchart.

*A program flowchart describes in detail the specific computer processing steps and their sequence.*

program is extremely simple, a flowchart may not be necessary. However, for most programs, it is necessary to have a sequence of operations and decisions that detail the computer program steps. Otherwise, the programmer would have a difficult task in coding the program properly. In a similar manner, the program flowchart provides an excellent means of documenting the program. The program flowchart, then, has three important uses.

- aids program development
- serves as a guide for coding
- is a sound basis for documentation

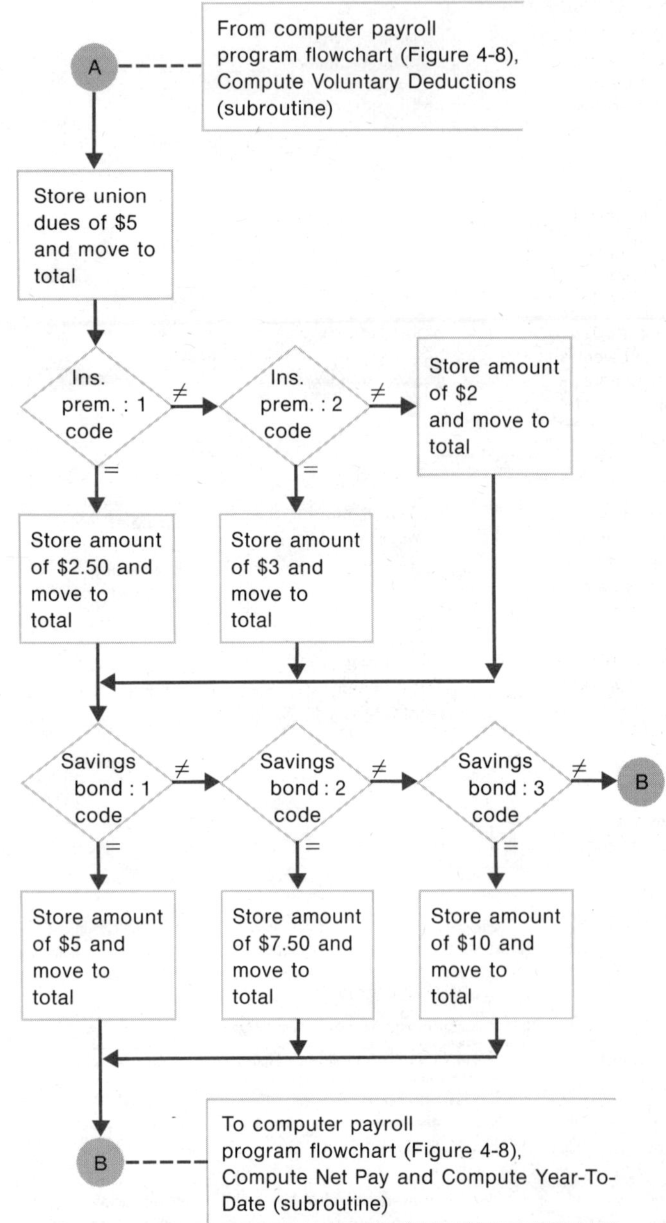


Figure 4-7 Compute Voluntary Deductions program (subroutine) flowchart.

***Payroll Illustration.*** Computer program flowcharts, comparable to the weekly payroll punched card system flowcharts in Figures 4-5 and 4-6, are depicted in Figures 4-7 and 4-8 respectively. The Compute Voluntary Deductions program (subroutine) flowchart (Figure 4-7) consists of a series of operations steps and decisions regarding the proper weekly payroll deductions. Comparisons are made to determine the deduction amount for insurance premiums and savings bonds while a standard union dues deduction of $5 is deducted for all employees.

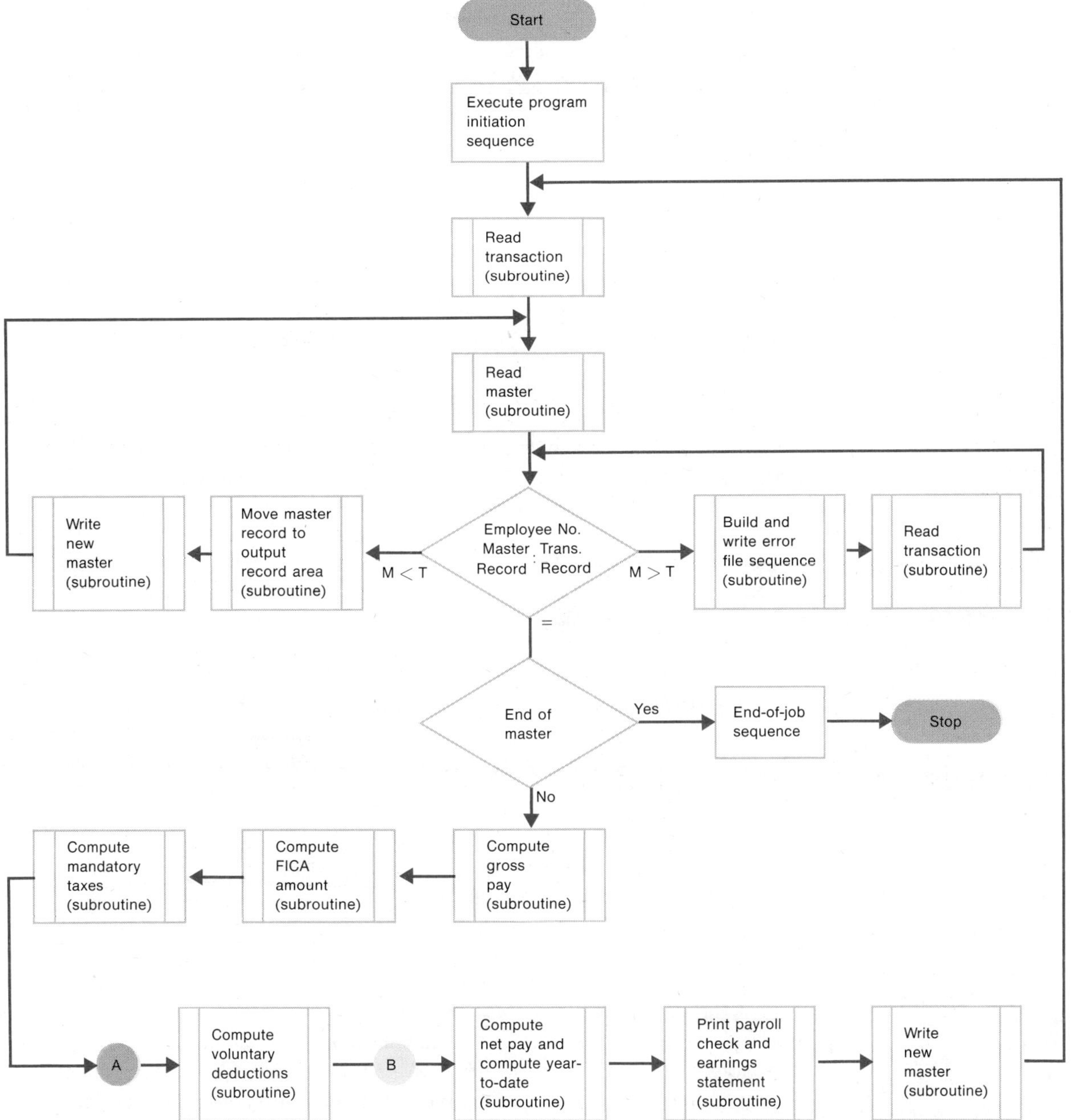


Figure 4-8 Weekly computer payroll program flowchart to compute net pay and print payroll check and earnings statement.

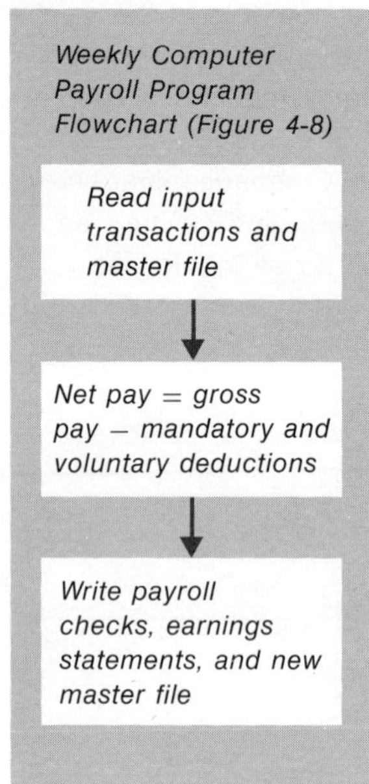


The overall computer payroll flowchart (Figure 4-8) shows the sequence of principal decisions and subroutines, such as Compute Voluntary Deductions, within the program. A principal decision is to compare the master record employee number to the transaction record employee number. Depending on the evaluation, the processing can take any one of three possible paths. If the master employee number of the first path equals the transaction record number, another comparison tests for end-of-job sequence. If not end-of-job, the employee's weekly pay is computed, a payroll check and earnings statement is printed, and a new master file record is written. The second path of the principal decision or the less-than condition signifies that the employee has not worked this week while the third path or the greater-than condition indicates an error condition. No matter what path is followed, appropriate action is taken by the program.

***Computer Prepared Program Flowchart.*** An extremely helpful flowcharting technique is utilization of the computer itself with a special flowchart writing program. Using asterisks and other special symbols, the printer plots the outlines of the symbols and converts them as if they were flowcharted manually. The advantage of such a method should be apparent—revisions can be easily made once the initial table is written and cards have been correctly punched. The updating process consists of repunching cards that represent program flowchart changes. This approach can keep the laborious task of updating complex program flowcharts to a minimum. An example of this approach is found in Figure 4-9.

*The modular program flowchart is a method of showing more detail on a succeeding flowchart.*

### Modular Program Flowchart

Another way of presenting the program flowchart is called *modular program flowcharting,* which is a technique of presenting a complete picture on each chart. This approach stresses the logic of a program, component routines, and subroutines. Any portion of the flowchart may be shown in more detail on a succeeding chart.

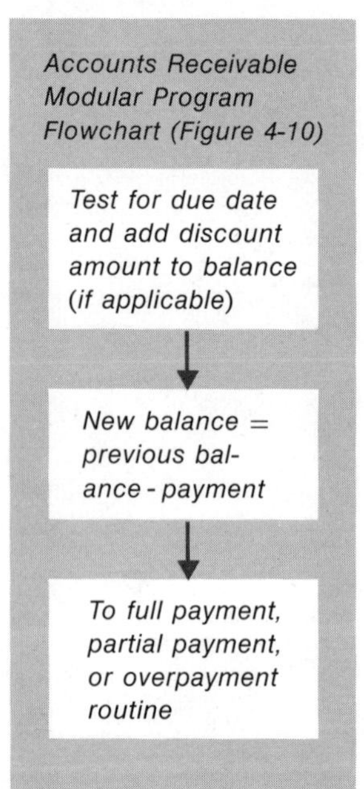


***Accounts Receivable Illustration.*** A modular program flowchart is illustrated for payments on open accounts receivable. Figure 4-11 is an expansion of the area "test due date and set date switch" program block (area enclosed by the irregular line) in Figure 4-10. Both flowcharts use the IBM Flowcharting Worksheet.

***Modular Program Levels.*** Within the framework of modular program flowcharting, there are three essential parts to the striping convention (the process of showing more detail on a succeeding chart). First, a horizontal line is drawn within and near the top of the symbol, as shown in Figure 4-10. Second, the detailed representation starts and ends with a terminal symbol. Finally, an identifier is placed above the stripe in the striped symbol. The identical identifier is placed in the entry terminal symbol of the detailed representation (JAA2 in the illustration).

An examination of Figure 4-11 indicates that this modular program flowchart is the final level for this level of flowcharts. Since no further detail is required, no blocks on this flowchart are striped. The legs of this chart return to the symbol immediately following the striped symbol on Figure 4-10.

*A document flowchart depicts the flow of forms, documents, or reports operating in a system.*

### Document Flowchart

The *document flowchart* technique shows the way various forms, documents, or reports move from person to person or from department to department. It is extremely helpful in understanding and obtaining an overview of paper flow within the firm for a specific function. Although no special flowcharting symbols are needed, normally the departments or individuals involved are labeled on the top of the sheet. An example of this flowcharting technique is found in Figure 4-12.

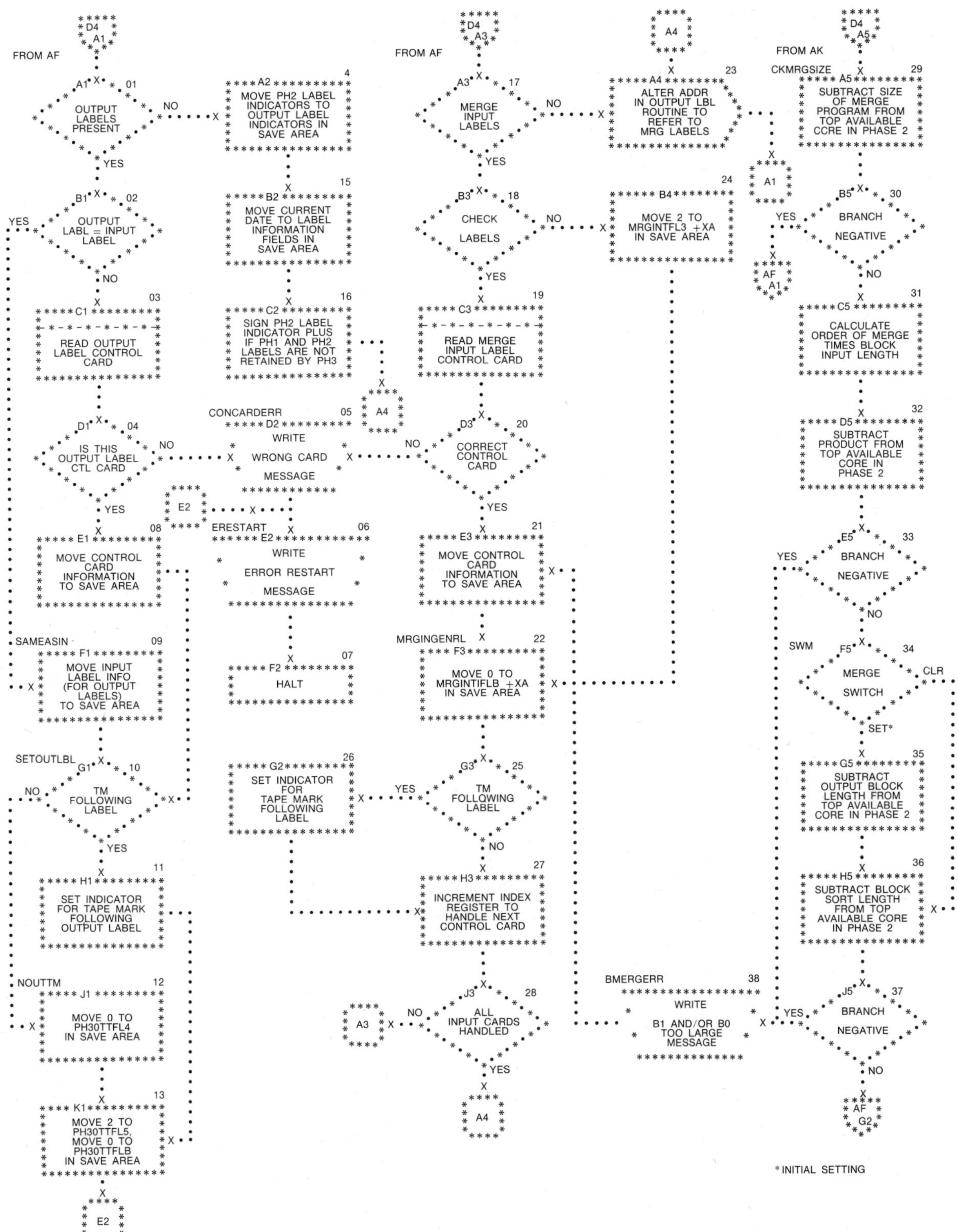


Figure 4-9 Machine-mode program flowchart. (Courtesy International Business Machines Corporation.)

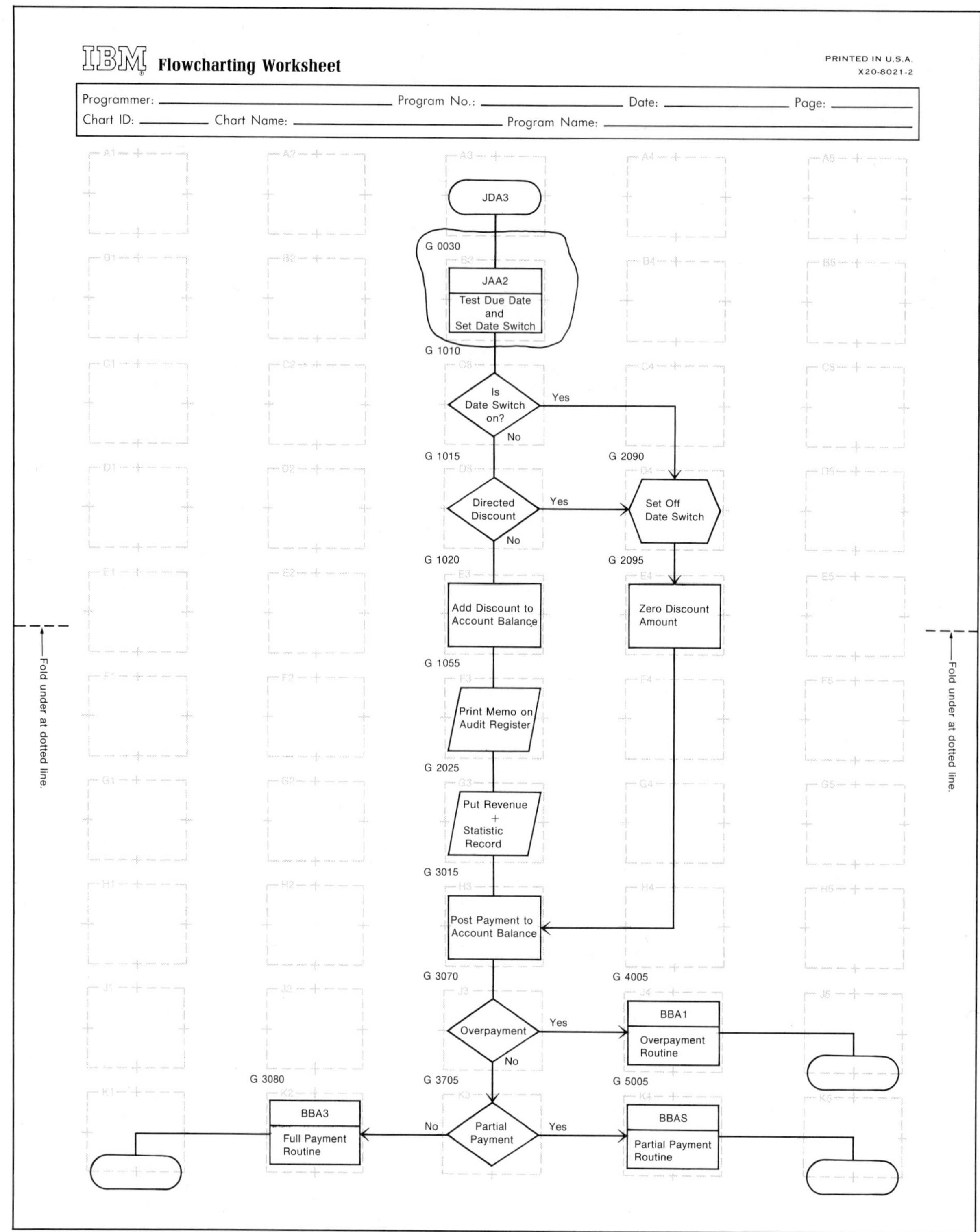


Figure 4-10 Modular program flowchart—higher level than Figure 4-11. (Courtesy International Business Machines Corporation.)

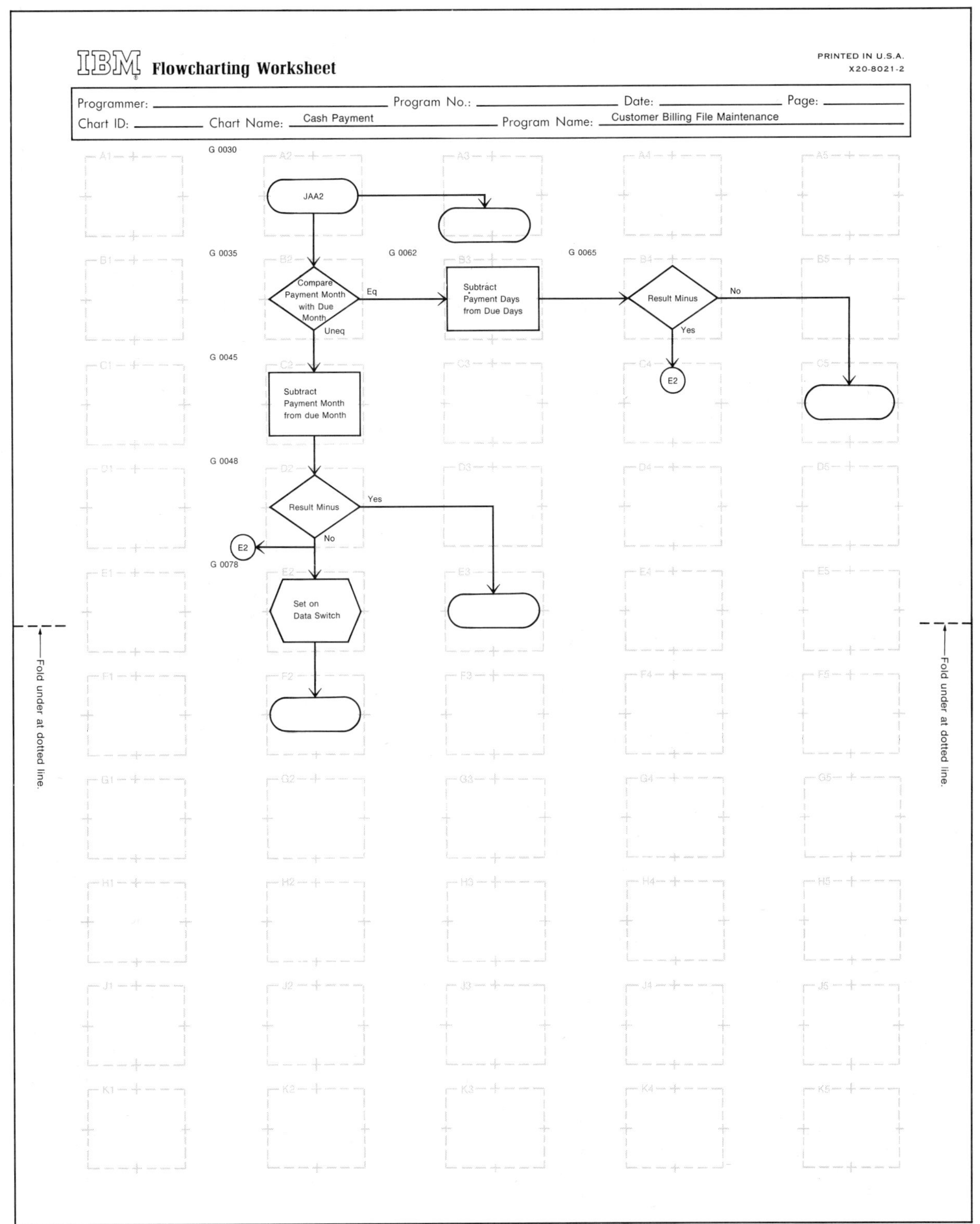


Figure 4-11 Modular program flowchart—expansion of processing block JAA2 from Figure 4-10. (Courtesy International Business Machines Corporation.)

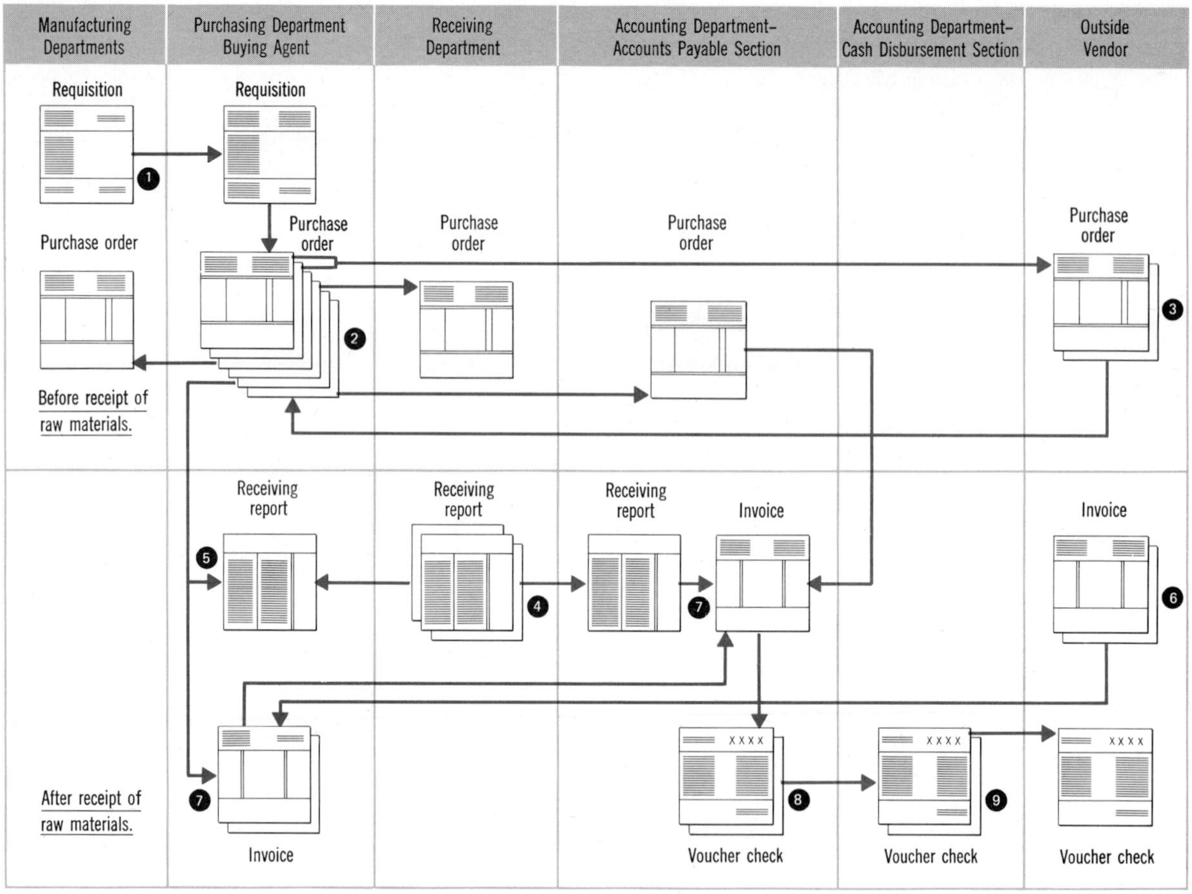

Figure 4-12 Raw material purchases—document flowchart.

*Figure 4-12 Documents Used in Raw Material Purchases*

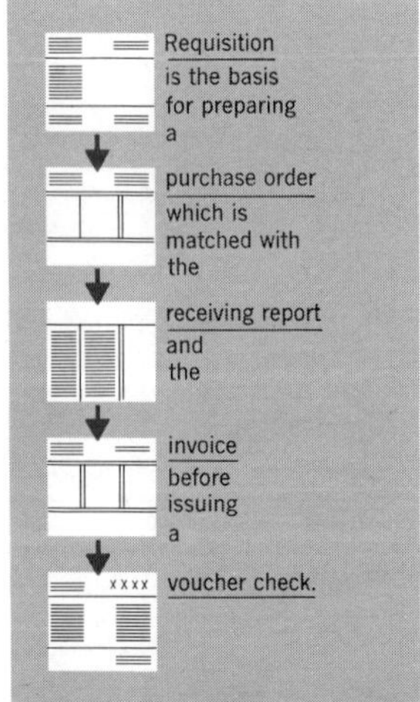

Requisition
is the basis
for preparing
a
purchase order
which is
matched with
the
receiving report
and
the
invoice
before
issuing
a
voucher check.


***Raw Material Purchases Illustration.*** Requisitions for raw material purchases are forwarded from the manufacturing departments by the respective plant formen to the purchasing agent (1). These form the basis for typing a six-part purchase order (2). One copy of the purchase order is sent to each of the following departments: manufacturing, receiving, and accounting (accounts payable section), while one copy is retained by the purchasing department. The original and duplicate purchase orders are mailed directly to the outside vendor. One copy of the purchase order is returned by the vendor to the firm in order to acknowledge receipt of the order and date(s) of future raw material shipment(s) (3).

Upon receipt of the raw materials, a three-part receiving report form is prepared (4). One copy each is forwarded to the purchasing department and the accounting departments (accounts payable section), leaving the final copy as a file copy for the receiving department. The purchasing department compares the purchase order against the goods received per the receiving report (5). The procedure allows the purchasing agent to control all outstanding goods on order. Once the vendor invoices are received (6), both are forwarded to the purchasing department for review of items shipped, terms, discounts, discrepancies, and similar items with the corresponding purchase order and receiving report. After making changes on the invoice if applicable, one copy of the invoice is sent to the accounting department (accounts payable section) for auditing the work of the purchasing department. Here, the accounts payable clerk compares the vendor invoice with the purchase order and the receiving report (7). Next, the invoice amount is typed on a voucher check (8). Twice a month (on the 10th and the 20th), the voucher check is prepared and mailed to the vendor while one copy is retained by the accounting department (cash disbursements section) (9). The above process completes the manual handling for raw materials purchases, shown in Figure 4-12.

## DECISION TABLES

There are inherent deficiencies in flowcharts although they are widely used for systems development work. The flowchart is generally difficult to follow for any type of complex program since one can get lost while tracing each path through the many procedures that comprise a program. Flowcharts take considerable time to draw the first time, not to mention the recharting necessary to effect changes for a completed program. Despite the fact that uniform flowchart symbols have been established, there is still confusion and lack of conformity in the field.

### Characteristics of Decision Tables

*A decision table shows conditions and corresponding actions that are logically related.*

As a result of the foregoing deficiencies and the very nature of data processing problems (decision-oriented), decision tables have been developed as a more efficient alternative to flowcharts in many cases. Basically, a *decision table* is similar to a flowchart in its use and construction. It can be used independently of or to complement a flowchart. A decision table shows conditions and actions in a simplified and orderly manner. By presenting logical alternative courses of action under various operating conditions, a decision table enables one to think through a problem and present its solution in compact notation. It allows a computer problem to be divided into its logical segments that provide a multilevel structure in the problem's analysis. At the highest level, decision tables can be used for an overall system by referencing to lower level tables as was accomplished in a previous section for modular program flowcharting. The purpose of a decision table, then, is to bring together and present complex decision logic such that its meaning can be readily understood.

Over the years, simplified forms of decision tables have been utilized. Tax rate and insurance rate tables are forms of decision tables. Likewise, the price list of various product lines, expressed in terms of quantity discounts, package sizes, and product specifications, is another example. These common examples are basically truth tables that have become the foundation of decision tables.

### Values of Decision Tables

*The important values of a decision table are:*

- *compact notation*
- *easy to modify program*
- *ability to produce a machine language program*
- *compatible with flowcharts*

Many values can be derived from the utilization of decision tables. Like flowcharts, decision tables force a complete statement of the problem from the outset. Several studies have shown that approximately 50% of total costs related to computer system development have been attributed to poor problem definition as well as ineffective documentation.

***Compact Notation.*** Many pages of a computer system program flowchart can be condensed in a single logic table. Studies indicate that persons with no previous computer experience have programmed applications in less time with decision tables than experienced programmers who fail to make use of decision tables.

Likewise, those who must review a program need not go through page after page of flowcharts to follow the logic of the program. Also, decision tables are easier for the nonsystems person to understand, and they are easier to check by observation for consistency and completeness.

***Easy to Modify Program.*** Another important value of the decision table's compact notation is that it is easier to modify and update the program for system changes. Adding new conditions or changing a given decision rule action will not require substantial reformulation that can be the case in flowcharts. In addition, introduction of new decision tables into an operating system will not require substantial revision to system flowcharts.

***Ability to Produce a Machine Language Program.*** Perhaps, the most significant value of decision tables is their ability to produce a machine language computer program (as set forth in a subsequent section). In such cases, a translator converts the decision rules into a programming language without human intervention and has the ability to convert this language into the appropriate machine language in the ordinary course of operations. Thus, this computerized process reduces the time to produce a completed program for testing sample input data.

***Compatible with Flowcharts.*** Although decision tables have many advantages over program flowcharts, they are not complete substitutes in a business data processing environment. Business processing is still primarily a sequential process of using input data to process controlled tasks, revise storage files, and prepare output. Flowcharts are still needed to show this sequential process and are useful when there are few conditions and simple decisions only or when presenting the combined system of decision logic, programs, and computers. Instead of showing each branch representing an individual decision, flowcharts can include a single block representing a complete decision table. From this viewpoint, decision tables and the various types of flowcharts complement and supplement each other in a business data processing system.

**Decision Table Components**

A decision table is divided into four basic elements with provision for other information that may be helpful for interpreting the final results. This is shown below.

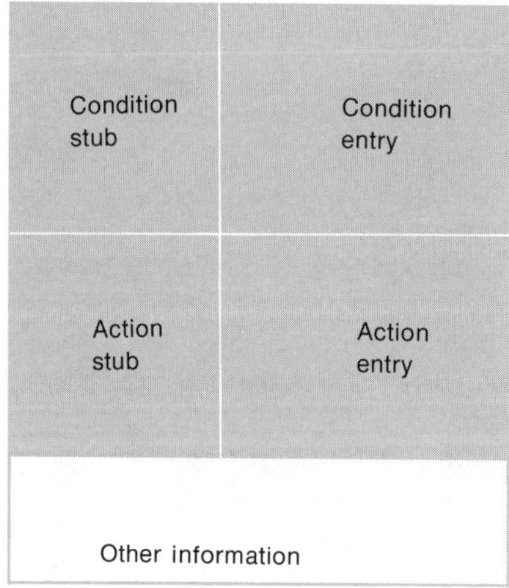

The basic components of decision tables are:
- condition stub
- condition entry
- action stub
- action entry

All conditions are listed in the upper part of the decision table and represent the contents of decision and branching symbols on the program flowchart. Since this represents the condition of the computer at a particular time or an "if" condition, it may be necessary to perform a specific operation on the data at this time. Actions taken correspond to the processing symbols on a flowchart or "then" action and are listed in the second half of the decision table. Thus, conditions and actions have an "if . . . then" relationship; that is, if a set of conditions exist, then perform the indicated actions. It should be noted that a condition cannot appear in the action area nor can an action appear in the condition area.

Condition entry symbols are:
- yes (Y)
- no (N)
- greater than (>)
- equal to (=)
- less than (<)
- blank (—)

Action entry symbols are:
- X
- blank (—)

***Symbols and Rules.*** Various symbols can be used in a decision table for the condition entry, namely, yes (Y), no (N), greater than (>), equal to (=), less than (<), and blank (—). The action entry to be performed is an X or a blank (—). A blank in either case means that the condition or action is not applicable. Each column in the decision table makes up a rule that corresponds to one of the many possible paths of a program flowchart. Basically, a decision table relates given conditions to the appropriate actions, with a column of entries that forms a rule. Alternative conditions which result in other actions that constitute other rules in a decision table are written side by side.

### Compute FICA Illustration

The decision table and the corresponding flowchart are depicted in Figure 4-13 for computing the current FICA amount.

In order to demonstrate the foregoing symbols and rules, consider the decision table in Figure 4-13*b* for computing the FICA amount of each employee plus the total FICA amount of the current pay period, shown originally in Figure 4-8 as a "Compute FICA Amount" (subroutine). (The corresponding flowchart for the decision table is illustrated in Figure 4-13*a*.) Rule 1 or column 1 states: if the old year-to-date tax paid (YTD) is greater than \$468, set current period FICA tax paid to zero for the individual being processed as well as initiate an FICA error routine to report this abnormal condition. Rule 2 reads as follows: if the old year-to-date tax paid from the prior pay period is equal to \$468, then set the current period FICA tax to zero. The rationale for this second rule is that there is no need to deduct FICA for the current period since the employee has already paid in a sufficient FICA amount for the entire year. Likewise, it is not necessary to add to the accumulated FICA tax paid for all employees (current period) if the current amount is zero.

Referring to rule 3, if the old YTD tax from the prior period is less than \$468 (even by \$.01), the current period FICA tax must be computed, which is gross pay times 5.2% for the action taken. If the new YTD tax computed (current period FICA tax computed + old YTD tax paid) is greater than \$468, the current period FICA tax paid must be determined. Also, the new YTD tax paid of \$468 must be stored for the employee. In a similar manner, the current period FICA tax paid must be added to the accumulated FICA tax paid for all employees.

Rule 4 is like rule 3 in terms of actions taken, but differs in one of its conditions; that is, the new YTD tax computed is less than or equal to \$468. Current period FICA tax will be the amount computed at 5.2% of gross pay. The new YTD tax paid will be equal to \$468 or some value less. In most cases, the latter condition will prevail. Thus the foregoing four rules adequately handle the FICA subroutine versus many symbols for the corresponding program flowchart (Figure 4-13*a*).

### Checking Inventory Level Illustration

Another example of a decision table, found in Figure 4-14, checks the inventory level for incoming orders. The decision table was first developed by determining

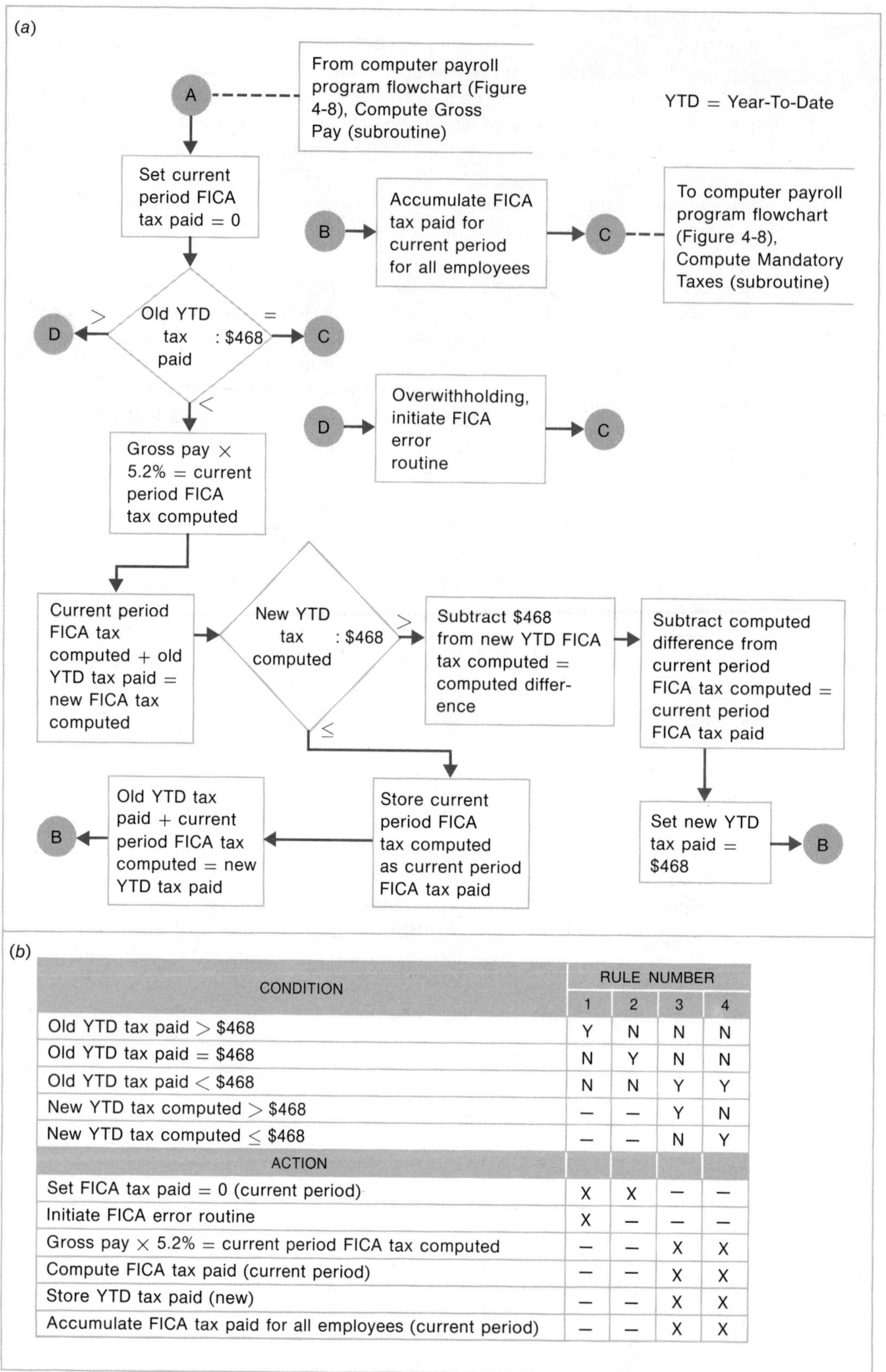


| CONDITION | RULE NUMBER | | | |
|---|---|---|---|---|
| | 1 | 2 | 3 | 4 |
| Old YTD tax paid > $468 | Y | N | N | N |
| Old YTD tax paid = $468 | N | Y | N | N |
| Old YTD tax paid < $468 | N | N | Y | Y |
| New YTD tax computed > $468 | — | — | Y | N |
| New YTD tax computed ≤ $468 | — | — | N | Y |
| ACTION | | | | |
| Set FICA tax paid = 0 (current period) | X | X | — | — |
| Initiate FICA error routine | X | — | — | — |
| Gross pay × 5.2% = current period FICA tax computed | — | — | X | X |
| Compute FICA tax paid (current period) | — | — | X | X |
| Store YTD tax paid (new) | — | — | X | X |
| Accumulate FICA tax paid for all employees (current period) | — | — | X | X |

Figure 4-13 Program flowchart (*a*) and decision table (*b*) for Compute FICA Amount—subroutine per Figure 4-8.

| DECISION TABLE | TABLE NAME: INVENTORY LEVEL CHECKING | | PAGE 1 OF 1 |
|---|---|---|---|
| | CHART NO: INVENTORY—5 | PREPARED BY: ROBERT J. THIERAUF | DATE: NOV. 5, 197– |

| CONDITION | 1 | 2 | 3 | 4 | 5 | 6 | 7 | 8 | 9 | 10 | 11 | 12 |
|---|---|---|---|---|---|---|---|---|---|---|---|---|
| Inventory available ≥ ordered amount | Y | N | N | N | N | N | N | N | N | | | |
| Inventory available < ordered amount | — | Y | Y | Y | Y | Y | N | N | N | | | |
| Partial shipment of goods | — | Y | Y | N | N | — | — | — | — | | | |
| Back order of goods | — | Y | N | Y | N | — | Y | N | — | | | |
| Additional goods due in next day | — | N | N | N | N | Y | N | N | Y | | | |
| **ACTION** | | | | | | | | | | | | |
| Item shipped | X | — | — | — | — | — | — | — | — | | | |
| Partial shipment | — | X | X | — | — | — | — | — | — | | | |
| Back order unshipped balance | — | X | — | X | — | — | X | — | — | | | |
| Out of stock notice sent | — | — | X | — | X | — | — | X | — | | | |
| Order held for entire day | — | — | — | — | — | X | — | — | X | | | |
| Other Information: | | | | | | | | | | | | |

(Column headers 1–12 are under RULE NUMBER.)

Figure 4-14 Decision table for checking inventory level.

the possible conditions. After exhausting the condition list, the action entries are listed. For the first rule, if the inventory is greater than or equal to the order amount (Yes condition), the item ordered would be shipped as noted by the "X" in the appropriate space. Since the remaining actions are not relevant for this condition, the "-" appears in the first column. The next eight rules are interpreted in a similar manner. In total, the decision table shows nine separate decision rules.

An investigation of Figure 4-14 indicates there is little difference between rules 6 and 9 since both result in the same action, that is, holding an order for one day. In such cases, the two rules can be combined into one rule. The combined rule is:

| *Decision Rule 6* | *Decision Rule 9* | *Combined Rule* |
|---|---|---|
| N | N | N |
| Y | N | — |
| — | — | — |
| — | — | — |
| Y | Y | Y |

## DECISION TABLE PROCESSORS

*Decision table processors are available that convert decision tables to computer code, thereby bypassing the programming phase.*

Because of the structure of a decision table, each table stands on its own. Any complex logic that is contained in a decision table is depicted in that table and serves as its own documentation. Because of this feature, computer programs are available that convert decision tables or original documentation to computer code, thereby eliminating the programming phase. Presently, these programs have obtained various levels of sophistication and vary greatly in their capabilities. Decision table translators include the Decision Logic Translator of IBM, DETOC of Information Systems Leasing Corporation, DETAP of Information Management, Inc., and TABTRAN of Westinghouse Information Systems Laboratory.

### TABTRAN Processor

Input to the TABTRAN processor is punched cards whose format follows the basic decision table structure. A table name card consisting of one or more words separated by hyphens precedes each table. Cards following the name card contain up to 150 conditions and actions. The left side of each card (columns 1 through 35) contains either a condition or action stub, the right side (columns 36 through 75) contains the entry characters. All condition cards are input first, followed by all action cards for this table structure.

The TABTRAN processor reads each decision table in punched card form and examines the relationship of each rule in the table to all other rules in the table. Through a preprocessing examination, any dependent rules are isolated and diagnosed as being either redundant or contradictory. Once the decision table has successfully completed the diagnostic phase, the processor selects condition stubs one at a time. With the selection of each condition, the table is subdivided into a yes and no component. Each successive subdivision further simplifies the table, until finally an appropriate action can be satisfied. A common business-oriented program that depicts this selection is generated as the table is reduced.

## SUMMARY

This chapter has concentrated basically on the methods of preparing flowcharts and decision tables. Although there are many values to be realized from flowcharts, greater values are obtained from decision tables for complex computer programs. Decision tables eliminate the need for flowcharts when programming while providing information for programming in a concise format that is easy to read and grasp. Instead of getting lost in a myriad of detail (numerous flowchart pages), decision tables can express very complex decision logic in much less space. They can be divided into logical segments that provide for a multilevel structure within the computer problem, similar to modular program flowcharting. In addition, decision tables can be keypunched and processed on a computer to produce an operational programming language program which, in turn, can be converted into the machine language of the particular computer for an operational computer program. However, for simple and straightforward computer programs, the use of program flowcharts might be the better method. Thus the utilization of flowcharts, decision tables, or a combination of the two revolves around the problem to be solved.

## QUESTIONS

1. What are the values of flowcharts when one is considering a punched card installation or a computer installation? Explain.
2. Distinguish among the following: basic symbols, specialized input/output and file symbols, and specialized processing symbols.
3. What are the basic differences between the USASI flowchart symbols and the ISO flowchart symbols? Explain.
4. Distinguish among the following: a system flowchart, a program flowchart, a modular program flowchart, and a document flowchart.
5. Can the computer be used in program flowcharting?
6. (a) What is the primary purpose of a decision table?
   (b) How does a decision table differ from a modular program flowchart?
   (c) Which should be preferred when coding and why?

## EXERCISES

1. Referring to the weekly payroll punched card system flowchart in Figure 4-6, develop an appropriate system flowchart for each of the following:
   (a) current payroll earnings cards,
   (b) current week's year-to-date payroll register,
   (c) current week's payroll earnings register,
   (d) current payroll check and earnings statements.
2. Develop subroutine program flowcharts and the corresponding decision tables for the following:
   (a) Compute gross pay (total hours = regular hours + overtime hours at time and a half).
   (b) Compute saving bonds deduction (amount equal to 5% of gross pay or $3.00 a week, whichever is less).
   (c) Compute credit union deduction (amount equal to 10% of gross pay or $15.00 a week, whichever is less).
3. Referring to the computer payroll program flowchart in Figure 4-8, develop an appropriate decision table for each of the following:
   (a) Compute gross pay (regular hours are based on a 35-hour week and overtime hours at $1\frac{1}{2}$ times the regular hourly rate).
   (b) Compute FICA amount (use current figures).
   (c) Compute mandatory taxes (state income tax rate of gross pay—2%, city income tax—1%, and federal income tax—consult current rate table).
   (d) Compute voluntary deductions (refer to Figure 4-7).
   (e) Compute current net pay and year-to-date amounts (refer to a, b, c, and d above).

## CHAPTER FIVE

# Input-Storage-Processing-Control-Output (ISPCO) Cycle Concept of Computers

*The input-storage-processing-control-output cycle is associated with the components of any computer system. (Courtesy International Business Machines Corporation.)*

A basic limitation of punched card equipment is the continuous human intervention and attention required. Even the simplest of output reports require card processing through several machines. The necessity to check and recheck each stage of operation is apparent in such a business data processing system. This approach is in contrast to a computer that can perform involved processing within its own system. There is no need to route the input data through several machines. Once the computer has been properly programmed, it can solve a business problem unaided and at an amazing speed. In order to accomplish the assigned data processing task, the computer must be specifically instructed. As will be seen in the forthcoming chapters, this is not always an easy task.

The basic types of computers—analog and digital—are initially explored in this chapter, followed by a discussion of the input-storage-processing-control-output (ISPCO) cycle concept in computer systems. The ISPCO cycle is related to the basic components of any digital computer. Other basic components of a digital computer are investigated for more advanced data processing systems.

## BASIC TYPES OF COMPUTERS

*Basic types of computers are:*

- *analog (slide rule accuracy)*
- *digital (generally 100% accuracy)*

The two basic types of computers are *analog* and *digital*. The analog computer is similar to the slide rule and the digital computer is comparable to the abacus. These comparisons should give some indication of their ability and accuracy. This book is directed toward a thorough and comprehensive discussion of digital computers.

Over the past few years, a third type of computer has been marketed, known as the *hybrid* computer. It combines the analog and digital capabilities into one computer system. The hybrid computer is designed to overcome the present problems of combining analog and digital computers for industrial manufacturing processes.

### Analog Computer

*An analog computer is essentially a measuring device since it operates on data in the form of continuously variable physical quantities, such as voltages and temperatures.*

The analog computer is used on those problems that generally originate as physical realities. The most common method of describing these physical problems is in mathematical form—algebraic equations, differential equations, or some arbitrary relationship. These problems are solved by substituting an analogous or equivalent relationship, expressed basically in the form of voltages. These voltages, in turn, may be manipulated—higher or lower—in order to correspond to the larger or smaller variables in the physical problem. Since the analog computer operates on data in the form of continuously variable physical quantities, such as voltages and temperatures, it is essentially a measuring device.

Because data are acquired through a measuring process, the analog computer accepts data as is, without the need for conversion to some internal operating code, such as the binary system for digital computers. This feature, in addition to its ability to process data at high speeds, makes it extremely useful for control purposes. However, the machine measures and compares quantities in one operation and has no storage. The answers to the problem are obtained by reading dials and cathode-ray tubes. Outputs of the analog computer may also be in the form of graphs. Other outputs may be in the form of voltages or pulses that may be used to control flows, pressures, and temperatures or to activate many different kinds of control devices connected to the computer.

As a result of its operational mode, the analog computer is not as accurate as the digital computer. Its accuracy is limited by the precision with which the continually variable physical quantities can be controlled and the capabilities of the equipment.

*A common application of analog computers is oil refinery processing where continued testing and checking of the manufacturing process is necessary.*

***Application of Analog Computer.*** A common application of the analog computer is control of output. For example, an analog computer is used in the automated control of an oil refinery process. Here, the specific gravity and other pertinent physical properties of crude oil are fed into the computer system for continual testing and checking. As the oil flows through for processing, several stages of differing pressures, vacuums, and temperatures are required to break the crude oil down into the refined products desired. By varying these factors, larger or smaller quantities of each given product (or combinations of products) can be produced as demand for the products change. Through the use of computers that are continually checking, on-line, the actual mixture of all factors versus the optimum mixture, it is possible to achieve 95% or better efficiency versus 75% efficiency with manual methods. It should be noted that a combination of analog and digital computers is used. The analog computers provide the input required for the digital computer which weighs all inputs against previously stored instructions and formulas. The digital computer performs the computations to determine the optimum function control required. This information is relayed back to the analog computers which make the necessary adjustments required of the control devices. In addition to being useful as controlling devices in oil refinery, analog computers are extensively used in cement, chemical, paper, and steel processes as well as in military weapon systems.

### Digital Computer

*The digital computer has the ability to calculate and manipulate discrete values which makes it adaptable to business operations.*

The analog computer operates basically by measuring while the digital computer operates on numbers by counting them. It is the ability of the digital computer to calculate and manipulate discrete values that makes it adaptable to business data processing problems. Even though both the analog and digital computers are used in making mathematical calculations, the accuracy of the analog machine is dependent on the precise control of voltages, pulses, and components. In the digital machine, accuracy is conditioned upon the number of value positions available for the manipulation of data—the more places available for an answer, the more accurate is the final answer. For the digital computer, it is only necessary in many cases to add an additional place position in order to increase its accuracy. For example, in calculating the weekly pay for an individual whose rate is $3.585 per hour and hours worked are 39 hours for the week, it is necessary to round the final answer from $139.815 to $139.82. This same type of processing is not available with the analog computer since dials and gauges are read for an answer.

*Digital computers are employed for* business, scientific, *and* process control *processing.*

***Major Categories of Digital Computers.*** Digital computer uses can be classified into three major categories.

1. business
2. scientific
3. process control

There is a continuing trend to market a general-purpose computer that is capable of performing all these tasks. However, a brief description of each major category will help classify the direction of this book, namely, data processing for business with meaningful information for management.

For *business processing,* much of the computer time is spent in reading input data, searching primary and secondary storage for associated data, processing data in a controlled environment, and preparing meaningful output that will allow "management by exception" to be practiced. By and large, relatively few internal computations are made. On the other hand, *scientific processing* is characterized by a small amount of input and output, but an extensive amount of internal calculations. While the scientific computer needs very fast internal processing, the business computer generally does not.

In *process control,* the computer accepts frequent to continuous inputs of data from the process being controlled. Data are tested according to a formula, a set of rules, or procedures and the computer feeds back the necessary data if the process is to be adjusted. The use of a digital computer with several analog computers was discussed in a previous section for an oil refinery where the analog computers fed input to the digital computer and accepted output data from it.

## INPUT-STORAGE-PROCESSING-CONTROL-OUTPUT (ISPCO) CYCLE CONCEPT

Basic data processing functions were enumerated in Chapter 1 and were applied to a computer system. They comprise input-storage-processing-control-output, known as the ISPCO cycle (Figure 5-1). Applying these functions to the individual components of a digital computer system, the following relationships exist.

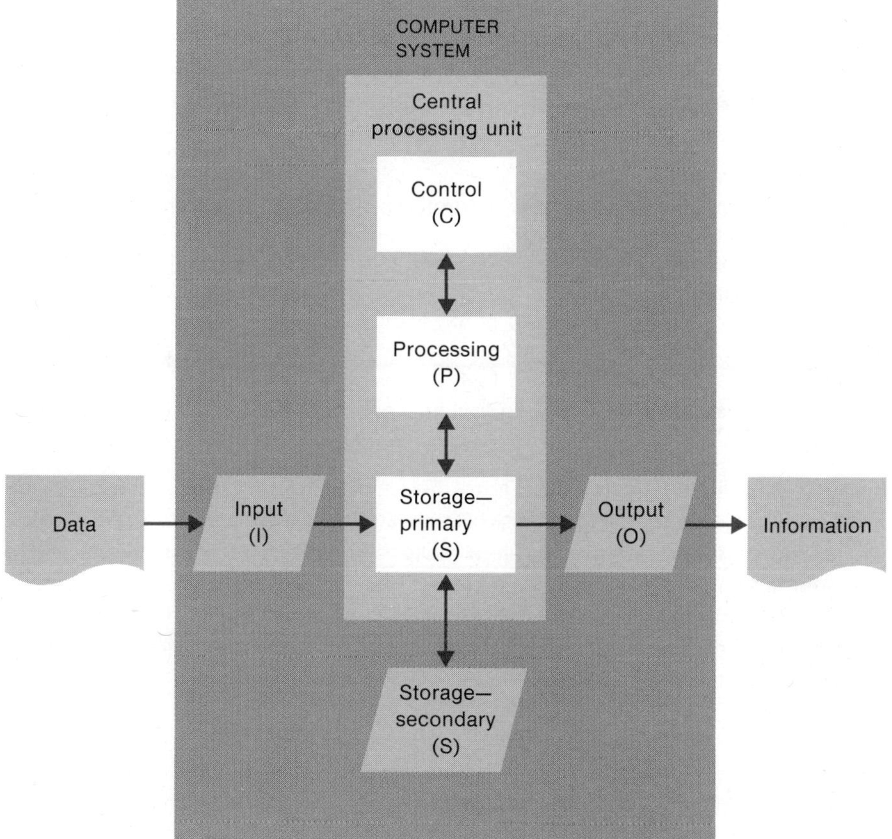


Figure 5-1 Input-storage-processing-control-output (ISPCO) cycle concept is a meaningful way of identifying the major components of a computer system.

*The ISPCO cycle concept is associated with the components of a computer system as follows:*

- *input—input devices*
- *storage—primary and secondary units*
- *processing—arithmetic/logical unit*
- *control—CPU control unit*
- *output—output devices*

1. INPUT data are read by various *input devices.*
2. STORAGE is available as high-speed, *primary storage* for storing program instructions and data or slower *secondary storage* for storing file data.
3. PROCESSING is accomplished through the *arithmetic/logical unit.*
4. CONTROL over processing is provided by the *CPU* (central processing unit) *control unit.*
5. OUTPUT information is produced by various *output devices* (recording and printing).

Each basic data processing function has one or more counterparts in a computer system. Basically, important information can be produced when accurate data are read into the computer system via input devices; processing is accomplished through the arithmetic/logical unit as determined by instructions and data in primary storage or memory; secondary storage or on-line files are properly interrogated; the computer is under the supervision of the central processor's control unit; and output information is presented in a usable format via output devices. These hardware components will be explained in subsequent sections of the chapter.

### ISPCO Cycle Concept Illustrated

Although digital computer systems vary in speed, size, and operating mode, they have the same basic components. Illustrated in Figure 5-2 is a small-scale computer system while a large-scale one is shown in Figure 5-3. Both systems utilize hardware that centers around input, storage, processing, control, and output. It should be noted that several of the computer devices serve several data processing functions, that is, magnetic tape and magnetic disk units serve as input, storage, and output devices (refer to Figure 5-3).

*Input-storage-processing-control-output units of a magnetic disk oriented computer system are illustrated in Figure 5-4.*

The input-storage-processing-control-output functions are applied to the individual hardware components in Figure 5-4. Each component performs an essential function and is as follows:

- *Input devices* convert instructions and data from man-readable code to machine-readable code.
- *Primary storage* (memory) stores instructions and data, and transfers them for use by the arithmetic/logical unit.
- *Secondary storage* (files) stores large amounts of data for on-line processing.
- *Arithmetic/logical unit* performs the necessary calculations and comparisons in response to signals from the CPU control unit.
- *CPU control unit* supervises and coordinates the computer system and data in accordance with the programmed instructions.
- *Output devices* convert processing results from machine-readable code to man-readable code.

The solid lines in the illustration (Figure 5-4) represent the flow of data and the dotted lines indicate the flow of control impulses by the CPU control unit.

Continuing advances of computers make it necessary to add more hardware components that take advantage of their fast internal operating speeds. Currently, control units (not the same as the CPU control unit), channels, and I/O interfaces are an integral part of many medium- and large-scale systems to speed up computer processing. Each will be explained later in the chapter.

## INPUT

If the computer is to produce information, data must be available in a form acceptable to its input devices. As was seen in the previous discussion on punched

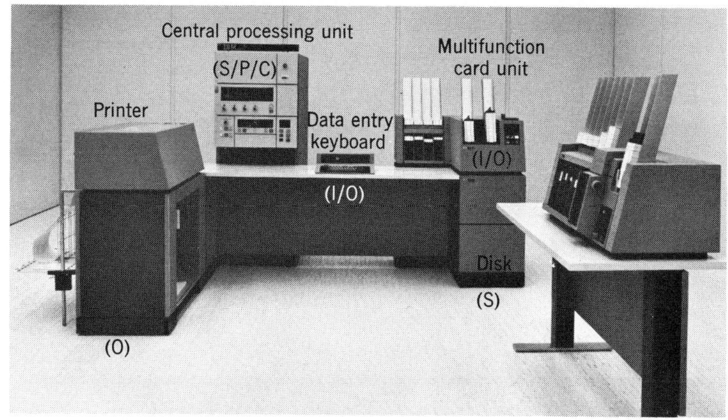


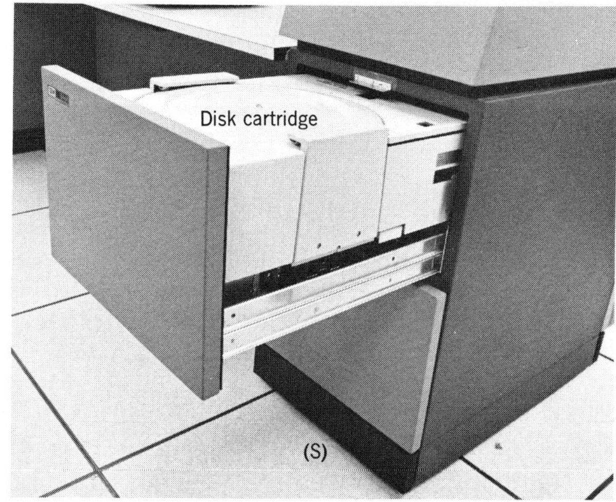


Figure 5-2 ISPCO cycle concept applied to the IBM System/3 Model 10—a small-scale computer system. (Courtesy International Business Machines Corporation.)

*Input data must be first converted from man-readable code to machine-readable code.*

card equipment, input data on cards are transformed into electrical pulses where different combinations of pulses represent different characters. These data can then be processed for some type of output. Much the same approach is utilized with computers. Most computer inputs are in a form that directly produces the pulse code itself. With such an input process, the data are converted immediately to a language that the computer understands. The overall input operation is thus speeded up immeasurably.

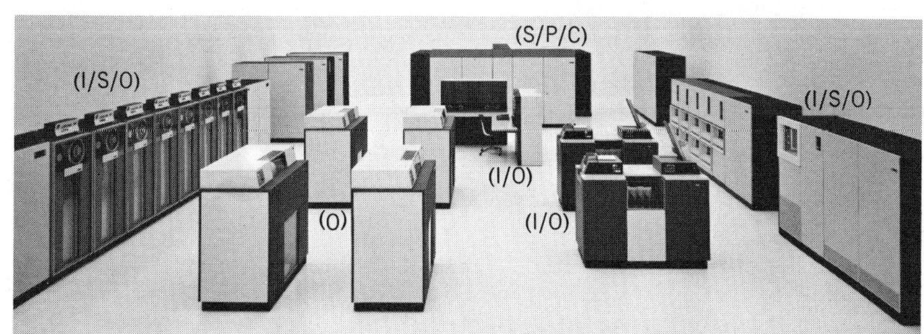


Figure 5-3 ISPCO cycle concept applied to the IBM System/370 series Model 165—a large-scale computer system. (Courtesy International Business Machines Corporation.)

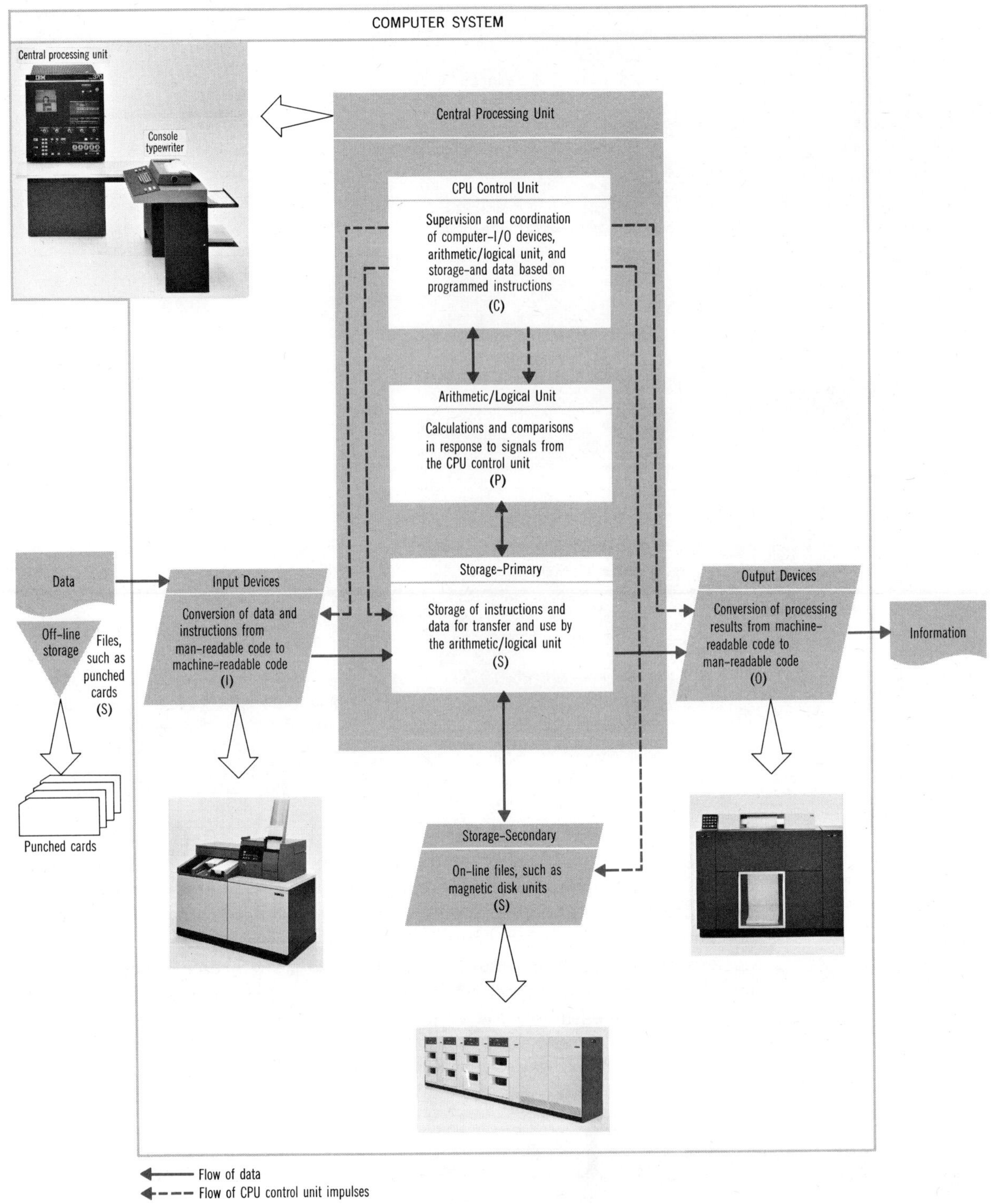


Figure 5-4 Input-storage-processing-control-output units of a magnetic disk-oriented computer system.

### Input Devices

*Input devices include:*
- *card readers*
- *paper tape readers*
- *magnetic tape units*
- *magnetic disk units*
- *communication devices*
- *time-sharing terminals*
- *optical scanning equipment*
- *CRT devices*
- *console typewriters*
- *human voice devices*

Among the various devices available for use as inputs to computers are: high-speed card readers, paper tape readers, magnetic tape units, magnetic disk units, communication devices, input/output terminals, optical scanning equipment, CRT (Cathode-Ray Tube) devices, console typewriters, and devices that accept instructions from the human voice. (All of these and other devices will be explained fully in Chapters 7 to 9). In a similar manner, there is always the provision for data to be entered into the system through console switches and buttons on the computer. Regardless of the input media, data must be converted into the machine's own language—a function of the computer itself.

*Input buffer storage holds data read in until needed by the program.*

***Buffer Storage.*** In order to speed up the slower units of input, manufacturers have developed additional hardware and software features on their equipment. For example, punched cards are a common method of input, but a relatively slow one for entering data into storage. Machine manufacturers have added temporary storage areas, referred to as buffer areas, to their input units. Their function is to store data temporarily that are read. Thus, when the computer is ready for data from a card, it is provided by the high-speed buffer rather than by the slow-speed card reader.

## STORAGE

*Storage consists of three types:*
- *primary (memory)*
- *secondary (files)*
- *off-line* files

The central processing unit (CPU) of a computer system is made of three distinct subunits. Residing within the central processor itself are primary storage or memory, the arithmetic/logical unit, and the CPU control unit, as shown in Figure 5-4. Data, read by input devices, are stored in primary storage until they are transferred for use by the arithmetic/logical unit under the direction of the CPU control unit.

Storage facilities of a computer system are not limited to primary storage only, but also include secondary and off-line storage. Primary storage (memory) and secondary storage (files) are both available for on-line processing while the third type is not under computer control. The first level of storage is smaller but much faster than secondary storage.

### Primary Storage (Memory)

*Primary storage holds the program instructions and data that will be executed by the arithmetic/logical unit.*

From the many input devices, information is entered into the memory of the machine, sometimes called primary storage, memory, or main storage, which is the information storage section. For all practical purposes, the computer's memory is analogous to the memory of a reference book. In order for the machine to recall information, it is necessary that it be told the location where the information is stored in memory. Most computer systems have at least 1000 storage locations where data are stored. It is necessary to identify each location with an *address* that is generally a four- or five-digit number.

*Storage locations can be identified as:*
- *words*
- *bytes*

***Storage Locations.*** The memory of the machine has many storage locations that are divided into cells. They are commonly referred to as so many *words* or *bytes* of storage. A word is a certain number of bytes or characters, depending on the computer system involved. (This material will be explained in the next chapter.) No matter what basis is used to describe storage capacity, memory location addresses generally start with zero and continue sequentially to the highest number in memory. For example, if the memory of the machine contains 10,000 ten-digit words (representing 100,000 digits of information), memory cells will be numbered from 0000 to 9999.

Primary storage operating speeds utilize measures, such as:
- milliseconds
- microseconds
- nanoseconds
- picoseconds

***Operating Speeds.*** Several types of storage systems have been developed and used over the years. Although they differ greatly in their mode of operation, their major differences are their speed. The magnetic drum memory operates in milliseconds (1 millisecond is 1/1000 of a second) while the magnetic core memory, even faster, is in the microsecond range (1 microsecond is 1/1,000,000 of a second). The operating time of thin film and some core memory is even faster. They are measured in nanoseconds (1 nanosecond is 1/1,000,000,000 of a second). The latest memory speeds are in the picosecond (1/1,000,000,000,000) range. The average time necessary for a computer to recall information from a single memory cell is called the *average access time* of the memory. As indicated, the average access time can be in milliseconds, microseconds, nanoseconds, or picoseconds.

*Destructive read-in and nondestructive read-out characteristics are found in most computer memory systems.*

***Special Characteristics.*** Most computer memory systems have the *destructive read-in* and *nondestructive read-out* characteristic. Data read into a storage location from an input device will erase their previous contents. On the other hand, when data are read out of a storage location, they are not erased. This unique feature enables the programmer to use the same piece of data several times within the program before moving onto the next record. To illustrate, a computer program for payroll requires that the gross pay be calculated and stored away for later use in the program. The gross pay calculation is needed again after legitimate deductions have been determined to arrive at net pay. This same figure is needed for totaling departmental figures and printing the amount on the payroll check and earnings statement.

*Two-level memory system is used to speed up internal processing.*

***Two-Level Memory System.*** In the IBM System/370 Model 165, for example, a two-level memory system is employed. It consists of a fast, large-size processor (main) storage used as backup storage for a smaller, very high speed buffer storage. The central processing unit works mostly with the buffer so that the effective access time for data is reduced to a fraction of the processor storage cycle time. Operating at 80 nanoseconds, the time-saving buffer sharply reduces the number of times data have to travel between the central processing unit and main storage.

### Secondary Storage (Files)

*Secondary storage data must be first brought into primary storage before processing can take place. It consists of:*
- *sequential access files*
- *direct access files*

One feature of computer data processing is the ability to reference files of information under machine control. This secondary storage is contained in separate storage devices that are available upon demand to the computer's CPU. These reference files are actually a type of memory, but must be distinguished from the main memory set forth previously. In general, file memory is considerably larger than main memory while its average access time is slower than the memory attached to the central processing unit. Also, information in the file memory cannot be processed without bringing it first into main storage. In this regard, file memory is an input device and can be segregated into two basic types, namely, *sequential* and *direct access* devices.

*Magnetic tape is used widely as sequential file devices*

***Sequential File Devices.*** The sequential file device is one in which all data are in some logical order—numeric, alphabetic, or some other combination. Generally, magnetic tape is utilized as sequential file devices since it has the advantage of low cost and almost unlimited capacity.

*Magnetic disk is used widely as direct access file devices*

***Direct Access File Devices.*** A direct access device has one distinguishing characteristic. It has the ability to skip around within the file in order to extract information without regard to sequence. Large volumes of data can be handled by magnetic drums, magnetic disks, and magnetic card file devices. They range in capacity from a few hundred thousand characters for magnetic drum to billions of characters of storage for the magnetic card device. Their average access time ranges in milliseconds for magnetic drums to about one-eighth second for magnetic card. For a fast file memory system, without regard to the high cost, the magnetic drum is the best approach. If the firm needs low cost, massive storage without the need for fast external files, the magnetic card device may be the answer. In effect, the determination of the appropriate file device will depend on the environmental factors of the computer system.

### Off-Line Storage

*Off-line storage is not connected to or directly usable by the computer.*

While primary storage is contained in the central processing unit itself, secondary storage is contained in separate devices outside the CPU. It is available on demand when requested by the CPU control unit. In addition to primary and secondary storage, there is a third type called off-line storage. This third category is not connected to or directly usable by the computer, on-line. Off-line storage data may or may not be in a machine-acceptable form, depending on the system's requirements. Magnetic disk packs, magnetic tapes, and punched cards are examples of off-line storage.

## PROCESSING

*Internal computer processing is accomplished by the arithmetic/logical unit.*

Data are entered from input devices and files into the computer's memory. They are ready to be manipulated by performing the appropriate arithmetic and logical operations. This is accomplished by the arithmetic/logical unit.

### Arithmetic/Logical Unit

*The arithmetic/logical unit calculates and compares data per program instructions that are in response to signals from the CPU control unit.*

The arithmetic section of this combination unit performs the normal operations of addition, subtraction, multiplication, and division. Also, the arithmetic section has the capacity to shift data to the right or left, compare the size or sign of data, and store or transfer data. These operations, performed in the arithmetic section of the central processing unit, occur one at a time with intermediate results being stored in the computer's memory.

*Logical tests center around determining whether one number is larger than, equal to, or less than another number.*

***Logical Tests.*** The logical part of this combined unit provides the machine's ability to test for various conditions under control of the program. Based on the processing procedures, it may be necessary to take a specific action as the result of the test. One test might be to determine whether one number is larger than, equal to, or less than another number. The next step in the program would be to execute the instructions for the specific path taken in the comparison test.

Since the arithmetic/logical unit is an integral part of the computer's hardware, there is little need to understand the electrical and engineering principles that cause this unit to operate. However, in the next chapter, the fundamentals of how the computer's hardware operates using Boolean algebra (truth tables) will be set forth. Also, the arithmetic unit will be related to the operations of the program register in order to demonstrate how a computer executes program instructions.

## CONTROL

*Control is necessary within a computer system in order to supervise and coordinate its many operations.*

Information is read from the input devices into memory where it can be combined with file information and manipulated by using the arithmetic/logical unit. The results, then, are produced by output devices. These operations in themselves, shown in Figure 5-4, are not complete. There is need for a *control unit* within the central processing unit that instructs the various components of the computer as to what is to be done and in what sequence. In essence, the control unit is the brain of the computer's components. It operates under the direction of program instructions, stored in memory.

### CPU Control Unit

*The CPU control unit instructs the I/O devices, arithmetic/logical unit, and storage (primary and secondary) what is to be done and in what sequence.*

The CPU control unit instructs the input devices concerning what data to read into memory and when to do it; it finds the information in the file and stores it in memory; it instructs the arithmetic/logical unit about what operations to perform, where the data are located in memory, and where the results are to be stored; and lastly, it tells the output devices what information is to be printed, punched, and the like. All of these operations are accomplished through the stored program.

*The computer console is the "face" of the CPU control unit.*

***Located in Central Processing Unit.*** The control unit is located in the central processing unit. For most computers, the computer console is the "face" of the control unit. It has many control knobs and lights that flash off and on as computer processing takes place. The many flashing lights have little function except to indicate the computer is operating. There are a few important lights that the operator should watch occasionally to insure that the computer is working properly. If trouble does develop, he may use some of them to help diagnose the problem. Shown in Figure 5-5 is the computer console for a large-scale computer.

Regardless of the size of the computer system, the console should be used only when necessary. Otherwise, the speed and accuracy of the computer will be

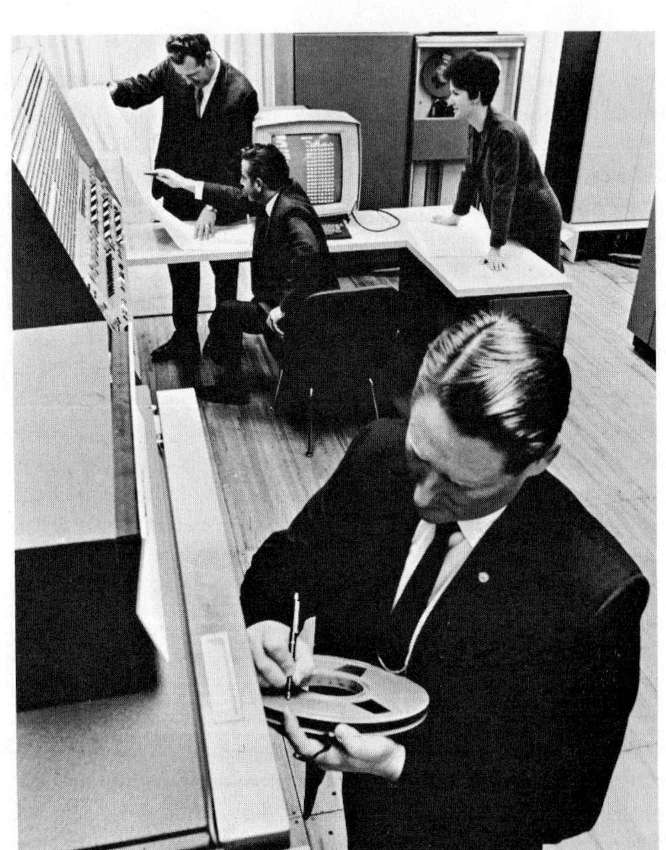

Figure 5-5 IBM 360/195 computer console with CRT station (main interface with the system). (Courtesy International Business Machines Corporation.)

lost when the computer is stopped for some type of manual entry. If the computer program has been properly written and tested, the control unit takes over the internal processing of data so output can be processed. There should be no need to utilize the computer console except to handle extraneous problems that develop during processing, such as equipment malfunctions, incorrect sequence of input data, or a wrong magnetic tape on a tape drive.

## OUTPUT

*Output data must be converted from machine-readable code to man-readable code.*

Once the data have been processed, it is necessary to communicate this information externally to the user in the form of output. The type of output device employed will depend on the information desired.

### Output Devices

*Output devices include:*
- *card punches*
- *paper tape punches*
- *high-speed printers*
- *magnetic tape units*
- *magnetic disk units*
- *communication devices*
- *time-sharing devices*
- *CRT devices*
- *console typewriters*

Some of the input devices mentioned previously—magnetic tape units, magnetic disk units, communication devices, input/output terminals, CRT devices, and console typewriters—can be used for output. In addition, card punches, paper tape punches, and high-speed printers serve as output devices. Output can also be in the form of electrical impulses that are used to direct other computers. The speed of these devices vary, the slowest being the electric typewriter and the fastest being the magnetic disk. Some of the output information can be used as it is, processed further on auxiliary equipment, or reentered into the same machine or compatible machine(s) for further processing.

Although the same equipment can be used for both input and output, both operations are separate and distinct from one another. The data read into memory may lose their tie with input since the data can be manipulated. Within the computer program, the input values may be changed, eliminated, or left as they were. For example, an inventory updating run might specify a beginning inventory figure for each item in inventory. After a computer updating run, the inventory item identification numbers will remain constant although the number of units available for shipment will change or remain the same, depending on the additions, deletions, and adjustments to inventory.

## ISPCO CYCLE CONCEPT APPLIED TO INVENTORY

*The ISPCO cycle concept, as applied to a weekly inventory program, is illustrated in Figure 5-6.*

The preceding discussion of the ISPCO cycle concept is applicable to any computer system. For example, consider a weekly inventory updating program that reads in weekly inventory cards and produces a weekly inventory report. Receipt, shipment, and adjustment cards for the week are fed into the high-speed card reader and are read into primary storage, one at a time, after the computer program has been previously read in. The arithmetic/logical unit executes program instructions in accordance with data extracted from primary storage. It adds weekly receipts to the balance from the previous week which has been read from secondary storage or magnetic tape. Likewise, the arithmetic/logical unit deducts shipments and adjusts for corrections to inventory. The new updated balance is written onto magnetic tape and the data are edited before being printed. All of these operations are under the supervision of the CPU control unit.

The computer system configuration to produce this weekly inventory report is illustrated in Figure 5-6. It consists of the central processing unit with an attached console typewriter, a high-speed card reader, magnetic tape units, and a high-speed

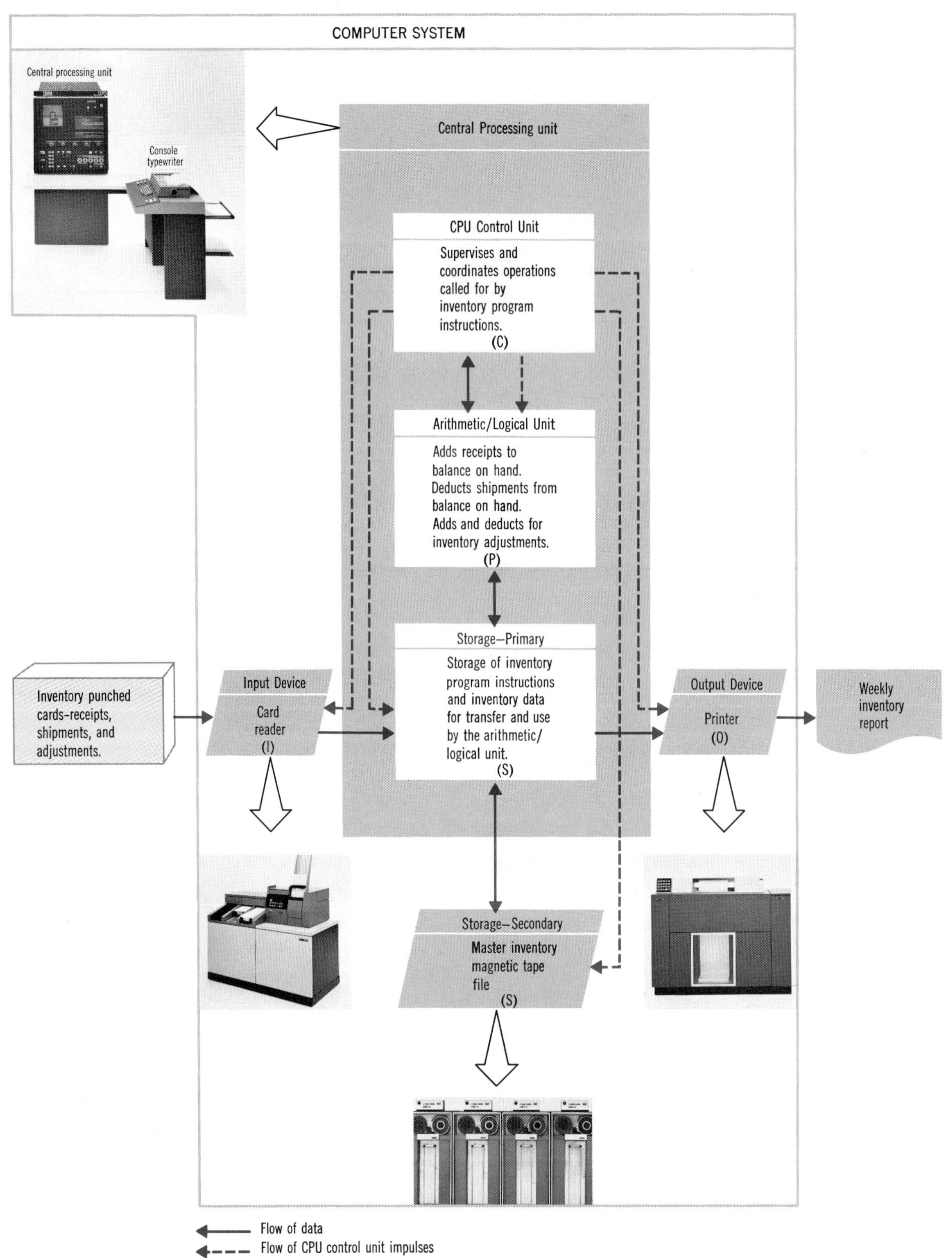


Figure 5-6 Computer system configuration of input-storage-processing-control-output units needed to process a weekly inventory updating program.

printer. Although additional computer components might be available, these are the requirements for processing the weekly inventory updating program.

## OTHER COMPUTER COMPONENTS

*Other important computer components are:*
- *control units*
- *channels*
- *I/O interface*

Computer input, storage, processing, control, and storage devices can be supplemented by other components for faster throughput performance. For example, the organization of a large-scale IBM System/360 Model 85, shown in Figure 5-7 (b), makes use of control units (not the same as the CPU control unit in Figure 5-6), channels, and an I/O (input/output) interface for controlling the computer's basic components. In addition, these systems have self-supervision capabilities, resulting in an interruption system that operates in conjunction with a control program. With the current IBM System/370 series, several refinements have been made to channels. Because of the importance of these advances in computer systems over the past several years, the functions of control units, channels, and I/O interface are discussed in the following sections. Likewise, reference will be made to the interruption system and control program.

### Control Units

*Control units provide the logic circuitry and the storage areas (buffers) to operate several attached I/O devices.*

An examination of Figure 5-7 reveals several control units that are not an integral part of the CPU per se. Control units provide the logic circuitry and the storage areas (buffers) needed to operate attached input/output devices. However, most control unit functions cannot be distinguished from I/O functions by the user.

A control unit may be a *single-path,* a *shared-path,* or a *multipath*. A single-path unit, usually integrated as part of an input/output device, controls only one device. Both shared-path and multipath units are capable of controlling more than one device and are usually stand-alone units (Figure 5-7). They differ in that a multipath unit permits several I/O devices to transfer data concurrently, whereas the shared-path unit does not.

### Channels

*Channels relieve the central processing unit of communicating directly with the various I/O devices, and are of two types:*
- *selector*
- *multiplexor*

The IBM System/360 series have two major types of channels—selector and multiplexor—which are the direct controllers of input/output devices and control units (Figure 5-7). They provide the system with the ability to read, write, and compute, all at the same time, by relieving the central processing unit of communicating directly with the I/O devices. Channels may be stand-alone units, complete with the necessary logical and storage capabilities, or they may time-share central processing facilities and be physically integrated with the central processing unit. In either case, the channel functions are identical.

*Selector channels are used primarily to control high-speed I/O devices.*

***Selector Channels.*** The selector channel (first type) is used primarily to control high-speed input/output devices, such as magnetic tape units and disk storage units. Selector channels can also handle lower speed I/O devices, but their burst-mode operation makes them especially suitable for high-speed devices. While operating in the burst mode, a single input/output device captures the channel and does not relinquish it from the time the device is selected until the last segment of data is serviced. In general, input/output operations on a selector channel are overlapped with processing. All channels can operate simultaneously, provided that the processing unit's data rate capabilities are not exceeded. Each selector channel attaches up to 8 I/O control units and can address as many as 256 input/output devices.

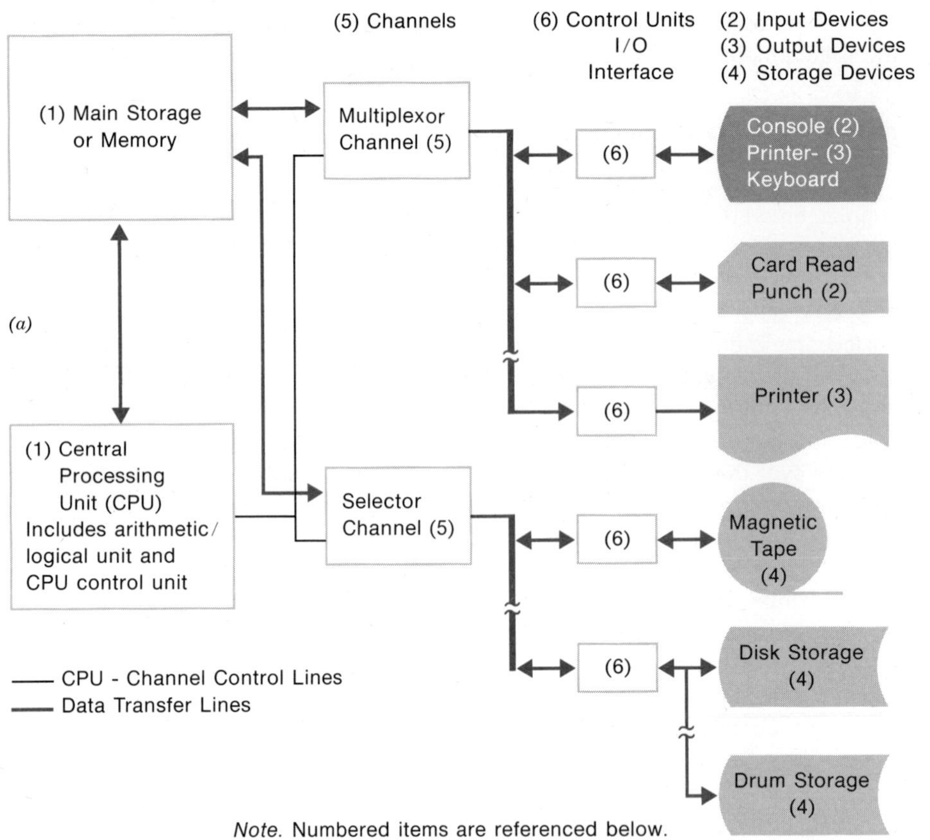


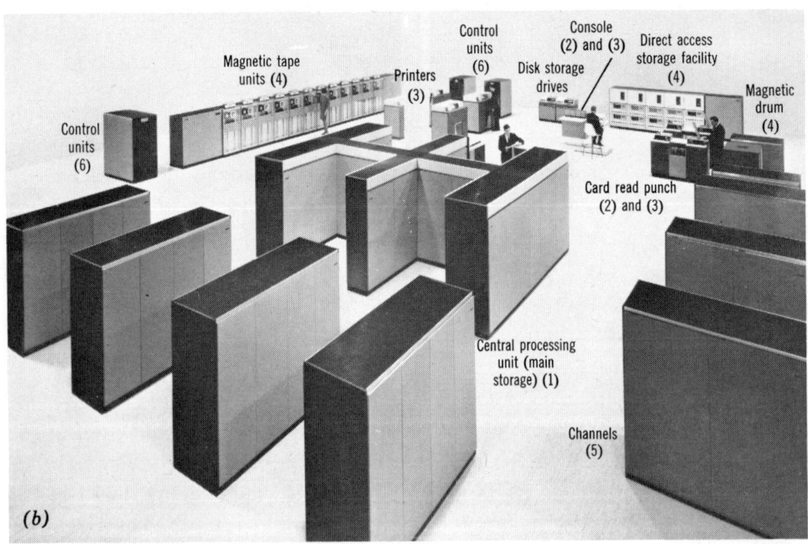


Figure 5-7 (*a*) Organization of a representative System/360 model or System/370 model with minor refinements, particularly channels, and (*b*) comparable units for the System/360 Model 85 (*b*). (Courtesy International Business Machines Corporation.)

*Multiplexor channels are used primarily to control lower speed I/O devices.*

***Multiplexor Channels.*** The multiplexor channel (second type) separates the operations of high-speed devices from those of lower speed devices. Operations of the channel are in two modes: multiplex mode for lower data rates, such as communication terminals, printers, and punched card devices, and burst mode for the higher data rates. In the multiplex mode, the single data path of the channel can be shared by a large number of low-speed input/output devices operating simultaneously. The channel receives and sends data to them on demand. This sharing has the effect of subdividing the data path into many *subchannels*. To a programmer, each subchannel is a separate channel and can be programmed as such.

Available channels in the current IBM System/370 Model 155, for example, include the *byte multiplexor* and the *block multiplexor*. The byte multiplexor channel is functionally identical with the one available on a comparable System/360 model. The block multiplexor channels are supersets of selector channels. They increase system throughput by permitting more data to enter and leave the system in a given period of time.

### I/O Interface

*I/O interface provides a method of attaching I/O devices through control units to channels.*

The foregoing channels and control units operate through the I/O interface which provides the system with a uniform method of attaching many different input/output devices. Both the channels and the I/O interface facilitate the attachment of various I/O devices (through control units), thereby making the system adaptable to a wide range of present and future devices and applications. To understand the usefulness of the I/O interface, the IBM System/360 and System/370 operate in the following manner (refer to Figure 5-7). An input/output operation transfers data between main storage and an I/O device. An input/output operation is initiated by a program instruction that generates a command to a channel. A control unit receives the command via the I/O interface, decodes it, and starts the I/O device. It should be noted that the information format and the control signal sequences provided by the interface are independent of the type of control unit and channel.

Both the IBM System/360 and 370 have self-supervision capabilities. This is due primarily to the interruption system and to the control programs. The interruption system permits the central processing unit to: (1) quickly change its state as a result of conditions in the central processing unit itself, in the input/output units, or external to the system; (2) identify the type of interruption; (3) store the current status information to permit later resetting of the status that the central processing unit had before the interruption.

The interruption system operates in conjunction with a control program. Most models are designed to operate with a control program. With a control program, data and programs processed are systematically organized, identified, stored, and retrieved. A continuous series of jobs can be performed with little or no operator intervention. Several data processing tasks can be performed concurrently, thereby increasing the total throughput.

## SUMMARY

This chapter has explored the inner workings of a digital computer system as they relate to the ISPCO cycle concept. In a computer system, the following operations occur.

- *Input* data are read by various input devices.
- *Storage* is available as high-speed, primary storage for holding program instructions and data or slower secondary storage for storing on-line file data.
- *Processing* is accomplished through the arithmetic/logical unit as determined by instructions and data in primary storage.
- *Control* over operations is provided by the CPU control unit.
- *Output* information is produced by various output devices.

The input-storage-processing-control-output cycle is augmented by additional hardware in more advanced computer systems. Control units, channels, and I/O interface devices are commonly found. Control units provide logic circuitry and the buffers necessary to operate the attached I/O devices; channels relieve the central processing unit of the direct handling of input/output operations; and the I/O interface provides a uniform method of attaching input/output devices through control units to channels. Their purpose is to increase internal operating speeds, thereby, speeding up the computer's throughput performance.

## *QUESTIONS*

1. What are the essential differences between analog and digital computers?
2. (a) Describe the function of each basic computer component.
   (b) Relate each basic component to the ISPCO cycle concept.
3. What is meant by the stored program concept?
4. Where are the arithmetic/logical unit, primary storage or memory, and CPU control unit located? Why?
5. Distinguish between primary storage and secondary storage of computer systems.
6. Specify the various types of files that are associated with a computer system.
7. (a) What activities are directed and coordinated by the CPU control unit?
   (b) What is the difference between the CPU control unit and control units?
8. What is the function of a multiplexor channel?
9. What is the function of the I/O interface?

## *EXERCISES*

1. Explain what functions are performed by the input, storage, processing, control, and output units of an accounts receivable program that operates in a batch processing mode. Magnetic tape units are used for secondary storage where the old and new master accounts receivable files are read and written respectively. Input cards include charges on account, payments on account, and adjustments to the various accounts.
2. Explain what functions are performed by the input, storage, processing, control, and output units of a monthly sales listing program. Individual sales transactions are stored on magnetic disk. The output desired is a monthly sales journal of all sales transactions.

# CHAPTER SIX

# Internal Operating Concepts of Computers

*The ability of any computer to convert data from one coding system to another makes it possible to enter alphanumeric data and receive it back in the same code. (Courtesy International Business Machines Corporation.)*

The internal operating concepts of computers, which are a logical continuation of the ISPCO cycle concept, are covered in this chapter. Initially, computer data codes are developed for past and present computer generations, followed by an explanation of the computer's logic. The stored program concept for a fixed-word length, a variable-word length, and a byte-addressable combination computer are set forth. Machine language instructions, as executed by the computer's arithmetic/logic unit, focuses on how a computer actually operates. The chapter concludes with a discussion of computer advantages and its basic limitations.

## COMPUTER DATA CODES

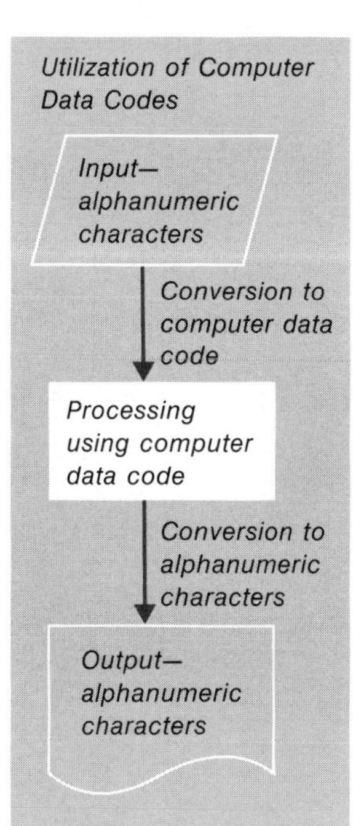


Data input and output for computer processing consists of the decimal number system, 26 alphabetic characters, and special characters. The same cannot be said for computations and manipulations that are made internally by the computer. Instead, data are represented by a special computer notation. Depending upon the design of the machine by the manufacturer's engineers, the computer data code can be any type system, the common ones being the binary and the binary coded decimal.

The computer data code systems are based upon an absolute value and a positional value. The radix or the base of the system determines how many absolute values are a part of that system. The positional values are found for the specific system by raising the base to the power of the position. These basic concepts of a number system will be illustrated below.

### Decimal Code

*Decimal system has a base or radix of 10 (0 through 9).*

The decimal coding system has 10 absolute values—0 through 9, indicating a system with a base or radix of 10. Once these 10 values have been used, it would be impossible to go any further without inventing more values if it were not for positional notation. The process of counting higher than 9 is obtained by moving one position to the left, writing down the number 1, and beginning all over again with the digits 0 through 9. Each time all possible combinations of values have been used, notation takes place again by moving one position to the left. For example, when the number 156 is written, the digits 1, 5, and 6 are written in sequence. This is actually shorthand notation for one times ten to the second power, $1 \times (10)^2$, plus five times ten to the first power, $5 \times (10)^1$, and plus six times ten to the zero power, $6 \times (10)^0$. Expressing the foregoing statement mathematically, the results are:

$$1(10)^2 + 5(10)^1 + 6(10)^0 = 156$$
$$(1 \times 10 \times 10) + (5 \times 10) + (6 \times 1) = 156$$
$$100 + 50 + 6 = 156$$

(Any number raised to the zero power equals 1)

In essence, as each place to the left is taken (positional notation), the digits are multiplied by increasing powers of 10 in order to find the actual value. If the number had included three values to the right of the decimal point, the first digit to the right (of the decimal point) would be multiplied by $10^{-1}$, the second digit by $10^{-2}$, and the third digit by $10^{-3}$.

***Decimal Positional Values.*** As stated previously, the base or radix of the decimal system is 10. Several of the positional values found in the base 10 system are found in Figure 6-1. The positive values are positioned to the left of the decimal point

| Position number | 4 | 3 | 2 | 1 | 0 | . | −1 | −2 | −3 | −4 |
|---|---|---|---|---|---|---|---|---|---|---|
| Base 10 position value | $10^4$ | $10^3$ | $10^2$ | $10^1$ | $10^0$ | . | $10^{-1}$ | $10^{-2}$ | $10^{-3}$ | $10^{-4}$ |
| Amount represented by position value | 10,000 | 1,000 | 100 | 10 | 1 | . decimal point | 1/10 | 1/100 | 1/1,000 | 1/10,000 |

Figure 6-1 Selected positional values in the decimal system.

and negative amounts to the right of the decimal. It should be obvious that this table of positional values was utilized in determining the above value, 156.

### Binary Code

*Binary system has a base or radix of 2 (0 and 1).*

One of the most widely used coding systems is the binary system. It has 2 as its base as opposed to 5 for the quinary system, 8 for the octal system, 10 for the decimal system, and 16 for the hexadecimal system. Although the binary system is comparable to the decimal system, the only two digits employed are 0 and 1. Thus the base of the binary system is 2 since only two symbols are utilized. Previously, the value 156 was used in explaining the decimal system. The same number, expressed in binary notation, is 10011100. Working out the value mathematically, the binary configuration is as follows:

$$1(2)^7 + 0(2)^6 + 0(2)^5 + 1(2)^4 + 1(2)^3 + 1(2)^2 + 0(2)^1 + 0(2)^0 = 156$$
$$128 + 0 + 0 + 16 + 8 + 4 + 0 + 0 = 156$$

Hence, the binary number 10011100 has a decimal equivalent of 156.

***Binary Positional Values.*** The concepts of absolute value and positional value are applicable to the binary system as they are to the decimal system. This should have been apparent in the above example. A comparison of decimal and binary numbers for 0 through 31 is given in Figure 6-2. These values plus more of the positional values in the binary system are depicted in Figure 6-3. The values of the binary bit are often called the "0 bit" and the "1 bit." In a similar manner, these two binary values can mean a "no bit," described by the 0 state, and the "bit," described by the 1 condition.

| DECIMAL | BINARY 16 | 8 | 4 | 2 | 1 |
|---|---|---|---|---|---|
| 0 | | 0 | 0 | 0 | 0 |
| 1 | | 0 | 0 | 0 | 1 |
| 2 | | 0 | 0 | 1 | 0 |
| 3 | | 0 | 0 | 1 | 1 |
| 4 | | 0 | 1 | 0 | 0 |
| 5 | | 0 | 1 | 0 | 1 |
| 6 | | 0 | 1 | 1 | 0 |
| 7 | | 0 | 1 | 1 | 1 |
| 8 | | 1 | 0 | 0 | 0 |
| 9 | | 1 | 0 | 0 | 1 |
| 10 | | 1 | 0 | 1 | 0 |
| 11 | | 1 | 0 | 1 | 1 |
| 12 | | 1 | 1 | 0 | 0 |
| 13 | | 1 | 1 | 0 | 1 |
| 14 | | 1 | 1 | 1 | 0 |
| 15 | | 1 | 1 | 1 | 1 |
| 16 | 1 | 0 | 0 | 0 | 0 |
| 17 | 1 | 0 | 0 | 0 | 1 |
| 18 | 1 | 0 | 0 | 1 | 0 |
| 19 | 1 | 0 | 0 | 1 | 1 |
| 20 | 1 | 0 | 1 | 0 | 0 |
| 21 | 1 | 0 | 1 | 0 | 1 |
| 22 | 1 | 0 | 1 | 1 | 0 |
| 23 | 1 | 0 | 1 | 1 | 1 |
| 24 | 1 | 1 | 0 | 0 | 0 |
| 25 | 1 | 1 | 0 | 0 | 1 |
| 26 | 1 | 1 | 0 | 1 | 0 |
| 27 | 1 | 1 | 0 | 1 | 1 |
| 28 | 1 | 1 | 1 | 0 | 0 |
| 29 | 1 | 1 | 1 | 0 | 1 |
| 30 | 1 | 1 | 1 | 1 | 0 |
| 31 | 1 | 1 | 1 | 1 | 1 |

Figure 6-2 Comparison of decimal and binary numbers, 0 through 31.

Arithmetic computations are performed with binary numbers following the same basic rules as for the decimal system. The only real difference is that the binary system requires more frequent carries since there is need for a carry to the next column every time the total exceeds one. This is in contrast to the decimal system where a carry to the next column is required whenever the total is greater than nine.

| Position number | 8 | 7 | 6 | 5 | 4 | 3 | 2 | 1 | 0 | . | −1 | −2 | −3 | −4 | −5 | −6 | −7 | −8 |
|---|---|---|---|---|---|---|---|---|---|---|---|---|---|---|---|---|---|---|
| Base 2 position value | $2^8$ | $2^7$ | $2^6$ | $2^5$ | $2^4$ | $2^3$ | $2^2$ | $2^1$ | $2^0$ | . | $2^{-1}$ | $2^{-2}$ | $2^{-3}$ | $2^{-4}$ | $2^{-5}$ | $2^{-6}$ | $2^{-7}$ | $2^{-8}$ |
| Amount represented by position value | 256 | 128 | 64 | 32 | 16 | 8 | 4 | 2 | 1 | . binary point | 1/2 | 1/4 | 1/8 | 1/16 | 1/32 | 1/64 | 1/128 | 1/256 |

Figure 6-3 Selected positional values in the binary system.

***Binary Addition.*** Binary addition is carried out in much the same manner as decimal addition. The difference is that this arithmetic calculation consists of four rules:

$$0 + 0 = 0$$
$$0 + 1 = 1$$
$$1 + 0 = 1$$
$$1 + 1 = 0 \quad \text{with a carry of 1}$$

*Binary addition is similar to decimal addition, except that it requires more frequent carries.*

Examples of addition in the decimal and binary systems are:

| *Decimal* | *Binary* | *Decimal* | *Binary* |
|---|---|---|---|
| 4 | 100 | 18 | 10010 |
| +3 | + 11 | +11 | + 1011 |
| 7 | 111 | 29 | 11101 |

The values for the binary system have been taken from Figure 6-2.

*Binary subtraction reverses the rules of binary addition.*

***Binary Subtraction.*** Binary subtraction is similar to binary addition except that the procedures are reversed. Instead of using a method by which one digit can be carried, it becomes necessary to subtract a larger digit from a smaller one. In binary subtraction, this can occur only when 1 is subtracted from 0. It is therefore required to borrow a 1 from the next position to the left and the remainder is 1. The rules for binary subtraction are:

$$0 - 0 = 0$$
$$0 - 1 = 1 \quad \text{with a borrow of 1}$$
$$1 - 0 = 1$$
$$1 - 1 = 0$$

Comparative examples for the decimal and binary systems are:

| *Decimal* | *Binary* | *Decimal* | *Binary* |
|---|---|---|---|
| 10 | 1010 | 25 | 11001 |
| − 6 | − 110 | −12 | − 1100 |
| 4 | 100 | 13 | 1101 |

***Complement Method (Subtraction).*** Internal computer operations generally perform subtraction by the complement method. The 1's complement of the subtrahend in a binary number is formed by changing all 1's to 0's and all 0's to 1's. The complement can then be added to the minuend using the addition logic circuit. After the addition, the higher order digit must be "carried around" and added to the low order digit to produce the correct answer.

An example of subtraction using the 1's complement is:

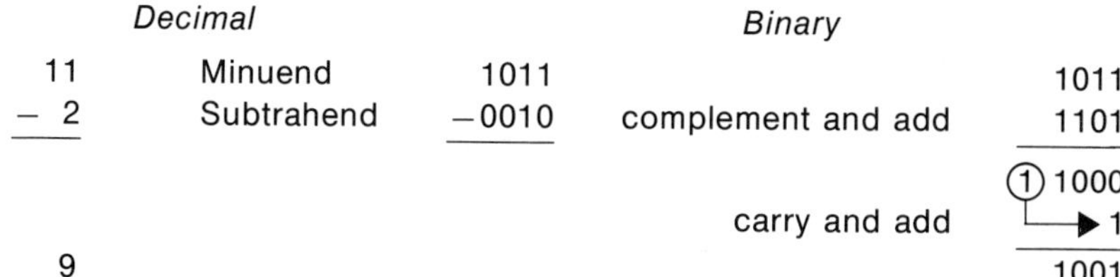

Decimal
Binary
11
Minuend
1011
1011
− 2
Subtrahend
−0010
complement and add
1101
1 1000
carry and add
1
9
1001


If the high-order digit is a zero, the result must be recomplemented (complement again) and a minus sign attached.

| Decimal | | Binary | |
|---|---|---|---|
| 11 | 1011 | | 1011 |
| −12 | −1100 | complement and add | 0011 |
| | | | (0) 1110 |
| | | add | → 0 |
| | | | 1110 |
| −1 | | recomplement | −0001 |

The 2's complement is another method used for subtraction. The 2's complement of a binary number is the 1's complement plus 1. When the 2's complement technique is used, the "end around carry" is unnecessary, but recomplementing is still necessary if the high order digit is zero.

An example of subtraction using the 2's complement is:

| Decimal | Binary | | |
|---|---|---|---|
| 11 | 1011 | | 1011 |
| − 5 | −0101 | complement and add 1 | 1011 |
| | | | 10110 |
| 6 | | | 0110 |

*Binary multiplication is performed by a series of binary additions.*

***Binary Multiplication.*** Binary multiplication is relatively simple because it is a matter of addition. Basically, the procedure is to write down 0's if the multiplier digit is 0 and copy the multiplicand if the multiplier digit is 1 and add these values using binary addition. The rules for binary multiplication, then, are:

$$0 \times 0 = 0$$
$$0 \times 1 = 0$$
$$1 \times 0 = 0$$
$$1 \times 1 = 1$$

Illustrations of the two systems are given below for multiplication:

| Decimal | Binary | Decimal | Binary | |
|---|---|---|---|---|
| | 1001 | 13 | 1101 | Multiplicand |
| | ×11 | ×12 | ×1100 | Multiplier |
| 9 | 1001 | 26 | 110100 | |
| ×3 | 1001 | 13 | 1101 | |
| 27 | 11011 | 156 | 10011100 | |

*Binary division employs the rules of binary subtraction and multiplication.*

***Binary Division.*** Binary division is comparable to division in the decimal system, except that the rules for binary subtraction and multiplication must be applied. The two rules for division are:

$$0 \div 1 = 0$$
$$1 \div 1 = 1$$

Examples of division in the decimal and binary systems are:

```
Decimal      Binary          Decimal      Binary
    4            100             12              1100
 6|24     110|11000         13|156      1101|10011100
   24           110              13             1101
   --           ---              --             ----
    0             0              26              1101
                                 26              1101
                                 --              ----
                                  0                 0
```

***Decimal to Binary Conversion.*** The decimal to binary conversion can be accomplished by taking the decimal number, dividing it by two each time, and writing the remainders each time until there is nothing left to divide. The binary answer is given by reading the remainders, starting with the bottom figure. Examples of these procedures are given below.

| *Decimal* | *Binary* |
|---|---|
| 31/2 = | 15 with a remainder of 1 |
| 15/2 = | 7 with a remainder of 1 |
| 7/2 = | 3 with a remainder of 1 |
| 3/2 = | 1 with a remainder of 1 |
| 1/2 = | 0 with a remainder of 1 |

| *Decimal* | *Binary* |
|---|---|
| 72/2 = | 36 with a remainder of 0 |
| 36/2 = | 18 with a remainder of 0 |
| 18/2 = | 9 with a remainder of 0 |
| 9/2 = | 4 with a remainder of 1 |
| 4/2 = | 2 with a remainder of 0 |
| 2/2 = | 0 with a remainder of 0 |
| 0/2 = | 0 with a remainder of 1 |

The binary equivalents for 31 and 72 are 11111 and 1001000 respectively. All binary values are read from bottom to top.

***Binary to Decimal Conversion.*** The binary to decimal conversion is accomplished by multiplying the higher order digit of the number by its base (2), adding the next digit to the product, and multiplying the sum by the base (2). This process is continued until the low-order digit has been added. Two examples are shown at left for binary to decimal conversion.

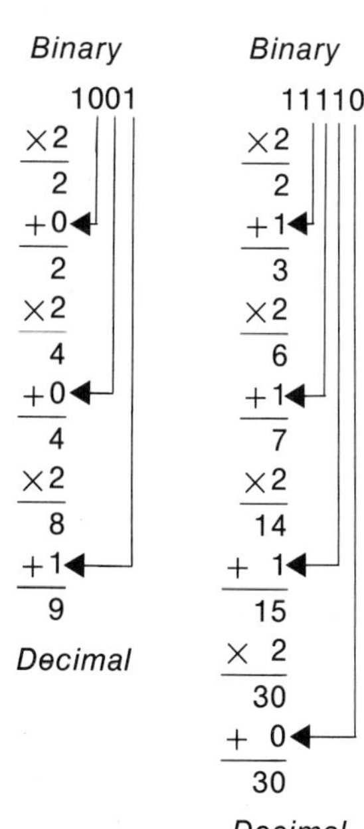


## Binary Coded Decimal

When the binary system is utilized, it represents two basic conditions: either 1 or 0, on or off, something or the absence of something. In the prior section, a numerical value was represented by a group of 1's and 0's. By using only four positions of place values—8, 4, 2, and 1—the decimal digits 0 through 9 can be represented. Going one step further, if this group of four-bit values are assigned units, tens, hundreds, thousands, and the like, any decimal number can be expressed. This extension of the binary system whereby a four-bit set can be used for each decimal digit is called the binary coded decimal (BCD). A comparison of the binary and BCD system for two values (53 and 163) is illustrated in Figure 6-4.

The binary coded decimal simplifies the task of programming business problems on the computer. This method provides fast conversion from and to decimal form for input/output conversion. However, this usually occurs at the expense of internal operating speeds within the central processor. It should be remembered that commercial applications typically involve very little manipulation for each record processed. This is in contrast to the straight binary computer where internal computational speeds are faster than with the binary coded decimal. Generally, the regular binary system is used in scientific computers where the accent is on fast internal

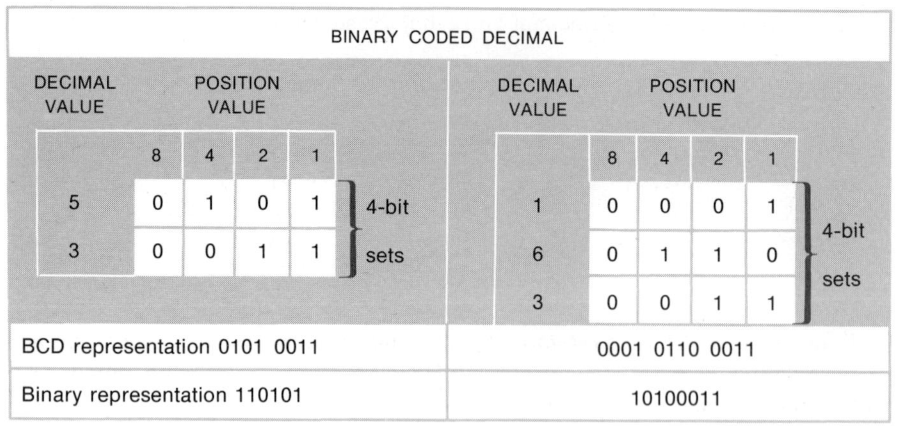

BINARY CODED DECIMAL
DECIMAL VALUE
POSITION VALUE
8 4 2 1
5 0 1 0 1
3 0 0 1 1
4-bit sets
DECIMAL VALUE
POSITION VALUE
8 4 2 1
1 0 0 0 1
6 0 1 1 0
3 0 0 1 1
4-bit sets
BCD representation 0101 0011
0001 0110 0011
Binary representation 110101
10100011


Figure 6-4 Comparison of binary coded decimal (BCD) and binary representation for decimal values 53 and 163.

*Binary coded decimal system uses four positions of place values—8, 4, 2, and 1—to represent 0 through 9.*

processing speeds and not on reading large volumes of input data or producing vast amounts of output.

The rules for binary coded decimal arithmetic, sometimes called decimal arithmetic or packed decimal, is not too different from binary arithmetic. The rules allow a decimal type carry when the results from adding two digits exceed 9.

### Six-Bit Numeric Code

A binary code that uses six positions of binary notation to represent numbers is the six-bit numeric code (Figure 6-5). These positions are divided into three bit

| DECIMAL DIGIT | | 0 | 1 | 2 | 3 | 4 | 5 | 6 | 7 | 8 | 9 |
|---|---|---|---|---|---|---|---|---|---|---|---|
| Check bit | C | 1 | 0 | 0 | 1 | 0 | 1 | 1 | 0 | 0 | 1 |
| Flag bit | F | 0 | 0 | 0 | 0 | 0 | 0 | 0 | 0 | 0 | 0 |
| Numeric bit position | 8 | 0 | 0 | 0 | 0 | 0 | 0 | 0 | 0 | 1 | 1 |
| | 4 | 0 | 0 | 0 | 0 | 1 | 1 | 1 | 1 | 0 | 0 |
| | 2 | 0 | 0 | 1 | 1 | 0 | 0 | 1 | 1 | 0 | 0 |
| | 1 | 0 | 1 | 0 | 1 | 0 | 1 | 0 | 1 | 0 | 1 |

Figure 6-5 Six-bit numeric code.

*Six-bit numeric code uses six positions of binary notation to represent numbers.*

sets. The first is a C or parity check bit that checks for the accuracy of data recorded and is normally an odd parity. This C bit of 1 is used only when the other five-bit positions are an even number of binary bits. The second position is an F or flag bit. It is a special-purpose binary bit that is generally used in two ways: it indicates a negative number in a numeric field or tells the computer when it has reached the end of a field or word. The last four-bit set is assigned the normal 8, 4, 2, and 1 place values.

In order to represent alphabetic or special characters in this code, two numeric value groupings (the same as illustrated in Figure 6-5) provide the storage space for the appropriate character. The first group of six-bit positions is the area reserved for the zone while the second six-bit positions store the digit values. The alphanumeric coding scheme for the six-bit numeric code is different from punched card coding, that is, eight zones (0 through 7) are utilized. The letter A, for example, is coded as a combination of a 4 zone digit and a 1 numeric digit.

*Standard Binary Coded Decimal Interchange Code is a seven-bit alphanumeric code, consisting of C-B-A-8-4-2-1 bits.*

### Standard Binary Coded Decimal Interchange Code

One of the difficulties with the six-bit numeric code is that it does not handle alphabetic and special characters too easily in terms of storing data compactly. In contrast, the seven-bit alphanumeric code, known as the Standard Binary Coded Decimal Interchange Code, provides for the alphabetic coding in punched cards. Having been widely used for second-generation computers, it is made up of the familiar binary coded decimal (8, 4, 2, and 1 bits), the A and B bits, and the check parity bit. The last bit, as previously, automatically checks the data as entered into the machine for valid data codes. As data are transmitted, each character is automatically checked to determine if the correct parity condition exists. Depending upon the equipment, it can be an odd- or even-number parity check.

The two zone bits (A and B) allow for three possible combinations: (1) A bit on, B bit off; (2) A bit off, B bit on; and (3) A bit on, B bit on. The last combination represents the same zone coding as the 12-punch in an 80 column card. Likewise, the B bit on alone represents the 11-zone punch and the A bit on alone, the 0-zone. Comparison of the alphabetic punched card coding and the seven-bit alphanumeric coding is set forth in Figure 6-6 for an even parity check machine. Not only is there

| PUNCHED CARD CODE | LETTER | PARITY CHECK BIT | ALPHA BIT POSITIONS | | NUMERIC BIT POSITIONS | | | |
|---|---|---|---|---|---|---|---|---|
| | | C | B | A | 8 | 4 | 2 | 1 |
| 12—1 | A | 1 | 1 | 1 | 0 | 0 | 0 | 1 |
| 12—2 | B | 1 | 1 | 1 | 0 | 0 | 1 | 0 |
| 12—3 | C | 0 | 1 | 1 | 0 | 0 | 1 | 1 |
| 12—4 | D | 1 | 1 | 1 | 0 | 1 | 0 | 0 |
| 12—5 | E | 0 | 1 | 1 | 0 | 1 | 0 | 1 |
| 12—6 | F | 0 | 1 | 1 | 0 | 1 | 1 | 0 |
| 12—7 | G | 1 | 1 | 1 | 0 | 1 | 1 | 1 |
| 12—8 | H | 1 | 1 | 1 | 1 | 0 | 0 | 0 |
| 12—9 | I | 0 | 1 | 1 | 1 | 0 | 0 | 1 |
| 11—1 | J | 0 | 1 | 0 | 0 | 0 | 0 | 1 |
| 11—2 | K | 0 | 1 | 0 | 0 | 0 | 1 | 0 |
| 11—3 | L | 1 | 1 | 0 | 0 | 0 | 1 | 1 |
| 11—4 | M | 0 | 1 | 0 | 0 | 1 | 0 | 0 |
| 11—5 | N | 1 | 1 | 0 | 0 | 1 | 0 | 1 |
| 11—6 | O | 1 | 1 | 0 | 0 | 1 | 1 | 0 |
| 11—7 | P | 0 | 1 | 0 | 0 | 1 | 1 | 1 |
| 11—8 | Q | 0 | 1 | 0 | 1 | 0 | 0 | 0 |
| 11—9 | R | 1 | 1 | 0 | 1 | 0 | 0 | 1 |
| 0—2 | S | 0 | 0 | 1 | 0 | 0 | 1 | 0 |
| 0—3 | T | 1 | 0 | 1 | 0 | 0 | 1 | 1 |
| 0—4 | U | 0 | 0 | 1 | 0 | 1 | 0 | 0 |
| 0—5 | V | 1 | 0 | 1 | 0 | 1 | 0 | 1 |
| 0—6 | W | 1 | 0 | 1 | 0 | 1 | 1 | 0 |
| 0—7 | X | 0 | 0 | 1 | 0 | 1 | 1 | 1 |
| 0—8 | Y | 0 | 0 | 1 | 1 | 0 | 0 | 0 |
| 0—9 | Z | 1 | 0 | 1 | 1 | 0 | 0 | 1 |

Figure 6-6 Comparison of alphabetic punched card code and standard binary coded decimal (BCD) interchange code or seven-bit alphanumeric code—even parity check bit machine.

a check bit feature for each character but there is also a parity check (known as two-dimensional parity) that can be performed on each bit channel by some computers. This is accomplished by adding the bits for a given unit of data and providing space for an odd- or even-check bit. In addition, some machines have the capability of automatically correcting the data for certain types of parity check errors.

### Hexadecimal Code

One of the difficulties encountered in communicating with a computer is the necessity of interpreting long strings of 0s and 1s. This process is prone to errors and very tedious. It can be simplified, however, by translating small groups of bits (3 or 4) directly into a more usable base. If a 3 bit string is used, it converts to an octal notation (base 8). This was the technique used in many second generation computers. Third generation equipment, which utilized an 8 bit (byte) interval code was more adaptable to a 4 bit string (base 16). Thus the hexadecimal system became the standard communication notation, especially for IBM equipment.

*Hexadecimal system has a base or radix of 16 (0 through 9 and letters A through F).*

By way of review, a numbering system requires as many different values as there are in the base of the system. Since the hexadecimal system has a base of 16, 16 different symbols are required. A comparison of this code with the decimal and binary system is illustrated in Figure 6-7. The hexadecimal code includes the familiar

| DECIMAL 10 | | BINARY 16 | | | | | HEXADECIMAL 16 | |
|---|---|---|---|---|---|---|---|---|
| 10 | 1 | 16 | 8 | 4 | 2 | 1 | 16 | 1 |
| | 0 | | 0 | 0 | 0 | 0 | | 0 |
| | 1 | | 0 | 0 | 0 | 1 | | 1 |
| | 2 | | 0 | 0 | 1 | 0 | | 2 |
| | 3 | | 0 | 0 | 1 | 1 | | 3 |
| | 4 | | 0 | 1 | 0 | 0 | | 4 |
| | 5 | | 0 | 1 | 0 | 1 | | 5 |
| | 6 | | 0 | 1 | 1 | 0 | | 6 |
| | 7 | | 0 | 1 | 1 | 1 | | 7 |
| | 8 | | 1 | 0 | 0 | 0 | | 8 |
| | 9 | | 1 | 0 | 0 | 1 | | 9 |
| 1 | 0 | | 1 | 0 | 1 | 0 | | A |
| 1 | 1 | | 1 | 0 | 1 | 1 | | B |
| 1 | 2 | | 1 | 1 | 0 | 0 | | C |
| 1 | 3 | | 1 | 1 | 0 | 1 | | D |
| 1 | 4 | | 1 | 1 | 1 | 0 | | E |
| 1 | 5 | | 1 | 1 | 1 | 1 | | F |
| 1 | 6 | 1 | 0 | 0 | 0 | 0 | 1 | 0 |
| 1 | 7 | 1 | 0 | 0 | 0 | 1 | 1 | 1 |
| 1 | 8 | 1 | 0 | 0 | 1 | 0 | 1 | 2 |
| 1 | 9 | 1 | 0 | 0 | 1 | 1 | 1 | 3 |
| 2 | 0 | 1 | 0 | 1 | 0 | 0 | 1 | 4 |
| 2 | 1 | 1 | 0 | 1 | 0 | 1 | 1 | 5 |
| 2 | 2 | 1 | 0 | 1 | 1 | 0 | 1 | 6 |
| 2 | 3 | 1 | 0 | 1 | 1 | 1 | 1 | 7 |
| 2 | 4 | 1 | 1 | 0 | 0 | 0 | 1 | 8 |
| 2 | 5 | 1 | 1 | 0 | 0 | 1 | 1 | 9 |
| 2 | 6 | 1 | 1 | 0 | 1 | 0 | 1 | A |
| 2 | 7 | 1 | 1 | 0 | 1 | 1 | 1 | B |
| 2 | 8 | 1 | 1 | 1 | 0 | 0 | 1 | C |
| 2 | 9 | 1 | 1 | 1 | 0 | 1 | 1 | D |
| 3 | 0 | 1 | 1 | 1 | 1 | 0 | 1 | E |
| 3 | 1 | 1 | 1 | 1 | 1 | 1 | 1 | F |

Figure 6-7 Decimal, binary, and hexadecimal equivalents.

0 through 9 and letters A through F whose place values, 0 through 15, are assigned in ascending order (0 through 9 and then A through F symbols).

***Hexadecimal Positional Values.*** The process of counting higher than 15 is obtained by carrying 1 to the next position to the left in order to represent the decimal number 16. The next number to the left is then 16 times larger or 256. This progression continues in a positive or negative direction, illustrated in Figure 6-8.

| Position number | 5 | 4 | 3 | 2 | 1 | 0 | • | −1 | −2 | −3 | −4 | −5 |
|---|---|---|---|---|---|---|---|---|---|---|---|---|
| Base 16 position value | $16^5$ | $16^4$ | $16^3$ | $16^2$ | $16^1$ | $16^0$ | • | $16^{-1}$ | $16^{-2}$ | $16^{-3}$ | $16^{-4}$ | $16^{-5}$ |
| Amount represented by position value | 1,048,576 | 65,536 | 4,096 | 256 | 16 | 1 | • | 1/16 | 1/256 | 1/4,096 | 1/65,536 | 1/1,048,576 |
| | | | | | | | Hexadecimal point | | | | | |

Figure 6-8 Selected positional values in hexadecimal system.

***Binary to Hexadecimal Conversion.*** Binary to hexadecimal conversion and vice versa is a straightforward process since there is a direct four to one relationship between the base 2 and base 16 systems. Every four binary digits become a single hexadecimal digit. In like manner, each hexadecimal digit becomes four binary digits. For example, convert the binary code 0011 1011 1000 to hexadecimal code:

```
0011  1011  1000
  3     B     8
```

The conversion of the hexadecimal 3B8 to the binary code is the same value as given above (0011 1011 1000). If there is any doubt about the conversion, refer to Figure 6-7.

***Decimal to Hexadecimal Integer Conversion.*** Decimal to hexadecimal integer conversion is accomplished by dividing the decimal number repeatedly by 16 until a zero quotient is obtained. Next, the decimal remainders 10 through 15 are converted into the appropriate hexadecimal symbols A through F. The first remainder is the least significant hexadecimal digit while the last remainder is the most significant digit. For example, the decimal values 210 and 1726, converted to hexadecimal notation, are:

| *Decimal* | *Hexadecimal* |
|---|---|
| 210/16 = 13 with a remainder of 2 | 2 |
| 13/16 = 0 with a remainder of 13 | D |
| 210 = D2 | |

| *Decimal* | *Hexadecimal* |
|---|---|
| 1726/16 = 107 with a remainder of 14 | E |
| 107/16 = 6 with a remainder of 11 | B |
| 6/16 = 0 with a remainder of 6 | 6 |
| 1726 = 6BE | |

***Hexadecimal to Decimal Integer Conversion.*** Hexadecimal to decimal integer conversion consists of expansion of the hexadecimal number in powers of 16, using decimal arithmetic for the calculations. Under this direct method, multiply the decimal equivalent of each hexadecimal digit by the place value of the digit, expressed in decimals, and add their products to obtain the equivalent decimal. To prove the validity of the hexadecimal values D2 and 6BE for decimals 210 and 1726 respectively, their values are:

$$\begin{aligned} D2 &= D \times 16^1 + 2 \times 16^0 \\ &= 13 \times 16 + 2 \times 1 \\ &= 208 + 2 \\ &= 210 \end{aligned} \qquad \begin{aligned} 6BE &= 6 \times 16^2 + 11 \times 16^1 + 14 \times 16^0 \\ &= 6 \times 256 + 11 \times 16 + 14 \times 1 \\ &= 1536 + 176 + 14 \\ &= 1726 \end{aligned}$$

*Hexadecimal addition follows the same rules as the decimal system, except that a carry results when the decimal value 15 has been exceeded.*

***Hexadecimal Addition.*** Hexadecimal addition follows the same rules as decimal and binary addition except that a carry does not result until the decimal value of 15 has been exceeded. To state it another way, whenever the sum of two digits exceeds F (the highest valued hexadecimal symbol), a carry of one is developed for the next higher order digit position. The hexadecimal addition table has 256 (16 × 16) entries, as shown in Figure 6-9. The sum of two digits in hexadecimal

| | 1 | 2 | 3 | 4 | 5 | 6 | 7 | 8 | 9 | A | B | C | D | E | F | |
|---|---|---|---|---|---|---|---|---|---|---|---|---|---|---|---|---|
| 1 | 02 | 03 | 04 | 05 | 06 | 07 | 08 | 09 | 0A | 0B | 0C | 0D | 0E | 0F | 10 | 1 |
| 2 | 03 | 04 | 05 | 06 | 07 | 08 | 09 | 0A | 0B | 0C | 0D | 0E | 0F | 10 | 11 | 2 |
| 3 | 04 | 05 | 06 | 07 | 08 | 09 | 0A | 0B | 0C | 0D | 0E | 0F | 10 | 11 | 12 | 3 |
| 4 | 05 | 06 | 07 | 08 | 09 | 0A | 0B | 0C | 0D | 0E | 0F | 10 | 11 | 12 | 13 | 4 |
| 5 | 06 | 07 | 08 | 09 | 0A | 0B | 0C | 0D | 0E | 0F | 10 | 11 | 12 | 13 | 14 | 5 |
| 6 | 07 | 08 | 09 | 0A | 0B | 0C | 0D | 0E | 0F | 10 | 11 | 12 | 13 | 14 | 15 | 6 |
| 7 | 08 | 09 | 0A | 0B | 0C | 0D | 0E | 0F | 10 | 11 | 12 | 13 | 14 | 15 | 16 | 7 |
| 8 | 09 | 0A | 0B | 0C | 0D | 0E | 0F | 10 | 11 | 12 | 13 | 14 | 15 | 16 | 17 | 8 |
| 9 | 0A | 0B | 0C | 0D | 0E | 0F | 10 | 11 | 12 | 13 | 14 | 15 | 16 | 17 | 18 | 9 |
| A | 0B | 0C | 0D | 0E | 0F | 10 | 11 | 12 | 13 | 14 | 15 | 16 | 17 | 18 | 19 | A |
| B | 0C | 0D | 0E | 0F | 10 | 11 | 12 | 13 | 14 | 15 | 16 | 17 | 18 | 19 | 1A | B |
| C | 0D | 0E | 0F | 10 | 11 | 12 | 13 | 14 | 15 | 16 | 17 | 18 | 19 | 1A | 1B | C |
| D | 0E | 0F | 10 | 11 | 12 | 13 | 14 | 15 | 16 | 17 | 18 | 19 | 1A | 1B | 1C | D |
| E | 0F | 10 | 11 | 12 | 13 | 14 | 15 | 16 | 17 | 18 | 19 | 1A | 1B | 1C | 1D | E |
| F | 10 | 11 | 12 | 13 | 14 | 15 | 16 | 17 | 18 | 19 | 1A | 1B | 1C | 1D | 1E | F |
| | 1 | 2 | 3 | 4 | 5 | 6 | 7 | 8 | 9 | A | B | C | D | E | F | |

Figure 6-9 Hexadecimal addition table.

addition is given at the intersection of the row and the column. Note that the highest entry is 1E (bottom right) which represents the sum of F plus F (decimal 15 + 15).

In order to understand hexadecimal addition with the foregoing table, four examples are set forth below. In the first two examples, the problems are straightforward since there is no carry. The appropriate values are read directly from Figure 6-9. In the third example, D plus B equals 8 with a carry of 1 into the next higher order position. Adding the next higher order digits, B plus E equals 9 with a carry of 1 plus the lower order carry equals A, with a carry of 1 into the next higher order digit position. Adding the next higher order digits or 4 plus 1 equals 5 plus the carry of 1 equals 6. The same type procedure is used in the last sample problem.

*Hexadecimal Addition Examples*

| | | | |
|---:|---:|---:|---:|
| 94 | 674 | 4BD | 7E86 |
| +39 | +348 | +1EB | +D55D |
| CD | 9BC | 6A8 | 153E3 |

*Hexadecimal subtraction follows the same rules as the decimal system, except that a borrow of 1 in the hexadecimal system represents the decimal value of 16.*

***Hexadecimal Subtraction.*** Hexadecimal subtraction follows the same rules as decimal and binary subtraction, except that a carry or borrow of 1 in hexadecimal notation represents the decimal value of 16. To determine the difference of two hexadecimal digits, Figure 6-9 can be used by locating the column heading that represents the digit to be subtracted (subtrahend). Next, go down this column to the digit(s) that represents the minuend. The heading of the row horizontally across from the minuend is the difference between the two digits. If the subtrahend digit is greater than the minuend digit, a 1 must be borrowed for the minuend digit before referencing the table.

To illustrate, four examples are shown below. The first two problems require no borrowing while the last two do. In the third example, B cannot be subtracted from 8 since it exceeds this value. A 1 is borrowed from the next higher order position at the left (A), reducing it to 9 (A − 1 = 9) and increasing the minuend digit for the first column to 18. To complete the subtraction for this column, the hexadecimal addition table is consulted. Under the B column (the subtrahend), the minuend digits, 18, appear in the D row, which means D is the answer for the first column. Moving onto the second column (next higher order position), D cannot be subtracted from 9. It is necessary to borrow at the left, reducing the digit 9 down to 8, and increase the minuend to 19. Going down the D column in the table, the minuend digits appear in the C row for the second value in the answer. Lastly, the difference between the higher order digit at the left, 8 minus 1 equals 7, as seen in the hexadecimal addition table. The last example is calculated in the same manner.

*Hexadecimal Subtraction Examples*

| | | | |
|---:|---:|---:|---|
| | | 19 | 12 |
| | | 8 ~~9~~ 18 | 8 ~~2~~ 15 |
| 16 | FD5 | ~~9~~ ~~A~~ ~~8~~ | ~~9~~ ~~3~~ 5 F Minuend |
| − 8 | −E63 | −1 D B | −4 7 D 1 Subtrahend |
| E | 172 | 7 C D | 4 B 8 E |

*Hexadecimal multiplication rules are the same as those for the decimal system, except that reference should be made to a hexadecimal multiplication table.*

***Hexadecimal Multiplication.*** Hexadecimal multiplication rules are the same as those for the decimal and binary systems. The fast way of determining the product of multiplying two digits is by referring to a hexadecimal multiplication table (Figure 6-10). In order to illustrate this table, two examples are used. In both examples, the values of the partial products are shifted one place to the left with respect to the prior one. These values are obtained by locating the insectional point of the multiplier and multiplicand in the hexademical multiplication table. In adding the partial products, hexadecimal addition is used. Any resulting carries are applied to the next higher digit positions, as indicated in the second example.

*Hexadecimal Multiplication Examples*

| | | |
|---|---|---|
| D84 | Multiplicand | |
| ×4 | Multiplier | |
| 10 | 4 × 4 | Partial products |
| 20 | 4 × 8 | |
| 34 | 4 × D | |
| 3610 | | |

| | | |
|---|---|---|
| 9E6 | Multiplicand | |
| ×3A | Multiplier | |
| 3C | A × 6 | Partial products of first multiplier digit |
| 8C | A × E | |
| 5A | A × 9 | |
| 12 | 3 × 6 | Partial products of second multiplier digit |
| 2A | 3 × E | |
| 1B | 3 × 9 | |
| Carries 111 | | |
| 23E1C | | |

## Extended Binary Coded Decimal Interchange Code

*Extended Binary Coded Decimal Interchange Code (EBCDIC) uses eight binary positions to represent a single character.*

The Extended Binary Coded Decimal Interchange Code (EBCDIC) employs eight binary positions to represent a single character of information (Figure 6-11) and is the basis for many third- and current-generation computers. Although the use of eight bits may, on the surface, appear to be inefficient, it has many advantages. Eight binary positions provide for up to 256($2^8$) different bit combinations. This additional bit configuration over the standard binary coded decimal (BCD) interchange code can be used for both uppercase and lowercase letters, numerals, and many special characters for programming. An 8-bit field can store two decimal values, which results in a greater utilization of primary and secondary storage than the BCD format. Also, any of the 256-bit configurations can be punched into a column of an 80 column card, providing the means for punching pure binary information into a card.

| 1 | 2 | 3 | 4 | 5 | 6 | 7 | 8 | 9 | A | B | C | D | E | F |
|---|---|---|---|---|---|---|---|---|---|---|---|---|---|---|
| 2 | 04 | 06 | 08 | 0A | 0C | 0E | 10 | 12 | 14 | 16 | 18 | 1A | 1C | 1E |
| 3 | 06 | 09 | 0C | 0F | 12 | 15 | 18 | 1B | 1E | 21 | 24 | 27 | 2A | 2D |
| 4 | 08 | 0C | 10 | 14 | 18 | 1C | 20 | 24 | 28 | 2C | 30 | 34 | 38 | 3C |
| 5 | 0A | 0F | 14 | 19 | 1E | 23 | 28 | 2D | 32 | 37 | 3C | 41 | 46 | 4B |
| 6 | 0C | 12 | 18 | 1E | 24 | 2A | 30 | 36 | 3C | 42 | 48 | 4E | 54 | 5A |
| 7 | 0E | 15 | 1C | 23 | 2A | 31 | 38 | 3F | 46 | 4D | 54 | 5B | 62 | 69 |
| 8 | 10 | 18 | 20 | 28 | 30 | 38 | 40 | 48 | 50 | 58 | 60 | 68 | 70 | 78 |
| 9 | 12 | 1B | 24 | 2D | 36 | 3F | 48 | 51 | 5A | 63 | 6C | 75 | 7E | 87 |
| A | 14 | 1E | 28 | 32 | 3C | 46 | 50 | 5A | 64 | 6E | 78 | 82 | 8C | 96 |
| B | 16 | 21 | 2C | 37 | 42 | 4D | 58 | 63 | 6E | 79 | 84 | 8F | 9A | A5 |
| C | 18 | 24 | 30 | 3C | 48 | 54 | 60 | 6C | 78 | 84 | 90 | 9C | A8 | B4 |
| D | 1A | 27 | 34 | 41 | 4E | 5B | 68 | 75 | 82 | 8F | 9C | A9 | B6 | C3 |
| E | 1C | 2A | 38 | 46 | 54 | 62 | 70 | 7E | 8C | 9A | A8 | B6 | C4 | D2 |
| F | 1E | 2D | 3C | 4B | 5A | 69 | 78 | 87 | 96 | A5 | B4 | C3 | D2 | E1 |

Figure 6-10 Hexadecimal multiplication table.

| CHARACTER | STANDARD CARD CODE | STANDARD BCD INTERCHANGE CODE | EBCDIC* | USASCII† |
|---|---|---|---|---|
| 0 | 0 | 100 1010 | 1111 0000 | 011 0000 |
| 1 | 1 | 000 0001 | 1111 0001 | 011 0001 |
| 2 | 2 | 000 0010 | 1111 0010 | 011 0010 |
| 3 | 3 | 100 0011 | 1111 0011 | 011 0011 |
| 4 | 4 | 000 0100 | 1111 0100 | 011 0100 |
| 5 | 5 | 100 0101 | 1111 0101 | 011 0101 |
| 6 | 6 | 100 0110 | 1111 0110 | 011 0110 |
| 7 | 7 | 000 0111 | 1111 0111 | 011 0111 |
| 8 | 8 | 000 1000 | 1111 1000 | 011 1000 |
| 9 | 9 | 100 1001 | 1111 1001 | 011 1001 |
| A | 12-1 | 011 0001 | 1100 0001 | 100 0001 |
| B | 12-2 | 011 0010 | 1100 0010 | 100 0010 |
| C | 12-3 | 111 0011 | 1100 0011 | 100 0011 |
| D | 12-4 | 011 0100 | 1100 0100 | 100 0100 |
| E | 12-5 | 111 0101 | 1100 0101 | 100 0101 |
| F | 12-6 | 111 0110 | 1100 0110 | 100 0110 |
| G | 12-7 | 011 0111 | 1100 0111 | 100 0111 |
| H | 12-8 | 011 1000 | 1100 1000 | 100 1000 |
| I | 12-9 | 111 1001 | 1100 1001 | 100 1001 |
| J | 11-1 | 110 0001 | 1101 0001 | 100 1010 |
| K | 11-2 | 110 0010 | 1101 0010 | 100 1011 |
| L | 11-3 | 010 0011 | 1101 0011 | 100 1100 |
| M | 11-4 | 110 0100 | 1101 0100 | 100 1101 |
| N | 11-5 | 010 0101 | 1101 0101 | 100 1110 |
| O | 11-6 | 010 0110 | 1101 0110 | 100 1111 |
| P | 11-7 | 110 0111 | 1101 0111 | 101 0000 |
| Q | 11-8 | 110 1000 | 1101 1000 | 101 0001 |
| R | 11-9 | 010 1001 | 1101 1001 | 101 0010 |
| S | 0-2 | 101 0010 | 1110 0010 | 101 0011 |
| T | 0-3 | 001 0011 | 1110 0011 | 101 0100 |
| U | 0-4 | 101 0100 | 1110 0100 | 101 0101 |
| V | 0-5 | 001 0101 | 1110 0101 | 101 0110 |
| W | 0-6 | 001 0110 | 1110 0110 | 101 0111 |
| X | 0-7 | 101 0111 | 1110 0111 | 101 1000 |
| Y | 0-8 | 101 1000 | 1110 1000 | 101 1001 |
| Z | 0-9 | 001 1001 | 1110 1001 | 101 1010 |

*Extended Binary Coded Decimal Interchange Code
†U.S.A. Standard Code for Information Interchange

Figure 6-11 Comparison of standard card code to selected computer codes.

*The numeric and zone positions of the EBCDIC system can be used to store two separate digits.*

***EBCDIC Character Codes.*** As pointed out previously, most character codes are a composite of zone and numeric segments. The EBCDIC system is no exception and divides each storage location, known as a byte, into equal parts. Each byte consists of 8 bits—4 zone and 4 numeric plus a parity bit. Referring to Figure 6-11, the extended binary coded decimal interchange code is similar to the numeric bit positions of the standard binary coded decimal interchange code (7-bit alphanumeric code). However, the zone positions are constructed and utilized differently. Figure 6-12 illustrates how the zone portion of the EBCDIC byte is used. The IBM System/360 and System/370 employ the 8-bit byte which is, actually, the EBCDIC character code.

The EBCDIC system allows for packing digits under programmed instruction, resulting in a more efficient utilization of storage. The packed format uses the numeric portion of a byte to represent one digit and the zone portion to represent

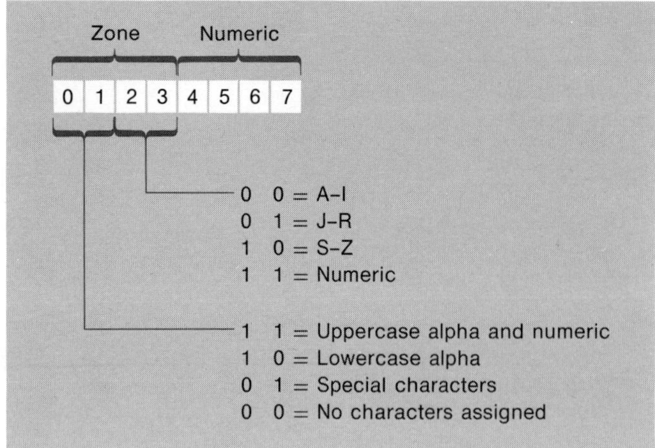


Figure 6-12 Various uses of zone portion of EBCDIC byte.

a second digit. Packing also speeds up arithmetic calculations and improves rates of data transmission.

### U.S.A. Standard Code for Information Interchange

*U.S.A. standard code for information interchange (USASCII) is widely used for data transmission devices.*

The U.S.A. Standard Code for Information Interchange (USASCII) is a 7-bit (Figure 6-11) or an 8-bit binary code that can be processed by many third- and current-generation computers. It is the basis for data transmission devices. While the EBCDIC formats are numbered from left to right, the USASCII is numbered from right to left. More will be said about this latter code in Chapter 9 on data communications.

## COMPUTER LOGIC

*Computer logic is based on the fundamentals of Boolean algebra or true-false propositions.*

The computer's hardware that operates on electrical pulses makes use of the binary 0 and 1. A binary 0 is represented by the lack of a voltage rise while a binary 1 is represented by a sharp voltage pulse. A comparable example with which the reader is familiar is a light that can be turned on or off at either end of a room. Every time the light is flipped on or off, a logic machine is operated, using the fundamentals of Boolean algebra—developed by a 19th century English mathematician named George Boole. It makes the light operate in basically the same way as an adding circuit in a digital computer. In essence, computer logic circuits employ some of the same rules of logic used to design home lighting circuits.

### True-False Propositions

*Algebra-like rules were developed by G. Boole for manipulating true-false propositions that use three connectives:*
- *OR*
- *AND*
- *NOT*

A Boolean proposition is either true or false. These two conditions can be represented by a two-state (binary) device, such as a simple on-off electrical switch, relay, vacuum tube, transistor, or comparable electrical component. Boole developed a set of algebra-like rules for manipulating true-false propositions, using the three fundamental connectives: OR, AND, and NOT.

***The OR Function.*** In its simplest form, an OR connective means that a condition C is true if A or B or both are true. The electrical circuit, shown in Figure 6-13*a*, illustrates the OR function. With two on-off switches in parallel, current flows and the light goes on when either switch 1 or switch 2 or both are closed. In Boolean

*The OR connective means that condition C is true if A or B or both are true.*

terms, this is generally written as: A ∪ B ≡ C where OR is the logical equivalent of addition and is represented by the ∪ symbol between A and B. (The column of three dashes means "identical to.") A logical truth table showing all possible combinations of values for this Boolean OR function is illustrated in Figure 6-13*c*.

*The AND connective means that condition C is true only when A and B are true.*

***The AND Function.*** A slight revision of the circuit, with switches 3 and 4 in series as in the second circuit of Figure 6-13*b*, illustrates a Boolean AND function. In this case, condition C is true (current flows and the light goes on) only when A and B are true (when both switches are closed). In Boolean terms, this is expressed as: A ∩ B ≡ C. This is the logical equivalent of multiplication, symbolized by an inverted ∪ between A and B. The truth table is illustrated in Figure 6-13*d*.

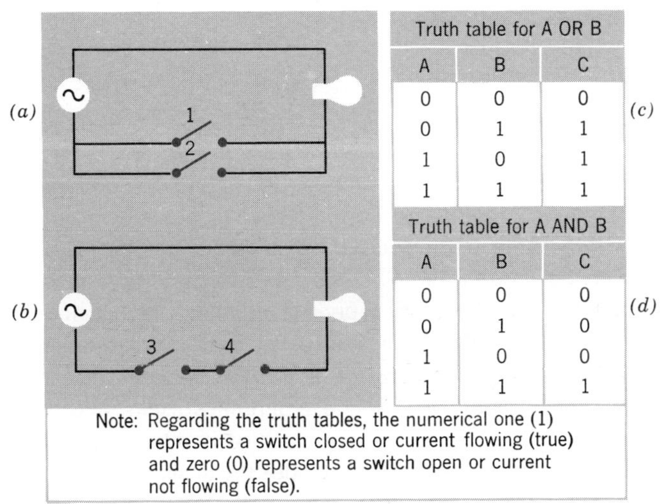


Truth table for A OR B

| A | B | C |
|---|---|---|
| 0 | 0 | 0 |
| 0 | 1 | 1 |
| 1 | 0 | 1 |
| 1 | 1 | 1 |

Truth table for A AND B

| A | B | C |
|---|---|---|
| 0 | 0 | 0 |
| 0 | 1 | 0 |
| 1 | 0 | 0 |
| 1 | 1 | 1 |

Note: Regarding the truth tables, the numerical one (1) represents a switch closed or current flowing (true) and zero (0) represents a switch open or current not flowing (false).

Figure 6-13 (*a*) The first electrical circuit is equivalent to a Boolean OR function—truth table A OR B (*c*). The light is on when either switch 1 or switch 2 is closed. (*b*) The second electrical circuit is equivalent to a Boolean AND function—truth table A AND B (*d*). The light is on only when both switch 3 and switch 4 are closed.

*The NOT connective represents a logical negation or not being.*

***The NOT Function.*** In addition to the OR and AND functions, Boole used the concept of algebraically representing logical negation or not being. This is symbolized with a bar above the letter representing the term, Ā, which is read "not A." The Boolean NOT operation inverts the logic of electrical signals in digital computer circuits, that is, it converts an input pulse to a no-pulse, a one to a zero, and vice versa. The truth table for the NOT function is shown at left.

*Truth Table for NOT Ā*

| A | Ā |
|---|---|
| 0 | 1 |
| 1 | 0 |

### How the Computer Adds

The above combinations of OR, AND, and NOT functions are carried out electronically. They enable the computer to handle the arithmetic and logic functions performed by the arithmetic/logical unit.

*The half-adder circuit employs the three Boolean connectives to add. However, it can add only two digits and has no provision for carry.*

***Half-Adders.*** The half-adder circuit, shown in Figure 6-14, uses the three basic Boolean relationships to add. However, it can add only two digits and has no provision for handling a carry digit. It can handle only one column or place value. Its logical truth table is depicted in Figure 6-15*a*. In Boolean terms, this is expressed as: (A ∩ B̄) ∪ (Ā ∩ B) = 1. This reads "(A and not B) or (not A and B) equal one." It describes exactly what happens in a room if you have two switches that control the same light. In the truth table, if you substitute "switch" for "digit" and "light" for "sum," you have a truth table that describes the operation of the light circuit.

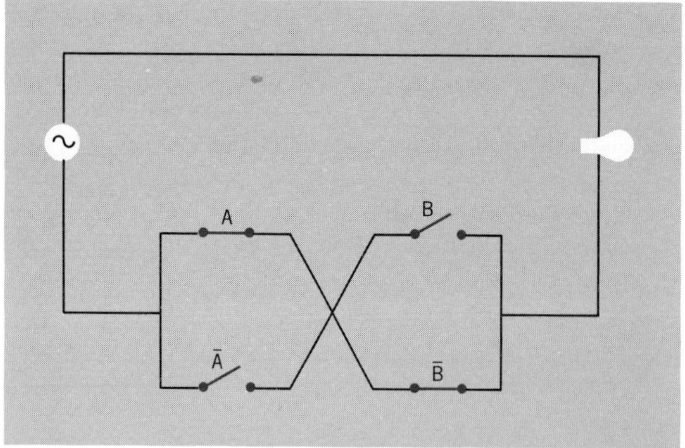


Figure 6-14 The conventional electric lighting circuit is equivalent to a half-adder in a computer.

A one (1) in the truth table means a switch or light is on while a zero (0) indicates an off condition. The revised truth table is shown in Figure 6-15*b*.

*Half-adders circuits are combined to form full-adder circuits for handling large numbers and providing for carry.*

***Full-Adders.*** In the computer, half-adders are combined to form full-adders that will handle large numbers and automatically carry digits from column to column (just like adding numbers with paper and pencil). The same devices can be used to subtract, multiply, and divide. In general, all computer arithmetic is reduced to addition. Multiplication can be accomplished by repetitive addition, which is handled at electronic speed in a computer. Subtraction and division, too, are reduced to addition by using complementary arithmetic. Electronic full-adders are also used to compare numbers by subtraction and cause the computer to take alternative actions, depending on whether the difference is a positive number, a negative number, or zero. Comparison by subtraction, then, provides the basis for a computer to make decisions and to take alternative actions.

| LOGICAL TRUTH TABLE | | |
|---|---|---|
| DIGIT A | DIGIT B | SUM |
| 0 | 0 | 0 |
| 0 | 1 | 1 |
| 1 | 0 | 1 |
| 1 | 1 | 0 |
| | (*a*) | |

| REVISED TRUTH TABLE | | |
|---|---|---|
| SWITCH A | SWITCH B | LIGHT |
| Off | Off | Off |
| Off | On | On |
| On | Off | On |
| On | On | Off |
| | (*b*) | |

Figure 6-15 Logical truth table (*a*) and revised truth table (*b*) for a half-adder circuit (refer to Figure 6-14).

## THE STORED PROGRAM

*The stored program concept refers to storing within the computer's memory a series of coded instructions that will accomplish desired processing.*

The foregoing discussion on Boolean algebra related to the computer's logic components. This section and subsequent discussions center on the computer's internal operations. The "stored program concept" refers to storing within the memory of the computer a series of coded instructions that will be used in accomplishing the desired processing. The program would be read into the computer, stored in memory, processed as directed, and its output would be produced according to some planned format. The function of the machine's memory is not only to accumulate data to be processed and associate it with other related data but also to instruct the computer as to what it must do in a very precise manner. The set of instructions represent basic operations that must be performed by the machine. When the computer begins operation, the first instruction is taken to the control unit and interpreted. The operation specified by the instruction is carried out. The second instruction is moved to the control unit where it is interpreted and executed. In a similar manner, all other instructions follow the same procedure. When the final instruction has been completed for the initial transaction, the process is repeated again for each transaction following. The method of instructing a computer will be described in the following sections. Before doing so, the word structure available with current computers is discussed.

**Fixed-Word Length**

*A fixed-word length computer is so structured that all its storage locations are capable of holding a specific number of digits, say ten.*

In fixed-word length computers, all storage locations in memory are capable of holding so many digits, say 10 digits and a plus or a minus sign. All stored data use the full 10-digit positions whether they are needed or not. If the number 4 is stored, for instance, it would appear as 0000000004 in a specified memory location. Just as data are stored in 10-digit lengths, so are the computer's instructions. In fact, the fixed-word length requirement for data and instructions makes it difficult, at times, to distinguish between the two in memory. It is only when the instructions reach the CPU control unit that they take on special significance.

*The lowest common denominator of storage is the bit.*

***Bit (Storage Unit).*** When referring to a fixed-word length computer, every storage location is identified by an address that specifies a certain number of storage representations. For example, a fixed-word length machine might be 24, 30, 36, 48, 54, etc. bits where a bit (binary digit) is a single character in a binary number. Once the computer designer determines the word size, all addresses are referenced by that number of bits. If a computer is developed as a 36-bit word machine, each reference to a single memory location will access the same number of bits.

*A byte is an 8-bit unit of data.*

***Byte (Storage Unit).*** For the IBM System/360 and System/370, these systems process data in multiples of an 8-bit byte (Figure 6-16). Each 8-bit unit of data is called a byte, the basic building block for both systems. A ninth bit is the parity or check bit that indicates whether the total number of binary "1" digits is odd or even. It is transmitted with each byte and carries an odd parity in the byte. Byte locations in main storage are consecutively numbered, starting with 0. Each number is the address of the corresponding byte. A group of bytes in storage is addressed by the left-most byte of the group.

*A word is a 32-bit unit of data. A halfword is 16-bits, and a double word is 64-bits.*

***Words (Storage Units).*** Bytes may be handled separately or grouped in fields. The halfword, word, and doubleword are fields of consecutive bytes. A halfword has two bytes (or 16-binary bits), a word has four bytes (or 32-binary bits), and the doubleword has eight bytes (or 64-binary bits), illustrated in Figure 6-16. These fields make up the basic fixed-length data formats.

*Fixed-word length fields (halfwords, words, and doublewords) must be located in memory on integral boundaries.*

***Integral Boundaries.*** Fixed-word length fields (halfwords, words, and doublewords) in most models must be located in main storage on *integral boundaries*. A boundary is integral for a unit of data when its main storage address is a multiple of that unit's length in bytes. For example, halfwords (two bytes) must have main storage addresses that are multiples of two (Figure 6-16). Sequential halfword addresses are shown as 0000, 0002, 0004, and so forth. Words (four bytes) must have addresses that are multiples of four (shown as 0000, 0004, 0008, etc.). Doublewords (eight bytes) must have addresses that are multiples of eight (shown as 0000, 0008, 0016, etc.).

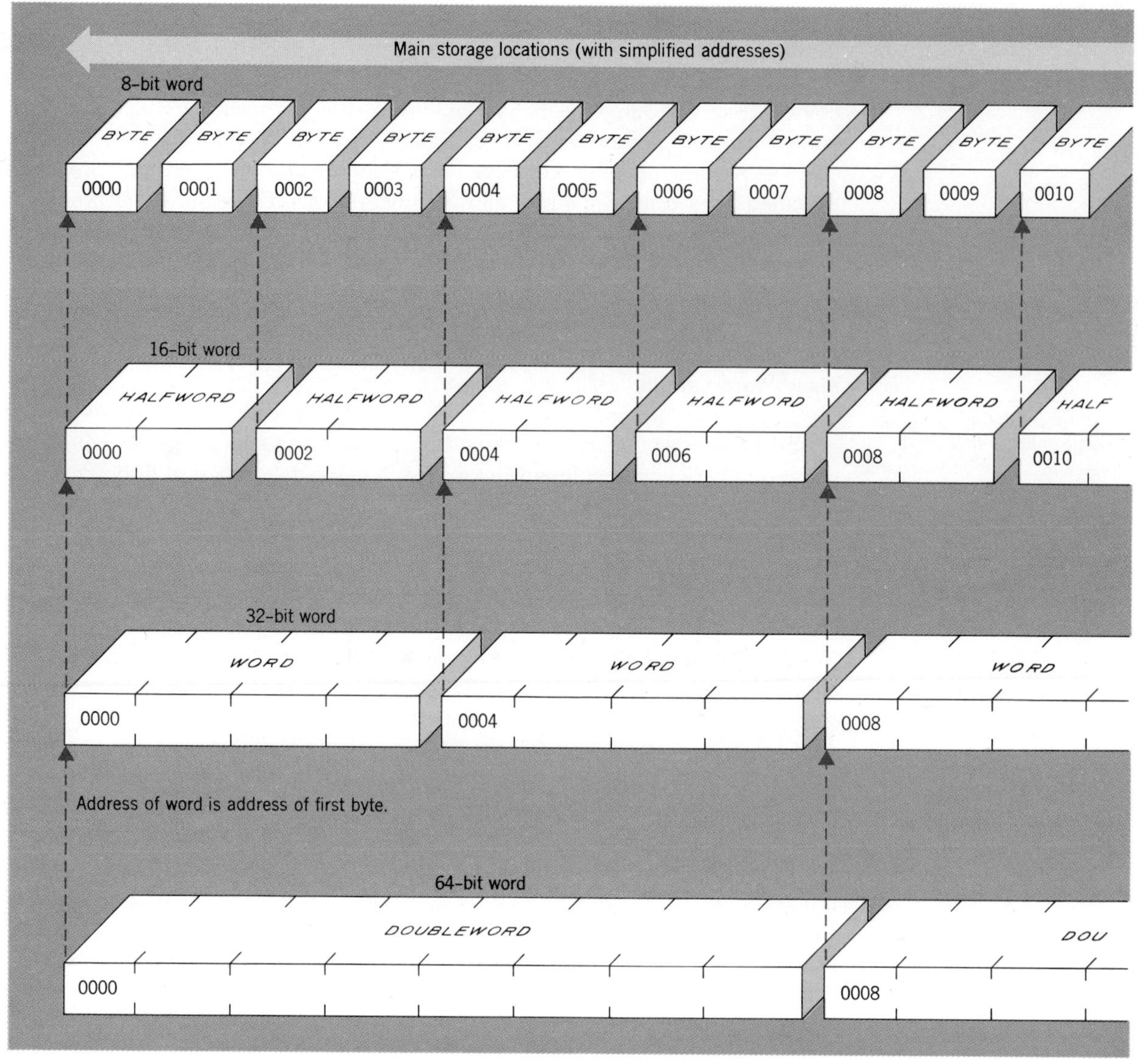


Figure 6-16 IBM System/360 and System/370 fixed-word formats-bytes, halfwords, words, and doublewords in main storage. (Courtesy International Business Machines Corporation.)

### Variable-Word Length

*A variable-word length computer handles each field, say a single character or many characters, as an individual unit of information.*

Instead of recording information in memory in words of a specific length, several computer systems are able to handle each field (a single character or many characters) as an individual unit of information. In some computers, a field is addressed by its right-most position (low order) in memory while, in others, the left-most position (high order) is designated. Regardless of the approach utilized in addressing the field of information, the end of the field can be indicated in several ways. One is that the length of the field can be specified in the instruction. Another method is to have the end of the field indicated by a special character, by a special bit position in the character, by sensing the sign of the field, or by some comparable scheme.

In order to illustrate two common approaches found in variable-word length computers, the example below is used for (1) specification of length method and (2) a word mark bit method. In the first approach, the instruction that denotes a variable-word length specifies the left-most beginning address and the number of location addresses for the specific word as shown below. The instruction begins in location 400 and the number of characters in the word is 8. With the second method, a special control bit is added to the group of bits. In the example, the instruction (5) defines one end of the word and the work mark bit (9) defines the other end.

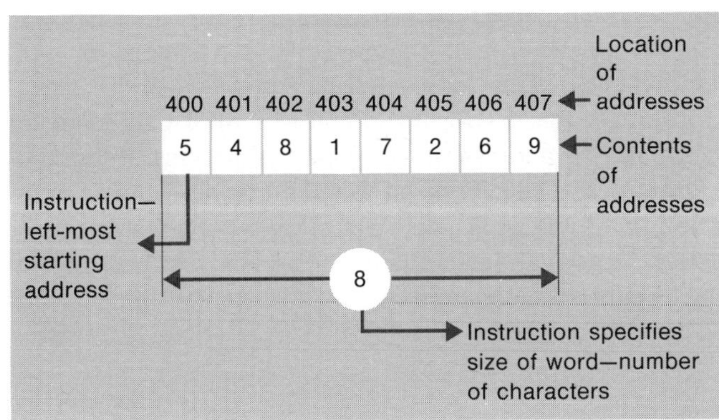


*Standard and packed decimal formats are available for fixed-word and variable-word lengths.*

***Standard and Packed Decimal Formats.*** The IBM System/360 and System/370 encode one character with each 8-bit byte for the variable-word format as is the case for the fixed-word format. The variable-length fields may start on any byte location and may contain up to 256 bytes, shown in Figure 6-17*a*. The binary coded decimal or packed decimal code can also be used for variable-word formats where each byte encodes two decimal digits in a 4-bit binary coded decimal. The address of the first byte plus length specifies the size of the word. This coding scheme is depicted in Figure 6-17*b*.

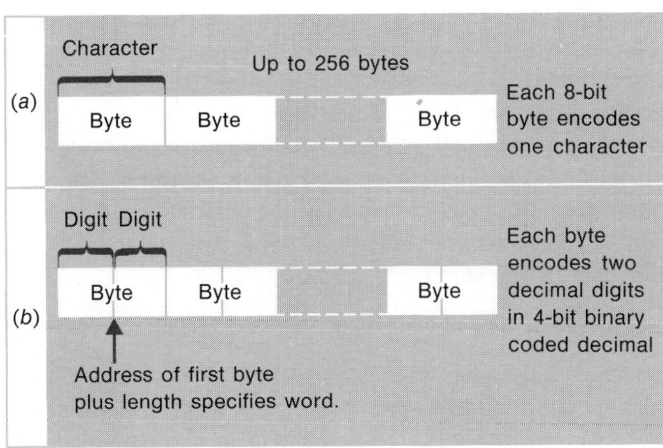


Figure 6-17 IBM System/360 and System/370 variable-length format—standard (*a*) and binary coded decimal or packed decimal (*b*).

### The Byte-Addressable Combination

*The byte-addressable computer has the capability of both fixed- and variable-word length formats.*

Both fixed- and variable-word length computers have their advantages and corresponding limitations. Fixed-word length is easier to program than variable-word length since the size of the field is always constant, thereby reducing the need for special methods to control word sizes. On the other hand, variable-word length can store more information in memory. Instead of allocating a certain size word length for one or a few digits of information, data can be packed into a smaller area of memory. The variable-word length computer, then, is capable of utilizing memory in a more efficient manner, which can be critical for larger programs. In view of these facts, several manufacturers have designed computer systems that have both fixed and variable address formats. This is accomplished by incorporating the byte-addressable combination in the computer's hardware.

***Current Trend in Address Formats.*** The IBM System/360 and System/370 are examples of both fixed- and variable-word address formats in a byte-addressable computer. As indicated previously, the fixed-word format is a word consisting of 4 bytes (each 8 bits long) where the address of a word is the address of the first byte. When an instruction refers to a specific fixed word, the computer brings in or stores 4 bytes. In addition to the full word, there are other word sizes as noted previously. For the variable-word format, instructions specify the first byte of the word and the number of bytes to be included, referred to above as the specification of length method.

## CPU FUNCTIONAL UNITS

*The basic functional units of a computer are found in the central processing unit.*

No matter what word length is used by the computer system, instructions must be executed by the program before output can occur. Before exploring computer instructions and how they operate within the CPU (central processing unit), the functional units of the central processor will be explored. These include registers, encoder, decoder, complementer, and comparator. Without an explanation of these elements, it would be difficult to understand the operations of computer instructions.

### Register Devices

*Register devices that receive, hold, and transfer data as directed by the computer's control circuits include:*
- *accumulator*
- *storage*
- *address*
- *instruction*
- *floating point*
- *general*

Registers are devices that are capable of receiving, holding, and transferring data as directed by control circuits. Acting as temporary memory for the central processing unit, they are capable of performing several different functions. For this reason, registers are named according to their functions. An *accumulator register* is one in which the results of arithmetic or logic operations are accumulated. In some central processors, any general register can be used for arithmetic operations. A *storage register* temporarily holds information taken from or being sent to storage. Two registers that are closely related are the *address register* and the *instruction register*. The former holds the address of a storage location or device while the latter holds the instruction being executed. A *floating point register* is used in floating point arithmetic operations. A register that performs the functions of several registers mentioned previously (such as accumulators, storage registers, and address registers) is called a *general register*.

### Index Registers

An important register that is capable of modifying an instruction address and indexing is the *index register*. With address modification, the storage address of data can be increased by one or more records each time the instruction is executed.

*Index registers are used to modify an instruction address and, thereby, reference sequential data.*

This causes the computer to read sequential records, one after another. In essence, an index register allows its contents to be added or subtracted from an address prior to or during the execution of an instruction. Indexing with this type of register is the most common form of address modification found in computers.

### Other CPU Functional Units

*Other CPU functional units include:*
- *encoder*
- *decoder*
- *complementer*
- *comparator*

The function of the *encoder* is to translate data from decimal form into the coding system used by the computer. The *decoder* is basically the reverse of an encoder, that is, it translates the computer internal code into decimal equivalents for output. In contrast to the encoder and the decoder, which translate information from one system to another, is the complementer and comparator. The *complementer* is special circuitry designed to perform complementing since computer subtraction consists of complementing the subtrahend and then adding for the answer. In addition to the complementer, hardware is needed that can compare instructions to determine the appropriate path when several are available. This is the function of the *comparator*. One such method compares small groups of data—in the form of bits—to determine the larger of the two values.

## COMPUTER INSTRUCTIONS

*Instructions must be in machine language for computer processing.*

Before processing occurs within a computer system, a program must be read into the central processing unit. To be more specific, the program must reside in the memory or primary storage under the direction of the control unit. The instructions of an operational program are in machine language as opposed to some type of symbolic or procedure-oriented language. Each computer system has its own set of machine language instructions based on its hardware. The format of the instructions, then, will vary depending on how the manufacturer designed the machine. As noted previously in this chapter, data and instructions, stored in the computer's memory, are indistinguishable. If data are called from a memory location in place of an instruction—caused by an error in programming—the CPU control unit would translate the data as an operating command. In such a case, the computer would enter into a loop, indicate an error condition, or show some other abnormal operating condition.

### Requirements for Each Computer Instruction

*Each computer instruction includes:*
- *operation code*
- *operand(s) or data address(es)*
- *instruction address*

The program, being a set of instructions for the computer to follow, processes data on this basis. Each instruction, generally, includes the following three items.

1. The operation code specifies the operation to be performed or what the computer is to do.
2. One or more operands, sometimes called data addresses, indicate the address or addresses of the data to be worked on or where data are to be taken. They designate the address or addresses of the data needed for the operation code.
3. The last part of the instruction is the location of the next instruction, sometimes referred to as the instruction address.

Based upon the foregoing general format, an instruction is basically an operation code plus operands and an instruction address. The operation codes for one computer will be completely different from all others. In like manner, the method of using operands and their number vary from computer to computer. Shown in Figure 6-18 are the machine language instructions for the current IBM System/360 and System/370 series.

| NAME | MNEMONIC | TYPE | OPERAND | CODE |
|---|---|---|---|---|
| Add | AR | RR | R1, R2 | 1A |
| Add | A | RX | R1, D2(X2, B2) | 5A |
| Add Halfword | AH | RX | R1, D2(X2, B2) | 4A |
| Add Logical | ALR | RR | R1, R2 | 1E |
| Add Logical | AL | RX | R1, D2(X2, B2) | 5E |
| AND | NR | RR | R1, R2 | 14 |
| AND | N | RX | R1, D2(X2, B2) | 54 |
| AND | NI | SI | D1(B1), I2 | 94 |
| AND | NC | SS | D1(L, B1), D2(B2) | D4 |
| Branch and Link | BALR | RR | R1, R2 | 05 |
| Branch and Link | BAL | RX | R1, D2(X2, B2) | 45 |
| Branch on Condition | BCR | RR | M1, R2 | 07 |
| Branch on Condition | BC | RX | M1, D2(X2, B2) | 47 |
| Branch on Count | BCTR | RR | R1, R2 | 06 |
| Branch on Count | BCT | RX | R1, D2(X2, B2) | 46 |
| Branch on Index High | BXH | RS | R1, R3, D2(B2) | 86 |
| Branch on Index Low or Equal | BXLE | RS | R1, R3, D2(B2) | 87 |
| Compare | CR | RR | R1, R2 | 19 |
| Compare | C | RX | R1, D2(X2, B2) | 59 |
| Compare Halfword | CH | RX | R1, D2(X2, B2) | 49 |
| Compare Logical | CLR | RR | R1, R2 | 15 |
| Compare Logical | CL | RX | R1, D2(X2, B2) | 55 |
| Compare Logical | CLC | SS | D1(L, B1), D2(B2) | D5 |
| Compare Logical | CLI | SI | D1(B1), I2 | 95 |
| Convert to Binary | CVB | RX | R1, D2(X2, B2) | 4F |
| Convert to Decimal | CVD | RX | R1, D2(X2, B2) | 4E |
| Diagnose |  | SI |  | 83 |
| Divide | DR | RR | R1, R2 | 1D |
| Divide | D | RX | R1, D2(X2, B2) | 5D |
| Exclusive OR | XR | RR | R1, R2 | 17 |
| Exclusive OR | X | RX | R1, D2(X2, B2) | 57 |
| Exclusive OR | XI | SI | D1(B1), I2 | 97 |
| Exclusive OR | XC | SS | D1(L, B1), D2(B2) | D7 |
| Execute | EX | RX | R1, D2(X2, B2) | 44 |
| Halt I/O | HIO | SI | D1(B1) | 9E |
| Insert Character | IC | RX | R1, D2(X2, B2) | 43 |
| Load | LR | RR | R1, R2 | 18 |
| Load | L | RX | R1, D2(X2, B2) | 58 |
| Load Address | LA | RX | R1, D2(X2, B2) | 41 |
| Load and Test | LTR | RR | R1, R2 | 12 |
| Load Complement | LCR | RR | R1, R2 | 13 |
| Load Halfword | LH | RX | R1, D2(X2, B2) | 48 |
| Load Multiple | LM | RS | R1, R3, D2(B2) | 98 |
| Load Negative | LNR | RR | R1, R2 | 11 |
| Load Positive | LPR | RR | R1, R2 | 10 |
| Load PSW | LPSW | SI | D1B1) | 82 |
| Move | MVI | SI | D1(B1), I2 | 92 |
| Move | MVC | SS | D1(L, B1), D2(B2) | D2 |
| Move Numerics | MVN | SS | D1(L, B1), D2(B2) | D1 |
| Move with Offset | MVO | SS | D1(L1, B1), D2(L2, B2) | F1 |
| Move Zones | MVZ | SS | D1(L, B1), D2(B2) | D3 |
| Multiply | MR | RR | R1, R2 | 1C |
| Multiply | M | RX | R1, D2(X2, B2) | 5C |
| Multiply Halfword | MH | RX | R1, D2(X2, B2) | 4C |
| OR | OR | RR | R1, R2 | 16 |
| OR | O | RX | R1, D2(X2, B2) | 56 |
| OR | OI | SI | D1(B1), I2 | 96 |
| OR | OC | SS | D1(L, B1), D2(B2) | D6 |
| Pack | PACK | SS | D1(L1, B1), D2(L2, B2) | F2 |
| Set Program Mask | SPM | RR | R1 | 04 |
| Set System Mask | SSM | SI | D1(B1) | 80 |
| Shift Left Double | SLDA | RS | R1, D2(B2) | 8F |
| Shift Left Single | SLA | RS | R1, D2(B2) | 8B |
| Shift Left Double Logical | SLDL | RS | R1, D2(B2) | 8D |
| Shift Left Single Logical | SLL | RS | R1, D2(B2) | 89 |
| Shift Right Double | SRDA | RS | R1, D2(B2) | 8E |
| Shift Right Single | SRA | RS | R1, D2(B2) | 8A |
| Shift Right Double Logical | SRDL | RS | R1, D2(B2) | 8C |
| Shift Right Single Logical | SRL | RS | R1, D2(B2) | 88 |
| Start I/O | SIO | SI | D1(B1) | 9C |
| Store | ST | RX | R1, D2(X2, B2) | 50 |
| Store Character | STC | RX | R1, D2(X2, B2) | 42 |
| Store Halfword | STH | RX | R1, D2(X2, B2) | 40 |
| Store Multiple | STM | RS | R1, R3, D2(B2) | 90 |
| Subtract | SR | RR | R1, R2 | 1B |
| Subtract | S | RX | R1, D2(X2, B2) | 5B |
| Subtract Halfword | SH | RX | R1, D2(X2, B2) | 4B |
| Subtract Logical | SLR | RR | R1, R2 | 1F |
| Subtract Logical | SL | RX | R1, D2(X2, B2) | 5F |
| Supervisor Call | SVC | RR | I | 0A |
| Test and Set | TS | SI | D1(B1) | 93 |
| Test Channel | TCH | SI | D1(B1) | 9F |
| Test I/O | TIO | SI | D1(B1) | 9D |
| Test Under Mask | TM | SI | D1(B1), I2 | 91 |
| Translate | TR | SS | D1(L, B1), D2(B2) | DC |
| Translate and Test | TRT | SS | D1(L, B1), D2(B2) | DD |
| Unpack | UNPK | SS | D1(L1, B1), D2(L2, B2) | F3 |

**DECIMAL FEATURE INSTRUCTIONS**

| NAME | MNEMONIC | TYPE | OPERAND | CODE |
|---|---|---|---|---|
| Add Decimal | AP | SS | D1(L1, B1), D2(L2, B2) | FA |
| Compare Decimal | CP | SS | D1(L1, B1), D2(L2, B2) | F9 |
| Divide Decimal | DP | SS | D1(L1, B1), D2(L2, B2) | FD |
| Edit | ED | SS | D1(L, B1), D2(B2) | DE |
| Edit and Mark | EDMK | SS | D1(L, B1), D2(B2) | DF |
| Multiply Decimal | MP | SS | D1(L1, B1), D2(L2, B2) | FC |
| Subtract Decimal | SP | SS | D1(L1, B1), D2(L2, B2) | FB |
| Zero and Add | ZAP | SS | D1(L1, B1), D2(L2, B2) | F8 |

**DIRECT CONTROL FEATURE INSTRUCTIONS**

| NAME | MNEMONIC | TYPE | OPERAND | CODE |
|---|---|---|---|---|
| Read Direct | RDD | SI | D1(B1), I2 | 85 |
| Write Direct | WRD | SI | D1(B1), I2 | 84 |

**PROTECTION FEATURE INSTRUCTIONS**

| NAME | MNEMONIC | TYPE | OPERAND | CODE |
|---|---|---|---|---|
| Insert Storage Key | ISK | RR | R1, R2 | 09 |
| Set Storage Key | SSK | RR | R1, R2 | 08 |

**FLOATING-POINT FEATURE INSTRUCTIONS**

| NAME | MNEMONIC | TYPE | OPERAND | CODE |
|---|---|---|---|---|
| Add Normalized (Long) | N ADR | RR | R1, R2 | 2A |
| Add Normalized (Long) | N AD | RX | R1, D2(X2, B2) | 6A |
| Add Normalized (Short) | N AER | RR | R1, R2 | 3A |
| Add Normalized (Short) | N AE | RX | R1, D2(X2, B2) | 7A |
| Add Unnormalized (Long) | AWR | RR | R1, R2 | 2E |
| Add Unnormalized (Long) | AW | RX | R1, D2(X2, B2) | 6E |
| Add Unnormalized (Short) | AUR | RR | R1, R2 | 3E |
| Add Unnormalized (Short | AU | RX | R2, D2(X2, B2) | 7E |
| Compare (Long) | CDR | RR | R1, R2 | 29 |
| Compare (Long) | CD | RX | R1, D2(X2, B2) | 69 |
| Compare (Short) | CER | RR | R1, R2 | 39 |
| Compare (Short) | CE | RX | R1, D2(X2, B2) | 79 |
| Divide (Long) | N DDR | RR | R1, R2 | 2D |
| Divide (Long) | N DD | RX | R1, D2(X2, B2) | 6D |
| Divide (Short) | N DER | RR | R1, R2 | 3D |
| Divide (Short) | N DE | RX | R1, D2(X2, B2) | 7D |
| Halve (Long) | HDR | RR | R1, R2 | 24 |
| Halve (Short) | HER | RR | R1, R2 | 34 |
| Load and Test (Long) | LTDR | RR | R1, R2 | 22 |
| Load and Test (Short) | LTER | RR | R1, R2 | 32 |
| Load Complement (Long) | LCDR | RR | R1, R2 | 23 |
| Load Complement (Short) | LCER | RR | R1, R2 | 33 |
| Load (Long) | LDR | RR | R1, R2 | 28 |
| Load (Long) | LD | RX | R1, D2(X2, B2) | 68 |
| Load Negative (Long) | LNDR | RR | R1, R2 | 21 |
| Load Negative (Short) | LNER | RR | R1, R2 | 31 |
| Load Positive (Long) | LPDR | RR | R1, R2 | 20 |
| Load Positive (Short) | LPER | RR | R1, R2 | 30 |
| Load (Short) | LER | RR | R1, R2 | 38 |
| Load (Short) | LE | RX | R1, D2(X2, B2) | 78 |
| Multiply (Long) | N MDR | RR | R1, R2 | 2C |
| Multiply (Long) | N MD | RX | R1, D2(X2, B2) | 6C |
| Multiply (Short) | N MER | RR | R1, R2 | 3C |
| Multiply (Short) | N ME | RX | R1, D2(X2, B2) | 7C |
| Store (Long) | STD | RX | R1, D2(X2, B2) | 60 |
| Store (Short) | STE | RX | R1, D2(X2, B2) | 70 |
| Subtract Normalized (Long) | N SDR | RR | R1, R2 | 2B |
| Subtract Normalized (Long) | N SD | RX | R1, D2(X2, B2) | 6B |
| Subtract Normalized (Short) | N SER | RR | R1, R2 | 3B |
| Subtract Normalized (Short) | N SE | RX | R1, D2(X2, B2) | 7B |
| Subtract Unnormalized (Long) | SWR | RR | R1, R2 | 2F |
| Subtract Unnormalized (Long) | SW | RX | R1, D2(X2, B2) | 6F |
| Subtract Unnormalized (Short) | SUR | RR | R1, R2 | 3F |
| Subtract Unnormalized (Short) | SU | RX | R1, D2(X2, B2) | 7F |

Figure 6-18 Machine language computer instructions for the IBM System/360 and System/370 series. (Courtesy International Business Machines Corporation.)

### Single-Address Instruction Format

*Single-address instruction format references an operand or data address for each instruction.*

A common instruction format is the one- or single-address that is generally associated with a fixed-word length computer. The instruction word is fixed at one and, sometimes, at one-half word. To simplify the discussion on a single-address instruction format, all storage locations for this computer (5000 word computer) are capable of holding 10 characters of information plus a sign (plus or minus). All data use the full 10-digit positions whether they are needed or not. This is contrasted with instructions that must contain 10 digits of information for a valid instruction. Each instruction is made up of three items: the operation code (positions 9-10), operand or data address (5-8), and instruction address (1-4) as described above.

***Single-Address, Fixed-Word Length Illustration.*** To illustrate the operation of a single-address, fixed-word length computer, the problem of adding A and B to obtain the value C, which then must be stored in a specified location, is set forth. Programming this problem in machine language requires four instructions as follows:

| *Operation Code* | |
|---|---|
| 20 | RESET accumulator to zero and LOAD contents of operand (data address) location into accumulator. |
| 25 | ADD contents of operand (data address) location to data in accumulator. |
| 40 | STORE contents of accumulator in storage location specified by operand (data address). |
| 10 | JUMP to another instruction of the program. |

The above instructions are for a hypothetical fixed-word length computer. Comparable instructions for the current IBM series are found in Figure 6-18 under the "Code" column.

In this sample problem, four storage locations, 2000 to 2003 (chosen arbitrarily) will contain the instructions. The value A will have been stored previously in location 0500 and the value B in location 0501. Both the values for A and B require ten-digit words as well as the value to be stored in location 1500 for C although their actual values will require less space in memory. The reason is that a fixed-word length computer is being utilized.

The four instructions that are required to solve for A + B = C are given below.

| | *Instruction* | | | |
|---|---|---|---|---|
| *Storage Location of Instruction* | *Operation Code* | *Operand (Data Address)* | *Instruction Address* | *Explanation* |
| 2000 | 20 | 0500 | 2001 | RESET accumulator to zero, LOAD A into accumulator, and GO to next instruction at 2001. |
| 2001 | 25 | 0501 | 2002 | ADD B to A and GO to next instruction at 2002. |
| 2002 | 40 | 1500 | 2003 | STORE contents of accumulator (C) in address 1500 and GO to next instruction at 2003. |
| 2003 | 10 | 3000 | — | JUMP to next instruction at 3000. |

Note that in the above program, the number to be added is not the number in the four-digit operand address segment of the instruction, but the ten-digit number in memory represented by those four digits. Thus, all data in this computer comes in ten-digit groups whereas the location of data is specified by only four digits.

### Multiple-Address Instruction Format

*Multiple-address instruction format references two or more operands or data addresses for each instruction.*

Another instruction format is the multiple-address system that is found in many computers currently on the market. The two-address instruction format contains two operands that normally reference two storage locations. For example, the instruction "add 1750 2060" would be interpreted (by some computers) to mean, "add the contents of storage location 2060 to location 1750 and store the results in 1750." In a three-address system, the first two addresses would reference the location of the data to be acted upon and the third address would specify where the result of the operation is to be stored. Generally, variable-word length and byte-addressable combination are used for the multiple-address instruction format.

***Two-Address, Variable-Word Length Illustration.*** Referring to the preceding example under the single-address format, the same set of instructions will be used for a two-address, variable-word length format (with a word mark bit), except that the 25 instruction needs to be modified. Assuming the values for A and B are stored in locations 0500 and 0501 respectively and the results, C, are to be placed in location 0501 instead of 1500, instructions start in location 2000 as follows.

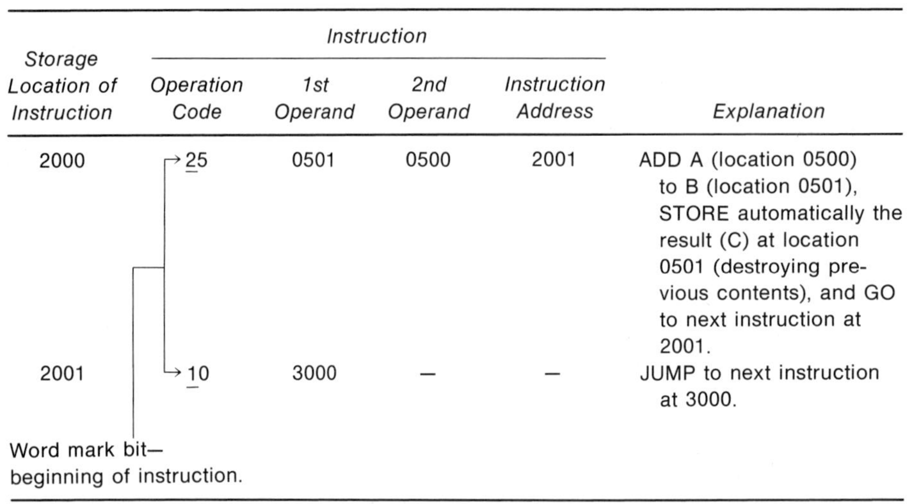

| Storage Location of Instruction | Instruction: Operation Code | Instruction: 1st Operand | Instruction: 2nd Operand | Instruction: Instruction Address | Explanation |
|---|---|---|---|---|---|
| 2000 | 25 | 0501 | 0500 | 2001 | ADD A (location 0500) to B (location 0501), STORE automatically the result (C) at location 0501 (destroying previous contents), and GO to next instruction at 2001. |
| 2001 | 10 | 3000 | — | — | JUMP to next instruction at 3000. |



If one of the values must be saved (B in the example), it would be necessary to have an additional instruction. This added instruction would store the value (B) in an appropriate location (for later use in the program) before specifying the storage-to-storage instruction indicated above. Storage-to-storage instruction concept means that data fields are brought out of primary storage, operated on by the arithmetic logical unit, and the results are stored back in primary storage.

***Single-Address Instruction Versus Multiple-Address Instruction.*** From the foregoing machine language instruction examples, the two-address instruction format does have an advantage over the single-address format. The number of instructions that must be executed to process a program is considerably reduced.

*The number of instructions to be executed with a multiple-address instruction format is less than with a single-address instruction format.*

In the example, the single-address instruction format required three lines of machine language to add A and B, storing the resulting value C, while the storage-to-storage approach required only one line of machine coding. However, the two-address instruction format destroys the initial value of the first operand by storing the answer in its place. Also, the multiple-address format is slower than the single-address method.

### Different Basic Instruction Formats

*Different basic instruction formats available on computers are:*
- *register-to-register*
- *register-and-storage*
- *immediate-operand-and-storage*
- *storage-to-storage*

In addition to the single- and multiple-address instruction formats, basic instructions may be of several different formats for many of the computers currently available. For the IBM System/360 and System/370, format codes RR, RX, RS, SI, and SS are available. The first byte of each of these formats gives the operation code that identifies the operation to be performed. Figure 6-19 depicts this feature for all basic instruction formats.

The RR format denotes a register-to-register operation. The operands are in general registers and the results replace the first operand. The second format RX denotes a register-and-storage operation. The first operand is in a general register and the second operand is in a main storage location. This format includes a factor for indexing the main storage address; the factor is contained within another general register, which is used as an index register and specified by the instruction. The results of an RX operation may replace the first operand, depending on the instruction. In the third format, RS denotes a register-and-storage operation. The first operand is in a general register, the second operand is in main storage, and a third may be specified by another general register.

For the fourth instruction format, SI denotes an immediate-operand-and-storage operation. The first operand is one byte of data carried in the instruction itself (the immediate operand), and the second operand is in main storage. The last instruction format SS denotes a storage-to-storage operation where both operands are in main storage. Reference to Figure 6-18 ("Type" column) indicates these basic instruction formats and their corresponding operands.

## EXECUTION OF COMPUTER INSTRUCTIONS

*Computer instructions are deciphered during the machine cycle, which can be divided into the instruction cycle and the execution cycle.*

Most stored computer instructions are executed in fixed intervals of time. A computer that utilizes fixed time intervals for determining the start of the next instruction is known as *synchronous*. On the other hand, a computer that initiates the next instruction based upon the receipt of a signal from the current operation is known as *asynchronous*. In both computers (synchronous and asynchronous), exact timing is needed for proper execution of the stored program instructions which is measured by regular impulses emitted from an electronic clock. The frequency of these pulses may be a billion or more each second. A fixed number of pulses measures the time of each basic machine cycle for a specific computer operation.

A *machine cycle* can be divided into two parts—the *instruction cycle* and the *execution cycle*. The first half of the machine cycle is necessary for carrying out the instruction while the second half actually performs the specified operation. The time for each cycle is known as instruction time or I-time and execution time or E-time, respectively. To illustrate the basic method of executing computer instructions, the prior example for a one-address and a two-address instruction formats will be utilized.

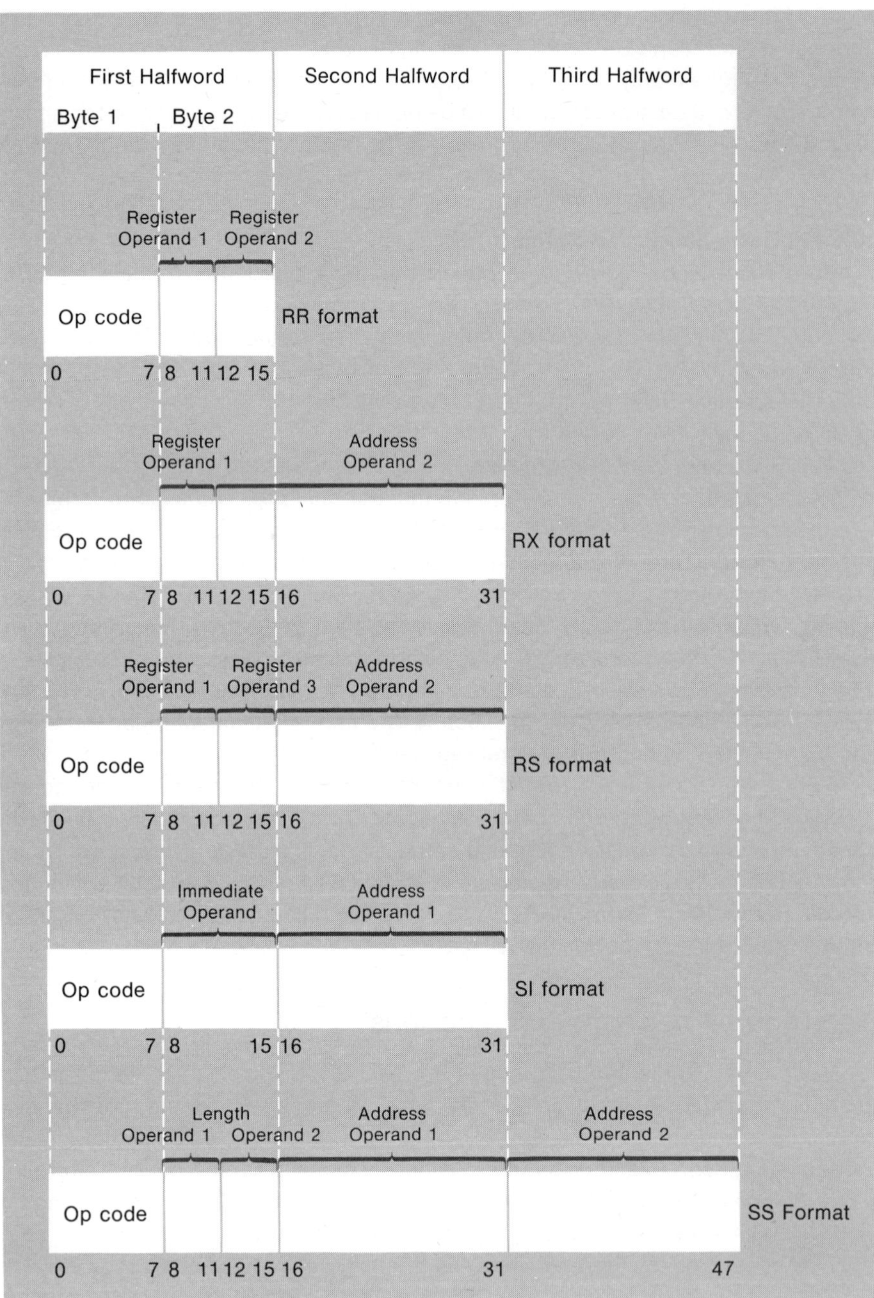


Figure 6-19 Basic instruction formats. (Courtesy International Business Machines Corporation)

## One-Address Instruction and Execution Cycles

*One-address instruction and execution cycles decipher the contents of an operation code register and a single-address register, and undertake the desired processing.*

The execution of an one-address instruction is illustrated in Figure 6-20. Assuming the machine has completed the first instruction—located at storage location 2000—it is now going on to the next instruction in memory location 2001. In Figure 6-20*a*, the 10-digit number is brought into the program register during the execution cycle. This data is the instruction (25 0501 2002) for adding the value *A* to *B* which has been previously stored in memory. We will let the value for *A* ($130.00) represent regular pay and the value for *B* ($20.00) be the employee's overtime pay for the week. The total amount *C* ($150.00) is the individual's gross pay for the week.

During the instruction cycle (Figure 6-20*b*) of the instruction located at 2001, the operation code (25) is brought into the operation register and the operand (0501) is brought into the address register. Nothing happens in the arithmetic unit during this cycle. However, in the next cycle (Figure 6-20*c*), the data in location 0501 (*B*) are brought into the arithmetic unit and added to the previous contents (*A*). While the arithmetic unit is adding *A* to *B*, the operation register and the address register are cleared. The number (2002) in the instruction address positions of the program register is loaded into the address register (Figure 6-20*d*).

Having completed the machine cycle for the instruction stored at location 2001, the computer locates the next instruction (40 1500 2003) which it brings into the program register (Figure 6-20*e*). The same machine cycle process is undertaken for this instruction as was performed for the previous one. The net outcome of this instruction will be the storage of the data (*C* or $150.00) contained in the arithmetic unit at location 1500.

*Machine cycles (instruction and execution) are directed by the CPU control unit.*

***Machine Cycles Directed by CPU Control Unit.*** The above machine cycles—instruction and execution—are directed by the CPU control unit. Not only is the control unit responsible for controlling input/output devices, entry, and retrieval of information from secondary storage but also routes information between primary storage and the arithmetic/logical section as well as directs the arithmetic/logical operations, as demonstrated above. The performance of these many operations requires elaborate circuitry over which data and instructions can be sent. Thus, routing the proper data through the circuitry, opening and closing the right electrical "gates" at the proper time, and determining timing sequences are vital functions of the CPU control unit.

### Two-Address Instruction and Execution Cycles

*Two-address instruction and execution cycles decipher the contents of an operation code register and two address registers, and undertake the desired processing.*

Using the illustration for the two-address instruction format set forth previously, the execution cycle begins by bringing in the contents of location 2000 ($\underline{2}$5 0501 0500 2001) to the program register from memory (Figure 6-21*a*). Assuming again that the computer uses variable-word length and word mark bit, it determines the first two digits to be $\underline{2}$5. Being the first two digits that have a word mark bit, it is interpreted to be the operation code that is loaded into the operation register (Figure 6-21*b*). The computer then looks at the following four characters of the instruction (0501) and automatically loads them in the A-address register. It checks for the presence of a word mark bit and, finding none, it loads the next four characters into the B-address register. This process ends the instruction cycle in Figure 6-21*b* even though no data has been processed.

The execution cycle adds the contents of *A* (0500) to *B* (0501). In this operation, the new value *C* is stored in the place of the *B* value at location 0501 (Figure 6-21*c*). Since the employee's gross pay is the value of interest, the loss of the original value in location 0501 or *B* will not cause problems later on as the program is processed.

In the next instruction cycle, the B-address register contains the location of the next instruction (Figure 6-21*d*). The computer goes to this storage location 2001 and finds $\underline{1}$0 with a word mark bit (Figure 6-21*e*). The machine language 10 is an operation code which orders the computer to jump to another instruction of the program. In payroll processing, the program would normally instruct the computer to perform other manipulations of data and output before going on to the next

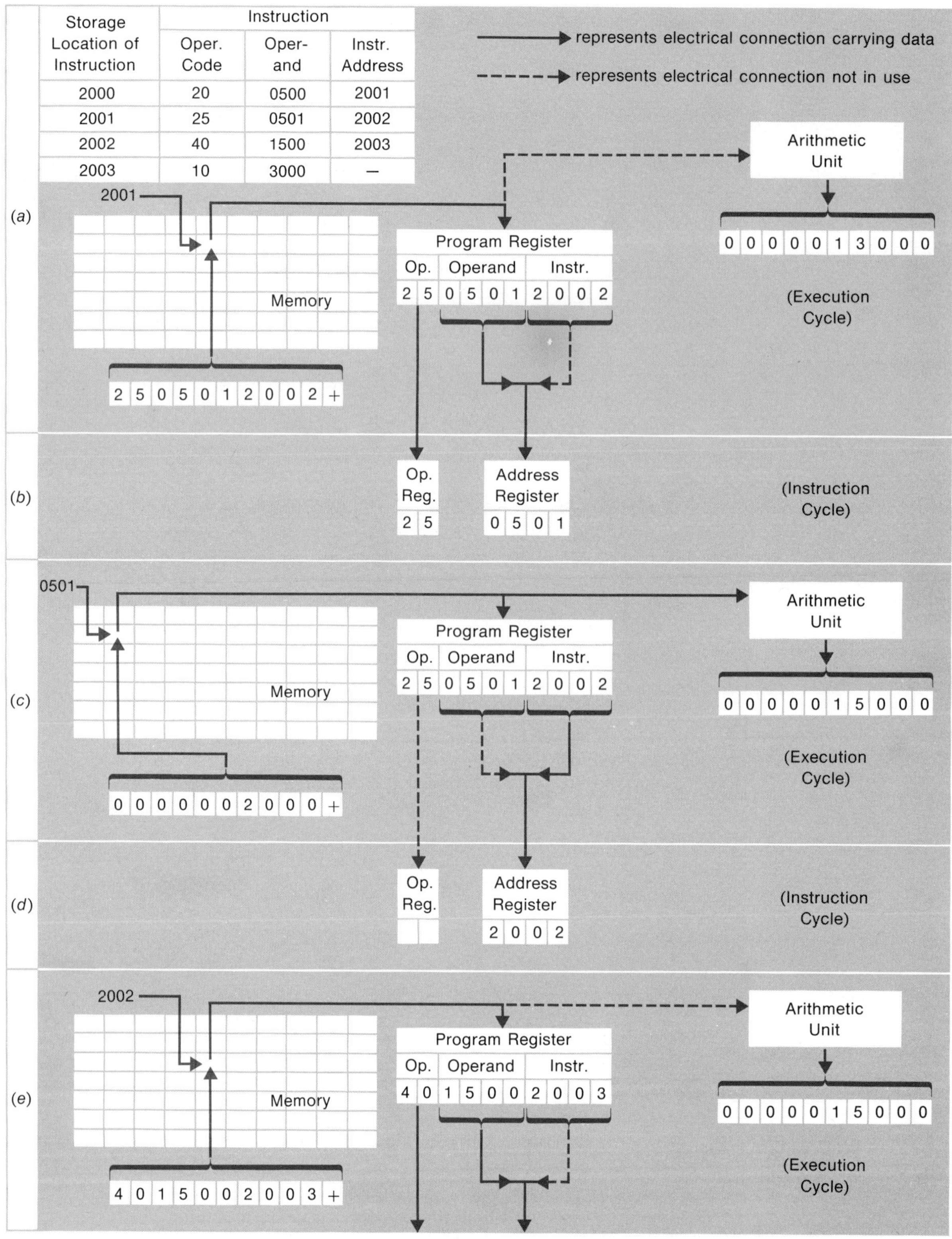


| Storage Location of Instruction | Instruction | | |
|---|---|---|---|
| | Oper. Code | Oper-and | Instr. Address |
| 2000 | 20 | 0500 | 2001 |
| 2001 | 25 | 0501 | 2002 |
| 2002 | 40 | 1500 | 2003 |
| 2003 | 10 | 3000 | — |

Figure 6-20 Instruction and execution cycles for one-address instruction format.

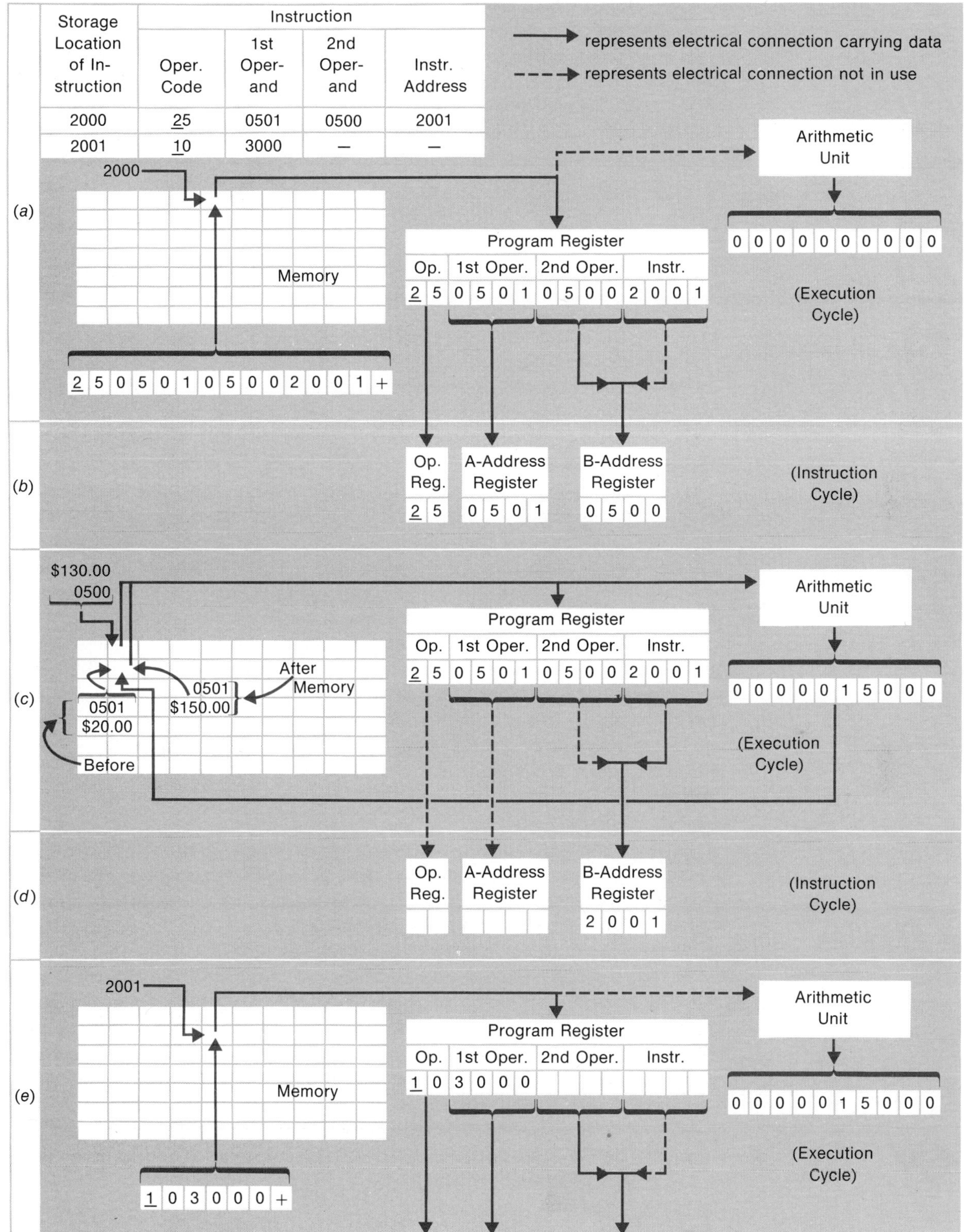

represents electrical connection carrying data
represents electrical connection not in use
Storage Location of Instruction
Instruction
Oper. Code
1st Operand
2nd Operand
Instr. Address
2000 25 0501 0500 2001
2001 10 3000 — —
(a)
2000
Memory
2 5 0 5 0 1 0 5 0 0 2 0 0 1 +
Program Register
Op. 1st Oper. 2nd Oper. Instr.
2 5 0 5 0 1 0 5 0 0 2 0 0 1
Arithmetic Unit
0 0 0 0 0 0 0 0 0 0
(Execution Cycle)
(b)
Op. Reg.
2 5
A-Address Register
0 5 0 1
B-Address Register
0 5 0 0
(Instruction Cycle)
(c)
$130.00
0500
0501
$20.00
Before
0501
$150.00
After
Memory
Program Register
Op. 1st Oper. 2nd Oper. Instr.
2 5 0 5 0 1 0 5 0 0 2 0 0 1
Arithmetic Unit
0 0 0 0 0 1 5 0 0 0
(Execution Cycle)
(d)
Op. Reg.
A-Address Register
B-Address Register
2 0 0 1
(Instruction Cycle)
(e)
2001
Memory
1 0 3 0 0 0 +
Program Register
Op. 1st Oper. 2nd Oper. Instr.
1 0 3 0 0 0
Arithmetic Unit
0 0 0 0 0 1 5 0 0 0
(Execution Cycle)

Figure 6-21 Instruction and execution cycles for two-address instruction format.

employee. It should be pointed out that all operations of the two-address instruction format are under the direction of the CPU control unit.

*Larger computers overlap machine cycles, allowing several computer instructions to undergo preparation concurrently.*

***Instructions in Large Computers.*** The larger computers—System/360, Models 85 and 195 and some System/370 series of IBM, for example—utilize a high-speed buffer that reduces the time it takes to get at stored data. Specifically, the operation of the instruction unit (program register) is overlapped, allowing up to three instructions to undergo preparation concurrently so that the next program-sequenced instruction is ready for execution. Thus current computers contain high-speed buffer storage that provides an ultra-high speed instruction processing rate.

## ADVANTAGES OF COMPUTERS OVER PUNCHED CARD EQUIPMENT

*The major advantages of computers over punched card equipment encompass:*
- *improve decision making*
- *reduced manual intervention*
- *better data processing control*
- *increased flexibility*
- *more intangible benefits*

An understanding of how the computer operates provides a background for evaluating its important advantages over punched card equipment. As will be seen in the following, many tangible and intangible benefits accrue to the computer user. A most significant feature is the computer's ability to provide managerial and operational information on a timely basis.

### Improved Decision Making

A computer provides for integration of many or all applications that cut across the entire firm as part of a total system. This approach makes it possible to implement a real-time management information system where "management by exception" can be practiced on a "now" basis. The timely feedback of data provides for adjustments where necessary in order to keep the firm's costs at a minimum. A computer system, then, assures better management control since timely data are available to management in a more complete manner, either on demand or at stated intervals, than a punched card system is capable of providing. Management is able to make decisions on current facts rather than on historical information. Computers have the capability to approach the "total systems concept" where all inputs and outputs are automatically coordinated. Punched card machines are not capable of obtaining such an ambitious goal.

### Reduced Manual Intervention

While a punched card system relies on several machines to perform individual functions, such as sorting, collating, calculating, and so forth, a computer performs these same operations by a series of programs. Data flows from one program to another without stopping or having the manual intervention of a punched card system. This is not to say that there is no manual intervention with a computer. A well-designed system keeps it to a minimum. The rationale for very little intervention after the computer input phase results from the capabilities of the computer itself. A computer system has the arithmetic and logical ability plus the capacity to store large volumes of data on-line either in primary storage or secondary storage and to operate on that data. A computer system is not tied to the number of columns in a card, but rather can form records on magnetic media in a length necessary for the specific application. Punched card equipment does not have the storage capability within its system. Its logical and arithmetic ability is limited in terms of what a computer can do.

### Better Data Processing Control

A computer, employing stored program logic, can do a more thorough job of editing and validating data before they are entered into the system than is the case with punched card equipment. The stored program concept is more precise than a combined plugboard, manual procedure method. In addition to being more accurate, it is faster than a punched card system. Basically, a computer system provides for a more complete processing system since it has a greater capacity, capability, and speed than a punched card system. Although most of the computerized business processing can be done on punched card equipment, the important differences are the method, the time, the cost, and the practicability that prevents a punched card system from matching a computer system.

#### Increased Flexibility and Immediate Response

An important feature of computers is the ability to increase capacity and capability by upgrading components—more memory, faster tapes, and similar hardware. This modular concept is in contrast to a punched card system where another unit of the same type (there are exceptions) is used to increase capacity. A computer system provides for immediate responses via input/output terminals whereas this capability is not available with punched card machines.

#### More Intangible Benefits

The cost of each data processing application on a computer, in general, can be lower than when alternative machine methods are utilized. Even though the initial cost of installing a computer is high, savings resulting from its speed and accuracy can justify the decision to install a newer generation computer. In most cases, computers cannot be justified on tangible benefits accruing to the firm. In these cases, intangible results from the computer will be the basis for a newer computer system. On-line real-time capabilities, for example, can reduce the time for handling incoming orders, which might be sufficient reason for acquiring a more advanced computer system. Also, the fact that competition has the same type of equipment for improving service might be reason enough.

### LIMITATIONS OF COMPUTERS

*Limitations of computers are:*
- *increased need for trained personnel*
- *machine breakdowns*
- *loss of audit trail*
- *carelessness of operators*

Although the above advantages are overwhelmingly in favor of EDP equipment versus punched card machines, there are a few limitations that cannot be ignored.

#### Increased Need for Trained Personnel

Computer installations require highly trained and competent personnel in order to reap the benefits of a system. Without competent personnel, it is doubtful that the firm will be able to design an efficient system to meet its needs. These people are not only hard to find because of the tremendous demand but also command high salaries. Smaller companies have difficulty competing with medium- and large-sized firms for employees in terms of the opportunities and salaries they can offer. This critical element, then, can spell success or failure for any EDP operation.

#### Machine Breakdowns

Machine breakdowns can be a real headache to users. This is particularly true if the computer system is an on-line real-time system or a time-sharing system. Even considerable downtime for a batch processing computer can temporarily put the firm out of business. Computers, being sensitive to heat, cold, and humidity, need controlled environments in which to operate. If trouble is experienced with air conditioning, a power failure has developed, or similar uncontrolled situations occur, the computer facility may be down for long periods of time even though the machine is capable of processing.

**Loss of Audit Trail**

One of the biggest problems with on-line systems is the loss of the audit trail. Data stored on magnetic disks, for example, is lost every time new data are written back on the storage media. This loss of data makes it impossible for the internal or external auditors to follow the flow of transactions on such items as inventory and accounts receivable. However, alternative auditing methods are available for satisfying the auditor as to the authenticity of these transactions.

**Carelessness of Terminal Operator**

In the past, the argument about insufficient volume was used frequently against the computer to warrant the expense involved. This may be true of the very small firm with a few people. However, the advent of time-sharing devices and service bureaus has, to a large degree, nullified this limitation. Those firms using time sharing-services must train their personnel in the proper use of these terminals. Otherwise, the accuracy of data stored on-line can be reduced by the carelessness of terminal operators.

## SUMMARY

An understanding of computer data codes—binary, hexadecimal, and related coding schemes—was presented in order to illustrate how the arithmetic operations are handled by a computer system. Other systems of data representation could have been explored, such as the bi-quinary, octal, and quinary. However, coverage was comprehensive enough to obtain an overview of how the computer operates internally. It should be pointed out that it is not necessary to comprehend the coding scheme used by the machine when programming if a programming language is the method of instructing the computer.

The inner workings of the computer's logic was followed by a presentation of machine language instructions and how they are executed. The concept of addressing as related to single-address and multiple-address instruction formats was discussed in terms of the word structure for the computer employed. While past- and current-generation computers have been either fixed-word length or variable-word length, the present trend is the byte-addressable combination that incorporates the advantages of both.

## *QUESTIONS*

1. What is the basic advantage and the basic limitation of the binary system?
2. Contrast the similarities and differences among the following computer data codes:
   (a) binary coded decimal (BCD)
   (b) six-bit numeric code
   (c) standard binary coded decimal interchange code
   (d) hexadecimal system
   (e) extended binary coded decimal interchange code (EBCDIC)
   (f) U.S.A. standard code for information interchange (USASCII)
3. Why is the hexadecimal system used as an operator notation form?
4. Of the several computer data codes illustrated in the chapter, which one results in the most efficient utilization of the computer's memory?

5. (a) State the rules for binary addition, subtraction, multiplication, and division.
   (b) Do the same for the hexadecimal system.
6. Explain the function of a parity check bit for transmitting data.
7. Explain the relationship of Boolean algebra (truth tables) to the computer's capability of performing arithmetic operations.
8. Distinguish among the following: a word, a byte, and a bit.
9. (a) What is a computer instruction? Explain.
   (b) Are computer instructions the same for all computers?
10. (a) What kind of registers are utilized by the central processing unit?
    (b) What are the functions of registers?
11. Differentiate between single-address and multiple-address instruction formats.
12. How does a byte-addressable combination computer differ from a fixed-word length or variable-word length computer? Explain.
13. What is the difference between the program register and the address register in the arithmetic/logical unit of the central processing unit?
14. (a) Explain briefly the execution of a one-address instruction in the arithmetic/logical unit.
    (b) Explain briefly the execution of a two-address instruction in the arithmetic/logical unit.
15. Of the many advantages given for computers, which one(s) is (are) most important from a management point of view and a data processing point of view?

## *EXERCISES*

1. Take the decimal values 74, 476, and 1076 and express them in the binary coded decimal system and in the hexadecimal system.
2. Add the following decimal values and express them in binary and hexadecimal codes.
   (a) 175 + 44 (b) 1420 + 175 (c) 4442 + 177
3. Subtract the values in Exercise 2 from one another, expressing them in binary and hexadecimal codes.
4. Multiply the following decimal values and state them in the binary and hexadecimal codes.
   (a) 175 × 20 (b) 250 × 25 (c) 1250 × 125
5. Take the following decimal values 25 and 145 and express them in the six-bit numeric code and in the standard binary coded decimal interchange code.

CHAPTER SEVEN

# Computer Equipment and Systems

- Data Buffering
  - Ideal Buffered Conditions
- Input/Output Devices
  - Card Readers and Punches
  - Magnetic Ledger Card Readers
  - Punched Paper Tape Readers and Punches
  - Tape Cartridge Reader
  - Magnetic Tape Units
  - Laser Optical Recorder/Reproducer
  - On-Line Printers
  - Microfilm Systems
  - Console Typewriter and Related Devices
  - Other Input/Output Devices
  - Summary of Input/Output Devices
- Central Processing Unit
- Primary Storage Devices
  - Magnetic Core
  - Magnetic Thin Film
  - Large-scale Integration (LSI)
  - Internal Operating Speeds
- Secondary Storage Devices
  - Laser Mass Memory
  - Magnetic Disk
  - Magnetic Drum
  - Magnetic Card
  - Magnetic Strip
- External Storage
- Summary of Internal and External Storage
- Computer System Configurations
  - Mini-Computers
  - Small Card-Oriented System
  - Small Magnetic Tape-Oriented System
  - Small Magnetic Disk-Oriented System
  - Medium-scale Computer System
  - Large-scale Computer System
- Modular Concept
  - Hardware Modularity
  - Software Modularity
- Summary

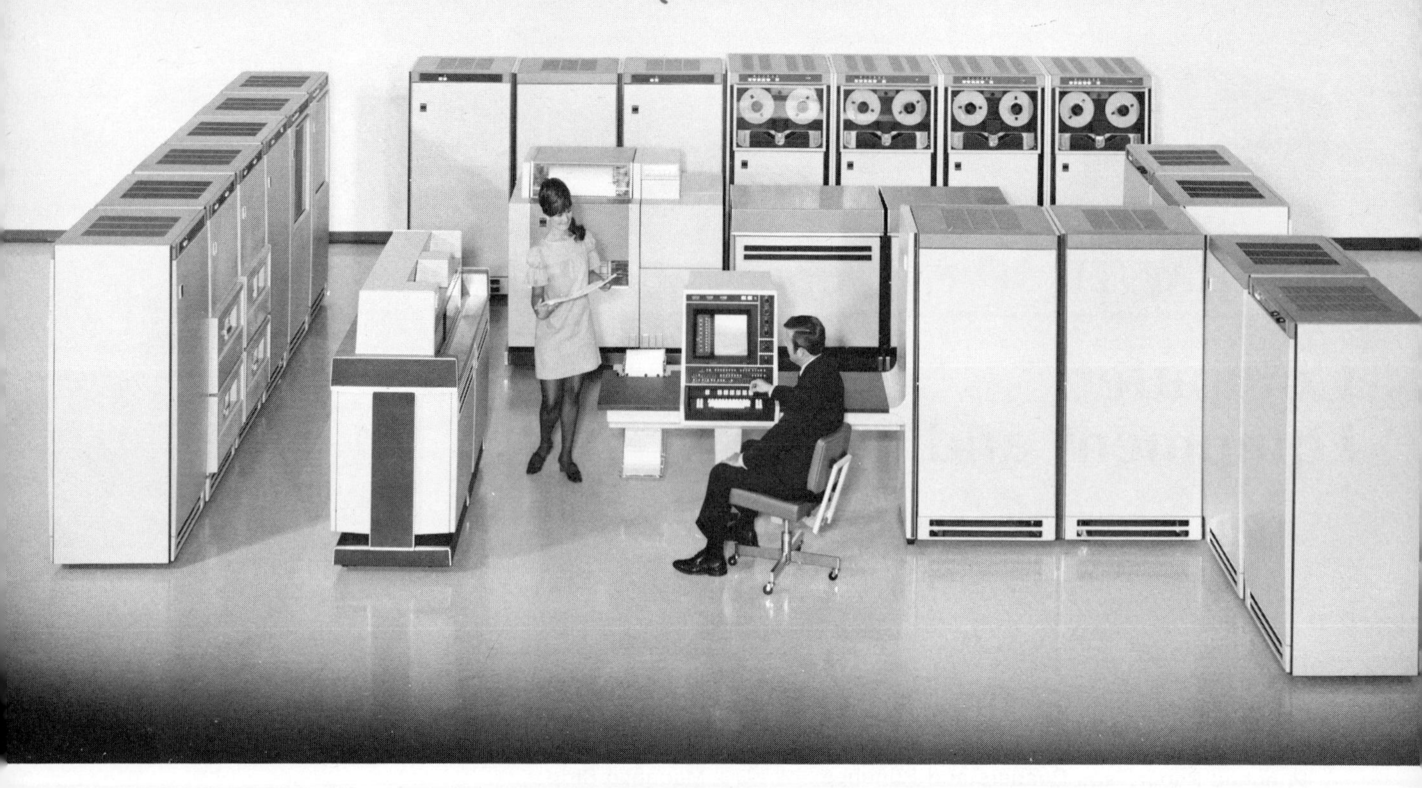

*The number of computer peripheral devices has grown in response to user needs. A central processing unit plus a configuration of computer devices comprise a computer system as illustrated above. Typical computer systems are presented in the chapter. (Courtesy The National Cash Register Company.)*

The major components of a computer system—input, central processor, (memory, arithmetic/logical unit, and CPU control unit), files (secondary storage), output, control units, channels, and I/O interface—are explored in more detail within this chapter. Other computer equipment, specifically optical character recognition (OCR) equipment and time-sharing devices are covered in Chapters 8 and 9, respectively. In addition to surveying various pieces of equipment, several computer systems, currently being marketed, are shown in order to illustrate the composition of equipment for business applications. These systems range from small scale to large scale, their differences being that of speed and ability to handle varying volumes of input, throughput, and output.

The process for determining which pieces of computer equipment are needed for a specific installation is based upon the amount and type of data processing operations being performed. Likewise, consideration must be given to the equipment available from the computer manufacturer. The task for the proper selection of computer equipment is an important part of a computer feasibility study, the subject matter for Part V—Implementing and Controlling Data Processing. Generally, the results of any computer system feasibility study will recommend that several pieces of equipment be utilized for a business data processing system. In the selection process, compatibility of equipment is essential. Data captured in one form must be processable by other equipment so that data processing is as free of human intervention as possible.

## DATA BUFFERING

*Data buffering is a method of overlapping computer operations in order to speed up processing.*

The importance of the data buffering concept will be apparent in the following discussion on computer equipment. Of greater importance is its impact on the computer system itself, in particular, the input-storage-processing-control-output (ISPCO) cycle. As previously discussed, input involves the various steps required to get data into memory using one or more of the available input devices. Processing involves controlled manipulation of the data between the central processor and storage to produce results. Output involves the transfer of those results to an output device. Basically, these phases are serial. In order to utilize all the components of the system efficiently, some means must be provided to overlap operations. Otherwise, much of the equipment will be idle for a considerable portion of its operating time, as shown in Figure 7-1*a*.

One method of overlapping operations is to place a temporary storage unit or buffer between the input/output devices and the central processor. For example, the physical movement and sensing of a single punched card may take as much time as thousands of arithmetic operations. If the processor waits for the card to be read or punched, time is wasted. Instead, the computer initiates a read command to start the card reader and then returns to computation. Meanwhile, the card is moved and sensed electromechanically while the data are transferred to buffer storage. When the processor returns its operations to the card reader, the card data are transferred to main memory electronically. This time is very short when compared with the electromechanical reading time. Therefore, if buffer storage is available to the card reader, data can be read and placed in temporary storage while the central processor manipulates internal data for meaningful output.

### Ideal Buffered Conditions

*The ideal buffered condition is overlapping simultaneously the input, processing, and output operations, as shown in Figure 7-1c.*

In Figure 7-1*b* and *c*, the data buffering concept is depicted. The ideal condition is shown as (*c*). As three operations are carried on simultaneously, the greater speed of the arithmetic unit becomes apparent. The arithmetic unit is being used only about half the time in the (*c*) illustration whereas the input and output units are being used full time. This further emphasizes that extremely fast memory access times may not be nearly as relevant as the speed of input or output devices.

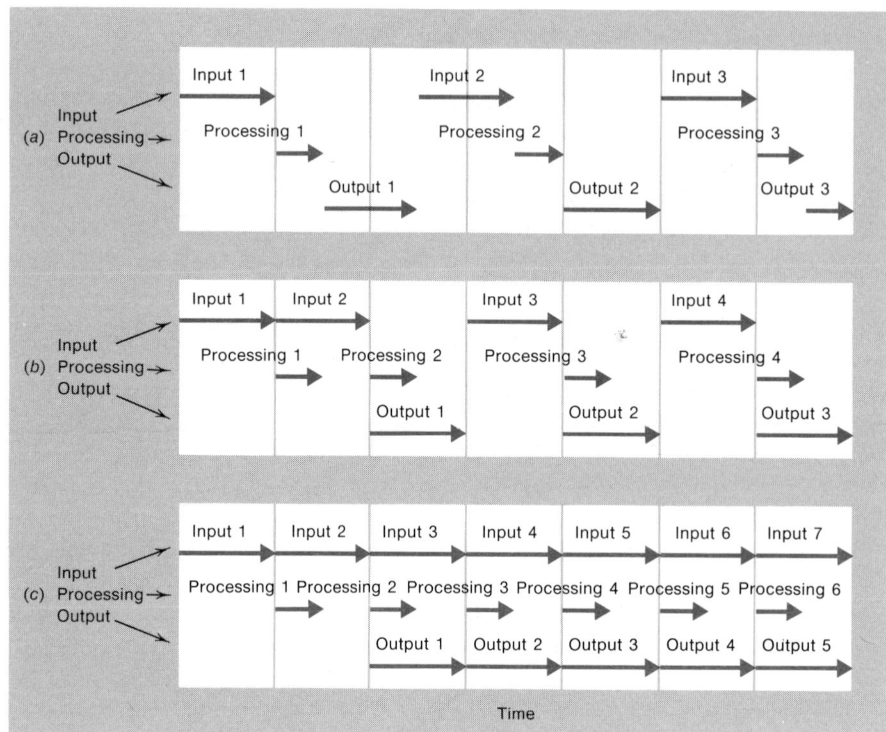


Figure 7-1 Data buffering—(*a*) not possible with serial processing, (*b*) and (*c*) possible with parallel processing where (*c*) is the ideal condition.

Since most business data processing requires very few internal calculations and manipulations by the central processor, the problem, then, is getting data into and out of the computer quickly in terms of its input and output devices. To speed up processing for current computers that are fully buffered, the transfer of data between input/output devices and memory usually takes place independently of one another through a channel. By way of review, an input/output channel allows for the buffering or temporary storage of data as well as the coordination and transfer of input/output data. Instead of the central processing unit stopping each time to read input or produce output data, the data are available in temporary storage for immediate processing by the CPU. In essence, the input/output channel allows the computer to process data internally while concurrently receiving input data and transferring output information.

## INPUT/OUTPUT DEVICES

An essential characteristic of input/output devices is that they are connected on-line to the central processing unit. They are activated under the control of the stored program and can transmit data to or receive data from the memory unit of the central processor. Many of these devices can be utilized as input and output devices, which will be pointed out in the following sections. In addition to the standard input/output devices, there is the increasing use of remotely located devices, such as teletype devices and visual display (CRT) units, to transmit data over conventional telephone lines to the computer. These devices are generally operated on-line. Other input devices, such as optical character recognition and magnetic ink character recognition, are capable of reading data directly into the computer. The discussion below will center around the standard input/output devices found in most computer installations.

### Card Readers and Punches

*Card readers and punches can be stand-alone units or combined read-punch units. Their function is to read and punch cards.*

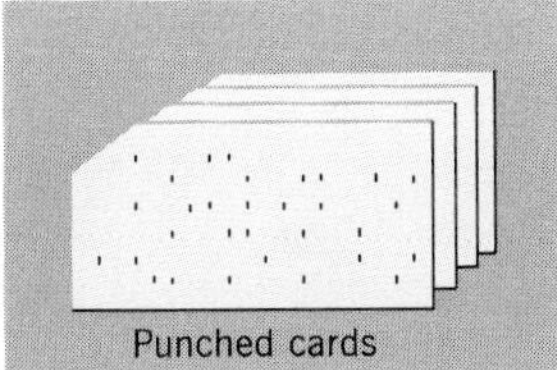


Punched cards are used as input and output to many computer systems. Card readers that serve as input devices vary widely in their reading rates. Reading speeds range from as low as 100 cards per minute up to 2000 cards per minute, the average speed being between 450 and 1200 cards per minute. Although this input rate seems high, the central processor is capable of processing at a much faster rate than the card reader can feed data into the computer system.

***Operation of Card Reader.*** Most computer card readers are similar in design to those used in punched card operations. In the brush type reader, cards are mechanically moved from a card hopper, through the card feed unit, and under reading brushes. The reading brushes sense the presence or absence of holes in each column of the card. This electric sensing converts the data to electrical impulses that can be utilized by the card reading unit for storing information. Some card readers have two sets of reading brushes (Figure 7-2) whereby each card is read twice as it moves through the card feed unit. This procedure checks on the validity of the first read station. After the cards are read, they are moved from the card feed unit and selected under program control in the appropriate stacker.

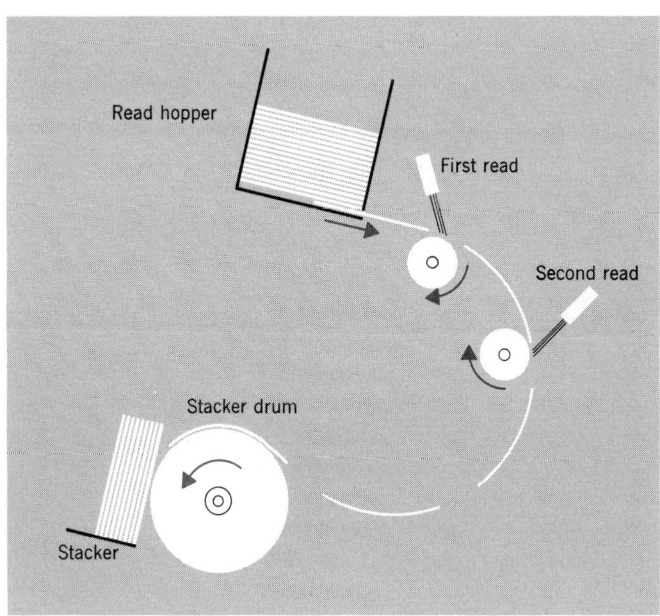


Figure 7-2 Schematic of card feed for computer high-speed card reader (brush type).

*Electromechanical card readers are slower than photoelectric card reading devices.*

A faster reader utilizes a photoelectric reading station, such as the one shown in Figure 7-3. The photoelectric card reader performs the same functions as the brush type, the difference being the method of sensing the holes. Photoelectric cells are activated by the presence of light. As the punched card is passed over a light source in the reader, light passing through the punched holes activates photoelectric cells (one cell for each column of the card) for recognizing and storing input data.

Figure 7-3 IBM 3505 Card Reader. (Courtesy International Business Machines Corporation.)

*The operation of the card punch is slower than that of the read unit.*

***Operation of Card Punch.*** The speed of output card devices, ranging from 60 to 500 cards per minute, are slower than that of readers, the average being between 100 to 300 cards per minute. As shown in Figure 7-4, the card punch unit moves blank cards automatically, one at a time, from the card hopper under a punching mechanism. The data received from storage is punched into the card. The card is moved to the checking station where the data are read and checked with the information received at the punching station. The card is then selected for the

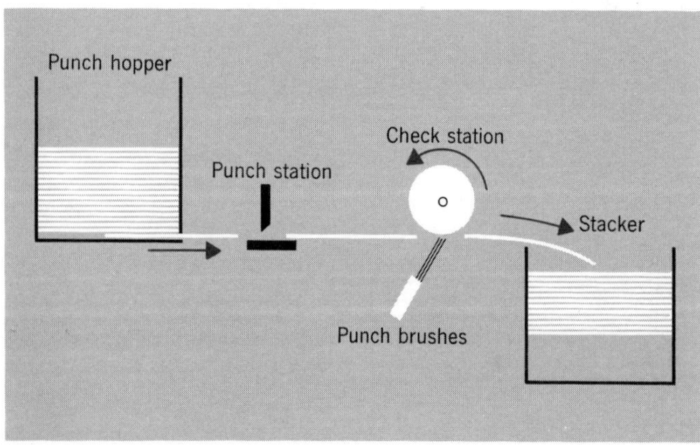


Figure 7-4 Schematic of card feed for computer card punch.

appropriate output stacker. Shown in Figure 7-5 is a typical card punch, operating at a rate up to 300 cards per minute.

*The trend continues toward combining the read and punch functions into one unit.*

***Combination Read-Punch Unit.*** A card punching machine may be combined with the card reader into one machine, shown in Figure 7-6 for the IBM System/360 and System/370 series. The long extension protruding from the read unit is known as a file feed, capable of holding up to 3100 cards. This card read-punch unit, with five output stackers, is capable of reading cards at a rate of 1000 cards per minute and punching at a speed of 300 cards per minute.

Figure 7-5 IBM 3525 Card Punch. (Courtesy International Business Machines Corporation.)

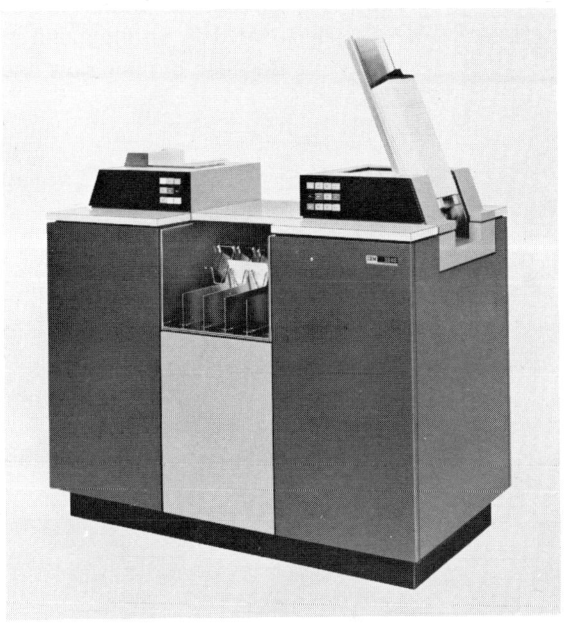

Figure 7-6 IBM 2540 Card-Read Punch. (Courtesy International Business Machines Corporation.)

Another combination read-punch unit on a small-scale computer system was previously shown in Figure 5-2. Depending on the Model—A1 or A2—it can read 96 column cards at the rate of 250 or 500 cards per minute and punch 60 or 120 cards per minute, respectively. This Multi-Function Card Unit (MFCU) consists of two input stations, a read station, two wait stations, single punch, cornering and print stations, and four output stackers. While under the control of the central processing unit, it can perform any of the following, individually, or in various combinations: read cards from two separate card files, collate, gang punch, summary punch, reproduce, interpret, punch calculation results, replace older master cards with new or updated ones in the proper file sequence, punch a card while the previous card is being printed, and print data on a card that are not punched in the card. Thus, a series of separate procedural operations on a punched card system can be consolidated and integrated into one or a few computer runs.

*The basic limitation of card read and punch units is their slow data transfer rate in and out of the computer.*

***Limitations of Card Input/Output Devices.*** Even though punched cards can be easily prepared and stored while being relatively inexpensive (approximately 0.1 cent each), the speed at which data can be transferred in and out of the computer is too slow for effective utilization of the central processing unit. This results in the

*Magnetic ledger card readers, the slowest of all input devices, read magnetic stripes on ledger cards.*

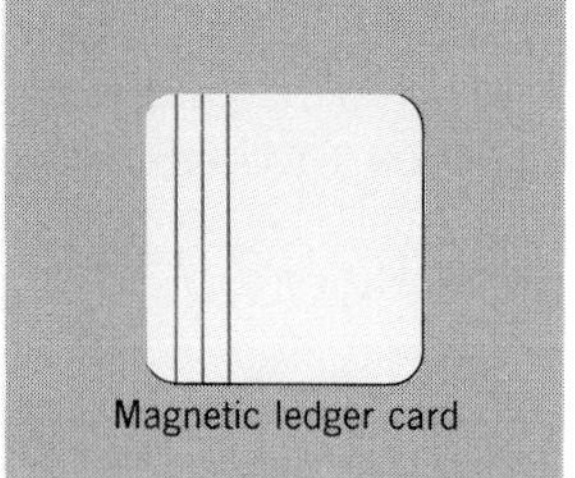


central processor being idle most of the time, waiting either on data being read or punched. Cards are limited to so many columns of information whereas a computer can handle long strings of information, say a thousand positions in length. In addition, cards are bulky to store for medium- to large-scale computer installations.

**Magnetic Ledger Card Readers**

Magnetic ledger cards are utilized in conjunction with some smaller computers, normally classified as electronic bookkeeping or accounting machines. Readers, such as the one illustrated in Figure 7-7, are available that automatically feed and read data on magnetic ledger cards at an average rate of 50 cards per minute. Because of their slow speeds, they are not widely used.

Figure 7-7 Burroughs Magnetic Ledger Card Reader. (Courtesy Burroughs, Inc.)

*Mechanical or photoelectric punched paper tape readers and punches can be stand-alone or combined read-punch units. Their function is to read and punch paper tape.*

**Punched Paper Tape Readers and Punches**

The paper tape reader reads data represented as punched holes in paper tape. The speed of reading ranges from 10 to as many as 2000 characters per second, depending on the type of paper tape reader. Mechanical readers can perform at speeds over 100 characters a second. For higher processing speeds, photoelectric-sensing techniques are generally employed. The tape reader moves or feeds the tape past a reading unit. The presence or absence of holes in the tape is sensed and converted to electronic impulses that are used as data by the computer system. Accuracy of reading is determined by making a parity check on each character.

Just as data can be read by a paper tape reader, data from the computer system can also be recorded as punched holes in paper tape by an automatic tape punch. Data received from main storage are converted to a tape code and punched in a blank tape as the tape is moved through a punching mechanism. Accuracy of data recorded is verified by a parity check for each character. Because of the electromechanical action usually required to produce the holes in the tape, the tape speed is approximately 300 characters a second.

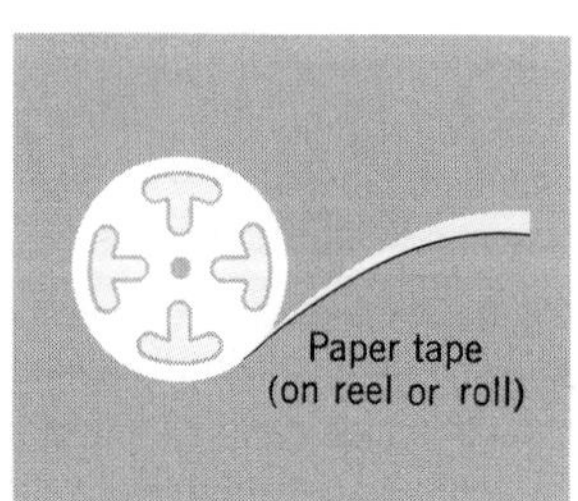


There are many punched paper tape readers, punches, and combination units available. Figure 7-8 shows a computer operator placing a punched paper tape onto

Figure 7-8 NCR Paper Tape Reader. (Courtesy The National Cash Register Company.)

the tape reader. It should be pointed out that output is not restricted to punched paper tape only. Several manufacturers are currently marketing paper tape to magnetic tape converters. Such a unit is illustrated in Figure 7-9. Conversion to magnetic tape is obtained by photoelectric reading of the paper tape input.

Figure 7-9 IBM 7765 Paper Tape to Magnetic Tape Converter. (Courtesy International Business Machines Corporation.)

***Advantages and Disadvantages of Paper Tape.*** Punched paper tape, when compared to cards, is a continuous medium of recording data since the length of any one record is not limited to the number of column positions. Secondly, punched paper tape is frequently a by-product of other machine operations. In effect, data are captured on punched tape at a very small cost when compared to keypunching and key verifying cards. Despite these advantages over punched cards, paper tape

*Punched paper tape data can be easily captured as a by-product of another data processing operation. However, its data transfer rate in and out of the computer is slower than punched cards.*

is not faster in terms of data transfer rate than cards and its output rate of punching is slower. Additional records cannot be inserted into the sequence of an already punched tape. They must be added on the end of the tape or a new tape must be prepared. Furthermore, punched tape cannot be sorted, collated, or reproduced by punched card equipment. As a result, paper tape for file applications is not as extensive as for punched cards.

*Tape cartridge reader is an input device for transferring data from tape cartridges.*

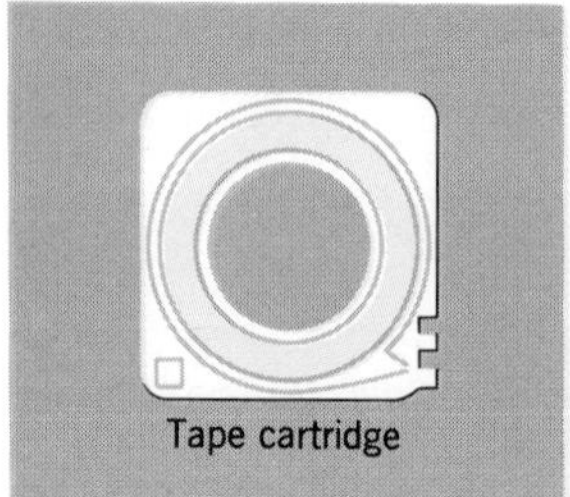


**Tape Cartridge Reader**

The IBM 2495 tape cartridge reader is the computer input device for data recorded by either the IBM 50 magnetic data inscriber or the IBM magnetic tape Selectric typewriter. It can read data into storage at the rate of 900 characters per second, being attached to a multiplexer channel. The machine accommodates as many as 12 cartridges (Figure 7-10).

**Magnetic Tape Units**

Most computer manufacturers have a series of magnetic tape units that are compatible with their own computer lines. They differ basically in two ways: the speed in reading or writing data on tape and the data density (number of bits, digits, or characters per inch) of the tape. Regarding the tape's speed, magnetic tape has a very fast data transfer rate with speeds ranging up to about 350,000 characters or bytes per second for either input or output. Many tape units can read tape as it moves in either direction.

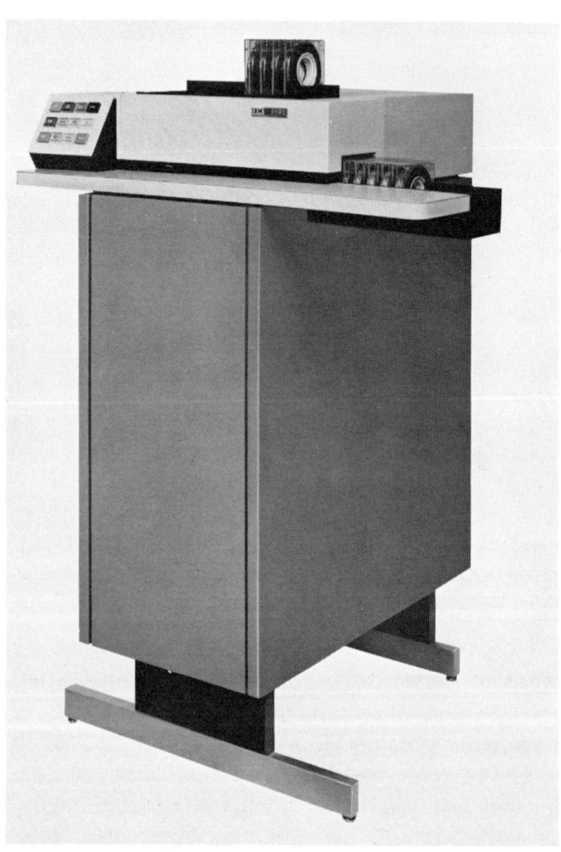

Figure 7-10 IBM 2495 Tape Cartridge Reader. (Courtesy International Business Machines Corporation.)

*Magnetic tape is used widely for input and output because of its fast transfer rate and low error rate.*

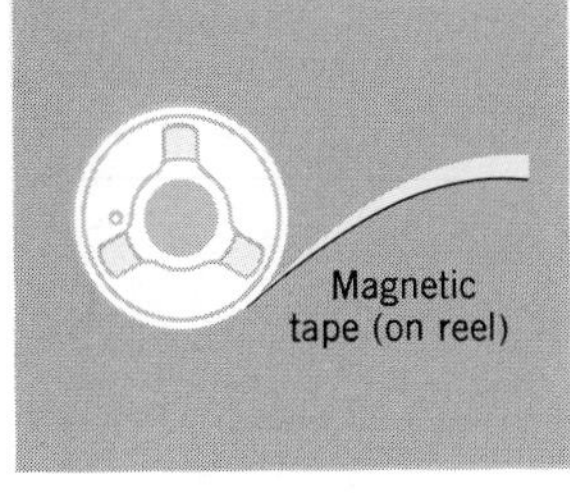


Referring to the tape's data density, early recording devices placed 200 parallel characters per inch on tape and had an error rate of one error in $10^5$ bits. Current systems allow 1600 parallel bytes per inch and provide error rates on the order of one in $10^7$ bits. The latest developments in serial recording provide capability for 16,000 bits per inch, with error rates less than one in $10^9$ bits. This increase in capacity and accuracy has been the result of improved magnetic tapes and magnetic heads, and to increasing sophistication of the methods used to record and recover data.

Magnetic tape drives read magnetic tape, which is made from a very strong and durable plastic. The tape is coated with a substance that can be easily magnetized. Data are recorded on the tape surface by means of magnetized spots. As indicated in Figure 7-11, numbers, letters, and special characters can be recorded by using the 7-bit alphanumeric code. A single reel of tape is usually $\frac{1}{2}$ to 1 inch wide and 2400 feet long.

Figure 7-11 Magnetic tape—7-bit alphanumeric code.

*Magnetic tape units utilize a coded pattern of 0 and 1 bits for reading and writing data.*

***Operation of Magnetic Tape Unit.*** Before the magnetic tape unit can be utilized for reading or writing tape, two tape reels—file and machine—must be mounted. The tape from the file reel is threaded through the tape feed mechanism (Figure 7-12). During reading or writing phase, tape is transferred from the file reel past the read-write head to the machine reel. To provide for high-speed starts and stops without tape breakage, a loop of tape is held in a vacuum column on either side of the read-write head and acts as a buffer for tape motion.

Writing takes place as the tape is moved across the magnetic gap of each of the seven recording (write) heads, one for each recording track. Electrical current flowing through each recording head coil at timed intervals magnetizes small areas along a channel in the oxide coating of the tape. These magnetized areas can be detected or sensed as a 0 or 1 bit condition.

During writing, current is flowing in some of the coils and not in others, establishing a coded pattern of 0 and 1 bits in a column across the width of the tape, as shown in Figure 7-11. Although the tape is moving at a high rate of speed, the electrical pulses to the write heads are so fast that it appears that the tape is motionless. Writing on magnetic tape is destructive, meaning that previous information on the tape is lost as new information is written.

Reading information from the tape occurs when the tape is moved past the read-write gap. As the magnetized areas pass the gap, small currents are generated in the read coil of the head. These electrical pulses from the magnetized tape represent data in electronic form which are made available by the tape drive circuitry

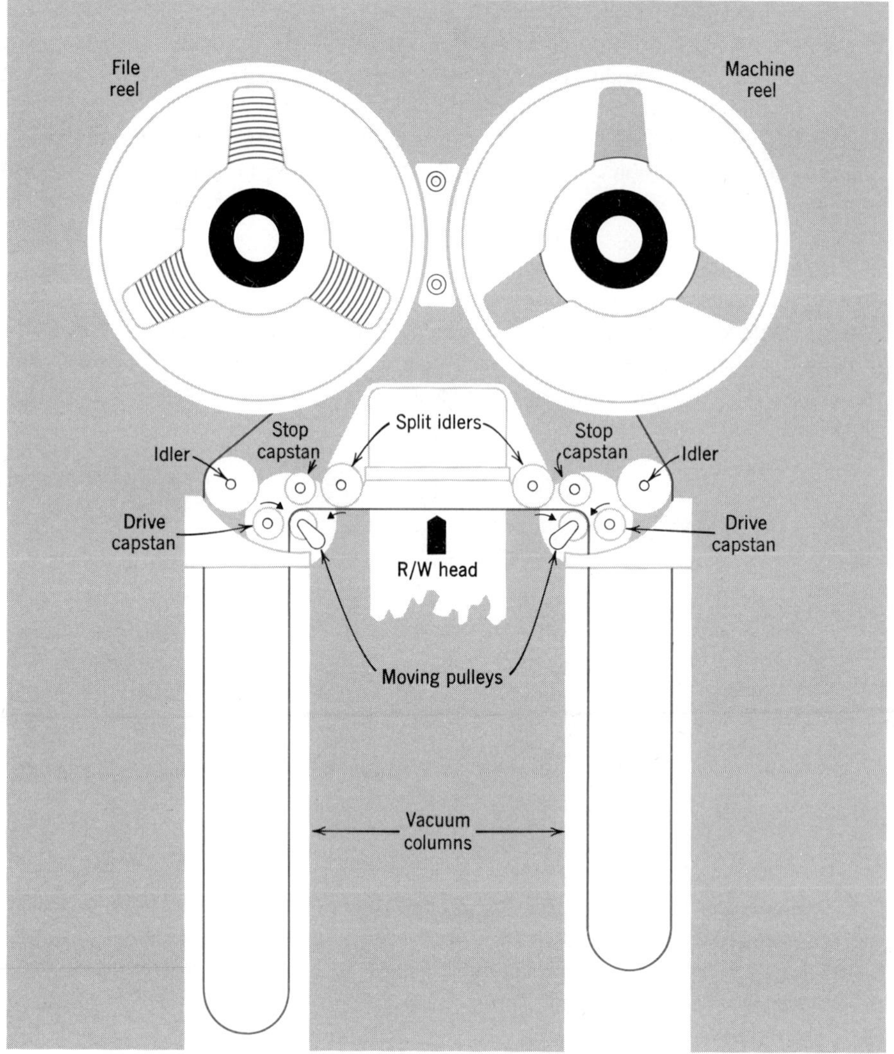


Figure 7-12 Schematic of magnetic tape feed unit.

to working storage. Reading is nondestructive; that is, the same information can be read again and again.

***Current Magnetic Tape Units.*** The foregoing fundamentals of magnetic tape units apply to all models on the market currently. For example, the IBM 3420 magnetic tape unit reads and writes data at densities of 800 or 1600 bits per inch on one-half inch magnetic tape. It is under the control of the 3803 tape control where several tape drives can be combined for a computer data processing system (Figure 7-13). The IBM 2415 (Figure 7-14) provides a tape service similar to and compatible with other tape drives. However, the tape drives are in the same housing unit as the control.

*Hypertape drives have the fastest performance speeds for magnetic tape input and output.*

For the highest performance magnetic tape input and output, the IBM 7340 hypertape drive Model 3 provides data rates up to 340,000 characters or 680,000 digits per second. A special feature of the 7340 is the automatic cartridge loader (Figure 7-15), mounted on the top of the hypertape drive. The automatic cartridge

Figure 7-13 IBM 3420 magnetic tape units and 3803 tape control. (Courtesy International Business Machines Corporation.)

loader reduces the time spent on tape handling, automatically unloading a processed cartridge and loading the next cartridge in less than 45 seconds under program control. While the current cartridge is being processed, the operator inserts the next cartridge and removes any discharged cartridge.

*File protection ring safeguards data written on magnetic tape.*

***File-Protection Ring.*** All of the magnetic tape drives utilize magnetic tape reels that are equipped with a file-protection ring—used to safeguard data already on the tape. If the ring has not been inserted, data cannot be written on the tape. On the other hand, if the ring has been inserted, data can be recorded. In either case, tape data can be read for processing.

***Advantages of Magnetic Tape.*** The most important advantage of magnetic tape is that it has one of the fastest data transfer rates of any input/output device. It

Figure 7-14 IBM 2415 magnetic tape unit and control. (Courtesy International Business Machines Corporation.)

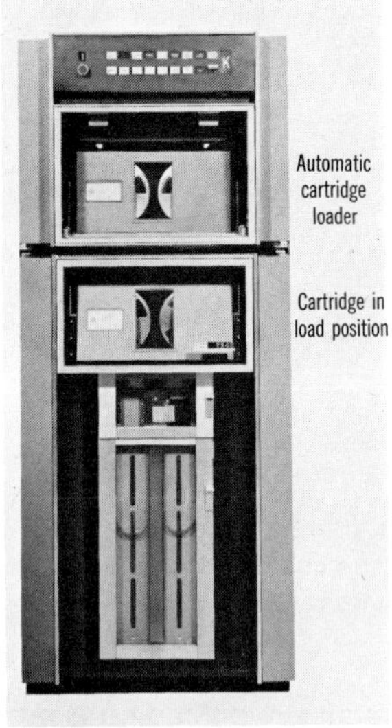


Figure 7-15 IBM 7340 Model 3 Hypertape Drive with automatic cartridge loader. (Courtesy International Business Machines Corporation.)

is capable of storing large amounts of data in a compact form that is readily available and easily erasable. From these viewpoints, magnetic tape can be utilized not only for input/output purposes but also as a major auxiliary storage medium. Tape reels are usable for up to 50,000 passes through a tape read-write unit, making tape a relatively inexpensive medium of storing data. Tape is widely used for storing intermediate results and information for computer programs, tables, and data needed in an EDP installation.

***Disadvantages of Magnetic Tape.*** Even though tape has many advantages, such as speed and compact storage, it possesses several disadvantages. Tape, like punched paper tape, requires the arranging of data stored on it in some meaningful sequence. This requirement makes it difficult to insert a new record into an already established sequence. Consequently, data must be batched in a large enough group to make processing feasible. Likewise, certain types of processing, such as inventory control (where it is desirable to process each transaction as it occurs) do not lend themselves to magnetic tape procedures. It is not economically feasible to tie up an entire computer system for minutes at a time while searching reels of tape for one specific item of information. Lastly, magnetic tape requires conversion to some other medium if it is to be visually readable.

**Laser Optical Recorder/Reproducer**

At first glance, the laser optical unit looks like any magnetic tape recorder. Instead of utilizing oxide tape, the laser optical system (Figure 7-16), capable of recording 180,000 bits on 36 discrete channels, uses an 8 mm microfilm. It has a transfer rate of up to 10 million bits per second. A total of 4.3 billion bits can be stored on a single $10\frac{1}{2}$ inch reel with 2000 feet of film.

***Operation of Laser Optical Unit.*** Both recording and reproducing functions are

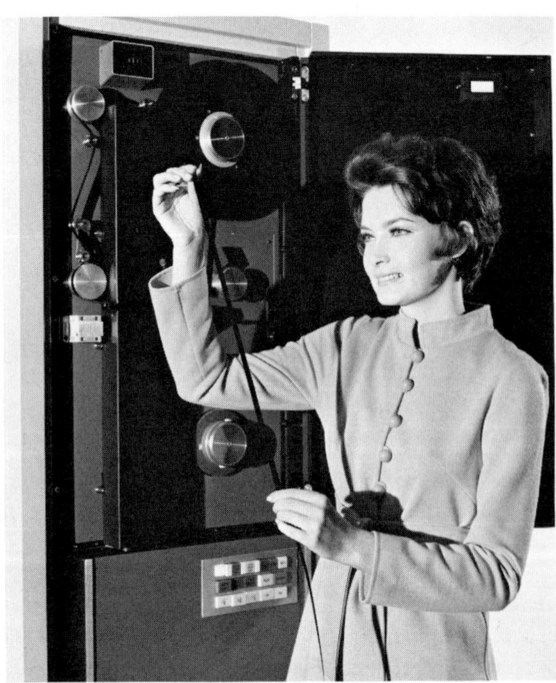

Figure 7-16 PDR-5 Laser Optical Recorder/Reproducer. (Courtesy Laser Microfilming, Inc.)

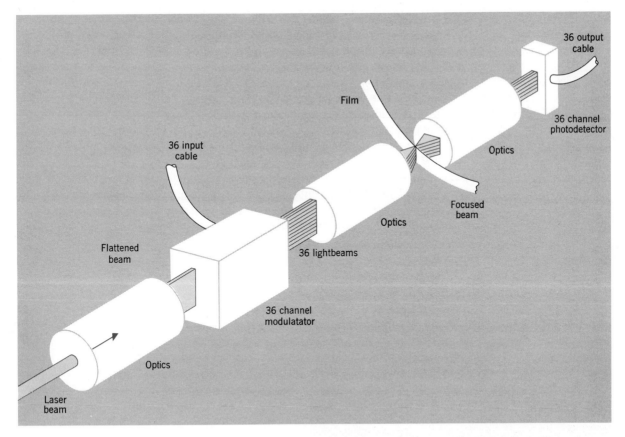

Figure 7-17 Schematic of PDR-5 Laser Optical Recorder/Reproducer. (Courtesy Laser Microfilming, Inc.)

*The laser optical unit is capable of recording data onto microfilm and reproducing it.*

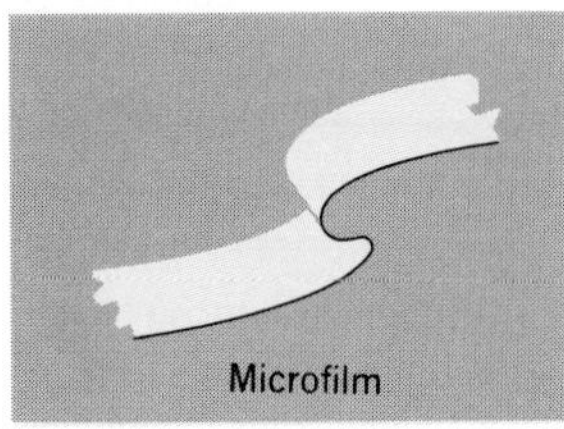


*The laser optical unit has the advantage of compact storage.*

accomplished by the optical system. In Figure 7-17, a beam, generated by a continuous gas laser, is shaped into a strip of light only .008 inch thick. A multichannel modulator separates this strip into 36 separate beams, varying the intensity of each in direct proportion to the input signal of its corresponding channel. The light signals continue through the transparent film base to a diverging lens system, where they are separated for pickup by a 36-element photodetector. This permits a real-time readout of the data being recorded. The reproduce mode operates similarly to the record mode.

***Advantage of Laser Optical Unit.*** One reel of film inscribed by this PDR-5 Recorder/Reproducer can store the same amount of information as approximately 40 magnetic tape reels. It can do the work of about five conventional magnetic tape recorders. The film can be replayed almost indefinitely without output degradation. The unit can record and reproduce at variable speeds with no loss in fidelity. It is intended primarily as a permanent digital data storage system, but low frequency analog data may also be recorded along with the digital information.

### On-Line Printers

A most important characteristic of an on-line printer is that it produces a large amount of readable output. With printing speeds of 100 lines per minute up to 2000 alphanumeric lines and 3000 numeric lines a minute, a computer system can literally

*On-line printers operate at different speeds. They print continuous paper forms and cards.*

bury a user in printed output. Generally, a print buffer holds data temporarily in storage, and thereby frees the computer for other processing while the line is being printed. Vertical spacing is generally under program control or punched tape loop (similar in design and function to the carriage tape used on a punched card accounting machine).

On-line printers are capable of printing cards in addition to continuous paper forms. Shown in Figure 7-18 is the IBM 1404 Printer Model 2 which can print continuous paper forms at a speed of 600 lines per minute or print cards at a maximum rate of 800 cards per minute. In the area of very fast on-line printers, the NCR EM-C5 High Speed Line Printer (Figure 7-19) can print up to 1500 lines per minute of alphanumeric data while printing numeric data at a rate of 3000 lines per minute. The IBM 3211 Printer (not shown) can print 2000 lines per minute using a 48 character set. When the character arrangement is optimized for specific printing loads, speeds up to 2500 lines per minute can be attained.

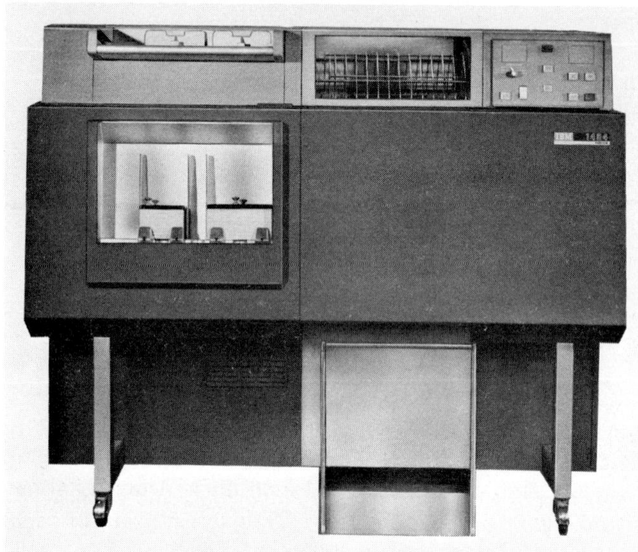

Figure 7-18 IBM 1404 Printer Model 2. (Courtesy International Business Machines Corporation.)

*Impact printers operate by pressing the paper and ribbon against the proper type.*

***Impact Printers.*** Many of the on-line printers are impact printers; that is, they print by pressing the paper and ribbon against the proper type as it passes in front of the paper. For each print cycle, all of the characters in the print set move past each printing position and a magnetically actuated hammer presses the paper against an inked ribbon at the instant the selected character is in position.

Impact printers go beyond furnishing the user with readable output. They are utilized for printing data on cards and forms that are designed to be returned by the sender, known as turnaround documents. Upon return, documents can be batched and fed into optical character recognition equipment. The data, in turn, can be read directly into a computer system or recorded on some magnetic storage medium.

*Nonimpact printers produce images by electrical charges.*

***Nonimpact Printers.*** Much faster printing, up to 5000 lines a minute, can be attained by use of nonimpact printers. Basically, these printers produce an image by electrical charges that are transferred to the paper for a visual record. Even

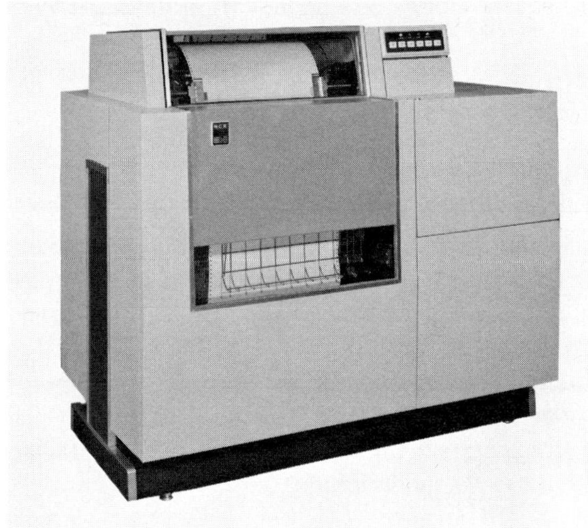

Figure 7-19 NCR EM-C5 High Speed Line Printer. (Courtesy The National Cash Register Company.)

though these devices are much faster than the impact printers, they are not capable of producing simultaneous multiple copies or printing high quality output.

*Microfilm systems capture data from the computer system onto microfilm. Desk-top inquiry stations are used to retrieve and display microfilm data.*

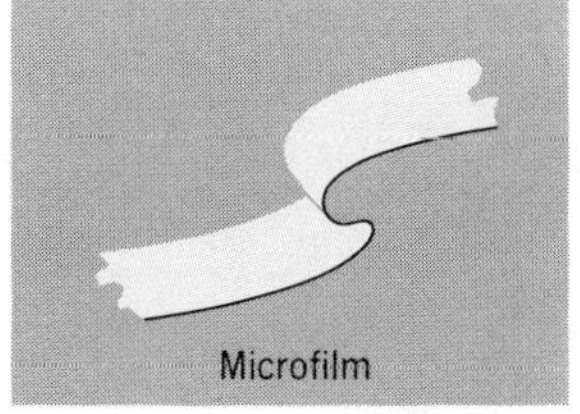


**Microfilm Systems**

In contrast to the foregoing speeds of on-line printers, microfilm systems, such as shown in Figure 7-20, can handle 7000 to 30,000 lines a minute as a new form of output. The basic method involves converting numbers and letters for display on a cathode-ray tube which, in turn, is then photographed on microfilm. Once the data are captured on microfilm, desk-top inquiry stations are used to retrieve and display selected information at the push of a button on the inquiry device.

The faster speeds of microfilm systems over on-line printers allow for considerably more processing if the computer is output bound by a printing device. The compactness of the data also facilitates storage and retrieval. Approximately 1500 pages of computer printed output from one of the newer microfilm systems can be held in the palm of one hand. Insurance companies, banks, retailers, and

Figure 7-20 Datagraphix 4440 Micromation Recorder. (Courtesy General Dynamics, Inc.)

manufacturers, among others, are saving money and speeding up data handling by this newer method.

### Console Typewriter and Related Devices

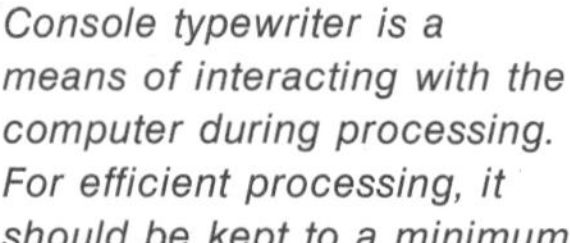
*Console typewriter is a means of interacting with the computer during processing. For efficient processing, it should be kept to a minimum.*

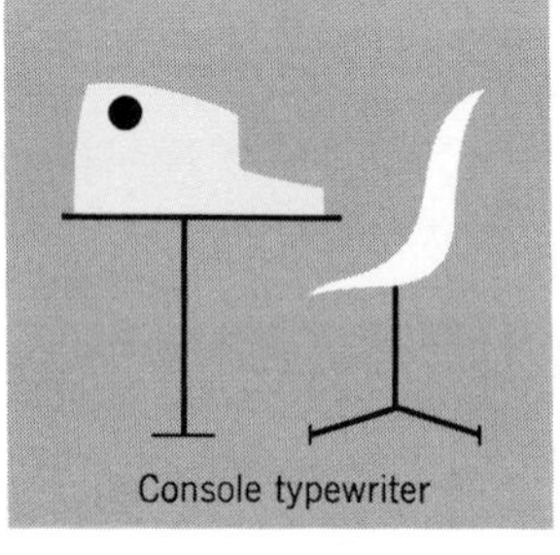


Practically every computer system has a typewriter device (cable-connected to the system) that permits some form of manual entry into, and control over, the central processor. The keyboard (Figure 7-21) allows the operator to instruct the computer and, in turn, the computer reports back in printed form the specific data requested. The typewriter can receive data sent under computer control in response to programmed instructions. The input speed of the typewriter console is dependent upon the ability of the computer operator while output is limited by the design of the equipment. This is usually around 10 characters per second.

For the IBM System/370 Model 165, a stand-alone system console unit is provided (Figure 7-22). This unit contains the main system control panel (buttons, switches, lights, and the like required for system operation) plus advanced console features: a cathode-ray tube and keyboard, an indicator viewer, a document viewer, a processor storage configuration plugboard, a system activity monitor, and a device for loading microcode and diagnostics. Certain of these features assist the customer engineer in detecting central processing unit malfunctions more rapidly than would otherwise be possible.

Figure 7-21 Console typewriter for the IBM System/370 Model 155. (Courtesy International Business Machines Corporation.)

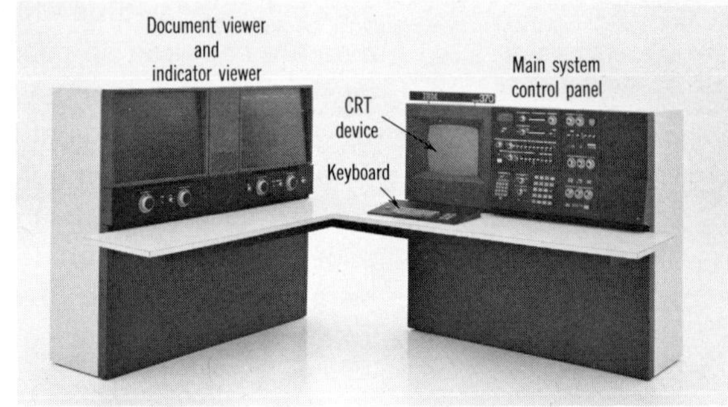

Figure 7-22 IBM System/370 Model 165 Console Unit. (Courtesy International Business Machines Corporation.)

### Other Input/Output Devices

*Other input/output devices include:*
- *transaction recorders*
- *CRT display stations*
- *voice response systems*
- *graph plotters*
- *display units*
- *large screen display systems*

There are many other important input/output devices available for business electronic data processing systems. Among these are magnetic ink character recognition (MICR) and optical character recognition (OCR). Magnetic ink character recognition provides for sorting documents automatically without the need to keypunch data initially. MICR equipment has the capability of transmitting data as they are sorted to the computer's memory for processing under programmed instruction control. In a similar manner, optical character recognition equipment is designed to handle input data—cards, forms, and paper journal tape—for transmitting data directly to a computer or some other machine-processable medium. Additional input/output devices include transaction recorders, cathode-ray tube (CRT) display stations, voice response systems, graph plotters, display units, and large screen display systems.

***Transaction Recorders.*** Point of origin transaction recorders can be operated off-line or on-line. In an on-line mode, the transaction recorder transmits data directly to a computer system. This permits updating available airline seats, account balances, payroll records, inventory records, and similar items that must be maintained on a current basis. While some transaction recorders come equipped with slots for inserting fixed input data and entering variable data by keys, dials, or levers, others have only a keyboard for entering input data (Figure 7-23).

***CRT Display Stations.*** Cathode-ray tube display stations are very similar in operation to typewriter terminals for input and output. Their basic difference is that they generally do not provide a printed copy. A decided advantage of a CRT display station (Figure 7-24) is the ability to check data for accuracy on the screen before sending it to the computer. More will be said about this important input/output device in Chapter 9.

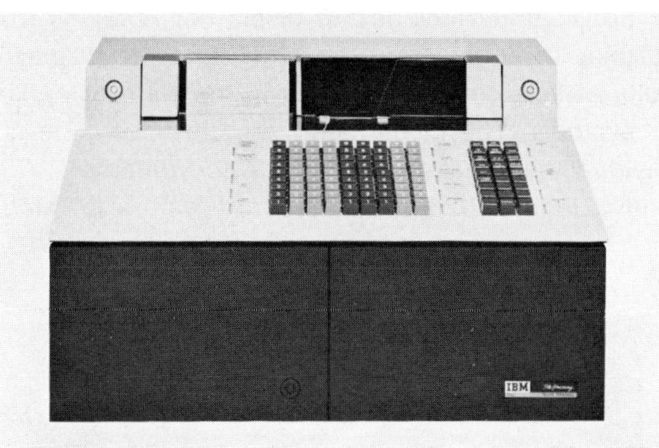


Figure 7-23 IBM 1062 Teller Terminal used to transmit transaction data. (Courtesy International Business Machines Corporation.)

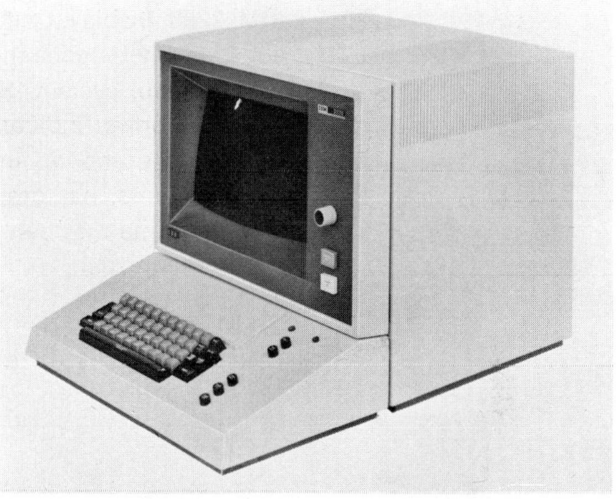

Figure 7-24 IBM 2265 Display Station provides direct man-machine communication. (Courtesy International Business Machines Corporation.)

***Voice Response Systems.*** A similar terminal communication device is the voice response system. This system consists of a message handling unit, a number of touch-tone telephone units, and standard telephone lines for an on-line mode. The audio response unit has a vocabulary tailored to the user's needs. A major advantage of a voice response system is the quick verbal response from a computer system by means of remotely located and multipurpose telephone terminals.

***Graph Plotters.*** Automatic graph plotters (Figure 7-25) are utilized where graphic or pictorial presentation of computer data are meaningful and easier to use than extensive alphabetic or numeric listings. They are indispensable for output when the volume of graphic presentation makes it uneconomical or impossible to perform the task manually. Generally, there is some restriction on format; however a pictorial representation may include any desired combination of axes, lines, letters,

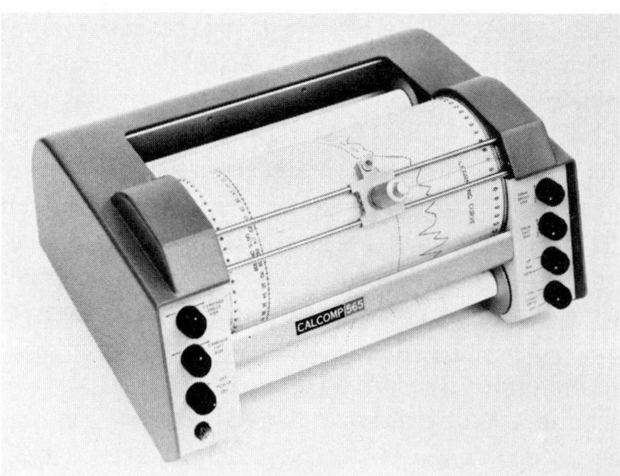


Figure 7-25 Cal Comp 565 Graph Plotter. (Courtesy California Computer Products, Inc.)

and symbols with an unlimited choice of scale factors, letter and symbol sizes, and printing angles.

***Display Units.*** A display unit that is capable of on-line displaying, updating, and manipulating drawings and alphanumeric data is found in Figure 7-26*a*. This IBM 2250 Display Unit also can be used as a system operator console, which substantially reduces the time needed for transferring messages between the operator and the system. Specific applications include the display of readings from process control indications; display of engineering drawings; and the display of intermediate and/or final results of scientific calculations in the form of curves, plotted points, bar graphs, or symbols. The display unit contains over 1 million display points that can be individually addressed by *X* and *Y* coordinates.

The light pen, as illustrated in Figure 7-26*b*, is a standard feature for Model

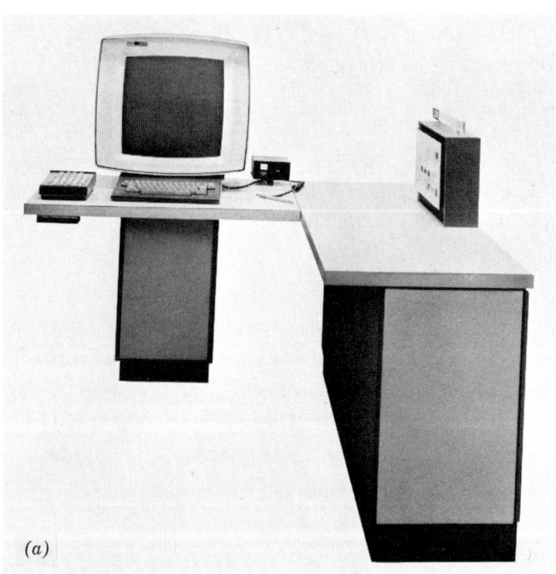


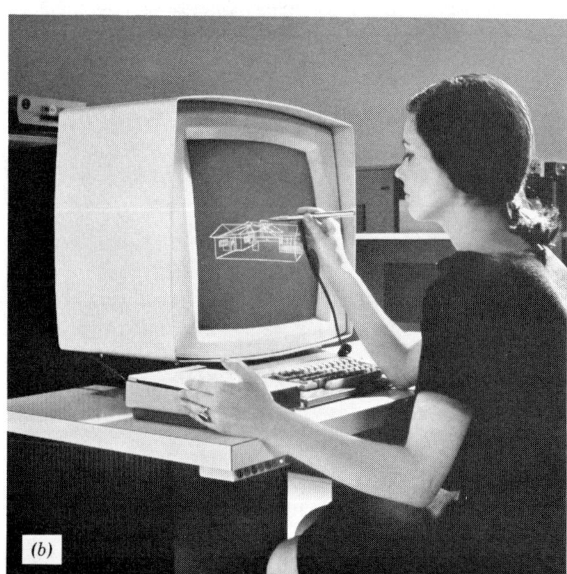


Figure 7-26 IBM 2250 Display Unit (*a*) and with light pen in use (*b*). (Courtesy International Business Machines Corporation.)

3. It is a device that enables the operator to identify a particular point, line, or character in the displayed image to the program. The operator moves the penpoint to the part of the image he wants to identify. The photodetector associated with the pen, sensing light at that point, generates a signal for the program. The light pen can be used alone or in conjunction with a keyboard to rearrange or delete information, or to add lines from a base point already lighted by the CRT beam.

***Large Screen Display Systems.*** With the recent advances in peripheral equipment technology, large screen display units, using laser display technology, are now showing information from a remotely located digital computer. One such system is the Management Information Display Systems (MIDS) which has a five feet by five feet screen for viewing critical data (Figure 7-27*a*). Each point on the 512-by-512 point display matrix may be independently energized to form a high brightness, three color, alphanumeric or graphical image (Figure 7-27*b*). Display format is determined by the user's applications and formats may be quickly changed using the system's internal processor.

Communication between the operator, display system, and remote computer is provided by a table-top inquiry unit. This typewriter-sized unit enables an operator to select, enter, modify, and delete information on the system's five-foot square rear projection screen. A special control allows the operator to select any point on the

(a)

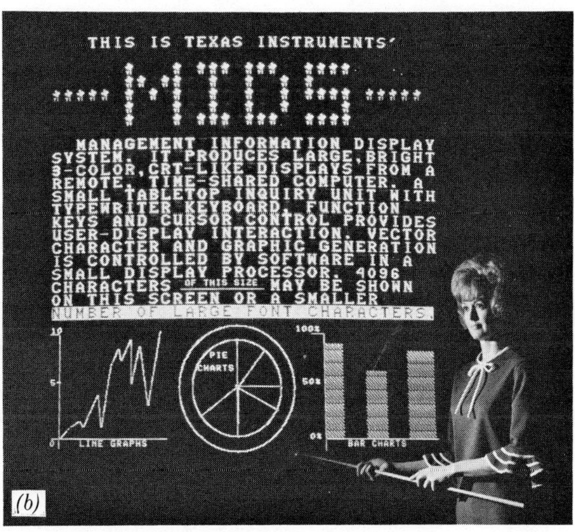

(b)

Figure 7-27 Management Information Display System (*a*) with 5′ × 5′ rear projection screen (*b*). (Courtesy Texas Instruments, Inc.)

screen and transfer the location of this point to the remote computer as the start point for updating or other desired action. In essence, this type of display combines the flexibility and performance of a cathode-ray tube display with the convenience of a large viewing format.

### Summary of Input/Output Devices

*The trend in input/output devices is toward faster entry and exit of data at a reasonably low cost.*

The number of input and output devices increases as newer equipment is found to handle the ever-growing input and output demands of a computer system. They will provide fast entry and exit of data at a reasonably low cost. A current list of input/output devices, depicted in the preceding material, is summarized in Figure 7-28. Although the trend in the past has been toward punched card and magnetic tape, the current trend is toward greater use of OCR equipment and time-sharing devices. As a result, separate chapters are presented to cover these subjects in some depth.

| INPUT EQUIPMENT | OUTPUT EQUIPMENT |
|---|---|
| Card reader | Card punch |
| Magnetic ledger card reader | Paper tape punch |
| Paper tape reader | Magnetic tape unit |
| Paper tape to magnetic tape converter | Laser optical reproducer |
| Tape cartridge reader | On-line printer |
| Magnetic tape unit | Microfilm system |
| Laser optical recorder | Console typewriter |
| Console typewriter | CRT display station |
| Magnetic ink character equipment | Voice response system |
| Optical character recognition equipment | Graph plotter |
| Transaction recorder | Display unit (including large screen display) |
| CRT display station | |
| Voice response system | |

Figure 7-28 Input and output devices for computer systems.

## CENTRAL PROCESSING UNIT

*The essential components of the central processing unit are:*
- *memory*
- *arithmetic/logical unit*
- *CPU control unit*

The central processing unit contains the memory or primary storage, arithmetic/logical unit, and the CPU control unit. Primary storage and the CPU control unit may be in the same or separate housing unit, depending on the computer system. Some CPU's have a control console as a part of the unit itself while other central processors have a separate console with a typewriter (Figure 7-29) and/or visual display device (Figure 7-22).

Advancements in computer design and programming has reduced the need to utilize the console in computer processing. Some of the functions once required of the computer operator are now contained in the system's circuitry and components, or are a part of the program itself. These improvements result in less set up time and running time for the user's data processing problems.

Figure 7-29 IBM System/370 Model 155 central processing unit with attached console. (Courtesy International Business Machines Corporation.)

## PRIMARY STORAGE DEVICES

*Internal memory devices must be capable of moving data at extremely fast rates. They include:*
- *magnetic core*
- *magnetic thin film*
- *large-scale integration*

Memory devices that are an integral part of the central processing unit must be capable of moving data at extremely fast rates. Early computers made great use of magnetic drums that operated in the millisecond range. Magnetic core, magnetic thin film, and large-scale integration (LSI) now operate at microsecond and nanosecond speeds. Faster memory devices currently under development will make it possible to operate in picoseconds, making internal processing speeds even faster. Each time there is an increase in operating speeds, the computer becomes even more input or output bound, depending upon the speed of the slowest unit. Thus the speeds of internal memory devices are not always the basis for selecting a particular digital computer for business and industrial applications. Consideration must be given to the throughput ability of the computer system.

### Magnetic Core

*A magnetic core plane is a series of tiny cores strung on wires, as shown in Figure 7-30.*

A magnetic core is molded from a ferrite powder into a doughnut shape, comparable to the size of a pin head. These tiny cores are, in turn, strung on wires in much the same manner as beads on a necklace in order to form a core plane (Figure 7-30). Several core planes are stacked on top of one another to form a core stack. Many thousands or millions of cores are used in main storage, depending upon the size of the computer's memory.

A core can be easily magnetized in a few millionths of a second and it retains its magnetism indefinitely. When a strong enough electrical current is sent through the wire, the core becomes magnetized. The direction of current determines the magnetic state of the core. Reversing the direction of current changes the magnetic state. The two states, then, can represent on or off, plus or minus, yes or no, 0 or 1.

*Four wires run through each core and are necessary for nondestructive read out capability.*

***Selecting a Core.*** Two wires run through each core at right angles to each other. When half the current needed to magnetize a core is sent through each of the two wires, only the core at the intersection of the wire is magnetized, illustrated in Figure 7-31. No other core in the string is affected. Even though there are a large number of cores strung on a screen of wires (Figure 7-30), a single core can be selected for storage without affecting the others.

A third wire, called a sense wire, runs through each core which is needed to read back the stored information (Figure 7-32). This wire is used to detect the small current created when an electric pulse reverses the polarity of a core. It can be

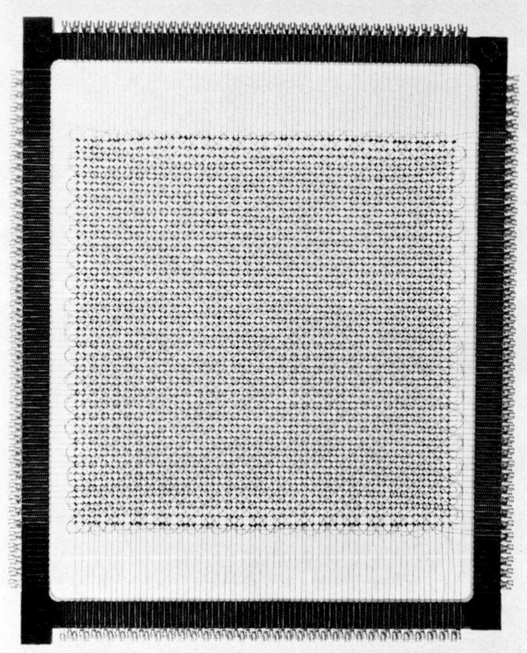

Figure 7-30 Magnetic core plane.

determined from the current whether the core was originally positive or negative. When a core is read by reversal of its polarity, the act of reversing the original positive or negative state of the core destroys the information stored in it. This is referred to as a "destructive read out," that is, all 0's are changed to 1's. To overcome this destructive read out, there is an automatic resetting of cores after they have been read out. The computer attempts to put 1's into all previously read

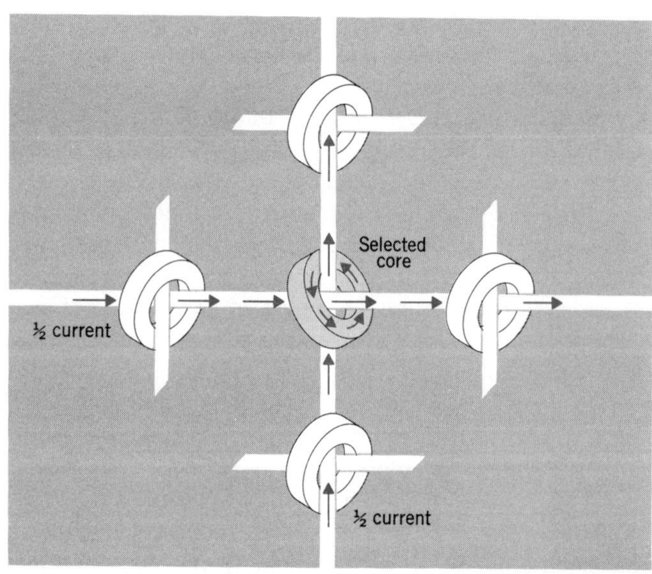


Figure 7-31 Selecting a core.

positions even though some of them may have been 0's. A fourth wire, called an inhibit wire, is run through each core to prevent the writings of 1's into those positions that previously contained 0's before they were read (Figure 7-33). The net result of the four wires passing through each core is a nondestructive read out, but destructive read in.

***Storing Data In Core.*** In order to represent a single BCD alphabetic character in the binary coded decimal system, say an A, the computer references seven core planes stacked on top of one another (Figure 7-34). Starting from the top, the C or check bit is (1) and the B and A bits are (1 1) while the 8, 4, 2, and 1 bits are (0 0 0 1). Each group of seven cores that is needed to represent a character is referred to as one-core storage location or position. Thus, every position of storage is assigned its own specific "address" and individual core positions can be selected by specifying the address.

***Advantages of Magnetic Core.*** Core storage is extremely fast since there is no waiting for a read/write head or rotational delay time of a magnetic drum. The only hindrance to the electric current, traveling at the speed of light, is the resistance it meets as it flows through the wires. Its reliability, coupled with speed, accounts for its wide usage which, in turn, has caused a drop in the costs of producing this type of primary storage.

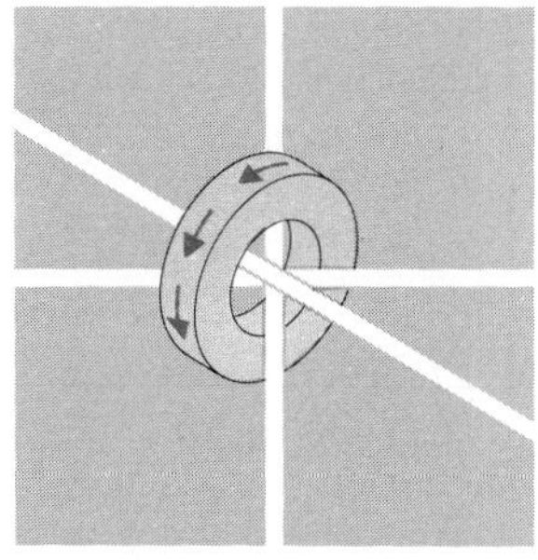

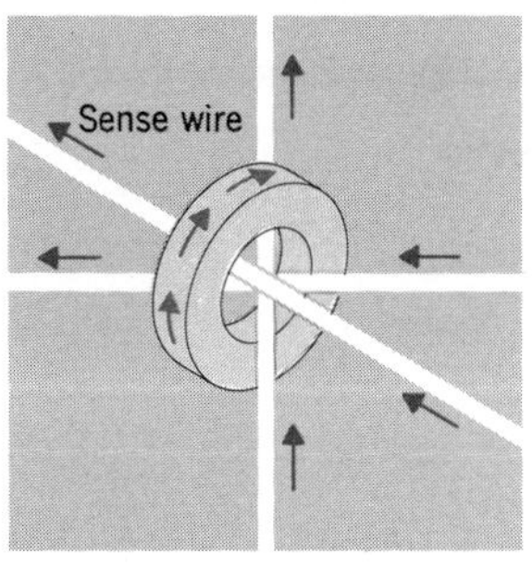


Figure 7-32 Core sense wire.

## Magnetic Thin Film

*Magnetic thin film varies from manufacturer to manufacturer. The two basic types of thin film are:*
- *cylindrical*
- *planar*

Magnetic thin film, which varies from manufacturer to manufacturer, is made of much smaller elements and in a different form from that of magnetic core storage. A common type of magnetic film is the thin film or planar film, consisting of very thin, flat wafers made of nickel-iron alloy. These metallic spots are connected by ultra-thin wires and are mounted on an insulating base, such as glass or plastic (Figure 7-35).

***Types of Thin Film.*** Magnetic thin film may be in the form of a *cylindrical film.* This means that the memory device may be a thin film, short rod or a plated wire memory. It may also be a *planar film* (described above) that is wrapped around a wire. Referring to the thin film, short rod memory, rods are made by depositing a thin metallic film and then a protective coating on copper wire. This process yields a plated wire that is cut into extremely short lengths to form the "bit rods." The basic memory plane is formed by inserting the bit rods into solenoid coils wound on a plastic frame (Figure 7-36*a*). Then the entire plane (Figure 7-36*b*) is sealed between two sheets of plastic and housed into units containing a 16,384 byte memory (Figure 7-36*c*). Automated processes are utilized to plate the wire, cut the rods, wind the solenoid coils, insert the rods into the solenoids, and seal the planes. The result is a high performance memory at a relatively low cost per byte.

***Thin Film Memories vs. Core Memories.*** Thin film memories and core memories are similar in that both have a plane or stack of magnetic elements with drive electronics and sense electronics. However, magnetic thin film has two important advantages over cores. They switch several times faster and have a nondestructive read-out ability. Regarding the last point, the read cycle needs to allow for only one switching time instead of two with core memories. (From the preceding discussion on core, you will recall that a second switching time is needed to restore the information that is destructively read out in the first switching period.) In total, thin film memories operate two to three times faster than core memories.

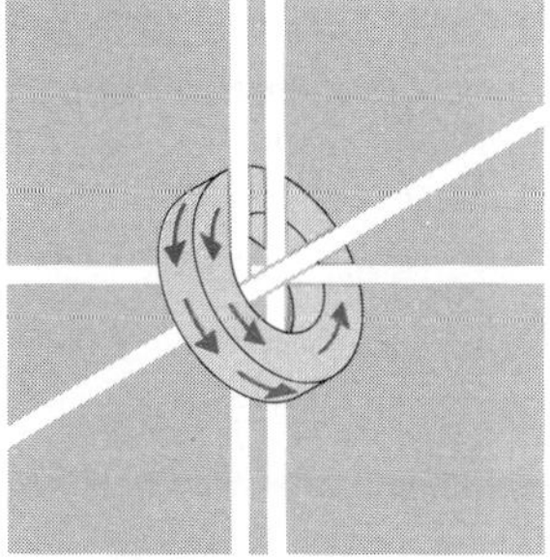

Core represents 0

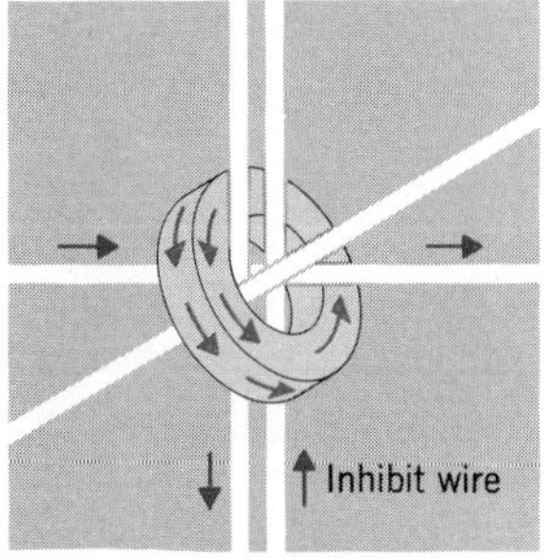


Core remains 0

Figure 7-33 Core inhibit wire.

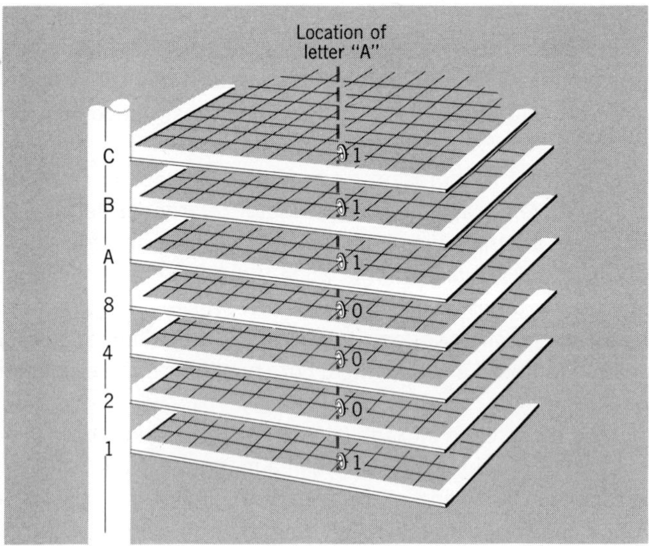


Figure 7-34 BCD character location for the letter A.

## Large-scale Integration (LSI)

*Large-scale integration (Lsl) memories employ two basic techniques:*
- *bipolar*
- *MOS*

Large-scale integration (LSI), sometimes called monolithic integrated circuits, has two basic approaches. One employs *biopolar integrated circuit techniques*. The other uses *metal oxide semiconductor* (MOS) *techniques*.

***Characteristics of LSI.*** The bipolar techniques are favored since their speeds give them an edge over slower MOS circuitry in main memory units of large-scale and scientific computers. However, MOS can compete with bipolar in the newer desk-top electronic calculators and in mini-computers to medium-scale computers where nanosecond speeds seldom are necessary. These were the key factors in IBM's decision to use MOS/LSI or MST (monolithic system technology) circuitry for the entire main memory of its System/370 Models 135 and 145.

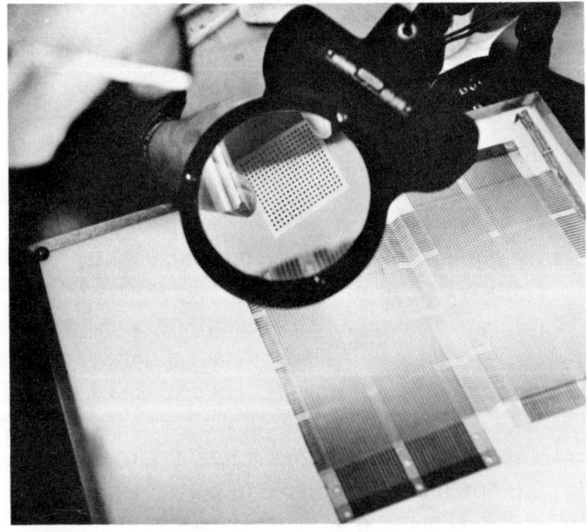

Figure 7-35 Thin film memory plane with overlay. (Courtesy UNIVAC Division of the Sperry Rand Corporation.)

MOS circuits are complex, precision-etched silicon slivers encased in metal, plastic, or ceramic. Some are the size of aspirin tablets, others as big as matchbooks. More important, while bipolar devices operate at higher speeds—up to 10 nanoseconds per function—MOS utilizes less power which means its components can be crowded more compactly onto the silicon.

The great attraction of MOS is their size. Since an MOS transistor is much smaller than its bipolar counterpart, you can place many more of them on the same size chip. In the System/370 memory, (Models 135 and 145), each MST chip contains 1434 microscopic circuit elements in an area less than an eighth of an inch square. These elements form 128 memory circuits and 46 support circuits, or a total of 174 circuits on each chip. In turn, multiple chips are placed on a ceramic plate and encased in half-inch square memory modules. Each half-inch square module contains 512 storage bits and is mounted on a storage array card containing

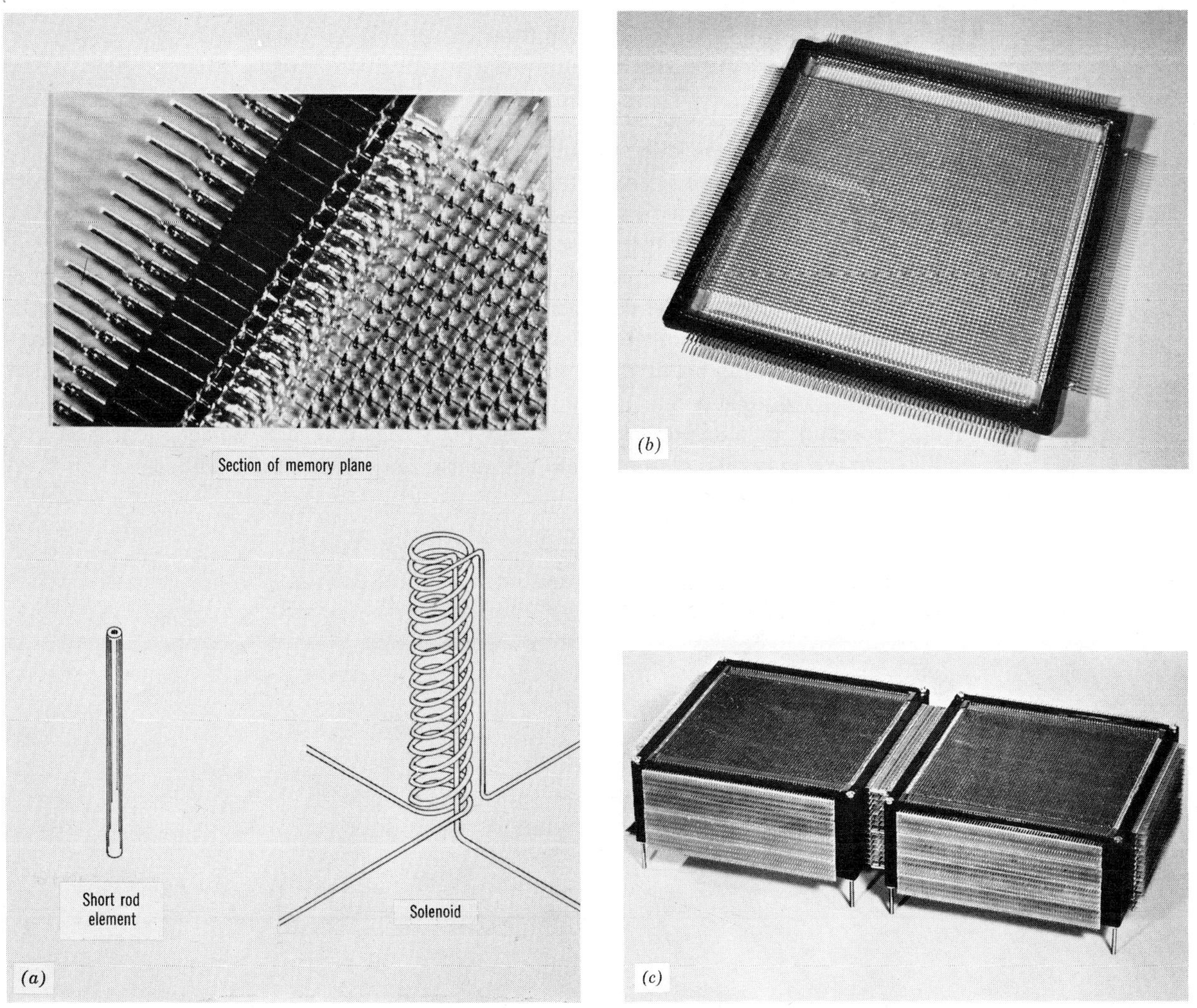


Figure 7-36 Thin film, short rod memory. (*a*) Bit rods, (*b*) memory plane, (*c*) 16,384 byte memory stack. (Courtesy The National Cash Register Company.)

Figure 7-37 Monolithic system technology (MST). (Courtesy International Business Machines Corporation.)

12K bits. These storage array cards, then, form a basic storage module that contains 48K bytes of monolithic storage (similar to that found in Figure 7-37).

*LSI memories have these advantages over thin film and core memories:*
- *more reliable*
- *smaller size*
- *faster speed*
- *lower cost*

***LSI Memories vs. Thin Film and Core Memories.*** LSI or monolithic integrated circuit memories have several advantages, one being higher reliability of digital circuits and insensitivity to environmental changes. Other important advantages are their smaller size, faster speed, and lower costs. In contrast to magnetic core and thin film memories, the cost per bit of an integrated monolithic circuit memory is almost independent of memory size. This permits the manufacture of many memory sizes without the cost penalties now incurred on smaller sizes. Although costs for magnetic core and thin film are remaining constant, the costs of manufacturing are dropping for LSI (Figure 7-38). For these reasons, large-scale integration will displace magnetic core and thin film memories rapidly in the future.

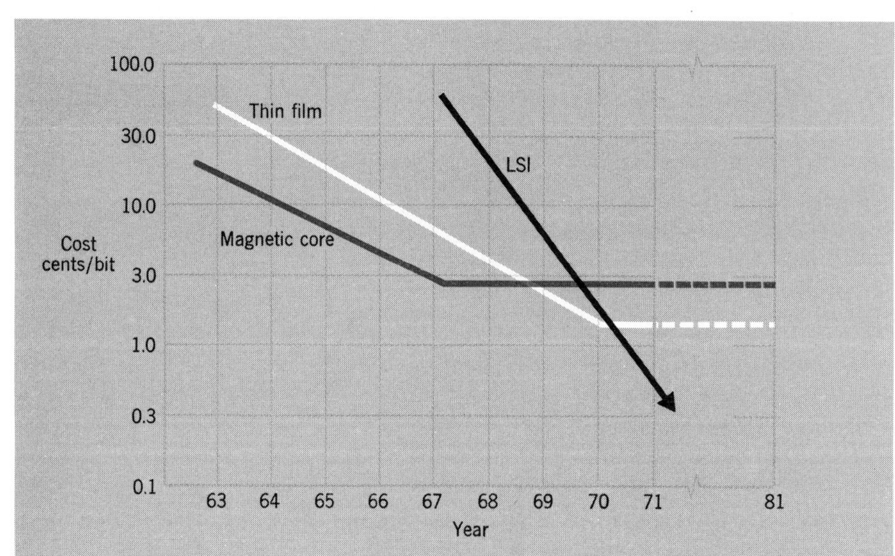


Figure 7-38 Comparative memory costs—magnetic core, thin film, and LSI.

### Internal Operating Speeds

*Internal operating speeds can be measured in microseconds, nanoseconds, and picoseconds. However, a better approach is using the number of instructions performed per second for throughput performance.*

Currently, core and thin film memories dominate the computers installed. Core memories have cycle times over 500 nanoseconds while thin film memories dominate the region with cycle times between 150 and 500 nanoseconds. Core has a minimum cycle time potential of approximately 350 nanoseconds. Planar and plate wire memories or thin film can be as low as 100 nanoseconds. On the other hand, integrated circuits or large-scale integration seem to have an average time under 150 (about 120 nanoseconds), the minimum cycle time being below 50 nanoseconds. These present speeds are truly remarkable when compared to prior generations of computers.

A more realistic approach in measuring internal operating speeds is to think in terms of "throughput performance" rather than in nanoseconds. Of great importance to the user is the number of instructions that can be performed within a certain period of time. The new benchmark for computer measurement in the 70's is mips (million instructions per second). Currently, IBM's 370/195 and CDC's 7600 supercomputers operate at the rate of approximately 15 mips. Other more advanced systems are operating between 100 million and 200 million instructions per second. While these speeds are most impressive, a 1000 mips computer will be in operation before the end of the 1970's.

## SECONDARY STORAGE DEVICES

The need for fast access storage, which serves as an extension of the computer's primary storage, has resulted in the development of several mass data files. Secondary (auxiliary) storage devices have the capability of storing several hundred million characters of data in either sequential or random sequence, depending on the type of storage unit. Their design is such that they may be directly accessed by the computer for use within the central processing unit. Data in secondary storage are not as accessible as information in primary storage since it must be routed through memory first before calculation and manipulation can occur.

Magnetic tape, one of the input/output devices described previously, can also serve as auxiliary storage devices. Applications, however, are limited for this storage device. The more universally used storage units are magnetic disks, magnetic drums, magnetic card and strips, and the data cell. A more recent addition to this listing is the laser mass memory system. All of these secondary storage devices are discussed below.

*The laser mass memory employs recording medium strips. It is capable of recording and reproducing up to one trillion bits of digital data.*

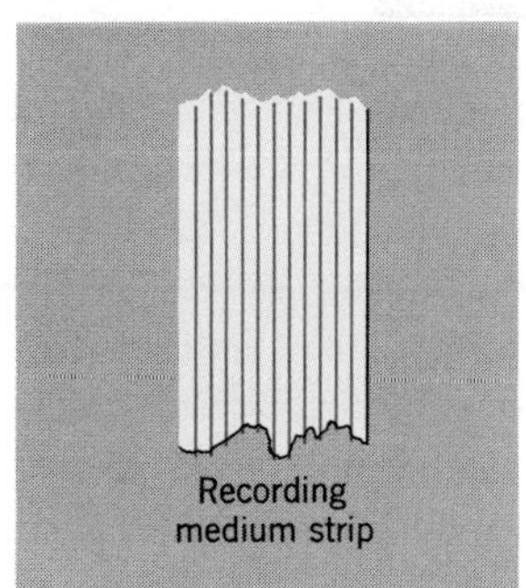


### Laser Mass Memory

A laser storage system, such as the one illustrated in Figure 7-39, provides the capability of permanently recording and reproducing up to $10^{12}$ bits (one trillion bits) of digital data under computer control. It utilizes the laser as its permanent recording process. The UNICON Laser Mass Memory System writes data along the length of the recording medium. Besides the laser recording unit, there is a recorder control unit that provides a hardware and software interface which is compatible with the user's computer. Its function is to provide for simultaneous processing of the data to and from each drum in either a read or a write operation. This subsystem also controls the automatic selection of recording medium strips to or from a common strip file and the loading and unloading of a strip from either read/write drum.

***Operation of Laser Mass Memory Unit.*** The laser recording unit is composed

Figure 7-39 UNICON 690-212 Laser Mass Memory System. (Courtesy Precision Instrument Company.)

*The laser beam records data in the binary code.*

of two read/record units, each with independent simultaneous read/write capability and with provision for automatic data selection from a common trillion bit mass file. Each of the two read/record units is composed of a rotatable drum unit, together with a loading and unloading mechanism for transfer of the selected data strip to or from the common mass file to a working position on the drum surface. Adjacent to the drum (Figure 7-40), a track selection mechanism is provided for

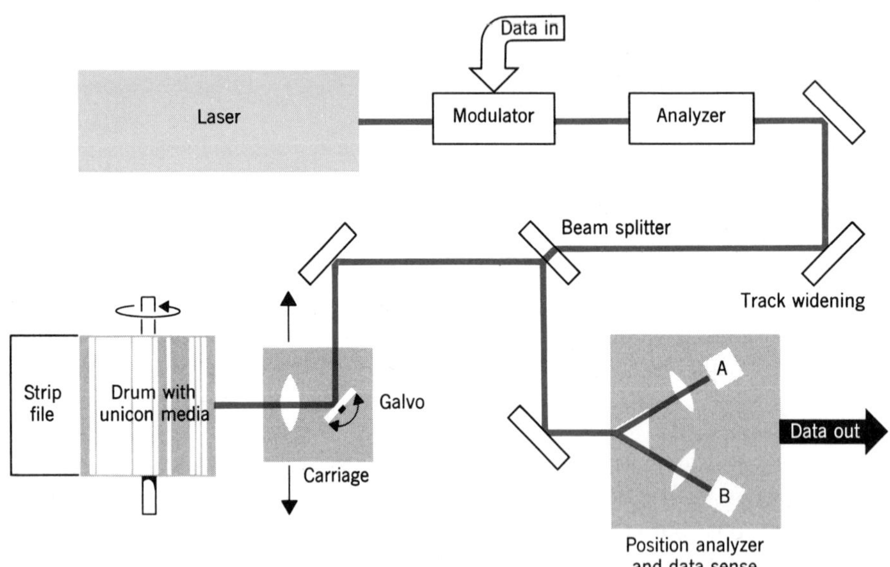


Figure 7-40 Flow diagram for laser recording/reading process. (Courtesy Precision Instrument Company.)

support of an optical head that directs laser light onto any selected region of the data strip which has been mounted and is rotating on the drum unit. A light modulator unit, together with suitable optical elements, provides control of the intensity of the laser light beam, in a manner suitable for recording of data. Additional optical elements and a data sense unit utilize the laser light reflected from a selected region of the rotating data strip for retrieval of the stored information.

Data are written in binary code on the recording medium in such a manner that the beam is focused onto the medium at the beginning of a series of ones. The beam continues to vaporize the recording medium until a "zero" is to be recorded, at which time the beam is turned off by the modulator. In this manner, it is possible to record data.

*The laser mass memory has the advantage of storing 25 reels of magnetic tape on one of its recording strips.*

***Advantages of Laser Mass Memory.*** The essential characteristics of the UNICON Laser Mass Memory System—high density, permanent, error free recording, and reproduction—permit its use in a number of applications in addition to that of an on-line $10^{12}$ bit mass memory. One of these is for the storage of data that would otherwise be stored on magnetic tape. Each strip can store the equivalent of 25 reels of conventional magnetic tape, yet costs about as much as one reel of tape. One of the strip packs with its 25 data strips has a storage capacity of 625 magnetic tape reels.

### Magnetic Disk

*Data are recorded on magnetic disk as magnetized bits on each side of its surface.*

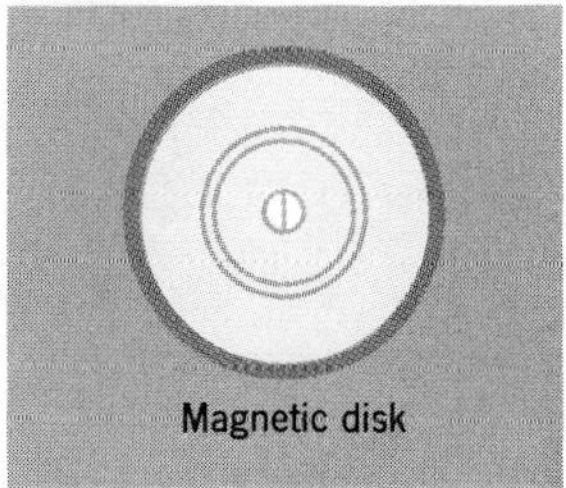

Magnetic disk

The magnetic disk, similar to a phonograph record, is coated on both sides with a ferrous oxide recording material. Information is recorded as magnetized spots on each side of the disk. On an IBM 2316 six magnetic disks are mounted together as one unit, commonly referred to as a disk pack (Figure 7-41*a*). The disk pack can be easily removed from the magnetic disk unit (Figure 7-42) and be replaced with a new disk pack. This has made disks very much like magnetic tapes.

Rather than storing data by columns of characters, it is recorded serially bit-by-bit, eight bits per byte along a track. In Figure 7-41*b*, data is stored serially, using the extended binary coded decimal interchange code (EBCDIC). The absence of parity bits in the illustration should be noted. The technique of checking for parity in each byte is generally not used with direct access devices.

*Data are read or written by positioning the access arm over the desired location. Generally, time to search disk storage includes access motion time and rotational delay time.*

***Operation of Magnetic Disk.*** As shown in Figure 7-41, enough space is available between each disk file to permit access arms to move in and read or record data. Access arms generally have two read/write heads for retrieving or recording on either side of a disk. To read or write data, an access arm must be positioned on the disk over the desired location. The arm moves in and out to locate the correct storage location. If there is no arm for each magnetic disk, the arm must move out from the stack of disks and up or down to the correct disk (shown as $T_e$ in Figure 7-41*c*). As might be expected, the greater the number of heads, the faster the data may be read or written.

Figure 7-41*c* depicts a simplified, single-module storage with one comblike access mechanism. Access to one specific track on a given recording surface is accomplished by the lateral movement of the whole access mechanism from a current track location. The time required for this movement is called *access motion time* ($T_a$) and is related to the lateral distance the arm moves. In addition to access motion time, there is another timing factor, known as *rotational delay time* ($T_r$). Rotational delay time is the time required for the disk to position the desired record at the selected read/write head. Maximum rotational delay time is slightly more than the time required for one full revolution, average rotational delay time being one-half the maximum. Typical disk speed is 1800 revolutions per minute. The selection of the proper read/write head is performed simultaneously with access motion time. This is performed electronically and the time is negligible. Total data search time for disk storage includes the access time and rotational delay time.

***Essential Features of Magnetic Disk.*** The storage capacity of magnetic disk packs varies; some have the ability to store many millions of characters of informa-

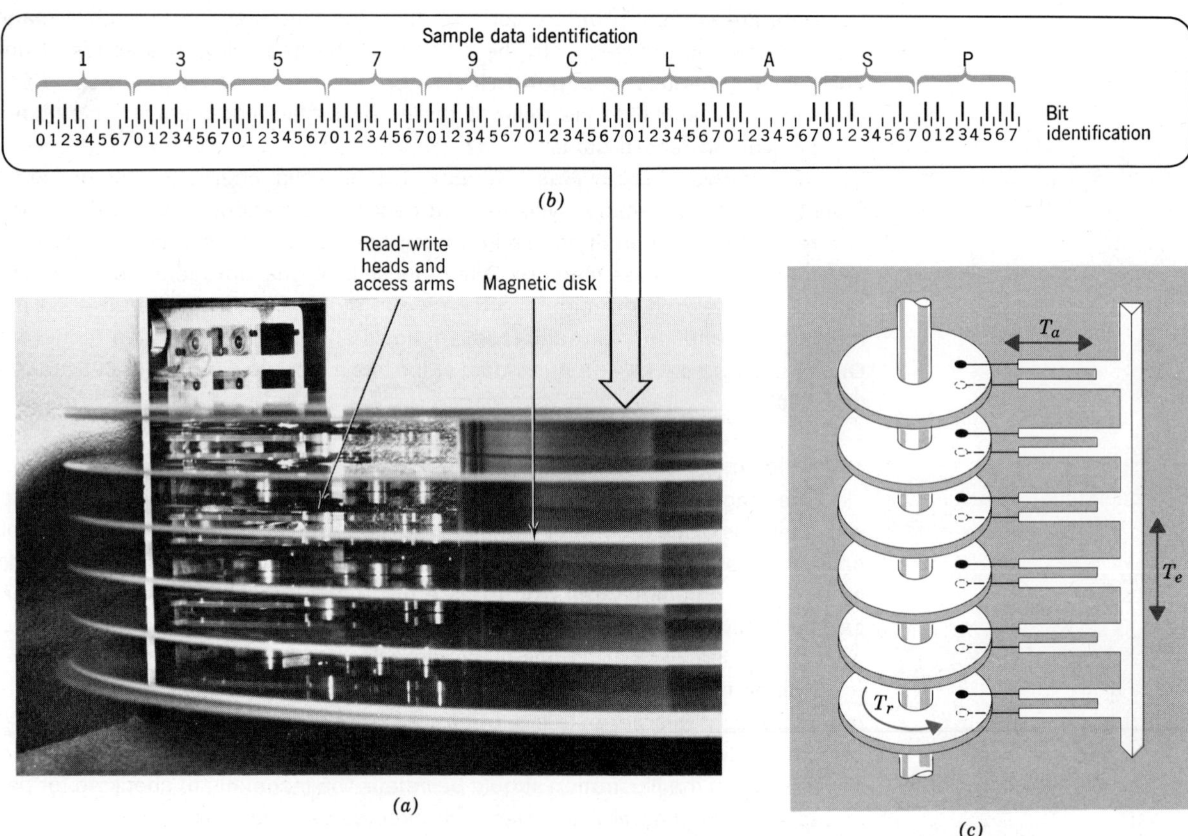


Figure 7-41 (*a*) Closeup picture of an IBM 2316 removable disk pack (utilizes six magnetic disks), (*b*) representation of data on disk, (*c*) and access motion time ($T_a$) and rotational delay time ($T_r$) to disk storage.

tion. Even though access time is restricted to the revolving action of disks and the arm movements, the average search time is about 75 milliseconds while the average rotational delay is about 12.5 milliseconds. The speed for the data transfer rate can be as high as 800,000 bytes per second (per storage device illustrated in Figure 7-44) once the data are located by the read/write head. It should be noted that these average times are much lower for the newer equipment on the market.

*Generally, data on magnetic disk are addressed by the disk number, the sector on the disk, and the track number.*

Data are addressed on the disks by the disk number, the sector on the disk, and the track number on the IBM 2316. The disks, numbered consecutively from bottom to top, are assigned sectors on each side. Generally, they are assigned sector addresses 0 through 4 for the top side and 5 through 9 for the bottom of the disk. There are 200 tracks of recorded data on each side of the disk, having addresses 000 through 199. In some disk files, record lengths may be flexible enough to allow recording variable lengths of data records. As pointed out in an earlier chapter, the advantage of variable record length capability is the more efficient use of storage space. Thus the number of characters available per sector for each track varies with the density of the data stored.

***Current Magnetic Disk Units.*** Magnetic disk units are found in all sizes. As was shown previously in Figure 5-2 for the IBM System/3, the disk unit is supplied without machine frame or covers and is intended for mounting within the frame of the computer system. Two 14-inch magnetic coated disks are mounted, one on top of the other, on a common spindle. The lower disk cannot be removed by the computer operator from the drive while the upper one is removable. This approach is designed to control data destruction and facilitate handling. The disks and recording heads are basically the same as those used on other disk drives, namely, the IBM 2311 shown in Figure 7-42.

*Magnetic disk units vary from single units to a multidisk storage facility.*

Figure 7-42 IBM 2311 Disk Storage Drive. (Courtesy International Business Machines Corporation.)

In addition to the single magnetic disk unit (Figure 7-42) and the dual disk units (Figure 7-43), there are multiple magnetic disk units. Such a system is illustrated in Figure 7-44. This IBM 3330 Disk Storage Facility has a maximum storage capacity of 800 million bytes. It features modular construction, allowing users to configure up to four dual disk modules as their requirements expand. Each 3336 disk pack holds 100 megabytes on its 19 recording surfaces while another surface holds timing marks. Two more platters, the top and bottom ones, are not used at all for recording—only for protection of the recording and timing surfaces.

Not only are there removable disks but there are also disk files that are permanently mounted in a cabinet. Each disk file may contain 25 to 50 disks in a module. One or more modules may be housed in one file unit. However, the trend has been toward disk packs that house several disks in one unit.

***Advantages of Magnetic Disk.*** An important characteristic of the disk is that any item of data is as quickly obtainable as any other. Because the access arms and the read/write heads move from the periphery to the inside of the disk and back out again, in addition to the way data are arranged on the disk, it is possible

Figure 7-43 NCR EM-J Series Dual Disk Units. (Courtesy The National Cash Register Company.)

*Magnetic disk is well suited for random order processing. Also, its vast storage capability and fast transfer rate have made it widely used.*

to skip over unwanted data. This is a decided advantage over magnetic tape as is the ability to process transactions without sorting the data previously. Also, several different but related data may be stored on disk files, thereby allowing a transaction to be processed against these files at the same time. For example, a customer order can be processed on-line against the following magnetic disk files: credit check, inventory, accounts receivable, and sales analysis. In essence, disk is best for random access operations where input data are not arranged in any particular sequence before they are written on the disk. This direct accessibility feature plus its vast storage ability and relatively fast transfer rate have made them widely used in computer systems.

***Disadvantages of Magnetic Disk.*** Magnetic disk files are more expensive than magnetic tape and certain operations do not lend themselves to random order processing. When a record is updated using a disk file, the record is read, processed,

Figure 7-44 IBM 3330 Disk Storage Facility and 3830 Storage Control Unit. (Courtesy International Business Machines Corporation.)

*Magnetic disk has the problem of losing the audit trail. Also, some operations do not lend themselves to random order processing.*

and written back on the disk, thereby losing an audit trail. If there are errors, the processing is not as clear as with magnetic tape since the old and new tapes are available for determining where the errors occurred. Magnetic tape, then, is better—cheaper and faster—for operations requiring sequential processing where transactions can be batched before being processed. The need for both magnetic disk files and tapes should be obvious. Tape devices have processing efficiency while disk devices have inquiry efficiency. The data processing environment is the deciding factor as to which one or both are used.

### Magnetic Drum

*Magnetic drum is a cylinder with a magnetized outer surface for storing data that spins at so many revolutions per second.*

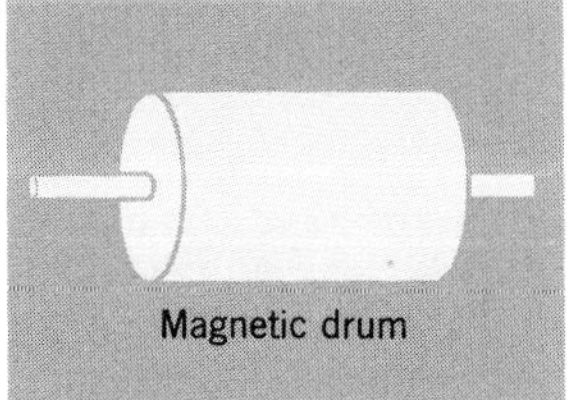


*Magnetic drum storage makes use of binary coded decimal for recording data.*

In the earlier days of computers, magnetic drums were the basic means of primary storage. Today, they are used as on-line storage devices where fast access to secondary storage is required. Basically, a magnetic drum is a cylinder with a magnetized outer surface. The size of the drum limits the quantity of information that can be stored. Some magnetic drum units are capable of storing several million characters of data. The IBM 2301 Drum Storage (Figure 7-45), which utilizes the 2820 Storage Control Unit, can store to 4,100,000 bytes or 8,200,000 digits. The data transfer rate to and from the central processor may be up to 1,200,000 bytes per second or 2,400,000 digits per second while the rotational delay to a specific part of the track ranges from 0 to 17.5 milliseconds, averaging 8.6 milliseconds.

***Operation of Magnetic Drum.*** Data are normally represented in standard binary coded decimal form, as depicted in Figure 7-46. Storage is in the form of invisible tracks around the cylinder as noted above. Each track is divided into sections which are, in turn, subdivided into character locations. The number of tracks, sections, and characters depends upon the size of the magnetic drum. As the drum rotates at a very fast speed, data are recorded or sensed by a set of read/write heads. These heads are close enough to the surface of the drum to magnetize it and to sense the magnetization on it.

Essentially, the operation of the read/write heads is similar to magnetic tape. Spots are magnetized by sending pulses of current through the write coil. The polarity of a spot is determined by the direction of the current flow. In effect, magnetized spots can be read as either 0 or 1, depending upon their polarity.

***Advantages and Disadvantages of Magnetic Drum.*** Drum storage is less expensive than core. It is slower because of the rotational delay time involved for the drum and read/write heads to be positioned over the data requested by the computer program.

Figure 7-45 IBM 2301 Drum Storage (utilizes the 2820 Storage Control Unit). (Courtesy International Business Machines Corporation.)

### Magnetic Card

Magnetic cards have the capacity for storing large quantities of data at a lower cost than with magnetic disk storage. The trade name for the magnetic card is CRAM (Card Random Access Memory). It is marketed by the National Cash Register Company.

***Operation of Magnetic Card.*** Data are magnetically recorded in tracks or channels on the surface of the magnetic card. For the unit pictured in Figure 7-47, cards are filed in random order in a cartridge holding 384 cards. Since the magnetic cards can be randomly selected, the desired card is released, under program control, from the rods on which it is suspended and is pulled by means of a vacuum onto a rotating drum. While positioned on the rotating drum, many read/write heads come into contact with the card. After data have been read or recorded magnetically, the magnetic card may be recirculated for reading other data or it may be released

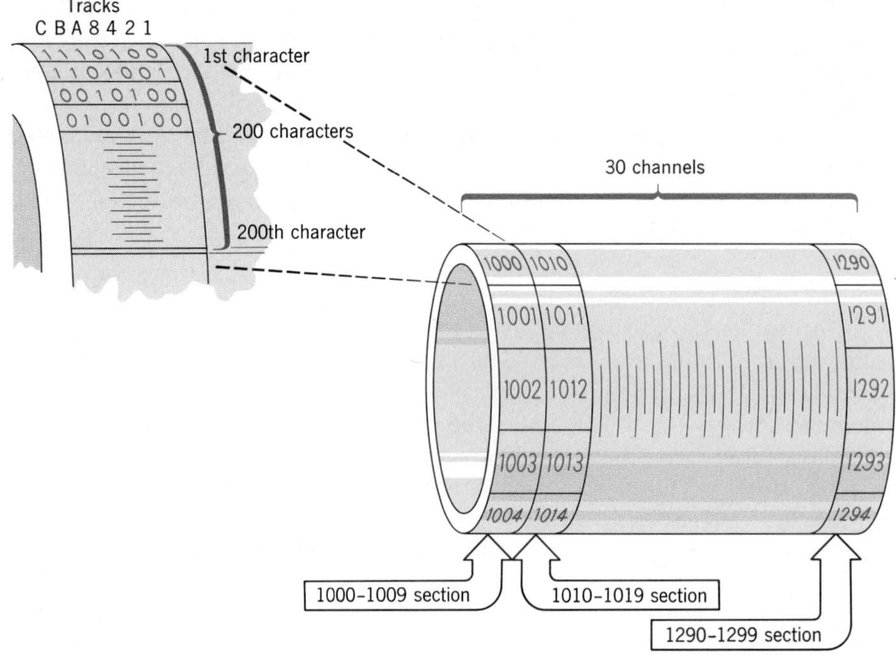


Figure 7-46 Schematic for a typical drum storage.

*Card random access memory can store large quantities of data on magnetic cards.*

for reading another card. If released, the card is returned to its original position and is suspended until selected again.

***Advantages and Disadvantages of Magnetic Card.*** The problem with magnetic cards is their speed. The physical movement of the cards from the cartridge to the rotating drum is relatively slow, that is, about eight per second. Once the card is ready for reading or writing, the transfer rates are comparable to magnetic tape. Magnetic cards are useful for storing large quantities of data on-line where a small volume of transactions occur. Thus, a relatively large inventory file that is updated

Figure 7-47 Card random access memory unit. (Courtesy The National Cash Register Company.)

daily on a batch processing basis is an excellent application to reap the benefit of this secondary storage.

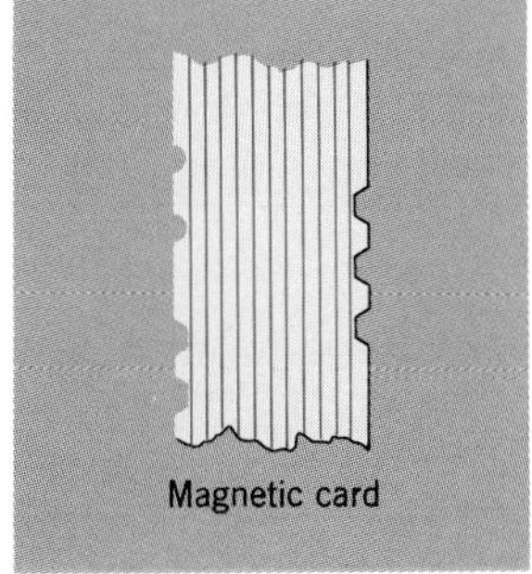


*The magnetic strip of the data cell is comparable to the magnetic card.*

### Magnetic Strip

The IBM Data Cell is comparable to the NCR CRAM system. The storage medium for the IBM 2321 Data Cell Drive (Figure 7-48) is a strip of magnetic tape $2\frac{1}{4}$ inches wide by 13 inches long. Each data cell contains 20 subcells of 10 strips each. Each 2321 offers space for 400 million bytes or 800 million packed decimal digits and signs of on-line data. The data transfer rate is 55 thousand bytes per second.

The data cells are all removable and interchangeable among 2321's, permitting an open ended capacity for data cell libraries. They provide a very large storehouse of readily available operating data, such as part-by-part inventories, shop schedules, customer accounts of large companies, and manpower records.

Figure 7-48 IBM 2321 Data Cell Drive (utilizes the 2841 Storage Control Unit). (Courtesy International Business Machines Corporation.)

## EXTERNAL STORAGE

*External storage is data stored off-line, but in a form suitable for direct entry into a computer system.*

External storage or off-line storage contains data in a form suitable for direct entry into a computer system. These include: punched cards, punched paper tape, magnetic tape, and magnetic disk packs. Magnetic disk units, magnetic cards, and magnetic strips may also be classified in this category if the storage devices are removed from on-line computer operation. Newer input media are magnetic ink character and optical recognition character documents and forms. Although external storage is not directly accessible by the computer, it can be an important input storage, or output medium when made a part of the on-line computer system. In essence, external storage facilities provide a means of retaining critical information before or after it has been processed by the computer system. It is not under the control of the computer until it is brought on-line.

## SUMMARY OF INTERNAL AND EXTERNAL STORAGE

*The major categories of storage are:*
- *primary (memory)*
- *secondary (on-line files)*
- *external (off-line files)*

The number of internal and external storage devices are increasing as newer ones are found to replace or supplement older units. These devices are not growing as fast as input/output peripheral equipment. The rationale is that bottlenecks are basically in the input/output area of the computer system. A listing of storage available is set forth in Figure 7-49. Also, a hierarchy of internal storage devices is depicted in Figure 7-50.

| *Internal Storage* | *External Storage* |
|---|---|
| Primary Storage: | Punched cards |
| Magnetic core | Punched paper tape |
| Magnetic thin film | Magnetic tape |
| Large-scale integration (LSI) | Magnetic disk pack |
| | Magnetic disk unit |
| Secondary Storage: | Magnetic card |
| Fast core mass memory | Magnetic strip |
| Laser mass memory | Magnetic ink character recognition |
| Magnetic tape | Optical character recognition |
| Magnetic disk | |
| Magnetic drum | |
| Magnetic card | |
| Magnetic strip | |

Figure 7-49 Summary of internal and external storage for computer systems.

As you will recall, the basic difference between internal and external storage is their relationship to the computer system. All internal storage is on-line and under the control of the computer while external storage is not. However, when the external storage medium is brought into direct contact with the computer system, it is considered to be an integral part of secondary storage.

## COMPUTER SYSTEM CONFIGURATIONS

*The configuration of a computer system is dependent upon the user's needs.*

Several of the basic equipment devices illustrated previously are brought together and integrated into a computer system. Computer configurations to be explored are:

- mini-computers
- small card-oriented system
- small magnetic tape-oriented system
- small magnetic disk-oriented system
- medium-scale system
- large-scale system

A small computer system can rent for as low as $1000 per month while a large computer system can carry a monthly rental of well over $100,000. In between these two monthly rentals, there are literally thousands of different computer configurations that can be developed for the specific requirements of the user.

### Mini-Computers

Currently, there is considerable interest in mini-computers. A mini-computer is one that can be purchased at prices ranging from $2000 to $20,000, can be mass

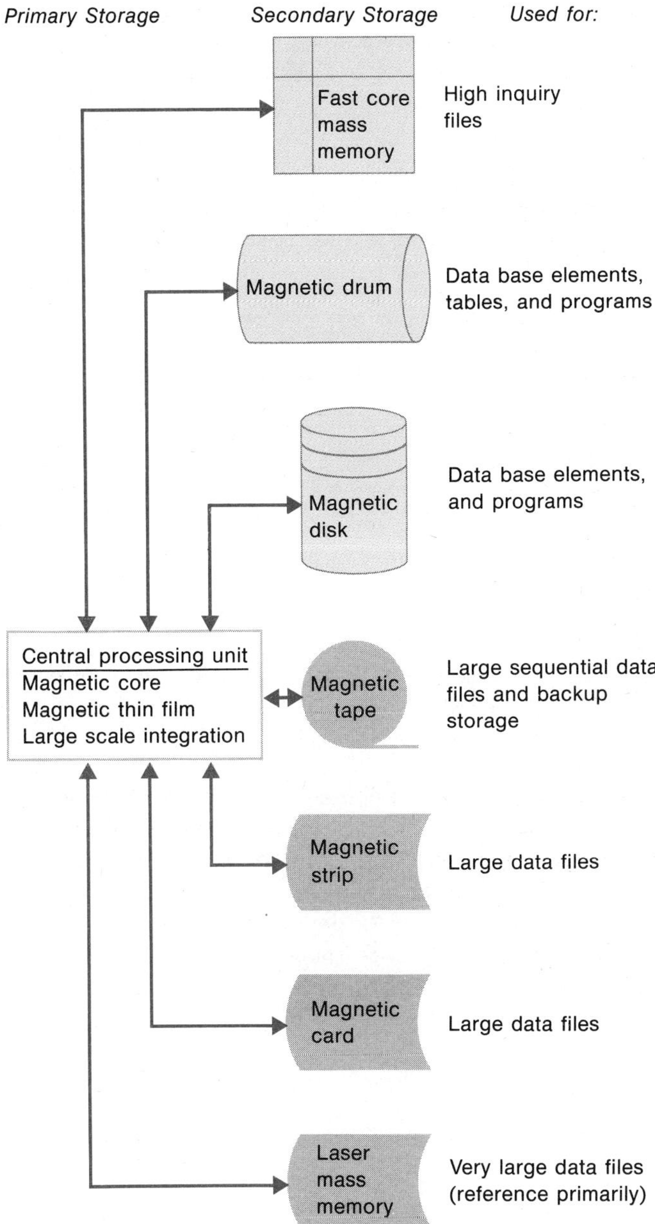


Figure 7-50 Hierarchy of storage devices in terms of usage.

*Mini-computers have experienced a fast rate of growth because of their range of uses.*

produced, can be maintained by the user's staff, and normally can be programmed and operated by people who are not computer experts. Typically, a mini-computer has a small bit word size and a small core memory. It is capable of accepting a wide variety of peripherals, such as magnetic tape units, disk storage, and line printers. Likewise, it can communicate with other devices, namely, other computers, laboratory equipment, and plant machinery.

***Importance of I/O Bus.*** The basic means for transfering data between the computer and the input/output devices is generally referred to as the I/O bus. Other names that may be used to designate this facility are Varian's Party Line and

*The I/O bus permits data to be transferred between the input/output units and the working registers of the computer.*

Interdata's Multiplexer Bus. The I/O bus is usually offered as standard equipment and included in the price of the basic processor. Functionally, the I/O bus permits the transfer of data between the input/output units and the working registers of the computer. Some computers have dedicated registers for I/O transfers, thereby reducing housekeeping requirements. Figure 7-51 shows how the I/O bus interfaces with various components of a mini-computer system. The number of devices that may be connected is determined by the size of the address field of the computer's I/O instruction, and correspondingly, the number of address lines in the I/O bus.

Mini-computer

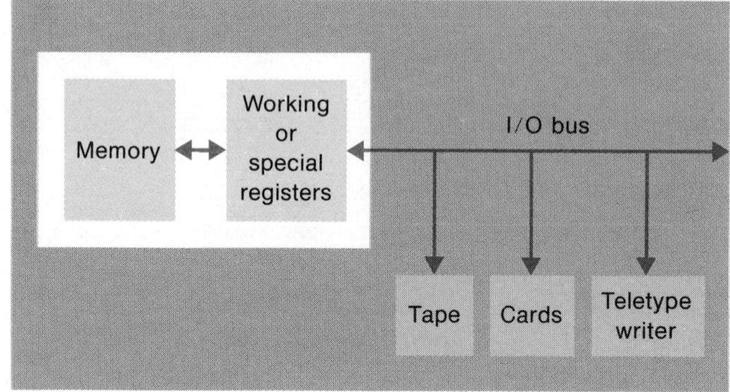


Figure 7-51 I/O bus—data transfer is by word under program control.

*Current mini-computers have these characteristics:*
- *utilize a memory*
- *are programmable*
- *operate at fast speeds*
- *control peripheral devices*
- *are low cost*

***Current Mini-Computers.*** A current mini-computer is the Varian 620f (Figure 7-52). With a core memory cycle time of 750 nanoseconds and a read-only memory (ROM) of 300 nanoseconds, it is a 16-bit machine with a 4K word memory (4000 of addressable storage locations or 4096 words of core memory). The core memory is expandable to 32K in 4K increments. Up to 32 peripheral controllers can be connected to the 620f's basic input/output bus. These peripherals include all standard input/output devices, such as disk drives, line printers, drums, plotters, and displays. The 4K core memory version is available for purchase at a price of approximately $10,000.

Another typical mini-computer is the Honeywell 316 (Figure 7-53) which sells

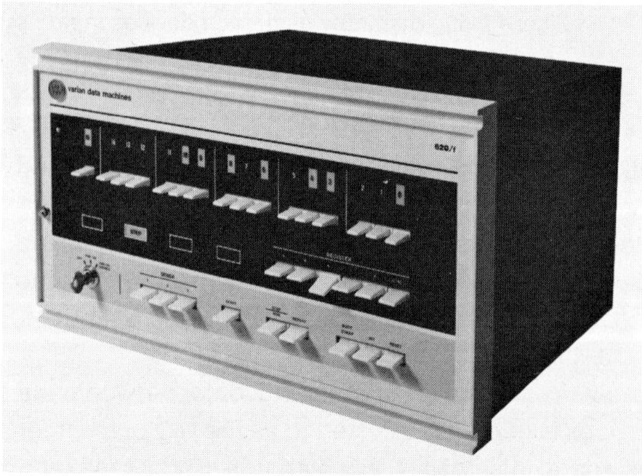

Figure 7-52 Varian 620f mini-computer. (Courtesy Varian Data Machines.)

Figure 7-53 H-316 mini-computer. (Courtesy Honeywell Information Systems.)

for under $10,000. It has a memory size of 4K, expandable to 16K. This 16-bit computer has a 72-command instruction set and has more than 500 field-proven software packages available for implementation.

*Mini-computers are not subject to the time delays found in some time-sharing systems.*

***Mini-Computers vs. Time-sharing Terminals.*** Many of the tasks commonly performed by a mini-computer in industry could be handled by a time-sharing terminal linked to a large computer. However, the original cost of a mini-computer can be less than the annual rental cost of a time-sharing terminal. Of equal importance to the user is the question of reliability. Control outputs from time-sharing terminals are wholly dependent on the large computer to which they are connected. Should a failure occur in that unit, all terminals and the machines to which they are connected are out of service until repairs are made. Should a mini-computer fail, only the one task to which it has been assigned is affected. It can be replaced with a spare mini-computer in a matter of minutes. A mini-computer, then, is not subject to the time delays prevalent in some time-sharing systems—delays that can not be tolerated in a variety of industrial applications.

*Mini-computers serve as links to other computers, as shown in Figure 7-54.*

***Mini-Computers in a Total System.*** In Figure 7-54, several mini-computers and a small time-sharing system can be linked to a centrally located computer in order to form a hierarchal network. The mini-computer on the production line, for example, may send data, such as part counts, rejection rates, and machine performance to a central computer for filing. In a similar manner, business and engineering data can be controlled from time-sharing devices by a mini-computer before entering the small time-sharing computer. All data within Figure 7-54 are finally directed to the larger computer. The larger computer, then, can issue commands to the different equipment connected on-line. Its reponses will be based upon information received. If irregularities, for example, are reported from a machine station, the central computer will immediately direct the mini-computer to shut down the machine or assign necessary corrective measures.

*Point-of-sale terminal utilizes a mini-computer in its hardware.*

***Mini-Computer—Point of Sale Terminal.*** An interesting application of the mini-computer is the point-of-sale (POS) system for retail stores, designed by NCR. At the heart of this system is the NCR 280 point-of-sale retail terminal (Figure 7-55),

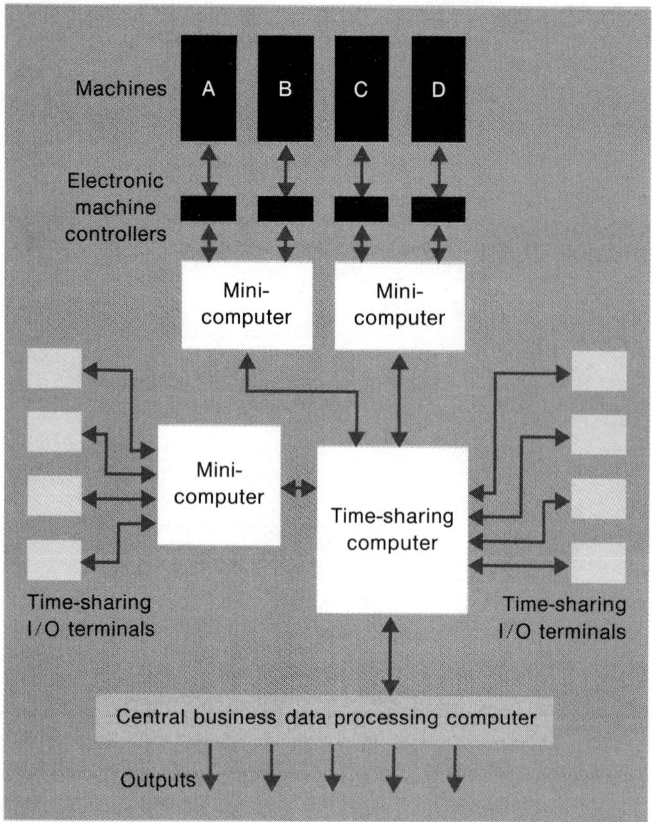


Figure 7-54 Hierarchal network using mini-computers.

an electronic descendant of the cash register that is a mini-computer (has a 256 byte memory). A wandlike device optically reads binary-coded media in the form of merchandise tags, ID cards, credit cards, and similar items in order to eliminate human error in gathering point-of-sale information. Data are read instantly and correctly with one simple pass of the penlike wand, containing light-sensitive glass fibers.

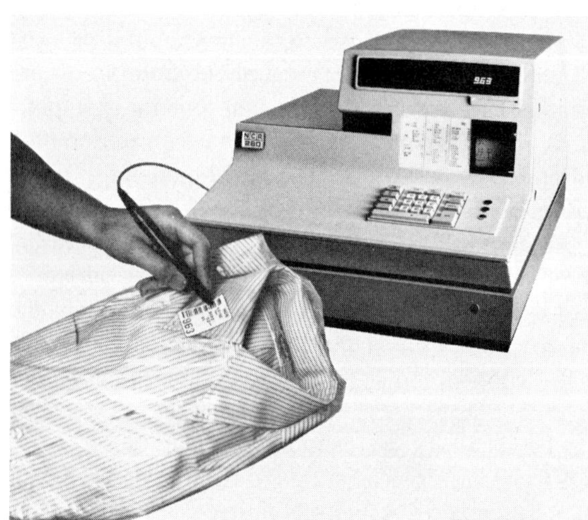


Figure 7-55 NCR 280 Point-of-Sale (POS) Retail Terminal with wandlike reader. (Courtesy The National Cash Register Company.)

At each step of every sale, the NCR 280 mini-computer instructs the clerk what to do next, leaving no room for error or omission. An electronic display of instructions on the terminal actually leads the clerk through the sequence of every transaction without lengthy training. The NCR 280 system reads the tags, records all the details of the sale, and does all the calculations. An on-line credit authorization system provides automatic, instant authorization of every charge sale. Also, an electronic data collector records the information from up to 48 electronic cash register terminals onto a single reel of magnetic tape for on-line processing. The system includes a printer to print merchandise tags on conventional tag stock.

### Small Card-Oriented System

*Small card-oriented computer allows the user to upgrade his system from punched card equipment.*

There are several small card-oriented systems currently available, the most popular one being the IBM System/3 Model 10. The system utilizes monolithic integrated circuitry and comes in the punched card (96 column) and the magnetic disk version (Figure 5-2). A basic punched card version can be rented for approximately the same price as many 407 accounting machines. For punched card installations currently using the 80 column card, there is a card reader/punch that will handle this size card.

***System/3 Model 10.*** The System/3 Model 10 has an 8K (expandable up to 32K) character memory and uses the extended binary coded decimal interchange code (EBCDIC) internally. The disk version, which requires at least 12K of core memory, comes with one or two drives, providing a capacity of 2.45 up to 9.8 million characters. Depending upon the model, cards can be read at the rate of 250 or 500 per minute, punched at 60 or 120 per minute, collated and printed at 60 or 120 per minute. Other peripherals include 100 and 200 lines per minute printers, 1000 and 1500 cards per minute sorters, a Selectric printer keyboard, and an off-line key data recorder. Most of this peripheral equipment was discussed previously. Also, the System/3 has telecommunication capabilities.

User programs are designed through a proprietary program, called the Application Customerizer Service. The programmer utilizes input forms (fill-in-the-blanks) to prepare program outlines, including flowcharts for coding RPG II (Report Program Generator—to be covered in Chapter 10) programs—the only language for the System/3. The Application Customerizer Service provides the customer with a well documented logical system design, makes the programmer more productive, gets more applications running faster, and is more economical. However, the more the programmer deviates from the basic application design, such as adding new reports, new card records, and the like, the more difficult it is to implement the system. In order to accommodate teleprocessing applications, the RPG II language has a special feature that includes a fill-in-the-blanks telecommunications specification sheet through which the user can describe the communications tasks he wants to perform. This information is then punched into cards and fed into the computer, along with other RPG II instructions that comprise the user's application program.

***System/3 Model 6.*** In addition to Model 10 in the System/3 series, Model 6 (Figure 7-56) is a low-cost direct entry disk system with multipurpose capabilities, renting for approximately $1000 per month. Its disk capacity is capable of handling 9.8 million bytes with a dual drive. A data recorder can be attached for batch input and the machine can be also utilized as a terminal/processor. The system is compatible with System/360's, System/370's, and other System/3's.

The Model 6 handles business applications, such as billing, accounts receivable, inventory control, and sales analysis, and is supported by RPG II programming.

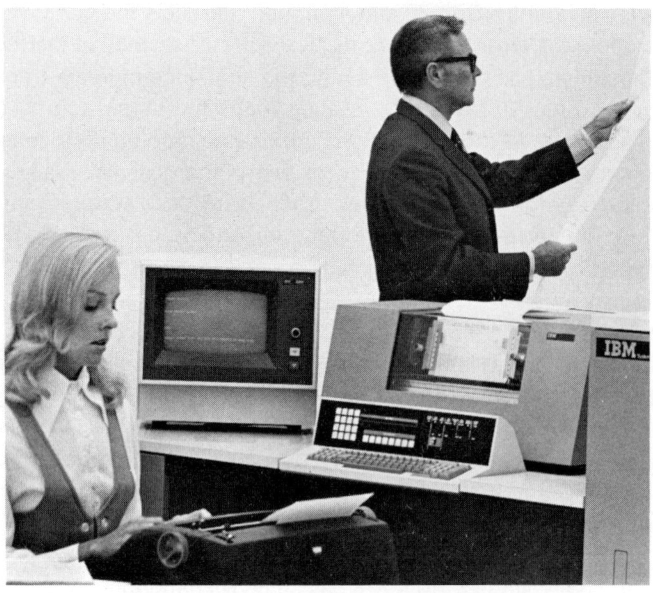


Figure 7-56 IBM System/3 Model 6 with 2265 Display Station (optional). (Courtesy International Business Machines Corporation.)

A quick switch can be made to mathematical problem solving by typing a command via the console keyboard. A basic programming language is provided for this function.

***Honeywell 58.*** Competition for the System/3 series includes the Honeywell 58 card-oriented system. The basic Model 58 (Figure 7-57) encompasses a central processing unit with 5K (expandable to 10K), a data entry station, a 200 line per

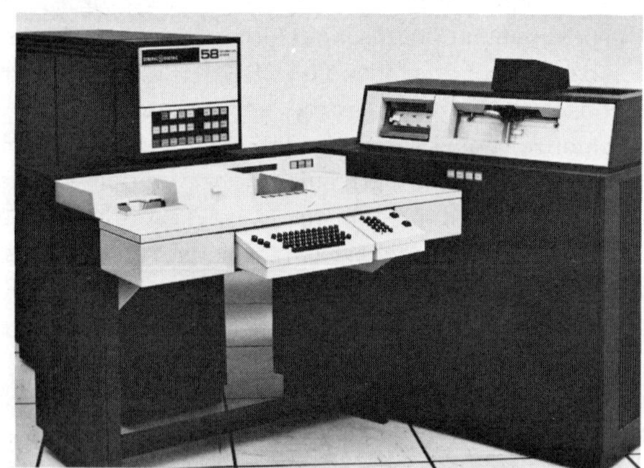


Figure 7-57 Honeywell 58 card-oriented computer system. (Courtesy Honeywell Information Systems.)

minute printer, a 200 card per minute reader, and a 30 card per minute punch. Enlargements can take the form of magnetic disk and data communications. Communications capability is through the Datanet-51, a 2400 band, single-line communications controller. The market for this system is basically divided between upgrading a punched card system and improving accounting machine operations. Thus the Model 58 can handle payroll, order processing, inventory control, general accounting, and other business applications.

## Small Magnetic Tape-Oriented System

*Small card-oriented computer system can be upgraded to magnetic tape for handling a firm's increasing data processing load.*

Punched cards can limit the speed and flexibility of a business computer system. For this reason, the next step is to a small-scale computer system that utilizes magnetic tape or magnetic disk for on-line file storage. Figure 7-58 shows a typical small magnetic tape-oriented system.

***UNIVAC 9200 II.*** The UNIVAC 9200 II can be expanded to 32K of memory and utilizes monolithic integrated circuits. A plated-wire main memory operates in a nondestructive read-out mode, obviating the rewrite cycle after each read cycle. The 9200 has on-line printers that range in speeds from 900 lines per minute up to 1600 lines per minute (with 43-character set). The computer system can be equipped with up to 12 tape drives, the average requirement being four. This is necessary in order to meet the sorting requirement. A typical 9200 II tape-based system will lease for about $3000 per month. Other systems will be as high as $5000 per month.

Figure 7-58 UNIVAC 9200 II—small magnetic tape-oriented system. (Courtesy UNIVAC Division of the Sperry Rand Corporation.)

## Small Magnetic Disk-Oriented System

*Small card-oriented computer system can also be upgraded to magnetic disk if growth warrants the move.*

A small magnetic disk-oriented system can be installed in place of a tape system. The decision will depend on the feasibility study. It is usually desirable to have at least two disk storage devices. Monthly rental prices are comparable to magnetic tape in that both systems lease anywhere from $2000 to $5000 a month, depending on the peripheral equipment.

***NCR Century 100.*** An NCR Century 100 Series disk-oriented computer system is illustrated in Figure 7-59. It uses a 16K thin film, short rod memory module with a memory cycle time of 800 nanoseconds. The basic unit of data storage, as in most computers, is the 8-bit byte. Bytes can be addressed and manipulated individually, or consecutive memory locations can be grouped to form decimal or binary fields up to 256 bytes in length. Instructions are either 4 or 8 bytes long and specify 1 or 2 memory addresses, respectively. The internal data code is USASCII.

Each installation gets a disk file with one pack designated as the "system disk." The basic disk drive houses two removable packs, each with approximately 4.2 million bytes of capacity. One of these packs is designated as the system disk. Up to 13% of the storage area on this pack will be dedicated for peripheral storage of software, diagnostics, peripheral identification tables, and a continuous log of software utilization and system malfunctions. Peripherals include CRAM whose access time is an average 125 milliseconds. Capacity per file is 125 million characters and several CRAM units can be linked with a single controller.

Figure 7-59 NCR Century 100—small magnetic disk-oriented system. (Courtesy The National Cash Register Company.)

*Medium-scale computer system has these attributes over its small-scale counterpart:*
- *faster processing*
- *increased storage (primary and secondary)*
- *more peripheral devices*
- *higher cost*

**Medium-scale Computer System**

If a firm has need for a larger system than those set forth above, it can acquire a medium-scale computer system. Not only are the central processor and peripherals faster but also the amount of storage and the number of attached units is larger. The price range for this category is quite wide, ranging from approximately $10,000 to $75,000 per month.

***System/370 Model 155.*** A typical medium-scale computer system is illustrated in Figure 7-60. Being one of the System/370 series, this Model 155 incorporates Monolithic Systems Technology (MST) in which the circuits are up to eight times more densely packed than the System/360. The machine has an associate buffer memory that makes the machine's memory just as fast as the central processing unit. Matching of the central processor and main memory cycle speed is achieved through the use of a buffer memory with an 80-nanosecond cycle time. The buffer memory has a size of 8000 bytes while the main memory is available in seven sizes,

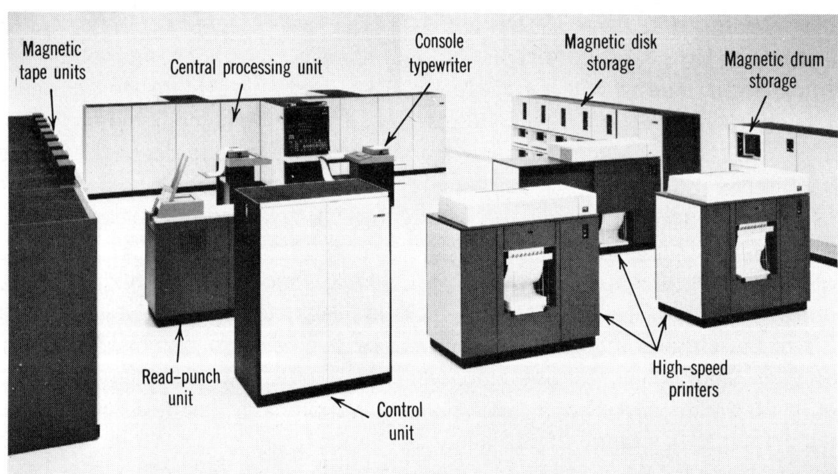


Figure 7-60 IBM System/370 Model 155—a medium-scale computer system. (Courtesy International Business Machines Corporation.)

ranging from 256,000 bytes to over 2 million bytes. The 155 has a processor cycle time of 115 nanoseconds although the main memory cycle time is 2.1 microseconds. Also included in the system are up to six high speed data channels that can accommodate up to 5.8 million characters per second.

The Model 155 can be equipped with the 3330 disk storage unit. The 3330 unit has access time of 30 milliseconds and achieves a data transfer rate of over 800,000 bytes per second. The unit uses new disk packs with 12 disks and 20 recording surfaces, 19 of which store data. A total of 800 million bytes of data are accessible on-line with the 3330 unit. Another piece of equipment available for this computer system is the 3211 line printer, operating up to 2500 lines per minute. Monthly rentals for the entire system range from $37,365 (256,000 bytes) up to $78,936 (2 million bytes).

### Large-scale Computer System

For firms requiring extremely powerful computing and manipulating capabilities, the large-scale computer system is generally the answer. A monthly rental price for such a system may well exceed $100,000 (Figure 5-7).

***UNIVAC 1110.*** The UNIVAC 1110 (Figure 7-61), leasing from $70,000 to $170,000 per month depending upon the equipment configuration, has the capacity to proc-

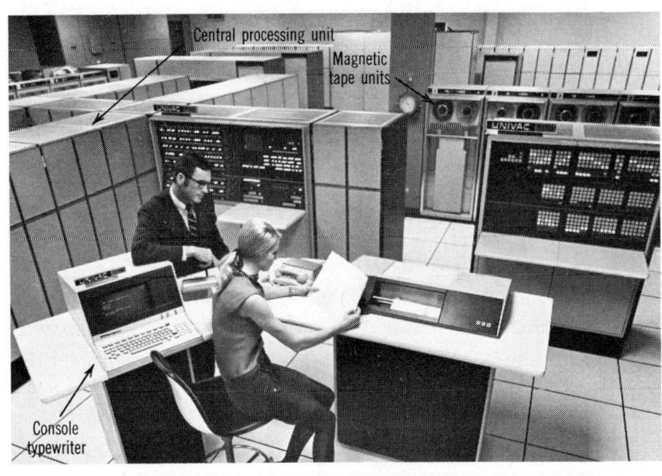


Figure 7-61 UNIVAC 1110 large-scale computer system. (Courtesy UNIVAC Division of the Sperry Rand Corporation.)

*Large-scale computer system is a powerful source of computing. Its capabilities normally include:*
- *real-time processing*
- *local batch processing*
- *remote batch processing*
- *time sharing*

ess more than 3 million instructions per second. It has the capability to perform local batch processing, remote batch processing, time sharing, and real-time processing of business and scientific applications. The number of terminals that can be supported by the system ranges from 150 to 300. Also, there is compatibility in hardware and software with other members of UNIVAC's large-scale computer family, resulting in a modularity for this large computer system.

Being a large-scale, general purpose computer system, its minimum configuration includes two command/arithmetic units (CAUs) and one input/output access unit (IOAU). Called a $2 \times 1$, this system can be expanded to a $2 \times 2$, $4 \times 2$, or $4 \times 4$ configuration. These units allow multiprocessing and multiprogramming. The processors operate simultaneously with each CAU rated at 1.7 million instructions per second (operating on 36-bit words). Each performs logical, control, and arithmetic functions, and has a four-deep instruction overlap; that is, four instructions can be in different stages of execution simultaneously. The IOAU performs the input/output functions and each may control 8 to 24 channels. Maximum channel rates are 600,000 words per second for data going directly to memory and 500,000 words per second if they are coming out.

Character-oriented instructions allowing decimal addition and subtraction, and editing and translation capabilities are also among the 186 basic machine instructions. There are 112 registers, 56 for systems usage and the other half for the programmer. Main storage is comprised of plated wire that can be read in 320 nanoseconds and written in 520 nanoseconds. Up to 256K words can be attached in 32K banks.

## MODULAR CONCEPT

The modular concept is an important one in data processing. It applies to computer systems as well as to their operational programs. These hardware and software modular aspects are investigated below.

### Hardware Modularity

*Hardware modularity allows the user to assemble an equipment configuration that can be added to at some time in the future.*

Present computers, as illustrated in the preceding sections, are "modular" or "building-block" machines. This means that the machine modules (hardware) can be assembled in different combinations in order to provide various machine capabilities. Not only can a computer system be tailored to meet the specific requirements of one user but it can also be expanded to meet his volume and tasks in the future. This is extremely important because both business and scientific computing expands in volume as more and more is learned about the machine's capabilities. By means of modular construction, a user can select from among several basic arithmetic speeds, memory sizes, a number of data communication channels, a number of input/output devices, and so forth. The modular concept can be expanded to interconnect two or more computers for multicomputer systems. In a similar manner, standardization of interface devices make it possible to combine components and machines from several equipment manufacturers in order to assemble a desired system.

### Software Modularity.

*Software modularity allows for expansion to a large computer system without the need for extensive reprogramming.*

Another important aspect of modularity is the compatibility of the machine language. If the number of input/output units are to be expanded, there must be sufficient memory space available to handle the additional number of units. But more importantly, the basic machine language used to instruct the expanded memory of a larger computer system should be the same as for other sized systems. The modularity concept provides for this expansion without the need for extensive reprogramming. Referring to earlier generations of computers (first and second generations), it was necessary to reprogram when a user outgrew a system and found it necessary to acquire a larger system. This is no longer true of most third- and current-generation computers. From a programming point of view, the building block concept, then, provides flexibility for most growth situations experienced by a firm as well as keeping the software cost to a minimum. This is important since software costs often exceed hardware costs for business data processing systems.

## SUMMARY

The basic components of computers, set forth in a previous chapter, were presented in more detail. These included input/output devices, central processing unit, internal memory devices, auxiliary storage devices, and external storage. Additional components of a computer system will be described in the next two chapters, namely, magnetic ink character recognition, optical character recognition, and time-sharing equipment. Although these components represent the hardware of the computer system, there are three other important elements in computer data processing systems. These are software or programming, procedures, and personnel which are the end result of a feasibility study. Each of these elements will be explored in some detail in subsequent chapters.

As a part of a general overview of computer systems, several typical configurations were illustrated. These ranged from mini-computers to a large-scale computer system. A firm can upgrade its installation by adding more input and output devices, primary storage, and secondary storage without reprogramming. The modular design concept of current computers makes this possible, a very decided advantage over punched card machines and earlier computers.

## *QUESTIONS*

1. (a) How important is data buffering for computer input/output devices?
   (b) Describe at least four types of computer input.
   (c) Describe at least four types of computer output.
2. How essential is an on-line printer and card punch in every computer installation? Explain.
3. Contrast the similarities and differences between a magnetic core and a magnetic thin film memory.
4. What advantages are available with a laser mass memory system versus other methods of storage?
5. What are the various forms of external storage?
6. How can the mini-computer be used for business data processing applications?
7. What applications would be preferable for a magnetic tape-oriented system versus a magnetic disk-oriented system?
8. What is meant by the building block concept when referring to computers?
9. Based upon the equipment surveyed in the chapter, what, in your opinion, will be the future trend in computer hardware?

## CHAPTER EIGHT

# Optical Character Recognition Equipment

*OCR equipment represents a faster data entry input method than keypunching. In addition, costs can be lower if there is sufficient volume. Pictured is an operator extracting cards from an OCR device. (Courtesy Control Data Corporation.)*

Although the price of computer throughput has decreased, the cost of input has increased. Firms have moved away from punched card equipment in order to circumvent the time and cost of preparing and manipulating data for computer input. One of the ways of effecting time and cost savings is the keyboard data entry system. A more promising method is the utilization of optical character recognition (OCR) equipment. Depending upon the model, data can be entered directly into the computer or into some machine processable form off-line. The number of machines available offers the user a specialized device to meet his particular applications.

This chapter will focus initially on magnetic ink character recognition and, then, on the major types of optical character recognition equipment. These include:

1. optical/magnetic sorter,
2. optical reader card punch,
3. optical mark reader,
4. optical journal tape reader,
5. optical page reader,
6. optical character reader.

Codes that are readable by these pieces of equipment are set forth in the appropriate sections of the chapter in order to make the presentation more meaningful. Numerous OCR applications will conclude the discussion of this fast growing area of computer input.

## MAGNETIC INK CHARACTERS

*Magnetic ink characters consist of:*
- *ten digits*
- *four special symbols*

The American Bankers Association has adopted a national standard code for the banking industry. This standard code is called MICR, magnetic ink character recognition, and consists of numerals and symbols of a distinctive type style. As shown in Figure 8-1, the MICR code or the E-13B type font consists of ten digits and four special symbols.

### MICR Inscribing

*MICR data are inscribed by using a key operated machine which prints magnetic characters on the document.*

Inscribing is accomplished by a key-operated machine (Figure 8-2) that prints on checks or other documents in magnetic ink containing particles of iron oxide. The machine combines the function of inscribing with those of an adding machine. When data are inscribed or printed, they are located $\frac{3}{16}$-inch from the bottom edge of the document. Characters are spaced eight to the inch.

In Figure 8-3, the position of MICR printing on a check is illustrated. Starting from left to right, the first two fields are the Check Routing Symbol and the ABA Transit Number which refer to the bank number for clearing checks through the Federal Reserve Bank System. These two numbers are the same ones located in the upper right hand corner of the check. Next is the account number, assigned to the customer. Since these three fields (check routing symbol, ABA transit number, and account number) are printed before the check is written or cashed, they are termed *prequalified*. Moving to the right again, the next field is Process Control which identifies the type of transaction. The last field of information contains the amount of the check. These last two fields are termed *postqualified* since they are inscribed after the check has been written and cashed.

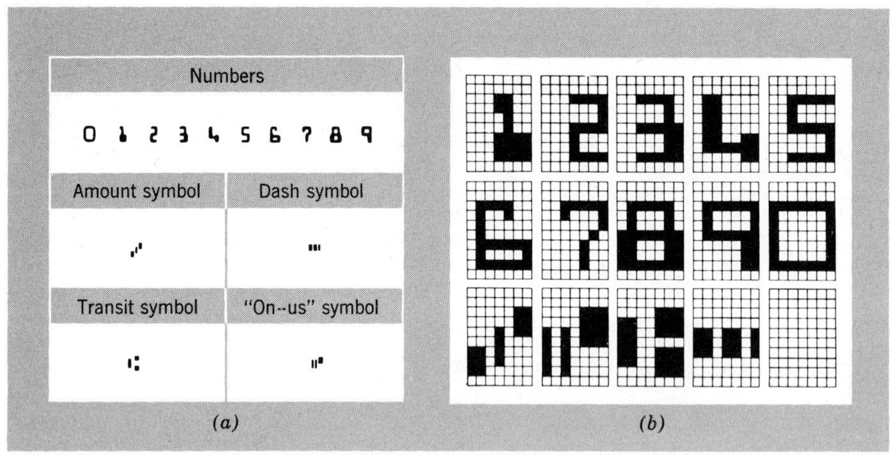


Figure 8-1 (*a*) Fourteen magnetic ink characters of font E-13B and (*b*) their matrix patterns.

## MICR Equipment

*MICR equipment is available from several equipment manufacturers.*

Specialized equipment, such as the IBM 1419 Magnetic Character Sorter-Reader (Figure 8-4) is utilized by banks for processing large volumes of daily transactions. Not only does the 1419 read both card and paper documents inscribed with the E-13B type font, but it also is designed to sort magnetically inscribed documents into as many as 13 classifications: A, B, 0–9, and R(reject).

Documents read may be of intermixed sizes and thicknesses, as typically encountered in check handling operations. The standard minimum length is 6 inches. Shorter documents, such as the 51-column postal money order, can be read by the system. These shorter documents can be intermixed with standard length documents and can also be sorted if a special feature for that purpose is installed. If this feature is not installed on the 1419, 51-column cards and other documents less than 5 inches long are sent to the reject pocket. If the feature is installed, the 1419 speed is reduced by an amount that increases slightly with the average length of the documents. Many special features are available on the sorter-reader, including

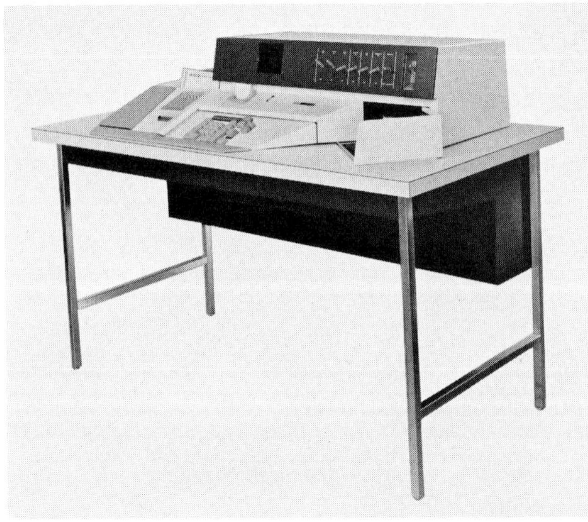

Figure 8-2 IBM 1203 Unit Inscriber. (Courtesy International Business Machines Corporation.)

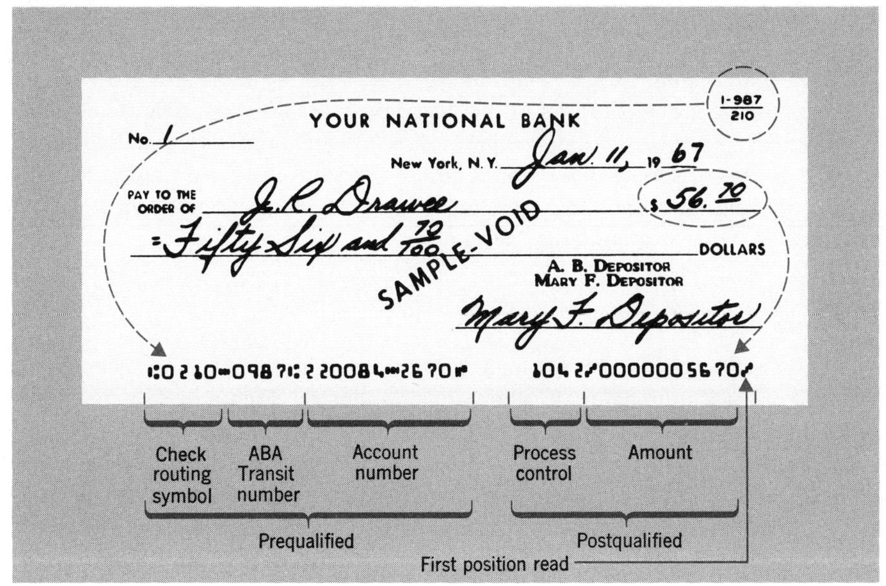


Figure 8-3 Magnetic inscription of characters and definitions of fields.

an endorser to print the bank's endorsement on the back of each document at no reduction in operating speed.

### Operation of MICR Equipment

*MICR equipment recognizes characters by comparing their matrix patterns (0- and 1-bit configurations) to stored matrix patterns.*

Typical operation of the IBM 1419 involves feeding documents over a read head where the characters are sensed. The sensing process is accomplished by transmitting electronic signals to a character matrix that has a storage location of 70 segments (Figure 8-1*b*). Lack of any appreciable signal from a character segment causes the machine to store a 0-bit in that storage location. The presence of a significant signal causes the machine to store a 1-bit in the proper storage location. After the entire character has passed under the read head and all segments (70) have been sensed, the pattern of the character shape is made up of 0- and 1-bit configurations. The reader is designed to recognize each of the 14 characters separately. If a character is slightly out of position as it passes over the read head,

Figure 8-4 IBM 1419 Magnetic Character Sorter-Reader. (Courtesy International Business Machines Corporation.)

the signals sent back to the storage matrix form what is known as a "folded" character. The machine can automatically "unfold" the character by shifting it vertically within the matrix to attempt recognition. After all data have been sensed, the document is directed to one of the 13 pockets for the illustrated machine.

Magnetic ink character readers may be used to enter printed information directly into a computer at speeds comparable to the speed of punched cards. Data may also be recorded on punched cards, paper tape, or magnetic tape which can be used later as input to a computer system.

## OPTICAL CHARACTER RECOGNITION

*OCR equipment has the capability of reading printed or handwritten source documents, thereby circumventing other means of data preparation, such as the key punch.*

Magnetic ink character recognition, as indicated in the previous section, is an important processing medium for the banking industry. Such a system has a relatively limited application in direct document recording since only 14 characters can be recognized. The need for other input processing devices, capable of reading printed or handwritten source documents and circumventing key punch or paper tape methods, has been evident from the beginning of automated business data processing. This direct input ability has important advantages to the user, namely, cost and error reduction. To fill this need, optical character recognition equipment has been marketed for input data processing.

In 1951, Dr. David H. Shepard invented the first practical optical reader, followed four years later by the first commercial installation at *Reader's Digest*. Since that time, there has been a profusion of new and different optical character recognition devices. There are mark sense readers, bar code readers, type font readers, character recognition devices, and readers of constrained handwriting. Documents that can be read include full pages, coupons, airline tickets, checks, journal tapes, tags, and print-on punched cards. Manufacturers of OCR equipment are producing a wide range of input devices to meet the demands of business and industry. Although their efforts are directed basically toward the elimination of punched cards, research indicates that both will continue to have broad application within its designated capabilities.

### Optical Font Types

*There are three basic optical font types.*

When classed by optical font types, OCR equipment falls into three categories. They are:

1. "pseudo" mark sense readers,
2. stylized font readers,
3. multifont readers.

*The GE COC-5 font (Figure 8-5a) makes it possible to operate in a mark sense mode with simple recognition logic.*

***GE COC-5 Font.*** Two manufacturers, the General Electric Company and the National Cash Register Company, are building machines in the first category. These machines are difficult to class as true OCR readers since they sense marks or bar codes arranged in the shape of numeric characters. The GE machines read the GE COC-5 OCR font, a font made up of vertical bars. The numerals are difficult for people to read. However, this font makes it possible to operate in a mark sense mode with extremely simple recognition logic. Figure 8-5*a* shows several of the COC-5 characters and the manner in which they are read. The missing bars in the characters generate a simple binary code in the reader's recognition circuitry. The Bull CMC-7 (proposed European standard) is a magnetic code which operates in much the same manner.

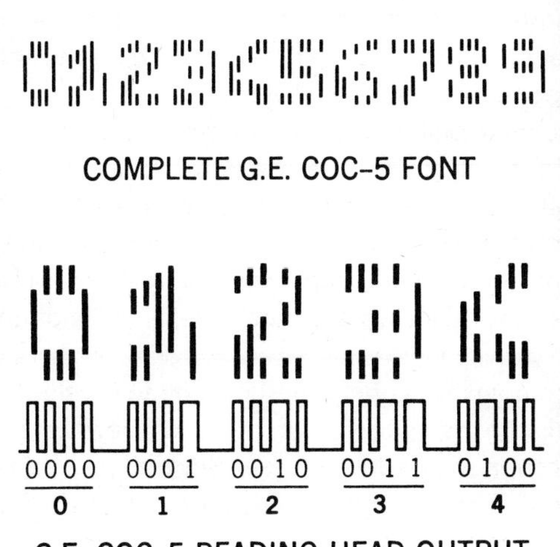


(a)

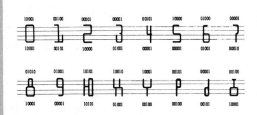

NATIONAL CASH REGISTER "NOF" FONT
(Lines show upper and lower reading tracks)

(b)

ABCDEFGHIJKLMNOPQRS
TUVWXYZ0123456789

USASCSOCR (USA Standard Character Set for Optical Character Recognition)

ÜÑÄØÖÆÅ£¥

ADDITIONAL CHARACTERS FOR INTERNATIONAL USE

(c)

Figure 8-5 Optical font styles—(*a*) GE COC-5, (*b*) NCR NOF, and (*c*) USASCSOCR and additional characters for international use.

The NCR NOF font (Figure 8-5b) utilizes the binary system to operate in a stylized font mode.

***NCR NOF Font.*** Compared to the GE COC-5 font, the NCR NOF font is easier to read manually. It is mechanically read by two separate photo cells, one scanning a track through the upper half of the character while the other scans a track through the lower half. As shown in Figure 8-5*b*, the binary numbers above and below indicate the bit pattern seen by each of the reading tracks. Except for several rather strange looking symbols, NOF appears as a normal numeric font.

USASCSOCR (Figure 8-5c) and other fonts are read in a stylized or a multifont mode.

***USASCSOCR Font.*** Many readers will accept one or more stylized fonts. This represents a second stage of complexity beyond the pseudo mark sense units. The most common font which almost all machines will read today is the USASCSOCR font, illustrated in Figure 8-5*c*. Probably the next most common font is the Farrington "Self Check." Beyond this point, machines accept almost any Gothic numerics. Some machines read hand-printed numerals while others accept a full alphanumeric type font.

The ultimate state of OCR complexity is encountered with the multifont reader. These machines accept, as a minimum, a small group of standard typewriter or printed fonts and will usually read both upper and lower case. Several will read certain hand-printed alphabetics. Many of the various machines currently available will be illustrated in the forthcoming sections of this chapter.

### Operation of OCR Equipment

Basically, an optical recognition character reader, as illustrated in Figure 8-6, consists of the following:

1. a document transport,
2. a scanner unit,
3. a recognition unit.

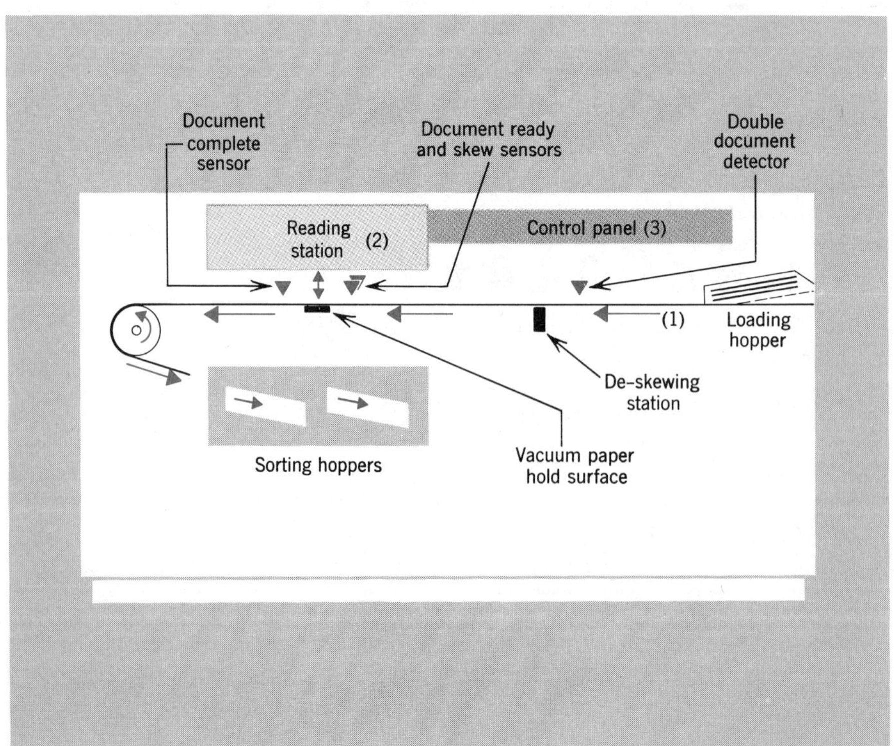


Figure 8-6 Schematic showing document-handling process for the CDC 915 Page Reader, illustrated in Figure 8-28. (Courtesy Control Data Corporation.)

*The OCR machine's transport sends the documents to a reading or scanning station where comparisons are made with storage images of the recognition unit. After reading and recording, the document is transported to an output stacker.*

The document transport or carrier unit is the mechanism needed to carry the document from the input stacker to the appropriate output stacker. In the process of this movement, the characters to be read are scanned by some kind of photoelectric device or scanning unit, sometimes identified as a reading station. This part of the OCR reader converts the characters on the input record into a representation that is analyzed by the recognition unit, in conjunction with a control panel for most OCR readers. This unit matches patterns from the scanner unit against internally stored reference patterns. Those patterns which are identifiable are recorded on some processing medium or are direct input to a computer. Those characters which cannot be identified can cause the input document to be rejected.

### Data Recognition Methods

*Generally, matrix methods are capable of reading a limited number of characters, while curve tracing and stroke analysis methods are capable of recognizing printed and handwritten characters.*

The more common methods of character recognition are:

1. matrix matching,
2. curve tracing,
3. feature or stroke analysis.

The first method (matrix matching) compares individual elements of the scanned character with the elements of all characters which can be identified. This method was explained previously for magnetic ink character recognition. In general, the matrix approach allows for more positive identification of a limited number of characters. Characters are read more economically on a low cost, high speed scanner.

The second method (curve tracing) is well suited for recognizing handwritten characters which vary in size and shape. Sometimes referred to as the topological approach, curve tracing identifies characters by observations as to vertical lines, horizontal lines, and the like. Under the third method (feature analysis), a character is recognized on the basis of its line or stroke formation. This method requires a special printing font.

*The type of detection and recognition system employed in OCR equipment is dependent upon the optical fonts to be read.*

***Detection and Recognition Systems.*** The detection systems of an optical character reader and optical mark reader are basically the same, but their recognition systems differ. In both systems, detection consists of recognizing a drop in reflected light arriving at a set of photo cells. For the optical mark reader, the recognition unit notices only the gross drop in light and determines the value of the mark by noting its position in relation to some reference point, such as the beginning of a line. The recognition system of many optical character readers notes not only the gross drop in light, but also detects on a two-dimensional grid the point at which the drop occurred. An analysis of these coordinates is then performed in order to determine the character read.

Detection errors are much lower for optical mark readers than for optical character readers. However, the information packing density is much higher for optical character readers. Optical mark readers are simpler and less costly to build than optical character readers.

## OCR EQUIPMENT

*OCR equipment is classified as follows:*

- *optical/magnetic sorter*
- *optical reader card punch*
- *optical mark reader*
- *optical journal tape reader*
- *optical page reader*
- *optical character reader*

There is a proliferation of input devices to handle the firm's data processing needs. Optical character recognition equipment can be connected on-line to a computer or can be used off-line. In the on-line mode, raw data are machine- or hand-printed on source documents of various sizes, including adding machine and cash register tapes. Off-line, the optical scanner can be connected to a magnetic tape unit, a punched paper tape device, or a punched card machine. Off-line and on-line OCR equipment is classified as follows: optical/magnetic sorter, optical reader card punch, optical mark reader, optical journal tape reader, optical page reader, and optical character reader. Each will be discussed in the following sections.

### Optical/Magnetic Sorter

*Optical/magnetic sorter is a combination optical reader and MICR sorter where a mixture of documents can be read and sorted at the same time.*

A current piece of equipment in this fast growing field is a combination optical reader and MICR sorter. A mixture of documents, such as utility bills, credit card slips, insurance premium notices, loan coupons, bank checks, and deposit slips can be read and sorted at the same time on the Burroughs Reader Sorter (Figure 8-7). Information can be read in the OCR A (United States standard) or OCR B

Figure 8-7 Burroughs Reader Sorter—optical and MICR characters. (Courtesy Burroughs Corporation.)

(international standard) optical fonts or may be recorded in the standard magnetic character recognition code E-13B. In a single pass of an on-line version of the system, the reader sorter can pull off two lines of similarly recorded information, a line of magnetic characters and one of optical characters, or one line of each type of optical characters. The maximum read rate for the system is 1625 documents per minute.

### Optical Reader Card Punch

*Optical reader card punch scans data on a card and punches the information into the same card.*

Self-punch readers read data imprinted on cards and punch the information back onto the same cards. For example, the IBM 1282 Optical Reader Card Punch (Figure 8-8) optically reads printed, imprinted, or handmarked information from a card and punches it into the same card. It reads and punches 51- or 80-column cards at a maximum rate of 200 per minute, thereby, eliminating manual key punching. A maximum of 32 characters can be read and punched during a single pass. The machine operates independently (off-line) while preparing invoice or statement data for rapid entry to a data processing system. Its ability to read imprinted credit card account numbers and hand-marked amount data makes it particularly applicable to credit card accounting. In all types of billing operations, the 1282 permits bills and statements in card form to be punched automatically with both account

Figure 8-8 IBM 1282 Optical Reader Card Punch. (Courtesy International Business Machines Corporation.)

number and total amount, either prior to mailing or after return with payment. Partial payment and other exceptions can be noted by hand marking.

### Optical Mark Reader

*Optical mark reader scans data marked by a standard type lead pencil and records it in a machine-processable form, such as magnetic tape.*

Preprinted forms that have been marked by a standard type lead pencil can be read by an optical mark reader. Marks (erasures are possible), easily recognized by the human eye, are also easily recognizable by the mark reader. This equipment is not to be confused with a mark sense reader whose documents must be marked with special pencils containing soft and highly conductive lead. Erasures can be made with mark sensing. However, there is a distinct risk that sufficient lead will remain even when it appears to the eye that the erasure is made fairly clean.

*Mark reader forms are designed so that they are compatible with the OCR equipment being used.*

***Mark Reader Forms.*** At one time, optical mark readers were used mainly to score test results. Today, they are employed as data acquisition devices in payroll, inventory control, order entry, and insurance claims. Order blanks, market research surveys, questionnaires, personnel evaluations, and testing forms are additional types that are input for optical mark readers. The document is generally a printed form containing an area for recording marks on items which must be read (account number, part number, quantity, etc.) and areas for recording information not read by the optical mark reader (customer name, address, etc.). Typically, forms are preprinted with header information and other required user data. Response areas where marks are to be entered appear to the right or below the preprinted information. Values are printed at the mark positions in an ink which is not detectable by the optical mark reader. Shown in Figures 8-9 and 8-10 are sample mark reader forms.

The IBM 1231 Optical Mark Reader Model N1 is illustrated in Figure 8-11. This reader can be attached to a System/360 or System/370 channel for direct reading of marks in specified places on $8\frac{1}{2}$ by 11 inch paper data sheets. The marks may also be made by certain IBM printers, provided that the standard dash is replaced with an enlarged dash.

Data sheets are fed through the reader from a 600-sheet hopper and are stacked, in reverse sequence, in a 600-sheet stacker or in a separate 50-sheet stacker if an error is detected. Each data sheet has, on one side, up to 1000

# WEEKLY PAYROLL
## — HOURS —

EMPLOYEE NAME

Soc. Sec. No. EMPLOYEE NUMBER

DEPT.

## ADDITIONAL VACATION TIME

BANK VACATION NO. OF WEEKS ______________

RATE

EMPLOYEE NUMBER

:0: :1: :2: :3: :4: :5: :6: :7: :8: :9:

:0: :1: :2: :3: :4: :5: :6: :7: :8: :9:

:0: :1: :2: :3: :4: :5: :6: :7: :8: :9:

:0: :1: :2: :3: :4: :5: :6: :7: :8: :9:

DEPT. NO.

:0: :1: :2: :3: :4: :5: :6: :7: :8: :9:

:0: :1: :2: :3: :4: :5: :6: :7: :8: :9:

:0: :1: :2: :3: :4: :5: :6: :7: :8: :9:

:0: :1: :2: :3: :4: :5: :6: :7: :8: :9:

SHIFT :1: :2: :3:

HOURS

:35: :28: :21: :14: :7: REGULAR HOURS

:10: :20: :30: :40:

:1: :2: :3: :4: :5: :6: :7: :8: :9:

:¼: :½: :¾: HOURS

:10: :20: :30: :40: OVERTIME HOURS

:1: :2: :3: :4: :5: :6: :7: :8: :9:

:¼: :½: :¾: HOUR

:1/3: :2/3: HOUR

:10: :20: :30: :40: DOUBLETIME HOURS

:1: :2: :3: :4: :5: :6: :7: :8: :9:

:¼: :½: :¾: HOUR

:1/3: :2/3: HOUR

DAYS :1: :2: :3: :4: :5: REG. VACATION

WEEK :1: VACATION-BANK

DAYS :1: :2: :3: :4: :5: HOLIDAY-BIRTHDAY

DAYS :1: :2: :3: :4: :5: BEREAVEMENT JURY DUTY

DED. HOSP. DUES

DAYS

:0: :1: :2: :3: :4: :6: :7: WORKED (SHOE)

:0: :1: :2: :3: :4: PENSION

Figure 8-9 A weekly payroll hours form—input for an optional mark reader.

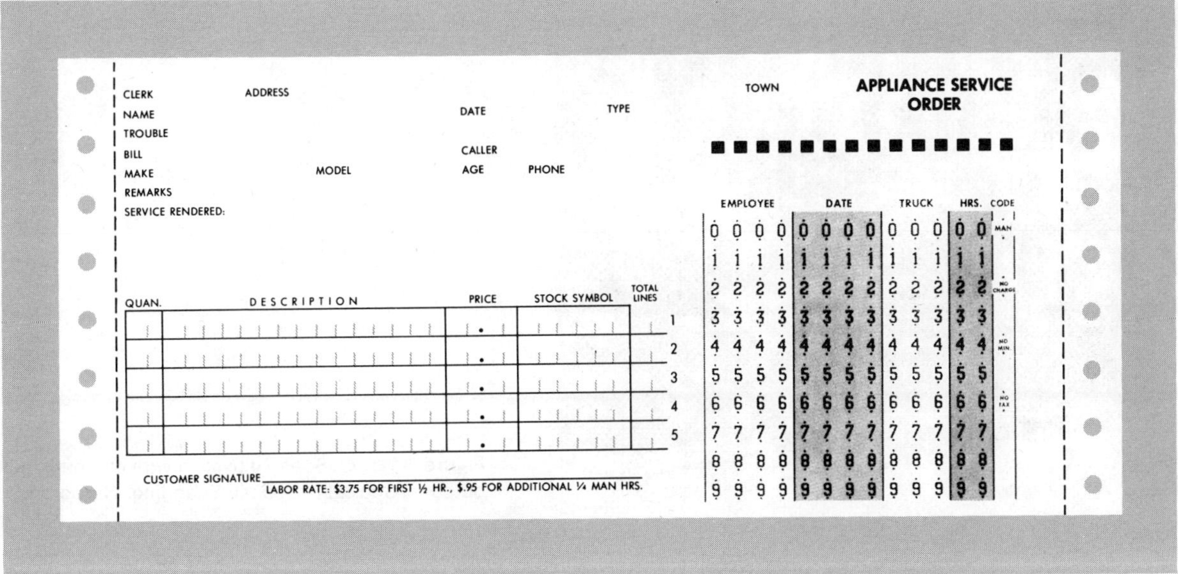

CLERK
ADDRESS
NAME
DATE
TYPE
TROUBLE
BILL
CALLER
MAKE
MODEL
AGE
PHONE
REMARKS
SERVICE RENDERED:

TOWN

APPLIANCE SERVICE ORDER

| QUAN. | DESCRIPTION | PRICE | STOCK SYMBOL | TOTAL LINES |
|---|---|---|---|---|
| | | . | | 1 |
| | | . | | 2 |
| | | . | | 3 |
| | | . | | 4 |
| | | . | | 5 |

CUSTOMER SIGNATURE
LABOR RATE: $3.75 FOR FIRST ½ HR., $.95 FOR ADDITIONAL ¼ MAN HRS.

| EMPLOYEE | | | | DATE | | | | TRUCK | | | HRS. | | CODE |
|---|---|---|---|---|---|---|---|---|---|---|---|---|---|
| 0 | 0 | 0 | 0 | 0 | 0 | 0 | 0 | 0 | 0 | 0 | 0 | 0 | MAN |
| 1 | 1 | 1 | 1 | 1 | 1 | 1 | 1 | 1 | 1 | 1 | 1 | 1 | |
| 2 | 2 | 2 | 2 | 2 | 2 | 2 | 2 | 2 | 2 | 2 | 2 | 2 | NO CHARGE |
| 3 | 3 | 3 | 3 | 3 | 3 | 3 | 3 | 3 | 3 | 3 | 3 | 3 | |
| 4 | 4 | 4 | 4 | 4 | 4 | 4 | 4 | 4 | 4 | 4 | 4 | 4 | NO MIN |
| 5 | 5 | 5 | 5 | 5 | 5 | 5 | 5 | 5 | 5 | 5 | 5 | 5 | |
| 6 | 6 | 6 | 6 | 6 | 6 | 6 | 6 | 6 | 6 | 6 | 6 | 6 | NO TAX |
| 7 | 7 | 7 | 7 | 7 | 7 | 7 | 7 | 7 | 7 | 7 | 7 | 7 | |
| 8 | 8 | 8 | 8 | 8 | 8 | 8 | 8 | 8 | 8 | 8 | 8 | 8 | |
| 9 | 9 | 9 | 9 | 9 | 9 | 9 | 9 | 9 | 9 | 9 | 9 | 9 | |

Figure 8-10 An appliance service order form—input for an optional mark reader.

preprinted positions for marks, and may be so printed on both sides. The sheets are read one side at a time and are read at a maximum constant rate of 2000 per hour or one every 1.8 seconds. Typical applications for the 1231 are payroll, order entry, accounts payable, inventory control, sales analysis, and general ledger work.

*In some optical mark readers, reading is accomplished by sensing differences of light via a revolving scanning disk.*

***Operation of Optical Mark Reader.*** In the OpScan 70 System (Figure 8-12), mark reading is accomplished by sensing differences in the reflectance of light by photocells mounted on a rotating scanning disk. As the light sweeps across the moving form, the photoelectric cell detects the drop in the reflected light caused by a pencil

Figure 8-11 IBM 1231 Optical Mark Page Reader. (Courtesy International Business Machines Corporation.)

Figure 8-12 OpScan 70 System with magnetic tape output. (Courtesy Optical Scanning Corporation.)

mark and sends a signal to the electric circuitry. The system's logic, then, interprets the mark as a number or letter, codes it into a computer language, and records it on magnetic tape at the rate of 2400 source documents per hour. If there are two or more marks in a given grid, the machine's logic will choose only the darkest mark.

*Perforated codes include:*
- *readable character code*
- *skeleton code*
- *in-line code*

*Nonperforated codes include:*
- *one code*
- *A-M bar code*
- *mark code*

***Perforated and Non-Perforated Codes.*** The Cummins 216-02 (Figure 8-13) Optical Mark Reader can read punched codes, printed codes, and embossed codes as well as pencil marks. Input codes recognized by the Scanak are three perforated codes (Figure 8-14) and three nonperforated codes (Figure 8-15). All of these codes are restricted to numeric data with a few special symbols available in the three perforated codes per Figure 8-14. The machine can read any four of these different codes during a single input pass. Primary areas in which this reader has been applied are accounting and production control plus special applications—bank drafts, credit receipt slips, time payment coupons, billing notices, and labor tickets.

### Optical Journal Tape Reader

Optical characters can be created by a number of devices that print or type with a specially stylized typeface. Adding machines, cash registers, and accounting

Figure 8-13 Cummins-Chicago Scanak 216-02 Optical Mark Reader reads six codes (any four on a single pass). (Courtesy Cummins-Chicago Corporation.)

| | FIGURES | SYMBOLS |
|---|---|---|
| Readable characters or Readable characters in reverse | | |
| Skeleton code of readable characters | | |
| In-line code | | |
| | 1 2 3 4 5 6 7 8 9 0 | ( * – ) sq. |

Figure 8-14 Perforated codes used on the Scanak 216-02. (Courtesy Cummins-Chicago Corporation.)

"ONE CODE" table of positional values.

| Digits | | 1 | 2 | 3 | 4 | 5 | 6 | 7 | 8 | 9 | 0 |
|---|---|---|---|---|---|---|---|---|---|---|---|
| V | 1 | 1 | | 1 | | 1 | | 1 | | 1 | |
| A | 2 | | 1 | 1 | | | 1 | 1 | | | 1 |
| L | 4 | | | | 1 | 1 | 1 | 1 | | | |
| U | 8 | | | | | | | | 1 | 1 | 1 |
| E | — | 1 | 1 | | 1 | | | 1 | 1 | | |

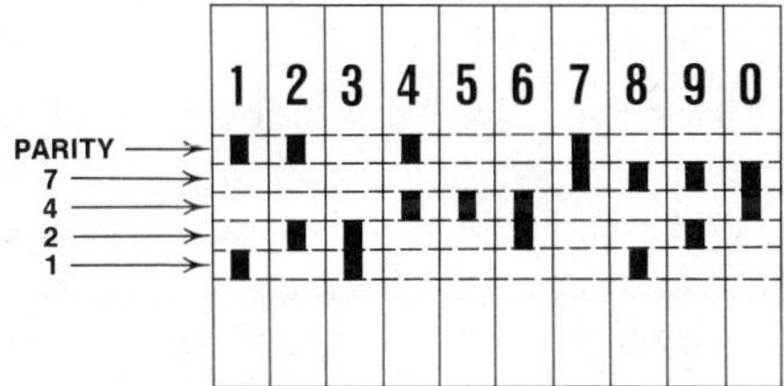


A-M BAR CODE table of positional values.

Mark code table for a ten digit number. Value indicated by marking through the desired numeral for each digit.

| | | | | | | | | | |
|---|---|---|---|---|---|---|---|---|---|
| .0. | .0. | .0. | .0. | .0. | .0. | .0. | .0. | .0. | .0. |
| .1. | .1. | .1. | .1. | .1. | .1. | .1. | .1. | .1. | .1. |
| .2. | .2. | .2. | .2. | .2. | .2. | .2. | .2. | .2. | .2. |
| .3. | .3. | .3. | .3. | .3. | .3. | .3. | .3. | .3. | .3. |
| .4. | .4. | .4. | .4. | .4. | .4. | .4. | .4. | .4. | .4. |
| .5. | .5. | .5. | .5. | .5. | .5. | .5. | .5. | .5. | .5. |
| .6. | .6. | .6. | .6. | .6. | .6. | .6. | .6. | .6. | .6. |
| .7. | .7. | .7. | .7. | .7. | .7. | .7. | .7. | .7. | .7. |
| .8. | .8. | .8. | .8. | .8. | .8. | .8. | .8. | .8. | .8. |
| .9. | .9. | .9. | .9. | .9. | .9. | .9. | .9. | .9. | .9. |

Figure 8-15 Nonperforated codes used on the Scanak 216-02. (Courtesy Cummins-Chicago Corporation)

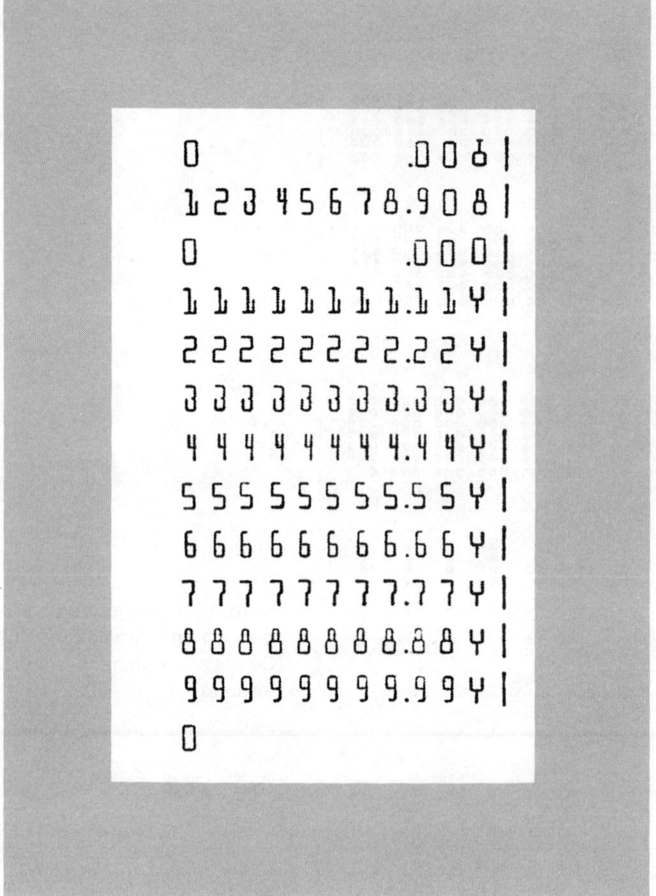

Figure 8-16 Cash register tape printed with optical numeric characters.

machines can be equipped with special type fonts to produce tapes that are readable by optical scanners. Figure 8-16 shows a cash register tape printed with optical numeric characters. Journal tape readers that read data in this illustration are marketed by several equipment manufacturers.

*Optical journal tape reader scans data created by a number of devices, such as adding machines and cash registers, and records data on a machine-processable medium.*

*Some optical journal tape readers utilize the binary system for recognizing data.*

Figure 8-17 shows an NCR 420-2 Optical Reader which is capable of reading data printed on rolls by adding machines, cash registers, and accounting machines. It has the ability to read journal tapes at the rate of 52 lines per second; it reads up to 32 characters per line. The 420-2 machine operates either on-line or off-line, creating punch paper tape or cards.

***Operation of Optical Journal Tape Reader.*** The 420-2 has a display panel for displaying the rejected line and indicating the rejected character or characters. The entire line is projected on the display panel $1\frac{1}{2}$ times the actual size. The rejected character is indicated by a light above the character. If more than one character in the line is unreadable, the rejected characters will be indicated sequentially until all have been entered manually. Corrections to the rejected characters are entered manually through a keyboard containing the ten numbers and the six special symbols (Figure 8-17).

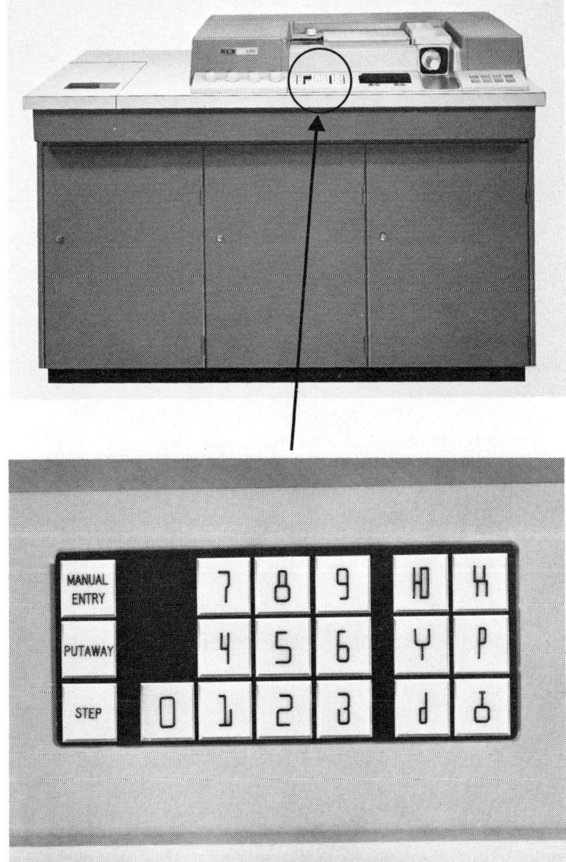


Figure 8-17 NCR 420-2 Optical Reader. (Courtesy The National Cash Register Company.)

The OCR device has a photoelectric reading system where the printed line is scanned through the apertures in the rotating drum. The printed line is projected by the light supply onto an opaque screen in the reading assembly. Electrical impulses are created when the photomultiplier tubes detect the darker vertical lines of a character instead of the lighter blank paper. To illustrate this process (mentioned briefly in a previous section), the reading of the numeric value 8 is depicted in Figure 8-18.

The character is divided into five vertical areas (Figure 8-18*a*). The OCR unit scans each character on two planes simultaneously (Figure 8-18*b*). It searches for a vertical line in each of the five zones on each plane since there are actually ten check points. The scanner does not read the whole character, only the vertical lines. The vertical lines which are read (Figure 8-18*c*) are decoded into a binary character by the OCR unit. The conversion for all numbers (0–11), Y, P, D, and spade symbol are made in this manner.

*Several optical journal readers are capable of reading different types of fonts on the same pass.*

***Multifont Optical Journal Tape Reader.*** A more versatile piece of equipment is the Farrington 4040 Optical Character Multifont Journal Tape Reader (Figure 8-19), recognizing Farrington, IBM, NCR, and ASA standard fonts. It utilizes flying spot scanning (topological approach) and has throughput speeds up to 6000 lines per minute. While magnetic tape is standard output, the unit can be interfaced directly with a computer. One of the machine's features is its ability to read

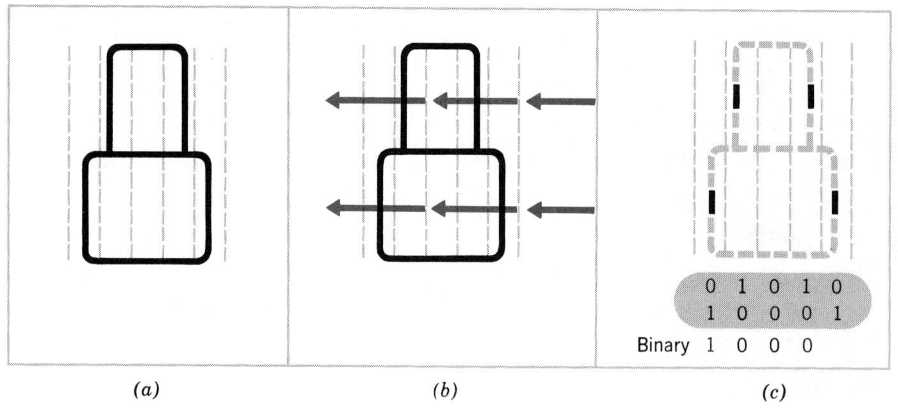


Figure 8-18 Reading process of the value 8 for an NCR 420-2 Optical Reader. (Courtesy The National Cash Register Company.)

tapes either forward or backward, making the rewinding of journal tapes unnecessary.

*Optical page readers have the capability of scanning entire pages of printed data and transcribing the information onto a machine-processable medium.*

**Optical Page Reader**

Optical character recognition goes beyond reading numeric values and is capable of reading alphabetic plus special characters. Shown previously in Figure 8-5*c* is the type style (USASCSOCR) which meets the specifications of the U.S.A. Standards Association. This OCR font is available on the IBM Selectric typewriter. Other typewriters can be obtained with optically readable type styles.

*The speed of the optical page reader is dependent upon the size of the forms read.*

**Reading Capabilities of Optical Page Readers**

Optical page readers are used widely to process typed or certain printed information. For example, the Farrington 3050 Optical Character Page Reader (Figure 8-20) reads documents up to $8\frac{1}{2}$ by 14 inches with either Farrington or USASCSOCR type fonts at speeds up to 400 characters per second. This machine is designed for applications that utilize input data in similar formats. The 3050 model is capable of displaying any questionable character on a screen, enabling the

Figure 8-19 Farrington 4040 Optical Character Multifor Journal Tape Reader. (Courtesy Farrington Manufacturin Company.)

Figure 8-20 Farrington 3050 Optical Character Page Reader. (Courtesy Farrington Manufacturing Company.)

operator to make the correction quickly and, thereby, maintaining file integrity. A built-in magnetic tape drive is included for output.

The IBM 1288 Optical Page Reader (Figure 8-21) reads data from cut-form documents that range in size from 3 by 6.5 inches to 9 by 14 inches. Because the 1288 can read mixed data from documents smaller than punched cards and as large as legal size forms, it can be used in a variety of applications. The OCR unit reads typewritten USASCSOCR font, alphanumeric data, optical marks, and pre-printed $\frac{3}{16}$'' Gothic font. Likewise, it reads hand-printed numbers 0 through 9, and five special hand-printed alphabetic characters—C, S, T, X, and Z. This OCR device also accepts printed numeric data from documents prepared on IBM high speed printers. Data can be read vertically and horizontally in a formatted mode. In one pass, the 1288 can read up to a full page of information directly to an IBM System/360 or System /370. Smaller forms, such as utility bills, can be read at a rate of 19,600 per hour. The 1288, then, forms a complete on-line data processing system which simplifies and speeds document handling.

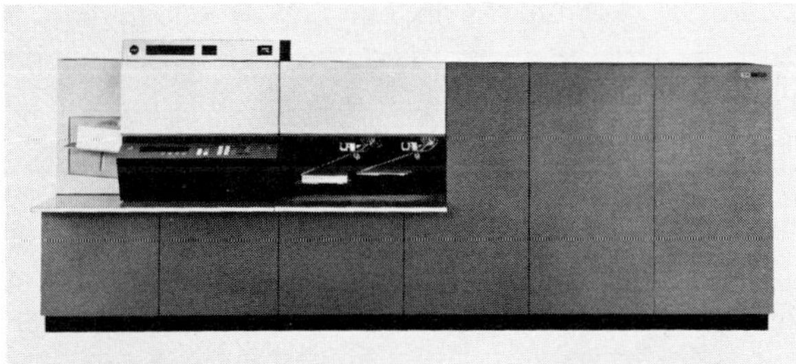

Figure 8-21 IBM 1288 Optical Page Reader. (Courtesy International Business Machines Corporation.)

Optical page readers are capable of reading mixed sized forms and different type fonts during a single pass.

***Multifont Optical Page Reader.*** Optical page readers are capable of handling multiple fonts and forms. Control Data's Multi-Font Page Reader (Figure 8-22) processes 14,000 characters per second of input submitted on mixed forms and recorded in mixed fonts. Scanning and recording on magnetic tape from an $8\frac{1}{2}$ by 11 inch form (single-spaced typewritten) occurs in two-thirds of a second. Five conventional fonts are read by the system: two typewriter fonts (IBM Prestige and Royal Elite), one card interpreter font (IBM 557), one adding machine font (Monroe 400), and a high speed printer font (IBM 1403). Likewise, the machine has a mark sense reading capability and can read text in standard magnetic ink font MICR E-13B. In addition, documents and continuous forms can vary from a 3- by 4-inch card to a 12- by 14-inch form with a copy width of 10 inches.

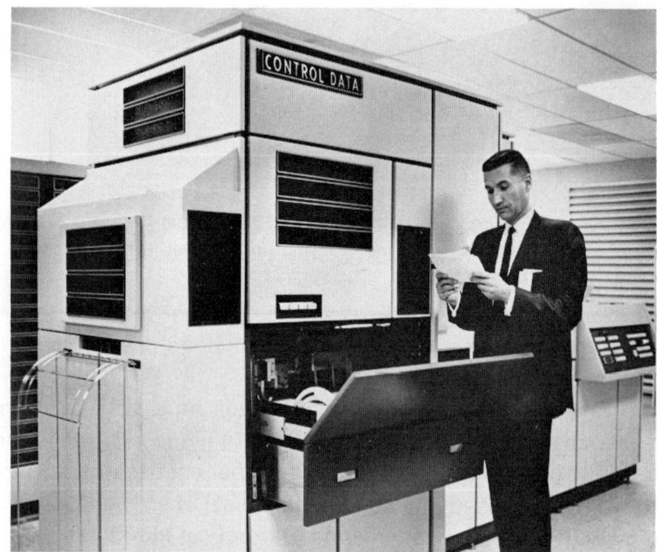


Figure 8-22 CDC Multi-Font Page Reader. (Courtesy Control Data Corporation.)

**Optical Character Reader**

Optical character reader has the ability to read handwritten characters as well as printed data and convert them to a machine-processable form.

Hand-written characters can be processed in a manner similar to marked cards, journal tapes, and printed pages. Several manufacturers are producing equipment to meet this need. While many of the high-priced alphanumeric multifont readers are capable of reading hand-printed characters, the most popular hand-printed character reader is the IBM 1287 Optical Reader (Figure 8-29—similar in appearance to the IBM 1288 in Figure 8-21). It should be noted that the 1288 can read the same typewritten and handwritten characters as the 1287.

***Operation of Optical Character Reader.*** As in other OCR equipment, the reading station (Figure 8-23) is the most important feature for the 1287, a curve tracing reader. The read station is a light-tight chamber in which the document or tape is stopped and registered. When the document is correctly registered, a cathode ray tube scans the document with a light beam. The document reflects the light into light sensors that carry the scanned image to the 1287's character recognition circuitry. If the trace formed by the character fits into the normal tolerance pattern for a particular character, then the machine will identify it correctly. This technique permits a rather wide variation in hand-printed numerals.

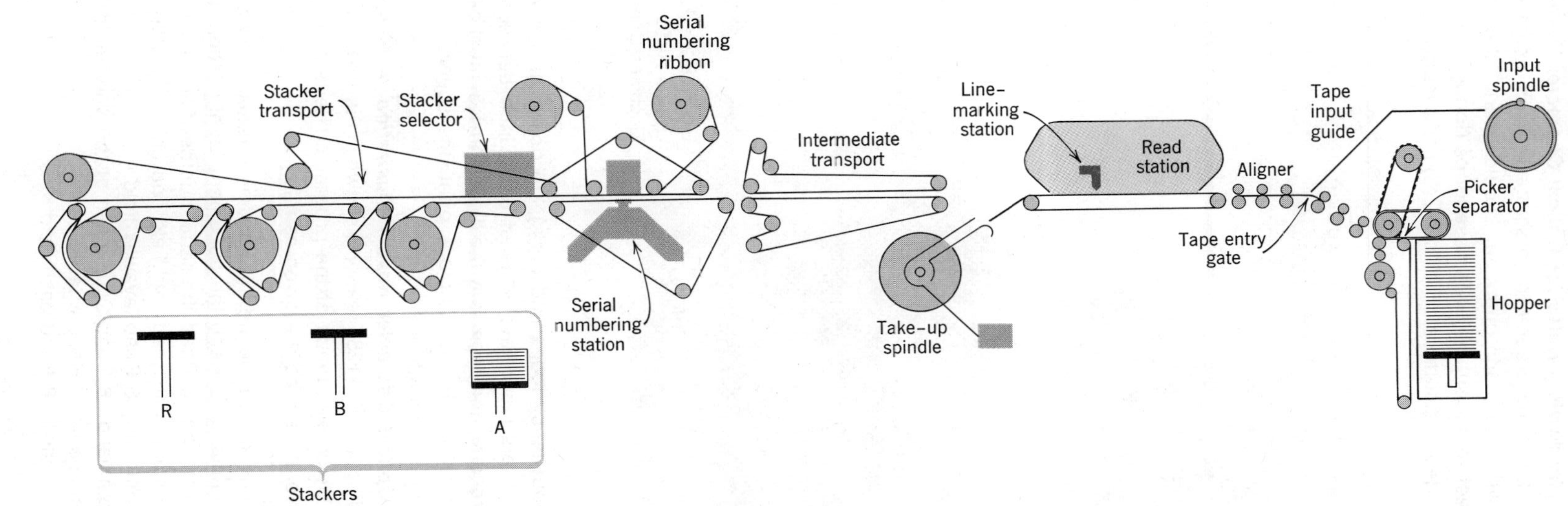


Figure 8-23 IBM 1287 document path (includes serial numbering feature). (Courtesy International Business Machines Corporation.)

*Special handwriting rules must be followed for acceptability and accuracy of input data.*

***Handwriting Rules for Optical Character Readers.*** Handwritten input data for the 1287 should conform to six basic rules, as depicted in Figure 8-24. They are: (1) write big (each character should nearly fill its box without extending into the reflective ink outline), (2) close loops (loops in digits 0, 6, 8, and 9 must be well-rounded and completely closed), (3) use simple shapes (characters must be formed

| RULE | CORRECT | INCORRECT |
|---|---|---|
| 1. Write big. | 02834 | 02834 |
| 2. Close loops. | 06889 | 06889 |
| 3. Use simple shapes. | 02375 | 02375 |
| 4. Do not link charac-ters. | 00881 | 00887 |
| 5. Connect lines. | 45T | 45T |
| 6. Block print. | CSTXZ | CSTXZ |

Figure 8-24 Handwriting rules for the IBM 1287 Optical Reader. (Courtesy International Business Machines Corporation.)

without fancy loops and curls), (4) do not link characters (horizontally adjacent characters must have at least 0.020 inch between them), (5) connect lines (all characters, and especially the digits 4 and 5, must be carefully written to avoid gaps between lines), and (6) block print (the special symbols, C, S, T, X, and Z must be carefully block-printed).

***Optical Character Reader Illustration.*** A sample sales check document for reading with the 1287 reader is shown in Figure 8-25. The numbered items represent the logical sequence of the program. The commands performed for each of the twelve items read are given as follows:

Command 1 Define the document registration mark.
Command 2 Read the document identification field.
Command 3 Read the serial-number field.
Command 4 Read void field and check for data.
Command 5 Read layaway field.
Command 6 Read COD (cash on delivery) field.
Command 7 Read charge field.
Command 8 Read cash field.

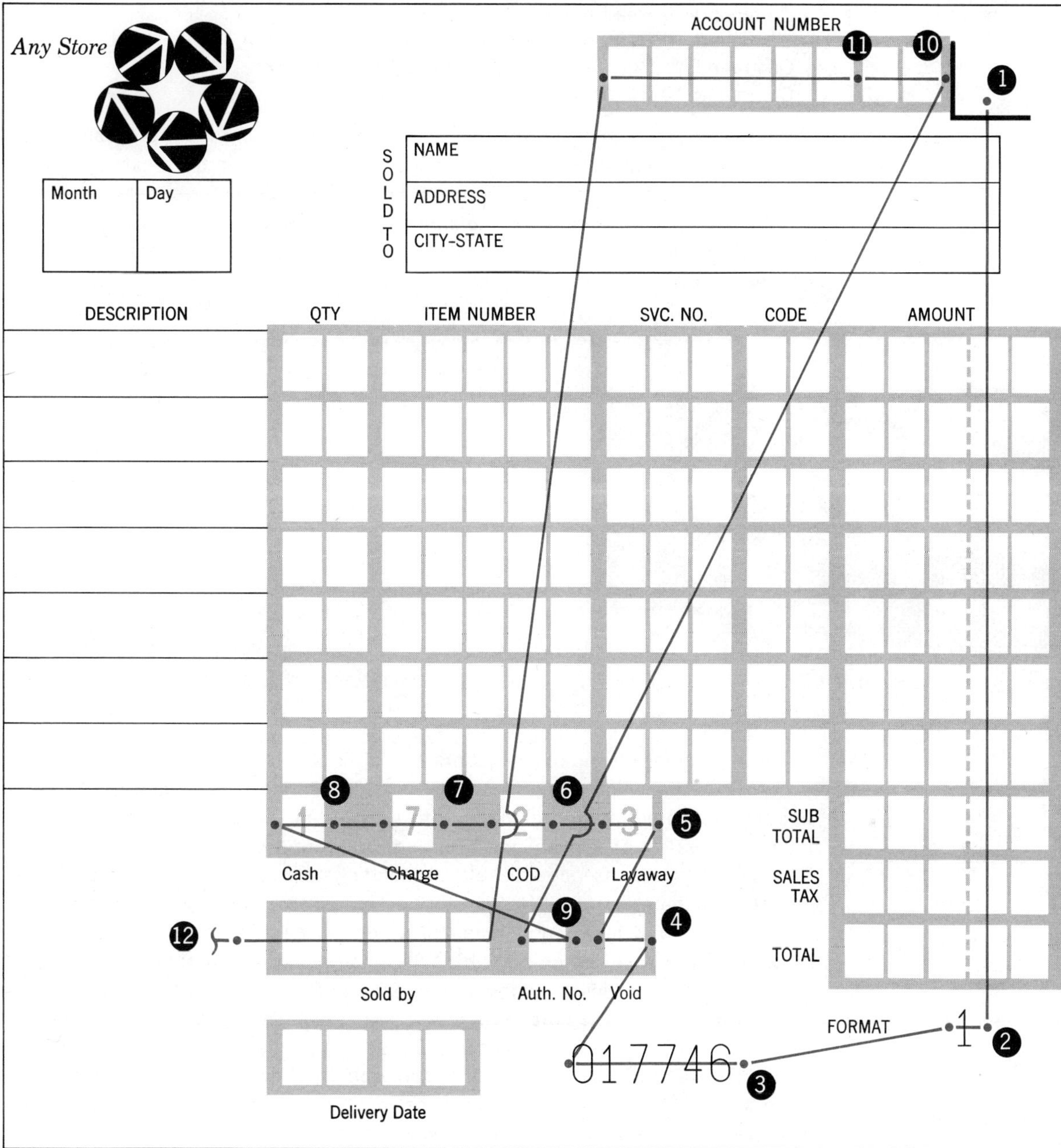


Note: Not to scale.

Figure 8-25 Sample sales-check document showing reading sequence of sample program for the IBM 1287 Optical Reader. (Courtesy International Business Machines Corporation.)

Command 9 Read authorization number.
Command 10 Read right-most two positions of account number field.
Command 11 Read handprinted account number field.
Command 12 Read sold by field.

Once the first document is read, control is returned to the main program. If the document is rejected, the same procedure is initiated for the next document. Otherwise, reading starts at command 2 for the second and subsequent documents.

***Optical Character Reader Equipment.*** Another optical character reader, the OpScan 288, processes source documents—paper stock or tab card—at the single-line rate of 600 forms a minute. The OpScan 288 (Figure 8-26) recognizes numbers from 0 to 9, plus these letters and signs: C, N, S, T, X, Z, — (minus), and + (plus). As it transfers characters directly to magnetic tape, it can alternate as needed from hand-printed characters to typewritten characters. This machine is ideal for a variety of applications involving turnaround documents, such as utility bills, charge sales, passenger tickets, dividend checks, and time payment coupons.

Figure 8-26 OpScan 288 Optical Character Reader. (Courtesy Optical Scanning Corporation.)

*The speed of OCR equipment and the types of characters that can be read are basically dependent upon the detection circuitry employed.*

When comparing the IBM 1287 to the OpScan 288, the 288 imposes a great deal of constraint in writing numerals. Detection circuitry need only determine whether or not a stroke or portion of the number passes through a given area. Because of this simplified recognition technique, the 288 is relatively inexpensive.

*Advanced optical character readers scan many types of fonts for recording onto a machine-processable medium.*

***Multifont Optical Character Reader.*** One of the more sophisticated systems for reading ordinary type face and hand-printed information is the Input-80 Optical Character Recognition System, manufactured by Recognition Equipment, Inc. (Figure 8-27). The machine basic type face vocabulary includes the upper and lower case alphabet, 0 through 9, and four standard business symbols. Its handprinted

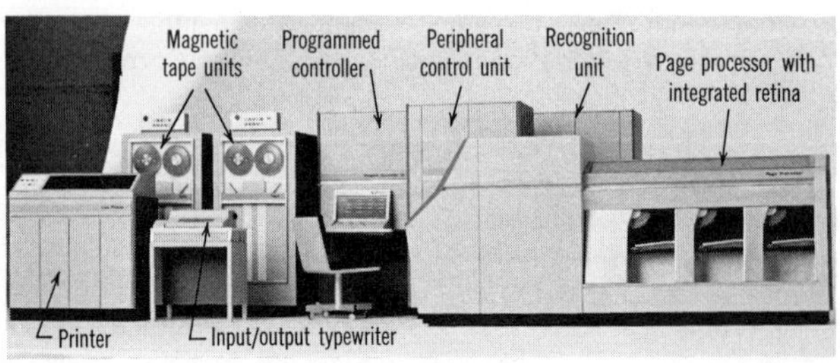


Figure 8-27 Input-80 Optical Character Recognition System. (Courtesy Recognition Equipment, Inc.)

character vocabulary recognizes numerals 0 through 9; the letters C, S, T, X, and Z; and plus and minus signs. With these characters, users can print as always because the machine defines characters by features, such as curved lines, sharp curves, and line intersections.

The basic system consists of a page processor to transport and scan the documents, a recognition unit to interpret the data, magnetic tape units to record the coded data, an input/output typewriter, a peripheral control unit, and a line printer. It is capable of reading many different fonts and can code characters at rates up to 3600 characters per second. The Input-80 system processes full typewritten pages at a rate of 38 per minute or it can process smaller pages up to 300 per minute. Page sizes can range from approximately 4-by-6 inches to 9-by-14 inches. Degraded documents (torn, folded, or smudged), carbon backed pages, and pasted labels can also be read. The system can be obtained with single font capability (any one of 14 common type styles) or with multiple-font capabilities where users can select up to 360 character patterns from virtually any type styles including hand-printed numbers and symbols.

A unique feature of this firm's OCR system is its integrated Retina, which works like the human eye. As a complete character is projected on the retina surface, a vertical analyzer catches misalignment up to one full character high. Another device distinguishes weak strokes, smudges, and other character imperfections and is able to adjust electronically characters of differing sizes to the correct reading size. It can also look ahead to the next lines to be read, identify any misaligned characters or lines, and read them as though they were perfectly placed.

*Some OCR equipment have the capability of operating in an on-line mode, comparable to a high-speed card reader.*

**OCR Computer Systems**

Most OCR equipment can be linked on-line with a computer system. When operating in an on-line mode, the OCR device acts like a high-speed card reader. The essential difference is their reading rate.

***On-Line OCR Equipment.*** An on-line OCR system is illustrated in Figure 8-28. A Control Data 915 Page Reader (schematic of reader was originally shown in Figure 8-6) is shown with one of its 3000 series computers. The 915 scans and reads

Figure 8-28 CDC 915 Page Reader in use with a 3000 series computer. (Courtesy Control Data Corporation.)

*Input data of on-line OCR equipment have the capability of being tested before their acceptance for computer processing.*

typewritten or preprinted data. Since the page reader operates in conjunction with a computer under programmed control, the data are directed by the program to any computer-driven recording device, such as a magnetic tape unit, a high-speed printer, or a card punch. Through a digital communications unit, the 915 can also be linked with other computers and peripheral devices at remote locations.

The 915 Page Reader's utility is enhanced by its programmable features. Programming limitations are dependent only upon computer memory size and the imagination of the programmer. The scanner sorts documents in programmed sequences, recognizes discrete symbols on a document for selective reading, and senses special markings (filled and unfilled circles) on a document. Under program control, it will mark documents with a marking pen at the reading station. The 915 can also process and read documents at very high speeds. Time is not wasted in scanning blanks, blank lines, or unwanted data. Processing can proceed at maximum speed since the page reader's output is buffered by the computer as it is fed to recording devices. Thus, the 915's capabilities can be fully utilized in simple or complex programs when part of an on-line computer system.

Another on-line OCR computer system is illustrated in Figure 8-29. The IBM 1287 Optical Reader is attached to a System/360 channel for direct reading of

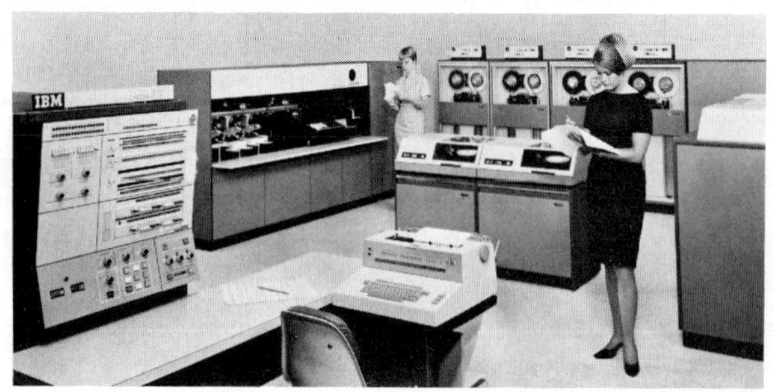


Figure 8-29 IBM 1287 Optical Reader Model 2, on-line with a System/360 computer. (Courtesy International Business Machines Corporation.)

source documents and is under program control. For a conservative approach to this on-line system, all fields of the document are read completely before the data are processed (validated against check digits and hash totals), and all processing completed before the document is dispatched to the appropriate stacker. Carrying out these functions in serial fashion precludes the opportunity to increase throughput by overlapping. Nevertheless, this slow programming method still allows reading about 60 to 120 documents a minute, a rate that includes the manual reading and on-line keyboard correction of rejected characters. Also, this time-independent approach simplifies the programming job and makes it easier to add new documents and formats to the system.

*Errors found during computer processing can be corrected later by utilizing an on-line CRT unit. Incorrect data can be displayed for making the appropriate correction to the on-line storage medium (disk).*

***On-Line OCR Computer System Illustration.*** A typical route accounting system that utilizes a conservative approach to an on-line OCR processing system operates as follows. Documents, entered into the 1287, are sorted into three different categories (stackers): those which are error free; those which contain characters that cannot be read; and those which have been read, processed, and found to contain an error. The data from error-free documents are written on the error-free disk. Unreadable characters are displayed by the 1287 for the operator who makes a judgment and enters the illegible characters through the scanner keyboard. The data from documents that have been read, processed, and found to contain an error are written, along with a description of the error, on the second disk for display terminal manual editing. These procedures are illustrated in Figure 8-30.

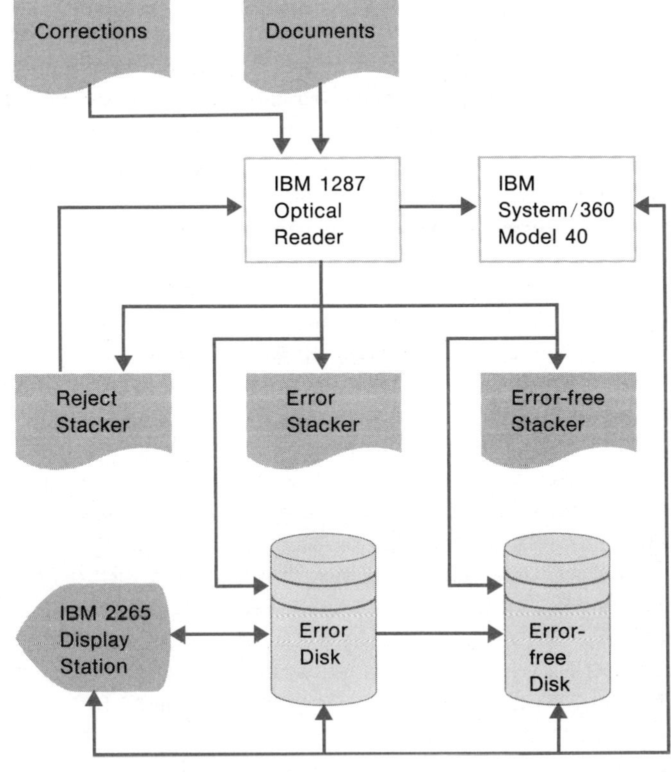


Figure 8-30 Typical on-line OCR processing system—further processing will be from the error-free disk.

Working from the original source documents and a display of the data and error, a clerk is able to handle over 100 documents per hour. Since most of error documents contain hash totals for which the computer has already generated a new total, most of the editing time is spent retotaling on an adding machine to insure that the scanner did not misread a character. The clerk keys in the total from the terminal and requests the data to be saved for reprocessing (which is done in batches). The data records for documents that pass the second processing cycle are deleted from the error disk and written on the error-free disk. Any documents that still contain an error are recycled through the edit/processing procedure for the second time. This happens infrequently. When it does, the error is always corrected on the second cycle.

Documents which contain units only cannot be handled by the clerks since they have no way of knowing what their product codes are. Consequently, these documents are returned to the appropriate department for correction. When returned, the data are processed on the 1287 Optical Reader. The data record goes through the same correction procedure explained previously.

**Cost Aspects of OCR**

Practically all OCR equipment on the market is relatively expensive. Most page readers are in the $160,000 to $400,000 bracket, with monthly rentals ranging from

*Cost per unit of data processed can be lower with OCR equipment than other input machines.*

$2500 to $6000. The most expensive page reader sells for over $1 million and leases for about $23,000 per month. Document readers are lower, priced generally from $100,000 to $220,000, and rent for $2000 to $6000 a month. Even journal tape readers carry price tags from $84,000 to $120,000, renting from $2000 to $3200 per month. For lower priced equipment, the purchase price of optical mark readers range from $7000 to $50,000.

***Utilization Factor.*** When data conversion capability of these systems is considered, the cost picture changes. Most of these readers are so fast that they can match the productivity of over a hundred key punches and verifiers when used to capacity. In other words, if there is a sufficient input volume, OCR machines can do the job much faster and at a much lower cost than keypunching or, for that matter, any other available means of data entry. Extensive employment, then, of OCR equipment can lead to a substantial reduction in overall input data processing costs.

***Breakeven Point.*** Several manufacturers have conducted breakeven studies on OCR machines.[1] Honeywell, for example, has conducted a study comparing a typical punched card system with an OCR system in a billing application. Based on average rentals for typical document readers, the firm found that the breakeven point for a $3000 per month OCR reader is about 17,000 bills a day. Another manufacturing firm, Control Data, lists the total systems cost for an 80-unit keypunch installation, including hardware rentals, tab card cost, and labor cost, as $14,950 per month versus $10,775 per month for a leased CDC 915 page reader plus 14 typewriters, 14 typists, and 5 proofreaders. IBM places the breakeven point for its 1288 page reader at 8 to 10 keypunches while Scan-Data says the workload for 10 to 12 keypunches would justify the use of its Model 200 page reader.

***Outside OCR Processing.*** For those companies that do not have sufficient input volume to justify the exclusive use of an OCR reader, a number of data processing service centers are offering OCR reading service. They include some of the well-established data centers, such as McDonnell Automation Company, Statistical Tabulating Corporation, and various localized service bureaus. Some of the data centers are subsidiaries of computer manufacturing firms or OCR hardware manufacturers.

Although optical character recognition allows some firms to achieve significant cost savings in data entry, it is valuable to others because of the efficiency it can add to a system. The high speed with which an OCR reader can read the documents often allows a company to achieve data processing efficiency unmatched by any other means. Several large- and medium-sized firms have been able to initiate faster service to customers. Although this intangible benefit cannot always be measured in dollars, it certainly helps to maintain customer goodwill.

*OCR equipment has gained a strong foothold in:*

- *utilities*
- *mail order houses*
- *insurance firms*
- *airlines*
- *oils*
- *banks*
- *credit cards*
- *foods*
- *graphic arts*
- *department stores*
- *government*
- *armed forces*
- *education*

### OCR Applications

The optical character recognition industry is growing currently at a much faster rate than the computer industry. The number of areas where the equipment can be applied will undoubtedly increase. Many of the present punched card installations are or will be replaced by OCR equipment. Basically, OCR will appeal to large volume users while punched cards will be utilized, for the most part, in all other installations where volumes are not sufficiently large to warrant optical readers. Thus, each will function within its range of capabilities.

[1] Albert L. C. Chu, "The Plodding Progress of OCR," *Business Automation,* March 1970, p. 51

***Utilities.*** Many utility companies have eliminated keypunching and key verifying by utilizing optical mark readers to handle their large volumes of data. Meter reading forms for customers are prepared on the computer from master customer meter magnetic tapes at the central data processing center. They are distributed to the meter readers who make the actual readings. Information that has been hand-printed by the meter readers is read by OCR equipment and written directly onto magnetic tape off-line. The tape becomes input for the monthly or periodic billing of customers.

The other major source of input is the statement stubs returned with payment by the firm's customers. Information concerning full or partial payments is hand-printed by clerical workers and processed on an optical mark reader. The data on payments is recorded on magnetic tape as input for billing. Not only is key punching eliminated for all input data in customer billing, but also it is eliminated for processing service work orders, customer service invoices, daily time cards, cashier stubs, and other computer input data. For the most part, OCR equipment serves to eliminate key punching within an utility firm.

***Mail Order Houses.*** Another industry that is benefiting from OCR devices, particularly in the accounting area, is the large mail order house. As remittances come in from a million or more customers throughout the year, the amount paid is verified and manually marked on the remittance slip before the check or money order is separated and batch totaled. The remittance amounts are then encoded on the line that identifies the customer, listed, and batch totaled. The OCR reader then scans them at very high speeds, recording the data on magnetic tape and printing out an audit trail listing and a batch total report for balancing to control totals. The OCR reader allows the mail order firm to update its customer accounts and to recheck its batch balances so efficiently that 95 percent of the payments received are posted the same day. Besides the payment system, the reader also helps maintain a sales solicitation file that contains millions of names and addresses, performs check reconciliations, and updates another solicitation file on a service basis. Even with these high volume applications, some firms report that the capacity of their OCR equipment is still not being utilized.

***Insurance Industry.*** The insurance industry is a logical candidate for advanced scanning equipment. The IBM 1287 document reader is being used quite widely to update master files of insurance policies in force. For this application, a tab card size "universal" form is used. When filled with column heads, it becomes many different forms for a variety of transactions from premium payments through changes in beneficiaries. The 1287 reads hand-printed numbers on these forms and transmits the information to a card punch. The application reduces many hours of key punching into a short daily run on the 1287.

***Airline Industry.*** The airline industry is making great use of optical character readers to process millions of airline tickets during the month. The OCR system reads pre-printed ticket numbers and imprinted route codes from audited coupons of original tickets at the home office. It records the data directly onto magnetic tape. The data, in turn, are used to update the unearned revenue on the computer. When the airline tickets are actually used, the system processes passenger coupons sent in for each leg of the trip on an optical character reader which are written automatically onto magnetic tape. This input tape plus the unearned revenue input tape are computer processed to determine the amount transferable from unearned to earned revenue. In this procedure, the airline knows exactly how much money it is earning currently. This is in contrast with the prior procedure where approximately 5 to 10% of all airline tickets were sampled to determine earned revenue. Most airlines have found a dozen other jobs for their optical equipment, such as sorting bank drafts and checks.

***Industries Using Credit Cards.*** OCR equipment for credit card processing by the *oil companies, banks,* and *credit card firms* is needed to process the large volume of charge tickets for customer billing. An oil company, for example, receives batches of charge tickets and dealer summaries from service stations and bulk plants daily. These data are read via the optical character reader, bar-coded, and written onto magnetic tape. Each account number is verified using the self-checking digit during this process just as other audit functions are performed. A magnetic tape for all properly read invoices is produced and edited before being fed into the computer for updating the accounts receivable file. A similar procedure is used for creating a magnetic tape on payments received. On the billing date (cycle billing basis), statements are bar-coded when produced (using an OCR credit card data processing system) and sorted with the charge tickets (bar-coded) before mailing to the customer. This OCR system, then, eliminates the need for extensive key punching.

***Food Industry.*** Many food chains are utilizing OCR readers to control inventory. Store personnel take inventory by marking simplified inventory forms with a regular pencil. Forms are optically scanned by the mark reader at a central location and the data are converted to magnetic tape. Computer analysis of this input data provides a printout of stock replenishment for the firm's warehouses. In this manner, the warehouses that supply merchandise to the firm's stores are replenished as soon as possible.

***Graphic Arts Industry.*** OCR is currently making headway in the graphic arts industry. Major printing companies are beginning to use OCR, such as the Scan-Data 100 which can be equipped to read a number of type fonts, including the conventional Gothic type font, in five sizes and in various pitches plus bold face, at the speed of 800 characters per second. This system can be used in conjunction with such typesetting and composition systems as the RCA Videocomp to automate completely the typesetting process from manuscript to positive or negative film. It has been demonstrated that a book normally taking seven days to typeset can be done in five hours. The link-up can also be used to read any common telephone directory and to extract and reset any information from it.

***Other Industries.*** By no means is OCR equipment limited to the foregoing areas. *Department stores, telephone companies, breweries, savings and loan associations, service bureaus,* to name a few, are making great use of optical character and mark readers. The *federal government,* too, is utilizing an optical page reader to read the names, social security numbers, and quarterly earnings of wage earners in the United States. The Model 1975, built by IBM for the Social Security Administration, is reading data on about half of the 70 million wage earners in the country. It reads upper and lower case characters in type fonts used by most business machines, including manual typewriters. The *postal system* is employing optical scanners to read mail and sort them by ZIP codes. In addition to industrial and governmental applications of optical character recognition machines, the *armed forces* and *educational institutions* are running optical readers alongside key punch machines to process even larger volumes of data.

The secret of reaping tangible economic benefits from OCR equipment in any application is having sufficient volume to keep the equipment busy at least half of the time and not having to retype the input source document. Concerning this last

*OCR equipment is usually economically justified if the equipment is utilized at least 50% of the available time.*

point, optical character recognition is the answer for turnaround documents, that is, output produced by the data processing system becomes input for the system at a later date. Telephone, utility, oil, credit card, insurance, and merchandising companies are prime examples. Another way to benefit economically from OCR is with specialized forms which eliminate unnecessary steps, save time, and enable the user to take advantage of character or mark readers.

**Future Direction of OCR**

*Future direction of OCR equipment encompasses:*
- *improved on-line processing*
- *remote processing*
- *newer technology*
- *general script reading*

Over the years, there have been two major reasons for the slow growth of optical character recognition equipment. First, OCR has been limited to reading simple, marked pre-printed forms or highly stylized fonts. However, flexibility of input fonts has increased and will continue to do so in the future. Second, OCR was originally developed as a data input device and not as a data entry system. The pioneers in using OCR equipment performed some monumental reprogramming. In recent years, manufacturers of the equipment have added a processing controller or computer so that the newer units are complete data entry subsystems of a larger computer system. Thus, optical character recognition technology has finally matured to the point where optical character recognition can be utilized for many input applications where a firm has reasonable control over the preparation of the input document. Newer technology will not only improve user acceptance but also will result in cost reduction of readers.

***Improved On-Line OCR Processing.*** Several future trends in the optical character recognition industry are emerging. One is the greater use of scanning units to process data in an on-line mode. Compact and relatively low-cost readers recognize information from source documents and transmit the data electronically to the computer. This approach surpasses the slow speed and inefficiency of key punch machines and keyboard to magnetic tape devices. The OCR on-line devices can be operated by semi-skilled clerical personnel. Documents are placed on an automatic feeder, control buttons are set, and the documents are later retrieved from conveniently located output pockets. Documents containing unreadable characters are automatically line-marked and rejected—allowing for immediate correction and reentry.

***Remote OCR Processing.*** With the foregoing advances in OCR on-line processing, the expansion of optical scanning systems via remote terminals is now and will continue to experience phenominal growth, due in part to the growth of computer utilities. In such a system, a central processing unit and a recognition unit are linked to a number of remote scanners via telephone lines. Each OCR device is a facsimile unit which scans input data, converts it into code, and transmits it to the central processing system. After character identification, the signals are transmitted either back to the originating point or to any other desired location for recording on magnetic tape or comparable storage medium.

***Newer OCR Technology.*** Perhaps, the brightest hope for the future of optical character recognition equipment lies in direct optical image processing which utilizes laser and holographic techniques. With direct optical image processing, it is possible to restore degraded images, thereby improving the signal-to-noise ratio present in the recognition circuitry. In other words, future equipment will have the ability to recognize certain types of patterns more easily.

***General Script Reading.*** The future of reading general purpose script, however, does not look as promising. The human being can read script only because he has knowledge about the English language. In essence, the individual guesses the identity of written words from minute clues. Until machines are developed which can store substantial information about the language and concepts described by language, true optical script readers will not be possible.

## SUMMARY

Many punched card installations, small scale computer systems, and input/output terminals are being replaced by optical character recognition equipment. The reason is that lower input processing costs for large volumes of data are available with turnaround documents. This keeps input preparation to a minimum with OCR equipment. Another important benefit of OCR is the broadening of the employment market. The firm can look to clerical typists and not just trained key punchers to prepare inputs for its data processing system. Optical reading equipment is a must in many industries to reduce cost and time factors for input documents. It makes no sense to acquire faster computer systems if computer input preparation is too time consuming.

Applications of OCR equipment will be increased undoubtedly as time passes. More industries that utilize considerable volumes of turnaround documents will recognize the potential of optical character recognition equipment. Also, lower equipment costs in the future will add to the growing number of firms switching to this newer method of input processing. It is no wonder that the rate of growth for OCR machines is approximately twice the entire computer market.

## *QUESTIONS*

1. Why are punched card records less desirable for banking applications than MICR documents?
2. How do mark sensing machines differ from optical mark readers?
3. (a) Distinguish among the various types of OCR equipment. Explain the function of each. (b) Which type is faster and why?
4. What are the basic optical font types? Explain each basic type.
5. What are the basic data recognition methods? Explain each method.
6. Differentiate between character and script recognition.
7. How can the utility or oil company utilize OCR equipment? Explain thoroughly.
8. List additional applications for optical character recognition equipment—either as off-line or on-line equipment.
9. In what direction is input data processing for a computer headed? Support your point of view.
10. One person in the computer industry made the following comment. "The firm(s) who controls data input entry will control the data processing industry." Explain what he meant by this statement.

CHAPTER NINE

# Data Communications and Time Sharing

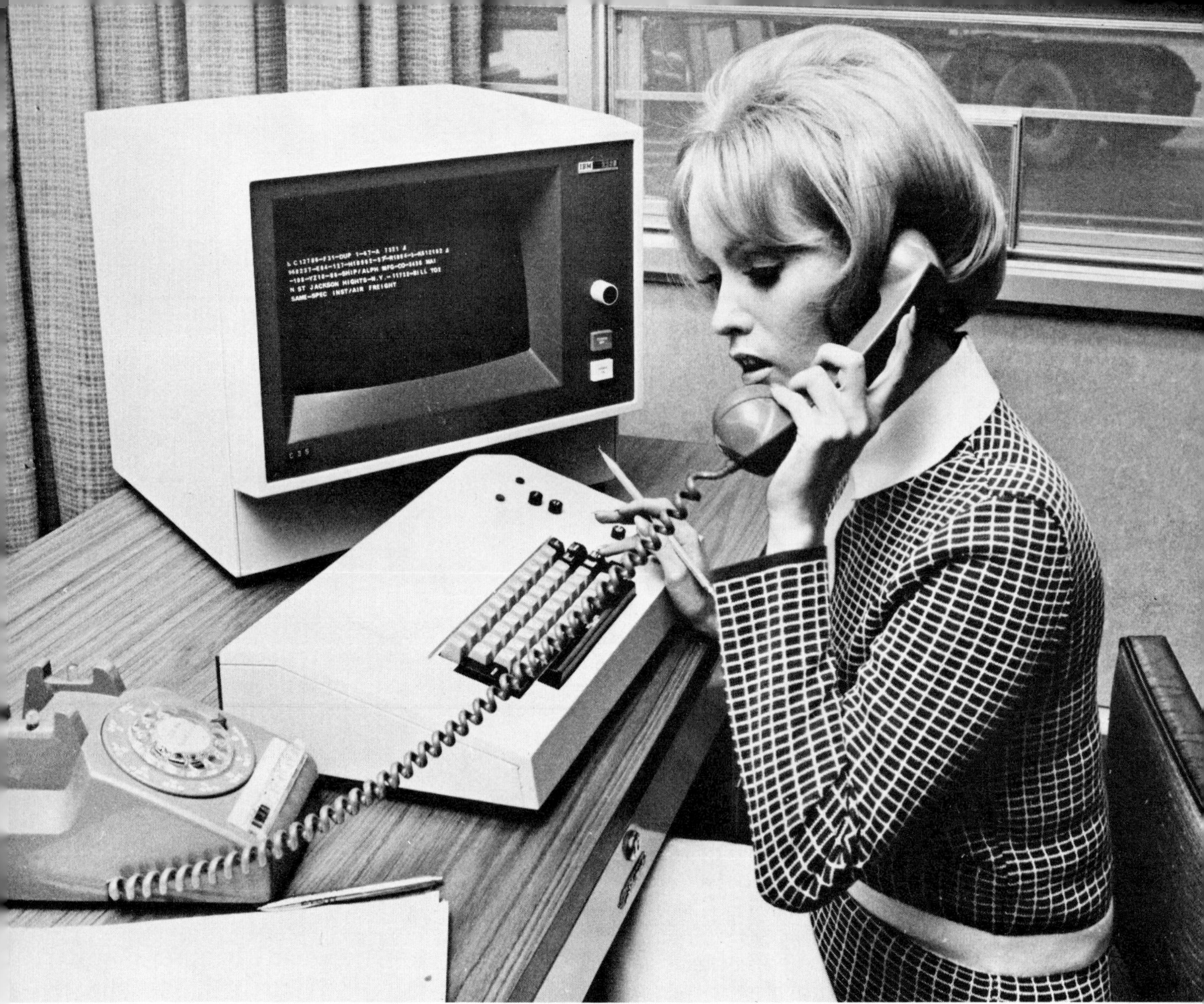


*The tremendous growth of data communications and time sharing centers around the need for timely information. A user can lease remote terminals that can be connected by telephone lines to a computer many miles away. (Courtesy International Business Machines Corporation.)*

In the past, electrical communications, such as the telephone and telegraph, have been utilized to transmit data for business purposes. Today, it has assumed a new role—one of linking men and machines in order that timely data can be received and sent as a by-product of a computer data processing system. The growth of data communications is reflected by the number of data sets in the A. T. & T. system, the number currently being about 100,000. The merging of high speed electrical communications and EDP has resulted in a data communication system which enables the firm to operate as if it is under one roof when, in reality, it is not. The area of data communications and material on computer time sharing will be explored in this chapter.

Basically, time sharing refers to a computer that is shared by users through a number of remote input/output terminals. Although some of the time-sharing terminals may be close enough to use direct cable connections, most terminals will not be joined in this manner. This means that a typical time-sharing system will rely heavily upon a data communication system for linking its terminals to a computer.

## DATA COMMUNICATIONS

Data communications, sometimes called telecommunications or teleprocessing, is an integral part of data processing activities. Without data communication capabilities, advancements, such as time sharing and real-time processing, would not have been possible. Its importance will be evident in the following sections.

### Importance of Data Communications

*The timeliness of information is an important factor when evaluating the kinds of data communications. Data communication equipment is capable of:*

- *linking data processing operations together*
- *making on-line inquiry processing possible*
- *facilitating data processing load balancing*

The real importance of data communications lies in the time factor. Instead of waiting long periods for other means of communications, such as air mail and special delivery, data can be communicated by electrical transmission in a matter of seconds or minutes. (The major common carriers providing interstate communication services are the American Telephone and Telegraph Company, Western Union Telegraph Company, and the independent telephone companies—General Telephone and Electronics Corporation being the largest.) This time reduction can mean more effective planning, organizing, directing, and controlling of the firm's activities. The information received now as opposed to tomorrow or the next several days can be used to change existing conditions when subsequent action will have been too late. Data communications should be utilized up to a point where the value of the immediate movement of information is greater than its cost (Figure 9-1). Also, the net benefit in dollars derived from information transmitted changes rather significantly as the time factor increases (Figure 9-2). In the final analysis, the timeliness of information transmitted is of vital importance to the firm.

***Links Data Processing Operations Together.*** Since data communications are capable of providing timely information, its applications to business are continually increasing. Data communications have and will continue to have an important role in keeping a firm in touch with its own regions, divisions, and plants as well as with its customers and suppliers. The transmission and collection of data to the home office from all possible sources provides management with instant information about the firm's overall operations. Likewise, data communications help the firm to reduce overall costs since billing, inventory, purchasing, payroll, and similar functions can be handled more efficiently on a centralized basis. By means of a

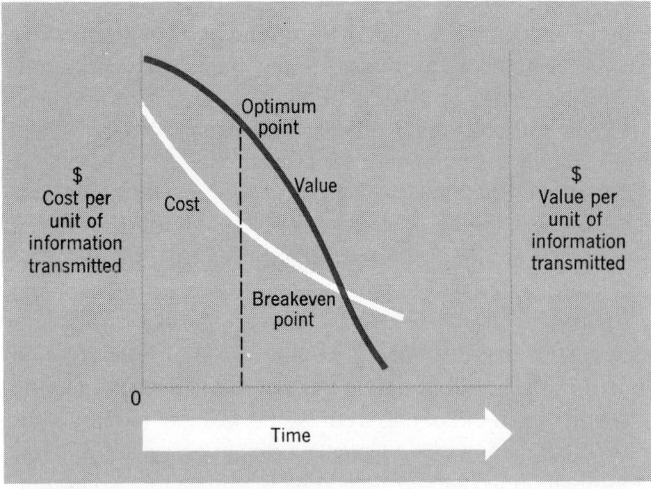


Figure 9-1 Data communications can be used up to a point where the value from the immediate movement of information is greater than its cost.

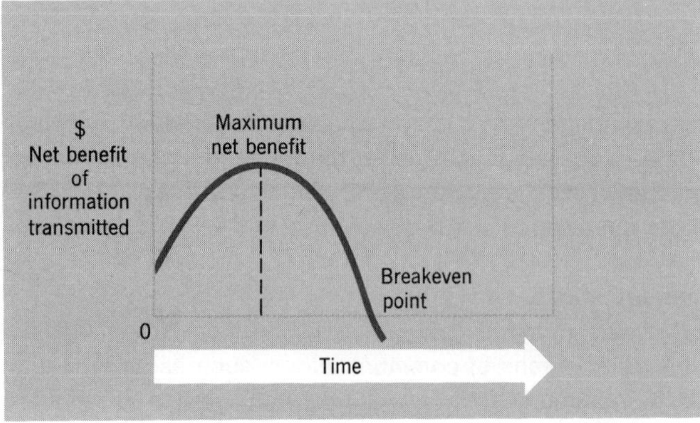


Figure 9-2 The net benefit in dollars derived from information transmitted changes over time.

data collection system, most business data can be communicated to and processed by a central facility.

***Makes On-Line Inquiry Processing Possible.*** Data communication systems have made substantial inroads into inquiry processing. Essentially, inquiries are sent to the computer from an inquiry device connected via communication lines. After the data have been processed, the data are transmitted back to the inquiring terminal. Examples of firms using on-line inquiry processing are airlines, banks, brokerage houses, hotels, and savings associations. Another example is a sales inquiry which automatically updates the inventory if merchandise can be shipped or initiates a production order if stock is not available. In this manner, the inventory file is always up to date.

***Facilitates Data Processing Load Balancing.*** In a data communication network, a central computer facility is linked and accessed by a number of remote terminals that are capable of input and output. In a similar approach, two or more computers, not in the same locations, are connected for the transmission of data in order to smooth out workloads. If one (or more) computer is overloaded, jobs on the one can be transmitted to another if time is available. Thus, computer load balancing can be very important as is the use of remote input/output terminals for computer time sharing.

## Data Communication Channels

*Two data communication methods for keeping the sending and receiving signals together are:*
- *synchronous (bit stream) transmission*
- *start/stop synchronization*

When data are sent by a transmitting station to a receiving station, the latter must be in synchronization with the former. This is necessary in order that the signals be received correctly. If the receiving station does not begin at the proper point or does not maintain the identical time interval of the sending terminal, the coded pulses will not be interpreted correctly. In view of these difficulties, several techniques have been devised to keep the sending and receiving terminals in step, the more common ones are *synchronous transmission* and *start/stop synchronization*. The synchronous or bit stream method keeps the receiving station in step with the transmitting device by means of a special timing circuit. This method insures that the data are synchronized for both receiving and transmitting stations. With the start/stop method, a start signal is sent initially and a stop signal at the end of the data transmission. This method allows the irregular transmission of data, but requires extra bits to act as start and stop signals.

## Types of Data Communication Channels

*1. Simplex channel allows one-way transmission of data.*
*2. Half-duplex carries data in both directions, but permits the transmission of data in only one direction at a time.*
*3. Full duplex transmits data in both directions simultaneously.*

Data communication channels or circuits are divided into three basic types. These are:

1. simplex,
2. half-duplex,
3. full-duplex,

The simplex channel allows one-way transmission of data while the half-duplex channel can carry information in both directions, but permits the transmission of data in only one direction at a time. A remote receive-only device is an example of a simplex data communication channel. On the other hand, a remote send-receive unit is one for use in a half-duplex data communication channel. The last major mode of operation for communication facilities is the full duplex which has the ability to transmit information in both directions simultaneously.

A variety of channels for data transmission are available from the telephone companies. When consideration is given to designing an effective data communication system, the capacity of the channel should match the speed capabilities of the equipment associated with it. Data processing equipment speeds in bits per second are depicted in Figure 9-3. These range from the slowest (typewriter) to the very highest (central processing unit), indicating a wide range of operating speeds.

## Data Communication Services

*Data communications services range from the slow speed of narrow-band, medium speed of voice-band, to the high speed of broad-band.*

Data communication services can be divided into three classes:

1. narrow-band,
2. voice-band,
3. broad-band.

These three bands are sometimes called circuit grades. The width of a band determines the maximum transmission speed since its width affects the frequency range. The higher the frequency rate, the faster is the transmission speed. Normally, bands are expressed as so many characters per second, bits per second (refer to Figure 9-3), or words per minute. Various combinations of signals or absence of signals form codes which represent numerics, alphabetics, and special characters. These individual impulses are called bits. Five to eight bits represent one character, while a word is defined as five characters plus a space.

| DATA PROCESSING EQUIPMENT | OPERATING SPEEDS BITS PER SECOND (bps) |
|---|---|
| Typewriter | 45 to 150 |
| Card Punch: | |
| 300 cards per minute | 3,200 |
| 500 cards per minute | 5,300 |
| Card Reader: | |
| 300 cards per minute | 3,200 |
| 600 cards per minute | 6,400 |
| 1000 cards per minute | 10,600 |
| Paper Tape Punch | 75 to 2,400 |
| Paper Tape Reader | 75 to 8,000 |
| Printer: | |
| 300 lines per minute | 6,000 |
| 600 lines per minute | 10,000 |
| 1000 lines per minute | 19,400 |
| Magnetic Tape Unit | 150 to 2,720,000 |
| Magnetic Disk Unit | 1,248,000 to 2,496,000 |
| Magnetic Drum Unit | 1,000,000 to 8,000,000 |
| Central Processing Unit | 2,000,000 to 16,000,000 |

Figure 9-3 Operating speeds of data processing equipment for data communications.

*Narrow-band class service or subvoice grade channel has a slower speed than that needed for voice transmission.*

***Narrow-Band Class.*** The narrow-band class of data communication service (first class) has a slower speed than that needed for voice transmission. For this reason, it is sometimes called a subvoice grade channel. The TWX (Teletypewriter Exchange Service) and the Western Union TELEX employed the narrow-band for many years. It is capable of transmitting data via five-channel paper tape. The narrow-band is used for data collection systems and data communication systems since it is relatively inexpensive. Typical speeds are 45, 57, 75, and 150 bits per second while the transmission rate can go as high as 300 bits per second.

*Voice-band class service has the capability of transmitting the human voice over public lines.*

***Voice-Band Class.*** Voice-band channels (second class) transmit the human voice over a range or band width of approximately 3,000 Hertz (cycles per second) for public lines and 4,000 Hertz for leased lines. Maximum data speeds range up to 2,400 bits per second. It is possible to obtain slower speeds by dividing into subvoice channels, consisting of bands of 150 to 200 cycles. The 100-Speed TWX Service makes use of the voice-band grade channel for reading, transmitting, and punching eight-channel paper tape at the rate of 100 words per minute. The Data-Phone (Figure 9-6) as well as other data transmission equipment use the voice-band to transmit data from punched paper tape, punched cards, and magnetic tape. The cost for this type data communication service is comparable to a long distance telephone call. Still another service available over voice-band grade channels is WATS (Wide Area Telephone Service). It permits long distance telephone service among a large number of telephones and is more economical than regular long distance for large volumes. WATS is billed at a fixed monthly rate, allowing a firm to make a large number of outgoing calls throughout the month. Its lines may also be used in conjunction with the Data-Phone for data transmission.

Telephone noise is the major error source in most systems. It originates within the telephone switching equipment and can sometimes be heard on the line as clicks. Noise prevents the receiving end from detecting a bit correctly sent from the transmitting end. Parity schemes are used to detect errors when they occur. Some codes are designed to detect the presence of errors, but more elaborate codes can actually identify what the error was, and even correct one or more errors.

The more elaborate the parity scheme, the less likely that double or multiple transformations of bits will produce acceptable codes. Thus, acceptance of bad data at the receiving end can be brought to a low probability. However, elaborate parity schemes reduce line efficiency, however, since time is lost in sending redundant bits.

*Broad-band class service has a higher-band width than the voice-band width. It employs several methods for data transmission:*

- *microwaves*
- *Telepak*
- *radio and TV bands*
- *millimeter waves*
- *tropospheric forward scatter propagation*
- *satellites*

***Broad-Band Class.*** The broad-band or wide-band class of data communication service (third class) has a higher band width than the voice-band width. It involves a microwave (radio relay) communication system that operates at frequencies above four million kiloHertz per second. Data must be continually amplified and repeated by stations (20 to 35 miles apart) which use dishlike antennas. Datran, a wholly owned subsidiary of University Computing Company, is building a microwave communication system. Thirty-five major metropolitan areas, each encompassing a 50-mile radius, will be initially serviced by a combination of 244 microwave repeater stations, 10 district offices with computerized switching, and tail-circuits to subscriber locations. Datran offers several advantages over methods now available to the public: subscribers will be connected in less than three seconds, compared to 20 seconds normally required: system induced transmission errors will be no more than one in 10 million bits, an improvement factor of 10 over normal telephone lines: and the customer is billed only for the actual time used, say seconds versus the standard three minute call.

Telepak, a private line service of American Telephone and Telegraph, is a wide-band program that can be leased on a milage basis per month with an unlimited usage basis. One telepak channel can carry 12, 24, 60, or 240 voice circuits, depending upon the user's requirements. Despite the high monthly cost of $15 per mile of leased circuit and the rental of a data communication unit, the cost per unit of data transmitted can be low if volume is high.

Other means of transmitting data over broad-band channels are radio bands, TV bands, millimeter waves, and tropospheric forward scatter propagation. This last method sends out multiple signals (as from the large end of a funnel). These signals scatter and bounce off the troposphere (five or more miles above the earth's surface) and one or more of these signals are picked up at a distant receiving point.

***Satellites.*** Another candidate to ease the ever increasing data transmission traffic is the use of satellites. However, there are high costs involved. A satellite operator will need to spend approximately $15 million for NASA's launching of one satellite. Despite the costs involved, A. T. & T. employs satellites for backing up its communications network. A current satellite model can accommodate 10,800 voice-grade channels. Little change in wide-band rates result from the use of satellites since rates must be based on the total investment in cables and microwave links as well as the satellites used in the Bell network.

### Data Communication Equipment

*The United States of America Standards Institute adopted the USASCII, seven level code (plus one bit for parity checking) as a standard for data communication equipment.*

In order to achieve coding uniformity of data transmitted, the United States of America Standards Institute adopted a new data processing code in June, 1967. It is known as the ASCII or the USASCII—U.S.A. Standard Code for Information Interchange (Figure 9-4). Although the adoption of this seven-level code (actually eight bits are used since the eighth bit is used for parity checking—verify that data transmission integrity has been maintained) is voluntary, it is expected that its application will be widespread. Presently, there are a number of variations of the seven-level code as well as five-, six-, and eight-level codes. The EBCDIC code, for example, can be transmitted on channels designed for ASCII. Standardization with

| | | | | | | 0 | 0 | 0 | 0 | 1 | 1 | 1 | 1 |
|---|---|---|---|---|---|---|---|---|---|---|---|---|---|
| $b_7$ → | | | | | | 0 | 0 | 0 | 0 | 1 | 1 | 1 | 1 |
| $b_6$ → | | | | | | 0 | 0 | 1 | 1 | 0 | 0 | 1 | 1 |
| $b_5$ → | | | | | | 0 | 1 | 0 | 1 | 0 | 1 | 0 | 1 |
| Bits | $b_4$ ↓ | $b_3$ ↓ | $b_2$ ↓ | $b_1$ ↓ | Col.→ / Row↓ | 0 | 1 | 2 | 3 | 4 | 5 | 6 | 7 |
| | 0 | 0 | 0 | 0 | 0 | NUL | DLE | SP | 0 | @ | P | \ | p |
| | 0 | 0 | 0 | 1 | 1 | SOH | DC1 | ! | 1 | A | Q | a | q |
| | 0 | 0 | 1 | 0 | 2 | STX | DC2 | " | 2 | B | R | b | r |
| | 0 | 0 | 1 | 1 | 3 | ETX | DC3 | # | 3 | C | S | c | s |
| | 0 | 1 | 0 | 0 | 4 | EOT | DC4 | $ | 4 | D | T | d | t |
| | 0 | 1 | 0 | 1 | 5 | ENQ | NAK | % | 5 | E | U | e | u |
| | 0 | 1 | 1 | 0 | 6 | ACK | SYN | & | 6 | F | V | f | v |
| | 0 | 1 | 1 | 1 | 7 | BEL | ETB | / | 7 | G | W | g | w |
| | 1 | 0 | 0 | 0 | 8 | BS | CAN | ( | 8 | H | X | h | x |
| | 1 | 0 | 0 | 1 | 9 | HT | EM | ) | 9 | I | Y | i | y |
| | 1 | 0 | 1 | 0 | 10 | LF | SUB | * | : | J | Z | j | z |
| | 1 | 0 | 1 | 1 | 11 | VT | ESC | + | ; | K | [ | k | { |
| | 1 | 1 | 0 | 0 | 12 | FF | FS | , | < | L | \ | l | \| |
| | 1 | 1 | 0 | 1 | 13 | CR | GS | — | = | M | ] | m | } |
| | 1 | 1 | 1 | 0 | 14 | SO | RS | ▪ | > | N | ∧ | n | ¬ |
| | 1 | 1 | 1 | 1 | 15 | SI | US | / | ? | O | — | o | DEL |

Figure 9-4 ASCII coding chart where each character is represented by seven bits.

USASCII will facilitate the conversion and interchange of data among the data communication equipment available throughout the industry.

***Data Communication System.*** No matter what code level is employed, data are transmitted in five stages through the use of data communication equipment and lines. Basically, the data are sent:

1. from an input device,
2. to a transmitting terminal,
3. through an electrical transmission line,
4. to a receiving terminal,
5. and to an output device.

This is represented in Figure 9-5.

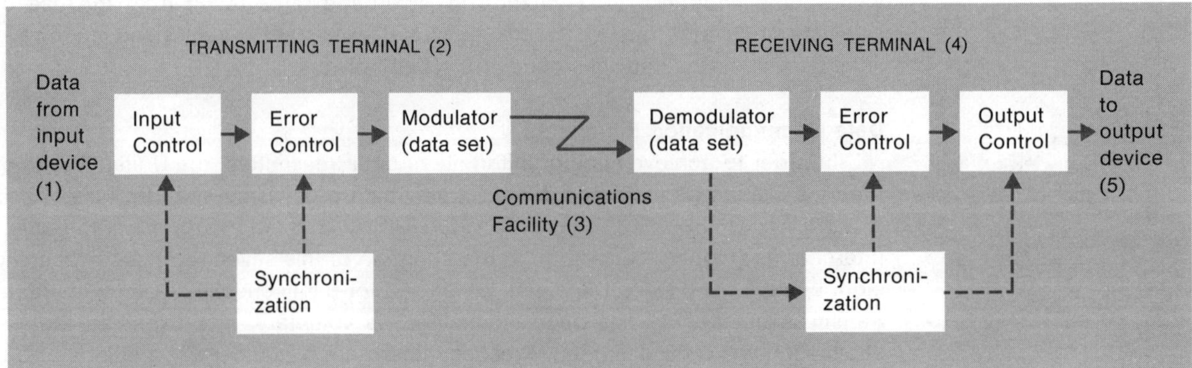


Figure 9-5 Data communication system—flow of data.

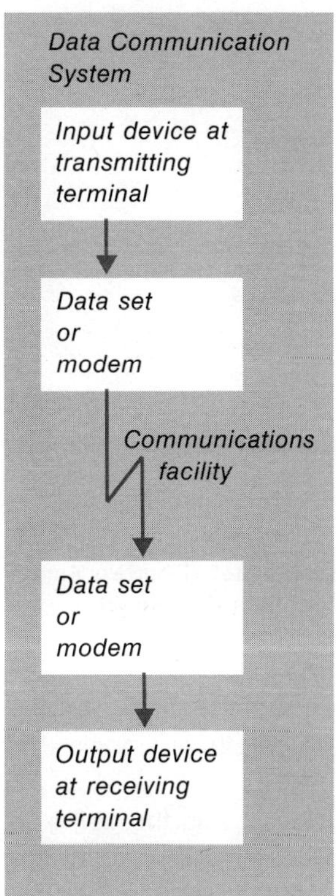


Referring to the five stages, the input device at the transmitting terminal may be a paper tape reader, card reader, magnetic tape unit, computer, keyboard, or special collection device (1). The sending terminal that transmits the data from the input device consists of several units, even though they are contained in a single cabinet and sold as a single communication terminal device (2). The input control unit accepts and stores data temporarily by means of a buffering device so that its speed is compatible with the communication facility. The error control unit detects and, sometimes, corrects errors that occur during transmission. The most commonly used methods for error control are validity checking and parity checking. While the former assumes the accuracy of character representation, the latter determines whether the number of bits received meets the established odd or even bit code. By means of the synchronization unit, transmitting and receiving units operate at the same frequency while data move. Before data can be sent over the communications facility, impulses generated by the terminal input device must be modified so as to be compatible with it. The transmitting terminal unit that performs the function is called a modulator (data set).

Once the data has been received over the communications network (3), the demodulator (data set) at the receiving terminal converts the signal back into a form acceptable to the output device. For two-way data communications, the data set is a combination modulator-demodulator unit, often called a modem (MOdulating-DEModulating equipment). The error control unit checks the data pattern to make sure it meets the validity check or parity check. The last unit or the output control unit accepts and stores the data temporarily for transfer to the output device at an appropriate rate. For the receiving terminal, the synchronization unit assures that it is operating on the same frequency as the transmitting instrument (4). Finally, the output device at the receiving terminal may be a paper tape punch, card punch, printer, magnetic tape unit, computer, or display device (5).

*Common data transmission equipment includes:*

- *data-phones*
- *push-button telephones*
- *portable terminals*
- *teletype terminals*
- *paper tape systems*
- *punched card terminals*
- *magnetic tape terminals*
- *computer systems*
- *CRT terminals*
- *data collection systems*

**Data Transmission Terminal Equipment**

Data sets cannot only perform the functions set forth in the above section, but also can be a means of dialing and providing a connection for the communications facility. Various types of data sets, used as data transmission terminal equipment, are furnished by communications carriers, depending upon their use. In the following material, several of the more common terminals and equipment will be explored.

*Data-phone permits data to be sent over public lines by depressing its voice capability.*

***Data-Phone.*** The best known transmitting system is the Data-Phone data set, manufactured by the Bell Telephone System. As shown in Figure 9-6, it is basically a modified telephone which can be used either for voice or data transmission. A method for utilizing the Data-Phone is to dial the appropriate number to which information is being sent. When the Data-Phone set is answered at the other end, the transmitting party indicates the start of an information transmission. At this moment, both parties depress the "Data" button which automatically depresses the voice capability and allows data to be sent over the wires. In this manner, Data-Phone data sets or modems can be either transmitters, receivers, or both.

*Push-button telephone allows data to be sent over public lines by depressing the desired button on the unit itself.*

***Push-Button Telephone.*** The push-button telephone is another commonly used data set, shown in Figure 9-7. A call is placed by depressing the buttons which correspond to the desired telephone number. Upon the completion of the call, the telephone can be used to transmit data or for normal voice communication. If data are transmitted to a receiving set connected to a recording device, such as a card punch or a punched paper tape, the receiving set accepts the call, transmits an answer tone, and connects the recording device to the transmission

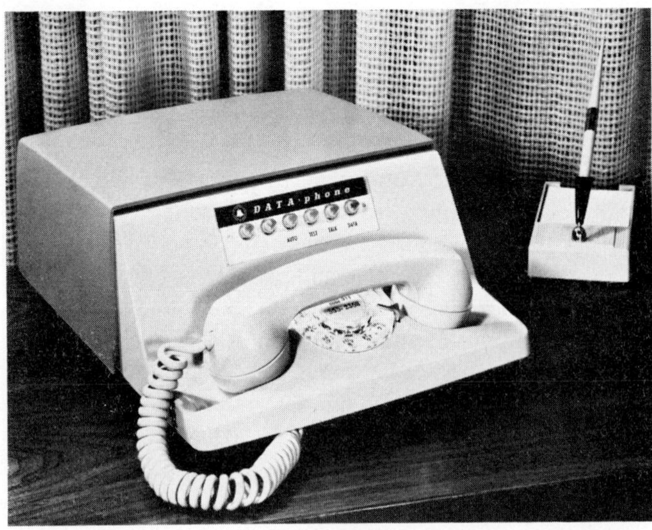


Figure 9-6 Data-Phone data set. (Courtesy American Telephone and Telegraph Company.)

line. Input data are entered by depressing the buttons on the telephone. As the buttons are depressed, the data set converts the tones to electrical signals that are captured by the recording device.

In addition to the above procedure, the telephone data set has the ability to use punched plastic cards. This added flexibility allows customers or company personnel to enter orders quickly and efficiently. For example, a customer wishes

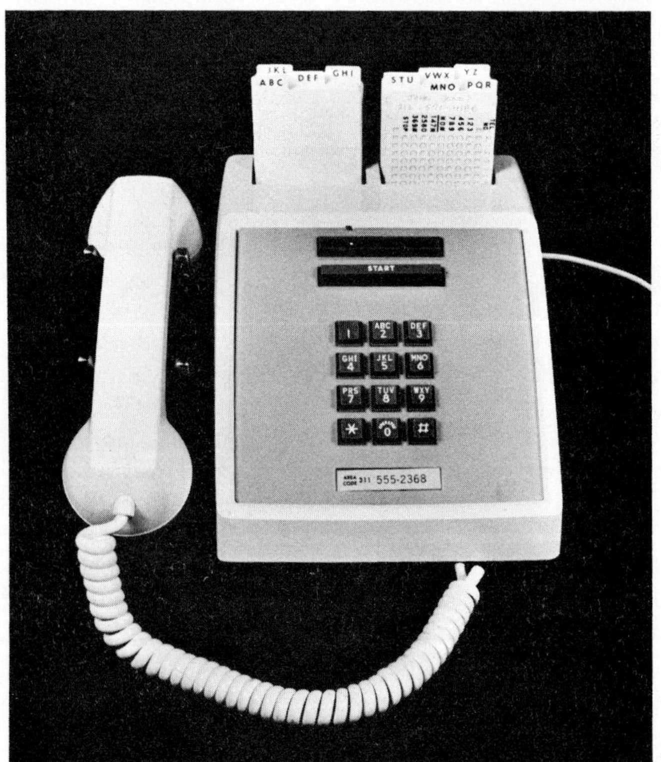


Figure 9-7 Telephone data set that allows dialing and data transmission by push buttons or punched plastic cards.

to place an order. He simply dials the number of the vendor and identifies his firm by inserting a prepunched plastic identity card into the reading device of the telephone. The customer then feeds into the reader a punched plastic card describing the first item he is ordering. Once the contents of the card have been transmitted via a tone signal to the sender, the quantity is entered by depressing the appropriate buttons. At the receiving end, a recording device produces a set of cards, punched paper tape, or other output. The same procedure is completed for the rest of the order. At the end of a certain time period, say a month, the vendor submits a listing of all orders entered and the amount billed for the customer. This procedure speeds up the ordering process and reduces the need for writing purchase orders.

***Portable Audio Terminal.*** Data communication equipment is not limited to stationary terminals. Portable computer terminals are becoming more popular since they perform the same functions as larger units and are reasonably priced. Some units rent for as low as $20 per month. For example, the IBM 2721 Portable Audio Terminal (Figure 9-8) allows the user to enter alphabetic and numerical data into

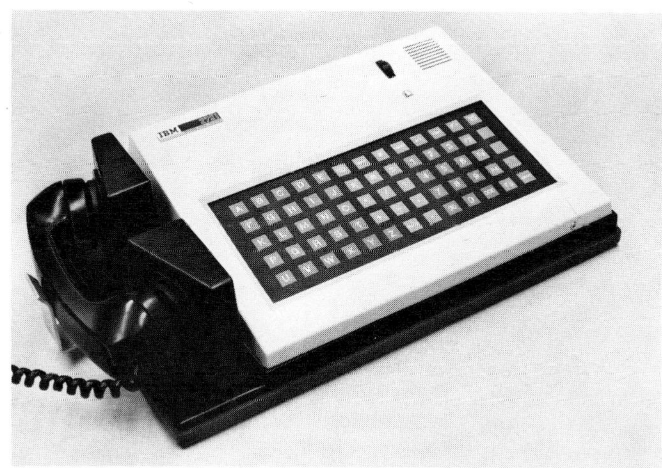

Figure 9-8 IBM 2721 Portable Audio Terminal. (Courtesy International Business Machines Corporation.)

*Portable audio terminal allows the user to enter numerical and alphabetical data through its keyboard and receive a reply from the computer over the terminal's built in speaker.*

a System/360 (model 25 and up) or System/370 from any standard telephone. The unit, priced at $600 (numeric code only), communicates to the computer through an IBM 7770 Audio Response Unit (Figure 9-9) and is designed for salesmen, insurance agents, personnel at manufacturing plants, and others with similar requirements.

An insurance agent, for example, fits a telephone handset at a prospect's home into the 2721's acoustic coupler, connecting it with a remote computer. With the keyboard, he would then enter the prospect's age, income, number of dependents, present insurance coverage, and other factors. The computer would then calculate the amount and type of protection needed to achieve the prospect's insurance needs. The computer's reply is heard over the terminal's built-in speaker or through a set of earphones. The spoken words are selected by the computer from a vocabulary stored in its audio-response unit. Words are chosen from a library of most frequently used words for the specific application. A 32-word vocabulary is provided with the basic 7770 unit and can be expanded in 16-word increments, up to 128 words.

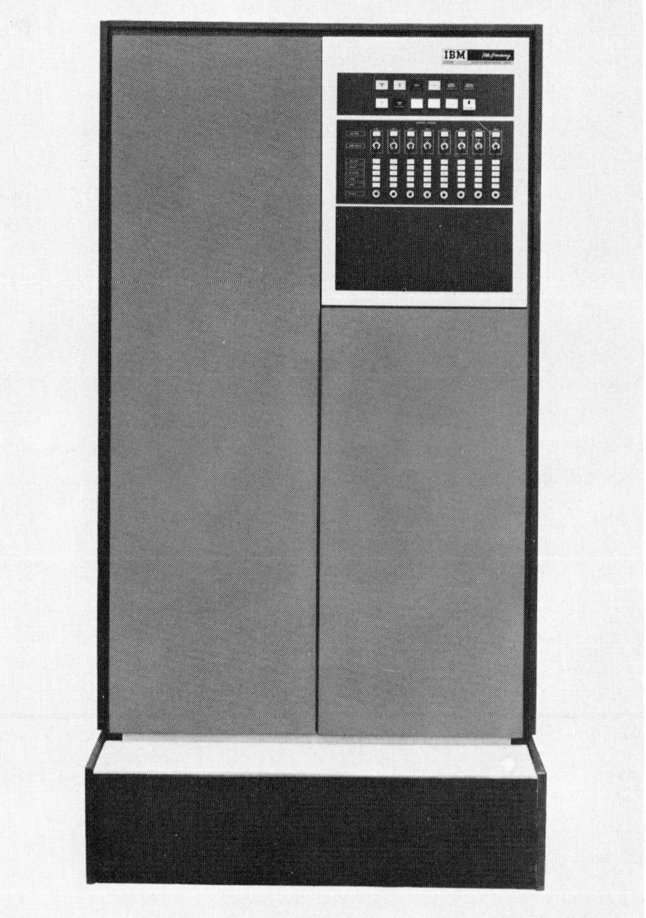

Figure 9-9 IBM 7770 Audio Response Unit. (Courtesy International Business Machines Corporation.)

In manufacturing applications, the unit allows workers to enter information on jobs in progress and tracks the status of jobs as they more from one department to another. Inventory clerks can use the unit to determine the nearest warehouse stocking a particular part. Other uses include: industrial salesmen checking critical delivery dates at the customer's office, solving engineering problems, and customer credit verification. In operation, touch-tone signals are communicated to the 7770 which then converts these signals to 8-bit bytes. Programming must be written to translate these signals into EBCDIC code meaningful to the computer. Unauthorized access to computer data can be prevented by assigning each terminal a special code number.

*Portable CRT terminal is capable of receiving and sending data in a half- or full-duplex mode.*

***Portable CRT Terminal.*** A recent addition to the category of portable computer terminals is the combination CRT/keyboard terminal (Figure 9-10). With this particular model, two operating modes are selectable by a front panel push button: Local mode—provides page transmission which allows local editing and On-Line mode—transmits character by character identical to a teletypewriter. In either mode, the user can select half- or full-duplex. When the screen is full, the top line is deleted and the information remaining on display is shifted upward to allow new characters to be entered on the bottom of the display, just as a teletypewriter rolls up paper.

Figure 9-10 Portable CRT/keyboard terminal. (Courtesy Bendix Corporation.)

This portable CRT/keyboard terminal utilizes semiconductor memory and an MOS character generator. A special power supply permits operation from any power line in the world.

*Portable printer terminal can produce full page computer printouts with carbon copies.*

***Portable Printer Terminal.*** Another portable computer terminal is the PortaCom, illustrated in Figure 9-11. The PortaCom portable terminal produces full page computer printout with carbon copies. It has its own built-in acoustic coupler and standard ASCII keyboard. Teletype compatible, it needs only a standard power outlet

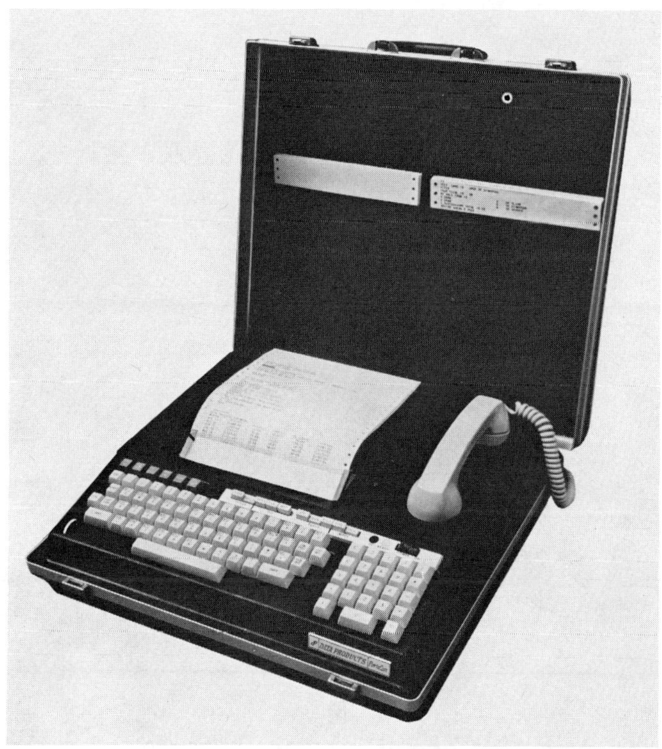

Figure 9-11 PortaCom portable computer communications terminal. (Courtesy Data Products Corporation.)

and a telephone to begin operating. The unit weighs 26 pounds, making it light enough to be hand carried, and leases for $80 per month.

*Teletype terminals are widely used since they permit the transmission and receipt of data between two points over telephone lines.*

***Teletype Terminals.*** Among the most widely used of all data transmission equipment today is the Teletype machine. What the telephone does for verbal data, the Teletype does for written data. It permits the transmission and receipt of data between two points by telephone lines. Teletype produces various models in order to meet the specific needs of its customers. Basically, their equipment includes:

1. RO (receive-only) set,
2. KSR (keyboard send-receive) set,
3. ASR (automatic send-receive) set.

*Receive only (RO) set is capable of typewriter output only.*

*RO set.* The Inktronic RO set (Figure 9-12) is a remote typewriter output. It prints up to 1200 words per minute which is much faster than ordinary page printers in its class. The method of printing is through electrostatic deflection. Ink literally leaps to the page to form a character. Ink droplets carry a negative charge and are drawn to the page through a series of electrodes that cause it to trace out the shape of the character desired. Each character, then, is made up of a number of dots.

*KSR set.* A teletype machine which will transmit data similar to that of a typewriter (keyboard input and output) is shown in Figure 9-13. The Inktronic KSR set

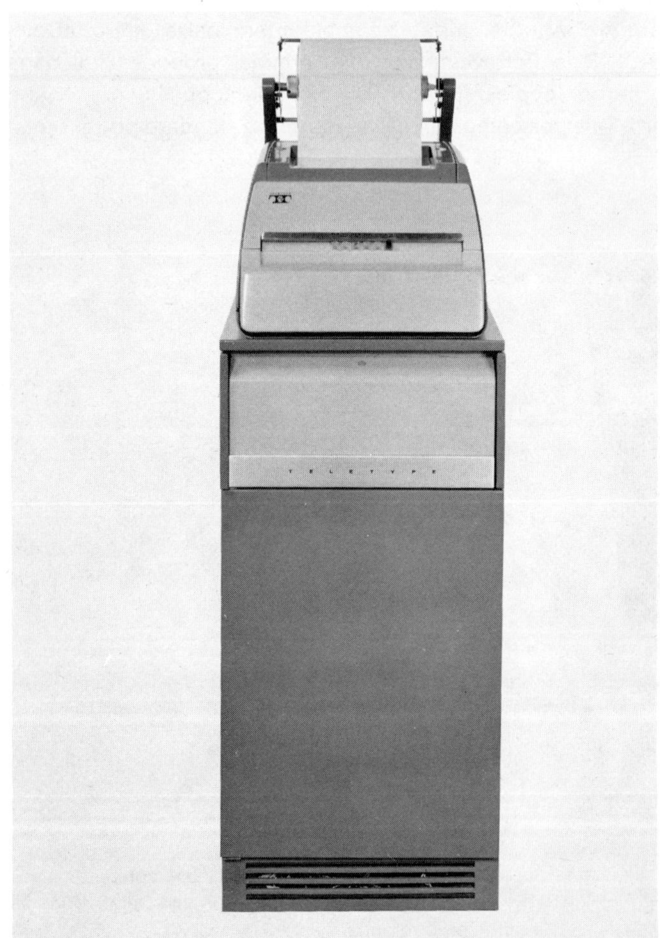

Figure 9-12 Teletype Inktronic RO (receive-only) set. (Courtesy Teletype Corporation.)

Figure 9-13 Teletype Inktronic KSR (keyboard send-receive set. (Courtesy Teletype Corporation.)

*Keyboard send-receive (KSR) set can produce printed output at both the sending and receiving ends.*

can produce a printed copy at both the sending and receiving ends. Also, data can be transmitted and received in eight channel punched paper tape for direct input to a data processing system on those models that have the capability, such as the Model 37 ASR set. This approach allows for preparing paper tapes in advance so that its accuracy can be checked as well as transmitting automatically at a more rapid rate than would be possible with manual typing.

*Automatic send-receive (ASR) set can send and receive printed data as well as punched paper tape.*

*ASR set.* The Teletype Model 37 ASR set is illustrated in Figure 9-14. It can be arranged to operate on a 5-, 6-, or 7-level code although it is basically designed to utilize the 8-level code with even parity. As indicated in the illustration, the control panel (1) is located above the keyboard and has 18 individual keys and lamps, offering a flexibility of controls for the Model 37. These controls include: interrupt, printer end-of-line, proceed, keyboard, printer, and punch commands for both local and on-line modes. The keyboard-printer console (2) can be used separately—for on-line computer access, for example—or may be used to monitor hard copy produced by the tape unit, or to prepare tapes for transmission. The paper tape module (3) contains both a punch and a reader. The reader can send to the punch, to the printer, and to other teleprinters or computer terminals. The punch can receive from its own reader or keyboard, or from remote terminals. It is possible to send, receive, and punch tape or print copy at the rate of 150 words per minute.

*Teletype data transmission equipment is widely used for controlling inventory that is scattered.*

*Teletype applications.* Numerous applications have been found for Teletype's data transmission equipment, namely, transmission of sales orders, invoices, production schedules, inventory, payroll checks, personnel data, quotations, internal reports, shipping data, and similar business data. Many firms have replaced their traditional inventory replenishment method with a communications network that ties its distribution outlets and warehouses to its computer center via a Teletype ASR set. Teletype equipment is used to send and receive inventory data among ware-

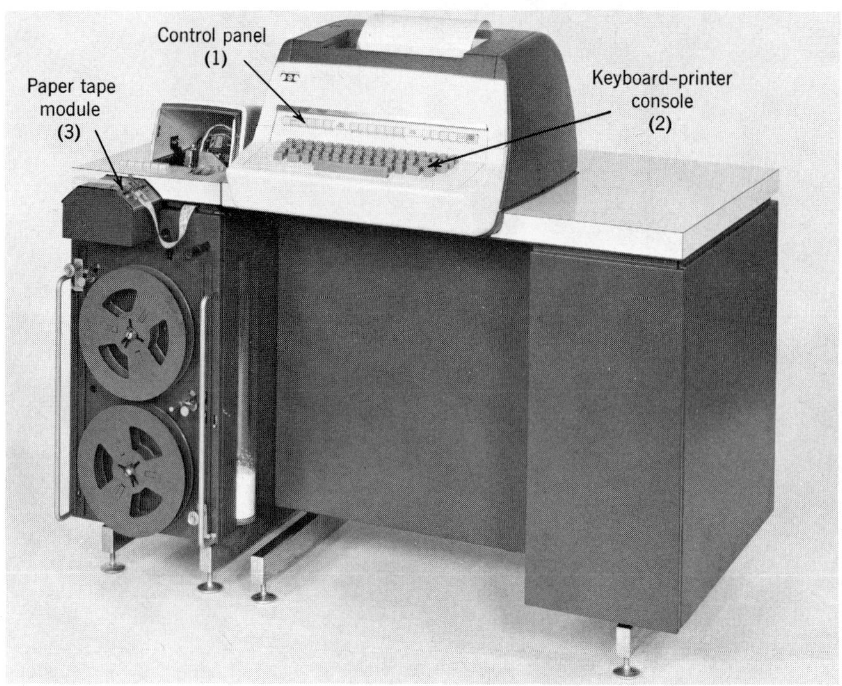


Figure 9-14 Teletype Model 37 ASR (automatic send-receive) set. (Courtesy Teletype Corporation.)

houses, distribution centers, and a computer center. The computer analyzes the inventory at each location and considers past stock requirements as well as seasonal demand and, where applicable, possible obsolescence. It determines the stock needs and material requirements of each warehouse and distribution outlet. The Teletype ASR set transmits stock replenishment orders quickly and accurately which results in keeping inventories current and costs at a minimum.

*Paper tape-to-tape system is capable of sending or receiving punch paper tape data at high speeds.*

***Paper Tape-To-Tape System.*** Telespeed high-speed tape-to-tape equipment, also manufactured by the Teletype Corporation (there are other manufacturers of similar equipment), is capable of communicating punch paper tape data at speeds from 750 to 1200 words per minute. It is strictly a punch paper tape transmission device and has no typewriter. Data can be accumulated throughout the regular work day and transmitted during nonworking hours or at other appropriate times. With this equipment, it is possible to alternate data transmission with voice communication on the same call.

As shown in Figure 9-15, the paper tape transmission terminals consist of two units—a sender unit and a receiving unit. The sender consists of a paper tape reader and a signal generator. As the tape passes through the reading device, the punched holes are sensed by pins connected to a signal generator. The latter device, in turn, sends signals representing the sensed holes to a data set for transmission over the communications channel. The operation is reversed at the receiving unit which consists of a signal interpreter and tape punch. As electrical impulses are received, the pins in the tape punch are activated and the proper holes are punched in the paper tape.

***Punched Card Transmission Terminals.*** Not only are business data capable of being transmitted via keyboard, and punched paper tape, but they can also be transmitted by a punched card transmission system. For a small number of data

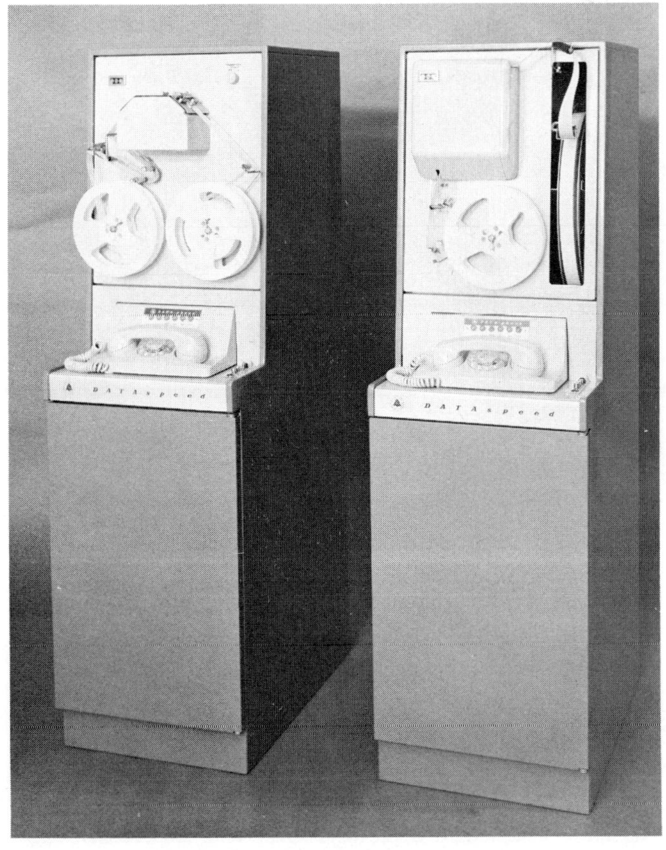

Figure 9-15 Telespeed Tape-to-Tape System. (Courtesy Teletype Corporation.)

*Punched card transmission terminals can transmit punched card data where the speed of transmission is dependent upon the type of terminal being employed.*

(punched cards) to be transmitted, a data transmission system, consisting of a Data-Phone, a card read, and a ten-digit keyboard, is utilized (Figure 9-16). After a connection has been made between the sending and receiving units, the sender lifts an exclusion switch located under the handset which disconnects the telephone and connects the transmitting terminal to the line. Numeric data can be entered manually through the keyboard or automatically by inserting a prepunched card. When a card is placed in the reader, the data are converted to audio-range frequencies that pass over telephone channels to a receiving station. Generally, the data are converted to punched cards. For example, many doctor offices, using the data transmission system shown in Figure 9-16, can send charge and payment information to a data processing center. A nurse dials the data center via a Data-

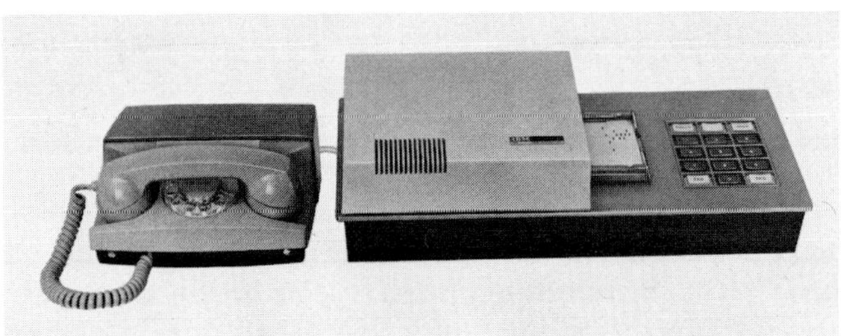

Figure 9-16 Data transmission system—combination telephone, transmitting subset, and transmission terminal. (Courtesy International Business Machines Corporation.)

Phone data set and inserts a pre-punched card which contains the patient's identity number. She, then, keys in data concerning the type of service provided and amount charged. At the processing center, punched cards are automatically generated which are fed later to a computer system that produces statements, transaction journals, and an aged trial balance.

Where large quantities of punched cards are to be transmitted to a receiving station, a high speed punched card transmission terminal is needed, shown in Figure 9-17. In this case, the transmission terminal is also capable of receiving data from another terminal. The speed of the sending unit is a function of the number of characters on each card, the type of circuit used, and the receiving unit employed.

Figure 9-17 IBM 1013 Card Transmission Terminal. (Courtesy International Business Machines Corporation.)

*Magnetic tape transmission terminal is designed to read or write tape during transmission and is used for large volumes of data.*

***Magnetic Tape Transmission Terminal.*** Another popular type of data transmission is one that uses magnetic tape transmission terminals. Each terminal is designed to read tape or write tape during transmission, depending on how a toggle switch is set. Magnetic tape terminals read or write tape with a high density of characters per inch. They are capable of utilizing magnetic tapes from or preparing magnetic tapes for the most popular tape devices. There is generally no limitation regarding the length of each record transmitted.

The Teletype Corporation, for example, is currently marketing a magnetic tape terminal. The Model 4210 Magnetic Tape Data Terminal (similar in appearance to the KSR set) has a send/receive transmission capacity of up to 2400 words per minute, twice as fast as most available punched paper tape equipment. The device is designed to add high speed on-line capability to existing low speed terminals. Data can be entered from the keyboard of a Model 33, 35, 37, or Inktronic input/output terminal which use the ASCII code, or on-line from a remote station or computer. The cartridge of re-usable magnetic tape has a storage capacity of approximately 150K words. The unit may be left unattended, arranged to answer calls automatically and either send or receive, depending on the mode selected.

***Computer-To-Computer Transmission.*** Computer-to-computer transmission of data is possible by connecting transmission control terminals to the respective computers. The sending transmission control terminal converts data from computer

*Computer-to-computer transmission is made possible by connecting transmission control terminals to the respective computers. This mode of operation allows one computer to back up another one.*

storage to the transmission language, used for common carrier communication. The data may have originated from on-line storage, punched cards, magnetic tape, or paper tape, then manipulated before sending through the data set. On the receiving end of the transmission, the data set picks up the signals while the data transmission control terminal converts data from the transmission language to the respective language of the computer for storage. The receiving computer is ready to manipulate the incoming data, such as update records in disk storage or prepare data for a printout. The real benefit of the computer-to-computer transmission is that it allows one computer center to back up another, especially during peak periods.

*Visual CRT terminal provides access to data stored within a computer system in the form of visual output.*

***Visual CRT Terminal.*** Visual display terminals have proved to be a necessity for many firms desiring up-to-date information. Such a terminal provides immediate access to information stored within a computer system. The hardware of a visual display terminal consists of a keyboard, a signal generator-interpreter, a buffer, and a visual display screen. An inexpensive CRT data terminal is shown in Figure 9-18.

Figure 9-18 Bunker Ramo 2210 computer CRT terminal. (Courtesy The Bunker Ramo Corporation.)

The Bunker-Ramo 2210 CRT unit leases for $39 per month including maintenance. In a typical installation, a complete work station can be outfitted for on-line processing at approximately $55 per month. This price includes the terminal, communications unit, and control unit full buffering, and interfacing to an IBM System/360. The unit's keyboard contains all alpha and numeric characters plus a selection of programmable function keys. A more expensive CRT display station, costing several hundred dollars per month, was illustrated previously (Figure 7-24).

*CRT terminal can provide printed output of selected visual data if the unit has printing capabilities.*

***CRT Terminal with Printed Output.*** For any CRT terminal, the keyboard is the means of inquiry for data which are stored on-line by the computer system. Coded signals are generated and transmitted by data sets and communication channels to the computer system. Once the computer interprets the signals and has retrieved the requested information, the data are transmitted again, using data sets, back over the communications channel to the visual display terminal in the form of coded signals. The signals, in turn, are interpreted and displayed on the TV type screen. Data that are displayed can be printed if the visual display unit is equipped with an attached printer or integrated within the CRT terminal per Figure 9-19. The applications for display stations are numerous. Among these are credit check, accounts receivable, production scheduling, inventory, shipping information, sales data, administration data, stock prices, and similar business data. The number of

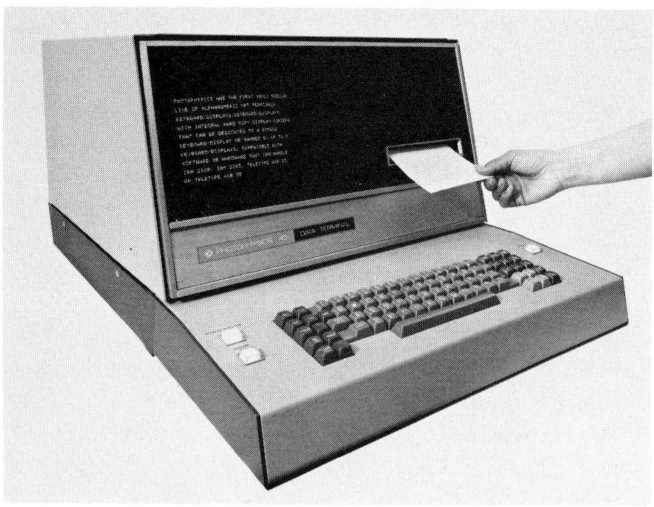

Figure 9-19 Photophysics "45" CRT Data Terminal with hard copy output. (Courtesy Photophysics.)

applications is as wide as the CRT terminals being marketed. A feasibility study is needed to determine what CRT units best serve the firm since their capabilities and prices vary from manufacturer to manufacturer.

*Common application of CRT terminals interacting with an on-line real-time computer system is the processing of customer orders.*

***CRT Terminal Illustration.*** A representative application of CRT data terminals is a customer ordering procedure. Although some customer orders arrive through the mail and via Teletype, many are phoned in to the firm's sales offices. Salesmen write up the orders and hand them to an adjacent order entry typist. Flashed on the CRT terminal are a series of questions to be answered by the typist: customer account number, customer order number, date of order, phone or mail order, tax code (type of customer), inside salesman, and job control number. Additional questions are flashed on the screen for an answer, depending upon the type of order. Sets of questions continue until the operator enters an L for "last." Each keyed-in answer appears on the screen opposite the question. There is one edit check for each item on the order and the operator verifies that an entry is correct by keying in OK (okay) or NG (no good). After an NG entry, she redisplays the particular item in question and enters changes. An editing program, stored in the computer, checks the answer against preestablished facts and limits, resulting in question marks being flashed on the screen when the program finds an answer unacceptable. When all questions have been correctly answered, the computer program checks the customer's credit. If credit is approved, a message is displayed on the screen. However, if the customer fails the credit check, a warning message is flashed on the terminal. Once the credit information is cleared, the computer program deducts stock requirements of the order from the firm's inventories or if inventories are insufficient, a production order is immediately placed. When the foregoing procedures have been completed, the computer prints out an order set for notifying the customer and actual shipment of the goods. The above process takes about 5 to 10 minutes, depending upon the complexity of the order.

***Data Collection System.*** While the foregoing terminals, for the most part, have transmitted data previously collected, recorded, or stored, a data collection and transmission system (Figure 9-20) is somewhat different. The more advanced ones feed the data directly into a real-time computer system in order to provide updated information. Such an approach can be illustrated by the following example—one relating to cost accounting and payroll.

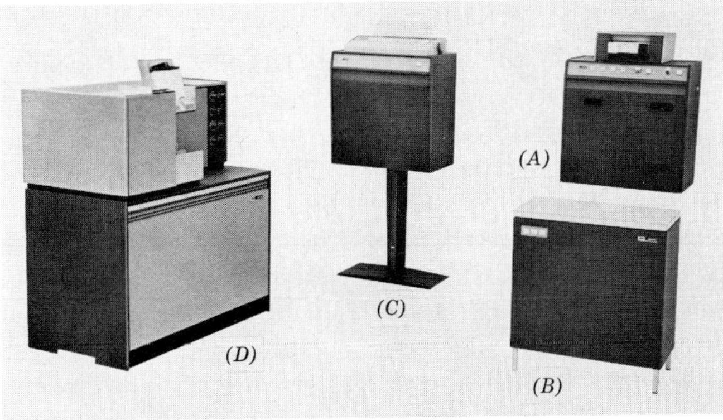


Figure 9-20 IBM 1030 Data Collection System. (*A*) 1031 Input Station, (*B*) 1032 Digital Time Unit, (*C*) 1033 Printer, and (*D*) 1034 Card Punch. (Courtesy International Business Machines Corporation.)

*Data collection system provides a means of maintaining production and payroll data on an updated basis via data collection units scattered throughout the plant.*

Under such a system, there are several data collection devices which are located conveniently for all job production personnel. When a factory employee starts a job, he inserts his own plastic identification badge into a reader (like the one shown in Figure 9-20*A*) which designates the employee's departmental number. He then places a punched card into the same reader which identifies the job being worked on. The data are transmitted to a centralized computer facility. Upon completion of the job, the above process is repeated along with keying in the number of units produced. The data are automatically transmitted to the central computer where they are stored by job number for cost analysis, paying the employee, and making the necessary adjustments to production schedules and inventory balances. In place of compiling data on the plant level and forwarding the data to the home office, all pertinent information is transferred to the central computer facility as it happens. In like manner, all other accounting data are stored on-line in real-time as they occur. Using an executive program that produces the required figures for an income statement, any of the firm's executives can interrogate the system for an up to the minute report on the profitability or lack thereof throughout the normal working day. Thus, the timeliness of keeping all data up-to-date (in an on-line real-time system) is necessary for an accurate presentation of the firm's financial condition at any time.

*The variety of data transmission terminals allows the user to select the equipment that will meet his needs.*

***Summary of Data Transmission Terminal Equipment.*** The various pieces of data transmission terminal equipment are summarized in Figure 9-21. Several of these devices are an integral part of any time sharing system, the subject matter for the next sections of the chapter. These include typewriter terminals and visual CRT display units whether they be stationary or portable units plus a multifunction terminal illustrated in Figure 9-25. In the final analysis, the application determines which equipment is suited best for the data processing operation.

- Data-Phone
- Push-button telephone
- Portable computer terminals:
  - Portable audio terminal
  - Portable CRT terminal
  - Portable printer terminal
- Typewriter terminals:
  - RO (receive-only) set
  - KSR (keyboard send-receive) set
  - ASR (automatic send-receive) set
- High speed paper tape-to-tape system
- Punched card transmission terminal
- Magnetic tape transmission terminal
- Computer-to-computer transmission
- Visual CRT terminal
- Visual CRT terminal with printed output
- Multifunction terminal
- Data collection system

Figure 9-21 Summary of data transmission terminal equipment.

## TIME SHARING

*Time sharing was developed to meet the programming bottlenecks created by a batch processing computer system.*

The idea of time sharing began to develop during the late 1950's. The impulse came mostly from the frustration that developed among scientists and programmers bottlenecked by the batch processing system. It was a British mathematician, Christopher Strachey who gave the first public paper on time sharing at a UNESCO congress in 1959. In that same year, Professor John McCarthy wrote an internal memorandum distributed at M.I.T. These two men, working independently, were the first to go on record with specific solutions to the problems of time sharing. Important research began at M.I.T. where Professor F. J. Corbató developed what has since become, in Project MAC (machine-aided cognition or multiple-access computer), one of the most advanced time sharing systems at work in the country. The idea of time sharing spread to other colleges, notably Dartmouth and the University of California at Berkley.

***First Demonstration of Time Sharing.*** The first demonstration of time sharing was at the M.I.T. Computation Center (November 1961) where four remote consoles in the same room were linked to an IBM 709 vacuum tube computer. The following September, Bolt, Beranek & Newman in Cambridge began time sharing on a Digital Equipment Corporation PDP-1. In May 1963, the System Development Corporation made its first tests of time sharing in Santa Monica. One year later, Dartmouth, using General Electric equipment, joined the time sharers.

*In retrospect, development of commercial time sharing is an outgrowth of the SABRE system (American Airlines) and Project MAC (military).*

***Important Time-sharing Developments.*** Other important developmental time-sharing systems were the SAGE and SABRE systems. SAGE (semiautomatic ground environment), which feeds the results of many radar observations into central computers and converts the data into displays of identified and unidentified planes in the air, was the first system with some of the elements of time sharing. Later IBM worked with American Airlines in establishing the SABRE reservation system where hundreds of American Airlines agents receive quick answers to as many as 2000 reservation queries a minute from a central processor.

In retrospect, the current stage of development for commercial time sharing is an outgrowth of the SABRE system and Project MAC. The SABRE system, an on-line real-time system, was instituted to coordinate a higher volume of passenger information at a shorter time interval than with manual methods. Project MAC was an attempt to reduce costs sufficiently which would allow a researcher to use a large scale computer as an extension of his reasoning power. The research required a turnaround time short enough to permit some degree of concentration on the problem. The SABRE project indicates the type of system that should be built while the other provides the broad base design techniques for implementing such systems. Basically, business time sharing is following the SABRE philosophy. It is one of coordinating and communicating information in an open-ended system that will serve as information storage and retrieval machine as opposed to being just a high speed calculator.

### Time Sharing Defined

*Time sharing permits users in different locations to share the same computer via I/O devices linked by telephone lines.*

*Time sharing* is defined as an environment in which many users in different locations share one computer at the same time via input/output terminals linked by telephone lines. The customer pays only for the time used, thereby, saving the individual considerable money for a computer available at all times. Within the time sharing environment, there are two basic approaches:

1. conversational processing,
2. remote batch processing.

Conversational processing is man interacting with the computer in an on-line processing mode.

***Conversational Processing.*** Conversational processing permits an individual to use a Teletype terminal or CRT terminal and dial the computer on his standard telephone. Basically, he places the receiver into an acoustical coupler interfaced to the terminal and is ready for on-line conversation with the computer. The high-speed response via typewriter input/output devices and cathode-ray-tube units provides a man/machine interactive relationship generally termed "conversational processing."

Remote batch processing is processing data accumulated for a period of time from a remote location.

***Remote Batch Processing.*** Remote batch processing is not time sharing in a conversational mode. Inherent is a time lapse factor which can be hours, days, or even weeks. However, in application, remote batch processing parallels time sharing processing. In this form of processing, the operator enters the data into a local processor. It processes the data and/or communicates with a larger central computer that responds to the local processor which, then, outputs the processed response. Operating in this type of mode, remote batch processing implies the use of entirely different types of terminals than are used in time sharing. Terminals used in remote batch can range from small, uncomplicated input/output devices, such as reader and printer, to another computer as the remote terminal.

**Reasons for Time Sharing**

The most frequently mentioned reasons for using time sharing are: convenience, flexibility, man-machine interface, and low cost.

Before exploring the basic characteristics of time sharing, it would be helpful to explore the rationale for its rapid growth. There are many reasons, the most frequently mentioned ones being:

1. convenience and ease of getting started,
2. application flexibility,
3. faster programming with man-machine interaction,
4. low cost.

***Implementation Factors.*** A remote terminal can be installed wherever there is electric power and telephone circuits. There are a number of portable terminals which can be operated from any standard telephone without special installation. In a similar manner, most users can acquire an on-line service in a matter of weeks or even hours while it may take months or years to install a conventional (batch) computer. Also, it is easy to divest oneself of this capability if it fails to meet the firm's needs.

***Application Flexibility.*** A time-sharing system has the added advantage of being a small computer to many users or a large dedicated system when required. One user may be using it as a desk calculator while another as a powerful system simulator. This application flexibility gained by the user is certainly not available with a batch processing system. Thus, flexibility can be a significant reason for utilizing time sharing devices.

***Faster Programming.*** With a conventional computer system, program development can be an extremely long, costly, and drawn out affair. The computer cannot be used for other processing when on-line computer debugging takes place. Time sharing can cut drastically into this delay of waiting for available computer debugging time. Many users report programs have been solved and running in much less time than required for a batch machine since the problem solver can communicate directly with the machine in a man-machine interaction mode. This is in contrast with a batch processing computer system where program cards must be converted to a computer input medium and proofed before entering the computer. An individual is not bogged down with intermediate steps, that is, he works directly with the programmed problem and the time-shared computer. This direct man-machine interaction frequently leads to ideas, insights, and an understanding of the relevant problem variables and interrelationships that are not possible with conventional methods. In essence, the programmer can ask questions that occur to him during the on-line debugging process which were not foreseen in the beginning. Also, he can alter the framework of the problem, if necessary while it is being solved.

***Low Cost.*** Low cost is an important reason for the growth of time sharing. A financial manager need not spend a considerable amount of time on a feasibility study. Quite often, he has the authority to expend several hundred to several thousand dollars per month for time sharing computer services. Since remote terminals, computer time-sharing services, and telephone lines are rented, everything is expensed monthly without the need to go through the formal organizational channels for large capital expenditures. Thus, some of the growth of time sharing can be ascribed to the ease of financial procedures in acquiring the system.

**Basic Characteristics of Time Sharing**

*Basic characteristics of time sharing encompass:*
- *real-time processing*
- *multiprogramming ability*
- *executive program control*
- *overhead time*
- *user data files and programs*
- *wide range of applications*

*Real-time processing allows the time-shared computer to respond in sufficient time to affect the operating environment of the user.*

*Multiprogramming ability permits the time-shared computer to work on many programs concurrently.*

The most basic of all time-sharing characteristics is the fact that remote terminals are connected directly on-line to the computer via a communication system (telephone lines usually). The on-line connection can be made or broken like an ordinary telephone call.

***Real-Time Processing.*** Time sharing is real-time in that it responds to user demands for computing service within specified time constraints. This allows the computer to become an "on-line" part of the operation being performed. Any time-sharing service, then, is basically an on-line real-time system that is shared by many user firms.

***Multiprogramming Ability.*** Time sharing is an extension of the multiprogramming concept which permits the computer to work on many programs concurrently. This is the reason why a time-sharing system is referred to as a multiple access system. Having this capability, each user has one or more input/output terminals connected by communication lines (telephone lines) to a central computer which responds as if the user is the only one utilizing the facility. Because of the speed of the central processing unit, the computer system can relay the output to the user almost immediately although the central processor is working on other programs at the same time. Thus, an essential characteristic of time sharing is the method of sharing the computer's main memory.

By and large, there are two methods for sharing the computer's central processing unit—*memory swapping* and *paging*. Under the memory swapping approach, the entire program is moved in or out of the computer's main memory. This results in having only one program in memory at a time. A very short period of time is allowed in main memory before the next program is brought in for processing. With the second approach, each program is segregated into a group of instructions called pages. These may range from a small number of instructions to a subroutine of a program, depending upon the size of the computer. When a specific program is to be run, a page (or group of pages) is (are) brought into the computer's main memory and executed. As a page is executed, its memory space can be released to the next page of the program. Pages from time sharing programs may be in memory simultaneously which allows the computer to switch back and forth among the programs.

***Executive Program Control.*** No matter what memory allocation approach is used, there is need for a supervisory program, sometimes referred to as an executive program. It schedules the processing of problems submitted by the terminals in

*Executive program schedules the processing of computer programs submitted by the I/O terminals and allocates memory in an optimum manner.*

use and copes with the problems of memory allocation between auxiliary and working storage areas. Furthermore, a larger high-speed memory is needed in a time-shared computer than in a batch processed computer for several reasons, one being a larger programming system has to be stored. For another, the problem and the corresponding data have to be stored in high speed memory not only while they are being processed, but also while the user is thinking at his terminal. In effect, a time-sharing problem occupies high-speed memory for a considerably longer period of time than it does with a comparable batch processing system.

*Overhead time which is approximately 40% for a time-sharing system consists of the following:*
- *swap time—20% to 30%*
- *overhead computation—about 5%*
- *relocation of memory—about 12%*

***Overhead Time.*** A characteristic of time sharing that is not found in batch processing systems is "overhead" time. This is defined as that part of the system's execution time which is not devoted directly to the execution of problems submitted by users. It is the time necessary for the system to engage in certain coordinating and recording activities each time the processing of a problem is interrupted for memory swapping or paging. Based upon past studies, swap time (time spent transferring data from main memory to auxiliary memory and back because of program interrupts) represents 20% to 30% of the total time in a time sharing system. Also, overhead computation is approximately 5% of the total available time, leaving normal computation time anywhere from 60 to 70%. However, the execution of a problem is increased by approximately 20% for the inclusion of relocatability of the memory. This means that additional overhead time on direct execution of user problems has to be considered. Hence, about 20% of the 60 to 70% of normal computation time mentioned above or approximately 12% must be added to the total overhead time. Total overhead time, then, is about 40% for a typical time-sharing system.

On the surface, the process of moving programs in and out of memory may appear to be slow in terms of waiting at time sharing terminals. Even though there is more main memory processing time for a time-sharing computer versus a batch processing computer, the machine will normally be waiting on the terminal operator. With a computer where the difference in speed between the machine and the human may be 1,000,000 to 1, the ratio of actual computing time to elapsed time may be extremely small. In a well-designed time-sharing system, the time lost for one user is filled up with the processing of other customers, say from 20 to 150, depending upon the size system. Such a system serves simultaneously many users, with each user feeling free to interact with the computer as if it was his own private machine. Thus, the inefficiency or overhead of a time-sharing system, for the most part, is not critical enough to cause the user to wait at the input/output terminal.

*User data files and programs are maintained on-line by the time sharing computer and are identified by the user's instructions or codes.*

***User Data Files and Programs.*** The user's data files are maintained at the time-sharing computer center where the user's instructions identify the files to be employed. This arrangement prevents a user from making unauthorized entry into the files of another user. In like manner, each user has his own set of programs which are stored by the time-sharing system or are read via the time sharing terminal through its punched paper tape attachment (if available). Also, there is a library of time-sharing programs which are available to users.

*A wide range of business applications are depicted in Figure 9-22.*

***Wide Range of Applications.*** Among the more prominent applications are: mathematical calculations (most common usage), statistics, programming, debugging, simulation, and operations research. Other areas include: accounting, budgeting, circuit design, data bank use, education, forecasting, investment analysis, market research, mechanical design, project planning, reliability, scientific research, sales analysis, and stress analysis. As shown in Figure 9-22, current business applications are certainly far reaching and will continue to increase in the future.

| FINANCIAL ANALYSIS | MANAGEMENT CONSULTING |
|---|---|
| Sales forecasting<br>Financial statement preparation<br>Rate of return analysis—current and future<br>Alternative project evaluation—decision tree analysis<br>Order entry processing<br>New product pricing analysis<br>Monthly sales analysis<br>Credit screening<br>Corporate wide long range planning<br>Accounts receivable analysis<br>Accounts payable<br>Product cost analysis<br>New product pricing strategy studies<br>Predictions on new products performance<br>Cash budgeting<br>Project evaluation analysis<br>Cash reconciliation<br>Depreciation and amortization | Facilities location<br>Pension plan funding projections<br>Cash budget model<br>Urban management studies<br>Analysis of capital investment<br>Acquisition and merger analysis<br>Personnel scheduling<br>Inventory system studies—simulation<br>Lease or buy analysis<br>Distribution system analysis<br>Transportation problem model<br>Queuing studies<br>Population projection programs<br>School projection models<br>Advertising expense allocation<br>Linear programming models<br>Non-linear programming models<br>Fleet scheduling<br>PERT/Time and PERT/Cost networks<br>Simulation studies<br>Optimization models<br>Economic ordering quantity models<br>Dynamic programming models<br>Markov analysis chains<br>Game theory models |

| FINANCIAL INSTITUTIONS |
|---|
| Evaluation of alternative savings interest plans<br>Financial lease analysis<br>Credit scoring (ranking) analysis<br>Cash flow forecasting<br>Installment loan program<br>Rate of return on capital investments<br>Financial statement preparation<br>Ratio analysis<br>Effective yield-to-maturity calculations<br>Pension fund performance<br>Portfolio analysis<br>Scheduling loan payments<br>Financial lease rate calculations<br>Financial statement analysis |

| INVESTMENT |
|---|
| Legal capital requirements evaluation<br>Corporate earnings projection<br>Bond redemption calculations<br>Bond bidding and pricing models<br>Portfolio evaluation and selection<br>Economic forecasting<br>Real estate financing<br>Merger analysis<br>Rate of return analysis |

| MANUFACTURING |
|---|
| Factory payroll<br>Machine utilization program<br>Overhead distribution program<br>Production scheduling<br>Facilities and plant location<br>Cost analysis<br>Cost estimating<br>Project control monitor<br>Project evaluation<br>Inventory control and analysis<br>Acquisition evaluation<br>Job shop simulation model<br>Production analysis<br>Direct labor planning<br>Lead time for purchasing<br>Make or buy determination<br>Long range production planning—linear programming<br>Quality control<br>Numerical control tape preparation<br>Critical path network analysis |

Figure 9-22 Selected time sharing business applications in use and under development.

*The type of terminal devices—portable, typewriter, CRT, and multifunction—used are dependent upon the time sharing environment.*

### Time-Sharing Terminal Devices

There is a wide range of terminal devices for a time-sharing system. The user operates with his own terminal devices which are connected by communication lines to a time sharing computer system. Data are inserted into the terminal from which output is obtained by means of programmed instructions. Basically, time-sharing input/output devices are divided into four types:

1. portable terminals,
2. typewriter terminals,
3. visual CRT terminals,
4. multifunction terminals.

***Portable Terminals.*** Portable terminals, previously shown in Figures 9-8 through 9-11, allow the user to travel to the problem itself and solve it right on the spot. For example, it allows one to take a physical inventory at some remote location and report the items after they have been counted for an immediate comparison to the perpetual inventory maintained on-line.

***Typewriter Terminals.*** A typewriter terminal for time sharing, operating at 10 characters per second, is depicted in Figure 9-23 (also portable typewriter unit per Figure 9-11). Teletype terminals are widely used for time sharing and can produce punched paper tape (Figure 9-23) as a by-product.

Figure 9-23 Teletype Model 33 ASR set. (Courtesy Teletype Corporation.)

***Visual CRT Terminals.*** A time-sharing terminal device, explored in a prior section, is the visual CRT display unit, shown in Figure 9-24. It is gaining in popularity due to its speed and flexibility, that is, the capability to display printed and graphic information at a much faster speed than typed information. An added advantage

Figure 9-24 IBM 2260 Display Station with alphanumeric keyboard. (Courtesy International Business Machines Corporation.)

is its ability to delete and change characters or words selectively in desired records or files. Its major disadvantages are slightly higher costs and lack of hard copy in most cases.

***Multifunctional Terminals.*** The foregoing time-sharing terminals may not be sufficiently flexible enough for many time sharing installations. For such systems, there are a few time sharing devices that combine a reasonably fast printout and card reading with the use of a typewriter and paper tape input/output. Shown in Figure 9-25 is a UNIVAC DCT 2000 remote input/output batch terminal which consists of a card reader, card punch, and a printer. As indicated in its name, it is capable of remote batch processing. Even though these input/output devices are slow when compared with similar computer equipment, their speeds approach the limit of the standard voice-band grade channels which are sufficient for the average time sharing user.

*A typical time-sharing computer system, such as the Honeywell Model 430, includes these hardware components:*

- *Datanet-30*
- *central processing unit*
- *console unit*
- *time sharing control terminal*
- *card reader*
- *printer*
- *disk storage units.*

**Time-Sharing Computer System**

A time-sharing computer system, connected to one or more of the above terminals, may be located nearby or hundreds of miles from the user's terminals. In Figure 9-26, a Honeywell Model 430 time-sharing computer system is pictured. An examination of the peripheral equipment indicates that the major unit peculiar to this time-sharing system is the Datanet-30. This piece of hardware enables terminal devices, up to 30, to communicate simultaneously with the computer system over common carrier channels.

***Datanet-30.*** The communications executive program resides within the Datanet-30. It may be divided into real-time and spare-time segments. The real-time

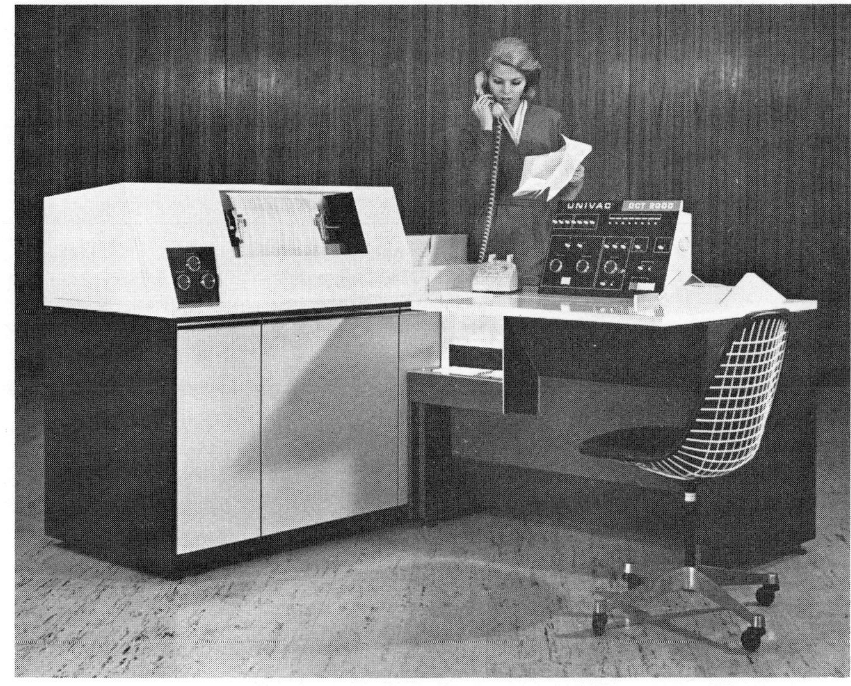


Figure 9-25 UNIVAC DCT 2000 Multifunction Remote Input/Output Batch Terminal. (Courtesy UNIVAC Division of the Sperry Rand Corporation.)

*Datanet-30 is responsible for the proper handling of all incoming calls from time-sharing terminals.*

portion has the responsibility for handling interrupts caused by the interval times (necessary to handle the swapping of programs), servicing the lines of the time sharing terminals, and setting up tasks for the spare-time segment. The spare-time segment is responsible for user validation, command analysis, servicing the computer interface unit, processing disk input/output, and communicating with the time-sharing executive. Functions, such as creating new programs, entry of source code, listing of old programs, creating data files are handled primarily by the Datanet-30. Figure 9-27 illustrates the allocation of core memory within the unit.

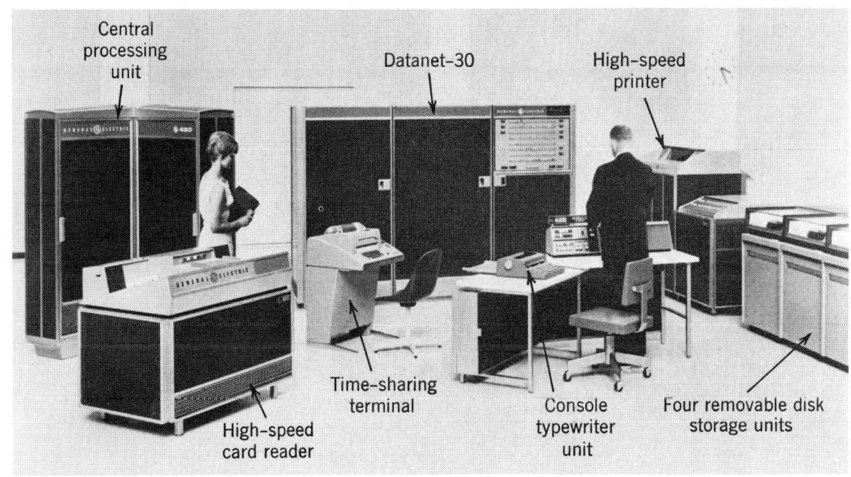


Figure 9-26 Honeywell Model 430 Time-Sharing Computer System. (Courtesy Honeywell Information Systems.)

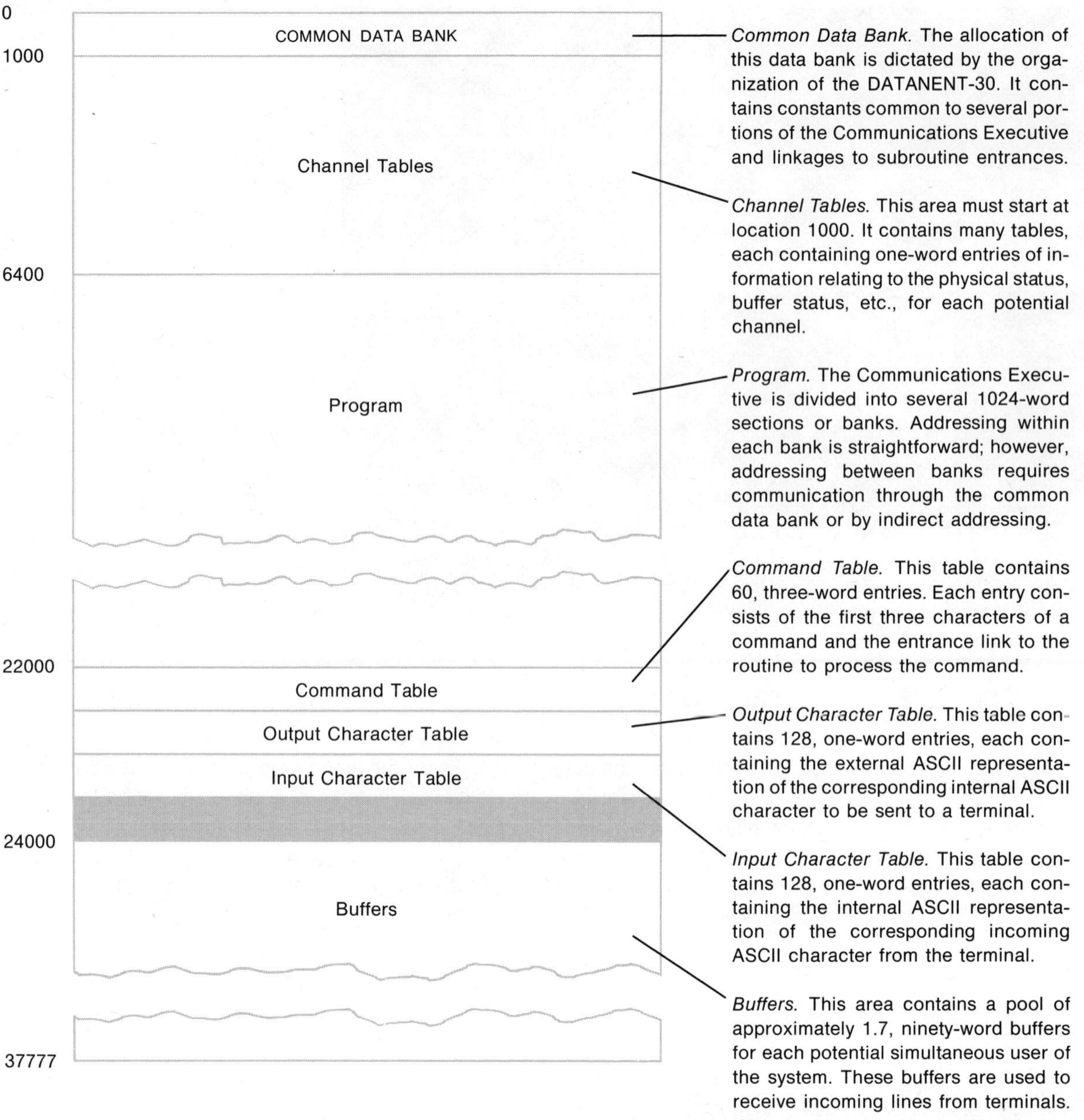

0
1000
6400
22000
24000
37777
COMMON DATA BANK
Channel Tables
Program
Command Table
Output Character Table
Input Character Table
Buffers
*Common Data Bank.* The allocation of this data bank is dictated by the organization of the DATANENT-30. It contains constants common to several portions of the Communications Executive and linkages to subroutine entrances.
*Channel Tables.* This area must start at location 1000. It contains many tables, each containing one-word entries of information relating to the physical status, buffer status, etc., for each potential channel.
*Program.* The Communications Executive is divided into several 1024-word sections or banks. Addressing within each bank is straightforward; however, addressing between banks requires communication through the common data bank or by indirect addressing.
*Command Table.* This table contains 60, three-word entries. Each entry consists of the first three characters of a command and the entrance link to the routine to process the command.
*Output Character Table.* This table contains 128, one-word entries, each containing the external ASCII representation of the corresponding internal ASCII character to be sent to a terminal.
*Input Character Table.* This table contains 128, one-word entries, each containing the internal ASCII representation of the corresponding incoming ASCII character from the terminal.
*Buffers.* This area contains a pool of approximately 1.7, ninety-word buffers for each potential simultaneous user of the system. These buffers are used to receive incoming lines from terminals.


Figure 9-27 Datanet-30, allocation of memory. (Courtesy Honeywell Information Systems.)

*The time-sharing executive program is composed of three parts:*
- *input/output supervisor*
- *processing supervisor*
- *file edit processor*

***Time-Sharing Executive Program.*** The time sharing executive program which resides in the central processing unit is shown in Figure 9-28 as part of the computer's memory. It is composed of three major components:

1. the input/output supervisor,
2. the processing supervisor,
3. the file edit processor.

Control of the interaction of peripherals and the file system is the function of the input/output supervisor. With regard to file control, it allocates and deallocates

| Memory area | Address | Register |
|---|---|---|
| | 0 | |
| Time-sharing Executive Program | | |
| | 11.5K | BAR#1 |
| Time-sharing Area #1 | | |
| | 21K | LR#1 |
| State Vector #1 | | |
| | 21.5K | BAR#2 |
| Time-sharing Area #2 | | |
| | 31K | LR#2 |
| State Vector #2 | | |
| | 31.5K | |
| Disk Allocation Table | | |
| | 32K | |

*Time-sharing Executive.* The "time-sharing executive" is completely core resident. It has no overlays other than system processors which are read into one of the time-sharing areas.

*Time-sharing Areas.* These two areas are used for compilation and execution of the users' programs and for certain miscellaneous functions within the "file edit processor." The occupants of these areas are called jobs. One job is active, being productive, while a job is being swapped in or out of the other area.

*State Vectors.* These two areas are associated with the time-sharing areas. Their major purpose is to hold the residue words from the beginning and ending sectors read from and/or written to disk-resident files.

*Disk Allocation Table.* This table is maintained to contain entries designating nonallocated space on disk. The disk allocator and deallocator routines maintain and use this table to optimize disk usage.

Figure 9-28 Honeywell Model 430, allocation of memory in the central processing unit. (Courtesy Honeywell Information Systems.)

areas on the disk while opening, closing, reading, and writing all files. The processing supervisor services interrupts from the central processor and serves as a job scheduler by swapping programs in and out of core. This section of the program performs functions, such as core allocation, job termination, and handles any overlaying that may be necessary. The third component of the time sharing executive—the file edit processor—has responsibility for inserting, deleting, and substituting lines within a file. It also processes part of the file commands.

*A comparable time-sharing entry from IBM is the System/360 Model 67.*

***IBM System/360 Model 67 Time-Sharing Computer System.*** A larger time-sharing computer system, illustrated in Figure 9-29, is the IBM System/360 Model 67-2 Duplex configuration. This duplex model allows shared use of the multiple processor storage units by two central processing units, making available as many as two million bytes of storage to either unit. It also allows the partitioning of the components into separate subsystems for maximum flexibility and availability. In addition to its time-sharing capability, the Model 67 can economically and efficiently handle huge libraries of data and can work around temporarily disabled components without disturbing critical jobs.

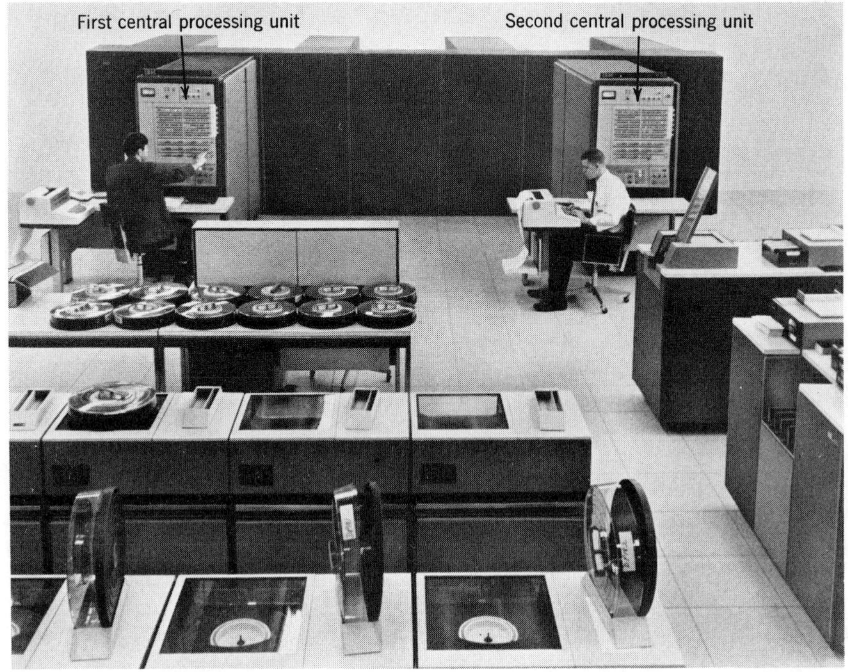


Figure 9-29 IBM System/360 Model 67-2 Duplex configuration. (Courtesy International Business Machines Corporation.)

### Computer Backup

*Computer backup with duplicated programs and files is the best protective step where reliability is a must.*

All computer systems fail occasionally while time sharing systems seem especially prone to reliability problems. (Of the many manufacturers of time sharing equipment, no one vendor is rated significantly more reliable than any other.) This appears to be the major criticism of time sharing based upon several studies. Many users of time sharing have found the system to be down at the most inopportune times. The best protective step where reliability is a must is a backup computer with duplicate programs and files of data. It may be years before the time-sharing industry is able to provide as reliable service as the utility and telephone companies.

Depending upon the type of application involved, there may or may not be a need for computer backup. For example, small savings and loan associations, utilizing a time shared computer, would have need for computer backup since customers are not expected to wait for service. In such a case, a backup computer is necessary. On the other hand, an engineer solving a mathematical problem can perform other productive activities while waiting for repairs to the machine. The need for backup services, then, is conditioned upon the necessity of having a computer available at all times for data to be processed.

### Programming a Time-Shared Computer

*Programming and debugging in a time-sharing conversational mode is faster for many programs than using a batch processing mode.*

When using a time shared computer, the user must define his problem, design his own computational procedure(s), and either use a time sharing library program or write his own. The programming aspect of time sharing is not that difficult since many programming languages are available to the user. Some of these programming languages can be learned in a matter of hours for programming simple programs. Of the many languages available, FORTRAN, BASIC, COBOL, PL/1, ALGOL, and

QUIKTRAN are the more frequently ones used by the various time sharing studies. In terms of use, they appear in the foregoing order.

For the most part, programs are run more quickly with the services of time sharing since an on-line conversational mode of writing and debugging programs is employed. The conversational mode allows for program statements to be examined, resulting in questions being asked or printed diagnostic errors by the computer. In turn, the user responds with answers, corrected statements, or questions. This interaction between the two continues until a correct program has been written. With a direct man-machine approach, much of the time involved in testing batch processing programs is eliminated.

*The procedural steps for developing a "yearly compound interest" program are relatively easy and straight forward in a time-sharing mode.*

***Time-sharing Program Illustration.*** A typical program per Figure 9-30 indicates the simplicity of using a time-sharing terminal. The programming language employed is BASIC. (This programming language is described in Chapter 10.) The steps involved in producing a "yearly compound interest" program are set forth below:

1. The user turns on the terminal typewriter device and dials the telephone number for the time sharing service.
2. When a high-pitched tone is heard in the handset, a connection with the computer has been made. The handset is placed in the acoustic coupler, a small box with two rubber insulated openings (attached to the terminal). If a busy signal is heard, the time sharing service should be dialed again after waiting 10 to 15 seconds. This procedure should be repeated until a high-pitched tone is heard in the handset.
3. When the handset is placed in the acoustic coupler, the time sharing system causes some identifying information (name of time-sharing service, time, and terminal number) to be printed by the terminal device (first two lines of Figure 9-30). Then, the terminal will type USER NUMBER—and stop (third line). The individual types in the appropriate number (X002 in this case) and depresses the RETURN button.
4. The system next types PASSWORD (fourth line) and positions itself on the next line (fifth line) for a response. The operator enters the password and depresses the RETURN button. The system conceals the password by typing X's over the password.
5. The system then asks the question—TYPE OLD OR NEW (sixth line). The operator responds by typing NEW for this particular program and depresses the RETURN button. On the next line (seventh), the system asks the PROBLEM NAME. The operator types INT, again depressing the RETURN button.
6. The system types out READY (eighth line) and stops. The individual depresses the RETURN button and is now ready to enter the program in BASIC—lines 10 through 60 as illustrated for calculating yearly compound interest. After entering the program, the operator types RUN and depresses the RETURN button. The system responds to typing the name of the program—INT and other identifying information (time, name of time sharing service, date, and day).
7. On the next line, the system prints ENTER VALUES FOR P, I, N. (These three names P, I, N, are extracted by the computer from the foregoing BASIC program. Also, a question mark (?) is printed by the system on the next line. The respective values, in the example, are entered by the operator which are 1000 (for principal), .06 (annual rate of interest), and 10 (number of years). Again the RETURN button must be depressed.
8. The system responds by calculating and printing out the results for the 10 years as indicated. It prints the running time in minutes and/or seconds. Also, it prints the word READY. Since the program has been completed, the operator types the word BYE (this command disconnects the terminal from the system) and

```
                         APPLIED CØMPUTER TIME SHARE CIN

ØN AT- 16:24  PØRT:12

USER NUMBER --X002

PASSWØRD

TYPE ØLD ØR NEW:NEW

PRØBLEM NAME: INT

READY

10 PRINT "ENTER VALUES FØR P, I, N"
15  INPUT P, I, N
20  PRINT
25  PRINT,  "CUMULATIVE"
30  PRINT "YEAR", "INTEREST", "TØTAL AMØUNT"
35  FØR J=1 TØ N
40  LET X = P*(1+I)
45  PRINT J, X-R, X
50  LET P=X
55  NEXT J
60  END
RUN

INT

                           16:26 ACTS 02/21/71 SAT.

ENTER VALUES FØR P, I, N
?1000, .06, 10.

                     CUMULATIVE
YEAR                  INTEREST              TØTAL AMØUNT
  1                    60.                     1060.
  2                    63.6                    1123.6
  3                    67.416                  1191.02
  4                    71.461                  1262.40
  5                    75.7486                 1338.23
  6                    80.2935                 1418.52
  7                    85.1111                 1503.63
  8                    90.2178                 1593.85
  9                    95.6309                 1689.48
 10                    101.369                 1790.35

RUNNING TIME: 01.0 SECS.

READY
BYE

ØFF AT 16:28
```

Figure 9-30 Sample output from a "yearly compound interest" program on a time-sharing service.

depresses the RETURN button. The final line to be printed by the system is the time signed off by the system.

It should be noted that there may be a programming error in one or more of the above program steps. If such a case should arise, the program is not executed, but diagnostic error messages are typed out.

### System Commands

*System commands instruct the time-sharing system as to what action is to be taken concerning the program itself. On the other hand, program instructions specify the mathematical and logical operations that must be performed within the program to accomplish the desired output.*

BASIC program instructions allow the programmer to instruct the computer in terms of his desired output program. In addition, to these programming elements—numbers, variables, arithmetic operations, statements, functions, and additional programming features (to be explained in the next chapter), there are system commands which instruct the computer as to what action is to be taken concerning the program. They permit the user to converse with the computer. A listing of these system commands for the Honeywell 430 Time Sharing System is depicted in Figure 9-31. Many of these commands are in response to questions asked by the computer, such as NEW or OLD. Others are initiated by the operator, such as RUN. These latter commands are sent to the computer by typing the command at the beginning of the new line (no line numbers needed) and depressing the carriage RETURN key. All commands are executed by the computer as soon as they are interpreted by the operating system.

### Economics of Time Sharing

*Economic justification for time sharing lies in the increased productivity of the individual's time.*

The economics of time sharing can be discussed from two points of view, namely, as an owner of a system and as a user of a system. If one is a supplier of time-sharing services to other users, the cost of a moderate scale system would be broken down as follows (approximate figures):

| | |
|---|---|
| Terminals and multiplexor (i.e., Datanet) | 40% |
| Central processing unit | 20% |
| Direct access storage | 20% |
| Peripherals (reader, printer, tape, etc.) | 20% |

A time-sharing computer system is not as efficient as a batch processing system because of the overhead time. Higher costs will be experienced with the time-sharing system due to the total overhead of the central processing unit. However, experience has indicated that most central processing units are idle a large percent of the time when solving business problems in a batch mode. The reason is that the system is either input or output bound due to the speed of the slowest peripheral unit. (The same generalization is not always true of engineering and scientific applications.) In fact, this is the rationale for using somewhat inefficient programming languages, such as COBOL since the CPU is idle so much of the time. The conclusion to be drawn from the foregoing are: both batch processing computer systems and time sharing computer systems utilize the central processing unit in an inefficient manner; and the total overhead time of the central processing unit does add to the cost of time sharing as does the cost of the terminals, multiplexors, additional memory, and communication channels. Furthermore, consideration must be given to overall efficiency in terms of human productivity for a higher cost time sharing computer system. The individual's efficiency, whether in the area of programming and debugging, requesting data from the system, or preparing data for the files of the computer, may improve so much that the increased costs yield economically justi-

| | |
|---|---|
| *Directive* | |
| • BYE | Disconnects from the system |
| • GOODBYE | Disconnects from the system |
| • HELLO | Change user number |
| • NEW: program name | Introduces a new temporary file and conditions system to operate on a new program. |
| • OLD: program name | Retrieves from the file system a previously saved program and conditions the system to operate on it. |
| • RESTART | Same as HELLO |
| • RETURN* | Terminates a program line, causes the system to take action based upon input entered, and acts as a normal carriage return. |
| • RUN | Compiles and executes the current program file. |
| • RUNBIG | Allows the user to run a program significantly larger than possible under standard RUN option. |
| • RUN: program name | Eliminates portions of the calling sequence formerly necessary to run a program. Cuts calling sequence by 50%. |
| • RUNNH: program name | Eliminates normal header line output of program name, time of day, time-sharing system identification, and date. |
| • SAVE | Permanently stores the current temporary program file in the file system. |
| • SAVE: password | Permanently stores the current temporary program file in the file system protecting that program file by a password. |
| • SAVE: , , E | Store the current program file with execute only permission. |
| • SAVE: , , W | Store the current data file with write only permission. |
| • SAVE: , , A | Store the current data file with append only permission. |
| • SAVE: , , R | Store the current file with read only permission. |
| • SCRATCH | Eliminates everything but the file name from the current temporary program file. |
| • STOP | Causes the system to stop whatever it is doing with the program (a BREAK character must be used when printing is occurring). |
| • UNSAVE | Used to release and destroy a previously saved program. |
| • UNSAVE: password | Used to release and destroy a previously saved program protected by a password. |
| *Edit* | |
| • CONTROL with X | Deletes an input line as if nothing has been typed. |
| • BACK ARROW (←) | Deletes the last character typed. The SHIFT key must be depressed. This is the character on the O key. |
| • LIST | To list current copy of working program. |
| • LISTNH | Lists the current temporary program file without heading information. |
| • LIST: nnn | Lists the current temporary program file beginning at line nnn, where nnn is one-to-five-digit line number. |
| • LISTNH: nnn | Lists the current temporary program file without heading information, beginning at line nnn. |
| • RENAME | Changes the file name but not the contents of the temporary file. |
| *Informative* | |
| • CAT | Lists a user catalog of files. |
| • LENGTH | To request number of characters in a working program. |
| • STATUS | Used to request present relationship to the system (idle, run, old, list, etc.) |
| • TTY | Requests the data communications processor number, channel, number, user number, file name, system name, and status. |
| *Mode* | |
| • KEY | Resets terminal operation to normal after reading in paper tape. |
| • TAPE | Informs the system that paper tape will be read in. |
| • SYSTEM:BASIC SYS:BAS | To denote BASIC programming language. |
| • SYSTEM:FORTRAN SYS:FOR | To denote FORTRAN programming language. |

*Special key on Teletype unit

Figure 9-31 Honeywell-400 Time Sharing System Commands. (Courtesy Honeywell Information Systems) fiable results for a time sharing computer. As noted previously, a time-sharing system eliminates most of the need for completing forms, key punching and verifying, batching, dispatching, and logging the data.

*Several bases have been developed to determine time sharing costs.*

***Typical Time-sharing Costs.*** The problem of establishing time sharing costs is not difficult since standard charges have been established. The pricing structure recognizes basic services. They are: number of terminals being served; communication or telephone line costs; total time for terminal linked to a computer; time which is spent by the terminal for computing; and memory, disk file, or tape file storage required to serve a terminal. Typical charges for time sharing services are:

| | |
|---|---|
| • Terminal equipment: | |
| Receive-Only (RO) Printer | $100.000 per month |
| Keyboard Send/Receive (KSR) | 113.50 per month |
| KSR plus RO | 170.000 per month |
| • Communication charges: | |
| Channel terminating charge | |
| first terminal | 30.00 per month |
| each additional terminal | 10.00 per month |
| Mileage charge (up to 100 miles) | 2.34 per month |
| • On-line file storage per 1000 words | 2.50 per month |
| • On-line transactions: | |
| Invoice header | 0.075 each |
| Bill lines | 0.025 each |
| Accounts receivable cash posting | 0.025 each |
| Miscellaneous inventory | 0.025 each |
| File maintenance | 0.025 each |
| Inquiries | 0.015 each |
| • Off-line reports per 1000 lines | 3.00 |

In many cases, the costs of the terminals, telephone lines, and communication data sets are the responsibility of the user.

Another method for determining time sharing charges establishes a minimum use charge of $100 per month with actual charges determined by the following formula:

Terminal units + line costs + data sets + hook-up fees + computing fees + file fees = total costs

Hook-up time is measured for the month, charged at $10 per hour, while computation time is $.04 per second. Disk file storage is based on actual usage in units of 1536 characters where the rate on a unit of storage is $2.50 per month. This pricing approach, like most, requires an internal computer program to collect terminal hook-up time to the minute, compute CPU times to the second, and determine the number of 1536 character units for file storage.

*Time-sharing costs can range from as low as $100 monthly to several hundred dollars where the usage factor is the basic determinant of cost.*

***Monthly Time-sharing Costs.*** The minimum fee, for a single terminal connected to a local time-sharing center over a switched toll line, is about $100.000 monthly. Depending upon the services and amount of time utilized, most time sharing devices cost from $200 to $600 per month for normal usage. The cost of a multipurpose input/output terminal (capable of reading and punching cards) is considerably more since its rental cost is $400 to $600 per month versus $50 to $200 per month for typewriter terminal devices. The cost of using CRT display devices is also higher than ordinary hard copy devices since their rental costs alone range up to $400 per month. No matter what approach is used by the firm, the user must provide the personnel, supplies, and programming (if library routines are not used).

*Generally, time-sharing equipment can be justified economically where there are a number of clerks performing manual tasks.*

***Time-sharing Feasibility Study.*** Case studies on the feasibility of time sharing has indicated that firms which have a number of clerks performing manual tasks is in an excellent position to employ time sharing services. On the other hand, those companies that have kept their clerical staff to a minimum will find it difficult to justify time-sharing devices. A case in point is the following study—time sharing costs are based upon the first set of data given above.

The firm has sales over one million. It services 300 retailers and has 900 inventory items. Formerly, all accounts receivable and inventory processing was performed by one working supervisor and six clerks. While the accounts receivable functions (invoice preparation, invoice postings, monthly statement preparation, credit check, and aging accounts receivable) were handled by a Burroughs machine and manual methods, the inventory was maintained on a Kardex file. Additional but less voluminous processing was performed in the following areas: ordering from suppliers, maintenance of accounts payable, payroll, and other general accounting functions. The annual cost of the previous manual system (excluding depreciation on the machinery) was:

| | |
|---|---|
| 1 working supervisor | $ 7,500 |
| 6 clerks—$5,500 each | 33,000 |
| Total annual costs (includes fringe benefits) | $40,500 |

Requirements for the time-sharing system include four persons—a working supervisor and three clerks plus three terminal devices. The costs associated with the new system are:

| | | |
|---|---|---|
| • Terminal equipment: | | $397.00 |
| 1 KSR plus RO device | $170.00 | |
| 2 KSR devices @ $113.50 | 227.00 | |
| • Channel terminating charges | | 50.00 |
| • On-line file storage | | 60.00 |
| 300 retailers | | |
| 900 inventory items | | |
| 1200 × 20 words (average) @ $2.50 per thousand | | |
| • On-line transactions | | 395.00 |
| 1000 invoices @ $.35 | | |
| (header @ $.075 + 11 items (average) @ $.025 | $350.00 | |
| 1000 receivable postings @ $.025 | 25.00 | |
| 300 customer statements @ $.025 | 7.50 | |
| 500 miscellaneous transactions @ $.025 | 12.50 | |
| • Off-line reports (estimated) | | 30.00 |
| 10,000 lines @ $3.00 per thousand | | |
| Total monthly service costs for time sharing | | $932.00 |

Restating the above monthly service cost on an annual basis, the cost is $11,184 or $11,200 approximately. The total amount per year for time sharing is:

| | |
|---|---|
| Service (as computed above) | $11,200 |
| Personnel: | |
| 1 working supervisor | 7,500 |
| 3 clerks—@ $ $5,500 each | 16,500 |
| Total annual costs (includes fringe benefits) | $35,200 |

Based upon a comparison of the two systems, the time sharing system has reduced costs by $5,300 or 13% yearly over the old manual system. It should be obvious why this particular study has resulted in favorable results to the firm, namely, a reduction in the number of clerks to perform the necessary data processing functions.

## VIRTUAL MACHINE OPERATION

The benefits of programming in a time-sharing environment versus a batch processing one can help relieve the programming bottlenecks within the firm. However, there are several problems with programming in a time sharing mode. Too often, programs are not transferable from one time sharing system to another or to an in-house batch system. It is still necessary to accept the time sharing company's language processor. Sometimes, the time sharing system is resource limited and the program must go to a larger batch oriented system. Thus, problems are associated with a time sharing approach to programming.

*Virtual machine operation allows a user to specify a machine configuration that he would like to use.*

***Virtual Machine Control Program.*** To overcome these difficulties, IBM developed a "virtual machine" control program that simulates a set of computers so that each user has a complete computer to himself.[1] A *virtual machine control program* allows a user to specify the machine configuration that he would like to use and to run his own choice of language processor and operation system simultaneously with other users on the system. No longer is the user stuck with limited languages and the need for program conversions. The virtual machine configurations can be different in memory size, number of input/output channels, and devices from any other user's virtual machine or from the real machine. In fact, the virtual machines can be larger than the real machine and possess simulated equipment not available on the real machine. For example, the real machine may have 512K of core memory and eight disk drives while one of the virtual machines may have 768K and ten disk drives.

For the virtual memory of each virtual machine, there are segment and page tables. The IBM System/360 Model 67, for example, has the necessary hardware to handle the segmentation and paging. With the 360/67, the page size is 4K bytes and there are 256 pages to a segment. With 24-bit addressing, there is a maximum possible virtual memory of 16 segments or approximately 16 million bytes for each user. However, the usual core sizes, specified by the users, range from 256K and one million bytes since larger sizes tend to be wasteful of core storage for control blocks.

In a typical virtual machine operation, the user is in a location remote from the computer. He communicates with the computer via a typewriter terminal which serves as the control console of his simulated machine. With a set of simple com-

[1] Jeffrey N. Bairstow, "Many from One: the 'Virtual Machine' Arrives," *Computer Decisions,* January 1970, p. 29.

mands, the user can create and operate his virtual machine as though he had the same control facilities as the operator of a real machine. When the user logs in, a virtual machine is created for him, each machine being represented by tables and blocks in the virtual machine control program. Since the virtual machine appears to the user to be a single machine, the user can operate as though he had a real machine. He can work interactively for program development or non-interactively for remote batch of production programs. In essence, each virtual computer user has a terminal which acts as his computer console.

## MULTIPROGRAMMING

*Multiprogramming is also applicable to a batch processing system. It allows the user to optimize his total available computer resources by using a:*
- *fixed number of tasks (MFT)*
- *variable number of tasks (MVT)*

The multiprogramming concept is found in a time-sharing computer environment, as noted previously. But just as important is its application to a batch processing mode of operation. The major objective of a multiprogramming system is to optimize the use of the total available computer resources. These resources include the core memory, the central processing unit, and the input/output devices in the system. To achieve this, jobs will not be organized into the type of sequential job streams used in a normal batch facility. Instead priorities will be set, and even hierarchies of priorities, to allow a job mix that most fully utilizes these facilities.

There are basically two types of multiprogramming systems. In the IBM System/360 and System/370, for example, there is multiprogramming with a fixed number of tasks (MFT) and multiprogramming with a variable number of tasks (MVT).[2]

*Multiprogramming with a fixed number of tasks allows allocating a fixed portion of memory to the processing of each job.*

***Fixed Number of Tasks (MFT).*** Multiprogramming with a fixed number of tasks consists of a set number of fixed sized core partitions. Each fixed sized core partition is dedicated to the processing of one job only. Quite often, the partition size will be much larger than the program size. In such a system, some core memory space is wasted. For example, a system with fixed partitions of 100K each would be half used while running 50K programs.

The users in such a system are responsible for determining the core memory partitions to be used by each program, the input/output device allocations, and various other functions. Because of this, the MFT system has a smaller portion of its core area dedicated to supervisory or operating system functions and can, therefore, offer the user control over a somewhat greater portion of his core memory space than would a system with a variable number of tasks.

*Multiprogramming with a variable number of tasks permits allocating memory in a manner that will optimize its capacity.*

***Variable Number of Tasks (MVT).*** A multiprogramming system with a variable number of tasks can optimize the use of the total resource available in a more efficient manner. Logic is provided to enable the system to direct the processing sequence according to the pattern it selects and to communicate with the system operator to indicate the input/output pattern that it is currently running. To accomplish this, the MVT system employs dynamic core partitioning techniques. The system selects the jobs it will run from the job queues that are in readily accessible storage, such as disk files. Depending on the pattern to optimize resources that the system selects, a multiprogramming job in process could consist of several tasks running concurrently. Each job step might consist of one or more tasks running concurrently.

In preparing programs for multiprogramming operations, two essential factors

[2] "Multiprogramming Does More for Less," *Computer Decisions,* June 1970, pp. 28–29.

are involved that differ from batch operations. One is the segmenting of programs so that they can fit into the partitions of memory. The second is the insertion of linkages to tie together segments of the programs in the proper sequences. Batch programs are often bigger than the partition size, so they must be broken into segments such that no segment is larger than the partition in which it will reside. These segments are then processed in a predetermined order, and each will follow or overlay its predecessor in the same partition. Thus, the complexity of a multiprogramming environment can create difficulty for data processing personnel.

## SERVICE BUREAU

*Service bureaus operate computer equipment for the purpose of processing data and providing meaningful output to its customers on a stated fee basis.*

Before examining the nature of the service bureau, it is useful to define the term itself. A large part of the industry today does not use the term in describing its operations. New names, such as data center and time sharing center have and are being added to the list that describes a service bureau. Despite attempts to distinguish or differentiate some of the newer forms of data processing centers, all of these organizations possess one thing in common—they all operate computer equipment for the benefit of firms other than their own on a stated fee basis. For all practical purposes, a service bureau can be defined as any organization whose principal purpose is to provide data processing functions for other firms, in particular, the actual processing of the data itself for some meaningful output.

The key factors in deciding whether a computer service bureau should be utilized or not are the needs of management and the cost aspects. Regarding the latter point, it is necessary to know how much is being spent presently on clerical operations which will be taken over by the computer service bureau. An important consideration is the additional volume that can be handled by the data center at a small increase in cost—less than the cost of adding more personnel to handle the same work in the customer's own office. Quite often, management will elect to use a data processing center even when little or no dollar savings are expected. Improved speed and accuracy of reporting are the determining factors. Thus, management's needs are generally a far more important consideration than slightly higher costs. The key question is, can the use of a data center improve the firm's ability to operate in a more efficient manner?

### Services Provided

*Services provided by service bureaus include processing of data as well as programming and implementation.*

Although computer service bureaus vary widely in their ability and size, their service is particularly suited to the needs of small- and medium-sized firms with or without electronic data processing equipment of their own. Of particular interest to this group is the fact that it is not necessary to prepare punched cards as data processing input. Input media, such as punched paper tape, MICR and OCR type font, and magnetic strip ledger cards can be produced on comparatively inexpensive office machines as a by-product of bookkeeping and accounting machines. By sending their by-product media to a data processing center, a business can give its management timely and updated reports.

***Complete Processing of Data.*** Services provided by an EDP service center go far beyond the familiar ones of payroll, sales statistics, and routine reports. It is possible for the data service bureau to process all the paperwork required from the receipt of customer order through shipment, invoicing, and updating of accounts receivable; from a bill of materials explosion for purchasing through production control schedules, costing records, maintenance of accounts payable, and updating of perpetual inventory records; and from cash receipts and disbursements ledgers through the posting of the general ledger. Many of the procedures can be handled by utilizing time-sharing devices for updated information in order to control the firm's operations.

***Programming and Implementation.*** When a time sharing device is used for routine accounting applications, such as customer billing, accounts receivable, and updating inventory records, certain prescribed procedures must be followed day by day. Specialized forms must be used, controls over procedures established, and comparable methods must be clearly set forth since change is not likely to occur. One method for getting a new user started on a time sharing basis with a service bureau is to define the processing and file requirement and let the service center design an appropriate system by working with the client. Programs are written or library routines are used while the client's records (programs and files) are recorded on a computer access medium. After terminal devices have been installed and clerks have been trained, a cut off point is established for converting to the new time sharing system. There should always be a short period of parallel operations as a safety factor so the new system can be thoroughly checked for deficiencies. Many times, the terminal devices are a teletypewriter and an auxiliary printer since this method allows for the typing of new information via the keyboard while other data are being printed on the printing equipment. The data entered through the console are transmitted, checked, and transmitted back for printing by the auxiliary printer. This procedure assures that invalid data are not being typed. If an operator notes an error before an entry is completed, it can be erased before transmission by depressing a control key. It should be noted that there is no need to dial the computer center to start processing since the leased line provides for a continuous connection to an on-line terminal.

**Evaluation of Service Bureaus**

*Evaluation criteria of service bureaus are:*

- *services offered*
- *experience of personnel*
- *equipment available*
- *input media that can be processed*
- *costs of services*

The major criteria for selecting a service bureau for time-sharing and batch-processing services are: type of services offered, experience of the center's management and personnel, equipment available, type of input media that can be processed, and costs of services. When considering a time-sharing service bureau, questions are asked concerning programming, languages available, assistance in systems design, response time of terminal devices, financial status of center, and control features. Regarding the last point, the user should be satisfied that proper procedures will be established to protect against unauthorized entry of confidential information, and file destruction, and provide for recovery from failure of time sharing equipment.

## COMPUTER UTILITY

*Computer utility is analogous to any public utility firm, such as gas and electric. It gives the user large scale computing power, common data banks, and a vast communication equipment network for meeting his data processing needs.*

Currently, the computer utility concept is gaining attention in the data processing service industry. In fact, there has been a steady evolution toward this concept since the early days of computers. A computer utility is basically a data processing service organization that provides a wide range of computer services. The computer services are far different from those of a traditional service bureau. However, some computer service organizations have expanded to the point where they are supplying computer utility services. By bringing together large scale computing power, common data banks, and a vast communication equipment network, the computer utility surpasses in capability what can be achieved with most in-house computer systems.

A computer utility, then, operates in a time-sharing environment as well as in a remote batch processing mode. The user initiates processing of his problems in a time sharing environment. The computer checks his input and issues any obvious error diagnostics for immediate correction and resubmission. Next, the user's job is placed in a queue to await the availability of the resources required to solve his problem, and the user terminates his communication with the computer. When the computer has processed his job, it reestablishes communication with the user, and returns the solution to his problem.

### Facilities Management

*Facilities management is an extension of the computer utility concept, that is, an outside data processing firm is responsible for normal in-house data processing operations.*

An extension of the computer utility concept is contracting the entire responsibility for a firm's data processing department to an independent "facilities management" group. This outside data processing firm or computer utility is responsible for normal in-house data processing activities. A contract, normally arranged on a five-year basis, would be signed for supervising all EDP operations, including equipment, people, and functions. Experience has indicated that facilities management is well suited for those firms who have problems procuring and keeping capable data processing personnel because of the tight labor market for good EDP people. A facilities management firm is in a better position to attract and hold qualified personnel since it is able to pay higher salaries as well as use the person's experience and talents on more than one processing facility. From this viewpoint, the facilities management organization is better able to guarantee the success of a new data processing operation than many small- and medium-sized firms are capable of doing by themselves.

### Computer Network

Since there is a need for large scale computing ability, computer utilities rely on large and powerful computer equipment. Many of the major computer manufacturers are currently providing the required large scale computing equipment as well as the advanced operating systems to permit multiple methods of access to remote users. Control Data Corporation, for example, has its supercomputers, which reflect their commitment to large computers serving the nucleus of a distributed network. Other computer manufacturers are capable of providing computer services in real-time, remote batch, and multiprogram batch on large scale computing equipment.

*The communications network of a computer utility is a vast one, as illustrated in Figure 9-32 for the CDC CYBERNET system.*

***CYBERNET.*** The Control Data Corporation has established a computer utility network, called CYBERNET, which links computers in 33 cities of the United States and countries abroad (Figure 9-32). This network enables the user to take full advantage of the firm's fast computer power, data bank capabilities, and many other data processing services through its CYBERPAK data service. With CYBERPAK, it enables users to purchase fractional portions of a CDC computer system with accompanying support services. Thus, customers can acquire up to a complete super-scale computer system with full support services and wide range of proprietary software application packages, such as programs for commercial applications, interactive data management, large-scale linear programming, engineering, and electrical analysis. Problems that normally take hours or days on medium-sized computers are solved in seconds or minutes with one of their supercomputers—a factor that could mean substantial savings in both time and costs to the user.

Another example of a computer utility is a widespread communications network

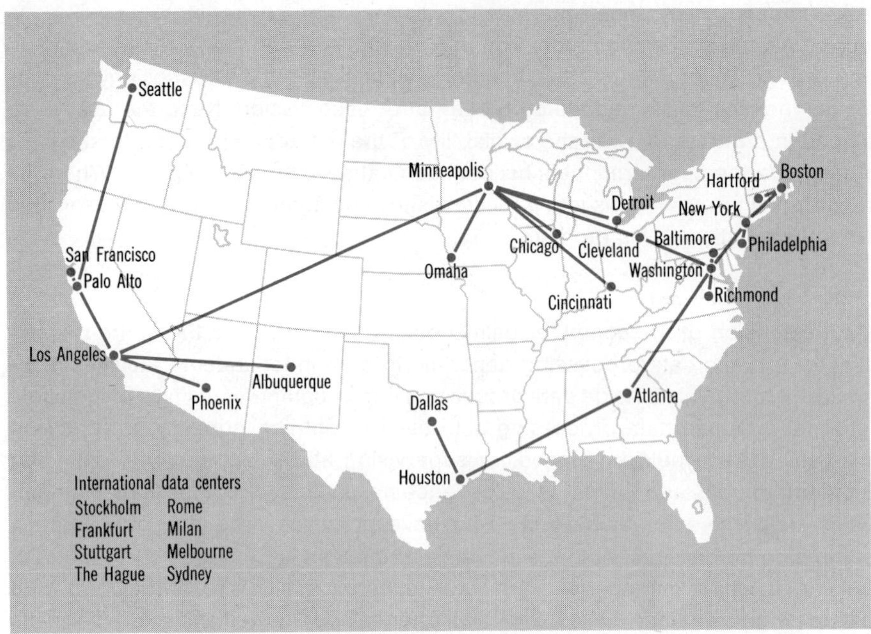


Figure 9-32 CDC CYBERNET System—a computer network linking 33 cities in the world. (Courtesy Control Data Corporation.)

on a service basis. The Planning Research Corporation established such a reservation system for Howard Johnson Motor Lodges and a number of other motel chains. This example of a specialized application in a particular industry involves the tie-in of many remote locations across the country through a computer service facility.

### Programming

*Computer utilities offer flexibility to their users since generalized packaged programs or user written programs can be employed for processing data.*

Within the programming framework of computer utilities, two approaches are currently available. One is the supplying of packaged programs while the other requires the firm to write its own programs.

***Generalized Packaged Programs.*** The computer utility develops and makes available to subscribers ready-to-use software systems. The problems normally associated with conversions to a computer system will partially disappear because the packages will have been in existence and operating for some time and their installation will be routine. Because of the greater economies in development, as well as in operation, the generalized application packages will become the most popular choice of the majority of small- to medium-sized firms. Even time sharing firms that originally started out as suppliers of computing power are seeking to develop proprietary application packages which they can offer their subscribers.

***User Written Programs.*** The second approach is making computer power accessible from a remote location without supplying the packaged programs to the user. For example, the University Computing Company which calls itself a "computer utility" has the user write and operate his own programs. The firm provides a link from small peripheral computers with high-speed card readers and printers at user locations that perform the input and output functions to a large central computer. One advantage of this approach is that it can accommodate high volumes of input and output automatically at the user's location, thereby eliminating delivery problems. However, the user retains the continuing responsibility and cost of developing the necessary software.

## SUMMARY

The introduction of data communication equipment and time sharing systems has greatly increased the flow of business information. Data communications have made possible the development of real-time management informations systems while a time-sharing environment has brought the on-line capabilities of computers to the smallest user. This timely flow of business data, sometimes referred to as "now" information, will undoubtedly add to a more efficient operation of the firm's activities. Information that tells what is happening now is generally more beneficial to management than one which produces needed operating data at a later date.

As time sharing continues to grow, it will reach a point where it will be used for all short problems. Whether it be in the academic, business, engineering, research, or other areas, time sharing will become an accepted way of life. It has the potential to enrich the quality of the environment by providing answers to problems on the spur of the moment which due to their complexity may not be solvable in days or weeks using manual methods. Time sharing, coupled with data communications, is one dynamic factor that has the potential of affecting the world in which we live. This man-machine interaction capability is available through an in-house computer system, a service bureau, a time sharing firm, or a computer utility, the last one being an important data processing service facility which will solve tomorrow's on-line real-time problems.

## *QUESTIONS*

1. How important is data communications in the field of business data processing today?
2. What is the function of a data set or modem?
3. Distinguish between data communication channels and services.
4. Describe the three basic types of communication channels.
5. What is the significance to a potential user regarding the types of communication channels and grades of circuits which are available? Explain.
6. Describe five types of data transmission terminal equipment.
7. (a) What is meant by time sharing? Explain thoroughly.
   (b) What are the important reasons for the rapid growth of time sharing? Explain.
8. State and explain the basic characteristics of time sharing.
9. Of the many basic types of time-sharing devices available, what are the advantages and disadvantages of each?
10. How does a time-sharing computer system differ from a batch processing computer system?
11. Why is a batch processing computer more efficient and faster than a time sharing computer?
12. How economical is a time sharing system when compared to a batch processing system? Explain.
13. What are the benefits of program writing and debugging using time sharing terminals versus a batch processing computer?
14. What is meant by the virtual machine concept? Explain.
15. What are the two basic types of multiprogramming systems? Explain each one.
16. What must the manager consider when selecting a computer service bureau for batch processing services versus time sharing services?
17. How does a computer utility differ from a traditional service bureau?
18. What is the future direction of data communications and the time sharing industry?

# IV

# PROGRAMMING LANGUAGES

## CHAPTER TEN

# Computer Programming and Languages

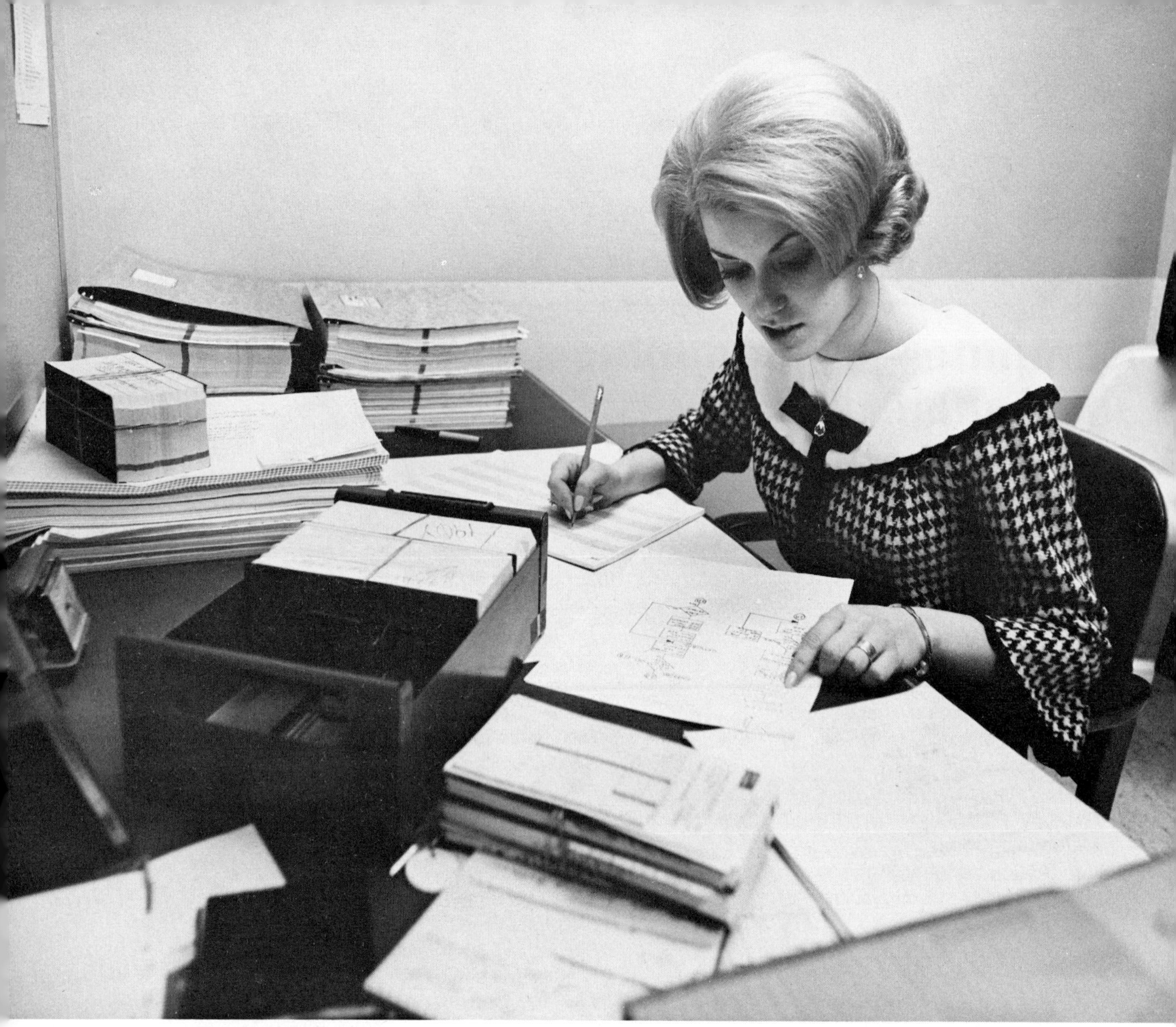

*COBOL, BASIC, PL/1, and RPG programming languages—the subject matter of this chapter—can be used for batch or real-time processing. Operating in a batch processing mode, they must be coded and compiled before sample data can be tested. (Courtesy International Business Machines Corporation.)*

The internal workings of a computer were presented in Chapters Five through Nine. An understanding of what a computer can do, how it performs, and how business problems must be expressed in machine language instructions for the specific computer being employed are necessary prerequisites for this chapter and two succeeding ones. Once a thorough knowledge of the problem to be solved has been obtained, the programmer must devise a step-by-step procedure that expresses this process as a sequence of instructions.

The purpose of this chapter is to build upon the previous presentation of computer data processing. The programming and implementing steps required for a batch processing system are described. Current programming languages, namely, COBOL, BASIC, PL/1, and RPG are presented. They provide an overview of the current direction in computer programming while the next two chapters will concentrate on FORTRAN in some detail. All five of these languages are expected to maintain an established place in the programming repertory of forward-looking business information systems, in particular, real-time management information systems. The chapter concludes with an evaluation of programming languages versus machine languages.

## PROGRAMMING CLASSIFICATIONS

A computer program is a set of *instructions*. It directs the computer to complete a certain sequence of program steps when processing a given set of data. Both the instructions and data that are required to solve a problem are stored in specific locations called *addresses*. Most instructions are composed of two basic parts—the operation to be performed and one or more operands. The operation indicates the action to be taken, such as read, write, add, compare, and so forth. The operand designates the location of data, an instruction, or a device designated by the program. In essence, the operand indicates what to add, where to store, what to compare, or similar operations.

*Programming, which is the process of instructing the computer to solve a specific problem can be subdivided as:*
- *applications programming*
- *systems programming*

The overall process from logical analysis through detailed program coding and testing is called computer programming. Although it has many steps which will be pointed out below, it can be divided into two parts: applications programming and systems programming. Both are essential for an efficient and economical computer system. As will be seen, they complement one another. Our basic concern is in the area of applications programming.

### Applications Programming

*Applications programming is oriented toward the solution of computer processing requirements for a particular problem.*

Applications programming efforts are undertaken by those programmers whose purpose is to accomplish specific data processing tasks for the firm. Programs may involve the major functions of the firm, namely, accounting, finance, engineering, manufacturing, marketing, personnel, purchasing, and research and development. Many general application programs have been written by the computer manufacturers in the form of program libraries and are available to users. Other general programs have been developed by software houses which are available on a fixed fee or on a monthly rental basis. Thus, applications programming is oriented toward the solution of the computer processing requirements for a specific problem.

The individuals are generally highly knowledgeable of the problems which they are analyzing. The programmers may have been hired and trained by a company. In other cases, the services of a software house or the assistance of the computer manufacturer may be used to accomplish the applications programming. No matter what the source of programmers, their task is to produce an efficient and effective program for the application under study.

### Systems Programming

*Systems programming is directed toward those routines that are common to many different computer programs.*

Systems programming is directed toward writing those programs which run the computer. Since there are many computer routines which are common to many different computer programs, these routines are developed by the equipment manufacturers and need not be developed by the user. Such programs are often referred to as control or supervisor program packages. They include control programs which operate the input and output equipment, such as read a block of tape and punch a card: utility programs which control output formats; diagnostic programs which examine electrical and mechanical malfunctions; and programs for conversion to a machine language.

From a programming standpoint, systems programming is an invaluable aid. When an applications programmer comes to a point in a program that requires reading or writing specific data, he can utilize the required control program which is obtainable from the computer manufacturer rather than writing his own control package. Without the need to write or test these program packages, the time to develop applications programs is speeded up considerably, thereby, making the job of the applications programmer much easier.

As indicated by the programming projects undertaken, the systems programmer is much closer to the hardware than the applications programmer. With the aid of such languages as COBOL, FORTRAN, and PL/1, the applications programmer, who possess only minimal knowledge of hardware functions, can put together an extremely efficient program. The systems programmer, however, must know how the machine functions; its memory capacity, retrieval and processing speeds; its input and output capabilities; and its electronic limitations. An academic background in the scientific disciplines is consequently valuable here.

Systems programming is one of the most challenging and rewarding careers in the entire data processing field. It is an intellectual exercise limited only by an individual's imagination. There are no tools or devices involved in systems programming—other than the use of computers to debug new programs. The men and women who bear the title "systems programmer" rely solely on their knowledge, skill, and ingenuity. In every sense of the phrase, they are an elite group of problem solvers.

## MAJOR PROGRAMMING LANGUAGES

*Currently, problem-oriented languages are commonly used for small-scale computer systems, while procedure-oriented languages are employed for larger size computer systems.*

An important part of systems programming today is the development of translator or processor programs. Instead of having the applications programmers code in some machine language, they can instruct a computer in a language closer to English and normal mathematical notation. Later the program can be translated into the machine language of the specific computer. Over the years, three major types of languages have been developed for these translator programs:

1. symbolic languages,
2. procedure-oriented languages,
3. problem-oriented languages.

**Symbolic Languages**

Symbolic languages resemble machine instructions but are expressed in a more convenient form. The assembly process ordinarily employs a one-for-one translation, assigning one absolute machine language program step for each symbolic label. The AUTOCODER (IBM) and S-4 (UNIVAC) are examples of this symbolic language.

**Procedure-oriented Languages**

Procedure-oriented languages allow the programmer to describe the set of procedures by which the problem is to be solved. Examples are BASIC, COBOL, FORTRAN, and PL/1, the subject matter for most of this chapter and the next two chapters.

**Problem-oriented Languages**

Problem-oriented languages describe the problem itself, that is, the programming language approximates the language of the problem to be solved by the computer. Examples are RPG and simulation languages.

## TRANSLATOR PROGRAM

Within each group of major programming languages set forth above, there are many different languages, each requiring a separate program assembler or compiler, sometimes referred to as a translator, to produce the desired machine language. Each programming language includes a set of allowable words, symbols, and characters as well as a set of rules for using this vocabulary to define the problem being programmed. Although each language requires a related translator program, the translation process is basically the same.

*The translator program converts the source program into an object program.*

As shown in Figure 10-1, programming language instructions are entered as input into the computer. The translator or processor program causes the computer

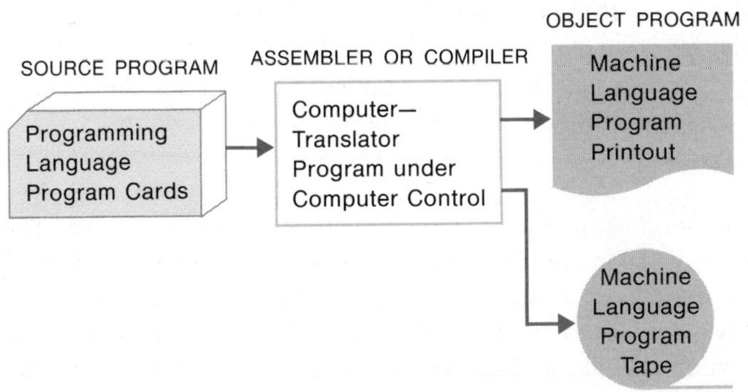


Figure 10-1 Translating a programming language program (input) into a machine language program (output).

to convert these instructions into machine language output. The machine language program, written on magnetic tape (can be written on magnetic disk or punched card output), is read into memory just as if it had been written directly by the programmer.

The programming language program as read in is known as the *source pro-*

*gram*. The computer program that performs the translation is referred to as the *assembler* (for symbolic languages) or *compiler* (for procedure-oriented and problem-oriented languages), depending upon the level of the language. The machine language program that results is called the *object program*.

## PROGRAMMING SYSTEM AIDS

*Programming system aids which are written by the systems programmer for the applications programmer include:*

- *utility programs*
- *subroutines*
- *macro instructions*
- *input/output control systems*

The development of powerful programming languages and the complexities of computer equipment have resulted in programming system aids. These include utility programs, subroutines, macro instructions, and input/output control systems, to name some of the more important ones.

### Utility Programs

*A utility program relieves the applications programmer of writing his own programs to accomplish routine tasks, such as reading input data and writing output information.*

Utility programs relieve the computer user of the need to prepare his own programs that accomplish routine tasks, such as reading or writing from tape to disk, tape to card, and the like. They can be grouped into several classifications: sort and merge routines, simulators (routines that run one computer which imitate the operations of another computer), translators (assemblers and compilers), housekeeping routines (set storage to a certain condition or cause data to be placed into or read out of storage), file conversion routines (move data from one storage device to another), and program testing aids (designed to aid in program testing and aids in error detection).

### Subroutines

*A subroutine is a set of instructions for carrying out a specified task within a computer program.*

An important programming system aid is the subroutine which is a standard sequence for directing the computer to carry out a specified operation. An *open subroutine* is included in the source program at the proper place and compiled along with the rest of the program. On the other hand, a *closed subroutine* requires that it be programmed only once since it can be entered several times during program processing. Control may be transferred to a closed subroutine from more than one place in the main routine. Linkage from the main routine to the subroutine is affected by a logical decision (branch) instruction. Some provision must be made for returning to the main program each time the subroutine is used. Consequently, the return instruction in the subroutine must be modified before branching occurs in order that a return to an appropriate point in the main routine occurs.

### Macro Instructions

*One macro instruction in the source program has the capability of generating two or more instructions in the object program, thereby reducing the number of lines to be coded.*

Macro instructions, another automatic programming language aid, have the capability of generating more than one machine language instruction. It is a method of defining a function or functions to be performed in the object program by writing a one-line statement. A macro instruction, for example, allows the programmer to write one instruction, such as read a card, read a tape, write a tape, and punch a card. The translator program automatically inserts the detailed series of machine language instructions to perform the designated task. Thus, macro instructions increase the productivity of the programmer. Series of instructions that are used frequently can be referenced by a single macro statement. Referring to subroutines, the macro instruction causes the automatic insertion of an open subroutine.

There are other forms of macro instructions. One that results in the inclusion of a fixed routine from a library is known as a *macro substitution*. Subroutines of this type are used to perform detailed operations, such as multiplication and division.

Another type of macro instruction is the *macro generation*. In these cases, the programmer need only specify the type of function he wishes to perform. He describes in a one-line statement the operation to be performed. The translator program selects the proper routine and generates the required number of machine language instructions to carry out the function desired. For both of these special subroutines, the instructions are merged into the source program as it is translated into machine language.

### Input/Output Control Systems

*The input/output control system provides control of the I/O functions during processing.*

The input/output control system (IOCS) is an extension of the macro instruction concept. It reduces the complexity of input and output programming and provides effective control of the input/output functions during processing. In addition to controlling the reading of input data and writing output data by means of programmed routines, it performs many other functions. The IOCS checks for equipment errors while reading and writing and initiates reread or rewrite procedures where possible. End of volume (EOV) and end of file (EOF) procedures are generated as required. IOCS processes labels on input tape or disk files and creates labels for new output files. The input/output control system controls the transfer of records to and from magnetic tape or disk files. Simultaneous reading, computing, and writing is performed on those computers capable of simultaneous processing. Lastly, it provides for priority processing and controls records to indicate the point at which an interrupted program should be restarted.

From a programming viewpoint, the input/output control system produces standard input/output routines and formats that are most helpful when several programmers are working on different parts of the same program or on several programs within one functional area of the firm. It can also be most helpful in adapting existing programs to a different configuration of the same computer or to a different computer. The programmer implements this system aid by writing a file definition which provides the IOCS system with the required information to function properly. If a record is needed for processing, the programmer writes GET and the file name. Correspondingly, when a record is to be written, the instruction is PUT and the file name. In addition to these macro instructions, OPEN is used to specify the operation for accessing a file and CLOSE terminates the use of a file.

## PROGRAMMING AND IMPLEMENTATION

*Fourteen steps comprise programming and implementation for a computer program in a batch processing mode.*

The task of preparing a computer program for daily operations is not simple and straightforward for a batch processing computer. As will be seen in the following sections, the steps are long and drawn out. The purpose of these detailed steps is to provide an accurate program when processing is complete. Only in this manner can the firm have reliable programs that handle all regular and exception items in conformity with the firm's objectives, policies, and procedures. Likewise, this overview of computer programming and implementation procedures will help the reader appreciate the efforts of the computer programming staff.

An important concept that will underlie the following steps is that no human intervention is necessary once the program has become operational. If there is only one possible condition or decision, the program will follow these established procedures. Similarly, if there are different program paths, the appropriate alternatives will be programmed for these conditions. A program, then, may contain single and alternative paths in order to complete the desired computer processing.

### Define the Problem

Step 1: *Accurate definition of the problem is critical to the success of the computer programming effort.*

Defining the data processing problem is the initial undertaking in developing a computer program (first step). This entails determining what its relationship is to the overall data processing system; what information is required from the system, particularly in the form of reports; where the input information is obtained; what files are involved; whether results are needed upon inquiry or otherwise; what exceptions must be considered in processing; and similar considerations. Even if a specific area is being converted as is, the answers to these questions must be obtained since any data processing system has far reaching effects on other parts of the system. The necessity to define the problem properly cannot be overemphasized. Without this process, the data processing problem may not be solved in a manner commensurate with the overall objectives of the data processing system.

### Prepare the Program Flowchart(s) and/or Decision Table(s)

Step 2: *Preparation of program flowcharts and/or decision tables includes all the possible alternatives of the defined problem.*

Expressing the problem in the form of a program flowchart(s) is essential. A decision table(s) is (are) a better alternative in many cases. Still in other situations, the combination of decision tables and program flowcharts are the answer (second step). This is particularly true where there is a myriad of decisions that must be undertaken by the program. By having them stated concisely and briefly in a decision table(s), an accurate flowchart(s) can be constructed that includes all of the possible alternatives.

Whether program flowcharts or decision tables or a combination are utilized, a set of these programming aids depict the overall flow of program steps. An overview approach is supported by one or more levels of detailed flowcharts or tables or both for a modular approach to programming. While programming aids allow the programmer to visualize the overall flow of work, they provide the necessary detail for coding the computer problem under study.

Generally, program flowcharts and decision tables will have been developed in their initial, basic form as part of the feasibility study. However, once a given computer system has been selected, these charts and tables may have to be reanalyzed in terms of the specific computer system requirements. This is necessary since every computer model and related equipment have their own special requirements. For example, only certain input and output devices are available, the primary and secondary storage capacity are of a certain size, the central processor has its own set of instructions and internal codes, and so forth. The net result of these requirements must be reflected in the steps to complete specific data processing tasks.

### Write the Computer Program

Step 3: *The computer program is written so that it conforms to the flowcharts and/or decision tables.*

Coding the computer program is the process of writing the actual computer instructions (third step). The programmer studies previously prepared flowcharts and decision tables in order to familiarize himself with the program to be written. He should think not only in terms of the problem to be solved, but also the end result—the computer's machine language. Even though he is coding in a symbolic language, a procedure-oriented language, or a problem-oriented language, consideration must be given to how the program will be compiled by the translator program. This approach is necessary if an efficient machine language program is to be produced. A lack of knowledge of the programming language, the machine language, and the computer itself can lead to inefficient programs that transform source data into output.

Before the programmer undertakes the detail coding, he should segment the program into a series of logically independent modules or subprograms. If these program modules can be compiled separately, there are many benefits that will accrue to the programming effort. Work can be divided among several programmers. Programs can be tested prior to all modules being written, thereby, reducing the testing time at a later date. Changes can be made independent of other unaffected modules. A modular approach to applications programming, then, is a preferred approach to program coding.

When writing a program, it should be pointed out that the programmer has resources available to help him develop the program. Program packages and special programs developed by equipment manufacturers, software houses, consulting firms, users groups, computer utilities, and service bureaus are available. Likewise, consulting services may be provided by many of these same sources. Thus, the programmer has the assistance of many firms operating outside itself for expert assistance.

In the final analysis, the second and third steps in preparing an operating program are closely related. The detailed program flowchart(s) and decision table(s) should be so written that program modules can be efficiently expressed in the language employed which, in turn, produces an efficient machine language program when compiled. The process of devising an efficient flowchart(s) and table(s) center around a certain amount of mental program coding. All factors that are deemed important in the object program are considered for these two programming steps.

### Desk Check the Program

Step 4: *Desk checking the program is recommended in order to uncover logical and clerical errors not evident to the preparer.*

Once the program has been written, it is highly unlikely that it will run the first time. The rationale is that programmers are human and make errors. For this reason, most computer programs are checked by another programmer or supervisor for errors. Basically, the above steps one through three are audited (fourth step). Despite the efforts of the most expert programmer, errors are generally found at this stage and appropriate corrections are made to the program. Two major types of errors are found in the typical program, namely, logical errors and clerical errors.

***Logical Errors.*** Logical errors are difficult to uncover since a thorough understanding of the program flowcharts, decision tables, and program is necessary. Basically, they refer to those conditions in the program that do not adequately represent the data processing operations required within the program. For example, the amount of an employee's deductions in a payroll program cannot produce a negative net pay even though the deductions may be legitimate. Additional logical tests are necessary to insure this negative condition never occurs.

***Clerical Errors.*** Clerical errors are the assignment of the same symbol for two different sets of data, the omission of an instruction, or the misuse of an operation symbol. No matter whether the errors are logical or clerical, the program will not process data correctly until these conditions are corrected. The time spent on this fourth step can save considerable testing time on the computer.

Although logical and clerical errors are applicable to all programs, they are noticeably apparent in complicated programs. Every program of any complexity should be checked carefully by another competent data processing person. A thorough examination of the logic should be undertaken. The program should be "desk tested" as well as possible in order to determine if it will accomplish the desired results. Next, a search for clerical errors and deviations from the program flowcharts and decision tables should be made. This may sound like a waste of time.

but experience has indicated that it is difficult for the original programmer to detect the simplest mistakes in logic, not to mention the numerous clerical errors.

### Keypunch and Verify Program Cards

Step 5: *Program cards are keypunched and key verified for a more accurate source program.*

Keypunching and verifying the program cards are the next step in programming and implementation (fifth step). Despite the fact that reliable key punch operators are used, key verification is recommended for more accurate results. Simple misreading at the keypunching stage can cause errors, especially if there are characters that look alike. There always seems to be confusion regarding O and zero, i and 1, and z and 2. It is recommended that the programming language program be printed after keypunching and key verifying. In this manner, the programmer can visually check for errors caused by illegible handwriting misinterpreted at the keypunching stage. One noticeable error that comes to light when a printed listing is available centers around the incorrect keypunching of data fields, that is, the wrong card columns being punched.

### Assemble or Compile Object Program

Step 6: *The source program is translated (assembled or compiled) into the object program.*

Assembly or compilation of the object program occurs under computer control (sixth step). By way of review, assembly refers to the translation of a program in a symbolic machine-oriented coding system to one of machine language instructions. Compilation is the translation of a procedure-oriented or macro instruction language into machine language. Although the term assembly and compilation are often used interchangeably, they do have slightly different meanings. Whereas a program written in AUTOCODER, S-4, SPS, ALC, and other symbolic languages are assembled, those written in BASIC, COBOL, FORTRAN, PL/1, and similar procedure-oriented languages are compiled. For both, the assembly or compilation process is carried out by the computer program (assembler or compiler) to produce an object program. The object program, in turn, is a machine language program which performs the instructions originally represented by the coding.

During the assembly or compilation process, the processor that translates from the symbolic or procedure-oriented language to the object program checks for clerical errors or omissions. An invalid operation symbol, symbols not properly defined, labels omitted in the program, various types of keypunching errors, and other errors can be brought to the attention of the programmer on the first try at assembly or compilation. For this reason, it is generally advisable not to punch an object program deck or write an object program magnetic tape. The normal procedure is to print the object program only.

### Correct Errors of Original Object Program

Step 7: *Errors shown on the object program listing are corrected before a second assembly or compilation.*

Once the original object program is complete, the debugging process begins (seventh step). Despite the amount of checking by other competent programmers during step four above, there are still clerical errors that are noted during the assembly or compilation of the first object program. These errors mentioned earlier, which are capable of being detected by the assembler or compiler, are reviewed by the programmer. Appropriate corrections are made to the programming language cards, thereby, making the program source deck ready for a second assembly or compilation.

### Reassemble or Recompile Object Program

Having made the necessary corrections to the program deck, reassembly or recompilation of the object program is undertaken (eighth step). During this second

Step 8: *The source program deck is processed again for an object program listing as well as card, tape, or disk output.*

computer pass, the printed object program should be devoid of any clerical errors that are capable of detection by the translator program. Since the object program is correct as possible at this point, a machine language program is produced for testing the sample data. It should be noted that for very simple programs, this step is generally not needed. However, for large and complex programs, many errors will be noted during the first pass which can be rectified by retranslating the object program during the second pass.

### Test (Debug) Object Program

Step 9: *Test data are processed against the object machine language program in order to test the program's accuracy. Memory dumps and trace routines are utilized to speed up the debugging process.*

In order to make each test session productive as possible, the programmer should have all materials necessary for efficient debugging (ninth step). These include an operating run manual, a machine language program of the problem to be tested, and the test data itself. Computer paper, blank cards, magnetic tape reels, and magnetic disk packs, required by the program, should also be readily available. An operating run manual should contain the original coding flowcharts, a list of operating instructions, input and output requirements, a complete list of all stop instructions and the reasons for reaching that portion of the program, and a list of the expected results from the test data employed. Thus, the exact testing sequence to be followed for each run, the purpose of each test, the data requirements, and the expected results should be determined before going on the computer.

***Program Test Deck.*** The ultimate test of the object program is to determine how accurate its results are when processed on the computer. This can be determined by applying hypothetical data which are representative of the real world. The data should be varied enough so that when the program has been successfully tested, all parts of the program will have been checked against every combination and sequence of data conceivable under actual operating conditions. Large quantities of test data do not necessarily insure good test data. It is the quality, not the quantity that is important.

Basically, these input data are designed to test the various branches and subroutines of the program. The correct output for these hypothetical input transactions should be predetermined. In this manner, a comparison can be made between the expected and actual results. In many cases, it is quite helpful to test for intermediate results within the computer's registers in order to detect various types of errors. The most important errors uncovered are those where certain program paths have been omitted.

***Test Procedure.*** The preparation of an adequate test deck should begin with those transactions which are straight forward in terms of the program's logic. Once these areas have been completely debugged, data should be introduced that test normal transactions which involve the complex logic of the object program. When these errors have been eliminated, representative data must be available to test the more common exceptions. Finally, the test deck should include unusual exceptions that must be handled by the program. Even after an exhaustive test of these sample data which contains most processing conditions, there is no guarantee that the program is one hundred percent correct. In some cases, certain extraneous conditions may arise in actual processing that were not contemplated by the programmer when devising the program. Still in other cases, a complex program may have so many branches that it is almost impossible to design test data that will insure that each instruction in the program will be executed in the debugging process. For example, a switch may be set at the wrong time which will cause erroneous processing of input data. These types of errors appear only after the program is put into actual use and may not be caught after several weeks or months of operation. Thus, the construction of an adequate test deck is a challenging task for any group of programmers.

***Test Modules.*** An important consideration when debugging a complex program is to break the program into component parts or modules and test each section separately. Even if a program does not use the modular approach, the major segments of a large complex program can be tested by entering intermediate results and starting at the beginning of the area(s) to be tested. The purpose of this segmented, debugging approach is to localize the clerical and/or logical errors in the program. Memory dumps and traces are utilized in the debugging process.

***Memory Dump.*** A memory dump does exactly what its name implies. It is a program that dumps memory. After the program being tested stops with an error condition, or at a specific instruction, the memory dump routine prints out the contents of any selected portion of memory as well as the contents at the various registers during the execution of the program instructions prior to the step. Such a selected printout of the computer's processing at a certain time provides the programmer with a picture of what has happened and/or what has caused the computer to stop.

***Trace Routine.*** In a similar manner, a trace routine takes control of the computer. As each instruction of the program is being executed, the instruction and the contents of the various registers are printed in order that the programmer can analyze what is happening within the computer. In effect, the trace is program testing that can be compared with the original coding to isolate errors.

Debugging routines are designed to eliminate costly computer time. Instead of sitting at the computer console and tieing up the computer for long periods of time, these routines permit the programmer to search for errors at his desk. Selected printouts of areas that are causing error conditions can be used effectively to correct problems within the program.

### Correct Errors of Original Program

Step 10: *Logical and clerical program errors are corrected as they are found.*

Program errors found during the testing or debugging phase are corrected (tenth step). Actually, the corrections are made as soon as they are detected. However, there is one word of caution: sometimes, changes are made which are not entirely correct. They may handle correctly the present data being tested, but may not process all test transactions properly. For this reason, it is advisable to rerun the test deck and compare predetermined results with changes for program accuracy.

Debugging procedures cannot detect all logical errors as indicated previously. Even if an adequate test deck is used, there is no guarantee that all errors have been found. The only conclusion to be drawn is that rigorous debugging methods eliminate most of the errors in the program and reduce the likelihood that others exist. The probability that program errors remain in complex programs is quite high.

### Reassemble or Recompile Program

Step 11: *The program should be retranslated for better documentation after all known errors are corrected.*

After the program is as error free as possible, it is advisable to reassemble or recompile the program (eleventh step). Generally, an extensive amount of patching is made to a complex program for the various errors found. Sometimes, the changes and documentation become very difficult to read and understand. In such cases, not only should a new object program be produced, but also the same test deck should be rerun for the program. Only in this manner can the programmer be assured of a program that is the same after numerous corrections have been made.

### Parallel Operations to Test Program

Step 12: *Parallel operations are necessary to test the computer program under actual conditions, in particular, how it handles the exceptions.*

Despite the many months of hard work by a group of experienced programmers, there is still the question of how well the program handles all normal and exception items. To gain confidence in the program and related data processing procedures, it is customary to run parallel operations for a period of time (twelfth step). Cross-checking between the old and new data processing systems will establish confidence in the ability of the new system. Discrepancies will be brought to light without the loss of valuable data and operating efficiency. Many times, the inadequacy of the old system is clearly demonstrated. Likewise, the errors and mistakes of the new program are highlighted for correction.

***Initial Conversion Activities.*** Initially, parallel operations are restricted to a small volume of data for comparing the old and new systems. For example, in a cycle billing accounting system, only one or two cycles out of twenty will be converted in order to test the accuracy of the new program and procedures. These dual operations may extend over a period of several months if major difficulties arise. The problems expected in all cycles are expected to show up when converting one or two cycles. Only after all difficulties have been resolved is it feasible to discontinue parallel operations.

***Personnel Considerations.*** The problems encountered in dual processing involve more than the program and related procedures. Personnel difficulties can be significant since someone must process the information in the old way while someone must handle it in the new manner. It is necessary to coordinate these operations for best results. A work force that may be reduced because of more computer mechanization may have to be increased for the period of dual operations. This duplication of effort may occur within or outside the data processing system.

The process of parallel operations can be very trying on people. A substantial resentment of newer data processing methods can be engendered by the changes taking place. Often, disgruntled employees seize this opportunity to discredit the new programs and procedures and all other changes associated with them. In such situations, it takes all the cooperation and efforts of programmers and department heads to overcome the "people problem." As stated previously, it is best to convert one area at a time so that disruption and confusion can be kept to a minimum. This approach allows people to adjust gradually to the changing business data processing environment.

### Conversion to Daily Operations

Step 13: *Conversion to daily operations is a more difficult undertaking than parallel operations. Sometimes, unusual exceptions show up that were not contemplated.*

Conversion to daily operations can be more hectic than parallel processing (thirteenth step). The reason is that large volumes of activities are involved versus a limited amount for dual operations. In addition, there is a problem that unusual exception items show up in large volume processing which is not always true of small volume operations during parallel processing. Likewise, the work habits of people have been changed which may not be to their liking. Only after a period of time can minor changes be undertaken to satisfy employees who are unhappy with the new data processing system.

Experience has shown that long hours required to convert the firm's daily operations can affect the performance of the average employee. Instead of being pleasant and agreeable, long hours tend to make employees irritable and unreceptive to necessary changes. For the most part, firms are extremely happy to have conversion activities behind them due to the strain on everyone involved. It is a necessary evil that must be undertaken before a new data processing system is operational.

### Documentation

Step 14: *Documentation is an integral part of the thirteen preceding steps and includes continual updating in a well managed EDP installation.*

Documentation is the final step in programming and implementation (fourteenth step). This phase is not a step in the same sense as the preceding ones since it is an integral part of those mentioned previously. It consists of gathering all documents associated with the program and placing them in a program manual. A typical program manual might include the following items: problem description, program flowcharts, decision tables, input and output record and file formats, printed copy of the program (in the coding language used), copy of object program, test data deck used during the debugging phase, and program change control log. Also, a copy of the operating instructions or computer run book used by the computer operator should be an essential part of the documentation process.

***Continual Updating Process.*** The documentation phase does not end once the program has become operational. It must be maintained on an up-to-date basis as changes occur within the system. At all times, documentation should represent the program in its current state rather than its previous status. As many firms have found out from experience, it is much easier to modify a well-documented computer program while it is almost impossible to modify a poorly documented or undocumented one. In many cases, firms have found it easier to reprogram the entire job from scratch rather than attempt to modify a program that lacks adequate documentation. Thus, the preparation of detailed documentation provides a ready reference manual for future data processing needs.

Many firms have found the quality of documentation indicative of the programmer's ability. Documentation must compete for the programmer's attention with the more challenging tasks of writing and testing programs. However, the competent and reliable programmer recognizes its importance in the long run. It is impossible to use programs that are not clearly understood and it is almost impossible to obtain an understanding of a program without excellent documentation.

Of all the arguments given for documentation, the turnover rate among programmers is sufficient reason for requiring adequate backup of programs written. The data processing manager that fails to require documentation will cause himself untold grief at some later date. When the various operational managers are demanding immediate results, he may not be able to satisfy their needs due to faulty or non-existent documentation by prior programmers. Although complete descriptions of complex programs are a chore to prepare, the data processing manager must ride herd on his people for program documentation if he expects to be known as an efficient and effective EDP manager.

### Relationship Among the Steps

*The foregoing programming and implementing steps (14) are summarized in Figure 10-2.*

The overall process of programming and implementation for an operational computer program has involved the foregoing steps. They are summarized in Figure 10-2. Although this process is rather lengthy, this systematized procedure leads to better results than some other haphazard method(s).

***Error Correction Process.*** A close examination of these steps reveals that they are a part of a correcting process. When a problem arises, the process loops back to a prior step which, in turn, means correcting all subsequent steps up to the point

1. Define the problem.
2. Prepare the program flowchart(s) and/or decision table(s).
3. Write the computer program.
4. Desk check the program.
5. Key punch and verify program cards.
6. Assemble or compile object program.
7. Correct errors of original program.
8. Reassemble or recompile object program.
9. Test (debug) object program.
10. Correct errors of original program.
11. Reassemble or recompile program.
12. Parallel operations to test program.
13. Conversion to daily operations.
14. Documentation.

Figure 10-2 Programming and implementation process for an operational computer program (batch processing).

*The fourteen programming and implementing steps constitute an error correction process, that is, the process loops back to a prior step or steps when a problem arises.*

where the problem occurred. With these interrelationships, it is necessary to return to an earlier step so that previous work can be redone. For example, during the coding phase, it may be necessary to break a major program into two separate ones since the original one exceeds the capacity of the computer being utilized. In a similar example, the use of macro instructions for a procedure-oriented language may cause the memory capacity of the computer to be exceeded when the object program is compiled. Depending upon the number of locations needed, recoding may remedy the problem or the program must be split for feasible processing. In such cases, considerable rework may be required. Sometimes, it is necessary to start with the initial step to redefine the problem.

Logical errors discovered during the testing or conversion process can force a return to the problem definition step. This means considerable reworking of all intervening steps in the process. Errors of this type are not only time consuming to correct, but also point out the need for a thorough and complete job from start to finish. Programmers who pay little attention to necessary detail will be made aware of this condition. Thus, data processing personnel, at times, must sacrifice speed in the interest of obtaining accuracy and getting the detailed information needed for the problem's solution. They must be capable and thorough in their efforts. This can be accomplished by utilizing the steps set forth previously for getting a batch processing program on the air.

## PROGRAMMING LANGUAGES

*Programming languages have these attributes:*

- *reduces programming time*
- *is associated with the English language*
- *is compatible with mathematical notation*
- *is easy to read and understand*

Higher level programming languages permit a data processing program to be written in a minimum of time. These various languages consist of abbreviated words or symbols that can be easily associated with the English language. This similarity, together with familiar mathematical notation, makes it quite easy to read and comprehend what is happening. Programming languages, then, facilitate the communications process for data processing personnel.

***Factors in Language Developments.*** According to some data processing enthusiasts, an effective programming language should be easy to learn, use, and implement. It should be machine independent, quick to compile, lead to efficient object programs, and be general purpose or applicable to a wide variety of problems. As the language is simplified so that it is easier to learn, it becomes less valuable to the experienced programmer. It is almost impossible to please the beginner in solving simple problems and the expert in solving very complex problems. The more machine independent and general purpose the language is, the harder it is to implement by writing an efficient compiler. Also more time and space are consumed by the compilation process. To obtain more efficient object programs, features which give preference to one or another computer and make assumptions about the class of problems to be handled must be incorporated into the language. In essence, a programming language that is suitable for solving all possible problems in the real world is not feasible at this time. For this reason, there is a variety of programming languages to serve a number of different problem areas.

*Higher-order languages to be covered:*
- *COBOL*
- *BASIC*
- *PL/1*
- *RPG*
- *FORTRAN*

***Higher-Order Languages.*** An overview of high-order languages will be set forth for COBOL, BASIC, PL/1, and RPG as well as for specialized programming and simulation languages. In the next chapter, FORTRAN IV will be presented. These four languages, excluding RPG, are procedure-oriented. They refer to a set of procedures by which the problem is to be solved rather than to the computer on which the program is to be processed. The procedural notation used to write a program in COBOL resembles English while BASIC is a compromise between English and pure computer languages. FORTRAN resembles algebraic procedures. The procedure-oriented language of PL/1 combines the features of other languages while RPG is a problem-oriented language suited for small computer users.

Restrictions that are present in English and mathematics also exist in the notation of these higher-order languages. Only a specified group of numbers, letters, and special characters can be used in writing a computer program. Likewise, special rules must be followed for punctuation and blanks. Despite these important constraints, a program written in a procedure-oriented language is more flexible in form than a machine-oriented language of a specific computer.

## COBOL Language

*COBOL language is oriented toward business problems.*

COBOL, an acronym for COmmon Business-Oriented Language, was the first major attempt to produce a truly business-oriented programming language. It was developed by the Conference on Data System Languages (CODASYL) Committee that consisted of several large users, computer manufacturers, the Federal government, and other interested groups. Their report contained the first version, called COBOL-60 where 60 represented the year of issuance. Since that time, several newer versions have been developed by the Programming Language Committee (PLC) whose job is to review and recommend changes.

***Recent Developments.*** A proposed development in 1969 is "COBOL Extensions to Handle Communications Processing." The proposal adds to the official COBOL specifications a set of language elements for acquiring, processing, and dispatching messages in a communications environment. Only after a shakedown period will CCF (COBOL Communications Facility) be incorporated in USA Standard COBOL. Further, additions to COBOL, such as this one, will be proposed and approved by the CODASYL's Programming Language Committee as specific needs arise.

*COBOL character set includes:*
- *0 through 9*
- *A through Z*
- *12 special characters*

***Language Components.*** The COBOL character set consists of the numerals 0 through 9, the letters of the alphabet, and 12 special characters. The language consists of names for identification purposes, constants and literals, operators that indicate some action or relationship, key words to establish the meaning of a statement, expressions containing the foregoing (names, constants, operators, or key words), statements using a verb and an item to be acted on, and sentences composed of one or more statements properly punctuated.

A COBOL program must always have four program divisions or else the program cannot be compiled.

***Program Divisions.*** A COBOL program is divided into four divisions, the hierarchy being:

1. Identification—identifies the program itself.
2. Environment—describes the equipment being used.
3. Data—specifies the form and format of the data files.
4. Procedure—depicts the processing steps to be undertaken.

Basically, the Procedure Division, being the actual processing instructions, are interpreted by the equipment described in the Environment Division as well as the files and records described by the Data Division. The Identification Division is required for documentation and is in no way affected by the other three divisions when producing an object program. In the next sections, the COBOL version describing this procedure-oriented language is based on COBOL-65.

1. The Identification Division of COBOL identifies the program and other pertinent information.

***Identification Division.*** The Identification Division is used to identify the program and to furnish other pertinent information. It can run from one to seven paragraphs long where each paragraph represents a sentence or a group of sentences and can be identified as follows:

```
IDENTIFICATION DIVISION.
PROGRAM-ID.—Program-Name.
AUTHOR.—Author-Name.
INSTALLATION.—Any sentence or group of sentences.
DATA-WRITTEN.—Any sentence or group of sentences.
DATA-COMPILED.—Any sentence or group of sentences.
SECURITY.—Any sentence or group of sentences.
REMARKS.—Any sentence or group of sentences.
```

Only the PROGRAM-ID paragraph is required and must appear as the first paragraph of the program. The other Identification paragraphs are optional. This first division is depicted in Figure 10-4 (lines 1–3) for the sample "HOUR-PAY" program.

2. The Environment Division of COBOL identifies basically the equipment to be used.

***Environment Division.*** The Environment Division has two main sections—the Configuration Section and the Input-Output Section, shown in Figure 10-4 (lines 4–11). The names of these sections are fixed and must start by the beginning of their respective sections. Likewise, the names of the paragraphs following each section are fixed and their names must be given at the beginning of any paragraph used. The structure of the Environment Division is given below. Note the use of periods as is the case for the prior division. It is required that they always be there.

```
ENVIRONMENT DIVISION.
  CONFIGURATION SECTION.
    SOURCE-COMPUTER. Computer-Name.
    OBJECT-COMPUTER. Computer-Name.
    SPECIAL NAMES. DEVICE-NAME.... Switch-Name.
  INPUT-OUTPUT SECTION.
    FILE-CONTROL. SELECT ...
    I/O-CONTROL. APPLY ...
```

*Configuration Section.* The Configuration Section identifies the computer on which the program is to be compiled (source computer) and the computer on which it is to be processed (object computer). Generally, they are the same. An optional paragraph, as indicated above, can be used to assign special names to equipment items, such as card reader, printer, and sense switches.

*Input/Output Section.* The Input/Output Section may consist of two paragraphs. The File-Control paragraph relates files with the devices on which they are to be read or written as well as the processing mode. While the first paragraph is required, the second paragraph or I/O Control is optional. The I/O Control paragraph defines special control techniques to be applied to the object program.

*3. The Data Division of COBOL defines the data to be referenced and processed by the Procedure Division.*

***Data Division.*** The Data Division is used to define the characteristics and format of the data to be processed. Every data name referred to in the Procedure Division must be defined in this division, except figurative constants. While items and records are described by record description entires, files are referenced by file description entires. The Data Division may consist of four sections. All of them, however, need not be used in a specific program. They are:

```
DATA DIVISION.
  FILE SECTION.
  WORKING-STORAGE SECTION.
  CONSTANT SECTION.
  REPORT SECTION.
```

*File Section.* Description of the files to be utilized follow the File Section heading and will be preceded by FD (File Description). The File Description will generally include a name for the file, a description of the input to the file, a description of the size of each individual record in the file, and the name of the tape (disk or drum) if the input or output is desired on magnetic tape (disk or drum). If the file record is a punched card or paper tape, the following statements should be written with the File Description—LABEL RECORDS ARE OMITTED. Referring to Figure 10-4, lines 13–37 illustrate the File Section.

*A picture clause references data as to their:*
- *size*
- *class (numeric, alphabetic, or special character)*
- *operational sign*
- *decimal point*

*Picture Clauses.* Each item of information, a record, and a file within the record must be given a distinct name so that it may be specifically identified. In addition, it is necessary to describe their format by picture clauses. A picture clause indicates the size of an item, its class, the presence or absence of an operational sign, and/or an assumed decimal point. The word PICTURE with identifying numbers and symbols follow each file description entry. The following characters are used for input items, working storage items, and constants:

| *Picture Character* | *Used to Represent* |
|---|---|
| 9 | A numerical digit |
| V | The position of an assumed decimal point (for internal calculations only) |
| S | The presence of an operational sign |
| A | An alphabetic character or a space |
| X | Any character in the computer's character set |
| Z | The zero suppression of the indicated characters |
| $ | A dollar sign character |

Examples of how different pictures might look when utilizing the above picture character symbols are found in Figure 10-3.

An entry name FILLER is used to indicate the unused portions of the record. This is required since the entire word must be taken into account. For example, when reading an 80-column card, the blank columns are referenced as filler pictures.

*Working-Storage Section.* The Working-Storage Section is used to describe the areas of storage where intermediate results and other items are to be stored temporarily. It describes the records and individual data items which are not part of input

| PICTURE | ACTUAL DATA | DATA WILL BE PRINTED AS | PICTURE CHARACTER CLASS |
|---|---|---|---|
| 99999 | 45921 | 45921 | Numeric |
| 99V99 | 8250 | 8250 | Numeric |
| S999V99 | −65921 | 65921 | Numeric |
| AAAAA | NAMES | NAMES | Alphabetic |
| XXXXX | 456AB | 456AB | Alphanumeric |
| ZZZ99 | 00045 | 45 | Numeric edited |
| $999V99 | 39521 | $39521 | Numeric edited |

Figure 10-3 Examples of picture characters.

or output files. However, these data values are developed and used when required by the program internally. The working storage locations required for Figure 10-4 are shown on lines 38 through 43.

*Constant and Report Sections.* The Constant Section describes the constants that will be used in the Procedure Division. These are permanent values which are assigned by the programmer and do not change during processing. The Report Section describes the content and format of reports to be generated by the COBOL report generator.

*4. The Procedure Division of COBOL specifies what processing steps are to be undertaken. The program is expressed in terms of:*
- *statements*
- *sentences*
- *paragraphs*
- *sections*

***Procedure Division.*** Basically, the Identification Division, the Environment Division, and the Data Division describe the program, the equipment, and the data to be utilized in a particular program respectively. It is in the Procedure Division where the actual programming of the problem takes place. In this division, the coder specifies what he wants to accomplish with the data described in the preceding division. His program is expressed in terms of statements, sentences, paragraphs, and sections.

*Program and Processor Verbs.* Action verbs form the basis of the Procedure Division where each COBOL sentence must end with a period. These verbs fall into two major categories—program verbs and processor verbs. These are listed as follows:

*Program Verbs*

| | | | |
|---|---|---|---|
| Input/Output | CLOSE | Data Manipulation | EXAMINE |
| | DISPLAY | | MOVE |
| | OPEN | Sequence Control | ALTER |
| | READ | | GO TO |
| | WRITE | | PERFORM |
| Arithmetic | ADD | | STOP |
| | SUBTRACT | *Processor Verbs* | ENTER |
| | MULTIPLY | | EXIT |
| | DIVIDE | | NOTE |
| | COMPUTE | | |

While program verbs revolve around the data processing steps that will be performed by the object program, processor verbs direct the processor in its works, such as utilizing existing routines written in a language other than COBOL. Examples of program verbs are illustrated in Figure 10-4, lines 46 through 64.

*Program Structure.* The smallest unit of expression is the statement when utilizing these action verbs. Sentences, paragraphs, and sections are the larger units of expression. A statement consists of a COBOL verb or the word IF or ON, followed by an appropriate operands (data-names, file-names, or literals) and other COBOL words that are necessary to complete a statement. On the other hand, a sentence is a single statement or a series of statements that is ended by a period and followed by a space. A paragraph consists of one or more sentences and a section is composed of one or more successive paragraphs. The latter must begin with a section-heading.

*Types of Statements.* There are four types of statements. The compiler-directing statements instruct the compiler to take certain actions when being compiled. Imperative statements indicate unconditional actions that are to be taken by the object program. Conditional statements contain a condition which is to be tested. They determine which alternate path is to be taken in the program. Lastly, note statements are allowed for comments about the program. They are not translated into the object program.

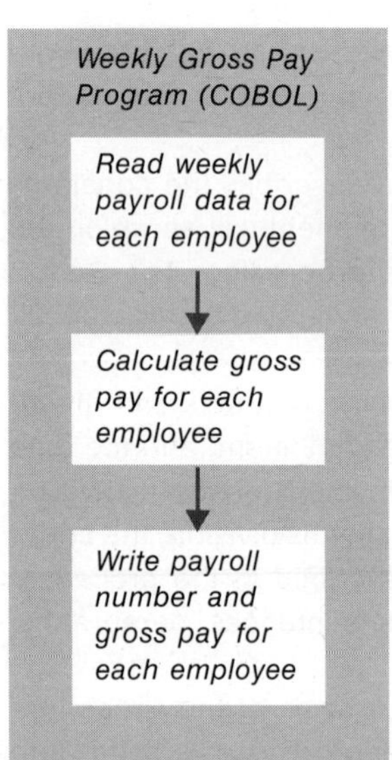


***COBOL Illustration.*** The foregoing divisions of the COBOL language are illustrated for computing gross pay in Figure 10-4 (as noted previously).

*Identification Division.* The Identification Division contains the name of the program (lines 1–3), namely, HOUR-PAY. A brief description of the program is found under REMARKS—PROGRAM TO COMPUTE WEEKLY GROSS PAY.

*Environment Division.* The Configuration Section of the Environmental Division, lines 5 through 7, indicates that an IBM 370 computer will be used to compile the program as well as process the object program. The Input-Output Section is used to name each file, identify its contents, and assign it to one or more input-output devices. Lines 10 and 11 identify the card-input device as a card reader, known as SYS007 (manufacturer number for this device is 2540) and the print-output device as a line printer, known as SYS009 (manufacturer number for this device is 1403).

*Data Division.* In the Data Division, the File Section, lines 13 through 37, has two File Description (FD) entries. The first, statements 14 through 18, describe the card input as a 80 column card where magnetic tape labels are not needed. The first entry is identified as a WEEKLY-PAYROLL-CARD-INPUT and is divided into several fields per lines 20 through 24. Card columns 1 through 5 contain the employee-payroll-number while columns 8 through 9 and 10 through 12 contain the hours-worked and hourly-pay respectively. The term "picture" identifies the coded description of the particular field. For example, the picture clause 9V99 on line 23 describes the hourly-pay as a three-position numeric field containing an assumed decimal point. In the second FD entry, the statements on lines 25 through 37 describe the print-output file named PRINT-LINE. The printed output with appropriate spacing contains the employee-payroll-number, hours-worked, and gross-pay for each person on the weekly payroll.

The Working Storage Section, lines 38 through 43, reserves storage locations for five fields—gross-pay, straight-time (amount), and overtime (amount, hours, and premium). It describes them as numeric fields containing appropriate decimal places. The number 77 was chosen for the COBOL-65 version to define a single variable in the Working Storage Section.

*Procedure Division.* The Procedure Division, starting on line 44 and ending on line 64, has no section headings but has three paragraph headings. The first paragraph, starting on line 45, reads START-PROG. Here, the input and output files are opened and the Print-Line is cleared of any data that may be present when the program is read in. In the second paragraph, READ-A-CARD, the following programming takes place. The statement on line 48 requires the program to read input cards and, when the final card has been read, go to (branch) the LAST-CARD paragraph (line 62) which is the third and final one in the Procedure Division.

```
LINE NO. SEQ. NO.          SOURCE STATEMENT                          CBD CL3-8 06/01/71

IDENTIFICATION DIVISION.
PROGRAM-ID. HOUR-PAY.
REMARKS. PROGRAM TO COMPUTE WEEKLY GROSS PAY.
ENVIRONMENT DIVISION.
CONFIGURATION SECTION.
SOURCE-COMPUTER. IBM-370.
OBJECT-COMPUTER. IBM-370.
INPUT-OUTPUT SECTION.
FILE-CONTROL.
    SELECT CARD-INPUT ASSIGN TO SYS007-UR-2540-S.
    SELECT PRINT-OUTPUT ASSIGN TO SYS009-UR-1403-S.
DATA DIVISION.
FILE SECTION.
FD  CARD-INPUT,
    RECORDING MODE IS F,
    RECORD CONTAINS 80 CHARACTERS,
    LABEL RECORDS ARE OMITTED,
    DATA RECORD IS WEEKLY-PAYROLL-CARD-INPUT.
01  WEEKLY-PAYROLL-CARD-INPUT.
    02 EMPLOYEE-PAYROLL-NUMBER PICTURE IS 99999.
    02 FILLER PICTURE IS X(2).
    02 HOURS-WORKED PICTURE IS 99.
    02 HOURLY-PAY PICTURE IS 9V99.
    02 FILLER PICTURE IS X(68).
FD  PRINT-OUTPUT,
    RECORDING MODE IS F,
    RECORD CONTAINS 133 CHARACTERS,
    LABEL RECORDS ARE OMITTED,
    DATA RECORD IS PRINT-LINE.
01  PRINT-LINE.
    02 FILLER PICTURE IS X.
    02 EMPLOYEE-PRINT PICTURE IS 9(5).
    02 FILLER PICTURE IS X(5).
    02 HOURS-PRINT PICTURE IS 99.
    02 FILLER PICTURE IS X(5).
    02 GROSS-PRINT PICTURE IS $$$9.99.
    02 FILLER PICTURE IS X(108).
WORKING-STORAGE SECTION.
    77 GROSS-PAY PICTURE IS 999V99.
    77 STRAIGHT-TIME PICTURE IS 999V99.
    77 OVERTIME PICTURE IS 999V99.
    77 OVERTIME-HOURS PICTURE IS 99V99.
    77 OVERTIME-PREMIUM PICTURE IS 999V99.
PROCEDURE DIVISION.
START-PROG.
    OPEN INPUT CARD-INPUT, OUTPUT PRINT-OUTPUT.
READ-A-CARD.
    READ CARD-INPUT, AT END GO TO LAST-CARD.
    MULTIPLY HOURLY-PAY BY HOURS-WORKED
    GIVING STRAIGHT-TIME ROUNDED.
    DIVIDE 2 INTO HOURLY-PAY GIVING  OVERTIME-PREMIUM.
    SUBTRACT 40 FROM HOURS-WORKED GIVING OVERTIME-HOURS.
    MULTIPLY OVERTIME-HOURS BY OVERTIME-PREMIUM
    GIVING OVERTIME ROUNDED.
    ADD STRAIGHT-TIME, OVERTIME GIVING GROSS-PAY.
    MOVE EMPLOYEE-PAYROLL-NUMBER TO EMPLOYEE-PRINT.
    MOVE HOURS-WORKED TO HOURS-PRINT.
    MOVE GROSS-PAY TO GROSS-PRINT.
    WRITE PRINT-LINE AFTER ADVANCING 1.
    MOVE SPACES TO PRINT-LINE.
    GO TO READ-A-CARD.
LAST-CARD.
    CLOSE CARD-INPUT, PRINT-OUTPUT.
    STOP RUN.
```

Figure 10-4 COBOL program to compute weekly gross pay for each employee.

The statements on lines 49 through 55 make the actual calculations for gross pay. This consists of determining the straight-time amount (statement on lines 49 and 50). Next, the hourly-pay rate is divided by two in order to give an overtime-premium rate (statement on line 51). The value 40 hours is subtracted from the hours-worked this week which results in overtime-hours (statement on line 52). Then, overtime-hours are multiplied by an overtime-premium rate for an overtime amount (statement on lines 53 and 54). Lastly, the straight-time amount and overtime amount are added for gross-pay (statement on line 55).

The next three statements (lines 56 through 58) cause data to be moved to the output print-line. It should be pointed out that these three names—Employee-Payroll-Number, Hours-Worked, and Gross-Pay are related directly to the names in the File Section of the Data Division. The statement on line 59 causes the data which were moved in the preceding three lines to be printed after spacing the paper. The last two lines (60 and 61) in this second paragraph cause the print-line to be cleared and the program to branch to the paragraph headed READ-A-CARD.

The instructions in the LAST-CARD paragraph are activated by a branch operation which occurs after the last card has been read. The statement on line 63 informs the system that processing of the files has been completed. The final statement on line 64 in this payroll program stops the processing run.

*COBOL has the following attributes:*

- *structure approximates business practice*
- *internal processing functions are in English*
- *documentation is found in the source program*
- *language is adaptable to batch processing*

***Evaluation of COBOL.*** Currently, COBOL is widely used for programming business applications. Its logical structure of files, records, and elements approximates business practice. One of its important characteristics is that internal processing functions are stated in English. This eliminates the necessity to learn the machine instructions of a specific computer. It has the added advantage of documentation in the source program itself. The quality of documentation is considered superior to other languages since programs are much easier to read. This should have been obvious in the Procedure Division of the illustrated Hourly Pay payroll program. Use of data names, maximum of 30 characters, allow more detailed description of the data. Lastly, COBOL is readily adaptable to batch type applications.

One of the major drawbacks of COBOL is its relatively elementary structure which can require extensive programming to accomplish relatively simple tasks. In the example, statements appearing on lines 49 through 55 for the READ-A-CARD paragraph could have been expressed as one line in FORTRAN, such as:

```
GROSS = (RATE * HOURS) + ((HOURS - 40.0) * RATE/2.0)
```

Thus, the COBOL language tends to be wordy and drawn out when compared to other programming languages.

When COBOL is again compared to FORTRAN, COBOL is more difficult to learn, but much easier to learn than some machine-oriented symbolic language or machine language. From the standpoint of efficiency, an experienced programmer can write a more efficient program in FORTRAN or a machine-oriented language than in COBOL. This statement is based upon numerous test results. Also, FORTRAN is a more efficient language than COBOL—both in the amount of preparation required by the programmer and in the amount of computer time necessary to compile identical programs. If a COBOL program is to be efficient, the programmer must be familiar with the characteristics of the computer on which processing will occur.

### BASIC Language

BASIC, an acronym for Beginner's All-purpose Symbolic Instruction Code, was developed in 1963 by a small group of undergraduate students at Dartmouth College

*BASIC language focuses on programming in a time sharing environment.*

under the direction of Professor John Kemeny. It was developed at a time when interest in time sharing was focused on large research oriented experimental systems. Since that time, many improvements in the BASIC language have occurred.

***Recent Developments.*** Many different BASIC versions, comparable to the surge in FORTRAN during the mid-50's, are available. They include Basic BASIC, Advanced BASIC, Extended BASIC, and Super BASIC. These newer versions are better suited for a very wide class of problems whether in an on-line or off-line mode and regardless of program size. The language has increased in power while retaining its simplicity.

*The structure of BASIC includes a simple English vocabulary and grammatical rules while resembling mathematical notation commonly used.*

***Language Structure.*** BASIC has a simple English vocabulary and few grammatical rules while resembling ordinary mathematical notation. Although the language is basically simple, it is a powerful language, providing arithmetic capabilities, logic comparisons, subscripting, common trigonometric functions, lists, arrays, and matrix multiplication. Provision can be made to use a particular part of the program many times by calling for it as a subroutine whenever needed. The structure of BASIC is somewhat similar to FORTRAN. The major elements of FORTRAN are constants, variables, expressions, statements, and subprograms. Comparable categories of BASIC are:

1. numbers,
2. variables,
3. arithmetic operations,
4. statements,
5. functions,
6. additional features.

The presentation in this chapter will center around Advanced BASIC for time sharing devices.

*Each BASIC statement must begin with a line number which specifies the order of execution by the computer.*

***Statement Format.*** Before discussing the fundamentals of BASIC, there are several rules to follow in terms of statement format. Each statement in the program begins with a line number. Not only do these numbers identify the statements within the program, but also specify the order in which the executable statements are to be followed by the computer. The choice of line numbers is arbitrary as long as they contain no more than five digits. However, consecutive line numbering is not recommended since it does not permit the insertion of additional statements which may have been overlooked during the original writing of the program. When adding a statement to an existing program, it is not necessary to place the statement in the proper sequential location since the computer does this prior to executing the program. Also, spaces have no significance since spaces are used arbitrarily to make a program more readable. The last consideration in terms of statement format is information listed in the data statements. It must be stored in data blocks by the computer in the same sequence as it is listed in the data statements. Otherwise, when the information is retrieved, the correct data will not be read. Thus, the programmer must store his input information in an order in which he desires to read it.

*1. Numbers in BASIC have these requirements:*
- *may be positive or negative*
- *may contain up to 11 digits*
- *may use exponentiation for values over 11 digits*
- *must be expressed in decimal form*
- *must be separated by commas for a series of values*

***Numbers.*** Numbers in BASIC may be positive or negative and may contain up to eleven digits, but must be expressed in decimal form. If the number exceeds eleven digits, the computer rounds off the value. However, further flexibility can be gained by using the letter E (exponentiation) which stands for "times ten to the power." Thus, values that exceed eleven digits can be written with the E notation. When a series of numbers are entered, they must be separated by commas. The comma following the last number is optional.

2. *Variables in BASIC represent values which change for either different executions of the program or at various points in the program. They are represented by a letter or by a letter followed by a digit.*

3. *Arithmetic operations in BASIC utilize certain priority rules that must be followed.*

4. *The more commonly used BASIC statements are:*
   - LET
   - READ
   - DATA
   - RESTORE
   - INPUT
   - PRINT
   - SET DIGITS
   - GO TO
   - IF–THEN
   - ON
   - FOR
   - NEXT
   - GOSUB
   - RETURN
   - END
   - STOP
   - REM

***Variables.*** Variables in BASIC are denoted by any letter or by any letter followed by a single digit. The computer will interpret A, X, I0, D5, and S4 as variables. A variable in BASIC represents a specific number although it is not usually known to the programmer at the time that the program is written. For example, a variable that represents hours worked can change from one employee to another as the payroll is processed for the week. Variables are given or assigned values by FOR, LET, READ, or INPUT statements. The value so assigned will not change until the next time a FOR, LET, READ, or INPUT statement is encountered with a value for that variable.

***Arithmetic Operations.*** One of the primary functions of BASIC language is to perform arithmetic operations. Evaluating formulas which are written as a part of the program is similar to those found in standard mathematical calculations with the exception that all BASIC formulas must be written on a single line. The five arithmetic operations that are used to write a formula are listed as follows:

| *Symbol* | *Arithmetic Operation* |
|---|---|
| + | Addition |
| − | Subtraction |
| * | Multiplication |
| / | Division |
| ↑ | Raise to the power |

When using the above arithmetic operators, care must be used in writing parentheses to make certain that terms are formed as intended for making the appropriate calculation.

*Priority Rules.* The rules that are followed in BASIC in terms of the order of priorities for arithmetic operations are:

1. The formula inside the parentheses is computed before the parenthesized quantity is used in further computation.
2. In the absence of parentheses in a formula involving addition, multiplication, and raising a number to a power, the computer first raises the number to the power, then performs the multiplication, and the addition last. Division has the same priority as multiplication, and subtraction the same as addition.
3. In the absence of parentheses in a formula involving only multiplication and division, the operations are performed from left to right as in the case for addition and subtraction.
4. If a term is negative, it is considered as being subtracted from zero.

***Statements.*** There were only 15 statements in the original BASIC. The number has since grown. In the following narrative, the more commonly used statements will be explored.

*LET Statement.* One of the most important statements is the Let Statement. It is a command to compute a formula and assign the answer as the new value of a specified variable. The format for this statement is:

LET variable = formula

Two examples are found in Figure 10-5 for the LET statement (lines 140 and 160).

*READ and DATA Statements.* Data obtained from the remote user console unit can be requested in one of two ways: it can be written as part of the program and entered as such or it can be entered upon program request. These two methods are employed in Read, Data, Restore, and Input statements. The Read statement causes the variables listed in it to be used (in order), according to the data sets found in the Data statement(s) in the program. Thus, a Read statement and a Data statement can not be used in a program except when they accompany each other. Their format is:

READ variable . . .
DATA variable . . .

*RESTORE and INPUT Statements.* Another statement for obtaining data is the Restore statement. It allows rereading the same data as many times as desired, its format being: RESTORE. The last statement for obtaining data is the Input statement which acts as a Read statement, but does not draw numbers from a Data statement. Frequently the Input statement is combined with a Print statement to clarify what value is being requested. Several examples are found in Figure 10-5 (lines 30 and 60, 70 and 90, 100 and 130 and 180 and 200).

*PRINT Statement.* Printing format control in BASIC is accomplished by the Print statement. The computer advances the paper one line when it encounters this command. The Print statement, then, has a number of uses which are: skip a line, print out the results of some computations, and print out verbatim a message included in the program. Its format is:

PRINT or PRINT (results or message)

Numerous examples of Print statements are found in Figure 10-5.

*SET DIGITS Statement.* A printing control statement is the Set Digits statement whose format is:

SET DIGITS formula

It provides a means for controlling the number of digits of a numeric value that must be printed. The value expressed by the formula in the statement is truncated (cut off) to its integer values, representing the number of print columns that are to be used in all future Print statements until another Set Digits statement is executed or until the program terminates. One to eleven printed columns may be specified.

*GO TO Statement.* Program branching and loop control statements are essential to utilize the logical ability of the computer. Often, it is desirable to execute commands in an order other than that in which they are written. In such cases, a Go To statement, whose format is:

GO TO line number

instructs the computer to do this or go to another executable statement rather than the next one in the program.

*IF-THEN Statement.* The If-Then statement is basically a conditional Go To statement since it allows jumping the normal sequence of commands. Its format is:

IF formula relation formula THEN line number

There are six mathematical symbols to be used in the If-Then statement when values must be compared. The six relational symbols are:

| *Symbol* | *Relational Meaning* |
|---|---|
| $=$ | Is equal to |
| $<$ | Is less than |
| $< =$ or $= <$ | Is less than or equal to |
| $>$ | Is greater than |
| $> =$ or $= >$ | Is greater than or equal to |
| $< >$ or $> <$ | Is not equal to |

One example of the If-Then statement is found in Figure 10-5 on line 210.

*On Statement.* The last of the program branching and loop control statements is the On statement whose format is:

ON formula GO TO line number, line number, . . .

It provides a means of combining several equality-type If-Then statements into a simple statement. The user must know the range of values that the formula can assume in order to provide the appropriate number of transfers.

*FOR and NEXT Statements.* Programmed logic loops are desirable in programs where one or more portions are to be repeated a number of times, perhaps with slight changes each time. Because loops are so important in programming, BASIC provides two statements to specify a loop very compactly. They are the For and Next statements. The For statement defines the beginning of the program loop and the Next statement indicates the end of a program loop. Their format is:

```
FOR variable = formula TO formula STEP formula
  .
  .
  .
NEXT variable
```

The For statement specifies the range of values its variable may assume during the repetitive execution of the loop and the formula which governs the stepping of the variable (i.e., the stepping factor). On the other hand, the Next statement is a command to add the algebraic value of the stepping factor to the algebraic value of the variable. It then causes the program to determine whether or not the value of the variable has reached or exceeded the specified range. Complicated For statements can be used where the initial value, the final value, and the step size may be derived from complex formulas.

*GOSUB and RETURN Statements.* Another type of loop makes use of the Gosub and Return statements. When a segment of a program is to be repeated more than once, it is better to treat it as a subroutine. The subroutine is entered with the Gosub statement and an appropriate line number while the last line of the subroutine directs the computer to return at the point where the subroutine jump occurred. Its format is:

```
GOSUB line number
  .
  .
  .
RETURN
```

The programmer must be careful not to write a program in which a GOSUB appears inside a subroutine which already refers to one of the subroutines previously entered.

*END and STOP Statements.* Program termination is provided in BASIC by two commands, namely, the End and Stop statements. The End statement (format:END) is the highest line number in the program which ends the program. The Stop command (format:STOP) is used in programs where there are more than one logical stopping points.

*REM Statement.* The last statement to be covered is the Rem statement whose format is:

REM comment or group of comments

It provides a means by which explanatory remarks may be included in a program. These comments appear on the program listing.

*5. Functions in BASIC are operations specified within statements. They can be mathematical or special purpose.*

***Functions.*** Functions are operations specified within statements which can be either mathematical functions or special purpose functions. In addition to the arithmetic functions set forth previously, there are several mathematical functions. They are:

| *Function* | *Mathematical Meaning* |
|---|---|
| SIN (X) | Sine of *X* |
| COS (X) | Cosine of *X* |
| TAN (X) | Tangent of *X* |
| ATN (X) | Arctangent of *X* |
| EXP (X) | Natural exponential of *X*, $E^x$ |
| ABS (X) | Absolute value of *X* |
| LOG (X) | Natural logarithm of *X* |
| SQR (X) | Square root of *X* |
| CLG (X) | Common logarithm of *X* (base 10) |

These functions can be used in a formula in place of a number or variable. Any number or formula may be used in place of *X*. The remaining five special-purpose functions are listed as follows:

| *Function* | *Mathematical Meaning* |
|---|---|
| TAB | Output tabulation |
| INT | Integer part of *X* |
| RND | Generates a random number between zero and one |
| DEF | Define additional functions |
| SGN | Sign of *X* (variable or formula) |

*6. Additional features in BASIC include:*
- *lists*
- *tables*
- *matrices*

***Additional Features.*** Additional features of BASIC include lists, tables, and matrices. Supplementing the ordinary variables are those variables which can be used to designate the elements of a list or of a table. These variables are employed where a subscript or a double subscript might normally be used.

*DIM Statement*. Whenever the programmer desires to enter a list or a table with a subscript greater than 10, the Dim statement must be used to inform the computer that ample space is available for the items. Its format is:

DIM variables (integer, . . .)

The following examples in a program,

```
30      DIM R (40)
80      DIM T (4, 30)
```

would allow the user to enter a list of 40 items in the first case and a table 4 by 30 in the second illustration.

*MAT Statements*. The matrix operation statements are very useful in solving matrix algebra problems. These special instructions for matrix computations are prefixed by the word MAT. The following is a list of available matrix commands:

| *Statement* | *Matrix Meaning* |
|---|---|
| MAT READ A, B, C | Read the three matrices *A*, *B*, *C* |
| MAT PRINT A, B, C | Print the three matrices *A*, *B*, *C* |
| MAT C = A + B | Add the two matrices *A* and *B* |

| *Statement* | *Matrix Meaning* |
|---|---|
| MAT C = A − B | Subtract matrix *B* from matrix *A* |
| MAT C = A * B | Multiply matrix *A* by matrix *B* |
| MAT C = INV(A) | Invert matrix *A* |
| MAT C = TRN(A) | Transpose matrix *A* |
| MAT C = (K) * A | Multiply matrix *A* by the number *K* |
| MAT C = ZER | Fill out *C* with zeros |
| MAT C = CON | Fill out *C* with ones |
| MAT C = IDN | Set up *C* as an identity matrix |

Referring to the prior chapter, system commands are used to instruct the computer concerning what action is to be taken by the program. It is by these commands that the user is able to converse with the computer. A complete listing of these commands is found in Figure 9-31. These system commands are in constrast with the program elements given in this chapter which are a series of instructions to the computer system for processing a particular program.

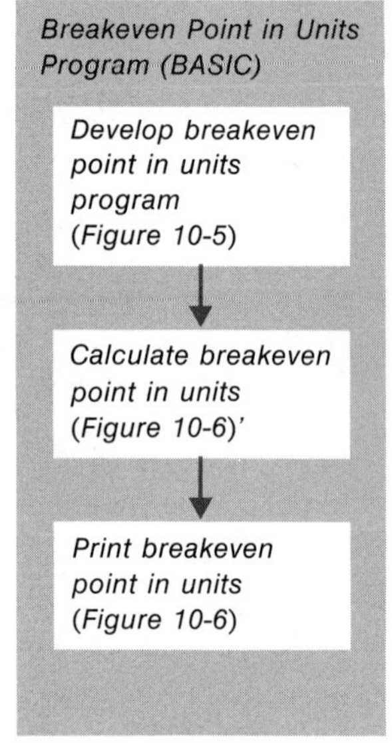


***BASIC Illustration.*** A sample BASIC program (Figure 9-30) was set forth in the prior chapter for computing compound interest on a yearly basis. In this section, the illustrative BASIC problem is a general purpose program for computing breakeven. As stated in Figure 10-5 per lines 10 and 20, "This Program Will Calculate the Breakeven Point, In Units, For a Single Product Organization." The Print statements on lines 30, 40, and 50 relate to the amount of total fixed costs for the firm. The Input statement (INPUT F) on line 60 is combined with the preceding Print statements to clarify what value is being requested, namely, the total amount of fixed costs, defined by the variable F. These combined Print and Input statements are found on lines 70 through 90 and lines 100 through 130 for selling price (S) and variable costs (V) respectively.

*Breakeven Program Calculations.* In the first Let statement (M = S − V) on line 140, the variable margin (M) or contribution to fixed costs and profit is computed. On line 150, the Rem statement provides a comment about the M value for use in the next Let statement (line 160). The Let B = F/M statement means that the answer obtained from the division (on the right side of the equation) is to be assigned as the answer for the specified variable (B). Thus, the Print statement on line 170 specifies an answer in "units."

If additional breakeven calculations are desired per the Print statements on lines 180 and 190, a "1" must be typed for the Input statement variable (E) per line 200. The next line (210) contains an If-Then statement that returns processing to line 30 of the program for an input value of "1." On the other hand, if the programs is to be ended, a "2" must be typed. The last line of the program is an End statement which formally terminates the program.

*Breakeven Calculated.* After the program has been entered per Figure 10-5, the operator types RUN (and depresses the RETURN key) and the system responds by typing the name of the program (BEVEN) plus other identifying information, as shown in Figure 10-6. Values are entered for each question. The values—fixed costs (F) of \$100,000, selling price (S) of \$350, and variable costs (V) of \$200 are entered manually through the keyboard of the teletypewriter. The breakeven point is found to be 667 (666.667) units, calculated as follows:

$$B = \frac{\text{F (Total Fixed Costs)}}{\text{S (Selling price)} - \text{V (Variable costs)}} = \frac{\$100{,}000}{\$350 - \$200}$$

$$= \frac{\$100{,}000}{\$150} = 666.667 \text{ units}$$

```
X

        APPLIED CØMPUTER TIME SHARE CIN

ØN AT- 09:10 PØRT:02

USER NUMBER--W804

PASSWØRD

XXXXX?

***XAVIER***

TYPE ØLD ØR NEW:ØLD

PRØBLEM NAME: BEVEN

READY
LIST

BEVEN     09:11  ACTS 09/16/71 WED.

 10  PRINT "THIS PRØGRAM WILL CALCULATE THE BREAKEVEN PØINT"
 20  PRINT "IN UNITS, FØR A SINGLE PRØDUCT ØRGANIZATIØN."
 21  PRINT
 30  PRINT "CALCULATE THE TØTAL FIXED CØSTS THAT MUST BE"
 40  PRINT "CØVERED BY THIS PRØDUCT. ENTER THIS AMØUNT AFTER"
 50  PRINT "THE QUESTIØN MARK."
 60  INPUT F
 70  PRINT "ENTER THE SELLING PRICE PER UNIT AFTER THE QUESTIØN"
 80  PRINT "MARK"
 90  INPUT S
100  PRINT "WHAT ARE THE TØTAL VARIABLE CØSTS ASSIGNABLE TØ EACH"
110  PRINT "UNIT SØLD? IE. CØSTS THAT WØULD NØT BE INCURRED IF A"
120  PRINT "UNIT WERE NØT PRØDUCED AND SØLD."
130  INPUT V
140  LET M=S-V
150  REM M IS THE VARIABLE MARGIN
160  LET B=F/M
161  PRINT
170  PRINT "THE BREAK EVEN PØINT FØR THIS PRØDUCT IS"; B; "UNITS"
171  PRINT
180  PRINT "IF YØU WANT TØ CØNTINUE THIS PRØGRAM FØR ANØTHER"
190  PRINT "CALCUALATIØN TYPE A 1 IF NØT, TYPE A 2."
200  INPUT E
210  IF E=1 THEN 30
220  END
```

Figure 10-5 BASIC program for calculating the breakeven point in units for a single product organization.

In Figure 10-6, the value 2 was manually typed for the final input value. This indicates no more calculations are to be performed. Also, running time and elapsed central processing unit time is printed, along with the word READY. Since we are finished with the program, a system command of BYE (per Figure 9-31) disconnects the terminal typewriter from the computer system.

***Evaluation of BASIC.*** While COBOL has been designed for batch processing applications, BASIC is designed for on-line processing in a time sharing environment. This on-line orientation results in a conversational mode with the computer. The immediate access to desk side terminals improves response time to information

```
RUN

BEVEN     09:13  ACTS 09/16/71 WED.

THIS PRØGRAM WILL CALCULATE THE BREAK EVEN PØINT,
  IN UNITS, FØR A SINGLE PRØDUCT ØRGANIZATIØN.

CALCULATE THE TØTAL FIXED CØSTS THAT MUST BE
  CØVERED BY THIS PRØDUCT. ENTER THIS AMØUNT AFTER
  THE QUESTIØN MARK.
  ?100000
  ENTER THE SELLING PRICE PER UNIT AFTER THE QUESTIØN
  MARK
  ?350
WHAT ARE THE TØTAL VARIABLE CØSTS ASSIGNABLE TØ EACH
  UNIT SØLD? IE. CØSTS THAT WØULD NØT BE INCURRED IF A
  UNIT WERE NØT PRØDUCED AND SØLD.
  ?200

  THE BREAK EVEN PØINT FØR THIS PRØDUCT IS 666.667 UNITS

  IF YØU WANT TØ CØNTINUE THIS PRØGRAM FØR ANØTHER
  CALCUALATIØN TYPE A 1 IF NØT, TYPE A 2.
  ?2

RUN TIME:    01.6 SECS   ELAPSED CPU:    02.2 SEC

READY
BYE

ØFF AT 09:14
```

Figure 10-6 Representative data used in BASIC program for calculating the breakeven point in units for a single product organization.

*BASIC has the following attributes:*
- *oriented toward a time-sharing environment*
- *fast response to information needs*
- *relatively easy to learn*
- *capable of solving simple and many complex problems*

needs and problem solutions. People who must solve problems quickly with a computer can by-pass the computer room and the programming staff if they know BASIC programming. This is an important consideration for a fast response data processing system. Since computer problem solutions are available when needed, company personnel utilize their time more efficiently and complete their projects more quickly.

A comparison of BASIC with COBOL, for example, indicates the simplicity of the former over the latter. Rather than getting bogged down in long and wordy sentences, paragraphs, and sections, BASIC allows the user to write programs that are straightforward. Not only is implementation quite easy with BASIC, but also the learning of the language is easy for the average person. After several hours with the language, an individual should be capable of some simplified programming. Thus, the ease of implementation and learning has made BASIC the fastest growing language for time sharing processing.

Since the language is basically used for writing programs at remote typewriter terminals, it is well suited for those company personnel who must write their own programs occasionally. Being a stripped down version of FORTRAN, the output takes a standard form and there is no distinction between integer and real values. This lack of advanced features which are available in FORTRAN makes the language limited when the programmer needs them. For this reason, FORTRAN is used for the more complex problems in a time sharing environment while BASIC is employed for less complex problems.

### PL/1 Language

PL/1 (Programming Language One), being a procedure-oriented language, was first introduced by IBM for its System/360 series. It was originally developed in 1963 and 1964 by a joint committee of IBM and the SHARE FORTRAN Project. The committee's initial intention was to extend FORTRAN by adding special features, such as character handling and array operations. Since this was difficult to do, a fresh start was made on a new language.

*PL/1 combines the features of ALGOL, COBOL, FORTRAN, and other special programming features into one language.*

***Business and Scientific Oriented.*** PL/1 is a general purpose language which combines the features of ALGOL,[1] COBOL, FORTRAN, and other special programming features. It is capable of handling business and scientific programming whether they be in an on-line or batch processing mode. Its technical significance is based on the consolidation into a single language many facilities which appear in separate languages. This simplifies the problem of the user who employs FORTRAN for scientific applications and COBOL for business applications. The major components of this business and scientific language to be covered are:

1. comments,
2. identifiers,
3. data,
4. expressions,
5. procedures,
6. statements.

*The 60 character set of PL/1 encompasses:*
- *0 through 9 numerics—10*
- *extended alphabetic characters—29*
- *special characters—21*

***Character Set.*** The PL/1 language has a 60 character set. These include the digits 0 through 9 and an extended alphabet of 29 characters, that is, the currency symbol ($), the commercial "at" sign (@), the number sign (#), and the 26 letters of the alphabet. In addition, there are 21 special characters which are:

| *Name* | *Character* | *Name* | *Character* |
|---|---|---|---|
| Blank | | Percent symbol | % |
| Equal or assignment symbol | = | Semicolon | ; |
| Plus sign | + | Colon | : |
| Minus sign | − | "Not" symbol | ¬ |
| Asterisk or multiply symbol | * | "And" symbol | & |
| Slash or divide symbol | / | "Or" symbol | \| |
| Left parenthesis | ( | "Greater than" symbol | > |
| Right parenthesis | ) | "Less than" symbol | < |
| Comma | , | Break character[2] | _ |
| Point or period | . | Question mark | ? |
| Single quotation mark or apostrophe | ' | | |

Special characters may be combined to create other symbols. For example, < = means "less than or equal to" and ¬ = means "not equal to." The combina-

[1] ALGOrithmic Language—used for expressing an algorithm which may be defined as a series of well defined arithmetic steps that are followed in order to obtain a desired result.
[2] The break character is the same as the typewriter underline character.

tion ** denotes exponentiation (X ** 2 means $X^2$). Blanks are not permitted in such character combinations.

1. *Comments in PL/1 are inserted into a program to clarify what action takes place at a given point.*

***Comments.*** Programmers frequently insert comments into their programs to clarify what action occurs at a given point. These comments enable someone unfamiliar with the program to follow the programmer's line of thought and are helpful to the programmer when looking back over program sections that were written earlier. Comments are permitted wherever blanks are allowed in a program. They may be punched into the same cards as statements, be inserted between statements, or appear in the middle of statements without affecting complication of the program.

The character pair, /*, indicates the beginning of a comment. The same characters reversed, */, indicate its end. No blanks or other characters can separate these two characters. The slash and the asterisk must be immediately adjacent. The comment itself may contain any characters, except the */ combination which would be interpreted as terminating the comment.

2. *Identifiers in PL/1 serve as names of data items, files, and special conditions as well as labels for statements.*

***Identifiers.*** An identifier is a combination of alphanumeric characters and break characters used in a program as names of data items, files, and special conditions, and as labels for statements. The actual words of the language, such as READ, WRITE, and GO TO, are also identifiers. Such language words are called *keywords,* and when used in proper context, have a specific meaning to the compiler. They specify such things as the action to be taken, the nature of the data, and the purpose of a name.

An identifier must begin with one of the 29 alphabetic characters and cannot contain blanks. No identifier can exceed 31 characters in length. Some compilers may restrict the length for certain kinds of identlfiers. Examples of identifiers from Figure 10-7 are:

```
MASTER_FILE      RATE
LOAN_#           PAY_#
```

Several of these examples illustrate the use of the break character to improve the readability of an identifier since blanks are not permitted.

3. *Data in PL/1 serve as a representation of information or values. Reference to data is made by using either a variable or a constant.*

***Data.*** Data—digits and characters—are generally defined as a representation of information or values. However they are used, they always represent values. A programmer is concerned with several different levels of data and different representations of the same values. These are: (1) raw data, the values to be processed and the information that states the problem to be solved, (2) the representation of values, which the programmer writes in his program, (3) compiler input data, the representations as they are punched into a card or is entered from a typewriter terminal (these data are translated into machine language data), and (4) internal data, the representations as they are maintained inside the computer.

Reference to a data item, numeric, or alphabetic is made by using either a *variable* or a *constant.* A variable is a symbolic name (identifier) having a value that may change during execution of a program. Since it is a name, a variable is not, in itself, a data item. The value of a variable at any specific time is the data item to which it refers at that time. On the other hand, a constant which is not given a symbolic name is unchanging. The data item is its name.

***Expressions.*** Any identifier, other than language keywords, written in a PL/1 program is called an expression. An expression may be a single constant or a name,

4. *Expressions in PL/1 may be single constants or names, or they may be a combination of these.*

or it may be a combination of them, including operators and other delimiters. An arithmetic expression combines arithmetic data identifiers and arithmetic operators. Arithmetic expressions may involve addition, subtraction, multiplication, division, and exponentiation. A number of arithmetic operations may be included in a single expression.

Parentheses within an expression indicate that the parenthesized portion is considered as a single value in relation to its surrounding arithmetic operators. The parenthesized portion of an expression is evaluated first, with innermost parenthesized material taking precedence. Also, although an expression may contain more than one data item, it represents the single value obtained after the expression is evaluated.

5. *A procedure in PL/1 is the basic building block of the language. It is a block of instructions designed to perform a specific function.*

***Procedures.*** The language handles problem solving through a modular design programming approach. This means that the program is divided into modules or building blocks for different applications and various levels of complexity. The basic building blocks in the language are called procedures. A procedure is a block of instructions designed to perform a specific function, say to calculate the gross pay in a payroll program. Programmers build application programs by employing these procedures. The important aspect of using procedures or building blocks is that it simplifies the task of reprogramming at a later date. Also, the programmer can write a number of short procedures and combine them into a larger program.

*PROCEDURE Format.* A program may consist of a simple procedure or of several procedures. During execution of the program, control can go from one procedure to another and can return to a previously executed or partly executed procedure. A procedure is headed by a Procedure statement and ended by an End statement, which appears as follows:

```
UPDATE: PROCEDURE;
   .
   .
   .
         END;
```

Each procedure must have a name or each Procedure statement must be labeled. A procedure name denotes an entry point through which control can be transferred to the procedure.

Control does not pass automatically from one procedure to the next. Each procedure, except the first, must be invoked or called separately from some other procedure. This usually occurs with the execution of a Call statement, such as:

```
CALL UPDATE;
```

Execution of this statement in another procedure would transfer control to the entry point of the procedure named UPDATE.

*PROCEDURES—External and Internal.* The first procedure of a program must have the OPTIONS (MAIN) attribute specified for it in its Procedure statement. At execution time, this procedure is called automatically to begin execution of the program. The different procedures in a program may be entirely separate from one another or some may be nested within other procedures. This should be apparent in the following two examples:

```
FIRST:    PROCEDURE OPTIONS (MAIN);        (First example)
          statement-1
          statement-2
          statement-3
          statement-4
          statement-5
          statement-6
          END;
UPDATE:   PROCEDURE;
          statement-a
          statement-b
          statement-c
          END;
```

The two procedures shown above are separate from one another. They are external procedures. All of the text of a procedure (except for its entry name) is said to be contained in that procedure.

```
FIRST: PROCEDURE                            (Second example)
       statement-1
       statement-2
       statement-3
       UPDATE: PROCEDURE;
               statement-a
               statement-b
               statement-c
               END;
       statement-4
       CALL UPDATE;
       statement-6
       END;
```

In this example, UPDATE is nested within FIRST where the former is an internal procedure and the latter is an external procedure.

Referring to the second example, execution starts with the FIRST: PROCEDURE statement. Statements 1, 2, and 3 are executed. When control reaches the UPDATE: PROCEDURE statement, that statement is ignored and execution continues with statement 4. Upon execution of the fifth statement, CALL UPDATE, control is transferred to UPDATE. Statements a, b, and c are executed. When the End statement is UPDATE is executed, control is transferred back to the procedure, FIRST, in order to execute the statement immediately following the CALL UPDATE statement or statement 6.

*6. Statements in PL/1 that comprise a procedure block include:*
- IF
- ON
- DO
- DECLARE
- GET
- PUT

***Statements.*** Statements are the major element of the PL/1 language since a number of them comprise a procedure block. There are *simple statements,* such as assignment, null, and keyword, and *compound statements,* such as IF and ON.

*Assignment Statement.* A simple assignment statement is illustrated in Figure 10-7 (line 17) which is:

```
INTEREST = PRINCIPAL * RATE/12;
```

The equal sign is used as an assignment symbol. What the statement means is that the expression to the right of the equal sign (PRINCIPAL * RATE/12) is to be evaluated and the result of the evaluation is to be assigned to INTEREST. It should be noted that the statement ended with a semicolon. The semicolon ends all simple and compound statements. Also, note that no special coding form was used since PL/1 is an unformatted string language. However, for the D version of the PL/1 compiler, entries begin in column 2 and extend through column 72.

*Null Statement.* A null statement, another type of simple statement, is simply the semicolon itself. What it means is a no-operation, that is, move on to the next statement in sequence. An example of a null statement usage might be:

```
ON UNDERFLOW;
```

Although ON UNDERFLOW is actually a part of a compound statement, it is truncated by the semicolon which then acts as the null statement requiring no action. The net result is that if there is an underflow interruption, it will be disregarded. The computer will move on to the next statement for execution.

*Keyword Statement.* A keyword statement, a third type of simple statement, is made up of a keyword followed by the body of the statement. One of the simplest forms of a keyword statement, illustrated in Figure 10-7 (line 22), is:

```
GO TO MASTER_FILE;
```

where GO TO is the keyword and MASTER_FILE is the body of the keyword statement. The semicolon at the end is the delimiter of the statement.

*IF Statement.* An example of the If compound statement is found in Figure 10-7. Toward the end of the program is the following compound statement:

```
IF BALANCE = 0
  THEN GO TO NEW_RECORD;
  ELSE PUT FILE (NEW_MASTER) LIST (LOAN_#, BALANCE, RATE);
GO TO NEW_RECORD;
```

If the balance is zero for the data being processed, go to a new record. If the balance is other than zero, perform the assigned task and go to a new record. In effect, this compound statement is made up of one or more simple statements where a semicolon ends the compound statement.

*ON Statement.* An example of the ON compound statement is:

```
ON OVERFLOW GO TO ERROR ROUTINE;
```

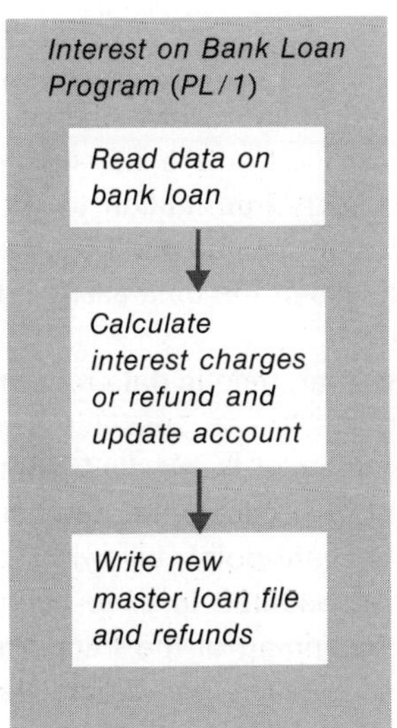


where two simple statements form a compound statement. Words like OVERFLOW and UNDERFLOW are keywords which are conditions. In essence, tests of conditions are set up and special paths are taken as a result of the condition discovered.

*Other Statements.* Other statements, such as Do, Declare, Get, and Put will be explained in the next section for the PL/1 illustration.

***PL/1 Illustration.*** To assist the reader in understanding the foregoing elements of PL/1, a sample problem is illustrated in Figure 10-7. It is a bank loan program that computes and updates interest on numerous bank loans of different amounts at varying rates of interest. The interest is compounded monthly, and in most cases, the borrower makes a monthly payment to reduce the principal of the loan as well as cover the interest charge.

The Procedure statement for this program is per the first line of the program. The UPDATE procedure for this PL/1 illustration is the entire program found in Figure 10-7. As far as the PL/1 compiler is concerned, the entire procedure could

```
01 UPDATE: PROCEDURE; /* BANK LOAN PROGRAM IN PL/1 */;
02         DECLARE PAY_# DECIMAL FIXED (7),
03              LOAN_# DECIMAL FIXED (7),
04              PRINCIPAL DECIMAL FIXED (8,2),
05              BALANCE DECIMAL FIXED (8,2),
06              PAYMENT DECIMAL FIXED (6,2),
07              REFUND DECIMAL FIXED (6,2)
08              INTEREST DECIMAL FIXED (5,2),
09              RATE DECIMAL FIXED (3,3),
10              MASTER FILE INPUT,
11              NEW_MASTER FILE OUTPUT,
12              INPUT FILE INPUT,
13              OUTPUT FILE OUTPUT;
14         ON ENDFILE (INPUT) GO TO MASTER FILE;
15 NEW_RECORD: GET FILE (INPUT) LIST (PAY_#,PAYMENT);
16 MASTER_FILE: GET FILE (MASTER) LIST (LOAN_#,PRINCIPAL, RATE);
17         INTEREST=PRINCIPAL * RATE/12
18         IF LOAN_#¬ = PAY_#
19           THEN DO;
20              PRINCIPAL=PRINCIPAL + INTEREST;
21              PUT FILE (NEW_MASTER) LIST (LOAN_#,PRINCIPAL,RATE);
22              GO TO MASTER_FILE;
23              END;
24           ELSE IF PAYMENT <= PRINCIPAL + INTEREST
25              THEN BALANCE = PRINCIPAL + INTEREST - PAYMENT:
26              ELSE DO;
27               BALANCE=0
28               REFUND = PAYMENT - PRINCIPAL + INTEREST;
29               PUT FILE (OUTPUT) LIST (LOAN_#,'REFUND:',REFUND);
30               END;
31   PUT FILE (OUTPUT) LIST (LOAN_#,PRINCIPAL,INTEREST,PAYMENT,BALANCE);
32   IF BALANCE=0
33      THEN GO TO NEW_RECORD;
34      ELSE PUT FILE (NEW_MASTER) LIST (LOAN_#,BALANCE,RATE);
35   GO TO NEW_RECORD;
36   END UPDATE;
```

Figure 10-7 PL/1 program to compute and update interest on numerous bank loans of different amounts at varying rates of interest. (Courtesy International Business Machines Corporation.)

have been written as one continuous string of statements and separated only by semicolons. In the sample problem, the format is designed to improve readability.

*Storage Locations.* An important part of a procedure is the Declare statement, starting on line 2. The Declare statement supplies necessary information to the compiler so that storage areas can be reserved for the data represented by the names used in the procedure. It describes the characteristics of the data assigned to each variable and tells the nature of each file.

A Declare statement specifies whether data assigned to arithmetic data names is to be binary or decimal, as noted on lines 2 through 9. It also specifies the maximum number of digits in any data item, and the number of those digits that represent a fractional portion. Regarding this latter point, it specifies the number of digits that should be considered to the right of the decimal point. Likewise, it specifies whether the value of the data item is to be represented in fixed-point (consists of digits and a single point that specifies the beginning of the fraction) or floating-point (used to specify values much larger or smaller than would be practical in fixed-point) notation. For example on line 4, PRINCIPAL is declared to be a variable representing decimal, fixed-point numbers, none of which will contain more than eight digits, with the two rightmost digits assumed to represent a decimal fraction. In a similar manner, PAY_# and LOAN_# (lines 2 and 3) are declared to be names that will represent fixed-point decimal numbers of no more than seven digits, with no fractional portion.

*File Names.* On lines 10 and 12 of the Declare statement, MASTER and INPUT are declared to be file names that represent files to be read. Referring to lines 11 *and* 13, NEW_MASTER and OUTPUT file names represent files to be written. The use of the words INPUT and OUTPUT as names for files is an example of the programming freedom with PL/1. Since the words OUTPUT and INPUT are also used as attributes, they are keywords in the language. Yet they are not reserved. They may be used as names without causing any ambiguity.

The On statement (line 14) instructs the computer to go to the master file after the last record in the input file has been processed. If there are other records in the master, they will be read and processed and the new master file will be updated for each. After the last record from the master file has been processed, an attempt to read from the master file will be unsuccessful and the program will be terminated. However, this will not happen until all processing is complete.

*Looping Procedure.* On the next line (line 15), the name NEW_RECORD starts a looping procedure which is related to the final If statement in the program. No matter what path is taken by this If statement, control (GO TO NEW_RECORD) per line 35 returns to the starting point of the loop. Referring again to line 15 or the first Get statement, it indicates the data to be read from the file name INPUT. The first input data item is to be assigned PAY_# and the second data item is PAYMENT. The second Get statement on line 16 indicates that data are to be read from the master file and that the list of data items is to be assigned LOAN_#, PRINCIPAL, and RATE. (The data might be read from punched cards, magnetic tape, or any other medium upon which data are recorded.)

*Interest Computation.* The assignment statement on line 17 computes the compounded monthly interest. Before this computed interest amount is posted, a check is made to avoid adding the computed interest and deducting a payment from the wrong loan (line 18). If the LOAN_# of the master file does not equal the PAY_# of the input file, the two records do not refer to the same loan. Since both files are ordered in ascending sequence according to serial number, the record from which PAY_#has been read refers to a loan that is listed later in the master file. Hence, no payment has been made during the current month for the loan referenced in the master file. In such cases, the new principal per line 20 is computed and written on the new master file (line 21).

Referring to line 22, control is returned to the Get statement (line 16) labeled MASTER_FILE. Another record is read from the master file and the LOAN_# from the new record is compared with the PAY_#. If the LOAN_# of the master file does not equal the PAY_#, the interest is computed per line 17 and a new principal amount is determined per line 20 (as indicated previously). Looping is repeated as often as it is necessary until the LOAN_# is equal to the PAY_#. At this time, the ELSE clause is executed, starting on line 24.

*Refund Calculation.* The ELSE clause is another If statement. If there has been no overpayment, that is, if the payment is less than or equal to the total amount due, the new balance is computed per line 25. If there has been an overpayment, the THEN clause is skipped and the DO group is executed, starting on line 26. The Do statement specifies that a refund is to be computed. The Put statement in the

Do group instructs the computer to write the serial number of the loan, the actual characters REFUND, and the amount to be refunded.

Once the foregoing steps have been properly executed, a Put statement on line 31 is added to write the results. This Put statement directs the computer to write the file named OUTPUT with the current values of the following variables: LOAN_#, PRINCIPAL, INTEREST, PAYMENT, and BALANCE. The If statement on line 32 (IF BALANCE = 0) has two possible paths. If the balance of the loan is zero, the data are not to be written on magnetic tape, but rather a new record (line 33) is to be read. The other alternative is found in the Put statement on line 34 which creates a new master file. This new master file will be used when the program is run the following month. It should be noted that the value of BALANCE will be the value of PRINCIPAL when the new master file is read next month.

The end of the program, like the end of a Do group, is indicated by an End statement. The beginning is indicated by a Procedure statement and the entire block of statements from PROCEDURE to END is called a procedure block.

*PL/1 has the following attributes:*
- *has more features than other procedure-oriented languages*
- *is divided into modules or building blocks*
- *utilizes free form coding*
- *can learn subsets of the language rather than the entire language*

***Evaluation of PL/1.*** PL/1 is about as widely used as COBOL or FORTRAN. Since it has additional features not found in either of these two languages, it is considerably more extensive in its potential applications. As noted previously, the language is divided in modules or building blocks for different applications and different levels of complexity. A programmer using one module need not know about the other modules. Also, PL/1 allows the programmer considerable freedom. There are no special indentations or reserved columns on the coding sheets since the language is basically free form.

One of the difficulties of the language is that it is more difficult to learn. Many users do not need the advanced features nor do they find it useful to be trained in their use. Despite these minor problems, PL/1 will undoubtedly play a major role in complex data processing systems, in particular, multiprogramming and multiprocessing environments. Its modularity concept will play an important role in future programming language developments.

### RPG Language

*RPG, a problem-oriented language, is widely used for small computers.*

The RPG (Report Program Generator) language is one in which the programmer writes the specifications for the problem and the compiler generates an output program from the specifications. There are four basic specification forms and two additional forms for the IBM System/3. Being a problem-oriented language, it is well suited for programs that are run on a small computer. Each version of RPG varies by manufacturer. The RPG program written for one computer generally is not compatible with another computer.

*RPG utilizes four specification sheets:*
- *control card and file description*
- *input*
- *calculation*
- *output-format*

***Procedural Steps.*** The detailed steps in developing a RPG program are given in Figure 10-8. Evaluation of the problem at hand includes the determination of the input files and the output reports (1). The programmer, then, must make the required entries on the various specification sheets, namely, control card and file description, input, calculation, and output-format (2). The source deck is key punched from the various specifications sheets (3). In the next step, the program specifications contained in the card deck are converted into machine language instructions. Storage areas are automatically assigned, constants and other reference factors are included, and linkage to routines for input-output operations and other functions are produced (4). The machine language instructions created in the prior step are executed under control of RPG. The user's input data files are used to generate the desired reports or output files (5).

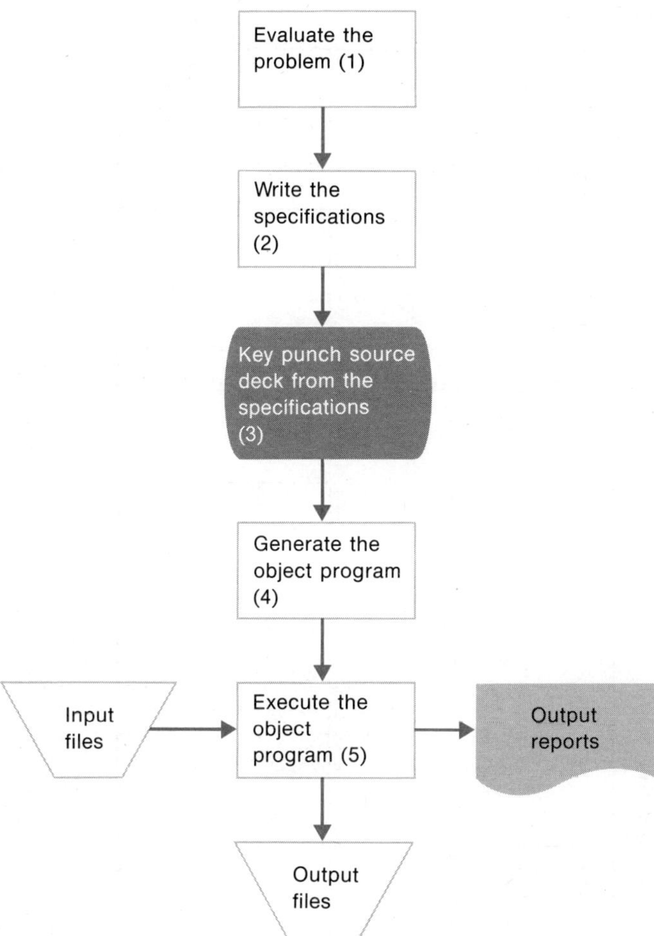


Figure 10-8 Report Program Generator preparation steps.

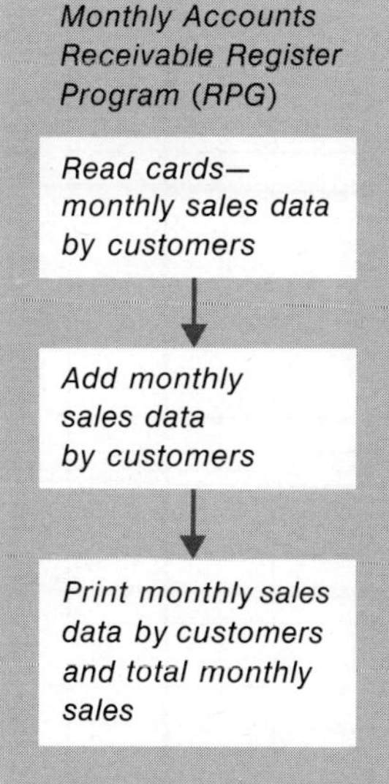


***RPG Illustration.*** The RPG illustration is a program designed to print a monthly accounts receivable register (A/RREG). The specification sheets to accomplish this printout from punched cards are found in Figure 10-9 through 10-12. Each input punched card contains summary data for sales made to customers throughout the month. Specifically, information in each 80 column card for this program is as follows:

| *Field Name* | *Description* | *Card Columns* |
|---|---|---|
| CARDC | Card code | 1–2 |
| INVNO | Invoice number | 3–7 |
| DATE | Billing date | 8–13 |
| NAME | Customer name | 14–33 |
| ADDRES | Customer address | 34–53 |
| CTYSTA | Customer city, state, and zip code | 54–73 |
| INVAMT | Invoice amount | 74–80 |

*Control Card and File Description Specifications.* The *control card specifications* sheet (Figure 10-9) contains an H (heading) in position 6. On the second half of this form or the *file description specifications* sheet, two files—input and output are

IBM

International Business Machines Corporation

GX21-9092-1 U/M050
Printed in U.S.A.

# RPG CONTROL CARD AND FILE DESCRIPTION SPECIFICATIONS

Date FEB, 197-

Program FIGURE 10-9

Programmer THIERAUF

| Punching Instruction | |
|---|---|
| Graphic | Φ O |
| Punch | NUM ALPHA |

Page (1–2): Φ1

Program Identification (75–80): A/RREG

## Control Card Specifications

| Line (3–5) | Form Type (6) | Core Size to Compile (7–9) | Object Output (10) | Listing Options (11) | Core Size to Execute (12–14) | Debug (15) | MFCM Stacking Sequence (16) | Sterling: Input--Shillings (17) | Sterling: Input--Pence (18) | Sterling: Output--Shillings (19) | Sterling: Output--Pence (20) | Inverted Print (21) | 360/20 2501 Buffer (22) | Number Of Print Positions (23–25) | Alternate Collating Sequence (26) | 27–74 Refer to the specific System Reference Library manual for actual entries. |
|---|---|---|---|---|---|---|---|---|---|---|---|---|---|---|---|---|
| 01Φ | H | | | | | | | | | | | | | | | |

## File Description Specifications

| Line (3–5) | Form Type (6) | Filename (7–14) | File Type: I/O/U/C/D (15) | File Designation: P/S/C/R/T/D (16) | End of File: E (17) | Sequence: A/D (18) | File Format: F/V (19) | Block Length (20–23) | Record Length (24–27) | Mode of Processing: L/R (28) | Length of Key Field or of Record Address Field (29–30) | Record Address Type: A/K/I (31) | Type of File Organization or Additional Area: I/D/T or 1-9 (32) | Overflow Indicator (33–34) | Key Field Starting Location (35–38) | Extension Code E/L (39) | Device (40–46) | Symbolic Device (47–52) | Labels (S, N, or E) (53) | Name of Label Exit (54–59) | Extent Exit for DAM / Core Index (60–65) | File Addition/Unordered: A/U (66) | Number of Tracks for Cylinder Overflow (67) | Number of Extents (68–69) | Tape Rewind: N/U (70) | File Condition U1-U8 (71–72) | (73–74) |
|---|---|---|---|---|---|---|---|---|---|---|---|---|---|---|---|---|---|---|---|---|---|---|---|---|---|---|---|
| 02Φ | F | CARDIN | I | P | E | | F | 8Φ | 8Φ | | | | | | | | READ4Φ | SYSΦΦ7 | | | | | | | | | |
| 03Φ | F | PRINTOUT | O | | | | F | 132 | 132 | | | | | OF | | | PRINTER | SYSΦΦ9 | | | | | | | | | |
| 04 | F | | | | | | | | | | | | | | | | | | | | | | | | | | |
| 05 | F | | | | | | | | | | | | | | | | | | | | | | | | | | |
| 06 | F | | | | | | | | | | | | | | | | | | | | | | | | | | |
| 07 | F | | | | | | | | | | | | | | | | | | | | | | | | | | |
| | F | | | | | | | | | | | | | | | | | | | | | | | | | | |
| | F | | | | | | | | | | | | | | | | | | | | | | | | | | |

Figure 10-9 RPG Control Card and File Description Specifications for printing monthly accounts receivable register (A/RREG).

described. The input file (CARDIN) is the primary (P, position 16) file which must provide for an end of file condition. The E in position 17 takes care of this condition. Input data are fixed (F, position 19) in length. Also, the block length is 80 (positions 22–23) as is the record length (positions 26–27). On the same first line, positions 40 to 52 show that the input device is a model 2540 card reader, assigned the symbolic name SYS007.

On the next line of the file description form, the output file (PRINTOUT) is defined as follows: format is fixed (position 19); block length is 132 (positions 21–23); and the records are 132 characters in length (positions 25–27). The entry OF (positions 33–34) allows for an overflow condition in the output file. Contained in positions 40–52 is the output unit or a printer, assigned the symbolic name SYS009.

*Input Specifications.* The *input specifications* sheet (Figure 10-10) describes the input requirements, such as the record layouts, fields used, and the like. In the illustration, if column 1 of the input card file contains the zone of a minus, the Record Identifying Indicator 01 is set on, indicated by the entries in positions 19–20, 24, and 26–27. The locations of the field names (set forth above) are entered in positions 44 through 51 while the names themselves are contained in positions 53 through 58.

*Calculation Specifications.* The *calculation specifications* sheet (Figure 10-11) describes the processing steps involved in the program: add, subtract, multiply, and divide. The sample problem specifies that the invoice amount (INVAMT, positions 18–23) be added (ADD, positions 28–30) to the total field (TOTAL, positions 33–37), storing the results in TOTAL. In positions 51 and 52, the field length and decimal positions are defined.

*Output-Format Specifications.* The *output-format specifications* sheet (Figure 10-12) identifies the printing positions, carriage control, and like items which will determine the final format of the report. The name of the file (PRINTOUT) to be printed is entered under Filename on the first line of the sheet. In position 15, the output types (H, D, and T) are entered which designate the heading, detail, and total lines respectively. The OR, entered in positions 14 and 15 of the second line, allows for printing the heading line (ACCOUNTS RECEIVABLE REGISTER) on the first page (1P, positions 24–25) *or* an overflow condition (OF, positions 24–25).

When the Output Indicator 01 is on per line 6 (positions 24–25), the detail fields entered in the Field Name (positions 32–37) will be printed on the high speed printer per the columns indicated (positions 40–43). The Z in position 38 means that zero suppression occurs on invoice number, date, and invoice amount. Referring to the last part of the program, zero suppression also occurs when printing the total amount of accounts receivable sales cards for the month. The final total is printed when the last record (LR, positions 24–25) indicator is on.

When the invoice amount and the total amount of all billed customers are printed, constants are used (positions 45–56) to improve readability. They include the dollar sign, the comma, and the decimal point. Lastly, an asterisk is used as a constant to set off the total monthly accounts receivable amount.

*RPG has the following attributes:*

- *intended for simple and straight-forward applications*
- *suited for small computers that do not have the storage capacity to handle procedure-oriented compilers*

***Evaluation of RPG.*** RPG is intended for straightforward applications. Those programs that require complex programming are not well suited for this language. The programmer would be much better off with one of the procedure-oriented languages. In terms of efficiency, RPG does not produce coding output as efficient as one written in a machine-oriented language. However, most of the problems that utilize RPG are limited by the speed of the input and output units, thereby, making this consideration relatively unimportant. The conclusion to be drawn about this

**IBM**

International Business Machines Corporation

# RPG INPUT SPECIFICATIONS

GX21-9094-1 U/M050
Printed in U.S.A.

Date FEB, 197-

Program FIGURE 10-10

Programmer THIERAUF

| Punching Instruction | Graphic | Ø | O |
|---|---|---|---|
| | Punch | NUM | ALPHA |

Page Ø2    Program Identification A/RREG

| Line | Form Type | Filename | Sequence | Number (1-N) | Option (O) | Record Identifying Indicator or ** | Record Identification Codes 1: Position | 1: Not (N) | 1: C/Z/D | 1: Character | 2: Position | 2: Not (N) | 2: C/Z/D | 2: Character | 3: Position | 3: Not (N) | 3: C/Z/D | 3: Character | Stacker Select | P = Packed/B = Binary | Field Location From | Field Location To | Decimal Positions | Field Name | Control Level (L1-L9) | Matching Fields or Chaining Fields | Field Record Relation | Field Indicators Plus | Minus | Zero or Blank | Sterling Sign Position |
|---|---|---|---|---|---|---|---|---|---|---|---|---|---|---|---|---|---|---|---|---|---|---|---|---|---|---|---|---|---|---|---|
| 01Ø | I | CARDIN | AA | | | Ø1 | 1 | | Z | - | | | | | | | | | | | | | | | | | | | | | |
| 02Ø | I | | | | | | | | | | | | | | | | | | | | 3 | 7 | Ø | INVNO | | | | | | | |
| 03Ø | I | | | | | | | | | | | | | | | | | | | | 8 | 13 | Ø | DATE | | | | | | | |
| 04Ø | I | | | | | | | | | | | | | | | | | | | | 14 | 33 | | NAME | | | | | | | |
| 05Ø | I | | | | | | | | | | | | | | | | | | | | 34 | 53 | | ADDRES | | | | | | | |
| 06Ø | I | | | | | | | | | | | | | | | | | | | | 54 | 73 | | CTYSTA | | | | | | | |
| 07Ø | I | | | | | | | | | | | | | | | | | | | | 74 | 8Ø | 2 | INVAMT | | | | | | | |
| 08 | I | | | | | | | | | | | | | | | | | | | | | | | | | | | | | | |
| 09 | I | | | | | | | | | | | | | | | | | | | | | | | | | | | | | | |
| 10 | I | | | | | | | | | | | | | | | | | | | | | | | | | | | | | | |
| 11 | I | | | | | | | | | | | | | | | | | | | | | | | | | | | | | | |
| 12 | I | | | | | | | | | | | | | | | | | | | | | | | | | | | | | | |
| 13 | I | | | | | | | | | | | | | | | | | | | | | | | | | | | | | | |
| 14 | I | | | | | | | | | | | | | | | | | | | | | | | | | | | | | | |
| 15 | I | | | | | | | | | | | | | | | | | | | | | | | | | | | | | | |
| | I | | | | | | | | | | | | | | | | | | | | | | | | | | | | | | |
| | I | | | | | | | | | | | | | | | | | | | | | | | | | | | | | | |
| | I | | | | | | | | | | | | | | | | | | | | | | | | | | | | | | |
| | I | | | | | | | | | | | | | | | | | | | | | | | | | | | | | | |
| | I | | | | | | | | | | | | | | | | | | | | | | | | | | | | | | |

Figure 10-10 RPG Input Specifications for printing monthly accounts receivable register (A/RREG).

IBM

International Business Machines Corporation

GX21-9093-1

Printed in U.S.A.

# RPG CALCULATION SPECIFICATIONS

Date FEB, 197-

Program FIGURE 10-11

Programmer THIERAUF

| Punching Instruction | Graphic | Ø | O | | | | | |
|---|---|---|---|---|---|---|---|---|
| | Punch | NUM | ALPHA | | | | | |

Page (1 2) Ø3

Program Identification (75 76 77 78 79 80) A/RREG

| Line (3–5) | Form Type (6) | Control Level (L0-L9, LR, SR) (7–8) | Indicators: Not (9–11) | Indicators: And, Not (12–14) | Indicators: And, Not (15–17) | Factor 1 (18–27) | Operation (28–32) | Factor 2 (33–42) | Result Field (43–48) | Field Length (49–51) | Decimal Positions (52) | Half Adjust (H) (53) | Resulting Indicators: Arithmetic Plus / Compare High 1>2 / Lookup Table (Factor 2) is High (54–55) | Arithmetic Minus / Compare Low 1<2 / Lookup Low (56–57) | Arithmetic Zero / Compare Equal 1 = 2 / Lookup Equal (58–59) | Comments (60–74) |
|---|---|---|---|---|---|---|---|---|---|---|---|---|---|---|---|---|
| 01Ø | C | | | | | INVAMT | ADD | TOTAL | TOTAL | 9 | 2 | | | | | |
| 02 | C | | | | | | | | | | | | | | | |
| 03 | C | | | | | | | | | | | | | | | |
| 04 | C | | | | | | | | | | | | | | | |
| 05 | C | | | | | | | | | | | | | | | |
| 06 | C | | | | | | | | | | | | | | | |
| 07 | C | | | | | | | | | | | | | | | |
| 08 | C | | | | | | | | | | | | | | | |
| 09 | C | | | | | | | | | | | | | | | |
| 10 | C | | | | | | | | | | | | | | | |
| 11 | C | | | | | | | | | | | | | | | |
| 12 | C | | | | | | | | | | | | | | | |
| 13 | C | | | | | | | | | | | | | | | |
| 14 | C | | | | | | | | | | | | | | | |
| 15 | C | | | | | | | | | | | | | | | |
| | C | | | | | | | | | | | | | | | |
| | C | | | | | | | | | | | | | | | |
| | C | | | | | | | | | | | | | | | |
| | C | | | | | | | | | | | | | | | |
| | C | | | | | | | | | | | | | | | |

Figure 10-11 RPG Calculation Specifications for printing monthly accounts receivable register (A/RREG).

**IBM**

International Business Machines Corporation

GX21-9090-1 U/M 050
Printed in U.S.A.
Reprinted 3/70

# RPG OUTPUT - FORMAT SPECIFICATIONS

Date FEB, 197-

Program FIGURE 10-12

Programmer THIERAUF

| Punching Instruction | | | |
|---|---|---|---|
| | Graphic | Ø | O |
| | Punch | NUMALPHA | |

Page (1 2) Ø4

Program Identification (75–80) A/RREG

Edit Codes:

| Commas | Zero Balances to Print | No Sign | CR | - |
|---|---|---|---|---|
| Yes | Yes | 1 | A | J |
| Yes | No | 2 | B | K |
| No | Yes | 3 | C | L |
| No | No | 4 | D | M |

X = Remove Plus Sign
Y = Date Field Edit
Z = Zero Suppress

| Line (3–5) | Form Type (6) | Filename (7–14) | Type (H/D/T/E) (15) | Stacker Select/Fetch Overflow (F) (16) | Space Before (17) | Space After (18) | Skip Before (19–20) | Skip After (21–22) | Output Indicators (23–31) | Field Name (32–37) | Edit Codes (38) | Blank After (B) (39) | End Position in Output Record (40–43) | P = Packed/B = Binary (44) | Constant or Edit Word (45–70) | Sterling Sign Position (71–74) |
|---|---|---|---|---|---|---|---|---|---|---|---|---|---|---|---|---|
| 01Ø | O | PRINTOUT | H | | | 2 | Ø1 | | 1P | | | | | | | |
| 02Ø | O | OR | | | | | | | OF | | | | | | | |
| 03Ø | O | | | | | | | | | | | | 53 | | ' A C C O U N T S R' | |
| 04Ø | O | | | | | | | | | | | | | | ' E C E I V A B L E R E ' | |
| 05Ø | O | | | | | | | | | | | | | | 'G I S T E R' | |
| 06Ø | O | | D | | | 1 | | | Ø1 | | | | | | | |
| 07Ø | O | | | | | | | | | INVNO | Z | | 2Ø | | | |
| 08Ø | O | | | | | | | | | DATE | Z | | 26 | | | |
| 09Ø | O | | | | | | | | | NAME | | | 53 | | | |
| 10Ø | O | | | | | | | | | ADDRES | | | 73 | | | |
| 11Ø | O | | | | | | | | | CTYSTA | | | 93 | | | |
| 12Ø | O | | | | | | | | | INVAMT | Z | | 11Ø | | '$ , . ' | |
| 13Ø | O | | T | | 2 | | | | LR | | | | | | | |
| 14Ø | O | | | | | | | | | TOTAL | Z | | 11Ø | | '$ , , . ' | |
| 15Ø | O | | | | | | | | | | | | 111 | | '*' | |
| | O | | | | | | | | | | | | | | | |
| | O | | | | | | | | | | | | | | | |
| | O | | | | | | | | | | | | | | | |
| | O | | | | | | | | | | | | | | | |
| | O | | | | | | | | | | | | | | | |

Figure 10-12 RPG Output-Format Specifications for printing monthly accounts receivable register (A/RREG).

programming language is that it is suited for simple problems that involve relatively uncomplicated programming. It is logically suited for those computers which do not have the storage capacity to handle procedure-oriented program compilers.

### Specialized Programming Languages

*Specialized programming languages are available to solve certain type data processing problems.*

The four languages of this chapter—COBOL, BASIC, PL/1, and RPG—and FORTRAN in the next two chapters are the most widely used programming languages today. Other programming languages have been developed in response to solving specialized problems. Several of these leading languages and their important characteristics are noted below.

- ALGOL—a procedure-oriented language for expressing and solving computational algorithms. An algorithm is a series of well defined mathematical steps that are followed in order to obtain a desired result.
- APL—a procedure-oriented language that describes many different mathematical processes precisely and concisely by employing array operations.
- COMIT—a language that searches a string of characters for a particular pattern and then transforms this pattern and/or the string into an entirely different form.
- FORMAC—a language that is an extension of FORTRAN IV adds the facility of formal algebraic manipulation—including differentiation—to an existing language.
- IPL-V—a list processing language that provides a wide number of instructions for manipulating lists, essentially at the assembly language level.
- JOVIAL—a procedure-oriented language that is an outgrowth of ALGOL with many of the data handling facilities of COBOL.
- LISP—a list processing language that is suitable for problems treating artifical intelligence and symbol manipulation since it employs certain mathematical concepts and ways of expressing computational processes.
- SNOBOL—a language that searches a string of characters for a specific pattern and transforms this pattern and/or string into a new form. Generally, SNOBOL is more efficient than COMIT.

### Simulation Languages

*Simulation languages are employed to manipulate a representation of the real world through some type of mathematical model.*

The programming of business simulation models (depict representations of the business world through mathematical models) has been simplified through the use of simulation languages. These languages include:

- GPSS (GPSS II)
- SIMSCRIPT
- GASP
- DYNAMO
- SIMULATE

The objectives of these simulation languages are to furnish a generalized structure for designing a simulation model and to provide a fast way of converting a simulation model into a computer program. In addition, these languages provide a fast and practicable way of making changes in the simulation model which, in turn, can be readily reflected in the machine language program.

The development of different simulation languages arose out of the need to solve a common set of problems. GPSS, SIMSCRIPT, and GASP, for example, are well suited for scheduling and waiting line problems. DYNAMO and SIMULATE are designed for simulating large-scale economic systems. A major benefit of using a simulation language to solve a specific problem is a reduction in programming time. However, there are problems of reduced flexibility in modifying the language and increased computer running time.

## Advantages of Programming Languages

*The advantages of programming languages far outweigh their limitations. As a result, machine language programming is rarely employed today.*

Programming that makes use of procedure-oriented languages has several important advantages over machine language programming. The more important ones are:

1. ease of making changes,
2. excellent documentation,
3. assigned memory locations,
4. program system aids,
5. lower time and cost factors,
6. ease of debugging,
7. program flexibility.

***Ease of Making Changes.*** Program changes can be made easily. With machine languages, it is necessary to add or delete the instructions and the data addresses referred to in these instructions. However, in procedure-oriented languages, memory locations are not assigned until the program is compiled. In these cases, it is a matter of crossing out the errors and inserting the proper instructions. This capability is of great help to the programmer during the coding phase when numerous changes are made.

***Excellent Documentation.*** There is improved documentation. Not only is the program easier to understand when written in some type of programming language, but also the printed output makes for a well-documented copy of the program. It is extremely important in any EDP installation that the programmer be able to understand what is transpiring within any given program. This is particularly true when programs outlast the personnel who prepared them, that is, the program must be modified by someone other than the original programmer. Likewise, control is improved since it is more difficult to make changes in a compiler-generated program. Unauthorized and undocumented changes generally show up when the program is recompiled.

***Assigned Memory Locations.*** The clerical job of assigning memory locations and converting symbols to operation codes are relegated to the computer, thereby, simplifying the task of programming. Having the compiler take care of the memory assignment, it is easier for several programmers to work on the program simultaneously. They must, however, coordinate the constants, numbers, and variables being used.

***Program System Aids.*** The programming task is simplified by use of the programming system aids. These include utility programs, subroutines, macro instructions, and input/output control systems.

***Lower Time and Cost Factors.*** Time and cost involved in these higher-level languages are lower. Being easier to learn, there is less time spent in training the firm's programmers as well as in the actual coding of the program. In view of these benefits, the time to place an operational program on the air can be lessened. But just as important is the cost of programming. In some cases, the costs per program can be reduced measurably. Even at a later time, lower reprogramming costs are available with a procedure-oriented language than with a machine language.

***Ease of Debugging.*** A problem written in a programming language is generally easier to debug. There are actually fewer instructions to be written because of the explosion factor. For example, $X = A + B/C * D$ would be translated into several lines of machine language coding. In comparison with a program written in machine language, the source program will be physically shorter. Since the number of errors is roughly proportional to the length of the program, obviously there should be fewer errors. Another reason for the program being easier to debug is that the notation itself is somewhat more natural and, therefore, more attention can be paid to the logic of the program with less attention to the details of the machine language code.

***Program Flexibility.*** Different computers owned or leased by the same firm can make use of the same program. This is certainly not the case with machine language programs. The coding of programs in such languages as BASIC, COBOL, FORTRAN, PL/1, and RPG makes the EDP operation less dependent upon one equipment manufacturer. If the firm desires to change computers, the conversion of programs is handled by recompiling on the new computer where changes in coding are relatively small. The same concept applies to the same manufacturer where models are not compatible.

### Limitations of Programming Languages

As with any area of EDP, there are inherent limitations in procedure-oriented languages. The more prominent ones are:

1. inefficient object programs,
2. excess assembly or compile time.

***Inefficient Object Programs.*** Inefficient object programs have been produced in the past with programming languages. However, compilers today generally produce machine language programs that are as good as the average programmer can produce. There are only a few really expert programmers who can write the most efficient machine coding. If the programmer understands the characteristics of the particular computer and has a working knowledge of the results that are produced by the compiler in the translating process, he can make choices in writing the source program that will minimize inefficient programming in the object program. Also, the program may be either input or output bound whereby the inefficient object program goes unnoticed.

***Excess Assembly or Compile Time.*** An important limitation is the computer time to translate the program into the required machine language. When changes are made to the program, it is translated several times before the program is considered to be operational. As with any new programming language, considerable rework and computer time may be necessary before the program is satisfactory to meet the firm's data processing needs.

The drawbacks of the higher level languages are being overcome by increased speeds of CPUs and large memories. In fact, it is difficult to find firms using machine language programming currently. If they are using machine language, it is caused by the lack of a compiler or one that is not reliable presently, but will be at some future time.

## SUMMARY

The use of programming languages to produce machine language instructions is taken for granted these days. Procedure-oriented languages allow the problem to be expressed in a form somewhat different from the machine language. This makes it possible to program with only a general knowledge of the computer itself and a minimum of training when compared to machine language programming.

An important consideration when selecting a programming language is the performance factor of the translator. Since languages vary widely in efficiency with respect to assemble or compile times, diagnostic capabilities, and running times, the performance of the compiler can be a most important part of a computer system feasibility study. No one wants to take on a new computer system if the manufacturer is experiencing difficulty with its translator which has been true in the past. Hopefully, the equipment firms will be doing a better job in the future.

The steps for programming and implementation for an operational computer program are long and drawn out in a batch processing mode. However, the use of remote on-line input/output devices can reduce the time and steps involved in programming. As was pointed out in the prior chapter, conversational programming with a time sharing computer is providing the needed thrust to break the programming bottlenecks in many firms today.

While nonprogrammers have been reluctant to employ computers in the past due to the complex languages, the same is not true today with the many simplified programming languages available. The ease of use and simplicity of languages, such as BASIC, allow company personnel the opportunity to solve short problems quickly and effectively via a time sharing terminal. Thus, time sharing capabilities fill the programmer's gap. It frees the experienced programmer for solving large scale computer problems while allowing non-programmers the ability to solve relatively simple problems in an on-line mode. Not only is there an awareness of the computer's capabilities with this enlightened approach to data processing, but it also brings a greater degree of computerization to the average firm.

## *QUESTIONS*

1. Define the following terms:
   (a) source program
   (b) translator
   (c) object program
   (d) assembler
   (e) compiler
   (f) symbolic programming
   (g) automatic programming
   (h) utility programs
   (i) subroutines
   (j) macro instructions
   (k) input/output control system
2. What are the essential differences among the following: machine language programming, symbolic language programming, procedure-oriented language programming, and problem-oriented language programming?
3. Distinguish among the following: applications programming, automatic programming, and systems programming.
4. What are the steps involved in getting a program on the air in a batch processing mode versus a time sharing mode?
5. What are the four divisions of COBOL and what purpose does each serve?
6. What are the major elements of BASIC?
7. How does BASIC compare to FORTRAN?
8. What types of applications are best suited for PL/1?
9. What is the purpose of specifications sheets in the RPG language?
10. Name the four basic types of instructions found in most programming languages.
11. Why are logical instructions so important to the operations of a computer?
12. Discuss the advantages and limitations for each of the following languages:
    (a) BASIC
    (b) COBOL
    (c) PL/1
    (d) RPG
13. Of what benefit are special programming languages and simulation languages to the average business user?
14. What are the advantages and limitations of procedure-oriented language coding?
15. What is the future direction of higher-level programming languages?

## CHAPTER ELEVEN

# FORTRAN IV Language

*FORTRAN IV, one of the most widely used programming languages, is presented in a batch processing mode. With minor changes, it can be readily adapted to real-time processing. Illustrated is a program testing session utilizing a batch processing computer. (Courtesy International Business Machines Corporation.)*

FORTRAN IV language is used widely for business, mathematical, and scientific applications.

FORTRAN which is the abbreviation for "FORmula TRANslation" was originally devised as an algebraic language. It was developed in 1956 by IBM for use with its 704 first-generation computer. In its first applications, FORTRAN solved many complex mathematical and scientific problems. Since that time, a number of variations of FORTRAN have been developed, the more common ones being FORTRAN II and FORTRAN IV. These later versions are more advanced in their application and permit the use of programming techniques to simplify complex problems. Basically, they take advantage of the computer's capabilities. For these reasons, FORTRAN languages are currently being utilized in business data processing systems as well as in mathematical and scientific computation. In this chapter, FORTRAN IV will be presented in a batch processing mode.

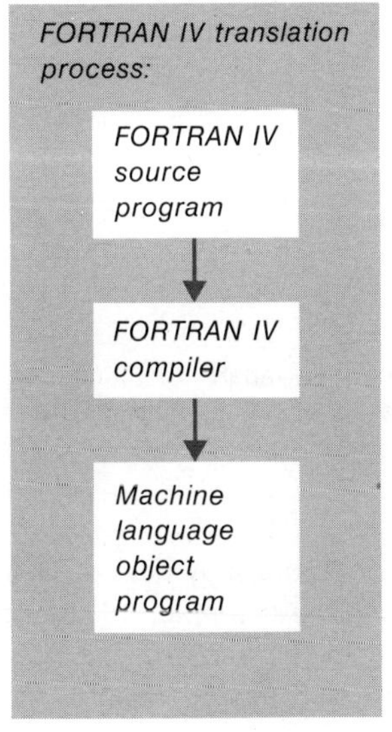


Since most well-structured business problems can be formulated as some kind of mathematical problem, FORTRAN is written in terms of the problem to be solved. From this viewpoint, FORTRAN is a procedure-oriented language. This is in contrast with the computer's own language (machine language) which is directed toward the machine operations. From a programming point of view, the programmer needs little knowledge about how the computer actually operates in the machine language mode. He can concentrate his efforts on the FORTRAN language and the problem to be solved.

As with all nonmachine languages, FORTRAN IV language cannot be employed as is to execute a computer processing run. It must first be translated into the computer's own machine language. This is accomplished by a FORTRAN IV compiler (translator program) which accepts the program written in FORTRAN IV (source program) as input and produces as output a machine language program (object program). In the process of compiling, the computer checks for programming errors, thereby, providing the programmer with information (computer diagnostics) about the validity of his program instructions. Since the process of compiling is very fast, it is customary to think of the FORTRAN program as the computer program, disregarding the short process of translation from source program to object program.

## FORTRAN CODING FORM

FORTRAN, being a highly structured and compact language, consists of a series of coded statements. These are written on a special coding form for punching cards as the input source program. The FORTRAN coding form not only assists the key punch operator in typing source program cards, but also aids the programmer in placing each statement (instruction) in its proper place. Generally, a card is punched for each line on the coding form.

EOQ illustration demonstrates many of the basic elements of FORTRAN IV.

A flowchart for calculating a series of EOQ's (economic order quantities) is shown in Figure 11-1. The FORTRAN coding form is utilized in Figure 11-2*a* for the EOQ illustration—its tabular listing is depicted in Figure 11-2*b*. The three basic program steps involved in the sample problem are:

1. reading five separate values from a high speed card reader,
2. calculating the economic order quantity (EOQ),
3. printing the inventory component part number and economic order quantity on a high speed printer.

***Column 1.*** A "C" placed in column 1 means that the FORTRAN compiler does not expect to find a statement on the card and, therefore, does not try to compile

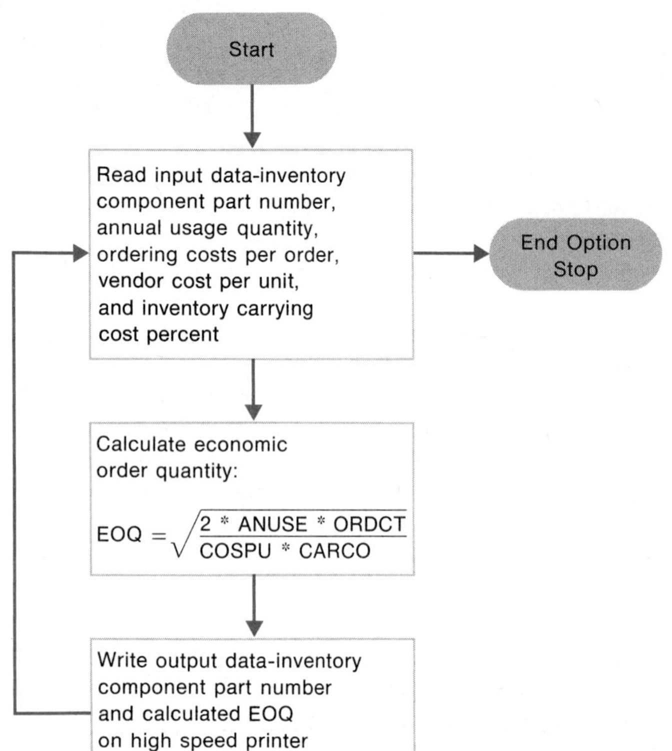
Start
Read input data-inventory
component part number,
annual usage quantity,
ordering costs per order,
vendor cost per unit,
and inventory carrying
cost percent
End Option
Stop
Calculate economic
order quantity:
EOQ = √(2 * ANUSE * ORDCT / COSPU * CARCO)
Write output data-inventory
component part number
and calculated EOQ
on high speed printer

Figure 11-1 Program flowchart for computing economic order quantity (EOQ) as programmed in Figure 11-2

*FORTRAN coding sheets reserve space for data as follows:*
- *col. 1—comments*
- *cols. 2–5—statement numbers*
- *col. 6—continue identification*
- *cols. 7–72—FORTRAN statements*
- *cols. 73–80—identification sequence*

it. Likewise, it indicates that the line contains a "comment" and may occupy any position from column 7 up to and including column 72. In the example, comment cards are used at the beginning of the program to explain the name of the program and its essential parts. They serve as visual aids when the program cards are listed.

***Columns 2–5.*** Columns 2–5 of the coding form contain the statement numbers. If no statement number is used, the positions are left blank. Under no circumstances are FORTRAN program statements written in these positions or punched in these columns on the program cards.

***Column 6.*** Column 6 serves those cases where a statement is too long to fit on one punched card. When this condition occurs, the statement is continued onto the next line or succeeding lines and some character other than zero is written in column 6 of that line. In this chapter, X will be used. For a very long statement, usually the first extra card has a "1" in column 6, the second extra card a "2," and so forth up to 9. However, the number of lines to which statements may be continued varies from one computer to another.

***Columns 7–72.*** In columns 7–72, the actual FORTRAN statements are written as shown in the illustration. Each character, whether it be a numeric, alphabetic, or other symbol, occupies a separate column on the coding form as well as when punched. Any blanks will be ignored by the FORTRAN compiler, except in a few special cases where blanks are meaningful.

***Columns 73–80.*** The last columns 73–80 are ignored by the FORTRAN compiler even though coding forms contain 80 positions. For long programs, the programmer can use these columns for identification purposes. Each of the program cards may be numbered serially for sorting purposes in case they become accidentally mixed up, say from dropping the cards.

## RECOGNIZABLE CHARACTERS

Input data processed by FORTRAN programs are generally numeric although alphabetic and alphanumeric data items are found. Numeric business data can be handled easily by FORTRAN while a certain amount of alphabetic and alphanumeric can be processed by a FORTRAN program. In this chapter, all data are assumed to be in the numeric mode unless otherwise indicated.

*Recognizable characters in FORTRAN are:*
- *numbers*
- *alphabetic characters*
- *special characters*

All FORTRAN *numbers* are written as numerical digits, 0 through 9. Commas are not used for setting apart large values, but are used to separate items. Periods are used for decimal points. All FORTRAN *alphabetic* characters (A through Z) are written in capital letters. In addition, all FORTRAN *special characters, such as* +, −, *, /, ( ), =, and $, have special meanings as will be discussed later. Thus, these special characters plus the combinations of numbers and alphabetics provide the necessary symbols for FORTRAN programming.

## ELEMENTS OF FORTRAN IV

*FORTRAN employs two kinds of numbers:*
- *integer or fixed-point (without decimal)*
- *real or floating-point (with decimal)*

In the FORTRAN language, there are two basic kinds of numbers—*integer* or *fixed-point* and *real* or *floating-point*. The integer or fixed-point mode means that the numbers will always be whole numbers and must be written without a decimal point. On the other hand, the real or floating-point mode indicates that numbers may be either whole numbers or decimal fractions and must be written with a decimal point. The floating-point mode is a more versatile means of representing data than the fixed-point mode. For this reason, it is used quite often where values are to be manipulated mathematically.

Calculations made with fixed-point values will have their results expressed in whole numbers since values are truncated (cut off) and not rounded. For example, $27/4 = 6$ and not 6.75. Values may be expressed as either positive or negative. If positive, the number is generally left unsigned while negative values are indicated by a minus sign next to their left-most character. It should be pointed out that computers can and do vary in the magnitude of values they can handle.

Within the framework of the FORTRAN language, there are five major classifications of FORTRAN elements. These are:

1. constants
2. variables
3. expressions
4. statements
5. subprograms

Each of these will be explored. Exposure to these areas will give the reader a working knowledge of FORTRAN.

## CONSTANTS

*FORTRAN constants include:*
- *fixed-point*
- *floating-point*

Numbers that do not change from one execution of the program to another are called *constants*. They can be used in computations or in certain control commands. The forms of the constants are always numerical which means they

**IBM** FORTRAN Coding Form

GX28-7327-6 U/M050
Printed in U.S.A.

PROGRAM FIGURE 11-2
PROGRAMMER THIERAUF
DATE FEB. 197-
PUNCHING INSTRUCTIONS — GRAPHIC / PUNCH
PAGE 1 OF 1
CARD ELECTRO NUMBER*

```
C     FORTRAN ILLUSTRATIVE PROGRAM FOR CALCULATING EOQ
C     INVCN = INVENTORY COMPONENT PART NUMBER
C     ANUSE = ANNUAL USAGE QUANTITY (R)
C     ORDCT = ORDERING COSTS PER ORDER (S)
C     COSPU = VENDOR COST PER UNIT (C)
C     CARCO = INVENTORY CARRYING COST PERCENT (I)
    1 FORMAT (I7,E8.0,F5.2,2F6.0)
    2 READ (4,1,END=10) INVCN,ANUSE,ORDCT,COSPU,CARCO
      EOQ = SQRT ((2.0 * ANUSE * ORDCT) / (COSPU * CARCO))
      WRITE (5,3) INVCN,EOQ
    3 FORMAT (1H ,I7,5X,11HTHE EOQ IS ,E8.0)
      GO TO 2
   10 STOP
      END
```

*A standard card form, IBM electro 888157, is available for punching statements from this form

Figure 11-2 (*a*) A FORTRAN program for calculating economic order quantity (EOQ), prepared on FORTRAN coding form. (*b*) A tabular listing for calculating EOQ.

```
C       FORTRAN ILLUSTRATIVE PROGRAM FOR CALCULATING EOQ
C       INVCN = INVENTORY COMPONENT PART NUMBER
C       ANUSE = ANNUAL USAGE QUANTITY (R)
C       ORDCT = ORDERING COSTS PER ORDER (S)
C       COSPU = VENDOR COST PER UNIT (C)
C       CARCO = INVENTORY CARRING COST PRECENT (I)
      1 FORMAT (I7,E8.0,F5.2,2F6.0)
      2 READ (4,1,END=10) INVCN,ANUSE,ORDCT,COSPU,CARCO
        EOQ = SQRT ((2.0 * ANUSE * ORDCT) / (COSPU * CARCO))
        WRITE (5,3) INVCN,EOQ
      3 FORMAT (1H ,I7,5X,11HTHE EOQ IS ,E8.0)
        GO TO 2
     10 STOP
        END
```

Figure 11-2 (*b*)

may be in the fixed-point or floating-point mode. Constants are contrasted with variables whose values change from time to time as new data are read in or computed within the program.

### Fixed-Point Constants

Whole number constants may be used as data in a FORTRAN program or may serve as a part of the instructions themselves. For negative fixed-point constants, a minus sign is written to the left-most position of the number. The size limit of the constant depends upon the computer. Some computers can handle up to a 10 digit fixed-point constant. Examples of integer or fixed-point constants are:

50
−1
20000
−80
598
1100000

### Floating-Point Constants

Decimal number constants refer to numbers in a FORTRAN program which contain decimals to the left, right, or between their digits. In the EOQ example (Figure 11-2), the value 2.0 is a floating-point constant. Up to seven significant numeric characters (some FORTRAN compilers allow up to eight characters) can be used to represent floating-point constants. If a number contains no decimal fractions, a decimal point is placed at the end of the number. The number 25, for example, is 25. in floating-point mode. As noted above, no comma can be included and a minus sign must precede negative numbers.

When the magnitude of the constant exceeds the capacity of its significant digit position, the value can be written as a mantissa and exponent. The exponent must always be preceded by the letter E. It must be an integer, a constant, and may be signed or unsigned. If unsigned, the exponent is assumed to be positive. A positive exponent indicates how many places to the right of the written decimal for the actual decimal. In a reverse manner, a negative exponent indicates the number of places to the left. For example, the constant 3.3E+9 or 3.3E9 would be written as 3,300,000,000 while the constant 3.3E−9 would be interpreted as .0000000033.

It should be noted that no more than seven significant digits can be written, excluding the exponent. The constant value 12345678901234, then, should be written as 1234568.E7. In the computer program, the constant would be read as 12345680000000 and the least significant digit positions would be lost. Also when using exponents, the decimal is assumed to lie to the right of the mantissa. The value 1234E5 and 1234.E5 are the same.

*Single-precision method will handle up to a 7 significant digit constant.*
*Double-precision method will accept up to a 16 significant digit constant.*

The foregoing examples are based upon seven significant digits in a single-precision operation. Some computers will accept up to 16 positions in double-precision for different versions of FORTRAN IV. (Single- and double-precision refers to the methods of handling input data.) Significant digits in the number must be followed without spacing by the exponent notation of the nature D $\pm$ ee. "D" denotes the value as being double-precision while the comparable value for single-precision is E as described above. The "ee" specifies the exact location of the decimal place.

Additional examples of actual numbers and their corresponding FORTRAN representations are illustrated in Figure 11-3. As indicated, the final FORTRAN output may be expressed in exponential terms.

| ACTUAL NUMBER | ACTUAL NUMBER IN FLOATING POINT MATHEMATICS | FORTRAN REPRESENTATION IN FLOATING POINT | FORTRAN OUTPUT |
|---|---|---|---|
| 5 | $5 \times 10^0$ | 5. | 5.000000 |
| 590 | $5.9 \times 10^2$ | 590. | 5.900000E+2 |
| 16,945 | $1.6945 \times 10^4$ | 16945. | 1.694500E+4 |
| −22,345 | $-2.2345 \times 10^4$ | −22345. | −2.234500E+4 |
| .000092 | $9.2 \times 10^{-5}$ | .000092 | 9.200000E−5 |
| 5,872,900,000 | $5.8729 \times 10^9$ | 58729.E5 | 5.872900E+9 |

Figure 11-3 Actual numbers and FORTRAN representation for floating-point values (single precision operation).

## VARIABLES

*FORTRAN variables encompass:*
- *fixed-point*
- *floating-point*
- *subscripted*

In contrast to constants which do not change from one execution of the program to another, there are variables which do change for either different executions of a program or at various points within the program. Variables refer to fixed-point as well as to floating-point numbers. They must be defined with alphabetic and numeric characters. The first character must be alphabetic. Variable names may be 1 to 6 characters in length while names differing in only one character are considered to be totally different.

Referring to the FORTRAN illustrative problem (Figure 11-2), several variables are utilized. In the FORTRAN statement,

```
2 READ (4,1,END = 10) INVCN,ANUSE,ORDCT,COSPU,CARCO
```

INVCN (inventory component part number), ANUSE (annual usage quantity), ORDCT (ordering cost per order), COSPU (vendor cost per unit), and CARCO (inventory carrying cost percent) are variables. More than one set of input values are being processed for each variable. As new data for each part are read in, new values are calculated for economic order quantities (EOQ's). The FORTRAN statement

```
WRITE (5,3) INVCN,EOQ
```

also represent variables. While the variable INVCN was referred previously as input, it will be printed with the corresponding economic order quantity.

### Fixed-Point Variables

*Requirements for fixed-point variables:*
- *first character must be alphabetic*
- *1 to 6 characters in length*
- *first character must be I, J, K, L, M, or N.*

A fixed-point variable can take on a value in a fixed-point mode. In addition to the foregoing requirements regarding the first character (must be alphabetic) and the number of characters (1 to 6), the first character must be either I, J, K, L, M, or N (unless a modifying type statement is used). Examples of fixed-point variables are:

```
ITEM
JOBNO
MANNO
N1000
NU18BC
```

In the FORTRAN illustration, INVCN is an example of a fixed-point variable. It changes as each new inventory number is read and printed.

### Floating-Point Variables

*Requirements for floating-point variables:*
- *first character must be alphabetic*
- *1 to 6 characters in length*
- *first character must be A through H or O through Z*

Just as a variable can be represented in a fixed-point mode, it can also be expressed in a floating-point mode. The same requirements regarding the first character and the number of characters apply. Instead of requiring the name to begin with some letter (I through N), the first letter must start with one of the other letters of the alphabet, namely, A through H or O through Z (unless a modifying type statement is used). In Figure 11-2, four examples are used in the Read statement and one in the Write statement for floating-point variables. Other acceptable examples for this type variable are:

```
C
TOT4
HOURS
TOTAL
GRANDT
SALARY
```

Where possible, it is desirable to assign variable names that suggest the data represented. This should have been obvious in the FORTRAN illustration. However, in order to conform to the FORTRAN compiler, certain restrictions must be placed on inventing variable names. The names of the mathematical functions, such as SQRT (square root), EXP (exponential), SIN (sine), COS (cosine), and LOG (logarithm) must be avoided since the compiler will recognize these words as requiring special mathematical treatment.

### Subscripted Variables

*Requirements for subscripted variables:*
- *variable name must be followed by a fixed-point character enclosed in parentheses*
- *variable name must be 1 to 6 characters, not including the character(s) in parentheses*

Variables may be subscripted in the common notation form $A_i$. This provides a method of sub-indexing a series of variables named A. In FORTRAN, this notational form of single subscripting is expressed as A(I). The compiler will recognize a subscripted variable (one that has several values) if the variable name is followed by a fixed-point character enclosed in parentheses. The variable name can contain from 1 to 6 characters, not including the character(s) in parentheses or the parentheses themselves. A subscripted sales variable, for example, could be expressed as SALES (I) for an analysis of 100 pieces of sales data. The subscripted variables could be written as SALES (J), SALES (K), and so forth.

Any set of data that makes use of subscripted variables is called an array while the individual quantities are called the elements. Subscripted variables can be used in the representation of arrays of either 1, 2, or 3 dimensions. The subscripted variable SALES (3) is an illustration of one-dimensional array where the value 3 represents a selected element in the array. In a two-dimensional array where there are rows and columns, a given position might be subscripted SALES (2, 3). The item would be located in Row 2, column 3, and represent some sales values assigned to this position of the array. Similarly, a specific position is subscripted SALES (2, 4, 2) in a three-dimensional array and represents some given value assigned to its array position.

## EXPRESSIONS

*FORTRAN mathematical operational symbols: +, −, *, /, and ** must be used in place of words, like: ADD, SUBTRACT, MULTIPLY, DIVIDE, and EXPONENT.*

Now that we have a way of representing constants and variables, we can place them in mathematical equational form. Any group of constants and variables can be connected by mathematical operational symbols to form an expression. The five basic operations utilized in the FORTRAN language for arithmetic expressions are given below:

| *Symbol* | *Operation* |
|---|---|
| + | Addition |
| − | Subtraction |
| * | Multiplication |
| / | Division |
| ** | Exponentiation |

The foregoing symbols must be used for arithmetic calculations since the words, themselves, such as ADD and DIVIDE would be treated as variables by the FORTRAN compiler and not as mathematical calculations to be undertaken.

### Arithmetic Statements

*FORTRAN permits only one arithmetic statement which uses the arithmetic symbol "=".*

There is only one arithmetic statement in FORTRAN which involves the use of the arithmetic symbol "=." The equal sign means "is replaced by" rather than "is equivalent to." It can handle very complex computations, consisting of any mixture of arithmetic manipulations. Consider the example C = A + B or the original illustration (Figure 11-2):

```
EOQ = SQRT ((2.0 * ANUSE * ORDCT)/(COSPU * CARCO))
```

The equal sign in the example or any mathematical equation tells the computer to do something very specific. It instructs the machine to compute the value of the expression on the right side of the equal sign and assign this value to the variable on the left-hand side. This is the procedure followed by the compiler and it is not to be reversed. Thus, expressions are not placed on the left side of the equal to sign, but always on the right side. The calculated value is always stored as a single variable on the left side.

### Arithmetic Expressions

*Requirements for arithmetic expressions:*
- *arithmetic symbols*
- *parentheses to indicate groupings of constants and variables*
- *two operations must be separated by parentheses*

Arithmetic expressions involve the arithmetic operators (+, −, *, /, **) set forth above. Parentheses must be used to indicate groupings of constants and variables in any mathematical expression. In the illustration, the constant 2.0 and the variables ANUSE and ORDCT in the numerator have been brought together by parentheses under the square root sign. The same is accomplished for the denominator COSPU and CARCO. Also, two operations symbols must be separated by parentheses. For example, X + −Y must be expressed as X + (−Y).

### Priority Rules

*Certain priority rules must be followed for accurate results.*

The first operation performed by the FORTRAN compiler in the compilation of arithmetic expressions is to analyze the statement for parentheses. Operations within the parentheses are performed first, followed by exponentiation as it occurs from left to right. Thirdly, multiplication and division are completed, starting from left to right. Addition and subtraction are performed last as they occur from left to right. Great care must be exercised when writing FORTRAN programs, especially in the area of parentheses. For example, the arithmetic expression X/Y + Z will not give the same answer as X/(Y + Z). The first expression will result in X being divided by Y and adding the results to Z. In the second, X will be divided by the summation of Y and Z.

Most FORTRAN compilers have specialized routines for computing commonly used mathematical functions. Among these are the square root, sine, and cosine. In the illustrative problem, the square root (SQRT) of the arithmetic expression must be taken. Before doing so, the following operations must be performed:

1. operations inside parentheses: `(2.0 * ANUSE * ORDCT)`<br>`(COSPU * CARCO)`
2. exponentiation—as it occurs from left to right: not applicable
3. multiplication and division—as it occurs from left to right: (value of numerator/value of denominator)
4. addition and subtraction—as it occurs from left to right: not applicable

An extra step (5) is added to handle the square root subroutine for a final answer (EOQ).

## STATEMENTS

*FORTRAN statements, along with expressions, are the program instructions for processing data.*

A record may contain several data items of varying lengths that occupy adjacent positions. In order to instruct the computer just how the record should be handled, a FORTRAN statement is utilized. In addition, a statement performs a single operation on a given problem, thereby, serving to direct the manipulation of desired data items. Thus, these two major uses of statements, together with expressions, form the basis for processing desired data in business and scientific programs.

### Format Specification Statements

*Format specification statements indicate:*
- *the format size*
- *placement of the decimal point*
- *location of variables in other statements*

Since data within a program may be needed in part or whole, Format statements with different specifications are provided in FORTRAN. This permits flexibility required by the data being processed within the program. The Format statement by itself does not cause the program to execute anything. For this reason, a Format statement with some type specification is called non-executable. However, when the Format statement is combined with an executable statement, such as READ or WRITE, the latter specifies how the data are to be transmitted either into or out of the computer program. Format statements, then, indicate the format size, where the decimal point is placed, and where the desired variables are to be located in other FORTRAN statements.

***Basic Types of Format Specifications.*** When using the Format statement, there are several basic types of format specifications. The most frequently used ones in business are:

| *Format Specification* | | *Description* |
|---|---|---|
| *Type* | *Format* | |
| I | Iw | Fixed-point numbers |
| F | Fw.d | Floating-point numbers without an exponent |
| E | Ew.d | Floating-point numbers with an exponent |
| X | wX | Skip columns |
| A | Aw | Alphanumeric (input oriented) |
| H | wH | Alphanumeric and/or blank fields (output oriented) |

The capital letters in the above format specification (I, F, E, X, A, and H) are recognized just as mathematical symbols are in FORTRAN expressions. The *w* indicates the width of the field while *d* refers to the position of the decimal point.

In a program, a Format statement is written on a separate line and is always preceded by a statement number in order to identify it from other Format statements. All format specifications on one line are enclosed in parentheses and are preceded by the word FORMAT. Also, Format statements may be placed anywhere in the program, except as the first instruction of a Do statement (to be explained later).

The basic concepts of Format statements with different format specifications can be explained by referring to the EOQ illustration. The two Format statements are reproduced below along with their related executable statements:

```
1 FORMAT (I7,E8.0,F5.2,2F6.0)
2 READ (4,1,END = 10) INVCN,ANUSE,ORDCT,COSPU,CARCO
  . . .
  WRITE (5,3) INVCN,EOQ
3 FORMAT (1H ,I7,5X,11HTHE EOQ IS ,E8.0)
```

Assuming the above input data are being read from an 80-column card, several fields of data from the card must be read into memory. Figure 11-4 shows such a card where values at the top represent the contents of a particular card. These numbers will be utilized below to clarify the meaning of format specifications.

The Read statement calls for reading five fields of data while the Write statement refers to printing two fields of information. The second number (1) in the Read statement refers to the Format statement above it. On the other hand, the corresponding number (3) in the Write statement is related to the Format statement directly below it. Each executable statement, then, has a corresponding Format statement that specifies the size of the data fields and where the decimal fields are to be placed. It should be noted that both Format statements cover all of the basic format specifications except for A. Each type of specification is explained below.

*I specification statement is used for fixed-point numbers.*

*Input I Specification.* The I specification is used to read input data in integer form and to produce the same data in some output form. The first variable (INVCN) which represents the inventory component part number is related to the I7 specification in the Format statement 1. The inventory number for the representative sample is 2206055 from Figure 11-4 and is identified as a seven column variable in a fixed-point mode. Thus, there are no decimal points in columns 1–7 of the punched card.

| 2206055 | 12555E+3 | 04725 | 0.0025 | 0.2550 | |
|---|---|---|---|---|---|
| Inventory Component Part Number | Annual Usage Quantity | Ordering Costs per Order | Vendor Cost per Unit | Inventory Carrying Cost Percent | |
| | Input Data | for EOQ | Calculations | | |
| 1–7 | 8–15 | 16–20 | 21–26 | 27–32 | 33–80 |

Figure 11-4 Sample input punched card for EOQ illustration (Figure 11-2), using FORTRAN IV.

Although seven columns will handle any inventory number in the example, other numbers may not have need for all seven digits. If the number 2206055 was 6055, the number would have been key punched as 0006055. It would be stored in memory as 6055 which results in dropping the three left-hand positions. It should be remembered that data are assumed to be positive unless a minus sign is present.

*F specification statement is employed for floating-point numbers without an exponent.*

*Input F Specification.* The F specification is designed to handle data in a floating-point mode. In Figure 11-4, the last three variables (ORDCT, COSPU, and CARCO) occupy columns 16–32 in separate fields. The first of these variables or ordering costs per order is specified in columns 16–20 by the designation F5.2. The 5 indicates that a five-column field is to be read while the 2 indicates that there will be two positions to the right of the decimal point. The representative value 04725 will be used in memory as 47.25, indicating that it costs $47.25 when an order is placed for each economic order quantity.

The next two variables which are vendor cost per unit and inventory carrying cost percent are located in columns 21–26 and 27–32 respectively. They both occupy six columns and are already in floating-point mode. Instead of writing the same format specification twice for both, the number 2 was placed in front of F6.0, indicating that both variables have the same size specification in floating-point mode. In format specification, the zero would seem to indicate that the decimal point would be at the far-right end of the number. However, Format statements do not override the decimal point punched into the card. The decimal point, then, predominates. Data in Figure 11-4 will be read and stored as .0025 for vendor cost per unit while the comparable value will be .2550 for inventory carrying cost percent.

The width specification in the Format statement may exceed 7 values. However, only seven data positions will be read from the input record, these being the seven most significant positions recorded in the field. If the value 123456789012 is read from an input record and the format specification is F12.6, the value stored would be 123456.7. Using the same value with a format specification of F12.2, the value would be stored as 1234567 since the decimal lies outside the seven positions.

*Input E Specification.* The E specification handles real numbers in floating-point mode. The E exponent (means "times 10 to the") is capable of providing for large

*E specification statement is utilized for floating-point numbers with an exponent.*

input and output numbers. This applies especially to mathematical and scientific applications. The E format specification should be used rather than the F format for very large values. The number preceding the exponent (E) may contain up to seven significant digits.

In the example, the annual usage is expressed in standard exponential notation since many small parts which cost less than one cent each are purchased in large volumes, that is, in million of units. The input data is 12555E+3 for annual usage of inventory number 2206055. The E+3 indicates that the decimal point should be moved three places to the right in order to obtain the actual size of the number. The resulting value is 12,555,000 units. If the input format specification had been E8.1 and the representative input was the same value, the actual number on the card would be considered as 1255500.0. The 1 in the format specification indicates that in memory there should be one position to the right of the decimal point. Since the value is zero, it would be dropped in memory because only significant digits are stored when floating-point variables are used. Of course, the correct positioning of the decimal point would be retained.

*X specification statement permits columns to be skipped.*

*Input X Specification.* The X specification indicates that specific columns of the input card are to be ignored. These columns may be blank or represent punched data which are not necessary for the computer program being processed. If the data are to be ignored, the number of columns to be disregarded must be ascertained and written before the X specification. For example, the Format statement for select reading of the first twenty columns of a punched card could be:

```
FORMAT (F5.1,10X,F5.2)
```

where the data in columns 6–15 would not be read. Columns 1–5 and columns 16–20 would be read.

*A specification statement is used to read alphanumeric data.*

*Input A Specification.* The A specification is used for reading all data that are contained in the computer's vocabulary. Although these vary from one computer to another, they usually include letters, numbers, and special characters. The A specification is written as "Aw" where the field width is more restrictive than the preceding specifications. The field width for some computers is 6 characters while in others it may be 4, 5, or some other size. For our purposes, the field width will be 6 characters.

If the field width is greater than 6, only the rightmost characters will be stored. The rest will be ignored. On the other hand, if the field width is less than 6, the data read in will be stored in the left-hand position of the memory word location. Blanks will be used to fill memory.

For example, the reading of a 24 character name would result in the following A Format statement and its corresponding Read statement:

```
1 FORMAT (4A6)
  READ (4,1) X1,X2,X3,X4
```

Note that the 24-character name is too wide for reading as a single A specification. Thus, it is necessary to define the four adjacent alphabetic fields when reading input data.

*Input D, G, L, and O Specifications.* Other specifications, including D, G, L, and O, are available for more sophisticated applications. As was shown for the foregoing, they all serve some basic need within the FORTRAN language. These additional specifications increase the capability of FORTRAN, making it a more flexible and a more powerful language. For additional information, an advanced FORTRAN manual or text should be consulted.

*Output format specification statements are similar to input specification statements.*

***Output Specifications.*** Output specifications are basically the same as those set forth for the format specifications I, F, E, X, and A. They are presented separately in order to clarify further the use of format specifications and some of the problems with producing output data. However, there is a basic difference—*w* and *d* have new meanings. The "w" specifies the data field to be "reserved" rather than the size field to be read. Similarly, the "d" indicates the number of digits to be retained to the right of the decimal point, regardless of the actual number of digits in storage for a specific number.

*Output I Specification.* The Iw specification which reserves space for a fixed-point number must include an additional space for a plus sign if needed. In like manner, the leftmost position in an output field must be reserved for the sign when outputing negative data. If "w" is set too small for handling data generated internally, the numbers on the left-hand end of a field will be dropped. If a number had been stored internally as eight positions and the Format statement were I5, the three numbers to the extreme left are lost when output occurs. When consideration is given to a sign (+ or −), four left-hand numbers would be dropped. In the EOQ example, the inventory component part number (I7) is printed out in the same manner as it was read in.

*Output F Specification.* As with the I specification, one space must be reserved for a sign position with the Fw.d specification. Likewise, one space must be reserved for a decimal point. Also, consideration must be given to (1) the number of answer positions to the left of the decimal and (2) the number of places to the right of the decimal. If the "w" part of the format specification (1) is not large enough to permit the output of the largest value, a size deficiency will cause an error condition to be noted for the field to be written, resulting in the answer not being written. On some computers, a message will be typed on the console typewriter to indicate that a floating-point number is outside the allowable range of values. (Manual intervention may be necessary to get the program running again.) When referring to the "d" part of the F specification or the number of digits to the right of the decimal point (2), extra places will be truncated without notice by the computer. Thus, these extra places are dropped without rounding.

*Output E Specification.* The output Ew.d format specification, being more flexible than the F type, helps avoid reserving unnecessarily large fields by using exponential notation. It is not necessary to calculate exactly the size of the results that are likely to occur. With this specification, the "d" again refers to the number of digits that must be retained to the right of the decimal. The "w" must allow spaces for the sign, the decimal point, and the exponent (usually three, can be four—E, sign, and one or two positions for size exponent). In the illustrative problem, the quantity for the economic order quantity will be in an exponential form since the firm purchases large quantities (millions) of parts at very low prices.

*Output X Specification.* Use of the wX specification for output is no different from its input application. It causes blanks to be placed in the output record. The 5X format specification in the EOQ example indicates that blank spaces are desired between the printing of the inventory component part number and "THE EOQ IS" for readability.

*Output A Specification.* The Aw specification for alphanumeric output operates in the same way as input. A six-place specification allows the computer to write the entire contents of the word location.

*Output H Specification*. Basically, the wH format specification is primarily output-oriented. It is used for alphanumeric information that must be printed. Referring again to the sample problem, the 11H refers to the number of spaces required to print "THE EOQ IS " with appropriate spacing (three).

**Input Statements**

*Input statements include:*
- *READ*
- *DIMENSION*
- *reading constants*

Statements which instruct the computer where to obtain desired data are known as input statements. These include the Read statement, the Dimension statement, and reading constants. There are other input statements, but these are the more important ones to be discussed.

*Read statement is the basic input command in FORTRAN.*

***Read Statement.*** The Read statement is the basic input command and is generally accompanied by a Format specification statement. Its general form is:

READ (integer constant, integer constant, END option) list of variables

The first integer constant in parentheses after READ refers to the specific input equipment-magnetic tape unit, magnetic disk unit, punched paper tape reader, high speed card reader, or similar units. Each is assigned a specific number by the manufacturer. The appropriate number must be used to designate the input unit desired. In our example (as well as others in this chapter and the next), the number "4" has been selected to designate the high speed card reader.

The second integer constant in parentheses refers to the preceding or following Format specification statement. A "1" in the illustration links the Read statement to the Format statement. The last item in parentheses is the END option which will be explained under the Stop statement.

The last part of the Read statement refers to the list of input variables. The five variables in the EOQ illustration are:

```
READ (4,1,END = 10) INVCN,ANUSE,ORDCT,COSPU,CARCO
```

As shown, the Read command must have a comma between the input device number (4), the Format statement number (1), and the END option of the Read command. All three are enclosed in parentheses. Also, the Read statement must have commas between items in the list of data names (five). No other punctuation is allowed. Spaces may be left between the elements of the command (command name, input device number, format number, and data names), but this is not mandatory.

The effect of the Read command is that data are read and the contents are transferred to the computer's memory. These data items are stored in primary storage at specific locations. They have been given names designated in the command. After the foregoing Read command has been executed, the inventory component part number will be stored in memory at a location called INVCN. Similarly, the annual usage quantity, ordering costs per order, vendor cost per unit, and inventory carrying cost percent will be stored at locations ANUSE, ORDCT, COSPU, and CARCO respectively. In reality, data names (constants and variables) are actually computer memory addresses after the object program has been compiled.

For larger computer programs, the Read command is used several times to bring in the same or additional data as required by the program. Generally, data are read in as needed rather than reading in all data and then using only a fraction of the data in a specific processing run.

***Dimension Statement.*** The Dimension statement, a nonexecutable type of

Dimension statement is a means of reserving storage locations for one or more dimension arrays.

statement (like a Format statement), provides a means of instructing the computer about data that will be read in later. It enables the computer to reserve ample storage space. Since the Dimension statement does allocate locations and positions in memory for data storage, it is generally advisable to insert all Dimension statements at the very beginning of the program. Also, the Dimension statement must appear before the subscripted variables are used.

*One-Dimension Array.* If only a single subscripted variable is to be stored in memory, a Dimension statement, such as

```
DIMENSION SALES (100)
```

would set aside 100 positions in memory for a variable name SALES—representing 100 values of sales information.

*Two-Dimension Array.* The Dimension statement for a two-dimensional sales data array could be:

```
DIMENSION SALES (12,100)
```

This would provide memory storage for 12 rows of sales values 100 columns wide if the data were set forth in a table. The 12 rows might represent the major geographic regions for a national firm while the columns might be the individual retail stores.

*Three-Dimension Array.* In a three-dimensional array of data, a firm might have a number of regions which are located in several states. These, in turn, consist of so many stores. Regions could represent the first dimension values, the states—the second dimension, and stores—the third dimension. An example of a three dimensional array is:

```
DIMENSION (5,25,100)
```

*Several Dimension Arrays.* Any number of arrays can be dimensioned in a single statement if several subscripted variables are used in the same program. They could all be written on the same line, for example:

```
DIMENSION SALES (100), RATES (12,100), Y (10,5)
```

It should be pointed out that an array should be dimensioned for its largest possible size. Otherwise, an attempt to store an array in a smaller space will cause problems later in the program.

Reading constants initially into storage allow their usage later in a program.

***Reading Constants.*** Reading constants into a FORTRAN program is relatively simple. Basically, they are defined in the statement where they are needed. If we desire, for example, to multiply a decimal fraction (S) by 100 to obtain a percentage value (SP), the following Arithmetic statement would be:

```
SP = S * 100.
```

The decimal point after the 100 makes it a floating-point number.

An alternative method for reading a constant into the program is to define 100 initially in the program as XP. This would be as follows:

```
XP = 100.
```

Referring to the foregoing example, the new statement for SP would be:

```
SP = S * XP
```

Either approach can be used. The final choice reflects the programmer's preference.

### Output Statements

Statements which instruct the computer to transmit data from memory to a designated output unit are termed output statements. Punch, print, and similar type statements need not be specified as such. Instead, a write statement is the basic output command used in FORTRAN. As in the Read command, the first number in the parentheses following the Write command specifies the output computer unit to be utilized while the second number refers to the Format statement. The designated output unit and the Format statement are separated by a comma.

*Write statement is the basic output command in FORTRAN.*

***Write Statement.*** The Write statement consists of the following general form:

WRITE (integer constant, integer constant) list of variables

The first integer constant in parentheses after the Write command refers to a specific piece of output equipment. Cards will be punched if the designated unit is a card punch, data will be printed if the output unit is a printer, and so forth. The number 5 will be assumed throughout this chapter and the next for a high speed printer. In a similar manner, all other output devices will be given a specific number. They are assigned by the computer manufacturer as are the input units.

The second integer constant in parentheses refers to the preceding or succeeding Format specification statement. Its number in the sample problem is 3.

A list of output variables to be written on magnetic tape, magnetic disk, and comparable devices must be separated by commas. The program locates and writes them out in the manner specified by the Write statement. As with the Read statement, the sequential order of the variables identifies the order of the output. Thus, the inventory component part number will be printed, followed by the economic order quantity.

In the illustration, the Write command and corresponding Format statement are:

```
  WRITE (5,3) INVCN,EOQ
3 FORMAT (1H ,I7,5X,11HTHE EOQ IS ,E8.0)
```

As indicated, the number (5) in the Write command refers to printing data on the high speed printer and the second value (3) in the parentheses refers to the Format statement below. The output for a specific inventory component part number per the data in Figure 11-4 is:

```
2206055     THE EOQ IS 1364E+3      (or 1,364,000)
```

When writing values, it should be pointed out that only data names may be included in the output list. It is not possible to write out constants by including them in the output instruction. The variables can only be written out if they have been previously defined, that is, assigned a value by either reading or calculating within the program.

Although the Write statement is comparable to the Read statement, in terms of rules to follow, there is one very important difference. While the Read command is destructive (destroys values previously stored), the same cannot be said for Write commands. The act of transmitting a value to an output unit does not disturb the item in memory. It is still available for additional calculations, editing, writing, and other uses. The value will remain unchanged until it is redefined by reading in or calculating a new quantity.

*Control statements include:*
- *GO TO (unconditional)*
- *GO TO (computed)*
- *IF (conditional)*
- *IF (logical)*
- *DO*
- *CONTINUE*
- *PAUSE*
- *STOP*
- *END*

### Control Statements

The foregoing statements and expressions are not sufficient to handle all problems in the FORTRAN language. Other important statements are needed, such as control statements. These allow the programmer to alter the execution sequence of a program. Basic control statements include the Unconditional Go To or Transfer statement, the Computed Go To statement, the If statement, the Logical If statement, the Do statement, the Continue statement, the Pause statement, the Stop statement and the End statement. Each of these will be discussed below.

*Unconditional Go To statement transfers control to some statement other than the next one in sequence.*

***Unconditional Go To Statement.*** The unconditional Go To statement provides a way of transferring control within the program to some statement other than the next one in sequence. The general form of this statement is:

```
GO TO n
```

where "n" is the reference number of the statement desired. In some instances, the command may refer to a preceding instruction while, in others, it may be linked to a following instruction.

The EOQ example illustrated the Go To statement. It caused a return to the beginning of the program by reading another card. Since this first statement happens to be a Read statement, the result is "read-a-card looping." The sample FORTRAN program will continue to calculate EOQ quantities as long as the high speed card reader has cards to read.

The statement to which reference is made in the Go To instruction must be executable. It may not be a Format specification statement, nor may it be the End statement discussed previously. In terms of punctuation, none is permitted. Also, spacing is unimportant, that is, GO TO 2 and GOTO2 in the sample problem have the same meaning. The former is preferred for readability.

The Go To statement is sometimes called an Unconditional Transfer statement. The rationale is that when the program reaches it, the program always goes to the statement where directed. This is in contrast to a Conditional Transfer statement.

*Computed Go To statement handles a multi-branch command.*

***Computed Go To Statement.*** The Computed Go To statement is useful in handling decision instructions. It is of the form:

GO TO $(n_1, n_2, n_3, \ldots n_m)$, i

where "n" represents the statement numbers and "i" is a nonsubscripted fixed-point variable. This command serves as a multichannel branch since the statement numbers enclosed in parentheses refer to executable statements appearing elsewhere in the program.

The statement numbers, being enclosed in parentheses, are separated by commas. The variable name (represented by "i" in the general form above) must be separated from the statement number set by a comma. Like most other instructions, spacing is unimportant.

To illustrate the computed Go To statement, the following

```
GO TO (10,15,25,40), K
```

directs the program to one of the four statement numbers (10, 15, 25, 40) depending upon the value of K. If the value K is 1 when this statement is executed, then transfer is made to the first statement (10). Depending upon the values of K—2, 3, or 4, the program will transfer processing to statement 15, 25, or 40 respectively. Inasmuch as only four statement numbers are specified in the set, K should never have a value greater than 4. If K would exceed 4, an error condition would be noted when the program is being executed.

A representative business application for the foregoing Computed Go To statement is a firm that sells merchandise to wholesale and retail firms. A variable K which is read in for each order indicates the type of customer. The number 1 instructs the computer to jump to a standard wholesale price discount subroutine, starting at statement 10. The number 2 stands for a special wholesale price discount subroutine which begins at statement 15. Numbers 3 and 4 are applicable to regular and special retail price discount subroutines, beginning at statements 25 and 40 respectively when orders are processed. Any value other than 1 through 4 would indicate an error condition.

*The If statement makes a conditional transfer based upon the value in the command.*

***If Statement.*** The If statement utilizes the computer's logical ability. This command makes a conditional transfer based upon the results of a computation. The If statement has the following general form:

IF (arithmetic expression) $n_1$, $n_2$, $n_3$

where "$n_1$, $n_2$, $n_3$" are statement numbers to which the program is directed, depending upon evaluation of the arithmetic expression in the parentheses. The expression may be an arithmetic expression, as simple or as complex as needed to handle the processing required. When the expression is evaluated, the program transfers to the statement number $n_1$ if the results are *negative*. If the evaluation produces a *zero,* the program transfers to statement $n_2$. Lastly, if the evaluation is *positive,* control is transferred to statement $n_3$. Thus, the If statement provides a three-way branch where the path is dependent upon the results of the expression's evaluation.

When the If statement is programmed, three statement numbers must be assigned even though the logic of the expression is such that one of them cannot be used. When only two of the three branches are necessary, the unused alternative may be assigned the same number as one of the active alternatives. Otherwise, there will be an error condition noted when compiling the program.

Punctuation must be provided when writing this conditional command. The arithmetic expression must be enclosed by a set of parentheses while the statement numbers must be separated by commas. No other punctuation symbols are allowed.

A common example of the If statement is the calculation of FICA taxes within a payroll program. If the gross pay year-to-date (YTD) of the employee has exceeded the $9,000 level, the firm stops deducting FICA taxes. The If statement for this payroll subroutine would be:

```
IF (YTD – 9000) 20,20,40
```

If the current gross pay year-to-date (YTD) minus $9,000 in the arithmetic expression results in a negative condition, statement 20 would be the next one executed. In such cases, FICA taxes would be calculated on the current pay amount. If the answer is zero, statement 20 would be executed since FICA taxes need to be calculated. If the answer to the arithmetic expression was positive, statement 40 would have some additional testing since none or some deduction for FICA taxes would be required. For example, if the previous year-to-date gross pay was $9,500 plus a current weekly pay of $200, there would be no need to make the deduction for FICA taxes. However, if the prior year-to-date gross pay was $8,900 plus a current weekly pay of $200, $100 only would be subject to the FICA tax deduction.

Those FORTRAN versions that do not accept the End option as a part of the Read statement (as noted previously) can terminate the program by using the If statement. This approach could have been used in the EOQ example. The inventory data cards, being processed in sequential order, could contain a last transaction card which has the number 9999999—a pseudo inventory number in columns 1 through 7. The If statement would be as follows:

```
IF (INVCN – 9999999) 2,10,10
```

A minus condition permits the program to continue looping through the program until the last card is read which contains all nines. This produces a zero condition which instructs the program to process statement 10, a Stop instruction. It should be noted that the test cannot produce a positive result because 9999999 is the largest integer which may be written in the seven place field. This logically impossible plus branch is assigned the number of the prior branch for convenience in compiling the object program.

***Logical If Statement.*** The Logical If statement evaluates a logical expression and provides two branches—true and false. Its construction is different from the above arithmetic If. The general form, shown in Figure 11-5, is:

*Logical If statement branches to a true or a continue (false) statement based upon the evaluation of its logical expression.*

IF (logical expression)        true-statement
continue-statement

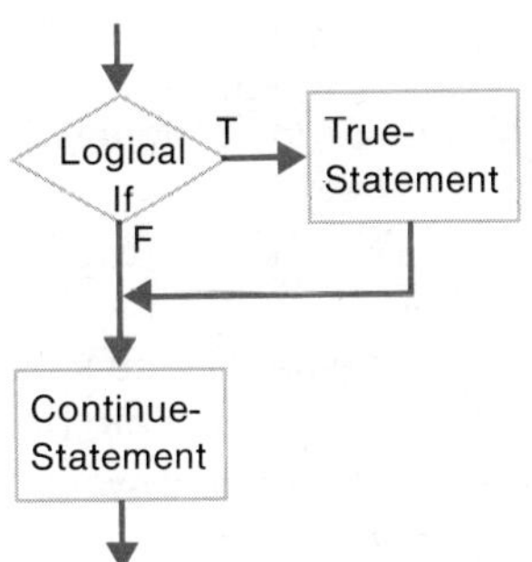


Figure 11-5 General diagram of the Logical If statement.

The "logical expression," enclosed in parentheses, may consist of any combination of numeric constants and variables, connected by logical operators.

There are six logical operators that can express the relation between two arithmetic constants, equations, or variables. These and their related meanings are:

| *Logical Operator* | *Meaning* |
|---|---|
| .LT. | Less than |
| .LE. | Less than or equal to |
| .EQ. | Equal to |
| .NE. | Not equal to |
| .GT. | Greater than |
| .GE. | Greater than or equal to |

Note that a period must precede and follow each logical operator in order to distinguish it from a variable name.

The "true-statement" can be any instruction other than a Format specification statement, a Do statement, or another Logical If command. The true-statement is executed if the expression in the Logical If statement is true. After this true-statement has been executed, the program normally proceeds to the statement following, namely, the "continue-statement" (to be explained below). However, a Go To instruction could be used for jumping to another part of the program.

In addition to the true statement, the logical expression might be false. If the statement is false, the program sequence leads directly to the continue-statement. This statement becomes the first on the false branch of the Logical If command.

An illustrative problem of the Logical If statement involves the discount allowed. Depending on the type of goods shipped (SALES), the discount can be 2% or 3%. If D is punched as 2. in the card, the discount rate equals (.EQ.) 2% while a value of 3. indicates a discount rate of 3%. The appropriate program segment for the discount calculation is:

```
      . . .
      . . .
      . . .
      READ (4,1) SALES, D
      IF (D.EQ.2.) GO TO 20
      DISC = SALES * .03
      GO TO 30
   20 DISC = SALES * .02
   30 WRITE (5,40) DISC
      . . .
      . . .
      . . .
```

In the program, if the D value equals 2., the Go To instruction will cause a jump to statement 20. Otherwise, the D value of 3. will go immediately to the next line. In both cases, the discount amount will be computed for a printout. It should be noted that Format statements were not included as well as other important subroutines. Basically, we were concerned with an understanding of the Logical If statement.

*Do statement causes certain parts of the program to be repeated and is often used as a counter.*

***Do Statement.*** The Do statement is a powerful one in the FORTRAN language. This command, often used as a counter, causes certain parts of the program to be repeated. The general form of the Do statement is:

DO n I = $m_1$, $m_2$, $m_3$

where the "n" after the DO stands for the number of the last statement in the loop and the "I" is the name of the integer variable which stands for an index or counter. The "$m_1$" symbol refers to the first value of the index (counter). The second symbol "$m_2$" is the final value of the index while "$m_3$" is the increment by which the index is increased each time the loop is performed. If a number is not inserted for the "$m_3$" position, the index will be incremented by one each time.

*EOQ problem illustrates the use of the Do statement by calculating 300 economic order quantities.*

To illustrate the Do statement, the original EOQ problem will be modified. Based upon the need to compute 300 economic order quantities, the program is modified per Figure 11-6. In the example, the Do statement requires that all instructions after it or program segment through the one numbered 6 be carried out. The I means that a counter (called I), starting with 1 and stopping with 300, will be incremented by 1 for each loop of the program. Notice that a number 6 had to be affixed to

```
C     FORTRAN ILLUSTRATIVE PROGRAM FOR CALCULATING 300 EOQ'S
C     INVCN = INVENTORY COMPCNENT PART NUMBER
C     ANUSE = ANNUAL USAGE QUANTITY (R)
C     ORDCT = ORDERING COSTS PER ORDER (S)
C     COSPU = VENDOR COST PER UNIT (C)
C     CARCO = INVENTORY CARRING COST PERCENT (I)
      DO 6 I = 1,300,1
      READ (4,1,END=10) INVCN,ANUSE,ORDCT,COSPU,CARCO
    1 FORMAT (I7,E8.0,F5.2,2F6.0)
      EOQ = SQRT ((2.0 * ANUSE * ORDCT) / (COSPU * CARCO))
    6 WRITE (5,3) INVCN,EOQ
    3 FORMAT (1H ,I7,5X,11HTHE EOQ IS ,E8.0)
   10 STOP
      END
```

Figure 11-6 A FORTRAN program for calculating 300 EOQ's.

the Write statement in order that the Do statement could be linked to it. Also, the Go To statement has been replaced by the Do statement.

*Certain priority rules must be followed if the Do statement is to function properly.*

*Priority Rules.* Certain rules must be followed in most FORTRAN systems if the Do statement is to operate correctly. The most frequently used rules are stated as follows:

1. The first statement in the range of a Do statement must be executable, that is, the statement on the next line after a Do command must be one that can be executed. It must not be a specification statement, such as, Format, Logical, Dimension, Common, or Equivalence.
2. Where multiple looping is desired, it is allowable for the range of one Do set to contain another Do set (called the inner Do). However, each inner Do loop must be within the range of the outer loop, as shown in Figure 11-7*a*.
3. No transfer of control by an If or Go To statement is allowed into the range of any Do statement from outside its range. Otherwise, such transfer would not permit the Do loop to be properly indexed. Reference is made to Figure 11-7*b* for the correct approach.

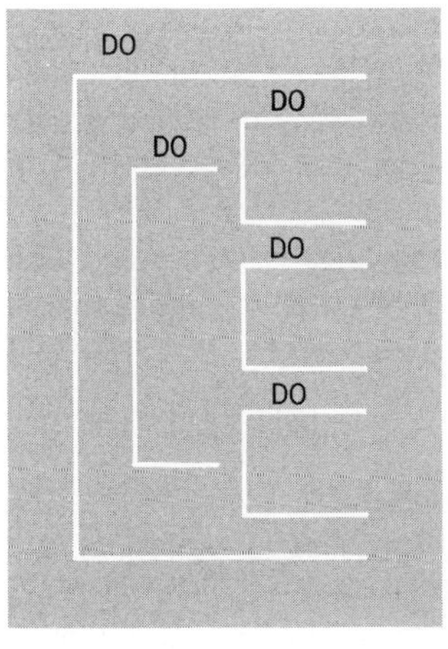


(*a*)

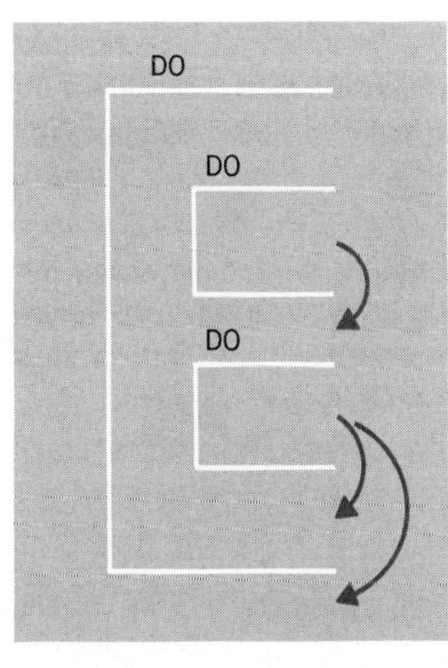


(*b*)

Figure 11-7 DO statement sets allowable under rule 2 (*a*) and rule 3 (*b*).

4. The last statement specified in the Do command must not be one that can effect a transfer. From this foregoing rule, Go To, Computed Go To, and If statements are excluded. Also, Dimension, Format, and other information statements cannot be used as a last statement.
5. The Do index may or may not be used as a data element. Whether or not it is used depends entirely upon the program's logic. In our example, the index value I was used as a data element. In another illustration, J, the Do index, may not be required as a data element in computation or output.
6. The values of $m_1$, $m_2$, and $m_3$ must be whole numbers in the fixed-point mode. Also, $m_1$ should be less than or equal to $m_2$.

*Continue statement is a last command in a Do program segment that transfers control back to the beginning of the Do statement.*

***Continue Statement.*** The Continue statement serves as a terminal command when a Do range would end with some type of transfer. Its general form is:

```
k CONTINUE
```

where "k" is a statement number. In the Do statement, the k value represents the statement number which terminates the Do program segment.

*EOQ problem illustrates the use of the Continue statement (employed three times).*

Referring to the EOQ example, the program can be modified to read initially 300 sets of data, calculate all the EOQ's at one time, and then print all the economic order quantity values. The revised program, utilizing Continue statements, is depicted in Figure 11-8. The first statement below the Comment statements defines the names and sizes of subscripted variables and reserves space for the 300 sets of data in memory. The next statements (down to the first Continue statement)

```
C     FORTRAN ILLUSTRATIVE PROGRAM FOR CALCULATING EOQ - 300 SETS OF
     XDATA
C     INVCN = INVENTORY COMPONENT PART NUMBER
C     ANUSE = ANNUAL USAGE QUANTITY (R)
C     ORDCT = ORDERING COSTS PER ORDER (S)
C     COSPU = VENDOR COST PER UNIT (C)
C     CARCO = INVENTORY CARRING COST PRECENT (I)
      DIMENSION INVCN(300),ANUSE(300),ORDCT(300),COSPU(300),CARCO(300),
     XEOQ(300)
      DO 7 I= 1,300,1
      READ (4,1) INVCN(I),ANUSE(I),ORDCT(I),COSPU(I),CARCO(I)
    1 FORMAT (I7,E8.0,F5.2,2F6.0)
    7 CONTINUE
      DO 8 I = 1,300,1
      EOQ(I) = SQRT ((2.0 * ANUSE(I) * ORDCT(I))/(COSPU(I) * CARCO (I)))
    8 CONTINUE
      DO 9 I = 1,300,1
      WRITE (5,3,END=10) INVCN(I),EOQ(I)
    3 FORMAT (1H ,I7,5X,11HTHE EOQ IS ,E8.0)
    9 CONTINUE
   10 STOP
      END
```

Figure 11-8 A FORTRAN program for calculating EOQ—300 sets of data.

provide the necessary program steps for reading all data elements. The index changes by 1 for each loop. INVCN (1), ANUSE (1), ORDCT (1), COSPU (1), and CARCO (1) would be read on the first loop. The index would change to 2 and the program procedure would continue until INVCN (300), ANUSE (300), ORDCT (300), COSPU (300), and CARCO (300) had been read by the high speed card reader and stored in the computer's memory.

The second Do set in Figure 11-8 which stops with statement 8 (second Continue command) computes the 300 EOQ values. The computed EOQ amounts are stored in the 300 positions reserved by the Dimension statement. The third Do statement provides for printing the 300 EOQ's in sequential order. As with the first set, updating the index (counter) and checking the last loop is handled automatically by the Do statement for both the second and third Do sets.

Although the program has increased in size due to the addition of three Do loops, the utilization of the Continue statement has been demonstrated. In some programming situations, Continue commands may be required for an efficient program. However, for this sample problem, the shorter and faster version is illustrated in Figure 11-2.

*Pause statement allows stopping the program temporarily.*

***Pause Statement.*** The Pause statement allows the programmer to stop processing the object program temporarily. After a Pause statement, the operator can resume processing by pushing the start button on the computer console. The computer will resume execution of the program at the statement following the Pause statement.

*Stop statement indicates the end of the program.*

***Stop Statement.*** The Stop statement is used at the end of the program. In the sample program, the last three lines are:

```
   GO TO 2
10 STOP
   END
```

The control statement, GO TO 2, instructs the computer to return processing to statement 2 for reading a new group of punched card data, similar to that found in Figure 11-4. The next statements will be executed, that is, a new EOQ will be computed and written by the high speed printer. Again, the GO TO 2 statement will transfer program control to reading a new set of data and so forth. This looping procedure continues until all the input cards have been processed. The End option of the Read command (END = 10) will transfer control to statement 10 where the computer will be halted per the Stop instruction. However, there is one word of caution. The End option is not available in all FORTRAN versions of the Read command. In our FORTRAN examples, this limitation is not applicable.

*End statement instructs the compiler to write the object program.*

***End Statement.*** The End statement is a requirement of the FORTRAN compiler. It is a signal to the compiler that the end of the source program has been reached. Thus, the End card must be the last card in the source program deck and, therefore, must be included. In addition to marking the end of the source program, the End card instructs the compiler to write the object program.

### Other Statements

*Other statements include:*
- *EQUIVALENCE*
- *COMMON*

Two other statements are normally found in FORTRAN programs and generally refer to subprograms (to be discussed below). These are the Equivalence and Common statements which are about the same. This similarity will be pointed out below.

*Equivalence statement permits giving more than one name to the same storage location.*

***Equivalence Statement.*** The Equivalence statement allows assigning more than one data name to the same computer storage location. All named variables must be in the same main program or subprogram but not in both. Its general form is:

EQUIVALENCE (variable names), (variable names)

As indicated, the statement may not have a statement number. Any number of variable sets may be specified after the command name by enclosure in parentheses. Similarly, any number of data names can be included in each set. Data names in sets must be separated by commas as well as enclosed in parentheses.

If the following Equivalence statement were given:

```
EQUIVALENCE(A,B,C), (HOURS,RATE,GROSSP)
```

the data names A and HOURS would be equivalent. In like manner, the variables B and C would be equal in storage to RATE and GROSSP (Gross Pay) respectively. The basic purpose of this or any Equivalence statement is to conserve memory space by having one data name refer to the same value in primary storage.

*Common statement allows data names in the main program and in subprogram(s) to have the same storage locations.*

***Common Statement.*** The Common statement is comparable to the Equivalence statement. It allows data names in main programs and subprograms to be assigned the same storage location. The general form is:

COMMON (variable names)

for both the main program and subprogram.

The following statements for both parts of a sample program are:

Main Program    `COMMON (A,B,C,D)`
Subprogram    `COMMON (PRICE,TAX,FRT,AMOUNT)`

The variables of a data name list (A, B, C, D) in the main program occupy the same memory location as their counterparts (PRICE, TAX, FRT, AMOUNT) in the subprogram. When the program is compiled, A and Price will be assigned the same storage location in order to conserve memory space. The other four values are related in a similar manner, that is, B and TAX, C and FRT (freight), and D and AMOUNT.

## SUBPROGRAMS

*Subprograms include:*
- *the arithmetic statement function*
- *the external function*
- *the subroutine statement*

When it is necessary to perform some standard calculation involving mathematic functions or it is necessary to perform a given set of calculations a number of times within a program, the FORTRAN language provides three subprogram techniques. These are termed the Arithmetic Statement Function, the External Function, and the Subroutine Statement. Each of these will be discussed below.

*The arithmetic statement function permits the substitution of a function name for an arithmetic computation.*

### The Arithmetic Statement Function

The Arithmetic Statement Function is so called because it must be created by a single, arithmetic-like command. It allows the substitution of a function name for an arithmetic computation which must be defined before it is used.

***General Form.*** The general form is as follows:

Function name (argument list) = Expression

The "function name" must conform to two requirements, namely, it must consist of 1 to 6 alphabetic characters in size and the mode of the function is determined by the name's first character (unless overridden by a Type Statement). The "argument list" which appears in parentheses is the set of variables used in the "expression." The variables must agree in mode, number, and order with the arguments. Commas are used to separate multiple arguments. Lastly, the expression may be any set of operators and operands (variables) that meet the requirements of an arithmetic expression.

*Standard mathematical functions are in addition to those that can be written by the programmer.*

***Standard Mathematical Functions.*** In addition to the programmer creating his own Arithmetic Statement Function, FORTRAN compilers have the following set of mathematical functions incorporated into them. These vary somewhat by compiler, but generally include the following ones:

| *FORTRAN Name* | *Mathematical Function* |
|---|---|
| LOG | Natural logarithm |
| SIN | Trigonometric sine |
| COS | Trigonometric cosine |
| EXP | Exponential |
| SQRT | Square root |
| ATAN | Arctangent |
| ABS | Absolute value |

The mathematical function SQRT was illustrated previously in Figures 11-2, 11-6, and 11-8.

*The external function is used for those functions which require several statements in their computation. It returns one value to the main program.*

### The External Function

It is more comprehensive than the arithmetic statement function which is limited to one statement and computes one value only. The External Function is used for those functions which require several statements in their calculations. From this viewpoint, the External Function is capable of producing one result from many differing conditions. Being capable of handling any set of commands, it is written and compiled as a separate program. The External Function returns the desired result to the main program where it is linked.

As with the Arithmetic Statement Function, arguments in the main program need not have the same names as those in the subprogram even though they must agree in mode, number, and order. Main program arguments may be subscripted variables. The External Function, being a separate program, is identified by its first statement which is unnumbered.

***General Form.*** The general form of the External Function is:

Type FUNCTION function name (argument list)

The word "Type" refers to the type specification—integer or real unless the first letter of the function name indicates the function's mode. In such cases, it may be dropped. The word "FUNCTION" must appear at all times. The "function name" provides the link between the function and the main program and should be the same data name used in the main program when referencing the function. It may be anywhere from one to six alphabetic characters. The last term in the general form is the "argument list" which may be any set of variable names. Commas are used to separate a list of arguments. Array names may be used as arguments although they may not be subscripted.

*The Subroutine statement can return any number of values to the main program or can operate independently by not returning any value(s) to the main program.*

### The Subroutine Statement

The Subroutine statement is more powerful than the External Function. While only one value can be returned with the latter, this limitation is not applicable to the other external subprogram called the "subroutine." Any number of values can be transmitted to the main program. Also, the subroutine can operate independently so as not to return any value(s) to the main program.

***General Form.*** The Subroutine's first statement for linking with the main program is:

SUBROUTINE subroutine name (argument list)

where the "subroutine name" is one assigned by the programmer and the "arguments" serve as communication channels between the main program and subprograms. The symbols in the parentheses can transmit data to the subroutine or return values to the main program. Just as with the External Function subprogram, the last executable command in the Subroutine is the Return instruction which transfers control to the statement following the Call instruction in the main program.

Referring to the Call statement just mentioned, Subroutines are linked to the main program by this statement which has the following form:

CALL subroutine name (argument list)

The requirements for this statement in the main program are the same as those for the Subroutine. While the Subroutine statement is located at the beginning of this external subprogram, the Call statement is inserted by the programmer where necessary to call in a specific Subroutine. In fact, various levels of Subroutines may call in other Subroutines which, in turn, may call in other Subroutines before returning to the main program.

The Subroutine is a sophisticated form of programming. It allows more than one value to be returned to the main program. But more importantly, this approach allows a larger program to be segregated into smaller parts for a modular approach to programming. Not only can these subroutines be written separately from other subroutines, but are capable of being compiled apart from the main program. This avoids the necessity to recompile long programs in the event of major and minor errors in one or more of its parts. Thus, the efficiency of the total programming effort can be increased by making extensive use of Subroutines for a modular programming approach.

*By way of review, the essential elements of FORTRAN are:*
- *constants*
- *variables*
- *expressions*
- *statements*
- *subprograms*

## RECAP OF FORTRAN IV ELEMENTS

The essential elements of the FORTRAN IV language are set forth in Figure 11-9. Basically, the five major sections of the language are summarized for the reader's convenience. They will be extremely helpful when working the sample problems at the end of the chapter. Although this listing is comprehensive, a FORTRAN IV language manual should be consulted for the specific computer to be utilized since variances do occur from one manufacturer to another as well as for specific models by the same manufacturer.

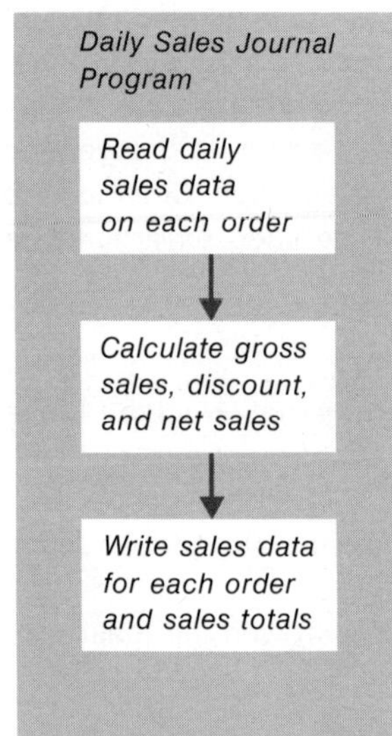


## FORTRAN IV PROGRAM FOR PRINTING A DAILY SALES JOURNAL

Although several examples were used in presenting the fundamentals of FORTRAN IV, a final one will be illustrated, that is, a program flowchart and the related procedure-oriented language program. The program flowchart for printing a daily sales (net) journal and the program itself are set forth in Figures 11-10 and 11-11 respectively.

***Data Names and Field Sizes.*** Before exploring the logic of the program flowchart and its program steps in FORTRAN, data names and field sizes, including the proper placement of the decimal, have to be specified. The field sizes have allowed for maximum values in printing the account number, sales, discount, and net sales amounts. Unused columns in the data fields will be key punched with zeros. The input and output data names with their respective size fields are:

| FIELDS—COLUMNS IN CARD | DESCRIPTION | FORTRAN NAME | FORTRAN FIELD SIZE |
|---|---|---|---|
| *Input:* | | | |
| 1–5 | Customer account number | NACCT | XXXXX |
| 8–11 | Number of items sold | UNITS | XXXX |
| 14–16 | Sales price per item | PRICE | .XX |
| *Output:* | | | |
| 6–10 | Customer account number | NACCT | XXXXX |
| 14–20 | Total sales per order | SALES | XXXX.XX |
| 25–30 | Total discount per order | DISC | XXX.XX |
| 34–40 | Net sales per order | SNET | XXXX.XX |
| 46–50 | Number of daily orders | JCOUN | XXXXX |
| 49–56 | Amount of daily sales (net) | SCOUN | XXXXX.XX |

| I *Constants* | *Examples* |
|---|---|
| Fixed-point constants | 50, -1, 20000, -80, 598, 1100000 |
| Floating-point constants | 5., 590., 16945., -22345., .000092 |
| II *Variables* | |
| Fixed-point variables | ITEM, JOBNO, MANNO, N1000, NU18BC |
| Floating-point variables | C, TOT4, HOURS, TOTAL, GRANDT, SALARY |
| Subscripted variables | SALES (3), SALES (2, 3), SALES (2, 4, 2) |
| III *Expressions* | |
| Arithmetic Statements | C = A + B, PAY = REG + OTIME |
| Arithmetic Expressions: | |

| *Symbol* | *Operation* | |
|---|---|---|
| + | Addition | A + B, RHOURS + OHOURS |
| − | Subtraction | A - B, SALES - DISC |
| * | Multiplication | A * B, HOURS * RATE |
| / | Division | A / B, COST / UNITS |
| ** | Exponentiation | A ** 2, VALUE ** 2 |

IV *Statements*

Format specification statements (input and output):

| *Type* | *Format* | *Description* | |
|---|---|---|---|
| I | Iw | Fixed-point numbers | FORMAT (I7) |
| F | Fw.d | Floating-point numbers without an exponent | FORMAT (F5.2, 2F6.0) |
| E | Ew.d | Floating-point numbers with an exponent | FORMAT (E8.0) |
| X | wX | Skip columns | FORMAT (5X) |
| A | Aw | Alphanumeric (input oriented) | FORMAT (4A6) |
| H | wH | Alphanumeric and/or blank files (output oriented) | FORMAT (11HTHE EOQ IS ) |

where w is width of the field
d is the position of the decimal point

| | |
|---|---|
| Input statements: | |
| The Read statement | READ (4, 1) INVCN, ANUSE, ORDCT, COSPU, CARCO |
| The Dimension statement | DIMENSION SALES (100), RATES (12, 100), Y (10, 5) |
| Reading constants | SP = S * 100. |
| Output statements: | |
| The Write statement | WRITE (5, 3) INVCN, EOQ |
| Control statements: | |
| Unconditional Go To statement | GO TO 2 |
| Computed Go To statement | GO TO (10, 15, 25, 40), K |
| If statement | IF (INVCN - 9999999) 2, 10, 10 |
| Logical If statement | IF (D .EQ. 2.) GO TO 20 |
| Do statement | DO 6 I = 1, 300, 1 |
| Continue statement | CONTINUE |
| The Pause statement | PAUSE |
| The Stop statement | STOP |
| The End statement | END |
| Other statements: | |
| The Equivalence statement | EQUIVALENCE (A, B, C), (HOURS, RATE, GROSSP) |
| The Common statement | COMMON (A, B, C, D) Main program |
| | COMMON (PRICE, TAX, FRT, AMOUNT) Subprogram |
| V *Subprograms* | |
| The Arithmetic Statement Function | GROSSP (A, B) = A * B |
| Mathematical Functions: | |

| *Name* | *Type of Function* | |
|---|---|---|
| LOG | Natural logarithm | Y = LOG (5) |
| SIN | Trigonometric sine | X = SIN (10) |
| COS | Trigonometric cosine | Z = COS (20) |
| EXP | Exponential | A = EXP (2) |
| SQRT | Square root | B = SQRT (A - C) |
| ATAN | Arctangent | C = ATAN (10) |
| ABS | Absolute value | D = ABS (100) |
| The External Function | | FUNCTION DISCA (X) |
| The Subroutine | | SUBROUTINE VALUES (X, Y, Z, SUM) |

Figure 11-9 Essential elements of the FORTRAN IV language.

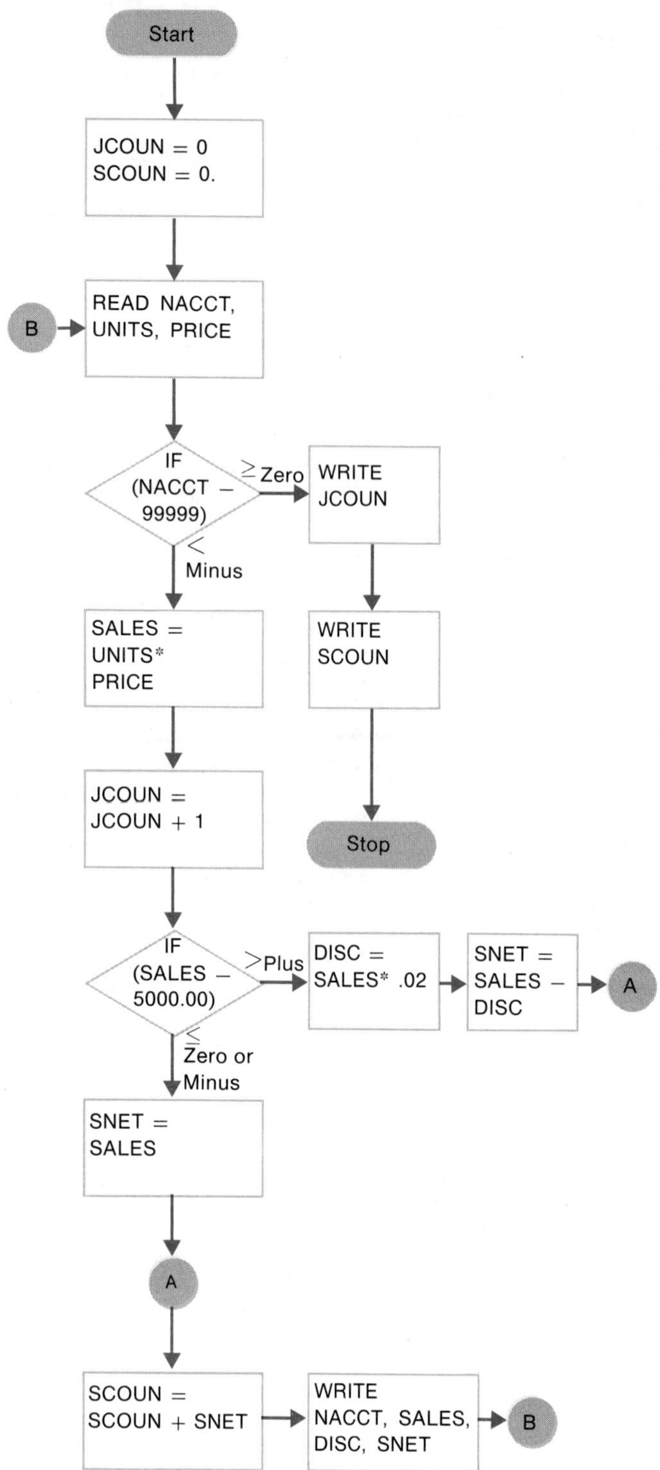


Figure 11-10 Program flowchart for printing a daily sales journal.

```
C     DAILY SALES (NET) JOURNAL PROGRAM - FORTRAN IV
      JCOUN = 0
      SCCUN = 0.
    1 FORMAT (I5,2X,F4.0,2X,F3.2)
    2 READ (4,1) NACCT,UNITS,PRICE
      IF (NACCT - 99999) 3,8,8
    3 SALES = UNITS * PRICE
      JCOUN = JCOUN + 1
      IF (SALES - 5000.00) 4,4,5
    4 SNET = SALES
      GO TO 6
    5 DISC = SALES * .02
      SNET = SALES - DISC
      GO TO 6
    6 SCOUN = SCOUN + SNET
      WRITE (5,7) NACCT,SALES,DISC,SNET
    7 FORMAT (1H  ,5X,I5,3X,F7.2,4X,F6.2,3X,F7.2)
      GO TO 2
    8 WRITE (5,9) JCOUN
    9 FORMAT (1H  ,15X,30HTHE NUMBER OF DAILY ORDERS IS ,I5)
      WRITE (5,10) SCOUN
   10 FORMAT (1H  ,15X,33HTHE AMOUNT OF DAILY NET SALES IS ,F8.2)
      STOP
      END
```

Figure 11-11 A FORTRAN program for printing a daily sales journal.

Referring to Figure 11-11, the first line describes the name of the program. The fixed-point counter (JCOUN) which will total the number of sales cards is initially set equal to zero (next line). Likewise, the floating-point counter (SCOUN) is set equal to zero (following line) for totaling the amount of net sales for the day. For the next two lines, the Format statement describes the format specification of the Read statement.

***Input Values.*** Since the numbers 4, 1 are found in the parentheses within the Read statement, the input data are read by the high speed reader unit (4) and reference is made to the Format statement (1) for data specifications. The first field (NACCT) is in a fixed-point mode where the account number can contain up to five integer values (columns 1–5). The next two columns are blank (2X), followed by the second field (UNITS) of information (columns 8–11). This represents the number of units sold which must be a floating-point variable. It will be multiplied by price (floating-point variable). Again, two card columns are skipped (2X). The last value to be read is the sales price per item (PRICE) which is a three digit value (includes one digit for a decimal point) in a floating-point mode. For all three input values, leading zeros have been key punched if the variables do not fill their respective field size.

***Discount Calculations.*** As shown in the program flowchart (Figure 11-10), the first logical juncture is the first If statement. If the account number read results in a minus figure (NACCT − 99999), normal processing will occur. This means going on to the next program line where units (UNITS) are multiplied by price (PRICE) for total sales (SALES). Next, the value 1 is added to the counter (JCOUN). The second If statement on the next line determines the amount of the discount. If gross sales (SALES − 5000.00) are equal or less than $5,000.00, no discount is given. Thus, gross sales equals net sales (SNET = SALES) per the next line statement. However, if sales are greater than $5,000.00 per the calculation in the second If statement, the discount program line allows a two percent (DISC = SALES * .02).

On the following line, gross sales less the amount of discount equals net sales (SNET = SALES − DISC). Whether a discount amount is allowed or not, both statements for net sales (SNET) go to (GO TO 6) the Arithmetic statement where the amount of net sales is added to the counter (SCOUN) before executing the Write statement on the next line.

***Output—Individual Sales.*** In this first Write statement, the account number (NACCT), the gross sales (SALES), the total discount (DISC), and the net sales (SNET) are printed on the high speed printer, indicated by the first number (5) in parentheses. The second number (7) refers to the Format specification statement on the next line. For all daily sales cards read, a separate line will be printed where the spacing between output values vary. Referring to the order of the Write statement, the first data element (NACCT) is a fixed-point variable while the other three are floating-point variables (SALES, DISC, SNET). All those in the floating-point mode have two places to the right of the decimal point. Once the data have been printed, the next line specifies a Go To statement (GO TO 2). Control is returned to the Read statement (2) where another set of values are brought in for the next card.

***Output—Total Number and Sales Amount.*** The above process is repeated until the last card is read by the input unit. When a final calculation is made for the first If statement, an equal condition occurs since the last card in the card reader unit is a pseudo account number (99999). Thus, 99999 − 99999 equals zero. This equal to condition, then, references statement 8, located toward the bottom of the program which is the second Write statement. As usual, the Write statement is accompanied by a Format specification statement. The second last line to be printed is: "THE NUMBER OF DAILY ORDERS IS ," followed by the integer value. Moving on to the next line or the last line to be printed is: "THE AMOUNT OF DAILY NET SALES IS ," followed by the floating-point amount. The last two values printed after the word "IS" are stored in counters JCOUN and SCOUN respectively. (It should be noted that the least significant digit of the SCOUN counter (F8.2) will be lost since only seven significant digits are available with a floating-point variable.) However, this means losing the units column only. The Stop command instructs the computer to halt its processing of the program. Finally, the End statement instructs the FORTRAN compiler to begin its machine language translation process.

## SUMMARY

The essential elements of FORTRAN IV programming in a batch processing mode have been covered in this chapter. They include constants, variables, expressions, statements, and subprograms. Although the language does vary for the various computers on the market, FORTRAN IV, as presented, can be programmed with a few minor modifications. These differences required by the specific computer can be learned in a very short time.

A most important advantage of FORTRAN is that it greatly facilitates programming for the average user. It can be learned in a short time, thereby, allowing more company personnel the opportunity of employing computers at all levels of operation. In the next chapter, FORTRAN IV is applied to representative business data processing areas. These program segments are an integral part of an overall real-time management information system (explained in some detail per Chapter 1).

## QUESTIONS

1. Distinguish among the following: a FORTRAN program, a FORTRAN compiler, and a machine language program.
2. Is there need for a programmer to concern himself with data locations in memory when using FORTRAN? Explain.
3. Is it necessary to include comment cards in a FORTRAN program deck? Explain.
4. (a) What is a FORTRAN statement number?
   (b) Is it necessary to use one for each program step?
5. (a) Distinguish between constants and variables.
   (b) Distinguish between fixed-point and floating-point numbers.
6. What is a variable in the FORTRAN language?
7. How do expressions and statements differ from one another?
8. What are the essential differences between the E and F Format specification statement?
9. Explain what the following Format specifications mean:

   ```
   Iw
   Fw.d
   wX
   wH
   ```

10. What short cut procedure is available for Format specifications that must be repeated two or more times?
11. Distinguish between the Read statement and the Dimension statement for controlling input data.
12. How do control statements differ from input and output statements?
13. Are the Stop and End statements one and the same? Explain.
14. What are the essential differences between an Unconditional Go To statement and a Computed Go To statement?
15. What FORTRAN statements are used for program looping and branching?
16. How does a Go To statement differ from a Continue statement?
17. How does the Equivalence statement differ from the Common statement?
18. How does the External Function differ from the subroutine in FORTRAN subprograms?
19. Which program is more efficient—one written in a machine language or in FORTRAN?
20. What are the main advantages of FORTRAN over BASIC and COBOL languages? Explain thoroughly.

## EXERCISES

1. Which of the following are not valid fixed-point variable names in FORTRAN and why?

   | | |
   |---|---|
   | (a) 2FOUR | (e) N5232 |
   | (b) I | (f) LOG2 |
   | (c) LARRY | (g) KEY |
   | (d) NR23 | (h) MANNO |

2. Which of the following are not valid floating-point variable names in FORTRAN and why?

   | | |
   |---|---|
   | (a) INVNO | (e) BOB |
   | (b) 3ONO | (f) B23CD |
   | (c) Sales | (g) NONE |
   | (d) CONT2 | (h) GO TO |

3. Using the algebraic expressions on the left-hand side, correct the corresponding FORTRAN expressions.

   | *Algebraic Expressions* | *FORTRAN Expressions* |
   |---|---|
   | (a) $\frac{(a+b)}{(c+d)}$ | (A − B)/(c + D) |
   | (b) $ax^2 + bx + c$ | (A * X) + (B * X) + C |
   | (c) $\frac{1}{2}\pi r^2$ | .5 * π * R ** 2 |
   | (d) $12x + 5y$ | 12·X + 5·Y |

4. Write valid FORTRAN expressions for the following algebraic expressions:
   (a) gross sales − discount + freight = net sales
   (b) maximize profits = $5 (N) + $12 (O) + $15 (P)
   (c) city tax = gross income × 1.5%
   (d) $\dfrac{\text{total fixed costs}}{\text{selling price per unit} - \text{variable cost per unit}} = \text{breakeven in units}$
5. Write Input statements plus Format specification statements to read the following cards.

(a)

| 154231 | 942012.55 | | 02275 | 5.005E+3 | |
|---|---|---|---|---|---|
| A | B | | C | D | |
| 1–6 | 7–15 | 16–24 | 25–29 | 30–37 | |

(b)

| 189765 | | 02100 | 100.25 | | 19580 | |
|---|---|---|---|---|---|---|
| Inven-tory Number | | Quan-tity | Price | | Purchase Order Number | |
| 1–6 | 7–10 | 11–15 | 16–21 | 22–25 | 26–30 | |

6. If the following data are printed on a high speed printer, correct the WRITE and FORMAT statements. Lower case b's indicate blanks, starting with print position 1.

b1929bbb9.6243bbb8436bbb8.436E+5

```
    WRITE (5, 10)
10  FORMAT (I4, 2X, E7.3, 3X, I5, 3X, E10.4)
```

7. Prepare a program flowchart and a FORTRAN program to read punched cards for any number of sales on account. Not only are individual sales to be printed, but also the total number of sales and amount of sales are to be printed. Use the following variable names:
   SALES = sales per each card (4 decimal value maximum, starting in column 20)
   NCOUNT = number of sales cards
   TOTAL = total sales amount
8. Prepare a program flowchart and a FORTRAN program to read a group of sales cards (not to exceed 999) containing customer number and amount. The customer amount field has the following floating-point mode—F7.2. Check all data cards and print those cards (including account number) whose value exceeds $5000. Also, print the total number and total amount of sales cards whose value exceed this amount. Use the following constants and variable names.
   999999 = pseudo account number
   NACCT = number of account (6 integer value)
   SALES = sales
   NACNT = number of sales over $5,000
   TOTAL = total sales over $5,000
9. Prepare a program flowchart and a FORTRAN program to calculate the payroll for all production workers whose payroll cards are read by the computer's high speed card reader. Each card contains the employee's payroll number (columns 1 to 5), the hours worked this week (columns 10 to 13), and his current hourly rate of pay (columns 15 to 18). All hours worked in excess of 40.0 hours are to be paid at the rate of one and one-half of the regular rate. The program is to print each employee's payroll number and gross earnings as well as the gross pay of all workers for the week. The following variables are to be used:
   MANNO = employee payroll number    OVERH = overtime hours
   HOURS = hours worked this week    OVERR = overtime hourly rate of pay

RATE = hourly rate of pay    OVERA = overtime amount
GROSS = gross earnings    TOTAL = amount of gross payroll for the week

10. Prepare a program flowchart and a FORTRAN program to calculate the annual amount of interest on loans and to print the amount of annual interest plus account loan number and principal. Also, the total interest on all loans is to be totaled. The problem is to be solved using the following equation:

$$\text{Interest} = \text{Principal} \times \text{Annual Rate of Interest}$$

Data are read from cards while output is in the form of a printout on the high speed printer. The variable names used are as follows:

NUMB = account loan number (card columns 1 to 5)
PRIN = principal (card columns 10 to 15)
RATE = annual rate of interest (card columns 20 to 23)
AMTI = amount of annual interest
TOTAL = total amount of interest

11. Prepare a program flowchart and a FORTRAN program to calculate the annual depreciation charges for a firm's production machines using the straight-line method. The formula to compute annual straight-line depreciation expenses is:

$$\text{Depreciation} = \frac{\text{Cost} - \text{Salvage Value}}{\text{Life in Years (per Federal Income Tax Code)}}$$

| Data read from cards are: | Variable names are: |
|---|---|
| Columns 1 to 5 machine number | NUMB |
| Columns 9 to 15 machine cost | COST |
| Columns 20 to 25 salvage value | SALV |
| Columns 29 to 30 estimated life in years | LIFE |
| Columns 32 to 35 year acquired | NYEAR |

The variable name for yearly depreciation is DEPR. Output is to be in the form of a printed report on the high speed printer showing individual total depreciation charges for the current year. Note: The firm has a policy of taking a full year depreciation in the year of acquisition.

12. Data and requirements for Exercise 11 remain the same, except that the method of depreciation is the double-declining method. This method ignores salvage value and uses a rate double that of the straight-line depreciation method. Current book value less current depreciation is the basis for computing the following year's depreciation.

3. Data and requirements for Exercise 11 remain the same, except that the method of depreciation is the sum-of-the-years-digits method. Also, the following card input data is to be added:

Columns 37 to 40 current year    IYEAR

This method considers salvage value in the same manner as the straight-line method. The number of the years digits are summed and form the basis for computing the current year's depreciation. For example, if the life of the fixed asset is 10 years, the sum-of-the-digits is 55 and is used as the divisor for the net cost. This calculated figure (net cost/55) is the basis for multiplying the remaining years of the asset which gives the annual depreciation expense.

## CHAPTER TWELVE

# Real-Time Management Information System—Selected FORTRAN IV Programs

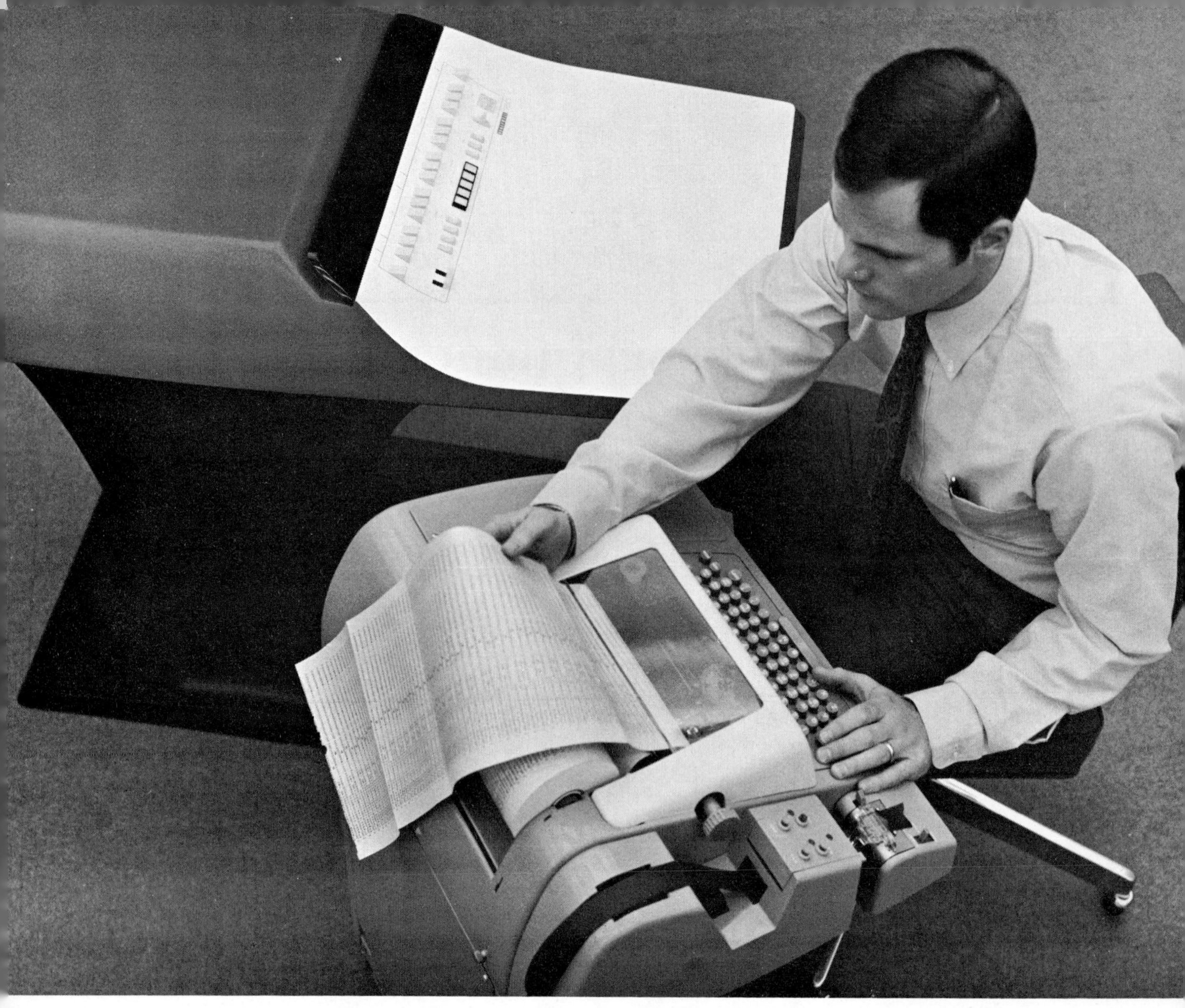

*Selected real-time MIS programs, written in FORTRAN IV, are programmed using a dedicated on-line terminal (shown at right). Depending upon the application, a mini-computer (shown at left) can be linked to an on-line system and utilized for real-time MIS programs. (Courtesy Honeywell Information Systems.)*

Within each major business function, there are many activities that must be performed if that area is to operate successfully. Correspondingly, most business functions have a series of interrelated activities that have an effect on others. Manufacturing, for example, does not operate without the assistance of marketing, engineering, accounting, and maintenance. Basically, these interworkings come about by the very nature of the tasks to be performed.

In this chapter, selected FORTRAN IV programs that are readily applicable to a real-time management information system in a manufacturing environment are explored. The interworkings of one function with another focus on the utilization of common data base elements that are stored on-line in secondary storage. Initially, sales are forecasted by the quantitative technique of exponential smoothing which, in turn, supplies the input for determining the number of finished goods to be produced. This process continues to the actual ordering of the required materials and issuing of factory orders on an optimum basis. These programs—sales forecasting, inventory control (finished goods and materials), and purchasing—are interrelated, thereby making is a necessity to share common data elements. However, other programs are presented that use the same information base while serving two different functions of the firm. This dichotomy is highlighted in the second half of the chapter.

As will be seen in the following material, not only is a common data base employed but also many of the FORTRAN elements found in the prior chapter are illustrated. Programs that concentrate on inventory inquiry, credit check, and comparable functions are not treated in the chapter since the program consists basically of Read and Write statements. Rather than present programs too simple in concept, more representative ones for a typical manufacturing firm are examined. For this reason, data are assumed to have been stored previously on-line in secondary storage and are available for immediate processing via some type of on-line input/output device. A real-time processing mode, then, is used for FORTRAN programs within the chapter versus the batch-processing approach of the prior chapter.

## REAL-TIME MIS CHARACTERISTICS—REVIEW

*By way of review, basic characteristics of real-time MIS are:*

- *on-line real-time processing*
- *forward-looking control system*
- *common data base*
- *I/O-oriented*
- *timely reports*
- *emphasis on exception reporting*
- *integrated subsystems*
- *output directed to lower and middle management*
- *use of operations research models*
- *remote batch processing*

The essential characteristics of a real-time management information system are reviewed briefly (as stated in Chapter 1) before presenting the various FORTRAN IV programs in the chapter. Being a forward-looking system, it shares up-to-date common data elements that are available to the central processor when needed. Data can be changed, that is, added or deleted as desired. In a similar manner, they can be retrieved in a variety of forms, manipulated or operated upon before presentation, and combined with material from other data bases. Also, data base information can be displayed in graphic form, selected so that only certain data meeting specified criteria will be issued, and transmitted in computer-compatible format. The firm's data base is capable of being interrogated by any remote I/O device that is connected on-line with the computer system.

With the ability to make inquiries of on-line files from any input/output device, the computer is capable of interacting with company personnel on a timely basis with essential information. It is possible to process data in real-time which results in feeding back information almost instantaneously. The various levels of management and operating personnel can be made aware of trends, exceptions, and results of recent transactions in order to initiate corrective action to meet predetermined plans. Feedback can alert company personnel about the internal and external factors affecting the firm's individual actions and overall performance.

## REAL-TIME MANAGEMENT INFORMATION SYSTEM PROGRAMS

The chapter's illustrated FORTRAN programs are applied to a typical manufacturing operation. The firm which has plants located throughout the country desires to grow with the national economy. It has found from past experience that up-to-date information is necessary for day-to-day operations as well as for overall direction. For this reason, the firm has numerous input/output devices located throughout its operations. They are connected on-line for an immediate response. Most of its functional business areas utilize these I/O devices continuously for more effective planning, organizing, directing, and controlling of the firm's activities.

For this firm, a logical starting point is forecasting monthly unit sales by product. Based upon past experience, the firm has found that it can accurately project future sales by utilizing exponential smoothing formulas. This approach provides the basis for producing several product lines that are sold exclusively by retail outlets. Raw materials and parts are purchased from the outside as input to the manufacturing plants while additional machining and assembly work are required to produce finished products. Large quantities of goods are shipped directly to large retail outlets while smaller quantities are handled by national distributors.

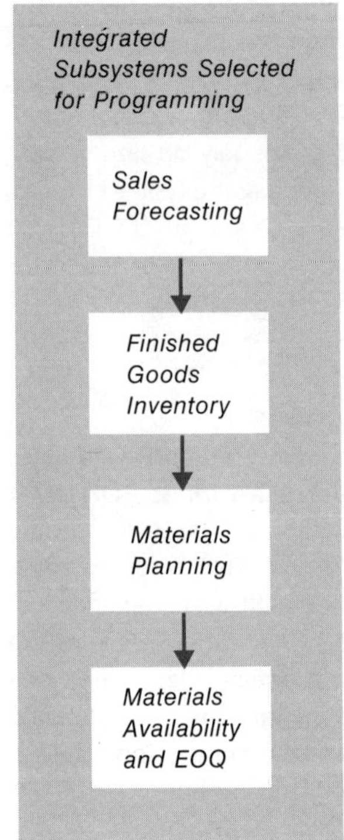


***Selected FORTRAN Programs.*** Four selected FORTRAN programs, found in the next sections of the chapter, are set forth in Figure 12-1 for this typical manufacturing firm. Basically, each function is interrelated. The sales forecast affects the quantity of finished goods to be produced which, in turn, affects materials to be manufactured within the firm and purchased from outside suppliers. Goods purchased or manufactured are produced on an optimum basis by using the economic order quantity formula. Although Figure 12-1 stops at this level, other integrated activities including scheduling, dispatching, and stock control of manufactured items can also be programmed. Similarly, purchased items are received and then sent to stock control. Both manufactured and purchased items are requisitioned for subassembly and assembly when required. Finally, finished goods are shipped directly to the customer or to the distributor, depending upon the size of the order. The number of programs to accomplish these activities is not small. Thus the programming effort as such is an arduous task.

Although the foregoing basic business operations have been concerned mainly with the physical aspects of the manufactured product, other areas, such as accounting, engineering, marketing, purchasing, personnel, and research and development direct their efforts toward supporting and servicing manufacturing activities. In order to understand how a procedure-oriented language affects these areas, several programs are included in subsequent sections of the chapter. They include purchasing and cost accounting variance reports as well as the areas of personnel and sales commissions.

### Sales Forecasting—Finished Goods Inventory

The first set of basic business functions that reference the same data base elements is sales forecasting and finished goods inventory. From past experience, the firm has found that it does experience upward and downward trends in its operations. Based upon this fact, trend adjustment is necessary in its sales forecasts

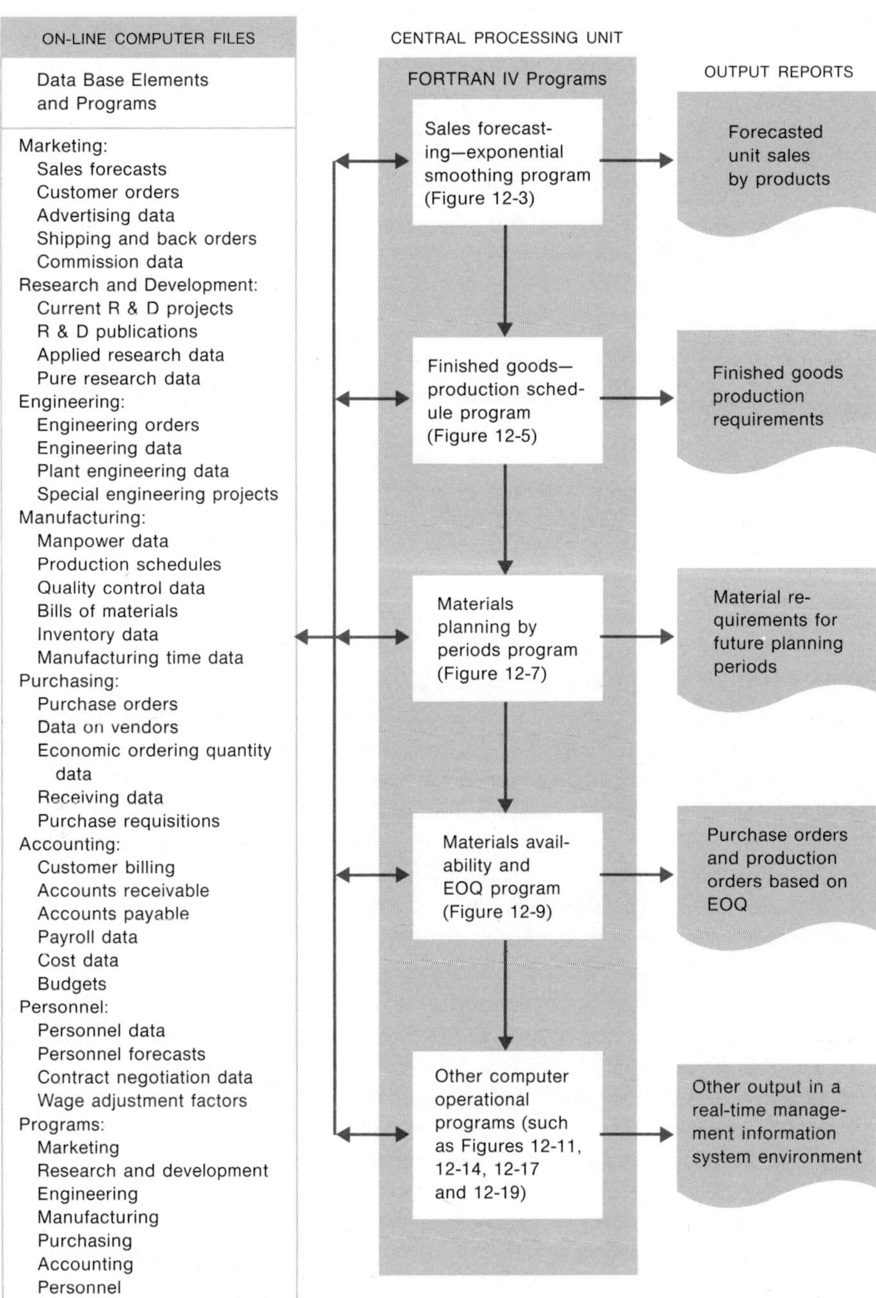


Figure 12-1 FORTRAN IV programs used to generate selected operational reports for a real-time management information system in a typical manufacturing firm.

since its sales prospects improve or decline, depending upon the nation's economy. On the other hand, it has found very little need for seasonal adjustment in its forecasted sales. Thus the firm includes trend adjustment and excludes seasonal adjustment in its sales forecasting method of exponential smoothing.

***Exponential Smoothing Formulas.*** Before the program flowchart and the FORTRAN program can be developed, an explanation of the various formulas that incorporate the technique of exponential smoothing with provision for the current trend is necessary. The basic forecast equation with trend included is

$$\bar{\bar{S}}_t = \bar{S}_t + R_t \tag{12-1}$$

where $\bar{\bar{S}}_t$ = forecast with the trend adjustment for the coming period, calculated during the current period.

$\bar{S}_t$ = forecast without the trend adjustment for the coming period, calculated during the current period.

$R_t$ = trend adjustment for the coming period, calculated during the current period.

Equation 12-1 is the summation of the nontrend sales forecast and the trend forecast that results in a trend adjusted forecast.

The basic formula for $\bar{S}_t$ is: sales forecast for the coming period ($\bar{S}_t$) equals the weighting factor ($A$) times the actual sales for the current period ($S_t$) plus (one minus the weighting factor or $A$) times the sales forecast for the current period ($\bar{S}_{t-1}$). The $A$ in this formula (sometimes called Alpha) is some value between 0 and 1 where the sum of these two weights ($A$ and $1 - A$) equal one. The equation can be written as

$$\bar{S}_t = AS_t + (1 - A)\bar{S}_{t-1} \tag{12-2}$$

The selection of the weighting factor ($A$) is very important for Equation 12-2. If $A$ is very high (close to 1), any fluctuations of actual current sales will have an important effect on the forecast for the next period. However, if $A$ is set close to zero, current sales will have relatively little effect on the upcoming forecast. The experience of several firms has shown that setting $A$ somewhere between 0.1 and 0.2 leads to favorable results. This setting smoothes the extremes of current sales while providing for fluctuations in sales forecasts.

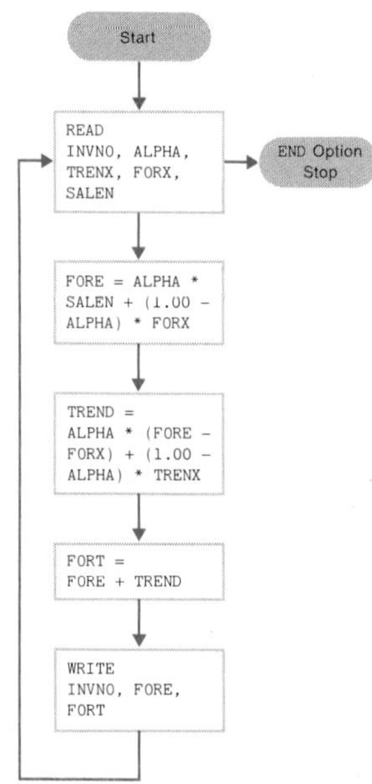


Figure 12-2 Program flowchart for a Sales Forecasting Exponential Smoothing Program..

The trend adjustment formula for $R_t$ is found in Equation 12-3. Instead of using the weighting factor $A$, a new one is defined as "$C$." Experimentation with the weighting factor ($C$) used for the trend equation shows that favorable results are obtained when it is in the neighborhood of $A$. For simplicity, $A$ and $C$ will be the same value. The basic equation for $R_t$ or the trend adjustment for the coming period is: the weighting factor ($C$) times [the forecast for the coming period ($\bar{S}_t$) minus the forecast for the current period ($\bar{S}_{t-1}$)] plus (one minus the weighting factor or $C$) times the trend adjustment for the current period ($R_{t-1}$). It is written as

$$R_t = C(\bar{S}_t - \bar{S}_{t-1}) + (1 - C)R_{t-1} \tag{12-3}$$

***Data Names and Field Sizes—Sales Forecasting.*** The program flowchart (Figure 12-2) and its corresponding FORTRAN program (Figure 12-3) are structured around these formulas for on-line processing. The input and output variable names required for processing sales forecast data are given on the top of the next page.

***Program—Sales Forecasting.*** The program reads current data[1] (compiled on a monthly basis), performs the necessary calculations per the exponential smoothing equations, and prints the forecasted results.[2] Output reads as follows: SALES FORECAST, FINISHED GOODS INVENTORY NUMBER where the appropriate sales

[1]For the Read statement, the first digit in the parentheses (next to READ) is "3" which reads data from secondary storage, specifically, from a magnetic disk.

[2]For the Write statement, the first digit in parentheses (next to WRITE) is "6" which prints data on an I/O terminal device, specifically, on a teletypewriter.

| Description | Name | FORTRAN Format Specification |
|---|---|---|
| Finished goods inventory number | INVNO | I5 |
| Weighting factor (between 0 and 1)—*A* or *C* | ALPHA | F4.2 |
| Trend adjustment (units) for current period | TRENX | F5.0 |
| Sales forecast without trend adjustment for current period (units) | FORX | F6.0 |
| Sales forecast without trend adjustment for coming period (units) | FORE | F6.0 |
| Actual net sales for current period (units) | SALEN | F6.0 |
| Trend adjustment (units) for coming period | TREND | F5.0 |
| Sales forecast with trend adjustment for coming period (units) | FORT | F6.0 |

```
READY
SYS:FØR

READY
NEW

PRØBLEM NAME: FIG123

READY
100C      SALES FØRECASTING - EXPØNENTIAL SMØØTHING PRØGRAM - FØRTRAN IV
110 1     FØRMAT (I5,F4.2,F5.0,2F6.0)
120 2     READ (3,1) INVNØ, ALPHA, TRENX, FØRX, SALEN
130       CALL EØFTST(3,J)
140       GØ TØ (3,5),J
150 3     FØRE=ALPHA*SALEN+(1.00-ALPHA)*FØRX
160       TREND=ALPHA*(FØRE-FØRX)+(1.00-ALPHA)*TRENX
170       FØRT=FØRE+TREND
180       WRITE (6,4) INVNØ, FØRE, FØRT
190 4     FØRMAT (48H SALES FØRECAST,FINISHED GØØDS INVENTØRY NUMBER ,
200&      I5,5X,F6.0,5X,F6.0)
210       GØ TØ 2
220 5     STØP
230       END
SAVE

READY
ØLD:FIG123

READY
RUNNH


RUNNING TIME:     .7 SECS

READY
```

Figure 12-3 A FORTRAN program for printing sales forecasts for all finished goods inventory items—utilizes exponential smoothing.

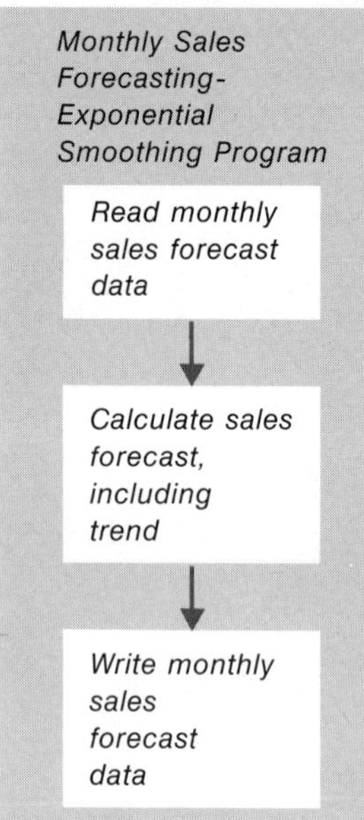


forecasts without trend (FORE) and with trend (FORT) adjustments are preceded by the finished goods inventory number (INVNO). It should be noted that the foregoing output data will be stored on-line for the next program. The coding to accomplish this is not included in the program.

***End-of-File Test.*** In the on-line processing program and subsequent ones in the chapter, an end-of-file test is required. It is necessary to call a subroutine EOFTST. The general format of this statement (for computer being used) is

```
CALL EOFTST (I, J)
```

where: I is an integer constant or variable representing the device number of file being tested.
J is an integer variable representing the condition indicator set during EOFTST.

Upon return from EOFTST, J is set to 1 if an end-of-file indication has not been encountered. J is set to 2 if end-of-file has been encountered.

***Data Names and Field Sizes—Finished Goods Inventory.*** In conjunction with the above on-line monthly program, a second program flowchart (Figure 12-4) and program (Figure 12-5) are developed for on-line processing. This second FORTRAN program determines the number of finished goods that must be manufactured next month. Two of the output variables (INVNO and FORT) in the first program are an integral part of the Finished Goods—Production Schedule Program. Three new variables, UNITS, ORDER, and PROD are needed to complete the FORTRAN program. The first two represent the number of finished goods on hand (UNITS) and on order (ORDER) while the last variable (PROD) refers to the quantity of finished goods to be manufactured next month. The format specification of these three variables is F6.0. Before this program can be utilized, physical adjustments to perpetual inventories stored on-line must have been made so that valid data can be the output of this second program.

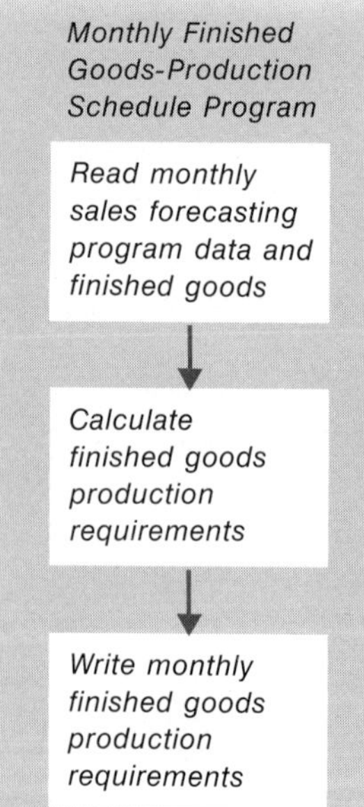


***Program—Finished Goods Inventory.*** The production requirement for next month (PROD) equals the forecasted number of units (FORT) less the physical units on hand (UNITS) and on order (ORDER). The If statement tests the results of the preceding computation. In those cases where the value tests to be minus or zero (units on hand and on order are equal or greater than the forecasted sales for the next period), the floating-point variable PROD is set equal to zero since present units on hand and on order are adequate to meet next period's forecast. On the other hand, if the PROD variable results in a plus evaluation, the production quantity is left unaltered. In either case, the inventory number (INVNO) is printed to the left of the wording FINISHED GOODS INVENTORY NUMBER—PRODUCTION, followed by the production quantity needed to meet the sales forecast for the next month. Thus, if there is sufficient inventory, a zero will be printed while an appropriate amount will be printed if the finished goods on order and on hand are not adequate to meet the coming period sales forecast. As noted for the first program in this section, coding necessary to store the output data is not included.

***Combining Programs.*** Although the above program is separate from the first program, they could have been merged into a much larger computer program. The process could have started with sales forecasting where the output served as input for finished goods inventory. In a similar manner, the output could be input for exploding bills of materials which are the basis for manufacturing and placing orders

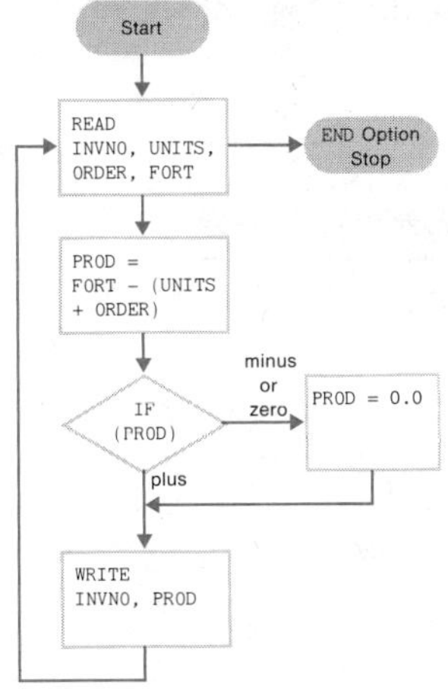


Figure 12-4 Program flowchart for a Finished Goods—Production Schedule Program.

with vendors. These results, in turn, could assist in the day-to-day scheduling and dispatching of the various manufacturing facilities. Thus, a sophisticated mathematical model could be built to coordinate several of the firm's operations automatically. The approach in this section and succeeding sections has been simplified since space does not warrant such a treatment.

### Materials Planning—Materials Availability and EOQ

Now that the monthly requirement levels of on-line finished goods inventories have been computed, the next phase is exploding bills of materials where there is an inadequate supply on hand or on order. The materials planning program multiplies the quantity needed of each component times the number of final products that must be manufactured. Also, it places these component requirements in the appropriate planning period since some parts will be needed before others. In the illustrative program flowchart (Figure 12-6) and the Materials Planning by Periods Program (Figure 12-7), three 10-day planning periods are utilized in an on-line processing mode.

```
READY
SYS:FØR

READY
NEW
PROBLEM NAME: FIG125

READY
100C      FINISHED GØØDS - PRØDUCTIØN SCHEDULE PRØGRAM - FØRTRAN IV
110 1     FØRMAT (I5,3F6.0)
120 2     READ (3,1) INVNØ, UNITS, ØRDER, FØRT
130       CALL EØFTST (3,J)
140       GØ TØ (3,7),J
150 3     PRØD=FØRT-(UNITS+ØRDER)
160       IF (PRØD)4,4,5
170 4     PRØD=0.0
180 5     WRITE (6,6) INVNØ, PRØD
190 6     FØRMAT (1H ,I5,45HFINISHED GØØDS INVENTØRY NUMBER - PRØDUCTIØN ,
200&      F6.0)
210       GØ TØ 2
220 7     STØP
230       END
SAVE

READY
RUNNH



RUNNING TIME:      .7 SECS

READY
```

Figure 12-5 A FORTRAN program for printing the number of finished goods units to produce next month.

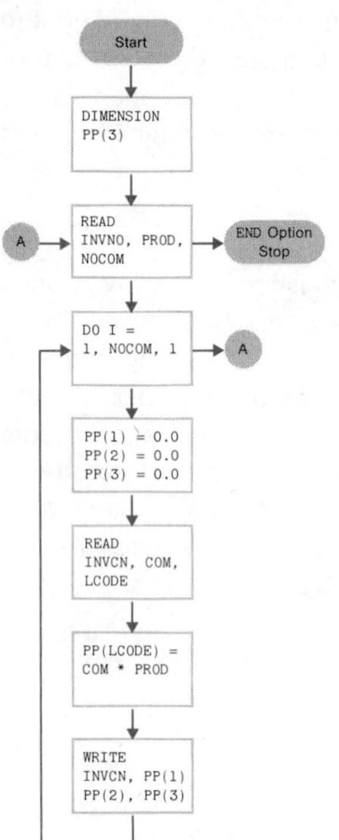
Start
DIMENSION PP(3)
READ INVNO, PROD, NOCOM
A
END Option Stop
DO I = 1, NOCOM, 1
A
PP(1) = 0.0
PP(2) = 0.0
PP(3) = 0.0
READ INVCN, COM, LCODE
PP(LCODE) = COM * PROD
WRITE INVCN, PP(1) PP(2), PP(3)

Figure 12-6 Program flowchart for Materials Planning by Periods Program.

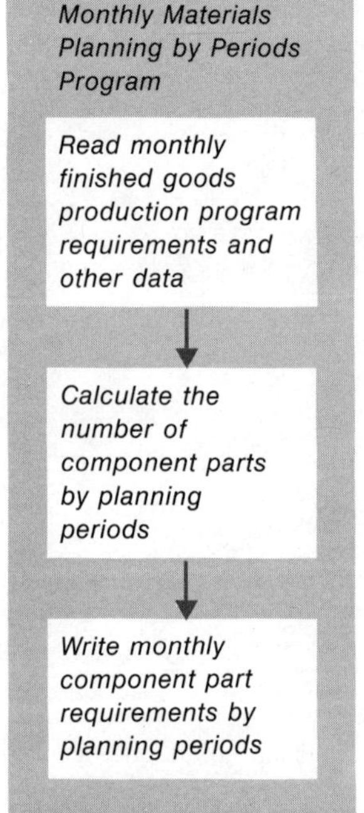
Monthly Materials Planning by Periods Program
Read monthly finished goods production program requirements and other data
Calculate the number of component parts by planning periods
Write monthly component part requirements by planning periods

***Data Names and Field Sizes—Materials Planning.*** The variables, defined in both Figures 12-7 and 12-8, are set forth as follows.

| *Description* | *Name* | *FORTRAN Format Specification* |
|---|---|---|
| Finished goods inventory number | INVNO | I5 |
| Finished goods production requirements | PROD | F6.0 |
| Number of components in each final product's bill of materials | NOCOM | I2 |
| Inventory component part number | INVCN | I5 |
| Number of component parts in final product | COM | F2.0 |
| Code level (planning period) for component part | LCODE | I1 |
| Planning period 1 (10 days)—component part requirements | PP(1) | F6.0 |
| Planning period 2 (20 days)—component part requirements | PP(2) | F6.0 |
| Planning period 3 (30 days)—component part requirements | PP(3) | F6.0 |

For the planning periods 1, 2, and 3, the first 10 days are associated with a code level of 1 while the second and third 10-day periods are related to code levels 2 and 3, respectively.

***Program—Materials Planning.*** The Dimension statement establishes PP as an array having three elements, representing the three planning periods for component part requirements. Read statement 2 provides for reading the finished goods production requirements (PROD) and the number of components in each final product's bill of materials (NOCOM) from secondary storage (3). Statement 3, the Do loop down to statement 5, provides for reading the detailed bill of materials from secondary storage. Basically, these lines of coding explode the requirements for the final product's bill of materials while spreading them to the appropriate planning periods. The NOCOM variable in the Do statement determines the number of loops that must be taken before the program goes on to the next final product or finished goods inventory item.

Within each Do loop, the following sequence of events takes place. Each element of the PP array is set equal to zero. Then, the inventory component part number (INVCN), the number required to produce one unit of finished product (COM), and the code level (LCODE) for each component part are read in. The code level identifies with which planning period the component part requirements are to be identified. For example, if a particular component part has a code level 2, the computed component part requirements are assigned to planning period 2. This means that the item must be manufactured or purchased within two periods or 20 days. Based upon past experience, this time period is sufficient to tie in with all other component parts so that the production deadline for assembly of the finished product component parts can be met. Thus, there is no need to order component parts until they are actually needed. Basically, this approach reduces the need to stock excess inventories throughout the year.

After the explosion calculation (COM * PROD) and the identification of the result as either planning period 1, 2, or 3, the data are printed by the teletypewriter device. Those planning periods that contain a zero value will be so printed. In

```
READY
SYS:FOR

READY
NEW

PROBLEM NAME: FIG127

READY
C       MATERIAL PLANNING BY PERIØDS PRØGRAM - FØRTRAN IV
        DIMENSIØN PP(3)
 1      FØRMAT (I5,F6.0,I2)
 2      READ (3,1) INVNØ,PRØD,NØCØM
        CALL EØFTST(3,J)
        GØ TØ (3,7),J
 3      DØ 5 I=1,NØCØM,1
        PP(1)=0.0
        PP(2)=0.0
        PP(3)=0.0
 4      FØRMAT (I5,F2.0,I1)
        READ (3,4) INVCN,CØM,LCØDE
        PP(LCØDE)=CØM*PRØD
 5      WRITE (6,6) INVCN,PP(1),PP(2),PP(3)
 6      FØRMAT (1H ,I5,3(2X,F6.0))
        GØ TØ 2
 7      STØP
        END
SAVE

READY
RUNNH


RUNNING TIME:      .4 SECS

READY
```

Figure 12-7 A FORTRAN program for printing material requirements for the next three planning periods.

addition, data are stored on-line for the next computer program although this coding has been ignored in Figure 12-7. Once the Write statement has been completed, the computer performs the same set of instructions for each of the components. Once the Do loop has been completed, the Go To (GO TO 2) statement tells the computer to read a new set of data for a final product and loop NOCOM times. The program terminates when the on-line data have been completely processed.

***Purchasing Versus Manufacturing.*** Continuing in an on-line processing mode, the output for the above program can take two paths. One is the purchasing of raw materials and parts from outside vendors while the other is the manufacturing of parts within the plant. The outside raw materials provide the basic means for manufacturing specific parts used in the assembly of the finished product. Likewise, outside purchased parts are used in the assembly of the final product. Before materials are manufactured or purchased, it is necessary to determine if present inventories and materials on order are capable of meeting the firm's needs for the next three planning periods. This will be the fourth program—Materials Availability and EOQ Program, flowcharted in Figure 12-8. At this point, it is important

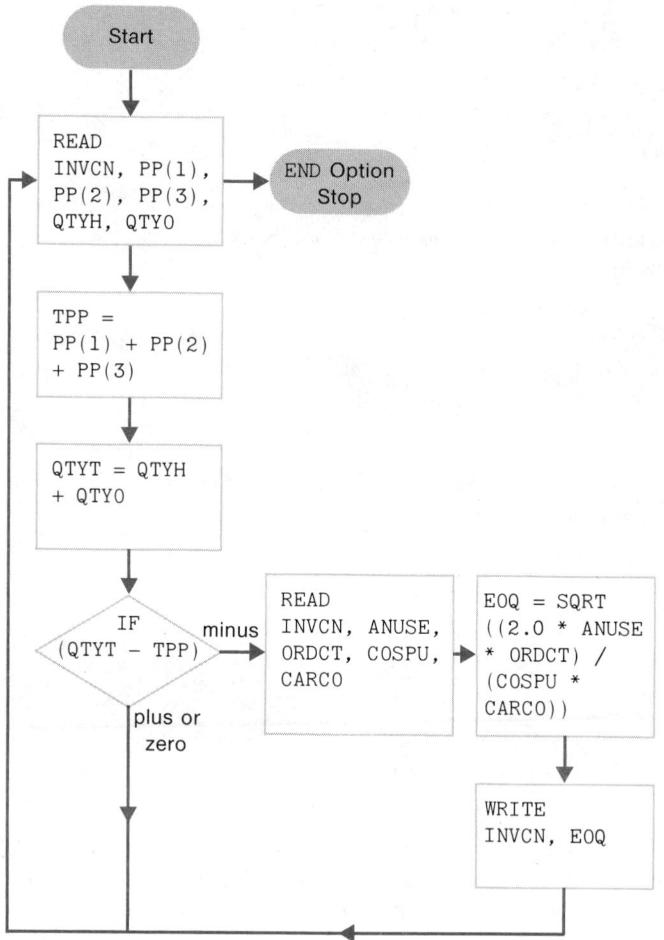


Figure 12-8 Program flowchart of Materials Availability and EOQ (economic order quantity) Program.

*Monthly Materials Availability and EOQ Program*

*Read monthly component part requirements by planning periods program data and other inventory data*

↓

*Calculate economic order quantity if current materials inventory is inadequate*

↓

*Write the inventory component part number and EOQ for production or outside purchase*

to note that perpetual inventories stored on-line must be adjusted to physical counts for accurate output of this program.

***Data Names and Field Sizes—Materials Availability.*** The variables–INVCN (inventory component part number), PP(1), PP(2), and PP(3) (planning periods 1, 2, and 3—component part requirements) which represent output from the preceding program provide input for the program found in Figure 12-9. The physical quantities of materials on hand (QTYH) and on order (QTYO) are also read from secondary storage.

***Program—Materials Availability.*** Two separate calculations are undertaken within the FORTRAN program. First, materials needed for planning periods 1, 2, and 3 are totaled (TPP). Second, the materials on hand are added to the quantity on order for manufactured or purchased parts, resulting in a total quantity of material available for use (QTYT). An If statement determines the need for issuing a new production order or purchase order for a specific inventory component part.

If there is sufficient inventory of materials on hand or on order, it is not necessary to issue a production order or purchase order. Current inventories are available to meet the next three planning period requirements. The evaluation of plus or zero in the If statement transfers control (GO TO 2) to the first Read statement. On the other hand, a minus result instructs the computer to read in data so that an economic order quantity (purchase order or production order) can be issued. In essence, present material availability is not sufficient to meet future planning requirements for the next three periods.

***Program—Economic Order Quantity.*** The program section to calculate the EOQ was discussed in Chapter 11 and will not be repeated here. As shown in Figure 12-9, it is essentially the same as that found in Figure 11-2, the differences being those of Format specifications, comments, and Stop statement. Regarding the variables that handle both a purchase order and a production order, they are the same except that the descriptions have changed. The appropriate purchase order variables are given below while the production order descriptions are given in parentheses. As with previous programs, another program is needed to write the output of this program into secondary storage (on-line).

| *Description* | *Name* | *FORTRAN Format Specification* |
|---|---|---|
| Annual usage quantity (same) | ANUSE | F7.0 |
| Ordering cost per order (set up cost per order) | ORDCT | F5.2 |
| Vendor cost per unit (factory cost per unit) | COSPU | F6.0 |
| Inventory carrying cost on finished goods (on raw materials) | CARCO | F6.0 |
| Economic order quantity | EOQ | F7.0 |

*Real-time MIS programs are:*
- *integrated*
- *stored on-line*
- *large*
- *timely*

***Characteristics of Real-Time MIS Programs.*** The FORTRAN IV programs in this section and the prior one illustrate several important points. First, the output of one on-line processing run provides the necessary input for the next program, resulting in an integrated approach for a real-time management information system. Second, all data are stored on-line in secondary storage and are brought into primary storage as needed. This allows for immediate response to questions being asked. Third, although the prior programs are explained separately, they are normally brought together with other subroutines or smaller programs for one large program. Fourth, the entry of physical adjustments to perpetual inventories where necessary allows the on-line computer program to feed back accurate and timely information on production orders and purchase orders for the coming month. Finally, an integrated data base references common data base elements. In this manner, there is no need to duplicate data that are capable of serving many information needs.

### Purchasing Report—Cost Report

Many other integrated programs, apart from the preceding four programs, can be written to produce the desired finished goods output. These include the loading of the manufacturing machine centers for the most efficient utilization of machines and manpower, the receipt of raw materials, and the issuance of materials for production. Rather than continue this approach, the programs in this section and

```
READY
SYS:FØR

READY
NEW

PRØBLEM NAME: FIG129

READY
100C      MATERIALS AVAILABILITY AND EØQ PRØGRAM - FØRTRAN IV
110 1     FØRMAT (I5,5F6.0)
120 2     READ (3,1) INVCN,PP(1),PP(2),PP(3),QTYH,QTYØ
130       CALL EØFTST (3,J)
140       GØ TØ (3,7),J
150 3     TPP=PP(1)+PP(2)+PP(3)
160       QTYT=QTYH+QTYØ
170       IF (QTYT-TPP)5,2,2
180 4     FØRMAT (I5,F7.0,F5.2,2F6.0)
190 5     READ (3,4) INVCN,ANUSE,ØRDCT,CØSPU,CARCØ
200       EØQ=SQRT((2.0*ANUSE*ØRDCT)/(CØSPU*CARCØ))
210       WRITE (6,6) INVCN,EØQ
220 6     FØRMAT (1H ,I5,5X,11HTHE EØQ IS ,F7.0)
230       GØ TØ 2
240 7     STØP
250       END
SAVE

READY
RUNNH


RUNNING TIME:        .7 SECS

READY
```

Figure 12-9 A FORTRAN program for determining materials availability before issuing production orders or purchase orders.

the next one are oriented toward different basic business functions within the firm. However, they share common data base elements.

Assuming data have been previously stored, that is, updated as the events occur, monthly data on items purchased are available on-line for the firm's purchasing and cost accounting functions. In the first program, variances of current unit prices from a base period are desired by the firm's purchasing agents for all monthly purchased items. This monthly review by inventory component part numbers permits them to evaluate the pricing structure of its suppliers throughout the year. Figures 12-10 and 12-11 contain the program flowchart and the corresponding FORTRAN program for a Monthly Purchasing Price Analysis Report.

***Data Names and Field Sizes—Monthly Purchasing Report.*** The necessary variables in producing this report are given on the top of the next page.

The output report that utilizes these variables is found in Figure 12-12. Each line on this Monthly Purchasing Price Analysis Report represents a summary of all purchases for a particular component part number by vendors. If there was more than one purchase during the month from the same source, these data are accumulated with prior data for the same month. Once the program in Figure 12-11 has produced the desired report, the data are transferred to other storage loca-

| Description | Name | FORTRAN Format Specification |
|---|---|---|
| Inventory component part number | INVCN | I5 |
| Outside vendor name | A1, A2, A3 | 3A6 |
| Unit price for the base month (standard) | PRICB | F6.2 |
| Unit price for the current month (actual) | PRICC | F6.2 |
| Monthly quantity purchased | QUANM | F7.0 |
| Monthly price index | PRICI | F7.2 |
| Total monthly purchased amount for each inventory component part | TOTAL | F7.0 |
| Monthly percent variance | VAR | F6.2 |

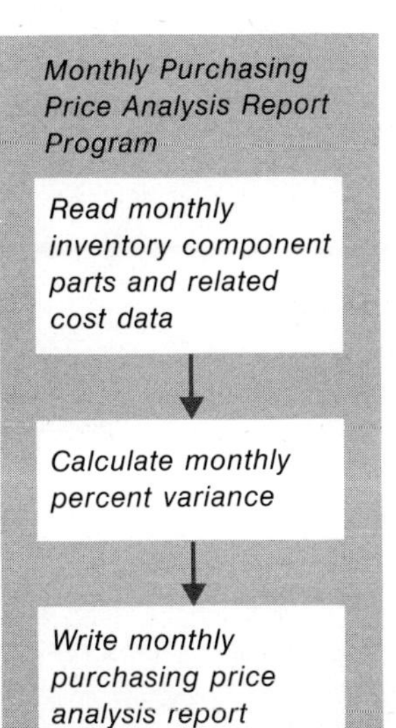
Monthly Purchasing Price Analysis Report Program
Read monthly inventory component parts and related cost data
Calculate monthly percent variance
Write monthly purchasing price analysis report

tions for longer period analysis while the current month's secondary storage locations are set to zero. In this manner, data can be processed in an on-line mode for the coming month.

***Program—Monthly Purchasing Report.*** The inventory component part number, vendor name, unit price for base month, unit price for current month, and monthly quantity purchased are read from secondary storage. With this data input, it is possible to calculate the monthly price index (PRICI), the total amount purchased monthly (TOTAL), and the monthly percent variance (VAR). The statements for these computations follow the Read statement. In the first Arithmetic statement, it is necessary to multiply the result on the right-hand side of the equal sign by 100., a floating-point constant. This multiplication converts the data to a percentage. Similarily, another floating-point constant is found in the third Arithmetic statement. The 10000. constant keeps the answer (VAR) as a percentage.

The most important part of this FORTRAN output is the last column in Figure 12-12. Monthly percent variances alert the firm's buyers to deteriorating price conditions, especially when two or more suppliers are competing for the firm's business. As noted in the illustration, two suppliers for part numbers 10315 and 10920 respectively should be scrutinized to determine the status quo regarding prices. In this situation or any other, an extremely high (unfavorable) variance might show up for an item. Likewise, a much lower unfavorable variance might be associated with a much larger total expenditure. From an overall buying viewpoint, it would be more beneficial to the firm if the purchasing agents spent their time on these items, or at least start with these items for critical appraisal.

***Additional Exception Reports.*** Additional purchasing reports could be prepared from the same common data base elements on a monthly basis or from data that have been updated for a longer period of time, say a quarter. Among these are vendor and product performance reports on a monthly or some other periodic basis as well as buyer performance reports. Other analytical reports could include those on buyer quality and delivery. While these reports are centered around the purchasing department, comparable ones can be developed for other departments. A Quarterly Cost—Standard Versus Actual Exception Report will be explored for the cost section of the accounting department. The program flowchart and FORTRAN program applicable to this report are found in Figures 12-13 and 12-14, respectively. A sample printout is illustrated in Figure 12-15.

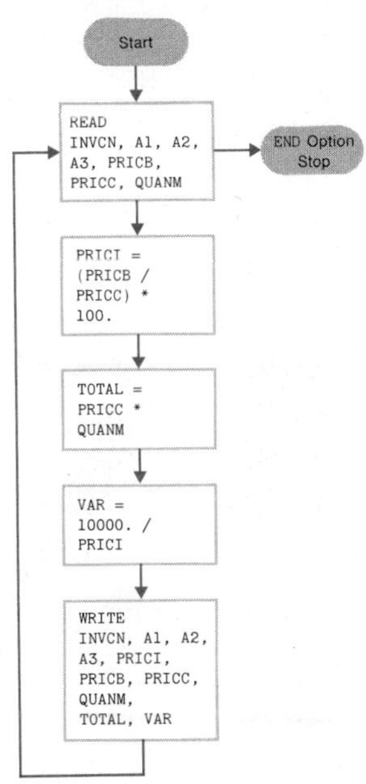
Start
READ INVCN, A1, A2, A3, PRICB, PRICC, QUANM
END Option Stop
PRICI = (PRICB / PRICC) * 100.
TOTAL = PRICC * QUANM
VAR = 10000. / PRICI
WRITE INVCN, A1, A2, A3, PRICI, PRICB, PRICC, QUANM, TOTAL, VAR

Figure 12-10 Program flowchart for a Monthly Purchasing Price Analysis Report Program.

***Program—Quarterly Cost Report.*** Several variables (INVCN, A1, A2, A3, PRICBQ, PRICCQ) are read from secondary storage. These are quite similar to the preceding program, except that the values have been accumulated on a quarterly basis and not on a monthly basis. (The program to update secondary storage is

```
READY
SYS:FOR

READY
NEW

PRØBLEM NAME: FI1211

READY
100C      MØNTHLY PURCHASING PRICE ANALYSIS REPØRT PROGRAM - FØRTRAN IV
110 1     FØRMAT (I5,3A6,2F6.2,F7.0)
120 2     READ (3,1) INVCN,A1,A2,A3,PRICB,PRICC,QUANM
130       CALL EØFTST (3,J)
140       GØ TØ (3,5),J
150 3     PRICI=(PRICB/PRICC)*100.
160       TØTAL=PRICC*QUANM
170       VAR=10000./PRICI
180       WRITE (6,4) INVCN,A1,A2,A3,PRICI,PRICB,PRICC,QUANM,TØTAL,VAR
190 4     FØRMAT (1H ,I5,3X,3A6,3X,F7.2,2(3X,F6.2),2(3X,F7.0),3X,F6.2)
200       GØ TØ 2
210 5     STØP
220       END
SAVE

READY
RUNNH


RUNNING TIME:        .8 SECS

READY
```

Figure 12-11 A FORTRAN program for determining the monthly variances of purchased material from a base period—unit price basis.

| INVENTORY COMPONENT PART NUMBER | VENDOR NAME | MONTHLY PRICE INDEX | UNIT PRICES STANDARD BASE MONTH | UNIT PRICES ACTUAL CURRENT MONTH | MONTHLY QUANTITY PURCHASED | MONTHLY PURCHASED AMOUNT | MONTHLY PERCENT VARIANCE |
|---|---|---|---|---|---|---|---|
| 10010 | AJAX MFG. CO. | 97.78 | 2.20 | 2.25 | 8,000 | 20,000.00 | 102.27 |
| 10315 | ARGO SUPPLY | 96.77 | 3.00 | 3.10 | 4,200 | 13,020.00 | 103.33 |
| 10315 | LINK SUPPLY | 96.15 | 3.00 | 3.12 | 1,000 | 3,120.00 | 104.00 |
| 10907 | LODGE CORP. | 104.55 | 23.00 | 22.00 | 900 | 19,800.00 | 95.65 |
| 10920 | AMCO STEEL | 61.90 | 6.50 | 10.50 | 100 | 1,050.00 | 161.54 |
| 10920 | INCO STEEL | 67.71 | 6.50 | 9.60 | 1,000 | 9,600.00 | 147.69 |
| ⋮ | ⋮ | ⋮ | ⋮ | ⋮ | ⋮ | ⋮ | ⋮ |

Figure 12-12 Monthly Purchasing Price Analysis Report.

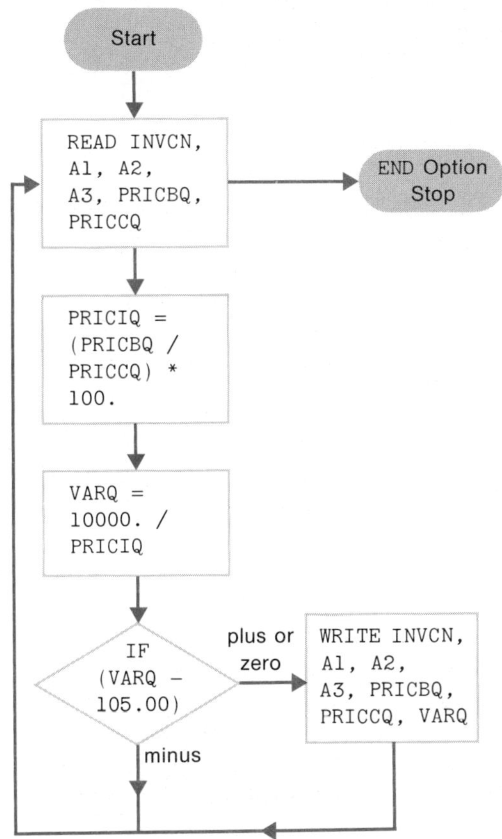


Figure 12-13 Program flowchart for a Quarterly Cost—Standard versus Actual Exception Report Program.

*Quarterly Cost-Standard Versus Actual Exception Report Program*

*Read quarterly inventory component parts and related cost data*

*Calculate quarterly percent variance and compare variance to 105%*

*Print quarterly cost exception report for those variances 105% and over*

not included in this section.) Comparable calculations for the price index (PRICIQ) and the percent variance (VARQ) are performed. However, an Arithmetic If statement evaluates the variance percentage. If the percent equals or exceeds 105.00, the program directs a printout on the teletypewriter unit. Otherwise, if the variance is less than 105.00, the value is to be ignored and the program starts reading another set of data from secondary storage as directed by the Go To statement.

The importance of this report to the cost accounting section should be somewhat apparent. Any time the actual cost of purchased materials (and manufactured items) exceed the accepted standard for a three-month period, the cost analysts must determine whether or not a change in the cost standard is warranted. It may be necessary to consult with the purchasing department on these higher costs in order to satisfy themselves of the need for changing standard costs. It is not necessary to alter a standard cost value if the situation is a temporary one. As shown in Figure 12-15, only those variances that have equaled or exceeded the 5% increase over the base value are reported for investigation. Thus the "management by exception" principle is readily applicable here as it is to many other reports.

**Personnel Search—Sales Commissions**

The last two examples of different business functions that utilize the same data base elements are the personnel department and the payroll section of the accounting department. The first program, applicable to the personnel department,

```
READY
SYS:FOR

READY
NEW

PROBLEM NAME: FI1214

READY
100C      QUARTERLY COST - STANDARD VERSUS ACTUAL EXCEPTIØN REPØRT PRØGRAM
110 1     FØRMAT (I5,3A6,2F6.2)
120 2     READ (3,1) INVCN,A1,A2,A3,PRICBQ,PRICCQ
130       CALL EØFTST (3,J)
140       GØ TØ (3,6),J
150 3     PRICIQ=(PRICBQ/PRICCQ)*100.
160       VARQ=10000./PRICIQ
170       IF (VARQ-105.00)2,4,4
180 4     WRITE (6,5) INVCN,A1,A2,A3,PRICBQ,PRICCQ,VARQ
190 5     FØRMAT (1H ,I5,3X,3A6,3(3X,F6.2))
200       GØ TØ 2
210 6     STØP
220       END
SAVE

READY
RUNNH

RUNNING TIME:       .7 SECS

READY
```

Figure 12-14 A FORTRAN program for selecting those quarterly unit costs that exceed the standard cost by 5% and over.

is designed to locate employees that have certain skills within the firm's multiplant operations. The Personnel Skill Search Program surveys the on-line computer files for specific skills. In the example, it is looking for employees who have skill numbers 15400 through 15402. This five-digit number indicates that they have the necessary skills to take on more advanced work. Instead of the firm making a manual search of personnel files and issuing numerous letters and notices about the openings,

| INVENTORY COMPONENT PART NUMBER | VENDOR NAME | UNIT COST | | QUARTERLY PERCENT VARIANCE |
|---|---|---|---|---|
| | | STANDARD | ACTUAL | |
| | | BASE QUARTER | CURRENT QUARTER | |
| 10920 | AMCO STEEL | 6.50 | 10.50 | 161.54 |
| 10920 | INCO STEEL | 6.50 | 9.60 | 147.69 |
| 19703 | AMERICAN METALS | 4.75 | 5.00 | 105.26 |
| 15500 | GLEN MFG. CO. | .50 | .75 | 150.00 |
| 21607 | ROSS VALVE CO. | .25 | .30 | 120.00 |
| 21607 | TRU-VALVE CO. | .25 | .31 | 124.00 |
| ⋮ | ⋮ | ⋮ | ⋮ | ⋮ |

Figure 12-15 Quarterly Cost-Standard Versus Actual Exception Report.

a computer file is interrogated for internal recruiting. Thus, manual methods can be replaced by an on-line computer approach before going outside to recruit the required personnel.

***Data Names and Field Sizes—Personnel Search.*** The data base elements for the Personnel Skill Search Program are given as follows.

| *Description* | *Name* | *FORTRAN Format Specification* |
|---|---|---|
| Individual skill number | ISKIL | I5 |
| Employee number | MANNO | I5 |
| Employee name | A1, A2, A3, A4 | 4A6 |

The first two numbers are integer variables while the last one is an alphabetic variable. In this program and the next one, these common data base elements are required for processing. By no means is their use restricted to these two programs. Numerous other programs can be written to answer the needs of the firm.

***Program—Personnel Search.*** The program flowchart and the FORTRAN program are found in Figures 12-16 and 12-17, respectively. The program instructs the computer to read in the skill variable for all employees. Those employees that

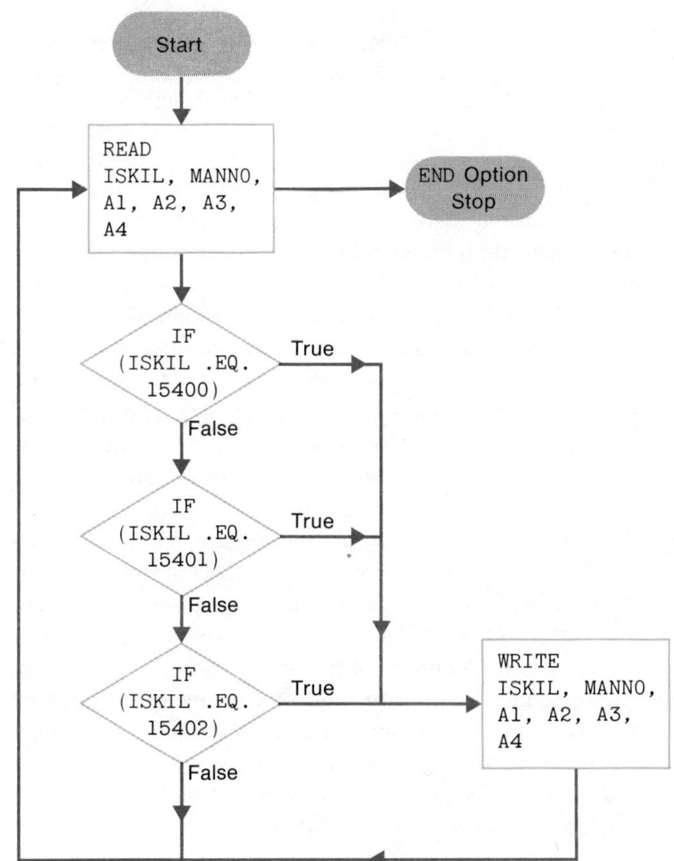


Figure 12-16 Program flowchart for a Personnel Skill Search Program.

```
READY
SYS:FØR

READY
NEW

PRØBLEM NAME: FI1217

READY
100C      PERSØNNEL SKILL SEARCH PRØGRAM - FØRTRAN IV
110 1     FØRMAT (2I5,4A6)
120 2     READ (3,1) ISKIL,MANNØ,A1,A2,A3,A4
130       CALL EØFTST (3,J)
140       GØ TØ (3,6),J
150 3     IF (ISKIL .EQ. 15400) GØ TØ 4
160       IF (ISKIL .EQ. 15401) GØ TØ 4
170       IF (ISKIL .EQ. 15402) GØ TØ 4
180       GØ TØ 2
190 4     WRITE (6,5) ISKIL,MANNØ,A1,A2,A3,A4
200 5     FØRMAT (1H ,2(I5,1X),4A6)
210       GØ TØ 2
220 6     STØP
230       END
SAVE

READY
RUNNH

RUNNING TIME:      1.0 SECS

READY
```

Figure 12-17 A FORTRAN program for printing names of personnel with specific skills (15400 through 15402).

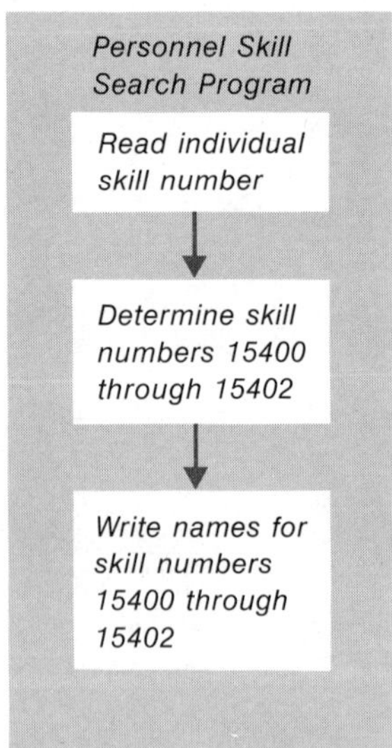
Personnel Skill Search Program
Read individual skill number
Determine skill numbers 15400 through 15402
Write names for skill numbers 15400 through 15402

have one of the following numbers—15400, 15401, or 15402—cause an equal (.EQ.) condition in one of the three Logical If statements. Where an equal to condition arises, a Write statement causes a printout of the individual's skill number, employee number, and name. Control is returned (GO TO 2) to the Read statement. On the other hand, if the input skill variable does not equal one of these skill number variables, the program returns to the Read statement without a printout on the I/O device. The end-of-file condition is recognized by calling the EOFTST subroutine and then testing the parameter J in a calculated Go To statement. The output of the teletypewriter, then, gives the requested information. The appropriate department(s) within the specific plant(s) can be contacted since the variable MANNO is a composite of plant, department, and employee number.

***Common Data Base Program.*** A second program that utilizes much the same data is the Monthly Sales Commissions Ledger Program. A listing of the salesmen along with their respective amount of commissions is to be prepared. In addition, the number of salesmen, the total monthly sales amount, and the total monthly sales commissions (including bonus) are to be printed at the end of the processing run.

As shown in Figure 12-18, commissions are paid at the rate of 10% for all salesmen. However, for those salesmen who possess certain skills, a bonus is paid. If the skill number is 10001, an additional bonus is 1% on sales while a skill number of 10002 will mean an added bonus of 2% on sales. The third skill variable or 10003 is to be ignored for a bonus computation.

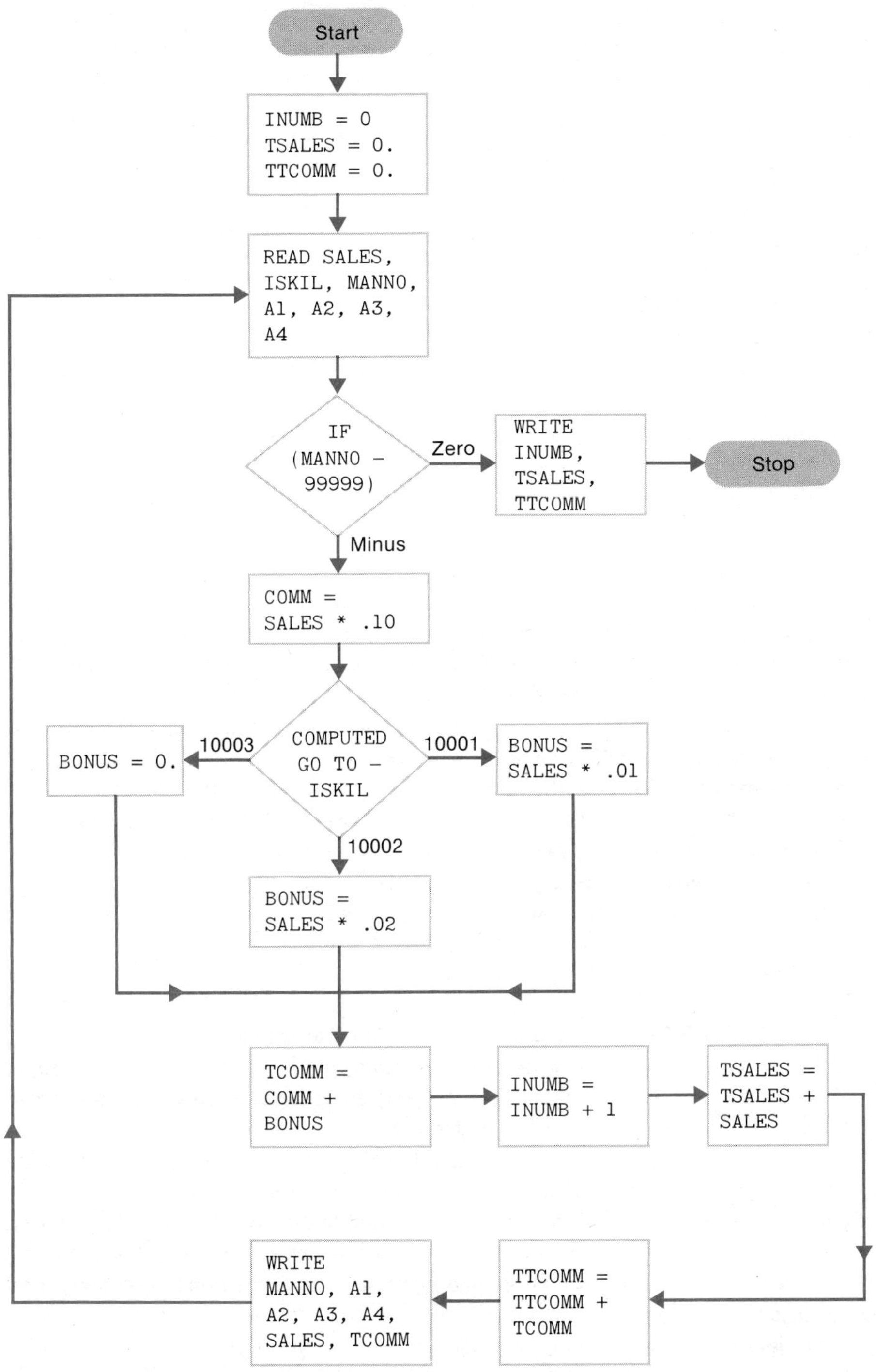


Figure 12-18 Program flowchart for a Monthly Sales Commissions Ledger Program.

***Data Names and Field Sizes—Sales Commissions.*** The input data are the same as the preceding program plus the addition of the sales amount. Also, many of these input items are needed for output which appear as follows.

| *Description* | *Name* | *FORTRAN Format Specification* |
|---|---|---|
| Salesman's monthly sales | SALES | F7.2 |
| Individual skill number | ISKIL | I5 |
| Employee number | MANNO | I5 |
| Employee name | A1, A2, A3, A4 | 4A6 |
| Salesman's monthly commission (including bonus) | TCOMM | F6.2 |
| Total number of salesmen | INUMB | I2 |
| Total monthly sales | TSALES | F9.2 |
| Total monthly commissions (including bonuses) | TTCOMM | F7.2 |

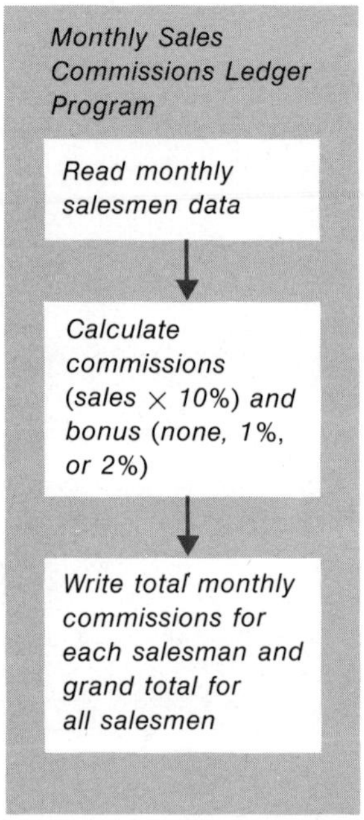

*Monthly Sales Commissions Ledger Program*

*Read monthly salesmen data*

↓

*Calculate commissions (sales × 10%) and bonus (none, 1%, or 2%)*

↓

*Write total monthly commissions for each salesman and grand total for all salesmen*

***Program—Sales Commissions.*** The important variable in calculating the monthly sales commission is the skill number (ISKIL) assigned to all personnel including salesmen. In the Monthly Sales Commissions Ledger Program (Figure 12-19), the bonus is calculated after determining the regular commission. When the last file number (containing all nine's) has been read from the magnetic disk storage, control is transferred to the last Write statement. This initiates printing of the total number of salesmen, the total monthly sales, followed by the wording—TOTAL MONTHLY SALES COMMISSIONS IS—and the appropriate amount. It should be pointed out that the pseudo salesman number (99999) provides an alternative method of detecting an end-of-file condition. This approach was prevalent in earlier computers. However, current programming languages enable the programmer to create and recognize end-of-file conditions as demonstrated earlier in this chapter and the prior one.

## SUMMARY

The first four FORTRAN IV programs have illustrated how the various functions of the firm can be logically integrated. This approach is a starting basis for a real-time management information system. The sales forecasts are developed into production and inventory planning that result in the placement of manufacturing and purchase orders. Although the presentation centered around a separate program for each function, normally these programs are integrated into a larger program. In such an approach, a set of many independent but compatible program modules (small program parts) are written. They are tied together by master control blocks written for each major functional area of the firm. Some firms have developed a set of several hundred program modules for making the most effective use of a large data base in a real-time management information system.

The last four sample programs have demonstrated how diverse functions can reference a common data base. Purchasing and cost accounting reports are prepared from the same basic data as is the case with compatible personnel and payroll programs. In essence, a large data base gives the systems analyst the ability to develop a wide range of programs that are closely interrelated or partially related.

```
READY
SYS:FØR

READY
NEW

PRØBLEM NAME: FI1219

READY
100C      MØNTHLY SALES CØMMISSIONS LEDGER PRØGRAM - FØRTRAN IV
110       INUMB=0
120       TSALES=0.
130       TTCØMM=0.
140 1     FØRMAT (F7.2,2I5,4A6)
150 2     READ (3,1) SALES, ISKIL,MANNO,A1,A2,A3,A4
160       IF (MANNØ-99999),3,4,4
170 3     CØMM=SALES*.10
180       GØ TØ (5,6,7),ISKIL
190 5     BØNUS=SALES*.01
200       GØ TØ 8
210 6     BØNUS=SALES*.02
220       GØ TØ 8
230 7     BØNUS=0.
240 8     TCØMM=CØMM+BØNUS
250       INUMB=INUMB+1
260       TSALES=TSALES+SALES
270       TTCØMM=TTCØMM+TCØMM
280       WRITE (6,9) MANNØ,A1,A2,A3,A4,SALES,TCØMM
290 9     FØRMAT (1H ,I5,4A6,F7.2,F6.2)
300       GØ TØ 2
310 4     WRITE (6,10) INUMB,TSALES,TTCØMM
320 10    FØRMAT (1H ,I2,5X,F9.2,34HTØTAL MØNTHLY SALES CØMMISSIØNS IS,
330&      F7.2)
340       STØP
350       END
SAVE

READY
RUNNH


RUNNING TIME:       .8 SECS

READY
```

Figure 12-19 A FORTRAN program for printing salesmen names and monthly earned commissions plus total monthly sales commissions.

The net result of these endeavors should be a real-time management information system where each programmed module performs a specific task, making each application unique.

## QUESTIONS

1. What are the benefits of a computerized data base in a real-time management information system?
2. What additional factors could be considered in the sales forecasting FORTRAN IV program?
3. The materials planning function is essentially one of sales forecasting. Why is materials planning needed if the sales forecasts have already been made?

4. How is the code level used in the materials planning function?
5. What is meant by exploding bills of materials?
6. Why do we explode component requirements into three planning periods, although we forecasted final product needs for only one period?
7. What are the advantages of utilizing the economic order quantity formula?
8. (a) Discuss the three types of products most inventory control systems handle.
   (b) Explain why we have been concerned with only two of the three types.
9. Explain where "management by exception" is used in inventory management.
10. Explain the need for human intervention in the purchasing function.
11. What additional reports can be prepared for accounting and purchasing over those set forth in the chapter?
12. How do the last two FORTRAN IV programs presented in the chapter differ from the preceding programs?

## EXERCISES

*Note.* The following problems are designed to demonstrate the use of real-time MIS. Where on-line files are not available, the programs may be written using cards as the input medium and the printer as the output medium.

1. Prepare a program flowchart and write a FORTRAN IV program to forecast total sales by simple exponential smoothing. Use the following variable names:

   NUMB = part number
   ALPHA = weighting factor
   FORX = previous period forecast
   TSALES = sales for current period
   FORE = forecasted sales for next period

   Input data are arranged in secondary storage as follows:

   | 1–8 | 9–12 | 13–22 | 23–32 |
   |---|---|---|---|
   | NUMB | ALPHA | FORX | TSALES |

   Output print format should be arranged as:

   | 1–8 | 10–13 | 15–24 | |
   |---|---|---|---|
   | NUMB | ALPHA | FORE | |

2. Prepare a program flowchart and write a FORTRAN IV program to forecast sales by the trend adjusted exponential smoothing method. The following data (variable names) are stored on magnetic disk (secondary storage):

   NUMB = part number
   AWAIT = "*A*" weighting factor used in calculating the unadjusted forecast
   CWAIT = "*C*" weighting factor used in calculating the trend
   TRENX = trend calculated in period $t - 1$
   FORX = sales forecast for period $t - 1$ (unadjusted)
   FORT = sales forecast for period $t$ (trend adjusted)
   SALES = sales for period $t$
   FORE = sales forecast for period $t$ (unadjusted)
   TREND = trend calculated in period $t$

   Input data are arranged in secondary storage as:

   | 1–5 | 6–9 | 10–13 | 14–19 | 20–26 | 27–33 | 34–40 |
   |---|---|---|---|---|---|---|
   | NUMB | AWAIT | CWAIT | TRENX | FORX | FORT (old) | SALES (current) |

Output data should be arranged in secondary storage as:

| 1–5 | 6–9 | 10–13 | 14–19 | 20–26 | 27–33 | 34–40 |
|---|---|---|---|---|---|---|
| NUMB | AWAIT | CWAIT | TREND | FORE | FORT (new) | SALES (next month) |

3. Prepare a program flowchart and write a FORTRAN IV program to calculate the new final product requirements based on a previously determined sales forecast. The following variables should be used:

   ONHAN = final product inventory on hand
   ONORD = final product inventory on order
   FORX = new sales forecast for final product
   NUMB = number of components in each final product's bill of materials
   IPART = final product identification number
   REQUIR = new final product requirements

   Input data in secondary storage (magnetic disk) are arranged as follows. (Do not read in any data that are not needed.)

| 1–7 | 8–16 | 17–26 | 27–34 | 35–41 | 42–45 | 46–54 | 55–64 | 65–74 |
|---|---|---|---|---|---|---|---|---|
| IPART | SIZE | FORX | AMOUNT | COST | NUMB | DATE | ONHAN | ONORD |

   Printed output should be of the following form:

| 1–7 | 9–18 | 19–23 | 24–27 | |
|---|---|---|---|---|
| IPART | REQUIR | | NUMB | |

4. Prepare a program flowchart and write a FORTRAN IV program to compute the exploded component part requirements for each of four planning periods. The following name variables are to be used:

   LEVL = code level of component part
   NUM = number of components of each final product's bill of materials
   IPROD = final product identification number
   IPART = component part identification number
   UNITS = number of units of this component in each final product
   REQUR = new final product requirements
   REQ(1) = exploded component part requirements for planning period 1
   REQ(2) = exploded component part requirements for planning period 2
   REQ(3) = exploded component part requirements for planning period 3
   REQ(4) = exploded component part requirements for planning period 4

   The input data are on-line in secondary storage and are arranged as follows:

| 1–7 | 8–14 | 15–18 | 19–25 | 26–32 | 33 |
|---|---|---|---|---|---|
| IPROD | REQUR | NUM | IPART | UNITS | LEVL |

   Printed output should be of the following form:

| 1–7 | 10–16 | 20–26 | 30–36 | 40–46 | |
|---|---|---|---|---|---|
| IPART | REQ(1) | REQ(2) | REQ(3) | REQ(4) | |

5. Prepare a program flowchart and write a FORTRAN IV program to calculate the monthly purchase performance index (PPI), allowing for variable weights. The following variables are to be used:

   WAITP = weight of the price index
   WAITQ = weight of the quality index

WAITD = weight of the delivery index
PPI = purchase performance index
DELIN = delivery index
QUALI = quality index
PRICI = price index

The indices, along with other important data, are on-line in secondary storage with the following arrangement:

PRICI positions 1–5
QUALI positions 26–30
DELIN positions 51–55
WAITP positions 61–65
WAITQ positions 76–80
WAITD positions 91–95

Print the following: "THE MONTHLY PURCHASE PERFORMANCE INDEX IS" and the appropriate value.

# V

# IMPLEMENTING AND CONTROLLING DATA PROCESSING

## CHAPTER THIRTEEN

# Feasibility Study—Exploratory Survey and Systems Analysis

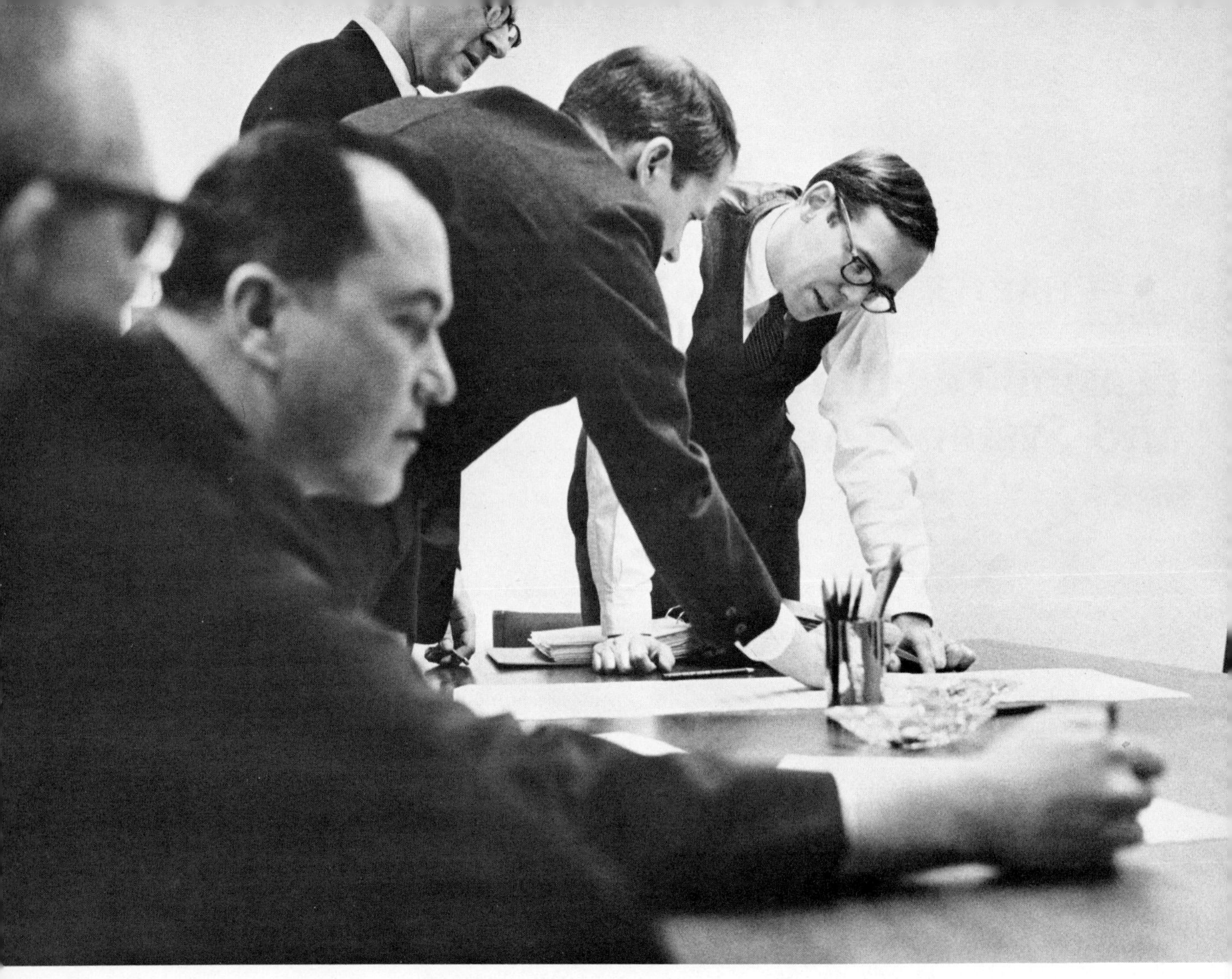

*The exploratory survey, the first step of the feasibility study, is basically an analysis of the present system (systems analysis). It culminates in a report that is reviewed by top management regarding the feasibility or nonfeasibility of undertaking a systems project. (Courtesy International Business Machines Corporations).*

The implementation of business data processing, as indicated in prior chapters, is not a simple task. In order to install a new system effectively, a detailed and carefully laid out plan must be initiated by management and followed by all personnel involved. The large outlays for equipment, programming, conversion, and related activities require a systematic procedure for implementation. Otherwise, vast sums of money can be wasted.

The purpose of this chapter and the next two are to explore the steps of a feasibility study in implementing and controlling a systems project. The feasibility study encompasses three major steps:

1. the exploratory survey including systems analysis,
2. basic systems design,
3. equipment selection.

The initial step of the feasibility study is discussed in this chapter. Basically, the function of this important phase is to determine whether a new system would be more beneficial to the firm than the present one. The feasibility or nonfeasibility of applying newer data processing equipment and procedures is established for the firm. An integral part of the exploratory survey is systems analysis which is a thorough and comprehensive review of the present system. This analysis allows the data processing committee to make a valid comparison among the many feasible systems alternatives. The chapter concludes with a discussion of the exploratory survey report to top management.

## DATA PROCESSING AFFECTS THE ENTIRE FIRM

*In a systems project, the most profound changes generally occur in the area of personnel.*

The introduction of automated data processing or the extension of newer data processing equipment and procedures has a far-reaching impact on the entire firm. When a firm considers a new systems project, the decision will affect more than established methods and procedures. The most important ones are:

1. personnel
2. basic business functions
3. communication process
4. organization structure
5. cash requirements

### Personnel

The most profound changes, in many cases, occur in the area of personnel. The work habits of individuals who have been accustomed to doing things a certain way over the years must be changed. Similarly, the methods and procedures to be followed by the firm's employees will change substantially. Present employees may have to be shifted to different jobs. New employees may be required to fill jobs that require a certain technical ability. Also, work areas of the employees may be altered which may not be to their liking. The decision to undertake a systems project, then, can have a great impact on personnel and their jobs.

### Basic Business Functions

An advanced computer system will drastically affect the basic business functions of the firm. Some of the traditional business functions can be relegated to the computer. Marketing analysis, inventory and production control, and budgeting are logical candidates for computer control. In a properly designed system, the output from one computer run serves as input for the next run. This succession of data processing runs provides an excellent way to carry out and coordinate the firm's basic business functions.

### Communication Process

The question of recentralization and decentralization is brought into focus since communications with the home office are possible on a "now" basis. Current established lines of communications that have come into being over the years may have to be revamped. New Lines of communications may have to be initiated.

### Organization Structure

The organization structure may need changing since some positions are replaced by the computer and new EDP positions are created. This is particularly true when an advanced data processing system is being contemplated. A flattening of the organization structure may occur since jobs of one or more organizational levels can be relegated to the computer.

### Cash Requirements

A very important area affected by a new data processing system is the firm's finances. The expenditure of large sums over a long period of time means that the firm must have the cash resources available when needed. During the programming and testing phase, rental is being paid on data processing equipment when little or no computer production is being generated. Also, the conversion phase from the present system to the new system can make great demands on the firm's cash resources.

A decision on data processing is of great importance to the present and future potential of a firm. Although the cost of the data processing system is critical to the firm, the monetary outlays are often over-shadowed by personnel considerations. A firm can change and control the physical requirements for an advanced computer system. However, the same cannot be said for the human element of the firm. This factor can be unpredictable if not handled properly.

## THE NEED FOR AN EXPLORATORY SURVEY

The exploratory survey is the first major step of the feasibility study. It includes several phases of investigation:

1. preliminary
2. overall
3. detailed
4. concluding

*The end result of the exploratory survey is the feasibility or nonfeasibility of implementing a new data processing system.*

After a period of preliminary investigation (first phase) or orientation, the exploratory survey pursues an overall investigation (second phase). This phase allows the data processing committee to comprehend the full magnitude of their undertaking. The big picture is emphasized at this time. Detailed investigation (third phase) revolves around the analysis of the present system, frequently referred to as systems analysis. In the concluding investigation (fourth phase), the data processing committee will reach one of two conclusions. One is that the present data processing system appears better than any one of the new systems studied. The other conclusion is that one or more new systems investigated appear to be superior to the present system. In the second case, the feasibility study proceeds to the next step—basic systems design, the subject matter for the next chapter. In the first case, the data processing group may go back and examine additional systems or study new equipment developments that have come on the market since the analysis was initiated. If the exploratory survey still indicates a negative answer, the feasibility study will cease, awaiting new developments in the field.

A detailed outline of an exploratory survey is found in Figure 13-1. These basic steps, the subject matter for this chapter, provide a logical framework for the initial step of the feasibility study. Also, they serve as a basis for preparing an exploratory survey report to top management.

*Preliminary Investigation*
- Selection of executive committee.
- Selection of data processing committee.
- Define the scope of the feasibility study.
- Obtain backing of top management.

*Overall Investigation*
- Organization of data processing committee.
- Training of data processing committee.
- Authority delegated to data processing committee.
- Selection of desired objectives.
- Definition of the problem.
- Determine a realistic schedule.

*Detailed Investigation of Present System-Systems Analysis*
- Historical aspects.
- Review of methods and procedures.
- Analysis of outputs.
- Files maintained.
- Analysis of inputs.
- Flowchart the current operations.
- Present work volume.
- Current personnel requirements.
- Internal control.
- Other requirements and considerations.
- Present costs and benefits of present system.

*Concluding Investigation*
- Feasible systems alternatives.
- Cost and tangible benefits for each alternative.
- Intangible benefits for each alternative.
- Cost and benefits of the present system compared to each alternative.

Figure 13-1 Detailed outline of an exploratory survey—the first step of the feasibility study.

The importance of doing a thorough exploratory survey, the initial step of a feasibility study, cannot be overemphasized. It is extremely essential for the future well-being of the firm that this time-consuming first step be done accurately and methodically. A fast and half-hearted attempt will often lead the firm to a premature conclusion about a new system. Only after installation do the real facts come to light, often resulting in major data processing problems and/or higher data processing costs. A careful and systematic approach to the exploratory study is a must for installing a successful data processing system. There are no legitimate shortcuts for this important phase.

## PRELIMINARY INVESTIGATION—EXPLORATORY SURVEY

*The initial phase of the exploratory survey is the preliminary investigation, which includes:*
- *selecting the executive committee*
- *selecting the data processing committee*
- *defining the scope of the feasibility study*
- *obtaining the backing of top management*

To initiate a study plan on data processing, there must be a reason. The present system may have some weakness, such as lack of reports for practicing "management by exception," data processing bottlenecks, or poor internal control. Whatever reasons are given by top management, the preliminary investigation of the exploratory survey should be undertaken first. Before this can be done successfully, however, an executive committee from top management should be established by the board of directors.

### Selection of Executive Committee

*The executive committee constitutes top management. It oversees the activities of the data processing committee.*

The purpose of an executive committee is to give direction to the data processing (DP) committee. Many times, members of the executive committee include one or more of the following: chairman of the board, president, executive vice-president, and vice-presidents—marketing, manufacturing, purchasing, finance, engineering, personnel, and research and development. This high-level committee not only oversees what the data processing committee is doing but also enhances the chances of success because of its rank and status.

Once the membership is established, the executive committee's initial task is to issue a written statement that a data processing committee has been formed to study the feasibility of applying newer data processing equipment. The statement should state that adjustments in personnel and jobs may be required to make the change. Some employees may have to be retrained and reassigned for new data processing jobs, some of which may be higher, lower, or the same as the present ones. It should be emphasized to all personnel that no one will be fired or asked to resign. This first memo to all employees should indicate that periodic written statements will be issued regarding the progress of the feasibility study. The failure to issue a memorandum of this type will cause alarm because of the possibility of data processing equipment replacing people.

### Selection of Data Processing Committee

*The data processing committee includes people from the functional areas of the firm, the data processing section, and outside personnel (if necessary).*

A concurrent task with the preparation of the written memorandum from the executive committee is the selection of a data processing committee. This latter committee will have the authority and responsibility for a data processing system. It, in turn, will be held accountable for its actions. The number of participants will depend on several factors, the following being the most important: the firm's size, the number of divisions and departments, the degree of centralization or decentralization, the number of business functions considered for new data processing applications, the required skills of the firm's personnel, budget constraints, and time considerations. Typical study groups range from four to six persons up to a dozen or more, depending upon the above factors.

Since a data processing system cuts across the entire organizational structure, a member from each of the firm's functional areas should be selected. If at all possible, each person selected should have several years of experience in his respective area, be objective in his thinking, and capable of creative thinking. Also, he should be familiar with his area's major problems. Generally, the individual who has the background and holds a responsible position in the firm has not had the opportunity to keep up with the latest developments in data processing equipment. For this reason, it is necessary to have persons with computer and programming experience within the data processing committee who, generally, do not know the methods and procedures utilized by the firm. This may mean going to outside consultants if the firm lacks the technical expertise in data processing. Whether the individuals selected are from inside or outside the firm, the data processing committee will function best when people with the required knowledge are present. It is recommended that one person within the firm devote all his time to the feasibility study. This individual will head the group and direct the study to maintain its momentum. Other members may work full time or part time, depending upon their current work assignments.

### Define the Scope of the Feasibility Study

*The scope of the feasibility study can range from very broad to very narrow.*

The determination of who will comprise the data processing committee leads to the question of what will be included in the exploratory survey of the feasibility study. It is up to the executive committee to define the scope of the data processing study. This top-level group might ask the data processing committee to restrict its activities to production, marketing, finance, or some other functional area of the firm. It might be very broad in scope so as to include a real-time management information system that employs mathematical models from operations research. Again, the scope might be somewhere in the middle of the above two approaches. Often, the data processing team will ask to enlarge or contract the area under investigation after a thorough investigation of all the facts. This can take place when the problem is defined precisely or may be redefined at a later stage in the exploratory survey. In essence, the overall scope is set forth by the executive committee at this time with more attention to the details of problem definition at a later time.

### Obtain Backing of Top Management

*A most important part of the preliminary investigation is obtaining the backing of top management. Otherwise, the feasibility study is placed in jeopardy if top management is not behind the project.*

One of the best ways for the data processing committee to secure the backing of top management initially is to include their names on the first written memorandum to all company employees. Such support from the outset is necessary since a feasibility study covers a long period of time. Generally, it is wise to include a statement on the objectives to be accomplished by the study and the broad scope of the study. Subsequent memos issued by the executive committee should be written in a manner that enhances the status and image of the data processing team. The content of these executive memos should be quite clear to all concerned, that is, top management wants effective results from the feasibility study undertaken by the data processing committee.

The data processing committee, which is constantly in touch with top management, acquires prestige from this association. Many times, the individuals are given important titles to help insure that all relevant data from the various departments will be made available when needed. This means that the data processing group has moved out of the middle management level to a higher organizational position. These changes are subtle ways of letting all personnel know that they have the backing of top management and results are expected of this select group.

The support of top management is important since the cost of the feasibility study is generally quite high. The president of the firm must usually give his approval. If the feasibility study is a failure, his job and those of the data processing team are in jeopardy. Self interest is an important issue.

Systems work which cuts across the entire firm needs the active participation and cooperation of all management levels to be completed successfully. The elimination or alteration of many departments can meet with forceful resistance without the strong backing of top management. This is particularly true when "little empires" have been allowed to build up over the years. The support of top management in critical problem areas can make the difference between success and failure.

## OVERALL INVESTIGATION—EXPLORATORY SURVEY

*The second phase of the exploratory survey or overall investigation consists of:*
- *organizing the DP committee*
- *training the DP committee*
- *delegating authority to DP group*
- *selecting desired objectives*
- *defining the problem*
- *determining a realistic schedule*

Once the data processing committee has been firmly established and is operating, it is ready to start the second phase of the exploratory survey, that is, the overall investigation. This consists of organizing and training the data processing group for certain tasks, delegating authority to the study team, selecting desired objectives, defining the problem in specific terms, and determining a realistic time schedule for the feasibility study.

### Organization of Data Processing Committee

*The DP committee should be split into several groups in order to carry out its assigned tasks.*

The leader of the data processing committee should devote full time to the feasibility study. He should hold a rank comparable to that of a vice-president since he will probably head the new system once it is operational. A survey of many firms indicates a positive correlation between the success of the study and the rank of the data processing manager. A rank high on the executive ladder where the individual has immediate access to top management means the systems project has a much better chance than if his rank is one of lower or middle management.

Depending upon the size of the undertaking, the data processing group can range from four to twelve persons (noted previously) from within or outside the firm. It is advisable to keep the number as small as possible to avoid the problems associated with large groups. All members need not be working on the study, but will be used at various times as needed. For the most part, the committee should be split into two or three smaller groups, sometimes called study or task groups. This will allow each group to investigate one aspect of the study and report its findings to the committee. Much time can be saved by the study group approach.

### Training of Data Processing Committee

*DP committee personnel from the functional areas need training in data processing. Conversely, data processing personnel require knowledge about the firm's functional areas.*

Generally, the data processing committee is a heterogeneous group. This means that some are knowledgable about the operations of the firm's functional areas while others are data processing experts. Both lack the necessary knowledge to carry a feasibility study to a successful conclusion. For this reason, both groups must receive additional training. The personnel from the functional areas should attend intensive data courses given by computer manufacturers, consulting firms, or software houses. These courses range from a week to several weeks. The growth of computer courses as part of university degree processing will tend to alleviate this general background problem in the future. Either approach should emphasize the background necessary to carry a feasibility study to a successful completion. Computer personnel, including outside consultants, will spend several weeks reviewing and understanding the present operations while the others are at a data processing school. This is the minimum amount of training the study group must have before it can get started on the proper selection of desired objectives and defining the problem in detail.

### Authority Delegated to Data Processing Committee

Authority must be clearly delegated to the data processing committee. This requirement is important for one reason: all those with whom the group comes

*The authority delegated to the DP group is necessary in order to lessen the resistance that may confront it.*

into contact must comprehend fully the need for their help and complete cooperation. Without the authority delegated officially to the group, many managers might not participate in a constructive way because they question the validity of newer data processing equipment, they do not understand the new system changes, or some other reason based on fact or fiction. The authority delegated from top management may have to be used at times to overcome the resistance that occurs anytime there is a change in systems. In these cases, the study group must use tact and diplomacy. Otherwise, the resentment may be detrimental to the entire feasibility study. Again, authority delegated and supported by top management is an absolute necessity.

### Selection of Desired Objectives

*Selection of desired objectives for a system project can take many directions as depicted in Figure 13-2.*

The formulation of objectives is the joint effort of the executive committee and the data processing committee. Not only do objectives force top management to do some serious thinking about the firm's future but they also bring to light problems that might otherwise have been overlooked. For the data processing team, it provides a framework from which to operate. The constraints and limitations under which the project must function are clearly set forth. Experience has indicated that a feasibility study has gone much more smoothly when a formal statement of objectives has been clearly defined.

The objectives desired by management can take many directions, as set forth in Figure 13-2. Objectives can center around a cost savings approach. In such

- Increased efficiency in the firm's operations.
- Reduction in data processing costs to the firm.
- More timely information for management decisions.
- Improved customer service and relations.
- Increased flow of data for meaningful information.
- Uniform and accurate handling of data with a minimum of human intervention.
- Elimination of conflicting and overlapping services within the firm.
- Improved internal control.
- Utilization of operations research to improve overall operations.
- Improved employee and public relations.
- Increased managerial development and efficiency.
- Efficient utilization of personnel and equipment.
- Increased overall net income from operations.

Figure 13-2 Selection of desired objectives for a systems project.

situations, consideration should be given to tangible and intangible benefits in order that the evaluation is complete and realistic. Other objectives can emphasize faster and more timely information for management decisions. In reality, this approach is aimed at cost reduction as well as faster service for customers. Ideally, a new system is one that is able to meet as many top management objectives as possible and, at the same time, reduce costs for the firm.

In addition to reduction in costs, more timely decisions, and improved service to customers, the following are also representative of objectives desired by management. The utilization of advanced data processing equipment speeds up the flow of data handled by the firm. This permits instantaneous information to be generated about the status of customer orders. It allows the firm to schedule production more effectively and notify the customer of any shipping changes or delays. Also, faster billing procedures are available. The uniform and accurate handling of data is available without the problems of human intervention. All these benefits improve customer relations and enhance the firm's competitive position.

Top management might consider other objectives, such as the elimination of conflicting and overlapping services within the firm. A very important objective is the employment of checks and balances as the data are processed, eliminating the need for manual checking. This would be part of internal control for the new system.

Another consideration for desired objectives is operations research. The use of mathematical models can reduce the amount of inventory carried as well as production costs. Operations research has been used successfully for most areas of the firm. The objectives of improving employee and public relations, increasing executive efficiency, and effecting efficient utilization of personnel and equipment have been accomplished by many companies. Also, major exceptions can be extracted and reported to a responsible person for immediate action.

The above listing of objectives is by no means complete, but is a cross section of objectives that can be set forth by the executive group for the data processing committee. The selection of many desired objectives usually results in the need for more advanced data processing equipment which can be more costly than the present system. No matter what objectives are included as a frame of reference, the primary one of any feasibility study is a resulting larger net income to the firm after consideration of all the tangible and intangible factors involved. It should be remembered that the desired objectives can be changed if they are found to be unrealistic later in the exploratory survey.

### Definition of the Problem

*At this point, the problem is defined in detail and set forth in writing.*

Once the objectives have been written, the data processing committee defines the problem more precisely. As noted previously, the scope of the feasibility study has been stated in general terms by the executive committee. It is the job of the study team to specify the areas that will be explored in greater detail. When doing so, the group must make sure that the scope of the feasibility study is compatible with the objectives. If the objectives and the scope of the study are in conflict, this is the time for the two groups to resolve the difficulties. For example, the objective—provide immediate information to customers on orders placed—is difficult to achieve with a batch processing system while it would be relatively easy for a real-time management information system. A conference between the two committees would resolve the problem.

Having defined the problem as accurately as possible within the scope of the study, the study team should have little doubt as to the areas to be covered by the investigation. It is advisable to state these findings in writing. A written memorandum by the data processing group ensures the accomplishment of what was originally intended and reduces the problem of "going off on a tangent." A carefully laid out plan for areas to be explored indicates where the study will cut across organizational lines and where authority is needed for changes in systems, methods, procedures, forms, reports, or organization.

### Determine a Realistic Schedule

*A scheduling technique, such as the Gantt chart and PERT/time network, is utilized to determine a realistic schedule.*

The final step in the overall investigation of the exploratory survey is the preparation of a time schedule for the entire systems study. Such a study may take place over a long period of time, ranging from many months to several years. Experience has shown that there is a tendency to underestimate the time element of the feasibility study as well as all other succeeding steps. The time factor is a function of the objectives desired and problem definition. For a successful study, it must be covered in sufficient depth and be as thorough as possible. This means the time factor is of secondary importance. If time becomes the important consideration, the results will usually mean that an optimum decision for the firm's data processing needs will probably not be made.

When developing a time schedule, the data processing committee must determine the amount of work involved in each step of the systems change and what resources in terms of personnel and skills will be needed. Likewise, consideration must be given to the following areas: training, programming, program testing, delivery of the equipment, physical requirements and installation of the equipment, files development, delivery of new forms and supplies, and conversion activities. The foregoing includes the major items that must be included in a realistic schedule.

*The two main parts of any systems project are:*
- *the feasibility study*
- *systems implementation*

***Major Parts of a Systems Project.*** An overview of the time, stated in percents, for the various steps in a feasibility study and systems implementation is given in Figure 13-3. These percents should not be construed as absolute values, but rather as a general guide for a typical systems project that would take approximately two years. Depending on the complexity of the systems project, the Gantt chart, PERT/Time, or PERT/Cost can be used to control the activities. It should be recognized that the steps in Figure 13-3 have been grouped and that many sub-activities are related to each one.

| | |
|---|---|
| *Feasibility Study:* | |
| Exploratory survey, including systems analysis | 12% |
| Basic systems design | 15% |
| Equipment selection | 10% |
| *Systems Implementation:* | |
| Training personnel—programmers and all others | 8% |
| Flowcharting and using decision tables | 10% |
| Programming and desk checking | 10% |
| Program compiling and testing | 20% |
| Parallel operations for checking new system | 5% |
| Final conversion to new system | 10% |
| | 100% |

Figure 13-3 Major steps of a systems project, stated in percent of total time.

***Feasibility Study.*** An examination of the time schedule in Figure 13-3 indicates that the feasibility study comprises more than one third of the total time for a systems change. This may seem excessive on the surface. However, an understanding of what a feasibility study is indicates the need for such time. To reduce the time of the systems project in this area generally leads to bad results.

***Systems Implementation.*** The first step of systems implementation is the training of personnel, in particular, the programmers. Programmers cannot be sent to the manufacturer's programming school until the equipment is selected, the final step of the feasibility study. Likewise, the equipment cannot be chosen until the firm has decided upon the basic systems design which forms the basis for the equipment bids. Thus, a logical sequence is found in the above listing for all steps enumerated. The failure to follow this ordered pattern can only lead to chaotic conditions.

The period required for systems implementation comprises about two-thirds of the total effort required for a systems change. This is where the hard work and long hours really begin. It is unfortunate that many in top management feel the real work has been completed when the feasibility study is over when, in reality, the reverse is true. This attitude by top management often explains the hurry to get the equipment installed and running during the systems implementation phase. This is particularly true when the rental on the equipment starts and management sees no production for the large cash outlays. The end results are incomplete, inefficient, and ill-conceived programs that are a disappointment to all involved in the systems project. The benefits, both tangible and intangible, will never be realized under these unfortunate circumstances.

***Feedback on Systems Project.*** The study group that is responsible for scheduling should not only prepare a realistic timetable but also be in a position at all times to report whether the study is ahead, behind, or on schedule. The data processing committee should issue reports periodically to the executive committee on the status quo of the project. Included in the reports should be information that is critical to the study, such as problem areas and delays. The utilization of the "exception principle" in progress reports is needed to control the project.

## DETAILED INVESTIGATION OF PRESENT SYSTEM—SYSTEMS ANALYSIS

*The third phase of the exploratory survey, commonly called systems analysis, includes a detailed study of the following present system areas:*

- *historical aspects*
- *methods and procedures*
- *outputs*
- *files*
- *inputs*
- *work volume*
- *personnel*
- *internal control*
- *other factors*

During the entire exploratory survey, whether it be the investigation phase or another phase, the executive committee and the data processing committee are constantly communicating. The top-level group has selected areas that are likely to derive the greatest benefits from a systems change. The data processing group is studying these areas in great detail in order to determine whether they merit employing newer data processing methods and equipment. If certain areas included in the original scope of the study are found to be poor candidates during the problem definition phase as well as later on or are not capable of meeting the firm's desired objectives at sometime during the study, there must be a meeting of minds to resolve these problems. The importance of the communication process for the two committees cannot be overemphasized.

The detailed investigation of the present system, commonly referred to as systems analysis, is the next job for the various study groups or systems analysts of the data processing committee. It involves collecting, organizing, and evaluating facts about the present system and the environment in which it operates. Generally, the study teams devote full time to this undertaking because it is so time consuming. Survey of existing methods and procedures, data flow, outputs, files, inputs, and internal control, to name the more important ones, should be more than a casual one. It should be an intensive review in order to understand fully the present system and its related problems. No area should be excluded unless it has no relationship to the scope of the study in terms of desired objectives and the problem definition. The search of the data processing group should be comprehensive and far-reaching.

### Objective of Systems Analysis

*The objective of systems analysis is to understand the present system, in particular, its exceptions and problems.*

The objective of systems analysis is to understand the workings of the present system in terms of equipment, personnel, demands, operating conditions, and its related problems. Systems analysis serves as a basis for designing and installing a better data processing system, providing it is economically feasible to do so. Basic systems design is concerned with systems development. The new systems design must be based on the facts obtained in the systems analysis stage and within the framework of the study. The systems implementation stage builds upon the systems analysis and basic systems design phases by devising programs, methods, and procedures; recruiting and training qualified personnel; selecting and installing the equipment; and putting the new system into operation. Even though systems analysis, basic systems design, equipment selection, and systems implementation are discussed separately, they are intimately related since each has some affect on the other. To isolate one important phase from another will generally result in a mediocre system. For example, ignoring important constraints and problems of the present system in the design stage tends to produce poor results.

### Methods of Obtaining Information

*Several ways of obtaining desired information about the firm's operations are:*
- *interviews*
- *company systems and procedures manual*
- *forms, documents, and reports used*

A systems analyst uses several tools to obtain the necessary data during the systems analysis phase. Among these are the interview; company systems and procedures manual; and forms, documents, and reports used. Each will be explained below.

***Interviews.*** Generally, the best way to understand what is transpiring is to talk directly with the individuals who are responsible for getting the job done. The analyst should study the activities of the department head, supervisor, or the person in charge. Attention should also be focused on the subordinates' work to confirm what has been said by their immediate superior.

For a successful interview, the analyst should be formally introduced to all supervisory personnel. From the outset, this approach immediately establishes the level for the entire study, that is, it is an official undertaking of the firm, backed by the executive committee and the board of directors. The interview should be friendly and informal. Notes about the interview should be taken as it progresses. The analyst should ask the supervisor his ideas on how the system can be improved. This is extremely important because the supervisor will feel that he has made a contribution to the study. In fact, the systems analyst should actively solicit his suggestions. A feeling of participation will make it easier when the systems changes are undertaken at a later date. The supervisor should be reassured that any changes made will be discussed with him first before implementation.

***Company Systems and Procedures Manual.*** Another excellent tool for the systems analyst is reviewing the firm's systems and procedures manual. Sometimes other names are used, but whatever the name, the manual contains a description of all procedures in use. Reference is made to inputs, outputs, and files employed in a specific procedure. This will be helpful in flowcharting the current operations at a later time. Caution is necessary when using the manual. Quite often, conditions have changed since the material was written. In a similar manner, existing procedures are different from those actually used without management being cognizant of this condition. When the procedures manual is not up-to-date or nonexistent, the analysts will have to spend more time during the interviews to obtain all necessary information.

***Forms, Documents, and Reports Used.*** Most procedure manuals contain actual copies of forms, documents, and reports used. If this is not the case, samples can be obtained during the interview period. The same caution mentioned above concerning the procedure manual applies here. So often, changes made on documents and forms are so insignificant that no one takes the time to insert the new ones into the procedures manual. Only after many changes is the difference readily apparent. Also, a review of all sample copies for the average firm may indicate a need to combine, eliminate, or design new ones.

### Historical Aspects

*A review of the firm's past history and its future potential identifies the likely areas for growth.*

A logical starting point for an analysis of the present system is a brief history of the firm. The historical facts should identify the major turning points and milestones that have influenced the direction of the firm. Emphasis should be placed on the industry in which the firm is operating, its markets, distribution channels, competitors, organization structure, future trends, goals and objectives, policies, government, and union regulations affecting the firm. A historical review of the firm's organization chart will identify the growth experienced by the levels of management as well as the development in the various areas and departments of the firm. Not only must historical data be analyzed but also current and future plans must be examined in order to understand the future thrusts of the firm and their corresponding implications. The systems team should investigate what system changes have occurred in the past. These would include operations that have been successful or unsuccessful with data processing equipment and techniques. There is no use in trying an advanced data processing system under the same conditions that has met with failure in the past.

### Review of Methods and Procedures

*A review of methods and procedures has a dual purpose—understanding and improving the present system.*

A review of the methods and procedures presently employed is necessary before examining in detail the firm's inputs, files, and outputs. A method is a way of doing something as contrasted to a procedure which is a series of logical steps by which a job is accomplished. A procedure specifies that action is required, who is required to act, and when the action is to be undertaken. To clarify the distinction between these two terms, a procedures review is an intensive survey of the methods by which a job is accomplished, the tools utilized, and the actual location of operations. Its basic objective is to eliminate unnecessary tasks in order to improve the present operation. Even though the purpose of the procedures review is improvement in the present system while an understanding of the present system is necessary for the feasibility study, both tasks can be accomplished at the same time. Often, the data processing group will make recommendations for immediate improvements in certain areas since the actual installation of newer data processing equipment may be years away. This allows immediate cost reduction and increased efficiency within the respective departments.

### Analysis of Outputs

*Analysis of outputs involves asking the questions—who, what, where, when, and why about current information being generated.*

The reason for the feasibility study may be to overcome inadequate management information being produced by the present system. Reports to all levels of management may not be timely enough to control effectively the firm's operations. In essence, the failure to meet the internal reporting needs of the firm constitutes a serious deficiency of many business data processing systems. Generally, the areas of external reporting to stockholders and governmental agencies do not cause the firm major problems.

***Questions About Outputs.*** The outputs produced by many departments of the firm become the inputs for other areas. For this reason, the firm's outputs or reports should be carefully scrutinized by the data processing committee to determine how well these are meeting the firm's needs. The question of what information is needed and why, who needs it, and when and where it is needed are ones that must be answered. Additional questions concerning the sequence of the data, how often the form is used, how long it is kept on file, and the like must be investigated. Often, too many reports are a carry-over from earlier days which have little relevance to current operations. During the interview, the many levels of management will request that certain reports be dropped or combined with others. The systems analyst will hear a "loud call" for timely management exception reports that detail only the significant deviations from the standard or budget. This is understandable because management does not have the time to go through mounds of paper that can be quickly summarized by a computer.

***Careful Analysis of Outputs.*** All reports, generated for internal use, should be timely, accurate, complete, concise, and useful. Attention to standardization of forms should be considered. The cost of preparation should not exceed their usefulness to the firm. Reports for all areas of the firm should be carefully scrutinized. A typical list of outputs for the three major functional areas of a manufacturing firm are shown in Figure 13-4.

*Marketing:*

Sales forecasting, marketing simulation study, PERT marketing study, marketing research study, marketing sales analysis (by region, territory, state, and city), sales by products and product lines, comparison of firm's sales to industry sales, monthly marketing budget and actual cost report, and salesmen commissions and salaries report.

*Manufacturing:*

Production control report, production shipping schedule, inventory control report, quality control report, exploded bills of materials, spoilage and scrap analysis, weekly departmental budget and actual cost report, factory personnel turnover analysis, economic order quantities—purchase orders, PERT/LOB (Line of Balance) report, and linear programming study.

*Finance:*

Cash flow analysis, management by exception reports, monthly balance sheet and income statement (in total and by departments), capital project study, financial stimulation study, stockholders listing, and aging of accounts receivable report.

Figure 13-4 List of typical outputs for three major functional areas of a manufacturing firm.

In summary, the data processing team should not accept the present forms as ideal or even usable in their present format for the new system. They should keep an open mind during this detailed investigation phase of the present system. When the time comes for determining new reports, they will be objective. This approach eliminates the problems associated with outputs currently being generated.

### Files Maintained

*A review of the files maintained center around the following:*

- *number and size*
- *location*
- *uses*
- *times referenced*

A review of the files maintained will reveal information that is not contained in the firm's outputs. It is always better to have too much information on file than too little. This is particularly true when specialized studies are undertaken periodically. The gathering and retaining of all potentially useful data has some merit. However, the related cost of retrieving and processing the data is another consideration. Files of information held for a long period of time may be difficult to store at a low cost and may result in a high processing cost for preparing meaningful reports. The maintenance of large files for extended periods of time is a function of its ultimate value in terms of future reports, its related costs of storing, and legal requirements.

The data processing team should note the number and size of files maintained by each department, where they are located, who uses them, and the number of times to which they are referenced. This information should be contained in the procedures manual. Information on files will be an important consideration when designing a new system. Files, depending on their static or dynamic nature, can be reviewed for a storage media that best suits them. This may be magnetic drum, magnetic disk, magnetic tape, laser, punched card, microfilm, or some other method of storage. Also, the size of the files can have an effect on the equipment selected. For these reasons, files can be the focal point in deciding which way to go on a systems project.

### Analysis of Inputs

*Analysis of inputs is compared to that of outputs since output for one area serves as input for another area in many cases.*

A detailed investigation of the present system is not complete until all inputs are reviewed since they are basic to the manipulation of data. Source documents are used to capture the originating data for any data processing system. The systems analyst should be aware of the various sources where data are initially captured, recognizing that outputs for one area may serve as inputs for other areas. The output of exponential sales forecasting, for example, may be the input for determining the levels of finished goods inventory which, in turn, establishes the level of goods to be manufactured and materials to be purchased.

Data processing personnel must understand the nature of the form, what is contained in it, who prepared it, where the form is initiated, when it is completed, the distribution of the form, and similar considerations. If these questions are adequately answered by the systems analyst, he will be able to determine how these inputs fit into the framework of the present system. A sample list of input records for the functional areas of a manufacturing firm are found in Figure 13-5.

*Marketing:*
Sales quotations, salesmen reports, sales forecasts, sales invoices, listing of customers, advertising budget, and customer credit information.

*Manufacturing:*
Production orders, receiving reports, shipping reports, purchase orders, time cards, stock records, stock requisitions, personnel records, and time standards.

*Finance:*
Vendor invoices, cash receipts, cash disbursements, fixed asset records, tax returns, stockholder listings, and insurance records.

Figure 13-5 List of typical inputs for three major functional areas of a manufacturing firm.

### Flowchart the Current Operations

*Flowcharting the current system is a basic method of bringing together all the data collected during the systems analysis phase.*

The best method to organize the facts obtained from the above investigation is to utilize some form of flowcharting. The system flowchart or the document flowchart are suitable for tracing the origin of input data, through each phase of processing and communication, into files, and finally out of files for desired outputs—many in the form of reports. The flowcharting of the present operations not only organizes the facts for the analyst, but also helps disclose gaps and duplications in the data gathered. It allows a thorough comprehension of the numerous details and related problems in the present operation. In essence, the knowledge, gathered to date, is brought together in a meaningful relationship for members of the data processing committee. It should be noted that flowcharting need not be undertaken separately, but generally is combined with the preceding sections of systems analysis. This allows the systems analyst to simplify his task because the data are fresh in his mind. The flowcharting of the areas investigated, then, is an excellent way of getting the information on paper.

The foregoing has indicated the need for flowcharting the origination of source documents, the files maintained, the flow of documents in the various processing steps, and the departmental output under study. In addition, there should be an overall flowchart that ties in the data from one department or section to another. This gives the data processing team an overview of the entire area under study and brings into focus the actual scope of the study. It makes the problem, as defined, more meaningful in terms of the desired objectives for a systems project. To attempt a study without adequate flowcharting is a formidable task.

### Present Work Volume

*Data on present work volume are compiled for average and peak loads, especially at month's end.*

Many firms require their departmental managers to keep an accurate tabulation on the volumes of inputs processed, files maintained, and outputs prepared within their respective departments. Other firms go a step further and compute an average cost for these items. Time can be saved if data on part and present work volume are available. Otherwise, these data must be compiled. It is important for the study group to determine reliable figures for average and peak days as well as the workload at month's end. In addition, accurate figures are necessary for the past five years to ascertain growth or reduction in volume. This data will be used to determine the present cost of operations and the projected costs for a new system.

Careful analysis of work volumes can be beneficial to the entire feasibility study. Where work volumes are small and the processing procedures are involved, the feasibility of applying advanced data processing equipment is unlikely. On the other hand, when large volumes of work require routine and straightforward processing, the likelihood of utilizing computers is very high. In addition, work volume analysis is helpful to the systems analyst in determining whether a particular work station is a control point, a storage area, or a terminal area. These observations can be translated into needs for visual display, storage, or processing capabilities when the time comes for the basic systems design.

An examination of existing files may well serve as a guide for their eventual reorganization. Current files may contain a certain amount of common data. Each time the common data are changed, all files must be changed. An example of this problem with files is a computer batch processing system that maintains magnetic tape files on inventory. Separate magnetic tape inventory files that vary in content are maintained for the marketing, manufacturing, and accounting departments respectively. This redundancy problem can often be overcome by a real-time management information system that has one inventory file available for on-line processing. An equal redundancy problem exists for the firm's outputs, namely, reports.

### Current Personnel Requirements

Current personnel requirements should be broken down by type, skill, and related cost. The efficiency of personnel working with or without equipment should be measured and analyzed. Most of this data can be obtained from personnel records, departmental statements, and departmental interviews. A resume of the

Important aspects when reviewing the firm's personnel requirements include:
• pay rates and fringe benefits
• local labor market
• labor union
• employee turnover
• management's attitude

firm's personnel resources can be utilized to appraise the cost and benefits of the present system. Information on local labor markets in terms of available data processing specialists is needed if the skills of current personnel resources are limited. Employee turnover, fringe benefits, and management attitudes toward the firm's personnel and labor unions should be collected and considered for any new data processing system. Every effort should be made to understand this element of the firm, which can make or break a systems project.

**Internal Control**

Reviewing internal control in terms of control points assists in visualizing the framework of the present system.

Many systems analysts fail to spend enough time on internal control of the present system. The reason for their ignoring internal control is that many of them have not been trained in this area. (Ample treatment will be given to this area in Chapter 16 on Computer Systems Controls.) Locating the control points helps the computer analyst to visualize the essential parts and framework of a system. At these critical points, some type of control is exercised. An examination of the present system for effective internal control may indicate weaknesses that should not be duplicated in the new system. The utilization of advanced methods and equipment in a new system means that greater control over the data is available as opposed, many times, to visual control within the present system.

**Other Requirements and Considerations**

The attendant circumstances will dictate other factors that are to be reviewed.

The major areas that should be analyzed in depth for a detailed investigation of the present system have been covered in the foregoing material. This has included the effect of exceptions and errors on the present system. Other requirements and considerations include what effect seasonal or other cyclical characteristics have on the present system. The firm's current financial resources and production facilities, including plant inventories, should be noted and analyzed; their future trends should be investigated. Information on the financial status of the firm is obtainable from the firm's financial statements. Data on land, buildings, equipment and tools, representing the firm's production facilities, should be included in the analysis by the systems group. Plans for new facilities and related equipment should be included in the study. Physical inventories should be ascertained as to total investment, number of items, turnover, and similar considerations. Of special interest to the study team is the data processing equipment currently in use, including communications facilities. Equipment utilization charts and tables should be reviewed for measuring efficiency and effectiveness.

Improvements through work simplification should be made to the present system if implementation is more than one year away.

***Work Simplification.*** Once the inputs, methods and procedures of processing data, and the outputs have been clearly delineated, the data processing group is in an excellent position to make recommendations regarding the present system. These include eliminating outright duplication, unnecessary reports, and useless activities; combining operations to reduce paper handling; and improving layout and methods. Others are revising and redesigning forms and reducing the number of procedural steps for an activity. Improvements of this type are commonly referred to as work simplification.

The question of whether or not make improvements to the present system at this time is one that must be answered by the data processing committee and the executive committee. Generally, the time factor is the basis for answering the question. If the actual implementation of the systems project is more than one year away, it is highly recommended that the data processing team issue reports to the departments with specific suggestions for improvements. For these reports to be effective, they must have the tacit approval of top management. Although this undertaking will lengthen the time of the feasibility study, it will provide a foundation for establishing a friendly relationship between the departmental managers and the data processing committee as well as smooth the path for the new system installation. These work simplification reports also establish the data processing team as a knowledgeable and competent group of systems people in the eyes of all involved. If the group does a poor job on this phase of the study, it gives top management the option of strengthening the group or cancelling the entire feasibility study. Otherwise, the final system recommended to the executive committee might be less than optimum.

**Present Costs and Benefits of Present System**

*A 5-year projection after completion of the feasibility study is a realistic approach for the present system.*

One of the major reasons for reviewing the present operation is to determine its cost. Cost should be analyzed by department since this is the most common basis for reporting and provides an excellent means of comparing new system costs. Typical departmental costs are found in Figure 13-6 which are determined by the firm's accounting section.

| | |
|---|---|
| Salaries and wages | File maintenance cost |
| Payroll taxes | Personal property taxes on equipment |
| Fringe benefits (such as life insurance, hospital care, and pensions) | Insurance on equipment |
| Equipment rental and/or depreciation of equipment | Forms and supplies |
| Repairs and maintenance of equipment | Utilities |
| Facilities rental | Outside processing costs by service bureaus and computer utilities |
| Training costs | Other departmental costs |

Figure 13-6 Feasibility study—sample listing of a firm's departmental costs.

***Tangible Versus Intangible Factors.*** Existing costs are not the only ones determined. Present system benefits must be set forth for comparison at a later date with each proposed alternative. These include the present level of service to customers, the value of reports, return on investment and profit, ability of the present system to grow with the firm, and inventory turnover. Many of these benefits can be measured precisely while others are intangible by their very nature which require subjective evaluation. For the final evaluation of the present system and the proposed alternatives, costs and tangible benefits are compared first for an answer. If the proposed alternative system meets the firm's established return on investment, there is no problem. However, if the proposed alternative falls below the acceptable level for the investment, the intangible factors are critical for a final answer.

***Five-Year Cost Study.*** The usual cost projections for the present system in a feasibility study is a five-year period, starting with implementation of the new system. The rationale is this: if a computer is selected, it will not be processing on a daily basis for about a year from the day of equipment selection (the final step of the feasibility study). Also, the equipment must be capable of handling the firm's workload from at least three years up to about five years. Thus, a five-year cost projection that starts after completion of the feasibility study is a realistic approach for the present and proposed systems. Attempting to go beyond five years is undesirable in view of the guesswork and assumptions that must be made about new generations of data processing equipment. The results would be much too unreliable even though some studies include a longer period of time.

## CONCLUDING INVESTIGATION—EXPLORATORY SURVEY

*The fourth and final phase of the exploratory survey concludes the investigation and consists of:*

- *determining feasible systems alternatives*
- *compiling important data on each alternative*
- *comparing data on present system to data on each alternative*

The final phase before preparation of the exploratory survey report to the executive committee is the concluding investigation by the data processing committee. Since each functional area of the present system that is germane to the study has been carefully analyzed, a feasible set of processing alternatives must be developed in order to select the best one from the set. Each alternative will not be developed in the same depth as was undertaken to understand the present system. Otherwise, such an effort would increase the time and manpower requirements of the study beyond its intended scope and budget.

### Feasible Systems Alternatives

*Feasible systems alternatives are developed that are within the constraints of the feasibility study. An important consideration is flexibility of systems alternatives.*

Proposed system specifications must be clearly defined before feasible systems alternatives can be developed. These specifications, which pertain to each functional area of the feasibility study, are determined from the desired objectives set forth initially in the study. Likewise, consideration is given to the strengths and the shortcomings of the existing system. Required system specifications, which must be clearly defined and in conformity with the study's objectives, are as follows.

1. Outputs to be produced, with great emphasis on managerial reports that utilize the "exception principle."
2. Files to be maintained with automated data processing equipment or otherwise.
3. Input data from original source documents for processing by the system.
4. Methods and procedures that show the relationship of input data to files and files to outputs of the data processing system.
5. Work volumes and timing considerations for present and future periods, including peak periods.

The starting point for compiling the above specifications is to work with the outputs first. After they have been determined, it is possible to infer what inputs and files are required and what methods and procedures must be employed. An alternative approach is to reverse the procedure by starting with the inputs. The output to input procedure is recommended since the outputs are related directly to the objectives of the firm, the most important considerations of the study. For this reason, the output approach is a logical way to get started. The future workloads of the new system must be defined for inputs, files, and outputs in terms of average and peak loads, cycles, and trends.

***Flexible System Requirements.*** The requirements of the new system may appear on the surface to be fixed. A closer examination often reveals that the study group should think in terms of these specifications having flexibility. For example, the objectives set forth in the study state certain computer files or a common data base must be updated once a day. Perhaps the best data processing solution is to utilize an on-line computer system where the files or a common data base are updated as actual transactions occur. This approach is within the constraints as initially set forth and introduces a new way of maintaining files. The important point is that alternative methods are available in data processing areas which may have the outward appearance of being fixed. With this approach in mind, it is possible to design a number of different systems with varying features, costs, and benefits.

In many cases, more processing systems will be investigated and analyzed when flexible system requirements are considered.

***Consultant's Role in Selecting Systems Alternative.*** A clear understanding of the new system requirements is the starting point for developing feasible systems alternatives. By far, this phase is the most important and difficult undertaking of the study to date. The experience of the outside consultant is of great value to the study group. His knowledge of many installations can help immeasurably to reduce the number of promising solutions for the firm. Too often, a study group "goes off on a tangent" about a specific systems approach that should have been discarded initially as not feasible. The outside consultant can exercise his influence to make certain that the study group does not get bogged down in time-consuming trivial matters. Also, he can point out the shortcomings of a certain approach that may have been strongly pushed by certain individuals. He can act with the head of the data processing committee to resolve conflicts that tend to divide the team when particular members like their approach over the others presented. The consultant's objectivity can enhance the firm's chances of selecting an optimum system when judging the merits and weaknesses of a new system. Thus the key to developing promising systems alternatives and selecting the optimum one is to employ the talents and experience of the data processing committee to its fullest capacity.

### Costs and Tangible Benefits for Each Alternative

*Net savings (losses) are developed for each alternative on a 5 year basis, computed as follows:*

| | | |
|---|---|---|
| *estimated savings* | | *xxx.xx* |
| *less: estimated one-time costs* | *xxx.xx* | |
| *estimated additional operating costs* | *xxx.xx* | *xxx.xx* |
| *net savings (losses)* | | *xxx.xx* |

The next step after developing feasible systems alternatives is to determine the anticipated savings and incremental costs for each alternative. Estimated savings, sometimes referred to as cost displacement, are enumerated as follows:

- reduction in the number of personnel—less salaries and wages.
- lower payroll taxes and fringe benefits with fewer people.
- sale or elimination of some equipment—depreciation and/or rental no longer applicable.
- reduction in repairs, maintenance, insurance, and personal property taxes.
- lower space rental and utilities.
- elimination or reduction in outside processing costs.

Incremental costs are segregated into two categories: "one-time" costs and "additional operating" costs. These are listed in Figure 13-7. The difference between the estimated savings and estimated one-time costs plus additional operating costs represents the estimated net savings (losses) to the firm before federal income taxes.

Accurate figures for a five-year period are of great importance to the data processing committee, indicating the need for the accounting department's assistance. Many times, the best way to increase the accuracy of the figures compiled by the study group is to have the outside consultant assist and review the data. His knowledge of current data processing equipment and ready access to equipment rental and purchase costs manuals maintained by his firm will save time for this phase of the study. His exposure to similar cost studies will add creditability to the final figures in the exploratory survey report to top management.

***Future Cost Considerations.*** When computing the estimated savings and incremental costs, it is not sufficient to base the estimates on the present data processing workload. Rather, the feasibility study group should review the operating work volume compiled during the detailed investigation. The trend of growth or cutback in the firm's workload should be analyzed and projected forward for the next five years. These data can, then, be utilized to project savings and costs,

*Estimated One-Time Costs:*

Feasibility study (includes exploratory survey, systems analysis, basic systems design, and equipment selection).

Training of programming and operating personnel.

Detail flowcharting of all feasibility study applications.

Programming of these applications.

Program assembly and testing of programs for new system.

Additional computer time (in excess of hours alloted free of charge).

Parallel operations (the old and the new system operate concurrently—duplication of personnel and equipment for a time period).

File conversion.

Site preparation (includes construction costs, remodeling, air conditioning, power requirements, and so forth).

Conversion activities (from existing system to new system).

Other equipment and supplies (includes forms handling equipment, files, magnetic disks packs, magnetic tapes, and the like).

*Estimated Additional Operating Costs:*

Data processing equipment (computer and related equipment)—monthly rental and/or depreciation.

Wages and salaries of data processing personnel (direct supervision, equipment operation, and other data processing jobs), payroll taxes, and fringe benefits.

Maintenance of equipment (if not included in the above).

Program maintenance (programmers).

Forms and supplies (for new data processing equipment).

Miscellaneous additional costs (insurance, repairs, maintenance, and personal property taxes on equipment purchased; power costs; and the like).

Figure 13-7 Feasibility study—estimated one-time costs and estimated additional operating costs.

similar to the analysis found in Figure 13-8. In this feasibility study for alternative #9, consideration has been given to higher future costs. Salaries and wages are generally increased by 5% per year. Cost reduction in the present system through work simplification has been incorporated in the analysis.

*The net savings (losses) less federal income taxes are discounted for each alternative on a 5-year period, resulting in a present value of net savings (losses).*

***Discounted Cash Flow.*** Since the projected savings and costs factors in a feasibility study are for five years (starting with systems implementation), the difference between the two sums after taking into account federal income taxes should be discounted back to the present time. The purpose of the discounted cash flow is to bring the time value of money into the presentation. This is shown for systems alternative #9 in Figure 13-9. Notice that the net savings after federal income taxes of $180,596 over the five-year period (anticipated life of the system), when discounted, shows a negative present value for this alternative, amounting to $22,897. On the basis of a discounted 20% return on investment for this alternative, it should not be undertaken (the firm's cutoff point for capital investments is 20%). Even though the revised discounted rate of return is approximately 16%, consideration should be given to additional benefits.

*Other tangible benefits, such as lower investment in inventory, are considered in the financial analysis for each alternative.*

***Other Tangible Benefits.*** Other tangible benefits may be available to the firm in order to justify the systems project. Among these are: reduced investment in the amount of inventory carried, less spoilage and obsolescence of inventory, lower purchasing costs through automatic reordering with data processing equipment, lower insurance costs and taxes on inventory, fewer number of warehouses needed, lower transportation costs, and less interest charges on money needed to finance inventories. More effective inventory control can have a pronounced effect on this large balance sheet item. In a similar manner, a more accurate projection of the firm's cash needs will reduce its charges for short-term money. Other large asset

Grosse Manufacturing Company
Feasibility Study Systems Alternative #9
Estimated Net Savings
Rental Basis—Five-Year Period
197–

| | YEARS FROM START OF SYSTEMS IMPLEMENTATION | | | | | FIVE-YEAR TOTAL |
|---|---|---|---|---|---|---|
| | 1 | 2 | 3 | 4 | 5 | |
| *Estimated Savings:* | | | | | | |
| Reduction in personnel (including payroll taxes and fringe benefits) | $120,200 | $400,500 | $440,300 | $490,500 | $540,500 | $1,992,000 |
| Sale of equipment | 120,000 | | | | | 120,000 |
| Rental (space) savings | 25,000 | 51,000 | 54,500 | 58,000 | 61,800 | 250,300 |
| Elimination of rental equipment | 2,050 | 4,380 | 4,690 | 5,000 | 5,300 | 21,420 |
| Other savings | 3,000 | 3,060 | 3,210 | 3,370 | 3,540 | 16,180 |
| Total Estimated Savings | $270,250 | $458,940 | $502,700 | $556,870 | $611,140 | $2,399,900 |
| *Estimated One-Time Costs:* | | | | | | |
| Feasibility study (for this year and prior year) | $95,000 | | | | | $95,000 |
| Training | 50,000 | | | | | 50,000 |
| Systems and programming | 255,500 | | | | | 255,500 |
| Master file conversion | 262,500 | | | | | 262,500 |
| Other conversion activities | 75,500 | | | | | 75,500 |
| Site preparation | 55,400 | | | | | 55,400 |
| Other one-time costs | 22,300 | | | | | 22,300 |
| Total Estimated One-Time Costs | $816,200 | | | | | $816,200 |
| *Estimated Additional Operating Costs:* | | | | | | |
| Data processing equipment rental (include maintenance) | $110,000 | $120,800 | $127,400 | $134,100 | $141,000 | $633,300 |
| Additional personnel for new system (includes payroll taxes and fringe benefits) | 34,000 | 60,700 | 62,300 | 63,400 | 64,600 | 285,000 |
| Program maintenance | 20,000 | 30,700 | 32,200 | 33,800 | 36,000 | 152,700 |
| Forms and supplies | 10,000 | 21,500 | 23,000 | 24,500 | 26,000 | 105,000 |
| Other additional operating costs | 4,400 | 12,400 | 12,800 | 13,200 | 17,600 | 60,400 |
| Total Estimated Additional Operating Costs | $178,400 | $246,100 | $257,700 | $269,000 | $285,200 | $1,236,400 |
| Net Savings (Losses) before Federal Income Taxes | ($724,350) | $212,840 | $245,000 | $287,870 | $325,940 | $347,300 |

Figure 13-8 Feasibility study systems alternative #9 for net savings (losses)—five-year period (rental basis).

items should be evaluated in order to determine if tangible savings are available through more effective control. All these values discounted to the present should be added to Figure 13-9. If the present value of net savings for a systems alternative is still negative after adding these tangible benefits, the intangible benefits must be explored. This situation will occur in most cases for a newer data processing system.

Grosse Manufacturing Company
Feasibility Study Systems Alternative #9
Cash Flow Discounted—20% Return After Federal Income Taxes
Rental Basis—Five-Year Period
197–

| YEAR | NET SAVINGS (LOSSES) BEFORE FEDERAL INCOME TAXES (PER FIGURE 13-8) | FEDERAL INCOME TAX @ 48% RATE | NET SAVINGS (LOSSES) AFTER FEDERAL INCOME TAXES | AT 20% PRESENT VALUE OF $1 | AT 20% PRESENT VALUE OF NET SAVINGS (LOSSES) |
|---|---|---|---|---|---|
| 1 | ($724,350) | ($347,688) | ($376,662) | .833 | ($313,759) |
| 2 | 212,840 | 102,163 | 110,677 | .694 | 76,810 |
| 3 | 245,000 | 117,600 | 127,400 | .579 | 73,765 |
| 4 | 287,870 | 138,178 | 149,692 | .482 | 72,152 |
| 5 | 325,940 | 156,451 | 169,489 | .402 | 68,135 |
| Totals | $347,300 | $166,704 | $180,596 | | ($22,897) |

Figure 13-9 Feasibility study systems alternative #9—cash flow discounted based on 20% after federal income taxes (rental basis).

### Intangible Benefits for Each Alternative

*Often, evaluation of tangible factors cannot justify a new systems project. Thus, there is a need to consider intangible benefits as a final evaluation measure.*

A number of intangible benefits or qualitative factors will be uncovered by studying the potential contributions of the new system to the firm's activities and problems. Generally, the use of advanced data processing equipment indicates that many qualitative benefits will accrue to the firm. A list of these factors is found in Figure 13-10. Even though qualitative factors are nonquantifiable initially, their ultimate impact is in quantitative terms, reflected in the firm's financial statements.

An analysis of Figure 13-10 indicates that the intangible benefits of a new data

Improved customer service by using better techniques to anticipate customer requirements, resulting in less lost sales, less overtime in the plant for rush orders, and similar considerations.
Better decision-making ability in the areas of marketing, manufacturing, finance, purchasing, personnel, engineering, and research and development through more timely and informative reports.
More effective utilization of management's time for planning, organizing, directing, and controlling because of the availability of timely data and information.
Ability to handle more customers faster with more automatic data processing equipment.
Closer control over capital investments and expenses through comparisons with budgets or forecasts.
Improved scheduling and production control, resulting in more efficient employment of men and machines.
Greater accuracy, speed, and reliability in information handling and data processing operations.
Better control of credit through more frequent aging of accounts receivable and analysis of credit data.
Reversal of trend to higher hiring and training costs arising from the difficulties in filling clerical jobs.
Help prevent a competitor(s) from gaining an eventual economic advantage over the firm.
Ability to utilize the many quantitative techniques of operations research.
Improved promotional efforts to attract new customers and retain present ones.
Greater ability to handle increased workloads at small additional costs.
Enhanced stature in the business community as a progressive and forward-looking firm.

Figure 13-10 Feasibility study—intangible benefits, considerations for newer data processing equipment.

processing system offer two major benefits ultimately to the firm. They are increased revenues and decreased operating costs. Better customer service and relations should enhance the firm's chances of increasing sales to its present customers and to many potential ones who are looking for these characteristics in its vendors. A new systems change not only affects the firm externally but also internally in terms of faster and more frequent reporting of results. In addition to accuracy, speed, and flexibility, automatic data processing equipment allows management more time to plan and organize activities and, in turn, direct and control according to the original plan. This is in contrast to many older systems that do not facilitate the functions of management. In summary, the qualitative factors, upon close examination, can have a pronounced effect upon the evaluation of each systems alternative.

### Costs and Benefits of the Present System Compared to Each Alternative

*There are two basic methods for comparing the present system to each alternative:*
- *identifying tangible and intangible benefits*
- *utilizing simulation techniques*

The data processing committee is in a position to compare the systems alternatives to the existing system once a thorough analysis of the important factors has been accomplished. There are two approaches to evaluation of alternatives: identifying and listing the relevant costs and benefits (tangible and intangible) or utilizing simulation techniques of operations research to determine the outcome of the systems alternatives. Either approach can be effectively employed for a definitive conclusion to the feasibility study.

*The first comparison method can take the form of a decision table, illustrated in Figure 13-11.*

***Decision Table to Evaluate Systems Alternatives.*** The first approach can take the form of a decision table, shown in Figure 13-11. The conditions in the upper part of the table represent the important facts assembled in the study while the middle part contains the possible courses of action. Each rule or systems alternative represents a set of actions corresponding to a certain set of conditions. Rule 3 (systems alternative #3) indicates a whole series of no (N) answers to the stated conditions with a low 16% return on investment. A similar situation applies to systems alternative #6. Further study for these systems alternatives should be discontinued. Rule 7 (systems alternative #7) indicates a high return for a real-time management information system when compared to the last two alternatives (#8 and #9). The important action required is a reevaluation of the values used in calculating the return on investment after federal income taxes for this systems alternative. The last rule or systems alternative #9 meets all the conditions except the one pertaining to return on investment. The action required for rule 9 is the employment of an additional consultant for the study. This is the result of considering optical character recognition equipment. No one on the data processing committee has sufficient experience or knowledge on this subject.

A decision table, similar to Figure 13-11, is helpful in resolving a complex management decision since all factors are assembled for all feasible systems alternatives. A complete summary of all pertinent factors on making the important decision should be a part of the decision table. Only in this manner can a decision table be an effective management tool.

*The second comparison method evaluates processing operations under conditions that approximate the real world as closely as possible.*

***Simulation to Evaluate Systems Alternatives.*** An alternative approach to estimating the overall performance of a proposed alternative through increased revenues or reduced costs is to utilize simulation. This operations research technique details the step-by-step events that are likely to occur. The simulation computer program uses past experience plus future forecasts to estimate the pertinent events that result in data input. The inputs can be simulated under the conditions of the proposed system. This simulation procedure monitors what happens as each order

| DECISION TABLE | TABLE NAME: FEASIBILITY STUDY—EXPLORATORY SURVEY | | PAGE 1 OF 1 |
|---|---|---|---|
| | CHART NO: FS-ES-1 | PREPARED BY: ROBERT J. THIERAUF | DATE: JULY 25, 197– |

| CONDITION | 1 | 2 | 3 | 4 | 5 | 6 | 7 | 8 | 9 | 10 | 11 | 12 | 13 |
|---|---|---|---|---|---|---|---|---|---|---|---|---|---|
| | RULE NUMBER | | | | | | | | | | | | |
| *Tangible Benefits:* | | | | | | | | | | | | | |
| Meets return on investment criteria —20% after taxes* | Y | Y | N | N | N | N | N | N | N | | | | |
| Reduced order processing costs | Y | Y | Y | Y | Y | Y | Y | Y | Y | | | | |
| Lower investment in inventory, all types | N | N | N | Y | Y | Y | Y | Y | Y | | | | |
| Less cash requirements in the future | N | N | N | N | N | Y | Y | Y | Y | | | | |
| *Intangible Benefits:* | | | | | | | | | | | | | |
| Improved customer service | N | N | N | N | N | Y | Y | Y | Y | | | | |
| Improved promotional efforts | N | N | N | N | N | N | Y | Y | Y | | | | |
| Ability to handle more customers faster | N | N | N | N | N | N | Y | Y | Y | | | | |
| Better decision making ability | Y | Y | Y | Y | Y | Y | Y | Y | Y | | | | |
| More effective utilization of management's time | N | N | N | N | N | N | Y | Y | Y | | | | |
| Improved scheduling and production control | N | N | N | Y | Y | Y | Y | Y | Y | | | | |
| Closer control over capital investments and expenses | N | N | N | N | N | Y | Y | Y | Y | | | | |
| Better control of credit | N | N | N | N | Y | Y | Y | Y | Y | | | | |
| Ability to handle more volume at low costs | N | N | N | N | N | Y | Y | Y | Y | | | | |
| More accuracy and reliability of data | N | N | N | Y | Y | Y | Y | Y | Y | | | | |
| Greater utilization of operations research techniques | N | N | N | N | N | N | Y | Y | Y | | | | |
| ACTION | | | | | | | | | | | | | |
| Utilizes a newer batch processing system | X | X | X | — | — | — | — | — | — | | | | |
| Utilizes a real-time processing system | — | — | — | X | X | X | — | — | — | | | | |
| Utilizes a real-time management information system | — | — | — | — | — | — | X | X | X | | | | |
| Minor changes of inputs and outputs | X | X | X | — | — | — | — | — | — | | | | |
| Substantial changes of inputs and outputs | — | — | — | X | X | X | X | X | X | | | | |
| Need for new files (common data base) | — | — | — | X | X | X | X | X | X | | | | |
| Moderate revision of methods and procedures | X | X | X | — | — | — | — | — | — | | | | |
| Complete revision of methods and procedures | — | — | — | X | X | X | X | X | X | | | | |
| Employ an additional consultant for study | — | — | — | — | — | — | — | — | X | | | | |
| Recruit new data processing personnel | — | — | — | X | X | X | X | X | X | | | | |
| Re-evaluate benefits of systems alternative | — | — | — | — | — | — | X | — | — | | | | |
| Discontinue feasibility study of systems alternative | — | — | X | — | — | X | — | — | — | | | | |

*Other Information:*

*1—22%; 2—20%; 3—16%; 4—18%; 5—18%; 6—16%; 7—19%; 8—17%; 9—16%

Figure 13-11 Feasibility study—decision table for appraising feasible systems alternatives.

is received, how long the order waits before being processed, how much more time the order takes when errors are found, how often inventory is available or not available for the order, how many back orders result, and how much time is needed to process the entire order. Other data can be compiled for the study, including those on revenue and costs. Keeping count on what happens in processing orders under simulated conditions will give the data processing team a realistic estimate on the performance of each systems alternative.

## EXPLORATORY SURVEY REPORT TO MANAGEMENT

*The contents of the exploratory survey report to top management should be objective as possible.*

At the conclusion of the foregoing studies, ample information should have been accumulated to make a final recommendation to top management. The exploratory survey report, authored by the data processing committee, should be a signed report to the executive committee. It should be financially oriented since large sums of money are involved. Important information that has a direct or indirect reference to finances must be included. Generally, the approval for one of the recommended alternatives must come from the board of directors or top management.

The contents of this report must be as objective as possible so that the best business data processing system is selected. The equipment should meet the needs of the system that has been developed rather than the system being altered to meet the capabilities of certain equipment. Consideration must be given to a fundamental fact that a computer oriented system is in a far better position to absorb growth in volume with a slight increase in operating costs as opposed to other systems. Comparable data processing principles should be embodied in the system recommended for a constructive report to management.

### Feasibility of Applying Data Processing

*An evaluation of systems alternatives should establish the feasibility or nonfeasibility of undertaking a new data processing system.*

The feasibility of changing to a different data processing system is a difficult undertaking when numerous alternatives are available. An analysis of the facts for one alternative is a job in itself. The comparison of many proposed systems is a formidable task. Using the data in Figure 13-11, the feasibility of a systems change is promising for all proposed systems, except alternatives #3 and #6 which are poor candidates when compared to the seven others. More benefits and higher returns are available with other proposals. When consideration is given to tangible and intangible benefits in the example, the remaining seven appear to be promising candidates. Thus the feasibility of applying newer data processing equipment and techniques has been established. The question, then, becomes one of determining which proposal is best when all critical factors are appraised.

### Recommend a New System From the Alternatives

*Generally, one systems alternative is recommended by the DP committee in its exploratory survey report to top management.*

The data processing committee's primary job is to select the best feasible systems alternative. The weighing of quantitative and qualitative factors with emphasis on the firm's future—growth patterns and related problems—can assist in resolving this dilemma. For the individual firm, the attendant circumstances must be analyzed for a definite conclusion.

In the example, an examination of the data in Figure 13-11 indicates that alternatives #7 through #9 are best. In terms of tangible and intangible benefits, there are more affirmative answers for a real-time management information system than for a newer batch processing system and a real-time processing system. The returns on investment are comparable for the most part, except for alternatives #1 and #2. Now, the question is, which one of these alternatives (#7 through #9) should be implemented? On the surface, all three have about the same benefits, except that alternative #7 gives a higher return on investment. However, a review of these three systems reveal that only alternative #9 utilizes optical character recognition equipment (also applies to alternative #3). Conversion today to OCR equipment will mean no or minimal conversion costs in the future for this area. With this added advantage in mind, the data processing committee feels the future cost savings justifies accepting a lower return. Its recommendation to top management has been finally resolved.

When agreement has been reached among the group about one particular systems alternative, a comprehensive report must be prepared that states this recommendation. A suggested listing for the final exploratory survey report is depicted in Figure 13-12. The report gives management an opportunity to examine the data and appraise their validity and merit. It also provides management with a sound basis for constructive criticism of the systems project.

1. Scope of the study in which the objectives are stated and the problem is clearly defined.
2. Overview of the existing system which points out its weaknesses and problems.
3. Adequate description of the recommended systems alternative, indicating its tangible and intangible benefits to the firm, its superiority in eliminating or reducing the deficiencies of the present system, and its general impact on the firm.
4. Financial data on the recommended systems alternative, similar to that found in Figures 13-8 and 13-9.
5. Reference to other feasible systems alternatives which were investigated, giving reasons for their final rejection. Decision table, similar to Figure 13-11, should be included.
6. Financial data on systems alternatives that were not selected, similar to that found in Figures 13-8 and 13-9.
7. Schedule of funds required for specific periods of time during systems implementation.
8. List of additional personnel needed to implement the new system and personnel requirements during conversion.
9. Accurate time schedule for the remainder of the systems project.
10. Other special factors and considerations.

Figure 13-12 Suggested listing for a final exploratory report to top management.

## Nonfeasibility of Applying Data Processing

*The nonfeasibility of applying newer data processing equipment and techniques can be caused by:*
- *limited scope of study*
- *little or nonexistent advances in hardware and software*
- *area does not lend itself to newer equipment*
- *other reasons*

A considerable expenditure of time, effort, and cost on the exploratory survey may result in the nonfeasibility of applying newer data processing equipment and techniques. This conclusion can be caused by initially limiting the scope of the study. Instead of extending the problem definition to many areas of the firm, the study was restricted to areas where progress in terms of new technical improvements has been slow or nonexistent, the area does not lend itself to newer data processing equipment, or some other reason. (When an opportunity exists for technical improvement, a broader approach is desirable for the most part.) This situation can be avoided with the help of outside consultants or personnel within the firm who are knowledgeable on data processing and are capable of suggesting fertile areas for a feasibility study. To blindly start on the exploratory survey without any idea of the results is wasteful and does not speak well of top management.

Waiting for future hardware and software developments may be a reason why the data processing group does not recommend a change in the present system.

This approach should be definitely discarded because the firm's competitors are "not standing still on such matters." To procrastinate too long is not desirable for the firm in the short run, not to mention the long run. If immediate benefits are improved service, better managerial reports, higher net profits, and other operational improvements, waiting for newer developments may be very costly to the firm in the long run.

The cost of conducting a thorough exploratory survey can be very expensive for the firm. A negative answer means that money has been spent unwisely while the firm's competitors may be receiving results from their respective studies. To produce negative results on this study and succeeding studies is definitely not recommended. After all, "over the horizon" is always the best data processing system. This is true any time a feasibility study is undertaken.

## SUMMARY

The exploratory survey is the first and most important step of the feasibility study. Its importance cannot be over emphasized since a thorough analysis of all promising and feasible data processing systems is undertaken. This permits the data processing committee to recommend the best system, under the attendant circumstances, to the executive committee. A quick and unsophisticated undertaking for this initial step will result generally in the selection and implementation of a mediocre system. The need for a thorough exploratory study is important to the firm's future success.

After the basis of the study has been determined—what will be covered, who will be involved, when it will be done, and how it will be accomplished during the preliminary and overall investigation phases—the data processing team, then, concentrates on the detailed investigation of the present system, known as systems analysis. This phase is the most time consuming and is immediately followed by the concluding investigation. Analysis of costs and benefits, both tangible and intangible, forms the basis of the exploratory survey report to top management or the executive committee. In this comprehensive report, the feasibility or nonfeasibility of applying newer data processing equipment and techniques is explored.

A careful analysis of the various phases of the exploratory survey indicates clearly that the planned approach of operations research (the scientific method) is an integral part of the study. The first step of the planned approach or observation is equivalent to systems analysis of the existing system. For the next step or the definition of the real problem, this is covered explicitly in the feasibility study while the development of alternative solutions is compared to the present system for the third step of the planned approach. In the fourth step, an optimum solution is obtained after an exhaustive analysis of all proposals. This solution can also be verified by using an operations research technique—simulation. The last two steps, namely, verification of the optimum solution and establishing proper controls, are not discussed in this chapter, but will be analyzed in later chapters. It should be noted that the material on the feasibility study does not follow verbatim the sequence of the planned approach. This is due to the nature of the undertaking and not the method. Application of the foregoing steps ensures top management that the best exploratory report will be compiled under the existing conditions.

## QUESTIONS

1. What is meant by a feasibility study?
2. (a) Why is it that the growth of the data processing system will lag behind the corresponding growth of the firm?
   (b) What effect does this have on the feasibility study?
3. (a) What are the steps involved in the exploratory survey of the feasibility study?
   (b) What are the steps involved in a systems project?
   (c) How do the steps in (b) differ from those of the planned approach of operations research (scientific method)?
4. Why is it necessary to obtain the support of top management before initiating a feasibility study?
5. Explain the relationship among the following: scope of the feasibility study, selection of desired objectives, and definition of the problem.
6. If you were assembling an ideal data processing committee for a typical manufacturing firm, who would be the members?
7. What part of the detailed investigation of the present system is most important from a managerial point of view?
8. (a) What problems can the firm expect when it has decided to convert to a real-time management information system from a batch processing computer system?
   (b) What are the problems a firm can encounter when converting from a manual or punched card system to a computer system?
9. What are the problems associated with calculating net savings after federal income taxes for feasible systems alternatives?
10. What questions must the systems analyst answer if he is going to improve the present system?
11. Why have an exploratory survey report? Why not save this expense and procure a newer generation computer to effect a systems change?
12. What are the essential contents of an exploratory survey report to top management?
13. Many firms have found that initial estimates of new system benefits are too high and costs too low. What are the major factors contributing to this condition and how may they be overcome?

CHAPTER FOURTEEN

# Feasibility Study—Basic Systems Design

*Basic systems design, the second and most creative step of the feasibility study, involves determining new system requirements. This includes working with people and resolving problem areas. (Courtesy International Business Machines Corporation.)*

Once a decision has been made to implement a newer data processing system, the details of the system must be specified. Imagination and creativity are a must for this phase. Otherwise, some of the basic weaknesses and related problems of the existing system will be duplicated unconsciously by the data processing group. The fundamentals of basic systems design, the second step of the feasibility study, are covered in this chapter.

Systems design is the creative act of inventing and developing new inputs, files, methods, procedures, and outputs for processing business data in conformity with the firm's objectives. Basic systems design differs greatly from systems analysis work even though they follow each other. Systems analysis is an intensive review of the present facts while systems design, the next step, is the creation of a new system. The systems designer is very much concerned about informational outputs required of the system. In essence, the job of the systems designer is an arduous task that requires special skills and talents.

## APPROACHES TO SYSTEMS DESIGN

There has been and still is a certain amount of controversy about the proper approach to systems design. One extreme is that the work involved in understanding the present system is a waste of time and tends to make the systems designer think in terms of the old system too much. This school of thought desires to develop an ideal system without regard to the present system. The other approach to systems design is to study the details of the present system and, then, design an improved system. When utilizing this approach to an extreme, too much reliance is placed on the present systems design work, resulting in only marginal improvements in the data processing system. Actually, very little creative work is performed since the new system is practically a duplication of the existing one, except for use of more advanced data processing equipment.

*The best approach to systems design is knowledge of the present system's exceptions and problems without letting these factors override the designer's creative talents in the new system design stage.*

Each viewpoint has its inherent weaknesses and should be avoided. The first fails to take into account the exceptions and peculiar problems of specific areas that may not be apparent unless some time is spent in examining the present system. These realities can make the best-designed system an undesirable one for any firm. The other approach is too conservative and lacks the creativity that is needed for an effective new systems design. A systems analyst who is capable of systems analysis and design is being short-sighted if he lets the present system continually cloud his thinking to the extent that his creative talents for a new one are not utilized. In view of these foregoing difficulties, the best approach takes the desirable aspects of both. Basically, it involves a thorough comprehension of the existing system with all of its exceptions and problems. By considering data of the present system where necessary and not letting them be the controlling and overriding factors, the systems designer can employ his imagination and creativity to the fullest extent in designing a new system. Thus, consideration for the existing system within reasonable limits allows the systems designer sufficient latitude to devise the best system.

## IMAGINATIVE SYSTEMS DESIGN

Even though a systems alternative has been established in the exploratory survey report, there are innumerable approaches available to the systems designer within this framework. These can be utilized to fit the particular circumstances and

*Imaginative systems design encompasses:*
- *creativity*
- *brainstorming*

can be adapted from past experience as well as from a broad knowledge of approaches that have been successful in other installations. The almost infinite variety of alternative designs makes the task a challenging one. For example, the decision to install a real-time management information system that cuts across the entire firm offers many possible design alternatives. In such a systems project, the systems analyst is offered countless opportunities for imaginative systems design.

The participants of the exploratory survey report to management are generally the ones to undertake the design of the recommended alternative. If systems designers are not part of the group, they should be brought in. Additional personnel to represent the various departments affected by the systems change are needed. This is necessary because participation and cooperation of all functional areas, represented by departmental personnel, is the key to implementing successfully a new system. It is much easier to redesign a system at this stage to accommodate their constructive suggestions than at a later date. Too many installations have faced embarrassing situations, only because appropriate departmental personnel were not given an opportunity to evaluate the systems design as it progressed.

### Creativity

*Creativity centers around a good analytical mind that is capable of reducing complexity to its essentials as well as trying new approaches to a problem's solution.*

Creative thinking is somewhat akin to the planned approach of operations research (scientific method). Emphasis is on creative work, that is, new and untried approaches of systems design. The unusual approach and the exploration of generally unaccepted methods and procedures can often bring the systems designer to a point where he can devise innovations for a proposed system. The incubation period where new design concepts are fermenting finally results in the illumination stage of creative systems design. Too often, time for creative thinking is restricted because there is the ever pressing demand for immediate results. This is typically the fault of top managers who feel that they alone have the capacity for creativity.

Good systems design requires a good analytical mind that can reduce a complex situation to its essential components. The systems designer must think logically and be highly imaginative in his approaches. Not only must he be able to visualize the possibilities of systems alternatives, he must be capable of communicating these ideas in an understandable manner. His ability must go beyond the systems analysis phase in order to conceptualize new systems design. He must take the initiative when required and answer valid objections to his work. In essence, he must operate effectively in two worlds—the conceptual one of imaginative systems design and the real one of effective business data processing systems.

Those initially selected for the data processing committee should possess the above attributes while additional personnel selected from each department should act as a sounding board for systems designers. A departmental representative, who has the answers to the proverbial questions of who, what, where, when, how, and why, should be imaginative enough to recommend improvements over the present system. Likewise, he should be objective in his thinking and should accept changes set forth by the data processing group. Facts that may be needed subsequently can be gathered under his direction. The departmental representative and the systems designer can complement one another. This combination can produce a more effective system than the systems designer working alone.

### Brainstorming

Brainstorming is an attempt to "storm" a problem quickly. Ideas concerning the problem's solution come off the top of one's head. The accent is on quantity

*Brainstorming is the development of new ideas, different approaches, better methods, and the like by a group for solving a specific problem.*

of ideas and not on quality. During the session, any idea is recorded no matter how ridiculous it may appear. There is no criticism allowed regarding any idea presented. Generally, one idea is useful in suggesting others. The session continues until the group has exhausted its ideas.

Once the session has adjourned, those whose problem area was discussed will evaluate the ideas presented. Most of the ideas will be rejected based on common sense and logical judgment. In fact, it may turn out that none can be considered as recorded. However, the creative process, possessed by systems designers, may provide the necessary impetus to modify one or more ideas as possible solutions to the problem under study. Thus, a specific problem area for a new system might not have the best solution if it were not for the brainstorming approach. A fresh look by an uninhibited and unrestricted free association can help solve problems where the proposed solutions are different from the existing ones.

## BASIC SYSTEMS DESIGN

*Basic systems design is the most creative phase of the feasibility study. It should be flexible enough to utilize equipment from most major computer manufacturers.*

Basic systems design is the most creative step in the development of an operational system. For a starting point, it involves reviewing data on the present system and data contained in the exploratory survey report, in particular, the new system recommendation. The requirements for a new system must be determined which include: policies, outputs, methods, procedures, files, inputs, and use of a common language. A thorough analysis of the foregoing areas gives the data processing team a basis for designing a new system. The preceding three steps, namely,

1. review appropriate data,
2. determine requirements for the new system.
3. design the new system,

and its sub-elements are summarized in Figure 14-1 and are the subject matter for the chapter.

*Review Appropriate Data*
- Review data on present system (Systems Analysis)
- Review data on new system (Exploratory Survey Report)

*Determine Requirements for the New System*
- New policies consistent with company objectives
- Output needs
- New methods and procedures
- Files to be maintained
- Planned inputs
- Common data processing language
- Human factors
- Internal control considerations

*Design the New System*
- Flowchart the new system
- Document the new system

Figure 14-1 Detailed outline of basic systems design—the second step of the feasibility study.

The scope of the basic systems design depends upon the recommended systems alternative. This can range from form simplification to an installation of a real-time management information system. A cross section of design approaches for data processing systems that are currently being devised include the following: management information system designed for real-time equipment, batch processing equipment, or a combination of both; data processing systems redesign to accommodate newer generation equipment; newer equipment, such as optical character recognition equipment; and improved processing procedures designed to replace older computers and punched card equipment as well as inefficient systems. The foregoing list is by no means complete, but is representative of a systems project for a firm.

***Starting Point for Systems Design.*** A logical starting point for basic systems design may be one of the following: working with an activity that dominates the entire system, an area that is the most costly for the new system, a most inefficient area of the existing system, or an area that will reap many intangible benefits, such as better customer service and improved managerial reporting. Based upon the area or activity selected, each important element must be analyzed and alternative ways of data handling must be developed. This involves creativity and, if necessary, brainstorming. After a considerable amount of mental activity and sketching feasible new systems within the framework of the selected systems alternative, the newly designed system will be documented with flowcharts and/or decision tables.

***Observe Principles of Systems Design.*** The systems designer must keep several objectives in mind no matter what systems project is undertaken. He must keep in mind that many groups of data are common to many functional areas under study. Inventory is a good example, especially in terms of the many files that contain duplicate information. Duplication of information, functions, and processing should be eliminated or kept to a minimum in a newly designed system. Methods and procedures devised should simplify data processing tasks, thereby, keeping the repetitive use of data and its manipulation to a minimum. There should be no need to undertake a work simplification study immediately following an installation. This has happened too often in the past and is caused by incompetent systems designers. Also, data files should be organized for reference at the proper time.

***Design System in General Terms.*** The systems designer should design a new system in general terms that is capable of utilizing equipment from most manufacturers. To design a system with only one equipment manufacturer in mind is restrictive, reduces the potential of the system, and often reduces the ultimate success of the systems project. Equipment is important at this stage, but only in terms of classes and types of equipment. The selection of a particular model number, however, is postponed until later (the subject matter for the first half of Chapter 15).

**Review Data on Present System**

*Reviewing data on the present system is best accomplished by reviewing material compiled during the systems analysis phase.*

Generally, many weeks have elapsed since data have been compiled on the present system. The purpose of the review is to recall pertinent facts about the system, in particular, its problems, shortcomings, and exceptions. This approach is keeping within the framework set forth initially in this chapter for creative systems design. A detailed listing of what should be evaluated in the review and avoided in the new system is contained in Figure 14-2. Notice the preponderance of the word eliminate. Too often, the weaknesses of the present system are found in the new one since this phase of systems design was performed superficially or entirely discarded. Sufficient time is necessary to implant these present system's weaknesses in the systems designer's mind for recall at a later date when creating the new system.

An evaluation of tangible and intangible benefits indicate too few for the present system, but will be increased with the new system.
Unnecessary inputs, reports, records, files, and forms of the present system will be eliminated with the new system.
Present duplication of operations, functions, and efforts will be avoided in order to achieve standardization among comparable data in the new system.
Excessive internal control or the lack of control procedures in the existing system will be eliminated.
Unnecessary refinement in the quality of data and superflous data on reports will be eliminated.
The flow of work will be reviewed by the systems designer. Present peaks and valleys of data flow can be overcome by eliminating systems bottlenecks, establishing new cutoffs, and rescheduling certain operations with the new system.
Excessive steps in the present methods and procedures will be reduced in the new one.
Waiting time between the steps involved in processing data currently will be reduced or eliminated.
Present system's inability to handle the firm's growth on a one shift basis will be eliminated.
Examination of how well the present system is practicing "management by exception" through feedback reporting.
The present uneven handling of "exceptions to the rule" data will be eliminated.
Overall, the systems designer will evaluate how well or how badly the firm has met its objectives when considering the deficiencies and weaknesses of the present system.

Figure 14-2 Basic systems design—review present system's weaknesses in order to avoid them in the new system.

An examination of Figure 14-2 indicates that the systems designer has certain questions in mind for determining the deficiencies and shortcomings of the present system. Basically, they are:

1. Can inputs, files, outputs, methods, and procedures be improved so as to accomplish the firm's objectives to the highest degree possible?
2. Are all operations necessary? Does this result in duplicate or overlapping operations, files, and the like?
3. Is there a faster, simpler, and/or more economical way of processing the data?
4. Are data recorded in a manner that is compatible with their final use?
5. Is it possible to reduce the work volume by modifying or changing policies, organization structure, files, departmental functions, or other established firm practices?
6. Can the system be improved through work simplification?

These may not be new or revealing to the reader, but are necessary for an in-depth review. These same basic questions will be asked time and time again by the systems designer as he devises the many parts of the system. He will discard many of his subsystems as a result of the above questions and comments per Figure 14-2 in order to devise a more efficient one. The creative talents of the systems designer can now be appreciated. His ability to create a system that is within the scope and requirements of the study and that will provide logical answers to the above questions is clearly a valuable one.

**Review Data on New System**

*Reviewing data on the new system is examining its basic framework as contained in the exploratory survey report.*

A review of data on the recommended alternative will assist the systems designer in obtaining an overview of what the new system is all about. The tangible and intangible benefits are explicitly enumerated in the exploratory survey report to the executive committee. All pertinent factors, such as the kind of changes in the organization structure and special factors to be considered, must be kept in mind. An intensive review is a must if all requirements and considerations of the new system are to be realized.

The exploratory survey report contains a basic framework of the new system. The overall system is defined and the related subsystems are stated in general terms. Subsystems are flowcharted for each area of the study, but only in general terms. Overall systems flowcharts depict the relationships among the many areas. An example of an overall flowchart is found in Figure 14-3 for a real-time management information system, operating in a typical manufacturing firm. (This illustration is similar to the one found in Figure 12-1.) Its related subsystems, as shown, are: sales forecasting, finished goods, materials planning, inventory control, production scheduling, production dispatching, data collection, and operations evaluation.

Even though system flowcharts are prepared for each major functional area, the most meaningful ones to the systems designer are those flowcharts that depict how the various subsystems are interconnected. This includes how the outputs from one area become the inputs for another. In the real-time management information system example, the output from sales forecasting and finished goods analysis becomes the input for materials planning which, in turn, produces output for inventory control (automatic purchasing). This succession of input/output activities continues through production scheduling, production dispatching, data collection, and finally to operations evaluation that employs the "management by exception" concept. Only exception items when compared to the current production schedule, budgets, and standards need be brought to the attention of management no matter what level is associated with the activity. An evaluation of Figure 14-3 indicates that management desires operational information as soon as it occurs. This will definitely assist the manager in keeping his operation under control and in accordance with the original plan. Thus, a review of all data, such as flowcharts, quantitative factors, and qualitative factors, provides a sound basis for determining the requirements of the new system.

## DETERMINE REQUIREMENTS FOR THE NEW SYSTEM

*Determining requirements for the new system include:*
- *policies*
- *outputs*
- *methods and procedures*
- *files*
- *inputs*
- *data processing language*
- *human factors*
- *internal control*

Specifying the requirements for the new system is a difficult undertaking, even for the most experienced systems designer. A logical beginning point differs from one system to another. No matter what area or activity is initially investigated, prime consideration is given to policies and outputs of the firm which are an integral part of the new system's tangible and intangible benefits. Basic questions used in determining the weaknesses of the present system are helpful to the systems designer in creating detail subsystems that start with outputs. These outputs are related to alternative methods, procedures, and files from which they are derived. Finally, all activities are directed back to inputs that are compatible with the new systems design.

Since the systems designer specifies the new systems requirements in more detail than the exploratory survey report, it is possible that alterations to the initial design must be undertaken. If the changes are minor, chances of them affecting the system's benefits are slight. On the other hand, if the revised design calls for major alterations, it is quite possible that the original savings and costs are erroneous, not to mention other factors contained in the study. This situation calls for immediate action on the part of the data processing committee. A meeting needs to be called with the executive committee to determine the best course of action.

This is the reason why basic systems design is a part of the feasibility study. There may be important factors discovered at a later date that affect the feasibility of applying newer data processing equipment and procedures to a specific systems alternative. It may be necessary to reevaluate the contents of the exploratory survey report for a final answer. If the analysis was thorough, the needs are low for a re-examination of all data compiled. However, if the report was deficient in critical areas of investigation, the Gigo principle again rises to the forefront of data processing activities. The accidental ommission of essential activities or areas can be just as embarrassing as those caused by willful commission.

### New Policies Consistent with Company Objectives

*Good systems design dictates that the firm's objectives be compatible with its new policies.*

The systems designer is often forced into a corner when he must meet the constraints of the firm's policies currently in effect. This condition can be overcome by examining those policies that will affect the areas under study. A close scrutiny of the data gathering on the new system will highlight those policies which are candidates for change. The need for further policy changes will become apparent as the systems design work progresses. Any policy changes approved by management should be consistent with the company's objectives as set forth in the final systems report.

Possible policy changes can be related to the following areas. Can the administrative policies be made more uniform in order to reduce the number of exceptions in the system? An example is the rate of sales commissions which can be too complex for any system. The same can be said of many pricing and discount policies. Basically, these complicated rate structures came into existence over the years to stimulate trade in special market segments. With the passage of time, the reasoning originally given no longer applies. Unfortunately, the higher data processing costs still remain. The problem can be resolved by determining whether customer dissatisfaction will result from simplification of the exceptions. If dissatisfaction does occur, the question of whether it will more than outweigh the data processing savings must be resolved.

A lucrative area for policy adjustment is a reduction in the work volume. A good example concerns the expensing of low value purchased materials initially rather than charging them to an inventory account and expensing them as they are withdrawn for production. Many firms have found the cost of maintaining inventory records in terms of pricing, making the entries for withdrawals, and charging them to jobs is greater than the value of the item. Another example is accounts payable where a firm's policy is to investigate overshipments and overcharges. The manpower required to straighten out these discrepancies is higher than their corresponding benefits since errors on both sides tend to balance out over a period of time.

### Output Needs

*Good systems design dictates that output needs be met as required and duplication of output be kept to a minimum.*

Output needs cover more than reports. They include listings, summaries, documents, punched cards, punched paper tape, updated files (common data base—magnetic tapes, disks, drums, and cards), computer display devices, teletype messages, responses from an I/O time-sharing terminal, and others. Many of the outputs provide the needed link between the data processing system itself and its ultimate user. These are the firm's customers and vendors plus the firm's personnel at all levels. The systems designer must develop systems output that meets the user's requirements. Otherwise, output will probably not be available or in the de-

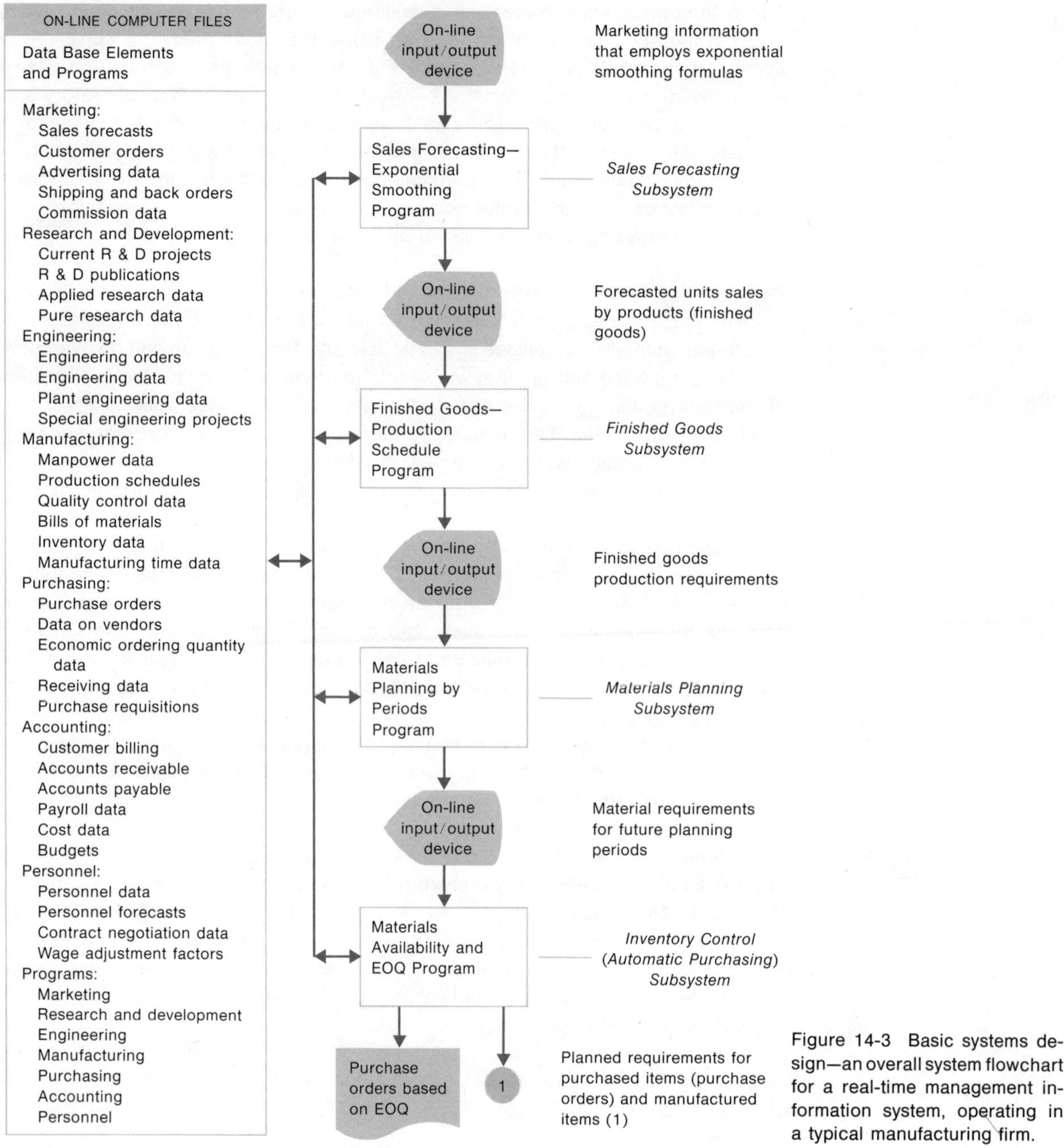


Figure 14-3 Basic systems design—an overall system flowchart for a real-time management information system, operating in a typical manufacturing firm.

sired format when needed. Information users or departmental managers and representatives, working with the systems analysts, will specify the format, detail desired, the degree of accuracy wanted, and the frequency of the report. The systems analyst may be able to improve on the output requirements of the user, especially if a real-time management information system is being designed.

During the detailed investigation phase or systems analysis, sample forms, documents, and reports were collected. These should be reviewed jointly by the

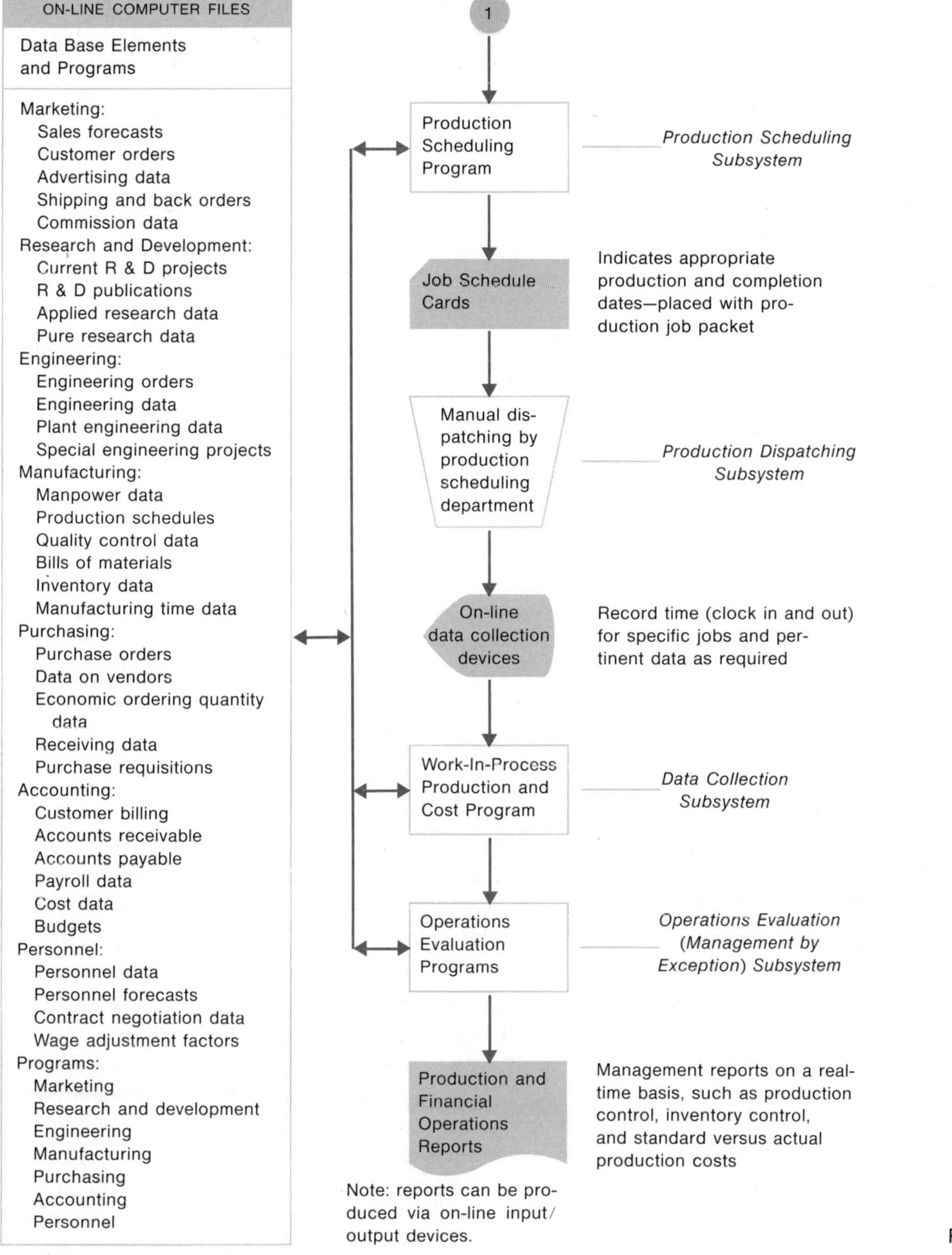


Figure 14-3 (*continued*)

systems designer and departmental representative. Two or more people will be in a better position to appraise the validity of the present output and its relationship to the output needs of the new system. A review method is to bring all samples of outputs together and sort them in appropriate categories. With this method, duplication of outputs should be apparent upon close examination. Experience of many firms indicates that 10 to 30% of all output records do not serve any valid purpose since many are a carryover from earlier days and are no longer needed or are a duplication of other reports. This excessive outpouring of data should not be duplicated with the new system.

If the above analysis is restricted to the present reports, questions can be raised regarding their validity. Appropriate questions are found in Figure 14-4. A discussion

Is the report necessary to make decisions to plan, organize, direct, or control the activities of the firm?
Is the "management by exception" concept incorporated in the report?
What would be the effect if operating personnel got more or less information than presently?
How would work be affected if the report was received less frequently or not at all?
Is all information contained in the report utilized?
How often is all or part of the information contained in the report utilized after its original use?
Can data on this report be obtained from another source?
How long is the report kept before discarding?
Is the report concise and easy to understand?
How many people refer to it?
Can the department function without the report?
Are there other reports prepared from pertinent data on the report?
Does utilization of the data justify the preparation cost of the report?
Is the report flexible enough to meet changes in the firm's operating conditions?
Is the report passed to someone higher or lower in the organization structure?
When and where is the report filed?

Figure 14-4 Basic systems design—questions to test the validity of a report.

of their merits will result in keeping some as they are, eliminating others, and combining data from other reports. (In general, consolidation of reports that have slightly different purposes into one report results in a standardization of the report's format.) Theoretically, the results of analyzing the present reports should coincide with the user's requirements as described above. However, there will be differences that must be reconciled in light of the proposed system and user's wants before the systems designer can finalize the output needs.

Once the systems designer has clearly defined the legitimate output needs for a specific area, he is in a position to devise the methods, procedures, files, and inputs that will produce the outputs. Basic design alternatives should be considered and evaluated for the best output. Here is where the true creative talents of the systems designer is needed. The systems designer must keep in mind that anything wanted as output must be planned and captured initially during the input phase. Actually, inputs, files, methods, and procedures limit the type of output. A data processing system cannot supply the output needs unless it has read and stored the necessary input data. Even though input data have been captured and stored, it must have the desired format for minimal processing.

### New Methods and Procedures

*Good systems design dictates that the number of methods and procedures be kept to a minimum for producing desired output.*

Now that the output requirements for the new system have been defined, the systems designer's attention is focused on new methods and procedures to produce these output needs. Consideration at this time must also be given to files and inputs since it is difficult to isolate methods and procedures from system's requirements. This phase requires intensive periods of creativity from the systems analyst. It is essentially a process of thinking logically and involves developing many systems design alternatives for a specific area. The new methods and procedures are tested for practicability, efficiency, and low cost. Attention must be given to those designs that meet the study's objectives (or, at least, come as close as possible). Once the many possibilities have been reduced to reasonable alternatives, say for one of the firm's functional areas, the alternative methods and procedures are examined thoroughly for the best one under the existing conditions. Included in these inventive steps is a recognition that each functional area or activity is not isolated, but rather a part of the entire system. Thus, each related part must be considered in the final evaluation of the area under study. This requirement for compatibility of methods and procedures is exemplified in Figure 14-3. The addition of this dimension to the systems designer's job increases the magnitude of his task.

In order for the systems analyst to perform the best job in designing new procedures, basic questions must be asked. These are set forth in Figure 14-5 and are comparable to the ones developed for testing the validity of a report. The validity of any procedure can be evaluated by these questions.

Can the procedure be improved to realize more fully the firm's objectives?
Are all steps in the procedure necessary?
Is it possible to simplify the procedure through modification of existing company policies, departmental structures, practices of other departments, or similar considerations?
Is there too much handling of the document in the procedure?
Does the procedure route the document through too many of the firm's personnel and departments?
Can the procedure be performed in a faster and a more economical manner?
Does the procedure make a contribution to the quality or flow of the work?
Is the cost of the procedure greater than its value to the firm?
Are all of the forms used in the procedure necessary? Can the forms be combined?
Does duplication of work exist in the procedure?
Are the steps in a logical sequence for the greatest efficiency in the procedure?
Are there parts of the procedure that functionally belong to another activity?
Is the new procedure really essential to the firm's operations?
What would happen if one or more steps in the procedure were eliminated?

Figure 14-5 Basic systems design—considerations for new procedures.

Probably the best method to determine the efficiency of the new methods and procedures is to create an information flow from the input point to the final output stage. Both the system flowchart and the document flowchart can be used to sketch rough drafts of the system. The former emphasizes the methods and procedures while the latter stresses the importance of input and output documents. Which one is best depends upon the area under investigation. Those areas where data processing is at a minimum are logical candidates for document flowcharts. In the final analysis, preference for one of these flowcharting methods or others is based upon the needs and wants of the systems designer.

### Files to be Maintained

*Good systems design dictates that files maintained be able to satisfy output needs.*

In designing files, the systems designer should remember that more should be contained in them than is required for output needs. However, efficient systems design dictates keeping storage data at a minimum. This should be consistent with the ability to meet and satisfy output needs now and in the future as well as those that arise unexpectedly. If output requirements are specified in detail as they should be, the problem of what files to maintain and the appropriate information to be stored is no problem for the systems designer. A problem occurs when output requirements are so inadequately specified that it is difficult to design organized files to meet the system needs.

An alternative approach is to design more files than are needed for the requirements under study. This additional information assures that many future report requests can be fulfilled. As noted above, extreme caution must be used in such cases. There is generally a high cost for constructing and maintaining files of questionable value to the firm. The cost of this added information versus value received is the real issue in question. The systems designer should refer to the six basic questions that were presented earlier in this chapter to determine the shortcomings of the present system and use them to evaluate files. He certainly does not want to duplicate present file deficiencies and difficulties in the new system.

**Planned Inputs**

*Good systems design dictates that inputs be carefully planned in order to keep processing at a minimum for meaningful output.*

Inputs must be planned carefully by the systems designer because much time, effort, and cost is involved in converting the data. They must be examined and evaluated from many viewpoints. Inputs may be handled in a more efficient manner on an individual or group basis. It might be possible to capture the data initially in a machine-processable form. The accuracy requirements of input data may call for editing and verifying methods. In some cases, inputs can be processed on a random sequence basis while, in others, there is need for a particular sequence before processing. The element of time constraints on the inputs and variations in input volume are important considerations when designing a new system.

Specific questions can be asked regarding how data are to be extracted from the source document. Will the data be read directly into the computer by means of optical character recognition equipment? Will information be keyed directly into a real-time processing system by input/output terminals located throughout the firm. Will data be keypunched and key verified for a remote batching operation? Or will input data be considered in light of the above plus other pertinent questions? These questions can be answered by referring to the outputs, methods, procedures, and files of the system designed. The inputs should be compatible as much as possible with their final use and interrelating parts of the data processing system. Otherwise, a less than optimum system will result.

Another approach to data input design is the provision for retention of raw data. This provides a basis for preparing future reports and answering questions not presently formulated. There is a word of caution since there is the high cost of retrieving and processing the data for meaningful output. Also, large amounts of raw input data must be stored, resulting in high storage costs. The same criterion used for storage of added file information is applicable to inputs, that is, the potential value from the stored raw data should be greater than the related cost of storing, retrieving, and processing the data.

**Common Data Processing Language**

*Good systems design dictates that a common data processing language be established in order to keep manual intervention to a minimum.*

One of the basic fundamentals of business data processing is to capture data automatically in a common data processing language as a by-product of a previous phase. This means that captured data are in an acceptable format for subsequent handling on data processing equipment and are capable of being processed without human intervention. When one thinks in terms of handling large amounts of data, only a common language will permit processing of data in a fast and accurate manner. Common data processing languages are: print code—optical and magnetic ink; card code—80, 90, or 96 columns; and channel code—punched paper tape and magnetic tape.

Most large data processing installations make use of more than one code. This is possible where the various codes are handled by data processing equipment and have no need for manual intervention. However, this should not be carried to the extreme. For example, the use of different card codes is not recommended since it may be necessary to devise costly procedures for further processing. The best method is to design a system where a language will be common to all parts of the firm.

### Human Factors

*Good systems design dictates that consideration be given to human factors in coding, data representation, and similar items.*

The foregoing requirements for a new system are not complete until the human factors in coding and data representation are considered. For example, research indicates that while a machine can read documents numbered "A4B" as easily as those coded "AB4," a human being cannot. Systems designers must consider the human element as well as procedures, data, and machines before finalizing any design. When trade-offs are deemed necessary, the human element should be given preference over the machines.

Error rates with various coding schemes increase as the number of characters in the data code increases. It is suggested that longer codes be divided into smaller units of three or four characters, such as 123–456 instead of 123456, to increase the reliability of coding. Characters used in data codes should be those in common use. Special symbols, such as Greek letters and diacritical marks, should be avoided. Also, wherever a number of data entry errors appears, the errors should be studied to see if there is a systematic pattern. Systematic errors, to the extent that they can be detected, should be identified. Factors that contribute to their occurrence should be considered in designing data codes.

Going a step further, a system should also be designed to interface with anyone who may come into contact with its results. This requirement applies equally to the needs of employees as well as the customers of the company. If employees can understand what the system requires from them and, at the same time, the system is helpful to them, the end result can only be improved operating efficiency for the company. If the customer can easily understand and process his bills, then improved customer relations will result. In the final analysis, less time and money will be spent dealing with customer inquiries and similar matters.

Too often in the past, the mechanical parts of the system have taken precedence over the human factor. Systems designers must constantly be on guard so as not to devise a total system completely in terms of technical factors. This requires that at every level of the new systems design the total human factor should be considered objectively. Otherwise, designers who have no concern at this point for internal and external human factors will cause problems when the new system is installed.

### Internal Control Considerations

*Goods systems design dictates that internal control be made an integral part of the new system in order to handle fraud, inaccuracy, and comparable problems.*

No systems design job is complete without adequate provision for internal control. Control over the firm's operations can take many forms, but all serve the same purpose. The systems analyst should make certain that his final design allows no one person full responsibility over an entire operation. This should be apparent in such areas as cash and payroll since one person with complete responsibility can defraud the firm without too much difficulty. The systems designer must build control points into the system. Checks at control points insure what has been processed agrees with predetermined totals. Controls of this type insure accuracy during processing, resulting in reliable output.

Design of new data processing systems encompasses one or more of the following controls: manual, punched card, computer—input, processing, and output, time sharing, security, and hardware. The number of controls needed is dependent upon the scope of the undertaking. A real-time management information system, for example, would have need for all of the aforementioned controls. The successful incorporation of internal control will keep auditing procedures to a minimum. Sufficient safeguards, built into the system, are necessary to handle fraud and inaccuracy. Chapter 16 on data processing systems controls presents a detailed study of internal control and auditing procedures. Reference should be made to this chapter for specific details on internal control considerations during the systems design phase.

## DESIGN THE NEW SYSTEM

*A modular or building block approach to systems design is recommended.*

Determining the above requirements is performed concurrently with designing the new system. After all, a system is nothing more than a total of all its parts. The design of a system involves making decisions about each of its parts—outputs desired, files to be maintained, planned inputs, and data processing methods and procedures that link input with output. An integral part of systems design work is answering the many questions set forth in the preceding sections so that no one item is left unexplored.

*Modular approach to systems design is a process of breaking down the system into its lowest component parts and examining for duplication. This functional breakdown also serves as a basis for designing system modules of the lowest level to the highest level.*

***Modular (Building Block) Concept.*** The design of a new system should be approached from the outset with modularity or the building block concept in mind. This involves identifying all of the foregoing system requirements. At this point, all of the requirements are placed in a functional block diagram, but these are only the highest level functions and seldom represent an optimum functional breakdown of a supporting computer-based system. Each of these functions are broken down into individual functions, applying the process iteratively from the top down. The resulting analysis is represented by an inverted tree diagram (Figure 14-6), wherein major functions at the top are successively broken into separate data processing functions in the lower branches of the tree.

As the breakdown continues, two important phenomena are observed: (1) the branches are beginning to terminate (they do not lend themselves to further breakdown) and (2) some of the functions are turning up in more than one place (duplicated modules). When the process is complete, a thorough functional analysis is obtained even though the system has not been fully designed. It should be noted that an analyst often finds alternative ways to break a function down into its component parts. He will spend a great deal of time changing his mind and filling in details which he considered unimportant on an earlier pass. But time spent here is worthwhile since this step forms the heart of the new system.

When the functional analysis is complete, the system designer creates a system structure for the functional modules that will operate within whatever hardware constraints are imposed. This modular approach allows the bringing together of individual modules that are capable of standing alone. The net result is that the complexity of an overall system is reduced since many of the duplicated modules are eliminated. Also, this modular approach facilitates modification or updating of

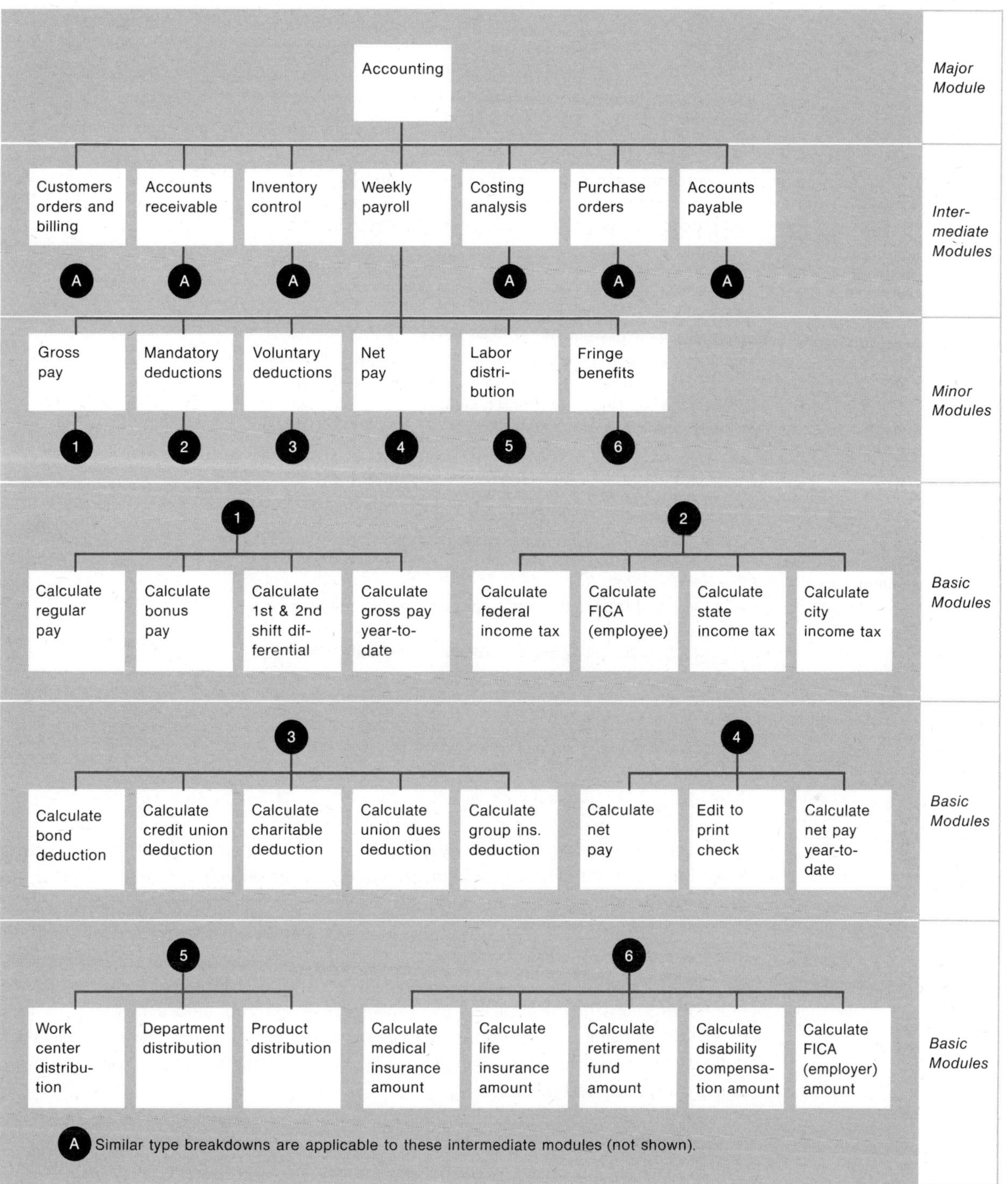


Figure 14-6 Modular (building block) concept applied to accounting, specifically, weekly payroll.

the system that may be necessary during succeeding stages of systems design as well as in the future.

***Steps in Systems Design.*** The various steps involved in the basic systems design are covered in Figure 14-7. The first two steps have been treated in determining and designing the new system. The remaining steps treat the method for resolving the final systems design. Basically, rough flowcharts are drawn to appraise the merits of many modular system alternatives with appropriate company personnel. After considering as many systems designs as possible, it will become apparent that some are more appealing than others. The more promising ones should be investigated further. It should be noted that alternative systems designs not covered in the original survey report are evaluated before selecting a final one. This permits a comprehensive review of all other promising systems alternatives that come to light when the creative talents of the systems designers are being employed to their fullest.

Determine tentative outputs, files, and inputs and their related basic content.
Devise many systems design possibilities through a modular or building block approach, including detailed methods and procedures as well as giving consideration to internal control and other parts of the system.
Prepare rough flowcharts showing the modular relationships of inputs, files, methods, procedures, and outputs for the various alternatives.
Review systems design alternatives with appropriate personnel.
Select the more promising alternatives with the aid of properly designated personnel.
Compare the tangible and intangible benefits of the promising alternatives with the final exploratory survey report. Cost factors, volumes, and requirements for equipment and personnel should be carefully analyzed to check the report's validity.
Select the systems design that best meets the study's requirements from among the promising alternatives.
Consider alternative systems designs which incorporate alternative functional modules, equipment, and techniques that were not covered in the exploratory survey phase. Many times, promising system approaches come to light during the creative design phase that were not investigated initially. (Disregard this step if not applicable.)
Determine the tangible and intangible benefits for these new alternatives. (Disregard this step if not applicable.)
Select the final systems design with the assistance of the firm's operating personnel. (Disregard this step if not applicable.)
Prepare final system flowcharts and/or decision tables for the recommended system design and relate it to all other parts of the business data processing system.
Consider the requirements for internal control, that is, has adequate provision been made for it in the final design.
Document the final design for bid invitations to equipment manufacturers.
Investigate potential problems during systems implementation.

Figure 14-7 Basic systems design—steps for one of the firm's functional areas.

***Exception Reporting.*** Once the final design has been resolved by the study groups based upon the existing tangible and intangible benefits, any significant deviations from the findings of the exploratory survey report must be reported to the executive committee. It is the function of these top managers to make a final decision on the feasibility or nonfeasibility of applying the recommended data processing system under changed conditions. This is why the feasibility study is a continuing one even though the data processing committee has endorsed a proposed system in the exploratory report. The feasibility study is formally concluded with equipment selection, the subject matter of Chapter 15.

## FLOWCHART THE NEW SYSTEM

*Flowcharts of the new system should be accurate, simple, and easy to understand.*

An important step, as stated in Figure 14-7, is preparation of final system flowcharts for the recommended new system. These flowcharts are drawn without specifying the equipment to be ordered. Accuracy, simplicity, and ease of understanding are the essential components since nontechnical personnel will be reviewing and evaluating them. An example of a system flowchart is found in Figure 14-8 for a computer raw material inventory updating procedure. This is an extension of the overall flowchart illustrated in Figure 14-3 for a real-time management information system.

Inspection of Figure 14-8 indicates that current transactions are updated as they occur. These include raw materials receipts from vendors, in-plant transfers to finished goods inventory, physical inventory count changes (physical inventory counting is performed on a rotating basis for counting raw materials once a month), and miscellaneous adjustments—based on spoilage, scrappage, obsolescence, shrinkage, and similar items. Also, automatic purchasing of raw materials is performed on-line. Cards are punched to signal excess inventory and certain inventory errors that are the result of previously mentioned on-line activities. In essence, this approach to raw material inventory allows inquiry into the system at any time for updated information that is critical to maintaining continuous manufacturing operations.

## DOCUMENT THE NEW SYSTEM

*Detailed documentation is necessary for submitting bid invitations to equipment firms.*

Detailed documentation is necessary since all data compiled on the new system will be needed for submitting bid invitations to equipment manufacturers and preparing program flowcharts. In regard to the first item, documentation is needed for the following: data origination and communications, planned inputs, files to be maintained (common data base), methods and procedures, output needs, and special requirements of the system. Also included in the bid invitation are system flowcharts depicting the interrelationships of the various parts to the entire system and those showing each area under study. Examples are found in Figures 14-3 and 14-8 respectively. Without this documentation, the data processing committee is vulnerable since data can be easily forgotten and personnel can leave for a number of reasons.

In order to prepare program flowcharts for coding at a later date, it is necessary to develop the appropriate logic. Although block diagrams or program flowcharts can be prepared for a detailed documentation of the new system, decision tables are preferred at this point for several reasons. They are easy to construct and give a more compact presentation than do program flowcharts which are accompanied by a written narrative. Decision tables are easy to modify and update. They show more clearly than flowcharts the effects of system changes upon the logic of the overall system. The more complex the logic is, the more appealing are decision tables to the systems designer. Thus, decision tables show conditions (if) and actions (then) in a clear and logical manner that facilitates programming during systems implementation.

## SUMMARY

The design of an effective new system is directly related to the creative ability of the systems designer. A fundamental basic systems design is to devise a large

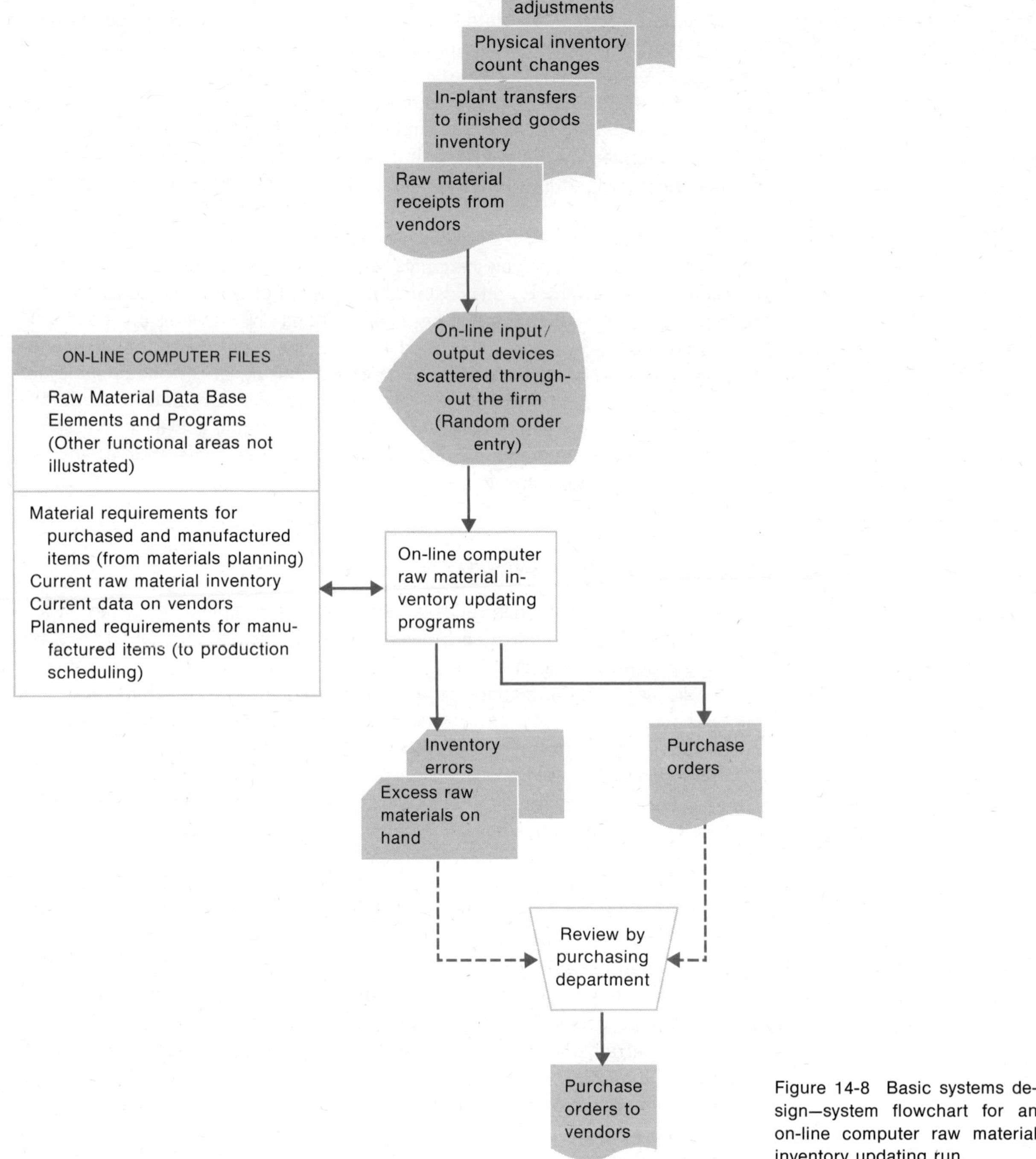


Figure 14-8 Basic systems design—system flowchart for an on-line computer raw material inventory updating run.

number of alternatives with varying inputs, files, methods, procedures, and outputs that conform to the systems alternative of the exploratory survey report. The systems designer relies upon his experience and inventive ability to develop promising systems alternatives incorporating these important components. Each alternative is analyzed by a representative group within the firm to determine its benefits and impact on the firm. The most promising systems alternative, then, is chosen and documented with system flowcharts and decision tables. The basis for selection is the successful accomplishment of the firm's objectives and attainment of quantitative and qualitative factors set forth in the exploratory survey report.

Numerous questions must be answered by the systems designer before placing his thoughts on paper. These, as enumerated in the chapter, determine the most suitable requirements of the new system. Any activity that touches the new system directly or indirectly is thoroughly investigated by these probing questions. The answers to these questions are used to develop the desired system. Intensive probing, hard work, and imaginative talents of the systems designer plus the constructive criticism of the firm's personnel are the key to designing promising new systems.

## *QUESTIONS*

1. Define basic systems design. How does this differ from systems analysis?
2. How important are creativity and brainstorming in systems design work?
3. What are the questions a systems man must ask himself when designing a new system?
4. (a) Why should the systems designer consider reporting requirements first when designing a data processing system?
   (b) What is the relationship between reporting requirements and file design?
5. What important factors must be taken into consideration when designing efficient and economical files?
6. What are the typical steps a systems designer should follow when designing a new system?
7. How important is documentation of the new system?
8. If a better system is determined during the basic systems design phase, what may have caused this to happen?

## CHAPTER FIFTEEN

# Feasibility Study—Equipment Selection and Systems Implementation

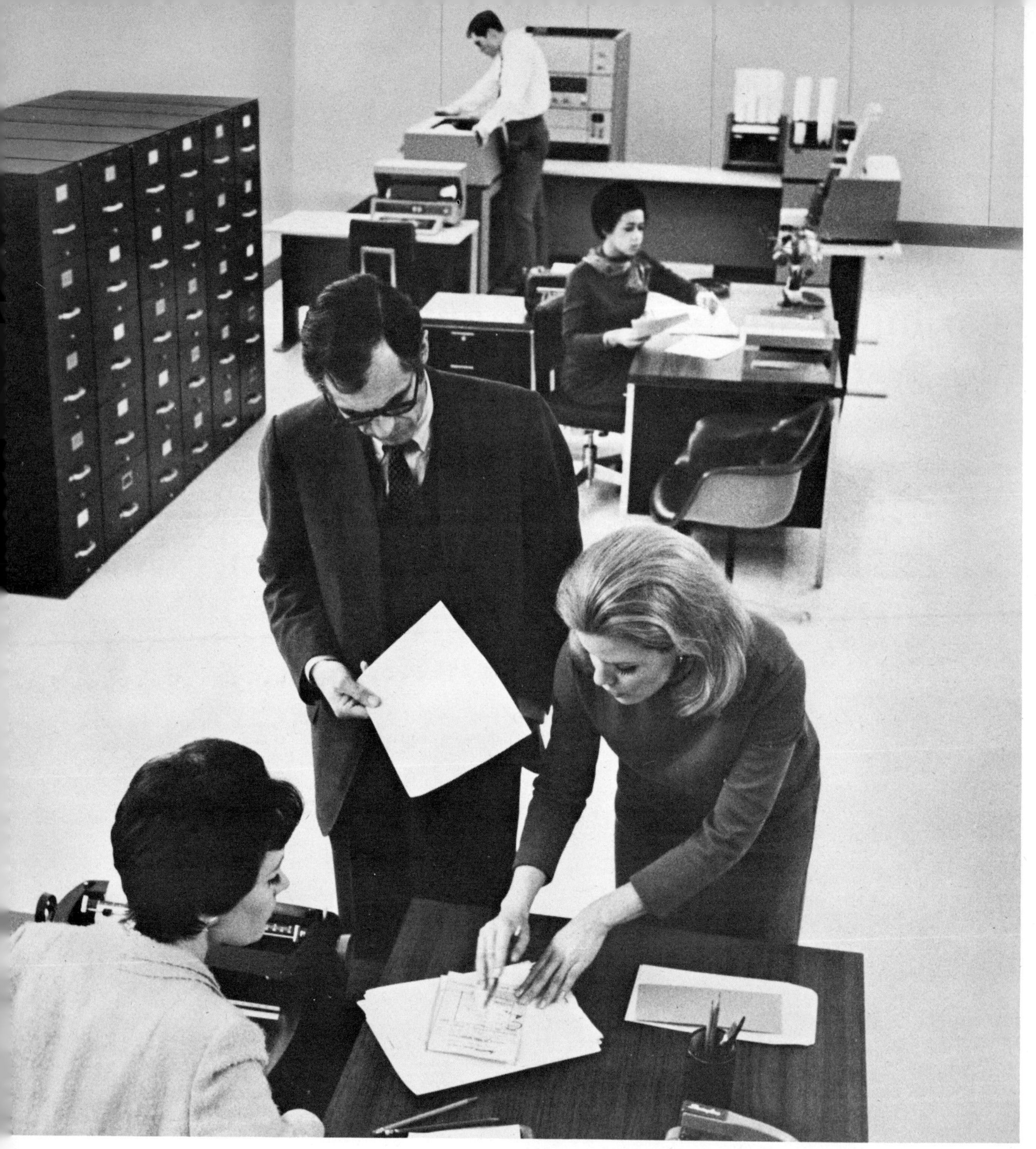

*The third and last step of the feasibility study is equipment selection. Once the equipment has become an integral part of a data processing system, it must be reviewed periodically for improvements. (Courtesy International Business Machines Corporation.)*

With the completion of the first two steps of the feasibility study, namely, the exploratory survey report and the basic systems design, the data processing committee is ready to undertake the last major step of the feasibility study which is the selection of data processing equipment. The final selection of the most suitable equipment will probably require some systems modification. In effect, the original exploratory survey report may have be modified sometime during this step. It is possible these modifications may be major, but generally they are not. This is the rationale for including equipment selection within the framework of the feasibility study. The feasibility or nonfeasibility of applying newer data processing equipment is not completely established until the order(s) is (are) placed with the respective manufacturer(s).

Significant factors involved in selecting data processing equipment are discussed as well as important data on systems implementation. Periodic review of the new system for possible improvements is another subject of discussion. The chapter concludes with an analysis of common problems that have become associated with systems projects. These problems must be solved if the computer, a major part of most new systems, is to be utilized effectively.

## EQUIPMENT SELECTION

Equipment selection should be undertaken by the data processing committee upon the completion of the basic systems design. Its basic steps, set forth in Figure 15-1, include:

1. determine equipment manufacturers,
2. submit bid invitations to manufacturers,
3. evaluate manufacturers' proposals,
4. select equipment manufacturer(s).

### Approaches to Equipment Selection

The equipment selection approach taken by the data processing committee is important for a successful conclusion to the feasibility study. There are two basic methods of selecting equipment. Only one is recommended.

*The recommended approach to equipment selection is submitting detailed systems information to each equipment manufacturer.*

***Recommended Approach.*** The recommended approach is to submit flowcharts and decision tables to each manufacturer where the specific areas of the new system are outlined. General information on the company, its future processing plans, and list of new system specifications should be forwarded to the competing manufacturers. The particulars of these specifications will be covered in subsequent sections.

*An alternative approach to equipment selection (not recommended) is having each equipment manufacturer conduct a lengthy systems review on the firm's premises.*

***Alternative Approach.*** The second approach is basically illogical since it disregards the data compiled by the feasibility study to date and requests that the equipment manufacturers start from scratch. Briefly, the manufacturers bring in their own systems personnel who will study the present system and devise a new system tailored to their own equipment. The operations will be timed and cost savings will be calculated on this basis. Generally, different approaches by each equipment manufacturer result in making a final evaluation virtually impossible when placed on a common basis. Most manufacturers will direct their proposals to highlight the specific features of their own equipment over their competition.

The problem of time is another important consideration since each manufacturer must conduct a lengthy systems review on the firm's premises. For example,

*Determine Equipment Manufacturers*
*Submit Bid Invitations to Manufacturers*
- List of new system specifications.
- Design of new system.
- Conferences with manufacturers.

*Evaluate Manufacturers' Proposals*
- Extent of automation proposed.
- Throughput performance.
- Type of equipment (modularity).
- Rental, purchase, or other basis.
- Delivery of equipment.
- Installation requirements.
- Manufacturer's assistance.
- Programming assistance.
- Training schools.
- Availability of software.
- Maintenance contracts.
- Other considerations.
- Compliance with terms of bid invitation.

*Select Equipment Manufacturer(s)*

Figure 15-1 Detailed outline of equipment selection—the third step of the feasibility study.

assume five manufacturers are involved and each spends a month to review the present system. This means about one-half year of lost time plus continuous disruptions to current operations. After department heads, supervisors, and operating personnel have been through the same set of questions five times, their attitude toward a systems change, needless to say, is negative. Likewise, their morale has reached an all-time low. Even after all the manufacturer's efforts, one month is still not ample time to learn a firm's system in sufficient detail, especially when it comes to exceptions and problem areas. Because of the manufacturer's inability to gather all the pertinent facts in the time allotted, their recommendations can be poor and, many times, impractical systems are advocated. Thus the second approach should be discarded. Specifications, prepared by the data processing group, should be submitted to likely equipment candidates.

### Determine Equipment Manufacturers

*An equipment manufacturer is determined on the basis of his interest in receiving a bid invitation.*

Before submitting necessary data to equipment manufacturers, their representatives should be contacted and invited to an orientation meeting on the proposed new system. During the course of the meeting, they should be instructed about the applications to be converted, general problems that will be encountered, approximate volumes—present and future, and other pertinent data. Each manufacturer should indicate in writing whether he wishes to receive a bid invitation. The reason for this approach should be obvious. There is no need to prepare a packet of specifications, flowcharts, decision tables, and comparable material if the manufacturer has no interest in bidding on the newly designed system.

Most firms, undertaking a data processing systems project, have some type of computer equipment under consideration based on the exploratory survey report. Since most firms have computer and related perpherial equipment salesmen calling on them at various times, they have had previous contact with most of the manufacturers. The major manufacturers of complete business computer systems are: Burroughs Corporation, Control Data Corporation, Honeywell Information Systems,

International Business Machines Corporation, National Cash Register Company, and Sperry Rand Corporation (UNIVAC Division). All these organizations have sales offices in the larger cities. Chances are that outlaying cities and towns are close enough to be handled by an office in a large city.

### Submit Bid Invitations to Manufacturers

*Bid invitations submitted to equipment manufacturers include a list of new system specifications and design of new system.*

Now that letters of intent are on file from equipment manufacturers, the company submits bid invitations to the interested equipment suppliers. The preferred approach, when sending bid invitations, is to mail the same set of data to all competing manufacturers. This permits bids to be placed on an unbiased basis, informs the manufacturers what requirements they must meet, keeps the number of questions to a minimum, and is a valid basis for comparison of equipment. The manufacturers will probably need additional information and assistance from the prospective customer as they progress with the preparation of their proposals. Generally, one person from the data processing group will perform this consultative function for a specific manufacturer.

Utilizing this approach, the respective manufacturers should have ample information to familiarize themselves with the company and its peculiar data processing problems. The recommendations made in their proposals should show clearly how the equipment will meet the customer's needs. If the specifications lack clear definition from the beginning, the bid invitations will come back as proposals with standard approaches that are applicable to any and all potential customers. In essence, all the firm's preliminary work has been a waste of time. The equipment manufacturers cannot prepare proposals tailored specifically for a particular customer if the data contained in the bid invitation are deficient. It is of utmost importance that data submitted to manufacturers be as complete and self-explanatory as possible.

*A list of new system specifications contained in a bid invitation is taken directly from the systems analysis and systems design phases.*

***List of New System Specifications.*** Much of the material needed for the bid invitation can be taken directly from the data contained in the exploratory survey report and developed during the basic systems design. The contents of the bid invitation include these areas:

1. company general information,
2. future data processing plans,
3. list of new system specifications,
4. new system flowcharts,
5. data to be forwarded by each manufacturer.

The detail for each major topic is shown in Figure 15-2.

In Sections I and II, the narrative should be brief so that attention can be focused on the remaining parts of the bid invitation. Data that are necessary for a thorough study are contained in Sections III and IV and form the basis for the manufacturer's proposal. Section III is composed of five essential parts: planned inputs, methods and procedures for handling data, files to be maintained (common data base), output needs, and other requirements and considerations for the new system. Material developed for Section IV was discussed in Chapter 14. If proper documentation was undertaken for basic systems design, the time to complete this area will be at a minimum since much of the material can be used in its present form.

***Design of New System.*** New system flowcharts are contained in Section IV of Figure 15-2. Not only are system flowcharts needed for each functional area under

I. *Company General Information*

- Description of the company and its activities.
- Overview of present data processing equipment and applications.
- Unusual data processing exceptions and problems.
- Other important general information.

II. *Future Data Processing Plans*

- Listing of areas encompassed by the new system.
- Target date for installation of new system.
- Deadline date for submitting proposals.
- Equipment decision date by the company.
- Criteria to be employed in analyzing and comparing manufacturers' proposals.

III. *List of New System Specifications*

(A) Planned Inputs:

- Where data originate within the system.
- Name and content of input data, such as documents and forms.
- Hourly rates of input data.
- Volume of inputs, including high and low points.

(B) Methods and Procedures for Handling Data:

- Transmission of local and distant data.
- Types of transactions handled.
- Computations and logical decisions required.
- New data generation within the system.
- Control points to test accuracy of data and eliminate processing of fradulent data.

(C) Files to be Maintained:

- Where data are to be stored—on-line and off-line.
- Name and contents of files to be maintained.
- Methods and procedures for updating files.
- Size of files to be maintained.

(D) Output Needs:

- Name and content of output, such as reports and summaries.
- Timely distribution of output data.
- Hourly rates of output data.
- Volume of outputs, including high and low points.

(E) Other Requirements and Considerations:

- Changes in policies to conform with new system.
- Compatibility of common data processing language.
- Special internal control considerations.
- Ability to handle the company's future growth.
- Lease or cost of equipment not to exceed a stated figure.
- Additional special requirements and considerations.

IV. *New System Flowcharts*

- Brief description of the systems approach for each functional area under study.
- System flowcharts and accompanying decision tables (if applicable) for each area.
- System flowcharts that show the interrelationships of the various areas for the new system.
- A flowchart that gives an overview of the new system.

V. *Data to be Forwarded by Each Manufacturer*

(A) Processing time for each area on the equipment.

(B) Proposed Computer Hardware:

- Basic equipment and components—its capabilities and technical features.
- Peripheral equipment—its capabilities and technical features.
- Expansion ability of the data processing equipment (modular concept).
- Purchase price and monthly rental figures on an one, two and three shift basis for basic and peripheral equipment.
- Alternative purchase and lease option plan (third party leasing).
- Estimated delivery and installation data.
- Number of magnetic tapes and/or disk packs required and their cost.
- Equipment cancellation terms.

Figure 15-2 Contents of a bid invitation to an equipment manufacturer.

(C) Site Preparation and Installation Requirements:
- Amount of space needed.
- Electrical power, air conditioning, and humidity control requirements.
- Flooring requirements and enclosure of equipment.

(D) Extent of Manufacturer's Assistance:
- Cost of manufacturer's personnel to assist in the installation and for how long.
- The availability and location of programming classes.
- The possibility of on-site training classes.
- Availability of procedure-oriented languages, compilers, programming aids, and program libraries.
- Nearest testing facilities and on what shifts.
- Amount of equipment time for compiling and testing programs without charge.

(E) Maintenance service to be provided.

(F) Equipment support for emergency processing.

(G) Other pertinent information.

Figure 15-2 (*continued*)

*Flowcharts and decision tables accompany each bid invitation. They depict the new system design for each functional area as well as the interrelationships among the subsystems.*

study, but also for showing the interrelationships among the areas. Decision tables should accompany the bid invitation. This will enable the manufacturer to have a complete understanding of the programming effort envisioned and help determine the hardware that is needed under the existing conditions. The New System Flowcharts section of the bid invitation should contain a flowchart that depicts the overall aspects of the new system. This allows the equipment manufacturer to obtain an overview of the system and its subsystems.

In the final section (V) of the bid invitation, data to be stated in each manufacturer's proposal are listed. Specifying in advance what the proposals should contain insures that comparable information for a final evaluation will be forthcoming.

*Conferences with equipment manufacturers are desirable since questions will be raised concerning the contents of the bid invitations.*

***Conferences with Manufacturers.*** Even though bid invitations specify the numerous details of the new system, legitimate questions will be raised by the various equipment firms. Many of the questions center around those areas which may have need of modification. This is necessary sometimes to take advantage of the equipment's special features. The result may be favorable benefits to the firm in terms of cost savings. Conferences between the manufacturer and the potential customer, then, can prove beneficial to both parties. However, caution is necessary during this period since salesmen may use this time to sell the firm and not the final proposal. The members of the data processing group must be careful in this respect. Otherwise, the final evaluation of the manufacturers' proposals will not be objective, but subjective.

### Evaluate Manufacturers' Proposals

The manufacturers should be given a reasonable amount of time to prepare their proposals. In most cases, approximately 60 days is adequate although large and advanced systems may take several months. When the proposals are completed, several copies are mailed to the customer for review which is, then, followed by an oral presentation by the manufacturer's representative. At this meeting, the salesman will hit the important points of the proposal and answer questions. After this procedure has been followed by all competing manufacturers, the data processing committee is prepared to evaluate the information contained in the various proposals.

There are many criteria that can be developed for evaluating a manufacturer's proposal. Among these are: extent of automation proposed, evaluation of through-

*The criteria for evaluating manufacturers' proposals are:*
- *extent of automation proposed*
- *throughput performance*
- *type of equipment*
- *rental, purchase, or other basis*
- *delivery of equipment*
- *installation requirements*
- *manufacturer's assistance*
- *programming assistance*
- *training schools*
- *availability of software*
- *maintenance contracts*
- *other considerations*
- *compliance with terms of bid invitation*

put performance, type of equipment, method of acquiring equipment, delivery of equipment, installation requirements, manufacturer's assistance, programming assistance, training schools, availability of software packages, maintenance contracts, and other considerations. (These criteria were extracted from Part V of Figure 15-2.) Finally, the proposals are evaluated in terms of how well have they complied with the bid invitation. Only after an intensive analysis of the facts can the data processing group intelligently select the manufacturer(s) for basic and peripheral equipment.

*Extent of automation proposed gives the data processing committee an overview of the approach advocated by a manufacturer.*

***Extent of Automation Proposed.*** A logical starting point for evaluation of the various proposals is the extent of automation proposed. Is the proposal a restatement of the present system, except for newer generation equipment? Is it an entirely new approach, utilizing the latest equipment? Or is it an approach somewhere between these two? Does the proposal extend beyond the functional areas contained in the bid invitation. Does it concentrate on only selected areas? Or does it cover the areas as requested? These are the type of questions that must be asked to determine how much automation is being proposed for the costs involved. This approach gives the data processing group an overview of what is being advocated by each competitor.

*Manufacturer's time estimates must be modified to reflect actual throughput performance.*

***Throughput Performance.*** Having a good understanding of how much automation has been proposed, the study team should make a thorough analysis of the equipment time required to process the data. This is a most critical area of evaluation since processing times, as stated, are generally much too low. The problem is not the hardware. No equipment supplier is going to give false information about equipment speeds, capacity, and similar hardware specifications. The real reason for these fast and incorrect speeds is that programming is not apt to be perfect. Seldom does a program utilize the computer's components in an optimum manner. Inefficient programming and compilers cause higher processing times as do jobs which are input or output bound. Times for reruns, loading the program, error stops, rewinding tapes, input and output units out of cards or paper, card and paper tape jams, temporary malfunctions of the computer's components, and similar considerations often cause much higher times.

In view of the foregoing difficulties, most experienced data processing personnel add 50% to the manufacturer's time estimates. This may seem high to a person inexperienced in data processing, but actually it is not. This 50% figure is low when contrasted to the 100% figure used for first- and second-generation computers.

There should be an independent evaluation of the manufacturer's times after a 50% time adjustment. This can be accomplished by utilizing benchmark problems and test problems. The benchmark problem approach consists of selecting a representative job to be performed by the new system. The results of the benchmark test are evaluated on how well the equipment meets the specified application. The test problem approach is aimed at measuring the functional capabilities of the equipment. The results of the equipment tests can be compared and cost performance can be evaluated. An alternative approach to testing equipment is the use of simulation and mathematical modeling techniques. In evaluating computer times, the final criterion for measuring system performance is throughput, the amount of data that can be processed within a specific period of time.

*The amount or lack of equipment compatibility with other equipment by the same or competing manufacturer is an important evaluation criterion.*

***Type of Equipment.*** The manufacturer must not only specify the make, model number, serial number, and quantity of basic and related peripheral equipment but he must also state their capabilities, operating characteristics, and technical features. Data on internal memory, operating speeds, storage capacity, and hardware controls are a part of the manufacturer's proposal on computers and related equipment. Supplies to implement the system are normally included in the proposal.

*Modularity allows the user to enlarge his computer system without having to reprogram his present system.*

*Modularity.* Modularity can be an important point when evaluating electronic data processing equipment. Computer modularity make it possible to expand the present system in terms of building blocks by adding more main storage, increasing magnetic tape speeds, enlarging secondary storage capacity, increasing the speeds of input/output devices, and similar additions. When the company has grown beyond the capabilities of the present model, the next size or larger model can be installed without having to devise a new system and reprogram. Compatibility of machines makes this possible. Thus, the new computer system can be upgraded, and added to, rather than completely replaced. Most newer generation equipment incorporates this modularity concept.

*The problem with nonmodularity is that present computer programs may be emulated or stimulated on the new equipment without taking advantage of its enlarged capabilities.*

*Nonmodularity.* Important considerations about nonmodular machines cannot be overlooked. Too often, a large-size computer is installed because one (or possibly more) program has exceeded the present equipment's internal memory. This means that the problem program(s) and all other existing problems must be converted to another computer whose machine language is not compatible with the present one. Rather than reprogram, which is much too costly, the firm will use emulation, simulation, or both. An *emulator* is hardware that translates the machine language instructions of the present computer into revised instructions of the new computer. Basically, the emulation causes the circuitry of the central processor to act in the same way as the one being replaced would act in executing such computer instructions. A *simulator,* on the other hand, is a special program that translates instructions of a previous computer into the required language of the new computer. The new program, then, can be executed for processing data.

The most important point about the concept of nonmodularity is that the hardware of the new computer system may not be employed to its fullest capacity. This is caused by the emulator or simulator which translates the new program on the basis of the replaced machine without considering the enlarged capabilities of the new machine. The result of not utilizing the new machine's special features, such as increased number of index registers and larger size of internal memory, is higher data processing costs. In essence, the rental of the new computer system is for a larger system that is being utilized only part of the time.

Difficulties encountered with emulation and simulation are well documented. One firm, for example, installed a larger computer model with nine index registers while the present equipment had only three. Needless to say, only three of the nine were used when the programs were simulated. The overall time of the program remained the same, but with increased cost to the firm. Another firm replaced their present computer with one that had considerably more storage capacity. The original programs were emulated in terms of previous storage which means the extra storage was not utilized.

*In addition to rental, purchase, option to buy, equipment can be acquired through third party leasing—the current trend.*

***Rental, Purchase, or Other Basis.*** Many financing plans are available to the firm when acquiring data processing equipment. These include rental, outright purchase, option to buy, and third-party leasing (lease back arrangements). Rental contracts, the most common method of acquiring equipment, state the specific monthly rate and number of hours for operating on a one, two, or three shift basis with rate adjustment for excessive downtime. The terms of the contract, including renewal, cancellation, and manufacturer's policy on overtime rental, are subject to careful evaluation by the data processing team. The policy of overtime rental can be a significant factor in the cost of the computer since some manufacturers base usage on 176 hours per month while others are much higher. The rates on a second shift rental also vary among manufacturers and can have a substantial impact on the final decision.

The decision to purchase must take into account these two important factors: obsolescence and availability of capital funds. Most firms that purchase equipment do so just after a new generation of computers has been announced. The rationale should be obvious. The newer line will be on the market for the next several years, reducing the problem of immediate obsolescence. Once another generation is announced, the problem of disposal can be significant since the firm will get a better trade in on a new system with the current manufacturer versus another one. This may prevent the study group from selecting the best equipment for the proposed system because of the financial factors involved.

The decision to purchase or lease is resolved sometimes by the number of shifts. An evaluation of a two or three shift operation gives a much higher return on investment, resulting in a buy decision. The study group should compare the return for this capital investment versus other potential ones. After all, the firm is well advised to spend its available capital funds for automating its factories, replacing old plants with new ones, and investing in comparable projects that provide a higher return to the firm.

Most rental contracts have an "option to buy" clause whereby part of the rental is applied toward the equipment. Terms of any purchase option include the initial deposit, percent of rental payments applied toward the equipment purchase, and option expiration date. This approach allows a firm to evaluate objectively the new system before investing in hardware. Another method of acquiring equipment is third-party leasing. The lease company, buying the equipment from the manufacturer, leases it back to the user. Experience has shown that many firms are better off with the third-party leaseback arrangement. In the final analysis, the equipment decision must be based upon the attendant circumstances and evaluated objectively by the data processing committee.

*Sometimes, manufacturers are dropped from the evaluation process due to long delivery times.*

***Delivery of Equipment.*** The manufacturer should specify a definite delivery date along with ample time to check out the equipment on the user's premises. Delivery dates run from several weeks to two (or more) years. This is contingent normally upon the manufacturer, the type of hardware, and the order date. Many manufacturers experience a virtual flood of orders when a newer generation of equipment is announced. This results in longer delivery dates. Occasionally, a competing manufacturer will be dropped from the evaluation process due to an abnormally long delivery date.

The time to check out the equipment can range from two weeks to several months, depending upon the equipment's sophistication. A tentative date for turning the system over to the data processing department should be stated in writing. A penalty clause for failure to meet the quoted dates which could cause the user financial loss should be agreed upon and written into the final equipment contract.

*Most manufacturers require air conditioning and humidity control for their equipment.*

***Installation Requirements.*** Installation requirements must be stated by the manufacturer so that the customer can prepare his premises. The dimensions and weight for each piece of equipment is specified along with the necessary power and wiring requirements. The latter refers to false-floor, underfloor, or overhead wiring necessary to connect the computer units together. Most electronic equipment requires air conditioning and humidity control.

Other requirements include room for files, supplies, repair parts, and testing equipment. Space must be allocated for all personnel involved in the system, namely, department heads, systems analysts, systems designers, programmers, operators, and technicians. In general, a location that is close to where data originate and are used is preferred for the new equipment.

*Manufacturer's assistance should be spelled out in writing in order to prevent disputes at a later date.*

***Manufacturer's Assistance.*** In the manufacturer's proposal, the amount of assistance that can be expected during systems implementation is clearly defined. Otherwise, needless disputes might develop that are detrimental to both parties. The assistance offered by all major equipment manufactures includes: programmers, analysts, and engineers to implement the new system; training schools for the client's managers, programmers, and operators; software packages to simplify programming; and equipment for program testing prior to the installation. Referring to the last item, each manufacturer normally furnishes free equipment time for compiling and testing programs before installation on the client's premises. The time (shift) available and the location should be set forth in the proposal.

*Since several of the manufacturers charge separately for equipment and services, the amount of free programming assistance, if any, should be set forth in writing.*

***Programming Assistance.*** Some equipment manufacturers will furnish experienced programmers and systems personnel for a certain period of time. Care should be taken that the manufacturer's personnel do not take charge of the programming effort. If this does occur, the firm's employees will not be capable of performing their jobs after the initial work is completed. Since programming and related systems work is a continuous job, the firm's personnel will have the task of maintaining the operation.

Not long ago, most manufacturers separated equipment pricing from the various services they offer. Charges for data processing education and systems engineering services are now billed separately to the user. Prior to this unbundling, the long-standing practice had been to charge customers a single price for its equipment and all connected services. Based on this current arrangement, it behooves the customer to have the amount of free programming assistance spelled out in the contract. Otherwise, the firm will be spending more for systems implementation than was included in the exploratory survey report.

*Because of the unbundling process, most training schools are no longer free and must be considered in this light.*

***Training Schools.*** Training programs are provided by most manufacturers for their customers. With the present method of unbundling for the most part—prices are stated separately for machines and related services—the training is no longer free. Classroom courses and seminars where the level of training varies are classified into the following categories: detailed instruction on programming the equipment; training of personnel for operating the computer and related peripheral equipment; instructing company personnel to perform preventive and machine maintenance if no service contract is signed on purchased equipment; and seminar training for executives, departmental managers, and staff personnel. On occasion, classes will be held on the user's premises if the equipment installation is large enough to justify it. The extent of training needed depends upon the complexity of the new system. When evaluating this area in the final analysis, quality and cost factors must be evaluated for each competing manufacturer.

*The availability of reliable software on newly announced computer systems is an important criterion.*

***Availability of Software.*** An important evaluation item is the availability of software to support the hardware. Software includes the following areas.

1. Programming languages for scientific and business applications.
2. Program packages for reading and punching cards, reading and writing magnetic tapes, sort and merge routines, and others.
3. Compilers or assembly programs to assist in writing the final programs.
4. Executive routines to aid the computer operator during program debugging and handle successive programs during production runs.

5. Monitor or dump routines for tracing execution of program instructions during program testing.
6. Routine programs, such as linear programming and random number generators, for handling specialized problems.

The availability of software cuts the user's time and expense since the programmer can work at a reasonably high level of programming efficiency. The task of duplicating software packages that are utilized by many hundreds and even thousands of users is eliminated. Software support for an early delivery of new generation equipment is an important consideration since it will be needed prior to installation of the machine. If the past is any indicator of the future, hardware has preceded software by many months on a new line of equipment. This has led to many embarrassing situations and penalities for equipment manufacturers.

Many who are not familiar with the complexities of software feel that a manufacturer's tested programs in such areas as inventory and payroll can be applied to all firms. For the most part, this is not true since each firm has its own peculiar characteristics which must be considered when programming. Even if the tested program is comprehensive enough to cover the firm's configurations, it has generally been written in such broad terms that it is inefficient in processing time for the typical firm. The availability and use of these tested programs for so-called routine areas of the firm must be carefully evaluated. In some firms, the manufacturer's tested programs are employed as a starting point, then appropriate additions and deletions are made to develop an efficient program.

*The amount of maintenance provided without charge depends upon the method of acquiring the equipment.*

***Maintenance Contracts.*** The maintenance required to keep the equipment in good operating condition is provided free under a rental contract but not when the equipment is purchased. Equipment rental normally includes machine engineers and servicing personnel plus parts and supplies for maintenance on the various shifts or a certain number of hours per month as specified in the contract. Scheduled time for preventive maintenance is generally performed at a time that does not interfere with regular computer operations.

The outright purchase of the equipment allows two methods for servicing the equipment. The firm can train its own personnel by sending them to the manufacturer's school for maintenance training or it can enter into a separate contract with the manufacturer. Either approach should be investigated by the study group.

For smaller equipment installations, the maintenance function will be performed from the manufacturer's sales office. The distance from the user, competence of the manufacturer's personnel, and their availability are important evaluation factors. For larger machine systems, the manufacturer may assign maintenance personnel to one or more systems. This is a plus factor in case of a machine malfunction during normal operating time. The evaluation group is advised to inquire from other firms in the area about the quality of maintenance for each competiting firm.

*Other considerations for evaluation include:*
- *ability to handle exceptions*
- *capability of handling fast growth*
- *nearness to compatible machines*

***Other Considerations.*** Other items may be of importance in addition to those set forth in Figure 15-2 (contents of a bid invitation). The question of retaining part of the existing system to handle exceptions and unusual items can have a bearing on the final decision. These items may represent a large portion of the data processed. If the firm is planning a forthcoming merger, can the new system handle a 50% additional load within a short period of time. The question of programming checks and controls not built into the hardware may add considerable time to production runs. An extremely important factor is the nearness to compatible machines that can process data on an emergency basis if a major systems breakdown occurs. Questions concerning overtime personnel costs in terms of whom will pay and similar considerations must be explored if they are applicable in selecting a specific equipment manufacturer.

*Compliance with terms of a bid invitation encompasses:*
- *completeness*
- *clarity*
- *accuracy*
- *responsiveness*

***Compliance with Terms of Bid Invitation.*** One last consideration must be investigated which revolves around how well each manufacturer has complied with the terms of the bid invitation. This involves completeness, clarity, accuracy, and responsiveness. Does each proposal cover all points set forth in the bid invitation? Is the proposal clear in every respect? Are all estimates of time and cost for peak, medium, and low workloads accurate? Does the proposal reflect a proper understanding of the bid? Failure on the manufacturer's part for any one of these points indicates a weakness that may be indicative of potential problems in the future. Final equipment evaluation, then, should include compliance with the original bid terms.

### Select Equipment Manufacturer(s)

*A decision table or a weighting method centers around a highest total points basis for selecting the equipment manufacturer(s).*

Selection of the equipment manufacturer(s) is a difficult task for the data processing committee. The selection process is much easier if the equipment proposed is identical for all practical purposes. In such cases, the choice is normally based on the lowest cost equipment. However, this approach is generally not used since most manufacturers have certain equipment features that differ from their competitors. This results in a slightly different approach to the customer's proposed system that can utilize somewhat dissimilar equipment. In order to resolve this dilemma among the various competitors, various methods have been developed for evaluating and selecting equipment.

***Decision Table for Evaluation Process.*** One method of evaluation is utilization of a decision table, shown in Figure 15-3. A decision table for a final evaluation not only defines the important criteria in compact notation, but also permits an objective evaluation since the values have been determined before receipt of the manufacturers' proposals. In the illustration, the highest possible score is one hundred points for each of the five competing manufacturers. A value of five points is deducted for each no answer while an additional five points is subtracted for an item that is checked. The checked questions represent criteria that have long run effects on the firm in terms of profits and return on investment. Thus, the deduction of ten points indicates greater importance attached to this particular criterion. Values for another firm might be different from those found in Figure 15-3. For the study currently undergoing evaluation, this is a realistic and precise approach in making this final decision for a real-time management information system. Thus, equipment manufacturer #2 with the highest score of 90 should be selected to receive the equipment contract.

***Weighting Method for Evaluation Process.*** Other methods exist for evaluating and selecting equipment. One is comparable to the method used in the illustration. This consists of assigning different weighting factors to each criterion. Each manufacturer is given a score for each weighting factor. In most cases, the score is lower than the absolute value of the weighting factor. The values of all criteria are totaled which represent the total points for each manufacturer. As with decision tables, the competitor with the highest score is selected.

***Performance Method for Evaluation Process.*** Another method in evaluating equipment superiority is its performance per dollar. Caution is needed here. All aspects of the machine's performance must be included, those being various hardware speeds, reliability of the equipment, efficient software, and similar consid-

| DECISION TABLE | TABLE NAME: CRITERIA TO SELECT EQUIPMENT MANUFACTURER | | PAGE 1 OF 1 |
|---|---|---|---|
| | CHART NO: FS-SEM-1 | PREPARED BY: ROBERT J. THIERAUF | DATE: FEB. 25, 197– |

| CONDITION | | RULE NUMBER 1 | 2 | 3 | 4 | 5 | 6 | 7 | 8 | 9 | 10 | 11 | 12 | 13 |
|---|---|---|---|---|---|---|---|---|---|---|---|---|---|---|
| *Major Criteria:* High degree of automation proposed | | Y | Y | Y | N | Y | | | | | | | | |
| Low-cost throughput performance | √ | Y | Y | Y | Y | N | | | | | | | | |
| Modularity of equipment | √ | Y | Y | Y | N | Y | | | | | | | | |
| Monthly rental within amount set forth in the exploratory report | √ | N | Y | Y | Y | N | | | | | | | | |
| Availability of equipment when needed | | Y | Y | N | Y | Y | | | | | | | | |
| Capable of meeting installation requirements | | Y | Y | Y | Y | Y | | | | | | | | |
| Adequate programming assistance available | | N | N | N | Y | N | | | | | | | | |
| Good quality training offered | | Y | Y | Y | Y | N | | | | | | | | |
| Dependable and efficient software for proposed equipment | √ | Y | Y | Y | N | Y | | | | | | | | |
| Available equipment for compiling and testing programs (initially) | | N | Y | Y | Y | N | | | | | | | | |
| Adequate equipment maintenance | | Y | N | Y | Y | Y | | | | | | | | |
| Equipment backup in local area | √ | N | Y | N | Y | Y | | | | | | | | |
| Availability of operating personnel | √ | Y | Y | Y | Y | Y | | | | | | | | |
| Compliance with terms of bid invitation | | Y | Y | Y | N | Y | | | | | | | | |
| **ACTION** | | | | | | | | | | | | | | |
| Subtract 5 points for each no (N) answer | | X | X | X | X | X | | | | | | | | |
| Subtract an additional 5 points for each no (N) answer checked | | X | — | X | X | X | | | | | | | | |

*Other Information:*
Total points = 100 (14 criteria × 5 pts. + 6 criteria × 5 pts. = 100)
Competitor's total points:
1—70; 2—90; 3—80; 4—70; 5—65

Figure 15-3 Criteria to select equipment manufacturer in the feasibility study.

erations. Otherwise, the scoring method will put too much emphasis on the machine's characteristics without regard for the supporting parts which may be just as important in the final analysis.

***Selecting Best Approach for Evaluation Process.*** As indicated previously, there are many factors to consider in equipment selection. In certain cases, some criteria are more important than others. Many of these are closely related to the hardware or software while others encompass the operating environment of the new system. Still other criteria revolve around the manufacturer or people. No matter what factors are deemed critical in the evaluation process, the method must be objective since a logical explanation is needed for selection of one manufacturer's equipment over the others. The data processing team will be in a better position when presenting its final recommendation to the executive committee if a logical basis is used. In the final analysis, the purpose of spending so much time, effort, and expense on the feasibility study is to obtain the best data processing equipment for the firm.

*The signing of the equipment contract brings the feasibility study to a formal close.*

***Signing of Equipment Contract.*** The signing of the equipment contract by a top-level executive, who has been the guiding force for both committees—executive and data processing—brings the feasibility study to a formal close. The exploratory survey report, basic systems design, and equipment selection, being the major steps of the feasibility study, represent approximately one-third of the total time expended on a systems project. In the period just ahead, not only will more time be involved than in the feasibility study but there will also be more involvement of the firm's resources in terms of its operations and personnel. The problem of how to coordinate and control the activities during this interim period is a challenging task even for the most seasoned data processing manager.

## SYSTEMS IMPLEMENTATION

*Systems implementation which approximates two-thirds of the systems project's time is generally a major undertaking if it cuts across the entire firm.*

The task of systems implementation is generally a major undertaking if it cuts across the entire organization structure. This results in a great need for implementation planning. A logical starting point for this type of planning involves knowledge of the following areas: personnel needs, programming, equipment selected, physical requirements, and conversion activities. An understanding of these areas establishes the specific tasks that must be undertaken and the relationship among them. Also, knowledge of the problems and exceptions is needed. This background permits the detailed planning of the various tasks that must be incorporated into a schedule with specific deadlines. The scheduling method should follow the natural flow of work to be undertaken. The usual questions of who, what, where, when, how, and why must be answered in developing the schedule. Implementation planning should include a method for reviewing completed and uncompleted tasks so that it can be a control tool for the entire systems project.

The major steps for systems implementation can be summarized as:

1. preparatory work of new system,
2. operation of new system,
3. periodic review of system for improvements.

These basic elements and their related subcomponents, the subject matter for the remainder of the chapter, are detailed in Figure 15-4.

### Preparatory Work of New System

Certain preparatory work must be accomplished before the new system can operate on a day-to-day basis. These include preparing a detailed time and activity

*Preparatory Work of New System*
- Scheduling the installation.
- Selecting qualified personnel.
- Training personnel.
- Realignment of personnel.
- Physical requirements and alterations.
- Testing and acceptance of new equipment.
- Programming and testing.
- File conversion.

*Operation of New System*
- Parallel operations.
- Conversion to new system.
- Provisions to make necessary changes.
- Scheduling personnel and equipment.
- Alternative plans in case of equipment failure.

*Periodic Review of System for Improvements*
- Examination of new system approaches
- Evaluation of new equipment.
- Cost analysis of system.

Figure 15-4 Detailed outline of systems implementation.

*Preparatory work of the new system is:*
- *scheduling the installation*
- *selecting and training personnel*
- *realignment of personnel*
- *physical requirements and alterations*
- *testing and acceptance of new equipment*
- *programming and testing*
- *file conversion*

schedule, selecting and training qualified personnel, realigning personnel, altering the premises, testing and acceptance of new equipment, programming numerous production runs, testing programs, and finally file conversion. The three basic steps of the feasibility study provided a starting point for completing these preparatory phases. System flowcharts, decision tables, and the manufacturer's proposal constitute the major material necessary to get the work started. Even though the data have been compiled and documented properly, the time and manpower requirements for the systems project are just beginning. Thus, it is necessary that the data processing manager be alert to keep costs at a minimum and within the confines of the exploratory survey report.

*Of the several methods available for scheduling, PERT/time is favored for lengthy and complex system projects.*

***Scheduling the Installation.*** Installation work should be scheduled in sufficient detail so that each important milestone can be controlled. Even though uncertainty may exist for certain activities, accurate times should be developed. Many times, the data set forth in the manufacturer's proposal can be used as a starting point in scheduling. (The user must consider increasing the delivery time since equipment manufacturers do experience difficulties.)

The scheduler must determine appropriate starting dates for each preceding or succeeding activity. Analysis of these times generally indicates that the systems project has ample time to complete all the necessary tasks before the equipment is delivered. On the other hand, overtime and additional personnel may be required to meet the equipment delivery date. The ability to foresee a problem today is a great help to the data processing group in controlling the project.

*The Gantt chart is recommended where the number of activities are at a minimum.*

*Gantt chart.* Several techniques are available for preparing installation schedules, the most popular ones being the Gantt chart, the Critical Path Method (CPM), and Program Evaluation and Review Technique (PERT). The planned time for each activity on a Gantt chart is represented by a bar or line whose length is proportional to time. Activities can be performed in parallel or can be placed end-to-end, depending on the need for overlapping. This graphical display of activities shows the start and stop times for each job, the relationship among the activities either in parallel or sequential order, and the total time from start to finish. The Gantt chart is recommended where the number of activities are not excessive (say 50). When the number of activities are numerous, it is advisable to utilize PERT since it shows the critical path for the entire length of the project and depicts how early an activity can be started or how late it can be completed without interfering with the project's completion date.

*A representative PERT/time network is illustrated in Figure 15-5 for a systems project.*

*PERT network*. PERT, a refinement of the Critical Path Method, is illustrated in Figure 15-5 for an entire systems project. The circled number in the illustration are events which represent the completion of activities. Events have no time associated with them while activities, depicted as arrows, do. The time within the triangles represent expected time ($t_e$) which is calculated by the formula, $t_e = (a + 4m + b)/6$ where $a$ equals the most optimistic time, $m$ equals the most likely time, and $b$ equals the most pessimistic time. The values developed from the formula have proven to be more accurate than utilizing any other method. Those appearing in Figure 15-5 were calculated on this basis.

Earliest expected times and latest expected times can be calculated, but are not shown in the example. The difference between these two times represent slack or extra time available for each activity within the project. In those cases where the earliest and latest times are equal, the event is on the critical path. Dummy arrows (dotted lines), used in the PERT network, do not represent activities, but rather allow for connecting events that are related in the network.

The heavy lines shown in the illustration represent the longest time path through the PERT network and the critical path. Any delays in starting or completing times on this path will delay the end completion date. This calls for careful scrutiny of the critical path as the project progresses. It also means that initial consideration should be given to working personnel overtime or reallocating qualified personnel to the critical activities. Those activities that are not on the critical path (heavy lines) have slack time for their completion even though it is not shown. If they should exceed their expected time, it is possible these activities may be on the critical path. In essence, all noncritical activities have the potential of becoming critical ones if not carefully supervised.

In Figure 15-5, there are only 50 events. Many of the important activities have been grouped for the sake of simplicity. Each computer program, in reality, should be a separate and distinct activity. The programming phase alone might constitute one hundred activities. A computer is recommended for controlling a large PERT project. In addition to determining the necessary level of detail, it is helpful to state the specific calendar days—earliest and latest expected times throughout the network. This gives the data processing manager an overview of where the systems project stands—favorable or unfavorable for its many activities.

*Sources of qualified data processing personnel are:*
- *data processing committee*
- *present data processing personnel*
- *present personnel interested in new opportunities*
- *personnel outside the firm*

***Selecting Qualified Personnel.*** The placement of the equipment order and scheduling its installation indicates the need for selecting qualified personnel for systems implementation and normal operations. Normally, the head of the data processing group becomes or is the data processing manager who is given the authority and responsibility for staffing the organization. Members of the data processing committee and those who have worked closely with the group are logical candidates. Even though these people have worked (full time or part time) on the feasibility study and have accumulated a wealth of information and experience, the entire undertaking was a temporary one. Perhaps some plan to return to their respective departments because they are not interested in the new data processing system, the challenge is too difficult, or some other valid reason. Even the ones who qualify for the key data processing positions should recognize that different

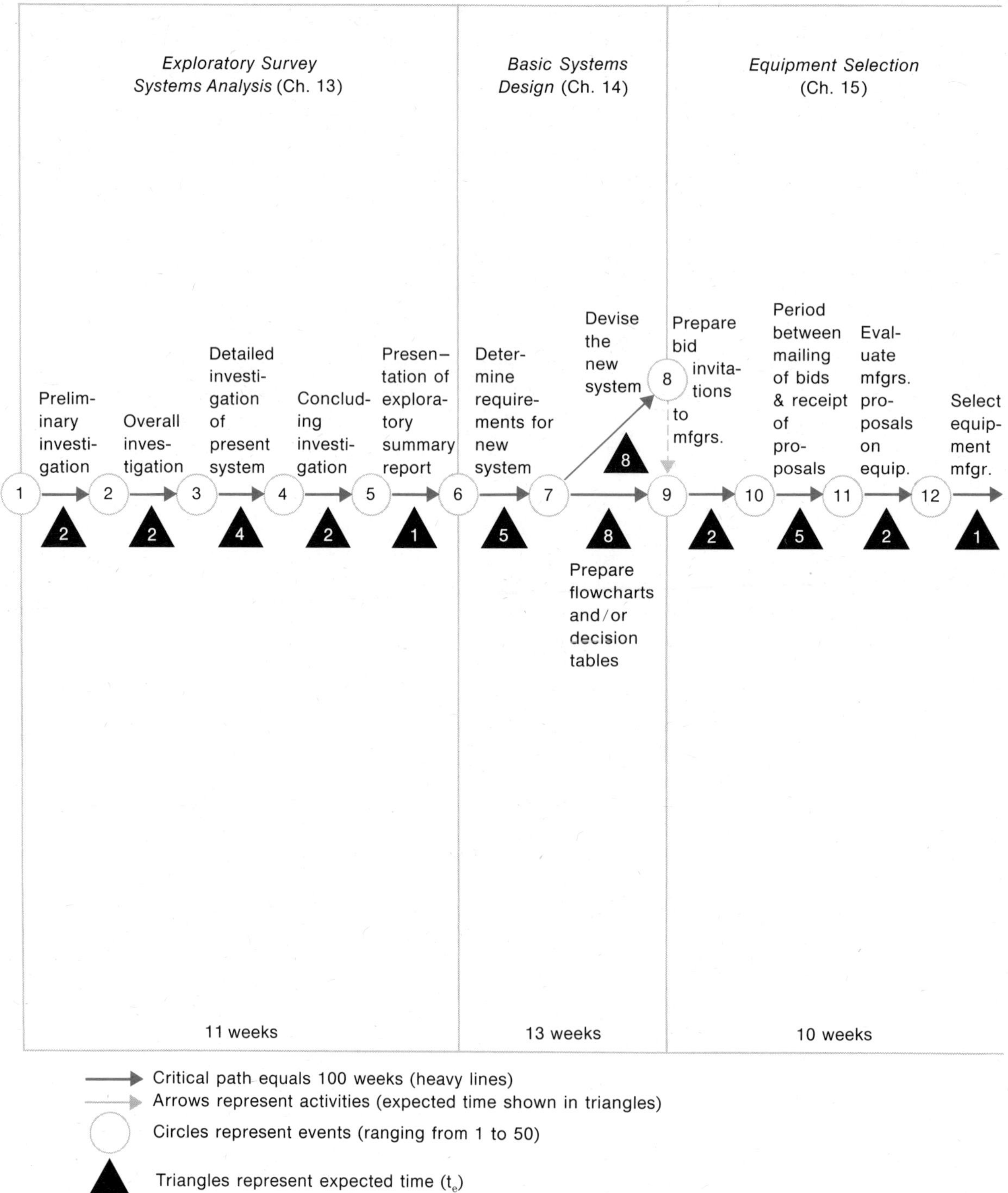


Figure 15-5 Simplified PERT network for a data processing systems project.

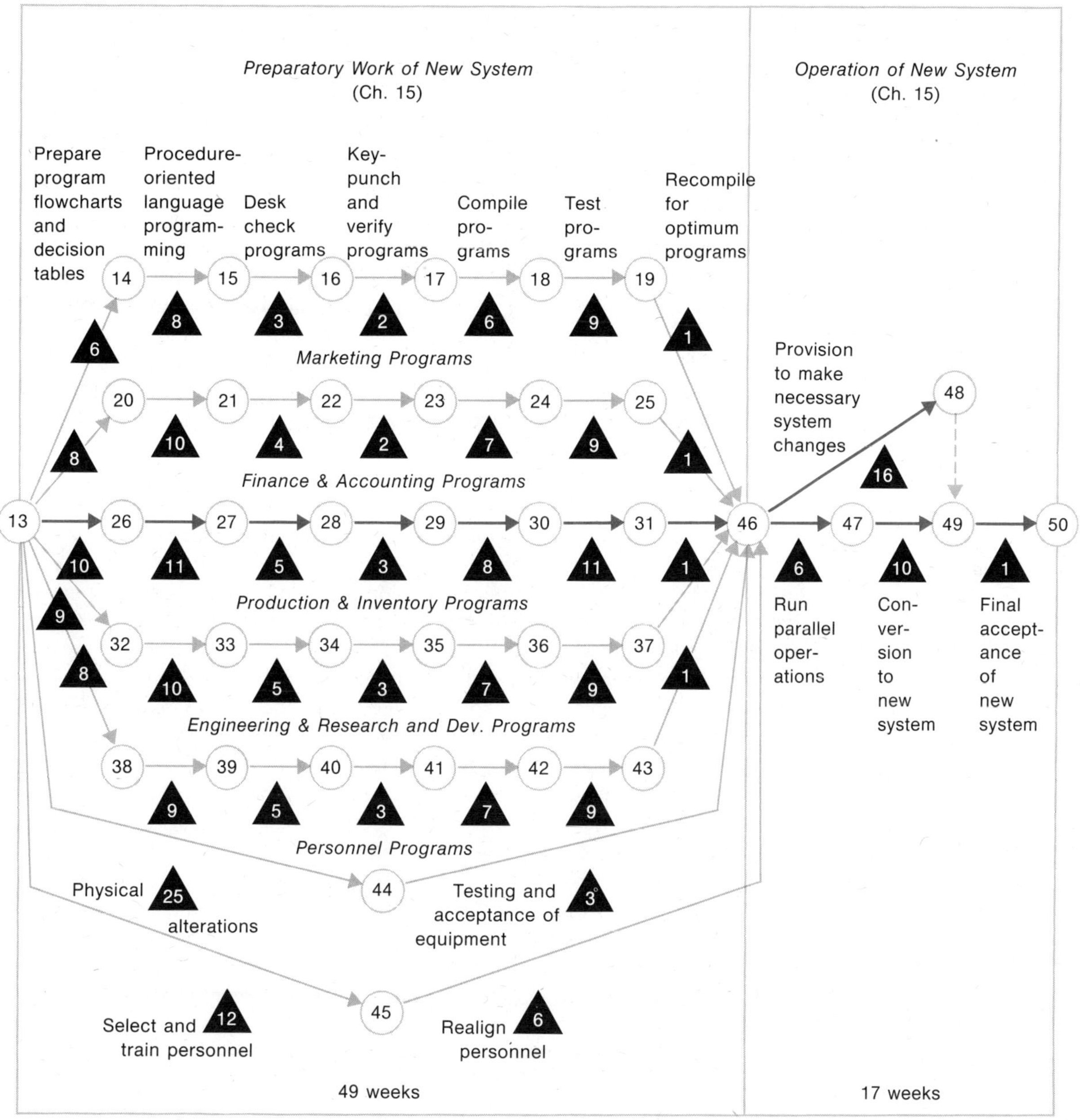


Figure 15-5 *(cont.)*

operating conditions will be faced in a new systems job versus those faced as a member of a study group. No matter what personnel are selected from within or from without the data processing committee, top management must reassure them that the firm's commitment to the newer data processing system is long range.

Source of additional personnel are those employees involved in existing data processing operations. There are many advantages to staffing under this method. Their background knowledge of the present methods and procedures is helpful in understanding the specialized tasks that must be accomplished with the new system. This understanding of procedural exceptions and problem areas can be of great assistance in complying with difficult system changes. The departmental managers know these people and what can be expected from them. For the most part, they are desirable employees and want training since it increases their professional status. Thus, management's interest in them should increase their loyalty in return.

If the many jobs set forth in the exploratory survey report cannot be filled from within by qualified personnel, the data processing manager has no alternative but to go outside the firm. This includes hiring trained personnel with prior data processing experience and people with formal training only in data processing. Applicants need to be tested and interviewed for their ability to handle positions in which they are interested. Testing scores, interviewers' evaluations, and personality traits should serve as a general guide for hiring data processing personnel. New personnel should be capable of contributing their experience, talents, and different viewpoints to the success of the installation. In addition to hiring from the outside, many firms have procured the services of software and consulting firms for assistance in systems implementation.

*Training personnel from the highest level to the lowest level includes:*

- *formal training courses*
- *on-the-job training*

***Training Personnel.*** Despite the sources of qualified personnel to implement the new system, training of personnel will still be necessary. All equipment manufacturers provide training courses for its customers. These range from several hours to several weeks, depending upon the subject matter and its depth. Courses on computer programming and related peripheral equipment are offered periodically at most sales-customer service offices by equipment manufacturers. Colleges, data processing schools, and associations also offer courses on the fundamentals of business data processing.

By no means is training limited to those who will operate the new system. Management must have a good grasp of what data processing is and how it can be applied effectively to the firm. Otherwise, there will be a gap between management and those involved in data processing. The full potential of newer methods and equipment will never be realized if this condition exists. It is suggested that management keep abreast of this fast-changing field after formal training by reading the current literature, in particular, books on the managerial aspects of data processing.

Formal training is not complete without on-the-job training. The best method for acquiring knowledge of data processing quickly is to have formal training supplemented by on-the-job training. An ideal situation, for example, is to send programmers to the manufacturer's school for two to three days while the other time is used on the job for flowcharting, programming, desk checking, and the like. This can be undertaken when the installation is large enough to warrant on-site training for the firm's personnel. Instead of using standard programming problems, the programmers can work on company programs which are simple and straight forward. This approach allows the data processing manager to observe and evaluate his own personnel, determine the validity of his implementation schedule, and obtain a general feel of the new system and its potential problem areas.

*Realignment of personnel is a most difficult undertaking in a systems project since a change in work habits must be effected.*

***Realignment of Personnel.*** The increasing number of studies on employee displacement following the installation of newer data processing equipment indicates very few persons have to be discharged. This is in contrast to automation in the factory where a sizable number of employees have been replaced by automatic machines. The chief reason why the discharge rate is at a minimum is the high turnover rate of young women whose jobs are being replaced by the computer. If the firm anticipates too many women in routine jobs when planning for personnel requirements in the future, normal attrition will eventually take care of excess personnel at this level. This is reason enough for the firm to state in all its memorandums that no one will be discharged.

Displacement of clerk and machine operators who perform routine tasks is generally no real problem; however, each level of employee above the office worker level presents different problems. Lower level supervisors and assistants to department heads, who are generally young, are quite capable of being retrained for new jobs that have not existed before. They are flexible enough to make the change with few problems. Some have become full time programmers. Their knowledge of the firm's operations plus the challenge of a new position have been an invaluable contribution to the new system. On the other hand, department heads and supervisors are generally older and less flexible in their habits. Not only may their respective departments or supervisory areas disappear, but also there will be fewer positions for middle management since there will be fewer clerical jobs for supervision. Many of the tasks performed by these middle level persons will be relegated to a computer. For example, automatic purchasing, production scheduling, and inventory control will be the normal output of a new system.

Those who are nearing retirement age can be requested to ask for an early retirement. However, there will be quite a few in the group who must face a demotion in job title, but not in pay. To cut both title and pay would be a serious blow to the morale of both the employees involved and the entire firm. For all levels affected by the new system, management should make every attempt to consider employee's interests in relocation since realignments are necessary and beyond their control. Concern for the individual should be manifest at all times during this difficult period.

The realignment of personnel occurs once the parallel operations begins. During this systems implementation step, both the new and old systems are running in parallel so that the new system can be checked out thoroughly. Personnel realignment begins on a massive scale once the firm is immersed in converting the many departments and areas as set forth in the original study. Generally, long hours will be required of all personnel for the conversion. The data processing newsletter should make every attempt to praise the efforts of all personnel involved in conversion and reemphasize that the organization has a challenging job for all employees.

*Physical requirements and alterations of many departments may be necessary, in particular, in the computer area.*

***Physical Requirements and Alterations.*** The actual installation of the equipment may require more, less, or the same amount of space as presently. However, requirements for conversion activities generally take more space since dual operations of the new and old system must take place within the same general area. Alterations may be needed to handle new inputs, files, common data base, and outputs. New methods and procedures may require physical modifications to many departments. New departments will replace old ones while other departments will have need of extensive modifications. Others will no longer be needed which may provide ample room for new departmental requirements.

The physical requirements and alterations necessary should be an integral part of the systems implementation schedule. Although the data processing manager will not personally supervise the new equipment installation and its physical environment alterations, he is, nevertheless, responsible and accountable in the final analysis. Adequate floor space for equipment and personnel, power supply, and air conditioning are important considerations for the data processing manager. It is best to determine as early as possible the layout of the new system. This permits the location of physical changes which may take a while to install. Too often, the data processing manager will ignore the physical aspects of a new system since prior system changes have gone smoothly without any need for large modifications.

*New data processing equipment should be accepted only after if has met the appropriate field service tests.*

***Testing and Acceptance of New Equipment.*** No matter what type of new equipment is being employed, the manufacturer's field service engineers must test it thoroughly before its acceptance by the user. Only the manufacturer has the necessary diagnostic routines to test the major equipment components. A common method is to utilize field service programs that are capable of testing the various pieces of hardware in the system. This method can be supplemented with a company computer program that has been thoroughly proven and operational at another location. Finally, long periods of operation without excessive downtime is an indication that the component parts are reliable for compiling and debugging programs. It is up to the data processing manager to accept the equipment after it has met the appropriate tests.

Quite often, the first models of a new line require more testing than those which have been in the field for a long time period. This is understandable since new engineering designs may be sound, but may give field service problems. Electrical and mechanical components may also need changing. Generally, special programs, developed by the manufacturer, are used to test the subsections of the system that incorporate new design concepts. Other special programs can be written by the user to determine the reliability of the new equipment. This may be one of the major programs that will be a part of the regular production runs. If the equipment fails to meet its stated specifications, the user is in a better position knowing about its deficiency now than at a later date.

*The major undertaking of any EDP system project is programming and testing, detailed in Figure 15-6.*

***Programming and Testing.*** The major task of any electronic data processing system is programming and testing computer programs. This point was highlighted in Figure 13-3. For the typical systems project of two years duration, major systems implementation phases consist of (1) training personnel, (2) flowcharting, (3) programming and desk checking, (4) and program compiling and testing. The time factors for each area are 8%, 10%, 10%, and 20% respectively, which total approximately one-half of the total project time. Referring to Figure 15-5, a further elaboration of Figure 13-3, the preparatory work for a computer totals 49 weeks out of an approximate two-year undertaking (100 weeks). Even though much time is allocated to other implementation areas, the task of programming and testing must be supervised effectively by the data processing manager in order to obtain best results.

The detailed steps involved in developing a computer routine were discussed at some length in Chapter 10. Reference should be made to that section for the specifics of programming and testing. Briefly, the steps involved are summarized in Figure 15-6. The detailed listing indicates not only the numerous steps involved

1. The problem is clearly defined in terms of system flowcharts, decision tables, and description of the run (inputs, outputs, files, logic, internal control, and other important considerations for coding).
2. The program flowcharts (block diagrams) and/or decision tables are the basis for detailed programming.
3. A symbolic, procedure-oriented, or problem-oriented languages are recommended over machine language for the entire programming effort.
4. The flowcharts, decision tables, and coded program are desk checked for logical and clerical programming errors.
5. Program cards are keypunched and key verified to keep manual errors at a minimum.
6. An assembler or compiler is used to assemble or compile the object program.
7. Errors, as indicated on the initial assembly or compiler printout, are corrected by punching new cards.
8. The program is reassembled or recompiled where a corrected printout plus punched cards, magnetic tape, or magnetic disk is used to store the machine language output.
9. Testing of the object program necessitates a sample transaction deck which is representative of the program being tested.
10. Logical and clerical programming errors are corrected as testing takes place.
11. An optimum program is reassembled or recompiled after all programming errors have been remedied during detailed testing.
12. Parallel operations are run for the new and old systems in order to detect programming errors that have not appeared in step (11).
13. Conversion to daily operations from the old system to the new system is undertaken.
14. Lastly, documentation of the computer program is essential for review and control purposes. This step should be an integral part of all phases of the systems project.

Figure 15-6 Detailed steps involved in developing an operational computer program.

in programming and testing but also is indicative of the formidable task in systems implementation.

Many times, a computer installation utilizes several methods to code and test programs if the conversion is from one computer to another. These methods include emulation, simulation, revision to present symbolic language programs, and utilization of the above steps for new programs. Depending on the manpower available, some applications may be emulated or simulated until time is available to reprogram, while other areas may be reprogrammed immediately. Generally, the program's frequency of use will determine whether it justifies reprogramming. Those programs used infrequently may continue to be run in the emulation or simulation mode so that programming efforts can be directed to achieve efficient programs for those utilized continually.

*Conversion to real-time MIS from a batch processing system is a monumental undertaking since there are few areas that are truly compatible.*

*Considerations for Real-Time MIS.* For the most part, programming and testing efforts become more difficult when a real-time management information system is installed. Even though the conversion is from one computer to another, there is a difference between a batch processing system and a real-time processing system. Many programs must be started from scratch since there is no counterpart available in the previous system for emulating, simulating, or revising present programs. The 14 steps enumerated previously must be undertaken, which will add time to the systems implementation phase. However, the next change from a real-time management information system (MIS) to a new one will not be as difficult.

When using the above programming and testing methods, the development cost of computer programs for the various functional areas of the firm may be as much as the total purchase or rental price of the equipment. This is particularly true when a comprehensive installation is planned, like a real-time MIS project. The initial cost of preparatory work does not stop once the system is installed. New computer applications and program revisions are likely to continue for a long period. Revisions of present programs are continually undertaken in order to decrease their total operating time, improve the contents of their reports, and handle more exceptions. Software cost, then, is a continuing one since new demands on the system must be changed through computer programming. In addition, the life of the average computer system is approximately five to six years which calls for some form of reprogramming when newer equipment is acquired.

*Close programming supervision is essential. Otherwise, programmers tend to take the most difficult approach instead of a direct one.*

*Programming Supervision*. Many data processing managers have found that close programming supervision is essential to meet the new installation deadlines. Too often, programmers take the most difficult route first instead of taking one that is relatively simple and straight forward. Invariably, they try their talents in utilizing the new features of the machine's hardware, in particular, the large number of index registers. This high level of sophistication can be undertaken at a later date when time is available to increase the machine's throughput performance. The data processing manager needs to remind his systems personnel that they must learn to crawl before they walk. They must be content with getting the system on the air and letting the intricate programming go to a later time if these programming techniques are not fully understood. Only in this manner can the systems implementation schedule ever be met.

*File conversion from one format to another can be a timely and costly undertaking for advanced data processing systems.*

***File Conversion.*** Because of the large files of information that must be converted from one medium to another, this phase can be started long before programming and testing is completed. The cost and related problems of file conversion are significant whether they be manual, punched card, magnetic tape, magnetic drum, or magnetic disk files. Manual files are likely to be inaccurate and incomplete where deviations from the accepted format are common. Punched card files also tend to be inaccurate and incomplete. Both files suffer from the shortcomings of inexperienced and, at times, indifferent personnel whose jobs are to maintain them. Computer generated files tend to be more accurate and consistent since they are under the control of a computer program. However, the format of the present computer files may be unacceptable for the new system.

Besides the need to provide a compatible format, there are several other reasons for file conversion. The files may require character translation that is acceptable to the character set of the new computer system. Data on punched cards, magnetic tape, and magnetic cards may have to be placed on magnetic disk or mass storage files for an on-line real-time-system. The rearrangement of certain data fields for more efficient programming may be desired. New tape or disk labels may be necessary. A new format that takes advantage of packed decimal fields may be reason enough for conversion. In order for the conversion to be as accurate as possible, file conversion programs must be thoroughly tested. Adequate controls, such as record counts and control totals, should be required output of the conversion program. Also, the existing computer files should be kept for a period of time until sufficient files are accumulated for backup. This is necessary in case the files must be reconstructed from scratch when a "bug" is discovered at a later date in the conversion routine.

Referring to Figure 13-8, the estimated one-time costs for conversion activities—file conversion, parallel operations, and similar items—are sizable. This can have an adverse effect on the firm's finances. A much lower return on the firm's investment in the systems project can be expected if personnel are not adequately supervised. This is applicable to file conversion routines that must be accurate. If

*Operations of the new system involves these areas:*
- *parallel operations*
- *conversion to new system*
- *provision to make necessary changes*
- *scheduling personnel and equipment*
- *alternative plans in case of equipment failure*

*Parallel operations allow a comparison of the old system and the new system in order to determine the accuracy and reliability of the new system.*

they are not, computer processing runs which make use of file data will not operate in an optimum manner.

### Operation of New System

Completion of optimum computer programs per step (11) in Figure 15-6 is shown as event 46 in Figure 15-5. Even though these programs have solved representative test data, there is no way to duplicate the actual flow of work with all its exceptions and timing considerations. The best way to prove the new system is to run parallel operations with the existing system.

***Parallel Operations.*** Parallel operations consist of feeding both systems the same input data and comparing files and output results. This is depicted as step (12) in Figure 15-6. Despite the fact that the best test deck possible was used during the preparatory work phase, related conditions and combinations of conditions are likely to occur that were not envisioned. Last minute computer program changes are necessary to accommodate these new conditions. Activity 46–48 represents this condition in Figure 15-5.

When implementing a real-time MIS project, the process of running dual operations for both new and old systems is more difficult than for a batch processing system. The problem is that the new system has no true counterpart in the old system. One procedure for testing the new real-time system is to have several remote input/output terminals connected on-line and to have them operated by supervised personnel who are backed up by other personnel operating on the old system. The outputs are checked for compatibility and appropriate corrections are made to the on-line computer programs. Once this segment of the new system has proven satisfactory, the entire terminal network can be placed into operation for this one area. Additional sections of the system can be added by testing in this manner until all programs are operational.

During parallel operations, mistakes often found are not those of the new system, but are the result of the old system. These differences should be reconciled as far as it is economically feasible. Those responsible for comparing the two systems should establish clearly that the remaining deficiencies are caused by the old system. A poor detailed checking job at this point can cause undue harm later when complaints are received from customers, top management, salesmen, departments, and other parties. Again, it is the responsibility of the data processing manager and his assistants to satisfy themselves that adequate time for dual operations has been undertaken for each functional area changed.

The data processing department must keep the entire firm posted on parallel operations and conversion activities. This can be accomplished via a series of bulletins which started at the inception of the feasibility study. Departmental personnel should be informed when they are to start on systems implementation and what specific activities will be required of them. Department heads should be informed before the actual date of conversion activities so that anticipated problems can be worked out before they occur. The time spent instructing personnel on parallel operations or conversion activities is well worth it. Otherwise, wasted motion and time will be the order of the day, resulting in a cost that will exceed the original study figures by a wide margin. Activities must be organized, directed, and controlled around the original plan of the feasibility study.

***Conversion to New System.*** After files have been converted and the new system's reliability has been proven for a functional area, daily processing can be shifted from the existing system to the new one. This is step (13) in Figure 15-6.

*Conversion to the new system can take place only after a cutoff point is established. Files and critical data must be updated up to this point.*

A cutoff point is established so that all files and other data requirements can be updated to the cutover point. All transactions initiated after this time are processed on the new system. The data processing manager and his delegated assistants should be present to assist and answer any questions that might develop. Considerations should be given to operating the old system for a short time. This permits checking and balancing the total results of both systems. All differences must be reconciled. If necessary, appropriate changes are made to the new system and its computer programs. The old system can be dropped as soon as the data processing group is satisfied with the new system's performance. It should be remembered that it is impossible to return to the old system if significant errors appear later in the new system. The operation of the existing system provides an alternate route in case of system failure during conversion.

*The system as initially designed should be flexible enough to accommodate necessary changes.*

***Provision to Make Necessary Changes.*** Operating procedures per the final step (14) in Figure 15-6 should be completely documented for the new system. This applies to both programming and operational procedures. Before any parallel or conversion activities can start, operating procedures must be clearly spelled out for personnel in the functional areas undergoing changes. Information on input, files, methods, procedures, output, and internal control must be set forth in clear, concise, and understandable terms for the average reader. Written operating procedures must be supplemented by oral communication during the many training periods on the systems change. Despite the many hours of training, many questions will have to be answered during conversion activities. Brief meetings where changes are taking place must be held in order to inform all operating employees of a change that has been initiated. Having qualified data processing personnel in the conversion area to communicate and coordinate new developments as they occur is a must. Likewise, revisions to operating procedures should be issued as quickly as possible. Consideration of these factors enhances the chances of a successful conversion.

Once the new system has been completely converted, the data processing section should spend several days checking with all supervisory personnel about their respective area. As with every new installation, minor adjustments can be expected. The system as initially designed should be flexible enough to accommodate the changes. Channels of communication should be open between the data processing section and all supervisory personnel so that necessary changes can be initiated as conditions change. There is no need to get locked into a rigid system when it would be beneficial for the firm to make necessary changes. Thus the proper machinery for making necessary changes must be implemented.

*Scheduling of personnel and equipment must be undertaken, daily, for maintaining an efficient data processing system.*

***Scheduling Personnel and Equipment.*** Scheduling data processing operations of a new system for the first time is a difficult task for the data processing manager. As he becomes more familiar with the new system, the job becomes more routine. The objectives of scheduling which relate to both personnel and equipment are depicted in Figure 15-7.

Many times before the data processing system is complete, there is need to schedule the new equipment. Some programs will be operational while others will be in various stages of compilation and testing. Since production runs tend to push aside new program testing, it is the task of the data processing manager to assign ample time for all individuals involved. This generally means second shift for those working on programs. Once all programs are on the air, scheduling becomes more exacting.

Schedules should be set up by the data processing manager in conjunction

- Maximize utilization of men and machines to further the objectives of the firm.
- Meet deadlines for reports and output desired.
- Increase productivity of personnel by including time for training and on-the-job training.
- Facilitate the planning of proposed new applications or modifications of existing applications for new and/or existing equipment.
- Reduce conflicts of several jobs waiting for a specific piece of equipment which may result in delays of important outputs or unnecessary overtime.

Figure 15-7 Objectives of scheduling personnel and equipment.

with the departmental managers of the operating units that are serviced by the equipment. The master schedule for next month should provide sufficient computer time to handle production runs that occur daily, weekly, semimonthly, monthly, or some other periodic basis. Daily schedules should be prepared in accordance with the master schedule and should include time for reruns if necessary, program compiling and testing, special nonrecurring reports, operations research programs, and other programs. In all cases, the schedules should be as realistic as possible.

Scheduling a real-time system is more difficult than a batch processing system. Even though the executive program handles the allotted time for each random inquiry of the system, the total time for these inquiries may vary from a few hours to a full operating day. The time to assign remote batch programs under these conditions is a problem since the number of interruptions that will occur is generally unknown. There is an alternative approach to this problem. It is to assign a block of time each day for operation of remote input/output consoles. If this arrangement is not feasible, the data processing manager must rely on past experience. When total random and sequential demands are not high, the machine will have sufficient capacity to complete all scheduled work even though batch processing runs will be stretched out by random system inquiries.

The practice of attaching recording clocks to keep track of the machine time in executing instructions and awaiting instructions is quite common. It allows the data processing manager to study the efficiency of each program and identify problem areas. The time clock is helpful in determining how the equipment's cost is to be charged to the firm's functional areas for statement purposes. However, for a real-time system, this is of no real value to the data processing manager. Executive programs are running continuously whether or not demands are being made for service. In essence, the total time for a real-time system has no real meaning. However, information can be accumulated internally by determining the input source and allocating this cost to the respective areas on the monthly departmental statements.

Just as the equipment must be scheduled for its maximum utilization, so must the personnel who operate the equipment. It is also imperative that personnel who enter input data and handle output data be included in the data processing schedule. Otherwise, data will not be available when the equipment needs it for processing. It is essential that each person follow the methods and procedures set forth by the data processing group. Noncompliance with established norms will have an adverse effect on the entire system. Effective supervision of personnel enhances compliance with established procedures and scheduled deadlines.

***Alternative Plans in Case of Equipment Failure.*** Alternative processing plans must be employed in case of equipment failure. It does not matter who or what caused it to happen. The fact is that the data processing system operation is down. Priorities must be given to those jobs that are critical to the firm, such as billing,

*In case of equipment failure, alternative processing methods and procedures must be effected until the EDP system is operating again.*

payroll, and inventory. Critical jobs can be performed manually until the equipment is functioning again. For obvious reasons, the preferred method is using identical hardware at another location. The failure of a real-time processing system for any length of time may mean starting over for certain areas, such as inventory and sales analysis. There is not sufficient time to enter all the information that is necessary to update the files, say for one week. This amounts to establishing a cutoff date and starting from there.

Documentation of alternative plans is the responsibility of the data processing manager and should be a part of the company's systems and procedures manual. It should state explicitly what the critical jobs are, how they are to be handled in case of equipment failure (use identical equipment at another location, manual methods, or some other data processing method), where compatible equipment is located (includes service bureaus), who will be responsible for each area during downtime, and what deadlines must be met during the emergency. A written manual of procedures concerning what steps must be undertaken will help expedite the unfavorable situation. Otherwise, panic conditions will result in the least efficient method being employed when time is of essence.

### Periodic Review of System for Improvements

*A periodic system's review for improvements considers these factors:*
- *examination of new system approaches*
- *evaluation of new equipment*
- *cost analysis of system*

Just after the system is installed, the data processing manager and his group should review the tangible and intangible systems benefits set forth in the exploratory survey report. The purpose of such a review is to verify that these benefits are, in fact, being achieved. Discussions with managers of operating areas being serviced will determine how well the new system is performing. Tangible benefits, such as clerical reduction and lower inventory, and intangible benefits of improved customer service and more managerial information are open for constructive criticism. Typical comments will be along the following lines: certain areas have been improved significantly, some are about the same, and others are not as good as before. The task of the data processing section, then, is to make the necessary adjustments to accomplish the quantitative and qualitative goals of the feasibility study. It may take from several months up to one year to effect the changes which include reprogramming the most frequently used programs for greater efficiency.

As time passes, the workload for the present data processing system increases. Factors that were not previously problems can become significant. Can the equipment run longer hours or should additional equipment be obtained? Can modification of methods and procedures be made to reduce processing time and cost? Can noncritical processing be shifted to another time? How does the time differential affect the manning of a real-time system that is operating within the continental limits of the United States? Answers to these questions must be evaluated by the data processing section through a periodic review of the existing system. The ultimate aim of such an investigation is system improvements. In essence, it may be necessary to undertake a feasibility study periodically in order to devise an optimum system for the firm's changed operating conditions.

*Examination of new system approaches may necessitate a new feasibility study when numerous changes are envisioned.*

***Examination of New System Approaches.*** Examination of new system approaches that lead to operational improvements must be explored by the data processing section. The reason should be obvious. Many systems projects are so complex that it is almost impossible to complete it in the most efficient manner for all functional areas the first time around. The efficiency of any large computer program is always open to question. Programming should be closely examined along with the inputs, files, common data base, methods, procedures, and outputs that are related to the program. Questions, such as can the input cutoff be set earlier through rescheduling of personnel and is there a need to redesign certain inputs, forms, and documents are typical ones for new input approaches that eventually affect programming. A common question for reducing equipment processing time centers around the ability of many computer programs to reference a common data base rather than maintain comparable or duplicated on-line or off-line files. The methods and procedures that route data for equipment processing and process them after machine processing are always open to question in terms of simplifying them. Can the regular work be separated initially from the exception items in order that each can be expedited faster and handled more accurately is another typical question. Regarding output, are the present reports and output adequate in view of the firm's growth, technological improvements, and increasing complexities of business? Numerous questions can be explored in areas that are related directly or indirectly to programming.

New system approaches should not be restricted to current applications, but to additional ones that seem promising in terms of changed conditions within and outside the firm. The areas that previously processed a low volume of data may have experienced a phenomenal growth, making them suitable for EDP equipment. A fundamental of data processing is that a computer operates best when handling large volumes of data. A promising area for review is a real-time management information system where data are stored on-line. Meaningful managerial reports can generally be prepared at a small additional cost since data are available at all times for processing. Also, operations research models for improving the firm's quantitative basis for decision making may be capable of utilizing the data stored on-line. The ability to access large volumes of current data as well as to compile statistics on the data changes occurring within the system provide new system approaches. An examination of these approaches may necessitate a new feasibility study when numerous changes are contemplated. This permits the implementation of a better system versus "patching" an existing system.

*Evaluation of new equipment may also lead to a new feasibility study.*

***Evaluation of New Equipment.*** Periodic review of the existing system for improvements includes keeping abreast of the latest developments in equipment. This refers not only to computers, but also to all related equipment. Even though the firm may utilize a small-, medium-, or large-scale computer with on-line capabilities for a real-time management information system, there is a constant parade of newer developments that can obsolete present equipment and are lower priced. New design concepts and circuitry permit the introduction of mini-computers, OCR equipment as input to a computer system, faster data communication equipment, and many other developments. If the past is any indication of the future, the introduction of new data processing equipment occurs at a faster rate than for most other industries.

One of the most significant trends in data processing equipment is to reduce the amount of clerical input activities and make them as automatic as possible. With increasing labor costs and need to handle complex business operations, time cannot be taken to keypunch and key verify data manually. The input/output terminals of a real-time processing system permits keeping the time element as low as possible. Unfortunately, this cannot be utilized by all firms due to the nature of their operations. Comparably fast and efficient equipment has been developed and will be further improved as time passes. Keying data from source document to magnetic tape and reading of printed and handwritten data with optical character recognition equipment are current examples. Developments will not be restricted to the firm, but equipment to handle supplier-manufacturer-distributor-retailer processing activities will be common in the future. The ultimate total system is the linking of all computer systems in the country for an electronic money system (to be discussed in Chapter 18).

*Periodically, the data processing manager compares the actual costs of the new system and estimated figures of the feasibility study. Unfavorable results need thorough investigation and appropriate action to remedy their causes.*

***Cost Analysis of System.*** New equipment developments are changing the cost of data processing. This is caused by the addition of many newer models whose capabilities and performance are better than previous models. Later computer models of the same generation and different generations of computers have proven this to be true. Even though internal hardware speeds are faster with increased miniaturization of circuitry and components, many computer programs are input- and/or output-bound, which means the new speeds of the central processor may be of no assistance in speeding up their operations. Thus the real criterion of lower data processing costs centers around throughput performance.

Estimated savings less estimated one-time costs and additional operating costs were computed for the estimated life of the new system in the exploratory survey report. Periodically, the data processing manager needs to compare these estimated figures with the actual amounts and evaluate the results with the firm's vice-president in charge of finance. The study's figures could be different from the actual results by a wide or narrow margin. Unfavorable deviations need assessment for possible courses of action to remedy the situation. It should be noted that fewer large differences are likely to occur when the data processing manager knows there will be a series of reviews, that is, a comparison of the estimated figures to actual amounts. Those data processing personnel who experience unfavorable results must be held accountable. For the most part, original estimates are stated realistically, but other factors have come into the picture that have distorted final results.

### Common Problems of Data Processing Systems

*Common problems encountered in undertaking a systems project revolve around the human element, that is, capabilities of personnel precede technical considerations.*

Tensions can run high within the data processing section of any firm when serious problems are confronting the group. Problem areas cover a wide range as set forth in Figure 15-8. An examination of this listing indicates that many of them can be attributed to the indifferences of top management. For this reason, top managers must set specific objectives that are focused on major business problems. Adequate resources in terms of personnel, equipment, and finances must be available as needed and all possible barriers must be removed for the systems project. Top management must take an active interest by reviewing and evaluating proposed plans, monitoring progress or lack thereof from beginning to end, and demanding results that are real and in conformity with the firm's objectives. Even though qualified systems personnel abound within the firm, they lack an overview of what must be done and lack the authority to make key decisions. In the final analysis, only management can make the new system a success since any firm can install newer equipment. The managerial and organizational aspects, then, must be handled effectively first before technical considerations can take on real meaning.

Common problems of installing newer systems do not stop at management, but are applicable to all personnel involved in the change. The need for capable personnel is necessary from the data processing manager down to the equipment operators. The cause of many system problems are average personnel who lack what it takes to accomplish the tasks successfully. The firm is better off with fewer capable people than many persons who occupy space. The extra cost of good personnel will more than pay for themselves in the form of tangible and intangible benefits from the new system. Only with qualified personnel can common problems become uncommon.

Failure to set realistic objectives based upon the existing conditions. Installation of data processing equipment requires goals, objectives, and schedules like any other business undertaking.
Lack of top management participation in the systems project. This usually results in superimposing a new system on the present one without significant changes.
Inadequate attention to the psychological factors of company personnel. The natural resistance to change and the impact of new equipment on their jobs must be taken into consideration.
Failure to evaluate available equipment properly. Hardware must be tailored to meet the needs of the system rather than the system tailored to the hardware's capabilities.
Breakdown in communications between the needs of the operating departments and the systems people. Frequent and constructive meetings between the two groups should alleviate this difficulty.
Under-utilization of equipment capability due to poor systems design and inadequately trained technical staff. Theoretical knowledge alone does not qualify one to cope with programming a sophisticated data processing system.
Inadequate monitoring of progress on the systems project. A well conceived plan provides adequate means of controlling the activities of the systems change.
Poor problem definition of individual computer programs. Incomplete definition of logic, inputs, files, common data base, outputs, and the like cause difficulty during the flowcharting and programming phases.
Failure to test programs adequately. This is caused by relegating the responsibility exclusively to the data processing section.
Inadequate documentation as the system project progresses. This can set the project back many months if there is a high rate of personnel turnover.
Poor supervision of conversion activities, in particular, file conversion. This may mean costly reworking to correct deficiencies or starting anew.
Inaccurate cost estimates in the exploratory survey report. Major causes of inaccuracy is an underestimation of time to program the various applications, convert from present system to new system, and process the programs on the equipment.
Poor selection of data processing personnel to implement the new system. Marginal data processing personnel should not be allowed to manage and program a complex system.
Ill-informed top management who have no concept of what is involved in the installation of a computer system. Top management should undergo some technical training to communicate effectively with the systems group.
Failure to incorporate adequate internal control in the new system and computer programs. This could make defrauding of the firm's assets possible as well as incorrect values being accumulated during the data processing flow.
Lack of operating personnel participation on problem areas and exception items. This results in a new systems design that does not reflect actual operating conditions.
Bypassing parallel operations in the hope that no problems will be encountered. The odds against this happening are extremely high.
Crashing a systems project results in a serious disservice to the firm. A crash program often produces serious long term effects and can adversely affect the firm's operations.

Figure 15-8 Common problems experienced when undertaking a systems project.

## SUMMARY

The final step of the feasibility study revolves around equipment selection. Bid requests or invitations which describe the important aspects of the new system provide the basis for receiving proposals from manufacturers. Proposals are, then, compared for selected criteria which have specific numerical values assigned to them. All things being equal, the manufacturer who has the highest score is awarded the contract. The ultimate responsibility for determining equipment, however, is not the manufacturer, but the user. The same is true for the advanced planning that is necessary to install the equipment.

Systems implementation begins after the formal signing of the equipment contract. While the feasibility study consists of three steps—exploratory survey including systems analysis, basic systems design, and equipment selection—systems implementation involves two steps—preparatory work and operation of new system with a provision for periodic review of systems improvements. Time for a typical systems project is one-third for the feasibility study and two-thirds for implementing the system. The number of operating personnel outside the data processing group is substantially increased for the latter phase. Also, the firm will experience high costs during systems conversion.

Programming and testing, the mainstay of the preparatory work phase, is time consuming and costly. Advanced programming techniques and programming languages should be utilized to assist in developing computer programs and reduce programming costs. Once a program has reached the operational stage, dual operations should be initiated to check for abnormal conditions that might have not been present during program testing. This phase culminates in conversion of all activities for daily operation. Consideration must be given to alternative plans in case of unforeseen difficulties during conversion as well as at a later date. Otherwise, the firm could be out of business temporarily.

Periodic review of the system should follow the installation which involves examination of new systems approaches, new equipment, and cost factors. Many times, an evaluation of the existing system may signal the need for a new feasibility study. In essence, the systems project cycle must start again. This permits making systems changes that reflect the existing business data processing environment.

## *QUESTIONS*

1. What are the steps involved in determining what data processing equipment the firm should procure?
2. Are there any problems associated with having various computer manufacturers draw up the new system specifications for a firm and having them submit bids on this basis?
3. What are the most important factors when selecting computer equipment?
4. In justifying a new system installation, is it a good idea to restrict company activities to the accounting function only? Explain.
5. (a) What kinds of personnel problems accompany the change from one system to another?
   (b) How can they be overcome?
6. Once the equipment order has been signed, what type of training problems are likely to occur? Explain.
7. Describe the kind of operating procedures that should be a part of efficient data processing.
8. (a) What programming difficulties can be experienced by the data processing section during the preparatory work phase?
   (b) Explain how each can be resolved.
9. How can the two major types of programming errors be located? Explain.
10. When installing a new computer system, what physical facilities are necessary?
11. How important is parallel operations for a simple computer program and a complex computer program? Explain.
12. Why should the firm review periodically its system for improvements? Explain.

## CHAPTER SIXTEEN

# Data Processing Systems Controls

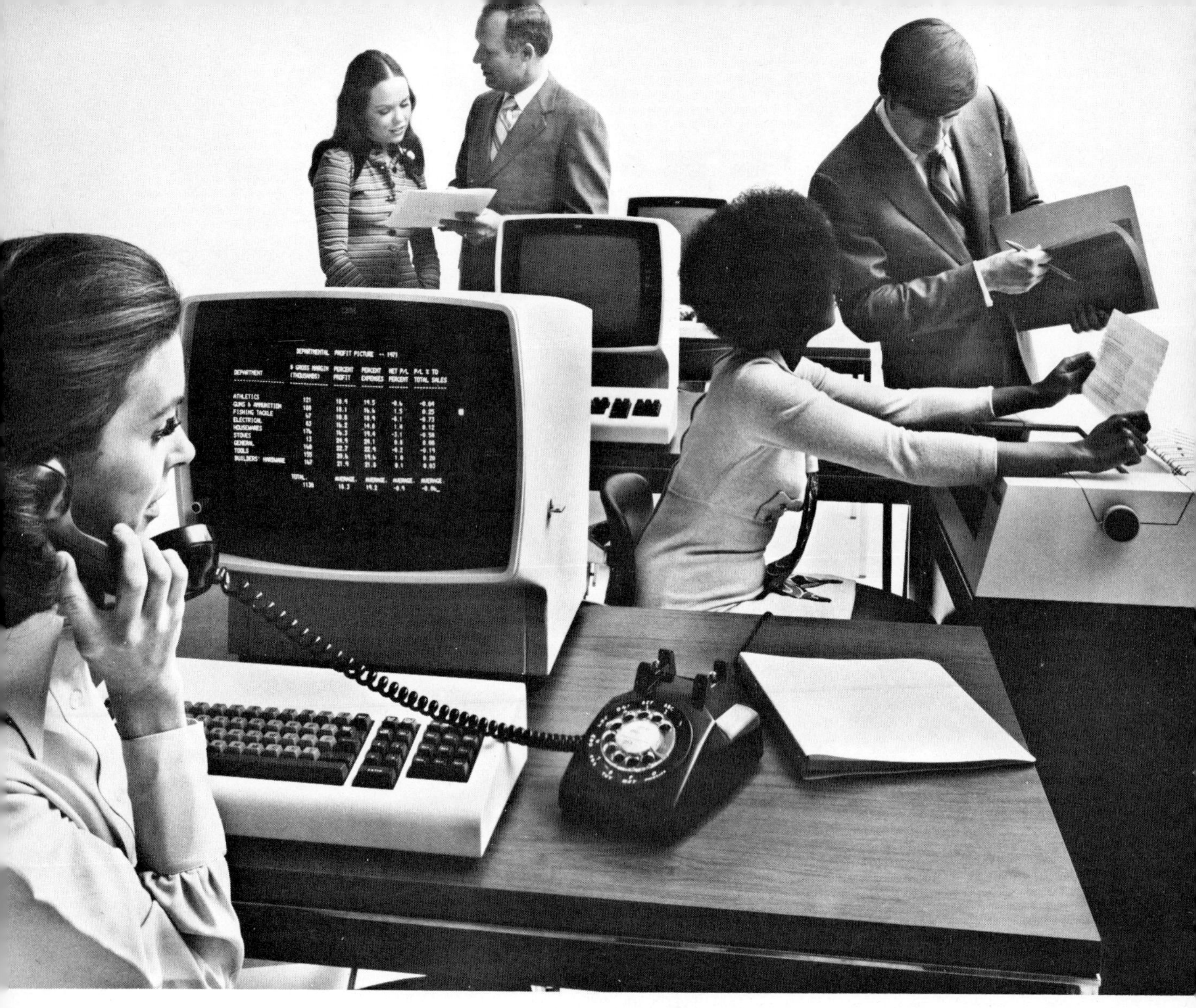


*For an accurate and reliable data processing system, internal control is required. As shown, the auditors work with the firm's employees when "auditing through the computer." (Courtesy International Business Machines Corporation.)*

Implementation of a systems project is not complete until adequate provision has been made for data processing systems controls. This need is more pronounced with advanced EDP equipment since fewer people will be involved in the new operation. The firm will rely more on machines than on people when processing data. Management must be assured that the new methods and procedures devised will control the required data in an accurate manner. Basically, this job is the responsibility of the systems designer who must consider internal control when finalizing the new system design. Failure of the systems designer to integrate internal control within the framework of the new system is an open invitation to future problems that could be detrimental to the system's success.

The individuals who have a special interest in the degree of internal control are the internal and external auditors, not to mention management, stockholders, creditors, and the government. They all want assurance that processed data are reliable when transmitted from one source to another. The establishment of control points for checking accuracy of processed information and the distribution of control over one specific area are vital for effective internal control. Controls for data processing systems are discussed along with the auditing procedures that are necessary to test the validity of transactions.

## NEED FOR ACCURACY

*There is great need for accuracy, otherwise, the Gigo principle predominates.*

With the complexities of the environment in which the firm must operate, the difficulties in achieving accuracy tend to increase. Newer methods and procedures must be invented to handle demands originating from adding new products, markets, or departments. This necessitates more control over inputs, files, methods, procedures, and outputs. The amount of accuracy and its related costs must be determined for these new operating conditions. The resulting errors and mistakes can be caused by the human element, incorrect instructions to personnel and machines, a malfunction of the equipment, or a combination of these at any stage from data origination through the reporting phase. Thus the systems designer must ascertain the reliability desired and devise the new system accordingly.

### Objective of Accuracy

*The objective of accuracy is to keep errors to a minimum and allow for their correction as detected.*

The objective of accuracy is to minimize the total costs associated with the detection and correction of errors as well as the extra costs caused by errors that are never corrected within the system. In contrast, eliminating all errors would be prohibitive in terms of cost. Additional personnel and machine time would be necessary to implement methods and procedures to test for 100% accuracy at the various data processing points. The systems designer must develop programs and procedures that keep errors to a minimum based on the cost constraints of the system and allow for correction after errors are detected. He must incorporate in the new systems design provisions for restarting when one or more errors are detected. Likewise, checks must be included in programs and procedures so that an undetected error(s) is (are) kept from producing erroneous results.

The relationship between the accuracy of information and its value to the firm is direct. When accuracy is low, its value to management is also small. As the degree of accuracy increases, the value of the information increases since it provides the required data for decision making. However, the value of information levels off as the point of 100% accuracy is approached. The rationale is that data used for decision making are not sensitive to marginal improvements for 100% accuracy. For this reason, the optimum accuracy for many firms is close to 100%, except for the accounting function which requires the highest accuracy for most of its activities.

The need for accuracy is quite apparent in outputs generated throughout the data processing system. Accurate reports serve as a sound basis for decision making while inaccurate ones may not. The degree of accuracy needed, then, is dependent upon the type of output. For example, a firm has an automatic inventory system whereby the computer automatically produces a reorder based on an economic ordering quantity. If the inventory on hand is different by two units from that stored on-line and the amount of the purchase order is 2000 units, the resulting inaccuracy of one-tenth of one percent is not critical. This inventory difference plus others will be adjusted as the inventory department makes their periodic check of physical quantities. Under these conditions, the firm can operate effectively with these minor differences. However, the same is not true for all activities of the firm. If the firm fails to post all sales invoices to their customer accounts, it is possible that an amount will never be paid. As with the two foregoing examples, a close look at the firm's outputs must be undertaken to determine the degree of accuracy needed.

### How Much Accuracy

*The amount of accuracy is dependent upon the requirements of the activity being studied.*

The question of how much accuracy is actually required to operate a reliable data processing system must be answered by the systems designer. A logical starting point is an examination of the firm's functional areas. The need for 100% accuracy in some areas will be apparent while the reverse will be true of other areas, as pointed out above. Activities, such as payroll, sales commissions, accounts receivable, and accounts payable, require the highest degree of accuracy. On the other hand, inaccuracies for low value inventory stock—cartons, supplies, and like items—can be tolerated since the cost of controlling these items is greater than their value. Based on these two extremes for accuracy, the systems designer needs a general guide. Basically, this is relating value of the data to the corresponding cost of obtaining it. The most desirable degree of accuracy is reached when the

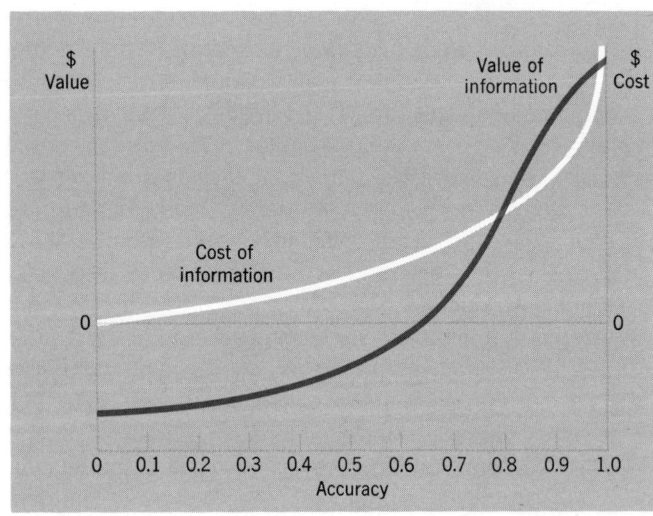


Figure 16-1 Relationship of value, cost, and accuracy to information. Accuracy can be increased up to the point where the value of information is still greater than its cost.

value exceeds the cost of acquiring the data by the greatest margin. Largely, output is produced up to the point where value derived from the information is still greater than its corresponding cost. (Figure 16-1).

In view of this value-cost relationship, the best methods for achieving a high degree of accuracy must: (1) eliminate most errors as they occur and (2) detect the remaining ones and provide the means for making the appropriate correction. The systems designer must develop control points to accomplish the degree of accuracy required. The receipt of payments by a large firm, for example, means establishing a control point for banking the firm's daily receipts. These same deposits must be balanced at a later time when posted to the customer accounts. Even though the control totals agree as the data move through the successive stages of the system (satisfies eliminating most errors when they first occur), there is still no assurance that the correct accounts were posted. The systems designer must make use of the self-checking digit or similar routines within the accounts receivable program so that all accounts are properly credited. Only in this manner will he be able to provide the accuracy required for a reliable system.

**Cost of Accuracy**

*Accuracy is desirable up to the point where the value of the information is still greater than its corresponding cost.*

The degree of accuracy, as indicated in Figure 16-1, depends upon the cost of obtaining the information and the value of having a certain percent of accuracy. Value for management is small or negative when accuracy of information is low. The rationale is that inaccurate information can lead to profit-losing decisions. As noted in the illustration, the value of information rises fast as the degree of accuracy increases, in particular, at the higher levels. More accurate information facilitates better decisions. However, as the value of information approaches perfect information, decision making is not sensitive to slight improvements of near-perfect accuracy.

*Generally, costs increase very fast as output accuracy goes beyond 95%.*

Costs increase rapidly for higher degrees of accuracy, in particular, as accuracy reaches 100%. The reason for costs growing at a faster rate when the degree of accuracy increases, say from 95 to 96%, is that more operations and control points must be set up for continuous checking of the data. Generally, costs increase very rapidly as output accuracy is pushed beyond the 95% point. The accuracy of keypunching data directly onto magnetic tape, for example, may be increased from 95 to 98% by having the operators reduce their rate of output. On the other hand, to increase keypunching accuracy even further requires extensive verification. In essence, costs increase at a much faster rate when the last mistake is eliminated.

In the preceding section, the accounts receivable example indicated the higher costs associated with 100% accuracy. Even in this area, it is possible to design a system with less than 100% accuracy. Instead of spending money on procedures that require the detail to equal the control figures, some firms employ accounts receivable adjusters to handle customer complaints on errors not corrected as the data are processed. This cost is considerably less than those programs and procedures which give 100% accuracy. The important point here or for any other activity of the firm is that increased accuracy adds to the cost of originating and processing the data. It is the job of the systems designer to devise a new system that meets the accuracy and cost requirements set forth by management. In absence of a company policy on this matter, a general rule is to increase accuracy up to the point where the benefit derived from the level of accuracy is still greater than its cost.

## INTERNAL CONTROL

*A desired goal of internal control is to promote overall efficiency and control of the data processing system.*

Once the systems designer has resolved the problem of how much reliability the new system will require, he is in a position to incorporate the necessary internal control into his systems design work that meets prescribed levels of accuracy. Even though the systems designer is not an accountant, he must be cognizant of the essential elements of internal control. Internal control, as defined by the American Institute of Certified Public Accountants, comprises the plan of organization and all of the coordinate methods and measures within a business to:

1. safeguard its assets,
2. check the accuracy and reliability of accounting data,
3. promote operational efficiency and encourage adherence to prescribed managerial policies.

This three-part division of internal control is referred to, respectively, as:

1. internal check,
2. internal accounting control,
3. internal administrative control.

A comprehensive system of internal control extends beyond the finance and accounting function. It includes promoting operational efficiency in the data processing system and control over the operating programs and procedures. In fact, all information developed by the system is covered by the concept of internal control.

Ideally, the ultimate in internal control is achieved when its essential parts are an integral part of the methods and procedures in processing the firm's data. The self-correcting mechanism of the system allows the data processing personnel to take appropriate action when errors, mistakes, or equipment malfunctions arise. In such a system, the amount of internal and external auditing is kept to a minimum. The adequacy of internal control, then, has a direct bearing on the amount of auditing required and serves as a measure of the system's effectiveness in following prescribed procedures.

### Internal Check

*Internal check is the segregation of functional responsibilities in order to safeguard the firm's assets against defalcation.*

Internal check is concerned with safeguarding the firm's assets against defalcation. It may be in the form of accounting procedures, physical controls, or other means that allow for the segregation of functional responsibilities. No matter what approach is used, the separation of data processing functions permits no one individual to have complete control over one area or activity of the firm. However, the use of computers tends to reduce the amount of activities that can be separated since many are under the control of the equipment itself and fewer workers are involved. Nevertheless, internal control procedures can be devised that will safeguard the assets of the firm.

Many firms utilizing EDP equipment have experienced large defalcations in the areas of payroll and inventory. This has been caused by the computer programmer who operates the program that he has written. If he has complete control, he can build a loophole into the system and carry out his fraudulent schemes. An example is a computer programmer who runs the weekly payroll program. He can create payroll checks for fictitious employees (removes checks before turning them over to a designated company employee), can pay extra overtime and wages to himself, and can deduct a few cents of income tax from every employee in the plant for payment to himself. Another example where the combination computer programmer and operator can steal without being caught is changing a few instructions in the computer inventory program. The machine can be made to report high inventory losses as normal merchandise breakage, enabling accomplices in the plant to take large amounts of goods from the firm's warehouses without the theft being noticed.

The problem of safeguarding the firm's assets has become more acute with real-time systems since data, such as inventory and supplies, are constantly changing. It is difficult for the auditors to reconstruct specific data for an audit trail, not to mention reconstructing what goes on inside the machine. In view of these existing conditions, the systems designer must keep several points in mind when devising data processing activities. These are set forth in Figure 16-2.

1. Establish the data processing section as a separate unit which has no direct control over the firm's assets—power to disburse funds, control over inventory, and so forth. This reduces attempts on the part of company programmers and machine operators to engage in fraudulent activity since several persons must be involved.
2. Require that systems specialists and programmers, equipment operators, and record librarians be distinct and separate groups.
3. Provide for the transfer of computer programmers and operators frequently to different machines and programs. The rationale is that the individual is less likely to undertake changes in the program or the data being processed.
4. Have a periodic surprise audit of the computer room where details are checked out thoroughly for irregularities. The fact that their work can be checked at any time is a deterrent to fraudulent activity.
5. Set up checking procedures to verify that data received by the user are accurate. This requirement can be accomplished by comparing batch totals as the data are processed.
6. Use any other means that is economically feasible to assign personnel to check on the activities of each other. The more persons involved in one activity lowers the possible collusion.
7. Require fidelity bonds for all data processing personnel in positions of trust.

Figure 16-2 Recommended procedures for effective internal check—safeguarding the firm's assets.

Several firms have built into their systems a means of printing out audit information. A computer executive audit routine is utilized that spots seeming irregularities in operating procedures which immediately triggers a printout of the questionable transaction for the auditor to examine. The output of the computer's console typewriter is locked and under the control of the internal auditor. Another method involves feeding test data into a computer and checking to determine whether anything interfered with the routine processing. The net effect of either approach is internal checking on the data processing system.

### Internal Accounting Control

*Internal accounting control checks the accuracy and reliability of data processed by the system.*

The systems analyst must devise methods and procedures that provide for internal accounting control. Accounting controls that check the accuracy and reliability of data processed by the system must be an integral part of the system. At certain control points in the system, batch totals, subtotals, grand totals, hash totals, record counts, count of prenumbered documents, or a combination of these are used to check the accuracy as data are moved from one stage to another. Within the data processing system, accounting control can be performed using manual methods, mechanical equipment, or electronic machines. The approach for checking accuracy and reliability of data is contingent upon the system designed.

The amount of processing performed at one time differs greatly for manual, punched card, and computer systems. Manual systems have a great need for more control points since their processing ability is limited. The output at one stage serves as input for the next stage. Since processing is performed for one small stage at a time, intermediate totals become an integral part of the audit trail. Much the same approach is utilized when designing a punched card system. However, the same cannot be said for computer systems since reliance is placed on hardware and software and not on people. More processing is performed at a time which results in fewer stages for intermediate totals. Many times intermediate results are not available in a readable format since they may be contained on a magnetic disk, drum, or tape file. However, printouts should be incorporated into the new systems design for internal control purposes.

Essential characteristics of internal accounting control can be classified as:

1. control total techniques,
2. control by comparison,
3. control by authorizations and approvals.

Each control technique is explained below.

*Control total techniques assure accurate processing of data from one processing run to another.*

***Control Total Techniques.*** Control total techniques assures that data have been processed accurately. Although the systems designer provides batching techniques and similar methods at various control points for noncomputer activities, computers require a different approach since they provide a means for obtaining unprecedented accuracy. Although computer control totals may no longer be needed to assure processing accuracy, they are still required to check accurate transmission of data from one processing run to another within the computer room as well as to and from the computer equipment.

*Control by comparison checks the accuracy of data by logical decisions.*

***Control by Comparison.*** Control by comparison takes a variety of forms. Comparisons can be made manually between vendor's invoices and receiving department reports to verify the receipt of materials, cash receipts can be compared with accounts receivable to determine the accuracy of incoming receipts, and so forth. Likewise, the computer can make logical decisions for a greater than, equal to, or less than condition which allows it to check the data as they are processed.

*Control by authorizations and approvals serves as a basis for acceptance or rejection of data being processed.*

***Control by Authorizations and Approvals.*** Control by authorizations and approvals can be performed manually or electronically. The most promising area is the computer with its logical comparative ability. Since the computer has been programmed for a set of predetermined criteria, it serves as a basis for acceptance or rejection. In effect, the computer is capable of performing routine tasks. These include reordering raw materials, checking the customer's credit status, approving vendors' invoices, and disbursing checks. By no means do the foregoing activities exhaust the computer's potential for control by authorization and approval.

When devising internal accounting control procedures, the systems designer must give preference to the outstanding features of the equipment contemplated and the system under consideration. He should not think in terms of the system's accuracy and reliability as the controlling factor during the basic systems design phase. On the other hand, he should not ignore requirements for internal accounting control. Otherwise, the Gigo principle may predominate.

It should be noted that the best time for reviewing the adequacy of accounting controls is during the basic systems design phase. The internal and external auditors can make suggestions at this time for improved controls to be built into the methods, procedures, and programs. These suggestions may be extremely expensive to implement if they are developed after the new system is in operation.

### Internal Administrative Control

*Internal administrative control promotes operational efficiency of the firm and encourages adherence to prescribed managerial policies. It is evaluated by a management audit questionnaire.*

Administrative controls comprise the plan of organization and all methods and procedures which are concerned with operational efficiency and adherence to managerial policies. They are distinguishable from the other two areas of internal control discussed previously since they originate in and are an essential part of all operating departments other than just finance or accounting. A popular method for reviewing the adequacy of internal administrative control with respect to the data processing system is a management audit. The emphasis in a management audit is on the location of problem areas. Its purpose is to identify those areas that require improvement through further detailed study. The management audit, then, is an interview tool for determining weaknesses. It forms the basis for making suggestions and recommendations for improving the firm's operations.

As in the case of internal check and internal accounting control, the basis of the investigation for a management audit is a questionnaire. (Reference can be made to any auditing textbook for contents of the questionnaire on internal check and internal accounting control.) The questions are so constructed that a "yes" answer indicates a favorable point while a "no" response is unfavorable. Most questionnaires provide ample room to explain a no answer since this represents a weakness that must be investigated. Many times, the question asked will not be applicable. In such cases, the column for "N.A." is checked. The answering of all questions provides a framework for a comprehensive evaluation of the firm.

*Management audit questionnaire for evaluating the functional areas of an EDP system includes:*
*I comprehensive evaluation of the entire company*
*II marketing*
*III manufacturing*
*IV finance and accounting*

Even though the management audit questionnaire includes a broad survey of the entire firm, discussion will be limited to those questions that apply to an electronic data processing system. A listing of sample questions that is effective for evaluating such a system is found in Figure 16-3. A review of these questions reveals the relationship of electronic data processing to its major functional areas. While the objective of any data processing system is to assist management in making decisions for the various areas of the firm, the function of the electronic data processing equipment is to go one step further by providing information on a timely and analytical basis. Correctly organized information available for the right people in any functional area is required. The objective of the management audit for internal administrative control, then, is to determine that the firm is realizing optimum utilization of its computer facility for operational efficiency; and that well-designed functional applications that adhere to managerial policies are meeting management information and control needs.

Although the questionnaire includes the major functional areas of the firm, specific questions relating to the EDP system itself and its equipment are excluded. A questionnaire (Figure 16-7) that complements the questions found in Figure 16-3 will be covered in a subsequent section of this chapter since it is a study of its own. Evaluation of the system's operational efficiency and its adherence to managerial policies is not required for certification of the firm's financial statements by the outside auditors. However, a questionnaire for evaluating internal check and internal accounting control is a part of the certified audit and forms the basis for the auditor's annual internal control letter to accounting and financial management.

## COMPUTER SYSTEMS CONTROLS

*Computer systems controls are applicable to all types of EDP systems.*

Data processing controls are applicable to both manual and punched card systems. The traditional questionnaires (with minor modification for a punched card system) provide an excellent way of evaluating the firm's internal control. However,

| | Yes | No | N.A. |
|---|---|---|---|
| I. Comprehensive Evaluation of the Entire Company. | | | |
| A. Organization: | | | |
| • Is data processing a separate department? | ____ | ____ | ____ |
| • Is the data processing system workload balanced? | ____ | ____ | ____ |
| • Is there a means of measuring the system's throughput performance? | ____ | ____ | ____ |
| • Are methods and procedures documented, communicated, understood, and followed? | ____ | ____ | ____ |
| • Is there an internal audit function performed to check compliance with the system's methods and procedures? | ____ | ____ | ____ |
| B. Long Range Planning: | | | |
| • Is there a standing plan for reviewing the EDP system to determine its operational efficiency? | ____ | ____ | ____ |
| • Is there a method of keeping key data processing personnel updated on new equipment developments? | ____ | ____ | ____ |
| • Is the data processing system meeting the long range needs of the firm? | ____ | ____ | ____ |
| • Is there an adequate equipment replacement plan? | ____ | ____ | ____ |
| C. Reporting: | | | |
| • Are computer reports being used by all managers at all levels for planning, performance evaluation, and control? | ____ | ____ | ____ |
| • Are managers satisfied with the computer reports? | ____ | ____ | ____ |
| • Are the number of reports worth the time and cost of preparation? | ____ | ____ | ____ |
| • Are reports: | | | |
| Timely? | ____ | ____ | ____ |
| Simple? | ____ | ____ | ____ |
| Standardized? | ____ | ____ | ____ |
| • Is the "exception principle" used to highlight favorable and unfavorable variances above a stated percent? | ____ | ____ | ____ |
| • Can something be done to speed up the reporting process? | ____ | ____ | ____ |
| • Is an organizational responsibility reporting used in preparing computer reports? | ____ | ____ | ____ |
| D. Budgeting: | | | |
| • Are company objectives, plans, and EDP system programs well understood so that they can be implemented in budgets? | ____ | ____ | ____ |
| • Is the budget an integral part of the total EDP system? | ____ | ____ | ____ |
| • Are budgets regularly updated by the data processing section for changing conditions? | ____ | ____ | ____ |
| • Are actual results processed on-line against budgeted figures in order that large variances can be investigated and necessary action taken? | ____ | ____ | ____ |
| E. Other: | | | |
| • Are mathematical techniques of operations research that lend themselves to computer manipulation being used? | ____ | ____ | ____ |
| • Is EDP equipment utilized in the firm's R & D programs? | ____ | ____ | ____ |
| • Are training programs adequate for understanding and operating the EDP system? | ____ | ____ | ____ |
| • Are data processing personnel competent in their respective areas? | ____ | ____ | ____ |
| • Has adequate consideration been given to contracting outside software services? | ____ | ____ | ____ |
| II. Marketing: | | | |
| A. Are computer sales forecasting techniques utilized by the firm? | ____ | ____ | ____ |

Figure 16-3 Management audit questionnaire—sample questions for evaluating the functional areas of an electronic data processing system.

| | Yes | No | N.A. |
|---|---|---|---|
| B. Are computer reports prepared showing contribution to fixed costs and profits by products and product lines? | ____ | ____ | ____ |
| C. Is there a market research program for utilizing the computer and its related equipment? | ____ | ____ | ____ |
| D. Is there a computer program to determine if the present sales mix is maximizing the firm's profits? | ____ | ____ | ____ |
| E. Does a sales order within the computer system automatically record the inventory change and issue a restocking order? | ____ | ____ | ____ |
| F. Is the present EDP system giving adequate customer service? | ____ | ____ | ____ |
| G. Are lost sales analyzed by the computer to determine why? | ____ | ____ | ____ |
| III. Manufacturing: | | | |
| A. Is there a centralized computer production control system? | ____ | ____ | ____ |
| B. Is there a computerized quality control program? | ____ | ____ | ____ |
| C. Can excessive inventories be reported periodically by the EDP system? | ____ | ____ | ____ |
| D. Has a computer program been undertaken to balance the cost generated by too small of an inventory against the cost of carrying excessive inventories in order to determine an optimum inventory turnover? | ____ | ____ | ____ |
| E. Are proper computer controls maintained for finished goods leaving the plant? | ____ | ____ | ____ |
| F. Have seasonal variation been programmed on the computer for determining inventory levels? | ____ | ____ | ____ |
| G. Have EOQ formulas been programmed in the computer system for the more critical and high volume items? | ____ | ____ | ____ |
| IV. Finance and Accounting: | | | |
| A. Are computerized financial statements prepared on a timely and meaningful basis? | ____ | ____ | ____ |
| B. Are statistical economic and financial reports prepared by the computer to supplement the balance sheet and income statement? | ____ | ____ | ____ |
| C. Is the cash flow forecast an output of the computer system? | ____ | ____ | ____ |
| D. Is there an effective computerized cost reduction program? | ____ | ____ | ____ |
| E. Is internal check and internal accounting control effective in the EDP system? | ____ | ____ | ____ |
| F. Is there a computer program for aging accounts receivable? | ____ | ____ | ____ |
| G. Does the computerized cost accounting system permit evaluation of individuals, jobs, processes, and the like? | ____ | ____ | ____ |

Figure 16-3 (*continued*)

traditional questionnaires must be updated to include computer systems that make use of batch and real-time processing. This was accomplished in Figure 16-3 for the firm's major functional areas which is actually part of the management audit questionnaire. A questionnaire will be developed in a subsequent section of this chapter for evaluating an electronic data processing system by itself without specific reference to the firm's functional areas.

Before an evaluation of internal control in an EDP system can be undertaken, it is necessary to explore the various types of controls. They include:

1. EDP department controls,
2. input controls,

3. programmed controls,
4. output controls,
5. on-line (real-time) controls,
6. hardware controls,
7. security controls.

The above listing and their component parts, shown in Figure 16-4, form a sound basis for evaluating internal control in an electronic data processing system.

*EDP Department Controls*
- Organization
- Methods and procedures

*Input Controls*
- Verification methods
  Key verification, visual verification, self-checking numbers, and tabular listings.
- Input control totals
  Batch controls, hash totals, and record count totals
- External labels

*Programmed Controls*
- Validation checks and tests
  Sequence checks, character mode tests, self-checking digit tests, limit checks, code validity tests, blank transmission tests, alteration tests, and check points
- Computer control totals
  Batch controls, hash totals, record count totals, balancing controls, cross-footing balance checks, zero balancing, and proof figures
- Internal labels
- Error routines

*Output Controls*
- Output control totals
  Batch controls, hash totals, and record count totals
- Control by exception
- Control over operator intervention

*On-Line (Real-Time) Controls*
- On-line processing controls
  Message identification, message transmission control, and message parity check
- Data protection controls
  Supervisory protection programs, lockwords, and authority lists
- Diagnostic controls

*Hardware Controls*
Parity checks, duplicate circuitry, echo checks, dual heads, overflow check, and sign check

*Security Controls*
Program control, equipment log, records control, tape rings, and preventive maintenance

Figure 16-4 Detailed outline of various controls used in evaluating internal control for an electronic data processing system.

*There is a hierarchy of computer system controls, depicted in Figure 16-5.*

The relationship of data processing systems controls to a computer is illustrated in Figure 16-5. Many of these controls center around the accurate and efficient processing of data. Even though input may be 100% accurate, output is conditioned upon the proper manipulation and handling of data within the program. For effective internal control in this area, programmers must have full knowledge of what these controls are and how they should be incorporated within a program. Otherwise, considerable program rework may be necessary after the program is considered operational.

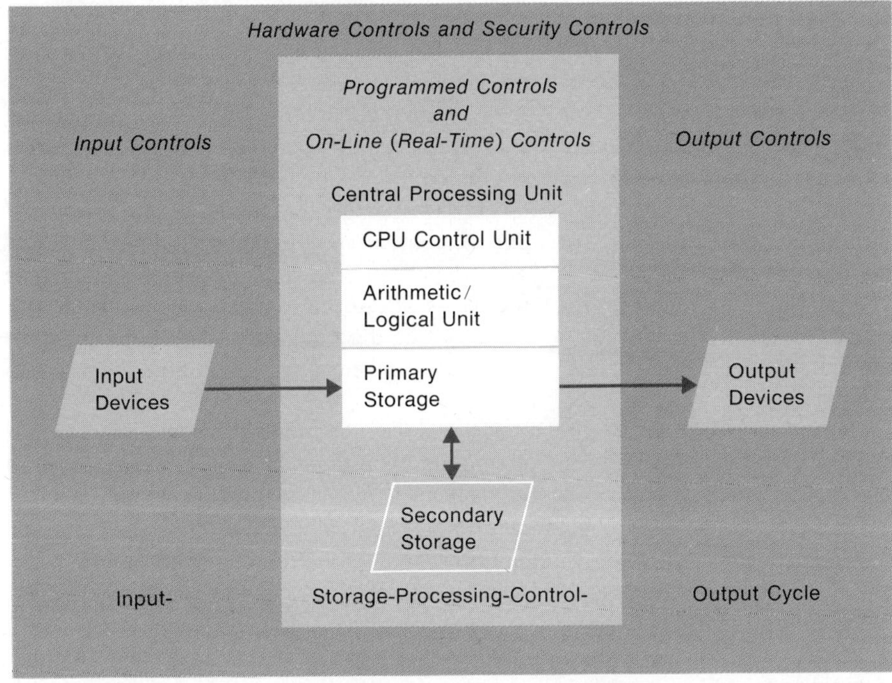


Figure 16-5 Relationship of data processing systems controls to a computer and the input-storage-processing-control-output (ISPCO) cycle.

*I. EDP department controls include those of:*
- *organization*
- *methods and procedures*

## EDP Department Controls

EDP department controls center around the data processing organization and its methods and procedures. The purpose of evaluating these two areas is to determine the department's operational efficiency or lack thereof. Lack of effective internal control here indicates potential problems in its related parts, as shown in Figure 16-5.

***Organization.*** The organization of the data processing department is usually the first section included in an internal control questionnaire for evaluating EDP. The relationship of data processing personnel to one another is scrutinized for possible collusion. Likewise, those personnel who program and operate computer programs they have written are investigated thoroughly. Effective internal control dictates that EDP organizational activities be separate and distinct from one another.

***Methods and Procedures.*** Methods and procedures within the EDP department are evaluated basically in light of standardization and documentation. Questions are asked concerning the established procedures in handling systems and operational activities. Of great importance is the degree of documentation practiced by the department. Too often, this important aspect is ignored by systems personnel in favor of more challenging EDP tasks. Poor internal control in EDP methods and procedures is a reflection on the department's management.

*II. Input controls that handle data before computer processing center around:*
- *verification methods*
- *input control totals*
- *external labels*

## Input Controls

Control of computer input data is defined as the procedural controls necessary to handle data outside the computer area. Extreme care must be undertaken in the handling of this data since input data are the most probable source of errors in the entire data processing system. If errors are created anywhere between the origination point and input into the computer equipment, they will be carried forward throughout the entire system. In order to keep errors to a minimum, the following procedural controls over input data are available for an EDP installation: verification methods, control totals, and external labels.

***Verification Methods.*** Some degree of input verification is absolutely necessary for consistently reliable results. The extent and methods employed are best determined by comparing the level of undetected errors against the cost of verification. Only in this manner can verification devices assure the accuracy and validity of input data. Several methods of input verification were given in Chapter 2. These included *key verification, visual verification, self-checking numbers,* and *tabular listings*. Although these verification devices are not associated electronically with the EDP system, they are just as important as the computer itself. Their function is to check the accuracy of raw data that are converted into a computer acceptable language.

***Input Control Totals.*** Control totals that aid in determining the accuracy of input data are generally obtained from adding machine tapes or from totals established in originating departments. Careful systems design can provide a high level of accuracy with very little additional effort and expense. Control totals (batch totals, hash totals, and record count totals) are usually taken on batches or groups of source documents. Batching with a control total is the most common method for insuring input accuracy.

*Batch controls* refer to source documents that are accumulated into batches, constituting feasible groups for processing data. The number of items within a batch should be limited in size so that reconciliation of discrepancies can be handled in an efficient manner. Generally, batches of approximately one hundred transactions are a convenient size. The transactions within the batch should be as homogeneous as possible since this provides compatibility for control totals. If volume necessitates the use of many batches, it may be advisable to have the batch number in all input data in order to permit reconciliation, especially after the continuity of the batch has been lost. Batch control totals should be attached to related input data when forwarded for processing. Consideration should also be given to computer verification of batch controls. Provision in the computer program allows for proving the detail against the control totals.

*Hash totals* may be used for control purposes where batch totals—dollars or units—cannot be calculated. They are items that are not normally added together, such as, account numbers, employee numbers, and unit prices. Hash totals represent totals of some data field which is common to all documents in the batch.

*Record count totals* can be found in several forms depending on the data processing system in use. Prenumbered forms are a type of record count because of the computer's ability to control them. Serial numbers of documents, such as vouchers and requisitions which constitute input, might be introduced along with account codes, quantities, and similar data for storage within the computer. At designated intervals, serial numbers of those documents that have not been processed, but should have been, can be determined by the computer program for immediate follow-up. This input technique assures that all data are processed through the computer system.

Minimum control for any data processing system should be some type of input count, such as a transaction count or a card count. This independent count assures that all input data have been processed off-line and are ready for computer processing. Record counts can also be used to check the accuracy of the data processed on-line. Likewise, record counts that are carried at the end of each on-line file can be compared before the computer program is terminated. This insures that file data are transferred from one source to another without loss of records.

***External Labels.*** External labels, another form of input controls, are visible ones attached to a magnetic tape or magnetic disk. Certain identifying information can be written on the tape or disk label. Information that may be a part of the label includes: name of run, type of information, density, reel number, number of reels in the file, frequency of use, date created, drive number, earliest date it might be reused, record count, and the individual's name responsible for the magnetic tape or disk. Thus the purpose of external labels is to make sure that the correct input file is being processed by the computer operator and data are not destroyed prematurely.

*III. Programmed controls for data being processed under computer control are:*
- *validation checks and tests*
- *computer control totals*
- *internal labels*
- *error routines*

**Programmed Controls**

A high degree of programmed controls is always advisable on the computer since undetected errors can have serious and far-reaching consequences. Programmed control steps should be included as a part of the machine's internally stored instructions. The extent of controls depends upon the increased costs in programming and machine time versus the related factor of increased accuracy. In addition to this consideration, the extent of on-line programmed controls includes the programming ability of the data processing section, the requirements of the particular run, and the capabilities of the equipment. Since most computer applications are slowed down by the speeds of input/output units, the central processor has generally more than sufficient time to perform the necessary control checks. Based on this consideration, the number of programmed controls is dependent upon the amount of program memory available. If sufficient space is available for program instructions, the programmer should include as many controls as is necessary. They can be classified as follows: validation checks and tests, computer control totals, internal labels, and error routines.

***Validation Checks and Tests.*** Validation comprises a series of checks and tests that can be applied to verify input, file, and calculated data during the computer processing run. It includes sequence checks, character mode tests, self-checking digit tests, limit checks, code validity tests, blank transmission tests, alteration tests, and check points. The inclusion of all or part of these processing controls is contingent upon the program itself.

*Sequence checks* are incorporated into a computer program so that data are checked for ascending or descending sequence while being processed. Data might be identified by customer number, inventory number, or another acceptable basis for processing. This programmed approach highlights data out of sequence, occurrence of duplicate numbers, and gaps in the sequence of processing.

*Character mode tests* are extremely valuable before manipulating data within the computer program. Fields that must contain numeric, alpha, zero, special characters, or some combination can be checked internally against a transaction code lookup table in order to detect erroneous data before executing detailed computer instructions. These tests are a must when working with programs calling for 100% accuracy. Addition of numeric and alphabetic data results in incorrect totals as with some other character combinations since their bit configurations are different.

*Self-checking digit tests* (covered in Chapter 2) should be verified by the computer, using the same formula as for input checking. Approximately 95% reliability can be expected. This technique is used extensively for code numbers that are recorded initially by hand and later converted into a machine acceptable language. As with most validation tests, provision should be made for reporting incorrect errors when located.

*Limit checks,* sometimes called *reasonableness tests* or *tolerance checks,* can be incorporated as part of a computer program. These are magnitude tests designed to determine whether processed data fall within predetermined limits. When processed data exceed or are less than these established value limits, the machine can be instructed to handle these exception items. Limits, for example, can be set for maximum and minimum levels of inventory, largest dollar amount for a payroll period, and highest amount of credit extension to a customer. Limit checks also include checking the capacity of equipment accumulators or registers when performing arithmetic calculations.

*Code validity tests* involve the testing of significant code numbers to establish their validity. The computer program will reject invalid codes by comparing the number of the input data with a list of existing accounts or file numbers stored within the computer's memory. For example, an invalid employee number that is read by the high-speed reader cannot be located within the payroll master file.

*Blank transmission tests* are utilized to monitor data fields at transfer points for blank or zero positions. They might be used to detect the loss of data and prevent the destruction of existing records in file storage.

*Alteration tests* indicate the failure to update a file properly. This can be determined by comparing the contents of the file before and after each posting.

*Check points* permit the computer to restart processing from the last check point rather than from the beginning of a run in the event of an error, an irregularity, or an interruption in the program. This can mean a considerable savings of time and money for extremely long processing runs. The best time to establish check points is during the flowcharting and programming phase. A typical check point procedure requires that processed data be dumped periodically into a temporary storage area that is available for immediate processing if a restart is necessitated.

***Computer Control Totals.*** Computer control totals are a continuation of the input control techniques described previously, which are: *batch controls, hash totals,* and *record count totals.* Errors uncovered by any one of these control techniques during computer processing may be handled as the program requires. The entire group of data may be rejected immediately, or it may be allowed to pass through for current processing. In the latter case, it is customary to store the error conditions and report it externally as a printout. There are additional computer totaling techniques that provide procedural control during processing. These are balancing controls, cross-footing balance checks, zero balancing, and proof figures.

*Balancing controls,* which are normally included in many accounting computer programs, are comparable to those used in controlling manual processing procedures. Beginning balances plus and minus the respective transactions produce a new ending balance for each record. The total of new balances for all records should agree with the manual control totals. Inventory, accounts receivable, accounts payable, and payroll are applications that rely on this computer control technique.

*Cross-footing balance checks,* long used by the accountants, are employed to check the accuracy of individual footings. This is accomplished by adding all figures in a horizontal direction and, then, in a vertical direction. When the computer has completed these footings, the sum of the horizontal totals should equal the sum of the vertical totals.

*Zero balancing* is a method to insure that a multiplication has been correctly calculated. The value of $x$ times $y$ equals $z$ may be checked by multiplying $y$ times $x$ and subtracting this value from $z$ to prove that the result is zero. Another method is adding a series of figures two different ways (see cross-footing balance checks above) and subtracting one from another for a resulting zero to determine the answer's correctness.

*Proof figures* can be used to check a series of multiplications. An arbitrary figure, larger than a multiplier, is selected. Each multiplicand is multiplied once by its true multiplier. It is then multiplied by the difference between the multiplier and the proof figure. Upon completion of a series of multiplications, the total of the products resulting from both multiplications is compared with the product of the total of the multiplicands and the proof figure. They should be equal.

***Internal Labels.*** The internal label of a magnetic disk or tape is an extension of the external data label. Certain identifying information can be written on the disk or tape. It is under the control of the computer program in the form of a lead record. Before actual computer processing begins, the program reads the lead record to ascertain that the correct magnetic disk pack or magnetic tape has been mounted on the proper input equipment. If the computer stops and indicates an incorrect input disk or tape, one of two possible errors could occur—either the wrong input device was utilized or the external label does not correspond to the internal label.

***Error Routines.*** There are several ways of handling error routines. The most common method is to treat the error routine as an integral part of the internally stored program. If errors are detected as a result of the validation checks, processing tests, and computer control totals, the program can instruct the computer to store the data, punch a data card, print the data, or to initialize some other method for bringing the error condition to light for external handling and correction. Under no circumstances would the processing run be halted. This is in contrast to other error routines which halt the computer for major problems. Examples for halting the computer are: magnetic tape file is out of sequence, input cards are out of sequence, magnetic bits of data are being lost, or incorrect magnetic disk is being addressed.

### Output Controls

*IV. Output controls that check reliability of computer results are:*
- *output control totals*
- *control by exception*
- *control over operator intervention*

The role of the computer as a center of control is accentuated even more when output controls are present. While input controls insure that all data are processed, output controls assure that results are reliable. The latter promotes operational efficiency over programs, processed data files, and machine operations. Output controls also insure that no unauthorized alterations have been made to data when under the control of the EDP equipment. They can be classified as follows: output control totals, control by exception, and control over operator intervention.

***Output Control Totals.*** The major categories for output control totals, which are set forth under input and programmed controls above, are essential for control of output data. The most basic of all output controls is the comparison of *batch control totals* with figures that preceded the computer processing stage. If the batch totals are in agreement, the output data must represent input data that have been processed accurately. In the absence of batch control totals for certain programs, the comparison of *output hash totals* or *record count totals* to predetermined figures will substantiate the validity of the data. No matter what output approach is used for control totals, the job of checking their accuracy belongs to the internal auditor or a designated employee.

Periodically, a computer processing audit should be made by the auditor of selected individual items. Individual transactions are traceable from the originating department, through the computer, and its related files, and finally to output control totals. Such tests assure that data are being processed accurately and in accordance with the firm's methods and procedures. More will be said about the auditing aspects of a batch processing system and on-line real-time systems in a latter part of this chapter.

***Control By Exception.*** The individuals responsible for output control would likewise be responsible for investigating exceptions. These exceptions could include recurring errors, excessive inventories, sales to customers who have exceeded their credit limit, higher prices for raw material purchases, and deviations from established sales prices. If computer programs are properly designed and programmed for controlling routine items and exceptions, time can be spent on the exceptional data for more effective decision making. Most advanced EDP systems make great use of this output control technique.

***Control Over Operator Intervention.*** Control over operator intervention is a problem common to all computer facilities. Generally, programmed controls do not prevent the console operator from interrupting the data being processed and manually introducing information via the computer console. Even if the internally stored program does possess a routine for printing out all information introduced, the operator still is able to suppress the printout on the console typewriter. However, if the typewriter is discovered turned off, the operator would immediately be suspect. In those systems where changes can be effected without a hard copy record, the need for supervising the computer's operation increases. However, research has indicated that unauthorized console interventions are kept to a minimum where there is rotation of computer operators and, in particular, when output controls are exercised over all computer printouts. Again, the need for effective internal check and internal accounting control are apparent.

### On-Line (Real-Time) Controls

*V. On-line (real-time) controls which center around the requirements of the system, the equipment, and security specifications include:*

- *on-line processing controls*
- *data protection controls*
- *diagnostic controls*

The foregoing computer systems controls are applicable to all systems whether they are batch processing or real-time processing systems. However, additional controls are necessary for a two way flow of information in an on-line real-time environment. In fact, on-line EDP systems create many new problems not found in batch processing systems. For example, how can confidential data be made accessable to only authorized personnel? What happens to data in the system when the computer is down for repairs? How can accuracy be assured with on-line real-time processing? Generally, controls will be dictated by such factors as requirements of the system, the equipment itself, and security specifications. The areas set forth below are not all-inclusive, but are representative of the control requirements found in a typical on-line real-time system. They include on-line processing controls, data protection controls, and diagnostic controls.

***On-Line Processing Controls.*** On-line processing controls are necessary since messages from and to the input/output terminal devices can be lost or garbled. It is possible that the terminal will go out of order during transmission or receipt of data. To guard against working with incorrect data under these conditions, the system should provide program routines for checking on messages. They are: message identification, message transmission control, and message parity check.

*Message identification* is used to identify each message received by the computer. Message number, terminal identification, date, and message code are the usual information sent which permits directing the data to the desired program for processing. If a message is received with an incorrect identification, it should be routed to an error routine for corrective action or rejection from the system. In general, rejection necessitates retransmission of the entire data.

*Message transmission control* requires that all messages transmitted are, in fact, received. One method is to assign a number to each message and periodically have the computer check for missing numbers and out of sequence messages. Unaccounted message numbers are printed for investigation. Another method is the confirmation of all messages received whether it be from the computer or an input/output terminal.

*Message parity check* is one that verifies the accuracy of the message sent. Since it originates at the sending terminal, a check digit is added to the end of the message, representing the number of bits in the message. In a similar manner, the receiving terminal compiles a check digit on the number of bits received in the message. If both check digits are equal, a "correctly received" signal is sent to the terminal or computer. If there is a difference, most systems will ask for a retransmission of the data.

***Data Protection Controls.*** Data protection controls provide answers to many on-line real-time questions. Questions include: What happens when two separate transactions are trying to update concurrently the same record? What assurance is there that program segments read into the computer's memory will not be accidentally read in over data currently being processed? The software for data protection controls include supervisory protection programs and data security—lockwords and authority lists.

*Supervisory protection programs,* like IBM's "exclusive control" program, solves the problem of concurrent updating and the resulting loss of data. It permits only one data transaction to update an on-line file at a time. Basically, this software package requires that each data set request permission of the supervisory program for updating a specific item. If the file is available, the proper machine instructions are executed. At no time during this updating process will the supervisory program allow other transactions access to this particular data file. Other equipment manufacturers have comparable routines.

*Lockwords and authority lists* are means of preventing unauthorized access to the on-line system. Lockwords or passwords, which are several characters of a data file, must be matched by the sender before access is granted to the file. Caution is necessary since the password may become common knowledge after a period of time. Hence, it must be changed periodically. Another type of security is an authority list. In this case, the lockword identifies the sender. When reference is made to the authority list stored in the computer system, it indicates what type of data the sender is permitted to receive. Whether the first or second method of data security is employed, a control routine should be established within the on-line system. Its function is to count the number of trys in sending a message. If the number of unsuccessful attempts have exceeded a certain number, say 3 or 4, it is possible that some unauthorized person is tampering with a terminal device. It should be noted that these methods do not exhaust the list of data security controls, but are the more popular ones.

***Diagnostic Controls.*** One of the difficulties with any real-time system is a malfunction of the equipment or a programming error that occurs during the system's operations. The best method is to keep the system operating if the trouble can be circumvented. This can be accomplished if diagnostic programs are used to detect and isolate error conditions for proper corrective action. However, once the problem has been determined, it is up to the supervisory program to make the necessary adjustments. It can restart the program in question, reexecute the faulty instruction, switch control to an error routine, initiate a switchover to another system, shut down part of the system, or halt the system. The first three are used to overcome software problems while the latter three are necessary to control hardware malfunctions.

Diagnostic programs, in an on-line system, are dependent upon the system's design and the equipment. They are a must when a terminal breaks down. While one diagnostic program checks the communication network and establishes that there is a problem in the network, another one checks each line until the down terminal(s) is (are) located. Having determined the problem, terminal control is returned to the supervisory program which can close down the line for repairs and route all output messages to an adjoining terminal.

When an on-line system must halt due to a breakdown of a major piece of equipment, emergency procedures must be set up to handle the work until the malfunctioning equipment has been repaired. Restart procedures must also be devised which include the use of a checkpoint record. This record, usually a magnetic disk or tape file, is a complete log of all messages and pertinent data processed up to a certain point in time. When a restart is necessitated, the checkpoint record restores the system to a time when this record was written. Every terminal is advised about the number of the last message that has been properly processed. All subsequent messages must be resent in order for the system to operate on a current basis.

### Hardware Controls

*VI. Hardware controls which are built into the equipment comprise:*

- *parity checks*
- *duplicate circuitry*
- *echo checks*
- *dual heads*
- *overflow and sign check*

Hardware controls, sometimes called built-in controls, are built into the equipment by the manufacturer. Parity checks, duplicate circuitry, echo checks, dual heads, and overflow check and sign check are the principal ones found in electronic data processing equipment. These hardware controls plus the software controls (programmed controls) enumerated in a previous section are the principal reasons why the computer is called a "center of control."

*Parity checks* are the most common of all machine circuitry controls and were described in Chapter 6. They verify each binary coded character by adding another bit, zero or one, when data are converted to the binary mode. The question of whether to add a zero or one bit depends on the design of the computer since some machines are even parity machines while others are odd parity ones. Whether the odd or even scheme is used is irrelevant. The important point is that the parity check is designed to check data every time they are transferred. Each time a character is rewritten, there exists a possibility that one of the binary bits will be lost or an extra bit added, creating an incorrect character in either case. Parity checking is designed to detect and report this type of error. The more common reasons why data fail to pass the parity check are: malfunction of computer equipment, dropping of magnetic tape reels, manufacturing flaws in magnetic tape, and the presence of dust particles on magnetic tapes.

*Duplicate circuitry* is used to assure a high degree of machine accuracy. In general, it is provided only for critical circuits since the cost and space requirements are too high for the entire system. The reliability of electronic circuits has eliminated the need for the double circuitry in most machines. In place of duplicate circuitry, many of the earlier computers plus a few today perform automatically every arithmetic computation twice, using the same circuitry. A few others perform the second set of calculations with the complements of the first data set.

*Echo checks* are used at information transfer points within the computer system. A feedback mechanism echoes a character back from the point of transmission to its original source. If there is a difference between the transferred data and the original data, this indicates a hardware failure somewhere in the system. For example, if data are transferred from the computer's memory to an output magnetic tape unit, the echoing device senses what has been received and its signal is echoed back to the central processor from the tape unit. This signal is, then, compared for accuracy.

*Dual heads* are hardware control devices. Even though they are similar to echo checks, dual heads represent a much more effective check since recorded information is checked, not just the electronic impulse. They permit data to be read and checked with the original data for agreement or they allow data to be read by two heads and checked for accuracy. The equipment necessary to perform this checking are combination read-write heads or dual read heads.

*Overflow check and sign check* are additional hardware controls found in most computer systems. The overflow check indicates that the capacity of a counter or accumulator in the computer's arithmetic unit has been exceeded. This hardware device prevents the loss of significant digits while calculating new data. The sign control check is used to indicate an arithmetic value that fails to have a required positive or negative sign. Both checks are necessary for an error-free computer system.

### Security Controls

*VII. Security controls offer a means of perserving data that may be needed later for reprocessing. Among these are:*

- *program control*
- *equipment log*
- *records control*
- *tape rings*
- *preventive maintenance*

Computer systems controls and hardware controls are essential for a successful electronic data processing system. The same can be said for security controls. Basically, these controls cover contingencies not adequately encompassed by other controls. They offer a means of preserving essential data when reprocessing becomes necessary and protecting against computer errors that might not otherwise be detected. For security controls to be effective, they must be standardized for day-to-day operations. When security procedures are not followed precisely, variable control follows, resulting in operational difficulties and inconsistent corrective action. Most computer installations have the following security controls; program control, equipment log, records control, tape rings, and preventive maintenance.

*Program control* is a necessity after each program has become operational. Computer programs that are generally stored on magnetic tape are duplicated and at least one copy is retained in a safe storage area as a backup tape for emergency conditions. Of equal importance when considering effective program control is the possibility of deliberate or accidental alteration as the program is being run. All programs that are properly controlled are not altered too easily. Control procedures over a program include making someone responsible for its safekeeping, usually the EDP librarian, issuing it to only authorized personnel, having the individual sign a log book, and similar control considerations. A computer-run book for each program should also be controlled as well as written instructions for the console operator that are necessary to meet any contingency during the processing of the program. The firm's auditors should check the various programs on a surprise basis by using test decks of input data whose outcome have been predetermined. This approach should detect changes that have been made without proper authorization.

A daily *equipment log* should be prepared so that computer operating time can be monitored. Some of the manufacturers have installed devices on the computer for recording time usage. This permits the auditor to check one source against another for falsification of computer time which may have been used for unauthorized program changes. Also, the auditor should check for any time discrepancies between the equipment log (when the run was completed) and the librarian record (when the program tape was returned) which may indicate that extra computer time was taken to alter the program for future processing.

In conjunction with the equipment log, a copy of the console typewriter printout should be delivered daily to the internal auditor. If at all possible, the auditor should check and initial the first typewriter console sheet and pick it up at the end of the day. One continuous printout should be available to him. If cuts appear in the printout, it may indicate unauthorized alterations were made during the day. Also, any unusual items, found on the printouts, should be fully explained by the responsible console operator.

*Records control* relates to master computer files that must be retained for future processing. They should be under the control of the EDP librarian as are the program tapes because of the cost incurred in their construction. EDP systems should adhere to the grandfather-father-son concept of file maintenance. Assuming daily updating, this approach requires the preservation of three days of successive output files along with the corresponding data transactions. Not only should magnetic disk and tape files adhere to the grandfather-father-son file maintenance concept, but also there should be a plan to store their related data away from the data processing center in a fireproof vault. This is necessary to reconstruct master files should magnetic disks and tapes be destroyed purposely or accidentally.

*Tape rings* are small plastic rings (Figure 16-6) which fit inside the reel holding

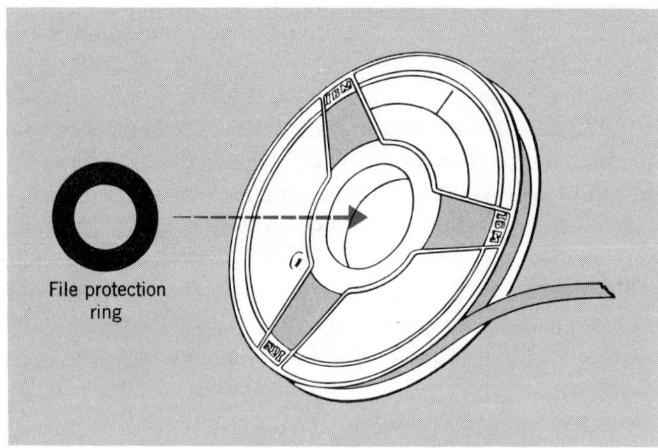


Figure 16-6 Magnetic tape file protection ring.

the tape. When not present, they prevent the contents of the file from being erased. With an inserted tape ring, old information can be erased and new information written when the internally stored program executes magnetic tape write instructions. It should be noted that some computers are designed on an alternative basis, that is, the lack of a ring allows data to be written while the insertion of a ring indicates the data will remain unchanged.

*Preventive maintenance,* although not a part of the hardware per se, is extremely important in keeping equipment downtime as low as possible. It consists of devoting a certain amount of time periodically, say once every other day, to routine hardware tests. Test problems that are run by the manufacturer's field maintenance staff are fed into the computer for checking the machine's circuitry. Under these test conditions, it is possible to determine the reliability of the system's components. Those that are beginning to show signs of weakness are replaced. This reduces the amount of lost production time and increases the reliability of the equipment during normal processing.

## QUESTIONNAIRE FOR EVALUATING INTERNAL CONTROL IN EDP SYSTEMS

*Questionnaire on EDP systems controls provides a basis for evaluating the degree of control over data processing operations.*

A questionnaire for evaluating internal control in electronic data processing systems provides a basic framework for determining the degree of control within the computer system. Extenuating circumstances usually relate to every EDP system, creating the need for questions and investigations not covered in the normal questionnaire. The individual reviewing the system must exercise his judgment in this regard. Whether or not additional questions are appended, the questionnaire is so designed that at least a minimum degree of control is being maintained in a system.

All questions in the questionnaire must be answered by checking the appropriate yes, no, or not applicable. A "yes" answer indicates good control while a "no" answer is indicative of poor control. (The same procedure was followed in the Management Audit Questionnaire per Figure 16-3.) The questionnaire follows basically the same sequence as found in the preceding control sections. Its major sections, contained in Figure 16-7, are as follows:

- EDP department controls
- Input controls
- Programmed controls
- Output controls
- On-line (real-time) controls
- Hardware controls
- Security controls

The EDP questionnaire is utilized by the outside accountants as part of their annual certified audit and serves as a basis for their letter on internal control. Specific recommendations should be made for corrective action where EDP controls are found to be inadequate or ineffective. Although the questionnaire in Figure 16-7 is utilized for evaluating the firm's internal control over its computer operations, it is necessary to supplement this questionnaire with others for a complete evaluation of the entire company, in particular, one on internal check, internal accounting control, and internal administrative control for noncomputer activities. Also, the management audit questionnaire for evaluating the functional areas of a computer system, shown in Figure 16-3, is needed to complement the questions in Figure 16-7.

## AUDITING PROCEDURES

Auditing, the subject matter for the remainder of the chapter, is treated from the certified public accountant's point of view. It is defined as a comprehensive

| | Yes | No | N.A. |
|---|---|---|---|
| I. *EDP Department Controls* | | | |
| A. *Organization:* | | | |
| • Is the EDP department operating as a separate unit without direct control over the firm's assets? | ___ | ___ | ___ |
| • Is the EDP department centrally located for best use? | ___ | ___ | ___ |
| • Are the following personnel groups, located within the EDP department, organizationally and physically separate from one another? | | | |
| (a) Punched card personnel | ___ | ___ | ___ |
| (b) Computer operators | ___ | ___ | ___ |
| (c) Systems analysts and programmers | ___ | ___ | ___ |
| (d) EDP supervisory personnel and auditor (control group) | ___ | ___ | ___ |
| (e) Programs and records (tapes and disk packs) librarian | ___ | ___ | ___ |
| • Are all computer programmers and operators frequently transferred to different machines and programs? | ___ | ___ | ___ |
| • Are systems and programming personnel forbidden to operate the computer for regular data processing runs? | ___ | ___ | ___ |
| B. *Methods and Procedures:* | | | |
| • Are there established written procedures for all EDP activities outside the EDP department? | ___ | ___ | ___ |
| • Is there standardization for system flowcharts and program flowcharts? | ___ | ___ | ___ |
| • Are programming techniques standardized within the EDP department? | ___ | ___ | ___ |
| • Are there established procedures for program testing? | ___ | ___ | ___ |
| • Have all standardized procedures been compiled in an EDP manual? | ___ | ___ | ___ |
| • Is the EDP manual current? | ___ | ___ | ___ |
| • Are there established procedures for making program changes? | ___ | ___ | ___ |
| • Are all program changes immediately documented, including the reason for the change? | ___ | ___ | ___ |
| II. *Input Controls* | | | |
| A. *Verification Methods:* | | | |
| • Are all important data fields verified for punched card or paper tape to insure accuracy of input information? | ___ | ___ | ___ |
| • If input media is not punched card or paper tape, is the degree of accuracy adequate? | ___ | ___ | ___ |
| • If conversion equipment and data transmission equipment is used to convert or transmit input data, is adequate verification being performed? | ___ | ___ | ___ |
| B. *Input Control Totals:* | | | |
| • Are batch control totals established before sending data to the computer? | ___ | ___ | ___ |
| • If no batch control totals are utilized, is there some other means of establishing input control, such as hash totals, record count totals? | ___ | ___ | ___ |
| • Are all input documents prenumbered and accounted for by an independent count so that all transactions received are processed? | ___ | ___ | ___ |
| • Is responsibility fixed for errors on input documents in order that corrective action can be taken? | ___ | ___ | ___ |
| • Are input error corrective methods properly controlled to insure actual correction and re-entry into the system? | ___ | ___ | ___ |
| C. *External Labels:* | | | |
| • Do external labels contain sufficient information for their effective use? | ___ | ___ | ___ |

| | Yes | No | N.A. |
|---|---|---|---|
| • Is there an adequate procedure for documenting magnetic tape and disk pack labels in the computer area? | ____ | ____ | ____ |
| III. *Programmed Controls* | | | |
| A. *Validation Checks and Tests:* | | | |
| • Is sequence checking used to verify the sorted input data? | ____ | ____ | ____ |
| • Are data fields checked for correct type of data—alpha, numeric, zero, blank, and special characters? | ____ | ____ | ____ |
| • Do code numbers (such as, account number and inventory number) make use of the self-checking digit technique? | ____ | ____ | ____ |
| • Are limit or reasonableness tests utilized where needed? | ____ | ____ | ____ |
| • Do programs test input data for valid codes and are printouts or halts provided when invalid codes are detected? | ____ | ____ | ____ |
| • Do programs make use of check points when processing must be restarted after its initial start? | ____ | ____ | ____ |
| • Do computer loading routines include tests which verify the successful loading of a computer program? | ____ | ____ | ____ |
| B. *Computer Control Totals:* | | | |
| • Do computer programs provide continuance of input control (batch totals, hash totals, or record count totals)? | ____ | ____ | ____ |
| • Are the following control techniques utilized in the various computer programs? | | | |
| (a) Balancing totals | ____ | ____ | ____ |
| (b) Cross-footing balance check | ____ | ____ | ____ |
| (c) Zero balancing | ____ | ____ | ____ |
| (d) Proof figures | ____ | ____ | ____ |
| • Is the completeness and accuracy of the various files checked during processing? | ____ | ____ | ____ |
| • Are changes in program rate tables and other data initiated in writing and under the control of authorized personnel? | ____ | ____ | ____ |
| • Are program changes retained for audit? | ____ | ____ | ____ |
| • Is there an on-line procedure for the detection and skipping of bad portions of magnetic tape? | ____ | ____ | ____ |
| • Are all halts, excluding end of job, recorded and retained for audit? | ____ | ____ | ____ |
| C. *Internal Labels:* | | | |
| • Do header labels have adequate information—program identification, reel number, date created, and date of obsolescence? | ____ | ____ | ____ |
| • Do trailer labels contain appropriate information—block count, record count, totals, and end of file label? | ____ | ____ | ____ |
| • Do programs test for header and trailer labels each time a new tape or disk is accessed or the end of the tape reel or disk is sensed? | ____ | ____ | ____ |
| D. *Error Routines:* | | | |
| • Is there an adequate program procedure for identifying, correcting, and reprocessing errors? | ____ | ____ | ____ |
| • Are all instructions to computer operators set forth in writing for effective processing control as well as handling error conditions? | ____ | ____ | ____ |
| • Are console operators cautioned not to accept oral instructions or to contact programmers directly when errors are found? | ____ | ____ | ____ |
| IV. *Output Controls* | | | |
| A. *Output Control Totals:* | | | |
| • Can output data be compared with predetermined totals (batch totals, hash totals, or record count totals)? | ____ | ____ | ____ |

Figure 16-7 Questionnaire for evaluating internal control in an electronic data processing system.

| | Yes | No | N.A. |
|---|---|---|---|
| • Are provisions made within the EDP system to reconstruct files in the event that the current files are damaged or destroyed? | ____ | ____ | ____ |
| • Are corresponding transactions being stored in reprocessible form for emergency operations? | ____ | ____ | ____ |
| B. *Control by Exception:* | | | |
| • Are all exception items immediately and properly investigated? | ____ | ____ | ____ |
| • Is corrective action undertaken for all exception items? | ____ | ____ | ____ |
| • Is there a periodic verification of master file balances (such as, inventory and payroll) to correct erroneous data and check for irregularities? | ____ | ____ | ____ |
| C. *Control Over Operator Intervention:* | | | |
| • Are procedures in force which prevent access of operators and other unauthorized personnel to programs for perpetuating fraud? | ____ | ____ | ____ |
| • Are typewriter console printouts controlled and reviewed by designated personnel (internal auditor)? | ____ | ____ | ____ |
| • Is there effective control being exercised over the operator's adherence to processing procedures? | ____ | ____ | ____ |
| • Is there a periodic surprise audit of the computer room to check for program irregularities by computer operators? | ____ | ____ | ____ |
| V. *On-Line (Real-Time) Controls* | | | |
| A. *On-Line Processing Controls:* | | | |
| • When input/output terminals are used for data transmission, are the following control techniques being employed? | | | |
| (a) Message identification | ____ | ____ | ____ |
| (b) Message transmission control | ____ | ____ | ____ |
| (c) Message parity check | ____ | ____ | ____ |
| • Is there adequate control over terminals in case it is necessary to retransmit the data? | ____ | ____ | ____ |
| • Is access to confidential information properly controlled? | ____ | ____ | ____ |
| B. *Data Protection Controls:* | | | |
| • Are supervisory protection programs in effect to handle the problem of concurrent updating and the resultant loss of data? | ____ | ____ | ____ |
| • Are lockwords (passwords) and authority lists utilized for data security? | ____ | ____ | ____ |
| • Is there a monitoring routine which counts the number of unsuccessful attempts (say 3 or 4) to enter the system and initiates a procedure to handle the difficulty? | ____ | ____ | ____ |
| C. *Diagnostic Controls:* | | | |
| • Are diagnostic programs, in conjunction with a supervisory program, used to detect and isolate error conditions for proper corrective action? | ____ | ____ | ____ |
| • Are there sufficient on-line programmed controls to handle the following conditions? | | | |
| (a) Restart the program in question | ____ | ____ | ____ |
| (b) Reexecute the faulty instruction | ____ | ____ | ____ |
| (c) Switch control to an error routine | ____ | ____ | ____ |
| (d) Initiate a switchover to another on-line system | ____ | ____ | ____ |
| (e) Shut down part of the system | ____ | ____ | ____ |
| (f) Halt the system | ____ | ____ | ____ |
| • Are checkpoint records developed as processing occurs in case of a restart? | ____ | ____ | ____ |
| • Are there manual emergency procedures to handle a halt in the on-line system? | ____ | ____ | ____ |

| | Yes | No | N.A. |
|---|---|---|---|
| VI. *Hardware Controls*<br>Hardware controls are outside the scope of the questionnaire since they have been predetermined by the equipment manufacturers. However, consideration can be given to adding specific pieces of hardware to effect better control over the EDP system. Prevailing circumstances must be evaluated for the best solution to hardware problems. | | | |
| VII. *Security Controls* | | | |
| • Are master files stored under conditions that provide reasonable protection against damage or destruction? | ____ | ____ | ____ |
| • Is there a schedule of all current programs which includes an identification number, date, and description? | ____ | ____ | ____ |
| • Are all computer programs properly documented? | ____ | ____ | ____ |
| • Are computer programs and supporting material maintained in the records library and issued to persons with written authorization? | ____ | ____ | ____ |
| • Are adequate daily equipment logs being<br>properly maintained? | ____ | ____ | ____ |
| reviewed for irregularities? | ____ | ____ | ____ |
| • Is entrance to the computer room limited to computer operators and authorized personnel? | ____ | ____ | ____ |
| • Are there procedures for preventing premature reuse of magnetic tapes and disks? | ____ | ____ | ____ |
| • Are there adequate controls to prevent premature erasures of data from magnetic tapes and disks? | ____ | ____ | ____ |
| • Is there an established policy for the retirement of magnetic tape reels which have excessive read or write errors? | ____ | ____ | ____ |
| • Is the computer system serviced by qualified service engineers on a regular basis? | ____ | ____ | ____ |
| • Are manufacturer's temperature and humidity requirements maintained? | ____ | ____ | ____ |

Figure 16-7 (*continued*) Questionnaire for evaluating internal control in an electronic data processing system.

*Auditing is a comprehensive evaluation of the firm's accounting records and its internal control with the purpose of expressing an opinion about the propriety of its financial statements.*

and critical review of the firm's accounting records and its related internal control with the purpose of expressing an opinion about the propriety of its financial statements. Although the external auditors (as well as the internal auditors) verify only a small fraction of data transactions for expressing an opinion, they place great reliance upon systems controls to produce accurate results. Normally, they test sample transactions to determine whether the system operates as planned. If there are variations operating within the data processing system, the auditor wants to know the nature, extent, and resulting consequences of these deviations. The number and amount of the variations may be material enough to change an unqualified opinion to a qualified one. In other cases, it may result in a complete disclaimer of any opinion regarding the validity of the firm's financial statements.

Many of the traditional business processing procedures have been either consolidated or eliminated with the introduction of computer equipment. As a result, the audit trail has been lost. Basically, the audit trail traces processed data from the final output stage back through its intermediate steps and finally to the originating document phase. This approach permits auditors to check the reliability of the data processing system.

## BASIC APPROACHES TO COMPUTER AUDITING

*Computer auditing approaches encompass:*
- *auditing around the computer*
- *auditing through the computer*

Since the audit trail cannot be followed step-by-step for an EDP system, auditors have adopted two alternative approaches for testing and verifying. They are usually referred to as "auditing around the computer" and "auditing through the computer."

### Auditing Around the Computer

Auditing around the computer (Figure 16-8) involves verifying the input and output phases without considering the actual computer programs used in the data conversion. The rationale is that if the output data agree with their corresponding input, it can be assumed that computer processing procedures are correct.

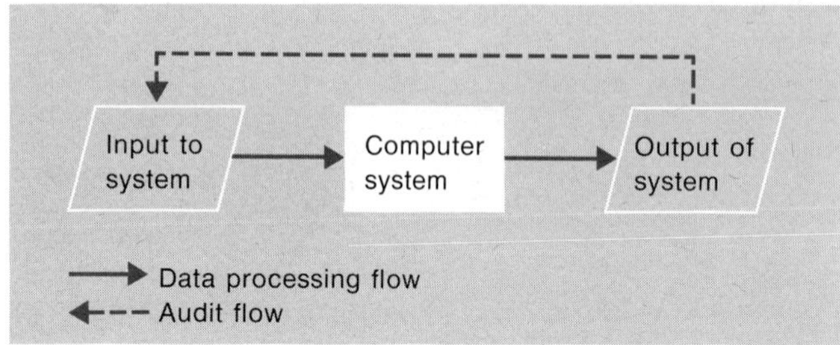


Figure 16-8 Auditing around the computer—first basic approach to auditing.

### Auditing Through the Computer

Auditing through the computer (Figure 16-9) is a detailed review of the computer processing programs and procedures in order to determine their accuracy. The reasoning for this method is that if correct data are processed within a reliable EDP system, there is only a very limited need to trace input data to output results.

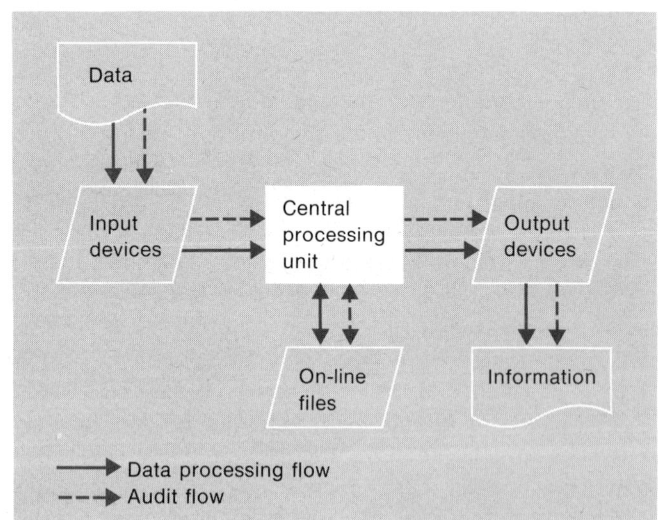


Figure 16-9 Auditing through the computer—second basic approach to auditing.

### Comparison of Basic Computer Auditing Approaches

Auditing around the computer approach is not only simpler to use and understand but also lessens the need for specialized training and knowledge of EDP systems. However, there are several problems, one being the inability to trace output data back to its corresponding input when many processing changes under program control have been effected. Another is that only large groups of data can be reconciled since output data are not compiled for small input audit samples. The problem with a wide variety of large volume transactions is that it makes this approach extremely difficult and, at times, impossible. Application of auditing through the computer requires a knowledge of computer operations as well as the ability to program a specific computer for a thorough EDP systems review. Its shortcomings include the cost of processing test transactions which may exceed the value that the auditor may obtain from them and the design of the system may make it difficult to test controls. In view of the foregoing difficulties, many auditing firms employ a combination of methods for effective auditing procedures. The attendant circumstances will dictate which parts of each is best suited for the firm.

## AUDITING SYSTEMS

The amount and type of auditing revolves around the type of data processing system and equipment employed. Basically, current equipment systems include:

1. manual and mechanical machines,
2. punched card,
3. computer batch processing,
4. computer on-line (real-time) processing.

Approaches to auditing each data processing system will be discussed below.

### Audit of Manual and Mechanical Machine Systems

*Audit of manual and mechanical machine systems involves the tracing of data through many detailed processing steps.*

Manual and mechanical (reference basically to bookkeeping machines) systems have several distinguishing characteristics. They rely heavily upon paper forms and documents that are processed through many steps before they reach the final stage. The large number of people handling the data as they are processed facilitates the detection of errors and their correction. Likewise, these numerous steps allow personnel to manipulate results purposely or accidentally. Unfortunately, these systems spend more time on paper handling than in the actual processing of data. Misapplication of procedures is a common occurrence since personnel rely too much on memory as well as suffering from the normal shortcomings to which every individual is subject. All in all, manual systems present a myriad of detail. Generally, the auditor has no difficulty in finding deficiencies or inefficiencies.

Auditing procedures for these type systems follow traditional methods. These include examining internal control of the accounting system, using an audit trail to trace data from their origination source to their ultimate destination, and observance of all other factors that are critical to the issuance of the accountant's certificate. A questionnaire is completed on areas that pertain to internal check and internal accounting control. Also, the client can request that an internal administrative control questionnaire be prepared and treated as a separate engagement.

### Audit of Punched Card Systems

*Audit of punched card systems centers around tracing data through several punched card equipment printouts.*

The audit of a punched card system is similar to a manual or mechanical machine system since there is little difference in the audit trail. The basic difference between the two systems is not the content of the audit trail, but its form. In a punched card system, the auditor encounters the need to trace data through several punched card machines printouts (or punched cards) to assure that a group of test data has been properly recorded. This is opposed to tracing data through several books of original entry where transactions are recorded via a manual or mechanical machine system. The questionnaires for both system approaches are the same, except for the addition of internal control questions on punched card equipment. However, greater accuracy can be expected with the punched card system since it is less subject to the whims of individuals.

### Audit of Computer Batch Processing Systems

*Audit of computer batch processing systems revolves around two basic approaches—auditing around and through the computer.*

Audit procedures for computer processing systems differ significantly from noncomputer system procedures. The stored program performs all data manipulation internally and does not provide intermediate output. When internal computer processing has been completed, data are not available for audit since no printout is produced for each major processing step. To produce a series of intermediate hard copy printouts for auditors would defeat the primary advantage of the computer's speed. Output is often in the form of magnetic bits on tapes or disks. For the auditor who wants to establish the reliability of the computer output, different auditing approaches are needed for computerized systems. The only evidence available to auditor, other than output results, is input data. The two basic approaches have been set forth previously, namely, auditing around the computer and auditing through the computer.

*Auditing around the computer (batch oriented) requires the selection of test transactions which are traced from the input phase to their final disposition (or vice versa) without regard to computer processing.*

***Auditing Around the Computer—Batch-Oriented.*** In auditing around computer batch processing systems, the auditor reviews and evaluates the degree of internal control. He does this mainly by interviews in order to understand the system. To confirm his understanding of the information gathered, he selects a few test transactions and traces them from the point of origination to their final disposition or vice versa. During this phase, he uses a questionnaire on the manual aspects of the system and a separate EDP questionnaire to evaluate its EDP aspects, skipping the section on programmed and on-line controls. On the basis of these questionnaires, the auditor comes to a conclusion as to the extent of internal control within the firm. This forms the basis for determining appropriate auditing procedures (audit program) which are validation tests and other procedural audit functions necessary to substantiate the balance sheet and the accompanying income statement. Since he is auditing around the computer, he will use computer printouts as a basis for audit procedures rather than testing computer programs directly. In virtually all computer batch processing systems today, the auditor performs selected data tests by tracing data from source documents and forms to reports and printouts as concrete evidence of effective internal control or lack thereof. In essence, the auditor utilizes computer printouts in much the same way as if they had been manually prepared.

Once the audit program has been completed, the auditor renders an opinion on the company's financial statements. Of equal importance is the internal control letter. The auditor, based upon his evaluation of internal control, should identify weaknesses that affect the scope of his audit procedures and control of the EDP system. He should suggest corrective action wherever internal control difficulties exist. Finally, the auditor should determine the need for a management audit and, if it exists, procure the engagement. It will be recalled that the functional aspects of the EDP system is an integral part of the management audit.

*Auditing through the computer (batch oriented) means verifying the logic and accuracy of computer programs by processing test data against these programs.*

***Auditing Through the Computer—Batch-Oriented.*** The alternative approach to auditing around the computer is auditing through the computer. If the auditor can satisfy himself concerning the logic and accuracy of the computer program, the amount of testing from the original source back to the final output can be kept to a minimum. Four general approaches for auditing through the computer are:

1. use computer test decks,
2. have the client write the computer audit programs,
3. code the computer audit programs,
4. use generalized computer audit programs.

As time pases, greater emphasis will be placed on the fourth approach.

*Computer Test Decks.* The first approach audits the accuracy of computer programs because the computer system cannot distinguish normal data processing from the test samples. Computer results are compared to results which have been predetermined manually. In like manner, test decks can be used to detail noncompliance with established methods and procedures since they can determine whether errors can occur without observation. To evaluate the extent of compliance or noncompliance with established methods and procedures, test decks must be designed for the specific computer programs of the EDP system. Since the firm's operational computer programs will be used for the test, each transaction must be designed to follow the program in all respects. Because of the computer program's complexity, considerable time is required for test deck design of several hundred transactions.

It should be recognized that it is often impossible to develop a test deck that tests every conceivable combination or condition. The auditor must judge for himself the extent and desirability of features to be incorporated in the test deck. It is recommended that the auditor design test decks with the cooperation of the client's personnel. Otherwise, he may be criticized for causing operational problems resulting from a poorly designed deck.

*Computer Audit Programs Written by Client.* The second method is having the client write the desired computer programs. This necessitates a certain amount of program testing for an operational program. The extent of testing depends on the reliance that the auditor can place on existing programs and operations control. Once the auditor has satisfied himself as to the adequacy of program testing, he should obtain a documented copy of the run and review for completeness. Finally, he should be present when the program is processed in order to establish control over the computer output.

*Computer Audit Programs Written by Auditor.* A third method is letting the auditor write computer programs to perform specified audit routines. The extent to which the auditor should perform this programming task is based upon his knowledge of EDP, competence in programming and testing programs, the language being employed, the complexity of the program, debugging time available, and client's assistance if problems are experienced. There is a problem with the third approach as well as the second one. These special audit programs are designed to perform a specific job for one client and may be applicable only to one computer with a certain sized memory.

*Generalized computer audit programs are the desired approach to auditing through the computer. They are utilized by CPA firms.*

*Generalized Computer Audit Programs.* In view of this limitation with the prior two approaches, the last approach utilizes a series of generalized computer audit programs for performing certain audit routines. These include: testing footings and extensions, selecting and printing audit samples (including confirmations), examining records for qualitative and quantitative factors, summarizing data and performing useful analyses, and comparing audited data with file records. Common characteristics of these routines are: what is to be computed, compared, and totaled can be defined clearly by the auditor; these audit functions change very little from client to client; and these same routines can be used on different phases of the same audit engagement. Based on this last characteristic, a generalized program can be written, for example, to review a file, select certain amounts (say over a stated amount), and total the file for not only accounts receivable, but also for inventory, accounts payable, and fixed assets.

*Program Developments by CPA Firms*. Generalized computer audit programs are being used by all progressive certified public accounting firms. They are written in a symbolic or procedure-oriented language since they can be translated into the machine language acceptable to their client's computers. Once the series of audit routines become operational on the client's computer, the auditor must complete a set of instruction or specification sheets for each audit routine. He might, for example, define selection interval criteria, specify what records are to be matched, or determine what footings are to be made. These sheets become the source document from which punched cards are key punched and verified. These input data plus the machine language program of the audit routine are the basis for auditing on-line as well as printing and punching selected data. As with the above approaches for auditing through the computer, the physical presence of the auditor is required to maintain control over the audit.

Generalized audit programs, such as Haskin & Sells "Auditape" and Lybrand, Ross Bros. & Montgomery's "Audipak," are helpful in most audits for a number of reasons. These computer routines result in a more effective audit since the computer can make the calculations, comparisons, and other audit functions much faster than a large group of auditors. It can replace time-consuming and repetitious audit tasks performed by the auditor. The ability of the generalized audit programs to handle most or all accounting computer programs discourages unauthorized alterations of programs. These generalized routines also reduce the time required for auditing as compared to one of the prior approaches.

**Audit of Computer On-Line (Real-Time) Processing Systems**

*Audit of computer on-line (real-time) processing systems makes it necessary to go through the computer since inputs cannot be matched with corresponding outputs.*

When auditing a computerized batch processing system, the amount of audit trail visability is a determinant of whether to audit around or through the computer. Good audit trails may mean the computer can be circumvented while poor or nonexistent audit trails indicate the need for going through the computer. In the case of an on-line real-time computer system, the auditor must go through the computer in most installations. He is no longer able to match inputs and outputs in all cases since data are capable of being fed from many different sources, literally a hundred or more on-line terminals in a real-time management information system. The question, then, is what computer audit approach should be undertaken.

***Test Deck Validation.*** The problem of the audit trail in an on-line system is comparable to any EDP system that has large-scale random access storage and is capable of processing transactions in the order of occurrence rather than by batch. After consideration has been given to using periodic printouts and remote batch processing for auditing, the auditor determines what procedures he can utilize for auditing through the computer. One of the most effective methods for checking the on-line system totally is processing test transactions through the system. The test deck should check on the operation and accuracy of input, programmed, and output controls. Incorrect data and irregularities should be an essential part of the test deck in order to test the adequacy of on-line real-time controls.

***Selective Validation.*** Apart from the test deck, which checks the functioning of programs and equipment during day-to-day operation, another approach is to review the separate areas of input, programming, and output. In the area of input, for example, transaction logs of inventory items could be maintained for the various input terminals during the day. A printout of all inventory items for the prior day plus all terminal transaction logs on inventory additions and subtractions for the current day should equal the inventory printout at the end of the day. Thus the validity of the on-line inventory program is checked. The next step is checking the physical count in the plant and/or warehouses to determine if all items were processed through the system. Missed or unprocessed receipts or issues from inventory can be the causes of differences between on-line figures and physical counts.

***Generalized Computer Audit Program Validation.*** In addition to the above auditing approaches for on-line computer systems, generalized computer audit programs can be used since much of the data is on-line and is available for extensive checking and testing. The amount of on-line testing is dictated by the degree of internal control. Also, the client can write specific audit programs or the auditor can do the same. In either case, the output from the system must be under full control of the auditor.

Questionnaires that were discussed at some length in this chapter are rightfully applicable to this type system. When an on-line, real-time system is the focal point of business data processing operations, it becomes the most important control center of information. A comprehensive evaluation of internal control, beyond that required by the annual audit, is a necessity.

## SUMMARY

The degree of accuracy needed within the firm varies by the particular functional area studied. In many cases, 100% accuracy is necessary. Certain areas of accounting require this degree of correctness. Still in other cases, accuracy for effective decision making may well be below 100%, say 90 to 95%. The question of how much accuracy can be answered by relating the value or benefits of data to the cost of obtaining it. Accuracy is desirable up to the point where the value of the information is still greater than its cost.

Once the systems designer has established the level of accuracy, he must devise a system that is compatible to it. This means implementing adequate verification and input control procedures to obtain the degree of accuracy needed for data processing inputs. The same must be accomplished for the processing and output stages. The entire system's design must embody the requirements for accuracy. The internal and external auditors can be of great assistance to the systems designer. It is more economical to incorporate these concepts now than after the system is installed.

A comprehensive review of any system, computer or noncomputer, is obtained by utilizing internal control and management audit questionnaires. The internal control questionnaire is concerned with evaluating internal check and internal accounting control while the management audit questionnaire examines internal administrative control only. Even though the outside auditor treats only the first two areas of internal control for issuing an opinion, this does not mean internal administrative control should be forgotten. In many respects, this evaluation is most important for improving the operational performance in the short and long runs. It should not be neglected although it is a separate engagement from the annual audit. Good internal control, then, can be defined as the process of safeguarding the firm's assets, providing reliable financial records, promoting operational efficiency, and maintaining adherence to managerial policies. It is essential for all data processing systems whether they be manual, mechanical, punched card, computer batch processing, or computer real-time processing systems.

Advanced EDP systems require different audit approaches. The auditor, instead of auditing from the originating sources, through intermediate steps, and finally to output results, must modify his procedural tests. Where sufficient visual audit trails are present in computer systems, he can audit around the computer. However, with the reduction of audit trail visibility, caused principally by real-time processing systems, he is forced to audit through the computer. Of the many approaches for auditing through the computer, generalized computer audit programs offer an efficient and acceptable solution. They are written in a symbolic or procedure-oriented language which can be applied to the client's computer equipment. As time passes, improved auditing techniques will be devised to cope with newer electronic data processing systems.

## *QUESTIONS*

1. How does the systems designer determine "how much" accuracy to be incorporated into a new system? Explain.
2. What are the principal causes of inaccuracies in a business data processing system? Explain.
3. (a) Define internal control and explain its essential components.
   (b) Who is interested in internal control and why?
   (c) Is there such a thing as too much internal control? Explain.
4. (a) What are the types of questionnaires that can be used to evaluate the firm's internal control?
   (b) What are the essential elements of each questionnaire?
5. (a) Distinguish between programmed controls and processing controls.
   (b) Distinguish between hardware controls and software controls.
   (c) Distinguish between batch processing controls and on-line processing controls.
6. Of all the computer systems controls given in the chapter, which group is the most important and why?
7. What affect do computer systems controls have on the internal auditor or the external auditor?
8. (a) Describe the checks and tests that can be built into a computer program.
   (b) What affect do these checks and tests have on the annual audit?
9. How important is control over operator's intervention in an EDP system?
10. Differentiate between "auditing around the computer" and "auditing through the computer."
11. (a) What is an audit trail?
    (b) Does the type of business data processing system affect the audit trail? Explain fully.
12. What is the relationship of accuracy to auditing in an EDP system?

# VI

# DATA PROCESSING AND ITS IMPACT ON THE FIRM

# CHAPTER SEVENTEEN

# The Human Element and Its Organization

*The growth of the computer industry has opened up numerous challenging career opportunities for high school and college graduates. The individual must be willing to learn new methods that are commensurate with his or her abilities. (Courtesy International Business Machine Corporation.)*

The process of introducing newer data processing equipment should include specific attention to the human element. Too often, firms have tried to ignore this critical factor which ultimately determines the success or failure of an EDP installation. Alienation of the human element within the firm results in increased human relations problems, employee turnover, and absenteeism, not to mention its impact on the firm's financial position. The net effect of ignoring the human element results in a change of employee attitude from positive to negative. It may take considerable work and time before employee efforts are properly redirected.

This chapter focuses on the human element, a common factor in all data processing systems. It covers those aspects dealing with human and morale factors plus those treating organization and conversion activities. Not only is each subject surveyed but attention is also given to related problems and constructive comments to alleviate these shortcomings. In the final analysis, the only successful approach to data processing is a positive one that involves imaginative people with leadership qualities and technical ability.

## HUMAN FACTORS

*The basic human factors of data processing are:*
- *the individual*
- *labor union*
- *management*

Once the decision has been made to order newer data processing equipment, a series of methodical changes must be undertaken. These procedural steps have already been enumerated in prior chapters. As firms install more and more newer generation EDP equipment, they are confronted each time with the human factor and its related problems. The lower level and middle level managers fear some part of their control will be lost because tasks will be assigned to the computer or advanced data processing equipment. Likewise, the fear of job displacement, the loss of job security, or the individual's inability to cope with a new job are faced by office employees. These attitudes create an environment that is not conducive to an efficient operation. It is up to management to anticipate these human problems and provide ready answers as they arise.

Even though management understands and anticipates the human aspects of a new system, a certain amount of dislocation and hardship will be encountered. By planning effectively for these conditions, the amount of hostility and dissension in the firm can be kept to a minimum. In general, management plans should include not replacing certain clerical personnel as they leave (starting with the time that the equipment is on order). Not only is normal turnover effective for reducing personnel but also routine jobs tend to have higher turnover of personnel than jobs requiring higher skills. Also, planned consideration should be given to increased data processing work caused by growth factors. Often, this results in a need for additional employees in supporting data processing activities. More new job openings may be created than were eliminated. Although many jobs will be different, management plans must consider what training is needed, who is to be trained, or what new personnel must be hired.

### The Individual

Office employees are generally group-oriented and less individualistic compared to their immediate supervisor and those above them. The individual is more susceptible to the influence of fellow workers, especially their opinions on the new data processing system. Other human factors that are important to the individual are: a need for recognition, affection, and attention; status in the eyes

*The economic (lowest), social, and ego (highest) needs of the individual are based upon Maslow's hierarchy of needs:*

- *physiological* — *lowest*
- *safety*
- *social*
- *esteem*
- *self-realization* — *highest*

of co-workers; the social need for working in groups; the necessity to lean on others for support and encouragement; and reassurance as to job security. Research has indicated that the individual has a natural tendency to resist changes, tends to believe rumors versus the real facts, needs continuous motivation, is concerned with short-range goals, and is influenced by key workers. In essence, the individual is more concerned about social and ego needs as opposed to economic needs when it comes to a system change (Figure 17-1). Social acceptance in a new environment by his fellow workers is of great importance. Will new working conditions mean isolation from the individual's present friends? In a similar manner, the office worker is wondering how the new job will meet his or her ability and talents. Will the newly created positions present too much of a challenge or will it mean that the individual must look elsewhere for work since he or she lacks the appropriate skills?

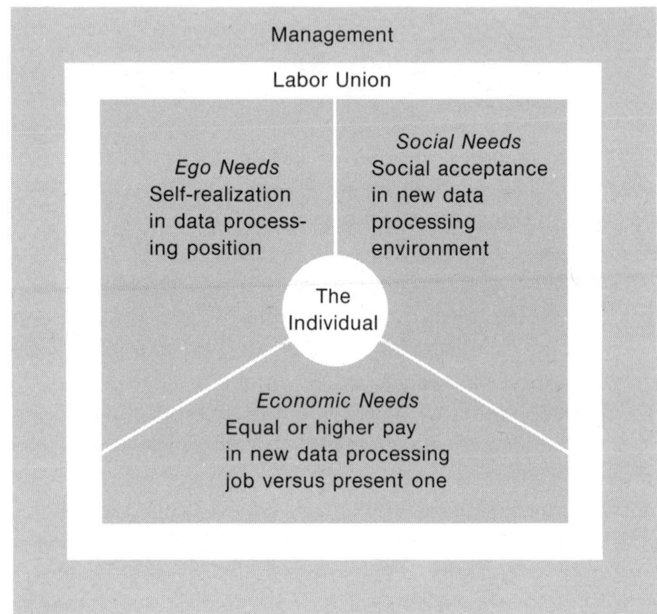


Figure 17-1 The focal point of any data processing system is the individual and his needs which are constrained by the labor union and management.

***Need to Keep Individual Informed.*** Based upon these human considerations, it is not surprising that employee resistance increases as time passes. The common fear of machines displacing office workers is ever present. The data processing group cannot prevent these basic human reactions from occurring since it will take a long time to substitute new values for old ones and satisfy the individual as much as humanly possible. However, if the data processing section is aware of these powerful forces at work (as it should be), it can offset them in certain cases and minimize them in others. This can be accomplished by several methods, one being an effective communication process. The importance of keeping the individual informed is paramount. They need reassurance as to their job security, opportunities under the new system, and procedural steps to be followed during the coming period.

An essential part of management's plans when deciding on more advanced data processing equipment, then, is advising all individuals whose jobs are affected as early as possible about the change. This gives the individual a chance to think over their future and how they fit into the firm and its training program. An early statement, preferably in writing, followed by subsequent ones should further clarify the firm's direction with newer data processing techniques and how this will affect the individual. Frank statements about groups that will be dislocated, jobs eliminated, and like matters permit the individual to develop his future plans with the assistance of his immediate supervisor. This planned approach is in contrast to saying nothing or very little to the employee until the time comes for actual conversion activities. Under these conditions the informal structure or the grapevine can give a distorted view of the true facts, especially in terms of personnel losing their jobs.

***Need to Gain Individual's Confidence.*** Perhaps the best way to gain the individual's confidence is to relate the firm's general system problems to his or her work area. Employees who are opinion leaders in the informal organization should be convinced of the present system's shortcomings and should be sold on the merits of the new system. They, in turn, can become salesmen to their fellow employees. In all cases, individuals should be given ample opportunity to air their views in formal and informal meetings as the systems project develops. This approach demonstrates to all individuals that the firm is concerned about their jobs and their future. By showing genuine interest in individuals, many of their initial and subsequent fears can be overcome. With an "open door" approach, personnel problems associated with dual operations, conversion, and day-to-day operations will be kept to a minimum so that the ultimate success of the new system will not be impaired.

With the introduction of newer data processing equipment, office employees should be advised and prepared for greater rigidity in their jobs. This is caused by the very nature of EDP equipment. Interdepartmental teamwork, which may have been unnecessary in the past, must be encouraged and enforced by the data processing section in order to insure a smooth work flow. Otherwise, bottlenecks will occur. Any tendency on the part of the individual to blame the system for errors can create serious operating problems, resulting in loss of confidence under the new system. This negative reaction on the part of company personnel can be avoided by including a provision for continuous checking during systems implementation. Any possible source of a system breakdown should be eliminated immediately before potential trouble spots become major problems. An alternative systems design technique that is effective in preventing previous system breakdowns in building some flexibility into the system. This approach permits adjusting to unforeseen contingencies without waiting for formal system changes.

### Labor Union

*Labor unions have and will continue to publicize the fears of the individual regarding office automation with newer data processing equipment.*

Any time a major new system is installed, top management must consider its effect on the labor union. Even though most office workers are not unionized, this is an opportune time for labor unions to publicize the fears and uncertainties that accompany further automation of the office. Thus, as time passes, more office unions can be expected since many data processing conversions have been far from ideal in the eyes of office workers.

***Need to Work with Union Leaders.*** Once management must deal with a union of office employees, it must clarify the systems project being undertaken and areas that are to be computerized. The systems impact on all union members must be candidly discussed. Management should not attempt to conceal pertinent facts since they will be eventually known to all employees. Having set forth all important data to the union's satisfaction, it is much easier to handle any permanent layoffs or job reassignments that are necessary during the conversion period. If management is tactful and honest in its dealings with the union, it can obtain the cooperation it needs to handle the forthcoming changes. To do otherwise will result in numerous problems that can be damaging to the firm.

Union leaders are crucial to the success of systems implementation since they often act as interpreters of the new system. They can be one of the most effective forces for securing cooperation and acceptance from the firm's office members. In order to obtain their individual support, management must see that they are receptive to its training programs. A well-directed training course provides an excellent opportunity for convincing union officials that newer EDP equipment is not to be feared. It can also provide a means of disseminating information about job opportunities and pay for its members.

Ideally, the union representatives will attend the same meetings and courses as those for the firm's supervisory staff. By placing them on the same level as supervisory personnel, the union leaders will be natural candidates for participating in system developments from the very outset. Although they will be looking out for the interests of their union members, they can be a tremendous help to management in seeing that system changes are adequately and carefully planned. Under these favorable conditions, union leaders can provide the necessary assistance during the many difficult phases of systems implementation.

### Management

*Lower and middle management present more problems to top management than their subordinates when considering a systems change. The rationale is that these two management levels are older and more set in their ways. Also, they fear the competition of younger personnel with more education and newer ideas.*

Just as an understanding of the human factors at work is necessary for the individual and the labor union, the same can be said of lower and middle management. Personnel at this level hold the key to the ultimate success or failure of the new system. Top management relies heavily on these two levels because they represent top management in the eyes of the firm's employees. Most nonsupervisory employees reflect the attitudes that flow downward from these supervisory personnel. Since their subordinates are quick to follow them, the data processing section must obtain their acceptance and complete cooperation. Otherwise, the implementation of a new system could turn out to be a waste of time.

Lower and middle management levels present a number of special problems to those engaged in the systems project. Often, these managing groups have a rather narrow perspective on the firm's overall operations. Since they are so immersed in their own respective areas, they lack the time and foresight to see what else is going on around them. Typically, there is an increased resistance to change as they grow older since they are reluctant to alter established work patterns. These management personnel fear their inability to compete with younger people. In a similar manner, lower and middle management levels fear a new system since any reduction in the number of employees is more than likely to reduce their span of supervision. Other human factors involved are: emotional barriers across departmental lines, inability to learn and supervise new procedures, tendency to blame the new system for errors, and an abnormal amount of pressure during systems implementation.

***Need to Reassure Lower and Middle Management.*** The previous listing of human problems for lower and middle management must be solved by the data processing group as early as possible. Even before the actual data processing study has begun, a written memorandum from top management is needed to allay their fears. The first announcement and subsequent reports must contain assurances of job security and other considerations that are deemed important by this group, such as reasons for the change and emphasis on the benefits available to all personnel. Reports to lower and middle management can be the same reports to their subordinates or can be separate ones, depending upon the attendant circumstances.

The same methods used for working with nonsupervisory personnel can be employed for these levels of management. The interview, in particular, gives data processing personnel one of its best opportunities to obtain their cooperation and reduce their fears. The systems man can lessen the manager's fears of loss of status by stressing his direct relationship to the new system. These include: receiving better information for more exacting decisions, increased role as a trainer of new methods and procedures, utilization of his years of experience, and treating him as an intelligent equal—capable of understanding the system and its problems. The process of winning over lower and middle management is a must since this group offers more resistance to system changes than all the employees reporting to them.

*Subordinates below lower and middle management reflect the attitudes of their superiors. Thus, it is necessary to evaluate the environmental factors before undertaking a data processing systems project. If necessary, the data processing group must undertake corrective action in attitudes before starting a project.*

Lower and middle management are quick to form their opinions about a new system project. Most of the time, their attitudes reflect those of top management. If the management at the very top has interest in the project and is actively supporting it, chances are that the same attitude will prevail at the various management levels below. This is the reason why it is extremely important for the data processing group to evaluate the top management climate immediately. If there exists an environment that is conducive to teamwork among the various functions and departments, delegation of responsibility with the corresponding amount of authority, and the challenge of problem solving, the group can concentrate on the technical aspects of the project. On the other hand, if there are rigid departmental barriers, reluctance to keep employees informed on company plans, and the communication process has been restricted, attention first must be focused on the human element. The data processing group must educate top management about the importance of "working through people" in order to accomplish a successful systems installation. To ignore the human factor under these adverse conditions and concentrate solely on the technical factors is a waste of time. The whole project is doomed to failure from its inception.

Top management must make assurances about job security, equal or better pay, opportunities about training, and guidelines to be followed for reassignment of lower and middle management jobs. An early statement of its policy on these critical matters to management and nonmanagement employees is an important plus factor in achieving a successful system. Top management's plan should include not only statements on the job area but also specific details on all other data processing changes that affect the entire firm.

## MORALE CONSIDERATIONS

Provision should be made in advance to handle any undesirable effects of a systems change on the firm's employees. Otherwise, the employee morale can be greatly affected. One of the several approaches to overcome morale problems is to consider the human element while designing the new system. The design of the system should be compatible with the abilities of those employees selected to handle the new system. A second approach to boosting employee morale and building their confidence is the dissemination of information on new positions created by the new system, many of which are higher paying and carry more prestige. Present employees should be encouraged to apply for the new positions as they are posted. Another morale booster is the utilization of formal training and on-the-job programs to enhance the competence of personnel under the new system.

*Proper selection and training of personnel reduces resistance to change and helps bolster morale.*

Experience over the years has shown that proper selection and training of the firm's personnel reduces resistance to change and bolsters morale. Most of the time it results in the firm's personnel doing a much better job than previously. The rationale is that the individuals finally realize that the firm is actively concerned about their welfare. For the first time, top management makes the statement that buildings and machinery do not make a firm "tick," but employees do. In essence, the firm's employees are its most valuable resource. By appealing to their higher needs, namely, social and ego needs as opposed to economic needs, the employees' morale is considerably higher with the new system.

## KEY TO SUCCESSFUL DATA PROCESSING—THE HUMAN ELEMENT

*The key to successful data processing includes:*
- *imaginative DP personnel with technical ability*
- *positive attitude toward data processing*
- *cooperation between top management and DP personnel*

Too often, many EDP installations have failed or have come to the brink of failing in the past. Management efforts to obtain acceptance of newer data processing equipment and procedures by its personnel were either lacking or ineffective. Cases where employees were slow in meeting deadlines, magnified the difficulties of conversion activities, and compiled data unwillingly were common. Group resistance or reluctance to cooperate fully led to disappointing results in terms of a new system. These problems were generally not connected to equipment difficulties, but rather were associated directly with the human element.

No system is an island unto itself; it needs people to run it efficiently. What kind of personnel are needed? There is a great need for imaginative people who have the required technical ability and have positive attitudes toward data processing. They, in turn, must have the necessary cooperation from all firm members who are directly or indirectly associated with EDP activities, in particular, top management.

The investment of time and effort in acquiring and maintaining good employee relations is actually not very great. The various methods set forth earlier in the book, that is, written memorandums, interviews, posting of new jobs, formal training, and on-the-job training, are necessary to avoid employee hostility and a complete breakdown in good employee relations. No system is capable of producing good results on its own. It must have the complete cooperation of those who are in a position to make it operational. Thus, it should be emphasized that the human element—a group of imaginative data processing personnel—interacts with the data processing environment in order to produce a successful data processing system (Figure 17-2).

### Imaginative People With Technical Ability

*Imaginative people generally concentrate their efforts on simplified approaches in terms of a new data processing system.*

Imaginative people with the required technical ability are a prerequisite for an efficient data processing system. Not only are imaginative personnel needed for daily operations but they are also needed for developmental activities, in particular, systems design. Systems designers should be the most creative and imaginative of all EDP personnel when it comes to developing newer data processing systems. If the firm has not selected capable systems designers, it will eventually show when the systems change is effected.

To build a successful data processing system, management should place its imaginative personnel who meet the technical qualifications of a specific job in

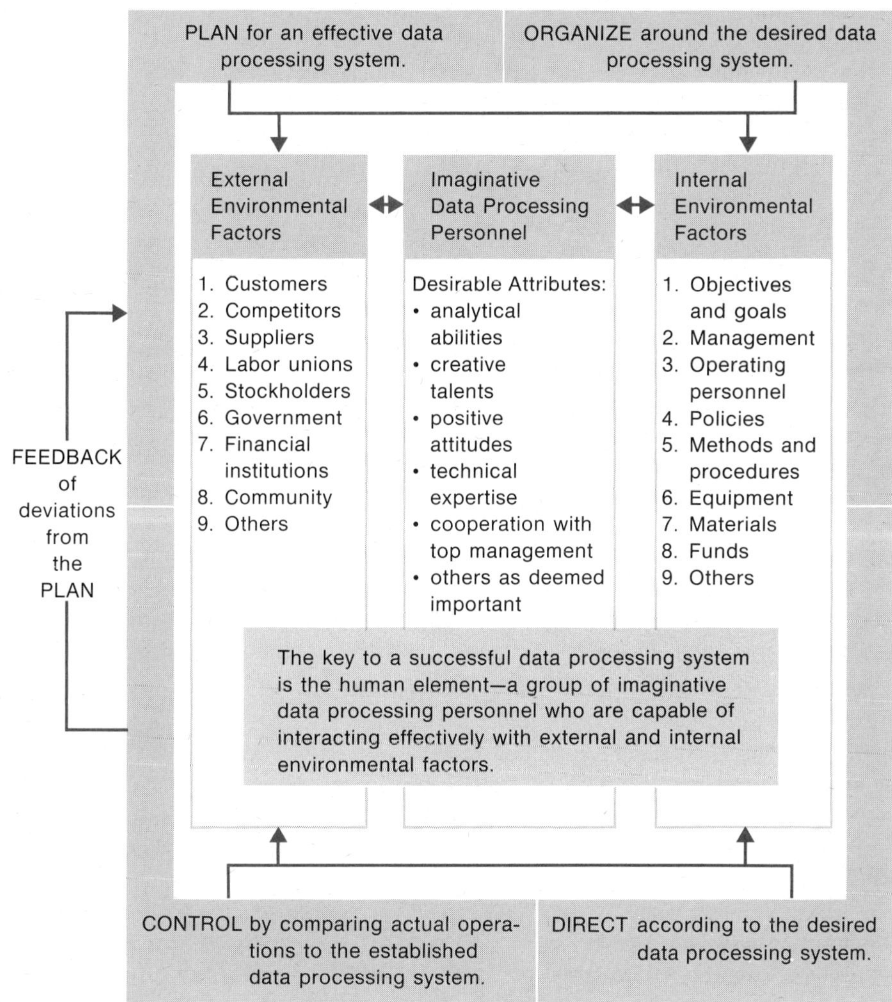


Figure 17-2 The relationship of important data processing system factors to the human element—the key to successful data processing.

key positions for several reasons. First, these people can sense in advance adverse conditions that can affect the human factor and other elements important to a smooth flowing operation. Being highly imaginative, they can correct the situation themselves or offer constructive comments for rectifying the problem immediately. Second, these high-caliber people can offer solutions that are highly practicable, but more importantly, ones that are simple to implement and use on a day-to-day basis. Instead of complex methods, procedures, and programs, imaginative people concentrate their efforts on simplified approaches, knowing that average people will be implementing these approaches. A simplified procedure goes a long way to establish good employee relations. A third consideration for strategically placing imaginative people is their positive attitude toward environment factors. If they take a positive approach toward their work and people around them, their subordinates will likewise reflect this same attitude since their supervisors are looked upon as the ultimate authority in their respective jobs. Lastly, imaginative people are not locked in their day-to-day habits, but have an open mind that is necessary for evaluating newer approaches to data processing. They are constantly on the look out for improvements. Also, they are the first to recognize that the ultimate system has not been obtained.

**Positive Attitude Toward Data Processing**

*A positive attitude toward data processing is acquired by being exposed to the area through formal education or on-the-job training.*

Of all the personnel in the firm, management must have a positive attitude toward whatever data processing system has been or is to be installed. It must be knowledgeable of what the new system is capable of doing for them. Management must overcome the fear that the machine poses a threat to their office and realize that a computer, when properly installed, can increase control by making new decision making information available when needed. They must recognize that their subordinates must work in a more disciplined manner in order to derive the maximum benefits of advanced equipment. Management's overview of the system should include a knowledge of the system's time and cost requirements which should be reviewed periodically. Otherwise, false expectations have a way of reappearing even when data on the new system have been clearly disseminated.

A positive attitude toward data processing is a requirement for anyone who desires to move up the management ladder, starting with the lowest level. It is acquired by taking formal courses, attending seminars, and working on the job. The aspiring individual is exposed to EDP experts whose enthusiasm will be instrumental is dispelling any negative opinions and attitudes on the subject. This is in contrast to company personnel who may have a negative outlook about newer data processing activities. The basic reason for this condition is that they have had little or no exposure in the data processing area, either through the firm's fault or their own. The individual's negative attitude is conditioned by his lack of EDP knowledge. By educating the employee and supplementing this education with other positive motivators, his fears gradually disappear. The changing of the human element from a negative outlook to a positive one provides an essential key to successful data processing.

**Cooperation with Top Management**

*Several studies have indicated that top management must not abdicate its control over data processing. Instead, top-level executives must form a team with the computer specialist in order to reap the benefits of data processing.*

Imaginative data processing personnel with technical ability and a positive attitude must be augmented by another important consideration, that is, cooperation with top management. Many computer studies have shown that rising computer expenses are not matched by comparable economic returns. The reason is that too many firms are leaving the job of computer implementation to the technician and not to top management. One study conducted by Booz, Allen & Hamilton, Inc. of 108 corporations has indicated one main reason for computer success—top management has taken charge of EDP operations.[1]

Another study by McKinsey & Company, Inc. examined the common denominator for a profitable computer operation and found there were three essential principles involved.[2] They include (1) the rule of high expectations (top management demands profitable results from its computer applications), (2) the rule of diversified staffing (assignment to the corporate computer staff, along with the usual operations research specialists and other professionals, of at least one capable person from each of the firm's major functions), and (3) the rule of top management involvement

[1] N. J. Dean, "The Computer Comes of Age," *Harvard Business Review*, January–February 1968, pp. 83–85.

[2] D. B. Hertz, "Unlocking the Computer's Profit Potential," *Computers and Automation*, April 1969, p. 33.

(the profit potential of computers is assured if top management is in charge versus computer technicians). Many computer installations are in trouble because top management has abdicated their managerial functions to computer specialists. Data processing personnel have neither the operational experience to know the projects that must be undertaken to further company goals and objectives nor the authority to get them performed in an efficient manner.

A most important key to successful data processing, then, is teamwork between management and data processing personnel. Top management must exert leadership and operating managers must actively cooperate with computer specialists in order to form an effective team to implement data processing systems. Only when managers get involved, cooperate with data processing personnel, and relate their problems to the computer equipment can the computer's potential be realized.

The initial cooperative efforts developed by both groups become the necessary stimulus for development of a more sophisticated data processing system. This cooperative effort is a must if the real profit potential of the computer is to be realized. To take any other path in the future will place the potential of the computer in danger. If a firm is not effectively utilizing its computer while its competitors are, there will be a greater danger of losing its market share. Advanced data processing systems will produce critical information to control the firm's internal operations that are consistent with the firm's markets. Competitors who do not have such systems may never recover their original market positions.

## ORGANIZATIONAL ASPECTS

*The number of levels within the data processing structure are greater for a large firm than for a small firm.*

The human factor as a part of the data processing system cannot operate in a vacuum, but must operate within an organization structure. As the firm grows, the degree of adherence to the EDP organization structure changes. The structure that was loosely knit in the past becomes more structured and formal, reflecting the larger number of people to be supervised. Also, more rigid lines of communication must be employed to accomplish the many tasks that must be undertaken.

The organizational changes necessary to accommodate a new system vary from one firm to another. How computer activities are organized depends on the size of the firm and the complexity of the system. A data processing system for a small company (say sales of $20 million) will be different from a medium-sized firm (say sales of $100 million) or a large-sized firm (say sales of $1 billion). Within every one of the foregoing categories, the application of the latest data processing equipment can vary because of the approach used. One may be a batch processing system, a real-time management information system, or some other system. The degree of hardware and software sophistication in an organization should be one that will best serve its needs.

### Organization Structure for Data Processing

The differences between the organization structures of a batch processing system and an on-line real-time processing system are not too significant. The on-line processing system still needs the same organizational units although they differ in size from a batch processing system. Despite the fact that there will be fewer personnel preparing input data in a comparably sized on-line real-time system, there still is need for input data on a remote batch processing basis. Personnel will be needed to send and receive data to and from the many on-line I/O terminals. There will be less need for computer console operators in an on-line processing mode since a continuous series of processing runs will not be scheduled. Rather, on-line real-time computer operations must perform a monitoring function in order to maintain an operational system. Even with these changes, the organization structure for an advanced on-line processing system is not too much different from preceding systems. The major difference is the number of personnel and the kind of equipment being employed.

*There is only one managerial data processing level in very small firms.*

***MIS Organization Chart for Very Small Firm.*** It is impossible to design a data processing organization that fits all firms and their respective needs. Nevertheless, it is worth-while to discuss and "EDP organization chart" for a typical firm of varying sizes. Illustrated in Figure 17-3 is a data processing organization chart for a very small firm whose total annual sales are several million dollars. Equipment rental is generally under $5000 per month. All operating personnel report directly to the management information system supervisor.

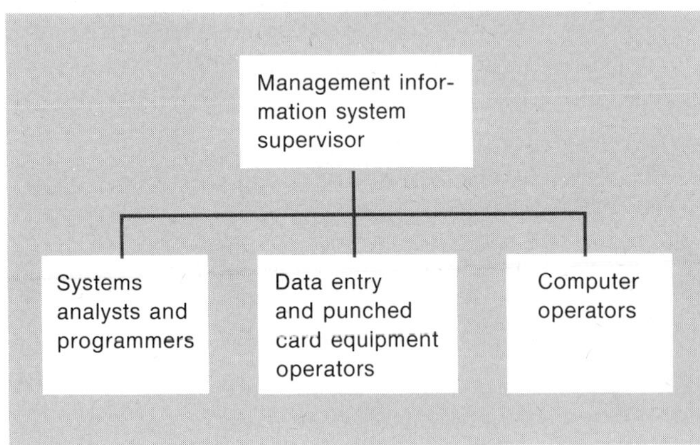


Figure 17-3 A typical MIS organization chart for a very small firm.

*There are at least two managerial data processing levels for small- to medium-size firms.*

***MIS Organization Chart for Small- to Medium-Size Firm.*** A management information system organization chart for a small- to medium-size firm is depicted in Figure 17-4 where equipment rental costs can range up to $20,000 a month. Four supervisors report to the management information system manager or his assistant. Two supervisors—systems development and computer programming—direct the systems and programming effort. Also, two supervisors—data entry & punched card equipment and computer operations—control daily operational activities. All supervisors are assisted by personnel who perform their assigned tasks. As noted in the illustration, the levels of management are kept to a minimum.

*There are at least three managerial data processing levels for medium- to large-size firms.*

***MIS Organization Chart for Medium- to Large-Size Firm.*** For a medium- to large-size firm, the MIS organization chart (Figure 17-5) becomes larger and jobs become more specialized. Also, the number of management levels increase as do the equipment rental costs. EDP installation rental can be in excess of $100,000 per month.

An examination of this management information system per Figure 17-5 shows that it is split functionally into two parts, namely, developmental and operational. These areas are controlled by the systems and programming director and the EDP operations director respectively. Developmental activities include:

1. feasibility studies,
2. systems analysis and systems design,

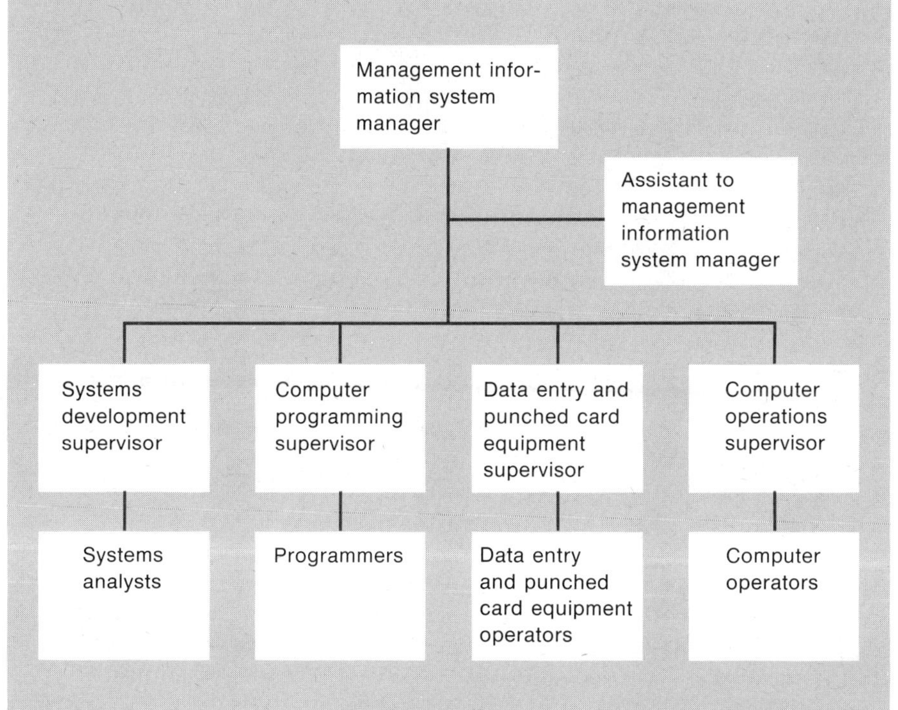


Figure 17-4 A typical MIS organization chart for a small- to a medium-size firm.

3. programming and testing new computer applications plus program maintenance,
4. operations research programs.

These are under the control of the assistant to the vice-president of the management information system, the systems development manager, the computer programming manager, and the operations research manager respectively. Operational activities or day-to-day activities encompass:

5. data entry and punched card equipment section,
6. computer operations area,
7. internal control activities.

These are directed by the data entry and punched card equipment manager, the computer operations manager, and the internal auditor respectively. Even though developmental and operational areas are shown separately on the organization chart, these two sections must work together for an efficient data processing operation. For example, after computer programs have been programmed and tested, development personnel must work with the operational people in implementing the new program for a smooth and efficient operation. Appropriate changes can be undertaken with a minimum of delay through their combined efforts.

The value of an organization chart, as depicted in Figure 17-5, is that it shows who has the authority and responsibility over one area, who will ultimately be held accountable, and what personnel resources are available to the person in charge. It indicates the span of control for managerial personnel and to whom they should report. The vertical and horizontal lines indicate the formal channels of command and the proper channels of communication. The highest level in any data processing

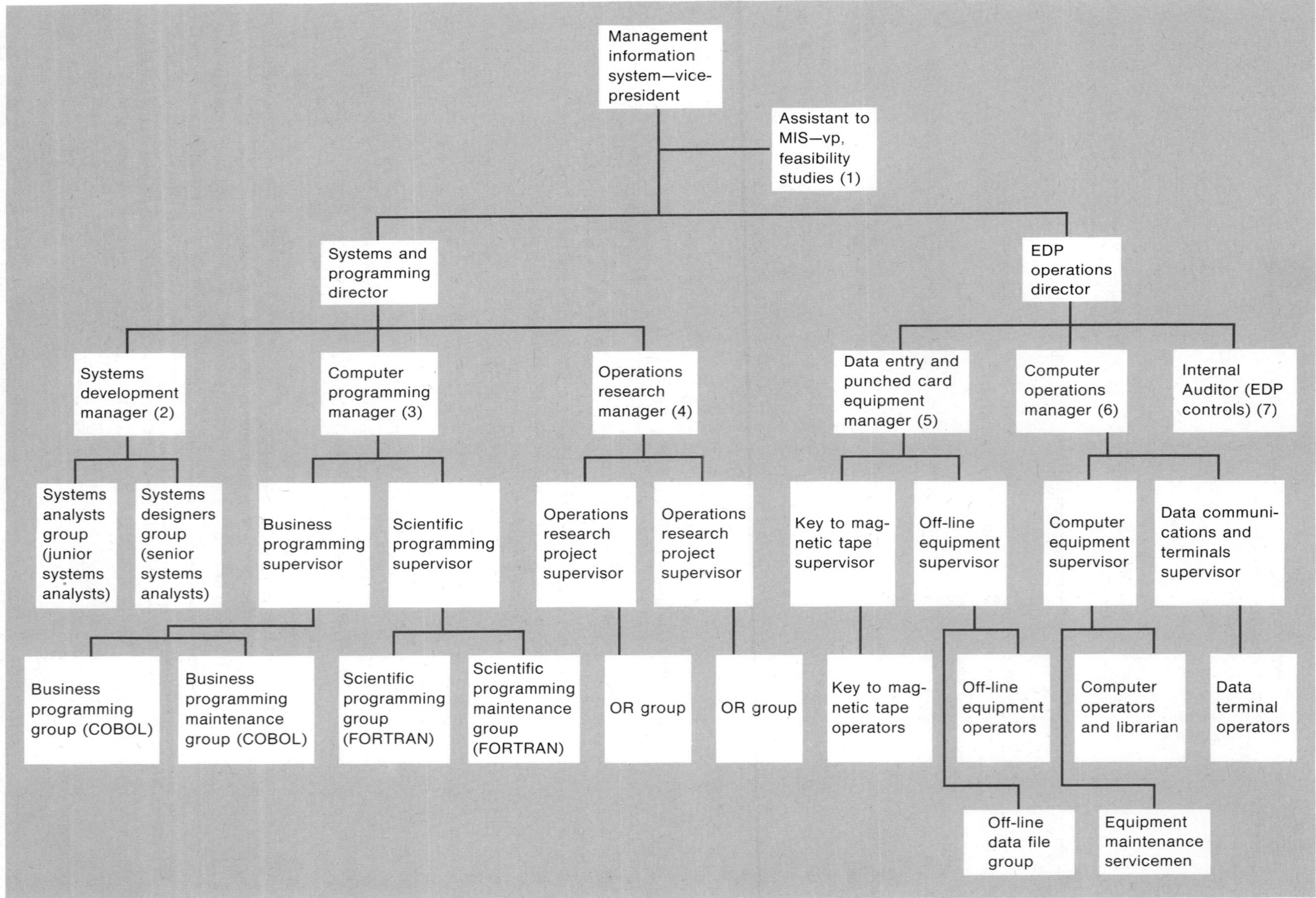


Figure 17-5 A typical MIS organization chart for a medium- to a large-size firm

organization is that of vice president which makes this individual a member of the top management team.

The reason for placing the head of the data processing operations so high in the organizational chart is that his activities cut across the entire firm. In order to implement and continually update a comprehensive and complex EDP system, he must have a high enough status to accomplish his overall objectives. Likewise, if the operations research manager is reporting to him, the vice-president of EDP needs a high office position to accomplish the projects that the operations research team must carry out. Just as in systems work, many times their activities extend beyond a few departments and encompass the entire firm. Hence, there is a definite need for a high-level executive to carry out effectively the demands of a data processing system, in particular a sophisticated and far reaching real-time management information system.

### Data Processing Personnel in a Medium- to a Large-Size Firm

Data processing positions, as found in Figure 17-5, are discussed below for a medium- to a large-size firm, starting from the top. The purpose of this in-depth job analysis is to give an insight into the actual operations of a management information system. In addition, a thorough study of this organization chart assists in understanding Figures 17-3 and 17-4 for other size firms.

*Management information systems vice-president (top management) has complete responsibility and authority over all data processing activities, thereby, being held accountable for their final results. He has an assistant and has two middle management personnel reporting to him, namely,*
- *systems and programming director*
- *EDP operations director*

***MIS—Vice-President.*** The management information system vice-president has full authority and responsibility over planning, systems analysis and design, programming and testing, OR activities, daily operations, and administration of all EDP activities within the firm. He is held accountable for the company wide management information system. Most of his time is spent reviewing newer equipment data and meeting with managers above and below him which gives direction and meaning to the firm's entire data processing activities. He is constantly consulting with his assistant on new proposals for equipment, especially in the area of feasibility studies. His assistant is involved in preparing cost data for current and proposed projects, reflecting the cost of equipment, men, and machine-hours required. All relevant data for feasibility studies are formally tied into the firm's annual financial plans (budgets). This myriad of detail is more than adequate to keep the vice president's assistant occupied full time.

In computer activities of significant size, there is need for two positions under the vice-president. There is a systems and programming director and an EDP operations director. Both report to and assist the management information system vice-president in carrying out his duties. While the former supervises and coordinates systems design and programming of all applications being developed, the latter is responsible for the daily operations of the EDP system. Generally, the systems and programming director is not concerned with routine operations of completed applications unless difficulties are being experienced.

*Systems and programming director has responsibility and authority over systems development and programming activities. He is assisted by:*
- *systems development manager*
- *computer programming manager*
- *operations research manager*

***Systems and Programming Director.*** The systems and programming director, in addition to his direct responsibility for EDP systems planning and design activities, coordinates contacts among the three managers reporting to him. He reviews recommended changes in data processing procedures which take full advantage of present equipment. These are forwarded to him by his subordinates.

***Systems Development Manager.*** The systems development manager, whose job consists of coordinating and controlling the activities of systems analysts and systems designers on new system developments, reports to the system and programming director. At the lower levels of the systems development section, systems analysts personnel (junior systems analysts) gather the necessary data on the present system as well as prepare flowcharts to assist the systems designers (senior systems analysts). New inputs, files, methods, procedures, and outputs are devised by the systems designers. Information from both of these groups is needed for the various feasibility studies under investigation which ultimately reaches the programming phase for implementation. In this area of systems development, there is a continual upward and downward flow of information from the systems analysts through their manager, terminating with the systems and programming director.

***Computer Programming Manager.*** The second manager, reporting to the systems and programming director, is the computer programming manager. His job consists of responsibility for the programming function. The computer programming manager assigns and coordinates the work of programmers engaged in writing and testing computer programs. Of great interest to his immediate superior is the development of programming procedures to increase the equipment's operating efficiency and maintenance of a capable programming staff.

In the illustration, two programming types are noted, namely, business and scientific. Each programming effort has its own supervisor with sufficient number of personnel for programming new applications and maintaining present programs. Programmers are not only responsible for developing program flowcharts and decision tables, based upon the designer's system flowcharts, decision tables, documents, and reports, but also for coding and testing programs to the point of being operational. Many times, senior programmers are assisted by junior programmers who code those areas that are straight-forward. They also perform detail checking necessary for good documentation. This allocation of work allows sufficient time for the senior members of the programming staff to handle the more difficult flowcharts, decision tables, programming, and program testing.

***Operations Research Manager.*** The third and last manager who reports to the systems and programming director is the operations research manager. His subordinates are concerned with applying standard or custom-made mathematical models (many of these will be noted in the next chapter) to many of the firm's operational programs, departmental activities, and overall operations. The wide scope of operations research means that all departments are potential users of OR services. Thus, OR personnel will be working with many of the developmental and operational groups found within the firm.

*EDP operations director has responsibility and authority over daily data processing activities. He is assisted by:*

- *data entry and punched card equipment manager*
- *computer operations manager*
- *internal auditor*

***EDP Operations Director.*** Data processing operations which tend to be straight forward are under the control of the EDP operations director. He is responsible primarily for daily operations in terms of scheduling and supervising EDP activities. Much of his time is spent on personnel functions since he has a larger staff than his counterpart. When a changeover to newer equipment and systems is contemplated, he must plan and coordinate his operations with those groups involved from the computer systems and programming area.

The EDP operations director has three managers reporting to him per the illustrated organization chart. They are the data entry and punched card equipment manager, the computer operations manager, and the internal auditor.

***Data Entry and Punched Card Equipment Manager.*** The data entry and punched card equipment manager is responsible for data preparation. His data preparation subordinates are production oriented whereby a certain amount of quality must be an integral part of their output. Depending upon the size of the system, a supervisor is needed to control the key to magnetic tape machines and one to supervise the off-line equipment. Without effective supervision, production and quality of work would be noticeably reduced.

***Computer Operations Manager.*** The second area under the direct control of the EDP operations manager is the computer area. It is under the direction of the computer operations manager who, in turn, is assisted by two supervisors. These include a computer equipment supervisor who is responsible for maintaining around-the-clock operation and a data communications and terminals supervisor who controls the many input/output terminals. The computer equipment supervisor controls the computer operators and the tape and disk librarian(s). Also, he has the equipment maintenance servicemen report to him directly since excessive downtime can be detrimental to an on-line processing system. All in all, the EDP operations manager has his work cut out for him. Equipment and personnel problems are enough to occupy his full day.

***Internal Auditor.*** A third individual reporting to the EDP operations director is the internal auditor. He is responsible for establishing controls before and after the data are processed by the computer system. Without internal control, the firm would not be able to safeguard its assets or rely on its financial records.

The various positions enumerated above for Figure 17-5 are normally assigned to personnel who have the necessary experience and talents for the particular job. Highly qualified individuals are difficult to locate on the open market. For this reason, many firms select new EDP personnel from their existing management team. Individuals from within the firm are already familiar with the firm and have earned the respect and confidence of other managers before assuming their new positions. If the organization must go outside, new data processing personnel must be given ample time to become familiar with the firm and its operations before issuing orders. As much as a year may be necessary for the individual to get "a feel" for his position.

*By and large, the college degree is a prerequisite for systems analysts and programmers. The high school diploma, on the other hand, is necessary for most data processing equipment jobs.*

### Training of Data Processing Personnel

Most firms require a college degree as a prerequisite for their systems analysis, systems design, and most programming personnel. They prefer personnel who have taken several courses on electronic data processing. A formal exposure assists the individual in deciding whether the data processing area really interests him. Firms require that prospective applicants take appropriate tests which measure mathematical and programming aptitudes. Computer manufacturers provide programmer's aptitude tests that assist the firm in making a final decision on applicants.

Once the firm has selected its applicants, it will send them to the manufacturer's programming school. Based upon the individual's performance in school, some will become systems analysts, systems designers, programmers, or placed where needed. No matter where they are placed in the organization, the new trainees are assigned to and guided by more experienced personnel. Within one year on the job after programming school, the individual should be capable of undertaking normal departmental activities of his group versus routine work presently assigned.

Operations personnel are generally recruited from within the firm and are given some formal training. However, most of their training will be on the job. Training for data entry equipment operators may be given by the respective manufacturer. In those cases where the manufacturer does not provide formal training, the firm's own supervisory personnel must develop and teach courses for the specific areas, utilizing the manufacturer's course materials for instruction.

Although personnel training in data processing activities is initially formal, acquiring new knowledge about their respective jobs should never end. Once the learning process stops, the firm will suffer since newer ideas and techniques are not being introduced to maintain an efficient system. A system which might be the answer today for the firm's needs, many times, will not be the ideal one for the firm's requirements tomorrow. Only by a continual updating process within the EDP section will the firm maintain an efficient system. To think that the ultimate system has been installed is unrealistic and can be a significant barrier to progress.

## CAREER OPPORTUNITIES IN DATA PROCESSING

*Challenging data processing career opportunities are available for:*
- *data processing management*
- *systems analysts*
- *programmers*
- *operations personnel*

In 1951, the first commercial computer (UNIVAC) was installed. The next year witnessed the installation of seven computers (4 UNIVAC, 3 NCR). Now that two decades have passed (1952–1971), approximately 70,000 computer systems have been installed. Within the next computer decade (1972–1981), the number of computer systems is expected to triple, mainly as a result of mini-computers.

A large number of systems personnel, estimated at well over one-half million people, are presently engaged in the data processing field. A breakdown of this estimate is as follows:

- data processing management—100,000,
- systems analysts—200,000,
- programmers—250,000.

It is estimated that there will be well over one million people employed in these three categories by the end of the third computer decade (Figure 17-6). This figure does not include the operational employees.

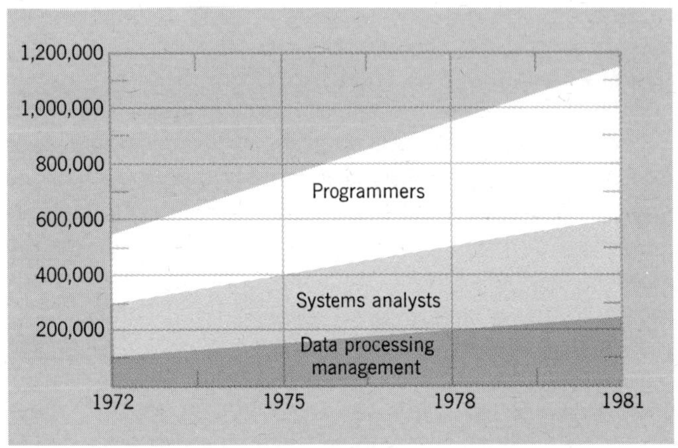


Figure 17-6 Projected estimates of systems personnel needs during the third computer decade (1972–1981).

Tremendous growth for this industry will provide college graduates with career opportunities in the systems development area. The operations area will accommodate high school graduates who are looking for opportunities in a relatively new field.

As more and more EDP systems are introduced, especially in the smaller firms, additional trained data processing personnel will be required at all levels. Major personnel categories, depicted in Figure 17-5, can be broken down as follows: management, systems analysts, programmers, and operations personnel. The appropriate background for these career opportunities are enumerated in the following sections.

### Management

*Requirements for data processing management include:*
- *creative and logical mind*
- *ability to get work done through others*
- *positive leadership qualities*
- *college degree (masters degree is desirable)*

The managerial category of an EDP system is responsible for the data processing activities occurring throughout the entire organization. A certain level of technical and administrative skills is necessary to supervise the work of others. Most of this management group have moved into their high-level positions after performing exceptionally well as systems personnel or programmers. Almost without exception, they have the ability to get work done through others with the minimum of problems occurring. DP management people should have a college degree; a master's degree is highly desirable. Without a college degree, other managerial candidates from within and outside the firm appear to be, at least on paper, better suited for an opening in data processing management. The required course of studies will be dictated by the type of installation, that is, a business-oriented computer system versus a scientific-oriented one. The former would require a major in some business area, preferably data processing, accounting, or management. The scientific installation would require a degree in mathematics, engineering, statistics, or some other field, depending upon the type of system. No matter what installation is being considered, all management personnel should have had management, higher mathematics, statistics, and data processing courses, supplemented by practical job experience. All candidates for EDP management jobs should possess leadership qualities.

### Systems Analysts

*Requirements for systems analysts include:*
- *creative ability*
- *exposure to the major functional areas of the firm*
- *college degree*

The number of systems analysts is almost equal to the number of programmers. Although system developmental tasks can be divided into those of systems analysis and systems design, as noted in Figure 17-5, the established trend is to use one title, namely, systems analyst. Generally, systems analysis work is undertaken by junior systems analysts while the senior members of the systems development section are responsible for systems design. The highly abstract work of devising new systems requires creative talents and the ability to think logically through the many alternatives and component parts. A college graduate is best suited for this creative job. As above, the course of college study is dependent upon the specific installation. A desirable background for a business installation includes courses on data processing, higher mathematics, management, and courses that explore the major functional areas of the firm. Formal exposure and experience in marketing, production, and finance are necessary to design systems that cut across the entire organization.

### Programmers

*Requirements for programmers include:*
- *logical mind*
- *knowledge of at least one programming language*
- *college degree (desirable)*

With the increasing number of computer installations, the demand for programmers is rising. Programmers can be split into two groups, namely, those dealing with business or scientific applications. Within each of these two groups is found another classification, namely, senior and junior programmers. The highly experienced personnel or senior programmers direct the efforts of junior programmers and other personnel involved in a programming project.

Because of the tremendous demand for programmers in the past, many business programmers did not possess a college degree. However, many firms use the college diploma as a screening device for applicants. In addition, since most colleges are offering some type of computer science or data processing area of concentration, the high school graduate or one from a private programming school are finding it more difficult to procure programming jobs in the better firms. No matter whether he is a high school or a college graduate, the essential requirements for programming is a logical mind that can determine the necessary detailed activities which are necessary to complete a specific program. Based upon this consideration, the need for a college business degree is not mandatory. Many of the best programmers have liberal arts and science degrees.

The background necessary for a scientifically oriented computer system is quite different from that required for business. In this area, a degree in mathematics, engineering, or a comparable discipline is a must. For highly sophisticated scientific applications, a master's degree is absolutely essential, especially when working with advanced engineering and operations research models. Thus, for a better position in programming scientific projects, the programmer must have the appropriate degree and experience if he expects to attain his long run career goals.

### Operations Personnel

*Requirements for operations personnel include:*
- *practical thinking*
- *manual dexterity*
- *high school diploma, junior college degree, or training as required by the job*

Data processing operations offer many career opportunities for high school graduates. Many openings are available for computer operators whose principal duty is to keep the machine operating in an efficient manner. Many computer operators formerly operated unit record equipment. Avenues of training for this job include: high schools, technical schools, private data processing schools, and junior colleges. However, many operators have obtained their skills through on-the-job training and schools conducted by equipment manufacturers.

Another area for high school graduates is working with unit record equipment. This can be as a tabulator operator whose principal task is controlling the operations of various off-line punched card equipment including the transfer of punched cards from one machine to another. The educational background is similar to that given for a computer operator.

An interesting career for a female high school graduate is being a keypuncher, a key to tape operator, or an input/output terminal operator. These jobs consist basically of working with original source data. Another promising opportunity in data processing is working with optical character recognition equipment for processing input data. The education desirable is a high school diploma although many girls have performed extremely well without one. A high level of manual dextermity, accompanied by practical thinking, is a prerequisite for doing an effective job.

## CERTIFICATE IN DATA PROCESSING

*The Certificate in Data Processing covers the following areas:*
- *data processing equipment*
- *computer programming and software*
- *principles of management*
- *quantitative methods*
- *systems analysis and design*

Just as the fields of accounting and law, among others, have programs for certifying the professional capabilities of its members, the same has been accomplished for data processing personnel. The Certificate in Data Processing (CDP) has been developed by the Data Processing Management Association. Ever since the first examination was held in June 1962 (New York City), the test has been offered each year (normally in February) nationally and in some foreign countries at a number of university and college test locations. It covers the following categories: data processing equipment, computer programming and software, principles of management, quantitative methods, and systems analysis and design. All candidates are advised of pass or fail. Those who fail are told in which sections they scored below passing and are permitted to retake those sections.

***Current Requirements.*** Current requirements to sit for the five-hour, 300-question exam include five years' proven experience in the field (or its equivalent in part-time work) and character references. Data processing management, systems

*Requirements for taking the CDP exam:*

- *five years' proven experience in computer-based information systems*
- *high character qualifications*

development work, programming, and data processing teaching count toward meeting the experience requirement while clerical, keypunch, and direct sales experience are not acceptable.

A complete study outline is available for the exam. Information may be obtained from the Executive Director, Data Processing Management Association, 505 Busse Highway, Park Ridge, Illinois, 60068 or from any local chapter of the association.

## REGISTERED BUSINESS PROGRAMMER

*The Registered Business Programmer exam has no formal requirements at this time.*

In addition to the annual examination for the Certificate in Data Processing, there is another called the Registered Business Programmer Examination (initiated in October 1970), which is administered yearly under the auspices of the Data Processing Management Association. Although no formal qualifications have been established at this writing, applicants are expected to have a level of training and experience equivalent to that of a senior programmer for this 150-question, two and one-half hour exam. The five general categories covered are: principles of programming, programming systems, problem-oriented languages, data processing systems design, and computational topics. The purpose of the exam is to identify practicing programmers who have reached a level of technical proficiency in programming tasks.

It should be pointed out that the Registered Business Programmer Examination has little relationship to the Data Processing Management Association's Certificate in Data Processing Program. The CDP Program is a higher level program intended to measure a broad range of knowledge in the total field of data processing. Furthermore, it requires a specified period of work experience. Those who take the Registered Business Programmer Examination are expected to develop their technological and managerial knowledge of data processing to a level that will enable them to qualify for the CDP examination.

## SUMMARY

Human factors, among other things, are important considerations for a successful systems project. The cost and time involved in developing and maintaining good employee relations are nominal as opposed to those that are necessary to rectify a bad management-employee relationship. Methods used to prepare employees for system changes are written memoranda, newsletters, posting of new data processing jobs, formal training, and on-the-job training. These methods are applicable to office employees as well as to lower and middle management.

The organization structure changes as newer EDP systems are installed. Likewise, organizational changes necessary to accommodate a new system vary from one firm to another. Comparable firms within the same industry and sales volume often have varying types of systems. Nevertheless, they have common personnel problems which can make or break any operating system.

The key to successful data processing for any type system is the human element. It takes more than imaginative people who work as a team with top management and have the required technical "know-how." It also requires a positive outlook toward data processing, especially when referring to all levels of management. This is particularly true for middle management levels since lower levels of management and nonsupervisory employees are quick to reflect attitudes that flow downward, especially if it is a negative one concerning a new data processing system. Thus company personnel must overcome the attitude that the computer is a threat to them. They must replace this outlook with a positive one, that is, the computer is a powerful tool for providing timely and useful information for greater decision making ability.

## *QUESTIONS*

1. Of the three human factors mentioned in the chapter, which one causes top management the most problems when converting to newer EDP systems? Explain.
2. What can the firm do to overcome morale problems when a newer data processing system has been formally announced within the firm?
3. Do organizational structures differ greatly for batch processing and on-line real-time processing systems? Explain.
4. Discuss the similarities and differences between the developmental and operational sections of an EDP system.
5. How important is the staffing and training of EDP personnel to the success of an EDP system? Explain.
6. What is meant by the statement, "The key to successful data processing is the human element"?
7. What are the educational requirements for management, systems, and operations personnel in a typical EDP system?
8. What are the current trends in the programming profession?

## CHAPTER EIGHTEEN

# Data Processing—Past, Present, and Future

*Although past data processing systems have been directed toward batch processing, present and future systems are oriented toward on-line real-time processing. Illustrated is a console operator of a supercomputer that can service many remote I/O terminal devices for man-machine interaction. (Courtesy Control Data Corporation.)*

Data processing activities within the firm must change in response to the environment in which it operates. The changing environment revolves around the complexities of new products, expanding markets, newer technology, aggressive labor unions, and increasing governmental authority. Likewise, it also includes newer generation computers that are capable of handling the increasing load of business data. Data and useful information extracted from the common data base have become a vital resource of the firm for coping with internal and external changes. The availability and the capability of computers to extract meaningful reports and analyses means that managers are able to function effectively in the ever-changing business world. In essence, the computer is a powerful tool for recognizing and changing with environmental factors that confront the firm.

In this chapter, the impact of computers on business now and in the future is presented. Initially, the effects of computers as they relate presently to the major functions of the firm are explored. The use of mathematical models of operations research with computers are analyzed. Future data processing developments are discussed in terms of hardware and software as well as electronic money and tele-purchasing.

## COMPUTERS—HOW THEY PRESENTLY AFFECT BUSINESS

*Initially, computers serviced the accounting function. Presently, they are utilized for:*
- *marketing*
- *manufacturing*
- *finance and accounting*
- *physical distribution*
- *research and development*
- *engineering*
- *personnel*

In the 1950's and the early 1960's, the computer was primarily a tool for specific operational problems. Generally, it was applied to one functional area of the firm, that is, to finance, accounting, manufacturing, marketing, personnel, or engineering. In fact, many large organizations were using separate batch processing computer systems at a particular location for each function. Under these operating conditions, it was common to have a computer used exclusively for accounting while another was employed for production. Complete autonomy of management for computer applications resulted.

In the late 1950's, it was recognized that the real potential of the computer was not being realized with this individualistic approach. The next step was the design of data processing systems that consolidated previously uncoordinated functional systems. The areas of marketing, manufacturing, finance, and other pertinent areas were brought together into an integrated system that provided management with a consolidated and consistent information base. Data banks in the form of computerized files were created as a part of the operating system since it enabled the various levels of lower and middle management to extract valuable information from multiple sources for making timely decisions. Basically, these systems were initiated in the 1960's and will continue in the 1970's, operating as real-time management information systems. As the total systems approach develops further, it will be accomplished within the framework of management information systems.

### The Marketing Function

*Typical marketing applications include:*
- *plan new products and markets*
- *forecast sales*
- *schedule finished goods requirements*
- *feedback to adjust supply to demand*

Presently, computers have made a significant impact on the marketing function. Many real-time management information systems have been designed to analyze the firm's products and markets through marketing research. The result of this research becomes the basis for forecasting sales several periods in the future. These forecasted figures can be used ultimately for scheduling day-to-day production. Included in the design of the marketing subsystem is a control mechanism for adjusting the forecasting model to reflect current sales. In essence, sophisticated computer marketing models are being employed by progressive firms to plan new products and markets, forecast their respective sales, schedule finished goods requirements, and provide feedback to adjust supply to demand. This approach provides the firm with a quantitative measurement of many products over their useful life, especially in terms of their contribution to the firm's profit.

Most firms have not reached this degree of refinement for marketing activities. Many are still producing routine outputs for marketing. These computer runs include: sales order processing, back ordering, sales analysis by market areas and products, sales commissions, sales budget versus actual values, and similar items. The degree to which the firm's marketing activities have been advanced by the computer is largely dependent upon the capabilities and competence of the systems development staff in this important area.

### The Manufacturing Function

*Typical manufacturing applications include:*
- *inventory control*
- *production scheduling and control*
- *automatic reordering of materials*
- *quality control*
- *allocation of manufacturing facilities*
- *selection and placement of factory personnel*

The manufacturing function is an integral part of marketing for a real-time management information system. The forecasted sales become the basis for calculating the finished goods inventory requirements which, in turn, determines the materials to be purchased from outside the firm and to be manufactured within the firm. This latter category forms the basis for production scheduling and the final dispatching of the order to the respective manufacturing department. The manufacturing subsystem process does not stop here but, rather, begins a series of events for managerial control. The budgeted or standard costs are compared to actual in order to evaluate current operations. If corrective action is necessary, it can be undertaken now to remedy unfavorable manufacturing conditions.

Computer activities for the manufacturing function presently vary from one firm to another as is the case for marketing. Inventories, scheduling, and production control are a part of the manufacturing data processing area. The following are also activities for a real-time management information system: automatic reordering of materials, quality control, allocation of jobs to specific machines, selection of factory personnel to certain jobs based on skills, placement of maintenance personnel for lowest costs, and determination of new capital equipment versus overtime. Still other progressive firms are utilizing PERT/LOB (line of balance) to plan production from the prototype phase, through the intermediate stage, and finally to large volume production. This technique, like most others found in advanced production systems, permits effective control in order to effect remedial action when required.

### The Finance and Accounting Function

*Typical finance and accounting applications include:*
- *cash flow analysis*
- *long-range capital requirements*
- *alternative investment analysis*
- *credit policy determination*
- *credit check analysis*

The finance and accounting function was the first to feel the real impact of computers. Initially, payroll, sales invoicing, accounts receivable, accounts payable, and fixed assets were applications commonly found on the computer. However, with the utilization of management information systems, the finance and accounting function has experienced more sophistication. Cash flow analysis, long-range capital requirements, alternative investment analysis, sources of capital, and dividend policies are an essential part of the finance data processing system. The determination of credit policies, delinquent account procedures, and credit risks have been computerized for better managerial control. Currently, the biggest change in the accounting area for a real-time system is the ability to obtain pertinent, updated information via I/O display devices for immediate decisions about customer and vendor accounts.

### All Major Functions

*Computer applications are shifting away from finance and accounting toward other major functions.*

Although the finance and accounting area was the first one to be programmed on most business computers, its importance in terms of current applications is still the largest. Based upon several estimates and studies of business activities, the classification per Figure 18-1 indicates the present dominance of the finance and accounting function.

| MAJOR COMPUTER FUNCTION | CURRENT (LATE 1960'S AND EARLY 1970'S) | FUTURE (MIDDLE AND LATE 1970'S) |
|---|---|---|
| Finance and Accounting | 45% | 30% |
| Manufacturing | 17% | 20% |
| Marketing | 13% | 16% |
| Physical Distribution | 9% | 13% |
| R & D and Engineering | 8% | 10% |
| Management Planning and Control | 6% | 7% |
| Personnel | 2% | 4% |
| | 100% | 100% |

Figure 18-1 Present and future computer applications for the firm's functional areas.

As more and more real-time management information systems are installed, the finance and accounting function, as a percent of total computer time, will decrease. The rationale is that newer systems are concerned with decision-making ability which affects the entire firm versus emphasis on one area only. An advanced management information system is concerned with improved sales forecasting, optimum marketing effort, efficient utilization of the plant, improved shipping schedules, increased vendor performance, and better negotiating position with unions, to name a few.

## COMPUTERS AND OPERATIONS RESEARCH

*Basic characteristics of operations research are:*
- *uses planned approach (scientific method)*
- *employs interdisciplinary (mixed) team*
- *examines functional relationships of a system*
- *uncovers new problems for analysis*

Starting with the introduction of digital computers, business firms have applied the knowledge and concepts of science to organizational and management decision problems. This scientific approach has been generally labeled operations research although the terms management science and quantitative business methods have been used widely. Operations research can best be defined in terms of its basic characteristics as follows: "Operations research utilizes the planned approach (scientific method) and an interdisciplinary team in order to represent complex functional relationships as mathematical models for the purpose of providing a quantitative basis for decision making and uncovering new problems for quantitative analysis."[1] This lengthy but inclusive definition of OR is concerned basically with the construction and application of mathematical models for solutions to recurring business problems that can be best handled by high speed computers. To try to solve these problems with manual methods would be costly and time

[1]R. J. Thierauf, edited by R. A. Grosse, *Decision Making Through Operations Research,* New York: John Wiley & Sons, Inc., 1970, p. 14.

consuming. In many cases, conditions would have changed before application could be effected.

*Standard or custom-made OR models and their appropriate data provide the input for computer processing, resulting in a quantitative basis for decision making.*

In view of these difficulties with manual methods, a model of the real world is constructed which possesses the essential characteristics of the actual situation. When constructing the model, the variables in the problem must be identified. A variable that obtains its value from some other element or variable is dependent. On the other hand, an independent variable is one whose value is determinable without reference to other elements or variables. Once these two broad categories are set forth explicitly in the problem, the relationship of these variables to one another or the effect each has on the others are defined. This relationship is necessary in defining an appropriate measure of effectiveness, that is, maximize profits, minimize costs, or some other criterion. Having the pertinent variables stated in mathematical notation and in equation form, the manipulative facility of mathematics now makes it an easy job for the computer. In essence, the mathematical language of the model allows a precise statement of the problem that lends itself to the fast, calculative ability of the computer (Figure 18-2).

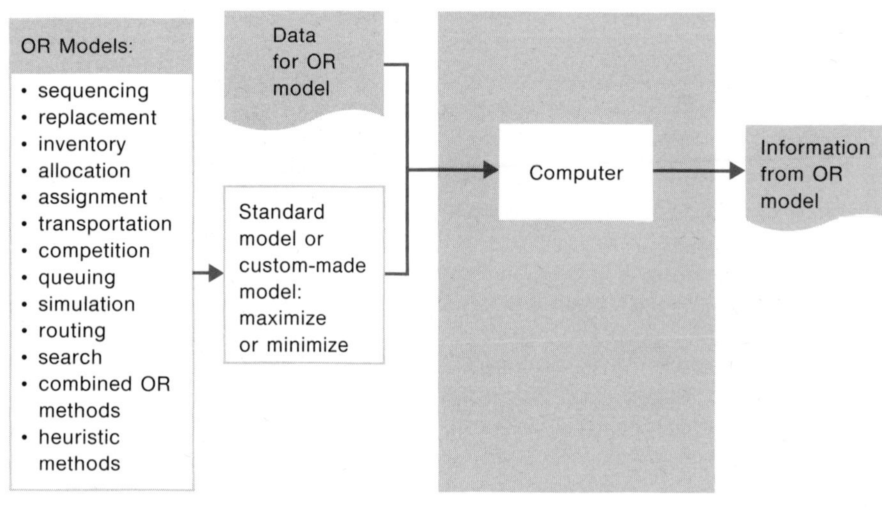


Figure 18-2 The appropriate standard or custom-made OR model is combined with the required input for computer storage, processing, and control, resulting in the desired output.

### Mathematical Foundation of OR

*The mathematical foundation of operations research is built upon:*
- *probability*
- *statistics*
- *higher mathematics*

The mathematical foundation of operations research is built upon probability theory, statistics, and higher mathematics. Understanding the essentials of probability theory is necessary in operations research since it is an integral part of many OR models. Probability is quite useful in the reduction of risk in many business situations. In a similar manner, Bayesian statistics is helpful in predicting the future with a minimum amount of information available.

Higher mathematics also provide a foundation for solving standard OR problems. Matrix algebra, vectors, determinants, differentiation, integration, partial derivatives, Lagrange multiplier, and differential equations, to name the major ones, are very essential in developing reliable OR models. Often, calculus methods are necessary to solve basic OR models since other mathematical approaches fail to solve the model or to give a satisfactory proof of the model. In addition, calculus methods provide a means for selecting the best solution without having to search through alternative course of action that is characteristic of the many OR techniques that follow.

### Overview of OR Models

*New standard OR tools are being developed for well structured problems, in particular, those that combine several OR techniques.*

The successful marriage of the computer with mathematical models has produced a rapid growth in the number of quantitative techniques for solving business problems. The number is still increasing as more techniques are developed for new business applications. Problems that have been successfully solved are not restricted to one functional area of the firm, but many times, cut across the entire firm. The principal types of problems that have been solved encompass the following:

- sequencing
- replacement
- inventory
- allocation
- assignment
- transportation
- competition
- queuing
- simulation
- routing
- search

Based upon the foregoing, combined OR methods have been developed for solving complex problems.

*Heuristics or rules of thumb are becoming increasingly important to solve poorly structured problems.*

The foregoing models are applicable to well-structured problems. Operations researchers have developed heuristic methods (to be explained in a subsequent section), capable of solving poorly structured problems. A problem is said to be well structured if the relationships between the variables and the objective function are known in the problem and if computational procedures exist for manipulating the values of the variables that optimize an objective. On the other hand, a problem is said to be poorly structured when it does not satisfy these conditions.

No attempt will be made to describe each quantitative area in great detail. Rather, an introduction will be given below.

***Sequencing.*** Sequencing models involve determining an optimal sequence for a set of jobs or events or the best sequence for servicing customers in order to minimize total time and costs. Sequencing problems are basically ones dealing with coordination of a large number of different tasks. Specific tasks must be performed in a certain order to complete a single project. Current techniques to handle sequencing problems include PERT (Program Evaluation and Review Technique)/time, PERT/cost, and PERT/LOB (Line of Balance). These are presently being applied to research and development, construction, new product planning, and similar areas. Other sequencing problems, such as machine scheduling, are solved by using simulation and heuristic techniques.

***Replacement.*** Replacement problems are generally of two types: those involving items that degenerate over a period of time and those that fail after a certain amount of time. The first group consists of the firm's fixed assets, such as machines and equipment, while the second type are inexpensive items, such as vacuum tubes and tires. Solutions to the high-cost items (first type) are obtained by the use of calculus and specialized programming methods. Indifference analysis (breakeven) provides another method for solving equipment selection and replacement problems. Statistical sampling and probability theory are used to replace low-cost items (second type) as they fail, at specified intervals, or a combination of these.

***Inventory.*** Inventory models are concerned basically with two decisions—"how much" to order at one time and "when" to order this quantity so as to keep total costs at a minimum. Carrying costs, ordering costs, and stock-out costs of inventory are determined so that a cost effectiveness relationship or model can be employed to select an appropriate balance between cost and shortages. Lowest cost decision rules for inventory can be obtained by algebra, calculus, probability theory, and simulation. The appropriate OR technique to implement will depend upon the attendant circumstances.

***Allocation.*** Allocation is applicable to problems dealing with limited resources. When there are a number of activities to be performed, alternative ways of doing them, and limited resources or facilities for performing each activity in the most effective way, there is an allocation problem. The approach to such problems is to combine activities and resources in an optimal manner so that overall efficiency is maximized, that is, profit is maximized or cost is minimized. This is known as "mathematical programming." When the constraints and the objective function (maximize profits or minimize costs) are expressed as linear equations, this is known as "linear programming." On the other hand, if any of the constraints or the objective function are nonlinear, this is called "nonlinear programming." Other types of mathematical programming techniques include integer, quadratic, convex, stochastic, decision, and parametric programming. They differ in the kinds of data that they handle and the kind of assumptions that are made.

A more recent outgrowth of mathematical programming is dynamic programming. It is extremely useful for processes that extend over a number of time periods or events. Instead of optimizing each decision as it occurs, dynamic programming takes into account the effects of current decisions on future time periods or events. Most problems of this kind require the use of a computer to manipulate the myriad of data.

***Assignment.*** Assignment problems involve the assignment of a number of jobs to the same number of resources (men). The desired assignment is one that will result in the greatest overall benefit to the firm. This problem type becomes more complex if some of the jobs require more than one resource and if the resources can be used for more than one job. Typical problems employing linear programming are those of scheduling jobs to machines or tasks to people for minimum overall cost or time.

***Transportation.*** Transportation problems are concerned with the most efficient shipping schedule for materials or products that must be moved from one location to another. Many times, there are excess products at the origins and deficiencies at the destination points. What is required is a minimum cost or time requirement for the problem's solution. The whole field of physical distribution where transportation is the only or major cost element lends itself to this situation. Linear programming, the stepping stone method, and similar quantitative techniques can be employed to solve this kind of problem.

***Competition.*** Competition models are used by business to develop advertising strategies, pricing policies, and timing for the introduction of new products. Statistical decision theory (probability) is an essential part of game theory to evaluate strategies. Since each competitor has many possible alternative courses of action, the problem is to determine the best method for making specific choices during the game. The optimum strategies are determined mathematically by computing the number of times each strategy should be played. Once the best strategies are calculated, the value of the game can be computed and, subsequently, read from a table.

Markov analysis can be included under the classification of competition models. The Markov process is a method of predicting competitive changes over time if customer brand loyalties and present market shares are known. Depending upon the loyalty of customers, Markov chains of the first, second, and higher order can be introduced for predicting future market shares.

***Queuing.*** Queuing models, sometimes referred to as waiting line theory, is concerned with uniform or random arrivals at a servicing or processing facility of limited capacity. The objective of this model is to determine the optimum number of personnel or facilities necessary to service customers who arrive when considering the cost of service and the cost of waiting or congestion. Not only are waiting lines applicable to customers, trucks, shop personnel, and airplanes, but also to inventory problems. Items in stock can be considered as an idle service facility waiting for customers. The demand for stock is an arrival for service while the outrage of stock can be looked upon as a queue of customers. Queues make great use of probability theory, calculus, and simulation.

***Simulation.*** Simulation, which can be used to simulate arrival and service times based upon random number tables in a queuing problem, lends itself to computer analysis. It is basically of two types. The first, Monte Carlo, generates factors like potential sales or delayed shipments by inspecting random number tables that are an essential part of the program. The second is systems simulation that employs historical data as input. The computer output shows the results that could have been obtained if the decision criteria had been used.

***Routing.*** Routing models are concerned with selecting a route that starts at a point of origin, goes through each city (intermediate point) on a trip, and returns to the starting point in the shortest distance in terms of time or cost. The routing model has been applied to production where the number of models or items produced is analogous to cities. Change-over production costs correspond to the cost of travel between cities.

***Search.*** Search theory makes use of prior experience and information in order to narrow down the areas that have the attributes of the desired objective. It has been applied to problem areas, such as exploration and quality control systems. Problems dealing with the storage and retrieval of information and the search pattern of customers in stores are also of this type.

***Combined OR Methods.*** Combined OR methods for well-structured problems indicate one of the future directions that operations research will take. Several of the above models, methods, and techniques are brought together to produce a new OR tool for managers. For example, a production control problem usually includes some combination of inventory allocation and waiting line models. While the usual procedure for solving combined processes consists of solving them one at a time in some logical sequence, appropriate models (where there are interrelationships) can be combined into one for an optimum solution.

***Heuristic Methods.*** Heuristic methods denote learning or self-adapting systems for problems that are poorly structured. The heuristic model uses rules of thumb to explore the most likely paths and to make educated guesses in coming to a conclusion. This replaces checking all alternatives to find the correct one that is characteristic of most approaches for well-structured problems. Heuristic programming appears to be very promising for the future of operations research.

The above classification does not encompass all operations research problems, but does include a great many that have been encountered up to this time. This listing is helpful to the manager in that it enables him to perceive what is common to all problems and reminds him that many quantitative methods are available for solving problems. The reader should not be too influenced by the name of the model, but rather keep an open mind in order to make analogies to comparable business situations. In essence, imagination can be an important key to the advancement of operations research as well as to the increased efficiency of the firm.

### Evaluation of Operations Research

*Operations research supplements the subjective feelings of the decision maker with objective output from mathematical models.*

With the solution of many problem areas by OR computer models for both well-structured and poorly structured problems, the utilization of operations research by all levels of management is increasing. OR methods provide management with solutions for many of its problems. Operations research gives the manager an opportunity to consider additional courses of action that were not available under older methods. Instead of looking at the problem, say from a two-dimensional viewpoint, a third dimension is added for a better understanding of the problem under study. This permits the manager to supplement his subjective feelings—hunch, intuition, and judgment—with the objective findings of the OR model for a better managerial decision. Not only does the quality of the managerial decision making process improve, but also frees him from spending so much time on current problems—their formulation and solution. His time is available to investigate new problems that arise and those poorly structured problems that have been ignored.

A significant factor that will aid the growth of operations research is continuing computer developments. Many problems that are considered presently to be insoluble will become capable of solution by OR methods. For example, mathematical models of the entire firm cannot possibly be handled by the present generations of computers due to their limited storage capacity. However, as newer technology increases storage capacity and lowers cost, it will permit the implementation of large-scale OR models that cut across the entire firm.

## PAST COMPUTER PERFORMANCE

*Internal operating speeds of computers have increased from one generation to another.*

Before exploring present and future computer developments, in particular, hardware and software, the internal operating speeds of computers are examined. They have increased from generation to generation, as shown in Figure 18-3 for selected computers.[2] As a result of these faster memories, the cost for performing the same number of calculations has dropped significantly over the years. Improvement in the number of operations per dollar between 1950 and 1962 has been at an average annual rate of 87% for commercial computation and 81% for scientific computation.[3] Research has also indicated that favorable cost calculations per dollar for the years 1963 through 1966 have averaged 160% per year for commercial computation and 115% for scientific computation.[4] Further research on this subject should indicate that equally promising performance can be purchased for different computer models whether they be from the same or competing equipment manufacturers.

[2]D. W. Brown and J. L. Burkhardt, "The Computer Memory Market," *Computers and Automation,* January 1969, p. 20.
[3]K. E. Knight, "Changes in Computer Performance," *Datamation,* September 1966, p. 40.
[4]K. E. Knight, "Evolving Computer Performance 1963–1967," *Datamation,* January 1969, p. 32.

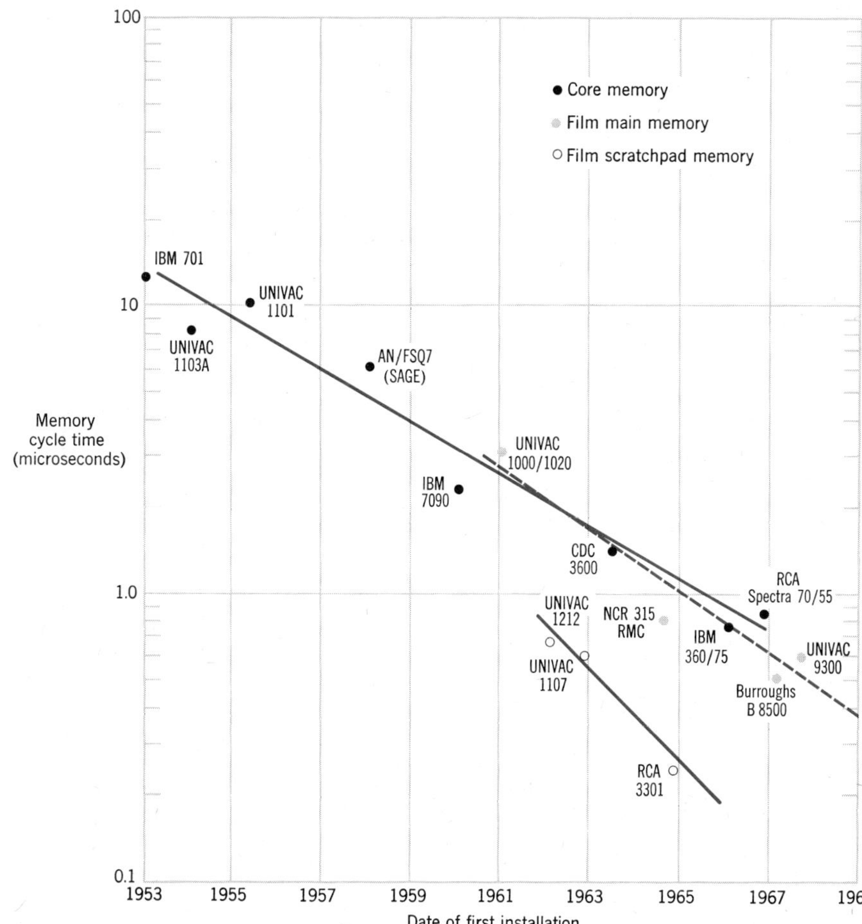


Figure 18-3 Memory cycle times for selected computers from 1953–1969.

*Grosch's law states that computing power increases as a function of cost squared.*

***Grosch's Law.*** The foregoing research continues to uphold *Grosch's Law*. His law predicts that computing power increases as a function of cost squared, that is, for twice the cost, the user should get four times as much computing power. For the two time periods stated, commercial computation results are: computing power = $K$ (cost)$^{2.2}$ for the 1950–1962 period and computing power = $K$ (cost)$^{3.1}$ for the 1963–1966 period where $K$ represents a constant derived from regression analysis—a yearly upward trend value. Comparable values for scientific computation are: $K$ (cost)$^{2.0}$ and $K$ (cost)$^{2.5}$ respectively.[5] When evaluating the periods studied, Grosch's law has been equaled or bettered. An important implication of this rule is that larger computers are lowest in cost when pricing per unit computations. Thus, there is an incentive to utilize large scale computer systems in order to handle the growing number of input/output devices and the large storage demands of massive data bases.

## PRESENT AND FUTURE COMPUTER DEVELOPMENTS

Analysis of hardware, software, and operating expenses, which are indicative of their future trend, have been undertaken by many reputable consulting

[5] *Ibid.*, p. 35.

firms. A composite of these studies (average values) is found in Figure 18-4. The most costly aspect of an EDP installation is the software expense which totals approximately 40% (24% for new applications plus 16% for current applications) versus about 36% for equipment rentals and/or depreciation charges. Thus the importance of software cost cannot be overemphasized.

| | AVERAGE (APPROXIMATE) |
|---|---|
| Equipment rental and/or depreciation costs | 36% |
| Systems development—systems analysis, systems design, and programming of new applications | 24% |
| Maintenance of current programs | 16% |
| Operating expenses for daily activities | 24% |
| | 100% |

Figure 18-4 Classification of computer expenses—based on several studies.

*The trend in computer costs is toward increasing software costs and decreasing hardware costs.*

With the present and future trends toward the installation of more sophisticated management information systems, software for these types of systems is getting more complex and expensive. Because software costs are continually increasing while hardware costs are declining for installing complex data processing systems, there is a marked tendency to acquire advanced hardware. This is in opposition to spending great sums of money creating software that will maximize the efficiency of the hardware. In essence, the cost factors of the equipment itself affects directly the amount of software that will be required in installing a new EDP system.

### Computer Hardware

*Computer deliveries are expected to be approximately 50,000 annually by 1980—small and mini-computers will predominate.*

The rise and significance of computers have been manifested during the first two computer decades (1952–1971). For example, in 1961, the computer industry had hardware sales in the neighborhood of $1 billion, with deliveries approximating 1000 systems. Within a short span of 10 years, deliveries were running at a rate of 18,000 to 20,000 units. By 1980, yearly deliveries are expected to be about 50,000 units. Most of the growth will be accounted for by small and mini-computers. These projections are based upon various research studies.

*Hardware expenditures for peripherals and terminals will continue to exceed those for central processors.*

***Major Hardware Components.*** As more and more large computers are installed which are capable of on-line real-time processing, there will be a growing number of remote terminal devices for each computer. By 1980, these devices will account for approximately half the total peripheral equipment market, reflecting a phenomenal growth in remote computing. This trend is depicted in Figure 18-5. In essence, the cost of computer hardware will be highest for terminals (teletypewriters, CRTs, and similar devices), followed by peripherals (input/output units, on-line files, and comparable units), and central processors (CPUs). Also, about 3 million terminals are predicted to be in use by 1980 and approximately half of these will be visual display units.

***Faster Peripheral Devices.*** Despite the unbelievable fast speeds of the central processor, it is only as fast as the peripheral equipment that feeds data in or out of the electronic data processing system. As a result of this phenomenon, there has been a virtual explosion of faster peripheral equipment by many independent equipment manufacturers today. This trend in faster peripheral equipment is expected to continue in the near future although the independent manufacturers

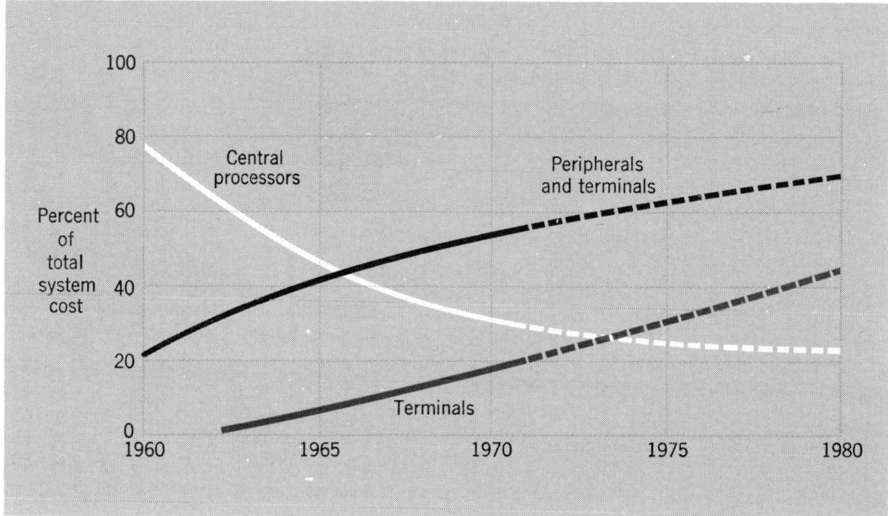


Figure 18-5 Expenditures on terminals will exceed that of central processors by a wide margin. Terminals will account for over half of the total peripheral and terminal market by 1980.

combined share of this emerging market is bound to decline. As the large computer manufacturers see a peripheral unit that has sufficient volume for mass production, they will take part of the market away from the independents.

*Microelectronics will further these hardware developments:*
- *large-scale integration*
- *associative memory*
- *laser*
- *magnetic bubble*

***Microelectronics.*** Microelectronics will continue to play a major role in future hardware developments. It permits faster and more efficient hardware and enables manufacturers to reduce production costs. In particular, microelectronics will be employed in computer memories where the new technology permits smaller, faster, and cheaper storage of data. In essence, microelectronics make use of smaller hardware components whereby electricity does not have to travel as far when compared to larger components that perform the same function. This approach permits a speedup in the processing ability of the central processor.

*Large-scale integration.* Past and current computers have employed integrated circuits (complete circuits or modules of memory are manufactured as single units) and thin film (produced by depositing very thin spots of metallic alloy on a ceramic or metal plate) for the computer's memory. Equipment manufacturers are currently utilizing LSI or large-scale integration circuits. Basically, this refers to the batch fabrication of memory elements and logical circuits. A large amount of logic hardware can be used for the same price of standard hardware. In effect, LSI circuits affect the amount of hardware and software that will be used in a computer system. Since there is a problem of losing information when power is turned off with large-scale integration, it will probably be reserved for high speed control memories or other special storage.

*Associative memory.* Another innovation in computer hardware is the associative memory. For this hardware concept, the data are addressed by association or on the basis of part of its contents since all data are searched simultaneously to locate specific data. This is in contrast with a standard computer system which requires that the specific location in memory be addressed for the desired information. Likewise, the conventional system requires that the user keep track of the memory locations. Even though associative memory costs are high, its most promising applications are information retrieval, report preparation, and inquiries from computer files. In these areas, the associative memory locates data, such as in tables and indexes, with a minimum of time.

*Laser*. Among the most promising hardware techniques for the future is the use of the laser. It has the ability to store data in a very compact manner. The laser has the capability of storing about one million bits per square inch on film. Laser-based computers, featuring many trillion bits of memory, will be common. Its basic principle of storage is the 0-bit and 1-bit combination of any binary system. It records a 1-bit by concentrating a very small beam of light for an extremely short period of time which results in "buring the emulsion." The laser reads data by sensing the white and black spots (0 or 1).

*Magnetic bubbles, pioneered by Bell Telephone Laboratories, are capable of compact and inexpensive data storage and processing.*

*Magnetic bubbles or domains*. An equally promising hardware development in the future are tiny magnetic "bubbles" or "domains," developed by Bell Telephone Laboratories. Like the transistor, the magnetic devices depend on basic solid-state physical phenomena. While transistors use the electrical characteristics of semiconductor crystals to amplify and switch signals, the new technology takes advantage of the magnetic alignment properties of crystals grown from mixtures of iron or lead oxides and rare-earth metals. Thin slices of such magnetizable crystals can store as many as a million bits of information per square inch. Stacks of slices might hold millions of words and numbers in a volume not much larger than a few cigarette packages. Currently, storing that much information takes units the size of clothes closets, packed with precision machinery.

Compactness is only one of the advantages Bell Laboratories researchers have found in devices made from their magnetic materials. The devices have no moving parts to wear out, generate little heat, operate on very low power, and need very little wiring to interconnect them. Once the crystals are grown, manufacture will be much simpler than making semiconductor devices. The potential is a vast reduction in the cost of storing and handling data.

These magnetic components have been nicknamed bubble devices since the technology is based on generating tiny magnetized areas known as magnetic domains in the thin crystalline slices (Figure 18-6). The domains—a fraction of a thousandth of an inch in diameter—move across the slices under the influence of electrical currents in printed conductors on the surface, or in response to changes in the magnetic fields surrounding the unit. Under polarized light, the domains are visible, and under a microscope look like tiny bubbles. If the circuits are operated very slowly, it is possible to watch the bits of data move through the storage and logic patterns that are printed on the surface of the crystal to guide them. The bubbles blend into a blur as the speed of data transfer increases toward the present maximum of 3 million bits per second.

### Computer Software

*Major trends in computer software encompass:*

- *improved programming languages*
- *more efficient compilers*
- *greater use of firmware and microprogramming*
- *limited human language programming*

Current hardware developments have been impressive when compared to earlier computer hardware. Unfortunately, the same cannot be said for computer software. The promises of software designers have not lived up to expectations. Often, the initial software capabilities for a particular generation of computers are realized only after another generation is announced to replace the existing one. Thus, another cycle of frustration with computer software begins since the next generation software, when implemented, does not live up to its original specifications.

***General Purpose Programming Languages.*** General purpose programming languages, such as COBOL and FORTRAN, have been widely used in the past and today. The trend seems to be toward some kind of combined programming language—one that utilizes English language words and statements plus mathematical

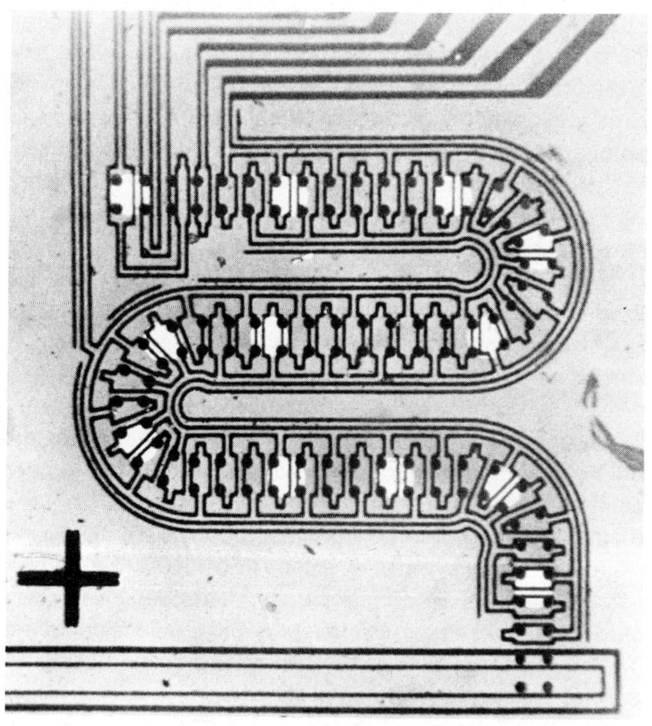

Figure 18-6 Tiny magnetic bubbles or domains. (Courtesy Bell Telephone Laboratories.)

formulas where needed. This approach has been apparent in the programming language PL/1 where there is an attempt to remedy the deficiencies of COBOL and FORTRAN. The net result is a greater standardization of computer software that allow programming packages to be used more widely. The dominance of IBM also permits greater standardization than if a different market structure existed.

***Compilers.*** Early compilers like FORTRAN required a large memory to handle them. Over the last several years, more efficient compilers have been written which now require only a small amount of storage capacity. The newer specification formats for programming languages are more user-oriented and less prone to errors than previously. In addition, the rapid developments in hardware speeds make the programming languages more attractive. Even though more time and instructions are needed to execute generalized software, 25 to 50% more, the central processor is still waiting on the computer's input and output devices.

***Firmware.*** Many of the functions now performed by software are now and will continue to be included in the firmware of the computer system. An example of firmware today is stored logic which allows the computer to accept instructions that are not included in its circuitry. When the instruction is actually decoded for execution, a routine is entered which instructs the central processor to undertake a series of steps that are included in the circuit design. The result of this set of instructions is that their execution has the same effect as if the circuitry of the computer was specifically designed to handle the instruction itself. Thus the computer is capable of executing a small number of elementary operations while the programmer writes all the instructions for a specific program.

Firmware has also been referred to as microprograms since the creator of a microprogram sequence is neither writing a software program nor designing hardware logic. Actually, he is performing an undertaking whose net result is a mixture of both. In essence, it may be possible (though not necessarily desirable) to separate completely the three functions—hardware, microprogramming, and software. This separation would dictate that the stored logic that implements the individual micro-instruction be designed first and be made compatible with the machine's hardware and software. The design of "microinstruction set" will influence the ease of computer programming. Even though firmware (microprograms) is currently being employed by many of the current computers, it is expected that this concept will be extended to include more applications in order to speed up the programming process.

*Sometime in the future, programmers will be taught phonetics, syntax, and semantics in order to converse intelligently and efficiently with computers.*

***Human Language Programming.*** Research is currently underway to ascertain the specific relationships between sentence structure and part of sentences used in normal speech and the ways in which the computer can handle them. This understanding will help equipment manufacturers in writing computer software languages that can better fit our human language. Hopefully, the ultimate of this research activity will allow the programmer to converse directly with the computer. Instead of sending the company's programmers to a special programming course, the individual will attend several sessions on how to instruct the computer for the most efficient program. Included in his training will be sessions on phonetics (conversing with the computer so that one is clearly understood) plus syntax and semantics (relating structure to the meaning of the language). In essence, language research may prove to be the most effective and fastest means of increasing the efficiency of computer software.

The results of research by Bell Telephone Laboratories in this area is a system that converts text input to synthetic speech. Words input through a Teletype are automatically produced as "nearly natural sounding" synthetic speech. The experimental work takes advantage of an improved understanding of speech patterns. The computer is provided with mathematical approximations for the shapes and motions the human vocal tract assumes when uttering common sounds and sound sequences. It is also provided with a basic dictionary of word categories and definitions in digital form. Rules of timing, pitch, and stress which people use naturally in everyday conversation are also approximated.

When words are inputed, the system analyzes the sentence, assigns stress and timing to each word, and finds a phonetic description of each word in the dictionary. Mathematical descriptions of vocal tract motions are then computed, converted to a signal, and generated as electrical speech signals which may be heard over a loudspeaker or telephone. Uses of this new technique include a doctor desiring the recitation of a page from a medical book, a stock manager seeking information about inventory, or an airline clerk looking for flight information.

While current and prospective software developments are headed toward more standardization, more efficient compilers, better firmware, and improved overall performance, software innovations have not taken advantage of hardware advancements. In fact, it may be quite a long time before software is on the same developmental level as its counterpart. The widening gap between hardware and software can be narrowed appreciably by an entirely different approach. This revolves around an effort to produce computers that will respond to the language of man, either directly or through a compiler.

### Computer Systems

The computer system of the 1970's is a real-time management information system. Basically, it is a computer based system that includes a comprehensive data

*Real-time management information systems will be replaced eventually by newer management information systems that solve complex problems for all management levels.*

base that can be used for managerial decision making. Real-time MIS provides valuable information routinely and upon request as well as avoids the duplication of files. Such a system is capable of integrating the managerial functions for timely feedback.

An important design feature of any real-time system is the integration of data processing activities. All the firm's major functions are operating in such a way that a change in one area will automatically trigger a change in other areas if they apply. With this system, all transactions are captured immediately upon their occurrence and are processed by a central computer system. Where necessary, the computer makes the required decision(s) and relays the instructions to responsible individuals for timely action. Likewise, computer report printouts, including exception items, are prepared promptly for appropriate action. In essence, a real-time management information system is a data center with capabilities of direct access for planning, organizing, directing, and controlling the functional activities of the firm.

***Data-Managed Systems.*** Once real-time MIS has reached its height in the late 1970's or later, the next step in the evolving maturity of computer systems will be the design of newer MIS systems, sometimes called data-managed systems. This new approach requires a broader viewpoint of the organization structure since it is directed toward the higher level of the firm's management. Instead of being concerned primarily with the functional areas or the management of business functions at the divisional level, the accent is on the management of the entire corporation at the corporate level. Standard data formats and procedures are needed to allow organization-wide use of shared data banks.

Since the primary role of top management is to allocate scarce resources among the various factors of production, general managers must be able to recognize and assess alternative actions at the highest level in the firm. The dynamics of business, such as the complexity of a firm's product mixes and the shifting of markets, dictates that top management must have the capability of assessing the effects of both internal plans and external business conditions on business objectives and operating performance. Top management's data information system must be capable of producing timely and accurate data on these critical issues.

The progression toward such a system will be slow. The development of this general management concept must be undertaken in a logical sequence. Basically, this systems approach must rely heavily upon the mathematical modeling concepts of operations research that result in overall optimization for the firm. Considerable developmental work is required before this new MIS concept can be implemented.

### Computer Utilities

Computer utilities will become more widespread as a result of the problems associated with operating an efficient data processing system. They will be capable of serving small, medium, and large firms with many remote I/O terminals connected to a computer system. The central processor, in such a system, shares a common memory that is quite large, highly efficient, and capable of handling many programs concurrently. Software, which is basic to a large EDP system, will be built into the hardware itself. The computer utility will integrate activities now undertaken on a separate basis. Systems development work, programming, time sharing, optical scanning, real-time processing, remote batch processing, financing, leasing, and the manufacture of peripheral hardware will be undertaken by one firm versus a series of firms as presently.

## ELECTRONIC MONEY (CHECKLESS SOCIETY)

*An electronic money system, sometimes called the checkless society, will have the entire banking system linked together by a vast communications network.*

Future computer developments in hardware, software, and systems make the feasibility of electronic money or the checkless society possible. The implementation of electronic money will drastically affect the banking industry. It will also affect credit card companies, finance companies, oil companies, department stores, and mail order houses, to name the major ones. Money transfers will be made instantaneously through electronic impulses and computers that utilize data communication channels. The present concept of money (passing paper from hand to hand and bank to bank) will become obsolete for the most part. However, paper money will be used to acquire small items and for those who will not accept this new method of handling money.

An electronic money system would have all firms and institutions linked together in a massive data processive system. The entire system would be linked by a vast communication network (Figure 18-7). A data processing banking center would be

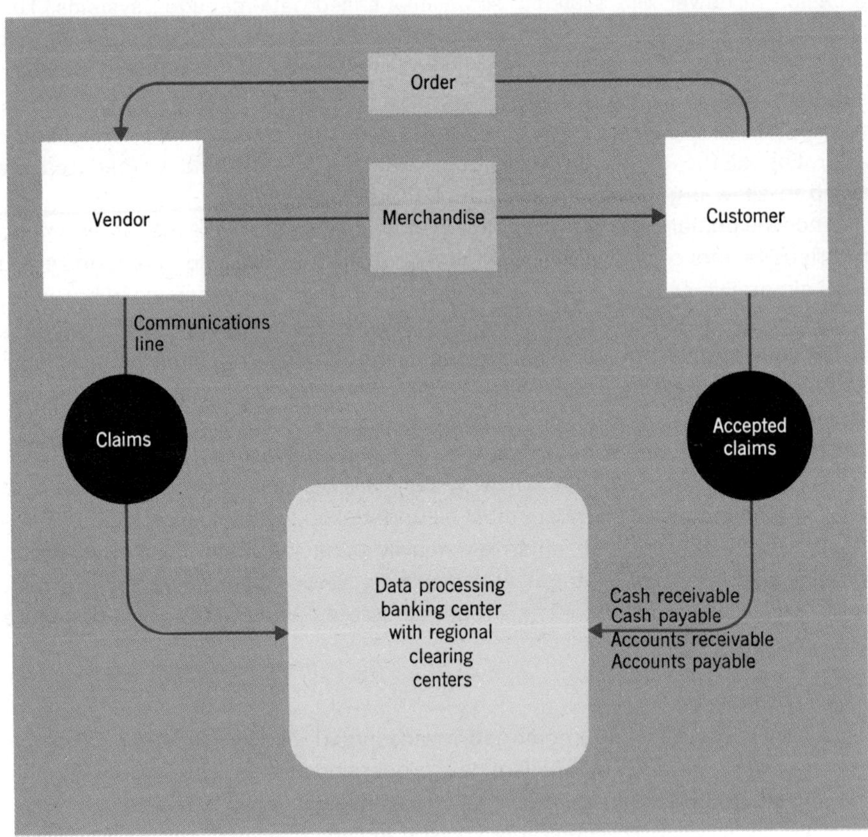


Figure 18-7 Relationship of the customer and vendor in an electronic money system.

used to clear claims (equivalent to invoices) against accepted claims (equivalent to payments). Basically, the system would operate as follows. The vendor submits invoices to one of the regional clearing centers. Similarly, the customer submits a list of claims that he is willing to pay. Both the claims and the accepted claims can be transmitted to the data processing banking center in machine language.

Payment could be made by means of a clearing operation. The net effect would be an elimination of checks.

An essential part of electronic money would be a firm's payroll. Instead of the individual receiving his payroll check periodically, his salary less all legitimate deductions would be written electronically on tape. This tape from the company's office would be fed to a computer at the payee's bank and entered as a deposit. The computer at the individual's bank would automatically pay all his recurring bills (generally on a monthly basis) which include payments on a home, a car, insurance policies, department store accounts, and similar items. Likewise, the computer will transfer the excess bank balance to a savings account, mutual fund, stock account, or some other authorized account.

*The individual will use a small plastic card (containing his or her voice pattern) for transacting business in a checkless society.*

***Plastic Money Card.*** Under an electronic money system, the individual would be able to handle daily transactions without physically utilizing paper money. This can be accomplished by having everyone carry a small plastic card that contains a voice pattern on the card itself. (Since everyone has a voice pattern—about unique as one's fingerprints, the bank's computer will test for the correct voice pattern before accepting a charge for goods or services.) The seller will insert the plastic card in a reading device that will identify the individual and voice at the customer's bank via the computer. If sufficient cash is available in the customer's account, the seller will ring up the sale which transfers the appropriate amount from the customer's account to the seller's account. If the customer has insufficient funds, the bank's computer can arrange a loan on the spot. On the other hand, if the customer prefers to let the bill run for a period of time, say to the end of the month (allowable by the seller), the transaction will be so recorded at the customer's bank. The seller will record the sale, but will not have funds switched until the date agreed upon.

To determine the balance of one's account, the individual would slip his plastic card into a videophone terminal (installed in his home) and key in the appropriate code numbers. After a quick identity check of number and voice pattern, the computer is ready for the request. The person would enter a request to view his up-to-the-minute bank balance which would be flashed on the viewing screen. The visual display unit would generally include: bank balance, saving account amount, mutual fund holdings, stock holdings, home mortgage balance, payments made in the last week, prearranged payments due the next week, and projection of deposits from employer for payroll check. This current visual information would assist the individual in deciding whether or not additional large purchases could be made without jeopardizing his financial position.

*Key to the acceptance of electronic money is the human element.*

Before this electronic money system can operate, there must be full acceptance of such a card by all banks of the country which must be linked into one credit card system. This is necessary since a store that keeps its account at one bank must accept the card of a person who keeps his account at another. The use of an "Interbank Card" whereby all banks in the United States would honor each other's cards is required. However, this problem is not as complex as obtaining public acceptance of this national system. For one thing, banks have been selling people on the idea of getting a receipt for everything they buy through cancelled checks. Now this concept must be undone. All in all, the psychological barriers are much greater than the technical problems. Perhaps in about 20 years all facets of the checkless society will have been assembled and operating in an efficient manner for most individuals in the United States.

## TELEPURCHASING

*Tele-purchasing is a method of viewing consumer products on a home CRT unit and placing an order for products viewed.*

The foregoing EDP advancement of electronic money need not stop with a checkless society. Perhaps, the most striking development of all can be expected with the mass arrival of the Bell Telephone's Picturephone. Basically, the Picturephone can be used as an inexpensive terminal since it has a screen (CRT) and can be connected to a computer. A housewife would be able to telepurchase or push-button shop from her own home. For example, she could call a department store and be connected automatically to the computer by inserting her "Interbank Card" in her phone set. She would request the store to display certain items on her Picturephone screen along with the code numbers for ordering. If she desires one or more items displayed, she taps out the code numbers for the item or items and the corresponding quantity. The department store's computer takes over from this point on, that is, it checks to make sure the customer can pay for the item and prepares the necessary forms for shipping the merchandise.

Another approach to telepurchasing is the expansion of cable television to serve as another outlet for inexpensive terminals. A keyboard or a Touch-Tone telephone could be linked to the television set. The housewife could, for example, switch to a cable channel and get the A & P, Safeway, or Kroger selection of the day. She could push a button when a certain item appeared on the screen and an order could be placed simultaneously with the warehouse. The end result would be comparable to that of the Picturephone.

An inexpensive terminal in most homes will lead to many other uses. Among these are: planning dinner menus, keeping track of the family budget, and printing an up-to-date financial position of the family finances. Income taxes could be figured on this low-cost terminal. Children could utilize this on-line device for solving business and mathematical homework problems as well as participating in games. Also, medical data on the family could be viewed on an emergency basis for any doctor having need of such information. This sample listing need not end here. Many more activities could be found for an on-line I/O terminal device in the home.

## SUMMARY

When data processing is viewed in terms of how it will affect the firm in the future, operational daily decisions will be affected greatly by the development of advanced data processing systems. The use of mathematical and heuristic models for well-structured and poorly structured problems will be commonplace for management. Likewise, advanced operations research models will be available for solving overall corporate problems. However, overall management responsibility for developing company plans and organizing for effective execution of the plans are not going to be dramatically changed by newer generation computers and systems. Top management will not be replaced by the computer in the future. Instead, the firm's key executives will become the firm's most enthusiastic computer supporters who will employ it as an important tool for managerial analysis and decision making.

Future developments in hardware (faster and smaller units with more storage capacity) and software (greater standardization and simplication in programming) will permit the use of more complex data processing systems. The real-time management information system, which deals basically with the management of the firm's major functions at the plant and divisional level, will be replaced by a higher level concept in business data processing. This new design will allow organization-wide use of shared data banks, in particular, for the top management level. There will be great need for systems analysts and operations research specialists attached to the corporate staff. Their primary function will be solving corporate problems with various computer models of operations research. The net result of this data-managed system concept is that top management will be able to assess alternative courses of action and select the optimum one for future planning.

Interesting future data processing developments include electronic money and telepurchasing. Although there are many barriers presently to a gigantic data processing banking system, acceptance or rejection of this innovation for the entire economy revolves around the human element. To ignore the "people factor" in implementing such a system is completely unrealistic. Because of its importance, the Epilogue takes a last look at data processing for business and management from this viewpoint.

## *QUESTIONS*

1. (a) How do computers presently affect the major functions of the firm?
   (b) How will computers in the future affect the major functions of the firm?
2. What is the relationship of operations research methods to computers? Explain.
3. State Grosch's Law. Is it valid based upon past research?
4. What is the future direction in terms of cost for the following?
   (a) central processors
   (b) peripherals
   (c) terminals
5. What major developments are expected in the future for the following?
   (a) computer hardware
   (b) computer software
   (c) computer systems
6. When consideration is given to future data processing developments, what impact will they have on the firm? Explain.
7. (a) After real-time management information systems have reached their peak, what is the next major direction in systems design?
   (b) What effect will new system concepts have on the individual within the firm and the firm itself?
8. Will our economy ever operate completely (100%) with electronic money sometime in the future?

EPILOGUE

# A Last Look at Data Processing for Business and Management

The Individual
Group
Management
Organization Structure
Firm
Society
Conclusion

*Computers do not operate in a vacuum, but are an integral part of our lives. They are capable of relieving us of boring and routine tasks. (Courtesy International Business Machines Corporation.)*

The epilogue concentrates on data processing as it affects:

- the individual
- group
- management
- organization structure
- firm
- society

The purpose of focusing attention on the human element is to indicate how present and future directions of data processing are and will affect our daily lives. An overview (Figure E-1) helps one recognize fundamental changes occurring and assists in understanding why they are happening. A basic understanding of innovations will, hopefully, help the individual adjust to the new data processing environment.

## THE INDIVIDUAL

*The individual will need to override computer answers due to extraneous conditions not contained in computer programs.*

With the growing number of data processing systems that rely heavily on computers and the increasing ability of such systems, there appears to be a danger that the creative talents of many company personnel are and will be stifled. If there are computer programmed decision rules that optimize performance for basic decisions of the firm, it would appear that there is a tendency to rely completely on these decisions. This approach results in a "depersonalizing" effect on the firm's decision making process. The individual carries out the decision determined by the computer program. Instead of discussing the factors that affect the decision with his immediate superior, he uses the computer decision since he does not have the capability of modifying the decision. The final result is that the hard and fast decisions of computers relieve the individual of all responsibility for an accurate decision and makes him feel frustrated. In effect, his creative talents are being restrained. Clearly, such a condition is undesirable.

Although sophisticated systems will abound in the future, there will never be one that is 100% accurate for all decisions. Why is this so? There are always future conditions that arise which were not initially contemplated by the computer decision model. Among these are changes in the economy, unexpected contracts or sales, strikes, floods, and similar conditions. In essence, there will always be a need for the individual to recognize the changed condition and to override or modify the computer answer. This process of changing must be kept to a minimum or else problems may result. Thus the individual does have the ability to utilize his creative talents by questioning computer decisions in light of changing business conditions that have not been considered by the computer decision model.

In the past as well as presently, there has been a substantial reduction in the number of routine clerical jobs. This trend will continue and the individual will become a specialist in some phase of the data processing operation. The daily routines of getting the work out has and will be replaced by feeding data efficiently into the computer system and directing its outputs to the proper section. Computer specialization will allow the individual to avoid routine and monotonous daily tasks for more imaginative ways of processing data throughout the system.

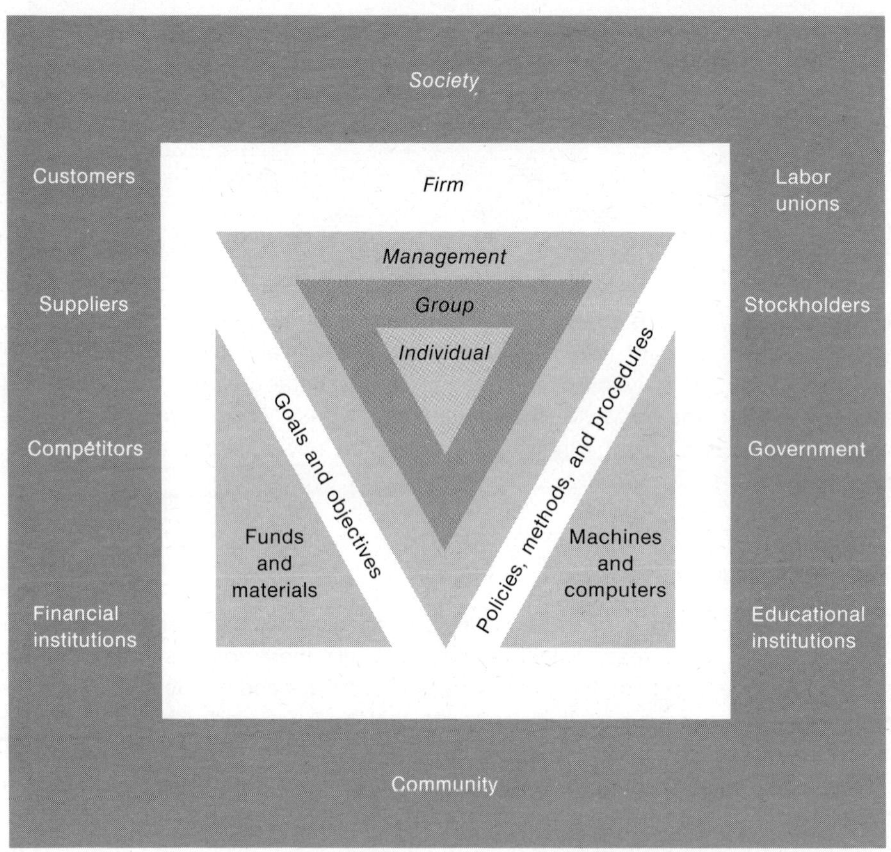


Figure E-1 An overview depicting the important factors that affect present and future data processing developments.

## GROUP

*A small nucleus of personnel will operate advanced data processing equipment, thereby reducing the cost of the operational activity.*

The group will also be greatly affected by the many sophisticated computer systems now and in the future. Instead of having large groups of personnel processing data in the various departments, they will be replaced by advanced equipment that utilizes a small nucleus of personnel to operate them. In this manner, the cost of processing will drop. With continued rising personnel costs and lower equipment costs, it is beneficial for the firm to employ more equipment and less people. Thus, data processing developments in the future will dramatically affect the size of the group and the job content for each individual within the group. This changing condition for the individual, a member of the group, will allow the firm to take advantage of the rising educational level of its employees who do not want routine jobs, but ones that are a challenge to their talents.

## MANAGEMENT

*Many of management routine tasks will be relegated to the computer. More time will be spent on the managerial functions, in particular, the planning function.*

Advanced data processing systems will have an impact on the format of information reaching top management in the future. Many managerial reports will be received on visual display devices and via a management control center which will be connected directly to the computer. Considerable improvement will be apparent in the computerized selection of pertinent management information along with a reduction in the amount of irrelevant information reaching management. Generally, great stress will be placed on exception items, favorable or unfavorable deviations from the current profit plan. This will allow all managers to practice "management by exception."

In addition to the timeliness of exception reporting, there will be new computer applications, especially to assist lower and middle management. The receipt of real-time information will be quite helpful at these management levels in controlling the firm's operations. It should be noted that real-time information is rarely needed by top management since their basic concern is long-range planning. Data for short periods of time, say one day, week, or month, are not critical to their important work.

In the future, the number of managerial operating problems reaching the top executive will diminish. Since computers will have the task of controlling many phases of the operation, top management will feel confident that some of its responsibility can be delegated to middle and, in some cases, to lower management under computer control. This will give management more time for solving poorly structured problems and, in particular, spending more time on the planning function of the firm.

Simulation models will be used by management at the higher levels to explore alternative courses of action. For top management, this means that operations research and computer specialists will be a part of their staff. High-level executives will want to evaluate alternative long-range plans, pricing decisions, advertising programs, product lines, and comparable business activities by having their assistants simulate these conditions on the computer. The use of I/O terminals, coupled with simulation models, will provide an acceptable solution to many complex management problems that defy exact mathematical formulation and solution by other methods.

## ORGANIZATION STRUCTURE

*The organization structure will tend to have fewer levels as a result of the accessibility of common business data stored on-line and available in a real-time processing mode.*

The future impact of computers on the organization structure will be pronounced as it is now. Currently, many middle management and lower management tasks have been relegated to the computer. As more and more areas are brought under computer control, more routine tasks, assigned to the various levels of management, will be computerized. The assignment of routine jobs to the computer will allow management personnel, especially the middle management level, more time to plan their activities, to instruct their personnel more thoroughly, and to motivate their subordinates toward the accomplishment of specific objectives. With more time available for creative tasks and less time required for routine matters, managers will hold positions that tend to be much more challenging and rewarding. Similarily, the manager will have the required time for running his department efficiently rather than being bogged down in a series of tasks that are capable of routine solution by the computer.

Middle management positions, as indicated above, will be upgraded with increased employment of advanced EDP systems. Since top management depends upon the specialization and skills of middle managers, the computer will allow an increase of this specialization and these skills. Middle management positions will be upgraded as a result of the increased complexities of the firm, its needs, and the greater amount of responsibility inherent in these new positions. Thus, greater computerization and systemation will restructure middle management jobs, organize work on a more logical basis, and free middle managers for more important tasks.

Although many firms will change and/or eliminate departments, management jobs, and clerical tasks as more applications are found for computers, there will be a great need to increase the number of computer specialists, operational specialists, and operations research personnel. The increasing level of computer sophistication will require specialists at all operating levels of the firm, including top management. The immediate access to a common data base by all company personnel necessitates the need for specialists who can perform the required manipulation of data using specialized computer programs and models. The rise of specialists and technicians will be commonplace as more complex data processing systems are implemented.

The restructuring of the organization away from traditional departmental lines for advanced computer systems will result in fewer departments because of the need to integrate activities around major functions. With this approach, the computer is the pivotal point around which the firm can operate. Not only is this structure compatible with real-time management information systems, but it is also a sound basis for future management information systems (data-managed systems).

### FIRM

*Advanced data processing hardware and software will make it possible to link suppliers-manufacturers-wholesalers-retailers in a data communications network.*

Future data processing advancements will have a very decided impact on the firm as now, especially when considering the degree of centralization and decentralization. Modern communications advances, in particular those employed in real-time MIS, make it possible to centralize decision making in a geographically decentralized organization. For the manager, it makes little difference whether the central data processing facility is in the next room or thousands of miles away. The computer system is always available via input/output terminals. Thus, important data for decision making can be centralized for use by administrative and operating managers. However, there is still need for local managers to cope with changing environmental factors in their areas and to solve their problems accordingly. For example, personnel behavior and motivation are still the responsibility of decentralized management while production, inventory, accounting, and similar functions can be easily planned and controlled centrally.

Advancements of data processing will not be limited to the firm itself, but will be extended to all firms in the marketing of goods. The supplier-manufacturer-wholesaler-retailer chain will be linked together in a common data processing system. Basically, this approach is an extension of the total systems concept. A replenishment of stock by the retailer will be automatically communicated via on-line programs to the wholesaler. He, in turn, will feed the order plus other orders received on a periodic basis (say hourly) to the manufacturer's on-line computer. The manufacturer's program will interrogate its present finished goods inventory. If goods are available, items will be shipped. A message will be relayed to the wholesaler and retailer in the marketing chain on the status of the item ordered. On the other hand, if goods are not available for immediate shipment, a production order will be initiated. If raw materials are not available for production, the manufacturer's computer will send a message to the appropriate supplier (several suppliers will be hooked on-line—costs and service will be the basis for selection of supplier) for issuing a production order in his plant or any other action that is appropriate to the situation. Again, an on-line message is relayed immediately concerning the shipping date to the manufacturer. This date plus other data on manufactured goods form the basis for a tentative shipping date which is relayed to the wholesaler and retailer in this on-line chain. This whole process may take from a matter of minutes up to a few hours, depending upon the computer system utilized and the availability of the required inventory at the various levels in the chain. In contrast, this process may take a few weeks if normal communication channels are used.

## SOCIETY

*The phenominal growth of data processing will continue to have a pronounced impact on society. It is estimated that the data processing industry will be the largest one by the 21st century.*

Greater utilization of advanced computer systems in the future will not be confined only to business and government areas, but will be extended to many phases of society. This was evident in the discussion on electronic money. It is also evident when applying for an office job. The computer industry has displaced many boring, repetitive, and uninteresting jobs with newer and more challenging ones. Total employment will not be affected as was the case with automation in the plant. Jobs, displaced by a computer installation, are generally offset by jobs created by this growing industry. The final effect of future data processing advancements is that newly created jobs are more specialized than their predecessors. Those who lack these new skills are going to be unemployable since our computer-oriented economy has few openings for unskilled and uneducated people. Thus, our present problems of hiring the hard-core unemployed for administrative and office jobs will be further compounded by the increasing need for specialists.

*Proper employment of computers is necessary for preserving the inalienable rights of the individual.*

Not only does society face additional problems of adapting to electronic money and continued technological unemployment resulting from computers but it also faces the problem of invasion of privacy. In the past, the cry of society has been, "I am tired of being an IBM number, I want to be treated like a person." In the future, the cry of the average citizen might be, "I want to control my own destiny despite my errors in the past." Since central data banks of governmental agencies, credit bureaus, banks, savings and loans, and similar institutions will be common, the individual's past might well be weighed too heavily. The individual will charge that the computer has painted him into a corner from which he may never recover. Invasion of privacy and infringement on the freedom of the individual may well cause large numbers of people to turn away from our capitalistic system. This unfortunate "computer plague on society" can be clearly avoided by an intelligent use of central data banks, that is, the banks can be employed only for statistical analysis without identifying specific individuals. In essence, confidential information should not be used for spying on the general populace.

## CONCLUSION

Advancements in data processing do not occur in a vacuum, but are implemented into a system that affects the individual, the group, management, the organization structure, the firm, and finally society. Society, in the final analysis, can accept or reject this new technology. It is interesting to note that this second technological revolution (automation was the first) is also meeting with opposition. Even though both are beasts of burden, computers are not being opposed because of unemployment problems as automation was and still is, but rather because of the impersonal nature of their operation. Ironically, this popular notion need not be true since computer data banks have the ability to centralize all pertinent data on the individual through government banks and credit bureau data files. In reality, the computer has the capability of being more personal than any type system in the past. Proper use of computers, then, is essential for preserving the basic tenets of a democratic society.

## *QUESTIONS*

1. What is the relationship of the individual, group, management, organization structure, firm, and society to computers? Explain thoroughly.
2. Are more changes likely to occur in management jobs or nonmanagement jobs? Explain.
3. From the human aspect, set forth a desirable approach to computers that is compatible with the basic tenets of our democratic society.

# APPENDIX

# Glossary of Terms

*Absolute coding.* Coding that uses machine language instructions and can be directly executed by a computer without prior translation to a different form.

*Access time.* The time interval between the instant at which data are called for from a storage device and the instant delivery is completed—the read time. Also, the time interval between the instant at which data are requested to be stored and the instant at which storage is completed.

*Accumulator.* A storage device in the arithmetic unit in which the results of arithmetic and logical operations are formed.

*Address.* A label, name, or number identifying a register, a storage location, or a device from which information is received or to which it is transmitted.

*Address modification.* The process of changing the address part of a machine instruction by means of coded instructions.

*Address register.* A register in which an address is stored.

*ADP.* Automatic data processing is a term used to describe a minimum of manual operations in processing data.

*ALGOL.* An abbreviation for algorithmic-oriented language, which is an international procedure-oriented language.

*Algorithm.* A prescribed set of well-defined rules or processes for the solution of a problem in a finite number of steps.

*Alphanumeric code.* A system in which characters may be either letters of the alphabet, numerals, or special symbols.

*Analog computer.* A calculating device that operates on numbers represented by measurable physical quantities, such as the amount of voltage, temperature, and the like.

*Analog signal.* A continuous signal whose magnitude is proportional to the effect it represents.

*Application package.* A computer routine or set of routines designed for a specific application, such as inventory control, on-line savings accounting, and linear programming.

*Applications programmer.* A programmer who writes programs for the needs of specific applications.

*Arithmetic unit.* The part of the computer processing section that does the adding, subtracting, multiplying, dividing, and comparing.

*ASCII.* American Standard Code for Information Interchange.

*ASR (Automatic Send Receive).* A teleprinter unit that allows messages to be prepared and edited off-line on paper tape for automatic transmission.

*Assembler language.* A language intermediate between machine language and English, but closer to the former.

*Assembly program.* A computer program that takes sequential instructions written by the programmer in a nonmachine language and changes them to a machine language used by the computer.

*Associative memory.* A storage device whose storage locations are identified by their contents rather than by positions, as in computer storage devices.

*Asynchronous computer.* A computer in which each operation starts as a result of a signal generated by the completion of the previous operation or by the availability of the equipment required for the next operation.

*Auditing around the computer.* A method of auditing involving the verification of the output from the source data without consideration of the method of conversion.

*Auditing through the computer.* A method of auditing involving the verification of computer processing.

*Automatic programming.* The process of using a computer to perform some stages of the work involved in preparing a final program.

*Auxiliary (peripheral) equipment.* Equipment not actively involved during the processing of data, such as input/output equipment and auxiliary storage utilizing punched cards, magnetic tape, disks, or drums.

*Auxiliary operation.* An operation performed by equipment not under continuous control of the central processing unit.

*Auxiliary storage.* A storage that supplements another storage.

*Background program.* A program, usually of the batch processing type, that can be executed whenever the facilities of a multiprogramming computer system are not required by real-time programs or other programs of higher priority.

*Backup.* Reserve equipment that takes over control when the computer is down.

*Band.* A unit of signaling speed equal to the number of signal events per second.

*Bandwidth.* The difference, expressed in the number of cycles per second, between the two limiting frequencies of a band.

*Base address.* A specified address (often held in a "base address register") that is combined with a relative address (usually contained in an instruction) to form the absolute address of a particular storage location.

*Batch processing.* A method by which a number of similar transactions or problems are grouped for processing during a single continuous machine run.

*Baudot code.* A system of coding for transmission of data in which five bits represent one character.

*Binary coded decimal* (*BCD*). A decimal notation in which the individual decimal digits are represented by a pattern of ones and zeros, that is, in the 8-4-2-1 binary coded decimal notation.

*Binary number system.* A number system using the base two, as opposed to the decimal number system which uses the base ten.

*Bit.* The smallest unit of information in the binary number system. It is the abbreviation for the "binary digit" where a bit refers to one (on) and a no-bit means zero (off).

*Block.* A group of machine words considered or transported as a unit. In flowcharts, each block represents a logical unit of programming.

*Block diagram.* A diagram of a system, instrument, computer, or program in which selected portions are represented by annotated boxes and interconnecting lines.

*Blocking.* Combining two or more records into one block usually to increase the efficiency of computer input and output operations.

*Block sort.* A sort of one or more of the most significant characters of a key to serve as a means of making groups of workable size from a large volume of records to be sorted.

*Boolean algebra.* A process of reasoning or a deductive system of theorems using a symbolic logic, and dealing with classes, propositions, or on-off circuit elements. It employs symbols to represent operators, such as AND, OR, NOT, EXCEPT, IF, THEN, and the like to permit mathematical calculation.

*Branching.* A computer programming term indicating that a sequence of steps has been completed or is to be broken and that the sequence is to be repeated or changed to a new one.

*Breakpoint.* A specified point in a program at which the program may be interrupted by manual intervention, or by a monitor routine.

*Broadband.* Data transmission facilities capable of handling frequencies greater than those required for high-grade voice communications.

*Buffer.* A temporary or intermediate storage unit used to hold data being transmitted between internal and external storage units or between input/output devices and internal storage.

*Bug.* A mistake in the design of a program or a computer system, or an equipment fault.

*Bulk memory.* Portion of the computer's memory located outside the central processing unit.

*Bus.* A circuit used to transmit signals or powers. It is used quite extensively for punched card equipment.

*Byte.* A sequence of adjacent binary digits operated upon as a unit. It is the basic unit used in determining the memory size of a computer.

*Calculator.* A device that performs primarily arithmetic operations based upon data and instructions inserted manually or contained on punched cards.

*Card code.* The combination of punches employed to represent alphabetic and numerical data on a punched card.

*Card design.* The technique of determining the pattern to be followed in punching data into cards which will be processed by a data processing system.

*Card feed.* A mechanism that moves cards serially into a machine.

*Card hopper.* A device that holds cards and makes them available to a card feed mechanism.

*Card jam.* A pile-up of cards in a machine whether it be on-line or off-line equipment.

*Card punch.* A device or machine that punches holes in specific locations of a card to store data.

*Card reader.* A device for inputting information from punched cards into the computer system.

*Card read-punch unit.* A device that carries out the functions of a card reader and a card punch.

*Card stacker.* An output device that accumulates punched cards in a deck.

*Card system.* A system that utilizes only punched cards as the processing medium.

*Cathode-ray tube* (*CRT*). An electronic vacuum tube containing a screen on which output data may be displayed in graphic form or by character representation. Essential for many on-line real-time processing systems.

*Central processing unit* (*CPU*). The unit of a computer system that contains the arithmetic, logical, and control circuits necessary for executing computer programs.

*Chad.* A portion of tape or card that is removed when a code is punched.

*Channel.* A path over which information is transmitted, generally from some input/output device to storage.

*Character.* A decimal digit, alphabetic letter, or a special symbol.

*Check digit.* One or more redundant digits in a character or word which depend on the remaining digits in such a fashion that if a change of digits occurs in data transfer operations, the malfunction of equipment can be detected.

*Checkpoint.* A reference point to which error-free operation of the program has been verified and to which the program may return for restart in the event of subsequent failure.

*Circuit.* A system of conductors and related electrical elements through which electrical current flows.

*Classify.* The identification of each item and the systematic placement of like items together according to their common features.

*Clear.* Program instruction to remove all information from a storage device of a machine and restore it to a prescribed state, usually zero or blank.

*Closed loop control.* The form of on-line control where the computer controls the instruments or controls certain valves without the intervention of the operator.

*COBOL.* Common business-oriented language is a coding language by which data processing procedures may be described precisely in a standard form. It is basically used for business programming.

*Code.* A set of rules that is used to convert data from one representation to another.

*Collate.* Two or more sets of related information, already arranged according to the same sequence, are merged into a single sequenced set.

*Collator.* A device to collate or merge sets of cards or other documents into a sequence.

*Command.* A group of signals or pulses initiating one step in the execution of a computer program—often called an instruction.

*Common processing language.* A coded structure that is compatible with two or more data processing machines or families of machines, thereby allowing them to communicate directly to one another.

*Communications executive.* A systems software component that resides in the data communications processor and services the remote terminals.

*Compiler.* A programming system that produces a program from a series of source statements. It is capable of replacing single entries with a series of instructions or a subroutine that produces an expanded translated version of the original program.

*Computer utility.* A time-shared computer system that is similar in concept to an electric utility.

*Computer word.* A sequence of bits or characters treated as a unit and capable of being stored in one computer location.

*Conditional transfer.* An instruction that may or may not cause a jump depending upon the result of some operation, the contents of some register, or the setting of some indicator.

*Configuration.* A group of machines that are interconnected and are programmed to operate as a system.

*Console.* The component of a data processing system that provides facilities for manual control and observation of the system's operation.

*Console operator.* An individual who operates a computer system.

*Constant.* Data with a fixed value that is available for use throughout a program.

*Continuous form.* Paper or card forms attached for continuous feeding in an accounting machine or computer printing device.

*Control card.* A punched card that contains input data required for a specific application of a general routine, such as a generator or operating systems; e.g., one of a series of cards that direct an operating system to load and initiate execution of a particular program.

*Control panel.* The panel that contains the external wiring to govern machine operations.

*Control program.* A routine, usually contained within an operating system, that aids in controlling the operations and managing the resources of a computer system.

*Control unit.* The portion of the central processing unit that implements the programs and thus controls all the other units.

*Converter.* A unit that changes the representation of data from one form to another so as to make it available or acceptable to another machine, such as from punched cards to magnetic tape.

*Corner cut.* A diagonal cut at the corner of a card to facilitate identification by sight.

*Counter.* A device, register, or storage

location for storing integers, permitting these integers to be increased or decreased.

*Cybernetics*. The comparative study of the control and communication of information-handling machines and the nervous system of man in order to understand and improve communication.

*Cycle*. An interval during which one set of events or phenomena is completed.

*Data*. A general term used to denote any facts, numbers, letters, and symbols, or facts that refer to or describe an object, idea, condition, situation, or other factors.

*Data acquisition*. The automatic collection of operating data.

*Data base*. Data items that must be stored in order to meet the on-line real-time information processing and retrieval needs of an organization.

*Data collection*. A system that records, in machine readable form, the data pertinent to a transaction at the time and place the transaction occurs.

*Data communications*. The transmission of data between two or more points.

*Data file*. A user file, either temporary or permanent, in which data information is stored.

*Data processing*. Any operation or combination of operations on data to achieve a desired result.

*Data reduction*. The transformation of raw data into more useful form.

*Data set*. A hardware device that provides the necessary interface between input/output devices and telephone or communication lines.

*Data transmission equipment*. Equipment designed to transmit either card code or channel code over long distances by means of telephone lines or by radio.

*Debug*. To detect, locate, and correct mistakes in a computer program.

*Decision*. The process of making comparisons by use of arithmetic to determine the relationship of two terms.

*Decision table*. A table that combines "conditions" (if) to be considered in the description of a problem, along with the "actions" (then) to be taken. Decision tables are sometimes used instead of flowcharts to describe and document problems.

*Deck*. A complete set of cards that have been punched for a specific purpose.

*Decoder*. A matrix of switching elements that selects one or more output channels according to the combination of input signals present.

*Demodulator*. A device that receives signals transmitted over a communications link and converts them into electrical pulses or bits that can serve as input to a data processing machine.

*Density*. The number of characters that can be stored per unit of length.

*Diagnostic routine*. A specific routine designed to locate a malfunction in the computer or a mistake in coding.

*Digital computer*. A calculating device that uses numbers to express all the variables and quantities of a problem. Its accuracy is generally 100%.

*Direct access*. A random access storage medium that permits direct addressing of data locations.

*Direct address*. An address that specifies the location of an operand.

*Disk file*. Form of bulk storage utilizing rotating magnetic disks.

*Disk pack*. A portable set of magnetic disks that may be removed from the disk drive unit, allowing another set of disks to be placed on the unit.

*Disk storage*. The storage of data on the surface of magnetic disks.

*Display station*. A device that provides a visual representation via a cathode-ray tube.

*Documentation*. Documents that describe the program and its contents during its preparation, its approval, and any subsequent changes.

*Downtime*. The elapsed time when a computer is not operating correctly because of machine or program malfunction.

*Drum memory*. Form of bulk storage utilizing a rotating magnetic drum.

*Dump*. A copying or printing out of all or part of the contents of a particular storage device. Synonymous with memory dump.

*Duplex channel*. A channel that allows simultaneous transmission in both directions.

*Duplicating*. The automatic punching of information from a card or tape into succeeding cards or tape.

*Dynamic relocation*. The movement of part or all of an active program from one region of storage to another, with all necessary address references being adjusted to enable proper execution of the program to continue in its new location.

*EAM*. Electrical accounting machine. Generally refers to punched card equipment.

*EBCDIC*. An abbreviation for Extended Binary Coded Decimal Interchange Code.

*Echo check*. A check upon the accuracy of a data transfer operation in which the data received are transmitted back to the source and compared with the original data.

*Edge-notched card*. A card in which holes have been punched around the edges. Notches made in the holes are used in coding information for a simple mechanical-search technique.

*Edge-punched card*. A card of fixed size

into which information may be recorded or stored by punching holes along one edge in a pattern similar to that used for punched tape.

*Edit*. Involves the deletion of unwanted data, the selection of pertinent data, and the insertion of symbols.

*EDP*. Electronic data processing. Generally refers to computer equipment.

*Electronic data processing system*. The term is used to define a system for data processing by means of computers as opposed to punched card equipment.

*Emitting*. Originating digits, letters, and special characters electrically within the machine rather than from a punched card.

*Emulator*. A device, generally used in conjunction with special routines, that enables a computer to execute machine language programs written for another computer of dissimilar design, without prior translation.

*Encode*. To apply a code, frequently one consisting of binary numbers, to represent individual characters in a message.

*Erase*. To replace all the binary digits in a storage device by binary zeros. To remove data from a magnetic surface or other memory unit.

*Error routine*. A prepared diagnostic program that searches for predetermined types of errors and advises, by computer output, the types of errors found.

*Executive program*. The principal program that supervises the implementation of all other programs.

*External label*. An identifying label attached to the outside of a file media holder identifying the file. For example, a paper sticker is attached to the reel containing a magnetic tape file.

*External storage*. The storage of data on a device, such as magnetic tape which is not an integral part of a computer, but is in a form for use by a computer.

*Facilities management*. All EDP operations (equipment, personnel, and functions) are performed by a computer service facility instead of having the firm operate its own in-house computer processing system.

*Feedback*. The process of returning portions of the output of a machine, process, or system for use as input in a further operation.

*Ferromagnetics*. In computer technology, the science that deals with the storage of information and the logical control of pulse sequences through the utilization of the magnetic polarization properties of materials.

*Field*. A set of one or more columns of a punched card consistently used to record similar information.

*File*. A collection of related records treated as a unit.

*File maintenance*. The processing of information in a file to keep it up-to-date.

*Firmware*. Software that is stored in a fixed or firm way, usually in a read-only memory.

*Fixed length record*. A record that always contains the same number of characters.

*Fixed point*. An arithmetic system in which all numerical quantities are expressed in a specified number of places with the radix point implicitly located at some predetermined position.

*Fixed word length*. A storage device in which the capacity for digits or characters in each unit of data is a fixed length as opposed to a variable length.

*Flip-flop*. A circuit or device containing active elements capable of assuming either one of two stable states at a given time.

*Floating point*. A system of representing numerical quantities with a variable number of places in which the location of the point does not remain fixed.

*Flowchart*. A graphical representation of the definition, analysis, or solution of a problem using symbols to represent operations, data flow, equipment, and the like.

*Foreground program*. A program that requires real-time responses or has a high priority and therefore takes precedence over other concurrently operating programs in a computer system using multiprogramming techniques.

*Format*. The arrangement of data on a form or in storage.

*FORTRAN*. Formula translator. A programming language designed for problems that can be expressed in algebraic notation as well as other mathematical notation. The FORTRAN compiler is a routine for a given machine which accepts a program written in FORTRAN source language and produces a machine language object program.

*Gangpunching*. The automatic punching of data read from a master card into the following detail cards.

*General purpose computer*. A computer that is used to solve a wide variety of problems.

*Generate*. A generator is utilized to prepare a machine language program from a set of specifications.

*Generator*. A program for a computer that generates the coding of a problem.

*GIGO*. A contraction of "Garbage In, Garbage Out," which refers to the uselessness of invalid input data.

*Group printing*. Printing group totals as cards pass through an accounting machine.

*Half-duplex channel.* A channel capable of transmitting and receiving signals, but in only one direction at a time.

*Hard copy.* A record presented in a permanent and readable form.

*Hardware.* A term applied to the mechanical, electrical, and electronic features of a data processing system.

*Hash total.* A sum of numbers in a specified field of a record or batch of records used for checking or control purposes.

*Head.* A device that reads, writes, or erases data on a storage medium. For example, an electromagnet is used to read, write, or erase data on a magnetic drum or tape.

*Header card.* A prepunched record of the basic information pertaining to a specific individual or form which is used to create automatically the upper portion of a document.

*Header label.* A machine-readable record at the beginning of a file containing data identifying the file and data used in file control.

*Heuristic.* Exploratory method using rules of thumb in problem solving.

*Hexadecimal numbering system.* A numbering system using the equivalent of the decimal number sixteen as a base.

*Hierarchical control.* Form of control in which computers are distributed at different levels of a system and each is controlled by the computer at the level above it.

*High-order position.* The leftmost position of a number or word.

*Hollerith code.* A standard 12-channel punched card code in which each decimal digit, letter, or special character is represented by one or more rectangular holes punched in a vertical column.

*Housekeeping routine.* Routine usually performed only at the beginning of machine operations which establishes the initial conditions for instruction addresses, accumulator settings, switch settings, and the like.

*Hub.* A socket on a control panel or plugboard into which an electric lead or plug wire may be connected in order to carry signals.

*Hybrid computer.* A computer system that combines analog and digital capabilities.

*Idle time.* The time that a computer is available for use but is not in operation.

*IDP.* Integrated Data Processing. Generally means the integration of several functional areas of data processing with the purpose of reducing or eliminating duplicate recording of data.

*Indexing.* A method of address modification that is performed automatically by the computer system.

*Index register.* A register whose contents can be added to or subtracted from an address prior to or during the execution of an instruction.

*Index word.* A storage position or register, the contents of which may be used to modify automatically the effective address of any given instruction.

*Indirect address.* An address that specifies a storage location containing either a direct address or another indirect address.

*Information retrieval.* The methods and procedures for recovering specific information from stored data.

*Initialize.* To set up program variables, such as addresses, counters, and program switches to zero or other starting values at the beginning of, or at prescribed points in, a computer routine.

*Input device.* The mechanical unit designed to bring data to be processed into a computer, e.g., a card reader, a tape reader, or a keyboard.

*Inquiry.* A request for information from storage.

*Instruction.* A set of characters which, when interpreted by the control unit, causes a data processing system to perform one of its operations.

*Instruction register.* The register that stores the current instruction governing a computer operation.

*Interface.* A boundary between two systems or devices.

*Interleave.* To insert segments of one program into another program so that during processing delays in one program, processing can continue on segments of another program; a technique used in multiprogramming.

*Interlock.* A protective facility that prevents one device or operation from interfering with another.

*Internal control.* The plan of organization and all of the coordinate methods and measures adopted within a business to safeguard its assets, check the accuracy and reliability of its accounting data, promote operational efficiency, and encourage adherence to prescribed managerial policies.

*Internal storage.* Storage facilities that are an integral part of the computer and directly controlled by the computer.

*Interpret.* To print at the top of a punched card the information punched in it, using a machine called an interpreter.

*Interrupt.* A break in the normal flow of a system or routine whereby an operation can generally be resumed from that point at a later time.

*Iterative.* Pertaining to the repeated execution of a series of steps.

*Joggle.* To align a deck of cards by jostling them against a plane surface.

*K*. 1 *K* equal 1024 units of storage capacity. The units are bytes for most business computers.

*Key*. One or more characters associated with a particular item or record and used to identify that item or record, especially in sorting or collating operations.

*Key punch*. A keyboard-operated device that punches holes in a card to represent data.

*Label*. One or more characters used to identify or describe an item of data, record, message, or file.

*Language translator*. A general term for any assembler, compiler, or other routine that accepts statements in one language and produces equivalent machine language instructions.

*Large-scale integration* (*LSI*). The accumulation of a large number of circuits on a single chip of a semiconductor—basically for read-only memories.

*Leased channel*. A point-to-point channel on line that is contracted for the sole use of a leasing customer.

*Library*. A collection of standard proven computer routines, by which problems or portions of problems may be solved.

*Limit check*. A check written into a computer program to call attention to any data exceeding or less than certain predefined limits.

*Line feed*. A teletypewriter control character that causes the rotation of the teletypewriter platen to the next line down.

*Line printing*. The printing of an entire line of characters as a unit.

*Linear programming*. A mathematical technique of operations research for solving certain kinds of problems involving many variables where a best value or set of best values is determined.

*Line speed*. The maximum transmission rate of signals over a circuit expressed in bits per second.

*Linkage*. Coding that connects two separately coded routines.

*Listing*. A record of a program in machine language and either assembler or compiler language.

*Literal*. A symbol that names and defines itself.

*Load*. To place data into a register or into internal storage. Also, means to place a magnetic tape onto a tape drive or to place cards into a card reader.

*Load-and-go*. An operating technique in which there are no stops between the loading and execution phases of a program and which may include assembling or compiling.

*Log*. A record of the operations of data processing equipment.

*Logarithm*. The exponent of a number, indicating how many times the number must be multiplied by itself to produce another given number.

*Logical operations*. Nonmathematical operations, such as selecting, sorting, matching, and comparing.

*Longitudinal parity check*. A parity check performed on the bits in each track of magnetic tape or punched tape.

*Loop*. The repetition of a group of instructions in a routine until certain conditions are reached.

*Low-order position*. The rightmost position of a number or word.

*Machine language*. The instructions written in a form that is intelligible to the internal circuitry of the computer.

*Machine-oriented language*. A language in which there is a general one-to-one correspondence between the statements of the source program and the instructions of the object program.

*Machine-sensible*. Term denoting information in a form that can be read by one or more machine(s).

*Macro instruction*. A symbolic instruction in a source language that produces a number of machine language instructions.

*Magnetic card*. A card with a magnetic surface on which data can be stored by selective magnetization of portions of the flat surface.

*Magnetic core*. A small doughnut-shaped piece of ferromagnetic material, about the size of a pin head, capable of storing one binary digit represented by the polarity of its magnetic field.

*Magnetic disk*. A storage device by which information is recorded on the magnetizable surface of a rotating disk. A magnetic disk storage system is an array of such devices, with associated reading and writing heads mounted on movable arms.

*Magnetic drum*. A rotating cylinder whose surface is coated with a material on which information may be recorded as small magnetic spots representing binary information.

*Magnetic film*. A layer of magnetic material, usually less than one micron thick, used for logic or storage elements.

*Magnetic ink*. An ink that contains particles of a magnetic substance whose presence can be detected by magnetic sensors.

*Magnetic ink character reader*. A device capable of interpreting data typed, written, or printed in magnetic ink.

*Magnetic ledger card*. A ledger sheet or card that has stripes of magnetic receptive material in which magnetic type coded data can be stored and read by machine.

*Magnetic tape*. A tape or ribbon of material impregnated or coated with magnetic material on which information may be placed in the form of magnetically polarized spots.

*Magnetic tape unit.* A device for writing information onto and reading information from magnetic tape.

*Magnetic thin film.* A layer of magnetic material used for logic or storage elements.

*Management information system.* A computer and communication system designed to furnish management personnel with data for decision making.

*Manual entry unit.* An elementary keyboard device for putting information into the system.

*Mark sensing.* A technique for reading special electrographic pencil marks on a card and automatically punching the data represented by the marks into the card.

*Mass storage.* An auxiliary storage medium whereby data are magnetically recorded in tracks or channels on the surface of cards or strips stored in demountable cells or cartridges.

*Master card.* The first card of a group containing indicative information for that group.

*Master file.* A file of records containing a cumulative history or the results of accumulation.

*Matching.* Checking two files to see that there is a corresponding card or group of cards in each file.

*Mathematical business model.* A mathematical representation of the behavior of the business world.

*Matrix.* An *n*-dimensional array of quantities. Matrices are manipulated in accordance with the rules of matrix algebra.

*Memory.* The part of a computer that stores the program and holds intermediate results plus various constant data. Also known as primary storage or main storage.

*Memory dump.* A copy of the contents of all or part of storage, usually from an internal storage into an external storage.

*Merge.* To combine items from two or more similarly sequenced files into one sequenced file. The order of the items is unchanged.

*Message switching.* The technique of receiving complete messages and forwarding the messages at a switching center.

*MICR.* Magnetic ink character recognition. Machine recognition of characters printed with magnetic ink.

*Microprogramming.* A method of operation of the control unit of a computer in which each instruction, instead of being used to initiate control signals directly, starts the execution of a sequence of "micro instructions" at a more elementary level.

*Microsecond.* One-millionth of a second.

*Microwave.* Very short electromagnetic waves used in high capacity communication networks for transmitting voice or data messages at ultra-high speeds.

*Millisecond.* One-thousandth of a second.

*Mnemonic.* Pertains to a technique used to assist human memory. Most symbolic assembly languages use mnemonic operation codes. For example, ADD is used for addition, SUB is used for subtraction, and so forth.

*Modem.* A contraction of MOdulator DE-Modulator. Its function is to interface with data processing devices and convert data to a form compatible for sending and receiving on transmission facilities.

*Modifier.* A quantity used to alter the address of an operand.

*Modify.* To alter in an instruction the address of the operand; to alter a subroutine according to a defined parameter.

*Modulator.* A device that receives electrical pulses or bits from a data processing machine and converts them into signals suitable for transmission over a communications link.

*Monolithic circuits.* Complete circuits produced in one manufacturing operation.

*Multiplexor.* A device that will interleave or simultaneously transmit two or more messages on the same communications channel.

*Multiprocessing.* A computer system consisting of multiple arithmetic and logical units for simultaneous use.

*Multiprogramming.* A technique whereby more than one program may reside in primary storage at the same time and be executed concurrently by means of an interweaving process.

*Nanosecond.* One-billionth of a second.

*Narrow band channel.* A channel that permits transmission of frequencies within the normal telegraph band of frequencies - lower than the voice-band channel.

*Needle checking.* Verifying that all cards in a deck contain the same data in a given column. The needle, when pushed through the punched holes, stops at a card containing a different punch.

*Nondestructive read.* A read process that does not erase the data in storage.

*Normalize.* In programming, to adjust the exponent and fraction of a floating point quantity so that the fraction lies in the prescribed normal standard range.

*Numerical control.* Pertaining to the automatic control of processes by the proper interpretation of numerical data.

*Object language*. A language that is an output from a translation process.

*Object program*. A program in machine language that has been converted from a program written in a programming language.

*OCR*. Optical character recognition. The machine recognition of printed and handwritten characters.

*Octal*. Pertaining to the number base of eight.

*Off-line*. Equipment or devices not under the direct control of the computer's central processing unit.

*Off-line storage*. A storage device not under control of the central processing unit.

*Off-punching*. Punching not properly positioned in a card.

*On-line*. Peripheral equipment or devices in direct communication with the central processing unit, and from which information reflecting current activity is introduced into the data processing system as soon as it occurs.

*On-line storage*. A storage under direct control of the central processing unit.

*Open loop control*. The form of on-line control where the operator is required to adjust the instruments on the basis of the computer's read-out.

*Operand*. An operand is usually identified by an address part of an instruction.

*Operating system*. An organized collection of techniques and procedures for operating a computer.

*Operation*. A defined action or one step in a procedure. The action specified by a single computer instruction. That which occurs when something is created, changed, or added to, such as writing, calculating, posting, or computing.

*Operation code*. The part of the command code of an instruction that designates the operation to be performed.

*Operations research*. The use of mathematical methods, models, and techniques for solving operational problems. The objective is to provide management with a more logical basis for making decisions.

*Optical character recognition*. The technique of using electronic devices and light in order to detect, recognize, and translate into machine language characters that have been printed or written on paper documents in a human-readable form.

*Optical scanner*. A device that optically scans printed or written data and generates its digital representation.

*Output device*. The part of a machine that translates the electrical impulses representing data processed by the machine into permanent results, such as, printed forms, punched cards, and magnetic writing on tape.

*Overflow*. On an arithmetic operation, the generation of a quantity beyond the capacity of the register or location that is to receive the result.

*Overlay*. To transfer segments of a program from auxiliary storage into internal storage for execution so that two or more segments occupy the same storage locations at different times.

*Over punches*. To add punches, usually control punches, to a card column that already contains one or more holes.

*Pack*. To store several short units of data in a single storage cell in such a way that the individual units can later be recovered.

*Padding*. Dummy characters, items, or records used to fill out a fixed length block of information.

*Page*. A segment of a program or data, usually of fixed length, that has a fixed virtual address but can, in fact, reside in any region of the computer's internal storage.

*Paging*. The separation of a program and data into fixed blocks so that transfers, such as between disk and core, can take place in page units rather than as entire programs.

*Paper tape*. A long strip of paper that carries information by means of holes punched into specific positions.

*Parallel*. To handle simultaneously in separate facilities. To operate on two or more parts of a word or item simultaneously.

*Parameter*. A quantity to which arbitrary values may be assigned but which remain fixed for each program. In a program generator, parameters specify certain machine hardware and data limits to be observed in the program being generated.

*Parity bit*. A binary digit appended to a group of bits to make the sum of all the bits always odd or always even.

*Parity check*. A check that tests whether the number of ones or zeros in a group of binary digits meets the established odd or even standard.

*Password*. A security feature used in time sharing that entails the use of a code known only to certain users.

*Patch*. A section of coding inserted in a program in order to rectify an error in the original coding or to change the sequence of operation.

*Peripheral equipment*. Units that work in conjunction with the computer but are not part of the computer itself. These include: tape reader, card reader, magnetic tape feed, high-speed printer, typewriter, and the like.

*Photo-optic memory*. A memory that uses an optical medium for storage. For example, a laser might be used to record on photographic film.

*Picosecond*. One-thousandth of a nanosecond.

*Picture clause*. Used in COBOL programs to indicate the size of an item, its class, the presence or absence of an operational sign, and/or an assumed decimal point.

*PL/1*. A procedure-oriented language designated to facilitate the preparation of computer programs to perform both business and scientific functions.

*Plugboard*. A removable panel containing an array of terminals that can be interconnected by short electrical leads in prescribed patterns to control various machine operations. It is also known as a control panel.

*Powers code*. A system of representing data by round holes punched in a 90-column card, invented by James Powers.

*Presumptive address*. An address that is altered through address modification to form an effective address that is actually used to identify an operand.

*Problem-oriented language*. A language whose design is oriented toward the specification of a particular class of problems, such as numerical control of machine tools.

*Procedure*. A precise, step-by-step method for effecting a solution to a problem.

*Procedure-oriented language*. A language designed to permit convenient specification, in terms of procedural or algorithmic steps, of data processing or computational processes.

*Process control*. A system in which computers, usually analog computers, are used for automatic regulation of operations or processes.

*Processor*. A machine language program that accepts a source program written in a programming language and translates it into an object program acceptable to the machine for which the source program was written.

*Program*. The sequence of machine instructions and routines necessary to solve a problem on the computer.

*Program card*. A punched card, punched with specific coding, placed around a program drum to control automatic operations in a card punch and a card verifier.

*Program Evaluation and Review Technique (PERT)*. A technique for planning and controlling system projects.

*Program file*. A series of programming language statements beginning with line numbers.

*Program flowchart*. Designed to portray the various arithmetic and logical operations that must be accomplished to solve a computer problem.

*Programmer*. A person who prepares the planned sequence of events contained within the computer program for solving a problem.

*Pseudo instruction*. An instruction that has the same general form as a machine instruction, but is not directly executable by a computer.

*Punched card*. A heavy paper of uniform size and shape suitable for being punched with a pattern of holes to represent data and for being handled mechanically.

*Punched tape*. A tape, usually paper, on which a pattern of holes or cuts is used to represent data.

*Queuing theory*. A form of probability theory useful in studying delays or lineups at servicing points.

*Quinary*. Pertaining to the number base of five.

*Radix*. The base or the fundamental number in a number system, e.g., 10 in the decimal system, 8 in the octal system, 5 in the quinary system, and 2 in the binary system.

*Random access storage*. A storage device, such as magnetic core, magnetic disk, and magnetic drum, in which each record has a specific predetermined address that may be accessed directly. Access time in this type of storage is independent of the data location.

*Raw data*. Data that have not been processed. They may or may not be in a form acceptable by machines.

*Read in*. To sense information contained in some source and to transfer this information by means of an input device to internal storage.

*Read-only memory*. A memory that cannot be altered in normal use of computer processing. Usually, a small memory that contains often-used instructions, such as microprograms or system software as firmware.

*Read out*. To transfer data from internal storage to an external storage device or to display processed data by means of a printer, automatic typewriter, and similar equipment.

*Real-time*. The processing of data derived from a particular operation in a sufficiently fast manner so that time is available to influence the continuing operation.

*Record*. A collection of related items of data treated as a unit.

*Record length*. The number of characters necessary to contain all the information in a record.

*Reentrant*. Pertaining to a routine that can be used by two or more independent programs at the same time.

*Register*. A device capable of temporarily storing a specified amount of data, usually one word, while or until it is used in an operation.

*Registration*. The accuracy of the positioning of punched holes in a card.

*Remote batch processing*. Entering batches of data from remote terminals into a time-shared computer system.

*Remote processing*. A method of using a computer system from remote locations. The direct access connection can be accomplished by using conventional voice grade telephone lines to exchange information between the computer and terminals. This is generally used in online real-time processing systems.

*Report generator*. A programming system for producing a complete report given only a description of the desired content and format of the output reports, and certain information about the input file and hardware available.

*Reproducing*. Duplicating punched information from one deck of cards into another.

*Resource sharing*. The sharing of one central processor both by several users and several peripheral devices. Principally used in connection with the sharing of time and memory.

*Responsibility reporting*. An accounting system based on the delegation of responsibility which provides control information for comparing actual results with planned or budgeted results.

*Roll-back*. A system that will restart the running program after a system failure. Snapshots of data and programs are stored at periodic intervals and the system rolls back to a restart at the last recorded snapshot.

*Routing*. A set of coded instructions arranged in a logical sequence and used to direct a computer to perform a desired operation or series of operations.

*Row binary*. A method representing binary numbers on a card where successive bits are represented by the presence or absence of punches in a successive position in a row as opposed to a series of columns.

*Run*. A single, continuous operation of a computer routine.

*Run manual*. A manual of documentation containing the processing system, program logic, controls, program changes, and operating instructions associated with a computer program.

*Secondary storage*. Storage that supplements a computer's primary internal storage.

*Security controls*. Safeguard techniques utilized in protecting computer programs, data files, and equipment.

*Selecting*. Removing cards from a file, or processing cards according to predetermined conditions.

*Selector channel*. A term used in certain computer systems for an input/output channel that can transfer data to or from one peripheral device at a time.

*Semiconductor memory*. A memory whose storage medium is a semiconductor circuit. Often used for high-speed buffer memories and for read-only memories.

*Sequence checking*. Checking items in a file to assure that they are all in ascending or descending order.

*Sequential processing*. The procedure of processing data records in the order that they occur.

*Serial*. The handling of data in a sequential fashion, such as to transfer or store data in a digit-by-digit time sequence, or to process a sequence of instructions one at a time.

*Serial access*. Pertaining to a storage device in which there is a sequential relationship between the access times to successive locations, as in the case of magnetic tape.

*Serial operation*. The flow of information through a computer in time sequence, using one digit word, line, or channel at a time.

*Servomechanism*. A device to monitor an operation as it proceeds and make necessary adjustments to keep the operation under control.

*Set-up time*. The time between computer or other machine operations that is devoted to such tasks as changing reels of tape and moving cards, forms, and other supplies to and from the equipment.

*Shift*. The process of moving characters of a unit of data to the right or left within a computer program.

*Short card*. A punched card of less than the regular number of columns.

*Sight checking*. Examining a group of cards for identical punching by viewing a light source through the punched holes.

*Simplex*. Pertaining to a communications link that is capable of transmitting data in only one direction.

*Simulation*. The representation of physical systems and phenomena by computers, models, or other means.

*Snapshot*. A dynamic dump of the contents of specified storage locations and/or registers that is performed at specific points or times during the running of a program.

*Software*. The programs and routines used to extend the capabilities of computers, such as compilers, assemblers, routines, and subroutines.

*Solid logic technology (SLT)*. A microminiaturization of solid logic components and associated circuitry into very small units or blocks.

*Solid state*. Refers to electronic components that convey or control electron flow within solid materials, such as transistors, crystal diodes, and ferrite cores.

*Sort*. To arrange items of information according to rules dependent on a key or field contained in the items.

*Source document*. The original paper on which are recorded the details of a transaction.

*Source language*. A language that is an input to a translation process.

*Source program*. A program usually written in some programming language and intended for translation into a machine language program.

*Special character*. A character that is neither a numeral nor a letter; for example, #, $, /, and &.

*Special purpose computer*. A computer designed principally to solve a restricted class of problems.

*Stacker*. A receptacle or hopper that accumulates cards after they have passed through a machine.

*Statement*. In computer programming, a meaningful expression or generalized instruction in a programming language.

*Storage*. A device into which data can be entered, in which they can be stored, and from which they can be retrieved at a later time.

*Storage allocation*. The assignment of specific programs, program segments, and/or blocks of data to specific portions of a computer's storage.

*Stored program computer*. A computer that has the ability to store, to refer to, and to modify instructions in order to direct its step-by-step operations.

*Straight line coding*. Coding in which the use of loops and/or closed subroutines is avoided by repetition of parts of the coding when required.

*String*. A set of records in ascending or descending sequence according to a key contained in the records.

*Subprogram*. A part of a larger program. Usually the subprogram can be converted into machine language independently of the remainder of the program.

*Subroutine*. A routine that is part of a program. A closed subroutine is stored in one place and connected to the program by means of linkages at one or more points in the program. An open subroutine is inserted directly into a program at each point where it is to be used.

*Subset*. A modulation-demodulation device designed to make the output signals of data processing equipment compatible with communication transmission facilities.

*Summarizing*. The accumulation of totals or amounts from data that have been classified and sorted into like groups.

*Summary punch*. A card-handling machine that may be connected to another machine, such as an accounting machine, and that will punch out on a card the information produced, calculated, or summarized by the other machine.

*Supervisor*. The general reference to the programs of a system that are responsible for scheduling, allocating, and controlling the computer system.

*Switch*. A point in a programming routine at which two courses of action are possible, the correct one being determined by conditions specified by the programmer.

*Symbolic address*. An address expressed in symbols that are convenient to the programmer.

*Symbolic coding*. Coding that uses the machine instructions with symbolic addresses.

*Symbolic program*. A program written in a language that makes use of mnemonic codes and in which names, characters, or other symbols convenient to the programmer are used instead of the machine language codes of the computer.

*Synchronous computer*. A computer in which each operation starts as a result of a signal generated by a clock.

*System*. A set or arrangement of entities that forms, or is considered as, an organized whole.

*System flowchart*. A flowchart that shows the sequence of major operations which normally summarizes a complete operation.

*Systems analyst*. A systems person who studies the procedures, methods, techniques, and the business in order to determine what must be accomplished and how the necessary operations may best be accomplished.

*Systems programmer*. A programmer who writes the programs that control the basic functioning of the computer.

*Table look-up*. The operation of obtaining a value from a table.

*Tabulating system*. Another term sometimes used to describe a punched card data processing system.

*Tag*. One or more characters attached to a particular item or record and used to identify that item or record.

*Telecommunication*. Any transmission or reception of signals, writing, sounds, or intelligence of any nature by wire, radio, visual, or any other electromagnetic means.

*Terminal*. Any input/output equipment that communicates with a central computer over a communications channel.

*Terminal management*. The ability of a time-sharing system to accept terminal data at top speed and its ability to respond to keyboard text entries with line feed responses.

*Test deck*. A set of cards representative of all operations performed in a particular application. Used to test control panel wiring and computer programming.

*Test routine*. A procedure that shows whether a computer is functioning properly.

*Thin film*. A layer of magnetic material, usually less than one-millionth of an inch in thickness, which is deposited by a vacuum process onto plate or wire.

*Throughput*. The total amount of work performed by a data processing system during a given period of time.

*Time sharing*. A computing system that permits many users to operate or use the system simultaneously or apparently simultaneously in such a way that each is unaware of the fact that the system is being used by others.

*Total systems concept*. The complete integration of all major operating systems within a business organization into one functional organized system operating under the discipline of a data processing facility.

*Trace routine*. A diagnostic routine designed to check or demonstrate the operation of a program.

*Track*. The part of a data storage medium that is influenced by one head.

*Trailer record*. A record that follows another record or group of records and contains pertinent data.

*Transaction code*. One or more characters that form part of a record and signify the type of transaction represented by the record.

*Transistor*. A tiny, solid electronic device that performs the same function as a vacuum tube. In a vacuum tube, current flows through the gas and space within the tube. In a transistor, the current travels through solid materials only, which explains the familiar term "solid state."

*Translator*. A device or computer program that performs translations from one language or code to another.

*Trap*. An unprogrammed jump to a preset location, activated automatically upon the occurrence of a particular condition.

*Truth table*. A table that describes a logic function by listing all possible combinations of input values and indicating all the logically true output values.

*Typer*. A device similar to an office typewriter that enters typewritten information into the computer.

*Unconditional transfer*. An instruction that always causes a jump.

*Unit record*. A record in which all data concerning each item in a transaction are punched into one card.

*Unpack*. To separate short units of data that have previously been packed.

*Update*. To change a master file caused by current information or transactions.

*User file*. A file entered into a time-sharing system by a user.

*User number*. A number assigned to users by the main-site installation to prevent unauthorized use of a time-sharing system.

*User program*. An object program file that has been loaded into memory for execution.

*Utility program*. Standard programs prepared and generally used to assist in the operation of a data processing system.

*Validity check*. A check based upon known limits or upon given information or computer results.

*Variable length record*. A record that may contain a variable number of characters.

*Variable word length*. Pertaining to a machine word or operand that may consist of a variable number of bits or characters. It is contrasted with fixed word length.

*Verify*. To determine whether a transcription of data or other operations has been accomplished accurately.

*Virtual address*. An address in a machine instruction that refers to a particular page that may be located in any region of the computer's internal storage.

*Virtual memory*. A technique that permits the user to treat secondary (disk) storage as an extension of core memory, thus giving the "virtual" appearance of a large core memory to the programmer.

*Voice band channel*. A channel that permits the transmission of frequencies within the voice band. A channel suitable for the transmission of speech, digital, or analog data.

*Word*. A set of characters that occupies one storage location and is treated by the computer circuits as a unit and transported as such.

*Word length*. The number of characters in a machine language word. In a given computer, the number may be constant, variable, or both.

*Word mark*. A symbol used in some variable word length computers to indicate the beginning or end of a word or item.

*Working storage*. A storage section set

aside by the programmer for use in the development of processing results, etc.

*X-punch*. A punch in the second row, one row above the zero row, on a Hollerith punched card.

*Y-punch*. A punch in the top row, two rows above the zero row, on a Hollerith punched card.

*Zero suppression*. The elimination of nonsignificant zeros to the left of the integral part of a quantity before printing operations are initiated.

*Zone punches*. Punches in the Y, X, and O positions on a Hollerith punched card—used in combination with digit punches 1 to 9 to code alphabetic and special characters.

# Data Processing Associations

**American Federation of Information Processing Societies (AFIPS)**
**345 East 47 Street, New York, New York 10017**

AFIPS, founded in May 1961, is devoted to advancing an understanding and knowledge of the information processing sciences through active engagement in various scientific activities and cooperation with state, national, and international (called IFPS) organizations on information processing

**Association for Computing Machinery (ACM)**
**211 East 43rd Street, New York, New York 10017**

ACM, founded in 1947, has over 20,000 members in more than 160 chapters. Its purpose is to advance the design, development, and application of information processing and the interchange of such techniques between computer specialists and users.

ACM's primary activities involve chapter and regional meetings as well as an annual conference. It publishes *Computing Reviews* (monthly), *Communications of the ACM* (monthly), and *Journal of the ACM* (quarterly).

**Association of Data Processing Service Organizations (ADAPSO)**
**947 Old York Road, Abington, Pennsylvania 19001**

ADAPSO provides data-processing services through systems its members operate on their own premises. A directory is published annually.

**Association for Educational Data Systems (AEDS)**
**1201 Sixteenth Street, N.W., Washington, D.C. 20036**

AEDS, founded in 1962 by professional educators, shares information related to the effect of data processing on the educational process. It acts as a clearinghouse of such information, recommends professional consultants, and organizes workshops and seminars on educational data processing. AEDS' main periodicals are *Monitor* (monthly) and *Journal of Educational Data Processing* (quarterly).

**Association for Systems Management (ASM)**
**24587 Bagley Road, Cleveland, Ohio 44138**

ASM, founded in 1944 as the Systems and Procedure Association, has over 7000 members through 105 chapters in the United States, Mexico, Canada, Venezuela, and other foreign countries. It purpose is to promote advanced management systems and procedures through seminars, professional education, and research.

Meetings are held regularly by the various chapters. An annual international meeting is held in the United States. ASM's monthly publication in the *Journal of Systems Management.*

**Business Equipment Manufacturers Association (BEMA)**
**235 East 42 Street, New York, New York 10017**

BEMA, founded in 1916, is comprised of the companies that manufacture computing equipment and office machines. Its main function is to guide users in solving problems and applying information for general benefit, and to sponsor the setting of standards for computers and information processing. It publishes a weekly *News Bulletin* and an *Annual Report.*

**Data Processing Management Association (DPMA)**
**505 Busse Highway, Park Ridge, Illinois 60068**

The National Machine Accountants Association (the name was changed to DPMA in 1962) was founded in 1951 and has membership of over 22,000 in the United States, Canada, and Japan. Its primary purpose is to develop and promote business methods and education in data processing and data-processing management. Through its many chapters, a professional attitude among its members in understanding and applying data-processing techniques is promoted.

Since 1962, the Certificate in Data Processing has been given to establish and maintain professional standards in data processing. The association also sponsors the "Registered Business Programmer" annual examination. DPMA's primary periodical is the monthly *Data Management*.

**Society for Management Information Systems (SMIS)**
**18 South Michigan Avenue, Chicago, Illinois 60603**

SMIS, founded in 1969, holds an annual meeting, sponsors research, and publishes papers on the new, emerging field of management information systems.

# Data Processing Periodicals

*Abstracts of Computer Literature,* Burroughs Corporation Plant Library, 460 Sierra Madre Villa, Pasadena, Calif. 91109.

Bimonthly abstracts on various aspects of computers (free).

*Automation-Data in State and Local Government,* Michigan Department of Education, Bureau of Educational Services, Library Division, 735 East Michigan Avenue, Lansing, Mich. 48913.

Monthly review of published EDP articles (free).

*Business Automation,* Business Press International, Inc., 288 Park Avenue, West Elmhurst, Ill. 60126.

Monthly publication on various EDP subjects.

*Business Automation News Report,* The Business Press, 288 Park Avenue, West Elmhurst, Ill. 60126.

Weekly report of topics of general interest.

*Communications of the ACM,* Association for Computing Machinery, 1130 Avenue of the Americas, New York, N. Y. 10036.

Monthly journal covering technical articles and subjects on computers.

*Computer Characteristics Quarterly,* Adams Associates, 128 The Great Road, Bedford, Mass. 01730.

Quarterly presentation of key characteristics on computers, peripheral devices, etc.

*Computer Decisions,* Hayden Publishing Company, 50 Essex Street, Rochelle Park, N. J. 07662

Monthly publication devoted to data processing articles of general interest (free to educators in data processing and other qualified individuals).

*Computer Design,* Computer Design Publishing Company, P. O. Box A, Winchester, Mass. 01890.

Monthly publication devoted to subjects on circuitry (free to qualified subscribers).

*Computer Education,* Data Processing Horizons, Inc., P. O. Box 99, South Pasadena, Calif. 91030.

A monthly magazine covering current developments in the teaching of data processing.

*Computers and Automation,* Berkeley Enterprises, Inc., 815 Washington Street, Newtonville, Mass. 02160.

Monthly magazine covering data processing topics of general interest.

*Computers and the Humanities,* Queens College of the City University of New York, Flushing, N. Y. 11367.

A journal published five times each year, covering topics related to computers and the humanities.

*Computerworld,* Computerworld, Inc., 129 Mt. Auburn Street, Cambridge, Mass. 02138.

A weekly newspaper oriented toward developments in the EDP field.

*Computing Reviews,* Association for Computing Machinery, 1130 Avenue of the Americas, New York, N. Y. 10036.

Monthly review presenting evaluations of books, articles, and films on various aspects of computing.

*Data Processing Magazine,* North American Publishing Company, 134 North 13 Street, Philadelphia, Pa. 19107.

Monthly magazine centering around topics of general interest in data processing.

*Data Processing Digest,* Data Processing Digest, Inc., 1140 South Robertson Boulevard, Los Angeles, Calif. 90035.

Monthly coverage of general topics on data processing.

*Data Processing for Education,* American Data Processing, Inc., 4th Floor, Book Building, Detroit, Mich. 48226.

Monthly publication devoted to general data processing topics in education.

*Data Management,* Data Processing Management Association, 505 Busse Highway, Park Ridge, Ill. 60068.

Monthly journal devoted to management and general topics on data processing (free to members).

*Datamation,* Technical Publishing Company, 1301 South Grove Avenue, Barrington, Ill. 60010.

Monthly covering current and prospective developments in the data processing field (free to educators in data processing and other qualified individuals).

*EDP Weekly,* Industry Reports, Inc., 514 Tenth Street, N. W., Washington, D.C. 20004.

Weekly developments in data processing are covered.

*Information Processing Journal,* Cambridge Communication Corporation, 1612 K Street, N. W., Washington, D.C. 20006.

Quarterly journal oriented toward a critical evaluation of articles and books on various aspects of data processing.

*Journal of the Association for Computing Machinery,* Association for Computing Machinery, 1130 Avenue of the Americas, New York, N. Y. 10036.

A quarterly publication devoted mainly to technical papers (free to members).

*Journal of Systems Management,* Association for Systems Management, 24587 Bagley Road, Cleveland, Ohio 44138.

Monthly journal covering analyses, procedures, and management systems (free to members).

*Software Age,* Press-Tech, Inc., 1020 Church Street, Evanston, Ill. 60201.

Bimonthly presenting software and other related topics at a nontechnical level (free to qualified subscribers).

**Other Periodicals**

*Computing Newsletter for Schools of Business,* University of Colorado, Cragmor Road, Colorado Springs, Colo. 80907.

*Data Processing for Management,* American Data Processing, Inc., 22nd Floor, Book Tower, Detroit, Mich. 48226.

*Data Systems News,* United Business Publications, P. O. Box 7387, Philadelphia, Pa. 19101.

*Digital Computer Newsletter,* Information Systems Branch, Office of Naval Research, Washington, D.C. 20360.

*EDP Analyzer*, EDP Analyzer, 134 Escondido Avenue, Vista, Calif. 92083.

*Honeywell Computer Journal,* Honeywell Information Systems, Inc., Deer Valley Park, P. O. Box 6000, Phoenix, Arizona 85005.

*IBM Data Processor,* IBM Corporation, Data Processing Division, 112 East Post Road, White Plains, N. Y. 10601.

*IBM Systems Journal,* IBM Corporation, Armonk, N. Y. 10504.

*Information Display,* Information Display Publications, Inc., 647 North Sepulveda Boulevard, Los Angeles, Calif. 90049.

*Journal of Computer and System Sciences,* Academic Press, Inc., 111 Fifth Avenue, New York, N. Y. 10003.

*Journal of Educational Data Processing,* Association for Educational Data Systems, 1201 Sixteenth Street, N. W., Washington, D.C. 20036.

*Management Services,* American Institute of Certified Public Accountants, 666 Fifth Avenue, New York, N. Y. 10019.

*Monitor,* Association for Educational Data Systems, 1201 Sixteenth Street, N. W., Washington, D.C. 20036.

*Scientific and Control Computer Reports,* Auerbach Corporation, 121 North Broad Street, Philadelphia, Pa. 19107.

# Bibliography


### Data Processing Fundamentals

Arnold, Hill, and Nichols, *Modern Data Processing,* New York: John Wiley, 1969.
Awad, E., *Automatic Data Processing,* Englewood Cliffs, N. J.: Prentice-Hall, 1970.
Awad E., *Business Data Processing,* Englewood Cliffs, N. J.: Prentice-Hall, 1971.
Bartee, *Digital Computer Fundamentals,* New York: McGraw-Hill, 1972.
Boyes, Shields, and Greenwall, *Introduction to Electronic Computing: A Management Approach,* New York: John Wiley, 1971.
Brightman, *Practical Data Processing,* New York: MacMillan, 1969.
Cardenas, Presser, and Marin, *Computer Science,* New York: John Wiley, 1972.
Carter, *Introduction to Business Data Processing,* Belmont, Calif.: Dickenson, 1968.
Claffey, *Principles of Data Processing,* Belmont, Calif.: Dickenson, 1967.
Crawford, *Introduction to Data Processing,* Englewood Cliffs, N. J.: Prentice-Hall, 1968.
Davis, G., *Computer Data Processing,* New York: McGraw-Hill, 1969.
Davis, G., *Introduction to Electronic Computers,* New York: McGraw-Hill, 1971.
Elliott and Wasley, *Business Information Processing Systems,* Homewood, Ill.: Richard D. Irwin, 1971.
Forsythe, Keenan, Organick, and Stenberg, *Computer Science: A First Course,* New York: John Wiley, 1969.
Gibson, *An Introduction to Automatic Data Processing,* Elmhurst, Ill.: The Business Press, 1966.
Gregory and Van Horn, *Automatic Data Processing Systems,* Belmont, Calif.: Wadsworth, 1963.
Hull and Day, *Computers and Problem Solving,* Reading, Mass.: Addison-Wesley, 1969.
Inman, *Fundamentals of Electronic Data Processing,* Englewood Cliffs, N. J.: Prentice-Hall, 1965.
Laurie, *Modern Computer Concepts,* Cincinnati, Ohio: South-Western, 1970.
Lott, *Basic Data Processing,* Englewood Cliffs, N. J.: Prentice-Hall, 1967.
Martin, *Electronic Data Processing, An Introduction,* Homewood, Ill.: Richard D. Irwin, 1965.
McCarthy, McCarthy, and Humes, *Integrated Data Processing Systems,* New York: John Wiley, 1966.
Ralston, *Introduction to Programming and Computer Science,* New York: McGraw-Hill, 1971.
Sanders, *Computers in Business: An Introduction,* New York: McGraw-Hill, 1972.
Saxon and Steyer, *Basic Principles of Data Processing,* Englewood Cliffs, N. J.: Prentice-Hall, 1967.
Scheid, *Introduction to Computer Science,* New York: McGraw-Hill, 1970.
Schmidt and Meyers, *Introduction to Computer Science and Data Processing,* New York: Holt, Rinehart and Winston, 1970.
Van Ness, *Principles of Data Processing with Computers,* Elmhurst, Ill.: The Business Press, 1966.
Wheeler and Jones, *Business Data Processing: An Introduction,* Reading, Mass.: Addison-Wesley, 1966.
Withington, *The Use of Computers in Business Organizations,* Reading, Mass.: Addison-Wesley, 1966.
Withington, *The Real Computer: Its Influence, Uses, and Effects,* Reading, Mass., Addison-Wesley, 1969.

### Data Processing Management

Brandon, *Management Planning for Data Processing,* Princeton, N. J.: Brandon/Systems Press, 1970.
Brink, *Computers and Management: The Executive Viewpoint,* Englewood Cliffs, N. J.: Prentice-Hall, 1970.
Canning and Sisson, *The Management of Data Processing,* New York: John Wiley, 1967.

Dearden, McFarlan, and Zani, *Managing Computer-Based Information Systems,* Homewood, Ill.: Richard D. Irwin, 1971.
Ditri, Shaw, and Atkins, *Managing the EDP Function,* New York: McGraw-Hill, 1971.
Flores, *Data Structure and Management,* Englewood Cliffs, N. J.: Prentice-Hall, 1970.
Hodge and Hodgson, *Management and the Computer in Information and Control Systems,* New York: McGraw-Hill, 1969.
Joslin, *Management and Computer Systems,* Arlington, Va.: College Readings, 1970.
Kanter, *The Computer and the Executive,* Englewood Cliffs, N. J.: Prentice-Hall, 1967.
Martino, *Information Management,* New York: McGraw-Hill, 1970.
Massey, *Computer Basics for Management,* Braintree, Mass.: D. H. Mark, 1969.
Montalbano, *Computing and Managing,* Scranton, Penn.: International Textbook, 1968.
O'Brien, *Management with Computers,* New York: Van Nostrand Reinhold, 1970.
Sanders, *Computers and Management,* New York: McGraw-Hill, 1969.
Shaw and Atkins, *Managing Computer Systems Projects,* New York: McGraw-Hill, 1970.
Sisson and Canning, *A Manager's Guide to Computer Processing,* New York: John Wiley, 1967.
Tomlin, *Managing the Introduction of Computer Systems,* New York: McGraw-Hill, 1970.
Wofsey, *Management of Automatic Data Processing,* Washington, D.C.: Thompson, 1965.

**Data Processing Systems**

Alexis and Wilson, *Organizational Decision Making,* Englewood Cliffs, N. J.: Prentice-Hall, 1967.
Blumenthal, *Management Information Systems,* Englewood Cliffs, N. J.: Prentice-Hall, 1969.
Bocchino, *Management Information Systems, Tools and Techniques,* Englewood Cliffs, N. J.: Prentice-Hall, 1972.
Boutell, *Computer-Oriented Business Systems,* Englewood Cliffs, N. J.: Prentice-Hall, 1968.
Brightman, et al., *Data Processing for Decision Making,* New York: MacMillan, 1968.
Chapin, *Computers: A System Approach,* New York: Van Nostrand Reinhold, 1971.
Cleland and King, *Systems, Organization, Management: A Book of Readings,* New York: McGraw-Hill, 1969.
Couger, *Computer Based Management Information Systems,* New York: John Wiley, 1968.
Dearden and McFarlan, *Management Information Systems,* Homewood, Ill.: Richard D. Irwin, 1966.
Dippel and House, *Information Systems Data Processing and Evaluation,* Cincinnati, Ohio: South-Western, 1969.
Elliott and Wasley, *Business Information Processing Systems,* Homewood, Ill.: Richard D. Irwin, 1971.
Enger, *Putting MIS to Work: Managing the Management Information System,* New York: American Management Association, 1969.
Glans, Grad, Holstein, Meyers, and Schmidt, *Management Systems,* New York: Holt, Rinehart, and Winston, 1968.
Greenwood, *Decision Theory and Information Systems,* Cincinnati, Ohio: South-Western, 1970.
Gregory and Van Horn, *Automatic Data Processing* Systems, Belmont, Calif.: Wadsworth, 1963.
Hartman, *Management Information Systems Handbook,* New York: McGraw-Hill, 1970.
Head, *Real-Time Business Systems,* New York: Holt, Rinehart, and Winston, 1964.
Heany, *Development of Information Systems,* New York: Ronald Press, 1968.
Hellerman, *Principles of Digital Computer Systems,* New York: McGraw-Hill, 1968.
Johnson, Kast, and Rosenzweig, *The Theory and Management of Systems,* New York: McGraw-Hill, 1967.
Kelly, J. *Computerized Management Information Systems,* New York: MacMillan, 1970.
Kelly, W., *Management Through Systems and Procedures,* New York: John Wiley, 1969.
Krauss, *Computer-Based Management Information Systems,* New York: American Management Association, 1970.
Lipperman, *Advanced Business Systems,* New York: American Management Association, 1968.
Martino, *Management Information Systems,* New York: McGraw-Hill, 1969.
Martino, *MIS—Methodology,* New York: McGraw-Hill, 1970.
Massey, *Management Information Systems,* Braintree, Mass.: D. H. Mark, 1969.
McCarthy, McCarthy, and Humes, *Integrated Data Processing Systems,* New York: John Wiley, 1966.
McDonough and Garrett, *Management Systems, Working Concepts and Practices,* Homewood, Ill.: Richard D. Irwin, 1965.
Meacham and Thompson, *Total Systems,* Detroit, Mich.: American Data Processing, 1965.
Murdick and Ross, *Information Systems for Modern Management,* Englewood Cliffs, N. J.: Prentice-Hall, 1971.
O'Brien, *Management Information Systems,* New York: Van Nostrand, 1970.

Prince, *Information Systems for Management Planning and Control,* Homewood, Ill.: Richard D. Irwin, 1970.
Rademaker, editor, *Business Systems,* Cleveland, Ohio: Systems and Procedures Association, 1966.
Rosove, *Developing Computer Based Information System,* New York: John Wiley, 1967.
Ross, *Management by Information System,* Englewood Cliffs, N. J.: Prentice-Hall, 1970.
Rothstein, *Guide to the Design of Real-Time Systems,* New York: John Wiley, 1970.
Schmidt and Taylor, *Simulation and Analysis of Industrial Systems,* Homewood, Ill.: Richard D. Irwin, 1970.
Schoderbek, *Management Systems,* New York: John Wiley, 1971.
Stimler, *Real-Time Data Processing Systems,* New York: McGraw-Hill, 1969.
Wendler, *Total Systems,* Cleveland, Ohio: Systems and Procedures Association, 1966.
Ziegler, *Time-Sharing Data Processing Systems,* Englewood Cliffs, N. J.: Prentice-Hall, 1967.

### Data Processing Systems Analysis and Design

Breipohl, *Probabilistic Systems Analysis: An Introduction to Probabilistic Models, Decisions, and Application of Random Process,* New York: John Wiley, 1970.
Churchman, *The Systems Approach,* New York: Dell, 1968.
Cleland and King, *Systems Analysis and Project Management,* New York: McGraw-Hill, 1968.
Clifton, *Data Processing Systems Design,* Princeton, N. J.: Auerbach, 1971.
Deutsch, *Systems Analysis Techniques,* Englewood Cliffs, N. J.: Prentice-Hall, 1969.
Gentle, *Data Communications in Business,* New York: American Telephone & Telegraph, 1966.
Hopeman, *Systems Analysis and Operations Management,* Columbus, Ohio: Charles E. Merrill, 1969.
Joslin, *Analysis, Design and Selection of Computer Systems,* Arlington, Va.: College Readings, 1971.
Laden and Gildersleeve, *System Design for Computer Applications,* New York: John Wiley, 1967.
Lott, *Basic Systems Analysis,* San Francisco, Calif.: Canfield Press, 1971.
Lyon, *An Introduction to Data Base Design,* New York: John Wiley, 1972.
Martin, J., *Design of Real-Time Computer Systems,* Englewood Cliffs, N. J.: Prentice-Hall, 1968.
Martin, J., *Systems Analysis for Data Transmission,* Englewood Cliffs, N. J.: Prentice-Hall, 1972.
Matthews, *The Design of the Management Information System,* Princeton, N. J.: Auerbach, 1971.
McMillan and Gonzalez, *Systems Analysis: A Computer Approach to Decision Models,* Homewood, Ill.: Richard D. Irwin, 1968.
Nadler, *Work Design: A Systems Concept,* Homewood, Ill.: Richard D. Irwin, 1970.
Optner, *Systems Analysis for Business & Industrial Problem Solving,* Prentice-Hall, 1968.
Parkhill, *The Challenge of the Computer Utility,* Reading, Mass.: Addison-Wesley, 1966.
Popell, *Computer Time-Sharing,* Englewood Cliffs, N. J.: Prentice-Hall, 1966.
Rothstein, *Guide to the Design of Real-Time Systems,* New York: John Wiley, 1970.
Stone, *Introduction to Computer Organization and Data Structures,* New York: McGraw-Hill, 1972.
Van Court Hare, *Systems Analysis: A Diagnostic Approach,* New York: Harcourt, Brace, & World, 1967.
Williams, *Principles of Automated Information Retrieval,* Elmhurst, Ill.: The Business Press, 1966.
Yourdon, *Real-Time Systems Design,* Cambridge, Mass.: Information Systems Institute, 1967.
Yourdon, *Design of On-Line Computer Systems,* Englewood Cliffs, N. J.: Prentice-Hall, 1972.

### Data Processing Programming

Andree, *Computer Programming and Related Mathematics,* New York: John Wiley, 1967.
Breuer, *Dictionary for Computer Languages,* New York: Academic Press, 1966.
Emerick and Wilkinson, *Computer Programming for Business and Social Science,* Homewood, Ill.: Richard D. Irwin, 1970.
Flores, I., *Computer Software,* Englewood Cliffs, N. J.: Prentice-Hall, 1965.
Flores, I., *Computer Programming System/360,* Englewood Cliffs, N. J.: Prentice-Hall, 1971.
Gruenberger and Jaffray, *Problems for Computer Solution,* New York: John Wiley, 1965.
Hughes, *Programming the IBM 1130,* New York: John Wiley, 1969.
Hull, *Introduction to Computing,* Englewood Cliffs, N. J.: Prentice-Hall, 1966.
Joslin, *Software for Computer Systems,* Arlington, Va.: College Readings, 1970.
Laurie, *Computers and Computer Languages,* Cincinnati, Ohio: South-Western, 1966.
Leeds and Weinberg, *Computer Programming Fundamentals,* New York: McGraw-Hill, 1970.
Martin, *Programming Real-Time Computer Systems,* Englewood Cliffs, N. J.: Prentice-Hall, 1965.

Sammet, *Programming Languages: History and Fundamentals,* Englewood Cliffs, N. J.: Prentice-Hall, 1969.
Schmidt and Meyers, *Introduction to Computer Science and Data Processing,* New York: Holt, Rinehart and Winston, 1966.
Sprowls, *Computer, A Programming Problem Approach,* New York: Harper and Row, 1966.
Stabley, *Logical Programming with System/360,* New York: John Wiley, 1970.
Stark, *Digital Computer Programming,* New York: Macmillan, 1967.
Thatcher and Capato, *Digital Computer Programming: Logic & Language,* Reading, Mass.: Addison-Wesley, 1967.
Webner, *Introduction to System Programming,* New York: Academic Press, 1965.

**Programming Languages**

*BASIC*

Barnett, *Programming Time-Shared Computers in BASIC,* New York: John Wiley, 1972.
Farina, *Programming in BASIC*, Englewood Cliffs, N. J.: Prentice-Hall, 1968.
Gately and Bitter, *BASIC for Beginners,* New York: McGraw-Hill, 1970.
General Electric, *GE-400 Series BASIC Language,* G.E. Publication, August 1968.
Kemeny and Kurtz, *BASIC*, Hanover, N.H.: Dartmouth College, 1971.
Van Court Hare, *Introduction to Programming: A BASIC Approach,* New York: Harcourt, Brace & World, 1970.

*COBOL*

Davis and Litecky, *Elementary COBOL Programming, A Step by Step Approach,* New York: McGraw-Hill, 1971,
McCameron, *COBOL—Logic and Programming,* Homewood, Ill.: Richard D. Irwin, 1970.
McCracken and Garbassi, *A Guide to COBOL Programming,* New York: John Wiley, 1970.
Raun, *Introduction to COBOL Programming for Accounting & Business,* Belmont, Calif.: Dickerson, 1966.
Saxon, *COBOL: A Self-Instructional Manual,* Englewood Cliffs, N. J.: Prentice-Hall, 1963.
Spitzbarth, *Basic COBOL Programming,* Reading, Mass.: Addison-Wesley, 1970.
Wohl, *The Use of Generalized "Packaged" Computer Programs,* Homewood, Ill.: Richard D. Irwin, 1967.

*FORTRAN*

Anderson, *Computer Programming, FORTRAN IV,* New York: Appleton-Century-Crofts, 1966.
Anton and Boutell, *FORTRAN and Business Data Processing,* New York: McGraw-Hill, 1968.
Couger and Shannon, *FORTRAN IV: A Programmed Instruction Approach,* Homewood, Ill.: Richard D. Irwin, 1968.
Couger and Shannon, *FORTRAN: A Beginner's Approach,* Homewood, Ill.: Richard D. Irwin, 1971.
Couger and Shannon, *FORTRAN IV: A Programmed Instruction Approach,* Homewood, Ill.: Richard D. Irwin, 1972.
Dimitry and Mott, *Introduction to FORTRAN IV Programming,* New York: Holt, Rinehart and Winston, 1966.
Farina, *FORTRAN Self-Taught,* Englewood Cliffs, N. J.: Prentice-Hall, 1966.
Ford, *Basic FORTRAN IV Programming,* Homewood, Ill.: Richard D. Irwin, 1971.
Golde, *FORTRAN II and IV for Beginners & Scientists,* New York: Macmillan, 1966.
Golden, *FORTRAN IV Programming and Computing,* Englewood Cliffs, N. J.: Prentice-Hall, 1965.
Hartkemeier, *FORTRAN Programming of Electronic Computers,* Columbus, Ohio: Charles E. Merrill, 1969.
Harvill, *Basic FORTRAN Programming,* Englewood Cliffs, N. J.: Prentice-Hall, 1966.
Healy and DeBauzzi, *Basic FORTRAN IV Programming,* Reading, Mass.: Addison-Wesley, 1968.
Kennedy and Solomon, *Ten Statement FORTRAN Plus FORTRAN IV,* Englewood Cliffs, N. J.: Prentice-Hall, 1970.
Ledley, *FORTRAN IV Programming,* New York: McGraw-Hill, 1966.
Lee, *A Short Course in FORTRAN IV,* System 360, New York: McGraw-Hill, 1967.
McCameron, *FORTRAN: Logic and Programming,* Homewood, Ill.: Richard D. Irwin, 1968.
McCameron, *FORTRAN IV,* Homewood, Ill.: Richard D. Irwin, 1970.
McCracken, *A Guide to FORTRAN IV Programming,* New York: John Wiley, 1965.
Organick, *A FORTRAN IV Primer,* Reading, Mass.: Addison-Wesley, 1966.
Pollack, *A Guide to FORTRAN IV,* New York: Columbia University Press, 1965.
Ralston, *FORTRAN IV Programming: A Concise Exposition,* New York: McGraw-Hill, 1971.

Smith and Johnson, *FORTRAN Autotester,* New York: John Wiley, 1965.
Stuart, *WATFOR, WATFIV FORTRAN Programming,* New York: John Wiley, 1971.
Weiss, *360 FORTRAN Programming,* New York: McGraw-Hill, 1969.

*PL/1*

Bates and Douglas, *Programming Language/One (PL/1)*, Englewood Cliffs, N. J.: Prentice-Hall, 1967.
Groner, PL/1 *Programming in Technological Applications,* New York: John Wiley, 1971.
Scott and Sondek, *PL/1 for Programmers,* Reading, Mass.: Addison Wesley, 1970.
Sprowls, *Introduction to PL/1 Programming,* New York: Harper & Row, 1969.
Weinberg, *PL/1 Programming Primer,* New York: McGraw-Hill, 1966.
Weinberg, *PL/*1 *Programming: A Manual of Style,* New York: McGraw-Hill, 1970.
Weiss, *The PL/*1 *Converter,* New York: McGraw-Hill, 1967.

# Index